HANDBOOK OF ARBITRATION PRACTICE

AUSTRALIA
LBC Information Services
Sydney

CANADA and USA
Carswell
Toronto

NEW ZEALAND
Brooker's
Auckland

SINGAPORE and MALAYSIA
Thomson Information (S.E. Asia)
Singapore

HANDBOOK OF ARBITRATION PRACTICE

PUBLISHED BY
SWEET & MAXWELL
IN CONJUNCTION WITH
THE CHARTERED INSTITUTE OF ARBITRATORS

LONDON 1998

Published in 1998 by
Sweet & Maxwell Limited of
100 Avenue Road
Swiss Cottage
London NW3 3PR
in conjunction with
The Chartered Institute of Arbitrators
Typeset by Wyvern 21, Bristol
Printed and bound in Great Britain by Athenæum Press Ltd, Gateshead, Tyne Wear

No natural forests were destroyed to make this product;
only farmed timber was used and replanted

First edtiton	1987
Second edtion	1993
Third edtion	1998
Reprinted	2000

A CIP catalogue record for this book is available from the British Library

ISBN 0 421 56540 3

HANDBOOK OF ARBITRATION PRACTICE

BY

Ronald Bernstein, Q.C., F.C.I.Arb., Hon. Assoc. RICS

John Tackaberry, Q.C., F.C.I.Arb.

AND

Arthur L. Marriott, Q.C., F.C.I.Arb.

CONSULTANT EDITOR

Derek Wood, C.B.E., Q.C., F.C.I.Arb., Hon. Assoc. RICS

WITH CONTRIBUTIONS FROM

Derek Kirby Johnson, M.A. (Cantab.), F.C.I.Arb. — Commodity Trade Arbitration
Bruce Harris, F.C.I.Arb., FRSA — Maritime Arbitrations
Professor Phillip Capper; Tony Bunch, B.A. (Hons) — Construction Industry Arbitrations
Ian V. Oddy, FRICS, F.C.I.Arb. — Rent Review and Property Valuation Arbitrations
Margaret Rutherford, Q.C., LL.B., F.C.I.Arb. — Documents-Only Arbitrations in Consumer Disputes
R. G. Greenslade, C.B.E., LL.B. — Small Claims Arbitrations in the County Court
Jan Paulsson, F.C.I.Arb. — International Commercial Arbitrations

Foreword by Lord Woolf

Introduction by the Lord Saville of Newdigate

Foreword

by
Lord Woolf of Barnes, Master of the Rolls

I am delighted to follow a well-established tradition and as Master of the Rolls provide a Foreword to this new edition. However I have an additional interest in welcoming the latest edition of the Handbook. It contributes to Access to Justice.

The recommendations which I have made as to Access to Justice are mirrored in the new Arbitration Act. They are kindred spirits. Civil proceedings and arbitration proceedings have been victims of the same excesses and in both cases management on the one hand by judges and on the other by arbitrators together with the absence of complexity are the only remedies. It is essential we adopt a proportionate approach.

The extremely distinguished and experienced contributors to each of the chapters in the Handbook recognise this to the full. They also have the ability to express themselves extremely clearly. The parties, their advisers and arbitrators will all find that the Handbook provides them with the information which they need in order to conduct arbitrations. However the Handbook provides more than this. It deals with the small claims arbitration process which is now such an important part of doing justice in the county courts. It provides a detailed account of the interface between the arbitration process and the court process.

The first and second editions justifiably had a high reputation. However I am confident that this edition will enhance that reputation. Bearing in mind who are the contributors, it is no surprise that this is in every way an excellent book.

Foreword

by
Lord Woolf of Barnes, Master of the Rolls

[illegible]

Authors' Note

In England the Arbitration Act 1996 came into force on January 31, 1997. It proceeds—at times unsteadily—towards the goal so lucidly stated by Lord Mustill and his colleagues in the Departmental Advisory Committee, of producing a statute in logical order, in simple language, and readily comprehensible to the layman. This is of considerable importance, both to the lay practitioner in England before whom, sitting alone, the majority of arbitrations are conducted, and to the lawyer abroad considering whether to specify London as a venue.

Arbitration is the principal means of dispute resolution in at least two fields of economic activity of great importance, namely, the construction industry and the development and letting of commercial property. But its influence goes far wider and arbitration is used, as this Handbook makes clear, in many fields ranging from agriculture to consumer disputes.

The authors have substantially revised the second edition to take into account the changes in practice which the new Act enables arbitrators to embrace. Various procedural ideas and concepts, some quite at variance with previous practice, have been advanced. It is to be hoped that arbitrators and practitioners will use the virtually unfettered freedom which the statute gives them to devise new and radical procedures which will promote the economic, expeditious and fair resolution of disputes. If they do so they will match the movement for reform which is now sweeping the courts.

The changes consequent upon the passing of the new Act have necessitated a major re-write and re-ordering of this Handbook. They have been accompanied by equally transformatory changes in the authorial team. Derek Wood, C.B.E., Q.C. has found that his responsibilities as Principal of St Hugh's College, Oxford prevent him from playing a full part in re-writing this edition. He has acted as Consultant to the new edition and has contributed Part 7 on Agricultural Property Arbitration. In his place have come John Tackaberry, Q.C., a past Chairman of the Chartered Institute of Arbitrators and Arthur Marriott, Q.C., who after his outstanding efforts as the mainspring of the 1996 Act has been appointed as one of the first two solicitors to be made Queen's Counsel.

The success of the first and second editions was in no small measure due to Lord Donaldson, who wrote a handsome Foreword and to The Right Hon. Sir Michael Kerr who wrote a magisterial Part 1. The authors are deeply grateful to them. For this edition their places have been taken by Lord Woolf who has written the Foreword and Lord Saville who has written Part 1. To them, too, the authors are deeply grateful. The authors also wish to record their appreciation of the contributions to the success of the earlier editions made by former contributors, each a past President or Chairman of the Chartered Institute of Arbitrators:

the late Michael B. Summerskill, Leslie W. M. Alexander, FRIBA, FRICS, and Maurice G. W. Pleasance, FRICS. We have been fortunate in persuading Bruce Harris (another past Chairman), Tony Bunch and Professor Phillip Capper to join the list of distinguished contributors.

This Third Edition has taken account of the fact that in large areas of the world arbitration practice is moving towards similar goals, a process receiving a powerful impetus from the growing adoption of the UNCITRAL Model Law (with more or less adaptation) and the splendid efforts of Gerrold Herrman, UNCITRAL's Secretary General in promoting it. The Authors have written this edition with the intention that it should be useful in many countries other than England and Wales. It is hoped that this process will be taken further by the publication, in conjunction with this edition, of Companion Volumes, written by lawyers distinguished in their own jurisdictions complementing the Handbook for use in their own jurisdictions.

Unlike its predecessors, the Arbitration Act 1996 applies to Northern Ireland as well as to England and Wales. To avoid tedious repetition, references in this edition to England should be read as including references to England, Wales and Northern Ireland; but not to Scotland, to which the English Act does not apply.

The authors' task could not have been accomplished without the devoted help, through more than the usual trials and tribulations, of June Elks (who also saw the first and second editions through to publication), Penelope Bryan, Victoria Bui, Jane Dederick, Pearl O'Brien, Jan Hammond, Lyle Jobling and Neil Midgeley. Also Kate Jones advised on the arcana of publishing contracts. The publishing and editorial staff at Sweet & Maxwell showed endless patience and courtesy when dealing with the unusual demands of a plethora of authors. We are truly grateful to them all, and also to all those others, too numerous to mention, whose brains, articles books and lectures we ruthlessly picked or from which we delightfully benefited.

Thank you all.

Ronald Bernstein
Derek Wood
John Tackaberry
Arthur Marriott
October 1997

Table of Contents

PART 5: CONSTRUCTION INDUSTRY ARBITRATIONS

By Professor Phillip Capper and Anthony Bunch, M.A.(Hons)

PART 6: RENT REVIEW AND PROPERTY VALUATION ARBITRATION

By Ian V. Oddy, FRICS, F.C.I.Arb.

PART 7: AGRICULTURAL PROPERTY ARBITRATIONS

By Derek Wood, C.B.E., Q.C., F.C.I.Arb.

PART 8: DOCUMENTS-ONLY ARBITRATIONS IN CONSUMER DISPUTES

By Margaret Rutherford, Q.C., LL.B., F.C.I.Arb.

PART 9: SMALL CLAIMS ARBITRATIONS IN THE COUNTY COURT

By R.G. Greenslade, C.B.E., LL.B.

PART 10: INTERNATIONAL COMMERCIAL ARBITRATIONS

By Jan Paulsson, F.C.I.Arb.

PART 11: ALTERNATIVE DISPUTE RESOLUTION

Arthur L. Marriott, Q.C., F.C.I.Arb.

APPENDICES

Table of Cases

Table of Statutes

(referenced to paragraph number)

Table of Statutory Instruments

Table of Rules of the Supreme Court

Table of County Court Rules

Table of International Conventions and Other Formulations

Part 1

INTRODUCTION

By the Lord Saville of Newdigate

Introduction

In Part 1 of the Second Edition of this book, Sir Michael Kerr observed that arbitration offers advantages that litigation, from its nature, can never provide. That was five years ago. Since then arbitration has boomed, both domestically and internationally. Other alternatives to court resolution of disputes have also appeared and become established. There have been many notable developments both in the domestic and the international scene. Most particularly, on the international front, there has been the steady spread of the UNCITRAL Model Law[1] (''the Model Law'') across the globe, with more and more countries adopting it, more or less unchanged, as their basic arbitration framework. On the domestic front in England there has been, relatively, an even bigger change with the passing of the Arbitration Act 1996 (''the Act''). The two particular events are linked. In the drafting of the Act it can be seen that the draftsman has kept a very close eye on the Model Law and many of its provisions are to be found in the sections of the Act. **1–01**

The Third Edition of this book has adjusted its aim accordingly. It focuses, of course, upon the Act. But it has also turned its face more outwards than before, and makes a start by looking at the Model Law. It also recognises that other means of dispute resolution must, in the future, go hand in hand with arbitration. Accordingly, there are sections on mediation and conciliation. But its main aim remains. That is the description of good practice in arbitration, whoever the participants may be and wherever the arbitration may be held. **1–02**

The function of arbitration

In the nature of human affairs disputes often arise. In a civilised society there are ways and means of resolving those disputes without recourse to violence or to other methods which are regarded as inconsistent with the principles which underlie such societies. One of those principles is the rule of law, which in turn requires there to be a state judicial system available to all and which is independent of the legislature and the executive. At the same time, in a free society **1–03**

[1] UNCITRAL Model Law on International Commercial Arbitration (United Nations document A/40/17, Annex 1) (As adopted by the United Nations Commission on International Trade Law on June 21, 1985) See Appendix 3.

those who want it should have the right by agreement to choose, if they wish, their own means of resolving their disputes, without recourse to the state court system, provided, of course, that this does not offend other basic principles of our society.

1–04 Arbitration is one means for resolving disputes, perhaps the oldest form of acceptable alternative dispute resolution, *i.e.* an alternative to the state court system. The essence of the type of arbitration under discussion is that the parties choose a third party whose decision on the dispute is binding on them. Where parties have a choice, any other form of dispute resolution will in practice be compared with litigation to see what advantages and disadvantages it offers.

1–05 In recent years judges have been ahead of arbitrators in their reform of procedures; see for example innovations introduced by Practice Directions in the Commercial Court and changes in practice introduced by Official Referees. But inevitably the wider range of disputes, the sheer volume of work and the need for predictability of procedure mean that civil litigation must be conducted according to formal and predetermined rules. So even if and when Lord Woolf's recommendations are implemented in England, arbitrators exercising the enhanced range of powers given to them by the 1996 Act will still have a much greater flexibility in devising, usually with but often without the specific agreement of the parties, procedures for ''obtaining the fair resolution of disputes by an impartial tribunal without unnecessary delay or expense''.

The Potential Advantages of Arbitration

1–06 Arbitration offers advantages that litigation, from its nature, can never provide. These vary from case to case. In many cases a major advantage is that the arbitrator or arbitral tribunal is so expert in the field of the dispute that the entire procedure can be conducted without the intervention of lawyers or other representatives, with major gains in speed and economy. Thus many disputes as to quality in the commodity trades, many disputes as to the rent of commercial property, and many small consumer disputes, are resolved in this way. But even where lawyers are instructed for one or both parties, arbitration can have many advantages, which—with any countervailing factors—are discussed in this book. The following are some of the advantages:

(a) The parties can choose the arbitrator or arbitration tribunal. If they cannot agree upon a particular person or persons, they can almost invariably agree upon some institution to make the appointment, and thereby agree upon the qualifications of the person or persons to be appointed. For example, the President of the Chartered Institute of Arbitrators or the President of the London Court of International Arbitration is likely to appoint someone known to be experienced as an arbitrator; the President of the Royal Institute of British Architects is likely to appoint an architect with experience of arbitration; and so on.

In the last resort, if the parties cannot even agree upon an appointing institution, the court will appoint an arbitrator and before doing so will consider any submissions as to what qualifications the person appointed should possess.

(b) Many disputes can be resolved on documents without a hearing. Thousands of disputes are resolved each year in this way, not only quality disputes (Part 4, below) and rent reviews (Part 6, below) but also a rapidly growing number of consumer disputes (Part 8, below).

(c) If a party to a contract does not wish to be exposed to the decision of one man, with the consequential possibilities of idiosyncrasies or ignorance, he can stipulate for arbitration by a tribunal of three, one of whom is to be appointed by him. This possibility is of particular importance where the parties to a contract are from different countries or cultures; each can be sure that the tribunal will include at least one member familiar with his country or culture.

(d) Except in the tiny number of cases in which the right of appeal to the courts has been agreed by the parties, or where leave to appeal has been given by the court, the procedure is private, self-contained and final. In comparison with court proceedings the risk of costs and delays due to appeals is minimal and (in England) has been reduced still further by the Act.

(e) The hearing (if there is to be one) and any preliminary meetings can be held in a place of the parties' choice. Apart from its great convenience in some cases, it can be in neutral territory rather than on what is perceived to be the home territory of one party.

(f) Arbitration by a tribunal chosen with speed in mind can be far quicker than litigation.

(g) The parties have a wider choice of procedure than in litigation; including, if they wish, replacing the traditional English adversarial procedure by an inquisitorial procedure for issues for which this is more appropriate, as used in other countries.

(h) The tribunal can take part in the preparation of the issues for adjudication; can help to strip out the inessentials; and can read the documents before, rather than at, the hearing. This can enormously shorten the hearing and reduce the costs.

(i) Parties can represent themselves or be represented by anyone of their choice. Rights of audience by representatives are not limited to lawyers as in the courts; and in particular a company or corporation an be represented by a director.

(j) Arbitration is acceptable to many states and state institutions which for reasons of national prestige would be unwilling to submit to the jurisdiction of any foreign court.

(k) The New York Convention provides, in many cases, a better means for enforcing awards in foreign countries than the equivalent enforcement procedures for judgments.

1–07 Arbitration has now developed to the extent that it provides a vital service for dispute resolution both domestically and internationally.

Special features of English arbitration

1–08 English law has the most developed law of arbitration of any country. Arbitration has been a popular form of dispute resolution for hundreds of years and the result is a system of rules and principles which has proved extremely popular throughout the world. England is, in fact, regarded as a leading world centre so far as international arbitrations are concerned. Its arbitration laws have been evolved over many years and provide a complete code available for those engaged in international trade and commerce who are minded to use arbitration as their chosen method of dispute resolution. In addition England has a highly developed system of commercial law which can also be chosen by the parties as the law to be applied by the arbitrators in deciding the substantive rights and obligations of the parties. English lawyers and arbitrators have built up an unrivalled reputation for the fair and impartial resolution of international trade and commercial disputes.

The UNCITRAL Model Law

1–09 They cannot, however, rest on their laurels. In 1985 the United Nations Commission on International Trade Law (UNCITRAL) adopted a Model Law on international commercial arbitrations. This in turn led a number of countries to consider whether they should adopt this Model Law in place of their own arbitral laws and procedures. In England a Departmental Advisory Committee chaired by Lord Mustill in 1989 advised against simply adopting the Model Law in place of existing laws, though there were a number of things in the Model Law which England could usefully adopt. The Model Law was also not a complete Code and would have in any event to be supplemented.

1–10 However, the Committee did not simply produce this negative conclusion. Instead it pointed to what was undoubtedly a defect in the existing law. This was not a defect of quality or content; but one of presentation. English law had built up over a very long time indeed. In the main the developments came from cases, but in addition, from as early as 1698, Parliament had passed legislation dealing with the law of arbitration. To a large degree this legislation was reactive in nature, putting right perceived defects and deficiencies in the case law. Thus it was not easy for someone new to English arbitration to discover the law, which was spread around a hotchpotch of statutes and countless cases. This meant that arbitration often involved unnecessary expense, in the form of employing lawyers who were expert in intricacies of our arbitration law and in where to find it. The position of London as the leading centre for international arbitration was being put at risk by the fact that English arbitration laws were not easily accessible.

The Mustill Committee in effect recommended that we should replace the hotchpotch with a new statute, comprising 1–11

> "a statement in statutory form of the more important principles of the English law of arbitration, statutory (and to the extent practicable) common law."

The Committee also recommended that the statute should be set out in a logical order, and expressed in language which was sufficiently clear and free from technicalities to be readily comprehensible to the layman; that it should apply to both domestic and international arbitrations; that it should not be limited to the subject matter of the Model Law, but that it should, so far as is possible, have the same structure and language as the Model Law.

After some false starts, which had the merit of attracting a large number of considered responses, I took over in late 1994 from Lord Justice (now Lord) Steyn chairmanship of the Departmental Advisory Committee. With the invaluable assistance of Toby Landau and Arthur Marriott (now a Queen's Counsel); of a draft Bill prepared by Basil Eckersley; and of Geoffrey Sellers as our Parliamentary Draftsman, the DAC published a draft Bill in July 1995. After months of further consultation and redrafting a bill was introduced in the House of Lords in December 1995, and with remarkably few amendments was passed in June 1996. 1–12

The Act embodies a change in presentation which should have a significant beneficial effect on arbitration in England. Unlike the past, it is now possible to read the legislation and to learn about what arbitrating in this country entails. Indeed, the three principles set out in section 1 of the Act, seek to encapsulate the basis of the English law of arbitration. 1–13

The changes introduced by the Arbitration Act

A great deal of time and effort was spent in an attempt to depart from the usual legalese of statutes of this kind and instead to speak in plain English. The 1996 Act aims to give arbitrators an enhanced range of powers so as to have a much greater flexibility in devising, usually with but often without the specific agreement of the parties, procedures for 1–14

(a) "obtaining the fair resolution of disputes by an impartial tribunal without unnecessary delay or expense".

This is the first of the three principles set out in Section 1of the 1996 Act, which seek to encapsulated the basis of our law of arbitration The others are:

(b) "the parties should be free to agree how their disputes are to be resolved, subject only to such safeguards as are necessary in the public interest"; and

(c) "the court should not intervene except as provided in the Act".

1–15 It is a feature of the Model Law that it proceeds in a logical way from the definition of the arbitration agreement to the recognition and enforcement of the arbitral award, and the new Act follows the same logic.

New duties of arbitrators and of parties

1–16 The new Act imposes on the tribunal a general duty when conducting the proceedings to act fairly and impartially, adopting procedures suitable to the specific case and avoiding unnecessary delay and expense, thereby providing a fair means of dispute resolution. And it imposes on the parties a corresponding general duty to do all things necessary for the proper and expeditious conduct of the arbitral proceedings. This includes complying without delay with any determination of the tribunal as to procedural or evidential matters, or with any order or directions of the tribunal and, where appropriate, taking without delay any necessary steps to obtain a decision of the court on a preliminary question of jurisdiction or of law.

1–17 The 1996 Act gives arbitrators greater powers to throw off the straitjacket of established procedures than Lord Woolf has been able to propose in proposals for the reform of litigation. So, for example, discovery has almost crippled the English system of civil litigation, and even more its US counterpart. Under the 1996 Act, unless the parties specifically agree to the contrary, the arbitrator has complete discretion as to whether there should be any, and if so what, discovery.

1–18 Again, the bane of English arbitration has been the so called "strict rules of evidence" often misunderstood by lawyers and impenetrable to most non-lawyers. Under the 1996 Act it is for the arbitrators (unless the parties agree otherwise) to decide what if any rules should apply.

1–19 A further important power now given to arbitrators by the 1996 Act, and not likely to be given to judges in the foreseeable future, is the power to cap costs under section 65. If, as will usually be the case, the parties have not agreed (in the arbitration agreement or in Rules adopted by that agreement) to exclude this power, the question whether either party wishes the arbitrator to exercise it can be addressed at the outset of every arbitration and a cap imposed. The quantum of the cap will be a matter for the discretion of the tribunal, and will mean that a party which chooses to spend more will not be able to recover the excess from the other party, whatever the outcome of the arbitration.

Responsibilities of participants

1–20 If arbitration is to offer an effective alternative the calibre and training of arbitrators must reach a high standard. It is important to face up to the fact that badly conducted arbitrations can lead to risks of injustice and frustration for either or both of the parties for which there will be no similar redress as in the courts. The calibre, experience and industry of the tribunal, and the nature and quality of the procedures employed in individual cases, are therefore of paramount importance.

Moreover, for arbitration to maintain its advantages as an alternative to litiga- 1–21
tion, all those concerned in it—parties, solicitors, barristers, other professional representatives, expert witnesses and above all arbitrators—must therefore become familiar with the special features of this process, both good and bad. They need to be aware not only of the procedures usual in their own particular field or expertise, but also of the general range of procedures available. For example, many arbitrations are conducted so formally as to have been called "litigation without wigs". This results more from an unthinking adherence to what has always been done by lawyers, than to a conscious decision that litigation procedure is the most appropriate to the needs of the case. Lawyers in arbitration do not follow litigation practice because they are determined to do so. They tend to follow it because they are used to it and because any departure which may be suggested involves unfamiliarily, the need for inventiveness, and above all the risk of something going wrong for which they may be blamed. But they are not fundamentally obstructive; merely cautious. Admittedly it may well be difficult for an arbitrator—particularly one who is not a lawyer—to bludgeon them into adopting a novel procedure. But they will respond to guidance from a firm tribunal which shows an understanding of their problems, and the resulting synthesis in dealing flexibly with individual disputes will often produce great benefits in terms of time and costs.

The basic duty of an arbitrator is to resolve the dispute between the parties 1–22
in a fair and impartial way. It is often the case that there is one particular issue which divides the parties and that the resolution of this issue will enable them to resolve the rest of the case. Part of the duty of the arbitrator is to ascertain whether this is so (which will require much preparatory work) and then to conduct the arbitration accordingly, *e.g.* by issuing sequential awards on specific issues, if it appears that this will aid the parties to compose the remaining issues without the expense of having to arbitrate the whole case.

Lessening the problems of Specialisation

One problem in this context is that most arbitrators are specialists, each operat- 1–23
ing in a single relatively narrow field such as the construction industry, or maritime contracts, or rent review. No doubt the procedure that has evolved in each field is that most appropriate for the majority of disputes in that field. But there will always be some disputes in each field for which a procedure used in some other field will be more apt. Some knowledge of the range of procedures available, and of how disputes are resolved in fields outside one's own, is an essential part of the equipment of an arbitrator in any field.

Changes in this edition

1–24 Litigation, arbitration and other forms of dispute resolution have moved on since the Second Edition of this Handbook was published in 1993. The authors and contributors have taken note of the changes not only in a major rewrite of the text to take account of the Arbitration Act, 1996 but also in adding contributions on Agricultural Property Arbitrations (by Derek Wood, C.B.E., Q.C.); Alternative Dispute Resolution (by Arthur Marriott, Q.C.) and on Arbitration in the County Court (by His Honour District Judge Greenslade).

Conclusion

1–25 Only time will tell whether English lawyers have succeeded in their objective to retain and enhance the reputation of England as the leading place for the form of dispute resolution known as arbitration, both domestically and internationally; and possibly by example to improve the practice of arbitration in other countries Whether our hopes will be realized we can only wait and see. However, this book justifies some confidence that we may succeed. As Sir Michael Kerr said in the Introduction to the second edition, it examines and discusses the practical workings of arbitration from both sides of the arbitrator's table. It does so in a way which will provide invaluable assistance to those who take part in, or are minded to take part in, or who want to know about the practice of arbitration. It provides the same service for alternative dispute resolution.

Mark Saville
July 1997

Part 2

GENERAL PRINCIPLES

By Ronald Bernstein, Q.C., F.C.I.Arb.
Derek Wood, C.B.E., Q.C., F.C.I.Arb.
John Tackaberry, Q.C., F.C.I.Arb.
Arthur L. Marriott, Q.C., F.C.I.Arb.

1. Arbitration—Nature and Objects

Arbitration is a method of resolving civil disputes

It is one of a number of available methods. Others include litigation, a publicly provided method, and conciliation and mediation. The phrase ''alternative dispute resolution'' or ADR is used in this book for all forms of mediation and conciliation. Neither ADR nor the words mediation and conciliation have widely established consistent meanings. It is necessary to check precisely how the user intends them.[1] 2–01

Moreover, there is a growing practice within publicly provided litigation systems of imposing on the parties to a dispute what amounts to statutory arbitration or mediation. 2–02

A legal definition

In English law, arbitration is a mechanism for the resolution of disputes which takes place, usually in private, pursuant to an agreement between two or more parties, under which the parties agree to be bound by the decision to be given by the arbitrator according to law or, if so agreed, other considerations, after a fair hearing, such decision being enforceable at law. Sometimes the submission instead of being voluntary is imposed by statute. In this work such arbitrations will be referred to as ''statutory arbitrations''. 2–03

Arbitration compared with litigation

What is litigation?

Litigation as used in this book means the process whereby disputes between legal persons are resolved by the use of publicly provided courts and tribunals. 2–04

[1] The following conventions are used in this book:
Tribunal—This term has generally been used, whether one is referring to an arbitration tribunal of one or more.
He/She/it—The text uses ''he''. The authors rejected the use of ''he'' and ''she'' alternatively as laboured: and the use of ''she'' throughout as (to their regret) too far removed from the reality. They regret any offence this decision has caused.
Court—This is used with a small ''c'' and nearly always means, in practical terms, the Commercial Court in London.
England—This term is used for England, Wales and where appropriate Northern Ireland.

No specific agreement is necessary between the disputants. Indeed the public legal system is well equipped to deal with situations where one of the parties is reluctant to take part in the procedure. However, the split between litigation and arbitration is not a total split. Under some public legal systems, "arbitration" is imposed on the disputants. This form of "arbitration" is public, and the "arbitrator" (a judge) is imposed on the parties, willy-nilly.

Arbitration as a public service

2–05 Lord Donaldson has said that arbitrators and judges are partners in the business of dispensing justice, the judge in the public and the arbitrator in the private sector.[2] The public legal system of any country represents a compromise between conflicting demands for quality, speed and cheapness of decision making. In many countries quality of decision making has usually been given the highest priority. Speed of decision, and cheapness, have suffered accordingly. Hitherto, in the United Kingdom the administration of civil justice has been commonly regarded as a loss making public service. Litigants are accordingly expected to queue up for the service, and to accept the delay, the inconvenience, and often the loss that such queuing involves.

2–06 Arbitration plays an important role already in the public civil justice system. Thus, the small claims arbitration service in the County Court has grown dramatically and is popular with litigants who want informal, speedy and inexpensive resolution of disputes now limited in value to £3,000. As radical change in litigation procedures gathers momentum, it may well be that arbitration plays a greater role as part of or as adjunct to the court system.

Public justice and private justice

2–07 In most countries it is considered essential that justice be administered in public. With the significant exception in England of statutory arbitration in the County Court anyone who seeks to enforce his rights by litigation must expect the litigation to be conducted in public. But there are many cases in which one or both parties may quite properly wish to resolve a dispute with as little publicity as possible; and in some cases this facility is a very important advantage that arbitration can offer. This privacy may be infringed if one party is or becomes dissatisfied with the arbitration process and seeks to involve the courts. However, such cases amount to a very small proportion of arbitrations.

2–08 The circumstances in which national courts may intervene in arbitration are moving towards standardisation, due in large part to the impact of the New York Convention of 1958, the UNCITRAL Model Law, and the UNCITRAL Rules (see Appendices 3–6). However, few countries have adopted the Model Law in an unqualified form and others which have drafted new legislation with the Model Law in mind have modified aspects of it, including the grounds upon which court intervention can be sought.

[2] *Arbitration*, December 1982, p. 98.

Differences between arbitration and litigation

Choice of tribunal

The freedom to choose the tribunal is an important advantage that arbitration has over litigation. The parties can take into account the personality, professional qualifications, experience, availability and cost of possible arbitrators before committing themselves. Even where the arbitration arises under an arbitration clause entered into before any dispute has arisen, and even if the parties cannot agree upon the selection of the tribunal, the appointor will in practice have regard to all these factors before making the appointment. In litigation, on the other hand, the vagaries of the court lists may result in an action being heard after a long delay by a judge with no experience in the field in which the dispute arises. In some parts of the world it is clear that the court system is quite unable to cope with modern commercial disputes and not infrequently there are difficulties caused by corruption and lack of independence of the judiciary. These difficulties are not confined to the developing world. The quality, speed and cost of obtaining redress in the courts of those countries which are members of the European Union varies considerably, as anyone who has attempted to bring a commercial law suit in, for example, Italy, Greece or Spain is well aware. **2–09**

The tribunal may be of mixed disciplines

In arbitration the composition of the tribunal is a matter for the parties to decide, provided that they can agree. So if they wish they can arrange a mixed tribunal, *e.g.* three technical experts from different disciplines, or two experts and a lawyer, or one expert with a legal assessor. **2–10**

However, in many arbitrations the parties do not choose the tribunal, because they cannot agree. Nonetheless, the parties opt for arbitration because, on the domestic scene, they believe that they will end up with a trade experienced arbitrator, probably appointed by a trade body; while in international arbitration it is the parties' reluctance or inability to agree on a court system to have jurisdiction over the dispute, that drives them to other forms of dispute resolution, including arbitration. In both the domestic and the international scene, there is also the expectation of finality and comparative economy; and finality, at least, is usually achieved. **2–11**

Control of the preparations

Another important difference arises from the fact that the arbitrator controls the preparations for hearing. Indeed under the Arbitration Act 1996[3] he is actively encouraged to do so, whereas in most cases the judge does not. Hitherto, few judges in the English legal system have dealt with the interlocutory stages of the cases that they try (Commercial Court judges and Official Referees try to be **2–12**

[3] See paras 2–36 *et seq.*, below.

an exception) though Lord Woolf's proposals for case management are likely to change this. An arbitrator is involved in each case during its interlocutory stages. If he makes proper use of his powers he has the opportunity to shape the preparations so as to eliminate unnecessary costs. In particular he can direct the advocates, the experts and even the parties to get to grips with identifying what the issues really are and how best to present them. He can decide a preliminary issue quickly; or it may be enough if he merely indicates his provisional views. In this way both the issues themselves, and the costs that have to be incurred in preparing for them, can be greatly reduced.

Technical evidence shorter before a technical arbitrator

2–13 If the arbitrator is a technical rather than a legal arbitrator and is an expert in the field in which the dispute arises—as to the merchantable quality of a machine, the strength of concrete structures, the quality of woollen cloth, or the applicability of an exception for subsidence in a buildings insurance policy for damage to a house—evidence before him should, and in most cases will, take a different form from the evidence given before a judge. The fact that they are addressing an expert should raise the question whether expert evidence is needed at all, shorten the length of any expert evidence which has to be given, shorten the time required for the experts to express their respective views and may even determine the nature of the hearing—is a legal presentation necessary?

Speed of decision-making

2–14 To a much larger extent than is generally realised, the rate of progress of an arbitration is in the control of the parties. They can take availability into account when choosing the arbitrator or arbitrators; they cannot do this in litigation. In particular, if they are content to be represented by technical men rather than by lawyers, and to have a technical arbitrator, they should be able to get a hearing far earlier than they could in court.

Wider choice of representation

2–15 If a private individual goes to court, and does not wish to conduct the case himself, he must be represented by one or more lawyers. In England, the extension to solicitors of rights of audience does not affect this point, because in practice most cases (other than the smallest) will require the services of two lawyers, one to prepare it and the other to present it. From the points of view both of speed and of cost, it will matter little whether one of the two is a barrister/trial lawyer.

2–16 In arbitration there are no restrictions upon a party's choice of representatives. While this has always been the rule, there have been occasional cases in domestic English arbitration where arbitrators refused to recognise the authority or role of a particular chosen representative. The matter is now resolved by section 36 of the 1996 Act.

Formalities

Flexibility of representation has been increased in England by what are called the Direct Access Rules. Under these rules, various professionals can instruct barristers direct in connection with arbitration proceedings. This direct access to the English Bar has long been available to foreign lawyers. Equally in international cases there are no restrictions on representation. However, such arbitrations are usually conducted by lawyers. 2–17

It is unusual in an English domestic arbitration for evidence of specific authority to be requested for a representative. However, in international arbitrations it is usual at an early stage for each side's principal representative to produce a power of attorney from the party. It is suggested that under most procedural laws, there would be some obligation on the representative to notify the tribunal and the other party if that power was modified or rescinded, either by the voluntary act of the party or by operation of law such as bankruptcy or liquidation. 2–18

Costs

The parties have to pay the arbitrator; whereas until recently court fees were merely nominal. This is a factor making arbitration more expensive. If the arbitration mirrors litigation, with a full scale hearing and lawyers on each side, it is likely to be appreciably more expensive than corresponding litigation. But now the arbitrator has the duty to keep the party-incurred costs within reasonable bounds and can do so because of his ability to control the preparations, because of the variety of procedures open to him, because he can cap recoverable costs under section 65 and because he is likely to be very experienced in arbitrations of the particular kind. An encouragement to an arbitrator to exercise his powers to control the length and therefore the cost of an arbitration can be generated by agreeing a lump sum fee with him, to cover the whole of his work up to and including the award. 2–19

Moreover, the decision of an arbitrator is more likely to be final than the corresponding decision of a first instance judge. The grounds for court intervention in an arbitration or an award are usually (and certainly so in England) much more constrained than the grounds of appeal from the judge; unless, of course, the parties have agreed to remove some of the constraints. 2–20

Moreover, if the parties have themselves chosen the arbitrator, the loser is more likely to accept his decision. Equally the arbitrator may be of such eminence that the parties are content to accept his decision without attempting to appeal. 2–21

Ease of enforcement

The enforcement of arbitral awards is dealt with in paragraph 2–882 onwards, but in general it is easier to enforce an award abroad then to enforce a court judgment. This is because most countries in the world have acceded to the New York Convention of 1958; whereas enforcement of court judgments is dependent either upon specific countries with reciprocal enforcement conventions or treat- 2–22 ies or upon the courts of one jurisdiction being prepared in the interests of comity to enforce by action the judgment of the court of another Sovereign State. The United Kingdom is a party to many conventions and treaties, but even so the network of jurisdictions available to United Kingdom parties under such agreements is far narrower than under the New York Convention.

When is litigation preferable?

Where one or both parties want legal aid

2–23 Legal aid is the name given to a system in England or Wales whereby the state funds a party bringing or resisting claims. The system is very limited and only really relevant to individuals of modest means. It is not available to corporate bodies at all. At present legal aid is not available in arbitration. If court annexed arbitration is introduced, legal aid ought then to be as available to the parties as in litigation. The non-availability of legal aid is not a ground upon which court proceedings will be stayed.

Multi-party disputes

2–24 In disputes between more than two parties, where the parties have not already contracted[4] for a consolidated arbitration (*e.g.* as in some JCT forms used in the construction industry), and the parties will not agree to arbitratiion, going to court is the only way of getting interlocking disputes resolved by the same tribunal. The courts of many countries have extensive powers, by way of third party procedure, consolidation of actions, and directions that actions be heard together, to ensure that interlocking disputes are heard (together or consecutively) by the same judge. Some jurisdictions, *e.g.* The Netherlands and Hong Kong empower the courts to consolidate arbitrations. Arbitrators and judges in England have no such powers (though an eminent English judge has said this lacuna is deplorable).[5] Institutional rules provide an opportunity to advance this aspect of arbitration.

Class actions

2–25 Where a number of actions raise substantially similar issues, such that a decision in one of them will probably enable the parties in the others to compromise their dispute, litigation will often be preferable. Moreover the decision of a judge is public and accessible, and therefore is likely to be followed by other judges and arbitrators deciding the same point.

[4] For drafting suggestions for a clause providing for determination of disputes between related contracts see drafting suggestion No. 55 in Appendix 1, below.

[5] Staughton L.J. in *The Amazonia* [1990] 1 Lloyd's Rep 240.

Authoritative decision required on common form contract

Similarly, where there is a difficult question of interpretation of a common form contract, or of the application of a common form contract to some event which affects a large number of similar contracts or the operation of a market, it may well be preferable to obtain an authoritative ruling of the courts on the point. Perhaps the best example in recent years is the scandal of Lloyd's. While comparable decisions can be made in arbitration and may well benefit from any technical expertise that the tribunal has, they have no general binding effect. In any event they may be appealable so that the case would ultimately come to the courts. It is the court's decision that will have the general effect. 2–26

County Court Arbitration

The County Court provides an arbitration scheme for disputes where (broadly speaking) the claim is less than £3,000.[6] It is always open to the parties to agree to refer disputes involving larger amounts. It is a statutory system and is obligatory, although the district judge has the power in limited cases to order trial in court. 2–27

Arbitration compared with determination by a third person acting as an expert

A contract may provide that disputes arising under it are to be resolved by some third person acting not as arbitrator but as an expert. Such provisions are used for example in the oil and gas industry for periodical redetermination of interests in unitised fields; in commercial real estate transactions; and in corporate valuations of shares or assets. Unless the contract or the accepted practice in disputes of that kind otherwise provides (which it frequently does), the third party so appointed is under no obligation to receive evidence or submissions and is entitled to arrive at his decision solely upon the results of his own expertise and investigations. The procedure involved is not arbitration, and relevant local statutes regulating arbitration will usually not apply to it. In considering when this procedure is preferable to arbitration as a method of resolving a particular dispute the following differences between them will first be discussed. 2–28

Material on which the decision will be made

Where a dispute is resolved by a third person acting as an expert, the primary material on which he acts is his own knowledge and experience, supplemented if he thinks fit by his own investigations and/or by material (which need not conform to rules of "evidence") put before him by either party. An arbitrator on the other hand, acts primarily on material put before him by the parties. 2–29

[6] See Pt 9, below.

Speed

2–30 Unless the contract under which he is appointed otherwise provides, an independent third party expert may make his determination without receiving evidence or arguments from the parties and is not bound to follow any set procedures. An arbitrator (except in the anomalous class of "look-sniff" arbitrations, as to which see paragraph 3–140, below) cannot. So third-party expert determination, if conducted without representations from the parties, is likely to be very much quicker. However, the determination is not an Award for New York Convention or domestic enforcement purposes, and accordingly enforcement overseas can raise problems.

Costs

2–31 If the parties do not have to instruct experts or lawyers to submit facts or opinions or arguments, the procedure is inherently cheaper than arbitration; except, again, for the anomalous class of "look-sniff" arbitrations.

Thoroughness

2–32 Third party expert determination may involve a less comprehensive investigation. Only one mind will be brought to bear on the problem. There will be no discovery of documents; there will not normally be any oral "evidence" or oral submissions. So in consequence, the justice may be rougher than might be the case in more formal procedures.

Clear rules of procedure

2–33 In many countries the relevant statutes and the decisions upon them have produced a well-defined procedure for arbitration with which many lawyers, as well as arbitrators, are familiar. But in most countries there are no statutory rules, and few decided cases, governing the procedure for determination by an independent third party expert. However, there may be trade or professional codes which give some guidance.[7]

No auxiliary powers in the court

2–34 The powers of the English courts to assist arbitrators in the exercise of their function are not available to aid a determination by a third-party expert. Thus witnesses cannot be subpoenaed; no order can be made for inspection of the property of persons who are not parties; the costs of the third party cannot be assessed by the court; the determination cannot be enforced as if it were a judgment of the court, as can an arbitration award (see paragraphs 2–825 *et seq.*

[7] *e.g.* in England the Guidance Notes for Surveyors acting as Arbitrators or as Independent Experts in Rent Review, published by the Royal Institution of Chartered Surveyors. Reprinted with a commentary in *Handbook of Rent Review* (Sweet & Maxwell).

below) and the procedures for enforcing an award in other jurisdictions[8] are not available.

Decision on point of law not binding

There is no right of appeal equivalent to the limited right of appeal on a point of law given (for example) by the Act. However, in some circumstances the determination can be set aside by the court, *e.g.* for fraud, or collusion, or because the determination is outside the terms of reference,[9] *i.e.* the expert has exceeded his instructions. Some contracts also provide that the expert's determination may be set aside for manifest error.[10] It should be noted that the power of the court is either to uphold or set aside; the court has no power to vary or remit the expert's determination. 2–35

2. The Arbitration Act 1996 and the UNCITRAL Model Law

In England the Arbitration Act 1996 came into force on January 31, 1997. It is referred to in this book either by its full name, or as "the 1996 Act". It applies to all arbitrations commenced after January 31, 1997 and, by agreement, can be applied to any arbitration commenced before that date. 2–36

The Mustill report and the UNCITRAL Model Law

The Arbitration Act 1996 is a statute without precedent in English arbitration law. It has not merely consolidated the principal Acts of 1950, 1975 and 1979 and codified the more important principles of English arbitration law; by the standards of traditional English parliamentary drafting it has done so in a radically innovative and unconventional way. Various improvements have been made to the law in the interests of clarity and party autonomy: and, importantly, certain statutory duties have been imposed upon tribunals and parties. 2–37

The new Act has its genesis in the report of the Departmental Advisory Com- 2–38

[8] See, *e.g.* Redfern and Hunter, *International Commercial Arbitration.*

[9] See, *e.g. Nikko Hotels (U.K.) Ltd v. MEPC* [1991] 28 E.G. 36, Ch.D. or *Jones v. Sherwood Computer Services*, *The Times*, February 14, 1990.

[10] *Heald Foods v. Hyde Dairies* (Potter J. unreported); *Conoco Ltd & Others v. Phillips Petroleum Company (U.K.) Ltd & Others*, Commercial Court (1996), unreported.

mittee (DAC) published in June 1989 and commonly known as the Mustill Report after its chairman, Lord Mustill. The DAC was appointed in 1984 in order to advise the Secretary of State for Trade and Industry whether the UNCITRAL Model Law should be enacted.

2–39 The Model Law establishes a regime for international commercial arbitration and reflects modern thinking and practice amongst international commercial arbitrators and practitioners. Although it has been enacted in only a handful of jurisdictions, it has undoubtedly influenced those concerned with the preparation of legislation in many more jurisdictions; and the 1996 Act is no exception.

2–40 The Mustill Report recommended that England should not enact the Model Law because, so the Report argued, to do so would be detrimental to English arbitration practice as it had developed over centuries by statutory enactment and decided cases.

2–41 Although these criticisms of the Model Law were somewhat strongly expressed, the Mustill Report was regarded in many quarters as conservative and timid. The criticisms made of the Model Law in the Report were somewhat weakened by the fact that contemporaneously with its rejection for England and Wales, the Model Law was recommended as suitable for enactment in Scotland.

2–42 But the Mustill Report did accept that even for the expert arbitration specialist and sophisticated commercial lawyer, it was often extremely difficult and at times almost a matter of chance, to ascertain precisely what the English law of arbitration was, with resulting confusion and uncertainty. This was felt to be detrimental to English arbitration and particularly to discourage the foreign lawyer and overseas businessman from designating London as a preferred venue for the resolution of international commercial disputes. The Mustill Committee was driven principally by the desire expressed in paragraph 109 of its report to make proposals which would serve to keep London in the vanguard of the preferred venues for international commercial arbitration. It would thus contribute valuable invisible earnings and help to maintain London as one of the leading financial and mercantile centres of the world.

Paragraph 108

2–43 Mustill rejected both the Model Law and an American-style Restatement of arbitration law. The Report concluded:

> "We need first a rational, logical, comprehensive, exposition of the more important contents of existing statute law. It will be time, then, to see where we should (or can) go from there."

The Mustill Committee made certain recommendations which are succinctly expressed in paragraph 108 of its Report as follows:

> "In these circumstances we recommend an intermediate solution, in the shape of a new Act with a subject-matter so selected as to make the essentials of at least the existing statutory arbitration law tolerably accessible,

without calling for a lengthy period of planning and drafting, or prolonged parliamentary debate. It should in particular have the following features:

(a) It should comprise a statement in statutory form of the more important principles of the English law of arbitration, statutory and (to the extent practicable) common law.
(b) It should be limited to those principles whose existence and effect are uncontroversial.
(c) It should be set out in a logical order, and expressed in language which is sufficiently clear and free from technicalities to be readily comprehensible to the layman.
(d) It should in general apply to domestic and international arbitrations alike, although there may have to be exceptions to take account of treaty obligations.
(e) It should not be limited to the subject-matter of the Model Law.
(f) It should embody such of our proposals for legislation as have by then been enacted: see paragraph 100.
(g) Consideration should be given to ensuring that any such new statute should, so far as possible, have the same structure and language as the Model Law, so as to enhance its accessibility to those who are familiar with the Model Law.''

The DAC as a matter of policy duly gave the consideration contemplated by sub-clause (g) of paragraph 108 and endorsed the approach of endeavouring to follow the same structure and language of the Model Law. In practice it proved easier to adopt the structure and express the spirit of the Model Law, than to adopt wholesale the specific language of specific provisions. Virtually every article of the Model Law is reflected in a section of the 1996 Act, in the same order and sometimes the same language, even if limited to key phrases. The result is far more than the ''intermediate solution'' contemplated by paragraph 108. 2–44

The recommendations of paragraph 108 were accepted by the then Secretary of State for Trade and Industry and various drafts both official and private were prepared and were the subject of extensive consultation and debate. A broad consensus was achieved as to the requirements of the arbitral community both here and abroad. 2–45

The structure of the 1996 Act and its main principles

It is a feature of the Model Law that it proceeds in a logical way from the definition of the arbitration agreement to the recognition and enforcement of the arbitral award. The 1996 Act follows the same logic. 2–46

The principle-based system

Unusually in a common law context, the law of arbitration is underpinned by general principles expressed as statutory duties, in a manner more usually found 2–47 in codified law systems. The introduction of this approach is perhaps the most remarkable aspect of the 1996 Act. These principles expressly apply to the process of arbitration itself as well as to the tribunal and the parties.

The principles underlying the arbitral process

2–48 Three principles are set out in the 1996 Act. The most important (although it is only mentioned second) is party autonomy:

> "The parties [shall] be free to agree how their disputes are resolved, subject only to such safeguards as are necessary in the public interest."[11]

Secondly, the role of the court is severely restricted:

> ". . . the Court [shall] not intervene except as provided by this Part."[12]

Thirdly, the object of arbitration is expressed to be to obtain

> "the fair resolution of disputes by an impartial tribunal without unnecessary delay or expense."[13]

Generally speaking it is for the parties to agree on the extent, greater or smaller, to which recourse can be had to the court.

Applicability of the principles

2–49 These principles are the foundation of Part 1 (Arbitration pursuant to an Arbitration Agreement) of the 1996 Act, and all its provisions are to be construed accordingly. There will therefore be a touchstone by which any proposed use of any of the provisions can be tested. Is the proposed use tending towards or away from the object of arbitration? Does it recognise or derogate from the principle of party autonomy? Does it limit the court's intervention to that spelt out in the 1996 Act or does it appear to go beyond? Answers in accord with the first of each of the above alternatives would suggest the proposed use was acceptable. Answers in accord with the second of each of the above alternatives must cause one to look suspiciously at the proposed use.

These principles apply to the tribunal

2–50 These principles are obligatory and apply to everything a tribunal does (or does not) do in the exercise of its function. As section 33 of the 1996 Act makes clear, the arbitral tribunal is bound to act fairly and impartially as between the parties. Each party must have a reasonable opportunity of putting his case and

[11] s.1(b).
[12] s.1(c).
[13] s.1(a).

dealing with that of his opponent. Equally, the tribunal must adopt procedures suitable to the circumstances of the particular case, and must avoid unnecessary delay or expense. By this route the tribunal is bound to provide a fair means for the resolution of the matter falling to be determined.

Application to the parties

Section 40, an innovative and extremely important provision, imposes on each party a duty to comply without delay with the directions and other orders of the tribunal as to the running of the Arbitration. The parties are also obliged, where appropriate, to take any necessary steps to obtain a decision of the court on a preliminary question of jurisdiction or law. 2–51

This is by stark contrast to litigation, where if he so wishes a defendant can with impunity lie low and say and do nothing if the plaintiff fails to progress the proceedings; though Lord Woolf's proposed reforms are likely to change this. 2–52

Domestic and international arbitrations

The legislative framework for arbitration in many countries distinguishes between "domestic" and "international" arbitration, and has different rules for each. Secondly, the definitions of "domestic" and "international" are not standardised, and care must be taken to determine the particular definition utilised by whichever legal system one is looking at. The distinction between domestic and non-domestic arbitration as drawn by the 1996 Act is no longer in force, principally due to doubts as to its validity in European Law.[14] Thus the same tests apply for stays of legal proceedings and agreements excluding the appeal jurisdiction of the court to both domestic and non-domestic arbitrations. Also the statutory powers and obligations of arbitrators and parties are exactly the same in both cases. Examples of different distinctions drawn by other jurisdictions are the Netherlands Arbitration Act 1986 and the French Laws of 1980 and 1981 on domestic and international arbitration respectively. 2–53

The seat of the arbitration

The seat of the arbitration is nevertheless a concept of considerable interest and importance to the practitioner of international arbitration. Section 3 of the 1996 Act provides that the seat of the arbitration means the juridical seat of the arbitration designated: 2–54

"(a) by the parties to the arbitration agreement, or
(b) by any arbitral or other institution or person vested by the parties with powers in that regard, or

[14] See Arbitration Act (Commencement No. 1) Order 1996 (S.I. 1996 No. 3146).

(c) by the arbitral tribunal if so authorised by the parties, or determined, in the absence of any such designation, having regard to the parties' agreement and all the relevant circumstances.''

2–55 Where the parties have not expressly designated a particular jurisdiction as the seat of the arbitration, then the arbitral tribunal or the court will have to determine the seat by applying the proper law of the arbitration agreement.[15] In a wholly English arbitration this question does not arise; the seat is clearly England absent express agreement to the contrary.

The role of institutions

2–56 An integral part of supporting party autonomy is the recognition of the role and importance of arbitral institutions. The 1996 Act gives full recognition and effect to the agreement of the parties to arbitrate according to institutional rules and subject to institutional supervision.[16]

2–57 The power of the arbitral institutions is also emphasised by the requirement that, before a court will exercise its supportive or supervisory powers, the agreed procedures of the institution must have been followed.

2–58 The leading England arbitral institutions are reviewing and, where appropriate, amending their institutional rules in the light of the new statute. Three matters upon which institutions might concentrate are rules designed to give effect to section 39, the power to make provisional awards, which can only be done by agreement; section 47, the power to make awards on different issues; and section 35, provision for consolidation in appropriate cases.

Statutory immunity

2–59 An important aspect of the support given to arbitral institutions is the grant of statutory immunity which is given by section 29 to arbitrators themselves and by section 74 to institutions.

2–60 The decision to give such statutory immunity and thereby remove the uncertainty as to immunity at common law, which had been provoked principally by the House of Lords decision in *Sutcliffe v. Thackrah* in 1974,[17] was a pure decision of policy. The DAC took note of the fact that, as the judicial right of review of arbitral conduct and arbitral awards was reduced, so institutions and arbitrators could be exposed more and more to personal suits. This was a particular concern in relation to the United States. It was felt that, given that most

15 *Sumitomo Heavy Industries v. Oil and Natural Gas Commission* [1994] 1 Lloyd's Rep. 45.

16 See, *e.g.* s.4(3).

17 [1974] 1 All E.R. 859 (See also the cases discussed in the February 1994 DAC Consultation Paper, *e.g. United Co-operatives v. Sun Alliance* [1987] 1 EGLR 126 (Mr Justice Hoffmann) and *Pratt v. Swanmore Builders* [1980] 2 Lloyd's Rep. 504 (Mr Justice Pain), where doubts were raised as to the immunity of institutions and appointing authorities.

institutions concerned with arbitration live something of a hand to mouth existence, it was unreasonable on public policy grounds to expect them to bear the cost of defending what might be an increasing number of challenges to the exercise of their function.

Procedural freedom

It is a major feature of the 1996 Act that it does not attempt to prescribe for arbitrators and parties a fixed and certain procedure. On the contrary, the 1996 Act expressly encourages arbitrators and the parties, consistent with the objectives of section 1 and the general duties of section 33 and section 40 to adopt, in the words of section 33(b) "procedures suitable to the circumstances of the case, avoiding unnecessary delay or expense". That is the yardstick against which arbitrators must assess the procedure to be followed and, subject to observing the rules of natural justice, and any agreement which the parties may themselves have reached, arbitrators are given the power to determine the procedures to be followed. **2–61**

In particular, arbitrators are neither bound to follow adversarial procedures, nor to apply strict rules of evidence as to the admissibility, relevance or weight of any evidence placed before them. Thus, the 1996 Act renders academic the discussion in the second edition of this work as to the power of arbitrators, absent agreement to the contrary, to depart from English adversarial principles. The way is now clear (even assuming it was not before) for arbitrators and parties to devise radical and innovative solutions to limit cost and reduce delay. The freedom given to arbitrators and the parties and the general duties imposed upon them to achieve the objective of a fair, expeditious and economic resolution of the dispute by the most efficient procedural means is buttressed by a number of other provisions of the 1996 Act which seek that same end. **2–62**

Jurisdiction: Separability: Kompetenz Kompetenz

The 1996 Act, for example, endeavours to cure many of the vices attached to challenges to jurisdiction, a feature which bedevils the conduct of so much arbitration both in this country and abroad. The cardinal principles of separability and Kompetenz Kompetenz are firmly established in the 1996 Act. Separability is found in section 7. The doctrine is a legal fiction essential to the efficient working of the arbitration process and developed in England in a long line of cases from the landmark decision of the House of Lords in *Heyman v. Darwin*,[18] culminating in the decision of the Court of Appeal in *Harbour Assurance v.* **2–63**

[18] [1942] 1 All E.R. 337.

Kansa[19] which for the first time established the principle as now enshrined in section 7.

2–64 The related doctrine of Kompetenz Kompetenz, namely the ability of the tribunal to decide upon its own jurisdiction, is found separately in the 1996 Act in section 30.

2–65 It is to be hoped that these two sections, combined with the procedures for challenge to jurisdiction found in sections 31 and 32 (loss of right to object), when taken in conjunction with section 67 and section 73, will be an effective barrier to the delays which have occurred, particularly in domestic arbitration by reason of challenges to arbitrators' jurisdiction. This is notwithstanding the clear guidance as to arbitrators' powers given by Mr Justice Devlin (as he then was) in the *Christopher Brown* case.[20] There is no doubt that challenges to the jurisdiction have often been an abuse of the arbitral process and have caused substantial delay and extra cost.

Power to the arbitrators

2–66 The principles of separability and the power given to arbitrators to decide in the first instance upon their own jurisdiction, is an example of one of the main purposes of the 1996 Act, which is to vest in the arbitrators, rather than in the courts, as much power over the conduct of the arbitration as is consistent with public policy. The powers of arbitrators are better defined and strengthened. The power to order a party to give security for the costs of the arbitration, now taken away from the courts and conferred on the arbitrator, is an example; see paragraphs 2–102 *et seq.* below.

Default provisions

2–67 Further, there are important powers given to the arbitrators to act in default, most notably in section 41 of the 1996 Act, where, subject to the agreement of the parties, the tribunal is given a range of powers, including the power to strike out, first given by the Courts and Legal Services Act 1990, in the event that there has been inordinate and inexcusable delay on the part of the claimant in pursuing the claim which will give rise to substantial risk of injustice or prejudice. If a party fails to attend or make written submissions where that is the means of resolution determined upon, then the tribunal is entitled to continue the proceedings in the absence either of the party, or of a written submission.

2–68 There are provisions entitling the tribunal to make peremptory orders and to proceed to make awards if peremptory orders are ignored. The 1996 Act therefore gives arbitrators and parties clear guidance as to the powers exercisable in the event of default and it is to be hoped that arbitrators will make robust and purposeful use of them when the occasion demands.

[19] [1993] Q.B. 701.
[20] *Christopher Brown v. Genossenschaft Österreichischer Waldbesitzer* [1954] 1 Q.B. 8.

The role of the courts

Central to the development of the English law of arbitration has been the relationship between the arbitral process and the court. Traditionally, the court's role has been both supportive and supervisory: and so it remains. The supportive powers are well and comprehensively set out in the 1996 Act. Thus, there are extensive provisions governing the appointment[21] of arbitrators designed to give effect to the intention of the parties as to the kind of arbitrator they wish to appoint and to ensure the impartiality or mental or physical competence of the tribunal, as well as to enforce the right of the parties to have the tribunal act with all due dispatch. **2–69**

In a series of sections from section 42 onwards, the court is given a wide range of supportive powers from the enforcement of peremptory orders, to securing the attendance of witnesses, the provision of necessary evidence and the making of protective orders whether by injunction or otherwise. The court may also, by section 45 of the 1996 Act, determine any question of law arising in the course of the proceedings which the court is satisfied substantially affects the rights of one or more of the parties. But the right to do this may be excluded by agreement and, in any event, may only be exercised if an application is made by agreement of all the other parties to the proceedings, or is made with the permission of the tribunal and if the court is satisfied that the determination of the question is likely to produce substantial savings in cost and that the application was made without delay. There is also another specific example of the general principle of expedition and economy in section 45(4) which permits the tribunal to continue with the arbitral proceedings whilst an application to the court is pending. Thus there need be no delay. **2–70**

Security for costs

Section 38 of the 1996 Act vests exclusively in the tribunal the power to order security for costs.[22] The decision of the House of Lords in *Ken-Ren*[23] gave rise to considerable controversy amongst international arbitration practitioners. The concern was two-fold, first that the English courts should seek to intervene to order security for costs in international cases subject to institutional rules (in the case of *Ken-Ren* to the rules of the ICC) and, secondly, because in so doing the English court was applying to an *international arbitration* principles with respect to the award of costs which apply in *English domestic* litigation. Section 38 of the 1996 Act vests the power to give security exclusively in the tribunal and further, makes it clear that in exercising that power the arbitrator is not bound to follow the procedures and practices of the English courts. Instead, the **2–71**

[21] See ss.15 to 27: these provisions are extensive, necessarily so, given the system of umpires and arbitrators which is a feature of commodity and maritime arbitration in London. See also s.19 which was designed to ensure that the court takes full account of the wishes of the parties.

[22] s.38(3).

[23] *S.A. Coppee Lavalin NV v. Ken-Ren Chemicals and Fertilisers* [1994] 2 W.L.R. 631.

arbitrator is subject to the overriding duty to act fairly and reasonably, having regard to the objective of arbitration set out in section 1 and to the general duties imposed upon him in section 33.

The supervisory powers of the courts

2–72 The supervisory powers of the court are also clearly defined in sections 66 to 71. An award may be enforced by leave of the court as though it were a judgment of the court, but this shall not be done where the award is defective in form or substance so that it is incapable of enforcement or, as one would expect, enforcement would be contrary to public policy. There is a further exception against enforcement where the award was given by a tribunal which lacks substantive jurisdiction.

Serious irregularity

2–73 Section 68 dispenses with the old rubric of misconduct and instead substitutes a provision for challenging the award on grounds of what is termed a "serious irregularity". By section 68(2) "serious irregularity" is defined as meaning one or more defined mistakes by the tribunal which have caused substantial injustice to the applicant. Those mistakes can range from a failure of the tribunal to comply with its general duty to act fairly and impartially, under section 33, to the making of an award which is uncertain or ambiguous. By section 68(3) the court, if satisfied that there has been serious irregularity may remit the award to the tribunal in whole or in part for reconsideration, set it aside in whole or in part, or declare the award to be of no effect in whole or in part. These latter powers must not be exercised unless the court is satisfied that it would be inappropriate to remit the matters in question to the tribunal for reconsideration. The effect of section 68 has been to replace the previous provisions on setting aside and rescission for misconduct with a comprehensive and closed regime for court interference. Only if a party comes within the specific categories of serious irregularity in section 68(2) will the discretion of the court under section 68(3) fall to be exercised. One important result will be that the old concept of technical misconduct will disappear.

Appeal on a point of law

2–74 Section 69 creates a right of appeal on a point of law and seeks to give effect in statutory form to the guidelines laid down by the House of Lords in *The Nema*[24] when their Lordships, particularly in the speech of Lord Diplock, pronounced on the corresponding provisions of the 1979 Act. The key provision is that the right of appeal shall only be granted, if on the basis of the facts found in the award, (i) the decision of the tribunal on the question of law is obviously wrong, or (ii) the question of law is one of general public importance and the

[24] [1980] 3 All E.R. 117, affirmed [1981] 2 All E.R. 1030.

decision of the tribunal is at least open to serious doubt. This is because, despite the agreement of the parties to resolve the matter by arbitration, it is just and proper in all the circumstances for the court to determine the question. The policy of the 1979 Act as interpreted by the courts in a series of landmark decisions in the 1980s remains fundamentally unchanged, but the opportunity has been taken to improve the language of the 1979 Act, to tighten the right to appeal somewhat more[25] and to include in statutory form *The Nema* guidelines.

Consolidation

The problem of consolidation is highly controversial and, despite considerable pressure from the construction industry and to some extent from the maritime industry, it was thought by the DAC that the topic was too difficult to legislate for and that it involved offending the fundamental principle upon which arbitration rests, namely that it is a consensual process. The DAC was not prepared to recommend that parties should be forced to arbitrate with others with whom they had not agreed to do so. However, section 35, whilst not providing for mandatory consolidation, or giving the court a discretion to consolidate, contains a statement of principle, emphasising that the parties are free to agree that the arbitral proceedings shall be consolidated with other arbitral proceedings, or that concurrent hearings may be held on such terms as may be agreed. **2–75**

Privacy and confidentiality

This topic is discussed in detail in paragraphs 2–656 *et seq.* below. As the Final Report of the DAC makes clear, the statute, while codifying rather important aspects of English arbitration law, does not seek to enact principles of privacy and confidentiality which have been generally accepted in this country as fundamental to the successful conduct of arbitration. Whilst the English courts in cases such as *Eastern Saga, Dolling-Baker v. Merrett, Hassneh v. Mew, Hyundai Engineering v. Active, Ins Company v. Lloyd's Syndicate* and *London & Leeds Estates Limited v. Paribas Limited* have sought to define limits of privacy and confidentiality, the existence of a general principle has been powerfully questioned by no less an authority than the High Court of Australia in the case of *Esso/BHP v. Plowman.*[26] As the Final Report makes clear, the DAC therefore considered that "the formulation of any statutory principles would be likely to create new impediments to the practice of English arbitration and, in particular, to add to English litigation on the issue". Far from solving a difficulty, the DAC was firmly of the view that it would create new ones. Accordingly the development and limitation of general principles of privacy and confidentiality must be left to pragmatic development in the courts. **2–76**

[25] A difference is that the rights of appeal are now limited by s.70(2) and (3). Another difference is the removal of the special categories.

[26] (1995) 128 A.L.R. 391

Conclusion

2–77 The 1996 Act is undoubtedly a major step forward in the history of arbitration law reform. It is clear and comprehensive, though inevitably many of its provisions and statutory duties will be the subject of interpretation by the courts in the next few years.

2–78 It is also inevitable that the courts will draw on the rich body of precedent which exists when interpreting the new provisions. But the intention could not be clearer; namely to vest in competent arbitrators and the parties the power and the obligation to promote the fair resolution of disputes, expeditiously and economically. It is greatly to be hoped that arbitrators and parties will take full advantage of the freedom which the new statute provides. It is the principal purpose of this book to indicate how they may do so.

3. The Arbitration Agreement

May relate to existing or potential dispute

2–79 An agreement to arbitrate may be made in respect of existing disputes between the parties or in respect of disputes that may occur in the future. In each case the agreement may be an "arbitration agreement" as defined below. The distinction between existing and future disputes is no longer important in the context of a domestic arbitration. If the parties to a domestic arbitration wish to contract out of the right to seek the court's assistance on a preliminary point of law, and/or the right to challenge the award in court on a point of law, they may do so in the same way as parties to a non-domestic arbitration agreement. The terms domestic and non-domestic arbitrations have no longer any legal meaning or effect in England.

2–80 Traditionally, an agreement to refer future disputes to arbitration has been referred to as an arbitration agreement. The arbitration agreement may be a wholly separate agreement not forming part of the larger primary agreement between the parties which expresses the purpose of the transaction. However, the usual case is that the arbitration agreement is contained in a clause or clauses of the primary agreement, though for legal purposes it is regarded by virtue of section 7 of the 1996 Act as a separate agreement which can survive the termination of the primary agreement of which it forms part.

2–81 An agreement made after disputes have arisen is traditionally referred to as a submission to arbitration or a submission agreement. It often stands alone: and is lengthy, addressing the particular procedures to be followed.

A well-drafted arbitration agreement will encompass both the agreement to arbitrate disputes, and an effective procedure by which this can be done. 2–82

The statutory definition

By section 6 of the 1996 Act in Part I an "arbitration agreement" means an agreement to submit to arbitration present or future disputes whether they are contractual or not. This rather skeletal definition is fleshed out substantially by other provisions of the 1996 Act. 2–83

The arbitration agreement must be in writing. Writing includes the following[27]: 2–84

(a) An agreement in writing, whether or not signed by the parties.
(b) An agreement made by an exchange of communications, provided they are in writing.[28]
(c) An agreement evidenced in writing. This includes an agreement made otherwise than in writing, but recorded by one of the parties or a third party and provided this recording is authorised by the parties.[29] Thus, the record of a secretary or a shorthand writer could suffice.
(d) An exchange of written submissions in legal or arbitral proceedings in which the existence of an agreement is alleged by party A against B, and not denied by B.[30]
(e) Any form of recording constitutes writing.[31] Thus an authorised tape recording of an oral agreement would do.
(f) Finally, reference in an agreement (oral or written) to a written arbitration clause or to a document containing an arbitration clause is sufficient to constitute an arbitration agreement, if the effect of the reference is to make the clause part of the agreement.[32]

Oral agreement to arbitrate

An oral agreement to submit present or future differences to arbitration may be valid and enforceable at common law. But it is not an "arbitration agreement" as defined by the 1996 Act which does not apply to it. It will be subject to many difficulties, both procedural and as regards enforcement of an ultimate award, as compared with the same agreement put into writing. In particular any party 2–85

[27] s.5(1).
[28] s.5(2).
[29] s.5(4).
[30] s.5(5).
[31] s.5(6).
[32] s.6(2).

to such an arbitration may unilaterally revoke the authority he has given to the arbitrator at any time. If an arbitrator is appointed under an oral agreement, he should invite the parties to enter into a written agreement at the outset. Arbitrations under oral submissions are so rare that they will not be separately considered in this work.

2–86 Since an oral agreement is not within the Arbitration Acts, it is highly desirable, though not always essential, that, if during an arbitration the parties agree to extend the jurisdiction of the arbitrator, such agreement should be put into writing.

Consumer arbitration agreements

2–87 The Consumer Arbitration Agreements Act 1988 has been repealed and replaced by sections 89 to 91 of the 1996 Act. Such agreements are dealt with in Part 8 below.

Constituents of an arbitration agreement

Essential constituents—the basic clause

2–88 To constitute an arbitration agreement in a contract, in the sense of an agreement to refer future disputes under the contract to arbitration, it is sufficient (though not desirable) to say merely "disputes to be settled by arbitration". Such a provision, in a written agreement governed by English law, would be an arbitration agreement and its defects of omission could be cured by the court if necessary. But such a clause could give rise to argument on the following, amongst other, matters:

(a) What degree of connection between a dispute and the contract is necessary before the agreement to arbitrate applies to the dispute?
(b) What kind of person is to be appointed as arbitrator?
(c) Who is to appoint him (other than the court) if the parties do not agree?
(d) What procedural rules are to apply to the arbitration?

2–89 The matter is further complicated if the contract is not governed by English Law and where the parties are from different legal jurisdictions. Here there may also be arguments as to what substantive law, and what procedural law, is to govern the arbitration. So it is both common and desirable for an arbitration clause to go into greater detail, and some of the additional constituents are considered below.

Incorporating rules of trade or institutional bodies

2–90 Many trade and professional institutions have published arbitration rules or codes. Most of them are periodically revised so as to meet practical problems as conditions change. In most cases incorporating an appropriate set of rules is likely to produce a result superior to the ad hoc rules of the average draughtsman; and also to save much time in negotiating the precise terms of the arbitration clause. For cases where the adoption of a ready made arbitration code is inappropriate, however, the following are some of the points to be considered in drafting a suitable arbitration clause. (Drafting suggestions for common clauses will be found in Appendix 1, below.)

Number of arbitrators

By section 15 of the 1996 Act the parties are free to agree on the number of arbitrators to form the tribunal. They are also free to agree on whether there is to be a chairman (who will take part in all the activities of the tribunal right from the beginning) or an umpire[33] (who may only be involved in the proceedings in certain circumstances). **2–91**

If the parties' agreement (oddly and undesirably) provides for an even number of arbitrators, it will be understood that an additional arbitrator is to be appointed as a chairman, unless the parties have agreed otherwise.[34] **2–92**

If there is no agreement on number, the tribunal shall be a sole arbitrator.[35] It follows that as a matter of good practice, when drafting an arbitration clause, if it is desired to have more than one arbitrator, the clause should state whether the reference is to be to two arbitrators and a chairman, or to two arbitrators and an umpire. **2–93**

The advantages and disadvantages of a three-man tribunal are considered in paragraphs 2–144 *et seq.* **2–94**

Method of appointment

The arbitration agreement should provide some method of appointing the tribunal, in case the parties are unable to agree on its membership. If the agreement does not so provide, then recourse can be had to section 16 of the 1996 Act. For the process put in place by this section, see paragraph 2–139. But appointment by the court can involve substantial costs and delay, and it is therefore preferable, in most cases, to provide for appointment by an appropriate third party such as the President or Chairman of a trade or professional association; the Chartered Institute of Arbitrators; the London Court of International Arbitration; the International Chamber of Commerce in Paris. A provision that the appointment is to be made by the institution or body will probably suffice; but it is preferable to provide that it should be made by the President or Chairman, as appropriate. It is better still to provide that the appointment shall be made by "the President (or Chairman as the case may be) of the institute or failing him by his duly authorised deputy". This can avoid delay if, for example, the President (or Chairman) is ill or is otherwise unavailable. It should be noted that **2–95**

[33] s.15(1).
[34] s.15(2).
[35] s.15(3).

appointment by an institution can take time. It may also involve considerable expense since some institutions will charge a substantial fee.

Procedural rules

2–96 If the arbitration agreement does not lay down any procedural requirements, and does not incorporate any body of rules which lay down such requirements, the procedure will be in the first place for the parties to agree. If they cannot agree it will be for the tribunal, which is master of its own procedure, to determine.[36] Under the 1996 Act, absent any other agreement of the parties, it may be desirable for arbitration agreements to specify agreed procedures with the objective of ensuring that the procedure is what both parties want. If it is desired to limit the tribunal's discretion as to the procedure, the agreement should specifically say so, *e.g.* by saying that the arbitration shall be conducted on documents only; or that legal representation shall not be allowed.

Award a condition precedent to litigation

2–97 An arbitration clause sometimes contains, or is associated with, a contractual provision known as a *Scott v. Avery* clause,[37] that is, a provision to the effect that the award of an arbitrator is to be a condition precedent to the enforcement of any right under the contract. For the purposes of this book it is sufficient to say that a *Scott v. Avery* clause, like most other clauses in a contract, should clearly specify what is to be the effect of a claimant's failure to obtain an award in his favour. A specimen form of *Scott v. Avery* clause will be found at No. 11 in the drafting suggestions at Appendix 1 below.

National law to be applied

2–98 Where a contract made in England between parties each of whom is a national of, or habitually resident in, England or is a company incorporated in, or whose central management and control is exercised in England, the presumption is that the parties intend the contract to be governed in all its aspects including the conduct of any arbitration by English law. In other cases, where there may be some doubt as to what is intended, the possibility of argument should be eliminated by stating that the arbitration is to be governed by English law.

The substantive law of the arbitration agreement

2–99 The substantive principles of law governing the agreement to arbitrate should be stated if different from the substantive law of the contract. (This is particularly important if the tribunal is to be required to determine disputes *ex aequo et bono*—see paragraph 2–213, below.)

2–100 In any case with any level of internationality, it is very important that the

[36] See, *e.g. Carlisle v. Wimpey* (1980) 15 B.L.R. 109, and s. 33 of the 1996 Act.
[37] See *Scott v. Avery* [1856] 5 H.L. Cas. 811.

contract expressly addresses the question of the governing law or laws. This applies to the contract itself. This is particularly important if it is desired to have a different law to govern the arbitration agreement and yet another law to govern the procedure of arbitration, though such complexities should be avoided.

A failure or ineffectiveness (*e.g.* choosing the law of the United Kingdom—ineffective—as opposed to the law of England or any one of the separate jurisdictions) in so doing may well lead to lengthy and expensive argument as to the appropriate substantive law (which may involve the Rome Convention, among other things, or identifying the jurisdiction with which the contract has the closest connection) and the appropriate procedural law (the starting point is to identify, if possible, where the parties intended the seat of the arbitration to be). **2–101**

"Arbitrator not to be bound by the law" clauses[38]

Arbitration clauses in international commercial contracts and in some domestic contracts sometimes contain a provision that the arbitrators need not apply the law, or a particular system of law. They may say that the arbitrator is "to act as *amiable compositeur*", or is to decide "according to equity and good conscience"; or "according to the customs and usages of the trade" or "so as to interpret this Reinsurance as an honourable engagement, and with a view to effecting the general purpose in a reasonable manner rather than in accordance with a literal interpretation of the language."[39] The existence of these clauses and their discussion in court decisions under English law probably derive from a mistaken belief that applying accepted rules of English law necessitates a strict adherence to the literal meaning of the words of the contract. This is not so, for as Lord Diplock pointed out in *The Antaios*[40]: **2–102**

> "I take this opportunity of restating that, if detailed semantic and syntactical analysis of words in a commercial contract is going to lead to a conclusion that flouts business common sense, it must be made to yield to business common sense."

The matter is now expressly dealt with in the 1996 Act by section 46(1) (b).[41] In any event the primacy given to party autonomy by the 1996 Act would seem to lead to the conclusion set out above. **2–103**

[38] See the discussion in Mustill & Boyd (2nd ed.), pp. 74–86, and the valuable paper by Stewart Boyd, Q.C. in the *Ronald Bernstein Lecture Series 1989* (available from the Chartered Institute of Arbitrators).

[39] See *Home Insurance v. Mentor Insurance* [1989] 3 All E.R. 74.

[40] [1989] 3 All E.R. 233.

[41] The intention of the DAC (para. 223 of the February 1996 Report) is that arbitrators can decide in accordance with such clauses, but the court cannot then determine any question of law.

Venue

2–104 The late Professor Schmitthof once said that to draft an arbitration clause without specifying the venue or seat of the arbitration was an act of professional negligence. It is clearly desirable to specify a venue, thereby indicating the juridical seat of the arbitration, the supportive and supervisory regime of the courts which is available to the parties and the mandatory requirements to which the arbitration will be subject.

Specifying the qualifications of the arbitrator

2–105 If it is desired to have an arbitrator with particular qualifications, it is clearly desirable so to specify in the arbitration agreement. The appointing authority, or in default the court, will thus know clearly the intention of the parties, should they be unable to agree upon a specific individual.

Time limits in the arbitration agreement

2–106 When drafting an arbitration agreement careful consideration should be given whether or not to include a time limit; and if so, what sort of sorts. The three types listed as follows and other matters relevant to time are discussed at greater length in paragraphs 2–123 *et seq.*, below:

(a) the giving of notice of claim;
(b) the giving of notice to appoint an arbitrator;
(c) the commencement of an arbitration.

4. Staying Court Proceedings

Three kinds of jurisdiction to stay

2–107 The policy of the courts and the legislature in recent years has been very much in favour of arbitration and the granting of stays. Indeed, in non-domestic cases where the criteria of section 1 of the 1975 Act (which enacted the New York Convention of 1958) were satisfied, the stay was mandatory. This policy has been taken further by the 1996 Act.

2–108 The existence of a relevant arbitration clause in a contract between parties to a dispute is no impediment to resolving the dispute in court if neither side objects. However, if one party goes to court but the other party wishes to enforce the arbitration agreement, then it is for the latter to seek an order from the court staying court proceedings. Such an order leaves the initiator of the proceedings with no option but to follow the provisions of the arbitration agreement if he wishes there to be a determination on the dispute.

The inherent jurisdiction to stay

The court has an inherent power to stay (*i.e.* to prevent from being taken any further) any proceedings which it considers to be frivolous, vexatious, oppressive, or an abuse of the process of the court. This power is for practical purposes irrelevant in the arbitration context; see sections 1(c) and 9 to 11 of the 1996 Act. **2–109**

Stay under the 1996 Act

The principal sections of the 1996 Act that deal with staying legal proceedings are sections 9, 10 and 11. These sections apply whatever the substantive or procedural law of the arbitration or the underlying agreement.[42] This gives the Act a certain extraterritorial element which in the consultative stages of the Bill was the subject of adverse criticism by foreign lawyers. The precise limits of the court's jurisdiction will no doubt be developed in decided cases. **2–110**

The basic situation which gives rise to relief under this section is as follows. Party A brings court proceedings against Party B. Party B is of the view that the dispute the subject of the proceedings is caught by an arbitration agreement between A and B. In these circumstances, Party B can apply to the court to stay the proceedings.[43] **2–111**

Application must be made before taking a step in the action

Any such application must be made after Party B has formally acknowledged the proceedings, but before taking any substantial step in the action to respond to the substantive dispute (*e.g.* by entering a defence). **2–112**

When court must stay the proceedings

In response to an application to stay which is made at the correct time the court's obligation is clear. It must stay the proceedings[44] unless the agreement is null and void, inoperative or incapable of being performed. The application to stay is not affected by a dispute resolution provision in the arbitration agreement which provides that other dispute resolution procedures must be exhausted before arbitration can commence. **2–113**

For example, an arbitration agreement may prohibit the initiation of the arbitration before there has been an attempt at mediation. At the time of the court **2–114**

[42] Sched. 1 to the 1996 Act.

[43] s.9(1).

[44] s.9(4).

proceedings and the application to stay them, there has been no attempt at mediation. In consequence, if the action is stayed for arbitration it will not be possible to start the arbitration (absent the agreement of the parties) immediately. This is not a ground of objection to the grant of the application to stay.[45]

Provision that arbitration not to be commenced until works completed

2–115 Construction agreements often provide that arbitration shall not be commenced, in the absence of agreement by both parties, until after the works are complete, or some other event (not being a dispute resolution procedure) has occurred. If one party starts court proceedings in relation to a dispute covered by that agreement, can the other party still apply to stay the court proceedings? The 1996 Act does not deal expressly with this situation where the arbitration is delayed pending an event or process which is not a dispute resolution procedure, unless it is (as the authors believe) by way of the application of the general principle expressed in section 9(4).

Where award is a condition precedent to proceedings in Court

2–116 A correlative provision[46] deals with the situation where the agreement between the parties contains a provision whereby an arbitration award is a condition precedent to bringing proceedings, but the court in fact refuses to stay the court proceedings that have been initiated (for example because the application to stay has been made too late). In that event the condition precedent is of no effect.

No provision where no application to stay is made

2–117 Although the 1996 Act deals with the situation where there is a condition precedent clause where the application to stay is unsuccessful, it does not provide for the situation where there is such a condition and no application to stay is made. Can either party object at the end of the court proceedings that the proceedings have been fruitless by reason of the condition precedent? It is suggested that the failure to apply for a stay or to raise the matter by way of defence would waive the condition precedent.

2–118 The 1996 Act goes on to deal with other situations where there may be court proceedings in the context of a relevant arbitration agreement.

Interpleader proceeding (Section 10)

2–119 In interpleader proceedings a party, usually a defendant to a claim, acknowledges some liability in respect of the claim, but asserts uncertainty as to whom

45 s.9(2).
46 s.9(5).

he must account. The potential claimants then have the opportunity in "interpleader" proceedings to resolve between themselves which is the one with the true entitlement. In this situation the court is obliged of its own volition to take notice and, if appropriate, enforce any arbitration provision. This occurs when the issue between the claimants in interpleader proceedings is covered by an arbitration clause between them. In that event the court granting interpleader relief *must* direct that the issue be determined in accordance with the arbitration agreement unless the situation is one where, if proceedings to resolve that issue had been brought (presumably by either or any claimant), those proceedings would not have been stayed, *i.e.* under section 9(4).[47]

The shift of the responsibility for initiating the "stay" investigation from a party to the court is unsatisfactory: and it is at odds with the party autonomy principles which underlie the 1996 Act. For example, it seems that if either or any of the claimants brings and fails in an application to stay, the proceedings are not stayed. Yet the position of each in the context of an application to stay may be very different. **2–120**

Should the matter in the event proceed in court, then any "award . . . condition precedent" in the arbitration agreement is of no effect[48] in like manner to the situation which obtains in connection with the general practice when stays are refused. **2–121**

Retention of security in Admiralty proceedings

Section 11 deals with the situation in admiralty proceedings where property has been arrested, or bail or other security has been given to prevent or obtain release from arrest. It may well be that the underlying dispute has to be arbitrated, and that a stay will be sought. If granted, the court may order that the property arrested, bailed, or given, should be retained as security for the satisfaction of any award given in the arbitration in respect of that dispute.[49] Alternatively, the court may order that the stay be conditional on the provision of equivalent security for the satisfaction of any such award.[50] This, however, will only work where it is the owner of the arrested or threatened property that wants a stay. This is a topic of relevance only to maritime cases and is commented upon more fully in Part 4 below. **2–122**

47 s.10 has a greater effect in the light of the abolition of the distinction between domestic and non-domestic arbitrations.

48 ss.9(5) and 10(2).

49 s.11(1)(a).

50 s.11(1)(b).

5. Time Limits and Extending Time

When are arbitral proceedings commenced?

2–123 In accordance with the principle of party autonomy, the parties are free to agree on what is to be regarded as commencing arbitral proceedings.[51] If there is no such agreement, then section 14 of the 1996 Act makes the following provision:

(a) Where the tribunal is named or designated in the arbitration agreement, a written notice by party A to party B requiring the latter to submit to the named or designated person a particular matter or dispute starts arbitral proceedings in connection with that matter or dispute.[52]
(b) Where the tribunal is to be appointed by the parties, the arbitral proceedings in respect of a matter or dispute commence when Party A serves on Party B a written notice requiring the latter to appoint an arbitrator or agree on the appointment of an arbitrator in respect of the matter or dispute.[53]
(c) Finally where the tribunal is to be appointed by a third party, arbitral proceedings commence in respect of a dispute or matter where Party A or Party B requests the third party to make an appointment in respect of that dispute or matter.[54]

2–124 Where there is no express provision in the arbitration clause (*e.g.* a very simple clause: "All disputes will be arbitrated") it would seem likely that the second of the above provisions applies, since Party A will have to start by inviting Party B to agree on an arbitrator. Parties should bear in mind that in all three cases the notice should identify the dispute/s or matter/s to which it relates.

Non-compliance with a time limit

2–125 Non-compliance with the time limit may result (a) in barring the claim itself or (b) in barring the right to assert the claim in an arbitration, or (c) in barring the right to assert the claim whether in arbitration or litigation. In the first case the right itself is extinguished. In the second case the right remains, and may be pursued by litigation, but may not be pursued by arbitration. In the third case the right remains, but although it may not be pursued either in arbitration or in litigation, it may nevertheless have some residual effect, *e.g.* by way of set-off.

2–126 In drafting an arbitration clause containing a time limit, therefore, it is highly

[51] s.14.
[52] s.14(3).
[53] s.14(4).
[54] s.14(5).

desirable to make it clear (a) from what moment time begins to run; (b) what is the act that has to be performed within the specified time from the starting date; and (c) what is to be the effect of non-performance of the specified act within the specified time.

Power to the court to extend time for commencing arbitration

By section 12 the court has a limited power to extend the time limit which the parties have put upon beginning the arbitration or beginning other dispute resolution procedures which are themselves a necessary precondition of arbitration.[55] The effect of an extension is to remove the bar to this claim or to revive an extinguished right as the case may be. 2–127

The court can only order such an extension in either of two situations: where, because the circumstances which have occurred were outside the reasonable contemplation of the parties, it would be just to extend the time[56]; or where the conduct of one party makes it unjust to hold the other party to the strict terms of the agreement.[57] This provision is a good example, perhaps, of the safeguards necessary in the public interest—see section 1 of the 1996 Act. 2–128

The court has a discretion as to the length of the extension and the terms upon which it makes the order.[58] The application must (presumably) be made as soon as reasonably possible after the applicant realises that there is a need to apply and the applicant must as a condition precedent have exhausted any available arbitral process for obtaining an extension of time. It is suggested that a court would be unlikely to give an extension where the arbitrator had refused to do so. The court, if it is otherwise entitled to make the order, can make it whether or not the relevant time limit has expired. The power is not a "one-off" power in the sense that the court can extend its own extension, although the circumstances in which this might happen are very rare indeed. The power is administrative. It has no effect on statutory bars, such as the Limitation Act.[59] Appeal from the decision of the court of first instance is only by leave.[60] 2–129

Substantive effect of time limits in the arbitration agreement

If the effect of the time limit provision is to bar the claim and the respondent raises this point at the outset, and the tribunal is satisfied that it is well founded, the tribunal should make an award at that stage to the effect that the claim fails 2–130

55 s.12(1).
56 s.12(3)(a).
57 s.12(3)(b).
58 s.12(4).
59 s.12(5).
60 s.12(6).

by reason of the time provision. But if the time provision bars not the claim itself, but the right to arbitrate on it, then the arbitrator has no jurisdiction.

2–131 This section does not apply to time bars which are not linked to the commencement of dispute resolution procedures. Thus such cases as *Babanaft International Co. S.A. v. Avant Petroleum Inc. (The "Oltenia")*[61] remain relevant. This is despite the criticisms of the lack of any power in the courts to dealwith such clauses expressed by Donaldson L.J. in the Court of Appeal in that case.

6. Constituting the Tribunal

2–132 The key to an efficient arbitration lies in the choice of arbitrator or arbitral tribunal. The chances of the arbitration being well conducted are greatly reduced if the arbitrator knows nothing of the field in which the dispute arises, or has little experience of the problems that face a judge or arbitrator.

Number of arbitrators

2–133 The tribunal appointed under an arbitration agreement will usually consist of one of the following:

(a) a sole arbitrator;
(b) two arbitrators with an umpire if they disagree;
(c) three arbitrators, of whom one will be a chairman as defined under the 1996 Act.

Theoretically speaking, the tribunal can be any number of people from one upwards. If the number of arbitrators provided for is an even number, it will be understood as requiring the appointment of an additional arbitrator as chairman of the tribunal unless the parties have expressly agreed that they want only the number provided for. An even number of arbitrators is both unusual and undesirable. The problem is that they may fall out as evenly as they were appointed. In that event the parties will either have to accept the status quo, or seek fresh relief in court—relief that it is unlikely to be available to them.

[61] [1982] 1 Lloyd's Rep. 448 (Bingham J.) and [1982] 2 Lloyd's Rep. 99.

Presumption that sole arbitrator is intended

In England the great majority of references to arbitration are to a single arbitrator[62] usually with no legal qualification. Many arbitration agreements expressly provide for arbitration by a single arbitrator, and every English arbitration agreement will be so interpreted unless a contrary intention is expressed.[63] 2–134

Agreement by the parties upon a sole arbitrator

In theory this is the most appropriate method. In practice there are some major difficulties. In the first place, once a dispute has arisen the parties may find it impossible to agree upon anything, and an eminently suitable nomination may be rejected simply because it emanates from the other party. Secondly, the result of this may be that when the default procedure is instituted, the persons best suited for the task may be disregarded merely because their names have already been proposed and rejected. Such disregard is more a matter of practice than a requirement of law. It is felt by some institutions that to appoint as arbitrator someone to whom a party has already objected may give rise to an enhanced unwillingness to co-operate in the process on the part of that party, and possibly also to challenges in court. However, there is no authority on the point, and it is the view of the authors that an institution should consider all eligible arbitrators when appointing, and not reject someone merely because he has already been considered and rejected by one of the parties. That said, in a final choice between equally suitable people, such a consideration may be taken into account. Thirdly, in many cases neither the parties nor their advisers have the range of knowledge and experience of individual arbitrators possessed by an appointing body such as, for example, the Chartered Institute of Arbitrators; London Maritime Arbitrators' Association; the Royal Institute of British Architects; or the Royal Institution of Chartered Surveyors in England: and the International Chamber of Commerce and the American Arbitration Association to name but two outside the U.K. Fourthly, professional advisers to the parties are often reluctant to advise their clients to accept a particular nominee for fear of being blamed if the result proves to be adverse. So in practice a high proportion of sole arbitrators are appointed by a third person—usually an appointing institution. It is clearly preferable to agree on a suitable candidate and professional advisors should encourage their clients to do so. 2–135

Most appointing institutions will, if asked, willingly help parties to make their own appointment, *e.g.* by supplying information about the qualifications and experience of members. 2–136

[62] In many other countries, and particularly in Continental Europe, most references are to a tribunal of three legally qualified arbitrators.

[63] s.15(3).

Nomination in the substantive contract

2–137 The objections to appointing the arbitrator or arbitrators in the substantive contract, before any dispute has arisen, are obvious, and it is very rarely done. The nature of the dispute, and consequently the qualities required to resolve it, are not yet known. Nor is it known whether a named person will be available, or indeed alive, when the dispute arises. Yet in some cases an initial nomination has advantages. One example is a complicated construction industry contract. The likelihood of some technical dispute arising is high, and so is the likelihood that when it arises a decision on it will be needed urgently. The fact that an arbitrator has been appointed in advance, and has to some extent already familiarised himself with the contract documents, may greatly facilitate a quick decision and, moreover, one that does not leave the parties at each other's throats for the remainder of the work. Nonetheless, such appointments by name in the original arbitration agreement are very rare indeed. Instead, parties in long running contracts have favoured adjudicators, or even, on very large projects, the creation of a disputes board. The adjudicator or board, as the case may be, is permanently available to address at very short notice any problem that occurs. The decisions of such individuals or bodies are usually temporary, binding until the end of the project, and then, if either party still considers the matter sufficiently contentious the decision can be taken to arbitration.

2–138 An alternative is to agree upon the qualifications required of the arbitrator such as "an experienced civil engineer", or "a Queen's Counsel in practice at the Commercial Bar"; "a commercial man"; "a solicitor experienced in commercial law".

Procedure for choosing a sole arbitrator

2–139 Where an arbitrator has not been nominated in the arbitration agreement and the parties do not or are not able to reach an informal agreement on a suitable person,[64] a formal procedure is necessary. The parties are free to agree on the procedure, even to the point of drawing a name out of a hat. If they do not have an agreed procedure, the 1996 Act provides for joint appointment by the parties not later than 28 days after service of a request in writing by one party to the other to do so.[65] If there is no agreement within the 28 days recourse must be had to the court under section 18, unless the parties have agreed on a fall-back procedure to cover this event.

Commercial judge as sole arbitrator

2–140 Provided that in the view of the Lord Chief Justice the state of business in the High Court and the Crown Court is such that he can be made available, a judge

[64] s.16(2).
[65] s.16(3).

of the Commercial Court may accept appointment as a sole arbitrator or umpire, or by virtue of an arbitration agreement. Given the state of business in the High Court and Crown Courts, this does not seem to be a likely eventuality. The procedure is now governed by section 4 of the Administration of Justice Act 1970. The differences between judicial arbitration and ordinary arbitration, and between judicial arbitration and litigation, are discussed in Mustill and Boyd (2nd ed.), Chapter 20.

Arbitration by Official Referee as sole arbitrator or umpire

In like manner if the Lord Chief Justice is of the view that in the light of the state of the Official Referees' business he can be made available, an Official Referee may accept appointment as a sole arbitrator or as an umpire or by virtue of an arbitration agreement. Given the state of business in the Official Referees' courts, this also does not seem to be a likely eventuality. If the parties consent, an Official Referee will have the same powers as are given to the arbitrator under an arbitration agreement in respect of which the Official Referee has been appointed.[66] 2–141

Regrettably, in the past, once an Official Referee was appointed arbitrator, the practice tended to be little different from that in an action before an Official Referee, even to the point of issuing and paying for summonses on interlocutory hearings, except that the hearing is held in private. It is unlikely that this approach will prevail in the future. 2–142

Tribunal of two or more persons

Given the English leaning in favour of a single arbitrator it is not surprising that, maritime arbitrations apart, arbitrations in England are usually heard by a single arbitrator. This is also generally true of other common law jurisdictions. In civil law jurisdictions, and in maritime arbitrations under the common law, the norm is three. Arbitral tribunals of other numbers are very unusual, unless there are a number of parties involved in the arbitration, and the tribunal has been formed by each party appointing an arbitrator. In this latter case a chairman will usually be appointed by the parties, or by the other arbitrators or by an institution. A three person tribunal can consist of two arbitrators and a chairman or two arbitrators and an umpire. 2–143

Some pros and cons of the three person tribunal

The role of a sole arbitrator in a very heavy arbitration with major consequences for the parties is a very lonely one. To have two colleagues with whom to discuss the case can be very reassuring. What is more, particularly where the 2–144

[66] Courts and Legal Services Act 1990, s.100.

parties come from different cultural and/or jurisdictional backgrounds, the presence on the tribunal of arbitrators from similarly different backgrounds can be reassuring to the parties; and can be positively helpful in understanding the case that is put forward by each party. Thus three arbitrators may make it easier for parties to accept the jurisdiction and authority of the tribunal and may assist them in the exercise of bringing themselves to comply with and even cooperate with the arbitral process. It may also be advantageous in a technical case if one or two of the arbitrators are technically rather than legally qualified. However, there can be drawbacks. There are often delays in convening meetings, effecting consultation between three arbitrators and in making interlocutory decisions; there can also be problems of personality and sometimes there are difficulties where one of the arbitrators is not impartial, or does not respect the confidentiality of the arbitrators' private deliberations. There are often delays once the deliberations are completed in getting agreement on the text of the award, particularly if the tribunal does not make a start on drafting an award immediately the hearings have finished. Difficulties can be compounded if the arbitrators have to come from far and wide and are busy practitioners with other demands on their time. The increasing availability of video conferencing may lessen, but will not eliminate, these difficulties.

2–145 The difficulties of selection are of much less importance where the arbitration is to be conducted by two arbitrators and an umpire, or by three arbitrators. In appointing "his" arbitrator the appointing party does not need to consent of the opposing party; and in many cases the umpire or third arbitrator (now nearly always a chairman) is appointed by the two party-appointed arbitrators. Yet even in such cases it is not unusual for an appointing institution to be asked to make, or to suggest, one or more appointments. This is particularly so where it is the parties who are choosing the third member of the tribunal.

2–146 The notion of a sole arbitrator is repugnant in many parts of the world.[67] A three-arbitrator tribunal is the norm under the Model Law. On the other hand, the costs of the three person tribunal are obviously greater than if only one arbitrator has to be paid.

Two arbitrators and a chairman

2–147 In this very common form of tribunal, it is usual for the parties each to appoint an arbitrator and the chairman is chosen by one of three methods—by agreement between the parties, by agreement between the party appointed arbitrators or by appointment by a relevant institution such as the ICC, LCIA, the CIArb, or one of the many other institutions around the world.

2–148 Although party appointed, each of the arbitrators is expected to be independent of the appointing party, and to reach decisions on the merits of the case.

[67] See Mustill J. in *Arbitration*, Vol. 48, p. 292 (May 1983).

Such an arbitrator is not an advocate for the appointing party and should not act as one.

The role of the chairman under English law

Where the parties have not agreed on a specific role for the chairman, his role is governed by section 20. In sum, decisions, orders and awards of the tribunal should, if possible, all be unanimous. If unanimity is unobtainable, then they shall be made by a majority.[68] If a majority is unobtainable then the chairman's decision prevails.[69] Thus his role corresponds with that of a chairman under many institutional rules, *e.g.* in ICC arbitration. Arbitrators should bear in mind, in reaching decisions, that the smaller the amount of agreement between the tribunal, the greater the chance that one or other or both parties will seek to challenge the award in subsequent proceedings. Since arbitration is intended to be final, it is permissible, even desirable, for an arbitrator to agree to a proposition which seems to him to fall short of an ideal analysis of the case or an issue in the case in the interest of achieving unanimity or at least a majority.[70] **2–149**

Two arbitrators and an umpire

The key difference between the three arbitrator tribunal and the tribunal composed of two arbitrators and an umpire is in the role of the umpire. Where there is an umpire, he does not necessarily become involved with the proceedings unless and until the two arbitrators have failed to agree on some aspect of or matter in the proceedings. By contrast, a chairman must be in place and active by the time that the appointment procedure is complete. **2–150**

Appointment and role of an umpire

An umpire is appointed by the two party appointed arbitrators. He may be appointed by them at any time[71] prior to a falling out; and must be appointed either forthwith, or before any substantive hearing, if the two party appointed arbitrators fail to agree on some matter. Whatever the time at which he is appointed, he does not have a decisive role until the party appointed arbitrators fail to agree on some matter,[72] although it is often helpful to have him sitting in on proceedings. Otherwise there will be a delay, which could be serious, while he familiarises himself with the disputes. Once the point is reached where he is involved actively, he usually conducts the proceedings alone and issues the award. **2–151**

68 s.20(3).
69 s.20(4).
70 For an authoritative discussion of these issues see Judge Schwebel's 1996 Freshfields Lecture.
71 s.21(1).
72 s.21(4).

The role of the party appointed arbitrators before and after the active involvement of the umpire

2–152 When appointed and after appointment the party appointed arbitrators must be and remain independent of the parties, and, subject to the desirability of achieving as large a measure of agreement as possible, must reach an independent and proper conclusion on the matters before them. This requirement continues after active involvement of the umpire. The contrary belief is that after the appointment of the umpire the party appointed arbitrators cease to act in an arbitral and independent role, but take on the role of advocates for their respective appointing parties. This is erroneous. The party appointed arbitrators are entitled and indeed obliged to continue to take part in the proceedings, and to tender their views to the umpire. When they disagree in those views, they are entitled to argue their respective views. However, it is their own views that they are arguing and not those of the appointing party—although of course the two may coincide. In such cases a relationship between the party and his appointee may be acceptable which would disqualify an arbitrator from appointment as sole arbitrator.

Selection by the parties where there are two or more arbitrators

Beauty parade and terms of appointment

2–153 Parties often wish to interview putative arbitrators. This practice has its dangers. Clearly there can be no objection to such interviews if conducted by both parties together; but where one party unilaterally approaches a potential arbitrator different considerations apply. Some putative arbitrators refuse to be interviewed and beyond supplying information as to their C.V., experience, possible conflicts, fees and availability and seeking information in very general terms as to the nature of the dispute, will not communicate with either party. Others are prepared to be interviewed and to be informed in some detail as to the nature of the dispute. A safe procedure to follow is that recommended by Gerald Aksen, the former General Counsel of the AAA and a very experienced arbitrator. He is prepared to see a party for no longer than 30 minutes on the strict understanding that the case is not discussed beyond the most general and neutral description of its nature. Mr Aksen also insists that the fact of and nature of the discussion be recorded in writing and in due course be given to the other party and, where applicable, his fellow arbitrators. This is good practice and should avoid problems of challenge.

Difficulties in making appointments

2–154 Inevitably, problems arise in the making of appointments. Parties are hesitant to agree on candidates, potential candidates are sometimes unavailable when asked to sit and therefore unwilling to accept appointments. Recalcitrant parties can cause delay and disruption to the process of appointment. Accordingly, the 1996

Act provides a comprehensive regime of assistance and support in default situations.

Sole arbitrator—appointment by the parties

The first question to ask is whether a specific method of appointment has been agreed upon by the parties, *e.g.* in the original arbitration agreement or under institutional rules which are to be incorporated into the agreement. If so, the parties should follow it; any arbitrator minded to accept appointment should check that it has been and is being followed. Absent such an agreement, and aside from any informal soundings which may lead to an agreement, the proposed claimant should write to the proposed respondent requesting agreement on an arbitrator and putting forward a name or names to the proposed respondent. The request should make clear that it is a formal one; and that the purpose of the suggestion is to agree on an arbitrator to resolve disputes. The disputes should be identified. **2–155**

By this means, the arbitral proceedings are commenced as is also the 28 day period allowed under the 1996 Act to agree the arbitrator.[73] If after the 28 days allowed no agreement has been reached, either side may, upon notice to the other apply to the court under section 18. In the event of such an application the Court has a variety of powers[74]: **2–156**

(a) it can give directions as to how an appointment is to be effected, *e.g.* by putting in place a procedure whereby the appointment is to be made by an appropriate institution;
(b) it can direct that the tribunal be constituted by any or all of any appointments that have been made;
(c) it can revoke any appointments already made;
(d) it can make any necessary appointments itself;
(e) it can combine two or more of these powers.

Where the court uses its powers under this section to make an appointment, it is to be treated as if made with the agreement of the parties.[75] As usual an appeal needs the leave of the court.[76] **2–157**

Minimising delay when applying to the Court for appointment

Given that invoking the assistance of the court will take time, should there be a reluctance on the part of the proposed respondent to get on with the arbitration, it is usually undesirable that much time be spent before initiating the default procedure. Even an appointment by a third party can take weeks if not months, **2–158**

[73] ss.14(4) and 16(3).
[74] s.18(3).
[75] s.18(4).
[76] s.18(5).

and during this time the parties are awaiting the outcome of the court proceedings or the application to the institution they have chosen. Nonetheless they can continue their attempts to agree. It is usually desirable, before putting forward a name, to ascertain whether the named person is willing to accept appointment, since delay may otherwise be caused.

2–159 Where the parties have agreed to appoint a person, the appointment is complete at the date of the agreement or (if later) the date when the agreed person consents to act.

Two arbitrators and a chairman

2–160 As with a sole arbitrator, the first step for parties, their advisers and the putative arbitrator is to see if there is an agreed method of appointment and/or an agreed method of dealing with a failure to appoint. If so, it should be followed meticulously. If there is no agreement on either matter, the 1996 Act provides remedies.

Appointment in the absence of agreed procedures (section 16)

2–161 Matters are initiated by a written request by one party to the other to appoint an arbitrator. Each side has 14 days in which to make the appointment.[77] In practice, the requesting party would normally make his appointment at the same time as, and by inclusion in, the written request. This notice should also identify the matters to be determined by the tribunal once appointed. The notice thus serves the purpose of commencing the proceedings as well as triggering the appointment procedure. If each party does so appoint its arbitrator, the two party appointed arbitrators will forthwith appoint a chairman.

2–162 A failure of the appointment procedure in such a case will almost always be because the proposed respondent has failed to appoint within the 14 days. He is now, for the purposes of the 1996 Act, the party in default. In that event, and provided he has himself appointed his arbitrator, the requesting party can give notice pursuant to section 17 to the other party—the party in default. The notice must be in writing and must be to the effect that he proposes to appoint his arbitrator as sole arbitrator.[78]

2–163 This notice effectively gives the party in default seven days only in which to do two things[79]: appoint an arbitrator, and notify the requesting party that he has done so. The notice is short: and many requesting parties will not mention the time limit in their notice or any covering letter. It will be up to the party in default to be aware of the time limit (it is seven clear days, so the date of receipt is not counted). The requesting party must wait until the eighth day to appoint his arbitrator as sole arbitrator.

[77] s.16(4).
[78] s.17(1).
[79] ss.17(2)(a) and (b).

Responses of party in default when appointed arbitrator has been successfully appointed as sole arbitrator

If the party in default fails to meet the time limit, and the requesting party appoints "his" arbitrator as sole arbitrator, the options available to the party in default are these: **2–164**

(a) Go along with the sole arbitrator regime. This is obviously more likely if the person in question is known or perceived to be fully independent.
(b) Seek an extension of the seven days from the court.
(c) Seek relief under section 18.
(d) Do both the latter.

If an application to court is made, no doubt the requesting party will seek confirmation of "his" appointed arbitrator as sole arbitrator—also under section 18.

Pros and cons of transforming appointed arbitrator into sole arbitrator

Whether to follow this route will be a nice question for requesting parties. There will be a great attraction in having a sole arbitrator, and particularly one in whom the requesting party has (presumably) considerable confidence. What is more there is no reason why the sole arbitrator should not press ahead with the arbitration. On the other hand, the simultaneous conduct of an arbitration of a substantive matter and a "procedural" battle in court against an attempt by the other party to unseat the sole arbitrator is not an attractive prospect. In particular, there is the danger of incurring the expense of the substantive hearing, when the court may accede to the procedural attack, with the risk of having to revisit the same substantive matters. At the end of the day, much will depend on whether the delays of the party in default are seen as tactical (in which case press ahead) or otherwise (in which case pause for thought may be the answer). In evaluating this particular choice, it may be important for a requesting party to remember that he must not assume that a "negative" course of action on the part of the opponent is a deliberate policy. Incompetence, procrastination and sloppy administration are more often the true explanation. **2–165**

Procedure for transforming a party appointed arbitrator into a sole arbitrator

Where the requesting party has decided to transform his appointed arbitrator into a sole arbitrator, and where the seven clear days have expired without effective response from the receiving party, then the requesting party (who has served the seven day notice[80]) should enquire of the arbitrator whether he is willing to act as a sole arbitrator, and if so write to him appointing him as such and notify the opposing party that the appointment has been made. Strictly **2–166**

[80] s.17(2).

speaking, this last step is not necessary: but for the sake of good order it should be done.

2–167 Absent such procedures, the process put in place by the 1996 Act is one for three arbitrators.[80a] The requesting party serves a notice in writing on the opponent requesting the appointment by the opponent of an arbitrator. As a matter of good practice this notice should normally also appoint the requesting party's arbitrator and of course identify the disputes to be resolved. Within 14 days of the service of this notice each party has to appoint an arbitrator.

Where the requesting party does not seek to transform his appointed arbitrator into a sole arbitrator

2–168 Where the requesting party does not seek to transform his appointed arbitrator into a sole arbitrator but the other party remains recalcitrant, then the requesting party will have to seek the assistance of the court to complete the tribunal under section 18.

The role of the court, where there are more than two parties, and/or an agreement for an uneven number of arbitrators greater than three

2–169 If there are more than two parties or if, for some reason, the parties have decided on an unusually large tribunal, the scope for problems to develop during the constitution of the tribunal is much greater. The 1996 Act accordingly provides for the application to these situations the default procedure of section 18.

Appointment by the court—date when effective

2–170 Where the arbitrator is appointed by the court, the appointment is complete when the order of the court is drawn up. In practice the court will not make the order unless it is satisfied that the person appointed is willing to act.

Ancillary matters of appointment

Umpire or third arbitrator—appointment by party appointed arbitrators

2–171 Before the Act of 1979, an agreement providing for a tribunal of two arbitrators together, if they disagree, with a third arbitrator to be appointed by them, took effect as if the third person was appointed as an umpire, and consequently had power to disagree with both the others. Section 6(2) of the Act of 1979 provided that failing any provision to the contrary such an agreement shall take effect as a reference to three arbitrators, so that the decision of any two of them is binding.

2–172 This approach has been continued by section 15(2) of the 1996 Act. The usual practice is for the notice to appoint, after formally calling upon the opposing

[80a] s.16(5).

party to appoint, to go on to suggest some names. Seven clear days means seven days not counting the day on which the notice is served on the addressee, or the day the application is made to the court.[81]

Default in appointment by appointing institution or person

Where an arbitration agreement provides for appointment by a person who is neither a party nor an existing arbitrator, it may be that that person fails to appoint within the time specified in the agreement or (if no time is specified) within a reasonable time or indeed at all. In this event, as always, the first thing to do is to see if there is already in existence an agreed procedure to deal with this problem. Although unusual such agreements are not unknown. An example is to be found in Article 6 of the UNCITRAL Rules. Given the growing popularity of these Rules, the situation will become more familiar. If such an agreement exists then it should be followed meticulously. If there is no such agreement then it is back to the court. **2–173**

Time limits

Statutory time limits

The Limitation Act 1980, which by section 34(1) is declared to apply to arbitrations, lays down a time within which proceedings must be brought, whether in court or by arbitration. In most cases the time limit is six years, but in the case of claims based upon a covenant in a lease or in any other document under seal, the period is 12 years. The defence that a claim is barred by the Limitation Act cannot be relied upon unless it is specifically raised in the arbitration proceedings. When it is raised the arbitrator has jurisdiction to determine it, subject always to such right of appeal (if any) as may exist under the 1996 Act. Accordingly, the fact that the claim appears on the face of it to have been brought out of time is not a matter that goes to the jurisdiction of the arbitrator. **2–174**

Contractual time limits

Likewise, some contracts containing an arbitration agreement provide a time limit upon notice of claim. In most cases the arbitrator will not initially know whether the time limits have been complied with. So here too he can proceed with the arbitration and, if a time objection is raised, he can deal with it as indicated in the preceding paragraph, and see paragraphs 2–123 *et seq.* above. **2–175**

[81] Service, for this purpose, means a general personal service on an individual addressee, or delivery to the registered office or principal place of business of a corporate addressee; see *The Supreme Court Practice*, Notes to Ord. 3, r.2.

What stops time running?

2–176 Statutory and contractual clauses imposing a time limit usually specify the act that must be done before the expiry of the time specified. For the purposes of the Limitation Act 1980 time ceases to run where an arbitration is commenced. By section 34 of that Act, an arbitration shall be treated as commenced when one party serves on the other or others a notice requiring him or them to appoint an arbitrator or to agree to the appointment of an arbitrator or (if the arbitration agreement provides for a reference to a named or designated person) to submit the dispute to such person. (The like tests are to be found in section 14 of the 1996 Act.)

2–177 If an arbitration agreement provides that the event which is to commence proceedings for the purposes of the 1980 Act is appointment by a person who is neither a party nor an existing arbitrator, and that person fails to appoint within the time specified in the agreement or (if no time is specified) within a reasonable time, the steps which are to be taken and the options which are available are set out above at paragraphs 2–123 *et seq.* above. Obviously this is a more serious situation where there is a time limit.

Disqualifications and challenges

2–178 It is of the essence of the function of an arbitrator that he should hold the scales of justice evenly between the parties and that he should be perceived by the parties to do so. His ability, or apparent ability, to do this may be in doubt:

(a) if he has, or is perceived to have, some personal interest in the outcome of the dispute; or
(b) if he has, or is perceived to have, some connection with one of the parties, or with the case presented by one of the parties, such as is likely to create bias.

2–179 But the matter is one of degree, it is not every interest, and not every connection, that disqualifies. At one extreme a person should not act as arbitrator when one of the parties is his spouse, or child, or a company which he wholly owns. But if the relationship is merely second cousin once removed; or he owns a minute fraction of the shares in a company party, the connection is too remote for any reasonable person to suspect bias absent evidence to the contrary. A comparable situation will exist in many Western countries in court proceedings. A judge may well have a portfolio of shares. It is unusual for a judge to offer to withdraw from a case because he has shares in a party or a related party before him. It is even more unusual for a party to check the share register of his opponent to see whether any judges (or indeed arbitrators) are on it.

Prior decision on the same issue

2–180 If the dispute raises an issue, whether of law or of fact, which the arbitrator has already decided in an earlier arbitration; or an issue so close that he could not decide it in one sense without in effect saying that his earlier decision was wrong; or if the earlier decision was by his partner and he could not decide the later dispute in one sense without in effect saying that his partner's decision was wrong, these are connections which might well raise a reasonable suspicion of bias or "prejudice". It is for this reason that if the same person is appointed as arbitrator in two concurrent disputes raising the same or a closely related issue, it is usually impossible for him to continue acting in both unless all parties consent. But the mere fact that an arbitrator has decided a previous dispute between the parties should not disqualify him.

The basic test

The basic test was summarised by Ackner L.J. as follows: Do there exist grounds from which a reasonable person would think that there was a real likelihood that the arbitrator could not, or would not, fairly determine the issue on the basis of the evidence and arguments to be adduced before him?[82] The reasonable person is not to be assumed to be someone with no knowledge of the facts; he is to be put in the position of the party raising the objection, having ascribed to him all that party's knowledge and experience of the field in which the dispute arises, and of the manner in which disputes are habitually resolved, but with no inside knowledge of the particular arbitrator. **2–181**

Removal of arbitrator by the court

The 1996 Act provides the following specific grounds upon any of which a court has power to remove an arbitrator[83]: **2–182**

(a) that circumstances exist that give rise to justifiable doubts as to his impartiality;
(b) that he does not possess the qualifications required by the arbitration agreement;
(c) that he is physically or mentally incapable of conducting the proceedings or there are justifiable doubts as to his capacity to do so;
(d) that he has failed or refused properly to conduct the proceedings and that injustice has been or will be caused to the applicant;
(e) that he has refused or failed to use all reasonable dispatch in conducting the proceedings or making an award, and that substantial injustice has been or will be caused to the applicant.

If there is an institution or person in whom the parties have vested the power to remove an arbitrator, recourse must be had first to that institution or person **2–183**

[82] See Lord Justice Ackner in *Hagop Ardatalian v. Umifest International S.A. (Elissar, The)* (1984) 2 Lloyd's Rep. 84 at 89; cited by Mustill J. in *Bremer Handelgesellschaft MbH v. Ets. Soules* [1985] 1 Lloyd's Rep. 160 at 164.

[83] s.24(1).

before application is made to the court.[84] An example of such an institution is the ICC, which regularly has to deal with challenges to arbitrators.

2–184 Where application has been made to an institution or person with the relevant power, and that institution or person has refused to exercise it, the task facing the applicant to the court will be all the greater. Why should the court interfere if the body vested with the power by the parties has refused to?

2–185 The following are some examples which arise in this context in practice.

Business connection with a party

2–186 A person may have a business or professional relationship sufficiently close to give him a personal interest in the outcome of a dispute. A naval architect who derives a large proportion of his income from a particular client would not be perceived by the reasonable outsider to be wholly free from bias towards that client. The connection may be direct; or it may be indirect, *e.g.* through a partner, or an associated firm. But as in the case of personal relationships, there comes a point when the relationship is so slight that a reasonable person knowing the facts would not think it likely to result in bias. No better test has yet been formulated than that of Lord Justice Ackner.

Connection with the subject-matter of the arbitration

2–187 A person may have a connection with the subject-matter of the dispute that affects, or would be thought by a reasonably minded outsider to affect, his ability to hold the scales evenly between the parties. Thus an agent who acts on behalf of the landlord of all the shops in a parade except one, might well be expected to be predisposed towards the landlord of that one as against the tenant, even though he has no other relationship with that landlord. An architect who is regularly consulted by an association of brickmakers might be thought likely to be biased towards a brickmaker in a dispute with a contractor or employer. But the effect of this kind of connection should not be exaggerated: indeed, it may well operate the other way.

Prior connection with a similar dispute

2–188 The proposition that a person involved (whether as party or advocate or presumably expert witness) in a dispute arising from a particular situation should not act as an arbitrator in another dispute connected with the same situation was rejected in the *Bremer Handelsgesellschaft* case. So, *e.g.* a valuer who has acted as advocate for a landlord in an arbitration in respect of property A is not thereby disqualified from subsequently acting as an arbitrator in a dispute in respect of property B to which the decision in respect of property A is said to be relevant.

[84] s.24(2).

Prior adoption of a point of view

A prior commitment to a point of view on one set of evidence and arguments cannot in itself be fatal to future participation as an arbitrator. What is required of an arbitrator, as of a judge, is to look at each case afresh. But a prior commitment as expert to a particular point of view may well be thought to be a disqualification from expressing the opposite view in a later case; unless of course there have been new facts justifying the change of view. 2–189

Time for challenge

A party who becomes aware of facts which entitle him to apply for the removal of the arbitrator should act promptly to raise his objection and to seek either the appointment of someone else (if the arbitrator has not yet been appointed) or the removal of the arbitrator (if he has already been appointed). This need to act promptly derives from section 73 of the 1996 Act. This section constitutes a code of waiver of objection to various aspects of the proceedings. One of the cases to which it applies is where there has been any irregularity affecting the tribunal or proceedings (other than specific ones not relevant to this discussion). The provision would cover objections to an arbitrator whose impartiality is doubtful. 2–190

The effect of this section is to deprive the complainant of the right to complain, if he takes part or continues to take part in the proceedings without objecting forthwith or within any specific time imposed by the arbitration agreement, the tribunal or the Act. Actual knowledge of the grounds of the objection is not necessary for the bar to relief to operate. However, if a complainant can show that he did not move because he did not know and could not with reasonable diligence have discovered, the grounds of this objection, the court has the power to intervene. The old test of involvement sufficient to create a waiver was taking "a step in the proceedings". "Taking part" is an appreciably less stringent test. Something less than a "step" will be enough, but there must be activity combined with a failure to protest for the section to bite. 2–191

Responses of the appointing authority to challenge

If a party wishes to delay the making of an effective award against him, his first step is sometimes to seek to interfere in the appointing process. By making representations as to who should or should not be appointed, he hopes to cause the application for appointment to be stood over for further investigations to be made, or for further consideratiion by the appointing authority, and thereby to be taken out of the ordinary machinery. The counter to this is for the institution to make whatever arrangements are necessary to ensure that representations of this kind do not in fact result in delay. In particular, since objections of this kind often make legal advice desirable, arrangements should be made for such advice 2–192 to be obtainable speedily. But it is preferable to accept that occasionally an appointment made speedily will be successfully challenged later, rather than to let it become known that an initial representation to the appointing authority will usually delay an appointment by several weeks.[85]

Other responses to challenge

Responses by the prospective arbitrator

2–193 If the appointment has not yet been accepted: and if after obtaining full particulars in writing of the objection/s the nominee considers that there is or may be some substance in the challenge he should refuse the appointment. If he has not yet accepted the appointment, and (again after obtaining the relevant information) considers that there is little or no substance in the challenge then he should seek the view of his nominating party: and having considered that view, make his own mind up as to what to do.

2–194 The need for written particulars of the complaint is particularly important if the arbitrator proposes to accept the appointment. This is because the grounds of challenge tend to mutate. The team presenting the challenge will experience a learning curve similar to that which exists in so many other fields of intellectual endeavour. Arguments that initially sound persuasive will, upon development, be found to be flawed. Another ground will be sought. Thus when a member of a tribunal hearing a claim under Swiss law, published, near the end of the proceedings, an article on claims for interest under Swiss law, one party complained to the ICC asserting that this evidenced lack of independence. Predictably, the ICC rejected this complaint. When the complaint was renewed before the Swiss courts, the objection had metamorphosed into the assertion that the article was an attempt to influence the other members of the tribunal.[86] A substantial mutation in the grounds of objection will weaken the credibility of the complaint in all its forms.

Where the appointment is already in place

2–195 This is an appreciably more difficult situation. The option of voluntary withdrawal used almost certainly not to be available to the appointee without the agreement of the appointor (even though previous editions of this book suggested otherwise). However the Act recognises (without declaring) that an arbitrator can resign. The side note to section 25 is ''Resignation of Arbitrator''. The section deals with the consequence of resignation. It does not expressly declare that the right exists.

[85] This problem arose so frequently in respect of appointment of rent review arbitrators that the President of the RICS issued a Policy Statement dated September 10, 1987; see *Chartered Surveyor Weekly*, Vol. 20, p. 67.

[86] Professors Sanders and Goldman.

Nonetheless, the option of resignation may now be available.[87] That said, it is a step to be taken only after very careful thought. Apart from anything else, resignation may do a great disservice to the non-challenging party. An example of this would be the unmeritorious challenge by a respondent bent on a delay. Resignation by the appointee is bound to result in some delay, especially if the appointee has to go to court to get appropriate relief; even if the same expedition to court is used to compete the tribunal. It will also involve some expense. In addition, any person who has accepted appointment as an arbitrator has thereupon accepted some obligations to each of the parties. Again the key factor must be whether the appointee considers that the challenge has some merit: and again, he should ascertain the appointor's view. 2–196

Powers of the court on application by resigning arbitrator

If the parties have not made an agreement which deals with the situation, an arbitrator can apply to the court for relief from any liability arising from his resignation and for an order in respect of his entitlement to or liability to repay fees and expenses. The court will grant such relief as it considers appropriate if it is satisfied that in all the circumstances it was reasonable to resign.[88] A timely challenge which has or might reasonably appear to have substance would appear to satisfy the court as to granting relief.[89] 2–197

Arbitrators have traditionally and correctly been warned against getting personally involved in court proceedings about their cases. The ideal response to a challenge to the person or the proceedings is to be found in *Carlisle v. Wimpey*.[90] There, the arbitrator wrote a very short letter of explanatiion to the court and left it at that. That advice—as little involvement as possible—was good advice and still is. An arbitrator should think long and hard before he exercises the rights given him by this section. 2–198

One other matter should be mentioned. The second edition of this book used as an example of objectionable behaviour and its consequences the arbitrator who, after giving directions in the arbitration, decided that he preferred to take a long holiday than to proceed with the arbitration. His resignation at that stage might cause one or both parties considerable damage and would probably found a claim for damages for breach of contract. It is likely that the court would impose terms upon his resignation including the repayment of fees and expenses should he apply to the court for relief. So also if a party—usually but not always the respondent—mounts a challenge for purposes of delay, the arbitrator may do a great disservice to the other party by merely resigning. 2–199

In sum the arbitrator should therefore proceed as follows: he should obtain full particulars, in writing, of the objection; he should consult with his appointing party or body; he should decide for himself whether he thinks that the objection 2–200

87 *cf.* para. 2–206 below.
88 s.25(4).
89 s.25(3).
90 (1980) 15 B.L.R. 109.

is well founded; or that there is a sufficient appearance of bias to merit resignation. If yes, he should offer to resign and leave it to the parties to sort out. If no, he should say that he considers that the challenge is unjustified, but that he will resign if asked to by both parties or the court. Only in an extreme situation should he resign without the agreement of his appointor: and only in an extreme situation should he enlist the aid of the court on this.

2–201 If in doubt at any stage, he should consider whether to seek advice. If the advice is that the objection is at least strongly arguable, he should offer to resign, telling the parties that he has done so upon advice; while if the advice is that the objection is unfounded, he should reject the challenge, and tell the parties that he intends to proceed with the arbitration unless and until the court otherwise orders.

Responses by the non-challenging party

2–202 If both parties agree that an arbitrator should resign he should normally do so forthwith. If there is a problem about fees and expenses then he has the option of asking the court for assistance. It follows that the first matter for consideration by a party faced with an objection to a proposed appointment, or a demand from the opposing party that an arbitrator already appointed be removed, is whether the delay, and possibly the costs, involved in opposing the request make it preferable to agree to it. This will in turn raise the question of how quickly a replacement can be appointed. So one course open to the non-challenging party is to ask the challenging party how he proposes that a replacement be appointed. If the challenging party at once submits some names for an alternative appointee and one of them is acceptable, it may be greatly preferable to concur and to ask the challenged arbitrator to withdraw. Alternatively, the non-challenging party may submit some names of possible alternatives and offer to agree that the challenged arbitrator should be asked to withdraw if the challenger will first agree one of the alternatives for appointment in his place. If the challenger though not submitting any acceptable name for a replacement, is willing to agree that some outside body (whether the original appointing authority or some other) shall forthwith be asked to appoint, the other party may think this preferable to the hassle and delay involved in opposing the challenge. In this case however, the possibility must be borne in mind that a new appointment may itself be challenged.

Resignation without challenge

2–203 It sometimes happens that after appointment an arbitrator becomes aware of facts which are not known to the parties but which, had he known them before appointment, might have made him doubtful about accepting appointment. For example he might discover that a company party is a subsidiary of his most regular client or that another partner in his firm is advising a party to the arbitration on an unrelated matter. In such a case he should notify the parties of the facts, and proceed as in paragraphs 2–200 to 201 above.

Waiver and "without prejudice" objection

A party who becomes aware of facts which ground an objection to the arbitrator and who does not raise the objection will be barred from objecting at a later stage. If with knowledge of the relevant facts he continues with the proceedings without raising the objection, he will be estopped (*i.e.* barred) from raising it later. Nor is it open to him (without the agreement of the other party, or the tribunal or the court—none of whom are likely to give their agreement) to raise the objection, and state that his continuing to take part in the arbitration is without prejudice to his right to maintain the objection later. **2–204**

If the opposing party accepts the objection, he should join with the objector in requesting the arbitrator to resign from the appointment. Whether this leaves the arbitrator entitled to fees for work done before he resigns will depend on the circumstances. **2–205**

Retirement and removal of arbitrator

Constraints on the right to retire

An arbitrator is (save for statutory arbitration) appointed in pursuance of a contract, namely the arbitration agreement. Whether the appointment itself creates a second contract, namely a contract between him and the parties to the arbitration agreement, is a matter of considerable doubt and little authority.[91] The 1996 Act confers powers on the court to remove an arbitrator, and these are discussed below. The 1996 Act implicitly confers a power on the arbitrator to retire, once he has accepted appointment. However, this is a power which should only rarely be exercised. On the contractual front it is difficult to envisage a contract of appointment under which the arbitrator has a right to retire at any time and for any reason. Retirement can involve the parties in great delay and expense, and if at the outset he had stipulated for an unlimited right to retire the parties might well have gone elsewhere. By accepting appointment an arbitrator by implication undertakes—among other things to conduct the arbitration with due diligence and at a reasonable fee.[92] Nonetheless, given the existence of the power to resign, it may be that appointments will include terms to deal with what is to happen in the event of a resignation. It is also possible that in the appointment parties will seek to include a term against resignation, in the same way as parties at present sometimes require an undertaking from a proposed arbitrator that he will not disqualify himself from completing an arbitration—as for example (and often the main object of the clause) by taking a judicial appointment. As a matter of English law such an undertaking will not be specifically enforced, though breach of it will leave him open to a claim in damages. **2–206**

But it is no less impossible to interpret the acceptance of appointment as **2–207**

[91] See Mustill & Boyd, pp. 219 *et seq.* and case cited at n. 95 below.

[92] *cf. K/S Norjari A/S v. Hyundai Heavy Industries Co. Ltd.* [1991] 3 All E.R. 211, *per* Leggatt L.J. at 221.

arbitrator as amounting to an unconditional promise that he will complete the reference and issue an award. Thus if the arbitrator dies, his authority ceases[93] and so does his obligation to complete. But there are situations less final than death which may prevent or hinder completion. Suppose he has a heart attack, and cannot resume for six months. It is suggested that he does not thereby commit a breach of contract. In such a case, he should discuss with the parties (if he is able to) what they wish to do. If they disagree, then he should consider the whole matter, the likely delay, the effect of that delay, and decide whether to resign or not. A consideration in such a matter must be the effect on his health of going to court. In the end he may (and very often should) leave it to the parties to go to court under section 24(1)(c) or not, as they see fit.

Access to medical records/advisers

2–208 While it is an intrusion on his privacy, an arbitrator in a particularly costly and lengthy case should be prepared to give the parties access to his medical advisers or if it is desired to insure him against failure to perform his duties through illness or death, submit to medical examination by a Doctor of the Insurers' choice. One has little choice about the health (physical or mental) of the publicly provided judges. One should not have the same problem with the tribunal of one's own choice in a lengthy and expensive case.

Change in the nature of the arbitration

2–209 The problem becomes more acute where there is a change in the nature of the arbitration. The example posed in the second edition was a reference that everyone expected would involve a five day hearing in the cool season in Southern India turns out to require a three-month hearing in the hot season? Would not the average quantity surveyor say to himself "*Non haec in foedera veni*", or perhaps "This is not what I agreed to do"? No doubt he would. Is he entitled to? One should first of all put aside the heat. Air conditioning has made even Texas endurable for substantial periods of time. One should also put aside a simple overrun in time, without a major change in the nature of the arbitration. That is the arbitrator's problem and he took it on when he accepted his appointment.[94]

2–210 The problem truly arises in situations such as those where he was clearly misled on appointment ("a couple of short legal points only") or where, whether or not misled, the arbitration has taken, as they sometimes can, a completely unexpected course. The consequence is a great increase in time, and embarrassment for the arbitrator. Here again, the implicit power to resign may provide an escape route. But this is a course which is not to be taken lightly and only after full discussion with both parties.

[93] s.26(1).

[94] In any event, hearing time should be strictly controlled—see, for example, paras 2–397 *et seq.* below.

The busy arbitrator

"If you want something done, ask a busy person". And everybody does. No one should accept an appointment if he knows that his existing commitments make it difficult or impossible for him to execute with reasonable diligence his duties under it and no reputable arbitrator would do so. But arbitration, like litigation, is beset with uncertainties. An Official Referee has said that nine out of 10 construction industry actions listed for hearing settle on or before the first day, but the tenth overruns madly its predicted hearing time. A judge can mitigate these uncertainties by taking a case transferred from another judge. An arbitrator cannot. If a hearing to which he is committed in Arbitration A seems likely to overrun greatly, and thereby to clash with a hearing already fixed for Arbitration B, or with some other commitment, he will usually consider whether he can escape from the other commitment so as to complete Arbitration A. Often he cannot. The problem will be eased if he has set aside—as he should have done—a reasonable period for preparing his award. Two points need to be made in conclusion. First, "overrun" should be avoided. An arbitrator is not and should not behave as English judges formerly did, sailing on to the end of an uncontrolled hearing, overrunning for days, weeks, months, notwithstanding the costs and the disruption to everybody involved by the failure to keep to a timetable. (Adjourning to another date is often an even worse solution.) Secondly, if the arbitrator has to set award preparation time as well as hearing time aside, he should consider cancellation charges. 2–211

Action by the arbitrator on appointment

Immediately upon appointment the arbitrator, if he does not already have a copy of the arbitration agreement, should call for one. If he has been appointed by agreement between the parties, he should call for the document or correspondence containing the agreement. If he has been appointed by a third party, he should ensure that the terms of the appointment conform with the terms of the arbitration agreement. If that agreement contains any time limit upon appointment, he should check that the appointment has been duly made within the specified time. If there is any problem or query on any of these matters, the arbitrator should immediately review it with the parties or if appropriate with the relevant appointing body. 2–212

Next, he should look to see whether the arbitration agreement, or any special terms of appointment, in any way widen or narrow the powers conferred on arbitrators by the general law. For example, it may widen the powers by expressly enabling him to decide *ex aequo et bono*, *i.e.* according to his own judgment as to what is a fair solution and not necessarily in strict conformity with law or with the contract. Or it may narrow his powers by specifying that any dispute is to be decided on documents only without a hearing; or that if there is to be a hearing lawyers are not allowed to be present. 2–213

If there are jurisdictional problems, it is highly desirable that they be raised 2–214 at or before the first meeting, if there is to be one, or otherwise in correspondence. At that stage the parties will usually welcome suggestions from the arbitrator designed to ensure that they do not spend time and money on a process which may become abortive because of some initial jurisdictional or procedural defect.

Can the arbitrator impose terms and conditions after appointment?

2–215 It is arguable that the joint request by the parties to the arbitrator is an offer, and that the arbitrator's unconditional agreement to act as arbitrator is the acceptance of that offer; so that thereafter it is too late for him to impose conditions, *e.g.* as to the basis upon which he will charge. In practice questions of fees, and sometimes of conditions of engagement, are often raised immediately after, rather than before, appointment.[95]

7. Miscellaneous Matters of Jurisdiction

Procedure when jurisdiction is in issue

2–216 The 1996 Act establishes a clear regime for resolving jurisdiction questions. The main sections are section 7 which enshrines the principle of separability; section 30 which provides that the tribunal has the power, absent contrary agreement of the parties, to rule on its own jurisdiction; section 31, which establishes the procedure for challenge; and section 67 which provides for challenges to the award on grounds that the tribunal lacks substantive jurisdiction.

2–217 If the parties, while disagreeing on the substantive issue of jurisdiction, are in agreement as to how to deal with it, the tribunal must follow the agreed course. If they are not in agreement, then the tribunal has a broad discretion as to how to proceed—see section 31 of the 1996 Act. The following is a suggested course.

2–218 The tribunal should first, if it has not already done so, establish whether it is empowered to rule on its own substantive jurisdiction—what is often referred to in continental treatises as Kompetenz Kompetenz. Under section 30(1) of the 1996 Act the tribunal will have such power, unless the parties have agreed otherwise. To put it another way, the default position is that the tribunal can determine whether there is a valid arbitration agreement, whether the tribunal is

[95] *K/S Norjari v. Hyundai Heavy Industries Co. Ltd.* [1991] 3 All E.R. 211. See para. 2–267 below.

properly constituted and/or what matters have been submitted to arbitration in accordance with the arbitration agreement.

In so doing it must pay particular regard to the timing of this objection. This is because section 31(1) of the 1996 Act lays an obligation on the challenging Party to raise any relevant objection at the outset of the proceedings. The sanction for failure to do so is dismissal of the challenge, although the tribunal has a discretion to admit a late objection if it considers the delay justified.[96] **2–219**

If the objection is duly taken, (and subject, as always, to the caveat that the tribunal must follow any procedure agreed between the parties) the tribunal has an option, it can either issue a ruling in an award (*N.B.* not a direction) specifically addressing the issue. Or it can deal with the issue in the award on its merits. **2–220**

It is suggested that if the tribunal does have the relevant power to rule on a question of jurisdiction it should usually proceed to a speedy determination of the issue. If it rules against the party challenging the jurisdiction, it should usually press on with the arbitration and leave the challenge to later (for example recourse to the court under section 32. If the tribunal is satisfied that the objection is well founded, it should refuse to continue further with the arbitration or the particular issue as the case may be. Alternatively, the arbitrator may continue with the arbitration and make an award in case the court rules that he has jurisdiction.[97] This is a matter of discretion; but it will usually be wiser to make a "ruling" when the point is first raised. As always these courses of action are subject to the right of the parties to agree on the procedure. In all cases it is essential that the tribunal should make it plain to the parties what it is doing. **2–221**

Action by arbitrator when jurisdiction or powers are questioned

The arbitrator should only take notice of any jurisdiction question if it is raised by agreement of the parties or is the subject of an objection or challenge by a party. In that event, it is incumbent on the party making the challenge to do so at the outset of the proceedings to contest the merits of any matter in relation to which he challenges the tribunal's jurisdiction; or later if and when the matter alleged to be beyond the arbitrator's jurisdiction is first raised; or later still if the arbitrator so rules. **2–222**

The arbitrator should require the challenge or objection to his jurisdiction to be clearly formulated in writing and he should ask the parties if they wish to enter into an agreement in writing expressly conferring jurisdiction upon him and thus withdrawing the challenge. If they will not so agree he should ask whether the claimant wishes to obtain a decision of the court on the question of jurisdiction before proceeding with the arbitration. **2–223**

If the claimant replies in the negative the arbitrator should then decide (after **2–224**

[96] See in this context ss.31, 32 and 73 of the Act.
[97] s.32(4).

taking legal advice under section 37 if he thinks fit) whether to rule on the question of jurisdiction as a preliminary point. If his ruling is that he has jurisdiction he should continue with the arbitration. Alternatively he can make no ruling on the question of jurisdiction, but state that he is continuing with the arbitration on the assumption that he has jurisdiction. It will then be open to the parties if either of them so wishes, either to apply to the court for an injunction restraining the arbitrator from continuing with the arbitration, or seek to dispute the validity of the award after it has been given.

2–225 If the respondent declines to take any part in the proceedings then unless the arbitrator is plainly of the view that he has no jurisdiction, he should continue with the arbitration ex parte. This is on the basis that the claimant takes his chance that the proceedings and the award are later held by the court to have been without jurisdiction. In this event the arbitrator should ensure that he has an undertaking from the claimant as to remuneration that will apply even if the court holds that he has no jurisdiction.

Widening the ambit of the arbitrator's jurisdiction

2–226 Frequently forms of arbitration agreements refer to arbitration claims or differences or disputes arising out of, or in connection with, or in relation to the contract. Parties believe that such a formulation is wide and comprehensive enough to bring all claims and disputes relating in any way to the formation, implementation and termination of the contract, before the tribunal. Although the courts lean towards giving general words of this kind the widest meaning that they can reasonably bear, there may remain some limitations upon the jurisdiction of the arbitrator.

Claim or procedure outside the arbitration agreement

2–227 It commonly happens that in the course of an arbitration a point is raised, or a procedure is followed, that falls outside the terms of the arbitration agreement. For example, the original pleadings may raise an issue that goes beyond those submitted to arbitration; or such an issue may be raised by amendment. This is what Lord Devlin once called "creeping jurisdiction". Objections to an extension of jurisdiction in this way must be made promptly if not to be caught by the provisions of section 73.

Desirability of recording the outcome of jurisdictional and powers issues in writing

2–228 If the arbitrator allows a new claim to be brought in, which may otherwise be outside his jurisdiction, and where the opposing party does not take a jurisdictional objection, the arbitrator should propose that the situation be regularised by an express written agreement, either varying the existing agreement or constituting a separate agreement. If the latter course is taken, a separate award on each agreement should be issued; alternatively, if a single award is to be issued, it should recite that it is made in respect of both agreements. Likewise if some extraordinary procedure is expressly agreed between the parties, it should be recorded in writing.

No power to order specific performance of a contract relating to land—section 48(5)(b)

The 1996 Act deals with the "default" powers of the tribunal to give relief. Unless the parties have otherwise agreed, the tribunal can grant declaratory relief, order the payment of sums of money, grant injunctive relief, and order the rectification, setting aside or cancellation of a deed. The tribunal can also in general order specific performance of a contract. However, if the contract relates to land, the tribunal will only be able to order specific performance if the parties have expressly agreed to give it that power. 2–229

8. Remuneration of the Arbitrator

The right to remuneration

There are few reported cases[98] either as to the precise nature of the arbitrator's right to remuneration (where there is no express agreement as to fees) or as to the basis upon which he may charge. There are perhaps three reasons for this. First, in many cases the non legally qualified arbitrator regards it as a tribute to his standing in his trade or profession that he has been asked to act, and any remuneration is of secondary importance. (This is most marked in arbitrations administered by the American Arbitration Association, a large proportion of which are conducted without fee or without a fee up to and including the first day—which of course is when they then settle). Secondly, in most cases the fee or basis of remuneration is expressly agreed before or immediately upon appointment so that the question of what right to remuneration is implied does not arise. Thirdly, the practice of requiring payment before issue of the award reduces the opportunity to use a dispute as to the amount of the fee as a means of delaying payment of the amount likely to be awarded, and the risk of a dispute as to the amount of the fee itself. 2–230

[98] See *K/S Norjarl v. Hyundai Heavy Industries Co. Ltd* [1991] 3 All E.R. 211.

Provisions of the 1996 Act

2–231 This area has now been addressed by the Act. Under section 28, the express contractual position (which is anyway the most usual arrangement) is preserved. Absent an agreement, the parties are jointly and severally liable for "such reasonable fees and expenses (if any) as are appropriate in the circumstances".[99] The concept of "such reasonable fees and expenses as are appropriate in the circumstances" is picked up when it comes to payment of the costs of the arbitration. Section 64 defines the costs (for the purposes of payment as between the parties) as including only such reasonable fees and expenses of the arbitrators as are appropriate in the circumstances. Thus what the arbitrators can recover from the parties, in a situation where there was no express agreement between the parties and the arbitrators, will match exactly what is recoverable between the parties when the final award on costs is known.

When arbitrators' fees differ from fees recoverable by a party

2–232 Where there is an agreement between the arbitrators and the parties, the inevitability of a match is lost. If the difference proves to be substantial, with the contractual rates at the high end, an arbitrator may find difficulty in obtaining payment, if he has not been paid in advance.

Limitations on the implied right to remuneration

2–233 There was an implied right to payment in respect of a completed award, and probably an implied right to payment for work done in a reference that is abandoned before an award is published. But there was and is no implied duty on the parties to continue the arbitration to any particular stage. If the arbitration is abandoned (*e.g.* by compromise) after the arbitrator has set aside a substantial period to deal with it, and he is unable to find alternative employment for that period, he may suffer loss. Under section 28 he has a statutory right to reasonable fees and expenses. Arguably this phrase does cover cancellation charges or reasonable fees. But it is suggested the courts will view such charges with great care. Extravagant claims for cancellation charges will almost certainly not be countenanced. The better practice for an arbitrator is to stipulate for such fees as a condition of his appointment.

The express contract for remuneration

2–234 It is highly desirable in an ad hoc arbitration that an arbitrator who regards remuneration as important should make an express agreement in writing with the parties as to his remuneration. Ideally, this should be done before he accepts the appointment. But in many cases he knows very little about either the sums in issue or the magnitude of the task involved. So in practice he often accepts

[99] s.28(1).

appointment and leaves the subject of fees to be dealt with at or shortly after the preliminary meeting. Where the arbitrator is appointed not by the parties or one of them but by some appointing body, *e.g.* the President of a professional institute, the position is more difficult. It is invariable practice for the appointing body, before appointment, to inquire whether the person concerned is willing and available to accept appointment. If he wishes to stipulate for a particular level of fees or for particular terms of engagement (such as payment at the outset, interim payments, payment for abortive hearing dates) he should do so before rather than after the appointment; or he should ask for the appointment to be made conditiional upon agreement of terms of appointment.

Sometimes remuneration and terms of engagement are prescribed

If rates of remuneration and terms of engagement are laid down by the profes- **2–235** sional body concerned or by the custom of the trade concerned, then the arbitration agreement itself may impliedly incorporate those terms so that the request for appointment may impliedly be a request for appointment on those terms. But otherwise it is open to either party, once the arbitrator has been appointed, to say:

> "You have been appointed without conditions as to fees. I am willing to pay you a reasonable fee for the services you perform, to be assessed by the court if we cannot agree it; but I am not willing to enter into any other agreement as to fees."

Nevertheless, it is common practice in many fields for an arbitrator, whether **2–236** appointed by the parties or one of them or by an outside body, to negotiate his fees after—usually immediately after—appointment; see drafting suggestion No. 44 in Appendix 1.

The decision in the Norjarl case

An interesting example of the difficulties which can arise if fees are not agreed **2–237** on appointment arose in *K/S Norjarl A/S v. Hyundai Heavy Industries Co. Ltd.*[1] After accepting appointment on terms which did not include provision for staged payments or for commitment fees, two of the three arbitrators propossed that they should receive commitment fees by instalments in advance of a lengthy hearing. One party was willing to agree terms for such payments, but the other party objected. It was held that failing the concurrence of both parties the arbitrators should proceed on the basis agreed at the time of their appointment. The result of the decision may be summarised as follows:

(a) An arbitrator who accepts appointment with or without any stipulation as to fees thereby enters into a trilateral agreement with the parties.

[1] [1991] 3 All E.R. 211.

(b) By that agreement the arbitrator assumes the status of a quasi-judicial adjudicator with all the duties and disabilities inherent in that status.
(c) Amongst those disabilities is an inability to deal unilaterally with one party for a personal benefit.
(d) It follows that an arbitrator who has accepted appointment on a particular basis as to the amount and payment of his fees (which may include a stipulation as to payment in advance or a commitment fee) cannot thereafter alter the basis of his remuneration unless all parties agree.
(e) An arbitrator who has accepted appointment without stipulation as to fees is entitled to a reasonable fee to be taxed, by him or by the court, at the conclusion of the arbitration, and cannot thereafter make any special agreement or arrangement about his fees unless all parties to the reference concur in it.
(f) So the arbitrator may not enter into any fee agreement or arrangement with a party to which any other party objects.
(g) These propositions apply to a sole arbitrator, a party-appointed arbitrator, an umpire, a chairman or a third arbitrator.

2–238 The above analysis has in effect been confirmed by the 1996 Act. None of it creates difficulty for an arbitrator appointed by agreement of the parties, for he can negotiate the fee arrangements before accepting appointment. But there are grave difficulties in the many thousands of appointments made by appointing institutions such as the Royal Institution of Chartered Surveyors or the Chartered Institute of Arbitrators. For in a large proportion of arbitrations one party would prefer to delay the proceedings. If that party's consent to a particular fee basis or arrangement is a condition precedent to the appointment of an arbitrator, the opportunities for delay, and the incentives for objecting to the fees proposed, are obvious. Yet if the prospective arbitrator agrees to accept appointment without agreement as to fees, he commits himself to an unspecified volume of work, to be performed at unspecified dates, for fees that are unspecified and that—if a party insists—are left to be determined by the court by a process that requires the arbitrator to justify his fees and that may not be completed for a considerable time after the end of the arbitration.

2–239 In practice disputes about fees are rare; the commitment fees proposed by the arbitrators in the Norjarl arbitration were considered by both Leggatt L.J. and Stuart-Smith L.J. to be "extravagant". So the lesser evil for the arbitrator may well be to accept appointment and immediately to notify the parties of the basis on which he proposes to charge. He accepts the possibility that one party will reject the proposals and thereby expose him to the risk that at the end of the arbitration either party will invoke its rights under sections 28, 56 and 63 of the Act of 1950 to have the fees determined by the court. If one party objects to the proposal, the arbitrator can notify the other party that having regard to the objection the fees are not agreed and are left to be resolved at the end of the arbitration.

Interim award for fees to date

Under the old law there may also have been the option for the arbitrator to issue an interim award in a long arbitration taxing and settling his fees to date. If done, this would have given him an opportunity to claim his interim fees on the award. If that remedy ever was available, it is available no longer. An arbitrator who wants interim payments should now specifically stipulate for them. If in the meantime the other party has paid, the arbitrator should consider refunding the payment.[2] 2–240

Contents of the express contract

In a simple case, where a reasonably accurate assessment of the difficulty of the case and the time likely to be required to deal with it can be made at an early stage, and the possibility of the dispute being compromised after the arbitrator has done significant work on it is slight, a lump sum payable on publication of the award may well be appropriate. But it will often be appropriate only in the most straightforward cases; and even so a case that seems straightforward when the basis of remuneration is being decided often turns into something for which the agreed lump sum is wholly inappropriate. However, with the growth of limited time hearings, the possibility of agreeing a lump sum, perhaps with stage payments, has increased, and should always be considered. 2–241

Some possible alternative bases of remuneration

Some alternative methods of remuneration are: 2–242

- (a) a percentage of the amount in issue between the parties at the outset;
- (b) a percentage of the mid-point between the rival figures; this is often adopted in rent arbitrations;
- (c) a single rate per hour or day spent;
- (d) one rate per hour or day spent in a hearing and another (usually lower) for time spent out of the hearing (*e.g.* on reading, or in writing the award);
- (e) some combination of the above.

The decision as to which basis to adopt will vary according to the weight and complication of the case; the likely time interval between appointment and hearing (including provision for inflation); the likely duration of the hearing; the effect of a possible overrun of the hearing; the effect of the commitment upon other earning capabilities; and the likelihood of compromise. 2–243

It has been suggested that fixing the fee as a percentage of the amount in issue should be conducive to the adoption of speedy and time-saving procedures, 2–244

[2] *Turner v. Stevenage Borough Council, The Times*, March 27, 1997, C.A.

as compared with hourly or daily rates which if anything encourage long drawn out proceedures, both in the interlocutory stages and at the hearing.[3] If this suggestion is to be adopted, it must presumably be applied to all professionals concerned, so that all have a like interest in finding the quickest and most efficient procedure for resolving the dispute. However, experience of rent review, where the arbitrator usually charges a percentage of the mean of the rival valuations of the property whereas the solicitors, and in effect counsel, charge on a time basis, does not suggest that anyone consciously or unconsciously spins out the work in order to charge higher fees.

Cancellation fees

2–245 Some arbitrators require the parties to agree to pay cancellation charges in the event that after time has been set aside for hearings, the case settles. If such charges are reasonable and have no element of ''windfall profit'' in them, then in principle it is unobjectionable to make such agreements with parties. But they should bear some real relation to the risk that cancellation will actually mean a loss of income either through having turned other work away, or being unable to get other work at short notice.[4] An alternative is to use the mechanism of booking fees, which avoids this problem.

Expenses of the arbitrator

2–246 The remuneration agreement should where appropriate deal with travelling and accommodation expenses, subsistence expenses, travelling time (not inconsiderable if there is to be a hearing and/or view in a faraway place) and special disbursements; possible inflation, if the time between appointment and award is likely to be considerable; currency of payment; interim or stage payments; security for payment; and time when payment is due.

2–247 See drafting suggestions Nos. 44, 82 and 84 in Appendix 1.

Time when monies are payable

2–248 It is desirable for the agreement as to remuneration to specify not only what sums will be payable but also the time at which, or the event upon which, monies become payable. For example, sums payable upon the completion of the award should be expressed to be payable upon notification that the award is ready, rather than on collection. In a long arbitration a tribunal will usually stipulate for interim payments. Sums paid in respect of expenses should be repayable as and when they are incurred (if they are not paid direct to the hotel, travel agent, etc.).

[3] See article by Dr Herman, Financial Correspondent of the *Financial Times*, in *Arbitration*, August 1985.

[4] For an indication of the problems of such arrangements and the attitude of the courts towards them see the *Norjarl* decision, above.

The quantum of remuneration

Arbitrations vary enormously in their complexity, in the amount at issue in them, and in the time required to conduct them. Arbitrators vary enormously in their experience and other qualifications. So it is difficult to give any useful guidance as to what is a proper level of remuneration. In England an arbitrator is entitled to "such reasonable fees and expenses (if any) as are appropriate in the circumstances"; which gives little guidance. Where the arbitrator is a professional man, perhaps the best guidance that can be given is that he should take the level of fees that he would charge for the most comparable type of work that he undertakes in his practice as, *e.g.* an architect, or dentist, or lawyer; and then adjust it (upwards or downwards as the case may be) according to the difficulty, complexity and importance of the issues that he has to resolve and the amount of his time that will be absorbed. In administered arbitrations the administering institution often fixes the level or basis of remuneration; and many may not regard the fees proposed above as appropriate. **2–249**

Remuneration where there are two or three arbitrators in an ad hoc arbitration

The basic principles affecting remuneration of the arbitrator apply whatever the number of arbitrators, and apply to an umpire or a chairman as to the arbitrators themselves. There are some practical difficulties. If the arbitrators are appointed more or less simultaneously, or if the parties jointly appoint two or three arbitrators, there is much to be said for consultation between the arbitrators to avoid great disparity between the fees charged. But in many cases one party—usually the chairman—appoints "his" arbitrator long before the other party makes an appointment. In such a case the appointing party may want the arbitrator to agree the basis of charging, and to start the process of arbitration—reading the papers, booking dates, and so on. In those circumstances it is open to the arbitrator to agree the basis of charge without awaiting any consultation with the other arbitrator. A chairman is often remunerated at a higher level than an appointed arbitrator to take into account the expected greater level of administration and the greater responsibility for controlling the arbitration to a successful conclusion. **2–250**

It is also open to the other arbitrator/s to seek and obtain agreement to a different rate or rates or different terms. Thus in a three-man tribunal, each arbitrator may receive a different amount. **2–251**

Remuneration of chairman or umpire

The position as regards remuneration of an umpire/chairman who has taken part in the proceedings is broadly the same as that of an arbitrator. Where an umpire is appointed he should agree with the parties the terms of his engagement, including his functions, duties, whether he should only involve himself when **2–252** the appointed arbitrators disagree, cancellation fees etc. If the parties have not agreed his function, then he will attend the proceedings and be supplied with the same documentation and materials as are supplied to the appointed arbitrators. If he has not entered into a specific agreement as to fees, then he is entitled to payment (on the statutory basis unless otherwise agreed) even though the two arbitrators agree so that he is not called upon to decide anything. The position is probably the same if the parties, without expressly requesting him to take part, acquiesce in his doing so.

Remuneration in administered arbitrations

Many institutional rules provide scales of remuneration

2–253 Where the arbitration is being administered by an institution, the liability of the parties to make payments (if any) in respect of the arbitrator's services will usually be governed by the rules of that institution, and the adoption of those rules by the parties will (unless some special agreement is made) constitute their agreement as to remuneration. For example, the Arbitration Rules of The Chartered Institute of Arbitrators (1988 Edition) provide in Rule 10(1) that the costs of the arbitration shall be in accordance with the Schedule of Costs, and in Rule 10(2) that from the commencement of the arbitration the parties shall be jointly and severally liable to the Institute for these costs until they are paid. Many trade or arbitration institutions require a deposit on account of fees.

Some institutions give guidance but not scales

2–254 Some institutions (the LCIA for example) specifically state that the Arbitrator cannot expect the same level of remuneration as he might expect to be paid in his primary profession. The LCIA leaves the arbitrators to fix their own rates, albeit with the assistance of a scale; these rates are then incorporated by the LCIA into the appointment. The fees charged by individuals vary considerably, but there is usually a loading in favour of the Chairman, who is expected to administer and to control the arbitration.

Fees in ICC Arbitrations

2–255 These are usually split 40 (Chairman): 30:30, but this can be varied by consent of all arbitrators. In long and heavy arbitrations, the tribunal sometimes formulates an estimate of costs and fees. If this estimate is likely to exceed the amount for which the ICC is likely to ask by way of contribution from the parties, the tribunal may ask the court of the ICC to seek an increased contribution. However, the ICC is understandably reluctant to do this.

VAT on arbitrators' fees

2–256 In a domestic arbitration the practice is relatively straightforward and, so far as anecdotal evidence is concerned, seems to be applied consistently. This involves the arbitrator, if he is registered for VAT purposes, charging VAT on his fees to the parties or treating his fees as inclusive of VAT. In either case he accounts for that VAT to the Commissioners for Customs and Excise. This practice also seems to be correct.

However, in September 1997 the European Court in *Hoffman v. Finanzamt* decided that VAT is to be charged by an arbitrator in full regardless of where in the world parties to the arbitration are situated or carry on business. This decision is potentially serious for international arbitrators. It is currently the subject of governmental discussion, and it is understood that in England the Commissioners of Customs and Excise will not seek to apply it pending discussions of a possible change in the relevant Directive. 2–257

What is terra incognita so far as the availability of any authoritative guidance or indeed the existence of a clear established practice is concerned, is what happens: 2–258

(a) where one or more of the parties are within the Union but outside England and Wales; or
(b) where the fees are determined and paid by an institution which is within the Union but outside England and Wales.

In this situation, all that can be recommended is that ad hoc arrangements are agreed with the parties or institution concerned; and that if any doubt remains in the mind of the arbitrator, he should seek to have those arrangements approved by his local VAT inspector, preferably before they have been concluded. 2–259

Enforcing the right to payment

Payment on delivery

Apart from statute, an arbitrator in England has a lien on the award to enforce payment; that is to say he is entitled to withhold delivery until he is paid.[5] 2–260

So in England the most common method of publishing an award is to enclose a note of fees and disbursements with the letters notifying the parties that the award is ready for collection, and to say that the award may be collected on payment of the amount specified.[6] If the award places ultimate liability on the opposing party, the party who has paid may recover from the opposing party. A well-drawn award will expressly so provide. 2–261

Statutory provision for payment into court

If there is no agreement in writing fixing the amount of the fee, a party who wishes to take up the award but to challenge the amount of the fee demanded 2–262

[5] This is not expressly referred to in the 1996 Act but *cf.* s.63(7) and s.64(4).
[6] See drafting suggestion No. 81 in Appendix 1.

may apply to the court under section 56 of the 1996 Act for an order that the arbitrator deliver up the award. On such an application the court may:

(a) order delivery up of the award on payment into court of the amount demanded or such lesser amount as the court may consider appropriate;
(b) order that the amount of the fee and expenses properly payable are to be determined in such manner as it thinks fit;
(c) order that the appropriate amount be paid out to the arbitrator from the moneys in court.

2–263 The amount that is properly payable is the amount that has been agreed, or if there has been no agreement, the statutory entitlement. No such application may be made until all other remedies are exhausted, and no appeal may be brought against the order of the court without leave. Disputes about fees between a party and an administering institution are subject to the same procedure.

Disadvantages to the arbitrator of disputes about fees

2–264 Apart from the possibility that the fees allowed may be much lower than the amount that the arbitrator has claimed, the procedure under the 1996 Act has the disadvantages first, that the arbitrator may be put to the trouble of justifying his charges in the minutest detail; second, that payment to him may be delayed for months whilst his proper entitlement is determined under section 64; and third, that he—a person appointed to resolve disputes—has succeeded in involving the parties, or one of them, in a fresh dispute. Hence the importance, to the arbitrator, of ensuring that the amount of the fees payable is regulated by a prior written agreement.

Disadvantages to the parties of dispute about fees

2–265 There is a further disadvantage to the parties of this procedure, since neither side will see the award in time to appeal it, or to take objection. It is also doubtful whether a court will extend the time for an appeal or other complaint, since it is always open to a party to pay up, collect the award and challenge the fee later.

Provision for assessment of arbitrator's fees as between parties

2–266 Section 64 of the 1996 Act is another provision that enables the court to consider the fees and expenses of the tribunal. Here, however, the dispute is between the parties as to what is recoverable the one from the other in respect of the fees and expenses charged by the tribunal. This will most usually happen where the parties are implementing a costs order made by the tribunal itself. What are recoverable are those reasonable fees and expenses as are appropriate to the circumstances. The court can either determine such a dispute or order that it be determined by some means other than itself—*e.g.* referred to an arbitral institution. The order may be made by the court on terms—*e.g.* as to the bringing into court of sums of money, or the payment of part of the monies sought to be recovered by a successful party. In dealing with this dispute, the court will take into account any order as to fees and expenses made under section 24 or 25 as a result of the removal or resignation of an arbitrator.

This section is not relevant to the arbitrator's own right, *vis-à-vis* one or both or more of the parties, to be paid his fees and expenses. Thus where he has agreed with the parties his terms of remuneration he is entitled to recover pursuant to those terms whatever the decision is in the "costs" dispute between the parties. **2–267**

Remuneration of arbitrator where he resigns or is removed

This is a new topic and, accordingly, guidance is speculative. **2–268**

Where an arbitrator resigns

Where the matter is resignation, it is thought that there will be less reason for refusing an arbitrator his remuneration up to date, if that can sensibly be calculated—*e.g.* it might be difficult, but not impossible, if he has quoted a lump sum for the whole arbitration. Something will depend on the reason for resignation and the point in time at which the resignation is announced. Where ill health, or a very substantial enlargement of the arbitration, or serious personal circumstances such as the sudden illness of a close relative, is the problem, it is likely that the courts will be reluctant to refuse an arbitrator his full remuneration to date. Equally, there will or should be little problem where the resignation is early on, or at a "natural" break in the arbitration, *e.g.* after the delivery of a decision on a preliminary point.[7] **2–269**

Where an arbitrator is removed

Where the arbitrator is removed, there must be a greater likelihood that he will be deprived of an entitlement to unpaid fees and may even be required to repay fees already collected. Again, all will depend on the circumstances. Physical or mental incapacity would not, at first sight, seem to warrant any deprivation, let alone repayment. The onset of Alzheimer's is hardly the arbitrator's fault; and anyway, it would lie hardly in the mouth of the judiciary to complain of such matters, given the fact that many of their predecessors were thought only to have been appointed to the bench on becoming blind, deaf and gaga. At the **2–270**

[7] This is not wholly satisfactory for the parties, since there is always room for a subsequent tribunal to understand the preliminary decision in a manner different to that which the maker intended; or where the tribunal is of three or more persons, for them to disagree about the meaning of the award.

other end of the spectrum, where the case is a refusal or failure to conduct the proceedings properly or to use all reasonable despatch, the matter is likely to be different. These are matters which lie at the heart of the appointment—see section 1 of the 1996 Act—and a failure here is likely to be viewed seriously by the court. The extent to which an arbitrator who has so failed should be entitled to retain any fees out of the matter must be questionable. Finally, lack of impartiality or qualifications seem likely to come in the middle of the spectrum. Involvement with a party, or the lack of a relevant qualification may have been overlooked perfectly innocently, and without fault on the part of the arbitrator. Why then should he not be paid for anything that he has done? On the other hand, he may be in the position of the barrister who succeeds in advising both sides to a dispute that each has a good case, without recognising the names of the parties involved or the facts of the dispute. Matters of this sort are unlikely to result other than from negligence, and may well lead to recovery by the parties of any fees paid to the tribunal.

2–271 It follows that an arbitrator who realises that he is in any kind of difficulty at all—*e.g.* if his diary has become much fuller than he expected, or he has found out a connection with one of the parties that may be a problem, or he realises that the dispute really takes him out of his professional depth—should be quick to offer to resign. Apart from saving him the embarrassment of being at the heart of a developing problem, such a step reduces the risk of having to find and repay substantial sums of money; and, of course, the parties may be so impressed by his integrity that they decide to keep him despite the problem.

Security for fees

2–272 The plainest obligation to pay fees will not avail if the debtor cannot or will not pay. In many cases the arbitrator is willing to rely upon the standing of the parties as a sufficient security that his fees will be paid. But where he has no indication of the standing of the parties it will often be wise for him to obtain some security other than the mere promise of the party. Various methods are available, for example:

(a) a deposit with the administering institution of the estimated fees; see, for example, ICC Rules, Article 9. The deposits are intended to be paid in equal shares by the claimant and the respondent but if either refuses to pay his share the other may pay it;
(b) a deposit with the arbitrator;
(c) a deposit with the Chartered Institute of Arbitrators;
(d) where the would-be appointor is a company of unknown means, a personal undertaking from a director or other officer of the company;
(e) an undertaking by a solicitor to be responsible for the fees. It should however be noted that a solicitor who makes an appointment on behalf

of his client does not, without more, become personally liable for fees due from the client;

(f) possibly by way of an order, upon his own motion, under section 38.

9. The Principles of Natural Justice

The fundamental requirements

Under English law there are two fundamental requirements of justice in deciding a dispute between two or more parties. The first is that the judge, arbitrator or other tribunal must be, and must be seen to be, disinterested and unbiased. The second is that every party to a dispute must be given a fair opportunity to present his case and to answer the case of his opponent. 2–273

These principles are helpfully embodied in section 33 of the Act as follows: 2–274

> "(1) The tribunal shall—
> (a) act fairly and impartially as between the parties, giving each party a reasonable opportunity of putting his case and dealing with that of his opponent, and
> (b) adopt procedures suitable to the circumstances of the particular case, avoiding unnecessary delay or expense, so as to provide a fair means for the resolution of the matters falling to be determined.
> (2) The tribunal shall comply with that general duty in conducting the arbitral proceedings, in its decisions on matters of procedure and evidence and in the exercise of all other powers conferred on it."

The arbitrator must be, and must be seen to be, disinterested and unbiased

As discussed earlier, the arbitrator must be on his guard with respect to connections with a party; connections in the subject matter of the dispute; and connections with the nature of the dispute. He should bear in mind at all times the test as formulated by Ackner L.J., namely 2–275

> "Would a reasonable man, not being a party to the dispute, think that the connection was close enough to cause the arbitrator to be biased?"

Duty to act impartially

The arbitrator has always been obliged to conduct the reference impartially in both actions and words and to decide each issue put to him—whether interlocu- 2–276 tory or final—fairly and impartially. Whatever the provocation—for example, where a party is obviously playing for time, or where a party or his representative is persistently discourteous—each decision must be made impartially. Even if a party is challenging in the courts some earlier decision of the arbitrator, and perhaps making unfair criticisms of the arbitrator, his overriding duty to act fairly and dispassionately remains—indeed, it is if anything increased.

Duty to be seen to act impartially

2–277 On the same principle, the arbitrator should take pains not to associate with one party or his representatives more than with the other. He should never, for example, lunch with one side only during a hearing. His confidence in his own probity may not be shared by a party who does not know him.[8] He should try to avoid even casual conversation with one side in the absence of the other. Examples of inappropriate behaviour are:

(a) An arbitrator received from party A a letter containing a powerful attack on the financial probity of Party B. There was no indication the letter had been copied to Party B: and in fact it had not been. The arbitrator did not check that it had gone to Party B, nor did he himself send it to Party B. When Party B found out about the letter the Arbitrator returned the letter to Party A at Party A's request rather than providing Party B with a copy. The arbitrator was removed.

(b) There was an apparently long conversation between a planning inspector and the chairman of the planning committee of the respondent council, immediately after a planning inquiry had been concluded. The decision of the inspector was quashed.

Where a relevant communication is forced upon the arbitrator by one side in the absence of the other, he should at once communicate it to the other side and give them an opportunity of commenting upon it.

Fair opportunity to present case

2–278 Each party must be given a fair opportunity to present his case; to know the opposing case; and to meet the opposing case.

Each party should know what case is being made against him

2–279 Since it is as fundamental a principle of arbitration as of litigation that each party shall have a fair opportunity to put his own case and to challenge the case put by his adversary, it must follow that, unless the parties otherwise agree, an arbitrator should not receive oral evidence or argument from one party in the

[8] And even less by one who does know him.

absence of the other, and should not receive any document from one party without ensuring that the other party receives a copy.[9]

No right to an oral hearing

A party can of course both put his own case, and challenge his opponent's case, without an oral hearing; many—perhaps a majority—of arbitrations are conducted without a hearing. Nevertheless before 1997 if neither the arbitration agreement nor any trade or other custom indicated the contrary, a party to an arbitration agreement governed by English law was entitled to demand that the arbitration be conducted by way of an oral hearing. A refusal to hear him would in most cases have amounted to a denial of justice. The present law is the reverse. There is no right to an oral hearing unless expressly so agreed in the arbitration agreement or by incorporating rules to this effect, or, of course, in terms of reference created as part of the arbitration. Absent such an agreement, the decision whether to have an oral hearing or not, and if so, how it is to be conducted and what it is to deal with is a matter for the tribunal.[10] 2–280

If there is to be a hearing, the arbitrator must ensure that each party is given notice of it, even if it seems likely that he will not attend, and even if he has already stated that he does not intend to attend. 2–281

Fairness in fixing dates

If there is to be a hearing, the date and place should be as far as is practicable convenient to both parties. This is of course a counsel of perfection, for the date of hearing is a frequent source of difficulty and dissension. Speed of decision-making is an important element in arbitration particularly to a claimant or counter-claimant and the maxim that justice delayed is justice denied is particularly apposite to many arbitrations. It is for the arbitrator to judge what is a reasonable opportunity for a party to present his case; but a party should not be deprived of that opportunity by a genuine mistake on his part, or on the part of his legal advisers.[11] Likewise the times fixed for delivery of pleadings or written submissions should not be so short as to deny to either party a reasonable period for preparing them. 2–282

Timetables set by Institutional Rules

Institutional or other rules which impose set timetables are almost bound to get it wrong, unless the arbitrations governed by such rules are consistently small 2–283

[9] It may not be enough that the other party knows that the arbitrator has received the document, if he does not know its contents—see *Renown Investments v. Mecca Leisure* [1984] 271 E.G. 989, C.A.

[10] s.34.

[11] See *R. v. Diggines, ex p. Rahriani* [1985] 1 All E.R. 1073.

and simple. Otherwise the sheer variety of the problems which any industry throws up are bound to call for different periods to resolve. Arbitrators must also bear in mind that a claimant who launches a claim well after the relevant events has had a very long time to prepare the case, whether or not that time has been used for that purpose. It follows that a defendant who asks for a long time to reply may be stalling; but may also be genuinely embarrassed by the difficulties of dealing with a stale claim: or a situation where there was no previous claim at all. A careful balance must be struck.

The arbitrator's own knowledge and experience

Opportunity to answer opposing case

2–284 The same principle of a party knowing the case which is put against him should apply where that case is made not by his opponent but by the tribunal. And it must apply whether the "case" in question is one of law or of expert opinion or of fact.

Arbitrator chosen for his experience

2–285 It can safely be supposed that no one ever chooses an arbitrator for his inexperience (though an inexperienced arbitrator can easily be exploited by an experienced respondent bent on delay). A major reason, often the most important single reason in domestic arbitration, for the choice of arbitration as an alternative to litigation, is the opportunity that it gives to the parties for choosing, as their tribunal, a person or persons experienced in the field in which the dispute arises. An arbitrator chosen for that reason is clearly expected to use, in some way, the knowledge and experience which is the reason for his being appointed. Arbitrators vary widely in the expertise they can bring to their task, and there is much confusion about the extent to which, and the ways in which, the arbitrator may apply his expertise.

Need for disclosure

2–286 It would be carrying the adversarial principle to an absurd length if a judge or arbitrator were required to disregard a fact within his knowledge and which is logically probative of the issue that he has to determine, merely because neither of the adversaries has put it before him. In many cases it would also be humanly impossible. In the theoretically possible situation where the parties are aware of a fact, and have consciously decided not to put it before the tribunal, but are unaware that the tribunal knows the fact, the proper course for the tribunal who suggests or realises that this fact is being deliberately withheld to take would be to inform them of the tribunal's knowledge.

When arbitrator's beliefs conflict with evidence

2–287 But what if the tribunal's knowledge experience and judgment conflicts with the evidence put before him? Suppose an arbitrator has great experience of the cost of repairing houses, and he is convinced that certain repairs can be carried out at a cost wholly different to that given in evidence by either of the experts called by the parties before him? There is here an apparent conflict, familiar to any experienced judge or arbitrator, between his function to adjudicate upon the material put before him by the adversaries, and his desire to do justice between the parties. A similar situation arises where the tribunal sees an apparently important point in a party's favour which his advocate has overlooked. The duty to do justice must prevail. The parties should be told of the tribunal's knowledge or experience, or of the point that it has seen, and of how in its opinion it bears upon the issue in question. They should then be given an opportunity of reshaping their respective cases accordingly or of explaining to the arbitrator why, in the opinion of one or both of them, the point taken by the arbitrator is irrelevant or mistaken. This latter exercise is a tricky one. The progenitor of an idea often has a strong emotional link with it. Arbitrators who volunteer new directions of enquiry must try particularly hard to understand any reasoned objection to them: and seek to avoid holding too tightly to the original idea.

Information obtained on an inspection

The purpose of an inspection is to enable the arbitrator to understand and assess the evidence put before him by the parties. The inspection should not be used to add to that evidence further evidence of which the parties are not fully aware. If on his inspection the arbitrator discovers or believes he discovers new facts which in his opinion are or may be material to his decision, he must notify the parties and give them an opportunity to deal with them, either in writing or at a further hearing. Thus in *Fox v. Wellfair*[12] the claimant's evidence (which was the only evidence put before him) was that some drains had not been properly laid. After the hearing the arbitrator, without reference to the parties, carried out his own tests, formed the opinion that they had been properly laid, and decided accordingly. In such a case it is his duty to notify the parties of his discovery, and give them an opportunity of putting questions to him, or leading further evidence, or both. If neither party wishes him to take the result of his investigations into account and they make this clear, he must ignore it. **2–288**

No obligation to accept unchallenged evidence

A tribunal is not obliged to accept evidence, even when it is unchallenged, if it falls short of establishing the allegation in support of which it is called; see *Lewis Emanuel v. Sammut*.[13] In *Fox v. Wellfair* above the arbitrator, in an arbitration at which the respondent did not attend, heard evidence from eminent experts as to what building work was necessary and what it would cost. His award was set aside, and he was removed, not on the ground that he had refused to accept unchallenged evidence, but on the ground that he had not given any indication that he was minded to reject it or why. The arbitrator told the court: **2–289**

[12] [1981] 2 Lloyd's Rep. 214.
[13] [1959] 2 Lloyd's Rep. 629.

> "I did not feel it was part of my duty to indicate at the hearing that I did or did not accept any particular evidence. That is in my submission a matter for subsequent consideration and decision and for the award."

That submission was rejected. O'Connor L.J. said at 680:

> "Not having had the arbitrator's thesis, whatever it was, put to the unchallenged and highly qualified witnesses is a grave miscarriage of justice".

Dunn L.J. said at 658:

> "An expert should not in effect give evidence to himself without disclosing it to the parties, and if there is only one, to that one."

2–290 This sentence gives the key to the problem. The arbitrator's knowledge should be treated as evidence given by himself, and should be subjected to the same scrutiny and the same "rules of evidence" as any other. Is the "fact" which he is minded to take into consideration something within his own knowledge, *e.g.* because he was personally present and himself witnessed it; or is it a belief which he has long held but which originated with something he was once told and which has never been wholly corroborated? If he is minded to take it into consideration he should inform the parties of it—perhaps by first putting it into writing—and he should submit himself to cross-examination upon it by each of the parties if they so wish. If the "evidence" that he gives to himself is subjected to such scrutiny, there is no cause for, and no sense in, excluding it.

2–291 The problem is acute when a witness at an *ex parte* hearing draws inferences, based upon his skill and judgment, with which the arbitrator disagrees. The arbitrator should put his own inferences to the witness. The witness may be able to adduce further facts or arguments to make the arbitrator change his mind. If the hearing is a contested one, it is usually preferable for the arbitrator to await the opposing side's evidence, to see if the inference is contradicted. If it is not, but the arbitrator is nevertheless minded to reject it, and the point is relevant to his decision, he should say so, and if necessary allow the witness to be recalled, or other evidence brought forward.

2–292 Another example of a failure to disclose his own view is to be found in *Zermalt v. Nu-Life Upholstery*.[14] In this case the arbitrator had to decide the rental value of a shop and the parties agreed that the matter should be decided upon an exchange of letters and evidence, without a hearing. Letters were exchanged and duly copied to the other parties. Points were raised in correspondence by the arbitrator, again with copies to both parties. A meeting took place at which the arbitrator and both parties were present. Points made by one party were answered in correspondence by the other. The arbitrator inspected the subject premises and certain comparable properties relied on. In his award the arbit-

[14] (1985) 275 E.G. 1134.

rator raised two matters that had not previously been mentioned by anyone. The landlord's application to set the award aside, and remove the arbitrator, under section 23 of the Arbitration Act 1950 was granted. Bingham J. said at 1138:

> "I fully accept and understand the difficulties in which an expert finds himself when acting as an arbitrator. There is an unavoidable inclination to rely on one's own expertise and in respect of general matters that is not only not objectionable but is desirable and a very large part of the reason why an arbitrator with expert qualifications is chosen. Nevertheless, the rules of natural justice do require, even in an arbitration conducted by an expert, that matters which are likely to form the subject of decision, in so far as they are specific matters, should be exposed for the comments and submissions of the parties. If an arbitrator is impressed by a point that has never been raised by either side then it is his duty to put it to them so that they have an opportunity to comment. If he feels that the proper approach is one that has not been explored or advanced in evidence or submission then again it is his duty to give the parties a chance to comment. If he is to any extent relying on his own personal experience in a specific way then that again is something that he should mention so that it can be explored. It is not right that a decision should be based on specific matters which the parties have never had the chance to deal with, nor is it right that a party should first learn of adverse points in the decision against him. That is contrary both to the substance of justice and to its appearance, and on the facts of this case I think that the landlords' case is made out."

The arbitration there was not conducted solely on written representations from the parties; the arbitrator had, and took, the opportunity of raising points with the parties both at a meeting with their surveyors and in correspondence. Yet he never raised two points which appear from his award to have been part of his reasoning. The same principle applies to legal arbitration and points of law. In sum the knowledge and experience must be disclosed at or before the (only) hearing. The problem is to know what knowledge and what experience need to be disclosed. If in doubt, disclosure is best. **2–293**

Circulating an award in draft

This is a controversial topic. Anecdotal evidence suggests that some very experienced construction industry arbitrators are prepared to circulate the award in draft to the parties. To show the parties a draft of the award before publication invites further submissions and a further draft and so on, as well as endangering the chances of payment to the arbitrator. Costs are already too high, and reconvening a hearing would in most cases lead to a quite unacceptable increase. Inviting written submissions on the draft is not practicable, because although it might appear less costly than reconvening a hearing, each side must be given **2–294** one chance to comment on the other's submission, and the delay would often be considerable. It follows that the circulation of the draft should be made subject to a very strict control as to what the parties are being invited to respond upon and the timing and procedure for so doing. An interesting example might be that of the ICC. The Court of Arbitration advised by the Secretariat vets awards on matters of form rather than substance but attention is drawn to apparent gaps or defects in reasoning and to other errors, perhaps of calculation. The quality of the Award is thereby improved.

The doctrine of legitimate expectation

2–295 An arbitrator who creates a reasonable expectation in the mind of a party that he intends to adopt a particular procedure should not depart from that procedure without giving reasonable notice of his intention so to do. The legitimate or reasonable expectation may arise from an express intimation or from the existence of a regular practice which a party may reasonably expect to continue.[15] But this should not discourage arbitrators from procedural innovation, having regard in particular to the obligations conferred on the arbitrator by section 33.

Summary

2–296 In arbitrations in which there is a hearing, the arbitrator should:

(a) enable himself, by his directions, to know what the issues are, and to read all the documents relating to them, before the hearing;
(b) do the maximum possible thinking about them before, rather than at or after, the hearing;
(c) ensure, at the hearing, both that he understands the cases being made on each side on each issue, and that the advocates know of any facts or arguments that he is minded to take into account that have not already been mentioned, and of which they might otherwise be unaware;
(d) give the parties an opportunity of controverting or challenging any such facts or experience;
(e) where he thinks it helpful to the parties and to himself, indicate to the parties any significant preliminary issue which he considers to be relevant and invite comment upon it;
(f) if, after the hearing, any point of importance occurs to him that the

[15] *CCSU v. Minister for the Civil Service* [1984] 3 All E.R. 395, *per* Lord Fraser at 943.

parties have not had an opportunity of dealing with, notify them and give them such opportunity.

(g) remember that at the end of the day, if the parties agree on a procedure he must follow it, even if it means discounting his own experience.

10. The Powers of the Arbitrator

Sources of powers

Derived from express agreement, implied agreement, or statute

The extent of his power is determined by the agreement between the parties. In that sense it can be said that the principal source of the powers of the arbitrator is the agreement between the parties. However, extensive powers are given to him under English law by the Act. These powers are given subject to the right of the parties to contract out of them. In the absence of such contracting out, the arbitrator has the powers. **2–297**

The agreement may confer powers upon him by virtue of: **2–298**

(a) express terms; or
(b) implied terms (particularly terms implied by the custom of a particular trade); or
(c) terms of some trade or professional institute incorporated into the contract, *e.g.* Arbitration Rules of the Chartered Institute of Arbitrators; or
(d) terms incorporated into the agreement by statute.

As an example of the first class, the arbitration clause may expressly authorise the arbitrator to order relief on a provisional basis: for example to order a Respondent to pay part or all of the claim to the claimant on account—subject to confirmation in a final award. An example of the second class is the power for the arbitrator to limit the whole of the investigative element of an arbitration to inspection of the goods the subject of the dispute in the absence of the parties, and to treat as evidence his observations of them—the "look-sniff" procedure. In the third class are the many contracts which expressly incorporate a set of arbitration rules, *e.g.* the rules of the Grain and Feed Trade Association or the UNCITRAL Rules.[16] The fourth class comprises the provisions expressed by the Act to be contained in every arbitration agreement unless a contrary intention is expressed in it. **2–299**

[16] *CCSU v. Minister for the Civil Service* [1984] 3 All E.R. 935, *per* Lord Fraser at 943.

The range of procedures available

The principal source of rules will be those adopted by the parties

2–300 Judges in municipal courts are bound by Rules of Court, and in the case of the High Court in England these, with accompanying notes, occupy over 4,000 pages of the Supreme Court Practice. All parties coming to court are bound by these Rules. They cannot even agree among themselves to dispense completely with the time scale imposed by the Rules. In other words, primacy in procedural matters is given to the tribunal, not the parties.

2–301 The reverse is true of arbitration in England. Within the (very broad) framework of the mandatory provisions the parties are free to concoct their own procedural recipe. They can "legislate" for liberality of procedure or for traditional methods: they can choose great formality or great informality: they can give to the tribunal a very wide jurisdiction of a very narrow one. Such agreement can be specific or effected by the process of incorporating a set of institutional rules. These tend to favour the liberal, informal, wide jurisdiction approach.[17] In the absence of agreement between the parties the Act provides a detailed set of default procedures.

Arbitrator is otherwise master of procedure

2–302 This is the general proposition. It is subject always to any restrictions imposed upon him by the arbitration agreement and to any constraints imposed by the mandatory requirements of the Act. In principle, in England, the arbitrator controls the procedure of the arbitration, and the courts have no inherent general power to direct him as regards what to do or what not to do[18] unless what he is doing or has done is manifestly unfair or contrary to natural justice.[19]

2–303 The wide range of his powers is of particular importance in enabling him to tailor the procedure to the needs of the particular dispute, rather than to take off the peg a procedure (*e.g.* litigation procedure) designed to cater for widely differing situations. He must always bear in mind the possibility that the parties may prefer a quick and cheap resolution of their differences to a meticulous, time-consuming and expensive search for perfect justice. If the former is what they both want, he should have no difficulty in devising a procedure that will produce it. If, as often happens, only one of them wants it, it is for him to determine a procedure which is both economic and fair.

2–304 The wide range of his powers is also important where he is satisfied that one party is deliberately and unreasonably seeking to delay the progress of the arbitration.

17 See s.4 of the Act and particularly 4(2) and 4(3).

18 Watkins L.J. in *Abu Dhabi Gas Liquification Co. v. Eastern Bechtel Corporation* [1982] 2 Lloyd's Rep. 425; Robert Goff J. in *Waring (F.R.) (U.K.) v. Administraccao Gerale Do Alcool E.P.* [1983] 1 Lloyd's Rep. 45.

19 *The Peter Kirk* [1990] 1 Lloyd's Rep. 154.

Autonomy of the arbitrator—does it extend to the inquisitorial approach

Doubts as to the extent to which an arbitrator may depart from the procedures usually used in English High Court litigation have now been removed by sections 33 and 34 of the Act. Section 33 imposes obligations upon the tribunal, and section 34 spells out the tribunal's powers, subject always to the right of the parties to agree any matter. **2–305**

Choice of procedures always available to the arbitrator

A. Where no hearing is to take place

The range of procedures available (whether before or after the Act) is as follows: **2–306**

(a) Documents only; no submissions beyond those contained in the correspondence that passed before he was appointed.
(b) Documents (as submitted by each party) accompanied by written representations which may function both as pleadings and as submissions. If required, these can be followed by written cross-representations.
(c) As (b), but with disclosure by each party of all documents in his control relating to the matters in issue.
(d), (e),
(f) As (a), (b) or (c) above but with an inspection of the subject-matter of the dispute (*e.g.* look-sniff arbitrations in quality disputes).

B. Where a hearing is to take place

(g) Oral hearing after pleadings; no discovery, but the parties prepare a common bundle of documents whose authenticity is admitted. In this connection it is important to distinguish between admitting the authenticity of a document (*i.e.* that it was written on the date it purports to have been written; and if it purports to have been sent that it was in fact sent) and admitting the truth of the statements contained in the document.
(h) As (g), but with Statements of Cases and Replies thereto substituted for pleadings.
(j) Oral hearing, after pleadings or Statements of Cases and Replies; no evidence except expert evidence; expert reports exchanged before hearing.
(k) As (j) but experts to attempt to agree after exchange of reports, and to

prepare a statement of points on which they agree and points on which they disagree.

(l) As (g), (h), (j) or (k) above but with full discovery of documents.

Procedures newly available to the arbitrator

2–307 The range of available procedures is now widened, particularly by the power given by section 34(2)(g) for the tribunal itself to take the initiative in ascertaining facts or law or both. Thus for example the tribunal can, after identifying the issues, decide that it will determine some issues without receiving any evidence; that it will determine other issues on documents only without a hearing; and that it will hold a hearing to determine yet other issues. The various options indicated above then need to be considered in relation to the method of determination to be chosen for each. If there is to be a hearing on any issue, it is increasingly likely to be limited in time.

2–308 Discovery is also likely to be sharply curtailed, in the interests of saving both time and costs. The circumstances in which, absent agreement of the parties, an arbitrator should order full discovery, should be very rare. Arbitrators, if they are to fulfill their duties under section 33 will need to be far more robust than hitherto in denying requests for full discovery.

Taking charge of the proceedings

Arbitrator is master of the procedure

2–309 As soon as he is appointed the arbitrator should take charge of the proceedings. In many cases the dispute is of a familiar nature; there is an established procedure for dealing with it; the parties and their solicitors (and perhaps counsel) are very familiar with the procedure. In such cases the directions will be stereotyped, and parties may well agree upon them without the need for a preliminary meeting. In all cases, however, the arbitrator must consider, in consultation with the parties, what procedure is most likely to produce a just, speedy and economical resolution of the issues involved. Arbitrators must guard against the slavish or automatic adoption of traditional procedures unless either that is what both parties want or the tests of section 33 are met.

2–310 Since arbitration is founded on the agreement of the parties, it is of course preferable that the procedure adopted be agreed between the parties and the arbitrator. But where necessary the arbitrator must decide. It is demeaning to his office to be seen to be going to almost any lengths to avoid having to make a decision. As the General Counsel to one of the world's largest multinational corporations once said (speaking from experience of arbitration practice in many countries):

> "It is difficult to make some people come to hard decisions, and act as judges, and say to somebody: 'You have 10 days to produce the papers, or

you are barred from presenting your evidence.' They try to be friends with everyone.''[20]

In similar vein the late Lord Roskill said: 2–311

''Rule 1 is—keep control of the proceedings and don't let cases drift. Remember you are the masters of your own procedure, then never try to fit every case into the same procedural strait-jacket because some won't fit. Be flexible, as flexible as you can in trying to meet the wishes of the parties, but above all be firm, politely firm, especially about delay. Why is it that some arbitrators seem frightened to grasp the nettle and take control of the cases and show that delay will not be tolerated? We all, I think, have some inbuilt fear of doing an injustice if we refuse to accept an excuse for seeking further time for pleadings or discovery or a request, attractively if unjustifiably advanced, for an adjournment of the hearing. A judge may feel inclined to take the risk because there is always the Court of Appeal to direct him if he has gone too far in a particular direction. But in matters like this an arbitrator has for all practical purposes both first and last word and I often think he fears that if he is firm someone may thereafter accuse him in the courts of 'misconduct', that dreadful word. I can understand the fear though I sincerely believe it to be unjustified. It has, I think, an historical basis and stems from the days when the courts were hostile to arbitrations, but I do not believe that any court would presume to criticize an arbitrator who was firm in dealing with disobedience to his orders, so long as he acted fairly.''[21]

Quality of decision making and the preliminary discussion

In many arbitrations the quality of decision-making is as important in the prepar- 2–312
atory stages as it is in the award itself. A bad arbitrator may fear that making a decision that is strongly opposed by a party will mean that that party will never agree to his being arbitrator again. But timidity—shrinking from decision—is the hallmark of a bad arbitrator, just as firmness, when accompanied by fairness and courtesy, is the hallmark of a good one. He must therefore be aware at the outset of the range of procedures mentioned above. But before deciding which is the most appropriate, he must inform himself of the general nature of the issues. The first step to doing this may well be the holding of a preliminary meeting.

The wisdom of having a preliminary dialogue in a meeting, even given the 2–313
inconvenience of arranging it to suit a number of people and the cost of holding it, will often outweigh the advantages of dealing with matters by correspondence

[20] Sheldon L. Berens at a meeting of the International Bar Association London, September 1981 (see *Forum London*, published by the IBA 1982).

[21] Third Alexander Lecture given by Lord Justice Roskill, March 8, 1977, reproduced in (1977) *Arbitration* 4.

(or even by conference call), which is the way interlocutory matters should usually be dealt with in arbitration. This is because it is an excellent opportunity to get the feel of the arbitration, the dispute, the parties and the advocates, to get agreement on outstanding matters (such as the arbitrator's terms of engagement) if this has not already been done; and to get agreement on procedures.

Powers of the tribunal

2–314 These fall into two categories. First those powers which the arbitrator or tribunal has unless the parties have agreed otherwise—the "contract out" powers. Second, those powers which the tribunal only has if the parties have so agreed—the "contract in" powers.

The contract out powers

2–315 Unless the parties have agreed otherwise either generally or in respect of any specific power or powers, the following are the statutory limits of the tribunal's powers to control the arbitration. Parties may widen or narrow these limits not only by specific agreement but by general or partial incorporation of rules promulgated by institutions; one example is the UNCITRAL Rules.

Specific powers of the tribunal

2–316 The tribunal

(a) may decide matters by a majority if the tribunal consists of more than one; and is not unanimous.[22] A chairman may decide alone, if there is no majority.[23]
(b) may rule on its own substantive jurisdiction, namely as to whether there is a valid arbitration agreement[24];
(c) may rule as to whether the tribunal is properly constituted[25];
(d) may rule as to what matters have been submitted to arbitration in accordance with the arbitration agreement.[26];
(e) may admit objections to the jurisdiction despite the fact that they were not raised at the outset of the proceedings,[27] or, if later, as soon as the matter the subject of objection surfaced in the arbitration,[28];
(f) may decide when and where any part of the proceedings is to be held[29];

[22] s.20(3).
[23] s.20(4).
[24] s.30(1)(a).
[25] s.30(1)(b).
[26] s.30(1)(c).
[27] s.31(1).
[28] s.31(2).
[29] s.34(2)(a).

(g) may decide the language or languages to be used in the proceedings and whether translations of any relevant documents are to be supplied[30];

(h) may decide whether any and if so what form of written statements of claim and defence are to be used, when these should be supplied and the extent to which such statements can be later amended[31];

(i) may decide whether any and if so what questions should be put to and answered by the respective parties and when and in what form this should be done[32];

(j) may decide whether to apply strict rules of evidence (or any other rules) as to the admissibility, relevance or weight of any material (oral, written or other) sought to be tendered on any matters of fact or opinion, and the time, manner and form in which such material should be exchanged and presented[33];

(k) may decide whether and to what extent the tribunal should itself take the initiative in ascertaining the facts and the law[34];

(l) may decide whether and to what extent there should be oral or written evidence or submissions[35];

(m) may decide the time within which any directions given by it are to be complied with, and may if it thinks fit extend the time so fixed (whether or not it has expired)[36];

(n) may appoint experts or legal advisers to report to it and the parties, or may appoint assessors to assist it on technical matters, and may allow any such expert, legal adviser or assessor to attend the proceedings[37];

(o) may order a claimant to provide security for the costs of the arbitration[38];

(p) may give directions in relation to any property which is the subject of the proceedings or as to which any question arises in the proceedings, and which is owned by or is in the possession of a party to the proceedings[39]:

for the inspection, photographing, preservation, custody or detention of the property by the tribunal, an expert or a party, or[40]

ordering that samples be taken from, or any observation be made of or experiment conducted upon, the property[41];

[30] s.34(2)(b).
[31] s.34(2)(c).
[32] s.34(2)(e).
[33] s.34(2)(f).
[34] s.34(2)(g).
[35] s.34(2)(h).
[36] s.34(3).
[37] s.37(1).
[38] s.38(3).
[39] s.38(4).
[40] s.38(4)(a).
[41] s.38(4)(b).

(q) may direct that a party or witness shall be examined on oath or affirmation, and may for that purpose administer any necessary oath or take any necessary affirmation[42];
(r) may give directions to a party for the preservation for the purposes of the proceedings of any evidence in his custody or control[43];
(s) may dismiss the claim for want of prosecution[44];
(t) may continue the proceedings in the absence of a defaulting party[45];
(u) may make a peremptory order.[46]

Powers relating to peremptory orders for security for costs

2–317 If a party fails to comply with a peremptory order against the claiming party for security for costs the arbitrator may dismiss the claim.[47]

Powers relating to peremptory orders other than for security for costs

2–318 The arbitrator may:

(a) direct that the party in default shall not be entitled to rely upon any allegation or material which was the subject matter of the order[48];
(b) draw such adverse inferences from the act of non-compliance as the circumstances justify[49];
(c) proceed to an award on the basis of such materials as have been properly provided to it[50];
(d) make such order as it thinks fit as to the payment of costs of the arbitration incurred in consequence of the non-compliance.[51]

Power to make more than one award

2–319 The arbitrator may make more than one award at different times on different aspects of the matters to be determined[52] and may, in particular, make an award:

(a) relating to an issue affecting the whole claim, or[53]
(b) relating to a part only of the claims or cross-claims submitted to it for decision.[54]

42 s.38(5).
43 s.38(6).
44 s.41(3).
45 s.41(4).
46 s.41(5).
47 s.41(6).
48 s.41(7)(a).
49 s.41(7)(b).
50 s.41(7)(c).
51 s.41(7)(d).
52 s.47(1).
53 s.47(2)(a).
54 s.47(2)(b).

Power to make a declaration or order

The arbitrator may make a declaration as to any matter to be determined in the proceedings[55] and/or may order the payment of a sum of money, in any currency.[56] 2–320

Powers corresponding to court powers

The arbitrator has the same powers as the court: 2–321

(a) to order a party to do or refrain from doing anything[57];
(b) to order specific performance of a contract (other than a contract relating to land)[58];
(c) to order the rectification, setting aside or cancellation of a deed or other document.[59];
(d) to strike out for want of prosecution.[60]

Powers relating to interest

The arbitrator may award simple or compound interest from such dates, at such rates and with such rests as he considers meets the justice of the case: 2–322

(a) on the whole or part of any amount awarded by the tribunal, in respect of any period up to the date of the award[61];
(b) on the whole or part of any amount claimed in the arbitration and outstanding at the commencement of the arbitral proceedings but paid before the award was made, in respect of any period up to the date of payment[62];
(c) from the date of the award (or any later date) until payment, on the outstanding amount of any award (including any award of interest under subsection (3) and any award as to costs).[63]

Powers relating to the award

The arbitrator: 2–323

(a) may decide what is to be taken to be the date on which the award was made.[64]

55 s.48(3).
56 s.48(4).
57 s.48(5)(a).
58 s.48(5)(b).
59 s.48(5)(c).
60 s.49(3)(a).
61 s.49(3)(b).
62 s.49(3)(b).
63 s.49(4).
64 s.54(1).

(b) may refuse to deliver an award to the parties except upon full payment of the fees and expenses of the arbitrators.[65]

Power to correct awards

2–324 The arbitrator may on his own initiative or on the application of a party:

(a) correct an award so as to remove any clerical mistake or error arising from an accidental slip or omission or clarify or remove any ambiguity in the award, or[66]
(b) make an additional award in respect of any claim (including a claim for interest or costs) which was presented to the tribunal but was not dealt with in the award.[67]

Security for costs

Power to order security for costs in an arbitration

2–325 The court has no power to order security for costs in an arbitration: but may order security in court proceedings connected with the arbitration such as appeals under section 69 or applications under section 68.

2–326 Unless the parties have agreed otherwise a tribunal has the power to order a claimant to provide security for costs including arbitrators' or institutional[68] fees. This is a general power applicable to any claimant. The only "restriction" on it is that the order cannot be founded on either of the following matters:

(a) the fact that the claimant is an individual ordinarily resident outside the United Kingdom: or
(b) the fact that the claimant is a confederation or association incorporated or formed under the law of a country outside the United Kingdom or whose central management and control is exercised outside the United Kingdom.

2–327 In consequence the power is a much wider one than that available to the court in litigation. In principle there is no reason why, as a matter of course, any respondent should not seek security for costs from any claimant. That said, it is likely that arbitrators will take a common sense view and will tend to exercise this power only where there is a real concern that there may not be the funds to honour an award at the end of the day.

2–328 There is another important difference between the position of an arbitrator

[65] s.56(1).
[66] s.57(3)(a).
[67] s.57(3)(b).
[68] Most institutional rules require payment or deposit of the institution's fees in advance. See, for example, Arbitration Rules of the Chartered Institute of Arbitrators.

and the court when it comes to awarding security for costs. In the court, care is taken in appropriate cases to ensure that the judge who hears the application for security does not try the case. This is because it is permissible for a plaintiff resisting such an application to point to payments into court and Calderbank offers to argue that the application is oppressive and/or that, in a sense, there is already substantial security.

There is no reason why a claimant in an arbitration should not exercise the same retort. Accordingly respondents who want security but do not wish the tribunal to know that a Calderbank offer has been made should where practicable apply for the security before making the offer. **2–329**

The same problem arises in much more acute form when a Calderbank offer at an early stage has had, as it sometimes does, the reverse effect to that intended. It is intended to speed resolution of the dispute, by forming a basis of settlement. Only if that does not succeed is it intended to provide protection at the end of the day against the ever-optimistic or greedy claimant. However a good offer early in a long case may actually make settlement later impossible—not because the parties cannot settle the substantive claim, but because the claimant cannot bring itself to accept the offer (now seen to be a good one), and thus pay all the costs incurred after the offer. The reaction of frustrated claimants in such a situation is to seek to wear down the respondent by lengthening the arbitration. **2–330**

If the frustrated claimant is also penniless, the respondent who at this stage wants security will have to accept that the tribunal will learn about the offer. On the other hand if the parties agree that the tribunal shall not have the power to order security for costs, then the respondent who wants security has no other remedy. The old power of the court to order security in connection with an arbitration has gone with the repeal of Part 1 of the Arbitration Act 1950. **2–331**

Determining the quantum of security to be given

A Commercial Judge, when sitting to decide a dispute as to the amount of security to be given in a court action, sometimes sits with a Taxing Master as an assessor. If an arbitrator has to decide such a dispute, and the amounts involved are large, it may well be appropriate for him to suggest to the parties that he sits with an experienced litigation solicitor as assessor appointed pursuant to section 37.[69] Arbitrators should also bear in mind, and should not hesitate to use if applications for security are made, their power under section 65 to cap recoverable costs. **2–332**

Power to order security for amount claimed

By section 39 of the Act the parties may agree that the tribunal shall have power to order on a provisional basis any relief which it would have power to grant in **2–333**

[69] s.37.

a final award. An arbitrator has no power to order such security save insofar as such a power is conferred upon him by agreement or by institutional rules incorporated in the contract. Many institutional rules give him such powers; see, for example, the JCT Arbitration Rules (1988), Rule 10.

Powers relating to costs and fees

Powers relating to costs

2–334 The arbitrator:

(a) may make an award allocating the costs of the arbitration as between the parties, subject to any agreement of the parties[70];
(b) may determine by award the recoverable costs of the arbitration on such basis as it thinks fit[71];
(c) may order that the recoverable costs of the arbitration be determined other than on the basis that there shall be allowed a reasonable amount in respect of all costs reasonably incurred[72];
(d) may direct that the recoverable costs of the arbitration, or of any part of the arbitral proceedings, shall be limited to a specified amount.[73]

Power of an umpire

2–335 An umpire decides matters alone as from and including the issue (whether substantive or procedural) on which the party appointed arbitrators are unable to agree.[74]

Powers to sanction applications to the court

2–336 The tribunal can sanction an application to the court, thereby greatly facilitating the task of a party who wishes to go there. Examples include the following.

2–337 The tribunal may sanction the use by a party to the arbitration of the procedures available in court to secure the attendance before the tribunal to give oral testimony or to produce documents or other material evidence.[75]

2–338 The tribunal may sanction an application for the assistance of the court in the matter of the taking of the evidence of witnesses by[76];

[70] s.61(1).
[71] s.63(3).
[72] s.63(5)(a).
[73] s.65(1).
[74] s.21(4).
[75] s.43.
[76] s.44.

(a) ordering the preservation of evidence[77];
(b) making orders relating to property which is the subject of the proceedings or as to which any question arises in the proceedings—for the inspection, photographing, preservation, custody or detention of the property, or ordering that samples be taken from, or any observation be made of or experiment conducted upon, the property; and for that purpose authorising any person to enter any premises in the possession or control of a party to the arbitration[78];
(c) ordering the sale of any goods the subject of the proceedings; the granting of an interim injunction or the appointment of a receiver.[79]

Without the tribunal's permission, seeking the assistance of the court in a non-urgent case is fruitless. 2–339

Powers exercisable only if the parties consent

The tribunal will not be able to take the following steps unless the parties to the arbitration have specifically so agreed: 2–340

(a) Exercising powers reserved to the court, *e.g.* extending time for the lodging of a claim beyond a time bar in the arbitration agreement[80];
(b) Consolidation of the particular arbitration with other proceedings, and holding concurrent hearings[81];
(c) Ordering relief (which it would have power to order in a final award) on a provisional basis. This includes injunctive relief.
(d) Ordering the payment of costs other than in accordance with the general principles upon which costs are ordered to be paid in court.
(e) Determining the dispute in accordance with other considerations than those derived from a system of law chosen by the parties to be applicable to the substance of the dispute.

In the absence of a contrary agreement between the parties the tribunal will usually have power to continue with the arbitral proceedings even if proceedings are in fact in court. Examples are where a party is seeking the determination of a preliminary point of law in court, or where a party is challenging an award on the basis of excess of substantive jurisdiction. 2–341

Specific obligations placed by the Act on the tribunal

In addition to the general obligations, particularly those imposed on the tribunal under section 33, there are some specific obligations. 2–342

[77] s.44(2)(b).
[78] s.44(2)(c).
[79] s.44(2)(d).
[80] *cf.* s.12 of the Act.
[81] s.35.

(a) The obligation to hear any representative chosen by a party (the parties can contract out of this freedom of representation).[82]
(b) Where the tribunal exercises its powers to appoint an expert, a legal adviser or an assessor, it must afford the parties a reasonable opportunity to comment on the information opinion or advice so obtained.[83]
(c) The tribunal must decide the dispute in accordance with the law chosen by the parties as applicable to the substance of the dispute. If or to the extent that there is no such choice or agreement, the tribunal shall apply the law determined by the conflict of laws rules which it considers applicable.[84]
(d) If it exercises its power to make awards relating to an issue affecting the whole claim, or to a part only of the claim/claims before it, it must specify in this award the issue, claim or part of a claim dealt with.[85]
(e) If the dispute is settled during the proceedings by the parties the tribunal shall terminate the substantive proceedings and, if so requested by the parties and not objected to by the tribunal, shall record the settlement in the form of an agreed award.[86]
(f) If there is no agreement between the parties as to the form of an award, the award shall be in writing signed by all the arbitrators, or all those assenting to the award.[87]
(g) The award shall contain the reasons for the award unless it is an agreed award or the parties have agreed to dispense with reasons.[88]
(h) The award shall state the seat of the arbitration and the date when the award is made.[89]
(i) If there is agreement between the parties as to the requirements as to notification of the award to the parties, then that agreement must be followed.[90]
(j) If there is no such agreement the award shall be notified to the parties by service on them of copies of the award, which shall be done without delay after the award is made.[91]
(k) If the tribunal proposes to exercise its power to correct an award or make an additional award, on the application of one party, then it must afford the other parties a reasonable opportunity to make representations first. Furthermore there are strict time limits on the exercise of this power, unless the parties agree to enlarge these.[92]

82 s.36.
83 s.37(1).
84 s.46.
85 s.47.
86 s.51.
87 ss.52(2) and (3).
88 s.52(4).
89 s.52(5).
90 s.55(1).
91 s.55(2).
92 s.57.

The tribunal must avoid the following: **2–343**

(a) failure by the tribunal to comply with section 33 (general duty of tribunal);
(b) the tribunal exceeding its powers (otherwise than by exceeding its substantive jurisdiction: see section 67);
(c) failure by the tribunal to conduct the proceedings in accordance with the procedure agreed by the parties;
(d) failure by the tribunal to deal with all the issues that were put to it;
(e) any arbitral or other institution or person vested by the parties with powers in relation to the proceedings or the award exceeding its powers;
(f) uncertainty or ambiguity as to the effect of the award;
(g) the award being obtained by fraud or the award or the way in which it was procured being contrary to public policy;
(h) failure to comply with the requirements as to the form of the award; or
(i) any irregularity in the conduct of the proceedings or in the award which is admitted by the tribunal or by any arbitral or other institution or person vested by the parties with powers in relation to the proceedings or the award.

Importance of the arbitrator conforming to his own directions

If an arbitrator, without objection from the parties, determines to follow a particular procedure it is important that he does in fact follow that procedure. Thus in *Control Securities v. Spencer*[93] the arbitrator (a surveyor engaged in a rent review) notified the parties that submissions should be in writing with the opportunity for counter submissions, that he would contact the parties to discuss whether there should be an oral hearing, and that comparables should be either in the direct knowledge of the party seeking to rely on them or supported by documentary evidence. In the event he failed to enforce the rules he had laid down in respect of comparables: he failed to copy one of the letters he received from one of the parties to the other party: and he failed to contact the parties to discuss whether there should be an oral hearing. The award was set aside. **2–344**

Under the Act the same result might be achieved on the ground that the arbitrator has failed to conduct the proceedings in accordance with the procedure agreed by the parties—but only if the complainant moved swiftly and the court was satisfied that substantial injustice has been done to the applicant. **2–345**

The power to seek advice

There appears to be a well-established practice amongst arbitrators in domestic arbitrations of seeking advice on matters both procedural and substantive which **2–346**

[93] [1989] 7 E.G. 82.

arise in the course of the arbitration. Anecdotal evidence suggests that arbitrators have sought advice both formally and informally from diverse sources, such as a professional body, another arbitrator, the Chartered Institute of Arbitrators, barristers, solicitors and sometimes friends. Sometimes the advice has been sought and given orally, at other times in writing. Sometimes arbitrators have told the parties in advance, or once the advice has been received; at other times they have not told the parties at all, either that they were seeking advice or the nature of the advice they received. Sometimes they paid for professional advice from their arbitrator's fees, on other occasions they have charged the cost to the parties as an expense of the arbitration.

2–347 While the practice of seeking advice in these various ways had something to commend it in that it could make for the more efficient organisation of an arbitration, the variety of practice was unsatisfactory and arguably unlawful. It could well be argued that for an arbitrator to seek advice on a procedural, and particularly, a substantive point of law without prior consent of the parties and subject to whatever conditions the parties might agree, was acting in breach of confidentiality. By taking such advice into account in making his decisions, without informing the parties, he was also acting in breach of natural justice. The 1996 Act expressly recognises that an arbitrator may wish to take advice on procedural and substantive matters. Section 37 gives him the power to do so, subject to conditions, the essence of which are complete disclosure to the parties of the intention to take advice, the advice being sought and the advice being given. Arguably, this is the only mechanism by which the arbitrator can now take advice.

2–348 However, in the authors' view, it would be unfortunate if the formal mechanism of section 37 had always to be invoked when an arbitrator merely required some procedural guidance which he could readily get from a colleague. Judges often discuss with their colleagues points of practice arising in their cases. No one suggests that this process is inimical to the due administration of civil justice and it would be unfortunate if arbitrators were deprived of this kind of assistance.

2–349 Accordingly, it is suggested that an arbitrator, upon appointment, should invite the parties to agree that he may take advice on a procedural point if he wants to and that he may do so, either at his own expense or as an expense of the parties and subject always to prior notification of his intention and full disclosure of the nature of the advice sought and the advice given. It should be emphasised that the difficulties of taking advice only occur once an arbitrator has been appointed. Thus, if an approach is made to a putative arbitrator, there is nothing to stop him taking advice from any source he wishes, other than the party seeking to appoint him, as to whether or not he should accept the appointment or, for example, as to the meaning of the arbitration clause pursuant to which he would be expected to act.

2–350 The variety of practice which anecdotal evidence has revealed suggests that it would be appropriate for institutions, when revising their rules in the light of the Act, to consider provisions entitling the arbitrator to take advice without full compliance with the formal requirements of section 37, but with nonetheless appropriate safeguards for the parties.

11. Expedition and How to Achieve it

The influence of trial by jury on pre-1997 arbitration procedure in England

Until about a century ago all English trials, in both civil and serious criminal cases, were conducted in public by judge and jury. Since the jury was selected only a few minutes before the trial began, it was not possible for its members to be told beforehand anything about the facts or the issues involved. Thus the whole trial effectively began when the jury was empanelled and sworn. This is still the practice in criminal cases tried on indictment. In civil cases except in the Commercial and Official Referees Courts, it is unusual for a case to be allocated to a particular judge more than a few days before the trial begins.[94] 2–351

Entire case must be presented publicly at the hearing, and not before

These administrative features necessarily shaped the way in which a case is prepared and conducted. The English civil trial has hitherto been prepared on the basis that the judge may know nothing about the case (not even what is pleaded) until he comes into court and that he may know nothing about the field. 2–352

Time wasted

In the more complex cases, the time wasted in opening a case and reading documents to the judge was enormous. Two persons were participating—one counsel and one judge—in a process that could be done by one of them alone, in the presence of possibly 15 persons many of whom have read the documents at least once and perhaps many times. If the judge has no special expertise in the field, much time is taken in explaining to the judge technicalities with which everyone in the room—including even the barristers—are by now familiar. The trial continues with evidence being given orally by a witness, and taken down in longhand by the judge, of matters which are not in dispute. That process might be interrupted by legal argument, wholly foreseen (or at least foreseeable), about admissibility of evidence of a particular kind. Only when the evidence reaches the point of facts which are in issue, with cross-examination of witnesses on those facts, can the assembly in one room of all those present begin to be justified. At that stage the adversarial system on which the English trial is based may justify itself. 2–353

Increasingly, cases in the English courts are better managed. In many of them the judge is acquainted with the issues before the substantive hearing begins; and orders as draconian as limiting cross examination to an hour and a half per factual witness and a day per expert are starting to be seen, even in what, in former days would have been 40 or 50 day cases. Lord Woolf 's proposals will make for further reform and savings of time and money. 2–354

[94] The practice is now changing rapidly under the influence of Lord Woolf 's report.

Arbitration practice often the same

2–355 Until recent years, if the matters in dispute in a civil action had been referred to arbitration rather than to the courts, the probability was that the procedure would have been the same, the waste of time the same, and the waste of costs even greater (in that the arbitrator's time would have been paid by the parties, whereas the judge's time was in large part paid by the state).

2–356 An arbitrator is, or should be, free of all this. He has no Lord Chief Justice or Clerk of the Lists switching him overnight from one court to another. He has no Department counting the hours in which he is sitting in court. He is not concerned that a stray member of the public should be able to understand the proceedings. And—perhaps more importantly—in a large proportion of arbitrations he is himself an expert in the field in which the dispute arises. In consequence he can read the documents with greater understanding than most lay judges, because he does not have to be led like a child through 500 or 5,000 pages of documents, having elementary trade or technical expressions explained.

2–357 The Act enables the arbitrator to be bold and innovative in deciding new procedures and not merely to continue to use the traditional procedures modelled on litigation. The idea that litigation or arbitration, even of complex technical disputes, needs to take weeks or months of hearings is being seriously questioned. The courts at all levels are anxious to reduce the time of hearings. The Woolf proposals for case management have as an objective the reduction of the time spent in hearings with a view to saving both time and money. There are many procedural devices for expedition and in the absence of agreement of the parties, arbitrators must opt for the most expeditious and economic procedural solution. That should be the objective in programming the arbitration and in particular in deciding the timing, length and purpose of hearings.

Advantages and disadvantages of an oral hearing

2–358 English arbitration procedure, other than in specialist fields, has traditionally been directed to the preparation and conduct of a single hearing. The Act gives the tribunal, absent agreement of the parties, considerable power to dispense with hearings unless considered necessary or desirable; and in any event to control what happens at the hearing and particularly its length.

Disadvantages

2–359 The first is that a hearing is usually the most expensive of the various procedures available, partly because it requires a relatively large number of participants to set aside a specific period of time and partly also because the presentation of a case at an oral hearing requires specialist skills which are usually costly.

2–360 The second is delay. Finding a date convenient for the assembly of the arbitrator(s), witnesses, parties, and (where they are instructed) advocates usually takes longer, and sometimes takes much longer, than the exercise of putting the tribunal together with the documents—even where the latter include submissions which have been professionally drawn, and the reports of experts.

Advantages

The first is in resolving conflicts of evidence. Usually, a conflict of factual evidence cannot be satisfactorily resolved without first, hearing and seeing the witnesses giving their differing accounts of the facts, and secondly, allowing cross-examination of each witness in turn. That "an adversarial or contradictory procedure guarantees a high quality of adjudication" is recognised even in countries whose basic procedure is inquisitorial.[95] A witness may often be persuaded to make a false statement in a document, when he would shrink from making it orally after promising (on oath or otherwise) to tell the truth. It is a commonplace of civil litigation in England that deliberate lying in the witness box is rare, and the ability to maintain a lie plausibly under competent cross-examination is very rare. But not all conflicts of evidence need to be resolved to enable the arbitrator to decide upon the dispute. **2–361**

The advantages of an oral hearing as a method of resolving a conflict of evidence are by no means confined to cases where the conflict arises from deliberate lying. The fallibility of human powers of observation, and of recollection, is another commonplace of litigation—civil or criminal. A very experienced judge once said: **2–362**

> "The courts are full of honest witnesses whose recollections as time passes becomes more and more certain and less and less accurate."

A difference of recollection can often be resolved by reference to contemporaneous documents. But even this is not satisfactory if the witness whose evidence appears to conflict with the documents is not given an opportunity of reconciling the two. Where a critical fact has to be resolved by the recollection of witnesses, the mere act of getting the witnesses together and letting each hear the other's version often results in the facts being agreed without the need for a decision by the tribunal. **2–363**

The second advantage is that it can facilitate the effective presentation of the rival cases. The degree of intercommunication between the arbitrator and the party or his advocate is usually far higher at an oral hearing than is possible on documents only. Many points arise in documents that the arbitrator wants to clarify. The answers to his questions may themselves raise further points. To conduct this process of clarification by correspondence, bearing in mind that each party must be allowed to see and comment upon, if he wishes, material provided by the other party would in many cases take far longer than summoning a hearing and seeking the clarification at it. **2–364**

[95] See, *e.g.* Robert and Carbonneau, *The French Law of Arbitration* (1983) 1, 3–12.

2–365 Moreover, at an oral hearing the arbitrator has the opportunity (of which too few avail themselves) of putting to each advocate in turn the difficulties that the arbitrator sees in finding for him on a particular issue. The discussion that results from this process can be of incomparable advantage in ensuring that the arbitrator fully understands the strengths and weaknesses of the rival cases.

2–366 Thirdly, an oral hearing can help in reconciling the loser to his defeat. A party who loses after his case has been presented at a fairly conducted hearing has at least the consolation that he has done all that could be done to win. Moreover, if the tribunal has taken part in a dialogue with his advocate, pointing out the difficulties of weak points in his case, and inviting him to deal with them, the party is more likely to understand—even if he does not agree with—the reasons that have led the tribunal to reject his case. In addition, there is the "day in court" syndrome. Many parties really only need an opportunity to sound off about their grievances in front of an audience to be reconciled to an adverse result. This is as true of the corporate executive as it is of the individual pursuing a personal claim. Provided the opportunity does not lead to disproportionate costs, arbitrators should seek to accommodate this need.

Chess clock arbitration

2–367 It is nowadays increasingly unusual to have an "open-ended" hearing, *i.e.* one in which time limits for various stages of the hearing have not been determined before the hearing starts. As far as practicable the arbitrator should resist holding hearings of this kind. Even the courts are increasingly likely to avoid such open ended hearings.

2–368 Time controls can be as simple as giving each party the same time; or as complicated as the timetable set out in Appendix 24 hereto. When using a limited time schedule, the tribunal must remember that it is even more important than in the traditional style of hearing that the tribunal should at the outset have a thorough knowledge of the documents and of the issues. Failure to ensure this may result in excessive intervention or sitting long hours which can be counter-productive and should be avoided.

2–369 If the tribunal decides to do some or all of the questioning itself, it should be careful to impose a time limit on itself and keep to it.

Requisites for a fair hearing

2–370 In *Carlisle Place Investments v. Wimpey Construction*[96] Robert Goff J. said:

> "I know of no requirement that an arbitrator must allow each party to call all the evidence which he wishes to call. It must depend on the circum-

[96] 44 B. L.R. 109.

stances of the particular case whether or not the arbitrator decides, in the exercise of his discretion, to conduct the arbitration in a particular way."

However, in *Town & City v. Wiltshier* an experienced Official Referee held, applying the views expressed in Mustill and Boyd, that the minimum requirements for a fair hearing were as follows: 2–371

(a) each party must have notice that the hearing is to take place;
(b) each party must have a reasonable opportunity to be present at the hearing, together with his advisors and witnesses;
(c) each party must have the opportunity to be present throughout the hearing;
(d) each party must have a reasonable opportunity to present evidence and argument in support of his own case;
(e) each party must have a reasonable opportunity to test his opponent's case by cross-examining his witnesses, presenting rebutting evidence and addressing oral argument;
(f) the hearing must, unless the contrary is expressly agreed, be the occasion on which the parties present the whole of their evidence.

On the assumption that there is to be a hearing, then points (a) to (d) remain good law and should be followed. But points (e) and (f), even assuming this was the law, are now no longer so. This results from the arbitrator's power under the Act as to the admission of evidence and conduct of the proceedings. Arbitrators must be mindful of the obligations imposed upon them by section 33 and must test any procedural application or proposal against the requirement of avoiding unnecessary delay or expense whilst remaining fair to both parties. 2–372

Importance of speed in arbitration

In arbitration speed of decision-making is one of the most important, and often *the* most important, advantage of arbitration as compared with litigation. This advantage derives from several differences: 2–373

(a) the courts cannot turn away a claimant because the lists are too crowded. They must accept the claim, but it is put at the end of a queue of constantly changing length. In arbitration on the other hand an arbitrator should not accept an appointment unless he is able to deal with the matter with a degree of expedition appropriate to its urgency;
(b) in many cases the arbitrator will himself be an expert in the field in which the dispute arises, as well as competent in arbitration skills and this should shorten both the time required to hear interlocutory applications, and the length of the hearing;
(c) in litigation, except in the Commercial Court or in cases of demon-

strable urgency, there is a queue for each interlocutory application—for directions, for further particulars, for specific discovery, etc. On each of these it may take days, weeks, even months to get an appointment before the master or district judge concerned. An arbitrator, should usually be able to deal with interlocutory matters on paper: and even where a hearing is needed may be able to deal with it by telephone or video conference. Even if the parties wish to have a formal meeting, he should usually be able to make himself available for a short application on a few days' notice at times of the day when courts do not sit;

(d) the arbitrator has the conduct throughout of the preparatory stages, so that by the time a hearing begins he should know a great deal about the facts and the issues; this should significantly shorten the time required for the hearings;

(e) at the beginning of the arbitration an arbitrator can fix a date for the hearing or hearings but in litigation this cannot usually be done until a great deal of the preparation has been completed;

(f) in many cases the arbitration agreement provides, or the parties subsequently agree, that the dispute shall be decided without a hearing—a procedure open to them in only a tiny proportion of cases in court.

(g) there is much greater flexibility for an arbitrator to break the case down into a series of defined issues which can be taken and decided at different stages, so that a long, complicated hearing of all issues can be avoided. At the moment the courts will usually only do that if there is some preliminary point of law which would be dispositive of all or some of the primary issues in the case. The Act expressly empowers arbitrators in section 39 to give provisional awards and in section 47 to make more than one award at different times on different aspects of the matters to be determined.

2–374 There are two procedural stages which in litigation are much speedier than in arbitration. The first is obtaining interlocutory relief by way of injunction or conservatory orders (particularly ex parte) and the second is the interval between the end of the hearings, and the pronouncement of the decision. In many cases the judge gives an extempore oral judgment as soon as the rival cases have been presented to him. In arbitration there is often a gap of weeks or months between conclusion of the presentations—whether written or at a hearing—and issue of the award. Many arbitrators take this as a matter of course. They should not; in doing so they negative one of the principal advantages of arbitration over litigation. Moreover, the quality of decision-making often suffers if a long interval is allowed to elapse between hearing the evidence and making the decisions based upon it. The practice of the Los Angeles Centre for Commercial Arbitration is to be commended. An arbitrator appointed under their rules loses a percentage of his fees for each month beyond a set period for which his award is outstanding after the end of the hearing.

Responsibility for the progress of the arbitration

In general it is not the function of the arbitrator to press for progress where both parties have made an informed decision to go slowly. But the emphasis here is on an informed decision of the parties. In a large proportion of cases the delay is attributable to some representative of the party—whether in-house employee, or solicitor or counsel—being occupied with other matters. So before allowing the arbitration to become dormant the arbitrator should take steps to satisfy himself that this is what both parties really want. 2–375

While the arbitrator is bound by the procedural agreement of the parties and has no power to override them, his sole remedy being that of resignation and the right to apply to the court under section 25 of the Act for relief from any liability incurred by him, he should be mindful of, and be prepared to raise with the parties, the principles of section 1 of the Act and the duties imposed upon him by section 33 and upon the parties by section 40. 2–376

The arbitrator's diary

In some cases the limitation upon speed is congestion of the arbitrator's diary. This is particularly so if the tribunal comprises two arbitrators and an umpire or three arbitrators. An arbitrator ought not to accept an appointment without satisfying himself that there is a reasonable prospect of his being able to perform his functions—the preliminaries, the hearing and the preparation of the award—with reasonable expedition. If there is any doubt as to his likely availability in the context of the anticipated order of the case he should make his position clear to the parties, or the appointing authority, before appointment or before entering upon the reference. Some appointing authorities (*e.g.* the President of the Royal Institution of Chartered Surveyors of London) before making the appointment, require the proposed appointee to state that if appointed he will be able to deal with the matter with reasonable despatch. The London Maritime Arbitrators Association Rules contain provisions for reconstituting the Arbitration tribunal with a view to avoiding delay which the parties or either of them consider unacceptable. 2–377

Under section 24 of the Act the court may remove the arbitrator if he fails to use all reasonable despatch and his failure has resulted, or will result, in substantial injustice to the applicant. 2–378

Target programming

The practice in litigation in England

In English litigation, the general practice is for counsel (or, in smaller cases the solicitor) to draft the statement of claim before or shortly after proceedings are initiated. Then the defence is drafted. Then if necessary for clarification of the opposing party's contentions further and better particulars are requested and given, and more or less concurrently, discovery of documents is requested and 2–379 given. Only when the issues have been clarified in this way do the parties, or rather their legal advisers, address their minds to the question of a hearing date.[97]

Consequences of this procedure

2–380 The process of settling the pleadings, including dealing with further and better particulars, and considering the documents, involves carrying out a substantial proportion of the preparation of the case for hearing. To carry it out the advocate involved and the expert witness, if there is one, may have devoted many hours or days work, including meetings with the client and perhaps a view of the subject-matter of the dispute. A change of advocate will involve a great waste of time and money, and is often unpalatable on personal grounds also. A change of expert witnesses is usually quite unacceptable. So in practice the hearing date is fixed to suit the diaries of the advocates and expert witnesses concerned. But the diaries of top-flight experts and specialist advocates are always congested, and the earliest date may be a very long time ahead—sometimes two years or more in complex commercial or construction industry disputes.

2–381 The matter is exacerbated by the English practice of having long oral hearings, and by the reluctance of judges to take steps to ensure that hearings are completed within the allowed time. The former means that very long periods in the relevant diaries are allocated to one case. The latter drives those who are involved either to have to withdraw from other engagements (because the judge has decided to go on with his case regardless of the arrangements of anybody else involved in the case) or to have to find a new date in already congested diaries so the case can restart.

2–382 There is often a conflict between unrestricted choice of advocate and speed of resolution. In such circumstances it cannot always be left to the parties to choose between an earlier result involving a change of advocate, or a delayed result so that each can be represented by the advocate of his choice. For often one party wants speed, and the other wants whatever delay is necessary to accommodate the advocate of his choice; and the arbitrator has to make the difficult decision between them. It is much more difficult to change advocates if there has been a substantial hearing or hearings, where the content or conduct of these earlier meetings is or may be relevant to later hearings.

2–383 These difficulties can often be lessened or eliminated, if at the outset of the arbitration procedures are adapted which keep hearings within manageable boundaries. Breaking the case down into discrete issues which are not interdependent is one such procedure. If this course is adopted and short, self contained hearings are decided upon, or one hearing is thought appropriate but with

[97] Nowadays in specialist work, or with a big city firm, all or at least much of the drafting is done by the solicitor wholly independently or for counsel's approval.

proper time limits, then, at or shortly after the preliminary meeting, a target date can be set for the hearing or hearings. The great majority of arbitrations are of a kind familiar to the lawyers and arbitrators concerned in them, and in such cases a sufficiently accurate estimate can be made of the length of the hearing or hearings. In other cases the exercise is a pure guesstimate. Nonetheless it is a valuable exercise since it gives the parties dates to work to. It is sensible, however, when fixing dates, in circumstances where the arbitrator suspects the estimates are ''seat of the pants'' estimates, to invite the parties to summarise what they expect the issues to be. This, at least, will give the arbitrator some sort of draft agenda against which to test any application for a new (and therefore probably longer and later) date. Fixing dates well in advance may raise difficulties, because some professional people do not like to clog their diaries with provisional entries which entail their refusing other work, unless there is some level of remuneration for the days so reserved. However, an increasing growth both in the use of sophisticated retainers and in competition has diminished the effect of such difficulties. In any event, they must be overcome if the arbitration is to fulfill its potential as a speedy method of resolving the dispute.

The four possible situations

Finding the right balance between giving a party the time that he requests for preparing his case, and the date that he requests for presenting it, without imposing on the proceedings a delay unacceptable to the other party, requires judgment. The problem usually falls into one of four classes, namely— **2–384**

(a) Where both parties want speed

In theory this should present no problem. In practice it often does, because expert witnesses or the advocates say that they are not available during the period otherwise suitable for a hearing. Where specialist advocates are instructed, the difficulty of finding a date on which both they and the arbitrator are available is perhaps the greatest single cause of delay. Moreover, there is an obvious conflict of interest between the client who wants his case heard quickly, and his lawyer who may have to return the brief or the instructions if the hearing cannot be postponed. For this reason it is often desirable for the arbitrator to request the presence, at any meeting at which the date of hearing is to be discussed, of the parties, or directors or other appropriate non-legal representatives; for it is for each party to decide, in the first place, whether he prefers a deferred hearing with X representing him, or an earlier hearing with someone else representing him. **2–385**

If the parties are agreed upon a suitable range of dates for the hearing, and the only obstacle is that the arbitrator is not available until a much later date, the arbitrator should consider offering to retire, in favour of someone with a more amenable diary. Such an offer should always be conditional, and not to **2–386** take effect until the parties have identified, agreed upon and conditionally appointed someone who has the requisite gap in his diary.

(b) Where both parties want delay

2–387 This should present no problems. An arbitrator who sought to impose on the parties a programme which both considered unacceptably fast will simply be ignored and in the process will lose authority over the proceedings. As a matter of practicalities, the parties could simply replace him at that stage: and if he objected under section 24 of the Act, the parties are able by agreement to revoke the arbitrator's authority.

(c) Where the claimant wants delay and the respondent wants speed

2–388 The general rule is that all disputes should be disposed of as rapidly as is possible concomitantly with a fair hearing (or in the case of documentary arbitration a fair consideration) of the issues. Previous editions asserted that in general the respondent's wishes should prevail. For a person against whom a claim is made is entitled to ask that the claim be adjudicated upon, and disposed of, with all practicable speed. However, this is merely one consideration in the exercise, albeit an important one.

2–389 The situation is of course an unusual one. It sometimes happens that the claimant has more to gain from the existence of a claim than from a decision upon it. For example, a company in financial straits may be depending on its bank for facilities to keep its business going in the hope of better times. The bank for its part may have over-optimistic expectations from the claim. Thus the claimant may not be keen for an early resolution. The matter may easily be further complicated, *e.g.* by the fact or allegation that the Respondent caused or substantially contributed to the claimant's financial problems.

2–390 It follows from the general rule, that neither party should be allowed to delay the progress of the arbitration to its conclusion without good cause. And the unavailability of a particular advocate is not of itself a good cause. The arbitrator may be put into the position of having to say to the claimant (or to the respondent):

> "The respondent (the claimant) wants this matter disposed of, and in the ordinary way I would fix the hearing for a date four months hence. I am willing to defer it by (say) one month so that you may be represented by the advocate of your choice; but I am not willing to defer it by six months."

(d) Where the claimant wants speed and the respondent wants delay

2–391 This is the most common problem. In arbitration as in litigation the proportion of claims arising from a bona fide dispute between the two parties either as to fact, or as to the legal position, is relatively small. In a high proportion of cases the defendant/respondent has refused to pay, for one or more of the following (as well as other) reasons:

(a) a determination to argue regardless of the costs as a result of fury at the situation ("it's the principle that counts");
(b) well knowing that he has no defence, he is anxious to put off as long as possible the day of payment;
(c) believing that he has an arguable defence which will gain delay in payment even if it does not succeed.

He accordingly argues it because he has nothing to lose by so doing except costs, and the gain to him outweighs the costs that he will probably have to pay. The speed with which cases of this kind, whether in litigation or in arbitration, can be disposed of is a measure of the efficiency of the legal or arbitral system involved. It must not be forgotten that a high proportion of such cases are compromised shortly before they are due to be heard. It follows that the shorter the delay imposed by the procedure up to the date of hearing, the sooner the reluctant debtor can be made to pay his debt. **2–392**

The most effective sanction, therefore, against the debtor who is using the arbitration process as a method of delaying payment is to reduce to the minimum the period of delay. The other sanctions, namely the award of costs and the award of interest, have a more limited effect. The amount of the costs may be comparatively insignificant in relation to the benefit to the debtor of delaying payment, particularly if there is a long gap between the appointment of the arbitrator and the date of the hearing, so that by paying shortly before the hearing date he gains a large delay for a small expenditure on costs. (Note, however in this context the problems of "paper heavy" cases, *e.g.* construction and patents, where the costs ultimately may exceed the value of the claim, let alone the amount awarded.) The award of interest, even at a rate equal to that at which the debtor can borrow money, is not so much a disincentive as the removal of an incentive to delay; the debtor is no worse off than if he had borrowed money from his bank to pay the debt sooner. Moreover, if the debtor is insolvent, or is a corporation run by people who have no remaining financial stake in it, delay in obtaining an award may mean that there are no assets available to meet it, so that the inclusion of orders for costs and interests is nugatory. **2–393**

Practical sanctions against delay

The displeasure of the arbitrator

In most cases the practical sanction against delay or default is the reluctance of a party who seriously intends to pursue a claim or defence to incur the displeasure of the arbitrator. So the first step to be taken by a party who wishes a speedy conclusion of the arbitration (usually but not invariably the claimant) is to obtain from the arbitrator clear directions as to the interlocutory steps to be taken, and the earliest practicable hearing date. If the other party fails to comply with the directions, prompt application should be made to the arbitrator for his assistance. In most cases a firmly phrased reminder from the arbitrator results in speedy **2–394** compliance. If it does not, the next step is to invoke the arbitrator's powers under the Act.

Costs and interest as sanctions

2–395 Nevertheless there are many cases in which the knowledge that if the arbitrator finds in favour of the claimant, it is likely that he will order the respondent to pay the costs (perhaps on an indemnity basis) together with interest at a full commercial rate, will operate as a disincentive to a defence put forward basically for purposes of delay.

Proceeding to a hearing

2–396 The most effective sanction against non-compliance by a respondent is often to fix an early hearing date. The disadvantages of this course are discussed in paragraph 2–398, below.

Powers of the arbitrator to deal with a recalcitrant party

At common law

2–397 An arbitrator has no general power to make an award in favour of a party on the mere ground that the opposing party has failed to comply with a direction. If the failure is by the claimant, the arbitrator can decline to proceed until it is remedied. If it is by the respondent, the arbitrator may not be able to impose a sanction.

Default powers in arbitration

2–398 Some institutional rules give arbitrators default powers, and sections 40 and 41 of the Act expressly give default powers to the arbitrator. If a respondent fails to comply with a direction that he deliver points of defence, or a Statement of Case, within a specified time, it is open to the arbitrator to fix a date for hearing, notify the respondent of it, and proceed with the hearing whether or not the respondent attends. In some cases this is the most expeditious way of dealing with the matter. But in practice it is often unsatisfactory. The date fixed for the hearing may have to be several weeks hence in order to give the claimant time to assemble his witnesses and prove his case. If a date is fixed three weeks ahead, for example, and the respondent then produces a defence three days before the hearing and announces his intention of appearing at the hearing to support it, the defence may be such that the claimant requires further time to prepare to meet it. The respondent will always have some explanation for the delay in delivering the defence. If the arbitrator is unimpressed by the explanation, he may rule that he will disregard the defence and continue the proceedings as if no defence had been delivered. The respondent may decide to apply to set aside the award on the grounds that by declining to hear his defence the arbitrator has breached section 68 of the Act; alternatively, under section 24 that the arbitrator has refused or failed properly to conduct the proceedings with resulting injustice or the likelihood of it. Given the reluctance of the courts to interfere in the exercise of the arbitrator's procedural discretion and powers, such an application is likely to fail, but there may be a substantial delay in bringing it to a hearing in the High Court. That delay may be greater than the delay occasioned by allowing the defence to stand and adjourning the hearing for the time that the claimant requires to meet it. So the short cut may in the end cause the maximum delay.

Non-compliance with a peremptory order for security for costs

A peremptory order is a "reinforcing" order, made where a party has ignored a previous order to the same effect.[98] Where the original order that has been ignored is for security for the costs of the other party, the arbitrator may make a peremptory order for security (in the same amount and by way of the like method as the original order). If the peremptory order is also not complied with, the arbitrator may make an award dismissing the claim of the non-complying party.[99] **2–399**

Non-compliance with any other peremptory order

The arbitrator has the choice of any or all of the following courses. **2–400**

(a) The arbitrator may[1] direct that the party in default should not be entitled to rely upon any allegation or material which was the subject matter of the order.[2] This power was available to the arbitrator before the Act but does not appear to have been greatly used. It is of particular assistance in dealing with a party who is reluctant to explain a positive case in reasonable detail and rational manner. It is a very powerful weapon and should be used with caution. In particular, care must be taken to identify clearly what cannot (and by implication what can) be relied upon.

(b) The arbitrator can draw adverse inferences, appropriate to the circumstances, from the refusal to comply with the peremptory order.[3] Again this power was available, it is submitted, to an arbitrator prior to the Act, but it is useful to have it spelt out. It is important to bear in mind that the adverse inferences are limited by the nature of the order in the particular circumstances.

[98] s.40(5).

[996] s.40(6) refers only to a claimant. It must, it is submitted, include a counterclaiming respondent against whom an order for security is possible if rare.

[1] s.41(7).

[2] s.41(7)(a).

[3] s.41(7)(b).

(c) The arbitrator can make an appropriate order as to costs.[4] This power undoubtedly existed before the 1996 Act. Again the Arbitrator needs to be careful to focus on the particular failure of the party in default when determining the appropriate order for costs. He should not see this power as providing an opportunity to manifest general dissatisfaction with the party in question.

(d) The arbitrator may apply to the court for an order requiring compliance with his peremptory order.[5] This power is new. It is given by section 41(2)(a). It can be excluded by the parties. Notice would have to be given to the parties to the arbitration. Indeed it is suggested that they would be necessary parties to the proceedings. No doubt there are extreme cases where an arbitrator might consider such a course justifiable and the risk of an adverse order for costs acceptable, but they must be very rare indeed. Any of the parties can itself make such an application if it has the approval of the arbitrator. Far better, it is suggested, from the arbitrator's point of view, to remind the parties of the existence of section 41(2) and to leave it to the innocent party, if so minded, to press forward. The advantage of going to court is that it makes available in the context of an arbitration sanctions against a party such as fines and imprisonment, which are not available to an arbitrator. However such a course is not to be adopted until all purely arbitral methods have been exhausted (section 41(4)).

2–401 It is suggested that he can act of his own volition if so minded. However, it would usually be sensible to await a request from the innocent party that he should take one or more of these courses. He is of course free to encourage the innocent party to act.

Want of prosecution

Power to strike out for want of prosecution

2–402 By section 41(3) of the Act the arbitrator or umpire has power to make an award striking out any claim in a dispute referred to him if it appears to him that the following conditions are satisfied:

(a) there has been inordinate and inexcusable delay on the part of the claimant in pursuing the claim[6]; and

(b) the delay will give rise to a substantial risk that it is not possible to have a fair resolution of the issues in that claim[7]; or the delay has

[4] s.41(7)(d).
[5] s.42(2)(a).
[6] s.41(3).
[7] s.41(3)(a).

caused, or is likely to cause or to have caused, serious prejudice to the respondent.[8]

Applications for extension of time

When considering an application by a party for an extension of the time specified in the directions for taking some interlocutory step, the most important consideration is whether any substantial detriment or hardship will be caused to the other party. The principles to be applied are similar to those governing an application for leave to amend. Arbitrators might do well to act similarly. 2–403

Availability of summary procedures

Summary procedure by consent

In litigation various summary procedures are available, and are often used; the application for summary judgment under Order 14 of the Rules of the Supreme Court in England is one example. A corresponding procedure (Order 29) enables a court to make a provisional order on a claim, based on the strong likelihood of the outcome. The generally received view, supported by previous editions of this book, was that the power to make a summary award was available in an arbitration only where the parties have agreed to it. 2–404

There is no doubt that the parties may expressly agree to the arbitrator making a summary award or provisional order. Their agreement to a summary procedure may take one of three forms: 2–405

(a) the pre-dispute arbitration clause may expressly provide for a summary procedure, *e.g.* by incorporating institutional rules which provide for it;
(b) some institutional rules provide an optional summary procedure which the parties may agree to adopt after the dispute has arisen; see, *e.g.* the Institute of Civil Engineers Arbitration Rules; the Joint Contracts Tribunal Arbitration Rules;
(c) even when no institutional rules are incorporated in the arbitration agreement, the parties may agree (with the arbitrator or independently of him) to adopt some form of summary procedure.

The question that arises is whether, absent agreement by the parties, an arbitrator has power to make a summary award (and therefore final in nature) in respect of a claim or claims when he considers that the claim is made out and there is no defence. Subject to the points made below, the authors consider that he can. Otherwise the reduction of the power of the court to require a stay would militate against the interest of the claimant who has an unanswerable claim in whole or in part—which cannot have been the intention of the legislature.

[8] s.41(3)(b).

2–406 That said, it is important that the tribunal constructs a fair procedure for claimant and respondent to put forward the claim and answer to an application for a summary award. He must also, in an international arbitration, invite both parties to address him on whether such an award will be accepted for enforcement by the courts in the jurisdiction where the claimant is likely to attempt to execute it.

Provisional awards

2–407 The arbitrator is given the power, but only with consent, to make provisional awards under section 39 of the Act.

More haste less speed

2–408 In all these cases the arbitrator should be cautious about entertaining an application for a summary or provisional award. In litigation, summary procedures, whether by way of an application by a plaintiff for a summary judgment or an application by a defendant to strike out or otherwise summarily dispose of proceedings, even if ultimately successful, often prove to be lengthier and more expensive than going the long way round. Judges are, in this context as in so many others, wary of the temptations offered by an apparent "short cut". There are similar dangers in arbitration. Consequently an arbitrator should consider the timetabling consequence of a summary procedure, and should draw these consequences to the attention of the parties. For in many cases a speedy hearing of the main claim will provide a more effective remedy for the applicant than any short cut. And in the ability to make himself available for a speedy hearing, the arbitrator has an advantage not usually available to a judge, who has far less control of his own engagements.

Summary award may not be as readily enforceable

2–409 Although the opportunities for delay by way of appeal to the courts are now greatly reduced, there is still the right to apply to set aside or remit under section 68. An attempt by the arbitrator to make an award without a full trial of the issues whether by oral hearing or on the documents may give the losing party an opportunity for great delay by applications to remit or set aside and in the meantime to stay enforcement of the award. Moreover, it may result in the claimant being unable to enforce the award in some foreign countries, where the procedure would be seen as a breach of due process.

Splitting the issues: interim awards

2–410 Nevertheless, some short cuts are available. If the claimant has two separable claims, of which one can and the other cannot be dealt with quickly, the arbitrator can direct a speedy hearing of the first and can issue an award which is final on that issue but interim within the arbitration as a whole. Section 47 of the Act gives the arbitrator power to do this but the award must specify the issue, claim or part of a claim, which is the subject-matter of the interim award. If the issue of liability can be dealt with quickly, but the assessment of damages (if any) cannot, he can direct a speedy hearing as to liability only. If the respondent admits liability on the claim, but raises a cross-claim in reduction of his liability, the arbitrator may be able to issue an interim award for any balance that cannot be eliminated by the cross-claim. Other examples can be found, that do not involve shutting either party out of the right to a fair and full hearing on the merits. However, it is important that split hearings be not arranged on assumptions of fact that turn out to be unfounded. For example in *Compagnie D'Armament Maritime v. Compagnie Tunisienne de Navigation*[9] the question whether the contract was governed by French law or English law was decided as a preliminary issue by the arbitrators, fought through three courts, and decided in favour of French law. The arbitrators later found as a fact that it made no difference, because there was no material difference between French law and English law on the subject.

12. Procedures where the Same Issue Arises Under Different but Related Contracts

Contract and sub-contract

There are many cases in which the same issue arises under a contract between A and B and under a related contract between B and C. Examples are: 2–411

(a) Where there is a quality dispute about goods that A has contracted to sett to B, and B has contracted to re-sell to C.
(b) Where there is a dispute about work which B has performed under a contract with A, and which C has performed under a sub-contract with B.
(c) Where A lets a building to B with a rent review clause, and B sub-lets the whole building (or a substantial part of it) to C with a corresponding clause.

[9] [1969] 3 All E.R. 589.

Power to amalgamate the adjudications

2–412 In such cases if A begins an action in the courts against B, and B wishes to raise the same issue against C, he can do so in England by means of "Third Party Procedure" (see Rules of the Supreme Court, Order 16). Alternatively B can commence separate proceedings against C, and ask the court to order that those proceedings be heard together with the proceedings by A against B. (See Order 4, rule 9.) In any decision as to the procedure to be adopted in such cases, the court will strive to avoid any procedure which raises the possibility that an identical issue may be decided one way between A and B, and another way between B and C.[10] In practice the court has ample powers to prevent this result.

2–413 Neither the court nor an arbitrator has comparable powers in the case of disputes which are submitted to arbitration. Thus:

(a) if the contract between A and B ("the first contract") provides for arbitration and the contract between B and C ("the second contract") does not, the court cannot order C to submit to arbitration on it;
(b) if each contract provides for the appointment of an arbitrator otherwise than by the court, and different arbitrators are appointed, neither the court nor the arbitrators can interfere.

Where both arbitrators are to be appointed by the same body

2–414 If the arbitration agreement in each contract provides for the appointment of an arbitrator by the same appointing body, *e.g.* a trade association, or the RIBA, or the RICS, it will be open to the appointing authority to appoint the same arbitrator in both arbitrations. The arbitrator can then hear the views of all three parties as to how the arbitration should be conducted. But unless all the parties have agreed, he has no power to order that the arbitrations be consolidated so that each party has the opportunity of hearing, and making submissions upon, all the evidence.[11] Nor can he take into account in arbitration A the evidence given in arbitration B, or vice-versa. That being the situation it is questionable whether the institutions are doing anyone a service when they appoint the same tribunal to related cases—but see paragraph 2–423 below.

Alternative procedures

2–415 In this situation there are broadly speaking four options, namely:

(a) one consolidated arbitration;
(b) two concurrent or consecutive arbitrations before the same arbitrator;

[10] See *Abu Dhabi v. Eastern Bechtel* [1982] 2 Lloyd's Rep. 425.
[11] See *Oxford Shipping Co. v. Nippon Yusen Kaisha* (*The Eastern Saga*) [1984] 3 All E.R. 835.

(c) two independent arbitrations before separate arbitrators;
(d) court proceedings including all three parties.

The first, one consolidated arbitration, with the arbitrator having before him when he makes his award all the evidence and all the arguments that any of the three parties desires to adduce, is the course likely to produce the highest quality of decision making. The fourth course is the most expensive and unsatisfactory. The second course, of two concurrent arbitrations, seems little more satisfactory. Even a trained lawyer would find it difficult, and perhaps impossible, to avoid being influenced in one arbitration by the proceedings in the other and only B, who is a party in each arbitration, would know the totality of the evidence that had been put forward. The real choice is therefore between one consolidated arbitration, and course (c). The first reaction of A and C to a proposal for one consolidated arbitration is that each will be faced with two opponents whereas in two consecutive arbitrations he would be faced by one only. That objection could be more apparent than real. The other objection is that of cost. An arbitration with three parties is likely to take appreciably longer, both in the preparatory stages and at the hearing, than one with two parties, and the costs per party are likely to be appreciably higher. But as between A and B it does not seem unfair if B has to bear all or most of the additional costs incurred by A and C, because: 2–416

(a) if the alternative course of two consecutive arbitrations had been adopted, B would have incurred, and been at risk as to, the costs of both arbitrations; and
(b) the need for consolidation is of B's making, not of A's or C's.

Two consecutive arbitrations before the same arbitrator

There is no particular disadvantage for the parties in whichever arbitration is taken first. The disadvantage is upon party A or C whose arbitration is taken second. For he is faced with the fact that the arbitrator has made up his mind on the evidence in the first arbitration, and it will take a man of clear head and great courage to admit that the evidence given in the second arbitration has persuaded him that his award in the first arbitration may have been "wrong". The inverted commas are necessary to emphasise that it may have been "right" on the material originally before him. Such qualities cannot be expected of the average arbitrator, however naturally they might be found in the retired Lord Justice of Appeal, who was the arbitrator appointed in the *Abu Dhabi* case. If the arbitrator delays making his award in the first arbitration until after he has heard the second, he exposes himself to criticism by A, the claimant in the first case, that the arbitrator will or may be influenced by evidence taken in proceedings to which A is not a party. 2–417

The fifth option used to be available by way of riposte to an application to 2–418 stay.[12] It is no longer possible other than by way of express agreement on the part of all the relevant parties—which may be very difficult to achieve. Since it is desirable that all related disputes be determined by the same tribunal, the Act is defective in having strengthened the "stay" provision without addressing in a positive manner the consolidation of related arbitrations.

Parallel claims by several claimants against the same respondent

2–419 It often happens that separate arbitrations are commenced more or less contemporaneously by several claimants against the same respondent, arising out of substantially similar facts. Examples are where several purchasers commence arbitrations against a contractor for defects in their houses arising from a common fault of design or construction; or where several purchasers of an insurance bond claim against an insurance broker or company for misrepresentation in the bond documentation; or where several tenants of separate but virtually identical premises in the same building (*e.g.* adjoining shops in a parade, or different floors in an office building) claim arbitration under identical rent review clauses.

In litigation the court takes control

2–420 The attitude of the courts in complex multi-party litigation is that the concept of a party being in charge of the litigation ought, as far as possible, to be subordinated to case management techniques controlled by the court.[13]

The starting point in arbitration—no general power to order concurrent or consolidated hearings

2–421 Arbitration is based on the consent of the parties, and an arbitrator has no general power to order that arbitrations be consolidated, or heard concurrently. So unless the terms of the arbitration agreement or of the scheme under which he was appointed give the arbitrator such a power, he must be prepared to conduct the arbitration separately for each party who insists on his so doing.

Should the same person be appointed for all the claims?

2–422 The first decision to be made where two or more claimants request arbitration in related disputes is usually that of the appointing institution; should it appoint different arbitrators or the same arbitrator? It is usual for the same person to be appointed for all the cases, for thereby it is at least possible that the parties in

[12] See for example *Berkshire Senior Citizens* (unreported).

[13] See *Chapman v. Chief Constable of South Yorkshire*, *The Times*, March 20, 1990, and the notes to Ord 15, r.12(6) in The Annual Practice of the Supreme Court.

all the cases will agree to a procedure which will avoid duplication of cases and of costs; whereas if different arbitrators are appointed duplication is inevitable.

The rights of the claimant

The next decision is that of the individual claimant: Is he willing to agree a procedure which minimises duplication and costs, or should he seek to remove the arbitrator and obtain the appointment of another arbitrator who will deal only with the claimant's case? In many cases the appointed arbitrator will be able, in consultation with all the parties, to devise a procedure acceptable to all of them, and thereby to minimise the costs of deciding the claims. But a claimant may wish to reserve his position as regards challenging the appointment, until he knows what procedure the arbitrator proposes, and can decide whether that procedure is acceptable to him. Given the provisions of section 73 of the Act the Claimant (and for that matter the Respondent) must be careful not to waive his rights. **2–423**

The rights of the respondent

The respondent, too, is entitled to challenge the appointment and to request that a different arbitrator be appointed for each claim. But in most cases the respondent will prefer that all the cases be dealt with by the same tribunal. Apart from any other consideration, once he has an award in one case, he may be able to negotiate his way out of the other. This is particularly so when he has managed to get brought on first a case which is favourable to his position. **2–424**

Procedure after appointment of a common arbitrator

Assuming no successful challenge, the arbitrator should proceed to discuss with the parties the procedure to be adopted. **2–425**

Contractual provision for third party situations

The party who is putting himself in the position of the middle man in two contracts (*e.g.* the contractor between employer and sub-contractor; the purchaser between vendor and sub-purchaser; the tenant between landlord and sub-tenant) can seek to protect himself by appropriate provisions in one or both contracts. Broadly speaking such provisions can take one of two forms. The first is to refer in the arbitration clause in each contract to the existence or prospective existence of the other contract, and to provide that if a dispute under the instant contract raises substantially the same issues as a dispute under the other contract, both disputes shall be referred to the arbitration of the same arbitrator. Precedents for a clause of this kind are at drafting suggestions Nos. 55, 56 and 62 in Appendix 1. The alternative method is applicable only to sale of goods contracts where the same goods are sold and re-sold on terms which are identical except as to date, price and parties. In such cases the contract may provide (or may incorporate the rules of a trade association which provide) that any dispute as **2–426** to quality only shall be resolved between the first seller and the last buyer, the award being binding on the intermediate parties.

Statutory or institutional provision for consolidation

2–427 Three or more parties, after a dispute has arisen between them, may agree upon consolidation as being the most practical way of resolving the various disputes between them. But there are at least three other ways in which two or more arbitrations involving overlapping issues may become consolidated.

(a) The statutes of the jurisdiction in which the arbitration arises may permit some form of consolidation, *e.g.* the Hong Kong Arbitration Ordinance.
(b) Institutional Rules adopted by the parties may authorise consolidation without consent.
(c) Standard form contracts between the parties may provide for consolidation, *e.g.* the JCT forms of contract (1988), discussed in Part 6.

13. The Preliminary Dialogue

Effect of the transformation of procedure

2–428 As appears from Part 1 of this Handbook and from many references thereafter, the 1996 Act introduces a transformation of the powers and duties of the arbitrator. In particular the Act imposes a positive duty to adopt procedures suitable to the particular case (section 33) and, subject to the right of the parties to agree any matter, gives the arbitrator power to decide all procedural and evidential matters (section 34). For the first time, the right to an oral hearing has been removed save insofar as such a right is conferred by the arbitration agreement, or rules which it incorporates, or express agreement of the parties. Post-1996 one of the first matters to be considered after the appointment of the arbitrator is whether or not there is to be a hearing.

The need for a preliminary dialogue

2–429 In the past a preliminary meeting has been usual in most arbitrations in which there was likely to be a hearing, and in many others. A preliminary dialogue is virtually indispensable in an arbitration which is proceeding to a hearing but can often be dispensed with in one that is to be determined on documents only. In the past this dialogue has taken the form of a meeting. But the development of telecommunications has in many cases made three-way discussions by telephone or video link a wholly acceptable substitute for a meeting, and one that can save much time and costs. So immediately on appointment the arbitrator should consider whether the terms of his appointment are such as to indicate whether the dispute is likely or unlikely to be determined on documents only. If the dispute is of a kind normally determined on documents only he should next consider whether there are any features of it making it practicable to dispense with a preliminary dialogue. In many cases it will be possible to issue provisional directions which will take effect after a specified time if neither party objects to any of them. But if the circumstances leave any doubt as to the usefulness of a preliminary dialogue he should proceed to arrange one.

The use of standard draft directions

It is open to an arbitrator practising in a particular field in which arbitrations follow a familiar pattern to have standard draft directions which can be issued, when notifying the parties of his appointment, with a covering letter to the effect that although he has little information at present as to the nature of the issues arising in this arbitration, the enclosed draft directions show the directions that are usually appropriate in matters of this kind. To get the arbitration under way without unnecessary delay he will issue directions in accordance with the draft unless either party notifies him within X days either that some other direction is appropriate at this stage or that no directions should be issued before a preliminary dialogue. If the directions require the delivery of Statements of Case with supporting documents, the arbitrator will be in a position either to take charge at the preliminary dialogue or to decide that no preliminary dialogue is necessary. **2–430**

Taking charge of the proceedings

There is a great advantage in obtaining even preliminary Statements of Case before any meeting. Before the 1996 Act the usual order of proceedings in most arbitrations has been that on appointment, the arbitrator notifies the parties of his appointment, and either waits for them to take the next step or arranges a meeting with them at which they will tell him what they want him to do. In either event, he learns in only a general way what the issues are, and directs pleadings or statements of case in times which begin to run only at or after the date of the meeting. One result of this is that at the preliminary dialogue each party and his advocate may have a clear idea of what they want, whereas the arbitrator knows nothing about the case. An opportunity to take charge of the conduct of the case at the outset is thereby lost. If at the very first meeting the **2–431** arbitrator has a reasonably clear idea of what are the issues between the parties, he can from the outset begin the selection of procedures best suited to resolving each of them. It is rare for an arbitration to be commenced without preliminary correspondence between the parties, and provided the arbitrator makes it clear that in principle he will not hold a party too rigidly to the first formulation of his case, in many cases this correspondence, or a selection from it, can with little or no addition suffice as a Statement of Case. Indeed, the arbitrator can state, in his Preliminary Directions Nisi, that this is all he wants at this stage, and that one of his objects in asking for it is to see whether he can help to limit the need for expensive advice from lawyers or other experts.

The use of draft directions

2–432 If, as we advocate, statements of case become the norm, there is nothing to prevent the arbitrator, as soon as he is appointed, from issuing provisional preliminary directions, that is, preliminary directions which will become operative after X days unless within that time either party notifies him of an objection to them. These provisional directions can provide for exchange of Statements of Case, accompanied by copies of the documents intended to be relied upon, within Y days.

Matters to be considered in the early stage of every arbitration

2–433 The following matters should be considered at the preliminary dialogue insofar as they have not already been clarified by the arbitration agreement or by some other agreement between the parties. This list is not exclusive. It should not substitute for the application of thought by those involved on how best to deal with the dispute.

(a) The appointment and remuneration of the arbitrator(s).
(b) Does the arbitrator have jurisdiction to decide all the issues over which the parties are in dispute?
(c) Is it desirable that any other parties be joined; if so is there any provision in the contracts making this possible, and do the parties want to do it?
(d) Does either party seek a direction under section 65 of the 1996 Act that the recoverable costs of the arbitration, or of any part of the arbitral proceedings, shall be limited to a specified amount and if so, what amount? [To be considered in conjunction with (y) below]
(e) What procedure is to be adopted to resolve the issues? In particular, is there to be an oral hearing, and if so should it deal with all or part of the issues and if part, which part and how are the remaining issues to be resolved?

(f) Are the issues already sufficiently defined, *e.g.* by correspondence? If not, how should they now be defined, *e.g.* by the exchange of Statements of Case and Statements of Reply; by allowing existing documents to stand as pleadings; by pleadings; or otherwise.

(g) Who is to present the case for each party, *e.g.* the party in person, lay advocate, solicitor or counsel?

(h) Does either party contend that discovery is really necessary to do justice in this dispute? If so in respect of what issues, at what stage, and to what extent?

(j) Does either party anticipate any particular problems in obtaining evidence, *e.g.* from witnesses overseas; and if so, how should these problems be resolved.

(k) What directions as to the timing of the various steps to be taken can best combine speed in obtaining an award with giving each party a fair opportunity to prepare his case?

(l) Are the arbitrator's powers adequate to deal with problems likely to arise, or is the case appropriate for application to the court for an order?

(m) Is any question of law likely to arise? If so which of the available procedures is most appropriate? (See paragraphs 2–508 *et seq.*, above)

(n) Do the parties agree that the arbitrator shall if so minded have power to take the advice of a lawyer engineer or other expert and if so, do the parties wish to agree upon the person or persons to be appointed.

(o) If there is to be a hearing, where is the most convenient place to hold it?

(p) Should all the issues be dealt with at once, or should they be split in some way?

(q) If expert witnesses are to be called, by what date should their proofs be exchanged?

(r) Do the parties wish to agree any particular rules of evidence; or do they leave it to the arbitrator to decide on the admissibility relevance or weight of any material to be tendered (see section 34(2)(f) of the 1996 Act)

(s) If there is to be a hearing or hearings, how much time should be allowed to each party for the presentation of its case, and should the arbitrator direct chess clock timing (see paragraphs 2–397 *et seq.* above and Appendix 24).

(t) If there is to be a hearing or hearings, a date should be set by which the advocates are to agree upon, and send to the arbitrator, a list of the issues that he has to decide. If they cannot agree upon a list, each should send his own formulation of the issues to be presented.

(u) Likewise, if there is to be a hearing or hearings, a date should be set by which a bundle or bundles of agreed documents is or are to be sent to the arbitrator so that he may read them, together with the pleadings or their equivalent and the list of issues, before the hearing begins.

(v) If it is thought that a second meeting or discussion is desirable—and if there is to be a single hearing it is very often of great advantage—arrangements should be made for it.

(w) Have the parties made, or do they wish to make, an agreement excluding the right of appeal?

(x) Will either party request the arbitrator to give reasons, or not to give reasons, for his award?

(y) How do the parties wish the arbitrator to deal with costs?

14. Identifying the Issues

Importance of early identification

2–434 Whatever procedure is to be adopted, it is essential that the points on which the parties are at issue be identified at the earliest practicable moment. One reason is that when both parties are clearly aware of the issues between them, they often see, just as clearly, a way to compromise some or all of them. A second is that the preparation for resolving the issues must begin with identifying them. A third is that the procedure for resolving the issues cannot sensibly be chosen until it is known what the issues are. Thus, for example, if the facts are agreed and the issue is solely one of law, the appropriate procedure may be for the arbitration to be conducted on documents only with power for the arbitrator to take the advice of a lawyer to be agreed between the parties and failing agreement to be selected by the arbitrator. But if the only issue is a technical one on which experts disagree, it may be wholly inappropriate for the parties to have a hearing attended by lawyers.

2–435 There are various procedural devices for identifying issues at an early stage of the arbitration. Thus, for example, most institutional rules require some form of pleading, often of law, evidence and fact by way of statement of case and statement of defence, usually to be accompanied by either a list or copies of relevant documents upon which reliance is placed.[14] In addition to compelling the parties to state their claims, defence, counterclaims and set-offs with clarity, many institutional rules empower the arbitrators to convene an early meeting or dialogue for review and appropriate directions. It is often a feature of such discussions that arbitrators, even when the institutional rules make no such

[14] See, *e.g.* LCIA Rules, Art. 6; ICC Rules, Arts. 3 and 4; the Model Law, Art. 23; UNCITRAL Arbitration Rules, Arts. 18 and 19.

requirements, try to identify with the parties the questions which the arbitrators will have to decide.[15]

Possible methods of identifying the issues

Pleadings: advantages and disadvantages

The classic procedure followed in arbitrations in England is derived from the courts and is the approach with which English arbitrators and practitioners are most familiar. However, there is no reason, either as a matter of law or practice, why, in attempting to define issues, arbitrators or parties are obliged to follow English litigation procedures. Indeed, there is a strong argument to the effect that they should not. A major criticism of an English court pleading is that it often obscures rather than clarifies and requires substantial amendment and particularisation before the fundamental issues in the case are clear. Many of these difficulties can be avoided, particularly in complex cases, by the parties being encouraged to plead in narrative form, as is customary in international commercial arbitration. The central object of any procedure to clarify the issues must be economy and expedition and the avoidance of litigation by ambush. **2–436**

In litigation the issues of fact are identified by pleadings. First, the plaintiff/claimant sets out the material facts on which he relies; secondly, the defendant/respondent states which of those facts he admits, and which of them he denies, and sets out any additional facts on which he relies; thirdly, the plaintiff/claimant having seen the defendant/respondent's defence delivers a reply if there are further facts that he wishes to rely upon. In most cases the pleadings stop at this third stage; but in some cases there may be a fourth, fifth or even sixth stage. This procedure has the theoretical advantage that when it has been completed each party knows what are the material facts that the other party will be putting before the tribunal, and he can prepare to meet the case thus stated. But it has many disadvantages. First, the stages are consecutive, and the process very time consuming. Second, the parties are not required to indicate any points of law that they intend to raise, and accordingly there may be no opportunity for the judge or arbitrator to consider such points in advance of their being raised at a hearing. Third, they encourage the defendant/respondent to take a negative attitude, by merely refusing to admit facts alleged by the plaintiff/claimant without indicating what the real nature of his defence is. Fourthly, matters of evidence are not revealed, until disclosure of documents and witness statements which does not occur until pleadings are closed. Forcing earlier disclosure of key evidence helps to clarify issues and may also encourage settlement. **2–437**

Statements of Case instead of pleadings

The alternative, which goes some way to meet these disadvantages, is the use of Statements of Case. Each party is directed to deliver to the arbitrator, on or **2–438**

[15] See, *e.g.* ICC Rules, Art. 13 which provides for the formulation of terms and reference.

before a stated date, a statement of his case setting out in narrative form the material facts on which he relies, any evidence which he considers important enough to mention at this stage and any arguments of law that he intends to raise. Then within a specified period thereafter each party is to deliver to the arbitrator a statement in reply to the other party's case, indicating which parts of it—law or fact—he accepts, and which he disputes. The object should be to convince, not to conceal. That object is defeated if the statement is too long, for undue length will make it difficult or impossible for the arbitrator to see the shape and the essential strength of the party's case. This procedure is usually quicker than pleadings, and usually gives a better idea to the arbitrator of the nature of the issues that he has to decide. In some cases exchange of Statements of Case is not practicable because the respondent has not yet been given a sufficiently clear idea of the basis of the claim made against him to be able to formulate his statement of case. In such a case the respondent's Statement of Case can be ordered to be delivered after he has had a fair opportunity of considering the claimant's.

Defining the issues in a schedule

2–439 Where there are many issues or potential issues, *e.g.* in many construction industry disputes, the claim on each issue, the defence to it, and the reply to the defence can be set out in schedule form so that the arbitrator can see, in one document and preferably on one sheet of paper, the opposing contentions on each issue. See drafting suggestions Nos. 59 and 61 in Appendix 1.

Where correspondence can stand as Statement of Case

2–440 In many cases the nature of the claim and/or of the defence to it will have been clearly conveyed to the respondent by correspondence before an arbitrator is appointed. If the correspondence in question consists of only a few letters, the arbitrator can save time by ordering that those letters stand as the Statement of Claim, and that the defendant deliver his defence in a relatively short time from the giving of directions. In some cases both the claim and the defence are clearly specified in the correspondence, and a direction identifying those which constitute the claim, and those which constitute the defence, will suffice.

Particulars and amendments

Further particulars

2–441 Some lawyers delight in asking for further and better particulars of something alleged in the opposing party's pleading or Statement of Case and, when they get those particulars, for yet further and yet better particulars. Sometimes the requests are justified. A common example is a pleading or Statement of Case which says merely that "it was agreed that" without saying when, or where, or how, or between whom it was agreed. The party faced with this pleading may truly be at a disadvantage if he is not given more details. He may need to know the date, or what representative of his is said to have agreed it, or whether it is said to have been agreed on the telephone or at a meeting, and if at a meeting, where the meeting took place and who else was present. Particulars of this kind may be truly essential to enable him to prepare his evidence in contradiction of the allegation; so much so that the party who pleaded merely "that it was agreed" was at fault in not taking the trouble to give the particulars there and then. On the other side of the line, if, given the particulars just mentioned, the party asks for yet further particulars, stating what words were used in the conversation, he is asking for something that no doubt it would be nice for him to have, but it is not essential for him to have in order to prepare his case.

When to direct further particulars

As a general principle, arbitrators should avoid directing further particulars and seek other ways, perhaps through fuller pleading in the first instance, discovery of documents or early disclosure of witness statements, to compel a party to identify unambiguously the matters upon which reliance is placed and to avoid litigation by ambush. **2–442**

In general, requests for particulars have three disadvantages. First, they tend to increase the costs of the arbitration. Secondly, they complicate the pleadings or Statements of Case, in that they increase the number of documents it is necessary to read in order to see what each party's case is and what the issues are. Thirdly, if they are accompanied by requests for more time, *e.g.* a respondent asking for particulars of the claimant's Statement of Case asks also that his time for lodging his Statement of Case be extended until after he has been given the particulars, they may cause delay. In most cases responsible advocates will agree upon whether, and if so what, particulars ought to be given and how they should be given, *e.g.* by appropriate discovery of relevant documents. Where they cannot agree, the arbitrator will have to find ways of letting the applicant for particulars have what is necessary to prepare his case. To avoid the multiple document syndrome, it is helpful to have the particulars merged (suitably identified) with the original document. **2–443**

Applications to amend the pleading or Statement of Case

There are many reasons why a party may desire to amend his case. His advocate may have been inadequately instructed at the outset. A change of advocate, or taking in a second and perhaps more senior advocate, brings a fresh mind to bear who wishes to take new points or present the case in a different way. Further information may have become available. Where pleadings are delivered consecutively, a pleading from the opposing party may make a change in the party's case necessary or desirable. There are countless others. **2–444**

Considering applications for leave to amend

Absent agreement to the contrary, it is for the arbitrator under section 34(2)(c) to decide whether amendments to a Statement of Case or Defence are to be **2–445** permitted. The first thing that the arbitrator must do when considering a claim for leave to amend is to consider whether the issue that would be raised by the amendment is one that he has jurisdiction to try. Just as he should, on appointment, and on reading the pleadings or Statements of Case, check that the issues that they raise fall within the jurisdiction conferred upon him by the arbitration agreement so, when the application for leave to amend is made, the arbitrator should check whether the issues raised by the amendment fall within his jurisdiction. If what has been referred to him is a claim for damages for breach of contract, and the claimant wishes to amend to add (either in the alternative or as an addition) a claim for damages for negligence based on the same facts, the arbitrator should first enquire of the respondent whether he consents to the new claim being determined by the arbitrator. If the respondent agrees, the arbitrator should cause the parties to record their agreement in writing, so that there is no doubt as to his jurisdiction. If the respondent will not agree then the arbitrator should follow the procedure set out in paragraphs 2–222 *et seq*. when confronted with an objection to his jurisdiction. Some institutional rules deal specifically with amendment of pleadings, particularly where it is sought to add new claims.[16]

Amendment not causing substantial delay

2–446 The general rule is that applications to amend a party's case should be allowed whenever this can be done without injustice to the opposing party. The disadvantage to the opposing party usually, though not always, takes the form of additional costs or additional delay. Disadvantage by way of additional costs can usually be met by an appropriate order that the amending party pay the costs of and occasioned by the amendment in any event. If there is reason to suppose that the amending party cannot or will not pay even if an order is made, the leave to amend may be conditional upon the amending party giving security for the costs.

Amendments causing substantial delay

2–447 Where an amendment is likely to cause delay in the ultimate conclusion of the arbitration the problems may be less easy to solve. If the application to amend is made at around the time of pleadings, many months before the fixed or provisional hearing date, and it does not wholly change the nature of the issues, there should be no problem. The difficult questions arise when an amendment makes a major change in the character of the arbitration, and in the time required for preparation, or for hearing, or both, or where the amendment is sought at a relatively late date—perhaps even during the hearing itself—and allowing it will inevitably involve delaying the award. The presumption should be to allow the amendment if this can possibly be done without injustice to the opposing party.

[16] See, *e.g*. LCIA Rules, Art. 13(d); ICC Rules, Art. 16; UNCITRAL Arbitration Rules, Art. 20; UNCITRAL Model Law, Art. 23(2).

The object of the exercise (and therefore the relevant part of the necessity for the amendment) is to ensure, if possible, that all the disputes between the parties are resolved; and that the disputes which are determined are the final disputes. Neither the parties nor the arbitrator should be trying to pin down a chimaera.

If it is the claimant who is seeking leave to make an amendment that will delay the award, it will be for the respondent to show reason why delay is prejudicial to him. He can always say "I do not like having this claim hanging over me" but in many cases this will carry little weight. But he may for example be able to say "I am an executor, and am ready to distribute the estate and am being pressed by the beneficiaries to do so—they need the money; but I cannot distribute until this claim is disposed of and this amendment will cause 6 months delay." And there are cases in which the claimant's main object is keeping a claim in existence rather than having it decided. **2–448**

Amendments not introducing new issues of fact

Where the amendment raises a new issue of fact, it will clearly be unjust to the opposing party to allow it without giving him a reasonable time to prepare and call evidence rebutting the new allegations of fact. But where, as quite often happens, the amending party merely wishes to formulate his case in law in a different way, without introducing any new facts, the amendment should normally be allowed even if raised during the hearing, provided that the opposing advocate is given a reasonable time—if necessary a short adjournment—to prepare his contentions upon it. Indeed, if no new facts are being introduced, an amendment may be unnecessary.[17] **2–449**

Applications for an adjournment

A request for an adjournment made shortly before the hearing date, with no indication of willingness to attend on any date shortly thereafter, and made on apparently flimsy grounds, is different in character from a request for an adjournment of a few days or weeks made for apparently good reasons well before the hearing date. The arbitrator's object will be to give each side a fair opportunity of presenting his case, and if one party asserts that the hearing date hitherto fixed will not allow him to do this, the arbitrator should be ready to change it provided—and this is essential—that the new date will not impose on the other party a disadvantage amounting to injustice, for example if his expert witness or counsel will not be available for the proposed new date. Where shortly before the hearing an application for an adjournment was made on the grounds that the respondent wanted to instruct new solicitors, and the arbitrator held that this was a matter that he could not take into account, it was held that he was guilty of misconduct. He should have taken this into account, and weighed the pros and cons of acceding to the request.[18a] **2–450**

[17] *I.O.C. v. Coastal* [1990] 2 Lloyd's Rep. 415.
[18a] *Thornes v. Official Solicitor* (1982) 265 E.G. 601.

The list of issues

Preparing the list of issues

2–451 A major disadvantage of the conventional English litigation system of pleading is that whereas the pleadings are almost the first stage in the preparation of a case for hearing, the list of issues becomes almost the last stage. Before the list can be finalised, each party must have decided what case it wishes to present. To make the necessary decisions under the conventional system each party needs:

(a) to have completed discovery and inspection of the opposing party's documents;
(b) to have made such further inquiries, and obtained such further evidence, as a perusal of the opposing party's documents may make desirable;
(c) to obtain the advice of his advocate or legal advisers as to which points should be fought, and which conceded;
(d) to have time to make his decisions in the light of that advice.

2–452 In too many cases this process is completed far too late, or is never completed at all—the dispute simply drifts into a hearing without either party reconsidering a decision to litigate made much earlier and on very different information. Effective case management by the arbitrator from the beginning, combined with procedures for early disclosure of relevant matters of fact, evidence and law should enable the preparation of a list of issues well before any hearing or hearings. Subject to questions of jurisdiction (*e.g.* what disputes were identified when the arbitration was commenced) the list of issues is not cast in stone and can itself be developed and refined as the case proceeds. Preparing a list of issues in this way confers two benefits on the parties. First, it leads to the compromise of claims, or issues, which would otherwise drift into a contested hearing. Secondly, it helps all concerned to concentrate on what is truly in dispute, and to cut out irrelevancies. And if the list is given to the arbitrator before the hearing, together with the relevant correspondence, it achieves a third benefit, in that it shortens the hearing itself. Where an issue is directly related to a money claim, the amount of the claim should be indicated along with an estimate of the time likely to be spent on it. This assists in identifying situations where the costs are disproportionate to the claim.

The pre-hearing review

2–453 In many cases whether conducted in conventional litigation fashion or in other ways, the view of the issues as seen at the preliminary dialogue is greatly altered in the course of the preparations for trial. So it is often useful, and in heavy cases usually desirable, that there be a further dialogue shortly before the hearing. The objects are: first, to identify the issues; secondly, to enable the arbitrator to do the maximum of reading before rather than at the hearing; thirdly, to clarify the evidence which the arbitrator will need to enable him to make an informed decision rooted in a sure foundation of fact, and thereby to programme the hearing so as to minimise the time for which witnesses—particularly expert witnesses—are required to attend; and generally to seek methods of shortening the hearing and reducing costs. The list of issues is the key to a successful review and, indeed to an efficient hearing.

The list of issues as an index

The management of his notes is an important technical problem for any arbitrator. Inadequate management is probably responsible for a substantial proportion of the delay in issuing awards, and of errors in them. One method of note management (and it is only one of many) is as follows: 2–454

(a) each issue in the list of issues is lettered;
(b) the pages of the notebook are numbered;
(c) a note is made at the time, in the margin of the notebook (or of the transcript if there is one), of the issue or issues to which this part of the evidence is relevant;
(d) at the end of each day an index is made up by entering the page references against the issue letter.

The final index might look thus: 2–455

ISSUE A (What was the contract?)
4 Jones X
7 Jones XX
12 Jones XXX
16 Smith X
27 Smith XX
31 Smith XXX

ISSUE B (Was the contract varied?) etc.

15. Discovery, Inspection of Documents and Interrogatories

Discovery in litigation

The basic rule

Hitherto the party ordered to give discovery in an English court action is: 2–456 "to make and serve a list of the documents which are or have been in his possession custody or power relating to any matter in question"; see Rules of the Supreme Court, Ord. 24, r. 2.

2–457 The inspecting party is not limited to documents which would be admissible in evidence,[18] nor to those which would prove or disprove any matter in question. Any document which may reeasonably be supposed to contain information which may enable the party applying for discovery either to advance his own case or to damage that of his adversary, must be disclosed. So must any document which may fairly lead him to a train of enquiry which may have either of these consequences. Thus the principle is wide. However, the case to be advanced or damaged is the case on a matter which is actually in issue. It is this limitation which is often forgotten or ignored.

The purpose of discovery

2–458 Clearly, what any party is looking for is admissions in the other party's documents which help the inspecting party to establish its side of a particular disputed issue. For example, in a dispute about workmanship, internal reports from the other party's foreman which complain about his men's poor workmanship, or identify poor attendance and drunkenness as serious problems, would be of particular assistance.

Discovery in the common law and in non-common law jurisdictions

2–459 The process of discovery is very valuable in assisting English courts and arbitrators to resolve issues of fact. But it has been severely abused and is regarded by many senior judges and practitioners as requiring urgent and radical reform. Lord Woolf has recognized the need for reform in his two reports and has made proposals for changing the basic rule as enshrined in Order 24. There is no doubt that the process does not generate the same enthusiasm or respect outside the Anglo-Saxon legal systems. Parties from non-common law systems who do not have a comparable process find the idea of disclosing one's internal and confidential documents incomprehensible and objectionable.[19] Consequently, in an international dispute between parties emanating from different legal systems an unmodified common law approach to discovery may be unsatisfactory. Apart from any other factor there is always the danger that parties from different legal systems will approach the process in a different way, so that the resulting discovery is not fair.

Difference between discovery and inspection

2–460 Discovery means the process of listing documents. The exercise of looking at the documents that the opposing party has disclosed is "inspection". All docu-

[18] See *Urban Small Space Ltd v. Barford Investment Co. Ltd* [1990] 28 E.G. 116.

[19] See the paper by Professor Claude Reymond in *Arbitration International.*

ments which come within the relevant principles must be listed, even if they are privileged. Inspection is allowed however, only of those documents which are not privileged; unless, of course privilege has been waived. One of the purposes of the exercise of listing is to enable each party to know the broad categories of documents in respect of which privilege is being claimed, so that in an appropriate case the claim of privilege can be challenged.

Privilege and public policy

There is a public interest in the admission of any evidence that assists in the just resolution of disputes, whether in litigation or in arbitration. On the other hand there are certain classes of material whose disclosure would be injurious to the national interest; for example, information relating to national security or to diplomatic relations with other countries. There are also certain classes of material in respect of which the private right to privacy is deemed to outweigh the general interest in disclosure. This material (which may be oral or written) is said to be ''privileged'', and falls under three heads: The privilege against self-incrimination; legal professional privilege; and communications for the compromise of a dispute. The rules are the same in litigation and in arbitration. **2–461**

Public policy immunity

Some classes of document are protected from disclosure on the grounds of public policy, *e.g.* Cabinet papers, Foreign Office dispatches, high level inter-departmental minutes, information relating to police informers, the proceedings in a jury room. The categories are not closed, but the courts are unlikely to expand them save by analogy with interests that have previously been protected.[20] **2–462**

Privilege against self-incrimination

As a general rule and subject only to certain statutory exceptions, no one is bound to answer any question, or to disclose any document, if the answer or the disclosure would tend to expose him to a real risk of a criminal charge or penalty. This privilege is that of the witness (or of any non-witness against whom disclosure is sought) whether or not he is a party. **2–463**

Legal professional privilege—whether or not litigation or arbitration is contemplated or pending

This privilege applies to confidential letters and other communications (oral or written) passing between a person and his legal advisers in their professional capacity and for the purpose of getting legal advice. The document must be **2–464**

[20] A recent attempt by a local authority to establish the proposition that a vast range of documentation had statutory protection against production rightly failed. See *Copeland v. Hayton* (1995), unreported.

written on a confidential basis, and it follows that not every communication between a person and his solicitor is privileged; for example, correspondence with his solicitor acting as his agent in selling a property is almost certainly not confidential and thus may not be privileged. It has even been held that communications between a party moving a Bill in Parliament and his parliamentary agent are not privileged[21]. On the other hand, where photo-copies of documents, not in themselves privileged, were sent to a Queen's Counsel for advice as to tax matters, and the Commissioners of Inland Revenue sought production of them, the Q.C.'s claim to privilege was upheld; see *R. v. Board of Inland Revenue, ex p. Goldberg.*[22]

Legal professional privilege—where litigation or arbitration is contemplated or pending

2–465 Any communication between a party and his legal advisers which came into existence at a time when litigation or arbitration was contemplated or pending, and which was made with a view to such litigation or arbitration (whether for the purpose of obtaining or giving advice, or of obtaining evidence, or of obtaining information which might lead to the obtaining of evidence) is privileged.[23]

2–466 Documents which have not come into existence for the purpose of the litigation, but which have been obtained by solicitors for that purpose, are likewise privileged.

Negotiations for the compromise of a dispute

2–467 To encourage the compromise of civil disputes, the courts recognise as privileged from disclosure any communication between parties or their lawyers or other agents which was made in a bona fide attempt to negotiate a settlement. This privilege is a joint privilege and cannot be waived without the consent of both parties. It operates whether or not the communication in question was expressed to be made "without prejudice". It is prudent to state expressly that such a communication is made "without prejudice"; but if it appears to be part of a bona fide negotiation for a settlement the absence from a document of a "without prejudice" endorsement does not prevent a successful claim for privilege. Equally the presence of such an endorsement does not conclusively or automatically render it privileged, if it is not part of a bona fide negotiation."[24] The test is whether the letter records a party as taking a position which is more detrimental to its interest than the one being formally maintained in the "open" proceedings. "Without prejudice" letters do not necessarily cease to be inadmissible even if a contract is concluded. They may however need to be referred to if there is a dispute as to whether a contract has been concluded.

[21] Sir Douglas Frank in *Pickin v. BRB*, unreported.
[22] [1988] S.T.C. 524.
[23] *The Italia Express* [1990] 3 All E.R. 157.
[24] See *Giacomo Ocsta v. British Italian Trading Co.* [1961] 2 Q.B. 201.

The privilege which attaches to such a letter is effective even outside the proceedings in connection with which it was written. Thus if, in proceedings between A and B, B writes to A a "without prejudice" letter, that letter is inadmissible (without B's consent) in any subsequent litigation or arbitration connected with the same subject-matter; see *Rush & Tompkins v. GLC*.[25] 2–468

Inadvertent disclosure of a privileged document

If a document in respect of which a party is entitled to claim privilege comes into the possession of the other party without any fraud or other improper conduct of that other party, the privilege will be lost. But the document will usually also be a confidential document, and the court has power to restrain by injunction any authorised use of it. Whether the court will exercise that power depends upon the circumstances. If the document was obtained by a fraud or by a trick, use of it will usually be restrained. But otherwise the court may decide that the interests of justice will be better served if the party who has without impropriety come into possession of the document is permitted to use it.[26] 2–469

Discovery in arbitration

The statutory power

In an arbitration under English law and subject to any restrictions or extensions of his powers in the arbitration agreement, the arbitrator derives his powers from section 34 of the Act. Section 34(2)(d) provides that the arbitrator may decide "whether any and if so which documents or classes of documents should be disclosed between and produced by the parties and at what stage". 2–470

This is an extremely wide power subject only to the protection against disclosure of privileged documents; to the overriding obligation of the arbitrator under section 33; and to the contrary agreement of the parties. Properly used, the power should enable arbitrators to prevent oppressive and expensive discovery and exercise greater control over the disclosure and production of documents. 2–471

Arbitrator's wide discretion

Thus, at one extreme it enables him to direct that there should be no discovery at all. At the other he can direct that there shall be full discovery along the lines of English litigation. The arbitrator should treat each case individually, and should look for the degree of discovery appropriate to the issues involved. It follows that he will be considerably assisted by an effective formulation of the issues, since he can if he wishes order discovery at different levels of intensity for different issues. Thus if there appears to be a direct conflict of evidence as to a material fact, he may think that every document relating to that issue should 2–472

[25] [1988] 3 All E.R. 737, H.L.

[26] See *Webster v. James Chapman & Co.* [1989] All E.R. 939, and the case there cited.

be disclosed; whereas if another issue turns mainly upon a difference of expert opinion, he may think that little or no discovery is appropriate on it.

2–473 Arbitrators should require parties to produce in good time documents upon which a party intends to rely. This can be done by requiring such documents to be supplied with the Statement of Case or Defence or separately. Many classes of dispute give rise to known and identifiable classes of documents. A stock exchange transaction will produce pro forma documentation, as will a dispute over variation orders in a construction case. Arbitrators should require the parties to produce documentation without which the arbitrator could not properly decide the dispute. This application of the principles of relevance and necessity should enable effective discovery orders to be made without the abuse which has characterised some cases hitherto.

Categorisation of the documents

2–474 Inter-parties documents are the letters and other documents passing between the parties themselves; for example, contracts, drawings, charts and plans, and general correspondence (by letter or fax or telex).

2–475 Internal documents are those internal to one party. From the point of view of advancing a party's case, these are often more important than the inter-parties documents. They often raise questions of privilege; for example, they may constitute advice from an in-house lawyer (in which case they may well be privileged) or may be an internal appreciation of the situation (in which case they are not).

2–476 Communications with other persons. Documents passing between a party and someone who is not a party, insofar as they are in the possession or power of the party, if material to any issue may be disclosable. But again these often raise issues of privilege; for example, if they are written to or by a lawyer for the purpose of obtaining or giving legal advice; or if they are written to or by a prospective witness for the purpose of obtaining evidence for use in probable or possible litigation or arbitration.

2–477 Documents in the possession of a related person. Documents in the possession of an employee of a party are deemed to be in the possession of the party himself. Documents in the possession of an agent (*e.g.* an architect, accountant, or broker) are in the power of the party if they emanate from him, and perhaps if they were obtained by the agent in his capacity as agent for the party. But documents emanating from the agent, *e.g.* his working papers, are not in the possession or power of the party, and the party cannot be compelled to disclose them. If considered important, it may be open to a party who wishes to put them in evidence to obtain production of them to the arbitrator by serving on the agent a subpoena duces tecum.

2–478 Documents in the possession of an unrelated person. Here there can be no question of the documents being in the possession or power of the party, for there is no relationship which gives the party either possession of or power over them. But as in the case of related persons, it is open to a party to compel their production by means of a subpoena duces tecum.

Subpoena duces tecum

Arbitrator has no power to apply for a subpoena

Application for a writ of subpoena can be made only by a party, not by an arbitrator. For this either the permission of the arbitrator is required or the agreement of the parties. An arbitrator may feel that access to some document or group of documents not in the power or control of either party is likely to be of substantial assistance to a party. If so, and if neither party seems to be taking the initiative, he should consider reminding both parties that either of them has power to issue a *subpoena duces tecum* with his permission. Issuing a subpoena involves costs, and can be upsetting for the recipient; hence the emphasis above is on "likely" and "substantial". Nevertheless the power is there and it is an important and valuable one.[27] **2–479**

Return date for subpoena duces tecum

In most cases the return date (*i.e.* the date of attendance specified in the *subpoena*) is the date fixed for the beginning of the hearing. But if a substantial number of documents is produced in response to the subpoena, it may be inconvenient to fit them into the bundles that the parties have already prepared and agreed upon for the hearing. Thus, any important documents produced in response to the subpoena should be available to both parties as early as possible. Note that the documents are produced to the court or the arbitrator (as the case may be) and not to the party serving the subpoena, and therefore both parties are entitled to equal access to the documents so produced. It is submitted that there is in principle no objection to, and powerful arguments for, having a *subpoena duces tecum* returnable earlier than the first day of the main hearing. To achieve an earlier date, the party seeking the documents should apply to the arbitrator for a preliminary hearing for the purpose of reception of the documents, and should serve the subpoena for that time and place. In many cases, the fact that production of the documents can be compelled by subpoena results in the documents being offered voluntarily, to save inconvenience to all concerned. **2–480**

Courts are becoming more reluctant to order what is in effect general discovery by way of *subpoena duces tecum.* Increasingly they seek specific identification of the documents which are sought and they are reluctant to entertain such applications until discovery in the action or arbitration, as the case may be, has **2–481**

[27] Section 43 of the 1996 Act.

been completed. In addition, the witness must be in the U.K. and the arbitration must be being conducted in England, Wales or Northern Ireland.

Interrogatories

What they are

2–482 Interrogatories are written questions put by one party to an opposing party, who is required to answer the questions in writing and upon oath or affirmation. Their object is to obtain the answers to contentious or disputatious matters where it is unlikely that the answer will be obtained by way of cross-examination from the witnesses who are likely to be called.

Interrogatories in litigation

2–483 They are not commonly used in litigation; and there are differences of opinion between judges both as to their usefulness and as to the extent to which they should be allowed. The principles are set out in *The Supreme Court Practice*, Ord. 26 and notes thereto. The most important general principle is that only such interrogatories shall be allowed as the court considers necessary either for disposing fairly of the cause, or for saving costs; see Ord. 26, r. 1(3).

Interrogatories in arbitration

2–484 An arbitrator had power under section 12 of the 1950 Act to order a party to answer interrogatories.[28] The power is now included in section 34(2)(e) of the Act. The power under section 12 of the 1950 Act was exercised even more rarely in arbitration than in litigation. Nevertheless it remains available, and if the arbitrator considers that (most unusually) they will truly assist in disposing of an issue fairly, expeditiously and cheaply, and are not being used merely for a fishing expedition or as a delaying or harassing tactic, or by way of anticipatory cross-examination,[29] he should be prepared to allow them. So far as the formalities are concerned, in most cases the same object can be achieved if they are administered and answered by letter, provided that it is made clear to the party answering them that he will be bound by the answers.

[28] The former power of the court to order interrogatories under s.12 of the 1950 Act was abolished by the Courts and Legal Services Act 1990.

[29] Cross-examination in writing is, of course, a useful and helpful technique in certain circumstances, and as part of a fully thought-out procedure.

16. Selection of Evidence for the Hearing

Selection by the parties

Contrary to what many seem to believe, identifying the documents relating to matters in issue in the arbitration is not the end of the matter. There are two further stages—selection and arrangement. In many cases this is not difficult. But in some business transactions—building and civil engineering contracts are obvious examples—enormous quantities of documents are generated. Selecting those that are or might be relevant to the issues in the arbitration is a difficult task. The time of the professional people qualified to discriminate between the relevant, the possibly relevant, and the irrelevant, is extremely expensive. In comparison the photocopier is immediately available and is cheap. So someone rather junior is asked to select. Because of his junior status he is inclined to operate on the principle that it is safer to have something in than leave it out. So every conceivable document relating to the dispute, but not restricted to the issues is picked out. The consequence is an agreed bundle, produced in an enormous number of copies, consisting largely of irrelevant documents that will never be used in the proceedings. Indeed, as the Court of Appeal has often pointed out, it is common for the lawyers who actually conduct the hearing to extract from the "agreed bundle" a "working or core bundle" containing only the documents likely to be referred to. So the apparent saving effected by employing a low-cost junior may be more than offset by the cost of copying and arranging far too large a bundle, and the consequential loss of time during the hearing. 2–485

The responsibility of the arbitrator

The arbitrator's control over this aspect of the case should not be limited simply to the identification of the categories of documents which are or are not to be discovered. His control should continue to ensure that a proper selection of documents is made for the hearing. Thus at some suitable moment—in the preliminary meeting, or in a second or subsequent such meeting in a heavy case—it may be appropriate for him to deliver a firm homily on the importance of an informed selection of documents for the agreed bundles. Particularly in heavy cases where the documents are voluminous he should not hesitate to indicate the classes or categories of documents he considers necessary. He may also consider giving a direction as to the number of copies that he considers necessary, so that a party who makes more than is necessary cannot expect to recover the additional costs so incurred. 2–486

Controlling the cost of unnecessary copying

2–487 If an arbitrator is of opinion that one party is seeking to put an unnecessary number of documents into the agreed bundles, it is open to him to exclude them or direct that the documents be marked in some way so that he can see which party asked for a particular document to be included and, if he thinks fit, make an appropriate order as to costs. Or he can ask that the costs of discovery be separately recorded by each party, to help him make an appropriate order for costs at the end of the hearing. He should also consider whether to make an order under section 65 capping the recoverable costs of discovery.

Admissible and inadmissible evidence

2–488 The Act has simplified the regime for deciding what evidence should be admitted for consideration by the Arbitrator and which should be excluded. Until the Act the conventional practice was that arbitrators, where the seat of the arbitration was in England and Wales, conformed to the English law of evidence, though this was subject to the contrary intention of the parties which could readily be implied particularly in international cases. Some commentators doubted whether arbitrators were so bound, but all doubts in the matter have been swept away by section 34(2)(f) of the Act. Now subject to the right of the parties to agree otherwise it is for the tribunal to decide:

> "whether to apply strict rules of evidence (or any other rules) as to the admissibility, relevance or weight of any material (oral, written or other) sought to be tendered on any matter of fact or opinion) and the time manner and form in which such material should be exchanged and presented."

2–489 This provision applies both to factual witnesses and to expert witnesses. There are certain criteria which it is suggested should be followed by arbitrators when seeking to exercise the powers given to them by section 34(2)(f). The first criterion should be that of relevance; the arbitrator should make it plain that no evidence will be received which is irrelevant to any issue in the arbitration; that is to say, which is not logically probative of a matter in issue. Thus, if the issue is whether the respondent supplied bad beer to the claimant, evidence that the respondent supplied good beer to other customers is inadmissible, because even if accepted it would not disprove the claimant's case that the beer supplied to him was bad. But evidence that the beer supplied to other customers out of the same batch on the same day was good would be relevant and admissible.

2–490 The second criterion is that evidence which is privileged should be excluded.

2–491 The third criterion is that arbitrators should ensure that any finding of fact which they wish to make is supported by evidence produced to them. They must consider and weigh evidence that is presented to them and upon which there factual findings must rest. If they do not, then they run the risk that the award may be challenged for irregularity. They must try to ensure that the award is rooted, to adopt Bingham J.'s phrase in the *Air Canada* case, in a sure foundation of fact.

Section 34(3)(f) should remove from the arena of arbitration any arguments of admissibility of factual evidence based on grounds other than relevance or privilege. The arguments should be confined to the weight to be given to evidence, rather than its admissibility. Arbitrators should in the context of admissibility, no longer be troubled by the rule against hearsay evidence, which in any case, for all practical purposes has been abolished in civil cases by the Civil Evidence Act 1995. **2–492**

It will effectively remain an objection to the admissibility of expert evidence, that the alleged expert is no expert at all qualified neither by study or experience. But such objections are rare; and argument on expert evidence is more usually on the weight to be attached to it and to the effect that preference should be given to the evidence of one expert witness rather than to another. **2–493**

Allowing evidence to be given de bene esse

Any remaining objection to evidence which may be voiced can be dealt with by having the objection reduced to writing (to present and preserve the position of the objector) and then hearing the evidence *de bene esse*. The practical effect of allowing evidence to be given de bene esse is that it is admitted on a provisional basis. If, for example, there is an objection to the admissibility of a document, the arbitrator can read it *de bene esse*; that is, on the footing that if later argument persuades him that the letter ought not to have been admitted, he will shut it out of his mind. In many cases an objection that looms large in the mind of the objector at the time is seen to be of no or virtually no importance by the time the other evidence has been heard. In the relatively unusual case where this is not so, the arbitrator can hear the submissions on both sides, and deal with it by one of the methods discussed below. **2–494**

It is not possible to admit evidence *de bene esse* if the objection to it is on the grounds that the material, whether oral or documentary, forms a part of negotiations for a compromise, made "without prejudice". **2–495**

The problem with which arbitrators are often faced is the refusal by one party to admit facts which are clear from documentary evidence; such as where a party refuses to admit facts as set out in a letter written by an apparently independent person. In those circumstances, if the objector insists on the author being called as a witness the arbitrator can either agree and so rule, putting the objector on risk as to costs; or refuse and admit the facts subject to argument as to relevance and weight. **2–496**

Pointing out the costs consequences

In some situations a sustained objection is likely to increase the costs of a hearing without any real likelihood that it will significantly affect the outcome of the arbitration; for example, refusing to admit the facts set out in a letter **2–497** written by an apparently independent witness on a point not central to the arbitration. In these circumstances the arbitrator must be firm and reject the request.

Taking legal advice

2–498 If the arbitrator wishes to take legal advice it is suggested that he discusses with the parties whether they wish him to proceed under section 37 or in some less formal manner. He should remember that the lawyer can only advise; it is for the arbitrator himself to make the final decision.[30]

Applying for the determination of the court

2–499 The admissibility of evidence is a question of law. Hence theoretically at least it would be open to a party with the consent of the arbitrator or of all other parties to apply to the court for a ruling under section 45 of the Act. Given the arbitrator's wide powers under section 34 and the narrow ground on which admissibility points may now be raised, it is however difficult to think of a situation which would justify using this somewhat "sledgehammer" procedure to crack what should be a fairly straightforward "nut".

Inadmissible evidence—privilege

Privileged communications are inadmissible

2–500 The classes of document that are privileged from discovery have been considered above. The same principles apply to protect privileged information during the hearing. If a document or oral statement is "privileged" it may not be put in evidence (whether by the person who made it or by the person to whom it was made) nor can a witness be asked about it during cross-examination, without the appropriate consent. What consent is necessary varies with the nature of the privilege, and is mentioned below.

Waiving the protection

2–501 Public policy immunity can be waived only by a Minister of the Crown. Legal professional privilege can be waived only by the client whom it protects, or an agent duly authorised to act on his behalf. The privilege attaching to without prejudice communications prevents their admission in evidence without the consent of both (or all) parties.

Inadvertent disclosure of a privileged document

2–502 If a document in respect of which a party is entitled to claim privilege comes into the possession of the other party without any fraud or other improper conduct of that other party, the privilege will be lost. But the document will usually also

[30] *South Shropshire District Council v. Amos* [1986] 1 W.L.R. 1271.

be a confidential document, and the court has power to restrain by injunction any unauthorised use of it. Whether the court will exercise that power depends upon the circumstances. If the document was obtained by a fraud or by a trick, use of it will usually be restrained. But otherwise the court may decide that the interests of justice will be better served if the party who has without impropriety come into possession of the document is permitted to use it.[31]

Contested application to use confidential documents

An arbitrator asked by the party to rule that a privileged and/or confidential document may be used in evidence should proceed carefully. If the other party reacts angrily, as it often does, his first task will be to introduce some calm. He should then, if at all possible, refuse to allow the immediate use of the document until a procedure has been established (*e.g.* written submissions to be delivered, with authorities annexed, and/or very exceptionally a trial within the trial, on affidavits with a right to cross-examine, etc.) to resolve the issue. The procedure should be as simple as possible and any hearing longer than two hours should be avoided. If it is possible to deal with it out of normal sitting hours, then very little time will be lost. He should warn the parties that at the end of this procedure he will make a separate order as to the costs involved in it. **2–503**

As far as possible the arbitrator should not examine or read the document itself until the issue is resolved. But in many cases he cannot determine the issue of admissibility without reading it. **2–504**

Effect of disclosure to arbitrator of without prejudice offer: should he resign?

It not infrequently happens that an offeror requests the arbitrator to resign because the offeree has disclosed to the arbitrator the content of a without prejudice offer. See for example *Brown v. CBS Contractors*[32] where His Honour Judge Hawser, Q.C. (sitting as a Deputy Judge of the High Court) remitted the matter to the arbitrator for argument, and reconsideration, of the question whether he should continue as arbitrator notwithstanding that evidence of without prejudice discussions had been put before him. An arbitrator should only resign if both parties require it, or in wholly exceptional circumstances where he cannot do justice. **2–505**

The following guidelines are suggested. **2–506**

(a) When he becomes aware that information about "without prejudice" discussions has been put before him without the consent of all parties, the arbitrator should notify all parties and ask whether any of them objects to his continuing the arbitration.

[31] See *Guiness Peat Properties Ltd. v. Fitzroy Robinson Partnership* [1987] 2 All E.R. 716.
[32] Unreported, 1986.

(b) If both request him to resign he should do so, subject where appropriate to his being paid for his services to date.
(c) If one requests him to resign, but the other opposes his so doing, he should give each of them an opportunity of making submissions on the matter.
(d) In the light of those submissions he should consider whether the information has created a serious risk that he will be unable to approach the substantial issue in the arbitration with an open mind. For example, if the substance of the arbitration is the assessment of damages, and the arbitrator is told by the claimant of a substantial offer made "without prejudice" by the respondent, the arbitrator may think that it will be impossible for him not to be influenced by the offer when arriving at his figure; but such circumstances should be very exceptional as in most cases the arbitrator should be able to disregard the knowledge of the actual amount when reaching a decision, considering as he must all the evidence and the weight to be given to it.

Initial directions should include a reminder

2–507 The principle that a without prejudice offer should not be disclosed to the judge or arbitrator (or, in the case of a Calderbank offer, not before his decision on all matters except costs) is an important one. A reminder of it should be included in the initial directions of every arbitrator.

17. Resolving Issues of Law

What is an issue of substantive law?

2–508 For present purposes an issue is one of substantive law if it satisfies the following criteria. First, it must concern the rights of the parties vis à vis each other under the agreement the subject of the arbitration. Secondly, after all the facts relating to it have been determined or agreed, what remains is the question as to what is the legal effect of those facts. The issue may be an issue of construction of a particular contract or other document peculiar to the instant case, or one of general law, *i.e.* not arising from the wording of the contract or other document in question. Lord Diplock pointed out in *The Nema*[33] that Continental systems of law regard a dispute as to the meaning of a contract or other docu-

[33] *Pioneer Shipping Ltd. v. B.T.P. Tioxide (The Nema)* [1981] 2 All E.R. 1030, at 1035.

ment as one of fact, but because of the influence of the jury the common law system regards it as one for the judge and therefore one of law. The decision of an issue of law often disposes of the case, such as whether, even assuming the claimant is correct on the facts, the respondent is protected against liability by an exclusion or limitation of liability clause.

By section 46 of the Act: **2–509**

> "(1) The arbitral tribunal shall decide the dispute:
> (a) in accordance with the law chosen by the parties as applicable to the substance of the dispute, or
> (b) if the parties so agree, in accordance with such other considerations as are agreed by them or determined by the tribunal.
> (2) For this purpose the choice of the laws of a country shall be understood to refer to the substantive laws of that country and not its conflict of laws rules.
> (3) If or to the extent that there is no such choice or agreement, the tribunal shall apply the law determined by the conflict of laws rules which it considers applicable."

This section is wide enough to cover the arbitrator acting "*ex aequo et bono*" or "in equity" or as "*amiable compositeur*". Thus, an award given by an arbitrator so acting will be an award within the Act and enforceable as such. The phrase "other considerations" is, it is suggested, wide enough to cover such concepts as "general principles of law" or "*lex mercatoria*" rather than a recognised municipal system. But decisions so made will not be subject to review or appeal under section 69. **2–510**

The issues raised by this section are of greater interest to international practitioners than to domestic. For example, unless the parties otherwise agree, section 46 does not allow the use of the "*voie directe*" to establish the applicable law. Arbitrators must apply recognised rules of conflict of laws to arrive at the applicable law. Arbitrators in an international case sitting in London need to bear this in mind. **2–511**

Formulating the issue

When a party raises an issue that appears to be one of construction or of general law, the first step for the arbitrator to take is to ensure that the party raising it clearly formulates it in writing and the second is to try to obtain an agreed formulation of it. A surprising proportion of supposed "points of law" disappear during this process. Once all concerned can see what the point is, they can consider how it is to be resolved. At this stage it may be useful for the arbitrator to warn the parties that the costs involved in resolving the point may be dealt with separately from the other costs of the arbitration. Thus, the party who "wins" the arbitration as a whole may nevertheless be ordered to pay the costs **2–512** of resolving the issue of law if he fails upon it. Such a warning causes the parties to consider whether the importance of the point justifies the expense likely to be incurred in deciding it.

Possible ways of deciding the issue

2–513 The point having been thus formulated, the parties in conjunction with the arbitrator can consider the following possible procedures for resolving it:

(a) submitting a joint case for the opinion of a barrister or solicitor, to be agreed between them or failing agreement to be nominated by the arbitrator, the parties to be bound by the opinion given;
(b) raising the point to be determined by the arbitrator as a preliminary issue (with or without a right of appeal to the court);
(c) as (b), but the arbitrator to determine the point with the assistance of a legal adviser, who failing agreement shall be appointed by the arbitrator. (As to the use of a legal adviser see section 37(4) of the Act and paragraph 2–516, below);
(d) leaving the point for argument at an appropriate stage of the hearing, to be determined by the arbitrator as part of his award, and with no right of appeal;
(e) as (d), but the arbitrator to determine the point with a legal adviser as in (c) above;
(f) leaving the point for argument at an appropriate stage of the hearing, on the footing that the arbitrator will determine it as part of his award but will also make an alternative award in case on appeal the court reverses the arbitrator's decision on the point of law. This course cannot be adopted if the parties have excluded or propose to exclude the right of appeal to the court;
(g) as (f), but the arbitrator to determine the point with a legal adviser as in (c) above;
(h) remitting the point to be decided by the court as a preliminary point of law under section 45(1) of the Act.

The choice between these courses

2–514 If the parties are content to accept the arbitrator's decision, and not to appeal, course (b) will be the cheapest and quickest. But if the arbitrator is not a lawyer, legal argument before him is often unsatisfactory, and many lay arbitrators dislike having to decide question of law. In such cases, the broad choice is between course (a), which will usually be the cheapest, and courses (c) or (e), which are probably quicker, a little more expensive and permit oral argument; or courses (f) or (h), which will probably be the slowest and the most costly. However, in a substantial case which is likely to be taken to court whatever the result, it may be preferable to adopt course (f) or course (h) at the outset.

Appointing a legally qualified chairman or umpire

If the arbitration tribunal is in any event to comprise two arbitrators with a chairman to be appointed by them, or two arbitrators and an umpire, the fact that the chairman or umpire is legally qualified and experienced in the field in which the arbitration arises will usually make it unnecessary to adopt any of the above courses. By section 20(4) of the Act the view of the Chairman shall prevail in relation to a decision, order or award in respect of which there is neither unanimity nor a majority. **2–515**

The uses of a legal adviser

Function is to advise not decide

Section 37 of the Act provides (*inter alia*) that unless the parties otherwise agree, the tribunal may appoint a legal adviser to report to it. The parties may allow the legal adviser to attend the proceedings and give to the parties a reasonable opportunity to comment on any information opinion or advice offered by the legal adviser. The appointment of a legal adviser under section 37 is subject to the same rules of procedure as the appointment of a technical assessor. The function of a legal advisor is to advise. It is for the arbitrator to make the decision, and for the legal adviser to assist him by analysing and summarising the opposing arguments on the legal issues and expressing his view as a lawyer upon them. In many cases the initial reaction of the arbitrator to a suggestion that a legal adviser be appointed to assist him is an adverse one. But the reaction is more often founded on ignorance than on experience. With few (but significant) exceptions, lay arbitrators are not well qualified to decide questions of general law without expert assistance. Even on questions of interpretation of contracts or other documents, most lay arbitrators who have experience of sitting with a legal adviser have found the assistance welcome. The fear of having the conduct of the hearing or the decision or both taken out of the arbitrator's hands is for the most part unfounded. It should not happen, and it will not happen if the arbitrator makes it plain from the outset that he is, and intends to remain, in charge. It will usually be convenient, during legal submissions, to permit the legal adviser to take part in a dialogue with the advocate. Even then, the object of the dialogue should be to clarify matters for the assistance of the arbitrator, and he should intervene if he wishes to clarify a point there and then rather than wait for the legal adviser to explain it to him later. **2–516**

In the first instance the use of a legal adviser will increase the cost of the arbitration, by the amount of the legal adviser's fees. But the overall object is either to reduce the total cost of resolving the dispute, by lessening or eliminating the costs involved in appeals against the award or in challenges to the award **2–517** on the ground of technical misconduct; or to improve the quality of the decision making process, by giving the arbitrator the assistance of (usually) a lawyer with special experience within the particular field. Either a barrister or a solicitor may be approached. In England the arbitrator may now appoint a barrister direct under the Direct Access rules without going through a solicitor.

2–518 If the hearing on the issues of fact is to be a long one, there is no need for the legal adviser to be present throughout; a time can be fixed for the legal argument, and he can attend for that argument only.

Estoppel arising out of an award

2–519 This subject is discussed in paragraph 2–788, below.

18. Settling and Offering to Settle a Dispute

2–520 It is a cardinal feature of Lord Woolf's reforms of English litigation procedure that parties should be encouraged and assisted to settle their disputes at the earliest possible stage of litigation, and if that fails, at later stages of the procedure. It is to some a controversial approach, but one which reflects public policy that the public interest is served by settlement. So too in the private sector of arbitration. Arbitrators should be conscious of the desirability of settlement and should take steps to promote it, by, for example, enquiring of the parties at regular intervals whether they have tried to settle and whether the arbitrator can be of assistance.

Litigation or arbitration as an incentive

2–521 Most disputants turn to litigation or arbitration only after other methods of settling their differences have failed. It is also a commonplace that the process of litigation itself has the effect of bringing parties closer together. A greater awareness of the expense and inconvenience of fighting a case, and a better realization of the uncertainty of the outcome, will encourage a settlement. The process of pleadings, discovery and taking proofs of evidence can reveal weaknesses in one's own case or strengths in that of the other side which had not previously been appreciated. Legal and expert advice from independent sources becomes more concentrated once proceedings are on foot. Of the actions started in the courts, only a tiny proportion reaches trial. The same must be true of references to arbitration. The litigation procedures of most countries encourage settlement by virtue of the costs, executive time, and delay involved, and this is particularly so where (as in England) the litigation system puts the loser at risk of having to pay the winner's legal costs. But this encouragement takes the form of making the parties become aware that the burdens of costs, risks, executive time and delay are disproportionate to the amounts in issue. Settlements arrived at on this basis often do little or no justice to the intrinsic merits of a party's case and represent a failure rather than a success of the dispute resolution system. Section 33 of the Act imposes on the arbitrator, in his decisions on matters of procedure and evidence, and in the exercise of all other powers conferred on him, the duty of

> "adopting procedures suitable to the circumstances of the particular case, avoiding unnecessary delay or expense, so as to provide a fair resolution of the matters falling to be determined."

This in itself is not enough. Given the public policy to promote settlement, the arbitrator should actively encourage settlement. It should therefore become standard practice for arbitrators at various stages of the arbitration to enquire of the parties whether they have tried to settle and whether the arbitrator, consistent with the arbitral mandate, can be of assistance. In making this enquiry the arbitrator can, and usually should, state that he asks this question in every arbitration and is not doing so because he thinks that the particular arbitration before him ought to be settled. This should help to get over what is often the principal impediment to settlement discussions, which is that each party is reluctant to initiate approaches to settle for fear of appearing to be weak. **2–522**

There are various ways by which the arbitrator can help the parties. He can, for example, express a preliminary and tentative view on the merits of the case which may focus the minds of the parties on their respective prospects of success or failure. Another way is to suggest in appropriate cases that an interim award on a point of law or construction of a contractual provision might assist. Another way may be to decide all issues of liability from quantum and thus enable the parties to negotiate in the context of a binding decision. **2–523**

More controversial is the system known in the jargon as Med-Arb; and enshrined in some statutes as for example the Arbitration Ordinance of Hong Kong, section 2B. The arbitrator with the consent of the parties can become the conciliator and if the conciliation fails can resume his role as mediator. The conceptual objections to such a course are obvious, but Med-Arb has been found to work in practice and is extensively used, for example, in both litigation and arbitration in China. **2–524**

Attempts to settle a dispute in which arbitration has begun raise the following among other questions: **2–525**

(a) in what form should an offer of settlement be made;

(b) what procedural steps follow after an offer has been accepted;
(c) what is the position if the offer of settlement is refused?

Without prejudice offers, Calderbank offers and open offers

Without prejudice offers

2–526 The policy of the law is to encourage settlements. If a party, directly or through an agent, makes an offer to settle a legal dispute, that offer will normally be treated as made "without prejudice". It will thus be privileged, and may not be mentioned to a court or arbitrator unless both parties (and not merely the offeror) agree that it may be mentioned; or the offer is accepted and thus becomes part of a binding contract. Likewise, all negotiations forming part of a mutual attempt to reach an agreement will usually be carried out on a without prejudice basis and treated as privileged. To ensure that privilege attaches to such offers or negotiations it is advisable and usual for them to be expressed to be "without prejudice"; but even if they are not expressed to be made "without prejudice", privilege will still attach, if in substance they constitute a genuine attempt to reach a compromise. The object of this procedure is to facilitate the compromise of disputes by making it possible for a party to make an offer of compromise free from the fear that it will be brought to the attention of the judge or arbitrator and might cause him to draw inferences adverse to the offeror. Neither party should bring either the existence or the contents of the offer to the attention of the arbitrator in any way. A without prejudice offer should not be mentioned in any subsequent letter that is not intended to be without prejudice. So if it is desired to communicate to the opposing party something without prejudice, and something else not intended to be without prejudice, two separate communications should be made. If the parties copy open correspondence to the arbitrator and number their letter, the without prejudice letter should not be numbered or should be part of a different numbering option.

The term "without prejudice"

2–527 The writing of a letter or the holding of meetings on a "without prejudice" basis ensures that privilege attaches to those communications oral or written in which a party expresses a position which is less beneficial or more damaging to itself than the one it is formally taking in open correspondence or meetings. It is this "reduced" position that would be prejudicial to the party if taken openly and it is this that is covered by the label "without prejudice" and is privileged.

2–528 Matters which are not prejudicial to the party's position are not privileged. Accordingly a threat to wind up the company rather than pay the debt is not privileged and can be brought to the attention of the arbitrator even if made in a without prejudice letter or meeting.

Calderbank offer: "without prejudice save as to costs"

2–529 This is a mechanism which only works in jurisdictions whose approach to costs starts from the general principle that the winner's costs should be paid by the loser. An offer expressed to be made "without prejudice save as to costs" or words to that effect, may not be disclosed to the arbitrator until he has issued an award on all matters except costs. Such an offer is commonly called a "Calderbank offer" after the name of the case in which the procedure was first approved by the English courts.[34] Once he has issued his award or awards dealing with all matters except costs, the offer may be brought to his attention, and he may, if he thinks it appropriate, treat it as having much the same effect as a payment into court in litigation given that the money is not necessarily available. The principle in litigation is that where the defendant to a money claim makes a payment into court which exceeds the amount ultimately awarded to the plaintiff, the defendant is entitled to be awarded his costs incurred after the plaintiff received notice of the payment-in. A Calderbank offer cannot have precisely the same effect, because a payment into court is more than a mere offer: it is an offer backed by actual deposit of the sum offered. Nevertheless it may be of great assistance to, and may therefore exert great influence upon, an arbitrator who is looking to see whose conduct has brought about the arbitration or the continuance of the arbitration.

Open offers

A party may make an offer which is not intended to be privileged, and will therefore be admissible in evidence before the arbitrator. Such offers are called "open offers". In order for an offer to be treated as "open" it must be expressly written on those terms, and cannot refer, even by implication, to previous negotiations which are privileged. Open offers are sometimes made for tactical purposes, to put pressure on the other side, the object being to let the arbitrator know which party is unreasonably prolonging the dispute, if the offer is refused. But they also carry the risk that, if the arbitrator knows of the terms of the offer, he will infer that the offeror is not fully confident in the merits of his case and will treat it as tantamount to a concession of part of the claim, or a partial admission of liability. **2–530**

Either party may make an open offer

Any party to an arbitration is entitled to make an "open" offer (that is, one that may be brought to the attention of the court or tribunal by either party) to settle the dispute on whatever terms it thinks proper. The function of such an offer, which should always be made in writing, is the beneficial one of highlighting, *inter alia*, the amount in difference between the parties and/or the willingness of that party to endeavour to dispose of the matter amicably. Many arbitrators feel embarrassed by such letters. Indeed, where the letter is an open letter from the claimant, offering to take less than the full amount of his claim, some arbi- **2–531**

[34] *Calderbank v. Calderbank* [1975] 3 All E.R. 333; and also see *Cutts v. Head* [1984] 1 All E.R. 597. For a form of Calderbank offer, see drafting suggestion No. 53 at Appendix 1, below.

trators have been known to seek to rule them out. The reasons for such resistance to what may be a useful step towards settlement have never been clearly expressed.

The effect of an open offer

2–532 An offer to settle is not usually relevant to any issue in the arbitration, as distinct from questions of costs which arise after the arbitrator has decided the issues. But it brings pressure on the parties in that it forces all concerned to address their minds to the question whether it is advisable to incur the level of costs that will be incurred if all issues are fully contested. A pound in the hand before a long hearing starts is worth two or three pounds at the end of it, and everybody knows it. This is particularly so since an order for costs in favour of a party usually leaves a shortfall on what that party has actually spent. The longer the case goes on, the greater the shortfall.

The role of the arbitrator in negotiations for a settlement

2–533 An arbitrator should face the fact that open letters are likely to come to his attention, and he should not seek to rule them inadmissible or refuse to read them. He should always have a keen eye for an amicable resolution of the dispute, and if the consequence of his becoming acquainted with open offers (as distinct from without prejudice offers, as to which quite different considerations apply) is that he feels embarrased or under pressure, that is something that he should be willing to accept. He should always be prepared to suggest to the parties that they should seriously consider compromising any part of the dispute. Yet at the end of the day his function is to decide matters that the parties cannot resolve.

Offer should deal with costs

2–534 An offer of settlement, in any of the above forms, will not be fully effective unless it deals with costs, including those of the arbitrator. If the offer fails to mention costs, but is accepted, the question of costs remains in dispute, and, it is submitted, will have to be resolved by the arbitrator, who will no doubt base his award on the agreement which has been reached. If the offer is not accepted, a failure to mention costs is likely to deprive the maker of any of the advantages which he might otherwise claim if the arbitrator's award is more favourable to him than the terms he offered.

Keeping the offer open

2–535 When an offer of settlement is made, in whatever form, the party making the offer has to decide how long the offer should be kept open. Should it remain open for acceptance within a fixed period, after which it lapses or is withdrawn? Should it be kept open throughout the proceedings, including the period between the close of submissions and delivery of the award? What is to happen to the costs if the offer is made at the time when they are relatively low, for example just after the preliminary meeting, but it is not accepted until they have become relatively high, for example during the hearing when, perhaps the recipient of the offer realises that his case is going badly, and would like to accept? If the offer is to be unlimited as to time one method of dealing with the costs is to stipulate that if the offer is accepted within, for example, 21 days, the offeror will pay the other side's costs, but if it is accepted later, the party accepting the offer will pay the additional costs which are incurred by both sides and the arbitrator after that date.

Recipient entitled to a reasonable time to consider offer

In the case of payment into court in an action, the Rules of Court in England provide that if within 21 days of receiving notice of a payment into court the plaintiff accepts the payment he is thereupon entitled to recover his costs up to the moment when notice of acceptance was given. If the plaintiff does not accept the payment-in, and at trial he recovers less than the amount paid in, the defendant is entitled to his costs from the date of payment-in. But if the payment-in is less than 21 days before the commencement of the hearing, and is not accepted, the court will have a discretion as to what weight should be given to it.[35] **2–536**

It is suggested that the weight to be attached to an offer (whether open or Calderbank) made shortly before a hearing begins is lessened if in the arbitrator's opinion the period between the receipt of the offer and the beginning of the hearing does not give the party to whom the offer is made a reasonable time to consider it.[36] **2–537**

Acceptance of offer

Dispute as to acceptance

When a properly constituted offer is accepted, a binding contract results, and the parties are prevented by their contract from pursuing any further so much of their dispute as they have compromised. Whether negotiations have in fact resulted in a binding contract must therefore be determined in accordance with the ordinary legal rules governing offer and acceptance. If there is a dispute over the question whether an offer has been accepted, that will be a fresh dispute arising between the parties outside the arbitration agreement, and the arbitrator himself will have no jurisdiction to decide it save in the event of both parties asking him to do so. **2–538**

35 See *King v. Weston Howell* [1989] 2 All E.R. 375, disapproving *Bowen v. Mills & Knight* [1973] 1 Lloyd's Rep. 580.

36 See the judgement of Sheen J. in *The Vasiliy Shelgunov* [1988] 2 Lloyd's Rep. 34; approved on appeal [1989] 1 Lloyd's Rep. 542.

Acceptance of offer "subject to contract"

2–539 Offers of settlement are sometimes made "subject to contract", particularly in cases in which one of the terms involves the transfer of land, or the grant or surrender of a lease, or the execution of a deed, such as a deed varying an existing formal document. In such a case neither party will be bound until the formalities have been completed, and the final documents have been executed and exchanged. Until that event occurs no binding agreement has been concluded, and the arbitration remains on foot.

Incorporating settlement in a consent award

2–540 Once a dispute is settled, technically the arbitrator has lost jurisdiction because there is no longer any dispute before him. It is however the usual practice to request him to make an award by consent embodying the terms of the settlement; this is required by some institutional rules such as Article 17 of the ICC Rules. This has the advantage of bringing the reference to a certain conclusion and, if the award involves payment by one party to the other, it can be properly enforced. Section 51 of the Act recognises this practice and enables a consent award to be made which is enforceable in all respects as any other award on the merits of the case. Such an award is essential if the costs are to be dealt with by the court, on an old fashioned taxation of costs.

Settling on undisclosed terms

2–541 It may be a term of the settlement that the bargain remains confidential to the parties. The compromise will then be embodied in a private document prepared by the parties or their lawyers, and not disclosed to the arbitrator. In cases of this kind in court, it is possible to draw up an order staying the proceedings on the terms agreed, without disclosing them, but reserving the right to either party to apply to the court for the purpose only of carrying the agreed terms into effect (a so-called "Tomlin" order). Arbitration procedure does not lend itself to orders of this kind, if only because the arbitrator is an individual, who cannot be expected to remain in office indefinitely in order to hold himself available for applications to enforce the agreement. Further, there may be doubt whether in given circumstances an arbitrator will have jurisdiction to make some kinds of order likely to be required to enforce the agreement, such as an injunction. If the settlement is not to be contained in a consent award, it is advisable to have the reference withdrawn by consent, on payment of the arbitrator's fees and expenses (if any). The settlement will then constitute a new contract between the parties, enforceable in the courts, unless it too contains its own arbitration clause.

Terms of settlement to contain an arbitration clause

2–542 The more complicated the dispute, the more complicated the terms of settlement may be and the greater the risk of a new dispute arising over those terms. It may therefore be advisable to write a fresh arbitration clause into the terms of settlement, and perhaps even to appoint the original arbitrator to determine any dispute arising out of the settlement, if he will accept the office. Examples of cases in which this device might be useful are construction industry and shipbuilding disputes, where the terms of settlement may include an undertaking by the contractor to carry out further works; complex commercial disputes in which the arbitrator has become familiar with much of the detail, so that he will have a ready grasp of any issues arising under the terms of settlement; long term agreements such as joint ventures or partnerships; and transnational disputes in which the parties have already made a conscious preference for arbitration over court proceedings in any jurisdiction.

Settling part only of a dispute

Offer to settle whole dispute cannot be accepted in part

As a general rule, if an offer is made to settle an entire dispute, it cannot be accepted in part only. A purported acceptance of part only of an entire offer is in law a counter-offer, not an acceptance. **2–543**

Offers to settle part of a dispute

An offer may be made expressly to settle part only of a dispute, or an offer to settle an entire dispute may be expressed as being open, in addition, to acceptance in distinct parts. Once a valid offer to settle part of the dispute has been accepted, the case is removed from the jurisdiction of the arbitrator to the extent to which it has been settled but otherwise it remains in being. Obviously the arbitrator will be informed of the settlement; and the parties may wish to ask him to deliver an interim award by consent dealing with the settlement, or to include it in his final award; or to deal with it otherwise than by means of an award. **2–544**

Rejection of offer

The rejection of a "without prejudice" offer has no effect on the course of the arbitration: it continues as if no offer had been made, and the arbitrator can never know about the existence or terms of the offer. The rejection of an open offer has already been discussed: the existence of the offer and its terms are admissible in evidence, and the arbitrator can take them into account at any time and for any purpose, including the exercise of his discretion as to costs. **2–545**

Calderbank offers

The purpose of a Calderbank offer is to enable the party making the offer (if it is rejected) to bring it to the arbitrator's attention at the end of the reference, **2–546** after the delivery of an award on the main issues in the case, when costs have to be considered. It is therefore admissible in evidence at that point in the proceedings, but not at any earlier time. It is accordingly essential to arrange for the arbitrator to consider the offer before he decides on the order for costs. A convenient and common way is to ask him to reserve all questions on costs when he issues his award on all other matters in dispute. Another way is to provide him with an envelope containing the offer, with instructions not to open it until he has decided everything except costs.[37]

Effect on costs

2–547 The effect of an open or Calderbank offer on the arbitrator's decision on costs is discussed in paragraphs 2–822 *et seq*., below.

19. Preparing for a Hearing

2–548 It cannot be emphasised too strongly that section 33 of the Act clearly imposes upon arbitrators a duty to find the most economic and expeditious means of resolving the dispute consistent with natural justice. Given the discredit which attaches to current procedures of both litigation and arbitration, arbitrators must seek new solutions. If the arbitrator takes charge of the case at an early stage, provides for the issues to be properly identified and rigorously controls the presentation of evidence, both oral and documentary, it ought to be possible for the arbitrator to limit oral hearings to an examination of points central to the determination of the dispute. Thus, key witnesses could be examined on key points, key documents can be considered, oral and written submissions made on the evidence and the law, discrete issues focused upon and proper time limits established for their consideration. Measures for expedition, economy and fairness are readily to hand. Arbitrators are now under a duty to use them.

Some general points on the reception of evidence

Relevance of the arbitration agreement

2–549 Because the arbitration agreement limits the scope of the arbitration, and because the guiding rule is that evidence must be relevant to the issues in the arbitration, the arbitration agreement in a broad and fundamental way controls the scope of

37 See *Tramountana v. Atlantic Shipping Co.* [1978] 2 All E.R. 870.

the evidence to be adduced in the arbitration proceedings. Such matters as whether the evidence may be directed to claims in tort as well as in contract will depend on the scope of the submission to arbitration.[38] In *Fillite v. Aqua-Lift*[39] it was held that the phrase "disputes arising under a contract" is not wide enough to include disputes which do not concern obligations created by or incorporated in that contract. Accordingly it was not wide enough to cover claims for misrepresentation under the Misrepresentation Act 1967, or for negligent misstatement. On the other hand, in *Ashville Investments Ltd v. Elmer Contractors Ltd*,[40] it was held that the words "any dispute or difference as to the construction of this contract or as to any matter or thing arising thereunder or in connection therewith" were wide enough to cover a claim for rectification of the contract. The modern tendency is for the courts to give effect to the parties' intention to arbitrate and to give disputes which arise by virtue of a contractual relationship a rather wide meaning. It is clearly undesirable for the resolution of such disputes to be divided between the arbitrator and the courts. One forum, one proceeding and one set of costs is to be preferred.

Equally fundamental is the fact that the arbitration agreement may expressly **2–550**
or by necessary implication establish rules of procedure which limit the evidence to be adduced or indeed exclude the need for any evidence at all, other than that which the arbitrator derives from his own inspection. Thus in *Mediterranean and Eastern Export v. Fortress Fabrics*[41] Lord Goddard C.J. said:

> "If an arbitrator has acted within the terms of his submission and has not violated any rules of what is so often called natural justice the court should be slow indeed to set aside his award."

In that context he held that an arbitrator who had been appointed because of his **2–551**
knowledge and experience in the textile trade was entitled to assess damages without hearing any evidence on their quantum. But note that he said that the lack of evidence:

> "would be a formidable, and indeed fatal objection in some arbitrations. If, for instance, a lawyer was called on to act as arbitrator in a commercial contract, he would not be entitled, unless the terms of the submission clearly gave him power to do so, to come to a conclusion as to the amount of damages, without having evidence before him."[42]

38 See *Woolf v. Collis Removal Service* [1948] 1 K.B. 11; *The Damianos* [1971] 2 Q.B. 588.
39 [1989] 45 Build. L.R. 28.
40 [1989] 2 All E.R. 577.
41 [1948] 2 All E.R. 186.
42 *ibid*, at 187.

Reducing the volume of oral evidence

Changing the balance between written and oral evidence

2–552 The arbitrator is not bound by the traditional manner of putting evidence before the tribunal, which can be seen in the courts on any working day—that is, oral evidence elicited by question and answer. The arbitrator should actively seek with the parties ways in which oral evidence may be most economically and expeditiously presented. There are now well established means, such as exchange of witness statements, compelling the identification in advance of uncontroversial factual matters and limiting parties to a specified number of witnesses and specified time limits in which to present oral evidence. Particularly where the issues are complex, he should try to ensure that written statements have a greater part to play. But it is important to provide safeguards against surprise and disingenuousness.

Exchanging proofs of witnesses of fact

2–553 The arbitrator should always consider how far it is possible to provide that proofs of evidence of witnesses of fact should be exchanged well in advance of the commencement of the hearing. For this to be effective the parties must previously have effectively identified the issues, and have agreed a proper working bundle. Provided these steps have been taken there is no reason why in most cases a direction for the exchange of proofs should not be issued; and it should be standard practice for the arbitrators so to order.

Methods of exchange

2–554 One method is simultaneous exchange. Proofs are exchanged on a date specified in the direction. The direction is generally to be preferred on grounds of speed and given that the issues have been identified so that both sides' proofs are focused on the same point, should then provide a later date upon which supplementary proofs are exchanged, to deal with any point upon which a party has been taken by surprise by material contained in the opposing party's first proof.

2–555 Consecutive delivery is an alternative. This follows the order in which oral evidence would be given in a court hearing. The claimant is directed to serve his proofs first, and the respondent to serve his proofs in answer after a suitable period to give him time to consider them. Provision should be made for the claimant to serve evidence in rebuttal if so minded.

2–556 There are other possibilities. None should be rejected on the grounds of novelty, though novelty is a good reason for caution. Thus skeleton proofs may be preferable to full proofs. Where there is a counterclaim, the order used in some States in the United States may be thought preferable, thus:

(a) claimant's evidence on the claim;
(b) respondent's evidence on the claim;

(c) respondent's evidence on the counterclaim;
(d) claimant's evidence on the counterclaim.

Obviously stages (b) and (c) can be amalgamated if so desired.

Delay before delivery to arbitrator
A sufficient period should be allowed between delivery of a proof to the opposing party, and delivery of a copy to the arbitrator, to allow the recipient to object to its being seen by the arbitrator; for example, if it refers to "without prejudice" discussions. 2–557

Parties not limited to proofs

No party should be limited to the evidence contained in the statements so exchanged. To protect the compliant party against the advantage seeker, the direction for exchange of proofs should define the degree of details required—full, skeleton, and so on. The arbitrator should make it plain that if at the hearing a whole tranche of factual evidence is sought to be given which is not in the statements that have been exchanged, he may exercise his powers to exclude or ignore such evidence or penalise late presentation by appropriate cost orders, adjournments, etc.; and he is likely to be sceptical unless there is a good reason for the evidence not being included earlier. 2–558

Status of the proof
If the person who made the proof is called as a witness, and confirms its contents, its status will be the same as if he had given the evidence orally, subject to the caution which would inevitably attach to evidence that might have been given in answer to a series of leading questions. He will then be subject to cross-examination in the usual way. If it is not reasonably practicable for the maker of the proof to be called as a witness, *e.g.* because he has died, or is too ill to attend the hearing for cross-examination, the proof can be admitted on the footing that the arbitrator will attach such weight to it as he thinks fit, or under the Civil Evidence Act 1995. 2–559

Proof exchanged but witness not called
If in litigation a witness statement has been delivered to the other party, but the party delivering the statement does not call the maker to give evidence, it has been held[43] that the proof remains confidential until: 2–560

(a) the maker makes it public in the witness box; or

[43] *Fairfield-Mabey v. Shell* [1989] 1 All E.R. 576.

(b) the party who delivered it waives the privilege attaching to it; or
(c) the privilege is waived by the contents of the statement being put, in cross-examination, to the opposing party's witness.

2–561 In arbitration, failing agreement to the contrary, it is for the arbitrator under section 34(2)(f) and (h) to decide what use may be made of the statement. A sensible approach is for the arbitrator to make it clear that once a witness statement has been supplied to the other party, either party may rely upon it, and the arbitrator may place such weight upon it as he thinks fit in the light of any submissions he may receive. If the arbitrator intends to follow this or any other approach, then he should spell out his approach when directing when statements are to be exchanged.

Notice to admit facts or documents

2–562 Another way in which the volume of evidence at the hearing may be limited is by prior admission of facts or documents. Processes by which the parties may agree facts, or documents, have been discussed. However, a party who cannot obtain the agreement of the other side may seek to advance the issue by delivering to the other party a notice to admit the relevant fact or document. If the other party unreasonably refuses to make the admission he may, when the arbitrator comes to consider the costs of the arbitration, be ordered to pay the costs of proving the fact or document in question, whatever order the arbitrator makes as to the other costs of the arbitration. This possibility can be an effective sanction where the cost of proving the fact or document is high (*e.g.* because a witness will have to be brought a considerable distance) and the party asked to make the admission has no reason to suppose that the facts are otherwise.

Expert evidence

When is it needed

2–563 In England an arbitrator is often appointed because of his expertise in the field in which the dispute arises. He is therefore presumably expected to use this expertise; after all, the parties are paying for it. If the parties have agreed that each is entitled to call expert evidence, so be it, but otherwise it is sensible for the arbitrator to consider, and to ask the parties to consider, whether expert evidence is necessary, and if so whether and how it can sensibly be limited. It is always worth reminding the parties at a preliminary meeting, and the experts when they first appear, about the nature of the experts' role. This has been well and succinctly stated by Lord Wilberforce in *Whitehouse v. Jordan.*[44]

[44] [1981] 1 W.L.R. 246, at 256.

"It is necessary that expert evidence presented to the court should be, and should be seen to be, the independent product of the expert uninfluenced as to form or content by the exigencies of litigation. To the extent that it is not, the evidence is likely to be not only incorrect but self-defeating."

Exchanging proofs

It is normal procedure in litigation, and it should be normal procedure in arbitration, for proofs of experts to be exchanged a sufficient period before the hearing to give each side an opportunity to consider them and, if thought fit, to make further inquiries or tests. **2–564**

Proof should contain the whole of the expert's evidence

An expert's proof should contain the whole of his evidence and not merely the bare bones of it. See *Kenning v. Eve*,[45] where the expert had set out in a letter to solicitors additional views to those expressed in his formal report. A copy of this letter was sent by accident to the other party. The other party was permitted to amend its pleadings to rely on information contained in the letter. **2–565**

Meetings between experts

In litigation a direction is usually given that before or after the experts' reports have been exchanged the experts meet to see how far they can agree, and to formulate clearly the points on which they disagree. When such a meeting is being arranged, it is important to establish that all participants are operating on the same basis. So the arbitrator should establish and record: **2–566**

(a) whether the meeting is to be open or "without prejudice".[46] Unless otherwise directed or agreed, all discussions between experts are without prejudice, unless and to the extent that they result in a concluded agreement. At that stage the agreement becomes admissible in evidence, but the discussions that preceded it remain privileged. It follows that nothing that takes place at such a meeting should be disclosed to the arbitrator save the concluded agreement, if there is one.
(b) whether or not it is to be attended by lawyers (preferably not);
(c) whether the participants are to have power to reach agreements binding on the respective parties (preferably yes);
(d) how the discussions at the meeting, and any agreements reached, are to be recorded.

[45] *The Times*, November 29, 1988.
[46] Preferably open; after all the experts are supposed to be independent and the problem with a "without prejudice" meeting is that the conclusions which are reached may be filleted by the lawyers before being presented to the court.

Expert cannot accept instructions from both parties without consent

2–567 It is reasonably clear that an expert who has reported to one party cannot without that party's consent accept instructions from another party in the same or a connected dispute. Even though his evidence should be wholly independent (see the previous paragraph), he may well have received privileged information from his first client, and it would be difficult or impossible for him wholly to excise such knowledge from his mind when preparing a report for the second client.

Making meetings of experts productive

2–568 It should be relatively simple for each expert to mark, in the Report of his opposite number, the statements with which he agrees and those with which he disagrees; and for the two reports so marked to be combined at the meeting so as to result in a Statement of Agreed Facts and a Statement of Issues. In practice so little progress is made at most meetings between experts as barely to justify the expenditure of time and costs involved (which are often considerable). Four suggestions are made to improve the usefulness of such meetings.

(a) Each expert should approach the meeting on the footing that his Report is now evidence ready for submission to the court or arbitrator as the case may be. So his duty now is to assist the tribunal; he is no longer (if he ever was) an advocate or negotiator for the party who has instructed him.
(b) The arbitrator's directions should require the experts to prepare and sign, before the end of the meeting, a note of the points on which they agree and the points on which they disagree.
(c) An expert who considers that his opposite number is refusing to cooperate in producing for the tribunal a helpful summary of where they agree and where they disagree should make his own summary, based on the reports that have been exchanged.
(d) An arbitrator faced with experts should at an early stage notify the experts that if they fail to produce a statement of agreed facts and of agreed issues and if in due course he is satisfied that the failure is the responsibility of one of the experts or of the legal advisers to a party, then he will order the party of the expert responsible to pay the other party's costs of the experts' meeting and any work necessary as a consequence of the wilful failure to agree.

Repetitive evidence

2–569 An arbitrator may face a situation in which the like evidence applies to a series of events or objects. In a building dispute, for example, there may be allegations of like defects on all the floors of a multi-storey building, or in a large number of identical houses on a housing estate. Thus in *Carlisle Place Investments v.*

Wimpey Construction[47] the claimant alleged defects in the roofs of 83 houses. The respondent applied to the arbitrator for an order that the issues of liability and quantum be determined upon evidence in respect of a limited number of roofs, a set number to be nominated by each party and by the arbitrator. The arbitrator partly so ordered; but he gave liberty to both parties to apply, stating that it was open to either party to raise issues about other roofs if they raised any additional questions requiring his attention. On an appeal by case stated, Robert Goff J. held that the arbitrator had acted within his powers and said:

> "I know of no requirement that an arbitrator must allow each party to call all the evidence which he wishes to call. It must depend on the circumstances of the particular case whether or not the arbitrator decides, in exercise of his discretion, to conduct the arbitration in a particular way."

That the matter is one for the exercise of the arbitrator's discretion is now plain from section 34(2)(b) of the Act.

Examination of witness abroad

If for some reason it is impossible to get to the arbitration a witness whose evidence is considered essential, the question arises whether the arbitration can go to the witness, or whether there is some other method whereby the witness' evidence can be obtained. In general, if the parties have agreed (whether before or after the dispute arose) that the arbitration shall be held in a particular place of country, each is entitled to have the evidence taken there. Many institutional rules give the arbitrator power to take evidence, hear argument and deliberate elsewhere than the seat for reasons of convenience and to save costs. This is commonplace in international commercial arbitrations where frequently the deliberations of the tribunal and the drafting and consideration of the award do not take place in the seat of the arbitration at all. It would be unwise for the arbitrator in a domestic case to impose on one of the parties the obligation to go along with a change (albeit temporary) of the effective base of the arbitration to another place or country. **2–570**

The parties can agree to evidence being taken elsewhere, in the presence of both parties but in the absence of the tribunal. This could be made available to the tribunal by transcript and/or video tape. The evidence can be given directly to the tribunal by telephone or video conference. It is not essential but it is desirable for both parties to be represented at both ends of the link. If such is not the case at the far end of the link, telephone conference evidence should carry less weight than oral evidence before the tribunal: and the tribunal should ensure (if necessary by two cameras) that the video picture covers the whole room at the witness end. **2–571**

[47] [1980] 15 Build. L.R. 109.

Power of the court to order the examination of a witness abroad

2–572 The English courts have power to order the examination of a witness on oath before a special examiner appointed either by the court or by the British Consul in the country involved; Rules of the Supreme Court, Order 39, rule 2. See too the Hague Convention on the Taking of Evidence Abroad in Civil or Commercial Matters (March 18, 1970) and *Re State of Norway's Application* (1 & 2).[48] A helpful introduction to the practice under this Convention and to the allied Hague Convention on Service Abroad of Judicial and Extra Judicial Documents in Civil or Commercial Matters—(November 15, 1965) can be found in Edwin Aley's Article in the International Business Lawyer (published by the International Bar Association) for September 1989.

2–573 These expedients should really only be necessary for important and seriously contested evidence.

2–574 Paragraphs 2–280 *et seq.* and 2–358 *et seq.*, above, deal with the need to minimise hearings by considering whether any, or indeed all, of the issues can be adequately decided without a hearing.

One hearing or several?

2–575 The key question is whether the issues can best be resolved at one continuous hearing—as is the present practice in English litigation and in English arbitration—or at a series of hearings. The conventional English litigation practice of a single trial or hearing is expensive and time consuming, and should not be automatically followed in arbitration. Arbitrators and parties should be alive to ways of improving upon it. The traditional hearing involves:

(a) Oral opening submissions from advocates;
(b) Reading the agreed documents;
(c) Reading proofs of witnesses;
(d) Cross-examination and re-examination of witnesses;
(e) Closing submissions from advocates.

A hearing is only essential for the fourth and perhaps the fifth of these. Arbitrators (in the absence of agreement to the contrary) are entitled to so order. It should be standard practice for arbitrators to read the relevant documents and witness statements including expert reports and other submissions in advance of any hearing at which they will be considered.

Disadvantage of long hearings

2–576 Lengthy and complex hearings are not a good way of reaching informed and fair decisions. Arbitrators, advocates, parties and experts are sometimes over-

[48] [1989] 1 All E.R. 746.

whelmed by documents, to the point that even the most experienced find it difficult to see the wood for the trees. Unless the parties have otherwise agreed, the arbitrator can decide for himself the admissibility, relevance or weight of any material (oral, written or other) sought to be tendered on any matters of fact or opinion, and the time, manner and form in which such material should be exchanged and presented. The arbitrator also has the power under section 34(2)(h) to decide whether and to what extent there should be oral or written evidence or submissions. These are powerful weapons in an arbitrator's hands to ensure expedition, economy and overall efficiency.

Effective conduct of the hearing

Experience in international commercial arbitration shows that the most effective way of shortening hearings is the making of written submissions of argument and evidence in advance, combined with limitation of time available to each party for presentation of oral evidence and arguments. Much experience has now been gained in the use of time limits and the practice is growing. Most lawyers in continental Europe view with amazement the idea that a witness may be examined and cross-examined for days or weeks; or that an advocate should open or close a case for days on end. Certainly the quality of justice is not impaired by sensible and fair time limits. If all the relevant documents are identified exchanged and read in advance, this will enable the arbitrator to decide the issue without lengthy hearings. It should become standard practice for the arbitrator to allocate a fixed period of hearing to each party, leaving the party to decide how to allocate it between opening, examination in chief, cross-examination of the opposing party's witnesses, and closing submissions. The heavier and more complicated the case, the greater the need for the discipline which proper time limits impose. Directions for time limits will not amount to serious irregularity under section 68 of the Act, unless the time allotted is so plainly inadequate that no reasonable arbitrator would impose it. Arbitrators should be much readier than hitherto to impose time limits and to enforce them. **2–577**

The increased volume of irrelevant documents

In recent years there has been a massive increase in the volume of documents put before the tribunal in substantial cases, whether in arbitration or litigation. This has resulted from a combination of two factors. First, there has been a substantial increase in the hourly cost of the specialist litigation solicitors or counsel who alone are capable of making an informed selection of documents relevant to the issues in the case. Secondly, there has been a substantial reduction in the labour cost of copying documents. The current practice is for all the documents relating to the subject-matter of the dispute, whether or not they have any bearing on the issues being litigated or arbitrated, to be copied and bundled for the hearing. The selection has to be made at some time, but it is now made on each side, and in isolation, by counsel in his final preparation for the hearing. **2–578**

The result often is that of perhaps 1,000 documents in the bundles, only 50 are ever referred to.

Disadvantages of unnecessary copying

2–579 The waste of time and costs involved in copying and bundling, though substantial, is perhaps the least of the mischiefs resulting from this practice. There are two major disadvantages. The first is that any documents put forward by one party have to be read by the other party's lawyers to see whether they are relevant, and this is a time consuming and expensive exercise. The second is that because the judge or arbitrator does not know before the hearing what each party considers to be the truly relevant documents, he cannot do more than a superficial reading of the mass of documents submitted to him. This disadvantage is magnified if, as happens under the present practice, the respective cases have been submitted in the form of pleadings rather than of statements of case. If the judge or arbitrator knows neither what the issues truly are, nor which of the 1,000 or so documents that have been delivered to him are really relied upon by each party, he cannot sensibly read and digest the relevant documents before the hearing. Thus the hearing has to begin with an opening by counsel for the claimant, in which he tells the tribunal the nature of the dispute, and what the issues are, and what is his case on them, and he then reads the documents that he considers to be relevant. So the hearing may have occupied one or two weeks before the first witness is called. That witness is then taken through his connection with the dispute, by oral question and answer, at the speed (if no daily transcript is being provided) at which the arbitrator can write his note. Much of what the witness says will not be challenged and the only reason why it has not already been admitted by the respondent is because the respondent has not previously been given a copy of the witness' proof. It is only when the first witness has completed his evidence in chief—days or weeks after the hearing began—that the oral hearing begins to be effective, in that testing of the witness's evidence by cross-examination is now possible. This way of proceeding is wholly unacceptable. It is contrary to the spirit and the letter of the Act. No responsible practitioner should propose it; and no responsible arbitrator should countenance it.

How these disadvantages can be lessened

2–580 To reduce this often enormous waste of time and, particularly, costs, arbitrators in fulfilling their duties under section 33 should direct their minds to four specific topics.

(a) How best to define the issues.
(b) How best to identify the relevant documentary evidence and to organise and present it.

(c) How best to identify the relevant witnesses and to organise the submission and examination of their evidence.
(d) How long the parties should have to enable them to present their cases fully but economically.

Defining the issues

The arbitrator should direct, at the outset, that a list of issues be agreed and delivered to the arbitrator at an early stage of the procedure. Failing agreement both parties can submit their respective lists. **2–581**

The procedure for defining the issues must vary according to the nature and complexity of the dispute. Thus, where there are a large number of issues or potential issues, *e.g.* in many construction industry disputes, the claim on each issue, the defence to it, and the reply to the defence should be set out in schedule form so that the arbitrator can see, in one document and preferably on one sheet of paper, the opposing contentions on that issue. This procedure is often appropriate where a claim for damages involves a large number of items; though if it is likely to be time consuming it may be desirable to defer the preparation of such a schedule until questions of liability have been decided. **2–582**

The selection of documents

It is essential that the selection of documents to be referred to at any hearing be made before the hearing, and be the responsibility of the advocate who is to conduct the case. It is suggested that to bring this about the arbitrator should be prepared to become closely involved in and should monitor the selection of documents in cases proceeding to a hearing. Directions which the arbitrator could make, include the following: **2–583**

(a) that discovery in the arbitration should proceed initially on the basis of what is sometimes called "reliance discovery". Thus, arbitrators should require the parties to list or produce at a very early stage, the documents upon which they choose to rely and further discovery should be provided or ordered only where it is self-evident that the documents required are material.
(b) that the advocate who will conduct the case shall be responsible for the selection of the documents to which he intends to refer;
(c) that the consolidated and paginated bundle(s) of the documents selected should be delivered to the arbitrator by a specified date before the hearing;
(d) that at the hearing all the documents so submitted shall be taken as read (because he will in fact have read them); and
(e) that at an appropriate stage the arbitrator will specifically consider the question whether a substantial number of irrelevant documents has

been selected, and if so whether a special order should be made in respect of the additional costs thereby occasioned.

Exchanging proofs in advance

2–584 It is also essential that proofs of all witnesses be exchanged, and copies delivered to the arbitrator, before the hearing. Exchanging proofs will increase the proportion of cases that are settled before rather than during a hearing, and by reducing the length of the hearing it will also reduce the costs of those cases that do not settle.

Preparation at an earlier stage

2–585 These procedural changes will involve a radical change in the present practices in the preparation for determination of long cases. Take first the pleadings stage. The plaintiff/claimant will have to formulate and express the propositions of law for which he contends at the outset, instead of (as now often happens) expressing them for the first time when the hearing begins. The defendant/respondent will have to do the same when drafting his defence, instead of perhaps half way through the hearing. The advocate will therefore have to do more work at this stage than under the present practice. Likewise, if a list of issues, proofs of witnesses, and an agreed bundle of documents likely to be referred to have to be delivered to the arbitrator well before the hearing. The advocate will have to prepare his case even earlier, rather than two or three weeks (or even days) before the date fixed for a hearing. If the lawyers or other advocates on both sides refuse to co-operate in the earlier preparation involved, there is little that the arbitrator can do to make up the time and costs thus lost. But he is not altogether powerless.[49] In an appropriate case he can state at the hearing, when representatives of the parties are likely to be present, that in his opinion the length and cost of the hearing has been substantially increased by the failure to comply with his directions. If the failure is by one party only, and that party is in the result successful, the arbitrator has power to deprive him of some of his costs and he could, in an appropriate case, order him to pay (or allow by way of set-off) the amount by which the losing party's costs have been increased by the failure.

Incidence of costs changed

2–586 Another result of this change in practice is to change the incidence of costs in the various stages of preparation for a hearing. If more thought and time—particularly on the part of the advocate—are to be involved at an earlier stage, a larger proportion of the total cost of preparation will be incurred earlier than the date when the substantive instructions are delivered to the advocate. This will be unimportant if the case does eventually reach a hearing, for the total

[49] s.61.

costs will not be increased. But in some fields—construction industry disputes are an example—only a small minority of cases in which proceedings are begun (whether by arbitration or litigation) actually reach a hearing. In some of the other cases the costs up to the date of settlement may be higher than they would be under the present practice. It is suggested that it will be rare for any disadvantage to result from the change of practice. In most of the cases that are compromised before a hearing begins, the compromise is reached because of the thought and attention that one or both parties have been compelled to give to the issues by the preparation of the case and the need to comply with the directions, or to attend meetings with solicitors or counsel for that purpose. If in some cases these preparations now have to be made earlier, those cases will tend to be compromised earlier which is not a disadvantage, particularly when it is borne in mind that delay itself costs the parties money, not always compensated for in interest. There is much to be said for commercial concerns seeking early settlement, thereby enabling management resources to be employed on more productive activity.[50]

Advantages of a four-sitting-day week

The influence on arbitration practice of the procedure in a trial by jury may continue to be felt. Inevitably arbitrators and practitioners may wish to continue in traditional ways with interlocutory stages leading to one hearing of all the issues. However, it is very much to be hoped that parties and arbitrators will use the freedom given to them by the Act to avoid lengthy hearings of weeks or months. Much of the work necessary to decide a dispute can be done more speedily and more cheaply outside the hearing. **2–587**

However, where a long hearing has proved unavoidable there are certain steps which can be taken to make the hearing itself more effective. Thus, for example, if the arbitrator spends the fifth day, or so much of it as is needed, reading his note, indexing it, and noting the questions that occur to him, he may well be able to shorten the hearing by indicating to the advocates points that he is minded—however provisionally—to accept. When the hearing ends, the process of analysing the evidence and submissions will be greatly simplified, and the delay involved in the preparation of his award will be reduced. Moreover, in most long hearings points arise that can usefully be cleared up on a non-sitting day. Expert witnesses can meet to agree points that have emerged. The advocates can meet to narrow issues, to have schedules typed, and generally to reduce to a minimum the points that remain to be dealt with by the long drawn out procedure of oral question and oral answer. **2–588**

So there is no reason to suppose that a four-day, rather than a five-day week **2–589**

[50] The Court of Appeal, dealing with a similar situation in civil appeals, has expressly directed taxing masters, when taxing costs, to tax the costs of preparatory work separately from fees for the hearing.

will significantly increase the time that elapses between beginning the hearing and issuing the award. On the contrary, it may well reduce it.

Effect on costs

2–590 Nor should it increase the costs. In most cases the arbitrator, the solicitors and counsel, and the professional witnesses will be charging on a daily or hourly rate basis. In a few cases an overall fee will be charged. A weekly basis is almost unheard of, and in any case it need not be adopted where a four-day week is to be adopted for the hearing. So the parties will not have to pay any more in the aggregate, and may have to pay less, where a four-day week is worked.

Precedents for the four-sitting-day week

2–591 Long planning inquiries have for many years been conducted on the basis of a four-sitting-day week. Many courts in England which have work loads that involve reading considerable quantities of documents do the same. It is obviously more efficient for the tribunal to read them outside rather than during the hearing hours. It is suggested that this practice could usefully be adopted in arbitrations that involve a hearing longer than about eight days.

The pre-hearing review

2–592 In all but the simplest cases of arbitrations in which there is to be a hearing, a pre-hearing review, held well before the hearing date, is likely to save time and costs. How long before depends on the nature and complexity of the case. Three or four weeks should suffice for all but the heaviest cases, but it should be after witness statements and experts reports have been exchanged. The objects of the review are:

(a) to enable the arbitrator to satisfy himself that all previous directions have been or will be complied with;
(b) to consider whether any further directions, *e.g.* as to discovery, are required;
(c) to ensure that the issues between the parties have been identified, so that each will come to the hearing with his attention concentrated on what is really an issue;
(d) to explore ways of shortening the hearing, *e.g.* by admitting all or part of some of the witness statements, or by directing a further meeting between experts or by limiting the number of witnesses; and imposing time limits for witness evidence and oral argument;
(e) to consider whether it would be advantageous to decide any issue as a preliminary issue, *i.e.* one on which the evidence and arguments are adduced, and an interim award is given, before the hearing continues

on the other issues (for example, where the terms of the contract between the parties are in issue, it is often of advantage to decide that issue before proceeding with the others);

(f) if any issue is to be tried as a preliminary issue, to define it precisely and to record it;

(g) to consider the programming of any hearing, so that witnesses need not attend those hearings, or those parts of a hearing with which they are not concerned;

(h) to arrange for the appropriate bundles of documents, including the list of issues, to be delivered to the arbitrator in sufficient time to enable him to read them intelligently before the hearing begins;

(i) to ensure that the hearing will start in an efficient manner on the due date.

As with the preliminary dialogue, a telephone or video conference, may suffice instead of a meeting; see paragraph 2–429, above.

20. The Conduct of the Hearing

The right to representation

Where there is a hearing, each party has a right not only to be present, but to be represented by an advocate (lay or professional) of his choice unless that right has been excluded by agreement (section 36 of the Act). The rules of many trade associations exclude the right to legal representation (see Part 3, below). But even where such rules have been incorporated in a contract they can be varied by consent, if the nature of the dispute makes the intervention of lawyers desirable. **2–593**

Party acting in person

Unless the arbitrator has been informed in advance that one or both parties intend to present their case in person, without being represented, it is the usual practice to ask the unrepresented party whether he is content to present his case in this way. The arbitrator should make it clear that this is the actual hearing, when each side has the opportunity of calling its witnesses and explaining its case. The arbitrator should explain in some detail the procedure which will be followed. **2–594**

Proceeding ex parte

2–595 A litigant who is deprived of the opportunity of having his case presented because of the default of his own advisers has no ground of complaint that natural justice has been denied to him.[51] Merely explaining to a party in this situation that he will no doubt be able to sue his advisers is cold comfort. This prospect of commencing upon fresh proceedings after his experiences in the present proceedings may be both depressing and daunting. In any event, there can be no certainty in most cases that an action against the adviser will lead to a result which wholly remedies the loss occasioned by this failure. Accordingly, an arbitrator faced with the problem of a party let down by his own adviser should consider whether there is any action, without causing serious injustice to the other party, which will permit the matter to be brought to a satisfactory conclusion.

Absence without adequate reason

2–596 As section 41(4) of the Act makes clear the absence of one party from a preliminary meeting or from the hearing or some part of it in no way prevents the arbitrator from continuing with the proceedings without him (ex parte). This is subject to the requirement that the party has been given adequate notice and has given no reason, or a reason that the arbitrator considers unacceptable, for his absence. What is an adequate reason is a matter of judgment. A request for an adjournment made shortly before the hearing date, with no expression of willingness to attend on any date shortly thereafter and made on apparently flimsy grounds, is different in character from a request for an adjournment of a few days or weeks made for apparently good reason long before the hearing date. The arbitrator's object must be to give each side a fair opportunity of presenting his case. If one party asserts with apparently good reason that the hearing date fixed will not allow him to do this, the arbitrator should be ready to fix a different date, provided—and this is essential—that the new date will not impose on the opposing party a disadvantage amounting to injustice. An example would be if his expert witness or counsel who has been engaged in the case throughout will not be available for the proposed new date. Particularly where a time table has been agreed or ordered well in advance and a date or dates for hearings fixed, arbitrators should as a general rule be loathe to vacate dates and thereby cause delay to the arbitration, unless good reason be shown. Mere inconvenience to a party or his lawyers or other advisers in keeping to an agreed or ordered time table will rarely be a sufficient reason.

2–597 The policy in the courts is only to permit adjournments where to proceed would cause injustice. Judges are now much more robust in refusing applications to adjourn, conscious as they now are of the waste of time, money and other resources if cases are adjourned. Arbitrators would do well to emulate this robust approach and the Act encourages them to do so.

[51] *R v. Secretary of State for the Home Department, ex p. Al-Mehdawi* [1989] 3 All E.R. 843.

If a party who has given no previous intimation that he does not intend to appear, simply fails to appear at the time appointed for a hearing, it is usually unwise to proceed without first inquiring whether his absence is intended. Prior to the Act, once it seemed likely that the hearing would have to be conducted in the absence of a party the recommended procedures were as follows. The arbitrator would serve on that party written notice of his intention that he intends to proceed on the specified date whether or not that party attends and he would take steps also to ensure that evidence was available of the service of such notice on the party concerned, *e.g.* by an affidavit of personal service, or by a duly completed post office acknowledgment of receipt form. **2–598**

Taking evidence on oath

Power to take evidence on oath in arbitrations under the pre-1996 Act

Section 12(2) of the 1950 Act provided that unless a contrary intention was expressed therein, every arbitration agreement was deemed to contain a provision that the witnesses on the reference should, if the arbitrator or umpire thought fit, be examined on oath or affirmation. In practice it was very rare for an arbitration agreement to express a contrary intention, and the arbitrator took the evidence on oath or affirmation if either party so requested; some arbitrators required that evidence be given on oath even if neither party requested. **2–599**

In arbitrations to which the Act applies the provisions of section 12(2) of the 1950 Act have been repealed and (in effect) replaced by a discretionary power under section 38(5) to permit evidence to be given on oath or affirmation. Section 34(2)(e) also provides that, failing agreement to the contrary, it is for the tribunal to determine whether any and if so what questions should be put to and answered by the respective parties and when and in what form this shall be done. **2–600**

Forms of oath or affirmation

Two forms of oath or affirmation are in common use, namely: **2–601**

(Oath):

> I swear by Almighty God that the evidence I shall give touching the matters in difference in this reference shall be the truth, the whole truth, and nothing but the truth.

(Affirmation):

> I solemnly, sincerely, and truly affirm and declare that the evidence I shall give touching the matters in difference in this reference shall be the truth, the whole truth and nothing but the truth.

(Oath):

> I swear by Almighty God that I will true answer make to all such questions as shall be asked of me touching the matters in difference in this reference.

(Affirmation):

> I solemnly, sincerely, and truly affirm and declare that I will true answers make to all such questions as shall be asked of me touching the matters in difference in this reference.

2–602 It is suggested that the first pair of these forms is preferable, since the second might perhaps be taken as approving the practice by which a witness answers strictly a question put to him, but knows that by reason of facts known to him but not called for by the question, his answer is likely to mislead.

Procedure

2–603 By the Oaths Act 1978 the person taking the oath is to hold the New Testament (or, in the case of a Jew, the Old Testament) in his uplifted hand and say or repeat after the arbitrator the words of the oath. Any person who objects to taking the oath may give his evidence on affirmation instead. It is not now the practice to ask him why he objects to taking the oath.

2–604 In addition, if evidence is to be on oath, a tribunal should enquire at an early stage whether witnesses of various religions may be giving evidence. If so he should direct the parties to agree on the appropriate procedure and to arrange for any necessary book or other accessory to be available.

2–605 If the award is to be enforced abroad, he should ask the parties to confirm that an award following evidence on oath is acceptable in the courts likely to have this task.

2–606 As to the position where a witness declines to answer a question, see paragraph 2–679, below.

Equipment

2–607 The arbitrator should as a matter of course take to a hearing a copy of the Old Testament and a copy of the New Testament. When he knows that there is to be a hearing, his directions for it should include a direction that a party who intends to call a witness whose evidence, if given on oath, would require a form of oath otherwise than upon the Old or New Testaments, should make whatever arrangements are necessary to enable the oath to be taken in that form.

Notetaking

The objects of notetaking

An arbitrator will use his notes for one or more of the following purposes: 2–608

(a) to remind the arbitrator of the evidence, when he comes to make his findings of fact;
(b) to compare what the witness says at one part of his evidence with what he says at another;
(c) to compare what the witness says in his evidence with what he said on another occasion, *e.g.* as may be inferred from the pleadings, or what he said in an affidavit, or what he said as recorded in minutes of a meeting, or what he is said by another witness to have said;
(d) to compare what the witness says with what an earlier or later witness says;
(e) to record accurately the essence of the advocate's final submissions, both to help the arbitrator make up his mind and (if he is to give a reasoned award) to enable him to set out, so far as he thinks fit, in his award the case for the losing party and why he has rejected it.

The following are possible methods of notetaking: 2–609

(a) The arbitrator takes a full note.
(b) The arbitrator jots down some reminders.
(c) The arbitrator employs someone to take a note for him.
(d) A full shorthand note is taken, and transcribed at leisure.
(e) A full shorthand note is taken, by shorthand writers working in relays, so that a transcript of the day's evidence is produced by the following morning.
(f) Simultaneous transcription to a screen.
(g) The evidence is recorded on tape, and transcribed at leisure.
(h) The evidence is recorded on tape and then transcribed so as to be available very quickly.
(i) A video recording is made.

The choice between these courses

In most cases in court, course (a) is used. But in cases in court the judge has 2–610
had many years of experience in taking a rapid and accurate note, both as advocate and on the bench. He is thus able to mitigate the principal disadvantage of this course, which is its essential slowness. It has been said that the duties of an arbitrator are onerous enough without adding to them those of clerk, usher and (in particular) notetaker. Apart from the delay that this course imposes, by causing the hearing to take much longer than it otherwise would, it is responsible for another and less obvious source of delay. It is difficult to take an accurate

note of what is being said, and to think about it at the same time. In most arbitrations the arbitrator concentrates on taking an accurate note—in particular, of final submissions—so that he can think about it at leisure when the hearing has ended. This has two important disadvantages. First, it prevents him from effectively taking part in the dialogue with the advocates which is one of the great advantages of the peculiarly English practice of an adversarial process combined with oral advocacy. Secondly, because he has not really thought about the evidence or the submissions whilst they are being put before him, he has to do this thinking after the hearing has ended. Many points are likely to occur to him which he would have clarified had he thought of them earlier. Moreover, the task of refreshing his memory as to the issues and the evidence and then thinking through the submissions in order to decide which he prefers, is a great labour which a judge (who is after all the professional in this field) avoids by discussion with the advocate during the final submissions, and giving judgment extemporaneously, or after thinking about it over a short adjournment whilst the case is still fresh in his mind. So what the litigants lose in the additional length of hearing occasioned by the need for the judge to make a longhand note, is to some extent offset by the speed of decision when the closing submissions have been completed.

An abbreviated note taken by the arbitrator

2–611 This course is not really suitable for cases which involve or may involve a conflict of oral evidence as to fact. It can be wholly adequate if employed by an experienced arbitrator.

A full note taken by an assistant

2–612 This course will only work if the notetaker is intelligent, experienced in notetaking, fully aware of the issues in the case and of good and rapid handwriting. In the authors' experience, the only persons with these qualifications are barristers and litigation solicitors; their day to day experience involves taking an accurate note speedily. It can be a very useful by-product of appointing an experienced trial lawyer as legal adviser, that he can by arrangement with the arbitrator take a full note and thereby relieve the arbitrator from this function.

Shorthand note transcribed at leisure

2–613 This course is rarely used. It is fairly expensive, requiring probably two shorthand writers working in relays. It is rare for a shorthand note taken by any but a professional court shorthand writer to be useful. The note cannot achieve objects (a), (c) and (d) above, because it is not available when the apparently contradictory evidence is given.

Shorthand note transcribed immediately

2–614 This is perhaps the ideal in every respect except cost. It produces a transcript by about 9 p.m. each evening of the day's proceedings, but it requires a team of two to four highly trained court reporters, and is quite expensive. It is desirable that each day the errors in the previous day's transcript be corrected by agreement between the advocates. This should not be during hearing time.

A more sophisticated (and more expensive) version of this process throws up on to screens in front of the individuals or onto a large screen visible throughout the room what is being recorded. The process is virtually simultaneous with speech, and enables, if on individual screens, the tribunal, advocates, whoever has a screen, to mark it up, scroll backwards and forwards, to search it, etc. at will. A large screen version can be very distracting. **2–615**

Tape recording transcribed either overnight or at leisure

These methods are relatively untried. Those who have experienced them say that the rustling of papers, and other extraneous noises often make important passages inaudible and other passages are lost through mechanical malfunction. It is also difficult upon occasion to be certain who is speaking even when there is only one voice. These facts emerge only when it is too late to remedy the omissions. **2–616**

Tape recording not transcribed

The practice of making a tape recording which is not transcribed but available to be checked against recollection or a manuscript note of evidence, especially in case of uncertainty or conflict, is commonplace in international commercial arbitration. Video recording of the proceedings is a rare method, which overcomes some of the problems of tape recording. **2–617**

Managing the note

In complex arbitrations and particularly where a hearing lasts for several days, it is helpful to index the note or transcript first of all witness by witness, and secondly (within each witness's evidence) issue by issue. Doing this at the end of the day's evidence has several advantages. First, it facilitates finding the references when needed later in the hearing. Secondly, it begins to focus the arbitrator's mind on the salient features of the evidence of each witness. Thirdly, it is of inestimable benefit when the arbitrator comes to write his award. As the arbitrator gains experience, it will hasten the day when, in an urgent case, an arbitrator feels confident enough to give his award at the end of the hearing. In that case it can be issued in manuscript, and typed later or it can be recorded in shorthand or on tape, and the written award can follow shortly afterwards. **2–618**

Some general points on the reception of evidence during the hearing

Order of witnesses

If a hearing is expected to last for more than a day or two, a great deal of expense can be saved if the order in which witnesses are to be called is known **2–619** in advance, so that the opposing party can dispense with the attendance of his witnesses whilst evidence is being given with which they are not concerned. This should be standard practice. The arbitrator should consider directing the parties to indicate the order in which they propose to call witnesses. The list should distinguish between definite and possible witnesses. The arbitrator should not insist that the listed order be followed strictly, but he is entitled to ask for an explanation from a party who changes the order; recalcitrant or uncooperative parties should be reminded of the arbitrator's power under section 34 to control the submission of evidence to him.

2–620 Arbitrators might well follow the example of the Commercial Court which has ruled that it has power to override the parties' right to determine the order of evidence if the court considers it just to do so; see *Bayer v. Clarkson Puckle*.[52]

Taking evidence through an interpreter

2–621 An interpreter's function is merely to inform the tribunal or the witness of the meaning of the words spoken by or to a witness. Where the evidence is being given orally, the interpretation must be strictly controlled. In the first place a careful attempt should be made to ascertain whether, and if so to what extent, the witness understands or speaks the language in which the hearing is taking place. If the arbitrator decides to allow the witness to give evidence through an interpreter, he should make it plain to the interpreter that his sole function is to translate and that he should not change the question so that it becomes a leading one, nor should he prompt or pressurise the witness. The interpreter should not be allowed to discuss the question, or the answer, with the witness unless the arbitrator (or perhaps one or more members of the tribunal) speaks the witness's language and can ensure that the discussion is a proper one. The interpreter should not be allowed to arrogate to himself the role of the tribunal or the advocate, by himself cross-examining or instructing the witness.

Legal and non-legal texts and articles

Legal texts and articles

2–622 There used to be some diffidence in citing, in support of a submission of law, a textbook or article written by a living author. The modern practice is to refer freely to such works.[53] But unless a passage has been judicially approved, it is merely the opinion of its author. See for example *Johnson v. Agnew*[54] where a "well-known book of reference on conveyancing matters" was criticised.[55] Lord Wilberforce said of a passage in that book:

[52] (1989) 139 New L.J. 256.

[53] Passages from the first edition of the Handbook have been cited to the Supreme Court of India—by both parties! — and from the second edition in the High Court of India.

[54] [1980] A.C. 367.

[55] T. Cyprian Williams, *Vendor and Purchaser* (4th Ed.)

"My Lords, this passage is almost a perfect illustration of the dangers well perceived by our predecessors but tending to be neglected in modern times, of placing reliance on textbook authority for an analysis of judicial decisions. It is on the face of it a number of unclear propositions not logically related to each other. It is 'supported' by footnote references to cases (two of this House and one of the Privy Council) which are not explained or analysed."[56]

On the other hand Lord Wilberforce himself relied[57] upon Voumards' *Sale of Land* for a proposition which had been judicially approved elsewhere. **2–623**

Non-legal texts and articles

An expert witness may refer to views expressed in a text book or article in support of his opinion. The weight attached to an expert view which is dependent largely upon such material would normally be less than the weight attached to an opinion founded upon personal experience. One of the purposes of the exchange of reports of expert witnesses is to enable the parties and their experts to consider beforehand matters such as this, so that they can probe in cross-examination the strength of the foundations for the expert opinion, and if so minded call evidence in rebuttal. **2–624**

The arbitrator himself may refer to a textbook or article. If he does so however he should notify the parties of the relevant passage and give them an opportunity of dealing with it by calling further evidence or making submissions or both. **2–625**

Evidence of fact

Texts or articles put forward as evidence of matters of fact other than by the consent of the parties ought to be approached with great caution. **2–626**

Weight is a matter for the arbitrator

As a general rule the arbitrator should be prepared to consider any text, legal or non-legal. But at the end of the day it will be for him to decide what weight (if any) to give to it, subject perhaps to the helpful rule of thumb with such material that the opinions expressed are only as good as the arguments or research relied upon to support them. **2–627**

Evidence unlawfully obtained

The general rule in both civil and criminal proceedings is that where evidence is illegally obtained, that illegality is not a sufficient ground for excluding the relevant material as evidence. In criminal proceedings in England the judge has a limited discretion to exclude such evidence. In civil proceedings (whether **2–628**

[56] [1980] A.C. 395, at 395–396.
[57] *ibid* at 397.

before a judge or an arbitrator) no such discretion exists. Even documents that a party obtained by stealing them from another party are not intrinsically inadmissible. But a court might by injunction restrain the thief from using the stolen material in litigation. So where documents were obtained by a trick and within the precincts of the court, such of the documents as had been exhibited to an affidavit and used in evidence were admissible (though there might be a sanction by way of proceedings for contempt of court) but such of the documents as had not been used were made the subject of an injunction and an order for the return of the documents; see *ITC Film Distributions v. Video Exchange*[58].

No property in a witness

2–629 There is no property in a witness. Either party is at liberty to approach any witness. Of course, a factual witness might not want to talk to either party or may want to talk to one party only. An opinion witness who has been retained by one party and has given an opinion or report to him in pursuance of the retainer is under a contractual obligation not to give a copy of it to another party without the consent of the party who has retained him. Indeed, an opinion witness who, whilst retained by a party, acted for or advised the opposing party would in most cases be acting unprofessionally as well as in breach of contract, and might well be restrained by the court from continuing so to do. On the other hand, an expert who has been discharged by one party may be employed by another, but, he cannot convey any information about his original documentation nor hand over copies of his reports or drafts.

Access to a witness during his evidence

2–630 In litigation a witness who is under cross-examination is nearly always requested not to talk to anyone about the case unless the court expressly authorises him to do so. The reasoning underlying this practice is thought to be that if others are allowed free access to him they may prompt him as to how to deal with points that have been put to him in cross-examination. Moreover, a witness' evidence carries more weight if the tribunal is satisfied that he is speaking from his own unalloyed recollection and opinion. The practice is a sensible one, and it is suggested that arbitrators should follow it. Nonetheless it is not a rule of law, and indeed is not observed in, for example, proceedings in Parliament where parties are seeking to obtain private bills. If there is any doubt about whether the usual rule is to apply (*e.g.* if the attorneys involved do not all come from England) the sensible course is for the arbitrator to raise the matter at an early stage and seek to resolve it.

2–631 Provided both parties follow the same rule (whether that rule be the traditional one in England, or one allowing access on a limited basis, *e.g.* outside sitting

[58] [1982] 1 Ch. 431.

hours; or on a total basis, *e.g.* witnesses free to seek advice before answering a question) it is difficult to see any objection. Of course "advised" evidence may be of lesser weight than spontaneous evidence.

Whether the traditional rule applies during a witness' evidence in chief (if there is any such which there should not usually be) is more doubtful; many judges and barristers in England assume that it does. **2–632**

Order of events at the hearing

Usual order at a hearing

Traditionally, arbitrators and practitioners in English domestic arbitration have followed court procedures and this has led to the usual order of events being as follows: **2–633**

(a) Opening statement for the claimant.
(b) Evidence in chief of the claimant's first witness.
(c) Cross-examination of the claimant's first witness.
(d) Re-examination of the claimant's first witness.
(b), (c) and (d) are repeated for each successive witness.
(e) Opening statement (if any) for the respondent.
(f) Evidence in chief of respondent's first witness.
(g) Cross-examination of respondent's first witness.
(h) Re-examination of respondent's first witness.
(f), (g) and (h) are repeated for each successive witness.
(i) Closing speech for the respondent.
(j) Closing speech for the claimant.

However, arbitrators, in the absence of the parties' agreement to the contrary, are not bound to follow English court or adversarial procedure. The arbitrator's duty is to adopt procedures most suited to the fair, economic and expeditious disposal of the case. If issues have been properly defined, the arbitrator can order the production of written submissions and evidence focused upon the issues. If the arbitrator has read the relevant material in advance, it should be possible severely to limit the time taken in opening statements and the examination of witnesses and consideration of documents. It is also possible by use of skeleton arguments to save time, by indicating in advance to the tribunal the logical sequence and weight of the respective arguments and evidence. Such practices are becoming more and more used by the courts as evidenced by various practice directions which seek to reduce the time spent in hearings. Even therefore if arbitrators and the parties wish to follow traditional English litigation procedures **2–634** for the conduct of the hearing, they can and should use various devices to limit time and expense.

Opening for the claimant

2–635 Hitherto the advocate for the claimant could not assume that the arbitrator knew anything about the case unless and until the arbitrator told him to the contrary. The arbitrator should direct that before the hearing an agreed list of issues and the agreed bundle of documents, and the reports of expert witnesses (if any) be submitted to him. It should be standard practice for the arbitrator to read in advance all relevant material and this should make any detailed opening statement by the claimant unnecessary.

Evidence in chief

2–636 There is no point in the evidence being given orally if the examination in chief consists of the advocate putting to the witness, sentence by sentence, what is in the witness's proof of evidence, and waiting for the witness to answer yes or no as the case may be. The most which should be permitted is supplementary questions put for clarification rather than to raise wholly new topics. Examination in chief should therefore be non-existent or very brief.

Cross-examination

Can the arbitrator refuse to allow cross-examination?

2–637 *Chilton v. Saga Holidays plc*,[59] decided under the pre-1996 law, was a claim brought in the County Court for less than £500, and was therefore, under Order 19 of the County Court Rules, referred to arbitration by the Registrar. At the hearing the plaintiff appeared in person and the defendant by its solicitor. A request by the defendant's solicitor to be allowed to cross-examine the plaintiff was refused by the Registrar, who said:

> "In cases where one side is unrepresented I do not allow cross-examination. All questions to the other side will be put through me."

2–638 In setting aside the award, Lord Donaldson, giving the judgment of the Court of Appeal, said:

> "Both courts and arbitrators in this country operate on an adversarial system of achieving justice. It is a system which can be modified by rules of court; it is a system which can be modified by contract between the parties; but, in the absence of one or the other, it is basically an adversarial system, and it is fundamental to that that each party shall be entitled to

[59] [1986] 1 All E.R. 841.

tender their own evidence and that the other party shall be entitled to ask questions designed to probe the accuracy or otherwise, or the completeness or otherwise, of the evidence which has been given."

However, under section 34 of the Act this is now a matter for the tribunal which is not bound to follow adversarial procedures, unless the parties otherwise agree. In the absence of agreement to the contrary, Lord Donaldson's views on the applicability of the adversarial system no longer apply. 2–639

Cross-examination has, or may have, three objects: 2–640

(a) To put before the opposing party's witness (or the appropriate witness, if he is calling more than one) the substance of the cross-examining party's case insofar as it conflicts with the evidence given by that witness.
(b) To elicit from the witness facts favourable to the cross-examining party's case or adverse to the opposing case.
(c) Where the evidence that the witness has given in chief is disputed, to elicit facts relevant to the credibility of the witness, so as to show that he should not be believed; this is known as "cross-examination as to credit".

Object (a) does not apply where the witness has already had an opportunity of disputing or commenting upon the cross-examining party's case, *e.g.* because proofs of evidence have been exchanged, or because the witness has been present in the hearing while an earlier witness gave evidence that conflicts with his evidence. 2–641

Questions put to the witness under heads (a) or (b) must be relevant to some issue in the arbitration. Cross-examination as to credit is not limited in this way. 2–642

The art of cross-examination cannot be explored here. Nor can the no less difficult art of controlling a prolix cross-examiner without giving the impression that he is not being allowed a fair opportunity to cross-examine. But arbitrators and parties should remember that, failing agreement to the contrary, section 34(2)(e) of the Act reserves to the arbitrator the power to decide whether any and if so what questions should be put to and answered by the respective parties and when and in what form this should be done. Arbitrators should make it clear that questioning is expected to be brief and to the point and should be prepared to stop an advocate who does not comply. 2–643

Re-examination

The object of re-examination is to enable the advocate who called the witness to give the witness the opportunity to explain, supplement or qualify answers that the witness has given in cross-examination. A witness whose evidence seems to have been badly shaken in cross-examination can sometimes be rehabilitated by re-examination. Although the form and nature of the questioning is 2–644 for the arbitrator to decide, it is suggested that the old procedure may usefully be followed: Thus the points put to the witness should arise out of the cross-examination; unlike cross-examination, which is unlimited save in the respects indicated above. Leading questions should not be asked in re-examination any more than in evidence in chief. The arbitrator should intimate that answers that the advocate has put into the witness's mouth are unlikely to carry much weight.

Opening statement for the respondent

2–645 The advocate for the respondent should be allowed to make an opening statement if he thinks it really necessary. If a list of issues has been agreed before the hearing began, and has not been significantly changed by the time the respondent's case begins, in many cases little or no opening statement will be required; the nature of the respondent's case will be clear both from the list of issues and from the cross-examination of the claimant's witnesses. If the list of issues is to be amended—often by deleting some—it will usually be convenient to do this before the evidence for the respondent begins so that the claimant's advocate has the opportunity of cross-examining witnesses in the light of the issues as they now stand. Points of law should have been indicated in advance. It may be helpful for the advocate to summarise the points in opening the respondent's case, so that the arbitrator and the opposing advocate may know to what matters the respondent's evidence is to be directed. But detailed argument of a point of law is usually better left until the evidence is complete.

Interventions by the arbitrator

Interventions during evidence in chief

2–646 If the advocate is competent, it should rarely be necessary for the arbitrator to intervene in the course of evidence in chief. He should freely do so, however, if otherwise his note will be unintelligible. For example, if the witness says: "Then he said to him. It's too small". and it is not clear from the context who said it to whom, and the advocate does not immediately clarify the matter, the arbitrator should do so. Otherwise, it is usually better for the arbitrator to make notes of the questions he is minded to ask, and to ask them at the end of the re-examination if they have not by then been disposed of. Occasionally, the evidence in chief will deal with matters which the arbitrator thinks cannot possibly assist him to decide the issues before him. In that case, he should ask the advocate whether this part of the evidence can possibly be relevant or, perhaps, indicate, that at least provisionally, he is minded to accept something as a fact without any further evidence being given upon it.

Interventions during cross-examination

2–647 An experienced judge rarely intervenes in a cross-examination being conducted by competent counsel. An inexperienced arbitrator should very rarely intervene in a cross-examination being conducted by an advocate in whose competence he has confidence. To interrupt a cross-examination, *e.g.* to ask the advocate what point he is seeking to make, or to put some inconsistency to the witness, may be to stultify the cross-examination. It requires judgment and experience to distinguish between a competent advocate who is in the early stages of a coherent line of questioning, and an inexperienced or incompetent advocate who is asking a succession of uncoordinated questions partly to appear to be earning his fee and partly in the hope that something useful will turn up. The golden rule must be: subject to any time limits that have previously been agreed or imposed, leave the advocate alone unless the arbitrator is sure that a continuation of the cross-examination, or of the cross-examination on the particular point, cannot in the end assist him in deciding the issues before him.

The arbitrator should also be aware of his responsibility to protect a witness against unfair or bullying cross-examination. The witness is entitled to be treated with courtesy at all times. The arbitrator should always keep in mind the boundary between a stern but courteous cross-examination, and a rude or bullying one. He should intervene whenever he thinks that the advocate is exceeding the bounds of fairness. **2–648**

When considering whether to intervene to curtail cross examination particularly if it appears to be lengthy, the real question is: has the cross-examination, whether as a whole or on a particular point, reached a stage where its continuation cannot possibly help the cross-examiner's case, or the arbitrator in his task? Some time is wasted in most cross-examinations. Much time is wasted in some cross-examinations. Cross-examination is at the heart of the English adversary system and some waste of time, owing to the imperfections of advocates or witnesses, or both, is unavoidable. But efficiently and properly done and confined to the material issues, it is probably the best procedure for arriving at the truth. **2–649**

Intervention during re-examination

It often happens, in practice, that a question is put in re-examination which does not arise out of the cross-examination, but which has been suggested to the advocate by something that occurred during the cross-examination. If the advocate considers it important that the question be put, the arbitrator should not rule it out merely because it ought to have been asked when the witness was giving evidence in chief; he should allow the question to be asked, and if necessary give the opposing advocate an opportunity to cross-examine upon it. The rules regulating the order of the proceedings in a hearing are rules of convenience only. The arbitrator should depart from them whenever he thinks it is convenient, or helpful to him, subject only to the principle that too many departures from the usual order of proceedings may result in disorder, and in the end much inconvenience. **2–650**

Closing submissions

The final submissions by the advocates are important for a number of reasons. **2–651**
The final submission is the first and only opportunity that each party has for

putting before the arbitrator his comments upon the evidence taken as a whole, and upon the case finally presented by the opposing party. Secondly, it should help the arbitrator to see the shape of each case as finally presented. In the course of doing so, he can clarify his mind by a dialogue with each advocate in turn as to what the crucial issues really are and as to how if at all any doubt that the arbitrator has about accepting a particular argument may be dispelled. Third, the most satisfactory form of reasoned award is one that summarises the opposing cases and explains why the arbitrator has preferred one to the other. An intelligible note of the closing arguments on each side is the best possible starting point for an intelligible and fully reasoned award.

2–652 If an arbitrator intends to remain silent whilst final submissions are being made to him, there is little point in their being made orally; they can be made in writing, first on behalf of the respondent, then on behalf of the claimant.

2–653 A third option is to have written submissions, followed by a brief hearing (an hour/half a day) for the tribunal to ask questions or the parties to highlight key points.

Interventions during final submissions

2–654 If the arbitrator remains silent during final submissions, he cannot achieve the above objects, and he thereby negatives one of the main advantages of a hearing as compared with a determination on written representations only. Moreover, silence on the part of the arbitrator is perhaps the most common source of repetition. The advocate cannot be blamed for making the same point over and over again if the arbitrator gives no indication that he has understood it. The parties have not engaged him to listen; they have engaged him, and are to pay him, to decide the issues after giving a fair hearing to each side. If after hearing the first of the two final submissions (usually that for the respondent) he has made up his mind on a particular issue against that party, and is sure that he will not change his view on a reconsideration of the evidence and the submissions, he should not be afraid to say so without asking the advocate for the other party to address him on that point.

2–655 There are alternatives to the classic common law system of examination in chief, cross-examination and re-examination. Experience in international commercial arbitration shows that, if the Chairman, or sole arbitrator, is a skilled questioner and before the hearing has read and understood the submissions in evidence and the documents available to him, much time can be saved by allowing the Chairman to ask questions first, with the parties' advocates then allowed to ask supplementary questions to clarify matters or to deal with points not made by the tribunal. Properly done this technique combines examination and cross-examination and can be very effective in reducing time spent in hearings. There is however a potentially major disadvantage, namely that a party may well feel that rigorous questioning by an arbitrator is in effect showing bias or even hostility; and thus the appearance of impartiality can be damaged.

21. Privacy and Confidentiality in Arbitration

The position in English law

The principle

Every edition since 1911 of Russell on *Arbitration*, the standard English textbook on the law of arbitration, has contained this passage: 2–656

> "Arbitration is a private tribunal for the settlement of disputes. The public, therefore, may not be admitted if their admission is objected to by either party or the arbitrator."

Earlier editions of this Handbook repeated the above passage and continued: 2–657

> "No authority is cited for this proposition but it seems implicit in an agreement to refer a dispute to arbitration."

This remains the authors' view, and it is now supported by several decisions of the English courts[60] although occasional examples can be found of arbitrations in England held in public. But the existence of a duty of confidentiality in arbitration in Australia has been negatived by a decision of the High Court of Australia in the *Esso*[61] case. The UNCITRAL Arbitration Rules (1976)[62] provide that the award may be made public only with the consent of both parties. The content of the implied agreement for confidentiality has been the subject of several decisions in England and elsewhere. 2–658

Who may attend a hearing

Consistently with the principle of privacy, persons entitled to attend the hearing include the following: 2–659

(a) each party. If the party is a company, this will include an officer or servant whom the company desires to be present as the formal representative of the party;

[60] Including one by Colman J., a judge with long experience of domestic and international commercial arbitration, who said in *Hassneh* (see below) that the practice of holding an arbitration hearing in private has been universal in London for hundreds of years.

[61] *Esso BHP v. Plowman*, (1995) 128 A.L.R. 391.

[62] Printed as Appendix 4 below. These Rules are optional, and do not govern an arbitration unless adopted by the parties, by the arbitration agreement or otherwise.

(b) any person whom any party desires to represent him or it at the hearing. This may be counsel, solicitor, surveyor or anyone else. If it is the intention of the party to be represented by a lawyer, he should notify such intention in good time so as to enable the opposing party to obtain legal representation if thought fit;

(c) subject to any specific direction as to the giving of evidence any person whom a party reasonably wishes to have present as a witness, or otherwise to assist in the presentation of the party's case;

(d) a shorthand writer or other notetaker, if the party wishes to have notes taken for the proper presentation of his case in the instant arbitration.

2–660 So if, as often happens, the arbitrator wishes to have someone in attendance upon him, *e.g.* a clerk, or pupil-arbitrator, he should ask the parties if they have any objection.

Publishing information about the arbitration

2–661 There would be little point in restricting attendance at a hearing if it were open to anyone to make public, for example in the press, or on television, an account of what was said or done at the hearing. It is submitted that subject to the exceptions considered in paragraph 2–670 below, a party would be entitled to an injunction to restrain the other party from such publication.

> "The fact that a document is used in an arbitration does not confer on it any confidentiality or privilege which can be availed of in subsequent proceedings . . . But that the obligation exists in some form appears to me to be abundantly apparent. It is not a question of immunity or public interest. It is a question of an implied obligation arising out of the nature of arbitration itself."[63]

2–662 The same principle should apply to the arbitration as a whole, including the pleadings or Statements of Case, expert reports or witness proofs that have been exchanged, as well as to evidence given orally at a hearing. And the duty, it is submitted, applies to all concerned, whether or not they are parties. So, for example, a witness who for the purposes of the arbitration is given another witness' statement is under a duty of confidence as regards that other statement.

Effect on arbitration in England of the decision in the Esso case

2–663 The decision of the majority in the *Esso* case was expressly founded on arbitration practice in Australia and was expressed to be limited to arbitration in

[63] See Parker L.J. in *Dolling-Baker v. Merrett* [1991] 2 All E.R. 890 at 899.

Australia. It is not binding on the English courts, and in the authors' view is unlikely to be followed:

(a) because the practice as followed in Australia differs from the practice that has been followed in England for probably centuries;
(b) because even in Australia the decision of the High Court was a narrow one—three judges to two;
(c) because the general opinion of judges and arbitrators in England is that to remove the protection of confidentiality from arbitration proceedings would be to weaken gravely, and perhaps fatally, the institution of arbitration.

Arbitrator's duty of confidentiality

Information should not be disclosed to others

The duty not to disclose information obtained in the course of and for the purposes of an arbitration applies to the arbitrator as much as to anyone else. Thus for example it would be improper for an arbitrator, without the consent of the parties, to make available to one of his partners, or to a client, information contained in a witness's evidence in the arbitration. **2–664**

Where arbitrator is a partner or employee, the file is his own file

In almost every arbitration the arbitrator is appointed personally, and not as a member or representative of his firm or of a company which employs him. This applies whether or not the arrangements between him and his firm or company result in his fees being paid over. So he should retain personally his arbitration file; it should not be put into the possession or control of his firm or company. **2–665**

Disclosure for publication

If, as if often proposed, any register of arbitration decisions or awards is set up, the arbitrator should not without the consent of the parties insert or authorise the insertion in it of any information relating to the arbitration. **2–666**

Property in the arbitrator's Notes

In the absence of a specific agreement on the point between the arbitrator and the parties, any notes that the arbitrator chooses to make are made for his own benefit and are his property. So the parties are not entitled to copies of them, whether during or after the hearing. If a party requests a copy the arbitrator is not obliged to supply it. This should not however discourage him from complying with a request, often made during a hearing, that he read out his note of a particular answer or passage in a witness' evidence. **2–667**

It is thought that the court has no power to order an arbitrator to supply a copy **2–668** of his notes; section 1(c) of the Act provides that the court shall not intervene in arbitration save as provided in the Act, and there is no provision of the Act giving the court jurisdiction to order production of an arbitrator's notes.

Who is bound by the duty of confidentiality

What persons are bound

2–669 There is no clear guidance from English judges as to the persons who are within the ambit of the duty of confidentiality. It is suggested that the boundaries apply not by reason of the nature of the person concerned—whether or not he is a party—but by reason of the nature of the information and the circumstances in which a recipient receives it. So a person who finds in the street or on a rubbish dump a document marked "confidential" does not thereby come under any duty of confidentiality. But a witness in an arbitration who receives any document prepared for the purposes of that arbitration, *e.g.* a copy of a pleading, or of another witness proof, would be bound by the doctrine of confidentiality.

Limits to the general duty of confidentiality

2–670 Since 1990 there have been at least five decisions of the English courts upholding the existence of some duty of confidentiality.[64] But in accordance with an English court's reluctance to decide more than is strictly necessary for disposing of the particular case before it, each of them refrains from attempting to define more than part of the boundaries of the duty. The subject is not mentioned in the Act, perhaps because of the absence of a general consensus on the subject and consequently the considerable parliamentary time that would have been required to debate it. The most useful practical guidance is that given by Colman J. in *Hassneh Insurance Co. of Israel v. Mew*.[65] In general it may be said that the duty of the recipient of information to keep the information confidential is subject to exceptions where:

(a) Disclosure is under compulsion of law.
(b) Disclosure is reasonably necessary in the public interest.
(c) Disclosure is reasonably necessary for fulfilling the recipient's duties to other persons.
(d) Disclosure is reasonably necessary for protecting or pursuing the recipient's rights against other persons.[66]

[64] They are collected and discussed in a seminal lecture by Sir Patrick Neill, Q.C. reprinted in *Arbitration International*, May 1996.
[65] [1993] 2 Lloyd's Rep. 243.
[66] See *Tourneir v. National Provincial Bank* [1924] 1 K.B. 461; *Dolling-Baker v. Merritt* [1990] 1 W.L.R. 1205; *Hassneh Insurance v. Mew* [1993] 2 Lloyd's Rep. 243.

Special protection of documents disclosed on discovery

> "Those who disclose documents on discovery are entitled to the protection of the court against any use of the documents otherwise than in the action in which they are disclosed. It is a matter of importance to the public, and therefore of public interest, that documents disclosed on discovery should not be permitted to be put to improper use and that the court should give its protection in the right case."[67] **2–671**

This decision arose from discovery pursuant to an obligation imposed by the Rules of the Supreme Court in England. But a direction by an arbitrator for the disclosure of documents could if necessary be enforced by the courts, and it is suggested that the courts would apply the same protection to documents disclosed by direction of an arbitrator. **2–672**

There is no express decision extending this protection to documents disclosed voluntarily for the purposes of an action or an arbitration but it is suggested that the same principle applies. In *Church of Scientology of California v. DHSS*[68] the English Court of Appeal held that any use otherwise than for the purpose of the instant action was "improper". Templeman L.J. said: **2–673**

> "If a litigant makes use of information obtained on discovery for improper purposes, that is to say otherwise than bona fide in the course of the action, he is guilty of contempt of court."

It is suggested that information obtained by way of discovery in an arbitration should not without the consent of the parties be used for any other purpose, not even in another arbitration in which one of the parties is involved. **2–674**

Has arbitrator any power to permit or prohibit disclosure?

Power to order discovery

As already noted, an arbitrator has power under section 34(2) of the Act to order a party to disclose to his opponent all documents in his possession power or control relating to the matters in issue in the arbitration. He has no power to order disclosure on a wider basis. **2–675**

Imposing terms upon order for discovery

It is suggested that where an arbitrator is asked to order discovery, it is open to him to intimate that he will do so on terms (*inter alia*) that the party asking for **2–676**

[67] *Distillers Co. v. Times Newspapers Ltd* [1975] 1 All E.R. 41, *per* Talbot J. at 48, cited with approval by Waller L.J. in *Riddick v. Thames Board Mills* [1977] 3 All E.R. 677. See also *Home Office v. Harman* [1982] 1 All E.R. 532.

[68] [1979] 3 All E.R. 97.

it will not without the leave of the other party or of the arbitrator or order of the court use or disclose otherwise than for the purposes of the arbitration any document produced in pursuance of the order.

When a witness is asked to disclose confidential information

2–677 The mere fact that a witness has received information in confidence—whether in express confidence or in the implied confidence of a confidential relationship (*e.g.* between a surveyor and his client)—does not in law entitle the witness to refuse to disclose it in the course of court proceedings.[69] In some cases the private promise of confidentiality must yield to the general public interest.[70] For such a communication to be privileged from disclosure in the course of legal proceedings there must be, in addition to the confidential relationship, a substantial public interest in protecting the confidence. But different weight attaches to the conflicting considerations in arbitration as compared to proceedings in court. The fact that the arbitration is in private may make the consequences of disclosure less harmful. On the other hand, the public interest in a just result may be said to be less in the case of a private adjudication than in the case of an adjudication in court which is a matter of public concern.

2–678 In the authors' view, an arbitrator has no power to order a witness to produce a document in the witness's possession. He does have the power to order a *party* to do so, subject to the party's rights to raise legal objection such as privilege. If the party refuses, in the face of such an order, the arbitrator is thrown back on the various sanctions for dealing with an uncooperative party, and/or upon the remedy of drawing an adverse inference from this refusal.

Compelling a witness to answer

2–679 An arbitrator cannot compel a witness to answer a question. The power of a judge to order a witness to answer notwithstanding that he would thereby have to disclose information imparted to him in confidence is in theory enforceable by the exercise of the judge's power to imprison for contempt of court. It is very rare for a judge to insist upon a witness answering a question which the witness feels that he ought not in conscience to answer.[71] By contrast, an arbitrator has no power over a witness. Accordingly, if in an arbitration a witness feels that he would be breaking a confidence if he were to disclose it, it is open to him to refuse to answer; if he refuses, the cross-examining party's remedy—if any—lies in the courts.

2–680 The same applies to any attempt to compel a witness (even one attending under

[69] *D v. NSPCC* [1977] 1 All E.R. 589.

[70] *Per* Ackner L.J. in *Campbell v. Tameside MBC* [1982] 2 All E.R. at 796.

[71] See, *e.g.* the speech of Lord Simon in *D v. NSPCC* [1977] 1 All E.R. 589 and the judgment of the majority of the House of Lords in *British Steel Corporation v. Granada Television* [1981] 1 All E.R. 417.

subpoena) to disclose information which he considers it contrary to his interests to disclose. For example a surveyor witness may know that a particular property is about to be marketed and may be reluctant to let his rivals know that fact. His reluctance should be respected by the arbitrator, if only on the grounds that the arbitrator has no power to compel him to answer any particular question. A judge may have such power but the occasions on which he is likely to exercise it would be rare.

Can the award be made evidence in later proceedings?

The answer to this question appears to be "yes". The grounds on which documents are privileged from discovery are well established and they do not include so-called "confidentiality". So the mere fact that a party, or a witness, has contracted not to disclose a fact or a document will not necessarily override the duty to disclose where disclosure is needed to advance the public interest in the proper resolution of disputes.[72] **2–681**

Under section 34 of the Act, the arbitrator has power to decide whether any and if so which documents should be disclosed and produced by the parties. Whether he should order a party to produce an award notwithstanding an express or implied term prohibiting disclosure is a matter for his discretion. **2–682**

22. The Advocate in Arbitration

The role of the advocate in the adversarial system

Hitherto most English arbitration, like English litigation, has been conducted on the adversarial system. It has been for each party to carry out whatever investigation he thinks fit, to prepare his case as he thinks fit, to present it to tribunal, and to probe the case presented by his adversary. The primary function of the arbitrator is to weigh such material as is put before him. The primary function of the advocate is to persuade the arbitrator of the strength of a particular case and of the weakness of the opposing case. But in practice these demarcations are blurred. Although it is not his primary function, the arbitrator may, and **2–683**

[72] See *Shearson Lehman v. Maclaine Watson & Co.* [1989] 1 All E.R. 1056.

often does, suggest to the parties that an important point appears to have been overlooked, or an important piece of evidence is missing.[73]

2–684 The advocate in practice directs investigations that are to be made in preparing the case. The apparent exception to this proposition, arising from the separation in England of the functions of a solicitor and a barrister, is more apparent than real, for where the barrister does not direct the investigations from the beginning it is because the solicitor is experienced enough to be able to forecast what investigations the barrister would wish to have made. So the choice of advocate has important consequences as regards the substance of the case to be put forward, as well as the presentation of that case to the tribunal. The procedural freedom given in the new Act should encourage advocates to be prepared to depart from traditional adversarial court procedures and to find innovative procedural solutions which will save their clients time and money. Arbitrators, mindful of their duties under section 33 and their powers under such sections as 34 should be prepared to take the initiative and, in cases of procedural dispute to be bold in ordering new and cost effective procedural solutions.

The advocate's duty to the arbitrator

2–685 Whatever the procedure adopted some duties are overriding. Thus, an advocate appearing before a court has a duty never knowingly to be a party to deceiving the court.

2–686 It is, fortunately, hard to find examples of conduct which illustrate a breach. However, a barrister who called a police officer witness in plain clothes rather than in uniform and thus concealed the fact that the officer had been demoted was effectively misleading the court (in this case the judge and jury both).[74]

The knowing creation of such a misconception in the mind of the tribunal is a breach of the advocate's duty to the tribunal.

2–687 Such matters are to be distinguished from submissions as to the proper inference to be drawn from the evidence or the proper conclusion of law. Here, the advocate does not have to be of the view that the contention put forward is the correct contention. Indeed so to limit himself would be to attempt to arrogate to himself the role of the tribunal.

2–688 It has occasionally been suggested[75] that he owes no such duty other than to a court; so that the principle does not apply, for example, in arbitration. The suggestion is quite wrong. An arbitration tribunal, like a court, is engaged in trying to do justice between the parties who have agreed to submit their dispute to it. The machinery of justice is greatly weakened if the tribunal cannot, without checking, rely upon statements made to it by the advocate; or if the advocate

[73] See Lord Denning in *Jones v. National Coal Board* [1957] 2 All E.R. at 158; and the comment on that account made by Lord Devlin in "The Judge" at p. 61.

[74] See *Meek v. Fleming* [1961] 3 All E.R. 148 and now *Vernon v. Bosley (No. 2)* [1997] 1 All E.R. 614.

[75] See *Arbitration*, Vol. 55, No. 2, (May 1989), pp. 77–78.

treats the tribunal, or his opponent, or a witness, with discourtesy. All advocates—legal or lay—owe the same duty to all tribunals, and, as Lord Donaldson M.R.[76] has said:

> "Arbitrators must do their best to recognise and counter departures from the standards of representation which they are entitled to expect, as would a judge."

Advocacy in litigation and in arbitration

The particular differences between litigation and arbitration that affect the task of the advocate are that: **2–689**

(a) in domestic arbitration at least, the arbitrator will probably have been chosen by the parties (directly or through their choice of an appointing institution) for his expertise of some kind;
(b) the arbitrator will personally control the preparations for the hearing, or the assembly of information and arguments if there is not to be a hearing;
(c) in most domestic cases the arbitrator will not be a lawyer and he will prefer, if he can, to avoid having to decide issues of law;
(d) unless the arbitrator happens to be a barrister or retired judge the arbitrator will have less experience in absorbing oral evidence and oral argument than the average judge, and accordingly will gain far more assistance from written evidence and written argument, than would a judge;
(e) unless the arbitrator is a lawyer himself the arbitrator will have far more suspicion of lawyers, and far less understanding of how to get lawyer-advocates to help him in his task than a judge would have.

The task of the advocate

The function to be performed

In any arbitration each party, or someone on his behalf, has to decide what claim to make or (as the case may be) on what grounds a claim is to be resisted. In most cases one person is responsible on each side; and that person will be called "the advocate". The party himself, if an individual, may prepare and present his own case. He may employ an expert in the field, *e.g.* a structural engineer or quantity surveyor who will act as a lay advocate; or he may instruct a solicitor. If he does, the solicitor may conduct the case alone or (in England) instruct a barrister. Members of many other professions in England are entitled to direct **2–690**

[76] *Arbitration*, Vol. 55, No. 4, (November 1989), p. 228.

access to a barrister, without the interposition of a solicitor. But whoever is to prepare the case, or to conduct it, the work involved is substantially the same.

Investigation

2–691 The first step that has to be taken by someone minded to make a claim, or to resist one, is to ascertain the facts out of which the claim or the resistance arises. This may be clear from a file; or it may require the obtaining of further documents; or it may require inquiries of people who have dealt with the matter; or it may require expert opinion or investigation.

Identifying the issues

2–692 In most cases before the investigation has got very far the relevant facts will be found to have been buried in a mass of irrelevant material. The next stage, for a claimant, is to identify the facts which together found the claim (*e.g.* in a sale of goods claim, the contract of sale, and the delivery of the goods as required by the contract) or the defence (*e.g.* the description of the goods in the contract, and the failure of the goods to conform to that description). At this stage the issues may not have been positively identified. Which facts are agreed and which disputed may have to be gleaned from the discussions (oral or in correspondence) that have taken place. The investigations may not yet be complete so that neither the issues nor the facts relating to them are yet defined. If pleadings have to be delivered at this stage, each side will try to plead its case in as broad terms as possible, so that if the investigations produce new facts, those facts can be relied upon without any need to amend the pleadings. The tendency is for the points of claim to allege as much as possible in as few words and with as little detail as possible; for the points of defence to admit as little as possible; and for the issues apparent on the face of the pleadings to go far beyond the issues as they will ultimately be presented at a hearing.

The function of pleadings

2–693 If the pleading is not going to be read until the hearing begins it matters little that it does not convey to the mind of the judge or arbitrator a clear impression of a powerful case. But it should be standard practice for the arbitrator to study the pleadings closely. Indeed, if the arbitration is on documents only the pleadings may be the primary channel of communicating to him each party's case. In arbitration, therefore, more than in litigation the pleading is a vital part of the presentation of the case and shaping the pleading is an important part of the role of the advocate. This applies with even greater force if—as is suggested in paragraph 2–438, above—a Statement of Case from each party takes the place of the pleadings. At the end of the rival presentations on each issue, the arbitrator will have to choose between them. He will begin the process when he reads these initial presentations. To capture his mind at that stage and thereby to put on the opposing party the burden of making him change his (provisional) mind, is an important part of the role of the advocate.

Presentation

The presentation of the case may be documentary or oral or both. Even in the simple case where the contract and the file is sent to the arbitrator without even a letter setting out the party's case, it will assist the arbitrator if the critical clauses of the contract, or paragraphs in the correspondence or other documents, are flagged, and shown by highlighting and, if need be, cross-referenced. 2–694

The main object of the advocate should be simplicity. If the proposition put to the arbitrator is complex, he may not really grasp it at all, and if he does grasp it, its complexity may make him doubt its validity. The advocate must at every stage—and on his feet if necessary—simplify the concept and simplify the language, so that its clarity penetrates the mind of the arbitrator, and its logic captures his judgment. 2–695

Weeding out the "bad" points

Expert witnesses sometimes feel aggrieved at being told that they may not put forward views in whose validity they do not believe, whereas the advocate is free to do so. In so doing they confuse evidence with advocacy. On many points—of fact, of expert opinion, or of law—there are two tenable views. The advocate is often in the position that if he were the judge, he would reject the view that he is putting forward and adopt the other. But he is not the judge—he is the advocate, and his function is to put forward any view that he considers arguable and that advances his client's case. Indeed if appropriately instructed he must put forward views that he does not consider tenable. 2–696

What is a "tenable" argument is itself a matter of judgment. An appellate court not infrequently rejects the reasoning of the judge below as being not merely wrong but utterly untenable. And counsel often finds that an argument which he personally thinks weaker than the opposing argument is accepted by the tribunal and perhaps upheld on appeal. An advocate, unlike the expert witness, is under no obligation to express his own view. Indeed, it is unprofessional for him to do so, and the arbitrator should not ask him to do so. 2–697

Some advocates, alas, cannot tell an arguable point from a hopeless one. Others—fortunately fewer—can, but will still take a point believed to be hopeless in case by some miracle the tribunal thinks it good. It is bad advocacy to take a point, or advance an argument, which the advocate believes to be untenable. It is no part of the advocate's duty to do so unless specifically so instructed. 2–698

Getting the facts right

Most disputes turn, in the end, upon issues of fact. The first duty of the advocate is to recognise this point, and therefore to take meticulous care in collecting and collating the facts, and correlating them with the correspondence and other 2–699 external events. Whatever else the pleadings or statements of case may do, they should define and clarify the issues of fact. If it is thought that the opposing party cannot seriously be contending for an assertion of fact contained in his pleading, and if resolving the point sooner rather than later will save time and costs, various steps are open for achieving this. A request for further and better particulars is sometimes effective in highlighting the falseness of the assertion or denial. Notice to admit facts may be appropriate or, if an issue is crucial to the arbitration, it may even be appropriate for this issue to be determined (whether on documents or at a hearing) as a preliminary issue.

The choice of advocate

2–700 The case can be prepared and presented:

(a) by the party himself (or, in the case of a company or corporation by a director or employee of the party);
(b) if the dispute is a technical one, by an expert in the relevant field;
(c) if the arbitration agreement provides for two arbitrators and an umpire, and the arbitrators have failed to agree, by the party-appointed arbitrator;
(d) by a lawyer; he will usually be a barrister, but the distinction between solicitor and barrister is not important for present purposes.

2–701 There is no restriction upon who may appear as an advocate and moreover, a party (or director) appearing in person may have anyone he chooses to sit with him and help him. Where the amount involved is small there may be no practicable alternative.[77]

The party in person or a director or employee of a corporate party

2–702 The object of the exercise is to persuade the arbitrator that the case you are presenting is stronger than the opposing case. A cardinal element in this task is distinguishing between the strong points and the weak points in your case and in the other side's case. This is a matter which calls for the exercise of a dispassionate judgment. Few people can remain dispassionate about their own disputes. Hence the adage that a lawyer who acts for himself has a fool for a client.

The combined witness/advocate

2–703 In practice this means "the combined expert witness/advocate". There is a considerable degree of conflict between the role of the expert witness, and the role of the advocate. The role of the witness is to be objective; to tell the truth the whole truth and nothing but the truth, whether his evidence be given on oath or

[77] *cf.* (for magistrates' courts) *R v. Leicester City Justice* [1991] 3 All E.R. 935, C.A.

not. The role of the advocate is presentation—emphasising the good points, and minimising the bad ones. If the dispute is a straightforward technical dispute before an arbitrator who is himself an expert in the field, a hearing at which each party is represented by a combined expert witness/advocate is likely to be the most satisfactory way of resolving the issue, and is almost certain to be quicker and cheaper than any alternative procedure. The conflict in roles is there, but is relatively unimportant in a dispute of this kind. To the extent that the dispute is a complex one, or involves issues of fact, however, the conflict in roles becomes more prominent and the advantages of separating them more pronounced. In particular the role as an advocate weakens the objectivity of the evidence of the witness, and thereby lessens its weight.

There is the further disadvantage of combining the roles, that the opinion evidence of the expert witness will be tested for the first time at the hearing, by cross-examination or by questions from the arbitrator. If a weakness in it then emerges, it is almost always too late for anything to be done. A prime function of the lawyer-advocate is to probe the expert opinion at an early stage in the arbitration—indeed, if possible, before the arbitration has begun; so that if a weakness emerges, and cannot be cured, *e.g.* by further evidence or investigations, the dispute can be compromised before heavy costs are incurred.[78] This task is so important that even where a hearing is to be conducted without lawyers (*e.g.* under trade association rules which bar them) it is often well worth while to consult a lawyer experienced in such disputes to look for any defects that he can expose in the case intended to be presented. 2–704

The combined arbitrator/advocate

In practice the arbitrator concerned is usually an expert, qualified either professionally or by experience in a particular trade. The fact that the procedure has existed for so many years is evidence of its suitability for some types of dispute. It is suggested, however, that it tends to be used mainly where the dispute is a straightforward technical or trade dispute, or where speed is of paramount importance. 2–705

The lay advocate

Lawyers do not have a divine right, and far less a divine gift, of advocacy. Someone who is not a lawyer may act as advocate in arbitration if a party wishes him to. In practice he is likely to be an expert in the field in which the dispute arises and as such he starts with an initial advantage over the lawyer. Given a reasonable amount of experience in the preparation and conduct of cases in arbitration, there is no reason why he should not be an effective advocate. There are, however, few such.[79] 2–706

[78] See the illuminating (and entertaining) paper by John Anstey, FRICS, in *Arbitration*, Vol. 48, p. 276 (May 1983).

[79] See the interesting paper by Arthur O'Reilly in *Arbitration*, Vol. 48, p. 286 (May 1983).

2–707 In some types of case it is wholly sensible to be represented by a lay advocate. In quality disputes (whether in commodities, or shipbuilding, or construction industry) where the arbitrator is an expert in the field, representation by an expert in such cases is likely to be more effective and less expensive. Where the only issues in the case are issues of expert opinion, and are such that cross-examination of the opposing expert is unlikely to advance a party's case, representation can be left to the expert involved. Again, if for some reason the procedure being adopted is inquisitorial rather than adversarial, the advantages of representation by a professional advocate are diminished. Finally—though this is hardly a matter of choice—there are many cases where the client does not have enough funds to pay for a lawyer as well as an expert or where the amount in issue does not warrant the expense of employing one.

The lawyer advocate

2–708 The major benefit that lawyers can bring to the preparation and presentation of a case for arbitration lies in the identification of issues, and the marshalling of the facts relevant to those issues. The case may be one in which no issue of fact arises. But only a lawyer will know whether or not it raises an issue of law.

2–709 The second major contribution that the lawyer can make—and usually does, if he is consulted at a sufficiently early stage—is to uncover the weaknesses in his client's case, and the strengths of the opposing case. His expertise in this, coupled with his experience of fighting (and losing) many disputes in the past, attaches unrivalled weight to his advice as to whether, and when, to compromise. In many cases it is the lawyer's advice—amounting often to heavy pressure—that results in a compromise. This is a vital contribution to the dispute-resolution process, albeit that the arbitrator may never be appointed or, if he has been appointed, may know nothing of it.

2–710 Thirdly, the English tradition of cross-examination requires a skill or art that more than any other aspect of advocacy needs experience, so much so that in acquiring it a "lay" advocate ceases to be such—he will have become a professional.

Summary

2–711 We can do no better than quote the following:

> "In concluding this judgment I feel constrained to make some general observations about the conduct of this type of litigation. A feature which marks the professional in the field of litigation is the ability to explain the complex, to reduce apparent confusion to order and, above all, to identify the real issues, putting irrelevance to one side. To put it short, it is the function of the Bar to separate the wheat from the chaff. It is emphatically not its function to pour bag after bag of additional chaff into an already

overloaded machine.[80] The more extensive the facts and the more complex their inter-relationship may appear, the more important it is that this function should be competently performed. Again, traditionally the function of the pleadings is to identify the issues of ultimate fact. It is positively counter-productive for the pleadings to become a rag bag of evidentiary matter . . . the court is entitled to require of litigants who seek to be placed in this list, self-discipline and efficiency in the sense that they be prepared to isolate the real issues, avoid the dry gullies and present their cases expeditiously and clearly.''[81]

Advocacy in written representations

Principles are the same

The object of the advocate, and the methods that he should use to achieve them, **2–712**
are essentially the same whether or not his arguments are to be presented at a hearing. For his case to be understood it must be clear. For it to be readily absorbed it must be concise. For it to prevail its logic must be compelling.

Beginning the representation

A representation should begin by saying what it is, who is submitting it, and on **2–713**
whose behalf it is being submitted, *e.g.*:

> ''Submissions made on behalf of the Claimant by John James FRIBA in support of the claim for £8,750 set out in the Points of Claim dated 20 June 1986.''

or

> ''The following submissions are made on behalf of the Respondent by John James FRIBA in amplification of the Points of Defence dated 12 July 1986.''

Say what you are asking for

If the hearing or opening sentence has not told the arbitrator what the submission **2–714**
is asking him to do, say so next. In the first of the two beginnings given above it does. In the second it does not. It is irritating to have to look right through a document (or for that matter to listen to a long oral argument) before being told what the argument is addressed to. So a suitable second sentence would be:

> ''The Respondent says that nothing is due to the Claimant, for the following reasons.''

[80] One might say the same of the claims consultant!

[81] Connolly, J. *ANI v. John Holland Constructions*, Supreme Court of Queensland, May 1989.

The representation should be clear

2–715 Clarity and brevity are the foundations of an effective argument. Many written submissions give the impression of having been dictated at top speed by someone who has not made time to think them through beforehand or to revise them afterwards. Clarity of thought, or of expression, comes naturally to a tiny minority; the others have to work for it. Take the following extract from a report in *The Times* newspaper of court proceedings:

> "Mr John Rew told the court that he objected when Mr Paul Evans brought dogs to his kennels where he had housed a favourite three-legged Labrador called Bramble, which had recently died.
>
> He said that Mr Evans, whose cottage is on the estate he owns, had no rights on his land and that the action over the dogs had increased a frostiness in their relationship."

2–716 It usually pays to begin by writing out the heading of each stage of the argument, and marshalling them into logical order, before explaining each in turn. In many cases the headings can remain in the draft as cross-headings, so that the reader can if he wishes get an overall view of the reasoning by looking at the cross-headings. It often helps, too, for the cross headings to be grouped at the outset, to form a kind of Table of Contents.

The representation should be concise

2–717 Conciseness can be achieved in three ways. First, by eliminating altogether words that are unnecessary for the purpose of making a point. Secondly, by eliminating altogether points that do not advance or strengthen the argument. Thirdly, by relegating to an appendix or annexure material that is too important to be eliminated altogether, but of which a summary is sufficient for inclusion in the main body of the representation.

2–718 An essential tool in drafting written representations is a "blue pencil", of whatever colour; a tool with which to delete from the draft unnecessary words. Most first drafts will benefit from a revision whose object is to retain the meaning but to reduce the length.

The representation should be compelling

2–719 It has to be assumed that the opposing party will be submitting representations to the opposite effect. The object of each of the representations is to persuade the arbitrator that the case presented in it is stronger than the opposing case. If the representation is being submitted before the opposing representation has been seen, a judgment has to be made as to how far the opposing case should be answered in advance, and how far it can be left to be answered by way of reply.

The arbitrator: "duty" to the advocate

Whether the advocacy is oral or written, computers are likely to creep in—word processing, spread sheets or whatever. The advocate must remember that it was possible to conduct cases without them for years; and that they only justify this role if they assist the aim of arbitration. We again quote from Connolly J: 2–720

> "The parties have agreed that I should not assess damages in relation to any head of claim by either of them but should rather direct an enquiry. In retrospect, I regret having agreed to this. The action has already taken an unnecessary time to try and, if the assessment of damages is also assisted by computers, that too is likely to take an inordinate time . . . A great deal of time was taken up in the course of this action with computer assisted assessments of the delay caused by various events in the course of the work . . . I was solemnly assured by learned counsel on both sides that the problems raised in this action could not be resolved without resort to computer programs. This would seem to suggest that every judge and every arbitrator who has ever had to resolve a building dispute of this sort before the days of computers must have miscarried. It must be remembered that the computer will furnish its answer in faithful compliance with any constraints to which the program is subject, whether they be real or unreal. If engineering contracts which come before the courts are all to degenerate into series of attacks and counter-attacks on the computer programs, the time taken for their trial will steadily blow out, as occurred in this case, and this type of litigation will rapidly become unmanageable . . ."[82]

It is unfair to the parties and their advocates if the arbitrator does not do the work necessary to master the case before him. Thus, arbitrators must read the necessary documents, pleadings, witness statements and submissions. Arbitrators ought to take an active role in questioning the advocate on the salient features of the case. Arbitrators must apply themselves and demonstrate thereby that they are competent to perform the task with which they have been entrusted. This is particularly true if arbitrators take an active role at all stages and seek to define issues and identify relevant documents in evidence. The objectives of expedition and economy and ultimately of fairness will be defeated if arbitrators remain passive and are content to have advocates explain everything at length on the basis that the arbitrator knows little of the case and may understand even less. 2–721

[82] Connolly J. in *ANI v. John Holland Construction*, Supreme Court of Queensland, 1989.

23. The Roles of the Expert Witness

2–722 The role of the professional expert witness has become a matter of concern in both litigation and arbitration; see for example Chapter 13 of Lord Woolf's Final Report (1996). Too often expert reports are overtly partisan, sometimes couched in uncompromising terms highly critical of other experts and heavily influenced by the lawyers, often to the point where the report is little more than special pleading or partial advocacy. Experts are not infrequently subject to constraint and direction from those retaining them, to the point where open, impartial and scientific discussion with the other experts in the case is rendered difficult or impossible. The judge or arbitrator is hampered rather than helped in the search for opinion evidence upon which he can rely. Change is required if confidence in the proper use of expert testimony is to be encouraged.

2–723 The Royal Institution of Chartered Surveyors has published a Practice Statement and Guidance Notes for Surveyors acting as Expert Witnesses (January 1997). Though addressed to members of the RICS the guidance that it gives could usefully be studied by experts of all disciplines. In particular it defines the duties of an expert witness thus:

> "(i) The primary duty of the Expert Witness is to the Court or other Tribunal to whom his evidence is given.
> (ii) The duty is to be truthful as to fact, honest as to opinion and complete as to coverage as to relevant matters. The duty is the same whether or not the Expert is giving evidence in Court on oath, or to a Tribunal on oath or to a Tribunal not on oath.
> (iii) The Expert's evidence must be independent, objective and unbiased. In particular it must not be biased towards the party who is responsible for paying him. The evidence should be the same whoever is paying for it.
> (iv) The duty applies as much to the preparation of a Statement of Opinion intended to be used as part of written representations in an arbitration or elsewhere where oral evidence is not given, as to a statement intended to be used in a Hearing before a Court or other Tribunal."

The differences between negotiator, advocate, and expert witness

2–724 It is important at the outset to distinguish between three distinct roles: the negotiator, the witness and the advocate. The negotiator is known to be partisan. He is expected to make statements of fact, and although he should never make any statement that he knows to be false, he is expected to be "economical with the truth". The duty of the witness is to tell the truth, the whole truth and nothing but the truth, and that is the criterion by which all his evidence should be prepared. The advocate is not giving evidence and should not make statements of fact save those that he can reasonably expect to be common ground. His fundamental tasks are first, to identify the issues, and second, to present the evidence relevant to those issues in any way most likely to persuade the tribunal of the strength of his client's case and the weakness of the opposing case. It is not his duty—though it may be in his client's interest—to present a balanced case. It is not his duty to put before the tribunal all the facts of which he is aware. It is not improper for him, if he so wishes, to pick out points from the evidence that appear to support his case, and omit all mention of points that controvert his case. To do so will usually be counter-productive, for he will forfeit the tribunal's confidence and thereby destroy the force of any good points he wishes to put forward. However, it is not improper.

The change of roles

In many cases the expert is expected either to act as negotiator, or to produce a report which will assist the client in negotiations. If this were his only role, no difficulties would arise other than the problems of conscience common to all negotiators. Difficulties arise when he has to proceed to the role of expert witness, and the difficulties are compounded in the many cases in which he also acts as advocate (whether in written representations or at a hearing). **2–725**

The expert's duty to the tribunal

Duty to tell the truth

There are surprising differences of opinion between professional men as to the principles they should observe when preparing, and ultimately giving, evidence before a court or an arbitrator. It has been said that an expert witness is under no duty to bring out facts which do not advance the case that his client is putting forward; that that is the duty of the expert on the other side. Many rent review valuers take the view that, having regard to the margin of error inherent in any valuation, if the best estimate of rental value that anyone could make for a particular building is £10,000–£11,000 per annum it is wholly legitimate for the valuer to value the building at £10,000 per annum if instructed by the tenant and at £11,000 per annum if instructed by the landlord) putting forward different arguments and sometimes different evidence in each case. **2–726**

This view is misconceived. A witness who states in evidence (whether or not on oath is irrelevant) that his opinion of value is 100, when his opinion in truth is that the value is a figure between 100 and 110 as to which he cannot be more certain, is not telling the truth; he is shading the truth, presumably because he thinks it will advance his client's interests. It cannot be right in principle that two valuers who in truth agree (as they so often do) that the right answer is a figure between 100 and 120 as to which they cannot be more accurate, should give evidence, on different sides, one saying that his opinion is 100 and the other that his is 120. Of course while a case is being prepared, the expert owes **2–727** a duty to his client to assist by every proper means in the preparation of the case and, if so requested, in negotiation. But once the witness begins giving evidence (and this includes submitting a proof or report before a hearing, or submitting a report intended to be used in a documents-only arbitration, as well as the oral evidence given during a hearing) his duty to his client is no more than that he shall use a reasonable level of professional skill and care. Subject to that duty, he owes a duty to himself to tell the truth, the whole truth and nothing but the truth. He also owes a duty to the arbitrator to assist him to arrive at a just decision. No greater tribute can be paid to a professional man than to have it said of him that his opinion remains the same whoever is paying for it; see the RICS Practice Statement and Guidance Notes referred to in paragraph 2–723, above.

Consequences of breaching this duty

2–728 Failure to observe these principles brings discredit not only upon the professional man involved but also upon litigation and arbitration alike. Thus the Secretary of the British Medical Association has expressed views which the authors do not wholly share, but indicate the extent of responsible and informed concerns:[83]

> "These Rules (of evidence) were designed specifically to establish facts and to protect the constitutional rights of persons appearing as witnesses. But as far as expert (or opinion) evidence is concerned the system permits important evidence to be concealed because the right questions may not be asked of the evidence by judge or counsel, and the expert himself may be misled because important evidence which might modify his opinion may be withheld from him. It is not suggested that this happens intentionally.
>
> Where Anglo Saxon law went wrong was to try to resolve the dilemma by subjecting the outside experts to the rules of an adversary procedure. The result has inevitably been a battle of the experts fought within rules which were never designed to deal with conflicts of scientific opinion. This compares most unfavourably with the way in which expert evidence is handled under the Civil Law system operating in most other European countries. In the first place only those experts recognized by the courts as experts in the subject matter concerned are allowed to give evidence. They are not subjected to destructive examination, cross-examination and re-examination and the result is that the evidence received by the court is truly independent and impartial."

[83] "The influence of the law on clinical decisions affecting life and death" by J.D.J. Havard, M.A., M.D., LL.B. Barrister quoted in July 1983, *Journal of the British Academy of Forensic Sciences, Medicine Sciencc and the Law*, and reprinted in *Arbitration* (May 1984).

Disadvantages to the client
A desire to please one's client is altogether human. So is a desire to win an adversarial contest. But an expert who allows these desires to colour his evidence is more likely to harm his client's case than to help it. Once the proceedings reach a hearing, the arbitrator will above all else be looking for signs of this colouring. In some cases, no doubt, the expert's attempts to conceal it will succeed. But in many more cases it will fail, and in failing it will do great harm to the client's case. 2–729

Exaggeration as a counter to exaggeration
It is sometimes said, in defence of a less than dispassionate opinion, that if one party's expert is exaggerating in one direction, the other party's expert has no option but to exaggerate in the opposite direction. This reasoning may or may not be sound at the stage of negotiations. It has some force if the conflict is to be decided on documents only, so that the tribunal never has an opportunity of hearing and seeing the witness under cross-examination. But it is unsound when the conflict reaches a hearing. For it assumes that the tribunal will not be able to perceive the exaggeration. It should be remembered that an expert opinion usually carries weight of two different kinds; first, the factual evidence on which the opinion is based, and second, the opinion itself. Once the tribunal is satisfied that an expert is exaggerating to strengthen his client's case, it is likely to give no weight at all to this second—and more important—element in his evidence. 2–730

Harmonising the approaches of advocate and expert witness in settling the proof

It will be clear from what has been said in paragraph 2-722 that the approach of the advocate, and the approach of the expert witness are very different. The problem when counsel comes to "settle" (*i.e.* to finalise) the "proof" of the expert, that is to say the document which will be presented to the tribunal as his evidence in chief and that will be disclosed to the opposing side before the hearing, is of harmonising the two approaches. The position of the expert is clear. The proof, as finalised, must contain his opinion in all the shades of emphasis that he considers appropriate. If there is any difference of opinion as to what should or should not be contained in the proof, his opinion must prevail. If counsel proposes that some parts of the draft be omitted the expert should consider the matter and should not agree if the deletion would, in his opinion, change the balance of the opinion he has expressed. Likewise, if counsel suggests that something be added, it is for the expert to decide not only whether he can make the statements that counsel would like to see made, but also whether the addition would distort the balance of the evidence that he is putting forward. 2–731

The danger of accepting suggestions from the lawyers
Where an expert's view is founded on his professional instinct or judgment, he should be particularly wary of accepting from the lawyers' suggestions as to 2–732

reasoning which would support his conclusion. If an experienced professional man is looking at a problem in his field objectively, his gut or instinctive judgment upon it should carry weight even though he cannot explain the thought processes which produce it. But if, having formed a judgment in this way, he then tries to rationalise it by adopting reasoning which in cross-examination is shown to be unsound, the soundness of his original judgment is infected with the unsoundness of his ex post facto reasoning. That is not to say that he should always reject counsel's suggestions as to the possible reasoning; it is to say he should not accept them unless he has satisfied himself that they are right. If, at the core of cross-examination he is reduced to saying "well, this idea was really counsel's, and on reflection I don't think it was a good idea" then his evidence is thoroughly and perhaps fatally discredited.

Cross-examination by your own advocate

2–733 There is however another function that the advocate can usefully and properly perform. It is to cross-examine the expert on the expert's draft so as to expose illogicalities, inconsistencies, obscure expressions, and passages in which the witness has not accurately stated his view. The object is not that counsel should re-write the proof, but that the witness should re-write it so as to remove, so far as he properly can, the fault thus exposed. The process is as unobjectionable, indeed as beneficial, as the re-writing of the first draft of an article in the light of comments that have been made upon it by a friend of the author. If the process is taken further, so that the proof contains views that are those of the advocate rather than of the witness; or so that matters which the witness considers material are deleted for no other reason than that the advocate considers them inconvenient for his purpose, the process has gone too far and is objectionable. The final product must be that of the expert; it is he who in the end must be prepared to say on oath that his proof represents the truth, the whole truth and nothing but the truth.

2–734 In relation to any issue which turns upon expert evidence, this role of the advocate in exposing any weaknesses in the expert evidence is perhaps the most important single function that the advocate has to perform. In a trial involving such an issue the result is rarely a draw. What happens in practice is that in cross-examination greater weaknesses emerge in the evidence of one expert than of the other, and the issue is decided accordingly. The result for that client is a total loss on that issue; and that issue may be the only or the only important issue in the case. Moreover, not only has he lost the case and all the executive time that it has involved, but he may also have to pay all the costs of the litigation. On the other hand, if the advocate in the process of settling the proof can detect flaws in the expert evidence, a range of alternatives is available to the client. There is often time to cause further investigations to be made to fill a gap in the evidence. If the flaw is the result of the expert witness's lack of experience of a particular problem, an additional expert may be instructed. If no way can be found of curing the defect in the evidence, the client can decide to withdraw his claim, or defence, at a time when the costs are relatively low. Or, most important, he may be able to compromise. The remarks of Lord Denning in *Whitehouse v. Jordan*[84], therefore, should not be taken as indicating that the expert must prepare his proof as on some olympian height unsullied by contact with the lawyers. Provided that each respects the other's role, and provided that the final product truly represents the final view of the expert, the process of joint consultation which produces that product is wholly legitimate.

Experts appointed by the tribunal

By section 37 of the Act unless the parties otherwise agree, the tribunal may appoint experts or legal advisers or assessors on technical matters. This practice is commonplace in civil law arbitration and in civil law litigation. But its use is becoming more widespread in common law jurisdictions, both in the courts and in arbitration. Some institutional rules, for example those of the ICC and the LCIA, specifically authorise arbitrators to appoint experts. Much time and expense can be saved by such appointments, particularly in complex technical cases; and experts can fulfill an important role not merely in reporting their own views but in focusing the attention of the tribunal, the parties and the parties' own experts on the issues which need investigation and decision. Thus, tribunal appointed experts can often chair meetings of the parties' experts, draw up agreed lists of issues and record views whether of agreement or conflict. This can be particularly helpful in very complicated technical cases where, for example, there may be multi-faceted issues not only of a technical nature, but of the extent of delay and amount of cost flowing from an alleged act of negligence or breach of contract. But by section 37 of the Act the expert reports both to the arbitrator and to the parties. An arbitrator cannot appoint an expert or legal adviser merely to report to him. **2–735**

There are certain guidelines which arbitrators would do well to observe in appointing experts. First, it is essential that any expert appointed by the tribunal meet the same standards of competence and impartiality as the tribunal itself. Second, it is desirable though not necessary that the parties agree upon the identity of the proposed expert and there are various mechanisms such as short listing procedures which can help in this way. Third, the matters upon which expert advice or assistance is required, should be clearly set out in writing. The mandate must be clear. Fourth, the mandate must be confined to the expert's competence. To take an obvious example, the technical assessor should not be asked whether such and such an act or omission by a party, constitutes an act of negligence or breach of contract; for that is a matter of law for the arbitrators to decide. Fifth, the procedures followed by the expert which may often involve site inspections, or the examination of physical evidence, should be conducted *inter partes*. Sixth, the expert's report should be provided to the parties and they **2–736**

[84] [1980] 1 All E.R. 650.

must be given the opportunity to comment whether orally or in writing and, if appropriate, to question the expert upon it.

2–737 It is vitally important, particularly in heavy technical cases, that the arbitrator pays close attention to the role of the experts both party and tribunal appointed. The arbitrator should at all times remember that he is charged with rendering an enforceable award. He is more likely to be helped (particularly if he has himself specialist or expert knowledge) if he participates in the choice of experts—which kind of expert is required—and in the drafting of the issues which the experts ought to consider. The test is whether the opinion to be expressed is necessary or desirable evidence which the arbitrator ought to have to enable him to come to a fair and just decision. That test should be robustly applied so that the use of experts is kept within acceptable bounds of subject matter, time and cost.

2–738 The arbitrator may find the cost capping provisions of section 65 particularly helpful with respect to the cost of expert testimony. The arbitrator should be prepared to discuss preliminary opinions of the experts and to chair meetings of the experts on both sides with or without lawyers present. He cannot prohibit lawyers being present but he can control their oral contribution, exercising his inquisitorial powers under section 34, sub-section (2)(f) and (2)(g). The arbitrator should not hesitate to penalise in costs the party who, or whose expert, abuses the system.

24. Some Techniques of Judging

Experience of judging

2–739 In countries where the English common law system prevails, judges are recruited from practising lawyers of experience and standing. Before appointment the new judge will have seen and heard trials conducted by many hundreds of judges of various ranks. This aural tradition consciously or subconsciously shapes the way in which each new judge in turn functions. An arbitrator, or the chairman of a tribunal, if he has not been a lawyer with a litigation practice, has no such experience or tradition to rely on. He may have appeared as an advocate, or an expert witness, in a few arbitrations or trials. But he has nothing like the depth of experience of a litigation lawyer. If he is often appointed as arbitrator, he will in most cases learn from his experience—that is to say, from his own mistakes—and his performance of the judicial function will improve as he goes along. But that improvement is in spite of, and not because of, his training or lack of it.

No judge or arbitrator or tribunal can be a good one without good judgment. No book can teach judgment, and this book does not try, But some of the techniques, and of the approaches to problems of common occurrence can be discerned and recorded, so that those new to the task of judging may be aware of how some of their more experienced predecessors perform the judicial function. **2–740**

Advocates need to understand the judicial process

Every advocate—whether lawyer or layman—needs to understand the judicial function and its techniques. It is trite to say that a good advocate tries to see the strong points in his opponent's case. It is less often appreciated that a good advocate tries to understand the problems facing the tribunal, and to shape his case so that it is the more likely to be accepted. **2–741**

Arbitrator needs to use the advocates

One of the hallmarks of a good judge is the intelligent use of the advocates appearing before him. He will be quite willing to admit ignorance—or indeed to pretend it—in asking for their help. The ideal situation, where each advocate has perfectly appreciated and perfectly presented the strong points of his case, and all that the judge has to do is to accept the one case or the other and then to say why he prefers it to the other, occurs but rarely. **2–742**

Under the adversarial system, the procedure when the evidence has been concluded and final submissions begun has many similarities to decision-making by a committee. And even the formal distinction—that the advocates speak in turn and not intermittently—is in practice often blurred by legitimate interventions to concede points or to correct errors of reference. The experienced judge will often turn each final submission into a dialogue. The inexperienced judge lacks the confidence to do this, and remains mute. A critic of arbitration has said "Arbitrators open their mouths only to yawn". **2–743**

Interventions by the arbitrator

The problem of unequal representation

In a perfect world every advocate would wholly master and perfectly present his or his client's case. All that the judge or arbitrator would be left to do would be to weigh the rival arguments—on the facts or the law as the case might be—and decide which was the more convincing. In the real world the respective cases are often unequally prepared, or unequally presented, or both. In such cases if the arbitrator adheres to the pure theory of the adversarial system, and does not intervene, justice will not be done. Yet if he intervenes to help a party in person, or a party with an incompetent advocate, then from the viewpoint of the other party justice may not be seen to be done. The situation calls for the exercise of tact and judgment in equal measure, and is perhaps the severest test **2–744** of the ability of the arbitrator himself. The English Court of Appeal[85] has been known to tell counsel that his case was unlikely to succeed unless reshaped, and to adjourn the hearing to allow him to reshape it. In general the desirabililty of achieving a just result should outweigh the undesirability of appearing to help one party more than the other.

Deciding issues of fact

2–745 An experienced High Court judge once observed:

> "The courts are full of honest witnesses whose memories as time passes become more and more certain and less and less accurate."[86]

2–746 The task of deciding a conflict of fact between two honest witnesses is often one of the most difficult that an arbitrator has to attempt. Most counsel would agree that some judges, even after many years on the bench, do not do it well.[87] Some pointers as to what to look for and what to guard against may however be suggested.

(a) Human recollection being so notoriously frail, and the difficulty of distinguishing between the quick-witted liar and the slow-witted honest man being relatively great, avoid relying upon recollection if better evidence is available.

(b) What people did and wrote and said at the time of an event is less subject to vicissitudes of recollection than oral evidence given from memory, several years after the event. Contemporaneous documents are much more reliable, in general, than subsequent recollection of events.

(c) Faced with two conflicting subsequent accounts of an event, the arbitrator should choose that which seems to be inherently more likely than the other. For example, if after an impact between the front of a coach and the rear of a car at a traffic light the car driver says that the coach rolled forward and collided with the car, whereas the coach driver says that he had halted at the traffic lights and the car reversed into the front of his coach, but the evidence is that the road at the relevant point was sloping downwards, it is inherently more likely that the coach driver would have relaxed his pressure on the brake than that the car driver would have inadvertently engaged reverse—the one action is momentary inattention, the other a positive mistake.

[85] Presided over by Lord Denning.
[86] *Arbitration* (December 1982), p. 104.
[87] Though it may be more difficult to get agreement as to who they are.

Any tribunal should be on its guard against preferring the evidence of A to that of B because A is more experienced as a witness, or more articulate, or a more likeable person, than B. 2–747

Avoiding judgments based on demeanour
A very wise judge once said:[88] 2–748

> "I question whether the respect given to our findings of fact based on the demeanour of the witnesses is always deserved. I doubt my own ability, and sometimes that of other judges, to discern from a witness's demeanour, or the tone of his voice, whether he is telling the truth. He speaks hesitantly. Is that the mark of a cautious man, whose statements are for that reason to be respected, or is he taking time to fabricate? Is the emphatic witness putting on an act to deceive me, or is he speaking from the fullness of his heart, knowing that he is right? Is he likely to be more truthful if he looks me straight in the face than if he casts his eyes on the ground perhaps from shyness or a natural timidity? For my part I rely on these considerations as little as I can help.
>
> This is how I go about the business of finding facts. I start from the undisputed facts which both sides accept. I add to them such other facts as seem very likely to be true, as for example, those recorded in contemporary documents or spoken to by independent witnesses like the policeman giving evidence in a running down case about the marks on the road. I judge a witness to be unreliable if his evidence is, in any serious respect, inconsistent with these undisputed or indisputable facts, or of course if he contradicts himself on important points. I rely as little as possible on such deceptive matters as his demeanour. When I have done my best to separate the true from the false by these more or less objective tests. I say which story seems to me the more probable, the Plaintiff's or the Defendant's."

The phenomenon of identification

What we call "team spirit" is a strong human impulse. Many groups of people form it both at work and at leisure. Thus the crew of a ship; the employees of a small firm; the people working in a particular office; the passengers on a coach tour, often acquire a group identity akin to that of members of a sporting team in that if the group becomes involved in some kind of contest, each member wants the group to win. 2–749

In a simple dispute such as a road accident with few people involved on each side, *e.g.* the driver, two pedestrian witnesses, a solicitor and an advocate the 2–750

[88] MacKenna J. in a paper read at University College, Dublin, February 21, 1973, printed in Iv. Jur., Vol. IX (N.S.) 1, adopted by Lord Devlin in his book on *The Judge*.

contact between these individuals is too slight for any team spirit to develop to affect the evidence given at the hearing. But in a complex action or arbitration, repeated consultations are held between the expert witnesses, solicitors and counsel so that contact is maintained over months or even years, followed perhaps by days of proximity at the hearing before the evidence is reached. A group spirit tends to emerge that can colour the evidence. Not, save on very rare occasions, to the point of causing a witness to tell lies. But to the extent of making him qualify evidence which favours the adversary, that he had not previously qualified, and to omit qualifications prejudicial to the party calling him, which he had previously made. The tone of the evidence can change and with it the likely impact on the judge or arbitrator.

The intra-cranial jury room[89]

2–751 Cases in which a judge or arbitrator has difficulty in deciding a conflict of evidence are relatively unusual. Where the problem arises, however, it is often helpful for the arbitrator to define the issue, and to summarise the evidence and arguments on each side, as if summing up the case to an imaginary jury; and then to put himself in the position of the imaginary jury and decide which of the rival versions of the facts carries the more conviction to him.

The burden of proof

2–752 After these principles have been applied the arbitrator may feel sure where the truth lies; or at least he may be satisfied that one version of the facts is more probable than the other. If, try as he may, he finds it impossible to say which is more probable, he should ask himself upon whom lies the burden of proving that issue. In general, the burden lies upon the person who asserts the fact and this will appear on the face of the pleadings or Statements of Case. As a last resort—and it should indeed be a course of last resort—the arbitrator who considers that the evidence on each side is so evenly balanced that it is simply not possible to say that one is stronger than the other is entitled to say:

> "This fact is alleged by (the Claimant). The onus of satisfying me that it is more likely than not to have happened lies upon him. On the evidence I am not satisfied and I cannot find it as a fact."

Avoiding errors of calculation

2–753 Errors of calculation are probably more common than any other kind of factual error in a judgment or award. It often happens that an advocate will put before the arbitrator a calculation based on certain assumptions, and will indicate that if the arbitrator makes findings different from those assumed, the calculation

[89] The phrase was first used by Goulding J. in *O'May v. City of London Real Property Co.* [1979] 249 E.G. 1065, and has been adopted in several later cases.

will need to be changed. If the number of possible permutations is small, the arbitrator should ask the advocate to prepare or cause to be prepared, calculations made on the alternative assumptions. Where the number of permutations is too great to make this practicable, but before the end of the hearing he has a fairly clear idea of what findings he is likely to make on the issues before him he can before ending the hearing ask for the calculations to be made on the assumption that he makes those findings, making it clear that he has not yet made up his mind. Alternatively, in some cases it is practicable for him to issue an interim award stating his decision on the issues before him, but without making the calculations that flow from those decisions. He can then invite the parties either to agree the calculations or, if they cannot agree, to address submissions to him, either in writing or at a further hearing. This is not leaving the issue of ''how much'' to be decided by a third person; it is merely incorporating agreed figures, if they are in fact agreed, and reserving the right to decide them, if they are not agreed. Finally, if he is computer literate, the parties may be able to provide him with a spread sheet which, given the appropriate software, will do the work for him.

Deciding conflicts between expert witnesses

The types of conflict that arise

2–754 Most hearings involving conflicting expert evidence fall into one or more of three classes.

(a) The experts are proceeding upon different factual bases, and they have failed to identify the differences.
(b) The experts are proceeding upon the same factual basis, but one of them is (or both of them are) stretching his or their opinions in the hope of pleasing his or their clients.
(c) The experts are proceeding upon the same factual basis, but there is a genuine difference of expert opinion between them.

Class (a): The different conclusions derive from different facts

2–755 Conflicts of class (a) should not reach a hearing, because it is now almost invariable practice to direct that experts meet before the hearing to agree facts and narrow issues, and at that meeting differences as to the facts (often arising from differing instructions) should be identified and noted. If they do reach a hearing, they are resolved at a relatively early stage in it, leaving no residual problems for the arbitrator, and only the embarrassment for the expert of explaining to his client why the facts were not identified at a much earlier and much less costly, stage.

2–756 If a hearing is reached, the arbitrator should consider whether it would be advantageous to adjourn the hearing—whether for an hour, a day, a week or a month—for the experts to see whether they can agree the position on each of the two factual hypotheses express or implicit in their reports; leaving the arbitrator to decide (if the parties cannot agree) which of the two hypotheses is correct.

Class (b): One or both experts exaggerating

2–757 An arbitrator should where possible avoid basing his decision on the demeanour of the witness. Nor is the certainty with which an expert expresses an opinion a very reliable guide to its validity. Academic qualifications may be some guide, but most arbitrators would place greater reliance on relevant experience than on professional qualifications.

2–758 The authors suggest the following as the most important matters to consider:

(a) the integrity of the witness;
(b) whether he has lost his objectivity;
(c) the extent of his experience with problems of this kind;
(d) whether he has done his homework on the problem;
(e) and finally, whether his opinion would have been the same if he had been instructed by the other party?

Class (c): Genuine conflicts of opinion between experts

2–759 In the authors' experience, conflicts of class (c) occur infrequently where experts are instructed. When they do occur, an arbitrator of like discipline will usually be a more appropriate tribunal than a judge or lawyer if—and this is an important qualification—he can approach the evidence of the experts with an open mind. In major disputes a tribunal containing both lawyer and expert, or a lawyer sitting with an expert as assessor, is an appropriate tribunal.

Deciding issues of law

Not necessary to be a lawyer

2–760 The different procedures available for deciding a question of law have already been discussed. In *The Nema*[90] Lord Diplock said:

> "It is not self-evident that an arbitrator or arbitral tribunal chosen by the parties for his or their experience and knowledge of the commercial background and usages of the trade in which the dispute arises is less competent to ascertain the mutual intentions of the parties than a judge of the Commercial Court, a Court of Appeal of three Lords Justices or even an Appellate Committee of five Lords of Appeal in Ordinary. A lawyer nurtured in a jurisdiction that did not owe its origin to the common law of England would

[90] [1981] 2 All E.R. 1030.

not regard it as a question of law at all. This, I believe, was all that Lord Denning M.R. meant to convey by his vivid, if somewhat less than tactful, phrase[91] 'On such a clause, the arbitrator is just as likely to be right as the judge, probably more likely.' ''

Many arbitrations involve an issue as to what the words of a contract mean. Yet many arbitrators shy away from deciding such an issue because it is said to raise a question of law. They should not; they should take comfort from Lord Denning's view that on such an issue, the arbitrator who is himself experienced in dealing with contracts of that kind is just as likely to be right as the judge, probably more likely. The problem lies in clarifying the opposing arguments rather than in making a choice between them. It has to be said that trial advocates are skilled in formulating arguments that cloak the fundamental weakness of the proposition being advanced. Uncovering the weakness is a process in which judges and legal arbitrators are more skilled than lay arbitrators, and in a substantial case this is a justification for asking for the assistance of a legal adviser to hear the opposing arguments and advise the arbitrator on them; or for proposing that the point be resolved by one of the other methods discussed above. But where the point is one of the interpretation of a contract or other document, and for reasons of, *e.g.* cost, or delay one or both parties wish the arbitrator to decide the point himself, he should have no qualms about doing so. The following paragraphs suggest possible methods of proceeding. 2–761

Are the parties legally advised?

In most cases where a point of law is raised, at least one party is represented by a lawyer. If the other party is not represented, but the arbitrator considers that there is no substance in the point, so that he does not need to hear legal argument to the contrary, he can dismiss the point then and there, leaving the party who raised it to such remedy (if any) as he may obtain from the courts. If only one party is legally represented, and the point of law seems to be one of some difficulty, the arbitrator should ask the unrepresented party (if he has not previously had an opportunity of doing so) whether he wishes to take legal advice on the point, or to obtain legal representation; if necessary being given an adjournment, or an extension of time for complying with some outstanding preliminary direction, for the purpose. 2–762

Making the advocates work

The first step for the arbitrator to take when a point of law is raised is to ask the party raising it to formulate it in writing. The second is to make sure that he understands it; a dialogue with the advocate raising it is usually the best way 2–763

91 [1980] 3 All E.R. 117 at 124.

of achieving this. It is a safe working rule that if, after this dialogue, the arbitrator cannot understand the point, it is unlikely to be a sound one; for sound propositions of law or of interpretation are always capable of being expressed intelligibly. The Arbitrator should follow the same procedure with the opposing party. His dialogue with the advocate should as far as possible be constructive rather than destructive. The point may be stronger than the advocate putting it forward has hitherto appreciated, and the arbitrator's object should be to explore its strengths as well as its weaknesses. It will often happen—indeed, more often than not—that in the course of the dialogue with both advocates the formulation of the point will change. This is not necessarily a sign that the point is fundamentally unsound.

Immediate decision, or deferred

2–764 At this stage the arbitrator usually has a choice of courses.

(a) He can decide the point, and announce his decision, before the hearing proceeds further, *i.e.* either immediately, or after a short adjournment to give him time to consider the point.
(b) If the hearing has not otherwise concluded, he can continue with it and announce his decision at some later stage.
(c) He can reserve his decision on the point, to be incorporated in his award. But if the hearing is to continue without his decision on the point being known, evidence and submissions will have to be put before him to deal with either possible decision on the point that he has reserved.

2–765 In some cases course (c) will cause such inconvenience, delay and expense that it is much preferable for him to take course (a) or (b) above, and to adjourn the hearing for whatever time he needs for that purpose. But conversely, if there is a strong possibility that his decision on the point of law will be the subject of an appeal to the court, it may be preferable for him to make findings of fact on the alternative bases of the opposing propositions of law, so that if his decision on the point of law is reversed on appeal, the court will be able to give a final judgment without having to refer the matter back to him for further evidence and argument.

Reconsidering ways of deciding the point

2–766 It follows from what has just been said that a stage may be reached at which a difficult point of interpretation has to be decided, with the possibility or indeed probability that the unsuccessful party may seek leave to appeal on it. Since even the application for leave may cause significant delay and costs, the parties may wish to reconsider the alternative courses open to them namely, obtaining the opinion of a specialist lawyer or authorizing the arbitrator to take legal advice (from a lawyer nominated by the parties, if they wish); or asking the arbitrator to sit with a legal adviser to be nominated by them or in default of agreement to be chosen by the arbitrator. If the parties wish that the matter be decided by taking the opinion of a specialist lawyer to be binding on them the parties' lawyers must draft an agreed case to him. If they wish the arbitrator to decide the point after taking legal advice, he should ask the advocates to summarize in writing their respective submissions on the point; the note that he has taken may be insufficient for this purpose. If they wish the arbitrator to sit with a legal adviser, the hearing should be arranged accordingly, and when the submissions on the point have been concluded the arbitrator and the legal adviser should retire to reach a conclusion. The decision should be that of the arbitrator; if he and the legal adviser disagree, the view of the arbitrator will prevail. But in practice this will be very rare.

Disputes as to the admissibility of evidence

In the past lay arbitrators sometimes faced special difficulties when a question was raised as to the admissibility of evidence. The problem is essentially a practical one, because an objection as to admissibility can be raised without warning during the course of the hearing. The Act has reduced considerably the scope for challenges on admissibility and arbitrators should now only be concerned with questions of relevance, weight and privilege. The way in which an arbitrator should deal with matters of this kind is fully discussed in paragraphs 2–488 *et seq.* 2–767

25. The Award

Requirements with respect to the form of the award

First, the parties may agree upon the form of the award[92] and the incorporation of institutional rules such as ICC, LCIA, or AAA, will determine the form which the award must take. 2–768

Secondly, in the absence of agreement as to form, it is now mandatory under the Act for the award to be signed by all the arbitrators or all those assenting to 2–769

[92] s.53(2).

it.[93] Unless it is an agreed award or the parties have agreed to dispense with reasons, the award must also be reasoned.[94]

2–770 This provision represents a change in English law, and was made first, because it was thought desirable to follow the UNCITRAL Model Law and secondly, because, it is considered to be a basic rule of justice that those charged with making a binding decision affecting the rights and obligations of others, should (unless those others agree) explain the reasons for making that decision.

2–771 The award should state the seat of the arbitration[95] and the date when it was made. ''Seat'' is not necessarily the same as the place where the award was made. As section 3 of the Act makes clear, ''seat'' means the juridical seat of the arbitration, it being understood that hearings or, for example, the deliberations of the arbitrators may take place elsewhere. This is particularly true in international cases where it is commonplace for witnesses to be heard in different jurisdictions and where the arbitrators themselves almost certainly come from different jurisdictions and may meet, deliberate and sign the award in a place quite different from the seat. Section 53 of the Act provides that failing agreement to the contrary) where the seat of the arbitration is in England and Northern Ireland any award in the proceedings should be treated as made there, regardless of where it was signed, despatched or delivered to any of the parties.

2–772 The tribunal (again in the absence of agreement to the contrary) is given powers to decide what is to be taken to be the date[96] upon which the award is made, and in the absence of such decision, the date of the award is to be the date on which it is signed by the arbitrator or, where one or more arbitrators sign the award, by the last of them.[97]

2–773 The parties may decide upon the requirements as to notification of the award to the parties[98] and, failing agreement, the award should be notified by service on them of copies of the award.[99] This should be done without delay after the award is made. It will still be possible for arbitrators to require full payment of their fees and expenses before delivery of the award to the parties.[1]

2–774 It is open to the parties to agree upon the power of the tribunal to correct an award or make an additional award[2] and, in the absence of agreement to the contrary, the tribunal may on its own initiative or on that of a party, correct any clerical mistake or error arising from an accidental slip or omission, or clarify or remove any ambiguity in the award, or make an additional award on a matter presented to the tribunal but omitted from the award.[3]

93 s.53(3).
94 s.53(4).
95 s.53(5).
96 s.54(1).
97 s.54(2).
98 s.55(1).
99 s.55(2).
1 s.55(3).
2 s.57(1).
3 s.57(3).

Substantive requirements

The award must be certain

It is preferable, though it may not be legally essential, that the award be certain on the face of it. Thus "I award the buyers £5 per ton" may be an enforceable award, if it is not disputed that the tonnage was 1,000; and an award that "I award that the rent payable as from June 24, 1984, be increased by 10 per cent over that previously payable" may be valid if there is no dispute as to what rent was previously payable. But an award in such a form is not immediately enforceable; for example, it probably cannot be enforced by execution as if it were an award of a stated sum of money. So it is greatly preferable that the award should say "I award the buyers £5,000" or "I award that the rent as from March 25, 1991, be £11,000 per annum". In short, if the award is of a money sum, state the sum rather than stating a method by which it can be calculated. If for some reason a figure which is essential to the calculation of the amount to be awarded has not been put before the arbitrator he should ask the parties to agree it and should if necessary reconvene the hearing so that the figure can be ascertained and so that he can award a specified amount. **2–775**

Interim or final

The award should be final unless the arbitrator has decided to issue an interim award, in which case he should state that the award is an interim one and should expressly reserve to himself all matters not determined by the award. As to the power to make interim awards see paragraph 2–410, above. **2–776**

When recitals are desirable

It is common for an award to recite: **2–777**

(a) the arbitration agreement;
(b) insofar as that agreement does not plainly identify it, the particular dispute referred to the arbitrator;
(c) the method of appointment;
(d) any special provisions of the appointment;
(e) the fact (if it be such) that there has been a hearing; alternatively, the fact that the parties agreed that the procedure should be on documents only, without a hearing.

In some cases these details are important; for example, if the award may need to be enforced through a foreign court, or if the award may bind successors in title to a party, as in the case of an award under a lease. But the longer the recitals, the more chance is given to the losing party of finding something wrong with them, or some inconsistency between the recitals and the substance of the award. It is particularly important that there be no internal inconsistency in an **2–778** award. So the recitals should be kept short. Indeed in many cases—particularly when a reasoned award is not required, and enforcement outside England most improbable, and the award merely awards a money sum with or without an order as to interest and costs—it may be sufficient to confine them to a simple statement of the nature of the dispute and the contract under which it arises.

When reasons should be given

2–779 The parties may agree that instead of giving a reasoned award as the Act requires the arbitrator shall give an award which does not contain reasons but shall accompany it by a statement of reasons given in confidence. Where they so agree they are precluded by their agreement from referring to the reasons on any application to the court; although of course it is always open to them to make a new agreement waiving the right to restrict the use of the reasons. Even where the parties do not expressly agree, there may be an implied agreement between them to follow the usual practice of a particular trade or type of arbitration, for example the usual practice of London Maritime Arbitrators to give reasons in this form.[4]

2–780 There are circumstances in which the overriding public interest requires that, notwithstanding the private contract of the parties that they will treat such reasons confidentially, still they may be disclosed to the court. For example, if the reasons extend to misconduct of such a nature that it ought in the public interest to be disclosed to one who had a proper interest to receive it, that interest might override the implied obligation not to disclose the reasons.[5]

Reasons for part only of the award

2–781 Where several issues have to be decided, the parties may want a reasoned award on some and an award without reasons on others. In particular, where there is an issue of law and one or more issues of fact, the parties may be content with findings of fact without reasons, but may wish a reasoned award on the question of law so that they may consider seeking leave to appeal to the court. If the parties agree upon what they want, the arbitrator should comply. If they do not agree, the arbitrator must determine the matter himself, giving reasons.

The discipline of reasons

2–782 Even if the award is to be given without reasons, the formulation of reasons is a powerful discipline. In a surprising proportion of cases the analysis involved in formulating reasons leads a judge or arbitrator to change his initial view as

[4] See *The Montan* [1984] 1 Lloyd's Rep. 389, at 393 and *The Ross Isle* [1982] 2 Lloyd's Rep. 589, at 593.

[5] See *The Montan*, *ibid.* at 393, citing Lord Denning M.R. in *Initial Services v. Putterill* [1967] 3 All E.R. 148.

to what the result should be. Many experienced arbitrators sketch out their reasons even where they are not to be published, and it is suggested that this is a practice well worth following.

Drafting a reasoned award

In *Bremer Handelsgesellschaft v. Westzucker (No. 2)*[6] Donaldson L.J. said speaking of the 1979 Act (but it is submitted that his comments are equally applicable to the 1996 Act): **2–783**

> "Yet another feature of the old special case procedure which made for delay was the form of the award. This was necessarily stylised, being divided into four parts—preamble, findings of fact, submissions of the parties and conclusions. It was not something which most arbitrators felt that they could draft without professional assistance and those who provided such assistance had other clients and commitments to consider. This produced still further delay.
>
> It is of the greatest importance that trade arbitrators working under the 1979 Act should realise that their whole approach should now be different. At the end of the hearing they will be in a position to give a decision and the reasons for that decision. They should do so at the earliest possible moment. The parties will have made their submissions as to what actually happened and what is the result in terms of their respective rights and liabilities. All this will be fresh in the arbitrators' minds and there will be no need for further written submissions by the parties. No particular form of award is required. Certainly no one wants a formal 'Special Case'. All that is necessary is that the arbitrators should set out what, on their view of the evidence, did or did not happen and should explain succinctly why, in the light of what happened, they have reached their decision and what that decision is. This is all that is meant by a 'reasoned award'."

Suggested structure of a short reasoned award

A. The arbitration agreement: date and parties (usually the parties to the arbitration). **2–784**

B. Date and method of appointment of the arbitrator(s).

C. The procedure adopted (documents only; or if hearing, give the dates)

D. The issues.

E. First issue of fact: I find as a fact that . . . because the evidence of Mr X was more closely supported by the contemporaneous documents than that of Mr Y or I preferred the evidence of Mr Z to that of Mr A; or as appropriate.

F. First issue of law:

[6] [1981] 2 Lloyd's Rep. 130.

Argument for Claimant ....
Argument for Respondent ....
I prefer the case for the ....because
(1) ....
(2) ....
I therefore find for the ....on this issue

G. Second Issue: (continue as first)

I therefore find for the ....on this issue
H. I therefore determine and award ....
with interest at per cent from to [the date of this award or as the case may be]
J. (i) This award is final as to all matters except costs.

(ii) If either party wishes to make any representations to me as to costs, it should send them to me, and to the other party, by noon of ....
If either party wishes to make any representations in answer to the other party's representations, it should send them to me and to the other party by noon on .. ..Thereafter I will make my final award.

ALTERNATIVELY

K. I AWARD AND DETERMINE that the .... shall pay to the .... the costs of this arbitration to be taxed (if not agreed) [by me] OR [in the High Court]

Date: Signature:

2–785 Another possible course is to set out the reasons in narrative form in a Schedule to the award. Drafting suggestions relevant to awards will be found in Appendix 1, below.

Correcting accidental slips

2–786 Section 57 of the Act gives the arbitrator power to correct typing or equivalent errors; errors of calculation; errors of description; and generally any error that has resulted from a "mental lapse".[7] But it does not give him power to change his mind; that is, to change anything in the award to which he addressed his mind before writing.[8] There are time limits of 28 and 56 days respectively for the making of corrections in arbitral awards.

2–787 Thus, sections 52 to 57 establish a simple and comprehensive regime for the form of the award. The object is to avoid the difficulties produced by cases such

[7] See *The Montan* [1985] 1 Lloyd's Rep. 189, at 198, *per* Sir Roger Ormrod.
[8] *R v. Cripps* [1984] 2 All E.R. 705.

as *Hiscox v. Outhwaite*[9] and to make it more difficult for awards to be challenged or their effect distorted by highly technical and often unmeritorious arguments on form.

Estoppel arising out of an award

The doctrine of estoppel by judgment

It is a principle of English law (known as the principle of *res judicata*) that there should be an end to litigation, so that no one should be harassed twice for the same cause.[10] Thus where a court of competent jurisdiction has made a final and conclusive decision on the merits of an issue between two parties, each party is "estopped" (*i.e.* precluded) from litigating the same issue again against the other in subsequent proceedings.[11] **2–788**

By section 58 of the Act the award is binding on the parties and any party claiming through or under them, unless a contrary intention is expressed. A decision by an arbitrator on the merits of an issue referred to him for determination, in respect of which he has jurisdiction, is for this purpose equivalent to a decision by a court of competent jurisdiction. Accordingly it will prevent the parties to the arbitration from re-opening the same issue in subsequent proceedings whether in court or before another arbitrator.[12] **2–789**

Cause of action estoppel and issue estoppel

Where a cause of action raised by a claimant has been conclusively determined in earlier proceedings (for example, where the claimant is suing for the same debt, or for damages for the same breach of contract) he is estopped by the previous decision from pursuing it, save where there has been fraud or collusion. This is known as a "cause of action estoppel". **2–790**

Different considerations arise where a new cause of action is raised between the same parties, but one of them wishes to rely in support of his claim or defence on an issue of law or fact which also formed part of his claim or defence in the earlier proceedings but which was decided, expressly or by necessary implication, against him. In those circumstances, unless there are special or exceptional circumstances which make it just that he should be allowed to raise the issue, he will be estopped from raising it. This is known as "issue estoppel". In *Arnold v. National Westminster Bank*[13] a judge of the Chancery Division in 1984 decided an issue of interpretation of the rent review provisions of a lease adversely to the tenant, and refused leave to appeal. Subsequent decisions of the **2–791**

[9] [1992] 1 A.C. 562.

[10] See the speech of Lord Upjohn in *Carl-Zeiss v. Rayner & Keeler Ltd (No. 2)* [1966] 2 All E.R. 536, at 572.

[11] See the speech of Lord Brandon in *DSV Sile-und-Verwaltungsgesellschaft mbH v. Owners of the Sennar, The Sennar* [1985] 2 All E.R. 104, at 110.

[12] *Fidelitas Shipping Company v. V.O. Exportchleb* [1986] 2 All E.R. 4.

[13] [1991] 3 All E.R. 41, HL.

High Court and the Court of Appeal in other cases held that that decision was "plainly wrong". In 1988 the tenant wished to raise, in respect of a later rent review under the same lease, the same issue of interpretation. It was held that the tenant should be permitted to do so.

Raising a point not argued in the earlier proceedings

2–792 Where a party could and should have raised a point in the earlier proceedings, but through negligence, inadvertence or accident failed to do so, he will not be allowed to raise it in later proceedings, unless there are special circumstances making it just that he should do so.[14]

26. Interest

Claims for interest

2–793 A claim for interest may come before an arbitrator in one of three situations:

Case 1: Where a debt has been paid before the arbitration commenced, and the claimant now seeks interest from the date the debt arose to the date it was paid.

Case 2: Where a debt is paid after the date it became due, and after the arbitration in which it is claimed commenced, but before the award.

Case 3: Where a debt remains unpaid at the date of the award.

Arbitrator's power to award interest

2–794 The award of interest is now governed by section 49 of the Act which establishes a regime under which arbitrators may award simple or compound interest. Thus, section 49 provides as follows:

"(1) The parties are free to agree on the powers of the tribunal as regards the award of interest.

(2) Unless otherwise agreed by the parties the following provisions apply.

(3) The tribunal may award simple or compound interest from such dates,

[14] *ibid. per* Dillon L.J. [1950] 1 All E.R. 535; Staughton L.J. at 541; Mann L.J. at 553.

at such rates and with such rests as it considers meets the justice of the case—

(a) on the whole or part of any amount awarded by the tribunal, in respect of any period up to the date of the award;

(b) on the whole or part of any amount claimed in the arbitration and outstanding at the commencement of the arbitral proceedings but paid before the award was made, in respect of any period up to the date of payment.

(4) The tribunal may award simple or compound interest from the date of the award (or any later date) until payment, at such rates and with such rests as it considers meets the justice of the case, on the outstanding amount of any award (including any award of interest under subsection (3) and any award as to costs).

(5) reference in this section to an amount awarded by the tribunal includes an amount payable in consequence of a declaratory award by the tribunal.

(6) The above provisions do not affect any other power of the tribunal to award interest.''

Debt paid before arbitration commenced

No power under the 1996 Act to award interest on money paid before arbitration commenced

If the respondent paid any money due to the claimant, or damages, before the arbitration commenced, the arbitrator has no statutory power to award interest on the sum paid; such interest is outside the scope of section 49(3). **2–795**

Interest may be recoverable as damages for breach of contract

Commercial agreements of all descriptions commonly require the payment of money on a particular day, or within a specified period after the happening of an event. Failure to pay on time is therefore a breach of contract. Neither arbitrators nor the courts have any power to award general damages for late payment of money due under a contract,[15] but interest may be recoverable as special damages. Special damage for this purpose is damage of a kind which, by reason of facts known to both parties at the time of making the contract, might reasonably be expected to be the consequence of a delay in payment. Thus in *Wadsworth v. Lydall*[16] the defendant knew, when he entered into a partnership dissolution agreement with the plaintiff under which the plaintiff had to vacate his home, that the plaintiff would probably be buying another property and using, to pay for it, the money that the defendant had promised to pay under the **2–796**

[15] *The Pintada* [1984] 2 All E.R. 733, HL.

[16] [1981] 1 All E.R. 401, approved in *The Pintada* above, at n. 315.

agreement. It was held that the plaintiff could recover both the interest that he had to pay to his vendor for delayed completion, and mortgage costs that he had to incur because of the delay.

Debt unpaid at commencement of arbitration

Payment before award

2–797 If the respondent pays the whole or any part of the sum claimed by the claimant after the arbitration has commenced but before the award, the arbitrator has a discretion to award interest under section 49(3)(b) of the Act.

Interest on sum awarded

2–798 Similarly, in addition to any other powers, the arbitrator may award interest on any sum awarded by him under section 49(4) of the Act.

Exercising the discretion to award interest

2–799 The object of an award of interest is not to penalise the party ordered to pay it. It is to compensate the successful claimant for being kept out of his money between the date it ought to have been paid, and the date of payment or the award itself (The right to interest from the date of award is governed by section 49(4) of the Act). So the general principle is that interest ought to be ordered unless there is good reason for not doing so; and if there is such a reason it should be stated in the award. Even delay by the claimant in bringing the claim is not of itself sufficient ground for refusing to award interest, unless the delay is both exceptional and inexcusable.[17]

2–800 Exercising the discretion not to award interest up to the date of the award would obviously be justified if payment of interest would result in the claimant being compensated twice over. Thus if, in a claim for damages for faulty construction of a building, the arbitrator awards damages based on the current cost of rectification[18] it would be inappropriate to award interest on those damages in respect of any period before the date of the award unless the work has actually been executed prior to the award.

Interest from date of award

2–801 Section 49(4) of the Act provides that the tribunal may award interest from the date of the award, or any later date, until payment. This can be at such rates and with such rests as the tribunal considers ''meets the justice of the case''.

[17] *Panchand v. Pagnan and Fontelli* [1974] 1 Lloyd's Rep. 394.
[18] As in *Dodd v. Canterbury City Council* [1980] 1 All E.R. 928.

The rate of interest where interest is awarded by the arbitrator

Where the arbitrator makes an award of interest under section 49, the rate of interest is in his discretion. The object is not to penalise the debtor but to compensate the creditor for being kept out of his money. Thus, if the creditors are trustees who, if they had been paid, would have left the money on deposit, the relevant deposit rate would be appropriate. Likewise, if the creditor is a business man who, if paid, would have reduced a bank overdraft carrying a high rate, the relevant overdraft rate might be appropriate.[19] **2–802**

Simple or compound interest?

The question whether to award simple or compound interest is one of discretion. In exercising the discretion, the arbitrator should bear firmly in mind the object of awarding interest. If the applicant can make out a case that compound interest is the only way he can be put in the position he would have been in if payment due to him had been made on time, then he should have compound interest. Thus, for example, if the applicant has had to borrow money from a bank and pay compound interest, an award by the arbitrator of compound interest would be justified. **2–803**

27. Costs

Statutory provisions

Sections 59 to 65 inclusive of the Act establish a regime for the award of costs in and of the arbitration. Costs are defined by section 59 as meaning the arbitrator's fees and expenses, the fees and expenses of any arbitral institution concerned and the legal and other costs of the parties. By section 60 it is open to the party to make an agreement that the party pay costs in any event but such an agreement is invalid unless it is made after the dispute has arisen. **2–804**

In the absence of agreement to the contrary, by section 61 costs must follow the event save where it appears to be tribunal that this would not be appropriate in relation to the whole or part of the costs. While this is easy to state, plenty of cases exist to show that determining the "event" is not straightforward. A tribunal would be wise, in any but the most straightforward case, to invite suc- **2–805**

[19] See the judgment of Forbes J. in *Tate & Lyle Food & Distribution Limited v. GLC* [1981] All E.R. 716.

cinct submissions, after issuing an award on all matters save costs, as to what the event is.

Capping the costs

2–806 The parties may agree as to what costs are recoverable and may agree, for example, to place a cap or ceiling on recoverable costs. The parties should be encouraged to do so. Unless the parties have agreed to exclude this power the arbitrator has the power under section 65 of his own motion to place a cap or ceiling on recoverable costs and to do so for parts of the proceedings as well as the whole. Moreover, even if the arbitrator places no ceiling on reasonable costs pursuant to section 65, and on the basis that the amount of costs recoverable should be proportionate to the amount in dispute, he can under section 63(3) limit recoverable costs to a sum or sums which the tribunal thinks appropriate. If the arbitrator does so, then he must specify the basis upon which he has acted[20] and the items of recoverable costs and the amount referable to each.[21]

2–807 These are new cost provisions and are potentially of great importance. First, if they are used properly, they should enable the balance which is now tilted in favour of the party with a deeper pocket to be redressed. Secondly, the new provisions should enable arbitrators to introduce some discipline in expenditure on the conduct of arbitration, so that the costs do not get wholly disproportionate to the amount in issue. There is great scope for the exercise of informed common sense by arbitrators when dealing with costs. It is quite absurd and brings arbitration into great disrepute that a claim, for example, in a construction industry dispute about £1 million, may cost more to arbitrate. Many of the procedural devices and practices discussed elsewhere in this book should help to reduce costs substantially, but there must be the sanction that the parties should be subject to ceilings on recoverable costs. As is made clear in paragraph 272 of the Report of the DAC:

> "It gives the tribunal power to limit in advance the amount of recoverable costs. We consider that such a power, properly used, could prove to be extremely valuable as an aid to reducing unnecessary expenditure. It also represents a facet of the duty of the tribunal as set out in Clause 34. The Clause enables the tribunal to put a ceiling on the costs, so that while a party can continue to spend as much as it likes on an arbitration it will not be able to recover more than the ceiling limit from the other party. This will have the added virtue of discouraging those who wish to use their financial muscle to intimidate their opponents into giving up through fear

[20] s.63(3)(a).
[21] s.63(3)(b).

that by going on they might be subject to a costs order which they could not sustain.''

Obviously any cap must apply to both parties. Equally obviously, the arbitrator must retain the power to vary or renew the cap for good cause shown. Finally, a cap may work injustice where one party's representatives are working on a contingent fee basis, related to the amount of the claim. When the arbitrator knows or believes that this is or may be the case, he must carefully review the pros and cons of a cap. 2–808

Principles to be applied in exercising a discretion as to costs

Sources of the discretion

Order 62 of the Rules of the Supreme Court[22] applies to the costs of an arbitration taxable in the High Court. By Order 62, rules 2(2) and 3(2) no party is entitled to recover any costs of an arbitration save by an award of the arbitrator. By section 61 of the Act, costs are in the discretion of the arbitrator. But although the discretion is wide, it is a judicial discretion and must be exercised according to rules of reason and justice, not according to the private opinion of the arbitrator, or from notions of benevolence or of sympathy. 2–809

The starting point

Costs follow the event: 2–810

> ''There is a settled practice of the courts that in the absence of special circumstances a successful litigant should receive his costs, and that it is necessary to show some grounds for exercising the discretion of refusing an order which would give them to him, and the discretion must be judicially exercised. Those words 'judicially exercised' are always somewhat difficult to apply, but they mean that the arbitrator must not act capriciously and must, if he is going to exercise his discretion (to depart from the usual practice), show a reason connected with the case and one which the court can see is a proper reason.''[23]

In most litigation or arbitration, the claimant claims a sum of money, whether liquidated or unliquidated. If he recovers the whole or a substantial part of what he claims, he has ''won''. If he does not, he has ''lost''. Applying the general principle that ''costs follow the event'', the ''event'' is that the claimant or the respondent ''wins''. If the claimant succeeds, the respondent is ordered to pay 2–811

[22] As substituted by S.I. 1986, No. 632 with the effect April 18, 1986.
[23] Lord Goddard L.C.J. in *Lewis v. Haverfordwest Rural District Council* [1953] 2 All E.R. 1599.

the costs of the arbitration; if the claimant fails, the claimant is ordered to pay the costs of the arbitration.[24]

Refusing costs to a successful party

2–812 As a general rule, a wholly successful party ought to be awarded his costs unless there is evidence that he:

(a) has done something connected with the arbitration calculated to cause unnecessary disputation and expense; or
(b) has done some wrongful act in the course of the transaction out of which the arbitration arises; or
(c) has acted unreasonably and oppressively.

Where a party is partly successful

2–813 Where the claim is for a money sum, and there is no offer from the defendant (whether open or in a Calderbank offer) and the claimant recovers a substantial sum, he may be said to have "won" notwithstanding that he recovers less than he claimed, for he had to pursue his claim in order to recover anything. So the mere fact that a claimant recovers less than he claimed does not justify a departure from the general rule that a "successful" party is entitled to his costs. If the costs would have been significantly less had the claim been limited to the amount awarded, or if the reduction results from the claimant losing upon an issue which substantially increased the costs, it is open to the arbitrator to award the claimant part only of his costs. If the claimant succeeds as to a relatively small amount, and on a basis quite different from that upon which the arbitration was commenced, the arbitrator may decline to award him any costs.

Misconduct by witness or advocate

2–814 The fact that a witness may have exaggerated, or even lied, or that an advocate has been discourteous, is not a ground for depriving a party of his costs. But if the party himself has exaggerated or lied, or has connived in lying or exaggeration by a witness, that would be misconduct and could justify a refusal to award him costs; the more so if the lie or exaggeration is the real cause of the dispute.

Costs where there is a counterclaim

2–815 If there is a claim and counterclaim, the one being set off against the other, then:

(a) if the claim and counterclaim are wholly or substantially independent

[24] s.61(2).

of each other, it may be appropriate to consider each separately and to make a separate order on each, *e.g.* claimant to have the costs of the claim; respondent to have [half of] the costs of the counterclaim.

If the parties or their solicitors are unable to agree upon the apportionment of the costs as between claim and counterclaim it would then be for whoever conducted the taxation—and preferably the arbitrator—to determine the apportionment. The apportionment can be difficult, and an order in this form should be avoided unless all other possibilities (such as a fractional order, or no order) are even more objectionable:

(b) if the claim and counterclaim have no independent existence, the counterclaim being in substance a defence to the claim (*e.g.* a builder claiming the price for his work to a house; the houseowner counterclaiming for work badly done or not done at all) it is usually more appropriate to treat the arbitration as one and to make a single order for costs, *e.g.* claimant to have [one half of] the costs of the arbitration. However such an approach may not be possible if there is a Calderbank offer against the claim or counterclaim only.

Interim award final as to all matters except costs

The right of a party to make a Calderbank offer has been discussed in paragraph 2–526. That right will be frustrated if the arbitrator's substantive award and his award as to costs are made simultaneously. So a party who has made, or who may wish to make, a Calderbank offer should ask the arbitrator to issue his substantive award as an interim award, final as to all matters other than costs. This leaves it open to the parties to agree as to the costs after they have read it, and if they cannot agree to ask him to make a further award.[25] At that stage the Calderbank offer can be put before him as a matter relevant to his decision on costs. **2–816**

Reasons for an unusual award

No reasons need be given for an award of costs which follows the event. Such an order is usual and needs no explanation. But if in the exercise of his discretion the arbitrator decides to make an order which does not follow the event, or is exercising his power under section 63(3), the award should explain the reasons that have caused the arbitrator to make an unusual order. **2–817**

[25] Section 57.

Costs after abandonment of claim or defence

2–818 Where a party withdraws his claim or defence, the usual rule is that he must pay the costs of the other party, because by his withdrawal he is conceding success to the other party. But if there are special circumstances where this is not the case, the arbitrator has a discretion to make some other order as to costs.[26]

Appealing against an award as to costs

2–819 The English courts will not interfere with an arbitrator's award as to costs merely because it would itself have made a different order.

> "In reviewing an arbitrator's discretion as to costs it is of the greatest importance to remember that the decision is within his discretion and not that of the courts. It is nothing to the point that I might have reached a different decision and that some other judge or arbitrator might have differed from both of us. I neither wish, nor am entitled to intervene, unless I was satisfied that the arbitrator had misdirected himself."[27]

2–820 But the courts may interfere:

(a) if the arbitrator's discretion has plainly been exercised on some wrong principle;
(b) if though the principle on which the award as to costs was made cannot be discerned, the award is one that no reasonable tribunal could have arrived at, and it must therefore be inferred that the arbitrator has acted on some wrong principle;
(c) if it is plain that the arbitrator has not exercised any discretion at all, *e.g.* because he erroneously considered himself bound by some rule of law or practice which in fact did not apply to the facts of the particular case.

2–821 The right of appeal to the court against an award as to costs is subject to the restrictions imposed upon appeals generally by the Act.

The effect of a Calderbank offer

What is a Calderbank offer?[28]

2–822 As noted in paragraph 2–526 above, a Calderbank offer is a firm offer to settle the proceedings or part of them, made in terms having the effect "without preju-

[26] See *Barretts & Baird v. Institute of Professional Civil Servants* (Court of Appeal, July 1989 reported in *C.S.W.*, August 31, 1989, p. 45).

[27] Donaldson J. in *Tramonatana Armadora v. Atlantic Shipping Co.* [1978] 2 All E.R. 870, at 875.

[28] See also paragraph 2–529.

dice except as to costs''. It is so called after the name of the case in which the practice was first approved by the courts.[29]

Payment into court, sealed offer, and Calderbank offer

A defendant who wishes to protect himself against having to pay the costs of litigating a money claim against him is entitled to make a payment into court of the amount that he is willing to pay. If he does so, the issue between the parties becomes: Is the plaintiff entitled to recover more than that sum?[30] By Order 22, rule 3 of the Rules of the Supreme Court, provided the payment in is made at least 21 days before the trial begins, the plaintiff may without the leave of the court accept the sum paid in, with any interest that has accrued on it, and may thereafter tax his costs up to the date of acceptance and recover them from the defendant. So the mere fact of payment into court of a sum of money amounts to an offer to the plaintiff of (a) the sum itself; (b) interest that may accrue on it; and (c) taxed costs up to the date of giving notice of acceptance. If the plaintiff does not accept the payment, and the sum awarded to him (excluding interest and costs) is less than the amount paid in, then he will be ordered to pay the defendant's costs from the date of payment in, unless there are circumstances connected with the case that justify the making of some other order. **2–823**

This procedure is not available, in proceedings in court, in respect of a claim that is not a money claim, *e.g.* claims for a declaration; or for rectification; or for an injunction and it is not available at all in arbitration. A procedure intended to have much the same effect has for many years been used in the Lands tribunal. It consists of a sealed offer, lodged with the tribunal in an envelope which is not opened until all issues other than costs have been disposed of. Such an offer is usually treated in that tribunal as having much the same effect as a payment into court. **2–824**

The sealed offer procedure has often been used in arbitration. But in the Lands Tribunal a sealed offer is lodged with the Registrar, so that the tribunal hearing the case is ignorant of the fact that an offer has been made, and cannot draw any inferences from that fact. It is not practicable to conceal from an arbitrator the fact that a sealed envelope has been lodged with him or his secretary. So the practice has grown, in arbitration, of making a ''Calderbank offer'', that is, a letter of offer, whose existence and contents are to be concealed from the arbitrator until he had decided all matters except costs. **2–825**

Differences between payment into court and a Calderbank offer

A Calderbank offer differs from a payment into court in many respects: **2–826**

(a) it is not backed by cash, and the claimant has less certainty as to when

[29] *Calderbank v. Calderbank* [1975] 3 All E.R. 333. The views expressed stated by Cairns L.J. were later approved by the Court of Appeal in *Cutts v. Head* [1984] 1 All E.R. 597.

[30] See *Findley v. Railway Executive* [1950] 2 All E.R. 969, *per* Somervell L.J. at 971.

the cash will be forthcoming or indeed that it will be forthcoming at all;

(b) for that reason it can be used as a negotiating tactic by a defendant who is unable or unwilling to put up the cash;

(c) there are no established rules of procedure governing it, corresponding to Order 22 governing payments into court;

(d) there is clear authority that a payment into court of less than the amount ultimately awarded is not normally taken into account at all in the decision as to costs. The position in respect of arbitration is much less clear; the subject is discussed below;

(e) a payment into court may not be taken out without leave of the court; a Calderbank offer may be withdrawn at any time before it has been accepted.

What effect should the arbitrator give to a Calderbank offer?

2–827 In *Tramountana v. Atlantic Shipping*[31] Donaldson J. said:

> "How should an arbitrator deal with costs where there has been a sealed offer? I think he should ask himself the question: Has the claimant achieved more by rejecting the offer and going on with the arbitration than he would have achieved if he had accepted the offer? That is a simple question to answer, whether or not the offer does or does not include interest. The arbitrator knows what the claimant would have received if he had accepted the offer. He would have received that sum and could not have asked the arbitrator to award any interest. The arbitrator knows what he has in fact awarded to the claimant both by way of principal and interest. In order that like may be compared with like, the interest element must be recalculated as if the award had been made on the same date as the offer. Alternatively, interest for the period between offer and award must notionally be added to the amount of the sealed offer. But, subject to that, the question is easily answered. If the claimant in the end has achieved not more than he would have achieved by accepting the offer, the continuance of the arbitration after that date has been a waste of time and money. Prima facie the claimant should recover his costs up to the date of the offer, and should be ordered to pay the respondent's costs after that date. If the claimant has achieved more by going on, the respondent should pay the costs throughout."

The contents of a Calderbank offer

2–828 A claimant who succeeds on a money claim is usually awarded all or part of the sum claimed, plus some interest, plus some costs. In order to compare the aggregate of these elements with the amount of a Calderbank offer, it is desir-

[31] [1978] 2 All E.R. 870, at 876; followed by Ralph Gibson J. in *Archital Laxfer v. Henry Boot Construction* cited at 332 below.

able, and usually necessary, that the offer include a term that if the offer is accepted the respondent will pay the claimant's taxed costs up to the date of the offer. Otherwise the arbitrator may be unable to say whether his award of £X plus costs up to the end of the hearing gives the claimant more than the respondent's offer of £Y without costs, or £Y plus £5,000 costs, made at some earlier date. An arbitrator is not expected or required to enter upon any detailed investigations in order to discover whether an offer made was such that a claimant has or has not achieved more by rejecting it.[32] So the onus is on the respondent, when making the offer, to ensure that it can easily be compared with the award if the offer is rejected. In the ordinary case the offer should be in the form:

> "£X plus interest to date [OR including interest to date] plus your costs to date to be taxed in default of agreement."

For a drafting suggestion for a Calderbank offer see No. 73 at Appendix 1 below. **2–829**

Should an arbitrator wholly disregard a Calderbank offer which is slightly less than his award?

It is settled practice that if a payment into court falls short, by whatever amount, of the amount ultimately adjudged to be due, it must be wholly disregarded when deciding questions of costs.[33] The position of a sealed offer in arbitration (as used before Calderbank letters came into general use) had to be considered against the background of the law relating to payments into court, although the Rules of the Supreme Court do not apply to arbitrations.[34] The Calderbank offer stands in the same relationship to payments into court as the sealed offer formerly did (and still does, where the procedure is used). If the Calderbank offer falls just short of the amount awarded, can the arbitrator take into account, when exercising his discretion as to costs, the fact that the respondent's offer was a "near miss"? It remains to be seen whether the courts in interpreting the Act will take the same view. A case can be made that a tribunal has an exceedingly wide power under section 63(3) to determine costs by award on such basis as it thinks fit; provided it specifies the basis on which it has acted and that basis is not irrational or perverse such that no reasonable arbitrator properly applying his mind to the question would have so decided. Such an interpretation of the tribunal's powers could be wholly in line with the policy of the Act and the principles of party autonomy. The practice of the court with respect to the basis of costs and the treatment of Calderbank offers is no doubt helpful, but there is no compelling reason for it to be mandatory particularly in international cases. **2–830**

"It is not clear to me that a fair and civilized body of law necessarily

[32] *Per* Ralph Gibson J. in *Archital v. Boot Construction* [1981] 1 Lloyd's Rep. 642, at 654.
[33] *Per* Ralph Gibson J. in *Archital v. Boot Construction* [1981] 1 Lloyd's Rep. 642, at 652.
[34] *Per* Donaldson J. in *Tramontana v. Atlantic Shipping* [1978] 2 All E.R. 870, at 877.

requires inclusion of a principle that if an offer or payment into court is too small by any amount or fraction of the amount recovered it must be wholly disregarded, but such a principle is clearly included in the law which I must apply.''

2–831 The question was considered in more detail by Judge Diamond, Q.C. (sitting as a judge of the Queen's Bench Division) in *The Maria*.[35] The claimants had claimed £74,828 but were finally awarded £16,216. The respondents had made a Calderbank offer of £15,000 plus interest and costs to date. Three highly experienced arbitrators decided that, having regard to the way in which the claimants had conducted part of their case, if there had been no Calderbank offer each party should bear its own costs. Then, taking into account their estimate of the costs which the claimants would thus have to bear, and deducting it from the amount awarded, the arbitrators took the view that the claimants had gained less by rejecting the offer than they would have obtained by accepting it. They therefore ordered the claimants to pay the respondents' costs after the date of the offer. The judge held that they were not entitled to make this order. Since the offer fell short of the amount awarded it had to be disregarded for all purposes, in the same manner as an inadequate payment into court. He therefore applied the arbitrators' initial reasoning, and substituted an award that each side should pay its own costs.

Time limits on making or accepting a Calderbank offer

2–832 By Order 22, rule 3 a plaintiff may, without leave of the court, take out a payment into court within 21 days of receiving notice of the payment. Thereafter he may only take it out if the court gives leave, and the court will refuse leave if it thinks it would be unfair to the defendant to do so. If the payment in is made less than 21 days before the hearing begins, it may still be effective, depending on the circumstances.[36]

2–833 If a Calderbank offer does not itself impose a time limit, it may be accepted at any time (but presumably not after the award is published). So it is prudent for the offeror to impose a time limit on unconditional acceptance. The 21 days allowed for payments into court is a useful guide to the period that should be specified. There is nothing sacred in the period. What is required is a reasonable time to consider the offer. The nearer the parties are to a hearing (and therefore the better prepared they are) the shorter the time that they should need to consider the offer.

2–834 The existence of a Calderbank offer may give rise to problems if the claimant or the respondent seeks to amend its case after the time for unconditional acceptance has expired. Since amendments which are allowed date back to the commencement of the proceedings, this may have a substantial effect on the evalu-

[35] *The Maria* [1992] 3 All E.R. 85.

[36] *King v. Weston-Howell* [1989] 2 All E.R. 375, disapproving *Bowen v. Mills & Knight Ltd* [1973] 1 Lloyd's Rep. 580.

ation of the offer. It is, however, difficult for the respondent to oppose an amendment on this ground without bringing to the attention of the tribunal the existence of the offer—which it may not wish to do. A tribunal should approach this particular minefield with great caution, at whatever time it encounters it. In particular, a respondent who asks for costs to be reserved when an amendment of financial substance by the claimant is allowed may have just this point in mind.

Since the period immediately preceding the hearing is usually one in which the heaviest costs are incurred, and since the plaintiff will be entitled to those costs if he accepts (say) one day before the 21 days of other period lapses, a respondent who is minded to make a Calderbank offer would be wise not to defer making it until shortly before the hearing. It should always be possible to accept a Calderbank offer after the expiry of the 21 days, subject to paying the respondents' costs from the date of the offer. 2–835

Protecting an offeree from a spurious Calderbank offer

A payment into court is an unequivocal offer made by the equivalent of putting cash on the table. So it may be accepted by taking out the money, without prior communication to the offeror. A Calderbank offer may be no more than a mere promise to pay, as distinct from payment. So an arbitrator should not take a Calderbank offer into account to the detriment of the offeree unless he is satisfied that it was a genuine offer that the offeror was ready willing and able to implement.[37] 2–836

Determining the amount of costs to be paid

Carrying into effect the order for costs

When an arbitrator awards that a party pay all or part of the opposing party's costs of an arbitration, or of a particular part of it (*e.g.* an interim award, or an application for further discovery), it is open to the arbitrator to make his award in the form of a money sum. For at least two reasons this may not be convenient. First, it should rarely be done without giving the parties an opportunity to make submissions as to the amount. Secondly, the party who is to receive the costs often wants time to make a more or less detailed account of his costs. So the more usual course is for the arbitrator merely to award that party P pay to party R his costs (or a fraction of his costs) of the arbitration (or of a specified stage of the arbitration) and pay the arbitrator's fees and disbursements (or a fraction of them). The next stage is for party R to formulate his claim for costs, and to invite party P to agree it. Where solicitors are acting for both parties, they more often than not agree upon the amount. But if they cannot agree, there is a dispute 2–837

[37] A party who was not able to implement the offer is unlikely to be able to implement the award and an order for costs, so the point may be academic—but this principle should be clear.

which has to be resolved. In a heavy case the amount in issue as to costs can be substantial. The process of resolving this dispute is called, in litigation "taxation of costs". The phrase is not used in the Act, and "determination of costs" is a more apt phrase.

Arbitrator determines method of determination

2–838 In litigation there are now two possible bases for the taxation of costs, the standard basis and the indemnity basis. Arbitrators are not bound to adopt either because in arbitration the receiving party is entitled to be paid:

> "a reasonable amount in respect of all costs reasonably incurred."

2–839 If arbitrators choose to follow the litigation precedent then any doubts as to whether the costs were reasonably incurred or were reasonable in amount applying a standard basis shall be resolved in favour of the paying party; whereas on the indemnity basis any such doubts shall be resolved in favour of the receiving party.[38]

When may costs be awarded on the indemnity basis

2–840 Although a judge or arbitrator has discretion to award costs on the indemnity basis, the usual practice is to award them on the standard basis unless there is a particular reason for departing from the usual practice.[39] Examples of such reasons are:

(a) where a party has been found guilty of fraud or gross impropriety either in the events out of which the proceedings arise or in the proceedings themselves;
(b) where a party or his representative has, by dilatoriness, greatly increased the costs of the other party;
(c) where a hearing has to be adjourned through inexcusable fault of a party or those acting for him.

2–841 In *Bowen-Jones v. Bowen-Jones*[40] Knox J. held that notwithstanding the change in the wording of the rule the principles on which the court would depart from the usual basis were unchanged.

Who should tax the costs—courses open to the arbitrator

2–842 As a general principle, now encouraged by section 63(3) of the Act, it is expected that the arbitrator will determine the costs himself. If the arbitrator makes no award as to costs, the court may intervene under section 63(4). When an arbitrator has decided to make an order as to costs, there are several ways in

[38] See RSC, Ord. 62, r. 12.
[39] *Preston v. Preston* [1982] 1 All E.R. 41.
[40] [1986] 3 All E.R. 163.

which he can provide for determination of the amount payable so that his order may become an enforceable award as to costs, namely:

(a) the award may specify the amount of costs;
(b) the award may direct that the costs, if not agreed, be taxed by the court;
(c) the award may direct that the costs, if not agreed, be taxed by the County Court;[41]
(d) the award may direct that the costs, if not agreed, be taxed by the arbitrator; or
(e) the award may direct that the costs, if not agreed, be taxed by the arbitrator assisted by a taxation assessor.

If the parties have consented to this course, their consent should be incorporated in a short written agreement. 2–843

Taxation of costs by the arbitrator

It is an unhappy fact of life that the costs of litigation or of arbitration are often high in relation to the amount in issue, and the 1996 Act is unlikely to change this overnight. The higher the proportion, the more important it is that there should be an efficient and speedy method of dealing with the costs. Moreover, where parties who are making a contract have a choice of the legal system by which disputes under the contract are to be governed, they may perceive as an advantage the fact that in arbitration under English law the arbitrator has power, which he usually exercises, to make an effective order for costs. Insofar as this power is thought to be an advantage the procedure for exercising it should be as swift and efficient as possible. A further point is that since the parties may have chosen to resolve their dispute by arbitration in preference to resorting to the courts, it is unfortunate, to say the least, if the arbitrator forces them to go to court before their dispute is finally resolved. 2–844

Fixed sum without taxation

For the arbitrator to fix a sum for the costs is apparently a simple, quick and cheap procedure. However, he ought not to fix the amount without giving the parties an opportunity of making submissions to him. If they have that opportunity, they obviously have the opportunity to agree a sum. It follows that in practice most of the cases in which the arbitrator will be asked to fix a sum will be cases in which the parties unsuccessfully attempted to agree. In such cases resolving the differences between them is in effect taxing the costs rather than fixing a particular sum. 2–845

[41] See *Perkins v. Brent-Shaw* [1973] 1 W.L.R. 975.

Taxation by the arbitrator

2–846 Taxation by the arbitrator has several advantages and should be preferred to taxation by the court. Arbitrators shall not shirk this responsibility. It is part of their duty under section 33. It must be remembered that before the taxation the party claiming the costs will have delivered to the opposing party an itemized bill of costs which need not be and should not be in High Court form, and the opposing party will, or should have, delivered an itemized objection to the bill. Given modern methods of time and cost recording in use by solicitors and the Bar, it should be comparatively straightforward even in heavy cases for the parties to supply computer printouts of time spent, work done, hourly rates and expenses incurred. The arbitrator will, by reason of his having conducted the arbitration, be able to understand both the claims for costs and the objections to them. The Taxing Master of the court, on the other hand, will require the bill to be presented in High Court form, will have to read some documents, and may have to read a great mass of documents before he can understand them, the claim, the objection, what work was reasonable, what witnesses it was reasonable to engage, and so on. Moreover, where the arbitrator is himself an expert in the field in which the dispute arose, he should be better placed than a Taxing Master to know what are the prevailing rates of remuneration for professionals practising in that field. The amount of additional reading required is so much less than in a taxation by a Taxing Master, and the queues for taxation are so much shorter, that the arbitrator should be able to give a much earlier appointment for oral argument (if required) than would a Taxing Master. Although the arbitrators' hourly fees may be higher than the corresponding court fees, the facts that an adjudication is made shortly after the award of costs, and is made by someone familiar with the course that the dispute has taken, may result in a saving of solicitors' costs of the taxation outweighing the additional fees of the arbitrator.

Taxation by the arbitrator with a costs assessor

2–847 A further course open to the arbitrator but preferably by agreement with the parties, is for the costs to be taxed by the arbitrator with the assistance of a Taxation Assessor, who could be perhaps a retired Taxing Master, or a solicitor or legal executive experienced in the taxation of costs in the High Court. An arbitrator may obtain the services of a lawyer to help him if he decides to tax the costs himself. If the arbitrator does so he must comply with the provisions of section 37 of the Act with respect to the tribunal's appointed assessors or legal advisers.

Taxation of costs by the court

Procedure in the High Court

2–848 Taxation in the High Court is conducted by the Taxing Masters, who are officers of the court. The procedure, in essence, is for the party in whose favour an order for costs has been made to serve on the opposing party ("the paying party") an itemized bill; the paying party then serves and lodges with the court his detailed objections; the parties (or almost invariably their solicitors) then appear at an appointment at which the detailed justifications and objections are put to the Taxing Master and decided by him.

Disadvantages of High Court taxation

In a heavy case the preparation of an itemised bill is time consuming and very expensive. It is common for the bills to be prepared, and in due course the objections formulated, by specialist costs clerks, whose services are themselves costly. Moreover, there is often a substantial delay in obtaining an appointment before a Taxing Master. Hence it is common for the claimant's solicitors to accept a substantial reduction in the amount of their bill in order to avoid the cost and the delay involved in having the bill taxed. This reduction, like the amount taxed off in a disputed taxation, is not borne by the claimant's solicitors themselves; it is passed on to their client. **2–849**

Taxation in the County Court

Taxation in the County Court is conducted by the District Judge, who has great experience of taxation of costs in cases within the County Court limits of jurisdiction.[42] (See also Part 9, below.) In general those cases involve substantially smaller sums than cases tried in the High Court, and there are various scales of costs governed by the amount claimed or, in the case of some property disputes the rateable value of the property. If the amounts involved in an arbitration are relatively small, and if (exceptionally) the arbitrator decides that they should be taxed in the County Court, the District Judge conducting the taxation will apply whatever Scale is appropriate to the amount awarded.[43] It is however open to the arbitrator, when directing that costs (if not agreed) be taxed in the County Court, to direct also that "the District Judge is not to be bound by scale fees". In that case the District Judge will use his discretion and experience in deciding what costs should be awarded. **2–850**

[42] This varies with the nature of the case but from 1991 can be as much as £50,000.

[43] The Scales are set out in *The County Court Practice*, and see also Pt 9 below.

28. Appeals and Applications to the Court

The two jurisdictions

2–851 Before the Act the courts had two separate statutory jurisdictions to control arbitrations. The first was the jurisdiction conferred by the 1979 Act, to hear an appeal on a question of law arising out of an award. The second was to remit or set aside an award, or remove an arbitrator, under the 1950 Act. These powers in a different form are now found in the Act.

2–852 There remains no power to intervene where the complaint is that the arbitrator has made an error of fact. Nor is it necessarily enough that he has made an error of law, for there is no right of appeal without leave, and leave will only be given in the limited class of cases indicated below. Hitherto, the courts however have sometimes intervened where there was an error of procedure (sometimes called "procedural mishap") which could have led to an unjust result. Now the court will only intervene in defined categories of serious irregularity as provided for in section 68 of the Act.

Appeals under the Act

Appeal on point of law

2–853 An appeal on a point of law is now regulated by section 69 of the Act. This section replaces the appeal provisions of the 1979 Act and seeks to enact in statutory form the guidelines for appeal set out in Lord Diplock's speech in *The Nema.*[44]

2–854 The right of appeal is limited to cases where the parties have not made an exclusion agreement as contemplated by section 69(1) of the Act. An agreement to dispense with the giving of reasons in an award is an exclusion agreement. Hitherto, in the case of a domestic arbitration agreement (as defined in section 85(2)) any agreement to exclude the court's jurisdiction to hear an appeal on a point of law was not effective unless entered into after the commencement of the arbitral proceedings in which the question arises or an award is made. But now that the distinctions between domestic and non-domestic arbitration agreements have been abolished by the Secretary of State under powers given to him by section 88 of the Act, exclusion agreements under section 91(1) may be made at any time whether before or after the referral to arbitration is made.

2–855 Appeal is only possible with leave unless all parties agree; and leave will only be granted if the court is satisfied:[45]

(a) that the determination of the question will substantially affect the rights of one or more of the parties,

[44] *Pioneer Shipping Limited v. BTP Tioxide (The Nema)* [1981] 2 All E.R. 1030.
[45] s.69(3).

(b) that the question is one which the tribunal was asked to determine,
(c) that, on the basis of the findings of fact in the award—
  (i) the decision of the tribunal on the question is obviously wrong, or
  (ii) the question is one of general public importance and the decision of the tribunal is at least open to serious doubt, and
(d) that, despite the agreement of the parties to resolve the matter by arbitration, it is just and proper in all the circumstances for the court to determine the question.

The court will determine the application on the documents without a hearing unless the court considers it necessary to have a hearing. **2–856**

The court, if it hears an appeal, may either confirm the award, vary it, remit the award to the tribunal for reconsideration in whole or in part or set aside the award in whole or in part. **2–857**

There are further restrictions on the right to appeal. First, "an application or appeal may not be brought if the applicant or appellant has not first exhausted— **2–858**

(a) any available arbitral process of appeal or review, and
(b) any available recourse under section 57 (correction of award or additional award)" (section 70(2)).

Secondly, no application or appeal can be brought unless the applicant has exhausted any available arbitral process of appeal or review and any available review under section 57. Thirdly, the application or appeal must be brought within 28 days of the award or the results of any arbitral appeal or review procedure. Fourthly, the court may order the applicant to provide security pending the outcome of the appeal.

There are miscellaneous powers of the court with respect to appeal such as the power to order the arbitrator to give reasons or more detailed reasons and to do so: **2–859**

> "If on an application or appeal it appears to the court that the award—[46]
> (a) does not contain the tribunal's reasons, or
> (b) does not set out the tribunal's reasons in sufficient detail to enable the court properly to consider the application or appeal,
>
> the court may order the tribunal to state the reasons for its award in sufficient detail for that purpose."

Control of awards under the 1996 Act

Remedying irregularity

Section 68 establishes a comprehensive regime for remedying "serious irregularity"—the old term "misconduct" has fallen into disrepute and is no longer **2–860**

[46] s.70(4).

used. A party may apply to the court to challenge an award on the grounds of serious irregularity affecting the tribunal, the proceedings or the award itself. By section 68(2) serious irregularity is defined as follows:

> "(2) Serious irregularity means an irregularity of one or more of the following kinds which the court considers has caused or will cause substantial injustice to the applicant—
> (a) failure by the tribunal to comply with section 33 (general duty of tribunal);
> (b) the tribunal exceeding its powers (otherwise than by exceeding its substantive jurisdiction: see section 67);
> (c) failure by the tribunal to conduct the proceedings in accordance with the procedure agreed by the parties;
> (d) failure by the tribunal to deal with all the issues that were put to it;
> (e) any arbitral or other institution or person vested by the parties with powers in relation to the proceedings or the award exceeding its powers;
> (f) uncertainty or ambiguity as to the effect of the award;
> (g) the award being obtained by fraud or the award or the way in which it was procured being contrary to public policy;
> (h) failure to comply with the requirements as to the form of the award; or
> (i) any irregularity in the conduct of the proceedings or in the award which is admitted by the tribunal or by any arbitral or other institution or person vested by the parties with powers in relation to the proceedings or the award."

2–861 The court has the power to remit the award to the tribunal in whole or in part for reconsideration, to set the award aside in whole or in part or to declare the award itself to be of no effect, in whole or in part.

2–862 The right to apply to the court may be lost under section 73 and is subject to the restrictions in section 70(2) and (3). Thus in order to challenge on the grounds of serious irregularity a party must come within one of the defined categories and also establish that the serious irregularity has or will cause substantial injustice to the applicant.

2–863 In paragraph 280 of the Final Report the DAC has made its intentions plain:

> "The court does not have the general supervisory jurisdiction over arbitrators."

2–864 Moreover,

> "It is only in those cases where it can be said that what has happened is so far removed from what could reasonably be expected of the arbitral process that we would expect the court to take action."

"Having chosen arbitration, the parties cannot validly complain of substantial injustice unless what has happened simply cannot on any view be defended as an acceptable consequence of that choice. In short [section 68] is really designed as a longstop, only available in extreme cases where the tribunal has gone so wrong in its conduct of the arbitration that justice calls out for it to be corrected."

Thus, many of the cases classified hitherto as misconduct should no longer be regarded by the courts as grounds for interference. The Final Report gives the example of cases before the Act where the court remitted awards to an arbitral tribunal because the lawyers acting for one party failed (or decided not to) put a particular point to the tribunal.[47] **2–865**

Jurisdictional challenges

Challenges to the substantive jurisdiction of the arbitrators now fall to be dealt with under sections 30 and 32 and sections 67 and 72 of the Act. Section 30 enables the tribunal to rule on its own jurisdiction. Thus: **2–866**

"(1) Unless otherwise agreed by the parties, the arbitral tribunal may rule on its own substantive jurisdiction, that is, as to—
(a) whether there is a valid arbitration agreement,
(b) whether the tribunal is properly constituted, and
(c) what matters have been submitted to arbitration in accordance with the arbitration agreement.
(2) Any such ruling may be challenged by any available arbitral process of appeal or review or in accordance with the provisions of this Part."

Section 31 provides for the timing of such challenges and for the powers of the tribunal when faced with such a challenge. Thus: **2–867**

"(1) An objection that the arbitral tribunal lacks substantive jurisdiction at the outset of the proceedings must be raised by a party not later than the time he takes the first step in the proceedings to contest the merits of any matter in relation to which he challenges the tribunal's jurisdiction. [A party is not precluded from raising such an objection by the fact that he has appointed or participated in the appointment of an arbitrator.]
(2) Any objection during the course of the arbitral proceedings that the arbitral tribunal is exceeding its substantive jurisdiction must be made

[47] *Indian Oil Corporation v. Coastal (Bermuda) Ltd* [1990] 2 Lloyd's Rep. 407; *King v. Thomas McKenna* [1991] 2 Q.B. 480.

as soon as possible after the matter alleged to be beyond its jurisdiction is raised.

(3) The arbitral tribunal may admit an objection later than the time specified in subsection (1) or (2) if it considers the delay justified.

(4) Where an objection is duly taken to the tribunal's substantive jurisdiction and the tribunal has power to rule on its own jurisdiction, it may—

(a) rule on the matter in an award as to jurisdiction, or

(b) deal with the objection in its award on the mertis.

If the parties agree which of these courses the tribunal should take, the tribunal shall proceed accordingly.

(5) The tribunal may in any case, and shall if the parties so agree, stay proceedings whilst an application is made to the court under section 32 (determination of preliminary point of jurisdiction)."

2–868 There is a power in the court to make a determination on a preliminary point of jurisdiction. By section 32,

"(1) The court may, on the application of a party to arbitral proceedings (upon notice to the other parties), determine any question as to the substantive jurisdiction of the tribunal. A party may lose the right to object (see section 73).

(2) An application under this section shall not be considered unless

(a) it is made with the agreement in writing of all the other parties to the proceedings, or

(b) it is made with the permission of the tribunal and the court is satisfied—

(i) that the determination of the question is likely to produce substantial savings in costs,

(ii) that the application was made without delay, and

(iii) that there is good reason why the matter should be decided by the court.

(3) An application under this section, unless made with the agreement of all the other parties to the proceedings, shall state the grounds on which it is said that the matter should be decided by the court.

(4) Unless otherwise agreed by the parties, the arbitral tribunal may continue the arbitral proceedings and make an award while an application to the court under this section is pending.

(5) Unless the court gives leave, no appeal lies from a decision of the court whether the conditions specified in subsection (2) are met.

(6) The decision of the court on the question of jurisdiction shall be treated as a judgment of the court for the purposes of an appeal."

2–869 But no appeal lies without the leave of the court which shall not be given unless the court considers that the question involves a point of law which is one of general importance or is one which for some other special reason should be considered by the Court of Appeal.

The DAC intended that the power under section 32 should be sparingly used for it is regarded as available "for exceptional cases only" (DAC final report, paragraph 147). 2–870

By section 67 of the Act: 2–871

"(1) A party to arbitral proceedings may (upon notice to the other parties and to the tribunal) apply to the court—
(a) challenging any award of the arbitral tribunal as to its substantive jurisdiction; or
(b) for an order declaring an award made by the tribunal on the merits to be of no effect, in whole or in part, because the tribunal did not have substantive jurisdiction.

A party may lose the right to object (see section 73) and the right to apply is subject to the restrictions in section 70(2) and (3).

(2) The arbitral tribunal may continue the arbitral proceedings and make a further award while an application to the court under this section is pending in relation to an award as to jurisdiction.

(3) On an application under this section challenging an award of the arbitral tribunal as to its substantive jurisdiction, the court may by order—
(a) confirm the award
(b) vary the award, or
(c) set aside the award in whole or in part.

(4) The leave of the court is required for any appeal from a decision of the court under this section."

The results of remission and setting aside

The position if the court remits the award to the arbitrator with the opinion of the court is plain. It is the duty of the arbitrator to reconsider the matter and in doing so to apply the law as expressed in the opinion of the court. The position if the court sets aside the award is less clear. Logically, the arbitration remains on foot, and with it the jurisdiction of the arbitrator: it is the award that has been set aside, not the arbitration. In practice, however, an order setting aside the award without also remitting it is rare. There is little authority on the principles to be applied in deciding whether to remit the award or set it aside. In *Windvale v. Darlington Insulation Company*[48] Walton J. decided to set aside rather than remit an award in a rent review arbitration, on the ground that the arbitrator had gone wrong so fundamentally at almost every stage that it was desirable that the matter should begin again with a clean start. But in general, where only a small part of the findings of the arbitrator has been successfully 2–872

[48] *The Times*, December 22, 1983.

attacked, and there has been no serious irregularity, remission is the more appropriate order.

Action by the arbitrator when his award is challenged.

2–873 If a party applies to the court to set aside or remit the award, or to remove the arbitrator, on the ground of serious irregularity,[49] the notice of motion should be served on the arbitrator as well as on the other party or parties. He can then choose between (a) doing nothing; (b) filing an affidavit for the assistance of the court; or (c) taking an active part in the proceedings, as a party to them. He should always take legal advice before deciding to take course (b) or (c). The court will be anxious to prevent unfounded slurs being cast on someone who is not before the court to defend himself against them. So broadly speaking (a) is preferable to (b), and (a) and (b) are preferable to (c). However, it sometimes happens that on reading the appellant's criticisms the arbitrator wishes to put some explanation before the court and in those circumstances course (b) is appropriate. If the circumstances of a particular case point towards course (c) he should bear in mind that if he takes an active part it is possible, though unlikely, that costs may be awarded against him.

Under the Act

2–874 Where an application is made under section 69 of the Act for leave to appeal, or for a direction that the arbitrator give reasons or further reasons, the summons must be served on the arbitrator. In other cases no notice of the proceedings need be served on the arbitrator, and he should not normally take any part in the proceedings unless of course the court directs him to do something.

29. Applications to the Court—the new Order 73

Which courts have jurisdiction

2–875 The coming into force of the Act has provided an ideal opportunity for an overhaul of the porcedures for relevant court applications. As the DAC's Supplementary Report made clear, the new Order 73 has been completely recast in

[49] s.68(1).

order to reflect the changes brought about by the Act and to simplify the procedure for court applications concerning arbitration. Such applications can be made to invoke both the supportive and supervisory powers of the court. Examples are applications for removal of arbitrators, for determinations of preliminary points of law, for enforcement of peremptory orders and for enforcement of awards.

The threshold issue about any application is the choice of the court in which it should be made. Naturally, any application to stay legal proceedings under section 9 of the Act must be made in the court in which the legal proceedings are pending.[50] Otherwise, any arbitration application may be made in the High Court. The High Court and County Courts (Allocation of Arbitration Proceedings) Order 1996,[51] however, permits certain applications to be made in an appropriate County Court. Applications to enforce an award may be made in any county court. Subject to this, the county court jurisdiction is vested in the Central London County Court Business List.[52] Proceedings commenced in the High Court may be transferred to the County Court, and vice versa.[53] In deciding which court is appropriate, the following factors[54] are to be taken into consideration: **2–876**

(i) the financial substance of the dispute. In particular, if the financial substance of the dispute is over £200,000, there is a presumption that the application should proceed in the High Court.[55]
(ii) the nature of the dispute referred to arbitration (for example, whether it arises out of a commercial or business transaction or relates to engineering, building or other construction work).
(iii) whether the proceedings are otherwise important and, in particular, whether they raise questions of importance to persons who are not parties.
(iv) whether the balance of convenience points to having the proceedings taken in the Central London County Court Business List.

The new Order 73

The new procedure for arbitration applications is laid down in the revised Rules of the Supreme Court, Order 73. This procedure applies both to proceedings in **2–877**

[50] High Court and County Courts (Allocation of Arbitration Proceedings) Order 1996, reg. 3.
[51] S.I. 1996 No. 3215.
[52] *ibid.* reg. 5.
[53] *ibid.* reg. 5(2) and (3).
[54] *ibid.* reg. 4.
[55] High Court and County Courts (Allocation of Arbitration Proceedings) Order 1996, reg. 4. The regulation provides that "where the financial substance of the dispute exceeds £200,000, the proceedings shall be taken in the High Court unless the proceedings do not raise questions of general importance to persons who are not parties."

the High Court and in the Central London County Court Business List.[56] The revised Order 73 does not change the procedure for applications under the Arbitration Acts 1950 to 1979.[57] These Acts apply to supportive and supervisory applications about arbitrations commenced before January 31, 1997. It also has a separate regime for applications for enforcement of arbitration awards.[58] The principal purpose of the new Order 73, however, is the introduction of a new and streamlined procedure for court applications under the Act.[59]

2–878 All court applications (other than applications to stay legal proceedings) under the Act must be made either in the Commercial Court or in the mercantile list of a district registry.[60] The application must be made by summons in the prescribed form.[61] The summons must include a concise statement of the relief claimed and (if appropriate) the questions on which the applicant seeks the determination of the court.[62] It must also, if appropriate, specify the section of the Act under which the application is brought, and show that any statutory requirements have been satisfied.[63] There are detailed provisions requiring service of the arbitration application[64] and acknowledgement of service.[65] A respondent who fails to acknowledge service on time may not contest the proceedings without leave of the court.[66] If it is to be served in England and Wales, an application is valid for one month.[67] The respondent generally has 14 days in which to acknowledge service.[68]

2–879 Order 73 lays down a procedural timetable[69] for handling arbitration applications, as follows:

Step	*Timing*
Issue of summons	
Filing of applicant's affidavit setting out evidence relied on	At issue of summons[70]
Service of summons and applicant's affidavit	Within one month of issue[71]
Acknowledgement of service	Within 14 days of service of summons[72]

[56] C.C.R., Ord. 48C, r. 16(4).
[57] R.S.C., Ord. 73, P. II.
[58] R.S.C., Ord. 73, P. III.
[59] R.S.C., Ord. 73, P. I.
[60] R.S.C., Ord. 73, r. 5(2) and (3).
[61] R.S.C., Ord. 73, r. 4(1).
[62] R.S.C., Ord. 73, r. 4(2)(a).
[63] R.S.C., Ord. 73, r. 4(2)(d) and (e).
[64] R.S.C., Ord. 73, r. 7.
[65] R.S.C., Ord. 73, r. 11.
[66] R.S.C., Ord. 73, r. 11(2)(a).
[67] R.S.C., Ord. 73, r. 7(5)(b).
[68] R.S.C., Ord. 12, r. 5.
[69] By automatic directions in accordance with r. 13, unless the Court otherwise directs. The applicant's initial affidavit is required in all cases by r. 9.
[70] R.S.C., Ord. 73, r. 9.
[71] R.S.C., Ord. 73, r. 7 and 9(1). The court has power under R.S.C., Ord. 6, r. 8 to extend the period for service. Service out of the jurisdiction is dealt with by R.S.C., Ord. 73, r. 8.
[72] R.S.C., Ord. 12, r. 5. Different periods will apply where the summons has been served out of the jurisdiction.

Service of respondent's affidavit in response	Within 21 days of time limited for acknowledging service[73]
Service of applicant's final affidavit (if any)	Within seven days of respondent's affidavit[74]
Fixing of hearing date	Within 35 days of time limit for acknowledging service[75]
Bundles and hearing estimates to be lodged	Five clear days before hearing[76]
Applicant's chronology, *dramatis personae* and skeleton argument to be lodged	Two clear days before the hearing[77]
Respondent's skeleton argument to be lodged	The day before the hearing[78]

The court may, however, derogate from these directions in appropriate cases. In particular, it may order oral evidence to be heard.[79] The court also has the power to order an applicant to provide security for costs of the application (but not of the arbitration to which it relates).[80] 2–880

The arbitrator should not normally take any part in the proceedings, unless the court directs him to do something. 2–881

30. Enforcement of English Awards

Legal effect of the award

The great majority of English awards are implemented without recourse to any enforcement procedure. Where this is not so, the courts will provide a choice of enforcement procedures. The award creates a new right or rights in favour of the successful party, which he can enforce in the courts in substitution for the rights upon which the claim or the defence respectively were founded. The award has two further consequences. First, it precludes either party from contradicting the decision of the arbitrator on any issue decided by the award, and also upon any issue that was within the jurisdiction of the arbitrator to decide 2–882

73 R.S.C., Ord. 73, r. 13(2).
74 R.S.C., Ord. 73, r. 13(3).
75 R.S.C., Ord. 73, r. 13(4).
76 R.S.C., Ord. 73, r. 13(5) and (6).
77 R.S.C., Ord. 73, r. 13(7).
78 R.S.C., Ord. 73, r. 13(8).
79 R.S.C., Ord. 73, r. 14(2).
80 R.S.C., Ord. 73, r. 17.

but which whether deliberately or accidentally he was not asked to decide. Secondly, the award can operate to bar the claimant, whether successful or unsuccessful, from bringing the same claim again in a subsequent arbitration or action.

Summary enforcement of the award

2–883 It has been said that the award of an arbitrator:

> "represents an agreement made between the parties, and is no more and no less enforceable than any agreement made between parties."[81]

2–884 But most of the objects of arbitration would be defeated if a claimant who had succeeded in an arbitration then had to take his place in the queue of litigants seeking to enforce their agreements. Hence, whilst it is open to the successful claimant to bring an action on the award in the same way as he could have brought an action on the original contract, many countries including England have provided a summary procedure for enforcement.

2–885 By section 66 of the 1996 Act:

> "(1) An award made by the tribunal pursuant to an arbitration agreement may, by leave of the court, be enforced in the same manner as a judgement or order of the court to the same effect.
> (2) Where leave is so given, judgment may be entered in terms of the award.
> (3) Leave to enforce an award shall not be given where, or to the extent that, the person against whom it is sought to be enforced shows that the tribunal lacked substantive jurisdiction to make the award. [The right to raise such an objection may have been lost (see section 73)]
> (4) Nothing in this section affects the recognition or enforcement of an award under any other enactment or rule of law, in particular under Part II of the Arbitration Act 1950 (enforcement of awards under Geneva Convention) or the provisions of Part III of this Act relating to the recognition and enforcement of awards under the New York Convention or by an action on the award."

2–886 In this section (and in Part 1 of the Act generally) "the courts" means both the High Court and the County Court. Thus the procedure for enforcement is found in the Rules of the Supreme Court and in the County Court Rules. The County Court has corresponding power if the amount sought to be recovered does not

[81] *cf.* the Judgment of Slesser L.J. in *Bremer Oil Transport GmbH v. Drewry* [1933] 1 K.B. 753.

exceed the current limit on jurisdiction in section 40 of the County Courts Act 1959. See also Part 9, below.

This summary procedure is not available: 2–887

(a) if the arbitration agreement is not in writing, and is therefore not within the Act;
(b) where the award is declaratory (*e.g.* in rent review arbitrations, the new rent is fixed or the amount of damages payable is determined subject to a later decision as to liability) and therefore does not constitute an award of payment of a sum of money;
(c) if the award is not in a form in which it can be entered as a judgment, *e.g.* it requires some calculation to be made before the amount payable is known.[82]

It is therefore important for a claimant who wants speedy payment of the amount due to him to ensure that the award (whether it is interim or final) is as far as possible in a form that will result, on an application under the Rules, in the court being able to order: 2–888

> "that it be adjudged that the defendant do pay to the plaintiff[83] £X."

An award that "the claimant was entitled to reject the goods"; or that "the claimant is entitled to an allowance of £500 per tonne"; or that "the rent is hereby determined to be £10,000 per annum" cannot be the subject of leave to enforce the award as a judgment. So a claimant who desires to enforce summarily such an award should ask for it to be remitted to the arbitrator with a direction that he put it into an enforceable form. But leave can be given to enforce an award which orders payment of an amount expressed in a foreign currency. 2–889

Defences to an action on the award or to an application for leave to enforce the award as a judgment

The main defence available when the successful party brings an action on the award or applies under the summary procedure of Order 73, rule 31 is that the arbitrator had no jurisdiction to make the award, or to make some part of it. The grounds relied upon may be: 2–890

(a) that there was no valid submission, so that the entire arbitration was a nullity;
(b) that the arbitrator was disqualified, in that he did not possess some

[82] *Margulies Bros v. Dafris Homoides* [1958] 1 Lloyd's Rep. 205.
[83] *i.e.* the respondent and the claimant respectively.

qualification that he was required by the arbitration agreement to possess such as membership of a specified association; or

(c) that the award, though valid when made, has ceased to be binding because it has subsequently been discharged, *e.g.* by a subsequent agreement between the parties.

2–891 Accordingly, in an action on the award the plaintiffs should plead, and be prepared to prove, the arbitration agreement; the references to the arbitrator of a dispute which was within the terms of that agreement; that the arbitrator was duly qualified and duly appointed; and the award itself.

Waiver, election and estoppel

2–892 The principles of waiver, election and estoppel have now received statutory recognition in the Act. By section 73:

"(1) If a party to arbitral proceedings takes part, or continues to take part, in the proceedings without making, either forthwith or within such time as is allowed by the arbitration agreement or the tribunal or by any provision of this Part, any objection—

(a) that the tribunal lacks substantive jurisdiction,

(b) that the proceedings have been improperly conducted,

(c) that there has been a failure to comply with the arbitration agreement or with any provision of this Part, or

(d) that there has been any other irregularity affecting the tribunal or the proceedings,

he may not raise that objection later, before the tribunal or the court, unless he shows that, at the time he took part or continued to take part in the proceedings, he did not know and could not with reasonable diligence have discovered the grounds for the objection.

(2) Where the arbitral tribunal rules that it has substantive jurisdiction and a party to arbitral proceedings who could have questioned that ruling—

(a) by any available arbitral process of appeal or review, or

(b) by challenging the award,

does not do so, or does not do so within the time allowed by the arbitration agreement or any provision of this Part, he may not object later to the tribunal's substantive jurisdiction on any ground which was the subject of that ruling."

Stay of enforcement pending a challenge to the award

2–893 A respondent who wishes to challenge an award will naturally object to complying with the award until his challenge has been finally disposed of. But the nature of the challenge may vary from the spurious, at the one extreme, to the apparently unanswerable at the other. In some cases the successful claimant can enforce the award subject to an obligation to repay (or its equivalent) if the challenge is ultimately upheld. This will rarely be possible if the arbitration agreement itself provides a right of appeal to some appellate tribunal as is the case in many commodity contracts. For in such a case unless the agreement provides to the contrary, the final decision is that of the appellate tribunal and not the tribunal of first instance.

Conditions imposed on leave to appeal to the High Court

Where the challenge takes the form of an application for leave to appeal on a question of law, under sections 67 or 68 of the Act, by section 70(6) the Court may order the applicant to give security for costs, and may direct that in default the application be dismissed. But the power to order security is not to be exercised on the ground that the applicant or appellant is an individual ordinarily resident outside the United Kingdom or is a corporation or association formed under the law of a country outside the United Kingdom or whose central management and control is exercised outside the United Kingdom. **2–894**

If the appeal is brought under section 69, the court has the power under the Rules of the Supreme Court, Order 32 to stay enforcement of the award if necessary on terms pending its decision. **2–895**

Cross-application for leave to enforce award

If the claimant believes that the application for leave to appeal is being made wholly or partly for the purpose of delay, he can issue an application under section 66 of the Act (for leave to enforce the award as a judgment) and ask for it to be listed together with the application for leave to appeal. Unless the respondent's word is wholly unreliable, however, it would be prudent to ask the respondent for an undertaking to pay within (say) seven days of his application for leave being refused, and to issue the application under section 66 only if such an undertaking is not forthcoming. **2–896**

Part 3

COMMODITY TRADE ARBITRATION

By Derek Kirby Johnson, M.A. (Cantab.), F.C.I.Arb.

Consultant, Hill Taylor Dickinson

This section deals with arbitration as conducted and administered under the rules of the Commodity Trade Associations situated principally in the City of London.

Commodity Trade Associations

What are they?

Commodity Trade Associations are, generally, non-profit-making organisations incorporated with limited liability under the Companies Acts. They are international in character and are formed by and for the trade, which is composed of producers, shippers, brokers, traders and manufacturers. Some of these may be multi-nationals, some smaller companies or partnerships. Typically, a producer may be a State-owned produce marketing organisation or it may be one of the big American grain traders, or a small rice grower in Pakistan. Brokers may be in London or Paris, Antwerp or New York. The shipper may be in Switzerland or the United States, the manufacturer in England or Holland. The traders may be, and usually are, everywhere and range from multi-national trading houses to smaller national companies. 3–01

The trades are usually very professional, dealing in large sums of money, involving shipping, banking and insurance arrangements and are definitely not for amateurs. Each trade house in London, Hamburg, Paris, Rotterdam, Antwerp, New York or Chicago is likely to trade in several fields at once, *e.g.* cocoa, coffee and sugar or barley, wheat, rice, animal feed stuffs and edible oils, and consequently these houses will have appropriate experience in these various fields, although the traders that they employ may be specialists, experienced in only one or perhaps two of these fields. 3–02

The objects of such associations are expressed to be the promotion of the trade concerned, which may include liaison with other trade associations in other countries, Customs and Excise, Ministries, the Bank of England, E.U. authorities, Lloyd's, chambers of commerce and the legislature. They also encourage uniformity in commercial use of forms of contract, charter parties, bills of lading and insurance terms, and their principal direct contribution to this field is by publishing agreed standard forms of contract and urging their use in the trade concerned throughout the world, for we are dealing here with international, not national associations. 3–03

Of course, the feature with which we are particularly concerned in this section is the provision of facilities by each association for the settlement of disputes by arbitration. There are three aspects to these provisions. 3–04

First, the standard forms of contract, which are kept continually under review 3–05 and updated from time to time, contain an arbitration clause (as to which see more at paragraph 3–37, below).

3–06 Secondly, the associations set up and administer a system of arbitration comprised of rules for arbitration (and appeal, where applicable; see below), codes of conduct (sometimes), and panels of arbitrators regarded as qualified to conduct arbitrations according to the rules and practice of the association concerned.

3–07 Thirdly, and perhaps most importantly for the purposes of this Part, the combination of the arbitration clause and the various association rules for arbitration comprise the agreement of the parties in respect of all the matters where the 1996 Act allows the parties freedom to make their own agreements, and together form the agreement referred to in section 5 of the 1996 Act. This Part analyses how the associations have taken advantage of the new freedoms to update their rules for arbitration.

3–08 In addition, some associations provide a measure of instruction for arbitrators whose qualification otherwise is length of experience in the trade (see for instance, paragraph 3–12, below).

Principal commodity trade associations

3–09 There are in the very nature of things a wide variety of commodities, and therefore a very large number of trade associations to promote the interests of those particular trades. However, not all of the trades represented by associations in the United Kingdom have provisions for arbitration and of those that do, there are some whose facilities are little used. At the other extreme, there are a few associations who conduct a great deal of international arbitration and, since their rules and practice cover nearly all the possible variations, this part will deal principally with those particular trade associations which handle a large number of arbitrations. They are as follows:

The Grain and Feed Trade Association (GAFTA)

3–10 This Association results from the merging in 1971 of the London Corn Trade Association with the Cattle Food Trade Association and it therefore promotes and protects international trade in grains of all descriptions, animal feedingstuffs, rice and pulses. GAFTA protects the interests of over 710 members in 76 countries. It is recognised worldwide for its expertise in contracts and arbitration, agricultural trade policy, market commentary and training and education.

3–11 GAFTA has over 80 different standard forms of contract specifying different terms of trade, methods of shipment, origin and commodity for use in the trade. All these standard forms of contract contain not only a domicile clause (see paragraph 3–37 below) but a provision that all disputes arising out of a contract incorporating a standard form shall be settled by arbitration under GAFTA's rules for arbitration and appeal, known as GAFTA Form Number 125, as to which see below.

GAFTA has long had a training programme for arbitrators, and requires all those who are to be members of the panel of appeal (from which boards are drawn) to pass a written test paper. However, GAFTA, recognising that there are few facilities available for training in trade expertise, and that the 1996 Act now places a greater responsibility on arbitrators in the management of a case, it has recently launched a Continuing Professional Development (CPD) Programme for the whole trade in which training courses are held worldwide from foundation to advanced levels, ranging from one week residential courses to workshops and one day seminars. Within its CPD Progamme, GAFTA has provided for refresher courses and an assessment panel for existing arbitrators, to ensure that they reach a standard known as Qualified Arbitrator. Aspirant arbitrators must complete a CPD Programme and obtain a certain number of points to become a Qualified Arbitrator. 3–12

The lengthy consultation process that led to a new Arbitration Bill coupled with the enactment of the 1996 Act some seven months in advance of its coming into force on January 31, 1997 has enabled GAFTA and most other associations to draft new sets of arbitration and appeal rules under the 1996 Act effective from January 31, 1997. However, it should be noted that whilst section 84 of the 1996 Act applies Part 1 to all arbitral proceedings commenced after the date the Act came into force (January 31, 1997), GAFTA and FOSFA (Federation of Oils, Seeds and Fats Associations Ltd, see paragraph 3–18 below) contracts contain a clause, which forms the arbitration agreement, requiring all disputes arising out of the contract to be referred to arbitration in accordance with the arbitration rules in force at the date of the contract. This means, therefore, that the new rules of those associations only apply to disputes arising out of contracts dated on or after January 31, 1997. In the case of The Cocoa Association of London Ltd (see paragraph 3–15 below), the new rules apply to contracts concluded after February 1, 1997. In the case of the two sugar associations, however, it is the arbitration rules in force on the date on which the association receives a request for arbitration that are applicable (see below). 3–13

A copy of the new GAFTA Arbitration Rules in the revision effective from January 31, 1997 are, by kind permission of the Association, reprinted in Appendix 15, below. 3–14

The Cocoa Association of London Limited (CAL)

This long-established trade association represents the interests of growers of cocoa in countries such as Nigeria, Ghana, Cote d'Ivoire, Sierra Leone and other West African countries, Malaysia and South America, especially Brazil; of traders and brokers in Europe and Great Britain; and of consumers, mainly chocolate manufacturers in Europe. It handles quite a number of quality arbitrations, but fewer technical ones, (as to which see paragraph 3–33 below). It 3–15 also has drafted a new set of arbitration and appeal rules pursuant to the 1996 Act and these are expressed to be applicable to contracts concluded on or after February 1, 1997, which makes them consistent with both GAFTA and FOSFA (see below).

Sugar associations

3–16 There are two Sugar Trade Associations run by the same personnel and from the same office. One deals with raw sugar from origin (usually shipped in bulk) and is called the Sugar Association of London Limited (SAOL) and the other deals with refined sugar (usually shipped in bags or poly-lined containers) and is called the Refined Sugar Association (RSA).

3–17 Their rules relating to arbitration are identical as many of the members of the trade deal in both sorts of commodity but, since raws are in practice different from refined, the associations remain separate. As explained in more detail below, the rules are basically those revised in December 1992, now amended in small but important respects to accord with the 1996 Act. Unlike the other associations, arbitrations are conducted in accordance with the rules in force, not at the date of the contract, but at the date when the association receives a written request for arbitration. Hence, the amended rules will apply to all arbitrations requested after January 31, 1997.

The Federation of Oil, Seeds and Fats Associations Limited (FOSFA—also known as FOSFA International)

3–18 This Federation results from the amalgamation of the London Oil and Tallow Trades Association and the Incorporated Oil Seeds and Fats Association, and deals with edible oils, such as soyabean oil, palm oil, and oil seeds such as soyabeans and oilseed rape. In the world scene, it overlaps a Dutch association called NOFOTA and disputes arising out of the same commodity, *e.g.* palm oil, would be arbitrated under FOSFA rules if the oil comes from a former British Empire country, *e.g.* Malaya, but arbitrated under NOFOTA if the palm oil comes from a former Dutch colony in South-East Asia. Again, its Rules for Arbitration and Appeal have been revised to accord with the 1996 Act and the new rules are effective from January 31, 1997.

The London Rice Brokers Association (LRBA)

3–19 This is not a limited company, but an association of firms of rice brokers in London and Antwerp who set a form of contract, requiring arbitration under the LRBA Rules and maintain a panel of persons qualified to act as arbitrators. Since August 1996 GAFTA has taken over the administration of its arbitrations, which are now conducted in accordance with GAFTA rules, as to which see above and paragraphs 3–61 *et seq.*, below.

Coffee Trade Federation (CTF)

Established in the early 1970s, it represents over 100 member companies including all leading roasters, merchants, brokers and wharfingers. It publishes its contract form in a booklet for incorporation by reference, as also its Rules for Arbitration. These are unique in this field in that (since May 1, 1989) they offer the choice of traditional two tier arbitration (as for GAFTA, CAL and FOSFA) or, provided the parties so specify in their arbitration agreement, a sugar association style single stage board of arbitration procedure. 3–20

The Federation of Commodity Trade Associations

All the above associations, together with others such as the Liverpool Cotton Association Limited, The London Metal Exchange (LME)(as to which, see paragraph 3–24, below), The Rubber Growers Association, The Timber Trade Federation and The United Kingdom Tea Association, together with some Futures Markets (see below) are members of the Federation of Commodity Trades Associations (the Federation) which acts as a central liaising body for contact with Ministries, Customs and Excise and, most importantly, the E.U., as well as other bodies. The Federation does not itself have any arbitration facilities; its role is one of liaison with all the commodity trade associations. 3–21

Physicals and futures markets

Distinctions

All the associations set out above deal with physicals, that is to say the commodities themselves, and contracts for the sale and purchase of such commodities for physical delivery. However, London is a centre of futures trading where what is bought and sold on the commodity futures (or terminal) markets are parcels of goods of a specified quantity and quality for delivery in certain specified months in the future. Whereas in physical trading all parties are dealing in goods which are expected to be delivered, in futures trading most of the traders 3–22 are buying and selling before the delivery dates arrive. However, those dates do arrive and a future can become a physical so that the persons who hold bought notes have to take delivery of actual goods. Likewise, those who have sold have to produce the goods for those who have bought and want to take delivery when the time arrives.

3–23 Each futures market specifies the quality of goods which are to be delivered to the market and the dealings are in specified parcels or lots. However, the goods, when received by a buyer, may not match the market's specification and there could be a claim for quality, and indeed this does arise when some buyers come to take their goods out of store, so that these associations do have arbitration rules, which, however, are seldom used since comparatively few disputes arise. This is because the London futures markets are very closely supervised and, to begin with, no one can trade on them without first becoming a member, a process that involves selection and election on proof of financial and business standing. Deposits may be involved and deals are done entirely through a clearing house.

The London Metal Exchange (LME)

3–24 The LME is a prime example of a separate and independent futures market. It is the world's leading futures market for base metals and dealings take place in minimum quantities of 25 tonnes for copper, lead, zinc and aluminium. Nickel is traded in lots of six tonnes and tin in lots of five tonnes. All sales for delivery are backed by warehouse warrants from listed warehouses throughout the U.K. and continental Europe as well as Singapore, Japan (aluminium only) and U.S.A. An arbitration service is provided for the settlement of disputes according to Arbitration Regulations revised in April 1992 to a form which almost exactly anticipated the 1996 Act. Now the new Act is in force, very little adjustment will be needed to what are an excellent and modern set of regulations.

Disputes procedures in futures markets

By association panel

3–25 All these futures markets lay down rules as to what is deemed to be incorporated in the members' contracts with the clearing house (apart from the procedures of the market itself) and one such is the provision for settlement of disputes by arbitration. Basically, this falls into two types of procedure: the first, and most universal, is the submission of the dispute to the association concerned, which appoints a panel, or board, to hear the dispute, and the parties have no right of nominating their own arbitrator. The parties submit their cases to the association which copies them to the other party and, unless the parties request a hearing, with or without witnesses, the panel has an absolute discretion to hear and decide the dispute on the written statements and documents delivered. There is little scope for advocacy in any such dispute and the parties are frequently perfectly happy for the dispute to be thus settled on documents. There is no right of appeal and the panel's award is final. Examples of this type of arbitration are found in the Futures and Options Markets formerly administered by the London Commodities Exchange now, since September 1996, merged into the London International Financial Futures and Options Exchange (LIFFE). The combined exchange offers trading in futures and options in (among other things) freight (through BIFFEX—The Baltic International Freight Futures Exchange), potatoes, barley, wheat, white sugar, robusta coffee and cocoa. The International Petroleum Exchange handle futures in mineral oils.

By party-appointed arbitrators

The other type of procedure, found in the London Gold Futures Exchange allows the parties each to appoint their own arbitrator either from a panel maintained by the association concerned, or from any member of the association. The third arbitrator, who will be chairman, is appointed by the association. The parties submit their respective cases direct to the arbitrators, who proceed on their own directions, rather than as a body under the direct control of the association. 3–26

The golden rule

The golden rule for anyone outside these trades who is about to become involved, perhaps as an adviser, in any arbitration, whether for physicals or futures, is that he should first obtain from the secretary of the relevant association a copy of the arbitration rules applicable to the contract, study them carefully, and seek clarification on any obscure points from the secretary of the association. 3–27

Historical Background to Commodity Trade Arbitrations

"Look-sniff" arbitrations

To understand how and why the soft commodity trades administer arbitrations as they do, it must be appreciated that they are based on the original "look-sniff" 3–28 arbitrations for quality and/or condition which were and are such an important feature of commodity trading. Goods shipped in bulk from far off origins could not be sent back if they were not to the liking of the buyer, so each trade quickly developed a system of experts in each commodity who could say whether or not goods were as required by the contract, or, if not, in what respect they fell short, and what should be the measure of damages. Such experts, knowing the market price of contractual goods, could say what the true value of the particular goods in question should be and therefore assess an allowance, payable by the seller, which amounted to a reduction in the price.

3–29 Since the only way a dispute between the parties was going to be settled was for it to be referred to experts, not in the employ of either of the parties, but outside, and therefore independent persons, the procedure developed whereby each party, the buyer and the seller, appointed his own expert, or ''arbitrator'', drawn from the trade to arbitrate the difference for him. So the two arbitrators, as recognised experts, but independent of the parties, would meet to examine a sample of the goods and try to agree on the allowance to be awarded. If they could not agree then they brought in a third person, an umpire, who made the decision as, in effect, a sole arbitrator. Both the arbitrators and the umpire would act as judiciously as possible to be fair as between the parties, but of course, they were primarily experts.

3–30 Their services, however, were unique, and not an alternative to the courts, for they would be assessing whether, say, wheat or barley was ''fair average quality'' (f.a.q.) for the month of shipment and country of origin specified in the contract or, if the contract warranted condition at discharge (known as a Rye Terms Contract), assess the depreciation compared to sound grain, or whether cocoa beans were good fermented or only fair fermented, or what was the percentage of broken or defective grains in rice or the amount of ''foots'' in edible oils and so on. These matters (which do not necessarily depend on laboratory analysis) are all highly technical to the layman and disputes on them are quite unsuited to the courts. Moreover, traders accepted that goods frequently failed either in quality or condition to match up to the contractual stipulation, and were anxious to keep all such matters for settlement within the trade and without the lawyers (an instinct that prevails to this day). After all, there is small opprobrium on a seller whose goods arrive defective, very little of a litigious nature in the buyers' claim for an allowance, just a recognition by all that, in the world of agricultural products, these things are facts of life to be settled fairly and amicably by the impartial services of experts in the trade, arbitrating the differences.

3–31 Further, since bulk commodities are rarely now the subject of a single sale direct from origin (*e.g.* Africa) to country of destination (*e.g.* Europe), but traded cost, insurance and freight (c.i.f.) through a string of intermediate traders, an allowance awarded by arbitrators at the end of the line can, if expressed as a percentage, *e.g.* two per cent, be applied throughout the string back to origin and this is, in certain trades expressly provided for in the contract. See generally as to string arbitrations at paragraphs 3–57 and 3–97 *et seq.* and paragraph 3–118, below.

Distinction between quality/condition and technical arbitrations

From these beginnings, it was but a short step to call in arbitrators to deal with default, which, in an area that is primarily concerned with shipment of raw materials and agricultural produce from far-off countries to Europe, meant (originally) failure by a seller to provide the goods. This type of dispute became known as "technical" as opposed to the quality/condition disputes comprised in "look-sniff" arbitrations, because it involved contract law and assessment of damages for breach of contract. Nowadays, the panels of approved arbitrators maintained by trade associations are commonly divided into a list of those who are qualified to conduct technical arbitrations and those who are also qualified to conduct quality arbitrations, with, in the case of GAFTA, a further division of the latter into the types of goods in respect of which such arbitrators are qualified, *e.g.* grains or proteins, pulses or fishmeal. With the exception of goods whose standard is assessed by laboratory analysis (*e.g.* sugar and palm oil) literally thousands of quality arbitrations take place, very few of which get beyond settlement by three arbitrators in the manner set out at paragraphs 3–140 *et seq.* below. 3–32

Technical arbitrations

Although the term is not so much used now as formerly, technical arbitrations means the whole field of disputes other than quality/condition that can (and do) arise in the buying and selling of bulk commodities such as wheat, barley and grains of all kinds, pulses, oil seeds such as soyabeans and a multitude of ingredients for animal feed (such as tapioca, fish meal and innumerable kinds of expellers), rice, cocoa, coffee, sugar (raw and refined) edible oils and metals. These goods may come from all corners of the world, be shipped for processing or manufacture in Europe or for consumption almost anywhere, and be sold free on board (f.o.b.), cost, insurance and freight (c.i.f.) or ex-store. Payment may be in cash against presentation of documents or by irrevocable letters of credit, and goods may be bulked by one f.o.b. shipper from several suppliers, may be sold and re-sold many times c.i.f., and cargoes may arrive at (say) Rotterdam destined for many different buyers, requiring delivery orders to be drawn out of bills of lading. There are generally export licences required, sometimes import licences, sometimes exchange control regulations. There are prohibitions of export, *force majeure* events and bankruptcies; failure to deliver or failure to pay: demurrage disputes when rivers are congested or supplies held up, discrepancies in documents, defects in documents: questions of waiver and estoppel to be decided. Experienced trade arbitrators are called upon to adjudicate in all such matters, drawing on their knowledge and experience in trade to lead them to a commercial decision, without being biased or influenced by the knowledge that the vast majority of such disputes arise from a movement in market prices 3–33 making the contract less profitable, or even a loss to the party seeking to avoid performance, or justify non-performance.

3–34 It is worth pointing out at this stage that the rules and procedures for commodity trade arbitrations are substantially the same, whether the dispute is technical or in respect of quality and/or condition and the particular factors relating to the latter are dealt with at paragraphs 3–140 *et seq*. below.

The Modern Format: Single Tier and Two Tier Systems

3–35 All the arbitrations described elsewhere in this Handbook consist of the one arbitral process resulting in a final award, which can only be taken to the courts if either party is dissatisfied with it. However, a fundamental and ancient feature of commodity trade arbitration is the two tier system, whereby the first arbitration is held speedily and relatively informally and results in the issuance of an award, which, subject to time limits, can be appealed by a dissatisfied party to a board of appeal of the relevant association. This gives a party two bites at the cherry and the arbitral process is not deemed to be concluded until the board of appeal has issued its final award.

3–36 Two tier systems are employed by GAFTA, CAL, FOSFA and CTF. The single tier system is favoured by the two Sugar Associations, SAOL and RSA for physical sugar, also by the LME and certain Terminal Markets for futures in sugar, cocoa, coffee and rubber and is optionally available in CTF arbitration. The procedure for single tier arbitrations will be examined at paragraphs 3–40 *et seq.* below and the stages in two tier arbitrations at paragraphs 3–61 *et seq.* and 3–111 *et seq.* below.

The Arbitration Agreement

Standard clauses in contracts

3–37 The standard forms of contract issued by each trade association for the use of its members (at their option) contain a clear and concise provision that any dispute arising out of or under the contract shall be settled by arbitration in accordance with the rules for arbitration of the relevant association. This provision will usually be followed by a *Scott v. Avery* clause,[1] forbidding resort to a court until the arbitration process has been exhausted. The GAFTA contract forms go further and, because contracting parties are most likely to be from different countries, contains a domicile clause whereby the parties agree that for the purposes of arbitration and settlement of disputes, the parties are deemed to be domiciled in England and agree that the contract and all disputes under it shall be governed in all respects by English law.

Mandatory and optional forms of contract

In some trades, it is considered mandatory for the official contract forms issued by the relevant trade association to be used for each and every contract, and this is common in, *e.g.* CAL and LRBA who only issue a few different contract forms. GAFTA contracts, on the other hand, are multitudinous and particularly long and comprehensive and originals are not always used. Much of GAFTA trade is done through Brokers who usually confirm the business by a brokers' confirmation note which the parties accept as the binding contract between them, and this is in shorter form and contains the vital information as to the parties, the goods, the price, the delivery date and special conditions, winding up with a statement as to the basis of the contract and a stipulation for arbitration (for in the commodity trades it is accepted that disputes should be referred to arbitration in the first instance and not the courts, and it is merely a matter of deciding which particular association's rules will apply). In such cases, therefore, it is not uncommon for the brokers' contract note to have a printed clause providing for these two stipulations to be filled in, so that the relevant GAFTA Contract form number can be stated, and arbitration stipulated as *e.g.* "London as per GAFTA 125" (GAFTA's Arbitration Rules being their Form 125). **3–38**

Who may use the standard forms of contract

As already noted above, in the case of the futures or terminal markets, only members of the market can trade, and, as such, they are bound by all the relevant rules of their particular association, including compulsory submission to arbitration in accordance with that market's arbitration rules by virtue of that membership and as a condition of trading. In the case of physicals, parties who are not members at all of the relevant association may opt of their own volition to trade on the contract terms of a particular association based in London and to refer all disputes to arbitration in London in accordance with that association's rules. **3–39**

[1] *Scott v. Avery* [1856] 5 H.L. Cas. 811.

Procedure in Single Tier Arbitrations

3–40 The best modern example of the single tier arbitration system in commodity trade arbitration is that adopted by the two physical sugar associations, the Sugar Association of London for raw sugar and the Refined Sugar Association for refined sugar. A copy of the latter's current rules (which are now identical to SAOL Rules), being basically the revision of December 1992 but with some small but important amendments to tke advantage of the 1996 Act, is reprinted in Appendix 23 below by kind permission of the Refined Sugar Association, and reference will be made to them in the following text. They serve as a clear general illustration of the close administration by a trade association of contract disputes.

The arbitration agreement

3–41 The RSA's rules relating to contracts contain an arbitration agreement in what is a fairly standard form, namely a stipulation that any dispute arising out of any contract subject to RSA contract rules shall be referred to the RSA for settlement in accordance with the rules relating to arbitration. Such contract is to be subject to English law and one of the new amendments provides that the contract rules in force at the time the contract was made apply to any reference to arbitration. Note the difference in this respect between the contract rules and the position with the arbitration rules set out at paragraph 3–45 below.

3–42 In addition, the RSA rules relating to arbitration start off with the same arbitration agreement wording quoted as a recommended arbitration clause, which parties not contracting under RSA contract rules can use if they wish to adopt dispute settlement under RSA arbitration rules.

3–43 Rule 1 then provides that any dispute arising out of or in connection with the contract which the parties have agreed (either in the contract or otherwise) to refer to arbitration by the Refined Sugar Association shall be determined in accordance with the following rules.

Claim procedure

3–44 A party who wishes to refer a dispute to arbitration under the RSA rules has first to serve seven days notice on the other party that the reference is to be made. After the expiry of the seven day notice, the claimant then refers the dispute to the council of the association by sending to the secretary a written request for arbitration.

3–45 An amendment to this rule stipulates that the arbitration rules in force at the time such request is received will apply to the reference, which is a somewhat different stance to that adopted by the associations operating two tier systems, who, as we have seen above , prefer to take the date of the contract as deciding the edition of the rules applicable to any dispute arising out of that contract.

The claimant must, either together with the request for arbitration or within 30 days thereafter (or such extended period as the council may allow), forward to the secretary in duplicate a clear and concise statement of his case in writing, together with a copy of the relevant contract containing the arbitration agreement, and any other documentary evidence which he thinks proper, together with details of names, addresses, telex and faxsimile numbers of the parties and a fee. The claimant may also, "without prejudice to the provisions of the Arbitration Act 1996 relating to security for costs" be required to make an advance payment on account of the association's fees, costs, and expenses, as referred to in rule 3, which contains a general power to this effect (rule 2). **3–46**

The same rule (rule 2) deals with jurisdiction by providing that, on receipt of the claimant's documents, the council thereupon has power to determine any such matter in dispute. A new amendment states that, without prejudice to the provisions in the 1996 Act relating to jurisdiction, where both parties are members of the association, the council shall have the jurisdiction to determine whether a contract has been made, whether there is a valid arbitration agreement and what matters have been referred to arbitration pursuant to that agreement. Presumably the fall-back provisions of section 30 of the 1996 Act will apply to cover the case where one or both parties are not members of the RSA. **3–47**

The secretary then sends one copy of this statement of claim, with copy documents annexed, to the respondent who then has 30 days (extendable at the council's discretion) after those documents have been despatched to him to send in his own statement of claim with supporting documents, again in duplicate, and again the secretary sends one copy on to the claimant. **3–48**

Each party then has a period of 21 days (or such extended time as the council may allow) to submit further written comments or documents. All submissions and documents must be in the English language, so that if foreign documents are included, translations must be provided. **3–49**

Appointment of panel of arbitrators

For the determination of a dispute, the council appoints a body of not less than three nor more than five persons (at the council's absolute discretion) drawn from its panel of arbitrators to act on its behalf, and that body appoints a chairman who, if necessary, has a second or casting vote so as to ensure that the award is of a majority. The council has power to fill vacancies and also to replace any member found for any reason to be unable to act. The body so formed acts on behalf of the council (rule 9). **3–50**

Determination on documents only, or with oral hearing

The council has a power in its discretion to decide the case purely on the written statements and documents which have been submitted under the procedure set **3–51** out at paragraphs 3–40 *et seq.* above, without the attendance of the parties or their representatives and witnesses. However, the council may call the parties before it and request the attendance of witnesses, and also consult the association's legal advisers, whose advice is for the council alone and not to be available to the parties. Should either of the parties require an oral hearing, they must make their request in writing to the secretary. The council may grant or refuse such request in their absolute discretion without assigning any reason. In the event of an oral hearing, with or without witnesses, the parties may appear personally or by counsel or solicitor. Neither party may make any oral statement in the absence of the other, excepting where his oppponent fails to appear after having been given due notice by the secretary. Without prejudice to section 34 of the 1996 Act, the council is not to be bound by the strict rules of evidence and is at liberty to admit and consider any material whatsoever notwithstanding that it may not be admissible under the law of evidence.

3–52 Unless both parties notify the secretary in writing to the contrary, the council shall issue a reasoned award (rule 10 amended). Although rule 8 declares that disputes are settled according to the law of England and that the seat of the arbitration is England, the rule further states that it shall not be necessary for the award to state expressly the seat of the arbitration. This negatives that provision in section 52(5) of the 1996 Act.

Award

3–53 The award, when drawn up, either by members of the council hearing the case, or by the association's legal adviser, is to be signed by the chairman alone and deemed to be the award of the council, final and binding in all cases (rule 9) (this negatives section 52(3) of the 1996 Act, suggesting that all the arbitrators, or at least, those assenting, should sign). It is recorded in a register, and the parties are notified that the award is ready for collection, on payment of the relevant fees, which are fixed by the council as it determines. As soon as one party takes up the award, on payment of the fees, a copy is sent to the other party, but if the award is not taken up by either party within 10 days, the secretary of the association may call upon either of the parties to take up the award and whichever party is so called upon must take up the award and pay the fees and expenses (rule 14).

3–54 By an amendment to rule 10, the council has the power to make more than one award at different times and on different issues in accordance with section 47 of the 1996 Act, but not to make provisional awards pursuant to section 39 of the 1996 Act.

Honouring the award

The rules provide (rule 15) that all arbitral awards must be honoured within 28 days after the date when it is taken up. There is a disciplinary provision at rule 16 that in the event of a party to an arbitration neglecting or refusing to carry out or abide by any award, the council may circularise members with a notification to that effect, and the parties to any such arbitration are deemed to have consented to the council taking such action. This, of course, is an important regulatory measure which is used by many commodity trade associations, as a protection and service to its members (but see further at paragraph 3–131, below). 3–55

Refusal to participate

An unusual provision is found in rule 5 to deal with a party who, being in dispute with another party, refuses to concur in the reference to arbitration. The claimant may forthwith obtain an award of the council on the question in dispute. This rule also allows the council, at its discretion, to refuse to arbitrate on any reference made by a member who has been suspended from the association or whose membership has been revoked. Such a party may then seek redress by action in the courts, a remedy permitted to him by the exclusion wording in rule 6 (see paragraph 3–58 below). 3–56

String arbitrations

There is a specific power (rule 7) for the council, in its absolute discretion, to arbitrate between the first seller and the last buyer in what is presumably a string of contracts (though the term ''string'' is not used) when the subject matter and terms of the contract are identical except as to date and price. Such a provision is often found in commodity trade arbitration rules but limited usually only to disputes in respect of quality and/or condition, where it is logical that such disputes should be so arbitrated (see paragraphs 3–31 *et seq.* above and paragraphs 3–97 *et seq.* and 3–118, below). However, it is difficult to see that such a provision can ever apply on a technical dispute, where the relations between the parties are governed strictly on a one to one basis. Although strings, either c.i.f. or f.o.b. may well be on identical terms save as to date and price, in practice technical arbitrations are usually held only between the parties to each contract and, although rule 7 of the Refined Sugar Association's rules does not say so, in practice, the council's discretion is likely to be exercised mainly where the dispute is restricted to quality and/or condition. 3–57

General

3–58 There are a number of other provisions in the rules to give them practical efficacy, for instance a form of *Scott v. Avery*[2] provision at rule 6 to the effect that, unless the council has refused to arbitrate in the circumstances set out in rule 5 (see paragraph 3–56 above) neither party shall bring any action against any other party to the contract in respect of any dispute arising out of it, until such dispute shall have been adjudicated upon in arbitration under the rules, and the obtaining of an award under the rules is stated to be a condition precedent to the right of either contracting party to sue the other.

3–59 There are also provisions as to the fees, which are to be settled by the council and recovered as set out above, and for withdrawal of a claim or counterclaim (rule 11).

3–60 A new provision, now becoming popular with commodity trade associations as part of their endeavours to inform and instruct their members, enables an edited version of the award or a summary of its points to be made available to members in a form approved by the parties, if they give their consent to such limited publication (see rule 17). GAFTA, for instance, has had such a practice for some time, not in the rules, but by means of a slip attached to all awards inviting the parties to agree to the publication to members of an anonymised version of the award.

Procedure in Two Tier Arbitrations

3–61 The essence of two tier systems is that there is first a fairly speedy and simple arbitration before a single arbitrator or a tribunal of three arbitrators, then secondly a right of appeal to a board of appeal of, usually, five persons. Originally, such appeal used to be only in cases where the arbitrators had made some error and the board of appeal was required to confirm an arbitrator's award unless a majority decided that it should be upset. Nowadays,the appeal is a complete re-hearing with the board of appeal generally free to make an entirely new award, as explained at paragraphs 3–111 *et seq.* below. Nevertheless, GAFTA's new rules contain, at rule 12:5, a stipulation that the award of arbitration shall be confirmed unless a majority of the board of appeal decide to vary, amend or set it aside.

3–62 For this section, particular reference will be made to the new GAFTA Arbitra-

[2] See para. 3–37, above.

tion Rules, Form 125, in the edition effective January 31, 1997, which, as noted above, are set out in Appendix 15 below, and all rule numbers quoted are from these GAFTA rules. For convenience, comparisons are made, where appropriate, to equivalent provisions in CAL and FOSFA rules.

The arbitration agreement

As already pointed out above, in most two tier systems, including GAFTA, the contract itself contains the arbitration agreement, together with the complementary *Scott v. Avery* clause,[3] so that the arbitration rules themselves start off by providing that any dispute arising out of a contract incorporating those rules shall be referred to arbitration in accordance with the following provisions. **3–63**

Preliminary matters

Rule 1 provides for the 1996 Act to apply, for the juridical seat of the arbitration, pursuant to section 4 of the 1996 Act, to be England and for arbitrations to take place at the association's registered offices in London or (without prejudice to the first two provisions) elsewhere if agreed by the parties. Similar provisions are to be found in FOSFA rules, whereas CAL rules content themselves with an English Law domicile and jurisdiction clause and a requirement that all hearings shall take place in London unless the arbitrators or board of appeal otherwise decide. **3–64**

Commencement of arbitration and time limits

Under rule 2, the arbitration is commenced by the claimant serving on the respondent a notice stating his intention to refer a dispute to arbitration, but within certain time limits. A traditional feature of most commodity trade arbitration is the imposition of sharp time limits within which a claim to arbitration must be made. If anything goes wrong with a contract, it is important that each party should know whether a claim is going to be made against him, and if the time limit expires without a claim being made, he can feel fairly safe in continuing business without making any provision for a claim. However, it is not uncommon for a claim to be made within the time limits and arbitrators appointed but further steps delayed, merely to preserve the rights of the claimant (but as to lapse of claims after too long a delay, see rule 4:9 below). **3–65**

So, in GAFTA Rules, the rest of rule 2 is devoted to a list of the relevant time limits. Rule 2:1 deals with quality and/or condition disputes where, because **3–66**

[3] See para. 3.37, above.

the nature of the claim requires speedy action before (further) deterioration sets in, the limits are necessarily short, ranging from 10 to 21 days. For monies due (rule 2:2), *e.g.* on a final adjustment of invoices for weight on out-turn or for demurrage, claims are to be made within 90 days after the dispute has arisen, which means that if a payer simply does not pay, the claimant must ensure that a dispute situation quickly arises so that time begins to run.

3–67 All other disputes relating to sale of goods are lumped into rule 2:3 where the limit is 90 days after the relevant period, *e.g.* for CIF, CIFFO and C&F shipment terms, from the expiry of the contract period of shipment or completion of final discharge at port of destination, whichever last expires, while for FOB terms, it is from the date of the last bill of lading or the expiry of the contract period of delivery, whichever first expires. For any other terms, it is 90 days from the last day of of the delivery, collection or arrival period as the case may be.

3–68 Any such failure to claim in time is a point that must be taken by the respondent in his submissions and not raised by the tribunal. Rule 2:4 makes it clear that unless this is done, no award can afterwards be questioned or challenged on the grounds that the claim was not made within the relevant time limits (see, however, rule 22 below for discretion to admit late claims).

3–69 In CAL, the claimant must notify the respondent within the time limits (if any) stipulated in the market rules or, if none is so stipulated, within 56 days of the dispute arising, and this time limit will apply to all technical claims. The relevant market rules stipulate only that quality claims must be notified within 28 days of landing or unstuffing or tender in/ex store and that arbitration shall be held no later than 56 days from such landing, unstuffing or delivery. In the past, CAL arbitrators have felt it incumbent upon themselves to check whether time limits have been observed, not leaving it to a respondent to raise the issue. Under the new rules, however, arbitrators are not to be obliged to take the initiative in ascertaining any facts or questions of law which are not raised by one of the parties. Therefore, if a claim is out of time, it is now up to the respondent to raise it, since there is no obligation on the arbitrators to do so.

3–70 Under FOSFA rules, a claimant has to give a notice claiming arbitration with the name of his appointed arbitrator within 21 days for quality and/or condition (14 days if supported by a certificate of analysis) and otherwise within 120 days in all those cases where GAFTA allows 90 days, except for moneys due, where the limit is 60 days.

3–71 The general rule is that anyone trading in any particular commodity must know by heart the time limits within which a claim has to be made, for if not, then most rules provide that any claims are deemed to have been waived and are absolutely barred, subject, however, to an absolute discretion for the arbitrators (or board of appeal, where approprate) to admit a claim nevertheless. In CAL and FOSFA, this provision appears in the rule dealing with time limits. In GAFTA, it is dealt with in a general rule on time limits, rule 22 as to which see below.

First tier arbitration—appointment of arbitrators

Rule 3 provides for the dispute to be heard and determined by a tribunal of three arbitrators, or, if both parties agree, by a sole arbitrator. 3–72

Sole arbitrator

If the claimant wants a sole arbitrator, he must, within nine days of his claiming arbitration under rule 2, (see above) serve a notice on the respondent seeking his agreement to the appointment of a sole arbitrator by GAFTA (rule 3:1(a)). The respondent must, within a further nine days, either agree to a sole arbitrator, or appoint an arbitrator to a tribunal of three arbitrators (rule 3:1(b)). If he agrees to a sole arbitrator, GAFTA will appoint one as soon as it receives the first statements and evidence to be lodged under rule 4 (see below) or on the application of either party where interlocutory or interim decisions are required (rule 3:1(c)). 3–73

Tribunal

If, however, the claimant wants a tribunal, then he must, within nine days of his claim, appoint one arbitrator and give notice of that appointment to the respondent, who, within a further nine days, must appoint a second arbitrator and give notice of that appointment to the claimant (rule 3:2(a) and (b)). Likewise, where the respondent has declined reference to a sole arbitrator and has appointed a tribunal arbitrator under rule 3:1(b), the claimant must, under rule 3:2(c), himself appoint a second arbitrator within nine days of receiving the notice of the respondent's arbitrator. GAFTA then appoints the third arbitrator in the like circumstances as it appoints a sole arbitrator (see above) and such third arbitrator is chairman of the tribunal so formed and his name is notified to the parties. 3–74

CAL has very similar provisions, save that the claimant appoints an arbitrator straight away and can ask the respondent to accept him as a sole arbitrator. If not, then the respondent appoints a second arbitrator and two officers of CAL appoint a third arbitrator who is chairman of the tribunal, as in GAFTA. 3–75

In FOSFA, the parties can agree a sole arbitrator or they can each appoint an arbitrator to enter upon the reference, and, if those two arbitrators agree, they can make an agreed award between them. However, if they disagree, they must appoint an umpire to decide the dispute as, effectively, a sole arbitrator. If they cannot agree on the appointment of an umpire, the Federation will itself make the appointment. 3–76

In all cases where a party cannot or will not appoint an arbitrator, the relevant association will make the necessary appointment (see GAFTA rules 3:3 and 3:4). 3–77

3–78 Rule 3:5 requires that any arbitrator to be appointed under the rules shall be a Qualified Arbitrator member of the association (see paragraph 3–12, above) and not be interested in the transaction in any of the ways set out in detail in the rule. His appointment is to be valid and effective provided that he has signified his consent (rule 3:6).

3–79 Advantage of the new provision in section 23 of the 1996 Act allowing revocation of an arbitrator's authority has been taken in rule 3:7, where there are the usual provisions for appointing a substitute arbitrator in certain events, such as death, refusal to act, resignation (this is new), incapacity, ineligibility or failure to proceed with the arbitration. To these is added "revocation of authority": nothing further is said as to the procedure by which such revocation may take place, so the fall-back provisions of section 23(3) and (4) of the 1996 Act must apply. In each such case, the party who originally appointed that arbitrator must forthwith appoint a substitute, with power to the association to appoint where any party fails to do so.

3–80 CAL and FOSFA both have similar provisions, but CAL does not provide for revocation of an arbitrator's authority. FOSFA has a long rule dealing with dilatoriness on the part of arbitrators or umpire which includes a power to remove either.

3–81 Rule 3:8 gives power to the association to require deposits on account of fees and expenses to be paid by any applicant for any such appointment and for the tribunal to call upon either party to deposit sums on account of fees, costs and expenses before the commencement of the arbitration hearing.

Arbitration Procedure

3–82 Having set up a sole arbitrator or a tribunal, the parties must now proceed as set out in Rule 4. Firstly, the claimant shall draw up a clear and concise statement of his case together with a copy of the contract and any supporting documents (rule 4:1) and serve them as set out in rule 4:4, namely, on the other party, with copies to the association, in 2 sets in the case of a sole arbitrator, in 4 sets in the case of a tribunal.

3–83 The respondent, on receipt of the claimant's case and documents, then has to draw up a statement of his defence (and counterclaim, if any) and, together with his documents, serve them as per rule 4:4 (rule 4:2). The claimant may serve further comments or submissions by way of reply (rule 4:3).

3–84 No time limits are set initially and nothing happens until the association receives the first set of papers served under rule 4:4, when, as noted above at paragraphs 3–73 and 3–74, the association either appoints a sole arbitrator (if such be required) or a chairman of the tribunal. Then, under rule 4:6, a time table for the proceedings will be advised to the parties by the tribunal (not forgetting that under section 15 of the 1996 Act "tribunal" includes a sole arbitrator) who are under a duty to ensure the prompt progress of the arbitration.

They may do this by making orders where appropriate and delays may be reported by the parties.

However, rule 4:5 introduces a new note taken direct from the spirit and the wording of section 33 of the 1996 Act. It provides that the tribunal may vary or depart from the procedure set out in rules 4:1,2,3 and 4 in order to give each party a reasonable opportunity of putting his case and dealing with that of his opponent and shall adopt procedures suitable to the circumstances of the particular case, avoiding unnecessary delay or expense, so as to provide a fair means for the resolution of the matters falling to be determined. 3–85

For the avoidance of doubt, rule 4:7 makes it clear that there is nothing to prevent the respondent from delivering his statement and evidence before receiving those from the claimant. A respondent, therefore, who perhaps has a counterclaim or other good reason to want to proceed with the arbitration, need not be delayed by dilatoriness on the part of the claimant. As soon as either party delivers its documents, GAFTA will appoint the Chairman of the tribunal (or sole arbitrator, as the case may be) and he is charged with the duty of ensuring the prompt progress of the arbitration (see rule 4:6). 3–86

First tier arbitrations will normally proceed on documents alone, but where the tribunal considers that an oral hearing is necessary, the association will arrange the date, time and place under rule 4:8. There is no provision for the parties to demand an oral hearing, which is to be entirely at the instigation of the arbitrators, who alone decide when it is appropriate. The subject of legal representation at hearings is dealt with separately in rule 16, as to which see below. 3–87

CAL procedure only stipulates that the claimant shall submit his statement of case and documents "as soon as reasonably possible" after the appointment of arbitrators, such being sent in four copies to the association and one to the respondent and one to each other party. On receipt of these, the respondent is likewise as soon as possible to send his statement and documents and if he makes a counterclaim, then the claimant only has 21 days to lodge his defence to such. 3–88

Under FOSFA rules, one copy of all submissions has to be sent to each arbitrator, one to the Federation and one to the other party. The claimant has to send his submissions and documents within 10 days of the claim to arbitration. However, the respondent, if he wishes to reply to the claim, must do so within 14 days, failing which the arbitrators shall proceed with the arbitration without delay. Draconian indeed! 3–89

CAL and FOSFA both provide for the parties to ask to be present at the arbitration, either in person or by representative, but not by a practising lawyer. However, CAL clearly envisages leave for such being given because then the arbitrators may order security for costs. 3–90

Lapse of claim

To deal with stale claims that have been made but not proceeded with, a provision at rule 4:9 provides for a claim to arbitration to be deemed to have lapsed 3–91 if neither party submits any documentary evidence or submissions within a period of one year from the date of the appointment of the sole arbitrator or of the first arbitrator to be appointed to a tribunal of three, unless the claim is renewed before the expiry of the year either by a notice served by either party on the other, or by the service of documentary evidence or submissions by either party. In either of these cases, the claim and counterclaim are each renewed for a further year. The claim may thus be renewed for successive periods of one year.

3–92 See rule 22 below for discretion to extend time limits generally.

3–93 FOSFA has a very similar rule, with discretion to the arbitrators (but not board of appeal) to admit a claim. CAL has no such provision.

3–94 Finally, glossing on section 28 of the 1996 Act, rule 4:10 makes the parties jointly and severably liable to pay all costs, fees and expenses of the tribunal and the association if the arbitration is abandoned, suspended or concluded by agreement or otherwise before a final award is made.

3–95 CAL approaches the problem by forbiding withdrawal of the submission to arbitration except by written agreement of the parties who must agree who is to pay the costs. FOSFA relies on a catchall rule obligating parties to arbitrations under the rules to be liable to the Federation for fees and expenses incurred.

Sampling and "Rye Terms" claims

3–96 In case either party wishes to submit samples for examination by the tribunal for quality or condition, the drawing, sealing and despatch of such must be done in accordance with GAFTA's Sampling Rules Form 124 (which are outside the scope of this Part). However, rule 5 lays down the procedure for the examination of the samples, to be done, generally, within 21 days after the completion of final discharge of the ship. The procedure for claims arising out of "Rye Terms" contracts, *i.e.* where the condition is warranted at arrival, is set out in rule 6.

String arbitrations

3–97 In respect of quality and condition, where there is a string of contracts on materially identical terms, save as to price, rule 7:1 allows a single arbitration to be held between the first seller and the last buyer in the string as though they were contracting parties. Any award so made is binding on all the intermediate parties in the string and may be enforced by any such party against his immediate contracting party.

3–98 Rule 7:2 allows parties in cases other than quality or condition to agree expressly to the tribunal conducting arbitral proceedings concurrently with other arbitral proceedings and even to conducting concurrent hearings, though of course separate awards are to be made pursuant to each contract. This rule exercises the freedoms given in section 35 of the 1996 Act as to consolidation and concurrent hearings.

CAL allows string arbitrations only for quality and condition, similar to GAFTA's rule 7:1. Under FOSFA rules, arbitration between first seller and last buyer is mandatory in all cases of quality and condition: in other cases, such may only be held if all the parties in the string agree in writing. 3–99

Jurisdiction

Prior to the 1996 Act, most associations' arbitration rules dealt with the question of the tribunal's own jurisdiction in the context of a provision for deciding whether or not there was a contract, by way of a preliminary point. Now that the 1996 Act provides, firstly, in section 7, for the separability of the arbitration agreement and, secondly, in section 30, for the tribunal to rule on its own jurisdiction, all the new rules have revised their approach to the problem. 3–100

By rule 8 the tribunal may rule on its own jurisdiction, that is, as to whether there is a valid arbitration agreement, whether the tribunal is properly constituted and what matters have been submitted to arbitration. If the tribunal holds that it does have jurisdiction, then it gets on with the arbitration, and there is no right of appeal against that determination. If, however, the tribunal determines that it has no jurisdiction, the parties are told and the claimant is invoiced for the costs. However, there is a right of appeal to a board of appeal. If it upholds the tribunal's determination, it so orders and the claimant is invoiced for the further costs incurred on the appeal. 3–101

If, however, the board of appeal reverses the tribunal's determination, then the board shall order that the dispute is referred to arbitration afresh, whereupon, the dispute is deemed to be one arising out of a contract embodying the rules, the tribunal formerly appointed ceases to act and cannot be re-appointed, and a new tribunal has to be appointed under rule 3 (see above), the time limits for such (unless extended by the board of appeal) running from the date of the board's order. 3–102

CAL has similar provisions in an extended form, save that if the either the arbitrators or the board of appeal rule that they do have jurisdiction, the original arbitrators are to continue to hear the dispute. 3–103

FOSFA rules provide for the arbitrators to decide the question, and if they agree that they have no jurisdiction, an appeal lies to the Appeal Panel of the Federation. Failing agreement of the arbitrators, they refer the matter to an umpire to rule on jurisdiction. If he decides that he does have jurisdiction, he proceeds with the arbitration. If he decides there is no jurisdiction, he tells the arbitrators who tell the parties without delay, and, again, there is a right of appeal to the Appeal Panel of the Federation. 3–104

Swept up into rule 8 are two miscellaneous matters: rule 8:2 declares that there is no right of appeal against any provisional relief ordered by a tribunal 3–105 until a final award has been made determining the issues between the parties. And in rule 8:3 advantage is taken of section 47 of the 1996 Act to empower tribunals to make awards on different aspects of the dispute (previously known as interim awards) each of which is to be final and binding, subject to any right of appeal, as to which see 3.8 below, where we shall see that there is a time limit within which any appeal might be lodged. This rule, therefore, helps to make clear when the parties must wait for a final award and when they already have a final award which may be appealed.

Awards of arbitration

3–106 In two tier systems, the awards of the tribunal, sole arbitrator or umpire are usually called awards of arbitration, to distinguish them from appeal awards, issued by boards of appeal.

3–107 Rule 9:1 requires all such awards of arbitration to be in writing and signed by the sole arbitrator or all three members of a three-man tribunal. This is marginally different from the fall-back provisions of section 52(3) of the 1996 Act requiring the signature of all those assenting to the award; nothing, however, is said to vary section 52(4) so it is a statutory implication that all such awards shall contain reasons. The tribunal has power to assess and award costs, including its own fees and expenses, and, on the application of either party made before the award is made, to extend the time for appealing, any such extension to be stated in the award (rule 9:2).

3–108 The signed (but not dated) award is sent to the association, which notifies the parties that the award is available on payment of the fees and expenses incurred by the tribunal and the association. If such are not paid within 14 days, the association can call upon one or more of the parties to take up the award and such party must then pay the fees and costs as directed. Upon receiving payment, the association then dates and issues the award, such date being the date of the award for the purposes of section 54 of the 1996 Act (rule 9:3).

3–109 Such award is final and binding on the parties, subject to any right of appeal pursuant to rule 10 (see below) (rule 9:4) and is not be questioned or invalidated on the ground that an arbitrator was not qualified to act unless objection was taken at the outset of the arbitration (rule 9:5).

3–110 CAL and FOSFA both require awards of arbitration to be written on an official form and their practice is to date the signed awards on receipt and then notify the parties. FOSFA rules further provide that if payment is not received by the Federation within 42 days of the date of the award, the parties forfeit their right to appeal.

Appeals Under a Two Tier System

If neither party appeals against the award of arbitration, then such becomes final and can be enforced in the usual way, but only after the time allowed for appeal has passed. 3–111

Procedure for claiming appeal

The rules of two tier systems provide that if either party is dissatisfied with the award of arbitrators, then the dissatisfied party may give a notice of appeal within a specified time limit, *e.g.* 30 days in GAFTA, 20 days in CAL and 42 days in FOSFA. Taking the GAFTA procedure as an example (see rule 10), the appellant must give written notice of appeal to the association, and to the other party, copied to the association. He has also to pay a fee to the association and it is a pre-condition of any appeal that the fees and expenses on the original arbitration award shall have been paid. There is also a provision at rule 10:1(c) allowing the association to call upon the appellant to pay such further sums as are required on account of the fees costs and expenses of the appeal. Where both parties appeal, the association has power to consolidate the appeals for hearing by the same board of appeal (rule 10:2). FOSFA makes such consolidation mandatory. If the appeal fee is not paid within 35 days, the appeal is deemed withdrawn, but there are provisions in case of difficulties with currency regulations (Rule 10:3), as there are in CAL and FOSFA. 3–112

The board of appeal

Each association maintains a panel or board of appeal being a list of persons qualified to sit on appeal boards. Rule 11:1 provides for boards to be elected and constituted in accordancs with the Rules and Regulations of the Association, and, when constituted, each board must appoint one member to be chairman. The board consists of three members where the appeal is from the award of a sole arbitrator, five members where the appeal is from the award of a tribunal of three. CAL and FOSFA have very similar provisions, save that boards are always of five members. 3–113

In addition to being Qualified Arbitrators (see paragraphs 3–12 and 3–78, above) all board members will be very experienced traders and persons who have performed many arbitrations at first tier level. 3–114

Appeal procedure

The appellant has to draw up his statement of case and serve it with his documents, which may include fresh evidence not before the the arbitrators, on the other party within 28 days of lodging his appeal, after which the respondent has 3–115

28 days to respond. Any reply must be served within a further 14 days. In all cases, the parties must at the same time furnish the association with copies of the documents they send each other, being three copies when the appeal is against the award of a sole arbitrator, five copies in an appeal against the award of a tribunal of three (rule 12:1 and 12:2). The board may set down some other timetable under rule 12:1. CAL allows 21 days in each case, with but a single copy to the association, whereas FOSFA merely provides for each party to present its case either orally or in writing, with no timetable laid down in advance.

Appeal awards

3–116 The association sets down a date for what is a new hearing of the dispute, when the board of appeal may confirm, vary, amend or set aside the award of arbitration (rule 12:4), but, by rule 12:5, an award shall be confirmed unless the board of appeal decide by a majority to alter it. The award is signed by the chairman alone as the award of the whole board and thereafter the procedure as to the dating and issue of the appeal award is the same as for awards of arbitration under rule 9:3, dealt with above (rule 12:6). This is reinforced by rule 15, which is largely to the same effect, for appeal awards, as rule 9:3. There are various strictures to prevent a party from making an appeal merely to gain time. Should the appellant, on learning of the date set down for the hearing, request a postponement of more than 14 days, the board has power to order him, as a condition of such postponement, to deposit with the association all or part of the money awarded in the first tier arbitration; failure to comply can lead to the appeal being deemed withdrawn, as can also happen if the board considers that the appellant has been guilty of undue delay in proceeding with his appeal (rule 12:7). CAL and FOSFA have similar provisions.

Withdrawal of appeals

3–117 The appellant has the right under rule 13 to withdraw his appeal before the board of appeal makes an award and may be entitled to a partial refund of the appeal fees if he is early enough. However, the respondent continues to have a right of appeal on the terms of rule 10 (see paragraph 3–112, above) on the basis that the 30 days allowed for him to lodge an appeal now commences with the date the respondent received notice of the appellant's withdrawal. Again, similar provisions are in CAL and FOSFA rules, save that FOSFA shortens the time from 28 to 21 days.

Appeals on string contracts—Quality and/or condition

3–118 Excepting for awards made on "Rye Terms" contracts (see paragraph 3–96 above), each party in a string award made under rule 7:1 has a right of appeal according to the terms set out in rule 14. These are largely practical arrangements to suit the rather curious situation of a string award being binding on all the intermediate parties.

Miscellaneous Matters

Legal representation and costs

Traditionally, commodity trades are not keen on allowing legal representation at arbitral hearings. Indeed, GAFTA used not to allow legal representation at all at first tier arbitrations; only at appeal, and then only with the consent of the board of appeal, given at its discretion. 3–119

Now we have section 36 of the 1996 Act allowing legal representation unless otherwise agreed by the parties. As shown at Section 31.1 above, the various trade association rules for arbitration examined in this Part form such agreement of the parties and GAFTA has therefore made a new provision at rule 16 that recognises and deals with present practice. 3–120

The rule allows the parties to agree expressly that they may have legal representation at the hearing and there is no suggestion of any permission required from the arbitral tribunal at either level (rule 16:1). It is implicit, though not expressed, that the winning party can therefore ask for an order for costs, which the tribunal is empowered to assess and award (see rule 9:1 above and rule 12:4 (d)). 3–121

Rule 16:2, however, states that, where there is no such agreement between the parties, they are nevertheless free to engage legal services in the drafting and preparation of their written documents, but the legal costs of so doing are not to be recoverable unless the tribunal considers that such costs were reasonably incurred. 3–122

This new provision should eliminate the problem of parties in the second category insisting on asking for their legal costs in the preparation of their statements of cases, which gave rise to the situation dealt with by Goff J. (as he then was) in *James Allen (Liverpool) Ltd v. London Export Corporation.*[4] 3–123

CAL rules do not permit legal representation at first tier, but envisage permission being given for such, whereupon a power to order security for costs arises. At appeal, the situation is as before, namely that parties may only have legal representation by leave of the board of appeal. FOSFA forbid any legal representation at first tier, but at appeal, such may be granted at the sole discretion of the board of appeal if the case is considered to be of special importance. 3–124

"Single Track" arbitration

Another new appearance in the GAFTA Form 125 rules is a provision at rule 17 for the parties to agree, in writing, to dispense with the two tier system in favour of a single tier arbitration. For this purpose, a tribunal of three arbitrators is appointed under rule 3:2 above, rule 16:2 as to legal assistance does not apply 3–125

[4] [1981] 2 Lloyd's Rep. 632.

and no appeal lies to a board of appeal, but either party may appeal directly to the court if leave under section 69 of the 1996 Act is granted.

3–126 It is worth mentioning here that GAFTA has a Simple Dispute Procedure contained in a separate set of rules called GAFTA No. 126. They are designed for disagreements not involving complicated legal issues, lengthy contentions or arguments and where a quick simple answer is required without a fully reasoned award. Basically, they provide for arbitration before a single arbitrator appointed by the association upon receipt of a printed arbitration agreement form signed by the parties which submits an existing dispute for settlement under the terms of GAFTA No. 126. The arbitration may take place in the domicile of the arbitrator (*i.e.* not necessarily in the United Kingdom) or elsewhere by agreement and a very simplified procedure applies, the time for claim, response and reply being seven days in each case. No legal representation is allowed and the award, with brief reasons, is to be ready, if possible, for publication to the parties seven days after the conclusion of the arbitration. Such award is final and binding with no right of appeal either to the association or the courts, for the arbitration agreement signed by the parties excludes both.

Tribunal's own evidence

3–127 A new provision at rule 19 authorises the tribunal or board of appeal, prior to the close of the proceedings, to take steps to ascertain the facts and the law on their own initiative, provided they give both parties reasonable opportunity to comment on and/or provide evidence in response. This rule is presumably encouraged by section 34 (g) of the 1996 Act, allowing a tribunal to decide whether and to what extent it should itself take the initiative in ascertaining the facts and the law. In other words, the tribunal may act inquisitorially.

Liability to pay fees and expenses

3–128 At rule 19 is a standard form in all the association's rules deeming an agreement by the parties engaging in arbitration or appeal, whether or not a member, to abide by the rules and be jointly and severally liable to the association for fees and expenses incurred. This gives the association power to require either party to pay the necessary fees, whether or not any award is taken up, as appears above. This is the same in CAL and FOSFA.

Non-compliance with time limits and rules

3–129 All provisions as to time limits and discretion to extend them are rolled up into a new rule 22. It states that if any time limit or provision in the rules are not complied with then the relevant claim, response or appeal, as the case may be, is deemed to be waived and absolutely barred. However, such matters have to be raised as a defence and if so then the tribunal has an absolute discretion whether to admit the claim on such terms as it thinks fit, or not to admit it. If it admits the claim, there is no right of appeal against that decision. If it declines to admit it then the claimant has a right of appeal pursuant to rule 10 (see paragraph 3–112, above) and the board of appeal has power in its discretion to overturn that decision and admit the claim (rule 22 (a)).

If, upon appeal, any of the provisions of rules 10 to 21 (see above) have not **3–130** been complied with, then the board has a complete discretion to extend the time for compliance or dispense with such and proceed to hear and determine the appeal. Any decision in this respect is to be final and binding (rule 22 (b)).

Power to post defaulters

A useful feature of commodity trade association arbitrations, mentioned above, **3–131** is the disciplinary power to notify members of the association if any party to an arbitration or appeal neglects or refuses to carry out or abide by a final arbitration award made under the rules. Rule 23, and similar rules in other associations, provide that parties to an arbitration or appeal are deemed to consent to the council of the association taking such action. In practice, if the winner of an award finds that the loser does not pay, he writes to the association and points out that the award has not been paid, and asks the council to consider "posting" the defaulter, by circulating all members.

As a matter of precaution, the association will communicate with the defaulter **3–132** and advise him that the application has been made and ask him whether he has anything to say, *e.g.* that payment is now being made or that a set-off is claimed. If the association is satisfied that a default has indeed taken place, then it may send out to all its members a bald notice to the effect that XYZ has failed to comply with an award of arbitration (or appeal). This, of course, has two main effects; one is that a defaulter knows that everyone will have been told that he has not abided by an arbitration award, so that his business standing is thereby diminished; secondly, members are to an extent protected by being notified of such default, so that they enter into further business transactions with that defaulter at their peril.

Of course, there are embarrassing circumstances sometimes where a perfectly **3–133** respectable party refuses to pay an award, for the simple reason that it is owed more than the amount of the award by the other party in another transaction, and refuses to be even more out of pocket by paying the award. Such reasons are often given to the association and the council then has to decide what it should do in the best interests of its members at large. The power to post is discretionary and the council is not compelled to post a defaulter.

The association may also post any party who does not pay the costs, fees or **3–134** expenses of the arbitration or appeal when called upon to do so by the association (rule 23:2).

Other provisions

3–135 There are a number of peripheral matters dealt with in all commodity association rules. One is mechanism to deal with a party who is prevented from paying money due to be paid because of currency regulations, where time can be extended upon certain proofs being suppied (rule 20).

3–136 Another is provision as to notices and service on parties and the association. Generally, such may be served by letter, telex, telegram or other method of rapid written communication (rule 21). Facsimile is not mentioned; it has the problem that at present machines cannot prove that a recipient did actually receive it. But, if he did, then it has been served.

Fees and Expenses of the Arbitrators

3–137 As seen at rule 9:1 (see paragraph 3–107, above) and rule 12:4, members of the tribunal and boards of appeal have the power (and duty) to assess and award their costs.

3–138 To assist them, the members of tribunals and boards of appeal will have (in GAFTA) a recommended hourly rate, and in other associations a rate that they set among themselves as the appropriate fee to charge, which will be related to the time consumed, the amount of time spent by the members of the tribunal or board of appeal reading the papers before and outside the actual hours of the hearing and perhaps the complexity of the case. In addition, of course, the association will itself have its own fees and expenses.

3–139 CAL rules are rare in that they set out details of the hourly rate to be charged by members of tribunals and boards of appeal (with discretion to vary such) and also the fees of the association.

Quality/condition arbitrations—usual procedure

Cocoa

3–140 The procedure for quality and condition arbitrations is a good deal simpler, and is peculiar to this type of arbitration. A sample of the goods is taken on arrival and sealed up and sent to the association. In the case of cocoa (cocoa beans or cocoa products), provisions for sampling are set out in the market rules. If the receiver considers that the cocoa is in poor condition, or of poor quality, and the parties cannot agree on an allowance,then he can claim arbitration on that alone. Thereupon three arbitrators are empanelled as described above. They attend at the association's offices, open the sample and cut the beans with a pen knife and examine the interior for slatiness, mould, insect damage or other defects, such as a smoky or hammy smell or taste. The three arbitrators do this together, each at a table with a pile of beans before him. On the results of their cutting, they agree whether an allowance should be given, and if so how much. This is entirely a matter of their personal skill and judgment.

Rice

In the case of rice, a similar procedure is followed. Each arbitrator takes a handful of the rice, and attempts to assess what is the percentage of broken, chalky, coloured or otherwise defective grains. The arbitrators between them agree on the standard of quality of the rice, and whether or not that accords with the contract description, which usually specifies the maximum percentage of brokens and other defects, *e.g.* 15 per cent, 20 per cent, 25 per cent, and so on, and also the crop-year. **3–141**

Grain or wheat

In the case of GAFTA arbitrations, many goods are sold f.a.q. (see section 3.1, above) in which case GAFTA has to set a standard for each type of grain or wheat for each month. GAFTA has a standards committee of qualified and experienced persons who select a sample of what is considered to be fair average quality for each month, and a quantity of this standard is maintained at the association's offices for use in quality arbitrations. At such arbitrations the sample of goods concerned is also delivered to the association, and the sample-room keeper prepares dishes into one of which is placed some of the standard and into another dish some from the sample concerned in the contract under dispute. However, they are not marked (only the sample-room keeper knowing which is which), and the arbitrators then enter the room and have to examine the goods blind (rather like a blind tasting of wines). They examine the dishes and decide which (if either) is better than the other, and if it turns out that the sample is better than the f.a.q., clearly there is a bonus for the buyer, who may be awarded a premium. If, however, the dish which is found to be superior is in fact the f.a.q. standard, then the arbitrators assess what is the allowance that should be given in respect of the inferior goods in the other dish. **3–142**

General

Parties may attend such examinations, and sometimes do, but in general, no one but the arbitrators attend (save for the sample-room keeper in the case of GAFTA) and in its very nature the procedure is very quick, and such arbitrations can be done in perhaps half an hour, so that the awards can be issued very speedily indeed. No association keeps its samples beyond a certain specified **3–143** time limit (*e.g.* three months or six months) after which they have to be disposed of, mainly because of space problems let alone because of deterioration or infestation problems. However, if there is an appeal against a quality arbitration, then the association should be notified in order that the samples may be retained for further examination by the appeal board. There is no appeal for condition in GAFTA where goods are sold on Rye terms. (See rule 6:4 above.)

3–144 Of course a number of quality determinations take place on laboratory analysis, *e.g.* for proteins, fats sand/silica and water, but if a defect is alleged which is not dealt with by analysis of an official sample, the parties may bring before the arbitrators unofficial samples for assessment of, e.g colour.[5]

Legal assessors

Most associations tend to have their own regular solicitor, who may be called upon to sit as legal assessor to any board of appeal requiring such, or indeed, even to arbitrators should they require advice on points of law, but the parties must be told, and in certain cases, the parties should be given an opportunity to comment on any advice or opinion given. An exception would be when such relates to advice given to assist the arbitrators to come to a conclusion.

3–145 He may be called upon to draw up any award on behalf of the board or tribunal, and his fees will be charged to the association and included as part of the costs of the award in the usual way.

3–146 CAL rules exploit section 37 of the 1996 Act and specifically provide for a board of appeal to be able on its own initiative to appoint experts or legal advisers to report to it and the parties, or to appoint assessors to assist it on any technical matters and such may attend the hearing. The parties are to be given a reasonable opportunity to comment on any information, opinion or advice offered by such person, and his fees and expenses are to be expenses of the board of appeal.

3–147 For the functions of legal assessors generally, see paragraph 2–516, above.

[5] See *Charles E. Ford v. AFEC Inc.* [1986] 2 Lloyd's Rep. 307.

Part 4

MARITIME ARBITRATIONS

By Bruce Harris, F.C.I.Arb., FRSA

Past Chairman, Chartered Institute of Arbitrators; Past President, London Maritime Arbitrators Association

What is a Maritime Arbitration?

The maritime arbitrations with which this Part deals arise under contracts. These contracts are most commonly for the use of a ship or ships (charterparties), but they may also be for the carriage of cargo (bills of lading), or for ship sales or shipbuilding. Less commonly such contracts may be for the repair of a ship, or for insurance. In most instances, the relevant contract contains an arbitration clause. 4–01

Some maritime arbitrations are not covered here, for example, the rare case of an arbitration concerned with a collision between ships, or between a ship and some other object. There the parties will invariably have agreed to refer the dispute to arbitration *after* it arises; and they will probably appoint a specialist Admiralty barrister as arbitrator and proceed much as they would in the Admiralty Court. Similarly, no attempt is made to deal with the (far more common) salvage arbitrations conducted under the auspices of Lloyd's. 4–02

Why is arbitration used in maritime matters?

Historically, the majority of contractual shipping disputes have long been resolved by arbitration rather than through the courts. As with other specialised businesses (*e.g.* the commodity trades and construction), those involved in shipping have generally preferred the judgement of their peers, as well as the privacy and flexibility of procedure that arbitration offers. 4–03

The most common type of maritime contract giving rise to disputes that are referred to arbitration is the charterparty. That is a contract for the use of a ship, either for a particular voyage or for a period of time ("voyage" and "time" charterparties respectively). For centuries such contracts have been broked through specialised markets, most notably the Baltic Exchange in London. There it became customary for the brokers of disputing parties to seek the views of a senior colleague by which, frequently, the parties would abide. This informal procedure is thought to have been the seed of more formalised arbitration practices. 4–04

Where does maritime arbitration take place?

Maritime arbitration is international

The Baltic Exchange is still regarded as at the heart of the world's shipbroking activities and, probably as a consequence, London is the main centre for mari- 4–05 time arbitration. There are, however, many other centres which provide the seat for a number of maritime arbitrations, notably New York, Paris, Tokyo and Hong Kong. The parties to maritime arbitrations are rarely of the same nationality. Frequently both are strangers to the venue chosen. The ventures with which the contracts are concerned often involve a ship flying one country's flag, owned by a corporation which is itself beneficially owned by the residents of another nation and is established in a third country, carrying cargoes between the ports of yet different countries. For all these reasons, maritime arbitration can truly be said to be international.

London—the centre of maritime arbitration

4–06 Nonetheless, London remains the most important venue for maritime arbitrations in the world. More than half of all such arbitrations are conducted there. Whilst the focus of this Part is London, some brief comments on the practice of maritime arbitration in other centres such as those named above appear in paragraphs 4–113 *et seq.*

Ad hoc v. administered arbitrations

4–07 The bulk of maritime arbitrations in the world are conducted on an *ad hoc* basis, *i.e.* no organisation administers them. The Chambre Arbitrale Maritime in Paris and the Japan Shipping Exchange in Tokyo are particular exceptions. Generally, however, the shipping world has not adopted administered arbitration schemes. Although in 1978 the International Chamber of Commerce ("the ICC") and the Comité Maritime International jointly set up the International Maritime Arbitration Organisation (known as "IMAO") in Paris, it has so far only been seized of nine cases. Bodies such as the International Court of Arbitration of the ICC or the London Court of International Arbitration ("the LCIA") are also very rarely involved in shipping cases. The arbitration clauses found in shipping contracts seldom provide for a particular administering body, or even for any particular rules to apply.

Why is maritime arbitration common?

4–08 Most maritime arbitration concerns what is called "tramp" shipping. To understand why this is so, it is helpful to appreciate the distinction between "liner" shipping on the one hand and "tramp" shipping on the other. The former business is regular and is generally run by substantial operators and used by fairly regular shippers. Contracts (booking notes or bills of lading) are on well-established and unamended standard forms. Disputes seldom arise (save in respect of loss of or damage to cargo) and when they do they are normally settled. Rarely do they lead to arbitrations.

4–09 Tramp shipping, on the other hand, is largely speculative. It often involves on both sides (*i.e.* owners and charterers) relatively small interests who are contracting frequently on a "one-off" basis. Elaborate terms are agreed—often under great time pressure—for the particular business in question, the shipowner seeking to maximise his returns and the charterer seeking to limit his liabilities. Many provisions are left ambiguous, often intentionally. The unexpected always happens, both at sea and in ports. Delays occur, damage is caused, losses are suffered; all with very great frequency.

Many tramp shipping contracts are performed each year. Consequently, many disputes arise and need to be arbitrated upon. There is little or no stigma attached to having an arbitration in this line of business: parties frequently do so whilst continuing to make new contracts with one another. 4–10

The result is a great deal of work. In London alone there are at least 10 individuals who can fairly be described as full-time maritime arbitrators and twice as many again who do a substantial amount of arbitration on a part-time basis. Between them they produce around 400 awards per year. Four or five times as many arbitrations are started each year: the majority settle. Ultimately the full implementation of the philosophy of the 1996 Act is likely to increase the burden on these already busy arbitrators: this is discussed in a little more detail in paragraphs 4–64 *et seq*. below. 4–11

Parties and Their Representatives

Parties

As will have become apparent, the parties involved in maritime arbitrations are mostly shipowners on the one side and charterers on the other. In some cases, of course, the parties to a dispute will be buyers and sellers of a ship, in others owners and repairers, and so on. Frequently an owner will charter his ship to a charterer who, in turn, sub-lets the ship to another charterer. The process may continue further down a sometimes fairly lengthy line. In such cases, the charterer who sub-lets will normally be referred to as a "disponent owner". (See also paragraphs 4–87 *et seq*., below.) 4–12

Representatives—P&I and Defence Clubs

Almost all shipowners, and nowadays many charterers (whether time-charterers or voyage charterers) enter the ships which they own, operate or charter in P&I Associations and Defence Associations. These play an important part in 4–13 maritime arbitration. They are frequently the paymasters for the costs involved, so it is useful here to consider briefly their functions. Both types of association are in fact mutual insurance organisations and hence are referred to as "Clubs", the insured being "members".

P&I Clubs

4–14 P&I ("Protecting and Indemnity") Clubs provide insurance against third-party liabilities. They insure, for example, liabilities for loss of or damage to cargo, oil pollution, damage to fixed and floating objects, wreck removal, death and personal injury and so on. In addition, as is usual in the case of such insurance, these clubs cover their insured's legal costs of defending or prosecuting any proceedings related to an insured peril.

4–15 Because of the nature of P&I cover and the fact that much of it concerns claims in tort or disputes arising under contracts where arbitration clauses are relatively uncommon (*e.g.* bills of lading), relatively few cases involving such cover go to arbitration. Nonetheless, quite frequently, for example, a shipowner will, through arbitration, seek an indemnity from his charterer in respect of some liability that he may have to cargo interests or even to an injured stevedore. In such cases the P&I Clubs are very much involved because they will normally be exercising subrogated rights in respect of any liability that falls upon their owner member.

Defence Clubs

4–16 Defence Clubs, in contrast, do not insure liabilities as such. They exist to provide their members (be they owners or charterers) with legal costs insurance in respect of the prosecution or defence of claims which are not otherwise insured. Defence Club cover is discretionary, in the sense that members do not have an absolute right to have all their costs paid. Usually a Club will cover the costs of a preliminary investigation with a view to an opinion being formed on the member's case; thereafter continued cover will be in the discretion of the Club, normally depending upon the view formed.

4–17 Usually in maritime arbitrations it is Defence Clubs that are in the background, because the disputes very frequently involve claims for freight, time-charter hire, damages for detention and other such matters that are uninsured. In those cases the sums in dispute are purely for the account of the members whilst, subject to the exercise of the Defence Club's discretion, legal costs may be for the account of such a Club.

Club Managers

4–18 The firms that manage both P&I and Defence Clubs are staffed by experienced claims handlers, many of them lawyers but others having commercial, nautical and/or technical backgrounds. They are thus particularly well equipped to handle the kind of disputes that arise. However, with rare exceptions, they normally only handle the initial stages of any particular matter, and thereafter keep a watching brief on behalf of their Clubs, the actual conduct of any particular dispute being put into the hands of lawyers. Interestingly, many of today's busier maritime arbitrators in London have Club backgrounds. This is probably because of the growing need for arbitrators to be able to understand increasingly legalistic disputes and to handle more procedural complexities than in the past (see paragraphs 4–50 *et seq.*, below). As a general rule, though, most parties and even many lawyers hitherto did not want to have professional lawyers (even retired ones) acting as arbitrators. There now seems to be less objection to lawyer-arbitrators, however.

Arbitrators are quite commonly appointed by Clubs because they handle the earlier stages of cases. This is perhaps another reason why arbitrators with Club backgrounds are popular. 4–19

Representatives—lawyers and lay claim handlers

The cases themselves are in most instances handled by lawyers. However, in recent years there has developed a (generally welcome) tendency to use lay claims handlers rather than lawyers. Particularly in matters which are dealt with on documents alone they can be at least as effective as many lawyers and no doubt cost less (many are based abroad and their fees do not begin to compare with those of City of London solicitors). Happily for them and the parties who use them it has now been established that their costs are recoverable by a successful party in arbitration.[1] 4–20

Arbitration Clauses

Standard form contracts

Most shipping contracts are based on standard forms or on previous contracts which are so based. There are numerous printed forms of charterparty and of bills of lading, and a few standard ship sale forms, of which one is in almost universal use. Ship repairers and shipbuilders will usually employ their own pro-formas. Most printed standard contract forms and pro-formas contain arbitration clauses. Examples of some of the clauses are set out below. Normally 4–21

[1] See *Piper Double Glazing Ltd v. D.C. Contracts* [1992] All E.R. 177.

such clauses will specify how many arbitrators there are to be (usually three, but sometimes two with the possibility of an umpire), how the arbitrators are to be appointed (usually each party appoints one) and where the arbitration is to take place (some clauses provide for options, but even when they do not, parties often change the printed venue in favour of another one).

The Baltime Clause

4–22 The Baltime form (a printed form of time charter) includes an arbitration clause which is often imported into charterparties concluded on other forms, either by reference or by being set out in full. It provides:

> ''ARBITRATION: Any dispute arising under the Charter to be referred to arbitration in London (or such other place as may be agreed according to Box 24) one Arbitrator to be nominated by the Owners and the other by the Charterers, and in case the Arbitrators shall not agree then to the decision of an Umpire to be appointed by them, the Award of the Arbitrators or the Umpire to be final and binding upon both parties.''

4–23 Such a clause does not limit in any way the choice of the parties' arbitrators.

The Centrocon Clause

4–24 Another common clause, which again is often imported into charterparties on different forms, is found in the Centrocon charterparty (a printed voyage charter form). It provides:

> ''All disputes from time to time arising out of this contract shall, unless the parties agree forthwith on a single arbitrator, be referred to the final arbitrament of two arbitrators carrying on business in London who shall be Members of the Baltic and engaged in the Shipping and/or Grain Trades, one to be appointed by each of the parties, with power to such Arbitrators to appoint an Umpire. Any claim must be made in writing and Claimant's Arbitrator appointed within three months [commonly amended to six or 12 months] of final discharge, and where this provision is not complied with the claim shall be deemed to be waived and absolutely barred. No Award shall be questioned or invalidated on the grounds that any of the Arbitrators is not qualified as above, unless objection to his acting be taken before the Award is made.''

4–25 This clause does impose limits on those who may be arbitrators under it. Whilst membership of the Baltic Exchange is easily proved, it is more difficult to know the exact meaning of ''engaged in the Shipping and/or Grain Trades'', and there is little authority to assist. It is thought, though, that the courts will normally take a fairly liberal view.

The New York Produce Exchange Form Clause

One very common arbitration clause—because the printed form in which it is found is widely used nowadays—is the New York Produce Exchange form of time-charter clause. It reads: 4–26

> "That should any dispute arise between Owners and the Charterers, the matter in dispute shall be referred to three persons at New York [commonly replaced by London], one to be appointed by each of the parties hereto, and the third by the two so chosen; their decision or that of any two of them, shall be final, and for the purpose of enforcing any Award, this agreement may be made a rule of the Court. The Arbitrators shall be commercial men."

What is worthy of note for present purposes in this clause is that it provides for three arbitrators (though, until the passing of the 1979 Act, that was deemed to be a reference to two arbitrators and an umpire).

The Asbatankvoy Clause

Another clause which provides for three arbitrators is found in a form very commonly used for the voyage-chartering of tankers, the Asbatankvoy form. This clause, which is extremely lengthy, provides for arbitration in New York or London (according to a choice to be made elsewhere in the charter form) before: 4–27

> "a board of three persons, consisting of one arbitrator to be appointed by the Owner, one by the Charterer, and one by the two so chosen. The decision of any two of the three on any point or points shall be final. Either party hereto may call for such arbitration by service upon any officer of the other, wherever he may be found, of a written notice specifying the name and address of the arbitrator chosen by the first moving party and a brief description of the disputes or differences which such party desires to put to arbitration. If the other party shall not . . . within 20 days of the service of such first notice, appoint its arbitrator . . . then the first moving party shall have the right without further notice to appoint a second arbitrator . . . In the event that the two arbitrators fail to appoint a third arbitrator within 20 days of the appointment of the second arbitrator, either arbitrator may apply to a Judge . . . for the appointment of a third arbitrator."

This clause has its roots in American law. One problem to which it can give rise (at least if a party wishes to take a technical approach) is that it may be awkward to comply with the requirement to serve a written notice upon an "officer" of the other party. Not infrequently the parties are Panamanian, Liberian or similar corporations and it is difficult, if not impossible, to identify and find the "officers", whatever that word may mean as a matter of law.

The Norwegian Saleform Clause

4–28 A further clause frequently encountered is contained in the most commonly used form of memorandum of agreement for the sale of ships, the Norwegian Saleform. In the 1993 version, this clause reads:

"(a)* This Agreement shall be governed by and construed in accordance with English law and any dispute arising out of this Agreement shall be referred to arbitration in London in accordance with the Arbitration Acts 1950 and 1979 or any statutory modification or re-enactment thereof for the time being in force, one arbitrator being appointed by each party. On the receipt by one party of the nomination in writing of the other party's arbitrator, that party shall appoint their arbitrator within fourteen days, failing which the decision of the single arbitrator appointed shall apply. If two arbitrators properly appointed shall not agree they shall appoint an umpire whose decision shall be final.

(b)* This Agreement shall be governed by and construed in accordance with Title 9 of the United States Code and the Law of the State of New York and should any dispute arise out of this Agreement, the matter in dispute shall be referred to three persons at New York, one to be appointed by each of the parties hereto, and the third by the two so chosen; their decision or that of any two of them shall be final, and for purpose of enforcing any award, this Agreement may be made a rule of the Court.
The proceedings shall be conducted in accordance with the rules of the Society of Maritime Arbitrators, Inc., New York.

(c)* Any dispute arising out of this Agreement shall be referred to arbitration at [ ], subject to the procedures applicable there.
The laws of [ ] shall govern this Agreement.
**16(a), 16(b) and 16(c) are alternatives; delete whichever is not applicable. In the absence of deletions, alternative 16(a) to apply.*"

The previous (1988) version of the clause provided, in effect, for arbitration in London unless the parties expressly agreed otherwise, and for the London Maritime Arbitrators Association (see paragraphs 4–34 *et seq*., below) to appoint a second arbitrator if the respondent failed to appoint, and the third arbitrator in any event.

The LMAA Clause

4–29 Lastly, the London Maritime Arbitrators Association (the "LMAA"; see paragraphs 4–34 *et seq.*, below) has published its own arbitration clause which is now incorporated into charterparties with increasing frequency. It provides for the parties to agree upon a sole arbitrator, failing which each party may appoint an arbitrator. The two arbitrators will appoint a third arbitrator unless the case is dealt with on documents only and the party-appointed arbitrators are in agreement, in which case their decision shall be final. It further provides for the President of the Association to appoint an arbitrator on behalf of any party that defaults in making an appointment within two weeks, and it expressly applies to any arbitration arising from it the LMAA Terms (see paragraphs 4–37 *et seq.*, below) current at the time when the proceedings are commenced. It further provides that where the amount in dispute does not exceed US$50,000 (or such other sum as the parties may agree) the dispute shall be resolved in accordance with the LMAA Small Claims Procedure (see also paragraphs 4–112 *et seq.*, below).

Which clause is preferable?

4–30 From the point of view of speed and economy, a sole arbitrator is undoubtedly preferable. However, clauses providing for sole arbitrators need to incorporate easily operated mechanisms for obtaining an appointment when the parties cannot agree on one (*e.g.* nominating an appointing authority such as the President of the LMAA). Otherwise they often create substantial difficulties, for in the absence of agreement application has to be made to the High Court. That can involve lengthy and expensive proceedings when the other party is—as is common—abroad and unco-operative.

4–31 Some clauses provide for an umpire in case of disagreement (see, *e.g.* the Baltime and Centrocon clauses). However, in practice nowadays, if a case under such a clause goes to an oral hearing, the arbitrators will ask (and the parties will normally agree) that the umpire should be agreed to be third arbitrator. This enables him fully to participate in the hearing (which he will, in any event, attend even if he remains in the capacity of umpire only). Party-appointed arbitrators can thus appoint someone for his or her particular expertise, and benefit from it. Hence, as between "umpire" and "three arbitrator" clauses, the latter seem clearly preferable. It is curious, therefore, that the current Norwegian Saleform clause has reverted to the "umpire" concept.

4–32 Some clauses impose particular requirements that the arbitrators must satisfy (see, *e.g.* the Centrocon clause). On the whole such limitations are undesirable, for many cases do not suit and are not best decided by individuals who have the required qualifications.

4–33 The LMAA Clause meets the requirements just mentioned, and does not suffer from either of the defects identified. In addition, it applies the LMAA Terms (and the Small Claims Procedure—"the SCP"—in appropriate cases) contractually. The Terms and the SCP are dealt with further in paragraphs 37 and 112.

The London Maritime Arbitrators Association (LMAA)

What is the LMAA?

4–34 The London Maritime Arbitrators Association (LMAA) is, as its name suggests, an Association of maritime arbitrators who practise in London. It was established in 1960 to bring together those who were then frequently practising as maritime arbitrators, most of whom were brokers. Until that date the Secretary of the Baltic Exchange had maintained a list of those willing to act as arbitrators. Once the LMAA was formed, that no longer was necessary.[2]

The LMAA's functions

4–35 The LMAA is essentially a body that brings together already-practising arbitrators. It does not seek to train or educate arbitrators, believing that to be best done by a body such as the Chartered Institute of Arbitrators, and through experience. It does, however, maintain a high standard for admission to membership, increasingly expecting applicants to have undergone training in the Chartered Institute, and certainly expecting them to have actual experience of acting as an arbitrator and to be able to show that they are capable of properly conducting themselves, writing adequate awards, etc.

4–36 The Association currently has 38 full members and 11 retired members, some of whom still arbitrate. In order to maintain links with the users of maritime arbitration and their representatives as well as with others involved (lawyers, experts and the like) the LMAA maintains a category of supporting membership which is open to those who do not normally hold themselves out as or practise as arbitrators. Currently there are over 700 members in this category.

[2] Further information on the LMAA, including its Terms and its internal Rules, can be obtained from the Hon. Secretary, The LMAA, 46/48 Rivington Street, London EC2A 3QP; tel. (0171) 613 5401; fax (0171) 613 5394.

The LMAA Terms

Apart from the natural advantages that arise from bringing together the arbitrators in one specialist discipline and from maintaining links with the users of and other practitioners in such arbitration (as well as with the judiciary), the LMAA's most substantial contribution has probably been the publication and the keeping up to date of the "LMAA Terms". These are terms on the basis of which members of the LMAA accept appointment and which now govern almost every London maritime arbitration. The 1997 Terms (revised to take account of the 1996 Act) are set out in Appendix 11 and some of their provisions are touched upon at various points below, as well as in paragraphs 4–34 *et seq.*, above. 4–37

In addition, the LMAA has published a Small Claims Procedure which parties may adopt for smaller disputes. The wording of this is set out in Appendix 000 and it is discussed briefly below.

The Association has also published Conciliation Terms for use by any parties wishing to submit their disputes to conciliation or mediation: the Association does not seek to distinguish between the two.

Starting a Maritime Arbitration

Appointing an arbitrator

As noted above, the majority of standard arbitration clauses in use in shipping contracts provide for each party to appoint its own arbitrator. The almost invariable practice is for the claimant to appoint its arbitrator first, giving notice of that appointment to the respondent and calling upon the respondent to make an appointment on its behalf. Very occasionally a respondent might start the proceedings by effecting an appointment itself, especially if it wants to obtain the services of a particular arbitrator. 4–38

Although quite often a claimant starts an arbitration in respect of one dispute only, and perhaps knows of no others, it is common form to appoint a claimant's arbitrator in respect of "all disputes arising" under the relevant contract. This ensures that all possible disputes are dealt with in one arbitration. It also helps to avoid prescription problems. 4–39

Sole arbitrator clauses

4–40 A few arbitration clauses provide for sole arbitrators, or effectively do so under section 15(3) of the 1996 Act because they do not spell out any other number of arbitrators. However, such clauses are not common. When they are found, or when a party seeks to vary an existing arbitration agreement so as to have a sole arbitrator, it has often proved difficult in the past for the parties to agree upon the identity of someone to take that position and, in the first case, an application to the courts has frequently been necessary. There is now, however, greater willingness to agree sole arbitrators: an acknowledgment, no doubt, of both economic realities and the fact that today's arbitrators are impartial (see paragraphs 4–53 *et seq.*, below).

Extending time for commencement of arbitration

4–41 Section 27 of the 1950 Act and now section 12 of the 1996 Act of course apply to maritime as well as to other arbitrations. However, certain charterparties contain clauses which bar claims not if arbitration is not commenced within a certain time, but if other steps—*e.g.* providing certain documents and the making of a claim—are not taken within a certain time. Such provisions are not covered by the statutory remedies and the court has no power to extend time when there is a failure to comply with them.

Notice of appointment

4–42 Notice of appointment of an arbitrator must be given in accordance with the requirements of the arbitration agreement, if any are spelt out. Otherwise, notice should be given to the respondent party itself. But in practice, in maritime disputes, notice is often given to a broker or other agent who may well have no authority, actual or ostensible, to receive it. This does not usually cause a problem, but it may do so, and many parties and their representatives would do well to take more care to ensure that they are serving notice properly.

4–43 In some cases there may be real difficulties in effecting service as required (see paragraphs 4–27 *et seq.*, above in relation to the Asbatankvoy arbitration clause).

Default in appointment

4–44 Many maritime arbitrations concern claims for money withheld, to a greater or lesser degree cynically, by respondents who wish to postpone as long as possible a more or less inevitable day of judgment. Such cases are largely debt-collecting exercises. Many such respondents fail to appoint an arbitrator in response to the claimant's notice of appointment in the hope of delaying matters. Provided the claimant has called upon the respondent to make an appointment, English law allows the claimant's arbitrator to be appointed as sole arbitrator in many instances, and for the claimant to apply to the court for the appointment of a second arbitrator in others (see paragraphs 2–95 and 2–156 to 164). Resort to these provisions is often required in practice.

Although it is often said that where a respondent fails to participate, it is preferable to have a "full" two- or three-man tribunal rather than a sole arbitrator by default, in maritime cases the court's power to make a default appointment in certain circumstances is relatively rarely employed and any option in favour of a sole arbitrator is more commonly resorted to. 4–45

Appointment of third Arbitrator or umpire

In most cases, though, respondents do appoint arbitrators. Some legislative and/or contractual provisions may require the appointment of a third arbitrator, or less commonly an umpire, once the parties' arbitrators have been appointed. In practice, however, it is normal to secure the agreement of the parties to postpone any such appointment until it becomes necessary (*e.g.* in case of disagreement, or upon the fixing of an oral hearing). This saves costs and allows the reference to be conducted more efficiently. In the case of three-arbitrator clauses, paragraph 8(b) of the LMAA Terms provides that the party-appointed arbitrators may, at any time after their appointment, appoint a third arbitrator so long as they do so before any substantive hearing or forthwith if they cannot agree on any matter related to the arbitration. 4–46

Normally, no third arbitrator will be appointed until shortly before an oral hearing takes place. Often interlocutory hearings for directions will be conducted without the tribunal having been completed, depending on the nature of the dispute and that of the hearing. 4–47

In general it is the first two (usually party-appointed) arbitrators who have the gift of the appointment of a third arbitrator or umpire. Occasionally a clause provides for some third party to make the appointment (see, *e.g.* the 1988 Norwegian Saleform clause referred to in paragraph 4–28 above). Even in such cases the first two arbitrators commonly invite the parties to agree that the appointment may be made by the arbitrators. They are usually in the best position to know whom to appoint. Such consent is generally forthcoming. 4–48

When it comes to making an appointment the first two arbitrators endeavour to choose someone whose particular qualities, experience and skills fit the case before them. 4–49

The Arbitrators

The arbitrators appointed are usually members of the LMAA, though there is no requirement to this effect unless (which happens rarely) the arbitration clause specifically provides for LMAA members. 4–50

4–51 Who are these arbitrators? Thirty or more years ago they were, almost entirely, brokers from the Baltic Exchange plus a few owners or charterers. Since that time, cases have become more complex, lawyers have been involved increasingly (the arbitration conducted by parties alone is now a rarity, whereas once it was common) and procedural matters have become correspondingly more important. Nowadays, most (though happily not all) of the busy arbitrators have some legal background or training, and many have worked for the managers of mutual Clubs (see paragraphs 4–13 *et seq*., above).

4–52 Many arbitration clauses contain a requirement that the arbitrators shall be "commercial men" (see, for example, the NYPE clause in paragraph 4–26, above), possibly "conversant with shipping" and sometimes "not lawyers". It is not altogether easy to define a "commercial man". In *Pando Compania Naviera S.A. v. Filmo S.A.S.*[3] it was held that a full-time maritime arbitrator who had, some years earlier, retired from practice as a solicitor but who also held directorships in shipping companies was a "commercial man". On the other hand, it has been held that a barrister practising at the Commercial Bar is not within the wording. An express exclusion of lawyers would raise a question as to whether a non-practising or retired lawyer would be disqualified.

Connections—Impartiality

4–53 The world of maritime arbitration is a relatively small one. Some parties appear time and time again. The numbers of firms of lawyers and the numbers of barristers specialising in this kind of work are limited. Only a small number of arbitrators do the great bulk of the work. In consequence the arbitrators frequently know many of the participants in arbitrations, sometimes quite well. This is unavoidable, but it is also a phenomenon that is well-known and all involved take care to conduct themselves appropriately in the light of these circumstances.

4–54 Maritime arbitrators occasionally have contact with one party or its representatives in the absence of the other party. However, that will only be to deal with formalities, for example explaining to an unrepresented party how to proceed, or giving availability for hearing dates and the like. Prior to 1996 there was no record of any attack on a maritime arbitrator's impartiality for many, many years. And the case which arose that year[4] involved a wholly misconceived

[3] [1975] 1 Q.B. 742.
[4] *Fletamentos Maritimos S.A. v. Effjohn International B.V. (No. 2)* [1997] 1 Lloyd's Rep. 302.

criticism, as the judge and—even more forcefully—the Court of Appeal made clear.

"My arbitrator"

Sadly, the notion of "my arbitrator" still exists in shipping circles. It was once perhaps true, to some extent at least, that certain arbitrators could be relied upon to do their best to look after the interests of the parties appointing them. Indeed, that was not surprising in the days when parties only rarely employed legal representatives, and when also the majority of arbitration clauses provided (or were deemed to provide) for two arbitrators and an umpire. Then the party-appointed arbitrators would commonly disagree and act as advocates before an umpire of their choosing. 4–55

In present times, however, where legal representation is the order of the day and where three-arbitrator clauses (which are very popular) mean what they say the *raison d'être* for the somewhat partisan arbitrator has largely ceased to exist. In addition, today's arbitrators come from backgrounds which tend to lead them to be impartial in any event. 4–56

Notwithstanding this, certain parties favour certain arbitrators and so seek to appoint them whenever they can. 4–57

Three-member tribunals

Some of the aspects of three-member tribunals in international arbitrations are dealt with elsewhere (see paragraphs 2–144 *et seq.*, above): the considerations that arise in London maritime arbitrations are generally somewhat different. 4–58

Even in the nowadays relatively rare case where there are two arbitrators and an umpire, arbitrators do not have any regard to the source of their appointment when forming and expressing their views. Consequently, a very substantial majority of awards now made in London maritime cases are unanimous. Umpires are rarely called upon, and third arbitrators rarely have to hold the balance. (The author remembers one particularly entertaining occasion when as chairman, he presided over a very heated discussion between arbitrators in which the owners' appointee was arguing for the charterers' case, and vice versa. Ultimately agreement was reached.) 4–59

An advantage of having more than one arbitrator is that different relevant disciplines may be brought to bear. For example, a case involving the sale of a ship might give rise to issues concerning broking practice, the technical condition of the ship, and law. A tribunal consisting of a broker, an engineer and a lawyer can then be ideal. In practice, in such situations, whilst forming their own views on all aspects of the case, arbitrators tend to pay particular attention to any special expertise enjoyed by another member of the tribunal. 4–60

Of course, having more than one arbitrator increases the tribunal's fees pro- 4–61 portionately (or almost proportionately) and it can lead to delay in two main ways. First, the need to consult on interlocutory directions slows things down. Secondly, it is often difficult to offer early hearing dates because of individuals' other commitments. The Fourth Schedule of the LMAA Terms (see paragraph 4–37, above) has, however, dealt with this satisfactorily.

4–62 Where a case is being conducted on documents alone, if the arbitration clause requires a third arbitrator the party-appointed arbitrators will usually seek—and generally obtain—the parties' agreement to waiving the requirement for the appointment of a third arbitrator if the party-appointed arbitrators find (as is usually the case) that they can agree an award.

Arbitrators' availability

4–63 Conscious that parties should not have to wait excessively long periods for their cases to be heard, the LMAA in the Fourth Schedule to its Terms has made provision for arbitrators to stand down and be replaced if they cannot fix hearing dates within periods of time which are deemed to be reasonable in all the circumstances, having regard in particular to the estimated duration of the hearing. The introduction of this Schedule has led to hearings taking place rather more quickly than was sometimes the case before, and probably to fewer appointments being made of busy arbitrators by cynical respondents who wish to slow down the arbitral process.

Proceeding with a Maritime Arbitration

Introduction

4–64 In London, at least, there is no set procedure by which maritime arbitrations are developed. Although the LMAA Terms have existed for many years, they have never sought to regulate the conduct of maritime arbitration proceedings. Parties and arbitrators have been and still are left free to choose their own procedures and to decide whether to have formal pleadings, informal submissions, lists of documents and so on. Each case is different, as is each practitioner. At least until now it has not seemed useful to attempt to lay down any firm rules, or even guidelines beyond those suggested for documents-only cases in the Second Schedule.

4–65 Indeed, maritime arbitrators have tended to leave the form of procedure very much in the hands of the parties (save where agreement is not reached, either tacitly or expressly) though even prior to the 1996 Act there was an increasing—and welcome—tendency on the part of some arbitrators to take a firmer hand and attempt to direct matters rather more than previously. This was no doubt in response to the relative lack of experience shown by many practitioners in the past few years, and the marked inclination on the part of some of them to lose sight of the substantive wood because of the procedural trees.

The following paragraphs outline some of the practices adopted in maritime arbitration to date. In the long run these are almost certain to be substantially changed as a result of the 1996 Act. However, it is thought that changes will occur only gradually. The two main reasons for this are, firstly, that most maritime arbitration is conducted by a relatively small number of individuals who are extremely busy full-time arbitrators (see paragraph 4–11 above), and secondly, that most tribunals consist of three members. **4–66**

The effect of a few busy arbitrators having so much work is that they are unlikely, at least in the short term, to have the time to be able to become proactive in most of their cases, and will have to continue to respond to developments as has been the practice in the past (see below). And having three members substantially increases the chances of a tribunal being extra-conservative, as well as slowing down the speed of response. **4–67**

Further, it is thought that many parties and practitioners will not speedily react favourably to any change in the patterns to which they have become accustomed, even if the arbitrators do seek to implement the 1996 Act policies. **4–68**

Accordingly, although the LMAA Terms have been revised in the light of the Act, they do not seek dramatically to change the approach to maritime arbitration, for the present at least. The more significant innovations are mentioned in paragraphs which follow. Before dealing with practices it is convenient to say one word about the busy arbitrator in the world of maritime arbitration. **4–69**

The busy arbitrator

Some of the ideals indicated in paragraph 2–212 above are not realistic in the world of maritime arbitration. There is a constant apparent shortage of arbitrators whom parties and their advisers are prepared to use. The probable increase in burdens on arbitrators as a result of the 1996 Act cannot help this situation. The obvious answer is that more arbitrators need to be identified, but in the long run this is something that can only effectively be done by the "the market", *i.e.* those who are making the appointments. There is very little that the LMAA can do. Experience has shown that membership of the Association does not help to advance the cause of an individual whose reputation has not otherwise attracted many appointments to him. Equally, a substantial number of individuals have become quite successful as maritime arbitrators before joining the Association. **4–70**

These considerations simply reinforce the suggestion made above that the busyness of the maritime arbitrators who are conducting the majority of cases **4–71** will slow down the implementation of changes that might appear elsewhere as a result of the 1996 Act.

4–72 It is now convenient to consider the kinds of procedure most commonly adopted under two broad headings, (i) arbitrations on documents alone and (ii) arbitrations with oral hearings. However, because of the flexibility of the procedures adopted, it is often impossible so to categorise a case at its outset. Characteristics of one type may well be found in an arbitration that ends up being of the other type.

Documents-only Arbitrations

Past practices

4–73 Even today, notwithstanding the substantially increased involvement of lawyers and the additional complexity of matters, a substantial majority (perhaps as much as 80 per cent) of maritime arbitrations are conducted on documents alone. The most common method of dealing with such cases derives from the practices of 30 or more years ago. Then, when parties were seldom represented, the claimant would normally send to the arbitrator appointed by him a short letter summarising his claim and attaching such documents as seemed to him to be useful in support. That arbitrator would then pass that letter (usually the original, since the photocopier was—happily—virtually unknown) to the arbitrator appointed by the respondent. He would pass it on to the respondent for comments and additional documents to be provided. Those in turn would then be passed back to the claimant via the arbitrator appointed by him. The claimant would then make final submissions and the arbitrators would discuss the matter and seek to reach an agreement, appointing an umpire and advocating the case before him if that was necessary.

Documents-only cases today

4–74 More recently, with the arrival of lawyers and efficient photocopiers, it is normal for claim submissions to be set out in a letter which is accompanied by supporting documentary evidence. That letter will probably be addressed to one of the arbitrators, and copied to the other and the respondents' advisers. The latter will then respond with defence (and possibly counterclaim) submissions and supporting documents, again copied to the arbitrators and the claimants' representatives, and so on. It is not uncommon for each side to provide more than one set of submissions. Sometimes arbitrators have to step in and demand that play be closed, since there is a limit to the number of profitable exchanges that can be written.

In such cases there will not commonly be any formal discovery procedure, though one party may ask the arbitrators to direct the other to produce certain documents. 4–75

Directions in documents-only cases

Arbitrators are often required, in such cases, to give directions for the timely service of submissions, though this is normally done only in response to a specific request from one party, and only as the case progresses. It is unusual to lay down comprehensive orders for directions at the outset of a matter. Indeed, both the LMAA Terms and, in practice, the arbitrators encourage parties to agree directions so far as they can, rather than requiring orders to be made. This is with a view to reducing the involvement of the arbitrators, and thus of course the costs (see also paragraphs 4–64 *et seq.*, above). 4–76

"Documents-only" into "formal" arbitration

Cases that are developed in this way are normally ultimately resolved without an oral hearing. Exceptionally, though, one of the outcomes of the exchange of the written submissions may be a realisation, or at least a desire, on one side that an oral hearing should be fixed, perhaps in order to hear a witness of fact, possibly because there are difficult questions of expertise or indeed even law involved, and sometimes in an attempt to delay matters or to put the pressure of threatened additional costs upon the other party. 4–77

Whereas previously arbitrators acceded to requests for oral hearings, considering themselves bound to do so, under the 1996 Act they will have to consider whether an oral hearing is consistent with their section 33 obligations and, if so, to what extent. Paragraph 12(c) of the Terms reiterates that in the absence of agreement, it is for the tribunal to decide whether and to what extent there should be oral or written evidence or submissions. 4–78

Formal Arbitrations

There are other cases where, from the outset, the parties exchange pleadings as if they were in court. Following that will normally be discovery, again along court-style lines (though lists of documents are, happily, often dispensed with). 4–79

Once more, the arbitrators may be called upon to make specific orders for the exchange of pleadings, the provision of discovery and the like, but again parties are encouraged to try to agree such matters.

Changing "formal" into "documents-only" cases

4–80 The majority of such cases will result in an oral hearing. In some instances, however, though a hearing may have been anticipated at the outset, it will become apparent that one is not necessary. The parties will then exchange written submissions which lead to a documents-only decision being made. That, inevitably, involves some duplication of effort and consequent waste of costs, though it must be observed that in the majority of such cases it is cheaper not to have an oral hearing. Again, in the light of the 1996 Act, unless the parties agree that there should be an oral hearing, it will be for the arbitrators to decide whether and to what extent there should be one.

Interlocutory directions

4–81 It is not always apparent to outsiders that maritime arbitrations are unusual in that procedural matters tend to be decided on a stage-by-stage basis. In other areas of arbitration life it is customary to lay down comprehensive orders for directions and often to fix hearing dates at the outset of a matter. Experience suggests that, at least hitherto, such an approach was not helpful in maritime cases, partly because the exigences of life make it difficult to adhere to such timetables and partly because the experience of the practitioners normally involved makes it unnecessary. As has already been mentioned, both the practice of arbitrators and the approach of the LMAA Terms has been, and for the present remains, to encourage parties to agree on directions (see, for example, paragraphs 12(b), 13(a) and 14(a) and (c) of the Terms).

Fixing hearing dates

4–82 Again, in contrast to procedures typical elsewhere, hearing dates are not usually fixed until "the preparation of a case is sufficiently advanced to enable the duration of the hearing to be properly estimated; this will normally be after discovery has been completed" (paragraph 14(a) of the Terms). And preliminary meetings are uncommon, though these are anticipated for more complicated cases, including those involving a hearing of more than five days' duration (see paragraph 16(b) of the Terms, and the Third Schedule which sets out a check-list of the matters to be considered before and possibly at such meetings).

Mode of communication

Where arbitrators have to deal with interlocutory directions, communication is normally made by fax or telex. Applications and submissions have to be addressed to the arbitrators and copied to opponents. Normally one arbitrator (if there are two or three on the tribunal) will take the lead in interlocutory correspondence, consulting his colleagues as may be necessary in order to reach agreement before orders are made. 4–83

Sundry New Provisions in LMAA Terms

Application of the terms

Paragraph 5 of the Terms purports to apply them whenever a dispute is referred to arbitrators who are full members of the LMAA, unless the parties have agreed otherwise, and whenever arbitrators are appointed on the basis that the Terms apply to their appointment. In case the provisions set out should be held not to amount to an agreement to which the Act applies, arbitrators are expressly given authority to confirm in writing on behalf of the parties that the Terms do in fact apply. The practice is developing of arbitrators so confirming once both parties have made their appointments. 4–84

Law and seat of arbitration

Paragraph 6 of the Terms provides that, in the absence of any contrary agreement, the parties agree that the law applicable to the arbitration agreement is English law and that the seat of the arbitration is in England. 4–85

Powers of arbitrators

By paragraph 15(a) of the Terms, arbitrators are given the power to limit the number of expert witnesses, or to direct that no expert be called on any issue, or that no expert evidence shall be called save with the leave of the tribunal. 4–86

"Chain" or "String" Arbitrations

4–87 It is not uncommon for a ship to be chartered from its owner and then to be sub-chartered by the charterer. The sub-charterer in turn may enter into a further sub-fixture, and so on. As a result, the same or a similar dispute may arise under each of the contracts. There are no provisions of law enabling any kind of consolidation of arbitrations in such circumstances even in the 1996 Act. In practice, though, certain techniques have been developed in maritime arbitration to reduce, if not eliminate, the risks of inconsistent decisions and cases proceeding "out of step" with one another.

4–88 For example, the "first" claimant may appoint his arbitrator and give notice of that appointment to the "first" respondent. He in turn will appoint that same arbitrator under his other contract (in which he will be claimant) and wait for a counter-appointment to come "up the line". The "first" respondent will then appoint that same arbitrator against the 'first' claimant. Especially when—as is often the case—this process takes place with a degree of co-operation, the outcome can be identical tribunals in two or more cases. Even if that does not happen, usually at least one member of the tribunals will be common. Or parties in a "chain" or "string" may agree to have the same sole arbitrator.

4–89 The LMAA Terms contain provisions enabling arbitrators to order the concurrent hearings of arbitrations where common issues of fact or law appear to be raised, even where the tribunals are not identical, and to make appropriate directions as the interests of fairness, economy and expedition require. These include directing that documents disclosed in one matter shall be made available to the parties in the other, upon conditions if appropriate, and that the evidence given in one arbitration shall be treated as evidence in the other subject to the parties being given an opportunity to deal with it and to any other conditions the arbitrators may impose (see paragraph 15(b) of the Terms). The arbitrators themselves try to achieve as much consistency as they can in the constitution of the various tribunals by making appropriate cross-appointments whenever possible. And where, for example, arbitration clauses are inconsistent (one may require an umpire whilst another, up or down the line, requires three arbitrators) the arbitrators urge the parties to agree appropriate variations to avoid difficulties that might otherwise arise. They frequently obtain the appropriate consents.

Default Cases

4–90 Quite frequently a respondent in a maritime arbitration fails to provide submissions or otherwise to participate, perhaps even from the outset. In such instances it has long been the practice, following non-compliance with an ordinary order, to make a peremptory order and to give notice that if that is not complied with the tribunal will proceed to an award on the basis of the claimant's submissions and documents alone without further notice and without a hearing. Section 41(7) of the 1996 Act will not alter this practice. Because experience has shown that in some countries an award will not be enforced where a party has not been given an opportunity to attend an oral hearing, such notices have commonly specified that if the respondent requires an oral hearing, he must apply for one before the date for compliance. No such application is normally made and the arbitrators can then safely proceed on documents alone. Despite the new power to dispense with oral hearings, this practice is unlikely to change.

Security for Costs

Under the LMAA Terms it has, for some years, been the position that applica- 4–91
tions for security for costs were to be made to arbitrators rather than to the High Court unless both parties agreed otherwise, or the tribunal gave leave for an application to the court. Those exceptions were seldom applicable. Consequently maritime arbitrators in London commonly dealt with applications for security for costs. In so doing they attempted to follow the approach adopted by the courts in relation to such matters. Now, of course, arbitrators alone have the power to deal with security for costs and are not apparently bound to follow the practice of the courts. It seems likely that there will be fewer applications, however, since the principal ground advanced in the past was the overseas residence or place of incorporation of a claimant, a ground which can no longer be relied upon.

Hearings

Oral hearings in maritime arbitrations are relatively informal. They usually take 4–92
place in one of the sets of arbitration rooms in central London that have been developed in recent years. It is uncommon to swear witnesses. Increasingly, submissions are put into writing and arbitrators are left to read documents rather than having them read out by counsel, all in an endeavour to shorten the hearings.

4–93 Unlike New York, where maritime arbitrations are commonly dealt with in a series of short hearings spread over a number of months, if not years, the practice in London is (so far as possible) to deal with everything in one go, just as it is in court.

Awards

Interim awards

4–94 Maritime arbitrators are often asked to make interim awards in circumstances which are perhaps unique to their business. Awards of the very particular type in question are normally sought by shipowners who are claiming hire (under a time-charter) or freight (under a voyage charter) from their charterers. Charterers often make deductions from hire or freight in respect of claims which they contend they have against owners. The law is such that deductions may only be made from hire where the alleged claim impeaches the owners' prima facie claim for hire in the sense that in some way the charterer can be said to have been deprived of the use of the ship in whole or in part, and where the charterer is acting bona fide and on reasonable grounds. If these tests cannot be satisfied, the owner is entitled to have paid to him the withheld hire. In the case of freight, on House of Lords authority no deductions may be made unless expressly authorised by the charterparty. Such provisions are rarely found.

4–95 It can therefore be seen that instances frequently arise where, deductions having been made from hire or freight, owners believe that these cannot presently be justified (whatever the ultimate merits of any counterclaim that charterers may advance) and therefore seek urgent interim awards on the basis that the charterers' claims can be resolved at leisure (and, the owners will hope, much later).

4–96 Occasionally urgent relief is sought by a party to a maritime arbitration, often in the form of a declaration, and maritime arbitrators are accustomed to responding very quickly in such circumstances. For example, a charterer may give an order which the owner contends is unlawful. A maritime arbitration tribunal may then decide, possibly within as little as 24 hours of the order being given, whether the owner is bound to comply with it or not.

Writing awards

There is no settled practice as to the writing of awards. Some individuals have particular views, *e.g.* that the chairman of a tribunal should do the first draft, or that the arbitrator appointed by the claimant should. On the whole, though, the initial drafting is undertaken by whichever arbitrator volunteers to do the work. He may do that because he has a particularly firm view whilst his colleagues are more tentative, or because he currently has more time to undertake the exercise, or because he thinks he writes better than his colleagues; or any combination of these factors. **4–97**

The draft will be circulated to the other arbitrators for discussion. In the case of a documents-only arbitration the arbitrators will seldom meet, but will exchange views in correspondence and on the telephone. At the end of an oral hearing the arbitrators will normally discuss the case, but will seldom find it necessary to meet in order to discuss any drafts that are subsequently prepared. **4–98**

Reasons

Maritime arbitrators have always made it a practice to issue reasons for their awards. But unless a reasoned award is requested (or, before the 1979 Act, a special case was requested) such reasons have been given separately from the award and on a confidential basis, *i.e.* that they are not to be used in or in connection with any proceedings on or related to the award, but are simply given for the information of the parties. **4–99**

Such confidential reasons can often be quite brief, not least because it is not necessary to set out the full background of the matter, nor the arguments in any detail (all these being known to the parties) and the arbitrators can largely confine themselves to their views on what seem to them to be the crucial points. **4–100**

"Confidential" v. "open" reasons

After the 1979 Act, reasoned awards became much more common. However, they were by no means the rule. In at least half of the cases decided by maritime arbitrators in London, unmotivated awards continued to be made. That is because, in practice and for whatever reasons, parties to maritime arbitration did not enter into exclusion agreements preventing appeals, save in a minute number of cases. They and their advisers took, and will no doubt continue to take, the view that it is better to decide at the close of submissions in a particular case whether or not to seek a reasoned award. Of course, without a reasoned award, there was no possibility of an appeal under the 1979 Act, and the same is true under the 1996 Act. **4–101**

Parties make this decision in the light of considerations of their own. It is **4–102** thought that these often include such questions as whether the party thinks it stands a better chance of succeeding before arbitrators alone or before the courts, whether the other side is likely to seek to challenge an award in court, and so on. The majority of documents-only awards are not motivated (though confidential reasons are normally given) whereas probably a majority of awards made following oral hearings are, because one or both parties request reasons.

4–103 Paragraph 23(b) of the LMAA Terms provides that the parties agree to dispense with reasons in all cases where no notice shall have been given to the arbitrators requesting a reasoned award before the award is made, and a note specifically points out that the effect of this is to exclude the court's jurisdiction to determine an appeal on a question of law arising out of the award.

"Open" reasons

4–104 "Open" reasons are generally longer, and thus more expensive to produce, than confidential ones. The background and the facts have to be spelt out in some detail so that any court faced with an application for leave to appeal, or even with an appeal, may be properly apprised of the matter. The parties' contentions have similarly to be dealt with more fully than would otherwise be the case so that all relevant considerations may be before any court that is concerned. And it is helpful for tribunals to give their alternative conclusions to cover the possibility that they might be wrong on one or more questions of law and that the court might upset their award on any such question. If alternative conclusions are indicated, the court is more readily able to substitute its own award without remitting the matter for further consideration by the arbitrators.

Publishing awards

4–105 Once awards have been signed by all the arbitrators, the last signatory will normally give notice to the parties of the publication of the award, announcing that it may be collected against payment of the costs thereof, which are specified in the notice. Following payment of the costs, the arbitrator in question will normally account to his colleagues for their part of the fees.

Arbitrators' Fees

Basis of fees

Maritime arbitrators exercise a lien upon their awards until their fees (and any expenses, which may include hearing room charges and related costs) have been paid. They do not seek security for their fees and expenses in advance. **4–106**

Generally, fees are calculated on the basis of work done. There is no established scale. None is fixed by the LMAA or any other body and the arbitrators seek to be remunerated on a reasonable basis for what they do. Charges are made, of course, not only for hearings, but for time spent perusing documents and considering cases, as well as for correspondence (*e.g.* in relation to directions). Whatever precise method of calculation is adopted, by and large any one maritime arbitrator will charge much the same as another for equivalent work. **4–107**

Appointment fees

The LMAA Terms require that, on appointment, an arbitrator be paid a fee in an amount which is fixed by the LMAA Committee from time to time. That fee, currently £75, is payable in consideration of the arbitrator accepting appointment only, and is intended to cover the costs involved in the opening of a file, the correspondence concerning the acceptance and so on. It is helpful to have such a fee payable on appointment, for a large number of cases go no further than the original appointment, and often arbitrators are not told of this until they ask. That may be years later, at which time it is difficult to get any fees paid. **4–108**

Booking fees

Booking fees are payable under the First Schedule to the LMAA Terms for time reserved for hearings. The amount is fixed from time to time by the LMAA Committee (and is currently £250 per arbitrator per day booked). These fees are payable in the first instance by the party asking for the hearing date and are payable within 14 days of confirmation of the reservation or six months in advance of the first day reserved, whichever is the later. **4–109**

If hearing dates are vacated the booking fees are forfeit if the dates are vacated less than three months before the start date, and forfeit as to 50 per cent if vacated three months or more before the start date. (Special provisions apply to hearings estimated to last more than 10 days). **4–110**

The amount of the booking fee is, of course, considerably less than what arbitrators are paid if they actually sit, but it and the forfeiture provisions are **4–111** fixed with a view to giving, on a broad basis, appropriate compensation for cancelled days without needing to inquire into actual losses. It has also been found that requiring parties to pay booking fees helps to focus their minds on the fact that, at the stage when such payment is required, they are about to begin incurring proportionately more substantial costs than they have incurred hitherto. This frequently leads to prompt settlements.

LMAA Small Claims Procedure

4–112 The LMAA has published a Small Claims Procedure which is increasingly commonly incorporated into charterparty arbitration clauses, and which many other parties also adopt on an *ad hoc* basis. The LMAA recommends its use for cases where the amount involved does not exceed a figure established from time to time by the Committee, currently US$50,000. It is not suitable where there are complex issues or there is likely to be examination of witnesses.

Its main features are as follows.

(i) A sole arbitrator appointed either by agreement or by the President of the LMAA.
(ii) A fixed fee (currently £750) for the arbitrator.
(iii) The exclusion of any right of appeal against the award.
(iv) A fairly tight timetable for the exchange of submissions and documents.
(v) The possibility of an oral hearing limited to one working day (though this, plainly, is discouraged).
(vi) The award is to be made within one month from the close of submissions.
(vii) The maximum costs one party may be ordered to pay to the other are £1,250, and the arbitrator may assess such costs on a commercial basis.

Each of the overseas centres mentioned in paragraphs 4–113 *et seq.*, below has procedures designed to facilitate and reduce the cost of arbitration in respect of small claims.

Maritime Arbitration Outside the United Kingdom

The following notes seek to highlight the distinctions between maritime arbitration as conducted in London and dealt with above on the one hand, and maritime arbitration as conducted in New York, Paris and Tokyo respectively. 4–113

New York

The bulk of maritime arbitrations in New York are conducted under the auspices of the Society of Maritime Arbitrators, Inc. ("SMA"). Parties and arbitrators customarily agree to apply SMA Rules. Some charterparties anticipate the application of these Rules, but *ad hoc* agreements to apply them are often required. Those Rules deal with many of the same matters covered by the LMAA Terms, as well as some of the procedural aspects dealt with in England in the Arbitration Acts. 4–114

The SMA Rules (which were revised in May 1994) provide, amongst other things, for consolidation of proceedings involving related contract disputes with others arising from common questions of fact or law. Unless all parties agree upon a sole arbitrator, or to a panel of three, the constitution of the tribunal in such cases is to be determined by the court. The Rules also now empower arbitrators to award legal and arbitration expenses (a practice hitherto little followed in New York). They cover points regarding the initiation of an arbitration, appointment of arbitrators and the notification of such appointments. They also stipulate that a claimant can require a respondent to appoint his arbitrator within 20 days, failing which the claimant can appoint a second arbitrator on behalf of the respondent, thus expediting the prompt constitution of the tribunal without recourse to the court. The Rules also provide a procedure for the replacement of an arbitrator in the event of inability to serve. They deal with the conduct of hearings, provide for the taking of a stenographic record (whereas in London transcripts of proceedings are extremely rare); the disclosure by arbitrators of personal or business relationships whether with the parties, related companies, counsel or other panel members (something which is almost unheard of in London); and the taking of oaths (by arbitrators and by testifying witnesses). 4–115

Although many arbitrations in New York are conducted on documents alone, in most cases hearings are held. Unlike what commonly happens in London, pleadings and discovery do not have to be exchanged before an oral hearing is arranged. The SMA Rules require that the parties deliver to the tribunal a statement identifying all the parties, and that each claimant submit a pre-hearing statement of its position and claim. Copies of any exhibits to be introduced at a particular hearing are to be supplied to the other party and to the arbitrators at least one week prior to the hearing. Whereas in the past hearings tended to be 4–116 held at lunchtime or in the evenings after business hours, the current practice favours full day or even consecutive day hearings, although not all arbitrators can divert so much time from their daily commercial endeavours. There are fewer full-time arbitrators than in London. Hearings tend to be more informal than in London, and are usually held in the offices of attorneys, parties or the tribunal chairman. Parties customarily submit post-hearing and reply briefs after evidentiary hearings have been held, although they may prefer to present their final arguments at an oral hearing. Under SMA Rules, decisions are to be issued within 120 days of the close of proceedings.

4–117 Virtually all New York arbitration decisions are final, subject only to reversal on extremely narrow grounds spelt out in the US Federal Arbitration Act. SMA arbitrators' decisions are fully reasoned and are published in the Award Service of the SMA which is distributed to subscribers on a quarterly basis. These decisions are also available through the Lexis electronic retrieval system.

Paris

4–118 The vast majority of maritime arbitrations in Paris are administered by the Chambre Arbitrale Maritime de Paris. Its rules contain detailed provisions for the conduct of arbitrations, from the seizing of the Chambre through to the signature and notification of Awards.

4–119 The Committee of the Chambre has considerable powers and duties, in particular in relation to the appointment of arbitrators: sole arbitrators (or occasionally a tribunal of three) where the parties are unable to agree on the identity of an individual, third arbitrators (unless—exceptionally—the parties have agreed that their nominees should make that appointment), and arbitrators on behalf of parties who fail to appoint.

4–120 The parties exchange written statements of case supported by the documents they rely upon, and provide these to the Chambre which normally only sends them to the arbitrators when the file is complete and, at least in theory, the matter is ready for hearing. The arbitrators are not involved in the administration of cases up to this stage.

4–121 Thereafter, the arbitrators fix a hearing (usually held at the offices of the Chambre). Arbitrations on documents alone are quite rare, although many of the hearings add nothing to the arbitrators' appreciation of a case to that which can be gleaned from the written exchanges. The hearings are usually brief. The parties' representatives seldom do more than reiterate the points made in writing, though occasionally a witness may be called.

4–122 Because the essential nature of the proceedings is inquisitorial, however, the arbitrators may ask questions and request further evidence or arguments.

4–123 The Rules require awards to be made within six months from the commencement of the case. Although this period can be extended, it is often respected. Consequently Paris maritime arbitration is frequently very speedy.

4–124 When a claimant's principal claim exceeds 100,000FF, a right of appeal against an award arises. The Committee has power to establish a ''second degree examination tribunal'' consisting of three members appointed by it alone, though either party may obtain the replacement of one arbitrator so nominated.

The costs of the Chambre and the fees of the arbitrators are fixed according to the amounts in dispute. They are made up of two elements: a lump sum which increases in accordance with the totals in dispute and a variable proportion calculated by adding together sums obtained through applying reducing percentages to successive levels of claim total. Thus, for example, where the total in dispute is no more than 50,000FF, the total fees and expenses will amount to 12,500FF, for 500,000FF the total fees and expenses are 47,000FF, and for 5 millionFF the total is 184,500FF. **4–125**

Arbitrators determine liability for these fees and expenses. Whilst it is not normal for arbitrators to order that one party must pay another's costs, they do have power (and often exercise it) to order a payment of a lump sum in this regard. The amounts so awarded, however, seldom approach the costs actually incurred, particularly when lawyers have been involved. **4–126**

Tokyo

Maritime arbitration in Tokyo is administered by the Tokyo Maritime Arbitration Commission of The Japan Shipping Exchange, Inc. At the start of an arbitration the Commission identifies three potential arbitrators who have the same kind of expertise in each of three groups (if the tribunal is to be made up of three arbitrators, as is usual) and submits this list of nine candidates to the parties who rank the candidates in each group in their order of preference and may also reject one from each group. The Commission considers the parties' preferences and finally selects and appoints one arbitrator from each group. **4–127**

Proceedings are normally conducted in Japanese, though if the parties agree, they may be conducted in English. **4–128**

The Commission's Rules contain detailed provisions for the exchange of written statements of case and documents and, as with Paris, most other matters. Hearings invariably take place (in Japanese, as a rule; though the parties may agree to use the English language). Once more, proceedings are essentially inquisitorial so that arbitrators may, for example, themselves request the presence of witnesses (fact or expert), ask for further documents and examine the parties. **4–129**

There is no appeal procedure provided for. Fees are fixed in accordance with an established formula. Where the amount claimed is up to ¥15 million, the fee is ¥350,000. Between ¥15 million and ¥100 million, the fee is the same ¥ 350,000 plus ¥10,000 for each additional ¥1 million. Above ¥100 million, the fee is the fee for that sum plus ¥20,000 for each additional ¥10 million. **4–130**

Part 5

CONSTRUCTION INDUSTRY ARBITRATIONS

By Phillip Capper

Partner, Masons Solicitors; Visiting Professor in Construction Law and Arbitration, King's College, University of London; Fellow of Keble College, Oxford

and

Anthony Bunch

Managing Partner, Masons Solicitors; Member of the Departmental Advisory Committee on Arbitration

Why Arbitration is Prevalent in Construction

The construction industry uses arbitration as its principal, final mode of dispute resolution for a number of reasons. These go beyond the usual attractions of arbitration, such as privacy, speed, flexibility, and choice and location of tribunal. There are three main reasons why arbitration has become the norm in the British construction industry: 5–01

- The prevalence of arbitration clauses in standard forms of contract. 5–02
- The technical content of disputes, leading to the use of arbitrators skilled in technical disciplines.
- The need in many disputes to have a tribunal empowered to open up, review and revise decisions, or certificates, arising from the professional judgment of the contract administrator during the project.

Arbitration Clauses in Standard Forms

A distinctive feature of the construction industry in Britain, as compared with many other industries, is the widespread—almost universal—reliance on a small set of published standard forms of contract conditions. There are, as we shall see below, two principal families of such forms. Both have their origins in the interest groups of the consultant professionals who have traditionally acted as construction contract administrators: architects and civil engineers. 5–03

The JCT Standard Form of Building Contract

The Standard Form of Building Contract has developed from the form originally promoted by the Royal Institute of British Architects. It is now produced by an 5–04 industry consensus body called the Joint Contracts Tribunal. The resulting JCT forms have been drafted reflecting the interests of employer clients, main contractors, sub-contractors, local authorities and of course architects. JCT forms are the contractual basis of a very substantial proportion of building works in Britain.

Civil Engineering: the ICE Conditions of Contract

5–05 The other principal family of standard forms of conditions of contract are those published by the Institution of Civil Engineers. These also are based on a degree of consensus drafting, through a drafting body representing interests in the civil engineering industry: the Conditions of Contract Standing Joint Committee (CCSJC). The resulting ICE forms of contract provide the contractual basis for most civil engineering works not only in Britain: they were also the basis of the standard international form of construction contract published by the Fédération Internationale des Ingénieurs-Conseils (FIDIC).

Other published standard forms of contract

5–06 There are other widely used published standard forms in particular sectors. For example, government contracts and those let by some major utilities have traditionally used the GC/Works/1. There is a model form of general conditions of contract recommended by the Institution of Mechanical Engineers, Institution of Electrical Engineers and Association of Consulting Engineers for use in connection with electrical, electronic or mechanical plant contracts: the form is called MF/1. Similarly, the Institution of Chemical Engineers publishes model forms of conditions of contract for Process Plant, called the *Red Book* and the *Green Book*. All of these provide for arbitration as the final form of dispute resolution.

A new approach: the New Engineering Contract

5–07 A new integrated set of standard forms suitable potentially for all works sectors is also published by the Institution of Civil Engineers. These are the NEC[1] forms comprising various components of the New Engineering Contract system. The NEC Contract achieved the encouragement and support from Sir Michael Latham's Final Report[2] of the Government/Industry Review of the Procurement and Contractual Arrangements in the United Kingdom construction industry,

[1] The Engineering and Construction Contract: a New Engineering Contract Document (2nd ed., 1995): available from Thomas Telford Services Ltd, Thomas Telford House, 1 Heron Quay, London E14 4JD.

[2] M. Latham, *Constructing the Team* (1994), HMSO, London.

''Constructing the Team'', published in July 1994. The NEC is unusual amongst standard forms of construction contract in the United Kingdom in not making arbitration the mandatory final mode of dispute resolution. Rather, though it does make provision for arbitration, this is optional and the choice of ''tribunal'' (court, arbitration, or whatever) has to be specified by the parties in the contract.

Arbitration as the de facto standard for final dispute resolution

All these forms provide for arbitration as the method of ultimate dispute resolution. The dominance of their use has produced a *de facto* universality of arbitration as the normal method, no doubt on many occasions without much critical thinking as to the choice of that method. We shall however see below that the nature of the multi-party involvement in construction procurement can militate against the appropriateness of the choice for certain kinds of dispute, unless a great deal of care has been taken in making prior provision for consolidation of arbitral proceedings. **5–08**

Technical Disputes Demanding Technical Arbitrators

The construction industry is not unique in generating disputes that arise from matters of considerable scientific or technical difficulty. However, two factors explored below combine to increase the technical content of construction disputes, and to increase the use of technically qualified arbitrators in their resolution. A further common factor lies in the degree of discretion vested by the traditional standard forms of contract in the consultant contract administrators: the architects and engineers. **5–09**

Issues dependent on opinion of the contract administrator

The first main factor is that the JCT forms, and the ICE forms even more so, tend to postpone matters of uncertainty under the contract, rather than seeking to determine them by prior contractual provision. They are therefore left to the later discretion and judgmental evaluation of the architect or engineer. Uncertainty may permeate matters so fundamental as the scope of the work to be undertaken, the schedule by which it should have been completed, or the **5–10** amounts of money that should be paid for it. Though legal and contractual issues may arise, disputes typically turn on these matters of technical evaluation. Those evaluations are likely already to have been the subject of a disputed determination by the architect or engineer, acting as contract administrator.

A secondary market for technical specialists

5–11 The second main factor flows inexorably from the first. These ex post facto technical evaluations, required by the contract style, involve not only the contract administrators and parties, but also—in Britain at least—an army of specialists and advisors skilled in various associated disciplines. These advisors promote, prepare, argue, defend and appeal from claims disputing technical evaluations. Such is the frequency and experience of these disputes that the participants themselves aspire to become more specialist in their resolution, and to make their careers in the pursuit of construction arbitration.

5–12 The circle is therefore completed: the contract style exacerbates the occurrence of technical disputes; the disputes require specialist technical support; the supporters aspire to become career dispute resolvers; and, construction arbitration can become an industry in itself. The principal recursive element in all of this is that the JCT forms, and the ICE forms even more so, are influenced in their drafting by professional interest groups strongly committed to the resolution of technical uncertainties arising on projects by the technical specialist themselves. This commitment affects both first stage resolution and ultimate dispute resolution by arbitration.

5–13 Even in those projects where the contract is not executed using the basis of one of these published standard forms, it is likely that the bespoke contract entered into will have derived from or be coloured by the style and practices of the published standards. Indeed so prevalent is the use in the industry of these standard forms that the tertiary education and in-service training of industry professionals proceeds largely on the assumption that these forms (and JCT or ICE especially) are not just contracts but descriptions of good (if not universal) practice. This again reinforces the tendency towards arbitrations being conducted on certain set assumptions flowing from practice in technical disciplines.

The challenge of new procedures post-1996

5–14 The challenge for the construction industry, particularly after the Arbitration Act 1996, is to keep these factors in proper balance and perspective. Undoubtedly construction disputes will frequently turn on technical issues and, of course, specialists will be required to facilitate their resolution. Indeed this is reflected even in English High Court practice, where construction disputes are dealt with by the specialist Official Referees. However, there remains considerable scope for improvement in the drafting of construction contracts for the prevention and avoidance of disputes; and where they do arise, for their better management and resolution. There is also scope for more rapid and effective arbitration of construction disputes by better attention to their technical elements and appropriate modes for their evaluation.

Empowering a Tribunal to Revise Project Decisions, Certificates, etc.

Courts' powers and arbitrators' powers

Arbitration has become the essential mode of dispute resolution for certain kinds of construction dispute since the decision in the Court of Appeal in *Northern Regional Health Authority v. Crouch*.[3] Until that decision it had been widely assumed that Official Referees were not fettered in their determination of construction disputes by the fact that an engineer or architect had issued a certificate or otherwise formally determined the parties' rights and obligations pursuant to powers vested in the engineer or architect under the contract. Indeed, Official Referees had come to judgments which contradicted the earlier such decision of an architect or engineer. 5–15

The effect of the *Crouch* decision

The decision in *Crouch* changed that, though its effects are in danger of being exaggerated.[4] The Court of Appeal drew a fundamental distinction between the powers of arbitrators and the powers of the court. Arbitrators were given by the standard forms of construction contract the express power to "open up, review and revise" certificates, decisions, etc., of the engineer or architect. In the view of the Court of Appeal, no such power was within the court's jurisdiction, nor could it—at that time—be conferred on the court by agreement of the parties. 5–16

[3] [1984] Q.B. 644.

[4] *Great Ormond Street Hospital NHS Trust v. Secretary of State for Health & others*, 1997 (unreported); *University of Reading v. Miller Construction Ltd* (1994) 75 B.L.R. 91; *John Barker Construction Ltd v. London Portman Hotel Ltd* (1996) 50 Con.L.R. 43.

Parties can now agree to give such powers to a court

5–17 More recently, Parliament has permitted parties to agree to confer such a power on the court.[5] However, most standard forms of construction contract continue to require reference to arbitration, and this explicit empowering of arbitrators, rather than of the courts.[6] Given the inherent unlikelihood of parties in dispute then to agree to confer such a power on the court, it follows that every construction dispute will under the current law have to be submitted to arbitration if it requires for its resolution the revision of an earlier certificate, decision, etc. of an architect or an engineer exercising professional judgment.

Distinctive Features of Construction Contracts

5–18 Whatever contractual documents are used, there are a number of characteristics which are common to, and largely distinctive of, almost all construction projects. It is generally in these characteristics that the seeds of eventual disputes lie, and they explain not only the higher occurrence of disputes in the industry, but also the traditional particular mechanisms for their resolution.

Construction procurement differentiated from other commercial supplies

5–19 The delivery of a product in construction is a process, not an event. The process requires many participating entities. Even where the main contractor takes on design responsibility, the client employer is likely still to have a consultant team. Also, key elements of supply, such as plant and machinery, may have to be sourced from a specified sub-contractor. Typically, in practice, the participants in a construction project will include at least the client employer organisation, advised by architects, engineers from various disciplines (civil, structural, mechanical, electrical, etc.) and costs consultants (or quantity surveyors); a main contractor perhaps with sub-consultants; and a host of sub-contractors and sup-

[5] S.43A, Supreme Court Act 1981: though all parties to the arbitration agreement must agree so to empower the court.

[6] For an example of an agreement to confer such powers on a court, unusually occurring in a published standard form of contract, see the I ChemE *Yellow Book*, clause 46.6 (Institution of Chemical Engineers, *Model Form of Conditions of Contract for Process Plant, Subcontracts* (2nd ed., 1997).

pliers—at one extreme, some specialist and more substantial than the main contractor itself and, at the other, individuals employed for their labour only.

The two most significant other approaches to construction procurement are management contracting and construction management. In both of these variants the construction contractor's expertise is harnessed more like a consultant team to manage the construction activities of other contractors carrying out particular works packages. In management contracting the management contractor still stands in contractual line between the client employer on the one hand and all the works package contractors on the other, but the management contract form relieves the contractor from many of the commercial and performance obligations that it would have in respect of its domestic sub-contractors on a traditional project. Construction management goes further, as there the construction manager is engaged like consultants by a side contract to advise: the works package contractors are then engaged directly in privity of contract with the client employer. 5–20

The unusual characteristics of construction works

Whatever contract may be used, the actual works on almost all construction projects exhibit recurrent distinctive characteristics: 5–21

- the prototypical nature of the works;
- split responsibility for specification and/or design;
- high degree of inter-activity between purchaser and supplier;
- expectation of, and provision for, substantial levels of change to the specified scope of work;
- complexity of sequencing of activities, and dependencies on other activities/supplies;
- site specificity;
- interaction with neighbouring fixed infrastructure;
- exposure to, and dependence on, weather conditions;
- longevity of the products, and lateness of revelation of defects.

Interactivity leading to change in scope of obligations

The high degrees of interactivity in the design and construction process, between employer client, his appointed consultants and agents, and the contracting team distinguishes construction from many other industries. Construction does not lend itself to a clear and fixed specification by a purchaser, which is then to be executed by a contracting organisation without further communication until completion and handover. Even so-called "turnkey" projects do not enjoy such simplicity. Communication during the course of the project is essential both for the developing definition of the eventual work and for the management of its 5–22 execution, relative to time and budget. The difficulty however that arises from such interactivity is a fluidity in definitions. The scope of obligations changes. But the causes and evidence of such changes may lie in a host of communications as often oral and informal, as formal and contractual.

The diversity and sheer volume of evidentiary material

5–23 Masses of record materials are produced even on relatively small construction projects, many of them as crucial as they are informal: such as, *e.g.* the pencilled scribblings of a gang member on daywork sheets, or the mud-stained cards recording a piling set. Project records may be as diverse as site investigation reports, feasibility studies, specifications, drawings, tender submissions, estimating and pricing details, diaries, minutes of meetings, formal instructions, test data, payment applications and certificates, weather records, job sheets, inspection reports, programming data and reports, and so on. To all of that is added great chains of correspondence between the participants, management reports in each of the entities, and the usual periphery issues of any business activity: from management accounting to press publicity. It is haphazardly in these various forms of contemporary record that are to be found the clues as to the causes of disputed matters.

Payment arrangements that may foster disputes

5–24 There are also structural elements in the payment arrangements for British construction which exacerbate the uncertainty of the sums eventually due. Fixed prices (or ''lump sums'') even for the initially contracted for scope of work are not the normal pricing method in many projects. On small projects, works of uncertain extent are let to contractors working on day rates; and arguments will arise as to the efficiency of the works carried out and the accuracy of the hours recorded to justify the rates claimed. Major projects for civil engineering works have traditionally been treated as so uncertain in their scope, by definition, that the traditional ICE forms are drafted on the basis that they will not be tendered for a fixed price. Rather, the payment system is based on ''remeasurement''.

The remeasurement system

5–25 In summary, the engineer, on behalf of the employer client, designs the works so far as is possible from information known as to the site. From those designs another specialist construction industry professional, the quantity surveyor, prepares a statement of the contemplated activities and materials. These are expressed in a bill of quantities. The relevant quantity is expressed, as a unit or item, and the estimated number or volume is shown. It is this document, the bill of quantities, which the tendering contractor quotes against by stating his prices—thereby binding himself on acceptance to a rate or price per unit for each of the components which go to comprise the overall works. Already this summary over-simplifies the technical expertise which has gathered around these practices: such bills will normally be prepared in accordance with a standard method of measurement which itself becomes an arcane field of expertise in its own right. The contract is called a "remeasurement" contract because the actual quantities of work and material supplied are remeasured as the project progresses. The price payable to the contractor is therefore the product of that actual remeasurement multiplied by the unit rates tendered in the priced bills of quantities. In other words, the tender price total has little real significance to the pricing of the actual work: the project proceeds with initial uncertainty and the sums eventually to be due to the contractor flow only from intervening professional activity and judgment. The latter, in hard cases, will be challenged.

The remeasurement system promotes a judgmental and interim approach to all payments during the progress of the works. The more they are interim, the more they may be argued over. 5–26

Interim measurement even applied to lump sum contracts

These specialised uses of bills of quantities, the resulting specialist expertise of quantity surveying, and the interim assessment of payments have permeated widely the British construction industry and its derivatives. They extend beyond remeasurement contracts into the normal practice also of building contracts, such as the JCT forms, even though the latter are let as lump sum contracts at tender time. So, even building contracts whose initial scope is agreed for a fixed price are paid for on account, during the progress of the works, by a system of interim measurement. Similarly the changes in the scope of those works are valued by reference to the rates stated in the bills of quantities. 5–27

Characteristics of the Disputes that Arise

Time, cost, and defects: multi-party issues

The archetypal disputes in the British construction industry arise of course from contractor's claim to be paid more for the increased time and cost of additional works; and the claims of building owners in respect of defects. The latter espe- 5–28 cially may involve many parties as responsibility is sought to be attributed between designers, suppliers and contractors; but even the former apparently more simple money claims are likely to be multi-party disputes as subcontractors' interests and responsibilities have to be taken into account.

Criticality of cash-flow

5–29 The low capitalisation of contracting organisations in the British industry has made cash flow critical to the life of the organisations and the projects they undertake. This has received the recognition of the courts. The construction industry is exceptional in being allowed by English law[7] to recover financing charges by way of damages for the late or non-payment of a money sum.

Accountability of settlements in the public sector

5–30 Conversely, until the exploration of private funding for infrastructure works, social services and utilities, many significant projects were public works. Public accountability and scrutiny by audit commissions allow less room for the resolution of disputes by commercial trade off. In the public sector, determination of a dispute by a competent tribunal through a transparent process may be more important to the public body than the extent of the financial responsibility thereby found against it.

Dispute Resolution Procedures

Independent powers of architect and engineer

5–31 Partly because of the public sector influence, the architect and engineer in traditional procurement under JCT and ICE respectively have come to be recognised by English law as having a dual role. They are not just the agent of the client employer. The contract forms give them independent powers of evaluation and decision. These latter powers must, as a matter of law, be exercised fairly. Indeed, it is precisely the evaluative and determinative characteristics of the

[7] *President of India v. Lips Maritime Corp.* [1988] A.C. 395; *Holbeach Plant Hire Ltd v. Anglian Water Authority* [1988] C.I.L.L. 448.

powers which by their contract the client employer and contractor have agreed to vest in the architect/engineer that have led to the perceived difficulties from the decision in *Crouch*.[8]

Conclusiveness preventing disputes arising

5–32 We have seen above that the perceived effect of the *Crouch*[9] decision is greatly to increase the significance in arbitration of the decisions, or certificates, of the engineer, architect or project manager. The powers of these contract administrators may go further. Their decision, or certificate, may in some circumstances be contractually conclusive: see, *e.g. Crown Estate Commissioners v. Mowlem.*[10] Attempts have even been made to achieve degrees of conclusiveness where an independent consultant professional is not being used as contract administrator: see, *e.g. Balfour Beatty v. Docklands Light Railway*[11]; *Tarmac Construction Ltd v. Esso Petroleum Ltd*[12]; and *Beaufort House Developments v. Zimmcor (International) Inc.*[13]

Engineer also acts as first-tier dispute resolver

5–33 The ICE contracts, and their FIDIC derivatives, go further. The engineer has a dispute resolving power beyond these initial evaluative and determinative powers. There is formal provision for a reference to the engineer of any dispute arising under or in connection with the contract for his decision. This procedure is a mandatory precondition for any subsequent reference of the matter to arbitration. In these traditional and still very widespread arrangements lies the basic structure of multi-stage dispute resolution that now characterises construction projects worldwide. The credibility of the independent aspect of this dual role is today challenged. NEC and FIDIC contracts have substituted a third party independent adjudicator for the formal decision stage which under ICE remains with the engineer.

Adjudication by third party neutral, as first-tier method

5–34 Adjudication as a first tier mandatory form of dispute resolution in construction contracts was made a statutory right by the Housing Grants, Construction and Regeneration Act 1996. The legislation flowed from some of the recommenda-

[8] See nn. 3 and 4 above.
[9] *ibid.*
[10] (1994) 70 B.L.R. 1.
[11] (1996) 78 B.L.R. 42.
[12] (1996) 51 Con.L.R. 187.
[13] (1990) 50 B.L.R. 91.

tions of Sir Michael Latham's Final Report of the government/industry review of procurement and contractual arrangements in the United Kingdom construction industry, *Constructing the Team.*[14]

Growth in multi-stage procedures

5–35 The growth in modern times of interest in other ADR techniques, such as mediation or conciliation, also influences the published revisions to standard forms of construction contract. The ICE forms provide for conciliation before arbitration. The contracts for the Airport Core Programme for the major new airport in Hong Kong provide for multi-stage dispute resolution,[15] including steps for mediation and for adjudication. In Britain, bespoke contracts for public infrastructure works provide for complex multi-stage procedures, with stepped opportunities for review by an engineer of decisions, followed by conciliation, and if necessary eventual arbitration by an appointed Official Referee, or even by a court empowered by the contract to open up, review and revise project certificates, etc.

Adjudication and expert determination

5–36 The movement towards adjudication as the mandatory first tier of dispute resolution by a third party neutral (instead of a formal decision by a traditional engineer) has been influenced by such a system for the Channel Tunnel.[16] The contract for the design and construction of the fixed link between England and France was derived from the FIDIC form. However, it provides for disputes first to be settled by a panel of experts. The contract for the second Dartford Crossing similarly provided for adjudication by a body appointed for the duration of the project. These models, reinforced by statutory right under the Housing Grants Construction and Regeneration Act 1996, have focused particular attention on the use of another ADR technique: expert determination. Just as architects and engineer's decisions have generated a substantial jurisprudence culminating with *Crouch*, so also the decisions from expert determinations have provoked some jurisprudence as to the extent of their reviewability (see, *e.g. Jones v. Sherwood Computer Services,*[17] *Nikko Hotels (UK) Ltd v. MEPC plc,*[18] *Mercury Communications v. Director General of Telecommunications1,*[19] and *British Shipbuilders v. VSEL*[20]).

[14] See n. 2, above.
[15] D. Lewis, "Dispute Resolution on the New Hong Kong International Airport" (1993) *International Construction Law Review*, 76.
[16] *Channel Tunnel Group Ltd v. Balfour Beatty Construction Ltd* [1993] A.C. 334.
[17] [1992] 1 W.L.R. 277.
[18] [1991] 28 E.G. 86.
[19] [1996] 1 W.L.R. 48.
[20] [1997] 1 Lloyd's Rep. 106.

Potential conflicts of jurisdiction in multi-stage procedures

Construction contracts normally provide for multi-stage dispute resolution procedures to be activated in an orderly sequential fashion, at least in regard to any one particular dispute. As with all dispute resolution, informal agreements will intervene to attempt parallel negotiations and other ADR techniques. The statutory imposition of adjudication, particularly on well-established traditional published standard forms of contract, may lead to some degree of parallel jurisdiction, *e.g.* as between adjudicators and arbitrators. Even with orderly prior provision, conflicts between the stages may still arise. 5–37

Conflicts of powers or jurisdiction between the elements of a multi-stage procedure are likely to be reduced if the recommendation of Sir Michael Latham's Report[21] is accepted, that final resolution of a dispute, *e.g.* by arbitration, is postponed until after completion or termination of the works. Such postponement of arbitration was required in the contracts for the Hong Kong airport and for some major infrastructure works in Britain. A degree of postponement is also provided for in the JCT form of contract, by allowing only some questions to be referred to arbitration before completion or termination of the works. There is a delicate balance to be judged in deciding whether such postponement is desirable in contract planning. It is said that references to arbitration during the progress of the works (as permitted by the Channel Tunnel contract) might unduly interfere with the satisfactory progress of the works and distract the participants from it. It might also diminish the force and value of interim stages such as adjudication. However, the postponement of the reference of dispute to arbitration until after the works has a number of disadvantages, including a festering of those problems, defensive conduct of the remainder of the works, and all the evidentiary difficulties that arise from the passage of time. 5–38

Arrangements for Arbitration in the Construction Industry

Standard forms, but standard decisions?

There is a curious tension and dilemma that arises from the dominant use of standard forms of contract in the British construction industry, and their provi- 5–39

[21] See n. 2 above.

sion for arbitration. On the one hand, it would much benefit the industry and its advisers to have guidance on decisions on the meaning and effect of provisions in the contracts, and practices arising therefrom. On the other hand, the very nature of arbitration, and its privacy save where matters are reviewed in the courts, prevents institutional dissemination of decisions.

5–40 This tension is mitigated somewhat by the substantial informal network of contacts of those servicing arbitration in the construction industry. There is a Society of Construction Arbitrators. Also, the Society of Construction Law brings together a great many individuals specialising in arbitration and the construction field, and its meetings and published papers assist in that regard. Similarly, the many meetings and publications of the Chartered Institute of Arbitrators, and its branches, contribute to understanding and learning in the field. It is also to the Presidents of the various professional institutions, Royal Institute of British Architects (RIBA), the Institution of Civil Engineers (ICE) and the Royal Institution of Chartered Surveyors (RICS), that applications are typically made for appointments of arbitrators in default of agreement by the parties. Membership, communications and networks that arise from these professional institutions again contribute to understanding and learning in the field.

A new sense of common purpose: CIMAR

5–41 Out of this diversity has arisen, particularly after the passing of the Arbitration Act 1996, a common sense of purpose in regard to arbitration rules. We have seen above that there are many features which particularly distinguish construction contracts in Britain, the nature of disputes likely to arise, and the procedures that are therefore appropriate to deal with them. There have been published in 1997 for the first time the Construction Industry Model Arbitration Rules (CIMAR).[22] These are for use with arbitration agreements under the Arbitration Act 1996. They were prepared following an initiative of the Society of Construction Arbitrators. In their published form, they have been produced with the approval of a very wide range of institutional bodies and interest groups across the breadth of the British construction industry. It is likely that they will be adopted by those drafting construction contracts, and in due course may well replace the published standard separate arbitration rules which each of the JCT and ICE presently issue for use with their respective contract forms.

5–42 Meanwhile, in very many cases the existing conventional arrangements will

[22] See Appendix 13.

continue for the incorporation of the JCT Arbitration Rules and the ICE Arbitration Procedure through the standard forms of contract. We therefore look at each of these in turn.

Arbitration under the JCT Contracts

The four elements of the JCT arbitration agreement

Provision by the parties for arbitration under the JCT contracts (for which illustration we take the traditional Standard Form With Quantities), one has to make reference to four elements comprising the arbitration agreement and the resulting incorporated procedure. These four elements are: 5–43

- the articles of agreement;
- the conditions;
- the Appendix; and
- the Arbitration Rules.

The articles of agreement are published by the JCT as a *pro forma* agreement with blanks to be completed by the parties. These identify the parties and the works, and provide for the appointment of the architect or contract administrator, and the quantity surveyor. Article 5 deals with the settlement of disputes by arbitration. It provides: 5–44

> "If any dispute or difference as to the construction of this contract or any matter or thing of whatsoever nature arising thereunder or in connection therewith shall arise between the Employer or the Architect/the Contract Administrator on his behalf and the Contractor either during the progress or after the completion of abandonment of the Works . . . it shall be and is hereby referred to arbitration in accordance with clause 41."

Clause 41: arbitration provisions in the JCT Conditions of Contract

The Conditions of Contract Part IV contains detailed and substantial provision on the settlement of disputes by arbitration. These are in over two pages of contractual terms comprising clause 41. 5–45

Clause 41.1 illustrates what a dispute or difference might comprise, and then 5–46 provides for the commencement of arbitration and the appointment of the arbitrator. The reference to the arbitration is by either the employer or contractor giving written notice to the other that the dispute is to be referred. It is to be referred to the arbitration and final decision of a person to be agreed between the parties as the arbitrator, or, upon failure so to agree within 14 days after the date of the written notice, of a person to be appointed as the arbitrator on the request of either the employer or the contractor by the person named in the Appendix. That appointing person named in the Appendix is also given the power, by clause 41.8, to appoint a further arbitrator in default of the parties agreeing one after the previous one dies or otherwise ceases to act before making his final award.

5–47 The Appendix is published with the JCT Conditions of Contract, but like the articles of agreement is in effect a *pro forma* with blanks to be completed by the parties, together with strike out options. There are default positions stated in the Appendix if the parties take no further action by deleting any of the options. In respect of arbitration, there are two significant provisions in the Appendix. First, there is the naming of the person to appoint the arbitrator, in default of agreement to do so by the parties. The Appendix states the appointor as the President or a Vice-President of one of the three following institutions, to be deleted as applicable. If no deletion is made then the appointor shall be the first of these. The three are: Royal Institute of British Architects, Royal Institution of Chartered Surveyors, or Chartered Institute of Arbitrators. The other provision of the Appendix in regard to settlement pursuits by arbitration is the statement that clauses 41.2.1 and 41.2.2 apply. This is the default, otherwise the parties strike out this statement in the Appendix.

JCT arrangements for consolidation of proceedings

5–48 Clauses 41.2.1 and 2 of the Conditions comprise the JCT arrangement for consolidation before one arbitrator of related disputes involving other parties. So, if a dispute or difference to be referred to arbitration under the JCT Standard Form of main contract raises issues which are substantially the same as or connected with issues raised in a related dispute between the employer or contractor and a nominated sub-contractor or supplier, and the related dispute has already been referred to arbitration, the employer and the contractor agree that the dispute or difference under this main contract shall be referred to the arbitrator appointed to determine the related dispute. Clause 41.2.1 goes on to provide that the JCT Arbitration Rule application to the related dispute shall apply to the dispute under this main contract; and that that arbitrator shall have power to make such directions and all necessary award in the same way as if the procedure of the High Court as to joining one or more defendants of joining co-defendants or third parties was available to the parties and to him. There is however a proviso in clause 41.2.2 that the employer or contractor may still require the dispute under this main contract to be referred to a different arbitrator if either of them reasonably considers that the arbitrator already appointed to determine the related dispute is not appropriately qualified to determine the dispute or difference under this contract.

Postponement of most matters until after completion

The Conditions of the JCT contract limit by clause 43.1 the matters that can be referred to an arbitrator until after completion or termination of the works. 5–49

Empowering the arbitrator to deal with project matters

Subject to certain conditions discussed below, the JCT Conditions gives by clause 41.4 the arbitrator, without prejudice to the generality of its powers, the power to rectify the contract so that it accurately reflects the true agreement made by the employer and the contractor. He is also empowered to direct such measurements and/or valuations as may in his opinion be desirable in order to determine the rights of the parties and to ascertain and award any sum which ought to have been the subject of or included in any certificate. It is of crucial importance following the *Crouch* decision that the arbitrator is also given by this clause the power to "open up, review and revise" any certificate, opinion, decision, requirement or notice and to determine all matters in dispute as if no such certificate, opinion, decision, requirement or notice had been given. The one qualification on this is that the arbitrator has no such power in respect of a decision of the architect/contractor administrator to issue instructions (pursuant to clause 8.4.1) in regard to the removal from site of work, materials or goods not in accordance with the contract. 5–50

The JCT Arbitration Rules[23]

The Conditions also provide that the arbitration shall be conducted in accordance with the JCT Arbitration Rules current at the base date stated by the parties in the Appendix. There is the further proviso that if any amendments to the Rules have been issued by the JCT after that base date the parties may, by a joint notice in writing to the arbitrator, state that they wished the arbitration to be conducted in accordance with those amended Rules. 5–51

The JCT Arbitration Rules therefore comprise the fourth element in regard to the JCT arbitration procedures. The Rules are of course the most substantial component. The Rules are drafted as a common form referred to in the arbitration agreement in 11 different published forms of contract within the JCT 5–52

[23] Arbitration Rules dated July 18, 1988: for use with the arbitration agreements referred to in rule 1 of those Rules: JCT Joint Contracts Tribunal for the Standard Form of Building Contract.

family. These go beyond the Standard Form of Building Contract (the main contract) to the design and build version, the intermediate and minor works forms, the form for management contracting, the sub-contract form for use with nominated sub-contractors and suppliers, and with named sub-contractors, and also a form of warranty by a nominated supplier.

Flexibility with alternative procedures

5–53 The JCT Rules have the advantage of relatively tight time periods (subject of course to contrary agreement). It is also encouraging that they do not use the language of "pleadings". The references are to statements of case, of defence, and of any counterclaim. Similarly, the formal language of discovery is avoided, the text using instead references to documents, *e.g.* on which reliance will be placed. The Rules focus on a preliminary meeting to be held within 21 days of the arbitrator's notification of his acceptance of appointment. This is the point at which the parties jointly decide, or if not, the arbitrator directs which form of procedure shall apply to the arbitration. The parties may decide one from three: Rule 5, procedure without hearing; Rule 6, full procedure with hearing; Rule 7, short procedure with hearing. If the parties do not jointly decide, then the arbitrator directs that the Rule 5 procedure without hearing shall apply unless, having regard to the information and/or representations of the party, the arbitrator directs that Rule 6 full procedure with hearing shall apply.

Arbitrator's powers under JCT

5–54 The Rules make provision for inspection of works, goods or materials whether on site or elsewhere by the arbitrator; provision in respect of the arbitrator's fees and expenses and on the payment by one party of any costs of the other party; and provision for payment to a trustee-stakeholder.

5–55 The arbitrator is empowered by the JCT Rules to publish an interim award. He is obliged to give reasons for his award only where and to the extent required by either party by notice in writing. In addition to any other powers conferred by law, the JCT Rules also confer express powers on the arbitrator:

- to take legal or technical advice;
- to give directions for protecting or disposing of property the subject of the dispute;
- to order security for costs and/or fees and expenses of the arbitrator;
- to proceed in the absence of a party;
- to direct, at his discretion, that the costs, if not agreed, shall be taxed by the arbitrator;
- to direct the giving of evidence by affidavit; and
- to order production of documents or classes of documents.

The JCT Rules conclude with a wide wrap-up empowerment:

> "If during the arbitration it appears to the Arbitrator to be necessary for the just and expeditious determination of the dispute that a Rule for the conduct of the arbitration other than that previously applicable shall apply, the Arbitrator, after considering any representations made by the parties, may so direct and shall give further directions as he may deem appropriate."

The JCT Arbitration Rules are published together with Notes. These are a substantial set of guidance notes, though parties will now need to be particularly careful as to whether under the transitional provisions for the Arbitration Act 1996, they are working under the old procedure or the new. 5–56

Jurisdictional issues in regard to the JCT procedures

The JCT procedure is, as we have seen above, a relatively straightforward one. 5–57
It is for most practical purposes presently a single stage procedure. The only formal provision for dispute resolution is through settlement by arbitration. To this extent, JCT is therefore to be contrasted with the ICE multi-stage procedures described in the next section. Some change is to be expected from JCT amendments to take account of the Housing Grants Construction and Regeneration Act 1996. Statutory adjudication introduced by that Act will require in effect a two stage procedure. Jurisdictional issues will thereby arise at the interface between adjudication and arbitration.

We have already seen that some jurisdictional issues will arise by the provi- 5–58
sion in clause 41.3 of JCT Conditions for the selective postponement of reference to arbitration on a number of matters until after completion or termination of the works. We also noted above that the empowering of the arbitrator under clause 41.4 is subject to certain conditions. Perhaps the most significant of these is as to the effect of the final certificate pursuant to clause 30.9. The final certificate shall have effect as conclusive evidence[24] of a wide range of matters in regard to the contract (*e.g.* quality of materials or goods, that the terms of the contract have been complied with, and that time and money entitlements have been given). That conclusiveness is prevented by the commencement of arbitral proceedings in respect of matters to which those proceedings relate. In order so to interrupt the conclusiveness, either party must within 28 days after the Final Certificate has been issued, start the proceedings. There is also provision for the Final Certificate to become conclusive if an arbitration has earlier been started but neither party has for a period of 12 months taken any further step in the proceedings.

[24] *Crown Estates Commissioners v. Mowlem* (1994) 70 B.L.R. 1.

The ICE Dispute Resolution Procedures

Arbitration is the final element in a multi-stage procedure

5–59 The provisions for arbitration in respect of the ICE conditions of contract comprise only two elements for the arbitration itself. There are, however, other stages in the dispute resolution process contemplated by the ICE conditions. The two elements for arbitration are clause 66 of the published Conditions, which incorporates the ICE Arbitration Procedure.[25] The Procedure is printed and published separately from the Conditions, though a copy is enclosed with the Conditions, as is a copy of the ICE Conciliation Procedure. Clause 66 of ICE, like the arbitration agreement under the JCT forms above, governs any dispute between the employer and the contractor in connection with or arising out of the contract or the carrying out of the works.

The ICE Notice of Dispute

5–60 ICE makes provision for the notice of a dispute. A dispute is deemed to arise when one party serves on the engineer a "notice of dispute" stating the nature of the dispute.

First stage: reference to the engineer for his decision

5–61 Before a dispute can be referred to arbitration it must go through the prior stage of a formal decision by the engineer. This includes disputes as to any decision, opinion, instruction, direction, certificate, or valuation which the engineer has already issued whether during the progress of the works or after their completion or termination. So, every dispute notified has first to be settled by the engineer who is required to state his decision in writing within one month after the service of a notice of dispute (or three months of a certificate of substantial completion of the whole of the works has already been issued). The parties then have three months after the engineer has given his formal decision (or after the date by which it should have been given) within which to refer the dispute to arbitration.

Optional conciliation stage

5–62 An optional procedure is interposed by ICE for conciliation. This may be required by either party giving notice requiring the dispute to be considered

[25] Institution of Civil Engineers, *Arbitration Procedure* (1997), principally for use with the ICE family of Conditions of Contract and the NEC family of Documents in England and Wales for arbitrations conducted under the Arbitration Act 1996.

under the ICE Conciliation Procedures. Conciliation can be invoked after the engineer has given his formal decision (or the time for giving it has expired) and no notice to refer to arbitration has been served.

Pre-arbitral stages can become final and binding

The decision of the engineer under this clause 66 procedure is final and binding upon the contractor and the employer unless and until the recommendation of a conciliator has been accepted by both parties or the engineer's decision is revised by an arbitrator's award. **5–63**

Appointment of the arbitrator

The appointment of the arbitrator under the ICE procedure leaves less room for party's choice than JCT. If the parties themselves failed to appoint an arbitrator within one month of either party serving on the other a written notice to concur in an appointment, then the dispute is referred to a person to be appointed by the President of the ICE. **5–64**

The ICE Arbitration Procedure[26]

The ICE Arbitration Procedure was revised in February 1997. It was prepared by the ICE principally for use with the ICE family of Conditions of Contract and the NEC family of forms in England and Wales for arbitrations conducted under the Arbitration Act 1996. The ICE states that it may be suitable for use with other contracts and in other jurisdictions. **5–65**

Consistent with the 1996 Act, the Procedure starts in rule 1 with a declaration of aims and objectives: "the object of arbitration is to obtain the fair resolution of disputes by an impartial arbitrator without unnecessary delay or expense". This rule also provides that the Procedure shall be interpreted and the proceedings shall be conducted in a manner most conducive to achieving the objectives. **5–66**

The rules in Part A then deal at some length with the commencement of the arbitration and the appointment of the arbitrator, though despite all the words they add little to what is provided in the ICE Conditions of Contract. **5–67**

Part B of the ICE Arbitration Procedure is concerned with the arrangements for the arbitration. Like JCT, but with less emphasis on time periods, it focuses on a preliminary meeting. Variants to a full procedure are available. Unfortunately they are made by the structure of the document to appear more exceptional. They are Part F (Short Procedure) and Part G (Special Procedure for Experts). The curious feature of the provision of rule 6 for the preliminary meeting is that it remains **5–68**

[26] *ibid.*

based on a consensus approach, without empowerment of the arbitrator in that section. So, the drafting phrases are "the parties and the Arbitrator shall consider whether and to what extent . . . Part F . . . shall apply . . ."

Powers of the arbitrator under the ICE Procedure

5–69 The powers of the arbitrator under the ICE Procedure are set out in Part C. In addition to the power to rule on his own substantive jurisdiction, the arbitrator is given power to decide all procedural and evidential matters including, but not limited to (in summary):

- what forms of statements of claim and defence should be used;
- what documents or classes of documents should be disclosed and at what stage;
- whether and in what form questions should be answered in advance of a hearing;
- whether the strict rules of evidence should apply;
- the time, manner and form in which fact or opinion material should be exchanged;
- whether and to what extent the arbitrator should take the initiative in ascertaining the facts and the law, and/or rely upon his own knowledge and expertise;
- whether and to what extent there should be oral or written evidence or submissions, expert evidence, evidence under oath or affirmation;
- the manner in which evidence of witnesses shall be taken; and
- whether and to what extent enquiries, tests or investigations should be conducted.

5–70 Also, the arbitrator is given power to decide, in default of agreement between the parties, when and where any part of the proceedings is to be held. The arbitrator may fix the time within which any directions given by him are to be complied with and may if he thinks fit extend the time so fixed whether or not it has expired. Part C also empowers the arbitrator to limit recoverable costs, to order security, and to order protective measures, for the preservation or evidence, or in relation to property which is the subject of the proceedings, and for preservation or disposal of the subject matter of the dispute.

5–71 The ICE Procedure therefore follows closely the language of the 1996 Act. By contrast with CIMAR, ICE does so by stating the substance in its own provisions: it does not quote, or incorporate by reference, the statutory language in the way that CIMAR does. The ICE style in this respect arguably makes it more user friendly, and more appropriate for foreign use where the substance of the English Act remains a good model though not having statutory application.

ICE arrangements for concurrent hearings

The ICE provides under Part D, in respect of procedures before the hearing, for a power to order concurrent hearings. This provision is weaker than that found in the JCT Rules above. Rule 9.1 provides: 5–72

> "Where disputes or differences have arisen under two or more contracts each concerned wholly or mainly with the same subject matter and the resulting arbitrations have been referred to the same Arbitrator he may with the agreement of all the parties concerned or upon the application of one of the parties being a party to all the contracts involved order that the whole or any part of the matters as issue shall be heard together upon such terms or conditions as the Arbitrator thinks fit."

Even where such an order for concurrent hearings has been made, the arbitrator must nevertheless make separate awards unless all the parties otherwise agree. The arbitrator may if he thinks fit prepare one combined set of reasons to cover all the awards.

Other aspects of ICE Procedure

Otherwise, both Part D, and Part E, Procedure at the Hearing, are rather wordy in their description of procedures, in a way which could more simply have been stated by reference to the powers of the arbitrator. In Rule 14 on evidence, the ICE Procedure falls back into traditional lawyers' language, with all the dangers of inviting thereby a heavy procedure which is both a pale and inadequate imitation of procedures before the courts. 5–73

Construction Arbitrations in the Modern Climate

Opportunities and challenges in multi-stage procedures

We have seen from the above that multi-stage procedures for dispute resolution are already normal in the ICE, NEC and FIDIC forms. The introduction by the Housing Grants, Construction and Regeneration Act 1996 of a statutory right to 5–74 adjudication is likely to impose a multi-stage procedure also in the JCT forms. The refinement of those processes produce opportunities and challenges. They are likely also to cause reconsideration of the true limits of the *Crouch*[27] decision, and the true nature of a "dispute".[28]

Appropriate procedures for different kinds of dispute

5–75 The opportunities are to recognise the appropriateness of different forms of dispute resolution to different kinds of dispute. The challenge is, in summary, to avoid the initial stages becoming expensive sideshows or cynical fishing expeditions before an eventual, old-fashioned style of litigation conducted before arbitrators in the private sector.

5–76 The distinctive features of construction contracts and their circumstances, discussed above, demonstrate that special consideration has to be given to the achievement of fair resolution of construction disputes without unnecessary delay or expense. The almost inevitable involvement in disputes of contested professional judgment on technical matters, set in a context of a mass of record material, calls for expert evidence.

5–77 The Official Referees have been in the vanguard, even before Lord Woolf's report, in encouraging expeditious procedures, and the Court of Appeal has also been pointing the way in construction cases.[29] It would be odd if any construction arbitrator did not go at least as far in seeking to streamline and simplify the procedures towards final resolution of a dispute. Part 2 of this work has already demonstrated the need for arbitrators to approach their task afresh, and not to be unduly influenced by English court procedures which themselves have anachronistic shadows of procedures more appropriate to civil jury trial. Most published procedures for arbitration, for use with the standard forms of contract, already encourage parties away from formal pleadings to more appropriate statements of case, and of defence, etc. Similarly, they already encourage parties to consider approaches to the disclosure of documents which is commensurate with the nature of the dispute, rather than encouraging the parties to embark on full scale discovery.

5–78 The provisions of the Arbitration Act 1996 in regard to costs and interim orders offer real potential for construction disputes to become managed in arbitration appropriately for the issues and sums at stake. The industry's experience of other methods of dispute resolution, such as adjudication and expert deter-

[27] *Great Ormond Street Hospital NHS Trust v. Secretary of State for Health* (1997), unreported; *University of Reading v. Miller Construction Ltd* (1994) 75 B.L.R. 91; *John Barker Construction Ltd v. London Portman Hotel Ltd* (1996) 50 Con.L.R. 43.

[28] *Hayter v. Nelson* [1990] 2 Lloyds Rep. 265; *cf. Cruden Construction Ltd v. Commissioner for New Towns* [1995] 2 Lloyds Rep. 387; *Balfour Beatty v. Docklands Light Railway Ltd* (1996) 78 B.L.R. 42.

[29] *British Airways Pension Trustees Ltd v. Sir Robert McAlpine & Sons Ltd* (1994) 72 B.L.R. 26; and see *GMTC Tools & Equipment Ltd v. Yuasa Warwick Machinery Ltd* (1994) 44 Con.L.R. 68.

mination will assist in this process. Many an arbitration in the construction industry might benefit greatly from the identification of preliminary technical issues, for reference to an expert determination in support of the overall arbitral procedure.

Conduct of Construction Industry Arbitrations before the 1996 Act

The construction industry as a user

In submissions for the consultation process that led to the passing of the Arbitration Act 1996, the Construction Industry Council stated that the majority of construction industry cases were resolved by arbitration, and of these approximately 60 per cent were presided over by an arbitrator who was not a lawyer. 5–79

The use of arbitration as a favoured process of dispute resolution for the construction industry was given a considerable boost by the decision of the Court of Appeal in *Crouch*.[30] The decision came at a time of increasing dissatisfaction with the law and practice of arbitration as it applied to construction industry disputes. Indeed, many parties took the view that it was preferable to strike out the arbitration clauses in standard forms of contract. 5–80

The perceived problems

Arbitration in this industry addresses, as we have seen above, substantial evidentiary material, technical expertise, and of course legal issues. However, there was all too often, even in arbitration, a slavish adherence to the processes of litigation giving rise to the justified criticisms that arbitration had become little more than ''litigation behind closed doors''. The major problems identified with construction industry arbitrations prior to the Act included: 5–81

- the inaccessibility of the legislation;
- the absence of wide powers possessed by arbitrators to control proceedings and in particular to enforce orders made;
- the need to readjust the balance between the arbitrator's powers and

[30] See nn. 3 and 4 above.

those of the courts whereby the court would support rather than intervene in the arbitral process; and

- the lack of a satisfactory procedure to regulate the conduct of related disputes.

The need for reform

5–82 An extensive consultation process preceded the Act and there is no doubt that the Act benefited enormously from the exercise. The construction industry participated actively in this process. The need for reform was great and the Act was warmly welcomed by the construction industry as going a long way towards meeting many of the problems which beset construction industry arbitrations.

Conduct of Construction Industry Arbitrations after the 1996 Act

The benefits of the Act

5–83 It is self-evident that the ability of construction industry arbitrations to provide a fair, economic and expeditious dispute resolution process depends primarily upon the manner by which the tribunal manages the arbitral process. This in turn concerns fundamental issues such as the manner by which arbitrators are appointed, and the training and education of arbitrators. However, what was abundantly clear prior to the Act was that if tribunals were to be urged to conduct arbitrations so as to the achieve the objectives referred to, and appropriately identified as general principles in section 1 of the Act, then the tribunal had to be given clear and wide powers. The tools had to be made available. The Act has provided them.

5–84 Below we consider a number of important issues which relate to how construction industry arbitrations are conducted. However, in addition to these more general matters of practice and procedure, the Act introduced a number of important changes and benefits which have particular application to construction industry arbitrations and we first discuss some of the more important examples of these.

5–85 It must be remembered that this discussion does not reflect the construction disputes in respect of which arbitral proceedings commenced before the January

31, 1997. Because of the size and complexity of many construction industry disputes, such arbitrations continue to be governed by the pre-Act regime for many years after 1996.[31]

The definition of an arbitration agreement

It is not uncommon for parties to agree orally to enter into a construction contract upon the terms of a standard form of contract. Whilst the Act requires an arbitration agreement to be in writing, the definition of "in writing" in the Act is very wide indeed.[32] For example, the agreement need not be signed, it can be by reference to terms which are in writing, it may be evidenced in writing or confirmed by subsequent conduct. If, in written submissions in arbitral or legal proceedings, a party argues for the existence of an arbitration agreement which is not denied by the other party, then it is deemed that an arbitration agreement exists. **5–86**

Prior to the Act, a number of cases concerning construction contracts, gave rise to conflicting authority on the question as to what is required for the effective incorporation of an arbitration clause by reference.[33] The Act makes it clear[34] that a reference in an agreement to a written form of arbitration clause, in a document such as a standard form of contract containing an arbitration clause, will be sufficient to constitute an arbitration agreement if the reference is such as to make that clause part of the agreement. **5–87**

Competence of tribunal to rule on its own jurisdiction

There is no doubt that recalcitrant parties have sought to delay the commencement of valid arbitration proceedings by challenging the jurisdiction of tribunals on spurious grounds. Institutions and arbitrators have been placed in a very difficult position by parties who have threatened or embarked upon court proceedings seeking an injunction to restrain the commencement or progress of the arbitration whilst declarations were sought in the court as to whether a construction contract existed or, if it did, whether it contained a valid arbitration agreement. Unless otherwise agreed, the Act[35] enables the tribunal to rule upon its own substantive jurisdiction, namely as to whether there is a valid arbitration agreement; whether the tribunal is properly constituted and what matters have been submitted to arbitration in accordance with the arbitration agreement. This doctrine, together with that of separability means that a party to a construction **5–88**

[31] *Great Ormond Street Hospital NHS Trust v. Secretary of State for Health* (1997), unreported.
[32] s.5.
[33] *Aughton v. M.F. Kent Services* [1991] 57 B.L.R 1; *Ben Barrett v. Henry Boot Management Ltd* [1996] ADRL.J. 33.
[34] s.6(2).
[35] s.7.

contract can no longer delay arbitration proceedings on the basis of an argument that a construction contract did not come into existence or has become ineffective.

Stay of legal proceedings

5–89 We have seen above that a common feature of claims in the construction industry is that disputes often arise between a number of parties in connection with the same subject matter. Such disputes might involve the employer; contractor; consultants; and one or more subcontractors or suppliers. The claims against the parties are likely to arise in circumstances where all of the relevant contracts do not contain arbitration agreements; and, if some or all of them do, those arbitration agreements are unlikely to provide for a consolidated arbitration. A further complication may well arise insofar as it may be a pre-condition to arbitration that the parties first use another dispute resolution procedure.[36]

5–90 A party who intends to proceed against a number of other parties in a construction dispute under different contracts in respect of which some but not all contain arbitration clauses, faces a considerable dilemma. Should he be forced to proceed by way of court proceedings and several separate arbitration proceedings? The approach often adopted has been to issue proceedings against all of the relevant parties and then to ascertain whether any of the parties applies to the courts to stay the proceedings to arbitration and/or takes a procedural step in the proceedings.

Abolition of the discretion in regard to the domestic stay

5–91 Prior to the Act, the court had a discretion in relation to "domestic arbitration agreements"[37] not to stay legal proceedings to arbitration. The ground usually relied upon was that the courts should ordinarily exercise its discretion to allow disputes to proceed to litigation together if amongst other reasons, a stay of the litigation in relation to one of those disputes would be liable to cause substantial injustice to the party which wanted them litigated together. A stay to arbitration would give rise to the prospect of inconsistent findings and decisions by the courts and the tribunal upon the same issues.[38]

5–92 The Act[39] initially preserved the ability of the courts to use its discretion to

[36] See adjudication, above; and see *Channel Tunnel Group Ltd v. Balfour Beatty Construction Ltd* [1993] A.C. 334; *Enco Civil Engineering v. Zeus International Development Ltd* (1991) 56 B.L.R. 43; *Drake & Scull Engineering Ltd v. McLaughlin & Harvey plc* (1992) 60 B.L.R. 102.

[37] s.85.

[38] *Taunton-Collins v. Cromie and others* [1964] 1 W.L.R. 633, *Bulk Oil (Zug) A.G. v. Trans Asiatic Oil Limited S.A.* [1973] 1 Lloyd's Rep. 129; *Great Ormond Street Hospital NHS Trust v. Secretary of State for Health* (1997), unreported.

[39] s.86.

stay legal proceedings albeit with the provision of allowing the Secretary of State to repeal or amend the provisions of sections 85–87. The DAC decided after the Act received Royal Assent, to recommend the abolition of the distinction between international and domestic arbitration agreements. Accordingly, sections 85–87 of the Act were not brought into force by the Commencement Order. The granting of an application of a stay of legal proceedings to arbitrations is therefore now mandatory unless the courts are satisfied that the arbitration agreement is null and void, inoperative or incapable of being performed.

The Act's support for contractual pre-arbitral dispute resolution processes

The court will also stay legal proceedings to arbitration notwithstanding the fact **5–93**
that it is first necessary for a party to exhaust another dispute resolution procedure prior to arbitration. This is a position commonly encountered in construction industry disputes where, as a pre-condition to arbitration, an engineer has first to decide upon the disputes or where a procedure has first to be exhausted such as a reference to a panel,[40] a dispute review board, a form of alternative dispute resolution or consensual or statutory adjudication.

Multi-party disputes

We have noted that multi-party disputes are extremely common in the construc- **5–94**
tion industry and that the orderly resolution of those disputes in one forum, namely the courts, can now be frustrated by a party whose agreement contains an arbitration agreement and who applies to stay any legal proceedings.

The relevant provisions of the Act concerning the stay of legal proceedings **5–95**
therefore emphasise the importance of an appropriate procedure being available for handling related disputes in arbitration proceedings. How does the Act deal with this vital issue concerning construction industry arbitrations? The answer is that it does not, and it is likely that the approach taken by the Act to multi-party disputes, coupled with the provisions regarding the stay of legal proceedings, represents the most important area of procedural difficulty for construction industry arbitrations.

Mechanisms for consolidation of arbitral proceedings

Absent consent by the parties following a dispute arising, there are three means **5–96**
by which two or more arbitrations concerning related issues can become consolidated:

[40] *Channel Tunnel Group Ltd v. Balfour Beatty Construction Ltd* [1993] A.C. 334.

- **Statutory.** The statutes of the jurisdiction may provide for some form of consolidation, such as, *e.g.* the Hong Kong Arbitration Ordinance and the Netherlands Arbitration Act.
- **Conditions of contract.** The contracts themselves may provide for some form of consolidation or other procedure for multi-party disputes.
- **Institutional or other applicable procedural rules.** Institutional rules adopted by the parties to the separate contracts may provide for consolidation with or without consent.

Pressure on the DAC for statutory power to consolidate

5–97 In the light of the importance of multi-party disputes in arbitrations concerning the construction and maritime industries, the DAC came under increasing pressure to include in the Act appropriate provisions for multi-party disputes. It was proposed that those provisions should allow for limited powers being exercisable by the courts where necessary so as to avoid inconsistent conclusions of fact or law. Further, it was proposed that in circumstances where the same tribunal was appointed in relation to two separate arbitrations, where it was convenient by reason of the nature of the dispute for both arbitrations to be heard concurrently, then the tribunal would have the power to so order.

The proposals were rejected

5–98 The DAC rejected those and other more limited proposals. It was felt by the DAC that to so provide would be a negation of one of the overriding principles namely that of party autonomy. Accordingly, the Act[41] does no more than provide that the parties are free to agree terms upon which there shall be the consolidation of arbitration proceedings or that concurrent hearings shall be held and that where no such agreement is reached a tribunal has no such power. This is therefore one of the sections of the Act where the parties have to ''contract in''.

Solutions for consolidating construction industry arbitrations

5–99 Parties to construction contracts therefore need to look to the other two remaining means of assisting multi-party disputes which were outlined above. The most obvious way of meeting the desired objectives is to clearly provide for the regulation of multi-party disputes in the contract itself. We have already referred to an example of this, namely Clause 41 of the JCT Form. An effective ''string'' arbitration clause giving effect to multi-party disputes needs very careful drafting. All the potential parties in the several related contracts need to

[41] s.35.

consent both to being joined in other arbitration proceedings and to having other parties joined in arbitration proceedings under their own arbitration agreement. It must be unlikely that parties will provide sufficiently for such circumstances where ad hoc agreements are entered into as opposed to contracting under standard forms of contract.

Scope for meeting the difficulties inherent in multi-party disputes can be provided by institutional or other applicable rules of arbitration. The London Court of International Arbitration (LCIA) Rules, for example, provide, in Article 13.1(c), that the tribunal shall have power to: "allow other parties to be joined in the arbitration with their express consent, and make a single final award determining all disputes between them". We have seen that the JCT form contains an applicable provision as a condition of contract. This form of contract incorporates the JCT Arbitration Rules but these rules contain no further provisions concerning multi-party disputes. The manner by which the ICE Procedure deals with multi-party disputes has been discussed above. **5–100**

Revision of Rules to Reflect the Act

Many of the institutions concerned with arbitration in the construction industry are revising their rules of procedure in order to reflect the Act. Reference has already been made to CIMAR. **5–101**

Construction Industry Model Arbitration Rules[42]

The CIMAR group's objective was to produce a model set of rules for consideration and adoption by all relevant construction institutions or other bodies having arbitration interests. Such a common approach across the industry was clearly highly desirable, and is receiving favourable reception from the institutions and users. CIMAR Rules are already being adopted for use by some bodies, and it is contemplated that they will in due course replace the JCT and the ICE rules. The CIMAR Rules are reproduced, with kind permission, at Appendix 13. **5–102**

[42] See n. 22 above.

Provisional awards

5–103 The powers and remedies available to the tribunal under the Act are extensive. The parties are free to agree to extend or curtail these powers and remedies. Such powers include the ability to make an interim award[43] upon an issue affecting the whole of a claim or a part of a claim or cross-claim.

5–104 As we have observed above, cash flow is of particular importance to the construction industry. It has been described as its very life blood.[44] It was for this reason that it was proposed that the Act should include a provision for the making of provisional awards akin to the relief of an interim payment pursuant to Ord. 29, r. 10 of the Rules of the Supreme Court. The granting of temporary or provisional financial relief needs to be exercised with enormous care and, as the equivalent power in the courts has shown, it is capable of abuse. In the light of these considerations, certain relevant authorities,[45] and other powers available to the tribunal to grant relief through interim awards, it was decided that the Act should provide for provisional relief being granted by a tribunal only when the parties so agree.[46] As with the power to consolidate arbitrations, unless the parties confer such power upon the tribunal no such power exists.[47] The Act makes it clear that section 39 does not affect the powers of the tribunal under section 47 to make awards on different issues.

An example on rules on provisional relief: the ICE Procedure

5–105 The ICE Arbitration Procedure (1997) includes a provision for "provisional relief":

> 19.3 The Arbitrator may also make a provisional order and for this purpose the Arbitrator shall have power to award payment by one party to another of a sum representing a reasonable proportion of the final net amount which in his opinion that party is likely to be ordered to pay after determination of all the issues in the arbitration and after taking into account any defence or counterclaim upon which the other party may be entitled to rely.
> 19.4 The Arbitrator shall have power to order the party against whom a provisional order is made to pay part or all of the sum awarded to a stakeholder. In default of compliance with such an order the Arbitrator may order payment of the whole sum in the provisional order to the other party.
> 19.5 A provisional order shall be final and binding upon the parties unless and until it is varied by any subsequent award made by the same Arbitrator

[43] s.47.
[44] *Gilbert Ash (Northern) v. Modern Engineering (Bristol)* [1974] A.C. 689.
[45] *The Kostas Melas* [1981] 1 Lloyd's Rep. 18 at 26, *per* Goff J.
[46] s.39.
[47] s.39(4).

or by any other Arbitrator having jurisdiction over the matters in dispute. Any such subsequent award may order repayment of monies paid in accordance with the provisional order.''

CIMAR provides for similar relief.

The Construction Arbitrator and the Appointment Process

Introduction

The initial and vital part of the process of arbitration concerns the appointment of the arbitrator. Often in construction disputes, parties pay insufficient regard to the nature and manner of appointment; or the appointing body nominates an arbitrator who is inappropriate in all the circumstances. **5–106**

If the process of arbitration is to respond to the needs of the parties to construction disputes, then it is of paramount importance that the process of agreeing or nominating an arbitrator is scrupulously transparent and that arbitrators are available for nomination who have suitable expertise in the practice and procedure of arbitration. The success of arbitration as an appropriate method of dispute resolution is almost wholly dependent upon arbitrators successfully discharging their powers and duties. **5–107**

Who and how many?

The parties are free to agree upon the number of arbitrators to form the tribunal. If the parties do not expressly agree to a single arbitrator but agree to institutional rules governing the arbitral process, it will vary as to whether one or three arbitrators will be appointed. This is illustrated by the following examples: **5–108**

- The ICC rules specify that if the parties do not agree upon the number of arbitrators then the court will appoint one arbitrator unless the court believes that three arbitrators are warranted.
- The UNCITRAL rules provide that three arbitrators shall be appointed if the parties cannot agree upon a single arbitrator.
- The LCIA Rules provide for the appointment of a sole arbitrator unless

the parties agree otherwise or the court determines that a three member tribunal is appropriate in all the circumstances.

5–109 The arbitration agreements in the standard forms of contracts discussed above provide for the appointment of a single arbitrator. In the absence of agreement as to the number of arbitrators or applicable governing rules, the Act provides that the tribunal shall comprise one arbitrator.[48]

Choosing the tribunal

5–110 The Act provides a comprehensive code for the appointment of an arbitrator; the failure of the appointment procedure; chairman and umpires; and the filling of vacancies arising as a consequence of the resignation or death of the arbitrator.[49]

5–111 It is clearly preferable that the parties should agree upon the identity of the arbitrator. On occasions, construction contracts identify in advance the arbitrator who will determine future disputes. However, as construction contracts increasingly demand the resolution of disputes by other means as a pre-condition to arbitration (in order to resolve disputes expeditiously) and thus, as arbitration becomes a process ordinarily undertaken after practical completion of the works, the need to agree upon the identity of the arbitrator to avoid delay in the appointment process becomes much less relevant. Ordinarily, therefore, the parties are left in the position of seeking to agree the identity of a suitable arbitrator once a party has commenced arbitration proceedings. Unfortunately, it is often the case that by this stage, the parties are reluctant to agree to anything, particularly something as important as the identity of the tribunal itself. This means that it is often left to institutions or nominating authorities to select and appoint an appropriate arbitrator.

How the arbitrator is appointed

5–112 It is in our view regrettable that the process of selection of an arbitrator is often shrouded in mystery. It is essential that the parties should have the utmost confidence in the arbitrator and thus how he came to be appointed. We believe that significant improvements could and should be made to the appointment procedures operated by many of the relevant institutions who regularly appoint construction industry arbitrators. These might include:

- Allowing the parties the right to address orally the relevant individual responsible for nominating the arbitrator as to the appropriate character-

48 s.15(3).
49 ss.15–27.

istics and expertise which it is felt ought to be possessed by the prospective arbitrator.

- The furnishing by the appointing body of a short list of proposed arbitrators with full details of recent relevant experience thereby enabling the parties to have a further opportunity to seek to agree one of those independently identified arbitrators.
- The ability to obtain references from parties and their advisers who have had disputes recently determined by the proposed arbitrator(s).

RIBA appointments

The Royal Institute of British Architects (RIBA) maintains a list of people whom it considers suitable for such appointments. The majority of the people on the list are architects, but the list also includes quantity surveyors, building surveyors, engineers and lawyers. Suitable names are chosen from this list and the RIBA secretariat then inquires whether the first person selected has any connection with the parties or the subject matter of the dispute, and is willing and able to accept appointment. On receipt of a notification that the individual concerned is willing to accept the appointment, the President completes a form of appointment and notifies the parties of the decision. **5–113**

Although the form used by the President refers to the "appointment" of the arbitrator, it is really only a nomination and does not become a formal appointment until the nominee has formally accepted the appointment and so notified the parties. The gap to accommodate this last stage of the appointment permits a nominated "arbitrator" who so wishes to advise the parties of any terms for his appointment and to receive the acceptance of these terms by the parties. On receipt of that acceptance the nominated arbitrator can formally accept the appointment and thereafter the appointment is complete. In *K/S Norjarl A/S v. Hyundai Heavy Industrial Co. Ltd*[50] the Court of Appeal supported the view that any conditions of appointment to be imposed by the arbitrator should be agreed before the appointment is accepted. **5–114**

Because of the preponderance of architects on the President's list of potential arbitrators, the President's nominee is likely to be an architect but in making his selection the President tries to select as a potential arbitrator a person possessing the expertise and qualifications appropriate to the dispute as described to him. **5–115**

ICE appointments

The arbitration clause in the ICE form similarly permits a party to apply to the President of the Institution of Civil Engineers but only after the Engineer has given his formal decision. Again, like the RIBA, the ICE maintains a list of **5–116**

[50] [1992] Q.B. 863.

potential arbitrators although in this case the vast majority of those listed are civil engineers.

RICS appointments

5–117 The Royal Institution of Chartered Surveyors membership covers a very wide range of different types of surveyors, who are suitable for appointment as arbitrators and the President in making an appointment will select a member of appropriate expertise.

Publication of lists of potential arbitrators

5–118 Neither of the lists maintained by the RIBA and the RICS is made public and so the names are known only to the institutions concerned. The ICE publish their list of arbitrators and a copy can be obtained from the institution by anyone and is frequently used by the parties or their legal advisers in an endeavour to agree upon an arbitrator.

The Hearing

5–119 Part 2 of this work has already considered the many important issues relating to the conduct of arbitration hearings. The matters raised are equally valid in relation to construction disputes and are to be reread in that context. However, because of the distinguishing features of construction disputes referred to earlier, there are several specific matters which are worthy of comment.

The choice of procedure

5–120 The very diversity of construction disputes means that it is inappropriate to adopt a uniform approach to the conduct of hearings. It has therefore become increasingly common for arbitrators to request a preliminary meeting or a pre-trial review at which agreement can be reached or in the absence of agreement, the arbitrator can in most cases determine, the applicable procedure to be adopted at the hearing.

As we have seen above, a welcome development in the drafting of the arbitration rules of certain institutes has been the provision of a flexible approach to hearings by identifying a series of alternative types of procedure, such as, for example: 5–121

- The Chartered Institute of Arbitrators Rules provide for the adoption of a simplified or expedited procedure.
- The JCT Rules provide for the three alternative forms of procedure summarised above:
  - — *Procedure without a hearing*. This method is suitable for a documents only arbitration but does not preclude an inspection by the arbitrator.
  - — *Short procedure with a hearing*. This method is appropriate to decide disputes on workmanship and quality.
  - — *Full procedure with a hearing*. This approach is suitable for larger cases where the issues are complex and testing of evidence may be necessary.
- The ICE Arbitration Procedure (1997) provides for:
  - — *A short procedure*. This procedure is appropriate for less complex matters and require submissions and evidence to be in writing followed by a one day hearing for the arbitrator to receive any oral submission which either party may wish to make and to enable the arbitrator to put questions to the parties.
  - — *A special procedure for experts*. This allows for the hearing and determination of any issues of fact which depend upon the evidence of experts. Once again most of the material is provided in writing with a day reserved for oral amplification by the experts of their opinion.
- CIMAR identifies three types of procedure which largely reflects the JCT approach:
  - — Short hearing.
  - — Documents only.
  - — Full procedure where neither the documents only nor the short procedure is appropriate.

Questions from the tribunal

It is important that the parties address relevant questions which the tribunal wish specifically to be answered. The parties should, where appropriate, have advance notice of these questions and tribunals should be encouraged to identify such questions prior to the hearing. By way of example, the LCIA Rules and the CIA Rules provide that the tribunal may provide the parties with a list of matters or questions which the tribunal wishes them to treat with special attention. 5–122

Time limits

5–123 Whilst there has been a welcome tendency to require the parties to deliver submissions and evidence in writing rather than orally, there remains a marked reluctance both in the courts and in many arbitrations to impose time limits upon the parties during the hearing. The length of the hearing is still, unfortunately, often fixed by reference to the parties' views as to how long it will take them to present their case. It is suggested that a more appropriate approach is to identify the length of time which the hearing ought to take and then to ascertain how the hearing can be managed so as to enable the hearing to be completed within the agreed time. Other forms of dispute resolution have clearly demonstrated that procedures can be managed so as to the enable parties, even in the most complex of cases, adequately to present their cases within a relatively limited period of time.

5–124 The Act does not expressly refer to the ability of the tribunal to fix time limits for the presentation of each party's case at the hearing. However, the accepted general principle of seeking to achieve a fair resolution of disputes without unnecessary delay and expense should encourage tribunals to take a more robust approach to the setting of time limits and ensuring that the parties adhere to them. It is suggested that an appropriate approach is to be found in rule 13.7 of the ICE Arbitration Procedure (1997):

> "The Arbitrator may at any time (whether before or after the hearing has commenced) allocate the time available for the hearing between the parties and those representing the parties shall then adhere strictly to that allocation. Should a party's representative fail to complete the presentation of that party's case within a time so allowed further time shall only be afforded at the sole discretion of the Arbitrator and upon such conditions as to costs as the Arbitrator may see fit to impose."

The Award

The form of the award

5–125 Part 2 of this work gives some guidance as to the drafting of an award. The parties are free to agree upon the form of an award, but in the absence of such agreement, an award:

- may be one of a number of awards in respect of different issues[51];
- must be in writing and signed by all the arbitrators[52];
- must contain reasons[53];
- must state the seat of the arbitration and the date when the award is made[54];
- may provide for simply or compound interest[55];
- may be expressed in any currency[56]; and
- is final and binding.[57]

The time for delivery of award and notification

The form of an award may also be determined by the incorporation of institutional rules, such as ICE, LCIA or UNCITRAL. However, these and many other rules broadly reflect the requirements of the Act outlined above. An interesting omission in many of these rules is a reference to the period of time within which an award should be published. The ICC rules refer to six months, though in practice this is often extended. CIMAR goes further and helpfully provides as follows: **5–126**

> "12.3 At the conclusion of a hearing, where the arbitrator is to deliver an award he shall inform the parties of the target date for its delivery. The arbitrator must take all possible steps to complete the award by that date and inform the parties of any reason which prevents him doing so. The award shall not deal with the allocation of costs and/or interest unless these have been addressed".

Once the tribunal has made its award it ordinarily notifies the parties in writing specifying how and where the award may be taken up, usually upon payment of the tribunal's fees and expenses. Difficulties have arisen in construction disputes in circumstances where a party has obtained an award without informing the other party, with the result that time limits as to, *e.g.* appeals may be exceeded. The Act provides that a copy of the award shall be served upon the parties[58] albeit that the original award may be withheld in case of non-payment of the fees and expenses of the arbitrators. **5–127**

[51] s.47.
[52] s.52(3).
[53] s.52(4).
[54] s.52(5).
[55] s.49(3).
[56] s.48(4).
[57] s.58(1).
[58] s.55(2).

Correction of award and additional award

5–128 The Act[59] enables the tribunal or the parties to correct an award on the basis of clerical or other accidental omissions and to make an additional award in respect of any claim which was presented to the tribunal but was not dealt with in the award. This is a feature of most if not all of the institutional rules. The Act[60] provides a strict time limit, not only for any such application but also in relation to the making of any correction or additional award.

5–129 The Act does not go as far as CIMAR which gives the arbitrator power to provide the parties with a draft of his proposed award for their comments within a specific period of time. In our view, the exercise of such a power would need to be handled carefully in order to avoid a party exploiting the opportunity to introduce fresh evidence or argument and to delay the publication of the award.

59 s.57.
60 s.57(4)–(6).

Part 6

RENT REVIEW AND PROPERTY VALUATION ARBITRATION

By Ian V. Oddy, FRICS, F.C.I. Arb.

Introduction

Disputes involving property

Arbitration has been used widely in the past as a means of resolving property valuation disputes. For example, the English Lands Clauses Consolidation Act 1845 provided that compensation in various circumstances should be settled by an arbitrator who was required to go before a Justice of the Peace to swear that he would: ''faithfully and honestly and to the best of (his) skill and ability, hear and determine the matters referred to (him).'' The declaration had to be presented and attached to the award. Nowhere now are Justices of the Peace involved in swearing arbitrators before they can perform their functions. However, statutes still make use of arbitration, for example, in connection with payments to be made under management schemes under the Wildlife and Countryside Act 1981; and more use is likely be made in the future of statutory arbitration in order to fulfil the objectives set out in the Woolf Report[1] aimed at speeding up litigation. 6–01

Valuation arbitration is employed privately in a variety of circumstances including options to purchase, the valuation of property within divorce settlements, agreements for partnership dissolution and in connection with the assets of retired and deceased partners, apportionments under wills and within the framework of leases, for example, in regard to service charges, repairs and other matters not least of which is rent review. 6–02

Normally the purpose of referring valuation disputes to arbitration is to determine the hypothetical value of the property or rights in property for letting or for sale. Ultimately, the valuation is always a matter of fact and expert opinion, but, particularly in the instance of rent review, there may be many complex legal issues which arise and which often have to be resolved either as a preliminary issue or in the reference or through separate court proceedings. 6–03

Alternative tribunals

The dispute mechanism is found in the agreement made between the parties, which agreement may be a lease, a partnership deed or some other binding 6–04

[1] *Access to Justice* (1996).

document. The reference under the agreement will be either to an arbitrator or an independent expert. Usually, provision is made for the parties to agree upon the choice of their third party or, failing agreement, the matter would be referred to the President of one of the professional bodies to make the appointment. Various summaries have been produced setting out the differences between a reference to an arbitrator and a reference to an independent expert; see for example the Code of Practice for Commercial Property Leases in England and Wales; Bernstein & Reynolds, *Handbook of Rent Review* (1993); and paragraphs 2–28 to 2–35 above. The essential differences, in rent review situations, are:

Arbitrator	**Independent Expert**
Bound to decide the dispute within the parameters of the figures submitted by the parties.	May make any determination he decides without regard to the figures (if any) put to him by the parties.
Will be bound primarily by the evidence submitted to him. May carry out his own investigations or research into matters of fact and law, but if he does so is bound to submit his provisional findings to the parties for their comment.	Is expected to carry out his own investigations. The contract he makes with the parties will determine what, if any evidence he may rely upon which has been supplied by the parties but generally he is not bound to have any regard to submissions made to him.
Is bound to conduct a hearing if the parties require it but he may order a hearing where no procedure has been agreed by the parties if he thinks fit.	Need not hold a hearing unless provision for it is included within his contract with the parties.
He must act fairly and impartially between the parties and tailor the procedures so that they are suitable to the circumstances of the particular case.	Must act with due care and diligence but is not bound by the rules of natural justice.
The requirement to act fairly will be interpreted so as to ensure that each side has full details of the other side's case and the opportunity to answer it in writing or orally at a hearing. An arbitrator will make directions at the outset as to how this is to be achieved.	He has discretion as to whether there should be any submissions but the instrument under which he was appointed may require him to invite submissions; alternatively, the contract he makes with the parties may require that submissions and counter-submissions will be employed.

Arbitrator	Independent Expert
Must order that costs shall follow the event except where it appears in the circumstances that this is not appropriate in relation to the whole or part of the costs.	The appointing instrument will state how costs are to be borne or whether the independent expert has discretion in this respect.
Awards shall contain reasons unless the parties agree otherwise.	Usually, no reasons have to be given for the decision but they may be required under the appointing instrument or the contract with the parties.
The award may be the subject of an appeal to the High Court on a point of law.	The determination is absolutely binding on all questions of fact and law unless the expert clearly went outside his terms of reference.
The arbitrator is immune from claims for damages for negligence in the conduct of the reference and in making his award.	May be liable in damages for professional negligence in carrying out his duties.

Selection of tribunal

The choice between providing for determination by an arbitrator or an independent expert may be a mixture of client expectation, perceived cost effectiveness, custom and precedent, the nature of the likely areas of dispute, the complexity of the issues involved and the likely availability of comparable evidence. 6–05

Where legal issues are likely to be involved or where genuine issues might arise involving mixed fact and law, then arbitration may be beneficial because of the body of law and procedure which will govern the proceedings, the fact that in the absence of an agreement to the contrary a reasoned award will be produced and that such an award will facilitate the possibility of an appeal if the requirements of the 1996 Act are met. However, in the case of a "one-off" property, or say an isolated out of town supermarket, an independent expert determination may be more appropriate. There are several reasons for this. The first is that the parties may have difficulty proving a case at a particular value if comparable evidence is widely scattered or simply not available. The second reason is that someone who is truly an expert would be able to put a figure on a property employing the background of his general knowledge and experience and from the deductions which he could make from the slender information which is available to him. In the event that an independent expert is the chosen 6–06 tribunal, it will be essential to formulate a firm contract between the parties and the independent expert to govern the relationship, the procedure to be followed, and the fee arrangements.

Further discussion of this subject will be found in the *Guidance Notes for Surveyors acting as Arbitrators and as Independent Experts in Commercial Property Rent Reviews* (7th ed., 1997) published by the RICS.

Growth of Rent Review Arbitration

6–07 Much post-war development was let on fixed 21 year leases but gradually it was seen that inflation denied the true value of the property to the landlord and unfairly placed a large asset in the hands of the tenant. Fixed increases in the form of stepped rents did little to ensure that the landlord's interest would keep pace with inflation and with the true value of his investment. Rent reviews to figures not pre-agreed but based on a series of assumptions became established.[2] The use of arbitration as a means of resolving disputes over rental values became common. The number of appointments of arbitrators and independent experts made by the President of the Royal Institution of Chartered Surveyors reached a peak in 1991 when just over 15,000 appointments concerning commercial property disputes of all kinds were actually made. However, there are no statistics covering the number of private appointments made by parties themselves or by other appointing Institutions.

Scope and purpose of this Part

6–08 The purpose of this Part of the Handbook is to say something of the nature of valuation arbitration and to bring out the special features of arbitration used for that purpose so far as users and practitioners are concerned. It is therefore necessary to identify what is actually attempted in a rent review arbitration; to consider how arbitrators are appointed for the purpose and indeed removed and the terms of their appointment; to consider the procedure which is appropriate, particularly bearing in mind that most of these arbitrations will be conducted by surveyors who are not trained as lawyers and may only have limited first hand experience of litigation; from a practical point of view to say something about the pitfalls of making inspections of subject properties; and finally, there are some short comments on some practical aspects of drafting awards and dealing with costs.

[2] For a historical note on rent review provisions see Bernstein & Reynolds, *Handbook of Rent Review*, sections 1–2.

Hypothetical characteristics

Most valuations proceed on the initial assumption that the subject property is available for sale or letting in the open market with vacant possession. Vacant possession may or may not be a fact. The purchaser or lessee is a hypothetical person whose characteristics may or may not conform to the actual owner or lessee.[3] Normally the vendor or lessor is also hypothetical, but that is not always the case. The premises are actual except that further assumptions may have to be made concerning the condition in which the property is being notionally sold or let. In the case of a lease, the terms of the hypothetical lease may well depart in various respects from the terms of the actual lease. In many fundamental respects there is no difference between contractual valuations and those made under statute, for example for estate duty or compulsory purchase purposes. The market background certainly in the case of a rent review, will be that current at the time the valuation falls to be carried out. **6–09**

The Arbitrator's Appointment

The arbitration agreement

The capacity to refer a valuation dispute to arbitration will invariably be found in the parties' agreement itself whether a partnership deed, option, lease or other document. There is no standard form because of the infinite variety of precedents now in use. Often, there may be reference to a time limit after which, if the parties have not agreed the matter, the dispute may be referred to arbitration. An opportunity is normally provided for the parties to agree the identity of the arbitrator or, alternatively, an application has to be made to a third party to make the appointment. This may involve the President of the RICS, the Incorporated Society of Valuers and Auctioneers, the Law Society, the Chartered Institute of Arbitrators or other suitable body. Practitioners should be aware that even where provision is made in the agreement for the appointment of an independent expert the parties may still decide that the matters between them should be dealt with by arbitration. Sometimes through a quirk in drafting, the independent expert is given discretion over the costs of the reference to him or at least as to how his fees shall be borne between the parties. Where discretion is given in such a matter, that discretion must be exercised judicially and at this point the functions **6–10**

[3] *F.R. Evans (Leeds) Ltd v. English Electric Co. Ltd* (1977) 245 E.G. 657.

of the independent expert become equivalent to those of an arbitrator and he must conduct himself accordingly. This will involve inviting the parties to make submissions to him, perhaps even counter-submissions. Then he will be responsible for exercising his discretion. Surveyors who find themselves in this position should recognise it for what it is and should not hesitate to apply the normal arbitration procedures.

RICS appointments

6–11 The RICS has developed a sophisticated computerised service with which to furnish the names of arbitrators and independent experts to parties seeking appointments. In 1995 the Arbitration Department obtained Quality Assurance certification. The President is free to call upon any member of the RICS to act as an arbitrator but in practice several hundred members have been identified as having appropriate knowledge and training in this area and are regularly called upon according to the variations in the market. Those who are invited to consider any particular appointment must respond to the RICS saying whether they or their firm have a conflict of interest and whether they can undertake the reference without undue delay. The recommendation is then made to the President who may subject the choice of person to further enquiry or otherwise sign the appointment. The appointee is from that moment appointed to act and the President has discharged his responsibility under the terms of the arbitration agreement unless the appointee dies or is unable to act. The RICS will continue to retain an interest in the performance of appointees in order to ensure that the general public receive a first class competent service. Thus, after a reference has been concluded, both parties to an arbitration are sent a questionnaire on which they may record their views on the conduct of the matter.

Fees

6–12 Arbitrators are entitled to require payment of a reasonable fee as a condition of their appointment (see section 28 of the Act). If remuneration is not based on an hourly rate it will usually be convenient to agree a schedule of fees in advance, including fees dealing with the different possibilities which might bring a reference to a close. The matter may proceed to an award; on the other hand, the parties have the right to settle at any time and this may be at any time between the preliminary meeting and the day before the publication of the award; a variable fee basis should be agreed to allow for these various possibilities. There may also be the need to fix a fee related to interlocutory hearings in order to deter parties who, for tactical reasons, seek to delay the progress of the reference. It is helpful if an arbitrator can agree a fair basis of remuneration for an uncompleted reference and this may include some charge for time set aside for a hearing that cannot be used for any other purpose. In a documents only arbitration reserved time is unlikely to be a critical issue. However, it should be borne in mind that the courts will only award a *quantum meruit* for work actually undertaken and not for work which has not been undertaken. The courts will not recognise booking fees or cancellation charges as part of the *quantum meruit.* If agreement with the parties on the issue of the arbitrator's fees has not been possible, then the 1996 Act makes certain provisions. The fees form part of the costs of the arbitration as set out in section 59 of the Act; but the arbitrator's fee shall only be such sum as is reasonable and appropriate in the circumstances; see section 64. Further reference to this matter will be found in paragraphs 2–230 *et seq.* of this Handbook. Arbitrators appointed by the RICS should not refuse to negotiate over the fee to be charged. If a party considers the fee to be excessive, upon an award being published it is possible to challenge the amount as provided for in section 64.

Style of the arbitrator

Section 33 of the 1996 Act requires that the arbitrator shall act fairly and impar- **6–13** tially between the parties, provide a reasonable opportunity for each party to put their case and to deal with their opponent's case and to adopt appropriate procedures suitable to the circumstances. Arbitrators should act as arbitrators and not attempt to act as judges. A degree of firmness with the parties and their advisers may be necessary from time to time but the arbitrator in settling the terms of his own appointment and also the directions which will govern the way in which the arbitration is to be conducted, must have regard to any procedure the parties have agreed between themselves. The style of procedure may be dictated by the magnitude of the issues involved. Most rent review arbitrations are dealt with by written representations; comparatively few require a hearing. Where legal issues are of paramount importance, a hearing may well be necessary and arbitrators should not hesitate to provide the opportunity for counsel to be heard. On the other hand, it may be inappropriate and unnecessarily costly to set up a hearing in respect of a small office suite or a corner shop on a housing estate. Even where a hearing is arranged to deal with legal construction, the valuation issues may be dealt with separately by written representations, and thus offer the opportunity for a saving of costs.

Duties and powers of the arbitrator

The general duties and powers of an arbitrator will be found in the 1996 Act. **6–14** (See also for example paragraphs 2–297 *et seq.*, above). Some of the general duties of an arbitrator have been particularly emphasised by decided cases. At the commencement of an arbitration, an arbitrator will agree with the parties or will impose upon the parties his directions for the conduct of the arbitration. The arbitrator's award is likely to be set aside where he considers inadmissible evidence contrary to his own directions.[4] Similarly, if the arbitrator directs that a statement of agreed facts shall be produced, he is not then at liberty to ignore what the parties have agreed without at least hearing them on the matter.[5] The arbitrator must deal with all the issues before him. The arbitrator is also bound to keep confidential all those matters that pass before him.[6]

Conflicts and bias

6–15 Surveyors giving advice to their clients on the choice of arbitrators may have to think carefully about the reputation of the people who are to be chosen and the reality of any conflict of interest disclosed. For example, the fact that a potential arbitrator or his firm had acted for the Department of the Environment or British Telecommunications plc, one or both of whom were a party to the arbitration, should not necessarily rule him out on the ground of conflict or bias; There will be many practices which will have found themselves acting for those clients. Circumstances may dictate otherwise however and it will be a matter of degree in terms of the number of cases or of the amount of personal involvement the potential appointee may have had with the particular party, or a question of how recent the involvement has been as to which will be the determining factor. Reference may be made to paragraphs 2–178 *et seq.* and 2–273 *et seq.* of this Handbook. If the arbitrator has information concerning the subject property or a comparable as a result of his previous activity in the market, then he should disclose that he has such information to the parties at the outset. The possibility of bias became an issue in a City of London case where an arbitrator appointed to deal with a rent review in a building had previously acted as an independent expert in giving a determination on a nearby building which could have been and which it was said was intended to be used as a comparable in the arbitration. The tenant's application to have the appointed arbitrator removed was dismissed.[7] Swift disclosure by the arbitrator is likely to resolve most problems. An arbitrator may be removed on the grounds of justifiable doubts as to his impartiality. Paragraph 15.5 of the Code of Practice[8] warns arbitrators to check carefully for potential conflicts of interest. Where there are justifiable doubts as to an arbitrator's impartiality, application may be made to the court for his removal under section 24(1)(a).

Removal of the arbitrator

6–16 Surveyor arbitrators should note that the court has removed an arbitrator where

[4] *Mount Charlotte Investments plc v. Prudential Assurance* (1995) 10 E.G. 129.
[5] *Techno Ltd v. Allied Dunbar Assurance plc* (1993) 22 E.G. 109.
[6] *London & Leeds Estates Ltd v. Paribas Ltd (No. 2)* (1995) 02 E.G. 134.
[7] *Moore Stephens & Co. v. Local Authorities' Mutual Investment Trust* (1992) 04 E.G. 135.
[8] RICS Business Services Limited, *Commercial Property Leases in England & Wales : Code of Practice* (December 1995).

it has been shown that through lack of experience, expertise or diligence, the arbitrator was incapable of conducting the reference in a manner which the parties were entitled to expect.[9] The grounds for removal of an arbitrator are now set out in section 24 (1) of the Act as follows:

"(a) that circumstances exist that give rise to justifiable doubts as to his impartiality;
(b) that he does not possess the qualifications required by the arbitration agreement;
(c) that he is physically or mentally incapable of conducting the proceedings or there are justifiable doubts as to his capacity to do so;
(d) that he has refused or failed:
  (i) properly to conduct the proceedings, or
  (ii) to use all reasonable despatch in conducting the proceedings or making an award,
and that substantial injustice has been or will be caused to the applicant."

Serious irregularity

6–17 An award may be challenged on the grounds of serious irregularity, affecting the arbitrator, the conduct of the proceedings or the award itself. Serious irregularity will be tested against matters identified in section 68 of the Act where the court considers substantial injustice has been caused or will be caused to the applicant. This topic is discussed at paragraphs 2–851 *et seq.*, above. Where there is serious irregularity, the court may remit or set aside the award or declare the award to be of no effect, in whole or in part.

Procedure

General guidelines

6–18 Where an arbitrator is invited by the parties or their advisers to accept the appointment, it is likely that the nature of the dispute, the issues to be decided, and the willingness to proceed to arbitration are all included as part of the

[9] *Bremer Handelsgesellschaft MbH v, Ets Saules* (1985) 2 Lloyds Rep. 199 C.A.

general circumstances put to the arbitrator. However, in the case of appointments from the President of a professional body it can often become quickly apparent that the appointment has merely been requested as a protective or tactical measure. In these circumstances, the arbitrator will find that he is a catalyst to the continuing negotiations, or even the means by which one party will pressure the other into beginning negotiations. Whether the arbitration will run or not it is appropriate for the arbitrator, following his appointment, to write to the parties to confirm that he has accepted the appointment and to enquire whether the matter should be proceeded with or whether it should be held in abeyance. If only one party is prepared to participate then it may be necessary for the arbitrator to proceed ex parte, but normally there is little difficulty in inviting both parties to attend a preliminary meeting. At this stage, either a letter setting out an agenda or a schedule of items to be decided can be sent or alternatively, in order to focus the minds of the parties, arrangements for the preliminary meeting can be confirmed together with a set of draft directions. Having the draft directions at an early stage enables the parties' advisers to take general instructions before beginning discussions with the arbitrator and therefore may reduce the time involved. (See paragraph 2–432.) Care should be taken at the outset to establish what has been agreed between the parties prior to the arbitration so far as procedure is concerned. Failure to comply with such procedure may amount to "serious irregularity". Tempting as it may be in hierarchical rent review arbitrations to press for consolidation, there is no power under the Act to force consolidation. For a review of the possible procedures refer to paragraphs 2–421 *et seq.*, above.

The preliminary meeting

6–19 One or more meetings may be needed to settle the form which the procedure will take. The structure of the arbitration can best be settled at a preliminary meeting and monitored by further meetings if necessary. Difficulties can arise where the parties or their representatives are geographically a long way apart, but this does not remove the desirability of holding the meeting. If the inconvenience or expense is thought to be too great then all the matters needed to be agreed will have to be cleared through correspondence. Separate telephone conversations with each party are unsatisfactory because of the misunderstandings and confusion which can result from them, to say nothing of the possible allegations of bias. The difficulty can be minimised if telephone or video conference facilities are available. Where telephone calls have to be employed with only one party it is preferable for them to be made or received by the arbitrator's secretary or assistant, who should keep a full note of what is said on each occasion. With the variations in modern lease drafting, not only landlords but tenants too can now often initiate a rent review by the service of notice. Where this happens the tenant will be the claimant and the landlord will be the respondent. The arbitrator should confirm the roles of the parties at the preliminary meeting. The parties should be reminded that any procedural or evidential matters not agreed will be determined by the arbitrator.

The conduct of a reference

An arbitrator must keep in mind the threefold nature of what is required of the proceedings. First, the main purpose is to inform the arbitrator of the facts, opinions and arguments from which he will determine the dispute. Secondly, each party must be able to assemble the evidence upon which he wishes to found his case and to rebut the opponent's case, and to present this evidence to the arbitrator. Thirdly, the procedural and administrative arrangements should be designed to facilitate that these objectives are attained. The arbitration must be organised to meet the requirements not only of the parties, but also of the arbitrator. He must be able to discern what the issues are and what material of importance should be placed before him so that he can apply his own experience and expert knowledge to assess the evidence. **6–20**

Agreeing directions

Directions should be confined to matters of procedure and will comprise orders made by the arbitrator for the proper conduct of the matter. The arbitrator's remuneration belongs to a separate document, most usually a letter written following agreement at the preliminary meeting or subsequently; there will need to be specific confirmation in writing that the parties themselves have agreed to those charges. The draft directions shown at Appendix A to this Part show the directions which might be appropriate for a rent review arbitration to be conducted by written representations. Where a hearing is required clearly different directions may be needed and appropriate draft directions are set out in Appendix B to this Part. These drafts should be adapted in order that, in the words of section 33, they lay down "procedures suitable to the circumstances of the particular case". The preliminary meeting should have given the arbitrator some indication as to whether he is dealing with a simple difference of opinion over value or whether the issues are very much more complicated. The arbitrator will need to distinguish between issues of law and issues of fact. Complicated issues of fact are matters which he will decide, and his decision will not be challengeable in the courts unless he is guilty of some serious irregularity. If the issues are complicated and involve both fact and law it may be appropriate for the arbitration to be conducted with a hearing. In any event, if one of the parties requests a hearing, then the arbitrator should agree to a hearing taking place if he believes that it is fair and reasonable to proceed in that way. For the most complicated of cases, following some shortened form of court procedure may be justified. An essential part of agreeing directions is to agree the timetable which will apply even though provision for "leave to apply" may be provided **6–21** for, so that parties may apply for adjustments to the timetable to take account of unforeseen events. As to the timing of the exchange of documents between the parties, see paragraphs 2–436 *et seq.* above. It may be wise to provide for a separate award in respect of costs. Very often in rent review matters an interim award dealing with value only is sufficient for the parties' needs, but the arbitrator will need to obtain the confirmation from the parties that a final award of costs is not required.

Saving time and cost

6–22 The process of arbitration should not be a specially made vehicle for printing money. The arbitrator can set a useful example to the parties and their advisers by the way in which the procedure is conducted. For example, in a complicated case where one set of issues will clearly depend upon the outcome of another set of issues, it might be useful and might save a great deal of time and expense, to deal with the issues at the beginning of the critical path first and separately. Under section 47, unless the parties otherwise agree, the arbitrator has the power to make more than one award at different times on different aspects of the matters to be determined. In a rent review case this might mean dealing with the construction of the rent review clause as one set of issues and dealing with that at a hearing; making a first interim award; and then leaving the parties either to negotiate a settlement in respect of value or to come back to the arbitrator so that the reference may continue. If the legal issues are resolved, whether by a hearing or by written representations, the valuation issues may be dealt with by written representations rather than the entire personnel involved taking several days to follow counsel examining witnesses on every comparable property. However, sometimes the circumstances dictate that the whole matter should be dealt with at a hearing. Another alternative would be for a hearing to be convened to deal with the cross examination of witnesses, as recommended elsewhere in the Handbook.

Documents only

6–23 Reference may be made again to Appendix A where suggested draft directions for an arbitration by written representations are set out. It will be noted particularly that the right is reserved to call for a hearing. This will need to be agreed by the parties; otherwise it will fall to be dealt with at the discretion of the arbitrator under section 34(2)(h) unless his discretion in that regard has been taken away by the parties. Where a documents-only arbitration is being held, a preliminary meeting is still to be preferred as settling the formal procedure, the timetable, and the evidence which will be treated as admissible, are all issues which need to be determined at an early stage. It should be stressed that whether or not the parties are continuing to negotiate behind the arbitration, they are present in the reference to assist the arbitrator to reach the right conclusion. The obligation on parties in a documents-only arbitration is still not to mislead the arbitrator and to tell the truth concerning their opinions and the evidence which they are giving. One way of emphasising this to the parties is to require that their submissions are accompanied by an affidavit.

Advice on procedure

Where the arbitrator requires advice in connection with the general procedure 6–24 in the reference there is the possibility of calling on informal advice from a wide range of sources including other arbitrators. So far as the actual conduct of proceedings is concerned, there is no obligation upon the arbitrator to disclose to the parties that he is taking advice. If the arbitrator requires expert or legal advice or assistance with technical matters, he may appoint appropriate people unless the parties have agreed otherwise; see section 37. Where the arbitrator takes such advice, he must give the parties a reasonable opportunity to comment on it. However, whether or not the arbitrator takes advice, the award will still be his and he must take responsibility for it. He will need to avoid the strictures referred to in paragraph 6.16 (see also paragraph 6–29 below).

Appointing legal advisers and assessors

Where the arbitrator considers it necessary and the parties have not agreed other- 6–25 wise, under section 37(1) the arbitrator may appoint experts or legal advisors to report to him or appoint assessors to assist him with technical matters. Those appointed may attend the proceedings and the parties are to be given a reasonable opportunity to comment on any information, opinion or advice offered by any such person. Section 33 requires the arbitrator to give a full opportunity to answer the case presented by the other side or produced through appointed experts or advisers under section 37. A failure to comply with section 33 may be a ''serious irregularity'' under section 68(2)(a). The fees and expenses involved in appointing experts and advisers form part of the expenses of the arbitrator; see section 37(2) and 59(1)(a).

Determination of a preliminary point of law

Unless otherwise agreed by the parties, a preliminary point of law may be deter- 6–26 mined by the court under section 45. An agreement between the parties to dispense with reasons will however, exclude the court's jurisdiction. The court shall consider an application under the section only if it is made with the agreement of all the parties or made with the permission of the arbitrator, and the court is satisfied that:

(a) the matter substantially affects the rights of one or more of the parties.
(b) determination of the question is likely to produce substantial savings in costs; and
(c) the application was made without delay.

For a discussion on this matter refer to paragraphs 2–508 *et seq*.

6–27 Generally, arbitrators should be prepared to tackle the legal issues in their arbitrations and will derive much assistance from the presentation of legal argument, either in oral proceedings or by way of legal submissions through written representations.

Evidence

The principles under the Act

6–28 Subject to the right of the parties to agree any matter, the arbitrator has the power to decide all evidential matters; these powers include determining:

(a) whether to apply strict rules or any other rules of evidence and the time manner and form in which such evidence should be exchanged and presented (section 34(2)(f));
(b) whether to take the initiative in ascertaining facts and law himself (section 34(2)(g)); and
(c) whether there should be oral or written evidence (section 34(2)(h)).

Applying rules of evidence

6–29 As stated above, if the parties have not agreed, it is for the arbitrator to decide all procedural and evidential matters. This will include whether to apply the strict rules of evidence or any other rules at all as to the admissibility, relevance or weight of any material whether oral, written or other which is sought to be tendered on any matters of fact or opinion. In dealing with evidence, as in other matters, the arbitrator will not be in danger of challenge if he follows the parties' agreed procedure, or that laid down by him in the absence of an agreement between the parties, or that which he agrees with the parties.

6–30 The Civil Evidence Act 1995 allows the admissibility of hearsay evidence, subject to the provisions dealing with notice and weight. Section 1 of the 1995

Act states that "in civil proceedings evidence shall not be excluded on the ground that it is hearsay". If the arbitrator's directions require that the normal rules of evidence are to apply, then hearsay evidence will be admissible. However, it is always open to the parties to agree, the arbitrator to determine, or both to decide (a) that all evidence shall be strictly proved or (b) that hearsay evidence shall be admitted or (c) for example, that the only hearsay evidence which will be admitted is evidence of property transactions in the form of pro formas signed by persons involved in those transactions. Much grief and aggravation can be avoided by means of a practical and sensible agreement between everyone concerned. In connection with (c) the arbitrator may also wish to invite the parties to use the pro formas for rental evidence found in the RICS *Appraisal and Valuation Manual* (The Red Book: Guidance Notes Appendices 4A, 4B, 4C).

Because of the possibility that new valuation evidence will arise during the course of a reference and the arbitrator will not wish to be found guilty of a serious irregularity by denying the opportunity for the parties to produce relevant evidence, some provision should be made in directions for the admission of late evidence. One form of words is shown in direction (9) in Appendix A and direction (11) in Appendix B. The essential point is that the party or parties receiving the new evidence should have a proper opportunity to comment on it, in compliance with the rules of natural justice, and the requirements of section 33. A failure to comply with section 33 may amount to a serious irregularity. **6–31**

Arbitrator's own evidence

A number of cases have dealt with the position where the arbitrator has provided himself with evidence or otherwise relied upon evidence which has not been put before the parties.[10] Section 34(2)(g) now provides a framework within which the arbitrator can take the initiative in ascertaining facts and law provided: **6–32**

(a) the parties agree that he shall act in that way or
(b) at least they have made no agreement that he should not, and
(c) he has decided that he needs to pursue that initiative.

This raises the question of when he should take the initiative and if he does, the lengths to which he should go in ascertaining facts and law. At least this power must enable an arbitrator to call a witness. As many arbitrators are themselves experts in their own right, it will be important for an arbitrator to guard against the selective accumulation of evidence which would support a particular conclusion which may lie somewhere in the back of the arbitrator's mind from an early stage in the reference. Reliance upon such an accumulation of evidence could **6–33**

[10] For example, *Top Shop Estates Ltd v. Danino* (1985) 273 E.G. 197.

become a "serious irregularity" within the terms of the Act (see paragraphs 2–851 *et seq.*, above).

6–34 The question of the extent to which the initiative should be pursued may depend upon the view taken of the aim of arbitration as referred to in section 1 of the Act; to provide for the fair resolution of disputes. The arbitrator might need to ensure that he had sufficient information to enable him to come to a conclusion with which he was satisfied. For example, in the case of an award dealing with shop premises, a considerable volume of evidence might have been produced concerning size, layout, return frontage, parking, loading and the like but the arbitrator may feel that he needs to have a pedestrian count taken outside the subject premises and also close to comparable premises in order to confirm his opinion of the relative values of the locations. Within the terms of section 34 there would be no objection to his obtaining such figures provided he informs the parties first and submits that new evidence to the parties in order that they may have a proper opportunity to address him on it. However, the prudent arbitrator will exhaust the possibilities of the Act before collecting his own evidence. He should inform the parties of his need for additional information. This will provide them with the opportunity to furnish that additional evidence and thus perhaps save on costs. The arbitrator has a duty to avoid unnecessary expense under section 33(1)(b). He may also make a peremptory order if the parties fail to produce the required evidence if ordered to do so under section 40. The answer to the question how far the arbitrator should go in exercising his initiative may be that the extent of the additional investigation should be sufficient to supplement the evidence and to fill any lacuna in the submissions of the parties, but it should be much less than attempting to become an additional primary expert in the arbitration. The extended power under the Act may have particular value in the case of ex parte hearings or where parties are not professionally represented. It will be a rare case that would justify the arbitrator taking a high profile inquisitorial role (see paragraphs 2–307 *et seq.*, above).

Identifying the physical property

6–35 The *Arthur Young*[11] case shows the importance of identifying what has to be valued. Whatever may be hypothetical about the valuation, the premises are real. The difficulty is that they may not be in a state in which they have to be valued for the purposes of the arbitration agreement. There are two main reasons why this may be so. The first is that the premises may not be in proper repair and the arbitrator may be required to assume that they are. The lack of repair may be due to neglect by the tenant, but this will have no influence in a rent review if the assumption is to be made that the tenant has complied with all the tenant's covenants including a covenant to keep in repair. In recent years draftsmen have included an assumption that the premises are fit for occupation so that, in a case

[11] *National Westminster Bank plc v. Arthur Young McCelland Moores & Co.* (1984) 273 E.G. 402.

where the cladding was defective at the date of a rent review, but where a rent review clause required the assumption to be made that the premises were fit for occupation and use, the arbitrator ignored the cladding defect and was upheld in doing so by the High Court.[12]

The second principal reason why the physical property may be different from that which has to be valued is that the tenant may have carried out improvements and, under the terms of the review clause, the tenant's improvements are required to be disregarded. Consideration of this point leads to underlining the importance of establishing that the arbitrator has seen all the relevant documentation, *e.g.* licences for alterations, before arriving at his conclusion. Twenty years after the grant of a 25 year lease, some of the details of the original premises which have to be valued can be very obscure. For rent review purposes, the general rule is that the premises must be valued as they exist at the valuation date unless this is displaced by the particular language of the lease or by other documents.[13] **6–36**

Directions on comparables

Appendices A and B refer to the submission of comparables. The arbitrator should emphasise the importance of being supplied with as much information as possible, which has preferably been agreed between the parties. It is a simple matter in directions to make provision for comparables which are not agreed, see Appendix A, direction (4) and Appendix B, direction (6). **6–37**

Discovery

The power to order discovery is set out in section 34(2)(d) and in common with the other parts of that section it is provided that the arbitrator may decide those matters not agreed between the parties. There is a discretion here and in exercising it the arbitrator may need to weigh cost and the relative size of the issue before him. If discovery is permitted in a particular arbitration, an order for discovery and for inspection may be made. It is unlikely in a valuation arbitration that there will be an order for general discovery such as might be attempted in litigation elsewhere. The usual circumstance is an application for an order for specific discovery. Such matters against a landlord might well include service charge accounts, leases of other premises within the building or elsewhere which might be cited as relevant comparables, correspondence passing between the landlord and those other tenants which has a bearing on the terms upon which rents were agreed, correspondence with the local authority or other statutory bodies or undertakers about the future of the building, its present condition or the provision of services to it and **6–38**

[12] *Lex Services plc v. Oriel House BV* (1991) 39 E.G. 139.
[13] *Laura Investment Co. Ltd v. Havering London Borough Council* (1992) 24 E.G. 136.

even complaints from other tenants. Discovery ordered against a tenant might include leases of other premises occupied by them, bills for expenditure for repairs and maintenance and other matters.

6–39 Valuation reports on both sides might be applied for, particularly regular portfolio valuations carried out for the landlord. In regard to a pre-arbitration report an arbitrator should consider whether or not the standing of the witness who prepared the report suggests that the report can be wholly relied upon. It will also be relevant to consider market movements between the date of the report and the date at which the property must be valued.

6–40 If an arbitrator orders discovery and the party does not comply, then the arbitrator may make a peremptory order under section 41(5). Such an order may be enforced by the court under section 42. The power to make peremptory orders may be excluded by agreement between the parties.

Comparables

6–41 The relevance of evidence concerning other properties in a valuation arbitration will depend entirely on their degree of comparability with the subject property. Where a comparable is wholly comparable in size and specification and valuation date and incorporates the same physical characteristics and an identical or near identical location, there will be no need for an arbitration; there should be no dispute. Most comparables are not like that. What the arbitrator will require is that the parties demonstrate to him the degree to which like is being compared with like. An example might help to show how this principle is to be applied in practice. It happened that the redevelopment of a building incorporated part of the original building and the licence for the works set out a schedule of floor areas which was to be used for the purposes of subsequent rent reviews. The parties to the arbitration agreed that the building according to the RICS/ISVA Code of Measuring Practice had different and smaller areas. The difference was the difference between net internal areas and gross internal areas. However, the comparable evidence produced to the arbitrator was on the basis of careful analyses of properties measured net in accordance with the RICS/ISVA Code. The arbitrator deduced his rental award from the unit values of the comparables analysed on the parties agreed code measurements, applied the figure to the agreed floor areas of the subject building measured in accordance with the Code and then devalued the resulting figure over the areas included in the schedule to the licence and then presented the valuation in his award in that form, thereby demonstrating that the areas in the schedule had been used. The arbitrator had compared "like with like" and the High Court dismissed an application for the award to be remitted on this point.[14]

[14] *National Westminster Bank plc v. Arthur Young McClelland Moores & Co.* (1984) 273 E.G. 402.

Assumptions and other considerations

6–42 The valuation arbitrator is not seeking only to make comparisons between the physical characteristics of different properties and those of the subject property. In the case of rental valuation he is also required to have regard to the terms of the leases concerned, both for the subject property and the comparables. He must therefore take into account those assumptions which are to be made which change reality and similarly the disregards which dictate that some factors will be ignored. The hypothetical tenancy will assume that there is a tenant prepared to take the premises even if there is a falling market with no likely alternative occupier in prospect. The arbitrator will invite the parties to guide him on how to deal with this issue. Planning and bye-law provisions may be relevant, as may environmental considerations that affect one property but not others. Obsolescence may be a factor. The arbitrator should ensure that his requirements of the parties will result in his having sufficient evidence in respect of all the material issues to enable him to make a fair award.

The art of valuation

6–43 Valuation has always been regarded as an art rather than a science. Often the judgements handed down by the courts, show that the credibility of the witnesses has been of paramount importance in carrying one or other side to victory. Even credible witnesses need to be supported by a body of opinion which they can demonstrate in evidence to a judge. It is interesting to contrast two cases brought against independent experts in negligence. In one case the judge accepted the independent expert's opinion that comparable evidence derived from catering establishments was not helpful in valuing shop premises because each was a separate market.[15] In another case in the Court of Appeal,[16] the independent expert concerned employed comparables derived from retail premises in valuing a restaurant and was able to show that in the circumstances he was justified in using such comparables and the case was dismissed. Arbitrators therefore will look for sound argument, backed by a rational analysis consistently applied and with some evidence that there is industry support for the method of valuation or devaluation which is employed. Discounted cash flow may be used in some instances and various specially constructed tables may also be employed by the parties in analysing and presenting their evidence.[17]

[15] *Wallshire Ltd v. Aarons* (1989) 1 E.G.L.R. 147.
[16] *Zubaida v. Hargreaves* (1995) 09 E.G. 320.
[17] *The Boston Gilmore Rental Equivalent Tables and Lease Incentives* by Davidson & Darlow are an example.

Other reported cases

6–44 Arbitrators should be wary of assuming that a finding of fact in one case, albeit accepted by a court, will necessarily hold good in another case involving a similar property but where the circumstances might be materially different. An example will make this clear. In a long dated rent review it might be found that an uplift of one per cent for each year over the normal five year rent review pattern should be added to what would otherwise be the proper rent for a five year review.[18] The fact that such an addition was appropriate in a particular case does not mean that it is a formula which can be applied to every long dated rent review. Each case will depend upon the facts and the market for that property at the material time. In another case where there was a restriction in the lease to the effect that the premises should not be used otherwise than as offices in connection with the lessee's business of consulting engineers, on the facts it was found by the arbitrator that a 32 per cent discount should be made for the restriction represented by the user clause against what would otherwise have been the open market value.[19] The arbitrator decided the level of discount to be made on the basis of the evidence put forward by the parties. It would not be correct to assume that where there is a restrictive covenant of this character there will always be a discount of 32 per cent. The parties may argue that a discount should be made; the arbitrator must be satisfied that the discount should be made on the basis of the evidence submitted to the arbitration and how much that discount should be.

Other Awards and Determinations

6–45 Until July 29, 1992 most rent review arbitrators would have been happy to admit the evidence of awards from other appropriate arbitrations as part of the evidence before them. Usually, they would have had some mental reservation as to the weight which they would give awards but they would have been happy to test them against the better evidence offered by open market transactions, or failing that, rent reviews agreed between professionally represented parties. In a judgment given by Hoffmann J. as he then was,[20] he ruled that awards from other arbitrations were not admissible because they were irrelevant. The judge said that to admit the award of another arbitrator in another case would involve a collateral inquiry as to whether the arbitrator had come to the right decision in that other arbitration. The result of such an inquiry would have insufficient relevance to the issue in the new arbitration. That dealt with the question of awards but it did not make clear what the position was with regard to the determinations of independent experts. Generally, rent review surveyors and arbi-

18 *National Westminster Bank plc v. Arthur Young McCelland Moores & Co.* (1984) 273 E.G. 402.
19 *Plinth Property Investments Ltd v. Mott, Hay & Anderson* (1978) 249 E.G. 1167.
20 *Land Securities plc v. City of Westminster* (1992) 44 E.G. 153.

trators had taken the view that these were of some value as evidence on the basis that they were careful third party valuations, often made after receiving detailed submissions from the parties themselves. Arbitrators tended to give them some weight depending upon who the independent expert was and the regard in which he was held. Hoffmann L.J. now in the Court of Appeal, when dealing with the appeal in *Zubaida v. Hargreaves* said:

> "A determination . . . is the opinion of another expert as to what someone in the real market would have paid. The accuracy of this opinion cannot be assessed without examining the materials on which it was reached. For this reason, if this had been a rent review arbitration, the determination would not even have been admissible evidence."[21]

The arbitrator will need to act fairly in accordance with his general duty, and safeguard himself against an error of law through relying upon evidence which the courts would declare irrelevant. While it is open to the parties to agree that awards and determinations shall form part of their evidence, arbitrators will have regard to the judgements of Hoffman L.J. **6–46**

Confidentiality and subpoenas

In the late 1980s and early 1990s many rental transactions were concluded and immediately encased in secrecy in so far as the landlord at any rate could effect it. The parties to the transaction were required to maintain secrecy and to keep the details confidential. Most surveyor agents assumed that such an agreement applied to them also. There may be some doubt as to whether that was correct in every case unless the client had insisted that his agent should keep the matter confidential and bound him specifically to do so in writing. How long such an arrangement should be continued might be a matter for agreement. Apart from that, the RICS itself has a regulation which says that client's affairs should be kept confidential and generally this is the normal rule as between an agent and a principal. The reason that confidentiality agreements were imposed was because the headline rent quoted in the lease document did not reflect all the terms of the transaction. In particular, large sums would be made available to the tenant as an inducement to enter into the lease; rent free periods sometimes extending for two or three years or even longer would be granted; fitting out works would be carried out to the tenant's specification but at the landlord's cost; and perhaps obligations in other buildings would be taken over by landlords in order to capture the tenant and obtain his signature on the lease of the landlord's new building. Some concessions were included in confidential side **6–47**

[21] (1995) 09 E.G. 320.

agreements and if the contents of those agreements was not known, the usefulness of the comparable would be negligible.[22]

6–48 The confidentiality problem is dealt with by means of a *subpoena duces tecum* which will require the *subpoenaed* witness to produce documents which show the true effect of the transaction or a *subpoena ad testificandum* which would require the witness to submit to examination. The power to grant a *subpoena* is not a power which can be exercised by the arbitrator, it is a power which can only be exercised by the courts and is discretionary. Clearly, a *subpoena* will override a confidentiality agreement and it will also override any regulation of the RICS. If a witness gives evidence on some matters but then claims that other connected information is subject to a confidentiality agreement, he will nevertheless be open to cross examination on the whole of the transaction.

6–49 The support of the court with regard to securing the attendance of witnesses or the production of documents is dealt with in section 43 of the Act. However, the parties may decide to be the architects of their own procedure; in the event that they have agreed that there shall be no discovery (section 34(2)(d)), section 43 will not be employed subsequently to circumvent that agreement. For further discussion on this topic see paragraphs 2–470 *et seq*., above.

Consistency

6–50 The credibility of witnesses is of immense importance in the sphere of valuation as in any other. Arbitration proceedings are private and therefore the proceedings are not available to other arbitrators or indeed valuers in other cases. In an unusual set of circumstances, through the disclosure of confidential information in the possession of an arbitrator, the evidence given by the same witness in two separate cases was challenged where in one case the witness had acted for the landlord and in the other case for the tenant.[23] Arbitrators should emphasise to the expert witnesses that they are involved in the reference in order to assist the arbitrator to reach a fair decision, not to argue an extreme case on their client's behalf. Since the publication in January 1997 of the RICS Practice Statement: ''Surveyors Acting as Expert Witnesses'', arbitrators should expect that chartered surveyors' reports and representations should be accompanied by a declaration similar to the following:

DECLARATION

This (Report/etc.) has been prepared on the basis:

1) that the matters set out are believed to be accurate and true;

2) that the (Report/etc.) includes all facts regarded as relevant to the opinion

[22] RICS Business Services Limited, *Commercial Property Leases in England & Wales: Code of Practice* (1995).

[23] *London & Leeds Estates Ltd v. Paribas Ltd (No, 2)* (1995) 02 E.G. 134.

expressed and that attention has been drawn to any matter which would affect the validity of that opinion;

3) that the (Report/etc.) complies with the requirements of the Royal Institution of Chartered Surveyors, as set out in SURVEYORS ACTING AS EXPERT WITNESSES : PRACTICE STATEMENT.

Signature: . . . .
Name of Surveyor . . . .
signing the (Report/etc.): . . . .
Date: . . . .

Inspection Pitfalls

Object of inspection

The primary purpose of the arbitrator's inspection of the subject property is not to take new evidence but to assist him in understanding the evidence put before him by the expert witnesses. Some arbitrators find it helpful to visit the subject premises before the hearing or before reading the submissions in a documents-only arbitration. It should be noted that under section 40 of the 1996 Act the parties are required "to comply without delay with any order or directions of the arbitrator", this will include making arrangements for the arbitrator to inspect the subject property, and the comparables. However, while the parties can be compelled to allow the arbitrator to visit the subject property, the same is not true in respect of the comparables adduced as evidence. It would be wise for the arbitrator to indicate to the parties in his award if he has been unable to inspect any of the properties put forward as comparables. When making his inspection, the arbitrator should also take the opportunity of checking the position on other representations made by the parties in respect of the locality. This could involve numerous allegations including such factors as the effect on value of derelict buildings in the immediate vicinity or the prevalence of a heavy, noisy traffic flow very close to the subject property, and such factors may not affect all the comparables. 6–51

New evidence obtained from inspections

Paragraphs 6–32 *et seq.* deal with the case of an arbitrator's own evidence. 6–52
Where at the time of inspection the arbitrator intends to employ his inquisitorial

powers under section 34(2)(g) he must exercise great care to ensure that he uses his powers carefully, wisely and within the statutory parameters. If the arbitrator intends to seek further evidence and this is the purpose of his inspection, then he should tell the parties what he has in mind. If, on making an inspection, the arbitrator observes a matter which he thinks is material, he should draw this to the attention of the parties and ensure that they both have an opportunity of making representations upon it. Failure to do so, is a breach of the requirements of natural justice and may be regarded as a serious irregularity which may result in the award being set aside and the arbitrator removed.

Accompanied inspections

6–53 Many arbitrators would prefer to inspect without the presence of either party. This gives them the opportunity of following their own methodical approach to the assessment of the case put forward by each party. In practice, difficulties will arise particularly if the arbitrator finds that the company secretary or office manager expects to accompany him on the tour of the building. This is undesirable because it means the inspection, in a sense, will be made with one party physically represented and one party absent. On the other hand, if representatives of both parties are present there is a possibility that some aspects of the arbitration will be rerun as the entourage moves from floor to floor or building to building. Perhaps the ideal situation is to make the inspection accompanied only by one of the occupier's security staff, messenger, or office "person". The arbitrator should take care in any event, to ensure that he is seen to act fairly between the parties and to avoid circumstances which could generate allegations of bias.

Drafting Awards

Interim and final

6–54 Where the issues between the parties are straightforward and perhaps only valuation elements are at issue, the arbitrator may agree at the preliminary meeting that he should proceed direct towards making a final award. The final award will of course, not only provide for his decision as to value, but also the shares in which his fees and costs will be paid by the parties. Where the issues are more complex and perhaps the sums involved are larger, the parties might wish to make representations on costs. In these circumstances, the arbitrator will agree from the outset with the parties that he will make an interim award as to value and then in the event that costs are not agreed by negotiation between the parties, he will issue directions concerning representations on costs. He will then be in a position to give his final award.

Clarifying the issues

Before starting to draft his award, the arbitrator should take stock of the position. Clearly, he is required to make an award at the valuation which the evidence supports, to do this he must identify the issues which he must decide in order to reach his conclusion. In his working papers, the arbitrator should identify each issue raised by the parties and will then need to cross reference those issues with the responses to them put by the other side. He must then decide which issues do not influence value and which do and by how much. If he is providing a reasoned award then it will be necessary to show how he reached his conclusion on each of the issues. In rent review arbitration these issues can involve the construction to be placed on the words included in the rent review clause; the effect on the market value of the building with obsolescent services or a congested traffic flow round the building; the size and shape of floors; importantly, the actual state of the market at the date of review and other matters. The arbitrator must deal with each of the issues raised by the parties together with any other issues he regards as important and upon which he has evidence. 6–55

Arbitrator's own knowledge

Expert arbitrators, for example, chartered surveyors who have been estate agents and rent review surveyors are appointed as rent review arbitrators because of their knowledge and expertise. This knowledge and their experience will guide them in knowing whether they are comparing like with like when it comes to the evidence. Such arbitrators should be able to detect whether witnesses have been carried away and exaggerated the strength of their cases or even nudged the boundary of perjury. Valuation arbitrators are expected to be experts in their field, but that expertise is used in the interpretation of the evidence and other material before them, not in manufacturing it. Paragraphs 6–32 *et seq.* deal with evidence supplied by the arbitrator. 6–56

Reasons

No arbitrator's award can be prepared without the issues being identified and the reasons deduced. The question is whether they should be added to the award or not. The parties are free to agree the form of the award they require. Under 6–57 section 52 of the Act, the award must set out the arbitrator's reasons, unless the award is an agreed award or the parties have agreed to dispense with reasons.

Identifying reasons

6–58 It may be necessary to chase each issue through the documents and other evidence in order to match the parties' contentions on a particular issue but this is what the arbitrator must do (see paragraphs 2–434 *et seq.*, above). Having focused on an issue, he must then set down which of the parties' reasons he finds most convincing and must then decide what weight each issue has in the overall scheme of the award. Preparing detailed reasons is both an essential and a helpful process whether or not those reasons are given to the parties in the award. It is a discipline which will ensure that the arbitrator is led by the evidence and he will be able to test whether the evidence makes sense from his expert knowledge. The arbitrator must also ensure that all his reasons are grounded in the evidence itself. Reasons are dealt with in detail in paragraphs 2–779 *et seq.*, above but the valuation arbitrator should bear in mind that the reasons he gives could form the basis from which an appeal on a point of law might be made to the court. The court will look carefully at reasons given in respect of the construction he places on legal matters; but will generally accept that the arbitrator is the final judge on matters of fact, for example, the state of the property market, rights of light, obsolete services, environmental matters and so on.

6–59 Under section 69(3)(c) leave to appeal an award shall be given if (*inter alia*) the court is satisfied that on the basis of the findings of fact the decision on the point of law given by the arbitrator is "obviously wrong". Sometimes, the distinction between fact and law can be obscure; thus where an arbitrator treated boat launching as ancillary to car parking, in making an award under a management agreement, he was found to have erred in law.[24]

Content of the award : issues

6–60 The range of issues which may be met with in practice and upon which the arbitrator will need to formulate a view will usually be identified in the submissions made to him by the parties. In a rent review arbitration examples of these issues may be as follows:

(a) the construction of the rent review clause;
(b) the assumptions which have to be made in making the valuation;
(c) the nature of the original specification of the building;
(d) what should be included as usable floor space;

[24] *Nature Conservancy Council for England v. Deller (1992) 43 E.G. 137.*

(e) whether car parking spaces are of extra value in a particular locality;
(f) whether alienation rights were restrictive;
(g) whether clauses were onerous;
(h) the range of uses to which the premises might be put;
(i) the state of the market;
(j) whether a quantum allowance was justified having regard to the size of the subject premises and market evidence;

and, having decided all those issues, the arbitrator must then make his award as to value.

Content of the award: style

6–61 Surveyors should remember that an award is an important document and it should be presented in a way which underlines its significance. Too many valuation arbitrators provide their award, even a reasoned award, in the form of a letter rather than setting it out as a report, and this is considered unsatisfactory. There are precedents which can be followed but many of them, particularly those from old text books use archaic language which is out of tune with modern usage and indeed the 1996 Act. Valuation arbitrators should not pretend to be lawyers but some formality is appropriate. The award should begin with the recitals as to the parties and the significant dates on which the hearings were held and representations and reports made. The award should go on to identify those issues which the arbitrator has found to be in dispute between the parties. In a reasoned award this list of issues should be followed by separate sections dealing with each issue, setting out briefly each parties' contentions on it and the arbitrator's conclusions. This may seem to be a pedantic way of dealing with the matter but it will have great benefits in demonstrating that the arbitrator has in fact discharged his duty of dealing with all the issues between the parties which may make a charge of serious irregularity much harder to ground. The award should conclude with a summary of the conclusions reached on the issues and showing how these are brought into a relationship with each other in order to influence the final figure. The award then states the value awarded. The award is then signed in the presence of a witness, dated, and the place at which the award is published should be given (*e.g.* London, Leeds, etc.). Some arbitrators believe that they should indicate the figure at the very beginning of the award as that is what the parties are immediately most interested in. Paragraphs 2–768 *et seq.*, above deal with drafting awards.

Publication

6–62 When agreeing fees it is likely to be helpful to the arbitrator to stipulate that the fees will be due on publication of the award. The publication date is the date on which the arbitrator communicates to the parties the fact that his award is ready for collection. His indication that the award is ready may be coupled with a reminder that it will only be released on payment of his fees in full. The parties have joint and several liability for those fees and so it is immaterial who actually pays. Any application to challenge an award or appeal an award must be brought within 28 days of the date of the award or as otherwise provided in section 70 (3). Arbitrators should therefore be careful to give the parties a reasonable opportunity in which to appeal and should avoid announcing the publication of their award immediately before major holiday periods (*e.g.* Christmas).

An award without reasons

6–63 The mechanics of producing an award are relevant whether reasons are provided or not, but the form in which an award may be given without reasons can be much simpler. It should still contain the recitals mentioned in paragraph 6–61. There will be no need to refer to the individual issues but the purpose of the reference should be stated. It will be necessary to say what work has actually been undertaken and mention will be made of having read the submissions, and inspected the subject property and the comparables. The valuation will be stated and the award will conclude with the arbitrator's signature and that of a witness, the date of the award, and the place of publication.

Costs in Property Valuation Arbitrations

Costs generally

6–64 The costs of the arbitration are:

(a) the arbitrator's fees and expenses, including those of any advisers appointed by him;
(b) the fees and expenses of any appointing institution; and
(c) the legal and other costs of the parties.

6–65 The arbitrator may make an award allocating the costs of the arbitration as between the parties but subject to any agreement of the parties. The general principle is that costs shall be awarded on the basis that they "follow the event except where it appears to the tribunal that in the circumstances this is not appropriate in relation to the whole or part of the costs" (section 61).

The "event"

In the case of valuation arbitrations, the claim and counterclaim may have no independent existence and therefore it may be difficult to establish what the "event" might actually be. In valuation disputes determined by arbitration, there is some support for making fractional awards in respect of costs. Reference may be made to Bernstein and Reynolds, *Handbook of Rent Review*. 6–66

The practice in rent review arbitration is to make fractional awards of costs in appropriate cases. This is supported by section 61(2) of the 1996 Act. 6–67

Calderbank offers

A Calderbank offer should be in a particular form which offers to compromise the proceedings, states the valuation proposed, says how costs are to be borne and states a time by which the offer should be accepted. The offer must be marked "Without prejudice save as to costs". If a Calderbank offer is made, then the party making it should ensure that it is received by the other party. Some measure of proof that such an offer was made may need to be demonstrated. Arbitrators should also be reminded that Calderbank offers are compromise offers to settle, not valuations and are inadmissible as evidence until costs are being considered. (See paragraphs 2–526 and 2–822 of this Handbook.) 6–68

Making room for Calderbanks

Each party has the right to make a Calderbank offer; this is expressed to be "without prejudice save as to costs" with the intention that when the arbitrator comes to deal with costs, the parties may influence him as to the amount of his award so far as each of them is concerned. The consequence of the operation of Calderbank offers is to place the onus on the arbitrator to remind parties that if they may wish to make Calderbank offers then he, the arbitrator, should proceed only to making an interim award so that he can receive their submissions in respect of costs before making his final award. He will also need to establish, if the award is to be made with reasons, whether the final award on costs is also to be made with reasons. Even where the parties have made a prior agreement that an interim award should be produced without reasons, they may still agree between themselves that the final award on costs shall be delivered with reasons. Appendices A and B both allow for this possibility. 6–69

Fractional awards

Where the only issue is one of quantum as in arbitrations which deal, for example, with damages only, compensation, or a rent review, the "event" is 6–70 not easily definable. Suppose that a landlord contends for a rent of £10,000 per annum; the tenant contends for £2,000 per annum; the arbitrator determines the rent at £6,000 per annum. Each side may claim that it has "won". The landlord will say that he has obtained £4,000 more than the tenant's figure, and the tenant will say that he has obtained £4,000 less than the landlord's figure. A more arguable position arises if, in the example given above, the arbitrator's award was £2,400 per annum. The landlord could say that he had to incur the whole costs of the arbitration to get more than £2,000 per annum and that he should be awarded his costs. The tenant could say that looking at the matter commercially, there was £8,000 per annum in issue in the arbitration; the landlord has recovered only one twentieth and the tenant has succeeded as to nineteen twentieths, so that in any real sense, the tenant has "won". On those facts, most arbitrators would consider that the landlord had to pay to the tenant a substantial fraction of the tenant's costs.

6–71 If the arbitrator makes a fractional award, it may have unforeseen consequences unless the arbitrator pays attention to the arithmetic. For example, if the arbitrator orders that party A should pay one half of the costs of party B it means that A would bear almost three quarters of the total costs of the arbitration. For example, suppose that the costs incurred by each party are £2,500, and the arbitrator's fees are £1,000. The effect of an order that party A shall pay one half of party B's costs and one half of the award is that party A has to pay £2,500 (his own costs); £1,250 (one half of party B's costs); and £500 (one half of the arbitrator's fees). This makes a total of £4,250 which is about 70 per cent of the costs of the arbitration.

Not following the "event"

6–72 There is further justification for not following the normal rule with regard to costs in litigation in the case of valuation arbitrations. First, unlike the position in most litigation or arbitration, the respondent may not be at fault in any real sense. Second, in some cases the question of who shall be claimant and who respondent is decided as a mere matter of convenience; the parties may have agreed upon a sale at a price to be determined by arbitration; in the case of a rent review, the matter may be decided merely by which party serves the notice to trigger the rent review.

Amount of the costs

6–73 With regard to the amount of the costs to be paid, the parties are free to agree what costs in an arbitration are recoverable. Under section 63(3), where there is no agreement, the arbitrator "may determine by award, the recoverable costs of the arbitration on such basis as [he] thinks fit". He will need to set out in his award the basis upon which he has acted and the items of recoverable costs and the amount referable to each. If the arbitrator does not determine the recoverable costs, any of the parties to the arbitration may apply to the court, who may either determine the recoverable costs on such basis as it thinks fit, or alternatively order that they shall be determined by such other means and upon such other terms as the court may specify.

Taxation

Different methods of taxation may be specified but in relatively small disputes, arbitrators should consider taxing their own costs and those of the parties. There is also power under section 37(1)(a) to appoint assessors, to sit with the arbitrator unless the parties otherwise agree. A legal advisor or assessor who specialised in the taxation of costs would be such a person who might be appointed by the arbitrator to advise him on these matters. However, if the parties agreed to the appointment of a taxing expert, it is not thought that their agreement would also run to questioning the amount of the costs awarded to each party which they might otherwise have the right to do under section 37(1)(b). Costs and taxation are dealt with in detail at pararaphs 2–804 *et seq*., above. **6–74**

Interest

An award of compensation or the determination of a rent review is a declaratory award. Under section 49 of the Act, the parties are free to agree on the arbitrator's powers with regard to the award of interest. If there is no agreement then the arbitrator may award simple or compound interest in such a manner as seems to meet the justice of the case. In particular he may award interest on an uplift in rent from the date of the rent review. This power may well be used by arbitrators in order to focus the minds of the parties towards making progress in arbitrations where otherwise there might be tactical delay. **6–75** the amount [illegible] to each if the arbitrator does not determine the recoverable costs [illegible] of the [illegible], the [illegible] may apply to the court, who may either determine the recoverable costs on such basis as it thinks fit or order that they shall be determined by such other means and upon such terms as the court [illegible].

Taxation

6-74 Different methods of taxation may be specified but in relatively small disputes arbitrators should consider taxing the relevant costs and those of the parties. There is also power under section 37(1)(a) to appoint assessors to sit with the arbitrator unless the parties otherwise agree. A legal advisor or assessor who was [illegible] in the taxation of costs would be such a person who might be appointed by the arbitrator to assist in the taxation. However, if the parties agreed to the appointment of a taxing expert, it is not clear whether their agreement would amount to [illegible] the amount of the costs awarded to each party which [illegible] have the right to determine [illegible]. Costs and taxation are dealt with in [illegible] paragraphs 7-304 et seq.

Interest

6-75 An award of interest on arrears following the determination of a rent review is a discretionary award. Under section 49 of the Act, the parties are free to agree on the arbitrator's powers in regard to the award of interest. If there is no agreement then the arbitrator may award simple or compound interest in such a manner as seems to meet the justice of the case. In particular he may award interest, simple or compound, from the date of [illegible]. This power may well be used by arbitrators in order to force the [illegible] of the parties [illegible] in arbitrations where otherwise there might be tactical delay.

APPENDIX A

IN THE MATTER OF THE ARBITRATION ACT 1996

AND IN THE MATTER OF AN ARBITRATION BETWEEN

CLAIMANT

AND

RESPONDENT

CONCERNING

THE FOLLOWING DIRECTIONS ARE GIVEN (AND AGREED)

(1) The landlord is to be the claimant and the tenant is to be the respondent.
(2) The parties have confirmed to me that there are no other matters dealing with procedure or evidence agreed between them which are not recorded in the arbitration agreement or in these directions.
(3) The parties are to prepare a schedule of agreed facts, to be forwarded to me, not later than 5.00 pm on [week 4]. The schedule is to be signed on behalf of both parties and to include a description, specification, plans, floor areas, floor loadings, amenities, service charges and business rates, together with a copy of the lease and all relevant licences and planning permissions.
(4) The parties are to agree particulars of any comparable transactions, including so far as practical: descriptions; plans; prices; costs; specifications; floor areas; floor loadings; details of amenities; service charges; business rates; and the relevant licence and lease details including the VAT status of any rent, all such information to be suitably scheduled and signed by both parties and submitted to me not later than 5.00 pm on [week 4]. Any comparables not agreed are to be included in the respective parties representations.
(5) Evidence of comparable transactions must be either within the direct knowledge of the surveyor concerned, or supported by documentary evidence , or agreed between the parties. Detailed transactions in a form signed by an agent instrumental in that transaction will be admissible. Arbitrators' awards and the determinations of independent experts shall be admissible as evidence in this arbitration, but I shall decide what weight to give them. ''Without prejudice'' correspondence and ''Without Prejudice'' offers must not be adduced as evidence.
(6) Copies of the claimants' written representations and the respondents' written representations are to be exchanged between the parties not later than 5.00 pm

on [week 5] with copies to me, not later than 5.00 pm on [week 6]. All paragraphs shall be numbered; this requirement is included to assist both me and the parties in connection with the parties' counter-representations.

(7) The representations referred to in direction (6) are to be accompanied by affidavits sworn by the surveyor for each party that the representations are a true record of the facts and opinions contained therein.

(8) Copies of the counter representations on behalf of each party are to be exchanged between the parties not later than 5.00 pm on [week 8], with copies to me not later than 5.00 pm on [week 9].

(9) If either party comes into possession of fresh evidence during the course of the reference, application for leave to present that evidence may be made to me and I shall give such directions, or make such orders as I think fit in all the circumstances. If the fresh evidence is to be admitted, it will be made available to me and to the opposing party in a suitable form so that a proper comparison may be made between the new evidence and the evidence already submitted. The party receiving the new evidence will be given time in which to inspect the relevant premises or other evidence concerned, and to make appropriate counter submissions and/or amend submissions previously made.

(10) I may wish to appoint experts or legal advisers or to take the advice of leading counsel and would give the parties notice accordingly. Any opinions, reports, or advice obtained will be made available to the parties and in that connection I shall give directions as to the time by which any representations or counter-representations shall be made. The costs involved in obtaining the opinions, reports, or advice shall form part of my costs and will be incorporated in my final award.

(11) I shall reserve the right to call for a hearing if, in my discretion, the circumstances justify it, or either party requests it, and all the costs incurred will form part of the costs of the award.

(12) In due course I shall require the parties to make arrangements for me to inspect the subject premises and also the properties cited as comparables. I shall not require to be accompanied on my inspection.

(13) Following my consideration of the matter I shall notify the parties that my reasoned interim award is available and thereafter, I shall give directions on submissions on costs.

(14) Leave to apply.

[Name] [date]
Arbitrator

APPENDIX B

IN THE MATTER OF THE ARBITRATION ACT 1996

AND IN THE MATTER OF AN ARBITRATION BETWEEN

CLAIMANT

AND

RESPONDENT

CONCERNING

THE FOLLOWING DIRECTIONS ARE GIVEN (AND AGREED)

(1) The landlord is to be the claimant and the tenant is to be the respondent.

(2) The parties have confirmed to me that there are no other matters dealing with procedure or evidence agreed between them which are not recorded in the arbitration agreement or in these directions.

(3) The statements of case on behalf of the claimant, and the respondent are to be exchanged between the parties before 5.00 pm on [week 5] with copies to me.

(4) Copies of the replies on behalf of each party are to be exchanged between the parties not later than 5.00 pm on [week 8] with copies to me.

(5) The parties are to prepare a schedule of agreed facts, to be forwarded to me, not later than 5.00 pm on [week 5]. The schedule is to be signed on behalf of both parties and to include a description, specification, plans, floor areas, floor loadings, amenities, service charges and business rates, together with a copy of the lease and all relevant licences and planning permissions.

(6) The parties are to agree particulars of any comparable transactions, including so far as practical; descriptions; plans; prices; costs; specifications; floor areas; floor loadings; details of amenities; service charges; business rates; and the relevant licence and lease details including the VAT status of any rent, all such information to be suitably scheduled and signed by both parties and submitted to me not later than 5.00 pm on [week 10]. Any comparables not agreed are to be included in the respective parties representations.

(7) Evidence of comparable transactions must be either within the direct knowledge of the surveyor concerned, or supported by documentary evidence , or agreed between the parties. Detailed transactions in a form signed by an agent instrumental in that transaction will be admissible. Arbitrators' awards and the determinations of independent experts shall be admissible as evidence in this arbitration, but I shall decide what weight to give them. "Without Prejudice"

correspondence and "Without Prejudice" offers must not be adduced as evidence.

(8) Copies of the claimant's written representations and the respondent's written representations are to be exchanged between the parties not later than 5.00 pm [week 12] with copies to me. All paragraphs shall be numbered; this requirement is included to assist both me and the parties in connection with the parties counter-representations.

(9) Written representations shall include the evidence of such expert witnesses as the parties intend to rely on. Neither party may adduce the evidence of more than [three] expert witnesses whose evidence shall not be duplicated.

(10) Copies of the counter representations on behalf of each party are to be exchanged between the parties not later than 5.00 pm on [week 14], with copies to me.

(11) If either party comes into possession of fresh evidence during the course of the reference, application for leave to present that evidence may be made to me and I shall give such directions, or make such orders as I think fit in all the circumstances. If the fresh evidence is to be admitted, it will be made available to me and to the opposing party in a suitable form so that a proper comparison may be made between the new evidence and the evidence already submitted. The party receiving the new evidence will be given time in which to inspect the relevant premises or other evidence concerned, and to make appropriate counter submissions and/or amend submissions previously made.

(12) I may wish to appoint experts or legal advisers or to take the advice of leading counsel and would give the parties notice accordingly. Any opinions, reports, or advice obtained will be made available to the parties and in that connection I shall give directions as to the time by which any representations or counter-representations shall be made. The costs involved in obtaining the opinions, reports, or advice shall form part of my costs and will be incorporated in my final award.

(13) The hearing will take place at [ ], commencing on [ ] with a maximum of [ ] days. Any change in the likely length of the hearing is to be notified to me promptly. I propose to allocate the time at the hearing as follows . . . .

(14) All correspondence with me is to be copied simultaneously to the opposing party.

(15) In due course I shall require the parties to make arrangements for me to inspect the subject premises and also the properties cited as comparables. I shall not require to be accompanied.

(16) Following my consideration of the matter I shall notify the parties that my reasoned interim award is available and thereafter, I shall give directions on submissions on costs.

(17) Leave to apply.

[Name] [date]
Arbitrator

Part 7

AGRICULTURAL PROPERTY ARBITRATIONS

By Derek Wood, C.B.E., Q.C., F.C.I. Arb.

Introduction

Arbitration is one of the longest established methods of resolving disputes concerning agricultural property, particularly between landlord and tenant. For centuries the standard form of letting agricultural land has been the tenancy from year to year, commencing either at the beginning of the growing season (Lady Day) or after harvest (Michaelmas). At common law such tenancies could be terminated by six months' notice to quit.[1] On quitting the tenant would by custom be entitled to claim compensation from the landlord for improvements made by the tenant which would benefit a successor—growing crops, other plantings such as fruit trees, fertilisation of the soil ("unexpired manurial values"), buildings and other works. The landlord might have had cross-claims against the tenant—dilapidations, waste or other deterioration of the holding. Disputes were normally settled by a local agricultural valuer acting as an arbitrator. The practice in these cases was informal. Much depended on the eye and professional skill and knowledge of the person appointed. The rules of procedure could be quite homespun.[2] 7–01

The Agricultural Holdings Act 1948 ("the 1948 Act") transformed the character of tenancies of agricultural holdings. Severe restrictions were placed upon the circumstances in which tenancies could be terminated. With few exceptions, lettings, whether periodical or not, and most licences (because they were converted into annual tenancies), required the (now) 12 months' notice to quit.[3] Notices to quit could then be challenged by tenants in a reference to the Minister, with an appeal to the Agricultural Lands Tribunal.[4] Later the jurisdiction of the Minister was dropped and the challenge went straight to the Tribunal.[5] If a notice was challenged, consent could be given to its operation in a limited set of circumstances only.[6] The right of the tenant to refer a notice to quit to the Minister (or Tribunal) could however be excluded in a number of special cases, originally seven.[7] Where the landlord sought to rely on some of these special 7–02

1 Extended to 12 months by s.25 of the Agricultural Holdings Act 1923.

2 *Re Hopper* (1867) L.R. 2 Q.B. 367.

3 1948 Act, ss.2, 3, and 23.

4 1948 Act, s.24(1).

5 Agriculture Act 1958, s.3.

6 1948 Act, s.25.

7 1948 Act, s.24(2). Customarily they were called "the seven deadly sins", although not many of them, such as the death of the tenant, could properly be described as sinful.

cases, the claim could be referred by the tenant to an arbitrator.[8] The grant of jurisdiction to arbitrators in the sensitive field of security of tenure called for a more formalised procedure.

7–03 The conferment of security of tenure brought with it necessary consequential changes in the law, most importantly a statutory right for either party to call for a rent review under what was now a virtually unbreakable contract of tenancy.[9] Parliament also took the opportunity to formalise the dispute-resolution procedure for the determination of other disputes, particularly over compensation payable to tenant or landlord at the termination of the tenancy.[10] A list of potential disputes was established in the 1948 Act for which arbitration was identified as the only permitted procedure for resolution. Schedule 6 to the 1948 Act laid down a special set of rules for the conduct of these arbitrations; and the Arbitration Acts had no application.[11] The 1948 scheme, with some important additions and variations (notably the rights of close relatives to succeed to a new tenancy on the death or retirement of the tenant), and other minor modifications, is still in force. Most recently it was re-enacted in the Agricultural Holdings Act 1986 ("the 1986 Act"). Section 84 of and Schedule 11 to the 1986 Act impose a mandatory set of rules for the conduct of arbitrations of disputes referred under the 1986 Act. Such arbitrations would rank as "statutory arbitrations" for the purposes of sections 94 to 98 inclusive of the Arbitration Act 1996, but the operation of the 1996 Act has been expressly excluded[12] and 1986 Act arbitrations stand apart as a separate mode of dispute resolution.

Milk quotas

7–04 The United Kingdom's accession to what is now the European Union imposed upon farming businesses the regime of the Common Agricultural Policy. One of the most significant measures has been the creation of milk quotas, first introduced into the United Kingdom by the Dairy Produce Quotas Regulations 1984.[13] In summary, occupiers of holdings identified as dairy holdings have registered against their holding an amount called a "reference quantity" or quota.[14] The effect of the registration is to establish a maximum quantity of milk or other dairy products so that, if the producer delivers for sale in any year a quantity in excess of quota, a punitive levy is imposed on the excess which destroys its commercial value. Despite the debate over the precise legal status

[8] The procedure was governed by regulations made from time to time under the 1948 Act, now superseded as stated in Table 1 below.
[9] 1948 Act, s.8.
[10] 1948 Act, ss.34–69.
[11] 1948 Act, s.77(1).
[12] 1986 Act, s.84 as amended by Arbitration Act 1996, Sched.3, para. 45.
[13] S.I. 1984 No. 1047, made under the European Communities Act 1972.
[14] The expression "holding" here is not limited to land let under a tenancy, but includes land of any tenure occupied by a dairy farmer.

of quota[15] it has in practical terms become a valuable asset. Changes in the occupation of entire holdings which have registered quota (for example on a sale of the freehold or the grant of a tenancy) carry a transfer of the entire quota with them. Changes in the occupation of parts of holdings require an apportionment which, if it is not agreed (as it usually is), is referred to arbitration, which may involve persons interested in the holding other than the transferor and the transferee.

The rules currently in force for the apportionment of milk quota in England and Wales are contained in regulations 8, 9, 10 and 32 of and Schedule 2 to the Dairy Produce Quotas Regulations 1997.[16] Milk quota arbitrations under these Regulations are also "statutory arbitrations" for the purposes of sections 94 to 98 of the Arbitration Act 1996, but the operation of the 1996 Act is excluded by paragraph 35 of Schedule 2. 7–05

Claims relating to milk quota can also arise between landlord and tenant at the end of a tenancy of land which has the benefit of quota. In a simple case, where the tenant is a registered producer in respect of a milk quota "holding" which consists exclusively of the land comprised in the tenancy, the benefit of the entire quota reverts to the landlord with the land itself, and no question of apportionment arises. But the tenant has the right under paragraph 13 of Schedule 1 to the Agriculture Act 1986 to receive compensation for such part of the quota as, in broad terms, is attributable to efficient farming practices or fixed equipment introduced by the tenant, or has been purchased by the tenant. Claims for compensation under this Act are settled, prospectively or at the end of the tenancy, by arbitration; and the procedures laid down in the 1986 Act apply to such arbitrations.[17] 7–06

The more complicated case is that of the tenant whose milk quota "holding" consists partly of let land which he is quitting and partly of other land which is being retained, or returned to another landlord. In this case any dispute over apportionment must first be settled by arbitration under the 1997 Regulations, and claims for compensation then have to be settled piecemeal under the 1986 Act. 7–07

Farm business tenancies

Since September 1, 1995 tenancies of agricultural land have not, except in special cases, attracted the protection of the 1986 Act, but have instead fallen within the purview of the Agricultural Tenancies Act 1995 ("the 1995 Act").[18] The main purpose of this Act is to enable landlords to grant what are called "farm business tenancies" without the burden of security of tenure or succession rights 7–08

[15] See for example *Faulks v. Faulks* [1992] 1 E.G.L.R.9.
[16] S.I. 1997 No. 733.
[17] Agriculture Act 1986, Sched.I, paras 10 and 11.
[18] For the exclusions see 1995 Act, s.4.

associated with the 1986 Act. Nevertheless a measure of statutory regulation is applied to these tenancies: the continuance and termination of tenancies; the tenant's right to instal and remove fixtures; rent review; and compensation on quitting.

7–09 Disputes arising under the 1995 Act are in varying terms referred to arbitration. These arbitrations are, just like 1986 Act and milk quota arbitrations, "statutory arbitrations" for the purposes of sections 94 to 98 of the Arbitration Act 1996. However, there is no provision in the 1995 Act equivalent to section 84 of the 1986 Act[19] which excludes the provisions of the Arbitration Act 1996. It follows that Part I of the Arbitration Act 1996, so far as it is consistent with the provisions of the 1995 Act,[20] applies to these arbitrations.

Other disputes

7–10 Quite apart from statute arbitration clauses are commonly found in many documents relating to agricultural property: farming partnerships, share-farming and agricultural contracting agreements, land options or even devises of land under wills. They are also found in tenancy agreements to which the 1986 or 1995 Acts apply. In so far as any of these disputes do not fall within the special statutory procedures already mentioned, the Arbitration Act 1996 will apply to them.

7–11 An unhappily complex picture therefore emerges.

(1) A significant group of disputes arising under tenancies to which the 1986 Act applies are referred to arbitration under that Act, and the Arbitration Act 1996 does not apply.
(2) Other disputes arising between the parties to a tenancy protected by the 1986 Act may be referred to arbitration if the tenancy agreement has an arbitration clause. If it does, the 1996 Act applies.[21]
(3) Disputes over the apportionment of milk quota are referred to arbitration under the Dairy Produce Quotas Regulations 1997. The 1996 Act does not apply to these arbitrations.
(4) Tenants protected by the 1986 Act who have claims for compensation for milk quota under the Agriculture Act 1986 must proceed under section 84 of and Schedule 11 to the Agricultural Holdings Act 1986.
(5) Disputes arising between parties to farm business tenancies to which the 1995 Act applies are referred to arbitration under the 1995 Act. Such arbitrations are "statutory arbitrations" within the meaning of the Arbitration Act 1996, and the provisions of that Act apply so far as they are consistent with the provisions of the 1995 Act.

[19] See n. 12 above.
[20] Arbitration Act 1996, s.94(2).
[21] See paras 7–16 and 7–17 below.

(6) Disputes over agricultural property arising under any other agreement or instrument containing a valid arbitration clause fall within the Arbitration Act 1996.

The scheme of this Part of the Handbook will be to examine first the arbitration procedures and practices under the 1986 Act, which have many special characteristics not paralleled in other fields of arbitration; and then to draw attention to the differences between these arbitrations and the other types of arbitration relating to agricultural property. **7–12**

1986 Act Arbitrations: Jurisdiction

Table 1 lists all the disputes arising between parties to tenancies protected by the 1986 Act which are compulsorily referred to arbitration under that Act. **7–13**

TABLE 1

Disputes which must be resolved by arbitration under the 1986 Act

Section, etc.	**Dispute**
Section 6 and Sched.1	Terms of tenancy: ascertainment of any terms not recorded in writing/settlement of terms making provision for matters specified in Sched.1 on which the parties have not agreed.
Section 7 and S.I. 1973 No. 1473 (as amended by S.I. 1988 No. 281), Sched. para. 13	Model clauses prescribed by the Minister: liability for the maintenance, repair and insurance of fixed equipment: determination whether any item of equipment is/was redundant to the farming of the holding.
ibid Sched. para. 15	Determination of all claims, questions or differences arising under the provisions of the model clauses.

Section, etc.	Dispute
Section 8	Terms of the tenancy: determination whether any terms substantially modifying operation of model clauses prescribed under section 7 are justified or should be varied. Consequential matters.
Section 9	Compensation or other relief when liability for maintenance or repair of fixed equipment is transferred from one party to another under sections 6, 7 or 8.
Section 10	Settlement of amount payable to tenant by landlord purchasing fixture or building removable by the tenant.
Section 12 and Sched.2	Triennial review of rent.
Section 13	Increase of rent for landlord's improvements.
Section 14	Variation of terms of tenancy as to permanent pasture.
Section 15(6)	Freedom to dispose of produce and of cropping: determination whether tenant is exercising rights in a manner likely to injure or deteriorate the holding.
Section 20	Compensation to tenant for damage by game.
Section 26 and Sched.3; Section 28; Section 29 and Sched.3; S.I. 1987 No. 710	Notices to do work and notices to quit served under Cases A, B, D and E: (i) Determination of tenant's liability for matters specified by landlord in a notice to do work. (ii) Determination of other questions arising under a notice to do work. (iii) Modification of a notice to do work. (iv) Extension of time for doing work, and of date for termination of tenancy in event of tenant's failure to comply. (v) Recovery from landlord of cost of work for which tenant is not liable. (vi) Where notice to quit given for any of reasons stated in Cases A, B, D or E, determination of any question arising under the provisions of the Act relating to those reasons.

Section, etc.	Dispute
Section 33	Reduction of rent where notice given to quit part of holding.
Section 48	Determination of terms of and rent payable under a new tenancy granted to a successor to a deceased tenant under Part IV of the Act.
Section 56	Determination of terms of and rent payable under a new tenancy granted to a successor to a retiring tenant under Part IV of the Act.
Sections 60–70 and 83	Compensation payable by landlord to tenant on termination of tenancy of holding or (section 74) part of holding.
Sections 71, 72 and 83	Compensation payable by tenant to landlord on termination of tenancy of holding or (section 74) part of holding.
Agriculture Act 1986 Section 13 and Sched.1	Compensation payable by landlord to tenant (prospectively or actually) for milk quota on termination of tenancy.

In the case of every type of reference the 1986 Act defines the circumstances or events which must be established before an arbitration can be started. Since these are statutory arbitrations the ability for the parties to waive the requirements of the Act is questionable. It is probable that a breach of a requirement which is purely formal or procedural, such as a minor deviation from a prescribed form or a failure to take a certain step within a strict time limit, can be waived by the party not in default.[22] By contrast, where a preliminary step has to be taken to establish the dispute itself, for example the service of a notice to remedy breaches or pay rent under Case D of Schedule 3, there is no subject-matter on which the arbitrator can adjudicate if the Act has not been complied with. Table 2 outlines in summary form the different first steps which give rise to the different categories of 1986 Act arbitrations. It is incumbent on the parties in the first instance to ensure that they have reached the stage at which an arbitrator can be brought into the picture. Table 2 is illustrative only: the relevant provisions must be consulted in detail to ensure that an arbitrator can be validly appointed. 7–14

[22] *Kammins Ballrooms Ltd v. Zenith Investments Ltd* [1971] A.C. 850, where the need for knowledge of the breach is discussed by Lord Diplock at 882–883.

TABLE 2

Method of reference to arbitration

Dispute	Action by	Procedure, time limits, etc.
Section 6	L or T	Reference to arbitration by party serving s.6 notice at any time after failure to agree.
Section 7 and Regulations, Sched. para. 13	L or T	Two month's notice in writing requiring arbitration if no agreement.
Section 7 and Regulations, Sched. para. 15	L or T	Arbitration at any time after failure to agree.
Section 8	L or T	Either party may request the other to vary the tenancy: arbitration at any time after failure to agree.
Section 9	L or T	Reference to arbitration to be requested within "the prescribed period", i.e. one month after date on which transfer takes effect: see S.I. 1959 No. 71.
Section 10	T L L or T	T gives one month's notice of intention to remove fixture, etc. L serves counter-notice within the month electing to purchase. Arbitration at any time if parties cannot agree price.
Section 12 and Sched.2	L or T	Written notice by either party to other demanding reference to arbitration of rent properly payable from "next termination date", i.e. next date on which notice to quit could expire; arbitrator to be appointed by agreement or on application made to President of RICS before that date.
Section 13	L	Notice of increase to be served within six months of completion of work.

Dispute	Action by	Procedure, time limits, etc.
Section 13 (cont.)	L or T	Arbitration of any dispute arising out of section 13 at any time thereafter.
Section 14	L or T	Written notice may be served by either party demanding arbitration on reduction of area of permanent pasture.
Section 15 (6)	L or T	Arbitration at any time on question whether exercise of rights is injurious to holding.
Section 20	T	Notice of damage within one month after T became aware or ought to have become aware of it; reasonable opportunity for L to inspect; notice of claim within one month after year ending on September 29 in which damage occurred.
	L or T	Arbitration at any time thereafter, including any claim by L to be indemnified by a third party.
Section 26 and Sched.3; Section 28; Section 29 and Sched.4; S.I. 1987 No. 710	L T	(i) Notice to do work served by L. Demand for arbitration served by T within one month of service of L's notice.
	L T	(ii) Notice to quit served by L under Cases A, B, D or E. T serves counter-notice on L within one month requiring arbitration on notice.
		(iii) Counter-notice ceases to be effective if no arbitrator appointed by agreement or application made to President within three months of counter-notice.
Section 33	L or T	Arbitration on reduction of rent if no agreement after L has resumed possession of part of holding.

Dispute	Action by	Procedure, time limits, etc.
Section 48	L or T	Either party serves notice demanding arbitration within "the prescribed period." Prescribed period is three months after later of "relevant time" as defined in section 46(1) or (2) or date of Tribunal's direction under section 45.
Section 55	L or T	Either party serves notice demanding arbitration within "the prescribed period." Prescribed period is three months after "relevant time" as defined by section 55(8) or date of Tribunal's direction under section 53(7).
Section 60 (1)–(4) and Section 63 (basic and additional compensation for disturbance)	T L and T L or T	(i) Notice of claim not more than two months after end of tenancy. (ii) Within eight months after end of tenancy, settle claim by agreement in writing. (iii) Arbitration if no agreement. (section 83)
Section 60 (1)–(3)(b)(5) and (6) (alternative basic compensation for disturbance)	T	In addition to section 83 procedure, (a) notice of claim not less than one month before end of tenancy and (b) reasonable opportunity for L to inspect goods before sale.
Section 62 and sections 64–69 and 79 (other claims by T for compensation)	T L and T L or T	(i) Section 83 procedure as above. (ii) Section 83 procedure as above. (iii) Section 83 procedure as above.[23]

[23] For additional rules relating to tenants who entered into occupation before March 1, 1948 or December 31, 1951 see Sched.12, paras 6–8.

Dispute	Action by	Procedure, time limits, etc
Section 70 (compensation for special system of farming)	T	In addition to section 83 procedure, (a) notice of intention to claim not less than one month before end of tenancy and (b) record of condition made under section 22.
Section 71 (compensation to L for deterioration of particular parts of holding)	L L and T L or T	(i) Notice of claim not more than two months after end of tenancy. (ii) Within eight months after end of tenancy, settle claim by agreement in writing. (iii) Arbitration if no agreement. (section 83)
Section 72 (compensation for general deterioration of holding).	L	In addition to section 83 procedure, notice of intention to claim not less than one month before end of tenancy.
Agriculture Act 1986 section 13 and Sched.1. (Compensation to T for milk quota).	L or T	(i) Sched.1 para.10. Prospective determination of amount of compensatable quota: either party may serve notice on the other at any time before termination requiring reference to arbitration. Arbitration if no agreement. (ii) Sched.1 para.11. Tenant's claim on termination of tenancy: (a) notice of intention to claim not more than two months after termination. (b) within eight months after end of tenancy, settle claim by agreement in writing. (c) arbitration if no agreement.[24]

[24] For special rules for deciding when tenancy has terminated see Sched.1, paras 11(3) and (4).

7–15 Apart from those disputes which must be determined under Schedule 11, the question is sometimes raised whether parties can, by agreement, have other disputes resolved under the same procedure.[25] It would for example be convenient and economical for parties who had one dispute to which the 1986 Act definitely applied and another to which it did not to refer both to the same arbitrator to be dealt with at one and the same time in the same proceedings.

7–16 It is submitted that this aim cannot be achieved in law although it might to a limited extent be achievable in practice. Parties cannot by contract make an Act of Parliament apply to a subject-matter which is outside the Act. At best they can, purely between themselves and as a matter of contract, agree to regulate their affairs "as if" the Act applies. They can therefore incorporate into a private arbitration agreement, relating to a dispute falling outside the 1986 Act, the procedural rules laid down in Schedule 11, for example by simply saying that "the Schedule 11 procedure shall apply". Such an agreement could not however prevent the mandatory provisions of the Arbitration Act 1996 from also applying to the dispute, because those provisions apply notwithstanding any agreement to the contrary.[26] One of the mandatory provisions of the 1996 Act is section 33 which requires the arbitrator to adopt procedures suitable to the circumstances of the case; and if he took the view that the Schedule 11 procedure was inappropriate he would be bound to overrule it even though the parties had agreed to it. No doubt, if he was dealing with two disputes, one within and the other outside the Act, he would try to run the two in harmony as much as possible, and to respect the parties' wishes. But his own duty under section 33 is paramount.

7–17 In any case such an agreement would break down completely at the point at which either party wanted to invoke the supervisory powers of the court. Points of law arising in 1986 Act arbitrations may be referred by way of case stated to the county court.[27] 1986 Act awards may be challenged on the grounds of "misconduct" or error on the face, again in the county court.[28] Judicial challenge to 1996 Act awards lies by way of appeal or application to the court (normally the High Court), with leave. Even if a non-1986 Act dispute were conducted by the arbitrator under 1986 Act procedures, the parties' agreement would be ineffective to confer on the county court the supervisory jurisdiction created by the 1986 Act. The provisions of the 1996 Act which prescribe the manner in which the courts may

[25] See for example Scammell and Densham's *Law of Agricultural Holdings* (8th ed., 1996), p.1064, where doubt is cast on the effectiveness of such an arrangement.
[26] Arbitration Act 1996, s.4 and Sched.1.
[27] See paras 7–52–7–54 below.
[28] See paras 7–80–7–87 below.

review proceedings to which that Act applies are also mandatory,[29] and apply notwithstanding any agreement to the contrary.[30]

Appointment of 1986 Act Arbitrators

Appointments made by agreement

Paragraph 1 of Schedule 11 gives the parties the right to appoint their own arbitrator by agreement. In default of agreement the arbitrator will be selected by the President of the RICS from a panel maintained by the Lord Chancellor.[31] The parties should always give careful consideration to the possibility of appointing their own arbitrator before applying to the President. Disputes referred to arbitration under the 1986 Act vary widely in character. Some involve technical questions of farm management and valuation. Others, especially those connected with notices to quit, may focus exclusively on questions of law. In *Johnson v. Moreton*[32] the arbitrator (a rural practice surveyor) had to determine the validity of a notice to quit in unusual circumstances. The tenancy agreement contained a covenant by the tenant not to serve a counter-notice to a landlord's notice to quit. When the notice to quit was served he did so, and the landlord then served a second notice to quit under Case E, claiming that the serving of the counter-notice to the first notice was an irremediable breach of covenant. The case progressed by way of case stated from the county court to the House of Lords which held the covenant in question to be contrary to public policy and unenforceable. The only acts of the arbitrator were to sign the case stated as drafted by the parties' lawyers, and the award which the House of Lords directed him to deliver. In *Troop v. Gibson*[33] the arbitrator had to decide (among other points of law) whether a landlord was estopped by convention from seeking to enforce the tenant's covenant against assigning or sub-letting. All the facts were agreed and the surveyor-arbitrator sat with a legal assessor. These cases imply no criticism of the arbitrators in question, but illustrate the point that the parties can and should decide for themselves what particular profes- 7–18

29 Arbitration Act 1996, Sched.1 (references to ss. 12, 24, 31, 32, 67, 68, 70 and 71).
30 *ibid.* s.4(1).
31 Sched.11, paras 1(1) and (5).
32 [1980] A.C. 37.
33 [1986] 1 E.G.L.R. 1.

sional expertise is called for, according to the nature of the dispute. They may want a rural practice surveyor who has a special knowledge of a particular kind of farming, or an agricultural scientist, or accountant or other consultant who is qualified to adjudicate between experts in the same discipline. The Lord Chancellor's list may not necessarily match their needs.

Appointments made by the President

7–19 The President appoints were there is a "default of agreement".[34] It is submitted that this phrase covers both a breakdown in negotiations after an attempt to agree, and an absence of appointment because there have been no negotiations at all.[35] The President is under a statutory obligation to appoint "as soon as possible",[36] and it has been held[37] that a delayed appointment is invalid. Whether there is a direct remedy against the President for a failure to appoint or for delay in appointing is open to question. In *United Co-operative Ltd v. Sun Alliance and London Assurance Co. Ltd*[38] it was held that no cause of action lay against the President in connection with a power of appointment arising under a lease; but the position may be different when he is required to act under a statutory duty.

7–20 Table 2 shows that in some cases a notice of claim must be given within strict time limits before the claim can be pursued.[39] In other cases two notices have to be served.[40] There are time limits for giving a notice demanding arbitration,[41] and time limits for appointing or requesting the President to appoint an arbitrator.[42] There are also dates before which a reference or appointment cannot be made: the President cannot appoint an arbitrator to carry out a rent review under section 12 earlier that four months before the review date[43]; and in compensation cases parties are given eight months after the end of the tenancy to settle their claims,[44] although if negotiations were completely to break down an appointment or request made within this period would probably be valid.

7–21 It follows that, where a request is made to the President, it should both state the nature of the dispute and set out the appropriate procedural steps which found the claim and the arbitrator's jurisdiction. The request should give the applicant's best assessment of the issues which are going to arise, so that the

34 Sched.11, para. 1(1).
35 *F.R. Evans (Leeds) Ltd v. Webster* (1962) 112 L.Jo.703.
36 Sched.11, para. 1(3).
37 In an unreported case referred to in Scammell and Denham, *op.cit.*, at p. 398.
38 [1987] 1 E.G.L.R. 126.
39 Ss.13, 20, 60–69 and 71; Agriculture Act 1986, Sched.1, para. 11.
40 Ss. 60(3)(b), 70 and 72.
41 Ss. 9, 12, 26 and 28 and Sched.3 and S.I. 1987 No. 710 (notices to do work and notices to quit); and ss. 48 and 55.
42 S. 12 and provision relating to notices to do work and notices to quit: see n. 40 above.
43 Sched.11, para. 1(3).
44 See Table 2.

President can give some consideration to the qualifications the arbitrator should possess. "Rent review of a mixed dairy and arable holding, with buildings sub-let for light industry", for example, is more helpful than "Rent review." "Notice to quit under Case E, landlord alleging that share-farming contract is unlawful sub-letting" is more helpful than "Case E notice to quit." The application will not be valid unless it is accompanied by the prescribed fee,[45] and if the application has to be made by a certain date it will not be effective unless the fee is sent before that date. If a Welsh-speaking arbitrator is required, that should be specified in the application.[46]

Date of appointment

In 1986 Act arbitrations establishing the exact date of the arbitrator's appointment is important not only for discovering whether a statutory time limit has been met, but also for fixing the date from which time runs for the delivery of statements of case and the award.[47] The appointment must be made in writing.[48] Where an arbitrator is to be appointed by agreement, the appointment is made when the arbitrator accepts the appointment; and acceptance is completed when the letter of acceptance is sent, not when the parties receive it.[49] If the arbitrator accepts conditionally (for example on condition that a completed form is returned) the appointment is not made until the condition has been met.[50] Parties attempting to appoint by agreement should allow for the possibility that the person they wish to appoint might impose conditions. He might accept on the condition that a case in which he is currently involved settles. He might require unconditional agreement of his fees.[51] For these reasons it is unwise to wait until the last minute to appoint; and the party who is anxious to meet a time limit should make a protective application to the President if there is a risk that an unconditional appointment cannot be completed in time. Appointments made by the President are complete when the President executes the instrument of appointment.[52] 7–22

Revocation of appointment

If the arbitrator dies or is incapable of acting, or for seven days after notice from either party requiring him to act he fails to act, a new arbitrator may be 7–23

[45] Sched.11, para. 1(3).
[46] Sched.11, para. 1(4).
[47] Paras 7–34 and 7–67 below.
[48] Sched.11, para. 5.
[49] *Robinson v. Moody* [1994] 2 E.G.L.R. 16.
[50] *Hannaford v. Smallacombe* [1994] 1 E.G.L.R. 9.
[51] See Sched.11, para. 6 and para. 7–24 below.
[52] Sched.11, para. 31. This provision appears to prefer the approach of the Court of Appeal in *Master and Fellows of University College Oxford v. Durdy* [1982] Ch. 413 to that adopted by

appointed as if no arbitrator had been appointed.[53] Where a new arbitrator is appointed (whether under these provisions or otherwise) in a rent review case the date of the appointment of the original arbitrator counts as the date of the appointment of the new arbitrator.[54] Neither party is entitled to revoke the appointment of the arbitrator without the consent of other party, and the appointment is not revoked by the death of either party.[55] All revocations and consents relating to the removal and substitution of arbitrators must be in writing.[56]

Remuneration

7–24 Where an arbitrator is appointed by agreement his remuneration is such amount as is agreed between him and the parties or, in default of agreement, fixed by the registrar of the county court, with an appeal to the judge.[57] It would be neglectful and potentially unfair to the parties if an arbitrator appointed by agreement did not have the question of his fees cleared up in advance. Some agricultural arbitrations, for example those involving notices to quit or rent review, involve considerable sums of money, but in others the amount at issue might be quite small, and arbitrators owe a duty to the parties, and the parties owe a duty to themselves, to make sure that costs are not running out of control. The fixing of a fair rate of remuneration in property arbitrations and expert determinations has been the subject of much discussion.[58] The consensus of opinion is that the charging of an hourly rate for all aspects of the work creates the least impression of unfairness. It also gives the parties an incentive to keep their proceedings moving as quickly and as economically as possible. The arbitrator is of course also entitled to reasonable disbursements such as fees incurred in taking legal advice[59] and the county court procedure is available to settle any dispute as to whether it was reasonable that they should be incurred, as well as their amount.

the court in *Richards v. Allinson* [1979] 1 E.G.L.R. 12, in which it was held that the appointment was not complete until both parties had received notice of it.

[53] Sched.11, para. 2.

[54] Sched.11, para. 3.

[55] Sched.11, para. 4.

[56] Sched.11, para. 5.

[57] Sched.11, para. 6(1)(a).

[58] See para. 6–12, above; RICS *Guidance Notes on Agricultural Arbitrations and Independent Expert Determinations*, para. 5.16; RICS *Guidance Notes for Surveyors acting as Arbitrators or Independent Experts in Rent Reviews* (7th ed., 1996), para. 3.9; and the commentary in Bernstein and Reynolds' *Handbook of Rent Review* (Sweet and Maxwell), section G.3-9.

[59] See paras. 50–51 below.

It is advisable for the arbitrator to indicate as early as possible that he thinks it necessary to incur special disbursements and obtain the parties' comments.

Where the arbitrator is appointed by the President the remuneration is the amount agreed between the arbitrator and the parties or, in default of agreement, fixed by the President.[60] Where the appointment is made by the President agreement of fees between the arbitrator and the parties cannot be made a condition of appointment, because the appointment takes effect when the instrument of appointment is signed by the President.[61] 7–25

In either case the arbitrator's fees and other recoverable payments constitute a debt due from either of the parties to him[62]; but it is submitted that, unless there has been an express agreement between the arbitrator and the parties for interim payments, no part of his remuneration is recoverable until the arbitration is complete. The question whether an arbitrator has a lien over the award in respect of his remuneration, that is to say whether he can withhold his award until he is paid, is discussed in paragraph 7–78 below. 7–26

Action on Appointment

Notice of appointment

The first duty of an arbitrator is to inform the parties of his appointment at the earliest possible moment. If he is appointed by agreement, he should communicate his acceptance by the shortest possible means. If he is appointed by agreement subject to a condition being met, he should notify the parties as soon as the condition has been satisfied. Where he is appointed by the President the parties will be unaware of the exact date of appointment until the arbitrator notifies them. Again, he should inform them by the quickest method available. The parties have to deliver their statement of case within 35 days from the date of appointment,[63] and any delay in notification will prejudice them by cutting down the amount of time which they have to prepare their statements. 7–27

[60] Sched.11, para. 6(b).
[61] Sched.11, para. 31.
[62] Sched.11, para. 6.
[63] Sched.11, para. 7.

Jurisdiction

7–28 The arbitrator's second task is to satisfy himself that he has jurisdiction. He may not at this early stage have all the facts available to satisfy himself finally, but he can carry out an initial check, if necessary by writing to the parties, on the sequence of events and their chronology to make sure that he has been validly appointed and to inquire whether any minor defects which are capable of being waived have in fact been waived.[64]

7–29 It is customary for arbitrators at this stage to remind the parties of their duty to ensure that any letters which they write to the arbitrator should be copied to the other side and to warn them of the consequences of disclosing privileged documents detailing "without prejudice" negotiations at any stage. It must be borne in mind that negotiations between parties to settle a dispute are legally privileged whether they are headed "without prejudice" or not, unless they are expressed to be open.[65] The letter might also raise some preliminary points about procedure, such as the need for a preliminary meeting, the scope of any documentary or other evidence, the date and venue of the hearing, and the need and optimum date for an inspection. If the arbitrator has been appointed by the President he will also wish to resolve the question of his own remuneration at this stage, if that is at all possible.

Challenges to Jurisdiction

7–30 There are two main grounds on which the jurisdiction of an arbitrator in a 1986 Act arbitration can be challenged: the invalidity of the appointment, and the personal disqualification of the arbitrator. An appointment will be invalid if there is some procedural defect in the appointment which cannot be or has not been waived, such as a failure by one of the parties to take in due time a statutory step which is a pre-requisite to appointment.[66] One example would be a failure by the tenant to serve within a month a counter-notice to a Case A B D or E notice to quit. An arbitrator may be personally disqualified on a number of grounds. If the President appoints, he is bound to select a member of the Lord Chancellor's panel[67] and cannot choose anyone else. Alternatively the arbitrator

[64] See para. 7–15 and Table 2 above.
[65] See paras 2–467 to 2–469 and 2–526 to 2–531 above.
[66] See paras 7–14 and 7–28 above.
[67] Sched.1, para. 1(1).

may have some connection with the parties or the subject-matter which raises a suspicion that he could not fairly decide the dispute.[68]

A party wishing to challenge the arbitrator's jurisdiction on any ground should do so as soon as the facts which give rise to the challenge come to light. Further participation in the proceedings after knowledge of the relevant facts may (depending on the objection to be raised) result in a loss of the right to challenge. The challenge may be set out in the statement of case or in a separate letter to the arbitrator and the other side. If the objection is to be made by letter, that should not be allowed to delay delivery of the statement of case, which can if necessary be delivered without prejudice to the right to challenge. 7–31

The procedure for resolving questions of jurisdiction is laid down in paragraph 26 of Schedule 11. It entitles the arbitrator at any stage of the proceedings, and requires him upon a direction given by the judge of the county court upon an application made by the other party, to state in the form of a special case for the opinion of the court any question raised as to his jurisdiction. This procedure does not however preclude the arbitrator from deciding the question of jurisdiction for himself first. In many cases it will be desirable for him to do so, or at any rate to make findings of fact to be included in the case stated for the court which are relevant to the question of jurisdiction. The issue may, for example, simply turn upon whether the tenant served in due time a counter-notice to a notice to quit, the landlord alleging that he received the counter-notice out of time. In such a case the arbitrator should hear the evidence himself and make up his own mind. His decision ought then to settle the matter. If his personal qualifications are being called into question he will probably not need to make findings of fact as such: he can simply set out in the special case the facts and matters which, in the opinion of one of the parties, disqualify him and leave it to the court to decide whether his appointment should stand. The procedure to be followed under paragraph 26 is discussed further in paragraphs 7–52 to 7–54 below. 7–32

Powers of the Arbitrator

Paragraphs 7 to 13 inclusive of Schedule 11 are headed "Conduct of proceedings and witnesses". Paragraph 8 provides: 7–33

> "The parties to the arbitration and all persons claiming through them shall, subject to any legal objection, submit to be examined by the arbitrator, on

[68] See the discussion in paras 2–178 to 2–189 above.

oath or affirmation, in relation to the matters in dispute and shall, subject to any such objection, produce before the arbitrator all samples and documents within their possession or power respecting which may be required or asked for, and do all other things during the proceedings which the arbitrator may require.''

However, the Schedule is in truth almost completely silent on how the proceedings should be conducted except on two points: the rules governing the delivery of statements of case, and the attendance and examination of witnesses at the hearing. It is submitted that the implication is that the arbitrator is otherwise the master of his own procedure, and has a wide discretion as to the manner in which the proceedings should be conducted, provided always that they are conducted fairly and in accordance with the rules of natural justice.[69] Part 2 of this Handbook, which is principally concerned with arbitrators appointed under the Arbitration Act 1996, emphasises the wide powers and duties which arbitrators are given under that Act to ensure that proceedings are conducted fairly, economically, and expeditiously. Although paragraph 8 obliges the parties ''to do all . . . things which the arbitrator may require'', none of the express provisions of the 1996 Act which are designed to secure that end—notably sections 1, 33, 34, 40 and 42—have an equivalent in Schedule 11. But even before the 1996 Act was passed it was always recognised that in general, and subject only to the restrictions imposed by the machinery under which the arbitration was set up, the arbitrator was in control of the procedure, and it was incumbent upon him to adopt a procedure which was best suited to the interests of the parties and would secure a just result.[70]

Statements of Case

7–34 One of the criticisms of the 1986 Act is that the procedure laid down for the delivery by the parties of their written statements of case is considerably less flexible than that available to parties to arbitrations under the Arbitration Acts, and the difference is even more pronounced since the passing of the Arbitration Act 1996.[71] Each party must deliver to the arbitrator a statement of its case ''with all necessary particulars'' within 35 days from the date of appointment,

[69] See generally paras 2–273 *et seq.*, above.
[70] See for example the 2nd edition of this Handbook (1993) ,p. 57, Part 2, para. 7.1.2.
[71] To understand the contrast see paras 2–434 *et seq.*, above.

and that period cannot be extended by the arbitrator.[72] This procedure may be satisfactory when each side is putting forward a positive case, for example on a rent review. It is more difficult when one side is presenting a claim, such as the right to enforce a notice to quit or to compensation, to which the other side is in effect a defendant. The requirement that the case should be delivered "with all necessary particulars" means in effect that each party has to anticipate as much as possible the case which is going to be advanced by the other side and ensure that all positive facts or arguments, except possibly purely legal arguments, are set out at this early stage.

The requirement that the parties should prepare their cases in parallel and submit them within a strict time limit is no doubt linked with the further requirement that, subject to an enlargement of time granted by the President, the arbitrator must make and sign his award within 56 days of his appointment.[73] It was clearly Parliament's intention that agricultural arbitrations should be progressed speedily and not get caught up in the lengthy processes often associated with litigation in court. Time is further saved if the submission of "all necessary particulars" includes attaching to the case the principal documents which the arbitrator will have to see: the tenancy agreement, all relevant notices and counter-notices and correspondence in which the parties have set out their contentions and claims. The documents can if necessary be put into a more convenient form at a later stage in the arbitration,[74] but their inclusion at this early stage gives the arbitrator the opportunity to become familiar with them. 7–35

Amendments and additions

Paragraph 7 also provides that: 7–36

"(a) no amendment or addition to the statement or particulars delivered shall be allowed after the expiry of the said thirty-five days except with the consent of the arbitrator;

(b) a party to the arbitration shall be confined at the hearing to the matters alleged in the statement and particulars delivered by him and any amendment or addition duly made."

The circumstances in which arbitrators should allow further particulars and amendments to statements of case are considered in paragraphs 2–441 to 2–449 in Part 2 of this Handbook. In agricultural arbitrations, arbitrators will wish to balance the need to ensure that justice is done to both parties, each side having a fair and full opportunity to present its case, against the underlying philosophy of Schedule 11, which is that these disputes should be resolved speedily and 7–37

[72] *Hannaford v. Smallacombe* [1994] 1 E.G.L.R. 9.
[73] Sched.11, para. 14; see para. 7–67 below.
[74] See para. 7–44 below.

economically. In *E.D. and A.D. Cooke Bourne (Farms) Ltd v. Mellows*[75] the Court of Appeal held that tenants should have been allowed to make significant amendments to their case when that would have caused no prejudice or injustice to the landlords.

7–38 The scope of the rule that the parties are "confined" at the hearing to the matters alleged in their statements and particulars, with any permitted amendments or additions, has not been fully explored by the courts. While it would prevent a party which has delivered no statement of case at all from putting forward any positive case at the hearing[76] it does not appear to preclude that party from appearing and challenging the case advanced by the opposition, cross-examining the other side's witnesses and making closing submissions to the arbitrator. Between those two ends of the spectrum a large range of intermediate cases can arise which can cause practical problems for arbitrators. Much will depend on the onus of proof. If a landlord is seeking to uphold a Case D notice to quit on the ground of non-compliance with a notice to pay rent, but fails to deliver a statement of case, it would seem that the arbitrator would be bound to dismiss his claim whatever may have been said by the tenant in his statement. If the failure to deliver a case is that of the tenant it is questionable whether he can nevertheless appear and cross-examine the landlord or his agent to show that the amount was in fact paid, or that the amount claimed was wrongly calculated or that the notice to pay was never served. Where the issue is the reasonableness of the time allowed to comply with a notice to do work and the tenant does not deliver a case it is not clear whether he can cross-examine the landlord's agent with a view to showing that the time allowed was unreasonable, by arguing that the burden of proof is with the landlord. In rent review cases, where each side must in effect prove its own case, the problem may be more easy to solve, and arbitrators will be able to detect and prevent the introduction of a positive case—rival comparables or farm budgets—under the guise of cross-examination.

7–39 Despite the strictness of the rule, in many cases written statements of case in 1986 Act arbitrations are sketchy and uninformative. Sometimes this is because the party in question is in the position of a defendant and is genuinely in the dark as to what case he has to meet. Sometimes the decision to submit a statement of case in general terms is tactical. It is not unknown in rent arbitrations for a party to recite the tenancy agreement, state the rent currently payable, give some description of the holding and the date of the demand for arbitration, and then simply request the arbitrator to fix a rent in accordance with the provisions of the 1986 Act. The case may not even state a figure. If a figure is stated the detailed calculations upon which it is based may not be set out although, by any measure, they must constitute "necessary particulars". The case may end with a routine paragraph that the party will submit further evidence at the hearing in support of its case. Paragraphs in this form are unlikely to satisfy paragraph 7,

[75] [1983] Q.B. 104.

[76] See *Hannaford v. Smallacombe* [1994] 1 E.G.L.R. 9.

and may not be sufficient to entitle that party to elaborate its case any further, unless the arbitrator gives leave to amend.

The Need for a Hearing

Apart from the strict rules concerning statements of case, Schedule 11 also differs from 1996 Act[77] in that it appears to expect every arbitration to proceed to an oral hearing. Paragraph 7 stipulates that parties are to be confined "at the hearing" to the matters set out in their statements of case, and paragraph 9 refers to "witnesses appearing at the arbitration". Before 1996 the conventional view was that in arbitrations governed by the Arbitration Acts the arbitrator was bound to arrange an oral hearing if either side wished.[78] That is probably still the position under the 1986 Act. But if both sides agree that a hearing is not necessary, for example because the case turns entirely upon a point of law or a consideration of documents based on agreed facts, or if the parties are content that the issues raised by their statements of case and particulars can be settled simply by a farm inspection, it is submitted that arbitrators need not feel obliged to require the parties to attend a hearing nevertheless. There would seem to be nothing to prevent the parties from sending any further written material to the arbitrator by agreement or on his direction. 7–40

Other Procedural Questions

In agricultural arbitrations there are a number of procedural and evidential matters which regularly have to be addressed before any hearing. Arbitrators should attempt to clear them up well in advance. Much of the advice given in this Handbook in relation to the 1996 Act can be adapted for the 1986 Act, although in the latter case the statutory time limit for the delivery of the award is an extra constraint. The key to an efficient arbitration is early and regular communication between the arbitrator and the parties. This can take place at a meeting, in 7–41

[77] S.34(2)(h).
[78] See 2nd edition of this Handbook (1993), para. 10.2.2.

writing or by a telephone or video conference. If both parties ask for a meeting the arbitrator is unlikely to refuse, but he may do so. Issues which commonly arise for decision are:

- discovery and use of documents
- use of other material, such as plans, maps and photographs
- expert evidence
- other witnesses
- how to deal with points of law
- date and place of the hearing.

In most cases arbitrators will also be anticipating the need to carry out a farm inspection and (in rent review cases) to inspect other holdings.

Discovery of documents

7–42 Paragraph 8 of Schedule 11[79] requires the parties (subject to any legal objection) to produce before the arbitrator any relevant documents within their possession or power which may be required, and to do all others things which the arbitrator may require. This paragraph is derived from clause (f) of the First Schedule to the Arbitration Act 1889.[80] Under the 1889 Act it was held[81] that these provisions in combination gave the arbitrator jurisdiction to order general discovery of documents, and to require the parties to answer interrogatories on oath.[82]

7–43 Before deciding to order a party to disclose its documents to the other side the arbitrator should be convinced that the documents called for will make a genuine contribution to resolving the issues raised in the statements of case. Although paragraph 8 gives the arbitrator a power to order general discovery, that is to require a party to disclose all documents within its possession or power which relate to the issues raised, the modern practice in arbitrations is to exercise that power sparingly.[83] There will always be some basic documents the relevance of which will be self-evident: the tenancy agreement, any relevant notices or counter-notices, and the details of claims submitted in open correspondence. There will also be relevant contemporaneous records kept by one party or the other—farm accounts, farm budgets, records of condition, stock movement records, MAFF returns, accounts with agricultural or building contractors. It is suggested that if one party wants disclosure of documents which go beyond

[79] See para. 7–33 above.

[80] Re-enacted in s.12(1) of the Arbitration Act 1950.

[81] *Kursell v. Timber Operators and Contractors Ltd* [1923] 2 K.B. 202.

[82] ''Interrogatories'' are written questions sent by one party to the other during the preliminary stages of proceedings, before the hearing. The object is to clarify issues, perhaps dispense with the attendance of certain witnesses, and to identify the need to call others. Their use in agricultural arbitrations is extremely rare, and they are not discussed in this Part.

[83] See paras 2–456 *et seq*., above.

those which the landlord or tenant must self-evidently possess which are relevant the arbitrator should listen carefully to both sides' arguments before ordering production. The process of obtaining and producing documents is one of the major sources of delay and expense in litigation. The 1986 Act requires arbitrations to be conducted expeditiously and inexpensively.

Documents to be used at the hearing

It is one of the characteristics of hearings before agricultural arbitrators (and the Agricultural Lands Tribunals) that the documents put in by each side at the hearing are never properly coordinated, but are produced in numerous small bundles with no systematic scheme of identification. This frequently leads to confusion and time-wasting at the hearing, and important evidence may get overlooked. To avoid this result it is suggested that arbitrators should take firm control of the documentation to be used at the hearing at an early stage. The arbitrator will be concerned broadly with two groups of documents: documents already in existence which the parties will voluntarily produce, or will be required to produce on discovery, as discussed in the previous paragraph; and documents which will be brought into existence by one party or the other as part of its evidence, particularly expert evidence. Documents in this second category may well include maps, plans, photographs, schedules or draft farm budgets or accounts. In a rent review case the tenancy agreements relating to comparable holdings may be produced, together with correspondence with the agents of other landlords or tenants, summarised in schedules of comparables. In order to avoid confusion and delay at a later stage, arbitrators should first encourage the parties to agree all the documents upon which they wish to rely as documents to eliminate the need for formal proof; to amalgamate them into as small a number of agreed chronological and paginated bundles as possible; and to agree as many facts arising out of those documents as they can. For example, in a rent review case there is no reason why both parties should not submit a joint schedule of comparables prepared on the understanding that either party will be free at the hearing to criticise any suggested comparable on the grounds that is irrelevant, distinguishable or unhelpful. In such a case it must at least be possible for the parties to agree the basic facts, even if the conclusions to be drawn from those facts are highly controversial. In a case involving improvements or dilapidations it must at least be possible to agree the cost of installation or remedial works and a basic description of the items in question. If the arbitrator does not take some initiative in these matters it is unlikely that the parties will. 7–44

Expert evidence

Most arbitrations under the 1986 Act involve expert evidence. This is most commonly provided by rural practice surveyors who are trained to prepare 7–45 reports for use in such proceedings, and are familiar with the practice that expert reports must be exchanged well in advance of a hearing. The use of expert witnesses generally is discussed in Part 2 of this Handbook, paragraphs 2–563 to 2–569 and paragraphs 2–722 *et seq*., above. In agricultural arbitrations arbitrators are sometimes reluctant to inquire of the parties in advance the number and identity of their expert witnesses. They should overcome any such reluctance, and insist not only that reports are exchanged well in advance but also, if it is at all possible, that the experts should meet and attempt to agree as many matters of apparently contested fact as they possibly can. Experts owe a duty to their clients to ensure that proceedings are conducted with a maximum economy of time and expense. If experts are reluctant to meet the arbitrator has jurisdiction, it is submitted, to order a meeting of experts under the general powers conferred under paragraph 8 of Schedule 11.

Other witnesses

7–46 Paragraph 8 would also appear to entitle arbitrators to require the parties to disclose to each other the written statements of any other witnesses (including the parties themselves) who will be giving evidence at the hearing. This is now standard practice in High Court proceedings, and there is no reason why it should not be adopted under the 1986 Act. The arbitrator will have to lay down a timetable if the parties cannot agree one.

7–47 Paragraphs 10–13 inclusive of Schedule 11 give parties the power, with the assistance of the county court, to compel the attendance of witnesses (including persons in custody) at the hearing. Persons on whom a witness summons is served may also be required to produce documents. The arbitrator himself would not seem to have the right to issue a witness summons, because the relevant County Court Rules apply to parties to litigation only.[84] It is however arguable that, under paragraph 8, the arbitrator would be entitled to ''require'' a party to issue such a summons. If the power exists, it is however likely that an arbitrator would wish to exercise it only in the most exceptional circumstances.

Enforcing the arbitrator's orders

7–48 Although paragraph 8 obliges the parties to the arbitration to produce documents (and samples) and do all other things which the arbitrator may require, Schedule 11 does not contain any machinery for enforcing orders made by the arbitrator under these provisions.[85]

7–49 Parties will not normally wish to incur the disapproval of the arbitrator by failing to comply with his requirements, because this will create an unfavourable

84 See para. 2–479 above.
85 Contrast s.42 of the Arbitration Act 1996.

impression which may be relevant to his assessment of the evidence in the case. It may influence him in fixing the date and place for the hearing or the exercise of his discretion in allowing amendments or additions to a statement of case, and it may be relevant to the exercise of his discretion in making orders as to costs. It is however doubtful whether these indirect sanctions can ever be as effective as direct support from the court.

Points of law

Points of law of considerable technicality and complexity can arise in 1986 Act arbitrations.[86] They can arise at any and every stage in an arbitration, and arbitrators should keep a watchful eye open for them. The various techniques for dealing with points of law are well recognised.[87] In every case it remains the duty of the arbitrator to decide all questions arising during the proceedings, both of fact and of law, even when he or the parties have obtained the opinion of the county court on a point of law under the case stated procedure (see paragraph 7–52 below), although in the latter case it would probably be misconduct to ignore or override the opinion of the court. An arbitrator can reach a decision on a point of law in any of the following ways: 7–50

(i) by hearing the arguments submitted by the parties, in writing as well as orally if the arbitrator so wishes, and deciding the point himself;
(ii) by sitting with a legal assessor and deciding the point after obtaining the assessor's advice;
(iii) by obtaining a written legal opinion from a solicitor or barrister; or
(iv) by stating a case for the opinion of the county court under paragraph 26 of Schedule 11.

It was pointed out in paragraph 7–18 above that the parties themselves should give some consideration to the particular qualifications which their arbitrator should possess, and if they know that the proceedings are going to turn mainly or exclusively on a point of law they might well have appointed a legal arbitrator by agreement. In such a case they would expect the arbitrator to adopt course (i) and he will have accepted the appointment on that understanding. If the arbitrator is not a lawyer, he can still adopt course (i), but will wish to consult the parties about that, and offer them a choice between (ii), (iii) and (iv). Whether he is sitting with a legal assessor or obtaining written advice he can if he wishes simply appoint a lawyer of his own choice, but the better practice is to tell the parties whom he has in mind to nominate, and invite their comments. If the parties themselves agree upon a named lawyer, the arbitrator is not bound to accept their nomination but will wish to give it careful consideration. Some 7–51

[86] See para. 7–18 above.
[87] *cf.* the position under the 1996 Act, discussed in paras 2–508 *et seq.*, above.

agricultural arbitrators simply instruct their own solicitor, who may or may not be an expert in the field, without giving the parties the chance to comment on the choice, but this practice can produce resentment and dissatisfaction. Legal assistance must be confined to the point of law upon which the arbitrator needs help, and a legal assessor who attends the hearing should not be permitted, in effect, to control it. The arbitrator must at all times preside over his own proceedings, but he may permit the legal assessor to enter into a limited dialogue with the parties' advocates. When legal advice is obtained from an assessor or in writing arbitrators ought normally to give the parties a reasonable opportunity to comment on the advice received.[88] The fees incurred in taking legal advice may, if reasonably incurred, be recovered from the parties as part of the arbitrator's disbursements.[89]

Stating a case

7–52 Paragraph 26 of Schedule 11 entitles the arbitrator at any stage in the proceedings, and requires him upon a direction given by the judge of the county court on the application made by either party, to state in the form of a special case for the opinion of the county court any question of law arising in the course of the arbitration, or any question as to his jurisdiction.[90] It is unusual for arbitrators to state a case without first consulting the parties, just as it is unusual for one party or the other to apply to the court without first consulting the arbitrator. The case stated procedure is essentially a collaborative exercise in which either the arbitrator or the parties or one of them will draft the case and put it in circulation for comment and agreement before it is signed by the arbitrator and submitted to the court. If this practice is not followed it can lead to problems later, for example if one party persuades the court that the question raised in the case is not the real question, or the only question, so that after argument the judge has to send the case back to the arbitrator for further consideration.

7–53 There is no special mystery in the drafting of a case. In *Camden London Borough v. Civil Aviation Authority*,[91] Megaw L.J. said:

> "It would certainly have very great advantages in saving time and money for all concerned if it were possible that the true questions of law which it is sought to bring before this court could be defined with reasonable precision in the case stated for the consideration of this court. It should, I think, be for the intended appellant to formulate with precision the question or questions of law which he regards as arising in the decision of the tribunal or which he wishes to contend have been wrongly decided. It would then

[88] Under s.37(1)(b) of the Arbitration Act 1996 the parties have this opportunity as of right.
[89] See para. 7–24 above.
[90] As to questions of jurisdiction see paras. 7–30—7–32 above.
[91] (1980) 257 *Estates Gazette* 273 at 277: case stated by the Lands Tribunal in a rating case.

be for the tribunal to consider whether or not that question or those questions is or are properly formulated as a question or questions of law and whether or not it or they can properly be said to arise in the tribunal's decision.''

The case will carry the heading of the arbitration and be entitled ''Case Stated by AB, Arbitrator, for the opinion of the court.'' Cases are normally divided into the following sections: 7–54

(i) the arbitrator introduces himself, the parties and the tenancy agreement, states the nature of the dispute which has arisen between them, and gives the particulars of his appointment;
(ii) the arbitrator sets out all relevant facts which have been agreed between the parties or have been found by him after hearing evidence which are relevant to the point of law upon which the court is being consulted;
(iii) the arbitrator records in summary form the rival submissions of the parties on the point of law in dispute; and
(iv) the arbitrator then formulates the point of law upon which the court's assistance is required usually by asking the court to indicate which of the rival contentions is in its opinion correct.

The parties may be expected to participate in particular in drafting sections (iii) and (iv) (see the remarks of Megaw L.J. above); but if the arbitrator cannot secure agreement he will then have to settle the wording of the case himself because it is ultimately signed by him and it is his document. The procedure in court is laid down in the County Court Rules 1981, Ord. 44, rr. 1 and 2.

The arbitrator may also have to decide, when a question of law arises, at what stage in the proceedings it should be decided. The power to make interim awards under the 1986 Act may be limited to the awarding of a payment on account of a sum which will finally be awarded.[92] It is however the fact that some points of law are of such importance that they will determine the whole case. The case stated procedure in particular is sufficiently flexible to enable arbitrators to follow that particular route before large sums of money are incurred investigating issues which might on one view never arise, and arbitrators should consult the parties on the timing as well as the method of getting points of law decided for this reason. 7–55

Date and place of hearing

Under the 1986 Act arbitrators have to balance the right of the parties to be given a fair opportunity to present their case within a reasonable timescale against the 7–56

[92] See Sched.11, para. 15 and paras. 7–69—7–71 below.

requirement of paragraph 14 of Schedule 11 that unless his time is extended by the President the arbitrator must deliver his award within 56 days of his appointment. Apart from some cases involving notices to quit, there are in truth few 1986 Act arbitrations which have to be treated with special urgency, and if the arbitrator were to ask the President for an extension of time on the ground that the parties needed more time to prepare their cases the application is hardly likely to be refused.[93]

Adjournments

7–57 The circumstances in which arbitrators should accede to requests for an adjournment are discussed in Part 2 of this Handbook, paragraph 2–450. The case of *Thomas v. Official Solicitor*[94] which is referred to arose under the 1986 Act.

The Farm Inspection: The Arbitrator's Knowledge and Experience

7–58 In most 1986 Act arbitrations the arbitrator's inspection of the holding is an important event. An inspection is not however necessary in every case, and it should not be treated as automatic. The object of an inspection is primarily to enable the arbitrator to understand the evidence, and it is generally advisable to delay the inspection until a date relatively close to the hearing when the arbitrator has read the statements of case, the parties' witness statements and the expert reports. There may sometimes be a special reason for an early inspection, for example because a state of affairs which is critical to one party's case is changing. Tenants faced with a notice to quit based upon a failure to comply with a notice to do work often make heroic attempts to put the matter right just before the hearing. Arbitrators should be sympathetic to genuine requests of this kind, but reserve the right to make a fuller inspection later.

7–59 To avoid any impression of unfairness the inspection should normally be unaccompanied. Sometimes arbitrators require assistance in locating particular features of holdings, and might need guidance from the farmer or one of his staff. The landlord should be told if that is going to happen, and be given the opportunity have a representative in attendance. Parties do not always appreciate

[93] See also the discussion in paras 7–67 and 7–68 below.
[94] (1982) 265 *Estates Gazette* 601.

that the sole object of the arbitrator's inspection is to inform himself of the subject-matter, and not to take evidence. It is less embarrassing if arbitrators warn parties against lobbying in advance rather than have to remonstrate with them when they meet.

Agricultural arbitrators are mostly appointed for their knowledge and experience of farming. Farms are large and complex pieces of property and expert arbitrators when they inspect will find out a lot more about the farmer and the landlord than has been referred to in the documents. Some of the things which they see may have a direct bearing upon the issues raised in the statements of case, although neither party has referred to them. Others may have an indirect bearing because they will indicate that the tenant is an efficient or inefficient farmer, or that the landlord is a responsible or neglectful owner. These impressions may reflect upon the parties' credibility when they come to give their evidence in due course. **7–60**

Arbitrators have to be clear in their minds how they are to deal with the impressions which they obtain on an inspection. There is a difference between happening to notice things which appear during the course of an inspection and making active investigations. Section 34(2)(g) of the Arbitration Act 1996 gives arbitrators under that Act a discretion to take the initiative in ascertaining facts themselves. 1986 Act arbitrators do not appear to have that power, although it has been noted that they do have a power under paragraph 8 of Schedule 11 to require the parties to assist them in various ways. In either case the guiding principles are the same. The arbitrator must confine his attention during his inspection to those matters which are relevant to the issues which he has to decide; and if he discovers on inspection anything which he thinks, in the light of his own experience, he ought to take into account because it is of direct or even indirect significance in the manner discussed above, it is his duty to disclose his observations to the parties for their comment, so that they have a fair opportunity to correct an impression which may be adverse to their case. This problem is discussed at length at paragraphs 2–284 to 2–293, above. If the arbitrator obtains apparently relevant information which for any reason he does not disclose, he must ignore it altogether. **7–61**

The Hearing

Order of events

Arbitrators under the 1986 Act normally follow the sequence of events which has become traditional in the courts, but they are not bound to do so. The **7–62** procedure which they select must be fair, guarantee that each party has a full opportunity to present its own case and to challenge the case advanced by the other side, and be designed to bring the hearing to a speedy and efficient conclusion. If the traditional pattern is followed, the arbitrator will decide which party should be treated as claimant and which as defendant. Normally this will be obvious: it will be the party which initiated the proceedings, although in some cases such as rent reviews there may be a genuine debate as to which party should go first. The party treated as claimant will make an opening statement and call its expert and lay witnesses whose written statements (if any) may now be treated as evidence in chief (as in court) without further examination by that party's advocate. Each of these witnesses will be cross-examined in turn by the advocate appearing on the other side. That party will then present its case and its witnesses will be examined, in like fashion. Each party will then sum up its case, the party which opened having the last word. Arbitrators may however wish to invite both parties to make opening statements, and to arrange the sequence of witnesses so that the witnesses on each side who are in direct conflict (especially experts) give their evidence the one following the other. The parties may in addition offer to submit skeleton arguments or lengthy written submissions; and if the arbitrator thinks that he would be helped if the parties were to reduce their cases (or parts of their cases) to writing he should ask them to do so.

Evidence on oath

7–63 Paragraph 9 of Schedule 11 entitles the arbitrator, if he thinks fit, to require witnesses to be examined on oath or affirmation, and he has the power to administer oaths or take affirmations. The procedure for taking evidence on oath is set out paragraphs 2–601 to 2–607, above. If the parties agree that it is not necessary to take evidence on oath or affirmation there should be no reason why the arbitrator should insist upon it.

Rules of evidence

7–64 Schedule 11 does not contain a provision equivalent to section 34(2)(f) of the Arbitration Act 1996, which gives the arbitrator a discretion "whether to apply strict rules of evidence (or any other rules) as to the admissibility, relevance or weight of any material" submitted.[95] Arbitrators in 1986 Act arbitrations are, it would appear, bound to follow the rules of evidence applicable to civil proceedings in court. In practice, since the virtual abolition of the hearsay rule by the Civil Evidence Act 1995, 1986 Act arbitrators will be concerned with a limited number of evidential problems. First, they should seek to confine evidence to that which is logically probative of the matters in issue, and exclude irrelevant

[95] See the discussion at paras 2–488 *et seq.*, above.

or purely prejudicial material.[96] Secondly, they should exclude evidence which is privileged, for example because it relates to a settlement of negotiations,[97] or consists of private communications between one of the parties and its lawyers. The weight to be attached to any evidence is then a matter for the arbitrator to decide; and the quality and manner of its proof will simply be one of the factors to be taken into account when deciding how much weight it should carry.

Experts as advocates

One of the features of agricultural arbitrations is that a party's case will often be presented in full by one professional agent, usually a rural practice surveyor, who will perform the functions of both advocate and expert witness. Many agents dislike this dual role, and recommend whenever they can that a lawyer is also employed, so that they can concentrate on the task of giving evidence. But in many cases it does not make economic sense to employ more than one professional, and great tact and discretion is called for in discharging both roles. Expert witnesses are expected and bound to state their honest opinion independently and without bias in favour of their particular client.[98] Advocates however are entitled and expected to present their clients' cases as attractively and persuasively as they can, within the limits of the available evidence and other material. It is suggested that this potential conflict of roles can be reduced if not avoided if the professional first considers what evidence he can honestly and properly put before the arbitrator as a witness, ignoring the role of advocate; and then considers how the issues in the case can be presented around that central core. Evidence which appears to spring from the exigencies of advocacy is liable to be easily detected and discounted by the arbitrator. **7–65**

Events after the hearing

After the hearing the arbitrator will assemble all the material which has been put before him, and start work on deciding the various issues in the reference. The arbitration is still in progress and the powers conferred by paragraph 8 are still exercisable. Thus, if the arbitrator requires further assistance from the parties, for example in the form of written submissions, or confirmation of evidence, or even a further hearing, he has the power to call for it. If he wishes to carry out a further inspection of the holding or other property he may do so, but the guidelines suggested in paragraphs 7–58 to 7–61 above should still be followed; and it would be advisable to inform the parties of the action being taken. **7–66**

[96] See para. 2–489, above.
[97] See para. 7–29, above and paras 2–467 to 2–469 and 2–526 to 2–531, above.
[98] See the full discussion at paras 2–722 *et seq.*, above.

The Award

Time for the award

7–67 Paragraph 14 of Schedule 11 requires the arbitrator to make and sign his award within 56 days of his appointment, but the President "may from time to time enlarge the time limited for making the award, whether that time has expired or not". Thus an application for an extension of time can be made even after the initial period (or any subsequent extension of it) has run out. The right to apply for an extension of time is exercisable by arbitrators appointed by agreement as well as those appointed by the President. But paragraph 14 raises some unresolved legal problems. The President is given a discretion whether to allow an extension of time or not. A refusal is practically unheard-of, and it is not clear what factors the President might theoretically take into account in deciding not to allow the extension of time. Secondly, the legal consequences of a refusal of an extension of time are not made explicit. Up to this point in the proceedings there will have been a valid arbitration, and a refusal to extend time will not, it is submitted, amount to a revocation of the arbitrator's appointment under paragraph 4. Can the parties then start before a new arbitrator, or does the claim simply lapse through lack of an award? It is submitted that if the arbitrator runs out of time for delivering a valid award he should be regarded as "incapable of acting" under paragraph 2 of Schedule 11, so that the parties can then proceed to appoint a new arbitrator under that paragraph.

7–68 The other unresolved question is whether the parties themselves are entitled to make representations to the President in support of or in opposition to an application for an extension of time. Arbitrators normally tell the parties, as a matter of form, that they are making the application, but the parties should be aware of the need to make an application anyway, simply by consulting the calendar. There are many possible reasons why a party would wish the arbitration to be aborted, even if that simply leads to the appointment of another arbitrator under paragraph 2. It is submitted that there is no reason in principle why representations to the President should not be made, although it would be improper not to send copies of any letter to the President both to the arbitrator and to the other side. However the President is the only person capable of ensuring that this has happened.

Interim award

7–69 Paragraph 15 of Schedule 11 gives the arbitrator the power if he thinks fit to make an interim award "for the payment of any sum on account of the sum to be finally awarded". This provision may be contrasted with the previous section 14 of the Arbitration Act 1950, now replaced by section 47 of the Arbitration

Act 1996, under which the power to make interim awards is expressed quite generally; and the more restrictive terms of paragraph 15 might imply that, apart from ordering the payment of sums of money on account, a 1986 Act arbitrator has no power to make interim awards.

7–70 If this is the legal position, it places a 1986 Act arbitrator and the parties under a severe handicap. The power to make interim awards in arbitrations is a useful device which enables arbitrators in appropriate cases to clear important issues out of the way before the parties incur time, trouble and expense on other issues which, on one possible view of the case, might not ultimately arise. It is particularly invaluable when dealing with questions of costs. The parties can ask the arbitrator to make an award which is final on all matters except costs (and therefore by definition an interim award), and then argue questions of costs when the arbitrator has announced his decision on the substantive issues. More specifically, the ability of a party to protect itself against an adverse order for costs by writing a *Calderbank* letter[99] depends entirely upon an assumption that the arbitrator does have this power. Paragraph 14, which requires the arbitrator to make and sign "his award" within 56 days of his appointment (subject to extensions of time) seems to proceed on the assumption that, apart from paragraph 15, there will be one award. Paragraph 18 which stipulates that 'the award' shall fix a day not later than one month after the delivery of the award for the payment of any money awarded may be regarded as neutral. There would appear to be nothing to prevent the parties from conferring a power to make interim awards by agreement. But if the parties cannot agree the arbitrator would, it is submitted, be taking a considerable risk in not dealing with all matters, including interest and costs, in one single award, even though it may be anticipated that the courts would be sympathetic to an argument that a general power to make interim awards is to be implied. A party seeking to protect its position on costs might be better advised to use the "sealed offer" procedure (that is to make an offer to settle and deposit a copy in a sealed envelope with the arbitrator, to be opened by him when he has decided all issues except costs) rather than rely on a *Calderbank* letter.

7–71 The 56-day time limit in paragraph 14 will apply both to an interim award made under paragraph 15 (or otherwise) and to the final award in any given arbitration, subject to any possible extension of time under paragraph 14 (2).

Form of award

7–72 The form of the award must follow the form prescribed by the Agricultural Holdings (Form of Award in Arbitration Proceedings) Order 1990,[1] which requires the award to be made in the form set out in the Schedule to the Order "or in a form to the like effect, with such omissions or modifications as the

[99] See paras 2–529 and 2–822 to 2–836, above.
[1] S.I. 1990 No. 1472.

circumstances may require.'' The prescribed form is easy to follow and contains simple wording applicable as appropriate to all issues and types of claim likely to arise in 1986 Act arbitrations. Where there are several claims, paragraph 16 of Schedule 11 requires the arbitrator to state in his award the separate amounts awarded in respect of each claim and (on the application of either party) ''the amount awarded in respect of any particular improvement or any particular matter the subject of the award.'' Paragraph 18 of Schedule 11, as noted above, requires the arbitrator in his award to fix a day not later than one month after the delivery of the award for the payment of the money awarded as compensation, costs or otherwise. The ''Notes for the arbitrator'' which are appended to the 1990 Order contain helpful advice to the arbitrator on how to use the form, and emphasise that the award must be endorsed with the date of delivery so that there is no doubt as to the date upon which payments are to be made, the date from which interest runs.

Interest

7–73 The entitlement of a party to a 1986 Act arbitration who recovers a sum of money to interest on that sum is limited. Paragraph 22 of Schedule 11 provides that:

> ''Any sum directed to be paid by the award shall, unless the award otherwise directs, carry interest as from the date of the award and at the same rate as a judgment-debt.''

The rate of interest on judgment-debts is fixed by orders made from time to time under section 44 of the Administration of Justice Act 1970. The rate of interest specified in the order which is in force at the date of the award continues to apply, notwithstanding that some other rate has been substituted by a later order.[2] The discretion of the arbitrator is limited to the question of principle whether or not the award shall carry interest. He does not have a discretion to fix a rate of interest other than the rate applicable to judgment-debts.[3] More importantly 1986 Act arbitrations differ from litigation in court and arbitrations generally in that there is no discretion to award interest in respect of any earlier period, prior to the award, during which the principal debt has been outstanding.

Costs

7–74 Paragraph 23 of Schedule 11 gives the arbitrator a discretion to direct to and by whom and in what manner the costs or any part of the costs incidental to the

[2] See *Rocco Giuseppe & Figli v. Tradax Export* [1984] 1 W.L.R. 742, [1983] 3 All E.R. 598.
[3] *ibid.*

arbitration and the award shall be paid. Paragraph 25 gives some guidance as to how that discretion might be exercised by requiring the arbitrator to take into consideration:

> "(a) the reasonableness or unreasonableness of the claim of either party, whether in respect of an amount or otherwise,
> (b) any unreasonable demand for particulars or refusal to supply particulars, and
> (c) generally all the circumstances of case."

Under paragraph 25(2) the arbitrator is entitled to disallow the cost of any witness whom he considers to have been called unnecessarily and any other costs which he considers to have been unnecessarily incurred.

The general principle to be followed is that costs should "follow the event",[4] 7–75
although paragraph 25 confers sufficient discretion upon the arbitrator to enable him to depart from that general principle whenever the circumstances of the case dictate. In some 1986 Act arbitrations it will be clear what the "event" is. If the case involves the validity of a notice to quit, either it will be upheld or overruled, and the landlord or the tenant will be the winner. In other cases, particularly those involving the payment of compensation or the fixing of a rent on rent review, there will or may be no dispute on liability—some money is due or some adjustment in the rent is appropriate—and the only question is how much. In these cases the "event" may be much less obvious. This problem regularly arises in property arbitrations of all kinds, and is discussed in paragraphs 6–70 and 6–71 in Part 6 of this Handbook. The practice relating to orders for costs in cases in which a *Calderbank letter* has been written[5] is discussed in paragraphs 2–529 and 2–282 to 2–836 in Part 2 of this Handbook.

On the application of either party any costs ordered to be paid are taxable in 7–76
the county court according to the scales prescribed by the County Court Rules for proceedings in the county court. The arbitrator may determine the scale upon which the costs are to be paid. In the absence of any direction from the arbitrator, the scale will be determined by the county court.[6]

Date and delivery of award

Paragraph 14 of Schedule 11 requires the arbitrator to "make and sign" the 7–77
award within 56 days of appointment, and paragraph 18 requires him to fix a day not later than one month after the "delivery" of the award for the payment of money awarded. The form of award prescribed by the 1990 Order requires the arbitrator to sign and date the award in the presence of a witness, and to

4 Explicitly set out in s.61(2) of the Arbitration Act 1996.
5 Assuming that this procedure is available: see paras 7–69 to 7–71 above.
6 Sched.11, para. 24.

specify the date on which it was 'delivered' to the landlord and tenant respectively. The date upon which the award is signed sets time running for an application to the county court to challenge the award under paragraphs 27 or 28 of Schedule 11.[7] An award is "delivered" to the parties, it is submitted, when it is sent rather than received. If delivery means receiving rather than sending, it is difficult to see how the arbitrator can comply with the requirement to specify the date of delivery in the award itself. Because of the significance of the date of signature arbitrators should send their awards to the parties, that is "deliver" them, as soon as they have been signed.

Arbitrator's lien on the award

7–78 In the case of *Trustees of the Sloane Stanley Estate v. Barribal*[8] it was held in the county court that an arbitrator appointed by the President was not entitled to exercise the usual lien over the award with respect to his own costs, that is to say he could not refuse to deliver his award until one party or the other or both of them had paid his costs. It was pointed out that an arbitrator appointed by the President is under a statutory duty to make and deliver an award under the 1986 Act within stated time limits, and cannot impose conditions on the parties which would or might qualify the performance of his statutory duty. It is submitted that this decision is correct in so far as it applies to arbitrators appointed by the President, and may also be correct in so far as it applies to arbitrators appointed by agreement, unless they have agreed with the parties in advance that, as a condition of their appointment, they will not be required to deliver their award until their fees have been paid. The position under the 1986 Act may be contrasted with section 56 of the Arbitration Act 1996, which expressly entitles an arbitral tribunal to refuse to deliver an award except on full payment of fees and expenses.

Reasons for the award

7–79 Section 10 of the Tribunals and Inquiries Act 1992 requires an arbitrator to furnish a statement of reasons for the award if the landlord or the tenant so requests "on or before the giving or notification of the decision". It would appear that a request is made "on" the giving or notification of the decision even if there is some reasonable delay while the party who ultimately makes the request considers what its response should be.[9] If the request is made before notification of the decision, the reasons can be set out in an appendix to the award as indicated by the form prescribed by the 1990 Order. Otherwise they

[7] See para. 7–87 below.
[8] Reported on an altogether different point in the Court of Appeal in [1994] 2 E.G.L.R. 8.
[9] *Re Poyser & Mills' Arbitration* [1964] 2 Q.B. 467 and *Scott v. Scott* [1921] P. 107.

will of necessity have to be set out in a separate document which will carry the same heading as that of the arbitration and should, apart from the statement of reasons itself, recite the formal award, identify the party from whom the request for reasons was received, state the date of the request, and define the point or points upon which reasons were asked for. Guidance on the drafting of reasons for an award is contained in paragraphs 2–783 to 2–785 inclusive in Part 2 of the Handbook. A lengthy and elaborate statement of reasons is not required. In *Re Poyser & Mills' Arbitration*[10] Megaw J. said (at 478) that "the reasons that are set out must be reasons which will not only be intelligible, but which deal with the substantial points that have been raised". In *Guppy's Properties Ltd v. Knott (No.3)*[11] which concerned the adequacy of reasons given by a rent assessment committee under the Rent Acts, it was again held that reasons must be intelligible; that although they do not have to deal with every point raised, they must deal with the substantial points, showing what matters were taken into consideration and what view was reached on them; and in so far as the tribunal decided to rely on its own knowledge and experience it did not have to explain further how it reached its valuation. The first two of these principles is directly applicable to the giving of reasons in 1986 Act arbitrations. The third is subject to the somewhat different approach which is adopted towards the use by the arbitrator of his own knowledge and experience as discussed in paragraphs 7–58 to 7–61 above, but remains relevant.

Challenging the Award

Paragraph 19 of Schedule 11 provides that the award is final and binding on the parties and the persons claiming under them. Paragraph 20 entitles the arbitrator to correct in the award clerical mistakes or errors arising from an accidental slip or omission. There is no appeal from any decision on the facts of the case, and the scope for legal challenge is confined to two cases: misconduct and errors of law on the face of the award. 7–80

Misconduct

Under paragraph 27 of Schedule 11 where the arbitrator has misconducted himself the county court may remove him, or alternatively set the award aside. 7–81

[10] [1964] 2 Q.B. 467.
[11] [1981] 1 E.G.L.R. 85.

There is also a power to set the award aside if the arbitration or award has been improperly procured. The latter type of case is virtually unknown, although the jurisdiction to intervene in such cases has a long history in the Arbitration Acts. It appears to be concerned with cases where the arbitrator, at least, and one or possibly both of the parties, is the innocent victim of another's improper conduct. In practice the jurisdiction under paragraph 27 is only exercised in cases where "misconduct" is alleged.

7–82 The concept of "misconduct" is also derived from the Arbitration Acts. In that context section 68 of the Arbitration Act 1996 has replaced the old concept of "misconduct" with "serious irregularity". The change may however be one of terminology rather than substance, and the definition of "serious irregularity" contained in section 68(2) of the 1996 Act gives a strong indication of what would also count as "misconduct" for the purposes of the 1986 Act.[12]

7–83 In *Bremer Handelsgesellschaft mbH v. Ets. Soules*[13] it was held that the High Court had power to remove an arbitrator for "misconduct" in three situations:

(a) where actual bias is proved;
(b) where the relationship between the arbitrator and the parties, or between the arbitrator and the subject matter of the dispute, is such as to create an evident risk that the arbitrator has been or will be incapable of acting impartially;
(c) where the conduct of the arbitrator has been such as to show that, quite apart from partiality he is, through lack of experience, expertise or diligence, incapable of conducting the reference in a manner which the parties are entitled to expect.

In property arbitrations misconduct may also arise if the arbitrator exceeds his terms of reference or fails to comply with them, in particular by failing to deal with one or more of the issues raised in the reference; or by failing to deal with it in the manner prescribed by the rules under which the arbitration is conducted. In a 1986 Act arbitration there may be technical misconduct if the arbitrator has failed to comply with the statutory requirements concerning the form and contents of the award. The arbitrator will also be guilty of misconduct if he has acted unfairly or failed to comply with the principles of natural justice, for example by carrying out his own investigations or taking into account the results of his own observations without giving the parties the opportunity to comment on these matters.[14]

[12] See paras 2–860 *et seq.*, above.
[13] [1985] 2 Lloyd's Rep. 199.
[14] See for example *Fox v. P.G. Wellfair Ltd* [1981] 2 Lloyd's Rep. 514, *Top Shop Estates Ltd v. Danino* [1985] 1 E.G.L.R. 9, *Zermalt Holdings S.A. v. Nu-Life Upholstery Repairs Ltd* [1985] 2 E.G.L.R. 14, *Control Securities plc v. Spencer* [1989] 1 E.G.L.R. 136, *Unit Four Cinemas Ltd v. Tosara Investment Ltd* [1993] 2 E.G.L.R. 29 and *Amego Litho Ltd v. Scanway Ltd* [1994] 1 E.G.L.R. 15.

Where the arbitrator has conducted himself in such a way that the parties might reasonably have lost confidence in his ability to act fairly, or in his expertise, it would be the normal practice to remove him. Where the misconduct is more technical, such as the failure to deliver an award in proper form or to include in the award a decision on all the matters in issue, it is more likely that the court will simply set the award aside or remit the award to the arbitrator for reconsideration under paragraph 28(1). 7–84

Error on the face

The case stated procedure established by paragraph 26 of Schedule 11 is intended to operate as the main channel through which questions of law arising during the course of the proceedings will be dealt with by the courts. Once an award has been delivered there is no general right of appeal to the courts, even on a point of law. At that stage the arbitration is over and the power of the court to intervene is limited to cases where there is an error "on the face" of the award. This right of challenge will arise only if an error of law can be deduced from the terms of the award itself, and any reasons annexed to it, and any documents which become part of the award by being incorporated into it. 7–85

In the case of errors of law the court has the power to set the award aside under paragraph 27. In the alternative it may remit the award, or any relevant part of it, to the arbitrator for his consideration under paragraph 28(1). In the further alternative it may under paragraph 28(2) vary the award "by substituting for so much of it as is affected by the error such award as the court considers that it would have been proper for the arbitrator to make in circumstances". The award as varied will then have the same effect as if it had been made by the arbitrator. If an award is remitted to an arbitrator under paragraph 28(1) the arbitrator must, unless the order otherwise directs, make and sign his award within 35 days after the date of the order, but that time may be extended by the court under paragraph 28(4). 7–86

Procedure

The procedure to be followed in challenging an award under these provisions is laid down in the County Court Rules 1981, Ord. 44. The application is made by originating application, and all parties to the arbitration, other than the applicant, and the arbitrator must be made respondents: Ord. 44, r. 3(2). The application must be made within 21 days from the date of the award, but the court may extend that time under the general powers conferred by Ord. 13, r. 4. The date of the award for these purposes would appear to be the date upon which it is signed by the arbitrator, and not the date upon which it is delivered to the parties. 7–87

The importance of ensuring that the award is delivered as soon as possible after it has been signed has already been emphasised.[15]

Milk Quota Arbitrations

7–88 Milk quota arbitrations, just as 1986 Act arbitrations, are conducted under their own set of self-contained rules, currently set out (for England and Wales) in Schedule 2 to the Dairy Produce Quotas Regulations 1997 (''DPQR'').[16] The rules are closely modelled on those set out in Schedule 11 to the 1986 Act; and paragraph 35 of Schedule 2 provides that the Arbitration Act 1996 shall not apply to an arbitration determined in accordance with that Schedule.

7–89 The disputes which DPQR arbitrators may be called upon to determine are highly technical. Given the currently high values which are attached to milk quota in the market, large sums of money are likely to depend upon them. The disputes referred to arbitration under the DPQR are:

(i) the apportionment of a quota or special quota relating to a holding where there is a transfer of part of a holding (regulation 8);
(ii) the prospective apportionment of quota submitted to the Intervention Board which the occupier has requested to be ascertained by arbitration (regulation 9(1)(b));
(iii) the apportionment or prospective apportionment of quota required by the Intervention Board where it is dissatisfied with information provided by a person applying for registration of a transfer of part of a quota (regulation 10); and
(iv) the apportionment of quota requested by a producer occupying part of a holding whose quota has been confiscated and who wishes it to be restored (regulation 32(5)(b)(iii)).

Basis of apportionment

7–90 The arbitrator is required by paragraph 3 of DPQR Schedule 2 to base his award on findings made by him as to areas used for milk production in the last five years preceding the relevant change of occupation or (in the case of a prospect-

[15] See para. 7–77 above.
[16] S.I. 1997 No. 733. In Scotland these matters are resolved by the Scottish Land Court under Sched.3, and in Northern Ireland by arbitration under Sched.4.

ive apportionment) preceding his appointment as arbitrator. Under regulation 32 the relevant period is the last five-year period during which production took place.[17] For the most part this requires a painstaking review of the history of the farming of the holding, and arbitrators will need to maintain a firm grip on the presentation of documentary and oral evidence: see paragraphs 7–41 to 7–46 above.

Multi-party proceedings

A disputed apportionment may affect persons who have an interest in the holding, or part of it, other than the transferor and transferee themselves. The interest of the Intervention Board has also been referred to in paragraph 7–89 above. The rules provide for the addition of those parties as parties to the proceedings. See paragraph 7–95, below. **7–91**

Appointment of arbitrator

DPQR arbitrators are appointed by agreement or by the President of the RICS in the same manner as 1986 Act arbitrators. The President must appoint a member of the panel drawn up by the Lord Chancellor for the purposes of Schedule 11 of the 1986 Act.[18] If the holding is in Wales and any party to the arbitration so requires, the arbitrator must possess a knowledge of the Welsh language.[19] **7–92**

In the case of a simple transfer under regulation 7(1) the parties have 28 days from the date of change of occupation in which to agree upon an appointment, and the transferee must notify the Intervention Board of the appointment within 14 days of the date of appointment.[20] The transferor or transferee may also, during the same period, apply to the President, and must give notice of that fact to the Intervention Board within 14 days of the date of application.[21] The Intervention Board itself may also apply to the President for an appointment where (i) the transferor and transferee have failed to appoint or apply for an appointment within the 28-day period[22] or (ii) it initiates a reference itself under regulation 10.[23] In the latter case the Board itself becomes a party to the reference. Appointments made for the purpose of regulation 32 are made by agree- **7–93**

[17] As to the manner in which the apportionment is made see *Pucknowle Farms Ltd v. Kane* [1985] 3 All E.R. 790 and Cardwell, *Milk Quotas* (Clarendon Press, 1996), pp. 122–128.
[18] Sched.2, paras 1(2) and 8.
[19] Sched.2, para. 7.
[20] Sched.2, para. 1(1). As to the date of appointment, see para. 22 above.
[21] Sched.2, para. 1(2).
[22] Sched.2, para. 1(3).
[23] Sched.2, para. 1(4).

ment between the producer and all other persons interested in the holding or by the President on an application made by the producer.[24]

Other formalities

7–94 The other formalities surrounding the appointment of the arbitrator, and the procedure for his replacement in certain circumstances, mirror those applicable to 1986 Act arbitrators discussed in the earlier part of this Part.[25] Applications to the President to appoint are invalid unless they are accompanied by the fee prescribed under the 1986 Act.[26] Where it is paid by the Intervention Board it can be recovered from the other parties.[27] The President must appoint as soon as possible after receiving the application.[28] If the arbitrator dies or is incapable of acting or for seven days after notice from either party fails to act a new arbitrator may be appointed.[29] No party can revoke the arbitrator's appointment without the other party's agreement, and the appointment is not revoked by the death of any party.[30] Every appointment, application, notice, revocation, and consent must be in writing.[31]

Action on appointment: joinder of parties

7–95 The guidance on the action to be taken by 1986 Act arbitrators on appointment set out in paragraphs 7–27 to 7–29 above is applicable to DPQR arbitrations. In addition the DPQR arbitrator has to consider whether to exercise his discretion under paragraph 13 of Schedule 2, described as ''absolute'', whether to join as a party to the arbitration any person having an interest in the holding, whether or not that person has applied to be joined, save that no person can be joined without their consent. Persons having an interest in the holding will include mortgagees, landlords, tenants and sub-tenants.[32] The exercise of this discretion carries important responsibilities, because there does not seem to be any remedy available to a third party who is excluded from the apportionment process but is adversely affected by its result. A party who has knowledge of the arbitration and is aggrieved by a decision to exclude him might be entitled to challenge the decision by way of judicial review in the High Court. The more difficult case is that of the third party whose existence is unknown to or concealed from the arbitrator. The best which the arbitrator can do is question the parties on appoint-

[24] Sched.2, para. 1(5).
[25] See paras 7–18 *et seq.*, above.
[26] Sched.2, para. 4.
[27] Sched.2, para. 5.
[28] Sched.2, para. 6.
[29] Sched.2, para. 9.
[30] Sched.2, para. 10.
[31] Sched.2, para. 11.
[32] See the discussion in Cardwell, *op.cit*,. pp. 128–133.

ment whether there are any parties who to their knowledge have any interest in the holding or any part of it whether as mortgagee, co-owner, landlord, tenant, sub-tenant or otherwise, and act on such information as he can obtain.

Any person who refuses to sign a statement under regulation 32(5) agreeing to an apportionment for the purposes of the restoration of quota to the register must be joined as a party.[33] **7–96**

Remuneration and powers of the arbitrator, procedure and supervision by the court

In all other respects the rules for the remuneration of the arbitrator and all other procedural matters follow the rules set out in Schedule 11 to the 1986 Act, already discussed in this Part of the Handbook. Table 3 shows the correspondence between the two sets of rules and refers the reader to the relevant parts of the preceding text. No form of award is prescribed. **7–97**

TABLE 3

Correspondence between rules for milk quota and 1986 Act arbitrations

	DPQR Sched.2, para.	**AHA 1986 Sched.11, para.**	**Discussion in text above, para. 7–**
Date of appointment	33	31	22
Remuneration of arbitrator	12	6	24–26
Conduct of proceedings: statements of case, etc.	14	7	34–39
Obligations of parties and powers of arbitrator	15	8	33,40–45
Examination of witnesses on oath	17	9	63
Witness summonses, etc.	18–21	10–13	46–47
Time for award and extension of time	22	14	67–68

[33] Sched.2, para. 13(2).

	DPQR Sched.2, para.	AHA 1986 Sched.11, para.	Discussion in text above, para. 7–
Award final and binding	23	19	80
Correction of errors	24	20	80
Reasons for award	25	21	79
Costs	26–28	23–25	74–76
Special case	29	26	52–55
Misconduct and error on the face of the award	30–32	27–28	81–87

1995 Act Arbitrations

7–98 Disputes arising between the parties to farm business tenancies to which the Agricultural Tenancies Act 1995 applies are (with certain exceptions) required to be resolved by arbitration. The application of the Arbitration Act 1996 to these arbitrations has not been excluded. It follows that its provisions apply so far as they are consistent with the 1995 Act.[34]

7–99 Most agricultural arbitrators will have learned their craft under the Agricultural Holdings Acts 1948–1986. Although many of the basic principles of fairness, and the methods for running the proceedings efficiently and economically, which have been discussed earlier in this Part of this Handbook will be as much applicable to arbitrations conducted under the 1995 Act as they are to 1986 Act and DPQR arbitrations, in other important respects 1995 Act arbitrators will be able to take advantage of the much wider powers given to them under the Arbitration Act 1996; and Part 2 of this Handbook is directly applicable to 1995 Act arbitrations. In paragraph 7–106 below the main practical differences for arbitrators specialising in this field are summarised. Indeed, a comparison

[34] Arbitration Act 1996, ss.94–98, see in particular s.94(2).

between the 1986 Act and 1995 Act procedures provides a vivid illustration of the changes in the law which the Arbitration Act 1996 has brought about.

Framework

The 1995 Act identifies three specific classes of dispute which are referred to arbitration, and has general dispute-resolution provisions in addition. The specific cases are: 7–100

(1) rent review under section 9;[35]
(2) the refusal or failure of the landlord to give consent to a proposed improvement under section 17;[36] and
(3) the settlement of a tenant's claim on quitting for compensation for improvements under section 16.[37]

Section 28 of the Act then provides generally that, apart from the specific cases, any dispute arising between landlord and tenant concerning their rights or obligations under the Act, under the terms of the tenancy or under any custom shall be determined by arbitration under section 28. Any matter required by the Act to be determined by arbitration is to be determined by a sole arbitrator.[38]

Section 28 is qualified by section 29, which does not apply to the three specific cases. Section 29 provides for the case where the tenancy agreement itself contains a provision for the resolution of disputes by a third person other than the landlord or tenant or a person appointed by one of them without the consent or concurrence of the other. In such a case, where both parties have jointly referred the dispute to that person, or one of them has, and has notified the other, and the latter has not required a reference to arbitration under section 28 within four weeks of receiving the notice, the dispute may be resolved by that person, provided that the relevant term of the tenancy enables the third person to give a decision which is binding in law on both parties. Section 29 clearly allows a decision to be made by an expert instead of an arbitrator. 7–101

Initiating a 1995 Act arbitration

1995 Act arbitrators are appointed by agreement or, if there is no agreement, by the President of the RICS. Table 4 sets out the procedural steps which lead to an appointment in each case. 7–102

[35] See 1995 Act, s.10(1).
[36] 1995 Act, s.19(1).
[37] 1995 Act, s.22.
[38] 1995 Act, s.30(1).

TABLE 4

Procedure for appointing a 1995 Act arbitrator

Section	Dispute	Procedure
9–14	Rent review	(i) L or T gives at least 12 but less than 24 months' notice requesting a review, expiring on a "review date" (section 10). (ii) Parties may at any time agree to appoint an arbitrator (or other person) to determine the rent (section 12). (iii) If no such appointment, either party may apply during six month period before review date to the President for appointment of arbitrator (section 12).
17–18	L's consent to improvements	(i) T makes written request for consent. (ii) L refuses consent *or* fails to give it within two months *or* requires as condition of consent variation in tenancy not acceptable to T. (iii) Parties appoint arbitrator by agreement. (iv) If no agreement L or T applies to President to appoint (section 19).
16, 20–21	Compensation for improvements at end of tenancy	(i) T gives notice of intention to claim not less than two months after end of tenancy (section 22(2)). (ii) Parties settle claim or appoint arbitrator. (iii) If no agreement or appointment after four months from end of tenancy L or T applies to the President to appoint (section 22(3)).

Section	Dispute	Procedure
28	All other disputes	(i) L or T gives written notice that a dispute has arisen. (ii) Notice states that unless arbitrator is appointed by parties within two months application will be made to the President (section 28(2)). (iii) If no appointment after two months L or T applies to the President (section 28(3)).

Appointments by the President

In paragraph 7–18 above it was pointed out that the parties should give careful consideration to the particular qualifications they require in an arbitrator, and make an appointment by agreement if that is at all possible. That comment holds good for 1995 Act arbitrations; but parties can also be more prescriptive in their application to the President, because he is not bound under the 1995 Act (as he is under the 1986 Act or the DPQR) to appoint a member of the Lord Chancellor's panel. Any application to the President must be made in writing and must be accompanied by such reasonable fee as the President determines in respect of the costs of making the appointment.[39] The President is not expressly obliged to appoint "as soon as possible",[40] although some such obligation may be implied. **7–103**

Revocation of authority and appointment of new arbitrator

Where a 1995 Act arbitrator dies or is incapable of acting and no new arbitrator is appointed by agreement, either party may apply to the President to appoint a new arbitrator.[41] The special procedure for giving sevens days' notice requiring an arbitrator to act, or be replaced,[42] is not available under the 1995 Act. Sections 23–25 of the Arbitration Act 1996 apply to the revocation, removal and resignation of 1995 Act arbitrators: see the discussion in Part 2 of this Handbook, paragraphs 2–178 *et seq.*, above. Unless otherwise agreed by the parties, the death of the person (or presumably one of the persons) by whom an arbitrator was appointed does not revoke his authority.[43] **7–104**

[39] 1995 Act, s.30(2).
[40] *cf.* paras. 7–19 and 7–94 above.
[41] 1995 Act, s.30(3).
[42] *cf.* paras. 7–23 and 7–94 above.
[43] Arbitration Act 1996, s.26(2).

Remuneration of 1995 Act arbitrators

7–105 The remuneration of 1995 Act arbitrators is governed by section 28 of the 1996 Act, and is discussed in Part 2 of this Handbook, paragraphs 2–230 *et seq.*; see also paragraphs 7–24 *et seq.*, above.

Action on appointment, conduct of proceedings, and supervision by the Court

7–106 It has been emphasised[44] that 1995 Act arbitrators enjoy much greater freedom of action than those appointed under the 1986 Act or the DPQR. In the conduct of references under the 1995 Act they should not feel bound to take the no-doubt tried and tested procedures of the 1986 Act as their starting-point and then consider what modifications to those procedures might be desirable. They should start with a fresh approach. The following main differences in practice and procedure should be noted. All these matters are discussed in detail in Part 2 of this Handbook. Paragraphs marked with an asterisk indicate that the procedures referred to may be overridden by agreement between the parties.

- **Powers and duties of the arbitrator and the parties.** In addition to the duty to act fairly and impartially the arbitrator is bound to adopt procedures suitable to the case which avoid unnecessary expense and delay (1996 Act, section 33) and the parties are bound to co-operate (section 40).
- **Procedural and evidential matters.** The arbitrator decides all such matters, subject to the right of the parties to agree any matter (section 34(1)) and has a general power to give directions (section 34(3)).*
- **Enforcement of arbitrator's orders.** The arbitrator (section 41) and the court (section 42) have extensive powers to enforce orders made by the arbitrator.
- **Statements of case.** There is no statutory requirement for the delivery of statements of case, much less a timetable laid down for their delivery. It is for the arbitrator to decide what form of written statements of case should be used, when they should be supplied and when amended (section 34(2)(c)).*
- **Documents.** The arbitrator decides whether any and if so what classes of documents should be disclosed between and produced by the parties and at what stage (section 34(2)(d)).*
- **Power to initiate investigations, or to appoint experts or legal advisers.** The arbitrator may decide whether and to what extent he should take the initiative in ascertaining the facts and law (section

[44] See para. 7–99 above.

34(2)(g))* and may appoint an expert or legal adviser to report to him and the parties (s.37).* The exercise of this power is subject to the overriding principle of natural justice that the parties must be given a fair opportunity to comment on the outcome of any investigations. In relation to the inspection of property the discussion in paragraphs 7–58 to 7–61 above remains relevant.

- **The need for a hearing.** The arbitrator not only decides when and where any part of the proceedings is to be held (section 34(2)(a)), but also whether and to what extent there should be oral or written evidence or submissions (section 34(2)(h)). He may also decide whether and if so what questions should be put to and answered by the parties and when and in what form (section 34(2)(c)).*
- **Rules of evidence.** The arbitrator may decide whether or not to apply "strict rules of evidence" and the manner in which any matter is to be proved (section 34(2)(f)).*
- **Reference of questions of law and jurisdiction to the court.** The case stated procedure is unavailable. The supervisory powers of the court in respect of matters of law and jurisdiction are discussed in Part 2 of this Handbook, paragraphs 2–216 *et seq.* and 2–851 *et seq.*
- **Time for delivery of award.** There is no statutory time-limit for the delivery of an award. If a timetable is agreed between the parties the court may extend time (section 50).
- **Interim award.** There is a general power to make interim awards (section 47). Among other things this is important in the context of *Calderbank* letters (see paras. 7–70 and 7–74, above).
- **Form of award.** There is no statutory requirement as to the form of the award, save that it must be signed, dated and state the "seat" of the arbitration (section 52). Guidance on drafting an award is contained in Part 2 of this Handbook, at paragraphs 2–775 *et seq.*
- **Reasons for award.** The award must contain the reasons for the award unless it is an agreed award or the parties have agreed to dispense with reasons (section 52(4)).*
- **Interest on sums awarded.** The arbitrator has a discretion to award simple or compound interest on any amount awarded in respect of any period up to the date of the award or, if the sum was outstanding when the proceedings started but was paid subsequently, the date of payment (section 49).*
- **Lien on award.** The arbitrator may refuse to deliver an award until all his fees and expenses have been paid (section 56).
- **Challenging an award.** An award may be challenged on the ground that the arbitrator lacked substantive jurisdiction (section 67) or that there has been a "serious irregularity" affecting the arbitrator, the proceedings or the award (section 68). There is a highly restricted right to appeal to the court (with leave) against an award on a point of law (section 69).

Challenges of the type available under the 1986 Act for misconduct or error on the face are inapplicable.

Other Agricultural Property Disputes

7–107 The other types of agricultural property dispute which are described in paragraph 7–10 are referred to arbitration outside the framework of the 1986 or 1995 Acts or the DPQR, and are governed by the 1996 Act, subject only to such procedures as may be agreed between the parties or set out in the instrument which establishes the right to arbitrate.

Part 8

DOCUMENTS-ONLY ARBITRATIONS IN CONSUMER DISPUTES

By Margaret Rutherford, Q.C., LL.B., F.C.I. Arb.

Past Chairman of the Chartered Institute of Arbitrators

Consumer Law and the Impact of the Arbitration Act

Consumer law, relating to the provision of goods or services, with its impact on economic and social development, affects all those involved "in the market place" and is of enormously wide application. In England, there is a mass of legislative provisions relating to consumer protection. However, the only one directly relevant to arbitration was the Consumer Arbitration Agreements Act 1988 (the 1988 Act) which was repealed in its entirely by the 1996 Act (Schedule 4). The 1988 Act was passed in order to correct what was perceived to be unfairness to consumers because of the incorporation of arbitration clauses into many traders' standard conditions. Essentially, it stated that an arbitration agreement between a person acting as a consumer and a supplier of goods or services would not be binding on the consumer provided that the sum in dispute did not exceed the limit for claims in the County Court. If, after the dispute arose, he chose to avail himself of arbitration, say under the ABTA Scheme, then once he agreed to have the dispute resolved by this method he effectively relinquished his right to litigate. 8–01

Relationship of the 1988 Act to other legislation

The 1988 Act contained several cross-references to other legislation, in particular the Unfair Contract Terms Act 1977. Neither Act was as well-drafted and comprehensible as the present Act. For example, it was unclear whether the 1988 Act covered contracts for building works or applied to contracts which had been let by competitive tender. In July 1995 the position was further complicated by the coming into force of the Unfair Terms in Consumer Contracts Regulations 1994 (S.I. 1994 No. 3159). These were introduced in compliance with Directive 93/13. It is inappropriate to go into details of the Regulations here. Suffice to say that an arbitration clause in a trader's terms is deemed unfair and therefore unenforceable against a consumer. A consumer is defined in the Regulations as "a natural person who, in making a contract to which these Regulations apply, is acting for purposes outside his business". The Regulations apply "to any term in a contract concluded between a seller or supplier and a consumer where the said term has not been individually negotiated". 8–02

The 1988 Act now repealed

8–03 Sections 89, 90 and 91 of the 1996 Act now, with certain necessary limitations, simply make arbitration clauses in consumer contracts unenforceable against the consumer by reference to the Regulations. The effect is basically the same as what had been intended by the 1988 Act but expressed in simpler, more easily understood terms, and with wider application. The definition of "arbitration agreement" is essentially the general definition contained in section 6(1). Section 89(2) provides that the term "the Regulations" includes any regulations amending or replacing them in the future. Section 89(3) states that sections 90 and 91 apply "whatever the law applicable to the arbitration agreement", in short, the protection is extended to consumers wherever they may be and whatever law applies to the agreement. This means that not only consumers in the European Union but in any country are given the same protection as United Kingdom citizens if an arbitration agreement is sought to be enforced against them in the United Kingdom. It matters not that the arbitration agreement may not be governed by our law.

Definition of "consumer"

8–04 The Regulations define a consumer as "a natural person." (see above). Section 90 states that a "natural person" for these purposes includes a "legal person" and thus could include a firm or company provided that it is acting "for purposes outside [its] business". Section 91 states that an arbitration agreement is unfair where a modest amount is sought. As to what is that monetary limit, this will be specified by order. It is thought likely to be the equivalent of the limit of claims in the County Court.

8–05 So, in a nutshell, if a consumer has contracted, say, to buy goods, and would be taken by surprise to discover later, when a problem concerning those goods arose, that the contract included an arbitration clause of which he would probably have no knowledge, not having had his attention drawn to the "small print", such arbitration clause in a contract for the supply of goods and services will be unenforceable against him provided his claim does not exceed the limit set down. If a supplier tries to obtain a stay of litigation started by the consumer his application will not be entertained by the court. On the other hand, should the consumer wish to avail himself of arbitration as a means by which his dispute might be resolved, he may of course do so.

Consumer disputes

8–06 There are some 360 million consumers within the single European market, and billions more in the rest of the world, who daily make transactions dealing with the provision of goods and services by manufacturers, retailers and commercial providers. Such contracts are as vulnerable to disputes as any other, and these must, in the interests of justice, be resolved. One of the five "categories of fundamental rights" of consumers is "the right to proper redress for . . . injury or damage by means of swift, effective and inexpensive procedures", (EC Resolution, April 14, 1976 [Preliminary Programme of the EEC for a Consumer Protection and Information Policy]). Thus consumers need fair, expeditious, effective and economic means by which to resolve disputes if there is a failure between the parties to reach a settlement.

Consumer Protection in England

Consumer protection is an important and ever-growing aspect of modern society. **8–07**
In the second half of the twentieth century a burgeoning of new law and practice affording safeguards to consumers began to emerge, particularly in Europe and America. This groundswell of consumer protection resulted from new business methods and changing social attitudes. For example, the Council of the European Communities issued a Directive in 1985 (Directive 85/37A) requiring Member States to implement a regime of strict liability for certain damage caused by defective products. The United Kingdom government responded by enacting the Consumer Protection Act, 1987, which is limited to United Kingdom territory. ("Product" is a wide term, including any goods or electricity, or goods comprised in another product or as a component or raw material, while "goods" includes substances, growing crops, things comprised in land by being attached to it, and any ship, aircraft or vehicle. The potential scope for liability is enormous, and complete insurance cover frequently unobtainable. Potential defendants include the manufacturer/producer, an importer into the E.U. and an "own brander").

Effective enforcement procedures

Inextricably linked to the question of rights is the provision of effective and **8–08**
economically viable procedures by which to enforce them and thus the resolution of disputes has been more urgently focused over the recent years. In the United Kingdom a surge of consumer protection legislation was passed in the 1960s and 1970s. In particular, the position of Director General of Fair Trading was created, with very extensive powers. Amongst other things he was put under a statutory duty to encourage relevant trade associations to prepare and dissemin-

ate to their members codes of practice. These are guidance documents whose function it is to safeguard and promote the interests of consumers by setting out minimum standards with which the various association members should comply. Over the intervening years many trade associations have done so and such voluntary or self-regulating codes have effectively improved standards. However, to give them "teeth", codes also set out complaints procedures whereby disgruntled customers can invoke resolution of their grievances. In such a case provision is often made for an arbitration procedure as an alternative to litigation. The costs of litigation (especially the possibility of being ordered to pay the defendant's costs, which cannot be ascertained in advance), the delays involved and the ordeal of a public hearing can combine to make litigation a worrying and possibly expensive matter for a consumer who may have a legitimate complaint against, for example, a travel agent. The Small Claims procedure in the County Court, whilst of benefit to the consumer, had a low financial limit. It is now up to £3,000. However, these days consumer disputes can involve considerably more than this sum, for example, it would not be uncommon to have a family holiday costing several thousand pounds. The objective of the alternative procedure is to reduce, possibly to eliminate, such objections.

Consumer Protection outside England

8–09 The United States and Europe are ahead of the United Kingdom in recognising and dealing with consumer problems. A discussion paper (*Access of Consumers to Justice and the Settlement of Consumer Disputes in the Single Market*, Commission of the ECC (93)576), the theme of which was the access of consumers to justice and out of court settlement of consumer disputes, described (*inter alia*) the means of resolving disputes in Member States and across national frontiers. Systems are already developing in the direction of certain desirable common features, for example, defined limits of claim, simplified means of referral, simplified procedural formalities, screening of claims through preliminary advice and conciliation procedures, and so on. Certain areas of concern remain, including cost, the need for preliminary information, delay, formality, complexity of procedures and the intractable problem of how to deal effectively with transfrontier disputes. All States are striving for improved management, administration and simplified procedures.

Code of Practice Arbitrations

Many codes of practice promulgated over recent years of the kind described above in paragraph 8–08 provide very effective machinery for the speedy resolution of disputes by simplified low-cost arbitration procedures. As an arbitration hearing can, in some circumstances, prove more costly than a court hearing, it follows that a simple and inexpensive method is not only preferable but essential for the protection of the consumer. An important feature of some of these codes is the provision of preliminary conciliation and mediation facilities as a precursor to arbitration, should the process fail. Most code arbitrations are dealt with on documents only, or by site visits plus documentary evidence. For example, under the Association of British Travel Agents (ABTA) scheme the file may be made up of a booking form, invoice, brochure, photographs, representatives' reports, letters from hoteliers and other guests, the complaint form written at the resort, and so on. The scheme for the National Association of Retail Furnishers, for example, is on documents which also include a report by an independent expert written after a visit to the furniture concerned. Some schemes, for example the one for the Glass and Glazing Federation (GGF) concerning disputes over double glazing installations, have an express provision for the arbitrator to make a site inspection to view the installation for himself. The National House Building Council (NHBC) scheme is built round a visit to the house in question by an expert arbitrator and the reception of evidence, which can be written or oral. 8–10

Existing arbitration schemes

There are many goods and services, from photography to funerals, covered by codes of practice associated with the Office of Fair Trading and which offer arbitration schemes. The schemes may be set up by the trade association to deal with disputes between members and customers, for example ABTA or, where there is no trade association such as Personal Insurance Arbitration Service (PIAS), by those members of the insurance industry who subscribe to the scheme. There are in the United Kingdom over 60 such schemes run by the Chartered Institute of Arbitrators, which include those for the travel industry, including ABTA but also individual tour operators who do not belong to ABTA, such as Starvillas Ltd, Passenger Shipping Association, Saga Holidays; household and general services, such as the Association of Manufacturers of Domestic Electrical Appliances (AMDEA), GGF, Mail Order Traders Association; communication services such as British Rail (B.R.), British Telecommunications, the Post Office, Mercury Pagings; construction, such as Building Guarantee Scheme, NHBC; financial and insurance services, such as Consumer Credit Trade Association, FIMBRA, London Personal Finance Association; personal 8–11 insurance arbitration service (PIAS); commercial schemes, such as B.P. Oil, Esso, Shell U.K., Hartlepools Water Company; and professional bodies.

Disputes in the tourism industry

8–12 Tourism, to select one consumer service, is said to be the biggest growth industry in the European Union. The European Directive on Package Holidays, concerning strict safeguards for minimum standards for package holidays and rights to compensation for consumers when things go wrong, has been adopted by trade ministers. Not only are holiday firms liable for loss or damage suffered by the failure of all or any part of the holiday sold, but it is no longer incumbent on the consumer to establish negligence by the tour operator before compensation can be awarded. Potentially the number of claims arising in the European Union could be enormous. Whether they are resolved by litigation, ombudsmen, alternative methods of dispute resolution or arbitration remains to be seen.

Documents-only Arbitrations

8–13 We have seen above that there are numerous ''code'' arbitrations, (often administered by the Chartered Institute so that they are often referred to as ''administered'' arbitrations, or ''administered schemes''). We have seen that these are usually, but not always, dealt with on documentary evidence alone. For example, it will be recalled that under the NHBC scheme the arbitrator will make site visits to inspect property and may have short hearings as well as, or in substitution for, giving consideration to various documents.

8–14 There will also be occasions when a consumer may pursue arbitration which is neither administered nor a code arbitration. This might be ''arbitration'' in the county court (which is not covered by the Act and which is subject to a low financial limit) or more usually under an arbitration agreement either embodied in a contract or made after the dispute arose. In these latter cases, the arbitrator will be aware of his obligation ''to obtain the fair resolution of the dispute without unnecessary delay or expense'' (section 1) and his mandatory duty to ''adopt procedures suitable to the circumstances of the particular case, avoiding unnecessary delay or expense'' (section 33 (1)(b)). Similarly the parties will be made aware by the arbitrator of their corresponding mandatory duty under section 40(1) to ''do all things necessary for the proper and expeditious conduct of the arbitral proceedings''. In these cases it is very likely that the arbitrator will suggest that the arbitration will be conducted on documents-only, without the need for an oral hearing, (statement of case and defence setting out facts relied on, full history of the matter, brief reference to evidence relied on, propositions of law, reference to authorities, lists of documents, copies of relevant documents attached to statements, etc.) or on documents plus a short hearing after the arbitrator has considered the written evidence. It is possible to resolve such disputes fairly without necessarily requiring cross-examination of live witnesses (and in many cases the calling of witnesses, perhaps from overseas in the case of a travel claim, some months after a holiday has occurred, is totally impractical). By foregoing an oral hearing costs are saved, and various other advantages to the consumer (see below) arise.

Advantages of documents-only arbitration

The disadvantages associated with oral hearings (difficulties of bringing parties, witnesses, lawyers and arbitrator together at the same time; difficulties of oral evidence adduced many months after the happenings in question; time off work for the parties and their witnesses; cost; delay, etc.), mirror the positive advantages of a documents-only arbitration. These include the superiority in some cases of documentary evidence written at the relevant time, contract documents, letters of novation, etc., over direct oral evidence of what was/was not agreed or did/did not take place some time ago; no time off work for parties or witnesses; no "once and for all" opportunity to express their case; no sense of grievance that a valid claim was demolished by adroit cross-examination aimed not so much at the ascertainment of the justice of the case as to its presentation to the best advantage; no anxiety about a court appearance; the advantage to the party in cost, speed and convenience; the advantage to the parties of being able to set out their cases at length, and to return and amend them if necessary during the period of preparation; the advantage of saving costs by not necessarily having to instruct solicitors. The Act, in emphasising the autonomy of the parties by encouraging them to decide their own procedures—"The parties should be free to agree how their disputes are resolved . . ." (section 1(b))—provides default procedures which the parties can include, exclude or modify. Thus they could decide on a documents-only procedure (or documents plus a site visit/short hearing, etc.). **8–15**

Where documents-only procedure is inappropriate

Cases in which compensation is claimed for physical injury or illness, or involving complicated facts or difficult points of law, are inappropriate for resolution on documents only. Many arbitration schemes expressly exclude this kind of claim and leave them to be decided either by arbitration with a hearing or by litigation. **8–16**

The structure of code of practice schemes

8–17 A code of practice arbitration differs from an arbitration under a contractual clause in that the contract out of which the dispute arises does not impose a legal obligation to arbitrate. When the dispute arises, the consumer is at liberty to litigate if he or she so wishes.

8–18 A code arbitration is a "real" arbitration in the sense that it it is based on the agreement of the parties to use this method of dispute resolution, it is governed by the Act and the final award is enforceable by the courts, should the other side refuse to comply with it. It normally arises at the consumer's option, the trader or other party normally being obliged by the relevant trade body to agree. However, as we have seen, the consumer may opt to refer the matter to court. The consumer's potential liability to contribute to the costs of the arbitration is both limited and known in advance, and the parties bear their own costs. Although there are variations between the various schemes, yet there is a set procedure which the parties agree to accept at the time they agree to arbitration, and that procedure is both informal and simple. Another feature of consumer arbitration is that such arbitration schemes are usually part of a more general scheme for self-regulation within a particular trade or profession and therefore compliance with the award will be axiomatic.

8–19 A code of practice may also offer the consumer the choice between a formal arbitration, including a hearing, and a documents-only arbitration. In general, either party to an arbitration is entitled to an oral hearing unless he has agreed, expressly or by necessary implication or by the incorporation of rules, to dispense with one. The rules covering most consumer arbitrations usually exclude the right to an oral hearing . A typical clause might read:

> "You have full legal rights to take any further action you may wish. You may commence proceedings in the appropriate court. You may also choose to use instead the special low-cost arbitration scheme which we have arranged with the Chartered Institute of Arbitrators. This offers arbitration on documents alone, a simple, inexpensive method with restricted client liability costs, or arbitration with a normal attended hearing under the Rules of the London Court of Arbitration. The restricted liability for costs, however, would not apply in this case."

Consumer may elect to enter into an arbitration agreement

8–20 If the consumer then chooses to proceed with a code of practice arbitration he is required to do so in writing and thereby a written submission to arbitration will come into existence. The arbitration agreement can be enforced against him since he has agreed to submit his dispute to arbitration in writing after the dispute has arisen.

Most United Kingdom schemes administered by Chartered Institute of Arbitrators

Almost all the code of practice schemes mentioned above are administered by the Chartered Institute of Arbitrators. The arbitrator is not appointed by the parties themselves, although they agree, by utilising the scheme, to the method of his/her appointment. This is made by the President/Vice President of the Institute from a special panel of suitably qualified and experienced arbitrators. (And note the provisions of section 74 of the Act, which provides limited liability for arbitral institutions, the immunity extending to the function of appointment/nomination of arbitrators.) 8–21

The National Small Claims Arbitration Service administered by the Chartered Institute of Arbitrators, provides for the settling of disputes between subscribers to the Service and their customers where ordinary dispute procedures have failed to achieve a settlement. The entitlement of parties to take advantage of the Service will be specified in the relevant contractual documents and the relevant code of practice, if any. The Institute has also initiated and inaugurated a new Consumer Dispute Scheme which is a composite process, with a formalized conciliation stage prior to arbitration, designed, as all arbitration procedures should be, to save time and costs, reflecting the spirit of the Act. 8–22

Procedure in a Documents-only/Code Arbitration

Where a consumer has chosen to submit a dispute to arbitration, either under a code of practice scheme or otherwise, rather than pursuing his claim in a court, he has probably done so because of considerations of speed, economy, simplicity, privacy and convenience. Thus it is not surprising to discover that most code arbitrations provide for documents-only procedure and that this would be the procedure most commonly used to resolve such a dispute, (albeit sometimes with the addition, say, of a site visit). The documents usually consist of a joint application for arbitration in a prescribed form (*i.e.* by the code or the Chartered Institute of Arbitrators), signed by both parties; a claim form fully setting out the nature of the claim; points of defence from the respondent, setting out the nature of his answer to each allegation in the points of claim; such supporting documents as the parties think relevant, for example, the contract, the brochure, reports from local representatives, invoices, manufacturers' specifications, letters between the parties after the dispute arose, survey or other expert reports, letters 8–23 from other witnesses, photographs, plans, and so forth, depending on the nature of the dispute; and (possibly) comments by the claimant on the respondent's case as contained in the documents of the kind mentioned above.

8–24 In a documents-only arbitration which is neither administered nor under a scheme, it would be for the arbitrator to explain clearly to the parties what it is he needs in order to be able to effect a speedy resolution of the dispute. In this case he might have a prepared list of his requirements which would be sent to the parties after his appointment. This would take the place of a preliminary hearing, thus saving time and cost, but would clearly set out which documents were required, dates by which they were to be exchanged or provided to the arbitrator, and so on. He may well order that only a full claim and a full defence (accompanied by as many other documents as are relevant) are required, that is to say, he may regard the traditional ''reply'' as unnecessary.

8–25 After that stage the 'pleadings'' (the word is used for convenience; there should be no formal pleadings but full submissions with no discovery and requests for further and better particulars discouraged) are normally closed but it is always open to the arbitrator to allow in further material, whether comments or documentary evidence, if he feels that to refuse to do so would unduly prejudice the party seeking to admit it. The object of arbitration, after all, is, by section 1(a) ''to obtain the *fair* resolution of disputes'' (emphasis added). What he must avoid, however, is to allow a dispute to become ''bogged down'' with what might amount to a request for ''further and better particulars'' from the respondent so that there is no ''unnecessary delay or expense''. This is not only an underlying principle of the Act, but, by section 33(b), a mandatory obligation is imposed on the arbitrator to ''adopt procedures suitable to the circumstances of the particular case, avoiding unnecessary delay or expense, so as to provide a fair means for the resolution'' of the dispute. Fairness, impartiality and the avoidance of delay (since justice delayed is justice denied) are the basic principles of justice.

Seeking further evidence

8–26 As to the production of additional evidence ordered by the arbitrator as opposed to additional evidence sought by the parties, the criterion he would use in deciding whether or not to do this would be whether he felt it would be impossible otherwise to dispose of the matter fairly. There will be occasions when he will conclude from his reading of the documents that there is in existence further material which, in his view, may be relevant for the purpose of enabling him to reach a just decision. In these circumstances he may ask for such material, making certain that copies are automatically given to the other side, so that comments can be made on them if necessary. However, he would have to balance this against his duty to avoid delay and expense. For example, were he to order further documents, the other side would have to be given the opportunity to comment of them, and this will delay the outcome.

Many schemes include a rule to cover further evidence. Under the Act, however, and in particular under section 34, the arbitrator has very wide powers to deal with all procedural and evidential matters (subject to the right of the parties to agree any matters). For example, section 34(2)(e) is drafted in such a way as to permit the arbitrator to order what are known as "interrogatories". However, it is framed in such general terms as to go beyond this. It would enable the arbitrator, for example, to gather up all the information he requires by sending the parties a list of questions to which he requires answers. This could help him to clarify issues or even, by drafting specific questions to which he required specific answers, to narrow those issues. (Such procedure could also be of help to the parties initially in drafting their statements of claim and defence.) The arbitrator must, of course, consider and evaluate the potential benefit or necessity of requiring such further evidence. The processing of the arbitration could otherwise be substantially delayed, thus not only defeating one of the prime aims of the scheme but, in a serious enough case, constituting serious irregularity under section 68 (failure by the tribunal to comply with section 33, which sets out the general duty of the tribunal). 8–27

Administration of codes of practice schemes

We have seen that code of practice schemes are usually administered by an institution such as the Chartered Institute of Arbitrators. It usually prescribes and collects fees payable. Parties communicate with the arbitrator through the institution. The institution or the particular trade organisation makes its own rules prescribing time limits for the lodging of documents. Usually the arbitrator is given the power to extend such time limits and of course he will exercise that power "fairly and impartially". 8–28

Arbitrator's Duty to Decide According to the Law

No power to disregard the law

An arbitrator has always had a measure of discretion to decide how to resolve a dispute, and this is considerably widened by the new Act. However, such resolution in the absence of agreement between the parties, must be according 8–29 to the law. An arbitrator is not a mediator (unless expressly so appointed by the parties), nor an adviser.

> "The duty of an arbitrator is to decide the questions submitted to him according to the legal rights of the parties and not according to what he may consider fair and reasonable under the circumstances."[1]

8–30 In a travel claim, for example, the fact that the claimant's expectations were unfulfilled, or that he was disillusioned with his holiday for reasons involving no breach of contract by the tour operator (*e.g.* it rained continuously), or that the disappointment sustained was due to circumstances falling within an exemption clause upon which the respondent is entitled to rely (*e.g.* the plane was delayed by adverse weather), will in themselves be insufficient to constitute a breach of contract. A misrepresentation in the brochure on which the claimant relied to his detriment, however, or a failure to provide certain promised facilities, will constitute such a breach. (And now see the stringent and comprehensive requirements of the Package Travel, Package Holidays and Package Tours Regulations 1992 which arose as a consequence of Directive 90/314.)

8–31 The Act gives parties total freedom to agree on all matters of procedure (although the relevant provision, section 34(1), is framed in such a way as to suggest that whilst party autonomy is paramount, the intention is that the tribunal takes the initiative in procedural and evidential matters). They can decide, for example, whether to apply strict rules of evidence. They may even authorise the arbitrators to decide the dispute on equitable, rather than on legal grounds. This may well be an attractive option in certain commercial disputes but the concept of free contractual bargaining does not apply in code arbitrations as the rules of the particular schemes set out procedures.

8–32 Difficult questions of law are rare. It is uncommon for code arbitrations, or other small claims on documents only to raise difficult points of law. The arbitrator's function is to decide, as a question of fact, to what extent, if at all, the claimant's complaints are justified within the framework of the particular contract, and, to the extent to which he finds them so justified, to quantify the amount of compensation payable.

Dealing with a point of law

8–33 If the arbitrator is faced with a difficult point of law it is open to him to proceed appropriately according to the particular circumstances. He might, for example, consider inviting both sides to make a preliminary submission of law in writing before dealing with the facts. He must, however, always be mindful of avoiding legal costs in arbitrations of this nature, and particularly in the light of the

[1] Singleton L.J. in *Taylor (Davis) & Sons v. Barnett Trading Co.* [1955] 1 W.L.R. 562.

general principles of the Act. But of course few of them will be appropriate in a consumer arbitration.

When an arbitrator is faced with a difficult point of law and one which is likely to arise, or has already arisen in a large number of other cases, he is in some difficulty. Clearly the claimant is interested only in his claim and possibly the amount of it would not justify the considerable expense of having the point decided either by the arbitrator at an oral hearing or by the courts. On the other hand the respondent, faced with dozens of similar claims which he considers to be unfounded in law, may require that the point is settled. Frequently there are provisions to deal with this contingency. For example, the Rules of the National Small Claims Arbitration Service provide: 8–34

> "If, in the opinion of the arbitrator, the dispute is not capable of proper resolution on documents only, he shall advise the parties through the Institute, with his proposals for how otherwise the arbitration should proceed. If the parties accept these proposals the arbitration shall proceed accordingly provided that the special cost provisions of the rules shall no longer apply. Failing such agreement the arbitrator's appointment shall be deemed revoked and the parties' application for arbitration deemed withdrawn and the parties' registration fees will be refunded. The claimant will then be at liberty to pursue the matter through the courts."

Further, the Act makes it clear that the parties are free to agree how their disputes are resolved, subject only to such safeguards as are necessary in the public interest, and that this includes the consolidation of arbitral proceedings. The arbitrator, however, has no power to order consolidation (or concurrent hearings) in the absence of the agreement of the parties. 8–35

Some Particular Difficulties in Documents-only Arbitrations

The need for clear directions

It is exceptional for there to be a preliminary meeting between the arbitrator and the parties at which to clarify both the issues and the procedure, thereby reducing or eliminating potential problems. Thus someone—be it the arbitrator or the administering institution—must discover, through correspondence and/or state- 8–36 ments of case, what are the facts out of which the claim or defence arises, what, if any, facts are admitted and what are the matters in issue. The Act allows the arbitrator to act inquisitorially, (section 34(2)(g)), but in order to avoid unnecessary expense it is all the more important for clear directions to be given in order that the parties know to what issues they should direct their evidence and submissions, and what procedure to follow. Standard directions, or instructions, can be very helpful, for example:

> "The Claimant is now directed to send the (administrator) within 28 days a Statement of Claim. This should be set out as indicated on the enclosed form and supported by any relevant documents/correspondence. All forms and documents included in the Statement of Claim must be submitted in duplicate."

8–37 There may be occasions when a chronology would be helpful, or where a particular document is thought to be essential, or something in the nature of a Scott Schedule required. In some cases a check-list of documents to be included might be helpful.

8–38 Since the tribunal is under a mandatory duty to avoid unnecessary delay or expense and adopt procedures suitable to the circumstances of the particular case, and since the parties may agree on whether or not to apply strict rules of evidence, hearsay evidence can be admitted. Institutional rules in such arbitrations, for example the ABTA scheme, may expressly provide that an arbitrator will make his award with reference to the documents. It is implicit in this, and indeed in the term "documents-only", that the arbitrator is not to be bound by the rules of evidence. However, in the absence of an agreement to this effect, an arbitrator who deliberately admits inadmissible evidence commits an error of law which could result in the unsuccessful party applying either for leave to appeal or to challenge it in some way, for example by alleging that there has been serious irregularity. Section 68(2)(c), for example, states that serious irregularity would include a failure by the arbitrator to conduct the proceedings in accordance with the procedure agreed by the parties. It would be wise to deal specifically in the award with such evidence, for example, "the three letters adduced by the claimant are irrelevant to the matters in issue and, being inadmissible, were not considered by me".

The inexperienced or inarticulate claimant

8–39 In most code of practice or other consumer arbitrations the claimant is a retail consumer and the respondent is a business organisation experienced in dealing with complaints and/or professionally advised. The claimant may not understand what points he must establish, and what evidence he should adduce in order to succeed. His claim may be exaggerated yet not without merit. The respondent, on the other hand will usually present a more professional case. It requires experience and judgment to recognise which of two conflicting accounts is the more likely, to resist prejudice against the less articulate party and partiality for the more professionally presented case. However, in these days of increased consumer awareness, with claimants freely able to receive advice from various consumer organizations, CAB, etc., and with numerous TV and radio programmes devoted to consumer protection, it is true to say that problems which arose when certain of the schemes started, such as those referred to above, have far less application today. The reality is that most consumers are not only aware of their rights but are readily able to set out their claims clearly, fully and professionally, supporting them with relevant documentation, photographs and the like. Although most code arbitration schemes will expressly discourage legal representation by their rules relating to costs, yet there will be occasions (for example in financial services disputes) when it is evident that legal advice has been provided. Often, for example, solicitors will assist the parties to draft the claim and reply to defence. Since there is no opportunity for the arbitrator to seek clarification of the evidence (absent asking for further evidence, as discussed above) it is essential it is clearly and fully set down, since all the other aids which an arbitrator has to help him (observing the witnesses' demeanour in reacting to questions, noting hesitations, contradictions in the oral evidence and suchlike) are missing.

Some classes of dispute raise questions which may be beyond the technical **8–40** expertise of the arbitrator. There are some schemes, for example in the furnishing industry, which authorise the arbitrator either to commission, or be provided with, an independent technical expert to inspect the goods in question and to issue a report. This regularly used power goes a long way to remove the disadvantage under which the consumer would otherwise labour. Some financial services schemes include the power for the arbitrator to seek expert evidence (*e.g.* from an accountant). Other respondents, particularly public bodies like the Post Office, or private bodies with high reputations to safeguard, like the major insurance companies, may make a practice of setting out in their defence a full case history, dealing with law as well as fact, which can assist the arbitrator to see points in the claimant's favour that the claimant has overlooked.

Clarifying the issues

To some extent this area has already been dealt with under paragraph 8–40 **8–41** above but it is worth reiterating certain points. The arbitrator must be prepared where necessary to request further evidence from the parties where he considers that an otherwise valid claim would fail for want of it, constantly bearing in mind his mandatory duty to avoid unnecessary delay or expense. However, he must bear in mind on whom the burden of proof lies. Before the 1996 Act, the arbitrator could not restrict the rights of the experienced/professionally represented party in an effort to reduce him to the level of the inexperienced/unrepresented party. Thus where a registrar, sitting as an arbitrator under the small claims procedure in the county court, declined to allow the solicitor for the respondent to cross-examine the unrepresented claimant, his award was set aside by the Court of Appeal for misconduct, *Chilton v. Saga Holidays*.[2] However, under the 1996 Act the arbitrator has power to conduct the hearing as he thinks fit, unless the parties have agreed to restrict his right to do so; see paragraphs 625 and 632 above.

The unsupported allegation

8–42 There are occasions when the complaint is unsupported by any cogent evidence. A mere statement by the claimant of facts which appear to be within his own knowledge is of course "evidence" for the peculiar purposes of a documents-only arbitration. It may be accepted by the arbitrator if it is not contradicted and is consistent with other proven facts. However, a mere assertion, *e.g.* that "the accommodation was disgusting" without supporting evidence (such as photographs, complaint forms filled in at the resort, etc.) and denied by the respondent, may be insufficient. The burden of proof lies on the claimant and it is for him to satisfy the arbitrator on the balance of probabilities that the facts are more likely than not to be as he alleges.

Failure of the respondent to submit a defence

8–43 A further area of difficulty lies in those cases where the respondent, after agreeing to arbitration, fails to submit a defence. There may be several reasons for this including, for example, that one company has taken over another and that a backlog of complaints not dealt with has built up. In arbitrations administered by the Chartered Institute of Arbitrators reminders are sent by Recorded Delivery and the Institute tries to be as helpful as is commensurate with fairness on both sides. An arbitrator would need to be satisfied that a respondent has been properly notified of the case against him before taking any steps to deal with the complaint. Having so satisfied himself, the question is, since nothing is denied, is the claim to be admitted in toto? It may be that within the bundle of correspondence there are answers to the claimant's allegations, notwithstanding no actual defence has been submitted. In the absence of something constituting a denial, the arbitrator must find on the evidence which is before him. The claimant must prove his case on the balance of probabilities, and evidentially the respondent's silence could amount to an admission. Again, however, something more than a mere assertion by the claimant may be necessary.

8–44 In a documents-only consumer arbitration, not being a code/administered arbitration, failure by the respondent to file a defence can present difficulties, particularly where the claimant's claim and supporting evidence indicate that it is

[2] [1986] 1 All E.R. 841.

likely to fail. For example, suppose that the evidence reveals that there is a reasonable exclusion clause on which the respondents could rely to avoid liability, or suppose the claimant, alleging negligence of the respondent, has failed to show any duty of care owed to the claimant by the respondent, or indicates damage which is too remote. The arbitrator, in dismissing the claimant's claim, should explain in his reasons why he did so. In the absence of a reasoned award, (the parties may have expressly excluded rights of appeal or stated that they did not want reasons), it might be unwise to dismiss the claimant's claim in the absence of a defence without more. A better solution might be to write to the parties saying that the arbitrator considers that a certain clause in the contract might possibly be of relevance and that they may wish to make submissions to him on this matter. Provide them with a time limit, and invite them to exchange their submissions, as well as sending copies to the arbitrator. A decision of the arbitrator on all matters of procedure and evidence must comply with the duty to act fairly and impartially, and to adopt procedures suitable to the circumstances of the particular case, avoiding unnecessary delay or expense.

Privileged correspondence or other material

Often in the bundle of documents in consumer arbitrations there will be references made to "without prejudice" offers, which is something the arbitrator would normally be unaware of. This difficulty can sometimes be avoided by making it clear at the outset of the arbitration that any offers made expressly "without prejudice" whether orally or in writing, must not be referred to in any way in the documents submitted to the arbitrator. In the case of such an offer being inadvertently included (because, for example, it was included in a letter containing an important admission) any arbitrator worth his salt should have no difficulty in identifying and evaluating such evidence, *i.e.* he would ignore it/instruct himself that any such offer does not constitute an admission of liability. Having had sight of it, however, it would always be prudent to refer to it in the reasons, for example, "I have totally ignored the letter dated 23rd March, stated to be 'without prejudice' ". 8–45

Ex gratia payments

Sometimes a respondent will make an offer expressed to be ex gratia and without prejudice to the claimant's right to claim more by arbitration or litigation. The use of the expression "without prejudice" in this context is quite different from the use referred to above. If a documents-only arbitration follows, either party may refer to the offer. It does not constitute an admission of liability (indeed it is frequently an attempt to terminate unconstructive, lengthy correspondence/preserve goodwill) but is frequently of relevance in the matter of costs. This will be the case, for example, where the award made is less than the *ex gratia* 8–46 offer and where the usual rule would be to award costs against the claimant, notwithstanding the success of his claim.

The intervention of lawyers

8–47 Whilst the advice of a lawyer as to what are the essential elements of the claim or defence, and as to what evidence to submit can be invaluable, the intervention and involvement of lawyers in relatively modest consumer claims sometimes does little to further their client's case. Formal statements of claim often merely paraphrase the client's sometimes graphic and authentic initial letter of complaint. An exchange of correspondence between solicitors seldom assists the arbitrator. As already stated, in the present climate of consumer protection, particularly with much media coverage, the average consumer is well informed and very aware of his rights and obligations. However, with more complex disputes which might arise, say, in cross border disputes concerning product liability, and where such arbitrations are conducted on documents alone, the reverse might be the case. The Act provides that, save agreement to the contrary, parties may be represented by lawyers or others chosen by them (section 36). The phrase "or other person" means literally anyone (and compare representation in the higher courts where although parties may appear in person, yet representation is restricted to lawyers).

The Award

General principles

8–48 The provisions of the Act which deal with awards in arbitration generally, apply equally to documents-only arbitrations. In such arbitrations, however, it is of even greater importance that the award and reasons are expressed in clear, simple language so that a claimant without the benefit of legal advice can understand what has been decided and why. Some drafting suggestions are given in Appendix 1.

Reasons

8–49 The rules or conditions under which the arbitrator is appointed may provide that the award will give reasons. Most code arbitrations require that reasons are given. The Act provides that parties are free to agree the form of the award: section 52(1). Section 52(4) states that the award shall contain reasons unless it is a consent award or the parties have agreed to dispense with reasons. These may appear in the body of the award or in a separate document which expressly states that it is given with, and forms part of, the award. The explanation for some arbitrators preferring to put their reasons in a separate document is that it is found to be more convenient to set out the reasons before writing out the more formal parts of the award. Also, from a practical point of view, the formal part can be put on a word processor, the details being completed separately for each case.

Reasoned awards in consumer disputes

It is rare for a point of law to be involved in a consumer dispute, and in any event many code arbitrations expressly provide that there is no appeal. The function of the reasons in this case is to state the arbitrator's view of the merits of the complaint and, if he finds them justified, to indicate on what basis he has assessed compensation. If a claim incorporates a number of separate complaints, upon each of which he has put a figure, the arbitrator should state why he has allowed/disallowed each head of complaint. In other cases it may be enough that an arbitrator states his overall conclusion on the evidence, without necessarily passing judgment on each and every matter raised. It is felt by some arbitrators that the giving of sufficiently detailed reasons to consumers is both a duty and a public service, and this is particularly the case in the writer's view with regard to travel arbitrations. In the travel industry "dreams are sold", and a consumer whose dream has failed to materialise may turn to a tour operator for recompense, even though his explanation for the failed holiday does not constitute a breach/breaches of contract. He will need to know why his claim has failed. **8–50**

Reasons should be factual, and comments or asides of a subjective or speculative nature should be avoided, as should observations which would give needless hurt or offence. Even if a claim is frivolous or grossly exaggerated, it is probably better to say less than more. However, where the submissions of one party contain imputations on the integrity or good faith of the other, the arbitrator should make it clear, in fairness to both, whether or not he considered such allegations to have any basis or indeed whether he considered them at all. **8–51**

Compensation

Limits on damages

8–52 There are three interconnected principles which limit the damages which a claimant may recover: causation (*i.e.* a respondent cannot be made liable for loss which was not caused by his breach of contract); remoteness (*i.e.* a respondent is only liable for damage which is not too remote, see below); and mitigation (*i.e.* once the claimant is aware of the breach by the respondent, he must take reasonable steps to avoid loss).

Foreseeability

8–53 Assuming the claimant's loss is attributable to the respondent's breach, the only loss which is appropriate for compensation is one which is reasonably foreseeable.

> "Where two parties have made a contract which one of them has broken, the damages which the other party ought to receive in respect of such a breach of contract should be such as may fairly and reasonably be considered either as arising naturally, i.e. according to the usual course of things, from such a breach of contract itself, or such as may reasonably be supposed to have been in the contemplation of both parties at the time they made the contract, as the probable result of the breach of it."[3]

Quantum of damages

8–54 The principle is restitution. The claimant must be restored to the position in which he would have been had the breach of contract not occurred, in other words, as if the contract had been fulfilled. He is entitled to the difference between what he was contractually entitled to receive and what in fact he received. (But see the paragraph below concerning an additional element for which compensation can be awarded in certain cases.)

Special and general damages

8–55 Special damages are those which are amenable to precise monetary quantification, *i.e.* the specific amounts which represent the actual financial loss to the

[3] *Hadley v. Baxendale* (1854) 9 Ex. 341.

claimant, for example the amount a disgruntled consumer has had to spend to rectify a defect in a purchased item. General damages are not amenable to precise quantification and are compensatory amounts. These have to be assessed by the arbitrator, for example, for diminution of the value of a holiday or for negligent financial advice resulting in loss. It is now established law that a holiday maker who establishes a breach of contact by a tour operator is entitled to recover general damages (in addition to special damages) for diminution in the value of the contract *and* for loss of enjoyment, mental anguish, inconvenience and disappointment.[4] The assessment of such damages is imprecise and difficult. Problems have arisen because a very large proportion of the cases dealt with have been unreported county court decisions so that clearly defined criteria for evaluating damages of this nature are unavailable. As a result different courts have adopted different criteria and there has sometimes been inconsistency of approach.

However, very broad outlines of the sort of factors the courts have considered when evaluating such damages have emerged. These include the proportion of the holiday which was affected by the breach; the extent to which the claimant obtained some enjoyment from his holiday and the effort he made, if any, to enjoy himself notwithstanding ; the cost of the holiday; whether the holiday maker made any attempt to mitigate the loss caused by the respondent's breach, and what precisely the brochure promised. 8–56

Interest

Power to award interest

The arbitrator has the power to award interest in a documents only arbitration in exactly the same way as in any other arbitration. Unless the arbitration agreement provides to the contrary, the arbitrator may award compound interest as well as simple interest on amounts successfully claimed and may award such interest on amounts awarded at rates other than the judgment debt rate. 8–57

[4] *Jarvis v. Swan Tours* [1973] 1 Q.B. 233; *Adcock v. Blue Sky Holidays Ltd*, unreported, May 13, 1980, CA.

Lump sum awards including interest

8–58 Some consumer disputes involve many thousands of pounds, for example a claim concerning the cost of fitted carpets and furnishings for a large house, a world-cruise holiday, or a financial services dispute. Specific provision should be made for the interest given on the sum awarded and the rate should bear some relation to the relevant circumstances. However, in view of the informal nature of some consumer arbitrations, an arbitrator might include an interest element in the lump sum amount which is awarded without specifically referring to it. Although simple and convenient this may not be appropriate, and it will never be appropriate where interest has been specifically claimed. A specific provision should ideally be made in order that the rate and period of interest, as distinct from the amount of compensation, should not be concealed. It will usually not be necessary to make detailed calculations, varying the interest rates during the relevant period. It will be enough in simple consumer cases to say, for example, "I award simple interest at the rate of X% from the first day of . . . to the date of this award."

Costs

General principles

8–59 The arbitrator in a documents-only arbitration has the same power and duty to provide for costs as he has in any other arbitration. Thus in a consumer arbitration, not being a code or administered scheme, the arbitrator must deal with both the costs of the arbitration and the fees/expenses of the arbitrator (often referred to as the costs of the award). By section 63(3) the arbitrator is given the power to determine what the recoverable costs of the arbitration are (*i.e.* in the old terminology to "tax" the costs).

8–60 In most code arbitrations on documents-only the matter of costs is considerably simplified by the provisions of the relevant rules. A registration fee is usually payable by each party when the application for arbitration is submitted—it is based on a scale and is used to defray the administrative costs incurred—and the arbitrator has a discretion to give such directions in his award as he considers appropriate concerning the reimbursement of the fee.

How the discretion should be exercised

The discretion should be exercised judicially, that is to say, not capriciously or arbitrarily but according to accepted rules of practice. Thus, if the claimant succeeds in his claim, he should usually be reimbursed his registration fee, on the principle that "costs follow the event". Any departure from the normal rule should be specifically referred to in the reasons. If the claimant fails in his claim, he should be ordered to pay an amount equal to his registration fee as a contribution towards the costs of the respondent. These administrative costs are usually the subject of a separate agreement between the Chartered Institute, the relevant trade, industry or professional body and its members. For instance, FIMBRA pay the costs of the arbitrator's fees and so their contribution is considerably higher than the claimant's registration fee. (They would also meet expenses incurred from the employment by the arbitrator of an expert.) The maximum for which the claimant can be held liable in costs in such code arbitrations is thus twice the amount of his registration fee. **8–61**

A claim should be treated as having failed if the arbitrator decides that the claimant has been adequately compensated by any sum which he has already received on an *ex gratia* basis (*i.e.* without prejudice to his right to arbitrate). Similarly, if the claim succeeds for an amount less than that offered in the course of negotiations (other than in negotiations wholly "without prejudice"), it would be appropriate, in the absence of special circumstances, to order the claimant to refund part of the respondent's registration fee (*i.e.* as set down in the relevant rules, for example under the ABTA Rules the most that such a claimant would be ordered to pay "as a contribution towards the costs of the respondent" would be the amount of his registration fee). It would be inappropriate to order the respondent to reimburse the claimant with the amount of his registration fee. Again, any departure from the usual practice should be explained in the reasons. **8–62**

Part 9

SMALL CLAIMS ARBITRATIONS IN THE COUNTY COURT

By R. G. Greenslade, C.B.E., LL.B.

Formerly a District Judge

Development of Arbitration in the County Court

Historical introduction and statutory framework

In England and Wales the ability of the county court to refer cases to arbitration has a long history. The County Courts Act 1888, s.104 provided: 9–01

> "The judge may in any case, with the consent of both parties, order the same, with or without other matters within the jurisdiction of the court in dispute between such parties, to be referred to arbitration, to such person or persons and in such manner, and on such terms as he shall think reasonable and just; and such reference shall not be revocable by either party, except by consent of the judge; and the award of the arbitrator or arbitrators, or umpire, shall be entered as the judgment in the action and shall be as binding and effectual to all intents as if given by the judge: Provided that the judge may, if he think fit, on application to him at the first court held after the expiry of one week after the entry of such award, set aside any such award so given as aforesaid, or may, with the consent of both parties aforesaid, revoke the reference, or order another reference to be made in the manner aforesaid."

A similar provision was included in the County Courts Act 1959, s.92. This still required the consent of the parties before any action could be referred to arbitration. In 1973 the Administration of Justice Act of that year, section 7, amended section 92 of the 1959 Act by substituting a new subsection (1): 9–02

> "A county court may in such cases as may be prescribed, order any proceedings to be referred to arbitration (whether with or without other matters within the jurisdiction of the court in dispute between the parties) to such person or persons (including the judge or registrar) and in such manner and on such terms as the court thinks just and reasonable."

For the first time the need for the consent of both parties was removed and the appointment of a judge or registrar (now district judge) as arbitrator recognised. The first rules enabled a matter to be referred to arbitration only on the applica- 9–03 tion of either party. The rules were refined over the following 18 years till the present regime was established in 1991 following the report of the Civil Justice Review in 1989. By this time the statutory framework for county court arbitration had been changed again. The County Court Act 1984, s.64 primarily provides authority for the making of rules relating to arbitration:

> "(1) County court rules—
> (a) may prescribe cases in which proceedings are (without any order of the court) to be referred to arbitration,
> (b) may prescribe the manner in which and the terms on which cases are to be so referred, and
> (c) may, where cases are so referred, require other matters within the jurisdiction of the court in dispute between the parties also to be referred to arbitration.
> (2) County court rules—
> (a) may prescribe cases in which proceedings may be referred to arbitration by order of the court, and
> (b) may authorise the court also to order other matters in dispute between the parties and within the jurisdiction of the court to be so referred."

9–04 The section was further amended by the Courts and Legal Services Act 1990 by the addition of subsections (2A) and (2B):

> "(2A) County court rules may prescribe the procedure and rules of evidence to be followed on any reference under subsection (1) or (2).
> (2B) Rules made under subsection (2A) may, in particular, make provision with respect to the manner of taking and questioning evidence."

The section ends with provisions redolent of the 1888 Act which deal with the award being entered as a judgment in the action and the power to set aside the award.

The County Court Rules (C.C.R.)

9–05 The current procedure for arbitrations is governed by the County Court Rules, Ord. 19, Pt I. This rule exercises the rule making powers given by the revised section 64 although no express provision is made to "require other matters within the jurisdiction of the court in dispute between the parties also to be referred to arbitration". There is therefore no method by which such matters can be arbitrated by the county court except by inclusion in a pleading whether it be particulars of claim, defence, counterclaim or defence to counterclaim.

Nature of County Court arbitration

It will be clear from the discussion that follows and from the cases cited that county court arbitration is intended to provide an easy and informal method of resolving disputes—"to get away from the rigid rituals which characterise ordinary litigation", *per* Beldam L.J. in *Afzal v. Ford Motor Co. Ltd.*[1] However, it does not follow that informality of procedure is intended to provide a system of "palm tree justice". The duty of the arbitrator is to discover the facts and apply the law of England to those facts in exactly the same way as when trying an action in court. 9–06

Relationship with mainstream arbitration

Although referred to as arbitration in both the County Court Act 1984 and the County Court Rules, county court arbitration has one essential difference from normal commercial arbitration. This is that there is no requirement for there to be any consent prior to the reference. As will appear, the jurisdiction to refer an action to arbitration in the county court will sometimes be exercised with the consent of the parties but the court retains power to make such a reference whatever the amount claimed provided that where the amount claimed exceeds £3,000 (£1,000 in the case of a claim for personal injury damages) one party applies for the action to be so referred. 9–07

Section 92 of the Arbitration Act 1996 disapplies Part 1 of that Act to county court arbitrations. 9–08

Stay of court proceedings where there is an arbitration agreement

The Arbitration Act 1996, s.9 provides for the stay of court proceedings where there is an arbitration agreement. Any party may apply to the court to stay proceedings in respect of any matter agreed to be referred and the court shall grant a stay "unless satisfied that the arbitration agreement is null and void, inoperative, or incapable of being performed." 9–09

However, the combined effect of the 1996 Act, ss.89 and 91, the Unfair Terms in Consumer Contracts Regulations 1994[2] and the Unfair Arbitration Agreements (Specified Amount) Order 1996[3] restricts the ability of a seller or supplier to enforce an arbitration agreement where the sum claimed is less than £3,000. 9–10

Where a contract is concluded between a seller and supplier and a consumer containing an "arbitration agreement" clause other than one which has been "individually negotiated" that agreement is deemed to be an "unfair term" and 9–11

[1] [1994] 4 All E.R. 720.
[2] S.I. 1994 No. 3159.
[3] S.I. 1996 No. 3211.

is not binding on the consumer in any claim for a pecuniary remedy not exceeding £3,000 (or such other sum as may be specified by order).

9–12 An "arbitration agreement" is an agreement to "submit to arbitration present or future disputes or differences (whether or not contractual)". A "consumer" may be either a legal person or a natural person. The provisions apply whatever the law applicable to the arbitration agreement.

The Place of Arbitration within the County Court System

Commencing proceedings

9–13 The recommendations of the Civil Justice Review in 1988 that there should be a self contained code for county court arbitration were not adopted. The position remains, as before, that the County Court Rules, Ord. 19, Pt 1 merely provide for the reference to arbitration of certain actions and by whom and in what manner such arbitrations should be conducted. These rules fall within the general framework of the County Court Rules providing for the manner in which proceedings are to be commenced, the method of service, the requirements for a defence and the ability to enter judgment in default of defence. It is only upon the filing of a defence that the "small claims code" of Ord. 19, Pt 1 comes into operation.

9–14 Actions in the county court are commenced by filing at a county court a request for the issue of a summons and a form of "particulars of claim". In practice a combined form of request and summons is commonly used. The request for issue of the summons contains details of the parties, names and addresses, and of any solicitor acting for the plaintiff. Save for a limited number of cases, which are unlikely to be arbitrated, a summons can be issued at any county court. However, there is provision for the "automatic transfer" of many actions to the defendant's court on a defence being filed (see below).

Particulars of claim

9–15 The particulars of claim should set out the facts on which the claim is based. C.C.R., Ord. 6, r.1(1) requires the filing of particulars of claim "specifying his cause of action and the relief or remedy which he seeks and stating briefly the material facts on which he relies''. There is no general rule as to the contents of pleadings in the county court but in practice the requirements of the R.S.C., Ord. 18, r.7 are observed. This rule states that every pleading:

> ''must contain, and contain only, a statement in a summary form of the material facts on which the party pleading relies for his claim . . . but not the evidence by which those facts are to be proved, and the statement must be as brief as the nature of the case admits.''

However, the county court regime is quite relaxed as to pleading and this is particularly the case in cases which will be referred to arbitration. The test very often is whether the parties themselves are aware of what the true nature of the dispute is rather than the formal way in which this is ''pleaded''. **9–16**

There are certain special requirements as to pleading. A claim for statutory interest pursuant to the Judgments Act 1838 must be made in the particulars of claim (C.C.R., Ord. 6, r.1A), as must a claim for aggravated, exemplary and provisional damages (C.C.R., Ord. 6, r.1B)—though such a claim is unlikely to be heard by county court arbitration. Where the plaintiff claims an injunction or declaration in respect of, or relating to any land, or the possession, occupation, use or enjoyment of any land the particulars should identify the land in question (C.C.R., Ord. 6, r.3(1) and 4). It is now clear that where a county court arbitration is heard, as is normally the case, by a district judge (including a deputy district judge) s/he retains the power under the rules to make an injunction or declaration or grant an order for specific performance: *Joyce v. Liverpool City Council*.[4] Such power is not exercisable by a ''non-judicial'' arbitrator as the power flows from the exercise by the district judge of the powers of the court in accordance with C.C.R., Ord. 21, r.5(2B). **9–17**

Where a claim includes a claim for damages for personal injuries (it being clear from the decision in *Afzal v. Ford Motor Co. Ltd*[5] that such actions *may* be heard by arbitration unless there is specific complexity of facts or one of the other reasons for rescinding the reference to arbitration (see below) applies) the particulars of claim must be accompanied by a medical report and schedule of special damages (C.C.R., Ord. 6, r.1(5)). There is no reason why a claim by an infant plaintiff or a patient which falls within the ''small claims limit'' should not be dealt with by arbitration. **9–18**

Interest: A plaintiff may claim interest either in accordance with the terms of any contract between him/her and the defendant or pursuant to the County Court Act 1984, s.69. A claim to interest under the Act—usually referred to as ''interest pursuant to statute''—must be pleaded in the Particulars of Claim, the amount claimed to the date of issue set out and a daily rate given so that the defendant can calculate the sum required to satisfy the claim (C.C.R., Ord. 6, r.1A). Interest so claimed is simple interest and may be allowed at ''such rate **9–19**

[4] [1995] 3 All E.R. 110; [1995] 3 W.L.R. 439, CA.
[5] [1994] 4 All E.R. 720, CA.

as the court thinks fit or as may be prescribed'' (County Court Act 1984, s.69(1)). For the purposes of obtaining a default judgment the rate must not exceed that prescribed by the current Judgment Debts (Rate of Interest) Order[6] which prescribes a rate of 8 per cent. In practice it is this rate that is claimed unless the plaintiff is able to claim a higher rate under contract. If so details of the contractual terms should be set out in the particulars of claim.

Service

9–20 The summons is prepared (and any separate particulars of claim annexed) and normally served by the court by post. If the plaintiff wishes s/he may serve the summons personally (C.C.R., Ord. 7, r.1). This must be by way of personal service on the defendant unless the claim includes a claim for damages for personal injury and the plaintiff is represented by a solicitor in which case postal service is permitted (C.C.R., Ord. 7, r.10A). There is also provision for service by the court bailiff but only if postal service has been attempted and failed (C.C.R., Ord. 7, r.1(4)).

9–21 The summons will state the court fee paid on issue of the summons and the scale costs of the solicitor on issuing the claim if the plaintiff is represented by solicitor.

9–22 With the summons and particulars of claim are served standard forms of defence and counterclaim, of admission in whole or in part, and a statement of means to enable a defendant admitting the claim in whole or in part to seek an order for payment of the judgment debt by instalments.

Defendant out of England and Wales

9–23 An action may be commenced against a person resident outside England and Wales. In many cases where the defendant is resident in a convention country such proceedings may be issued without leave. If not leave must be obtained prior to the issue of proceedings. The rules relating to service out of the jurisdiction are unfortunately complex but are to be found in C.C.R., Ord. 11. Where proceedings may be issued and served abroad without leave the request for issue of a summons and the Particulars of Claim require a certificate under C.C.R., Ord. 3, r.3(5)–(8). No default judgment (see below) may be entered without leave—such leave is obtained *ex parte* by affidavit giving the information set out in R.S.C. Ord. 13, r.7B as applied by C.C.R., Ord. 9, r.6(4).

Defence

9–24 The defendant is required to file any defence or counterclaim at the county court office within 14 days of the deemed date of service. This is seven days after the

[6] At present S.I. 1993 No. 564.

date of posting of the summons or of the date of personal service if that procedure is adopted.

A form of defence and counterclaim is provided but it is open to the defendant to use any form that s/he chooses. Indeed any written notification by the defendant to the plaintiff of a defence or counterclaim will prevent judgment in default being entered even though no formal defence has been filed (C.C.R., Ord. 10, r.6(1A)). 9–25

Admission and offers

The county court has a well developed system enabling the defendant to admit the claim either in whole or in part. An admission, if accepted by the plaintiff, can lead to judgment being entered. Frequently admissions are accompanied by an offer to pay by instalments and the rules give the plaintiff an opportunity to respond to such an offer. If there is a dispute only as to the time (or method) of payment decisions are made by court staff with the possibility of a review by a district judge (C.C.R., Ord. 9, r.3). Judgments for payment by instalments are a frequent occurrence in the county court. Failure to pay any instalment makes the whole balance due and enforceable. 9–26

Default judgments

In a substantial majority of cases no defence is filed and judgment is entered in default for payment forthwith, at a stated date or by instalments. However, as there is no procedure for entering a judgment in default of defence to counterclaim, an application would have to be made on notice. 9–27

Provision is made for applications to set aside a default judgment either as of right where there has been a failure of service or on showing that there is on the merits a defence with a realistic prospect of success (C.C.R., Ord. 37, r.4 and *Alpine Bulk Transport Co. Inc. v. Saudi Eagle Shipping Co. Inc., The Saudi Eagle*.[7] 9–28

Transfer of action

Upon the filing of a defence the court will decide whether the action should be transferred to the defendant's county court under C.C.R., Ord. 9, r.2(8). Any claim for a liquidated sum will be transferred to the court for the area in which the address for service of first defendant to defend (as stated in the defence) is situated, or, if represented by solicitor, to the court for the area in which the defendants address as shown on the summons is situated (C.C.R., Ord. 1, r.13). A claim for an unliquidated sum will not be automatically transferred. If the 9–29

[7] [1986] 2 Lloyd's Rep. 221, CA.

plaintiff objects to the transfer s/he may apply to the district judge of the court to which the action has been transferred, initially by letter, for the action to be transferred to another court (C.C.R., Ord. 16, r.4(2)(b)). The district judge can invite representations from any other party and will normally decide the question on the basis of any such representations, the pleadings and the plaintiff 's letter. This power is additional to the general power of the court under C.C.R., Ord. 16, r.1 to transfer any action to any other court if satisfied that ''any action . . . could more conveniently or fairly heard and determined in some other court''.

Summary judgment

9–30 The procedure under C.C.R., Ord. 9, r.14 for the plaintiff to apply for summary judgment does not apply to any action which is automatically referred to arbitration under Ord, 19, r.3.

The Reference

Automatic reference

9–31 Though the expression ''small claims court'' is used frequently, strictly there is no such court. Generally speaking such references are to claims not exceeding £3,000 (£1,000 in the case of claims for damages for personal injuries) which are automatically referred to arbitration under Ord. 19, r.3(1).

9–32 This rule provides that upon a defence being filed any proceedings in which the amount claimed or amount involved does not exceed £3,000 are automatically referred to arbitration upon the filing of a defence. In assessing the £3000 statutory interest is not to be taken into account (County Courts Act 1984, s.69(8)). However, if the claim is for a sum less than £3,000 but includes a claim for damages for personal injury exceeding £1,000, or a claim for possession, the automatic reference provisions do not apply: C.C.R., Ord. 19, r.3(1A). In practice the procedure is that upon a defence being filed the court file is placed before a district judge who will look at the summons and defence. S/he will consider whether any special directions are required or whether the standard directions (as to which see below) will suffice with or without any additional directions that s/he considers appropriate. S/he will make a broad assessment of the length of time that will be needed to hear the dispute and make a note of this. The court office will then send out a notice of hearing with the standard (and any specific) directions set out on the notice. Hearings are usually between six weeks and three months after the filing of the defence.

Inflated claims

In order to avoid an automatic reference to arbitration (and more particularly the "no costs" rule: see below) it is not unknown for plaintiff's solicitors to claim a sum in excess of £3,000 (or £1,000 personal injury damages). Deliberate inflation of the claim for this purpose may be treated as an abuse of process—see *Afzal v. Ford Motor Co. Ltd.*[8] In that case it was suggested that the defendant could apply on notice for the matter to be treated as automatically referred to arbitration despite the amount claimed. The defendant would have the onus of showing that the judgment could not reasonably be expected to exceed £3,000 (or £1,000, as the case may be). If such an application succeeded the defendant would appear to be entitled to the costs incurred to date if successful. If no such application is made and the action proceeds to trial the trial judge has a discretion to refuse to allow costs in excess of such (if any) as would be allowed under an automatic reference. The test was stated in *Afzal* to be "Could the plaintiff reasonably expect to be awarded more than [£3,000]?". The test should be applied on the basis of the information available to the plaintiff or his/her solicitor at the time proceedings were issued. 9–33

Effect of change in the sum claimed

It is clear from the wording of C.C.R., Ord. 19, r.3(1)—"Any proceedings in which the sum claimed . . . does not exceed £3000 . . . shall stand referred for arbitration . . . upon the receipt . . . of a defence to the claim"—that the automatic reference depends on the amount claimed as at the date of the defence. Any amended sum claimed at that stage should be taken into account. What will the position be where the sum claimed is reduced below or increased above the "small claims limit" after the delivery of the defence? In the absence of any specific rule it would appear open to any party to apply for the matter to be referred to arbitration if the amount claimed falls below £3,000 or for the reference to be rescinded if the amount is increased above that figure (or £1,000 in the case of personal injury damages). In making a decision the district judge should take into account the matters set out in C.C.R., Ord. 19, r.3(2). However, an action referred to arbitration because of a reduction could only be treated as an automatic referral so as to bring the "no costs" regime into play if it were considered that the original amount claimed amounted to an abuse of process and the district judge so declared. Simple reduction as a result of a change in 9–34

[8] [1994] 4 All E.R. 720, CA.

circumstances could not make the reference an automatic reference under Ord. 19, r.3(1).

Amount of counterclaim

9–35 If a counterclaim is made for a sum which exceeds the "small claims limit" this does not of itself prevent an automatic reference to arbitration although it may be a factor which will be considered by the district judge in deciding whether the reference should be rescinded.

Voluntary reference

9–36 If the claim exceeds £3,000 (or £1,000 personal injury damages) it is open to either party to apply for the action to be referred to arbitration. The forms of summons and defence provide a "tick box" for such an application. This will be considered by the district judge when the court file is placed before him. If both parties seek arbitration s/he will normally give directions as if it were an automatic reference. If only one party seeks a reference his/her decision will probably turn on the extent to which the claim exceeds £3,000 (or £1,000), if only a small amount above, particularly if both parties are in person, a reference is likely. The greater the amount of the claim the more likely the district judge will arrange for a pre trial review to be fixed to consider the application. The fact that one or both is legally represented may also influence his/her decision.

9–37 There are a number of significant differences between an action which has been automatically referred to arbitration and one where the reference is as a result of an agreement between the parties or an order of the court. The main difference is that the "no costs" rule of Ord. 19, r.4 (see below) does not apply to "voluntary" references. Furthermore on a voluntary reference the normal court procedures for payments in, security for costs and summary judgment apply—they do not where there is an automatic reference (Ord. 19, r.6(9) and Ord. 9, r.14(1)).

9–38 The rules do not lay down any specific factors for the district judge to consider in deciding whether to refer to arbitration against the wishes of one of the parties. S/he will normally consider the complexity of fact and law, the size of the claim and any counterclaim, the question of whether or not third parties might be affected by the decision, whether one or both parties are represented and whether either party would be significantly disadvantaged by a decision one way or the other.

Rescission of reference

9–39 These factors are not very dissimilar from the factors which entitle a district judge on application or of his/her own motion to order a trial in court even though the claim does not exceed £3,000 (or £1,000 for personal injury damages). These criteria are laid down in C.C.R., Ord. 19, r.3(2), namely:

(a) that a difficult question of law or a question of fact of complexity is involved;
(b) that fraud is alleged against a party;
(c) that the parties are agreed that the dispute should be tried in court; and
(d) that it would be unreasonable for the claim to proceed to arbitration having regard to
    (i) its subject matter
    (ii) the size of any counterclaim
    (iii) the circumstances of the parties, or
    (iv) the interests of any other person likely to be affected by the award.

Where a party applies for the action to be tried in court the district judge will be able to hear the views of both parties. If s/he considers of his/her own motion that the action is not suitable for arbitration the proper officer (the chief clerk) will give notice to both parties setting out the grounds on which the district judge is minded to order trial in court. 9–40

Either party may give written notice setting out his/her objections within 14 days after receipt of the notice from the court. 9–41

If the party objecting so requests a date is fixed for a hearing for the district judge to decide whether or not to order trial in open court and to give directions as to steps to be taken before any hearing whether or not s/he transfers the action to court. 9–42

While no statistics are available it is believed that the main class of applications to transfer to open court have been claims for damages for personal injury. Certain courts as a matter of principle directed that any such claim should be tried in open court. A number of such cases were reviewed by the Court of Appeal in *Afzal and others v. Ford Motor Co. Ltd*[9] in which the Master of the Rolls said: 9–43

> "The district judge cannot rescind an automatic reference to arbitration under Ord. 19, r.3(1) merely because a question of law is involved or the facts are complex. Rule 3(2)(a) makes it clear that the question of law has to be one of difficulty and a question of fact one of exceptional complexity if the claim is to be regarded as one which should be tried in court. It is not a proper interpretation of the rules to reintroduce these matters by themselves under r.3(2)(d) under the guise of subject matter which makes it unreasonable for the claim to proceed to arbitration. 'Subject matter' refers to the nature of the claim generally but in the context of the other provisions of r.3(2) we take it to refer to some quality of the subject matter of the

[9] [1994] 4 All E.R. 720.

claim of sufficient importance to the parties or to one of them to justify trial in court; for example a claim for damages for trespass which could have far reaching consequences for the rights of the parties or a claim involving ownership of a family heirloom. Cases which may be regarded as 'test' cases could be catered for under r.3(2)(d) as cases in which the interests of other persons are likely to be affected by the award.''

9–44 The reference to ''exceptional'' complexity relates to the rules as they then stood. The reference to ''exceptional'' has now gone but nevertheless the decision is of assistance in indicating the way in which the court should approach the question of rescinding the reference.

9–45 The court decided that there was nothing in personal injury cases (in the particular case, employer's liability) which as a class made them unsuitable for arbitration though leaving open decisions on particular cases. The court also held that inequality of representation was not a proper factor to be taken into account as one of the circumstances of the parties under r.3(2)(d) bearing in mind the wide ranging powers of the arbitrator under r.7(4) to give each party an opportunity to have his/her case presented having considered ''whether (or to what extent) they are represented''. Nor was the need for expert evidence a factor as this was also contemplated by r.7(6).

9–46 In his interim report Lord Woolf recommends that the test of *exceptional* complexity should be reduced to one of complexity and also suggests that inequality of the parties should be a major factor to be taken into account both in favour of arbitration where the some exceeds the ''small claims limit''—where a party might suffer from inability to afford to instruct a solicitor—and also in favour of directing trial in court in smaller cases where a party would suffer from legal aid not being available to enable him/her to be represented. His recommendation as to the removal of the need to show *exceptional* complexity of fact has been adopted and is reflected in the amended rule as set out above. Other changes proposed by Lord Woolf are unlikely to be implemented before October 1998.

9–47 While it is now clear that a district judge arbitrator may give non-monetary remedies, primarily an injunction, an order for specific performance and a declaration (*Joyce v. Liverpool City Council*[10]) the fact that such a remedy was sought might possibly be a factor to be considered by the district judge in rescinding a reference to arbitration.

Effect on costs of rescission of reference

9–48 Where an action automatically referred to arbitration is directed to be tried in open court the ''no costs'' regime applies up to and including the day on which

[10] [1995] 3 All E.R. 110; [1995] 3 W.L.R. 439, CA.

the order is made but thereafter the normal rules as to the incidence of costs (see below) apply (C.C.R., Ord. 19, r.4(4)).

Pre-hearing Procedure

Directions

The rules provide for standard directions as follows: 9–49

"(a) each party shall not less than 14 days before the date fixed for the hearing send to every other party copies of all documents which are in his possession and on which that party intends to rely at the hearing
(b) each party shall not less than 7 days before the date fixed for the hearing send to the court and to every other party a copy of any expert report on which that party intends to rely at the hearing and a list of the witnesses whom he intends to call at the hearing" (r.6(3)).

Unless there is to be a preliminary hearing these directions are sent out automatically (together with any other directions that the district judge thinks appropriate—*e.g.* preparation of a plan or photographs, production of any moveable item in dispute) with the notice of the arbitration hearing. At least 21 days' notice must be given (r.6(2)(a)). 9–50

Preliminary appointment

As mentioned above, once a defence is filed the court file is placed before a district judge. One point that s/he should consider is whether or not there should be a preliminary appointment. Under the former rules such appointments were common, indeed they took place unless the district judge directed otherwise. However there were complaints that this often meant two attendances at court, often with the loss of two full days' pay when very little was achieved at the first, preliminary, appointment. For this reason the Civil Justice Review recommended a single hearing procedure. 9–51

Their recommendation was taken up in the 1991 changes to the County Court Rules, and Ord. 19, r.6 now states: 9–52

"(4) A preliminary appointment shall only be held:

(a) where directions under paragraph (3) are not sufficient and special directions can only be given in the presence of the parties, or
(b) to enable the district judge to dispose of the case where the claim is ill founded or there is no reasonable defence.

In deciding whether to hold a preliminary appointment the district judge shall have regard to the desirability of minimising the number of court attendances by the parties''.

9–53 Despite this change practice varies considerably. A number of district judges consider that a preliminary appointment is of benefit because:

- it helps identify the issues;
- it enables an explanation to be given of the sort of evidence that will be required;
- the district judge can sometimes "mediate" a settlement;
- often only one party turns up and judgment can be entered for or against the plaintiff.

9–54 These are undoubtedly valid reasons but they fly in the face of the clear wording of the rule. The majority of district judges only occasionally hold a preliminary appointment primarily in cases in which it appears that there is no valid claim or defence, where one party appears seriously out of his or her depth or the not uncommon case where the wrong party is being sued, *e.g.* the other driver's insurers in a road accident case or a director of a limited company.

9–55 If there is to be preliminary appointment the court will give at least 8 days notice to the parties.

9–56 Under the rules the district judge has the powers that s/he would otherwise have on a pre trial review. These include the power to strike out the claim if the plaintiff does not appear, to give judgment if the defendant does not appear and the plaintiff is able to prove his/her case and generally to give directions as to the conduct of the case. Ord. 19, r. 6(6) requires the district judge:

(a) to give an estimate of the time to be allowed for the hearing (unless the parties consent to his deciding the dispute on the statements and documents submitted to him),
and
(b) whether of his own motion or at the request of a party, give such additional directions regarding the steps to be taken before and at the hearing as may appear to him to be necessary or desirable.

9–57 Such directions may include direction that a party shall clarify his/her claim or defence—the equivalent of an order for further and better particulars.

9–58 Instead of a preliminary appointment many district judges will fix an apparently hopeless case for a "five minute hearing". This will be the full arbitration so that a final judgment can be given but it is anticipated either that only one party will attend or that the matter can be disposed of as quickly on such a hearing as on a preliminary appointment.

Disapplication of County Court Rules

As has already been indicated the county arbitration procedure takes place within the general context of the County Court Rules. However, to apply all the procedural rules to arbitration would take away much of the simplicity and informality that the procedure is intended to provide. In *Afzal v. Ford Motor Co. Ltd*[11] the Master of the Rolls described the procedure in these words: 9–59

> "Court based small claims arbitration is intended to be a greatly simplified procedure for determining claims. The district judge remains an adjudicator and the process adversarial but, as the code makes clear, the aim, of the procedure is to get away from the rigid rituals which characterise ordinary litigation."

The following county court procedures are specifically excluded from all arbitrations: 9–60

- Further particulars of pleadings under C.C.R., Ord. 6, r.7 and Ord. 9, r.11.
- Discovery and interrogatories (C.C.R., Ord. 14, rr.1(2), 3–5A and 11.
- Notices to admit facts and documents (Ord. 20, rr.2 & 3).
- Exchange of witness statements (Ord. 19, r.6(9)).

In addition the following procedures do not apply to any claim referred automatically to arbitration: 9–61

- Payments into court (Ord. 11, rr.1, 1A, 3–5, 7, 8 and 10).
- Security for costs (Ord. 13, r.1(8)(a))) (C.C.R., Ord. 19, r.6(9))
- Summary judgment (Ord. 9, r.14(1)).

The reference to security for costs would not appear to apply to any application under section 726(1) of the Companies Act 1985—where it appears on credible evidence that there is reason to believe that a company may not be able to pay any costs awarded against it—as this is a statutory right which cannot be taken away by rule. However, the statute only provides a threshold requirement to be met before the court can exercise its discretion whether or not to make an order (see, *e.g. Sir Lindsay Parkinson Co. Ltd v. Triplan Ltd*[12]). It may well be that in exercising that discretion any court would take into account (a) the policy of 9–62

[11] [1994] 4 All E.R. 720, CA.
[12] [1973] Q.B. 609; [1973] 2 All E.R. 273, CA.

the County Court Rules and (b) even more practically the fact it would be unlikely to award significant costs against the plaintiff in a "small claims arbitration".

Third party procedure

9–63 One area of normal county court procedure that does apply is the ability to issue a third party notice seeking indemnity against another party or a stranger to the action. The general procedure for such an application is laid down by C.C.R., Ord. 12. The procedure is used occasionally in county court arbitration. Basically a defendant may issue third party proceedings without leave against any existing party. The defendant may also issue such proceedings against any other person without leave unless a date for hearing—either a preliminary appointment or the arbitration itself—has been fixed. Once that has happened a defendant wishing to issue a third party notice must apply on notice to all other parties for leave to do so. On issue it would be normal to direct that a preliminary appointment be fixed so that any problems over the introduction of new parties might be resolved and appropriate directions given.

9–64 One point about third party notices is that judgment in default may not be entered without leave against a defendant who issues a third party notice (C.C.R., Ord. 12, r.1(7)).

Procedural applications and appeals

9–65 While the intention is that arbitrations should be a "single hearing" occasionally one party will wish to seek some procedural order against the other. Such a party should apply on notice using the standard form of notice of application (N.244) obtainable from the court office. The form, should be completed giving details of the order sought and the reasons. It should then be presented to the court office which will fix an appointment and return a sealed copy for service on the other party. At least two "clear days" notice are required. At the hearing the district judge will consider whether to make the order, bearing in kind the need for informality. Applications of a formal nature even if permitted by the rules (see C.C.R., Ord. 19, r.6(9) and (10)) will be frowned upon. The district judge is likely to use any such application as a preliminary appointment and seek to ensure that then parties are aware of the procedure to be adopted at the arbitration and may give directions to assist them in the conduct of the arbitration.

9–66 Any order made by a district judge referring an action outside the small claims limit to arbitration, directing that an action within the limit should be tried or giving directions may be appealed to a circuit judge. The appeal should be on notice (the standard form of notice—N.244—may be used and is issued and served as described above) and must be issued at the court office within 14 days of the making of the order (C.C.R., Ord. 37, r.6(2)).

The Arbitrator

Appointment

The County Courts Act, s.64 is not specific about who may be appointed as arbitrator; indeed section 64(3) refers to "the arbitrator, arbitrators or umpire". However, the rules provide for three different possible arbitrators—the district judge, a circuit judge or an outside arbitrator. **9–67**

District Judge

By far the majority of arbitrations are heard by the district judge (including deputy district judges). Indeed any action referred automatically to arbitration under C.C.R., Ord. 19, r.3 (*i.e.* where the claim does not exceed £3,000—or £1,000 in the case of damages for personal injuries) is to be heard by the district judge (r.3(1)). **9–68**

Circuit judge

There is no positive provision for the appointment of a circuit judge as arbitrator, the only provision is the somewhat negative reference in r.5(2) that an order "shall not be made referring proceedings to the Circuit Judge except by or with the leave of the judge". It is understood that formal references to the circuit judge to act as an arbitrator are extremely rare though the provision may be of value in two particular cases. First, it enables a circuit judge to deal with arbitrations in the absence of a district judge, or where the district judge is heavily overlisted. Secondly, if there is an application to a circuit judge to set aside an arbitration award by a district judge or outside arbitrator the judge can hear the arbitration himself after setting aside the award without referring the matter back to a district judge or an outside arbitrator. One problem is that the rules do not make any provision as to who should hear an application to set aside a circuit judge's award—could it be dealt with as an award under the Arbitration Acts to be heard by a High Court judge, or might it be regarded as a quasi appeal from a circuit judge to be heard by the Court of Appeal, if the latter is leave required under the County Courts Appeals Order 1991[13]? Because of the infrequency of **9–69**

[13] S.I. 1991 No. 1877.

arbitrations by a circuit judge the problem may well have never occurred in practice and the Rules are silent.

Outside arbitrator

9–70 The rules clearly provide for the appointment of an outside arbitrator and such appointments are made from time to time. The wording of C.C.R., Ord. 19, r.3(1) would appear to prevent the appointment of an ''outside arbitrator'' in any action referred automatically to arbitration.

9–71 Apart from this apparent limitation, the major restrictions are that the consent of the parties is required (r.5(2)) and, perhaps more significantly, no order can be served, unless the court directs, until each party has paid into court ''such sum as the district judge may determine in respect of the arbitrator's remuneration''. In the majority of ''small claims'' the parties will probably prefer a free decision by a district judge arbitrator rather than paying for the appointment of an outside arbitrator. However there will be cases in which the cost of appointing an expert arbitrator will be less than the cost of each party employing expert an expert. A practical difficulty is that unless both parties themselves agree to the appointment of an outside arbitrator—subject to the approval of the district judge—there is no formal machinery to deal with the appointment and in practice a preliminary appointment will need to be fixed.

9–72 There is much sense in the use of outside expert arbitrators in technical matters. In his interim report Lord Woolf commends such appointments and hints that the cost ought to be met out of court funds on the basis that the time of a district judge or deputy district judge will be saved.

9–73 If an outside arbitrator is appointed his/her powers will be exactly the same as a district judge save that s/he would not appear to have the power to make any award other than for payment of money. The decision in *Joyce v. Liverpool City Council*[14] appears to be based solely on the district judge's powers under C.C.R., Ord. 21, r.5.

Conduct of the Arbitration

The Rules

9–74 County court arbitration has been said to be ''no more and no less than a procedure for resolving low value claims . . . with a minimum of formality and

[14] [1995] 3 All E.R. 110; [1995] 3 W.L.R. 439, CA.

expense'' (Sir Thomas Bingham M.R. in *Joyce v. Liverpool City Council*[15] and reference has already been made to the comments of Beldam L.J. in *Afzal v. Ford Motor Co. Ltd.*[16] Unfortunately it has taken a number of changes in the rules to reach a situation in which this aim is likely to be realised.

The conduct of each individual arbitration is in the hands of the arbitrator—usually the district judge or a deputy—and may (often necessarily) vary from case to case, as well as from district judge to district judge. However, C.C.R., Ord. 19, r.7 is intended to provide a basic framework to encourage, if not to ensure, informality. The rule provides that: 9–75

''(1) Any proceeding referred to arbitration shall be dealt with in accordance with the following paragraphs of this rule unless the arbitrator otherwise orders.

(2) The hearing may be held at the court house, at the court office or at any other place convenient to the parties.

(3) The hearing shall be informal and the strict rules of evidence shall not apply; unless the arbitrator orders otherwise the hearing shall be held in private and evidence shall not be taken on oath.

(4) At the hearing the arbitrator may adopt any method of procedure which he may consider to be fair and which gives to each party an equal opportunity to have his case presented; having considered the circumstances of the party and whether (or to what extent) they are represented, the arbitrator—

(a) may assist a party by putting questions to the witnesses and the other party, and

(b) should explain any legal terms or expressions which are used.

(5) If any party does not appear at the arbitration, the arbitrator may, after taking into account any pleadings or other documents filed, make an award on hearing any other party to the proceedings who may be present.

(6) With the consent of the parties and at any time before giving his decision, the district judge may consult any expert or call for an expert report on any matter in dispute or invite an expert to attend the hearing as assessor.

(7) The arbitrator may require the production of any document or thing and may inspect any property or thing concerning which any question may arise.

(8) The arbitrator shall inform the parties of his award and give his reasons for it to any party who may be present at the hearing.''

This rule gives rise to a number of points which require discussion. 9–76

[15] *ibid.*

[16] [1994] 4 All E.R. 720, CA.

Place of hearing

9–77 While the majority of hearings take place on court premises, the rule recognises the use of accommodation other than the "courthouse". The aim is to encourage informality in a way that use of a court room, even where robes are not worn, would not do. Most commonly hearings take place in the district judge's chambers. These vary considerably but normally provide a desk for the arbitrator and a table for the litigants. Generally they provide a fair balance between informality and the need to preserve some degree of order to the proceedings. The rule also envisages hearing "at any other place convenient to the parties". While this provision is extremely wide, in practice it is applied to enable the arbitration (or part of it) to take place at the premises at which work in dispute has been done. Thus in building disputes the hearing may take place at the particular property. Occasionally an arbitration may take place at a litigant's house because of age or infirmity. The undoubted value of this procedure is undermined by the additional time required to travel to and from such a hearing and, in view of increasing demands on district judge's time such hearings are now less frequent. The provision can be of considerable use where an outside arbitrator is appointed.

Rules of evidence

9–78 Hearsay evidence is common in small claims arbitrations and is often essential bearing in mind the relatively limited allowance made for witnesses' loss of wages in attending a hearing (see below under "costs"). However the mere fact that hearsay evidence is admissible, if relevant, leaves the arbitrator with the task of deciding what "weight" is to be given to such evidence, and frequently the weight to be properly given is slight.

Private hearing

9–79 Hearings will be in private in all but the rarest cases. The need to make hearings informal makes an open hearing impractical, However the rules permit the district judge to direct a hearing open to the public and this may occasionally be appropriate, primarily where a matter of public interest arises.

Oath not to be used

9–80 The use of an oath in county court arbitrations poses two problems. First, it tends to militate against informality. Secondly, in the majority of arbitrations it is difficult to draw a distinction between what is strictly evidence and what can more appropriately be regarded as argument or submission. However, the rule preserves the ability to require evidence to be on oath and this is occasionally helpful when there is a simple and direct conflict of fact, *e.g.* whether money was paid by way of a gift or loan.

Fair procedure

9–81 The choice of an appropriate procedure which can be regarded as fair by all concerned is often the most difficult task for the arbitrator bearing in mind the need for informality, the fact that many litigants will be conducting a court action for the first and, indeed, often the only time in their lives, and the great variation in their ability to gather together the evidence that is required to prove the case. The procedure, while still basically adversarial rather than inquisitorial, may best be described as interventionist.

The problem is increased by the fact that while the majority of arbitrations in the county court are conducted by the litigants themselves (or a "lay representative"—see below) some are conducted by lawyers on both side and there will be a number in which one side is represented and the other not. The latter create the greatest problems for the arbitrator. 9–82

Where both parties are represented the approach of the arbitrator may well be not dissimilar to that of an interventionist judge in an open court trial. The lawyers will be allowed to conduct their case but the arbitrator will intervene readily to indicate the points on which s/he particularly requires assistance and to cut short evidence and, more particularly, arguments or submissions when his/her mind is made up. 9–83

The position where either or both parties are represented by lay representatives (as well as the conditions upon which such representatives are entitled to act) are set out in the Lay Representatives (Rights of Audience) Order 1992[17] and more especially in the Practice Direction set out below. 9–84

Where both parties are in person the procedure will tend to follow a pattern in which the arbitrator outlines the dispute as s/he sees it from the "pleadings" making sure that s/he has understood the basis of each party's case. S/he may then explain any particular points of law that may be involved as well as the procedure that s/he will adopt. After that the arbitrator will question each party till s/he is satisfied that s/he has understood the nature of that party's case and then question the party or witness about the points put forward by the other party. While the arbitrator will ask each party whether s/he wishes to question the other party and/or witnesses the fact is that few are able to conduct anything approaching an effective "cross-examination". 9–85

In a simple case the arbitrator will probably take the evidence as a whole from each side. In more complicated cases, *e.g.* a building dispute, the arbitrator may well find it better to isolate each specific issue and question each party on that particular issue before proceeding to the next. This avoids the need for litigants to try to remember the evidence given on a particular point by their opponent some time before. 9–86

Where there are witnesses the arbitrator may follow the more traditional approach of hearing the plaintiff's case before the defendant's. However, some find it better to take the two parties' evidence first and then that of the witnesses—this has the advantage that the arbitrator is clear as to the full nature of each party's case before questioning the witnesses. 9–87

The most difficult situation is where one party is represented and the other is not—though it is easier to deal with this situation in an arbitration than in open court. Unfortunately no common practice appears to have evolved to deal with 9–88

[17] S.I. 1992 No. 1966.

this situation. The general approach is to follow the normal pattern of questioning by the arbitrator but inevitably the opportunity to cross examine will be used more effectively by the lawyer. At one time it was thought that the informality of the process entitled the arbitrator to refuse to allow a lawyer to put questions direct and would entitle the arbitrator to require that questions be put "through" the arbitrator. In *Chilton v. Saga Holidays plc*[18] it was said that on the rules as they then stood arbitrations were dealt with on an adversarial basis and that the right to prevent direct cross examination could not be excluded other than by agreement. The problem and the procedure to be adopted were described in the following words:

> "The problem which arises when you have one represented party and one unrepresented parts is very well known to all judges and particularly to judges who deal with small claims in the county court. It becomes the duty of the judge so far as he can, without entering into the arena to a point where he is no longer able to act judicially, to make good any deficiencies in the advantages available to the unrepresented party. We have all done it, we all know that it can be done and that it can be done effectively. That is the proper course to be adopted. The informality which is stressed by the rule and the requirement that the arbitrator may adopt any method of procedure which he considers to be convenient (it would be better perhaps if it had said 'just and convenient') covers the situation where, as so often happens, a litigant in person is quite incapable of cross-examining but is perfectly capable in the time available for cross-examination of putting his own case. The judge . . . then picks up the unrepresented party's complaints and puts them to the other side."

9–89 With respect the reality of this approach must be questioned and the correctness of the decision must be doubted—the rule after all said "convenient" and not "just and convenient". However, this decision lays down the procedure to be adopted unless the rules or any agreement provide otherwise. The rules have now been changed; do the present rules affect the situation?

9–90 The new rule expressly allows the arbitrator to "assist a party by putting questions to the witnesses and the other party". This alone is merely permissive and cannot affect any change in the principle. However, whereas the former rule merely permitted the arbitrator to adopt any procedure "which he may consider to be convenient" the present rule says "which he may consider to be fair and which gives to each party an equal opportunity to have his case presented". In its use of the word "fair" the rule appears to nod in the direction of the criticism by the former Master of the Rolls in *Chilton v. Saga*. He then referred to the decision in *Allen v. Allen and Bell*[19] in which it was said:

[18] [1986] 1 All E.R. 841, CA.
[19] [1894] P. 248.

"It appears to us contrary to all rules of evidence, and opposed to natural justice, that the evidence of one party should be received as evidence against another party without the latter having an opportunity of testing its truthfulness by cross examination."

However, the overriding test would appear to be that the procedure offers "each party an equal opportunity". In a situation such as that being considered only one party will normally have the opportunity of directly and effectively testing the truthfulness of the other party's evidence. The requirement to give each party an equal opportunity must mean seeking to put each party on a similar basis so that the unrepresented party does not suffer by lacking the ability to cross examine in an effective way. It is certainly arguable that while the arbitrator must ensure that the procedure is fair to the represented party if s/he is satisfied that the professional ability of one party to cross-examination places the other party at a serious disadvantage s/he could refuse to allow cross examination directly. This could enable the arbitrator to require all questions to be put through him. Fairness can only be decided on the facts of the particular case and not by any general presupposition about procedures to be adopted. It is clearly unsatisfactory that this point is still uncertain but we can only await the forthcoming revision of the rules as a result of Lord Woolf's inquiry into Civil Justice. 9–91

Absence of a party

As in all litigation there will be cases in which one party does not attend. The general procedure is that the party attending will be required to prove his or her case and judgment given accordingly. In hearing the case the court will naturally take into account the nature of the absent party's case and probe the evidence to ensure that no obvious injustice will be done by giving judgment on the case presented. In arbitration the duty of the arbitrator is greater and is assisted by the disapplication of the need for evidence to be on oath and the other rules as to evidence—and in particular the rule against hearsay evidence. S/he is required to take into account "any pleadings or other documents filed". Such documents—subject to the normal reservations about the weight to be accorded to untested hearsay evidence—will be evidence in the case and not merely a basis for the arbitrator to probe the evidence given. The difference may in practice be slight but it clearly makes it improper, *e.g.*, to dismiss a claim simply because of a party's absence. 9–92

Paper arbitrations

While the rules make no express provision for "paper arbitration" the rule referred to above lays the ground for an arbitration to be conducted on the papers before the court. Where one or both parties expressly ask for this to be done there is no problem. The difficulty occurs where, as is not infrequently the case, neither party attends and there is no request for a "paper arbitration" nor any explanation for non attendance. On the basis of the rule it would appear difficult 9–93 to ''strike out'' a claim merely because of non-attendance unless the court is satisfied on the papers that the claim has no realistic prospects of success. On the other hand the real reason for non-attendance may be that the parties have reached an agreement and to make a decision on the papers may create real problems only with the registration of judgments. The appropriate course may well be to adjourn generally. However, it is perhaps time for there to be a rule dealing expressly with ''paper arbitrations''. The objection in the past has been that in smaller cases laymen will frequently not appreciate the nature of the evidence that is required. If there is a hearing the arbitrator can deal with this by questions, s/he cannot do so in a paper arbitration save by correspondence—a procedure somewhat foreign to the court's approach. Nonetheless the advantages to some, though not all, litigants of such a procedure is clear.

Expert assessors

9–94 The power to appoint expert assessors is a valuable one and may well prove more so as the ''small claims'' limit is increased. The power is exercisable in any arbitration, unlike the power to appoint an outside arbitrator which does not apply to automatic references. The main stumbling block is the question of remuneration. In practice the effective procedure would be either to hold a preliminary hearing in a case where the use of an assessor would appear to be appropriate or to adjourn an arbitration once it became clear that there were technical issues which needed such appointment. The question of remuneration must be settled. The wording of C.C.R., Ord. 19, r.4.(3) allowing ''fees for an expert'' not exceeding £200 would appear to cover an expert assessor so that any payment by the successful party would be recoverable up to that amount. However the arbitrator/district judge would need to ensure that payment for an expert assessor or for an expert report was made before the appointment was made.

Production of documents or things

9–95 In many cases, as a matter of course, one or other party will bring along any item in dispute for inspection but the power to order this will prove useful in some cases.

Inspection of property

9–96 Such inspection will frequently prove sensible in straightforward issues of fact regarding, *e.g.* building works. Rather than hearing contested evidence, a visit to the property, or even the adjournment of the arbitration to be continued at the property will frequently prove the most effective means of resolving the dispute. In small cases the practical knowledge—and indeed common sense—of the arbitrator may be sufficient to decide issues as to quality of workmanship although caution will be required where more substantial sums are involved. The non expert arbitrator must be careful not to rely on his/her own judgment where there is a significant issue requiring expert evidence. The procedure—as well as the ability to hold the arbitration at the premises in question—is particularly appropriate to expert arbitrators.

Representation

While the intention of the small claims procedure is to provide an informal method of resolving disputes suitable for litigants in person there is no restriction on the use of lawyers by either party. **9–97**

In addition it has become customary for the arbitrator to use the wide powers of the Courts and Legal Services Act, s.27(2)(c) to grant a specific right of audience to other representatives, *e.g.* Citizens Advice Bureaux and similar agency workers. However this decision is entirely in the discretion of the arbitrator. **9–98**

Lay Representatives

The need for representation has now been recognised by the Lay Representatives (Rights of Audience) Order 1992,[20] made in pursuance of the Courts and Legal Services Act 1990, s.11. This Order applies only to proceedings which stand automatically referred to arbitration under C.C.R., Ord. 19, r.3. The right of audience does not apply to proceedings: **9–99**

> "(a) at any stage after the award has been entered as the judgment in the proceedings,
> (b) on any appeal brought against any decision made by the district judge in the proceedings,
> (c) on any application to set aside the award."

The restriction in (b) applies to an appeal against an order made by a district judge prior to the arbitration—no appeal lies against the arbitration award itself (see below). Furthermore, no lay representative may exercise a right of audience where his/her client does not attend the hearing, a limitation which can create problems that are discussed below. **9–100**

The regulations are the subject of a Practice Direction made by the Lord Chancellor as follows: **9–101**

"PRACTICE DIRECTION
LAY REPRESENTATION IN COUNTY COURTS

1. This Practice Direction is made under Order 50, rule 1 of the County Court Rules 1981 to secure uniformity of practice in the county courts in respect of new rights of lay representation conferred by the Lay Representatives (Rights of Audience) Order 1992. The Order is made under

[20] S.I. 1992 No. 1966.

section 11 of the Courts and Legal Services Act 1990 and came into force on 26 October 1992.

The scope of the new right

2. The Order entitles any person to speak at a small claims hearing on behalf of a part. The right is confined to a right of audience, that is, to appear before the court, to address the judge and, subject to the procedure adopted by the judge, to call and examine witnesses. The new right does not extend to the conduct of litigation.
3. Article 2(1) of the Order defines those small claims hearings where the new right may be exercised. These are the main hearings and (subject to the exceptions set out below) any interlocutory hearings. The Order does not allow a lay representative a right of audience in the following proceedings:
   (a) claims referred to arbitration voluntarily under Order 19, rule 9,
   (b) proceedings after an award has been entered as 'a judgment of the court, such as proceedings to enforce the award,
   (c) appeals against any decision of a district judge. These include appeals against an order that a case proceed to trial in open court (or against a refusal to make such an order),
   (d) applications to set aside an award.
4. A lay representative may not exercise a right of audience unless the party is present (article 2(2) of the Order).

Conduct of proceedings in which lay representatives take part

5. A key purpose in giving litigants a free choice of representative is to give them the confidence to pursue or defend their cases in court. This consideration should guide the court in the conduct of proceedings in which lay representatives take part, in its expectations of the standards of conduct and competence exhibited by lay representatives, and in its use of the sanctions under section 11(4) and 11(6) of refusing to hear, or of disqualifying, a lay representative (see paragraphs 9–16 below). The court is entitled to expect every representative to behave honestly, reasonably and responsibly. However, the standard of competence may vary greatly. A higher standard of competence may be expected of a person who provides such services commercially than of one who simply represents a friend or relative.
6. Judges now have a responsibility actively to conduct small claims proceedings in such a way as to ensure that they and the parties are fully aware of all the relevant facts and issues (CCR Order 19 rule 7, ...). The court's responsibility does not cease where a lay representative is acting, except to the extent that the lay representative is clearly capable of conducting the litigant's case without the help of the court.
7. Although the normal rule is that an advocate may not give evidence on behalf of the party s/he represents, the Order does not preclude a lay

representative from giving evidence as a witness in the proceedings to which it applies. In small claims hearings there may be occasions when it would be difficult to avoid this, for example where on spouse is representing the other and both have witnesses the events in issue. But parties should be warned that this may affect the weight which the court gives to the lay representative's representations.

Refusing to hear a lay representative

8. Under section 11(4), a Circuit judge or a district judge may refuse to hear a lay representative in particular proceedings if that representative behaves in an unruly manner. Examples might include ignoring directions of the court or otherwise impeding the proper progress of the proceedings.
9. If a judge is minded to exercise this power, he should tell the lay representative and the affected party what his reasons are and state them on form EX 83.
10. If the judge considers that a refusal to hear a lay representative may prejudice the client's case for the remainder of the proceedings, the judge should consult the affected party on the possibility of adjourning the proceedings to provide an opportunity for the party, or another representative, to take over the presentation of the case.

Disqualification of a lay representative

11. Under section 11(6) a Circuit judge or a district judge may disqualify a lay representative from exercising a right of audience in any proceedings in any county court where that person would otherwise have a right of audience under section 11. The judge may only order disqualification:
    (a) in the course of proceedings in which a right of audience under section 11 is being exercised, and
    (b) if he has reason to believe that the representative has intentionally misled the court or otherwise demonstrated unsuitability to exercise that right.

The judge may take into account conduct in the proceedings before him, or in any other proceedings where the person was exercising a right of audience. In practice, however, occasions are likely to be rare where the details of previous misconduct (such as, for example, conduct leading to a refusal to hear, or to being made a vexatious litigant) are sufficiently attested to support the making of a disqualification order.

12. A judge who is minded to disqualify a lay representative may well feel that he can deal with the matter on the spot. Before doing so, however, he should consider whether the client's case is likely to be prejudiced. If so, the judge should order an adjournment of the arbitration proceed-

ings to provide an opportunity for the affected party, or another representative, to take over presentation of the case.

13. The judge should also bear in mind that disqualification will in some instances deprive a person of his or her livelihood, or affect a person's standing in voluntary or paid employment, and he should consider whether the interests of natural justice may require the disqualification to be dealt with at a separate hearing.
14. Once he has determined the best course of action, the judge should warn the lay representative that he or she may be disqualified, and explain the reasons. Whether the disqualification is dealt with at the arbitration hearing or at a separate hearing, the lay representative should be given a reasonable opportunity of responding before the judge reaches a decision. If the judge makes an order of disqualification, the reason must be incorporated in the order.''

9–102 Few problems apply with regard to this procedure except with regard to clause 2(2) of the Order which prevents the exercise of rights of audience where the party is not present. This does not prevent the court exercising its powers under section 27(2)(c) of the Courts and Legal Services Act (above) in favour of a lay representative, merely his or her right to represent the litigant without leave of the court.

9–103 The problem is how a client which is a partnership, corporation or limited company is to be present. In the case of a partnership can an employee of the partnership represent the partnership in the absence of all (or even one of) the partners? The answer would appear to be ''no''. Certainly one partner must be present before any lay representative can have a right of audience. This can cause difficulties for small firms seeking to be represented by, *e.g.* a manager who may in reality have the knowledge required to conduct the case. Of course that manager can appear as a witness but cannot as of right conduct the case and would have to ask the court to exercise its discretion under the Courts and Legal Services Act 1990, s.27(2)(c). Similar problems will occur with regard to a corporation or a limited company. Such a body, having no physical existence, cannot appear except through an agent—can that agent be the lay representative or does there have to be another duly-authorised officer or other employee of the company present? To exercise a right of audience under the Order it would appear that the attendance of such an officer or other agent of the company in addition to the lay representative is necessary. However, it would appear to be the better view that in practice in county court proceedings a company can appear by any suitable agent it chooses without reliance on the provisions of the Order, see *Charles P. Kinnell & Co. Ltd v. Harding Wace & Co.*[21] in which it was said:

''As from its nature a company cannot appear in person, not having as a

[21] [1918] 1 K.B. 405.

legal entity any visible person, it must appear by counsel or solicitor, or by leave of the judge some other person may be allowed to appear instead of the company to address the court which includes the examination of witnesses and generally conducting the case. There is no limit or restriction imposed on the judge as to the person whom he may allow, or as to the nature of the cases in which he may allow some other person to address him instead of counsel or solicitor for the company. It is left to his discretion but except under special circumstances he would doubtless only sanction some director or officer or other employee of the company so appearing instead of the company and would limit his permission to cases which he thought could properly be disposed of before him, without the assistance of either counsel or solicitor.''

Thus, in order to appear as of right it would appear to be necessary for some officer of the company to attend with the lay representative but that officer or other employee of the company might, with the leave of the court, be permitted to conduct the arbitration simply as the agent of the company or corporation. **9–104**

The County Courts Act 1981, s.60 provides a special right of representation for an authorised officer of a housing authority to represent the council in connection with any claim for rent, mesne profits or damages arising out of the occupation of a council house. **9–105**

The Award

Form

Decisions are commonly made orally at the end of the arbitration. The arbitrator may well hear a significant number of relatively short arbitrations in a day and the task of preparing written decisions in all cases could prove unnecessarily demanding. Where a written decision is needed the arbitrator should be asked for this before giving an oral judgment. **9–106**

Remedies available

The most common award is a money sum directed to be paid at a particular time (usually within 14 days after judgment) or, if evidence of inability to pay a lump sum is provided, by instalments. A money award for a sum not less than **9–107**

£5,000 (probably including any costs awarded to the successful party) will carry interest under the Judgments Act 1838, s.17 (see the County Courts Act 1984, s.74 and the County Court (Interest on Judgments Debts) Order 1991[22]).

9–108 For many years an area of uncertainty has been whether the arbitrator had power to grant an injunction, or make an order for specific performance or a declaration. The common view was that the arbitrator did not exercise the full powers of the court and could only make a monetary award. This question was considered by the Court of Appeal in *Joyce v. Liverpool City Council.*[23] These appeals concerned housing disrepair proceedings. After analysing the powers of the district judge under the County Court Rules the court decided that as the district judge had power to grant such remedies in any other case within his or her jurisdiction there was no reason for differentiating his or her powers in the small claims jurisdiction. However, as the powers come from the general powers of the district judge it would not appear that such powers are exercisable by an "outside arbitrator". Furthermore these powers do not extend to the making of a *Mareva* injunction or *Anton Piller* order as the county court has no jurisdiction to make such orders: see the County Courts Remedies Regulations 1991.[24]

The effect

9–109 Once an award is made it becomes immediately enforceable as a judgment of the court. Such award may be enforced in the county court except that if the award exceeds £5,000 (inclusive of any costs awarded) it can only be enforced by seizure of goods in the High Court after an order for transfer: High Court and County Courts Jurisdiction Order 1991,[25] article 8(1)(c). A successful party is entitled to have any order enforced in the High Court (after transfer) except by charging order, by seizure of goods where the amount of the judgment does not exceed £2000 and any judgment arising out of an agreement regulated by the Consumer Credit Act 1974.

Costs

General principle

9–110 Costs in a county court arbitration may be awarded in the same way and upon the same principles as in any county court action, as to which see the Supreme

[22] S.I. 1991 No. 1184.
[23] [1995] 3 All E.R. 110; [1995] 3 W.L.R. 439, CA.
[24] S.I. 1991 No. 1222.
[25] S.I. 1991 No. 724.

Court Act 1981, s.51 and R.S.C., Ord. 62, r.3. There is in practice a presumption that the successful party will be entitled to the costs of the action but that presumption may be displaced in the particular circumstances of the case.

Small claims

However, where the action is one that is automatically referred to arbitration under C.C.R., Ord. 19, r.3, and in that circumstance only, there is a totally different rule. "Costs" for this purpose are defined as: **9–111**

"(a) solicitors' charges,
(b) sums allowed to a litigant in person pursuant to CCR Order 38 r.17,
(c) a fee or reward charged by a lay representative for acting on behalf of a party in the proceedings" (C.C.R., Ord. 19, r.4(1)).

In such a case no costs are recoverable by the successful party except

"(a) the costs which were stated on the summons or which would have been stated on the summons if the claim had been for a liquidated sum,
(aa) in proceedings which include a claim for an injunction or for an order for specific performance or similar relief, a sum not exceeding £260 in respect of the cost of legal advice obtained for the purpose of bringing or defending that claim,
(b) the costs of enforcing the award, and
(c) such further costs as the district judge may direct where there has been unreasonable conduct on the part of the opposite party in relation to the proceedings or the claim therein' (C.C.R., Ord. 19, r.4(2)).

The definition of "costs" is reasonably clear. The main issue that arises is whether any disbursements incurred by the successful party or his or her solicitor can be recovered: do they come under the definition of "costs"? The answer must be that with two exceptions no such disbursements can be recovered. The broad argument for this statement is that the expression "solicitor's charges" would appear to be apt to cover all expenditure incurred by the solicitor and recoverable by him/her in his/her bill—that is what s/he charges. This view is reinforced by the reference to sums allowed to a litigant in person. These include "such costs as would have been allowed if the work and disbursements to which the costs relate had been done by a solicitor"—C.C.R., Ord. 38, r.17(1). The exceptions are court fees and witness expenses. **9–112**

Costs of issue

Paragraph (2) as set out above allows the recovery of the court fees on issue of proceedings. Such fees are provided for by the County Court Fees Order 1982. **9–113**

There is only one relatively minor question arising out of this rule. What is the position where a plaintiff sues for, *e.g.* £900 and is awarded only £500. Had s/he sued for the lower sum there would have been a smaller court fee. Should the unsuccessful party be expected to pay the difference? While the rule tends to suggest that the actual fee paid is recoverable, there is a tendency for the district judge/arbitrator to limit the amount of fee recoverable to that which would have been paid had the plaintiff sued for the sum awarded. The authority for this lies in the general discretion of the court over the award of costs. In practice much will depend on the reasonableness of the plaintiff in claiming the sum that s/he did. If the amount was reduced by reason of the plaintiff's contributory negligence nor, possibly, where the plaintiff had a reasonable expectation of recovering the sum claimed, no reduction would be likely.

9–114 If a solicitor is involved his/her fixed costs on issuing proceedings will also be recoverable. It is customary not to insert solicitor's costs on a claim for unliquidated damages, hence the reference to the costs which "would have been stated", in that case the district judge/arbitrator will allow the scale costs and fees for the amount actually awarded (ignoring interest and any reduction in the award because of contributory negligence).

Costs of legal advice in injunction, etc. proceedings

9–115 Since the decision that claims for injunctive relief or specific performance fell within the jurisdiction of a district judge acting as an arbitrator the rules have been amended to enable some costs to be paid for obtaining advice in connection with bringing or defending such proceedings. This is limited to £260.

Costs caused by unreasonable conduct

9–116 The main area of difficulty in this rule relates to paragraph (2)(c). What amounts to "unreasonable conduct . . . in relation to the proceedings or the claim therein". There is very little authority to give guidance on this point and inevitably practice varies.

9–117 One area in which such costs might frequently be allowed is an unreasonable application for procedural direction or orders during the course of the proceedings. It has already been stressed that county court arbitration is intended to provide a simple and informal method of dispute resolution and is not be cluttered up with procedural applications which are only too frequently of a tactical nature. Thus in *Chilton v. Saga Holidays plc*[26] it was said:

> "while I have not actually invited counsel for Saga Holidays to defend his application for further and better particulars in this case, it is virtually

[26] [1986] 1 All E.R. 841.

indefensible. It was an attempt to turn this arbitration into a High Court hearing with detailed requests for information of which there was not the slightest need since they were already set out in a document prepared by the claimant. That is the sort of formality which should be disapproved of without qualification.''

Such applications are likely to be met with short shrift and an order that the applicant pay the other party's costs on the normal county court basis. **9–118**

Another area which creates little difficulty is where a party fails to attend a hearing or seeks a last minute adjournment. If the hearing is adjourned it is likely that that party will be ordered to pay the costs ''thrown away''—often primarily the other party's ''witness expenses'' but possibly including the costs of representation or preparing for the hearing. Where an application is made to set aside the decision by a party who failed to attend, that party would almost certainly have to pay the reasonable costs of the application and, if successful, of the previous hearing. **9–119**

It may well be that where a party quite unjustifiably brings or defends proceedings this would be regarded as ''unreasonable conduct'' though decisions on this point may well vary on the particular facts of the case. Plaintiffs are not expected to be lawyers and merely to bring a claim which is not in law justified would seldom justify a costs penalty. The position with regard to a defendant who puts in a defence but then does not turn up to support it may merit such an order, particularly if the defence is seen as simply an attempt to play for time. **9–120**

Where a defendant does attend and put forward an honest defence however mistaken in law the power to order costs would seldom be used. If such costs are awarded they are to be fixed by the arbitrator or the district judge and not taxed (paragraph (5)). **9–121**

Witness Expenses

Only limited witness expenses are recoverable, as provided for in paragraph (3): **9–122**

> ''Nothing in paragraph (2) shall be taken as precluding the award of the following allowances—
>
> (a) any expenses which have reasonably incurred by a party or a witness in travelling to and from the hearing or in staying away from home,
>
> (b) a sum not exceeding £50.00 in respect of a party's or a witness's loss of earnings when attending a hearing,
>
> (c) a sum not exceeding £200 in respect of the fees of an expert.''

Little comment is required with regard to this rule. Though the sums are inadequate in many cases (particularly that for the expert) there appears to be no discretion to exceed the amounts prescribed, as is the case with the majority of **9–123** prescribed county court costs. Furthermore the allowance for loss of earnings is just that and not a "witness allowance" in the general sense—an allowance which can go beyond mere financial loss (*Reed v. Gray*[27]). The recoverable fee for an expert is a total fee and covers both the preparation of a report and, if necessary, attendance at a hearing.

Costs of enforcement

9–124 Once an award has been made the restrictions in r.4 cease to apply. In fact the rule specifically states this with regard to the costs of enforcement. Such costs are usually recoverable on the basis of costs fixed by the rules (Appendix B, Part III). There is power under C.C.R., Ord. 38, r.18 for the court to make some other order as to the costs of enforcement proceedings—normally that they be taxed or fixed in some sum other than that prescribed and this power applies as much to arbitrations, whether for more or less than £3,000, as to other proceedings in the county court.

Costs on application to set aside

9–125 The position on an application to a circuit judge to set aside an award (as to which see below) is less clear. However in *Afzal v. Ford Motor Co. Ltd*[28] it was said that the circuit judge had power under C.C.R., Ord. 37, r.6(1) to award costs of such an application. Though some of the reasoning may be questionable this case is likely to remain authority for the proposition that costs can be ordered as in any other county court matter and that the restrictions of Ord. 19, r.4 do not apply to such an application.

Costs of action "voluntarily" referred to arbitration

9–126 The restrictions on costs described above refer only to an action which has been automatically referred to arbitrations, *i.e.* where the amount claimed does not exceed £3,000—or £1,000 if personal injury damages.

9–127 In all other cases the arbitrator must exercise the normal discretion as to costs, namely that costs follow the event unless there is some good reason for some other decision. Such costs may be ordered to be taxed or may be assessed by the arbitrator if the successful party is a litigant in person or, if legally represented, his solicitor or counsel asks for them to be assessed. Costs of a litigant in person are normally allowed at the rate of £8.50 an hour or a higher sum if he can show actual financial loss. The total sum allowed in respect of time spent

[27] [1952] Ch. 337; [1952] 1 All E.R. 241.
[28] [1994] 4 All E.R. 720.

by the litigant may not exceed two thirds of what might hypothetically have been allowed a solicitor for preparing and conducting the case. In addition a litigant is entitled to any disbursements which might normally have been paid by a solicitor is acting and the costs of any legal advice that he has obtained.

Challenging the Decision

No right of appeal on fact

There is no right of appeal against a judgment entered as a result of an award in county court arbitration. Such a decision is final as to the facts. **9–128**

Application to set aside the award

The award may only be challenged in the following way: **9–129**

(a) By an application to set aside an award made in the absence of a party. Such an application is made to the district judge under C.C.R., Ord. 37 r.2 as applied by C.C.R., Ord. 19 r.8(2). There are no limitations on the right to make such application but normally the applicant will be expected to show
  - that s/he acted diligently once s/he became aware of the judgment;
  - that s/he had good reason for not attending the hearing; and
  - that the applicant would have a realistic chance of success if the arbitration were reheard (this test is based on the test on an application to set aside a default judgment—see *Alpine Bulk Transport Co. Inc. v. Saudi Eagle Shipping Co. Inc., the Saudi Eagle*.[29]

(b) The second method is an application to the circuit judge to set aside the award on the grounds set out in C.C.R., Ord. 19 r.8(1) namely "on the ground that there has been misconduct by the arbitrator or that the arbitrator made an error of law". As these grounds are fundamentally the same as the grounds on which any arbitration award may be set aside by the High Court no further discussion is included at this point. Only two comments need to be made. First in view of the intention that the procedure should be informal and necessarily "brisk and effi-

[29] [1986] 2 Lloyd's Rep. 221, CA.

cient'' the task of persuading the circuit judge of misconduct merely from the manner in which the arbitration was conducted must necessarily be difficult—*Starmer v. Bradbury*.[30] In *Owen v. Nicholl*[31] use by the registrar of information obtained from evidence given by the son of one of the parties at his public examination in bankruptcy proceedings was held to be misconduct and the award set aside. It is not clear that such an approach would be followed under the present rules excluding the rules of evidence and giving the arbitrator a wide discretion as to the conduct of the arbitration in a fair manner. Much would depend on the extent to which the parties or either of them were put at a disadvantage by the introduction of such evidence. Further, the words ''on the face of the award'' do not appear as there is seldom any written award. In the circumstances the alleged error may be difficult to detect unless patent particularly as it is uncommon for lay litigants to record the terms of the oral judgment/award.

Procedure

9–130 An application to set aside an award where the applicant was not present is made by notice of application to the district judge. The notice must be served on the other party who is entitled to be heard. The factors to be considered are outlined above.

9–131 An application to set aside the award on the grounds of misconduct or error of law is made on notice to the circuit judge and the other party must be served and has the right to be heard.

9–132 If the circuit judge obtains any information from the arbitrator as to what took place at the arbitration

> ''it would be desirable, before he gave his actual decision, that the judge should inform the parties of what he had ascertained from the [arbitrator] so as to enable the parties, if necessary, to comment thereon or, in an extreme case, to tender evidence contrary to what he has been informed or to ask the [arbitrator] to make a statement in the presence of the parties as to what took place'.[32]

Setting aside the award

9–133 The rules provide merely for the award to be set aside if the circuit judge or district judge, as the case may be, is satisfied that this is appropriate. There is

[30] *The Times*, April 11, 1994, CA.
[31] [1948] 1 All E.R. 707, CA.
[32] *Owen v. Nicholl* [1948] 1 All E.R. 707, CA.

no rehearing as such and the only course is to set aside the award and give directions for a further hearing of the arbitration. In practice, particularly when the application is heard by a district judge it will be convenient not only to deal with the application to set aside but also to rehear the arbitration at the same time. Much must naturally depend on the time available and whether or not the parties are prepared for this to be done and do not wish time to further prepare or arrange for the attendance of witnesses. The circuit judge may adopt a similar approach but this is less common.

Part 10

INTERNATIONAL COMMERCIAL ARBITRATIONS

By Jan Paulsson, F.C.I.Arb.
Member of the Bar of Paris; Partner, Freshfields (Paris)

The Role of International Arbitration

Four immediate thoughts may strike a lawyer contemplating for the first time the prospect of international arbitration. First, it is possible that one or more of the arbitrators will be foreign. Secondly, the arbitration may, in whole or in part, be conducted abroad. Thirdly, evidence may be produced, or sought to be produced, from foreign sources. Fourthly, the logical place to enforce the award may be abroad. 10–01

It may further occur to the novice that each of these features of international arbitration, beyond endearing him to his travel agent, is potentially significant to the claimant's prospect of winning—and collecting. He would, of course, be quite right. So before examining the consequences of becoming involved in international arbitration, it may be useful to reflect briefly on the reason why parties agree to it in the first place. Are there clear benefits of international arbitration that outweigh the disadvantages of uncertainty inherent in the four factors mentioned in the introductory paragraph? 10–02

The answer is: not necessarily. International arbitration is generally chosen by the parties not so much because they like it as because they have no other realistic choice. There is much discussion about the intrinsic merits of arbitration: speed, confidentiality, finality, special expertise of the arbitrator, inexpensiveness—and whether these factors are real or illusory. Reasonable men differ; they prefer either arbitration or court litigation. If likeminded negotiators are at work in a national setting, there will be no difficulty; arbitration will be chosen over court litigation, or vice versa. But if the negotiators are of different nationalities, the option most often evaporates because of the simple fact that *the alternative court in the minds of the negotiators is not the same one*. A Frenchman and a Finn might—rightly or wrongly—both loathe arbitration, and neither would ever accept it when negotiating with fellow countrymen. When negotiating an international distributorship agreement, however, each finds it impossible to convince the other that the dispute should be heard by a judge in Paris or Helsinki, in the French or Finnish language, respectively. So they compromise, and their English-language contract is made subject to an arbitration clause calling for arbitration in London, Stockholm, The Hague, or some other neutral place. That is the reason that international arbitration—as opposed to domestic arbitration—is chosen. It prevails by default; there exists no neutral international court for private-law disputes. 10–03

A corollary of this observation is that international arbitration—along with more routine matters—gets the most intractable cases, where parties are not only 10–04 irreconcilable on the merits, but also separated by an unbridgeable gap of cultural and political misunderstanding. As a result, the lore of international arbitration includes a number of ghastly stories of deserving parties who had to face absurd delays and complications, to spend an unconscionable amount of money in litigating, and in the end found that their award could not be enforced. These unfortunate cases should not be allowed to obscure the fact that international arbitration is the typical means by which international contractual disputes are settled, and that in most cases the process operates smoothly.

Types of international arbitration

10–05 Some kinds of arbitration are not truly international in character even though parties of different nationalities are involved. There are many branches of trade or industry which have established arbitration procedures within professional bodies. Arbitrators, counsel, and the procedural law are all of a local variety. Thus, maritime arbitration in London is a distinctly English phenomenon: its cases are no less English, and no more international, because foreigners are involved than a High Court case becomes "international" due to the presence of foreigners. The significant international feature of the process is that the enforceability of the award is more likely to be tested abroad than in England; but the same is true for a court judgment involving similar parties.

10–06 What will be described here is a process that is not tied to a particular locale, but may be set in motion by parties from anywhere, who entrust their disputes to arbitrators of any nationality, and which is adaptable to any venue. There are two principal categories of this type of arbitration, namely institutional arbitration and ad hoc arbitration.

10–07 Since contemporary international arbitration gives the parties and the arbitrators wide latitude to establish whatever rules of procedure they deem appropriate, it would be wrong to suggest that the daily work of arbitrators is markedly different depending on whether they apply, say, the ICC Rules or the UNCITRAL Rules. The present discussion will concentrate on structural contrasts between the main types of international arbitration. A synthesis of the manner in which cases are generally presented by the parties and apprehended by the arbitrators will be attempted, beginning with paragraph 10–133 below.

Institutional arbitration

10–08 Although other arbitral institutions are also prepared to supervise arbitrations taking place in countries other than the one where the institution has its seat (such as the American Arbitration Association, which has panels of international arbitrators of various nationalities) and although some national institutions have a special role in particular contexts (such as the Arbitration Institute of the Stockholm Chamber of Commerce for US-USSR contracts or contracts involving the Peoples' Republic of China, and the Austrian Arbitration Centre of the Federal Economic Chamber for East-West European trade), the present description will be limited to the three best known international arbitration institutions: the ICC, the LCIA, and ICSID, and to an important recent entrant in the field, the WIPO Arbitration Centre.

ICC Arbitration

The International Chamber of Commerce created its Court of Arbitration shortly after the First World War. In 1989, the name was changed to the "International Court of Arbitration" in order to reflect its multinational membership (which includes 55 nationalities). The first ICC arbitration was decided in 1923. Since then, the ICC Court has become the leading international arbitration institution, both in terms of volume of cases and significance of disputes. In recent years, roughly 300 requests for arbitration have been submitted annually; since 1985 over 40 per cent of these cases have involved amounts in excess of US $1million—about one fourth of which have involved amounts in excess of US $10million.[1] Billion-dollar cases seem to come up at least once a year. Nearly one fifth of the cases involve international construction contracts, where the amount of money at stake on average tends to be high. 10–09

The international flavour of ICC arbitration makes itself felt dramatically when one considers the 1995 entries to the registry of new cases. In that calendar year, a record number of 427 requests for arbitration were received by the ICC. The parties involved were nationals of no less than 93 different countries, including 116 parties from Asia, 74 from Latin American, and 59 from Central and Eastern Europe.[2] The seat of the ICC Court is Paris, but only one-third of ICC arbitrations are actually held in that city. During the 1980–88 period, no less than 62 countries served as venues for ICC arbitrations.[3] 10–10

In most cases, the parties stipulate the place of arbitration. Otherwise, the ICC Court chooses the venue, taking into consideration the desiderata of neutrality, convenience, and enforceability of awards. 10–11

The parties are free to stipulate the number of arbitrators and their manner of selection. In the absence of such stipulation, the ICC Court will generally appoint a sole arbitrator if the dispute involves less than US $1.5 million, three 10–12

[1] W.L. Craig, W.W. Park and J. Paulsson, *International Chamber of Commerce Arbitration* (2nd ed., 1990), App. I, Table 8.

[2] See *The ICC International Court of Arbitration Bulletin*, May 1996, at p. 3.

[3] Precise breakdowns are found in Craig, Park and Paulsson, *op. cit.*, App. I, Table 7.

if the amount is greater. If a three-man tribunal is to be appointed, each party has the opportunity to nominate an arbitrator, who must be "independent" of the parties, for appointment by the ICC Court. Chairmen or sole arbitrators are not selected directly by the ICC Court, but are proposed by one of the various national committees that constitute the ICC. Most often, the ICC Court will turn to the national committee (if it exists) of the country where the arbitration is to take place (but not if one of the parties is of that nationality).

Terms of reference

10–13 One of the first tasks of an ICC tribunal is to draw up terms of reference to be signed by the arbitrators and the parties. (There are provisions ensuring that default by one of the parties does not prevent the case from going forward.) The terms of reference contain, *inter alia*, an exposition of the parties' respective contentions, particulars as to applicable procedural rules, and most important, the definition of the issues to be decided by the arbitrators.

10–14 The following comment has been made with respect to the terms of reference:

> "The Terms of Reference have been criticized as time consuming without bringing commensurate benefits. Many such critics come from common-law countries, particularly the United States, and their opinion may be coloured by their own rules of practice which encourage the discovery and development of facts after the exchange of initial pleadings and do not require an early definition of the issues by the parties. They may also underestimate the educational value of preparing the Terms of Reference when parties from widely differing legal and economic backgrounds are involved in the dispute. The authors have participated in some arbitrations where the meeting with the arbitrators to establish the Terms of Reference was the first effective realization by the defendant that an obligatory arbitral process was under way and that an award would ultimately be made on defined issues. Frequently, the discussion leading to agreement on the issues (or the effect on a party of the arbitrators' definition of the issues) has led to settlement. Thus the Terms of Reference may be useful as a protection of awards against attack, as a tool for organizing the future path of the arbitral proceedings, and sometimes as a means to rapprochement of the parties; it seems likely that they will remain in any future revision to the ICC Rules."[4]

10–15 The parties and failing them the arbitrators are free to establish procedural rules for the arbitration and to choose the substantive applicable law; in neither case need they follow the law of the place of arbitration (unless it uncharacteristically

[4] Craig, Park and Paulsson, *op. cit.*, p. 253. Indeed the 1998 ICC Rules of Arbitration retain the terms of reference (in Art. 18).

by its own terms is mandatory, with the result that non-compliance would endanger the award; see generally paragraph 10–83 below).

Awards rendered by ICC arbitrators cannot be directly communicated to the parties; they must be "scrutinised" and "approved" by the ICC Court. The process by which the ICC court occasionally requests the arbitrators to clarify, reconsider, or redraft their award is occasionally time-consuming, particularly in the case of three-man tribunals, and frustrating to the parties, because they sometimes spend many weeks and even months in a state of ignorance between the close of the case and their receipt of the award. Nevertheless, a recent study of the ICC arbitral process approves this practice[5]: 10–16

> "The Court never corrects alleged errors of fact or law; it simply acts to assure the formal sufficiency of the award. Most experienced ICC arbitrators can be counted on to render irreproachable awards. In all cases, however, the Court must give its approval after examination by a rapporteur from among the Court's membership. This is the stage at which an illogical, incomprehensible, or incomplete draft might be sent back to the arbitrators for clarification; here the quality control of the ICC arbitral process is exercised.
>
> This function seems to have been successfully carried out. According to one study, only four awards were set aside by local courts during the 1972–1975 period, which corresponds to approximately 0.5% of the awards rendered. Only around 6% of ICC awards, according to the former Director of the Court, are even challenged. This is a commendable record indeed given the multinational complexities of the cases submitted to ICC arbitration."

Advantages of scrutiny

The most persuasive argument in favour of the scrutiny process is that it ensures minimum standards notwithstanding the extraordinary diversity of arbitrators. In 1995, the ICC appointed arbitrators from 62 different countries, including sole arbitrators or chairmen from 40 countries ranging from Algeria to Argentina. If the scrutiny mechanism did not exist, there would be a powerful disincentive to the appointment of inexperienced arbitrators, no matter how talented, from emerging markets, no matter how important in world trade. That would certainly reduce the acceptability of ICC arbitration outside Europe and North America. (These observations illustrate the unfairness of comments to the effect that other arbitral institutions conduct no institutional scrutiny and yet—or so it is claimed—issue awards of a high standard. This is not an impressive feat if the awards are rendered by a homogenous group of arbitrators well known to the appointing authority.) At any rate, the disruptive potential of the ICC Court's 10–17

[5] Craig, Park and Paulsson, *op. cit.*, pp. 32–33.

scrutiny of awards should not be exaggerated. In 1994, only 19 of the 182 awards submitted to the court for approval were sent back to the arbitrators for reconsideration.[6]

Costs

10–18 The costs of ICC arbitration are assessed in a manner that has given rise to controversy: both the administrative charge of the ICC and the fees of the arbitrators are calculated with reference to the amount in dispute. It is the considered opinion of the present author that it is impossible to make a categorical statement as to whether this system is more expensive than one where costs are based exclusively on time charges. In practice, one hears many more complaints from underpaid arbitrators (whose effective hourly rates in complex cases can get discouragingly low) than from parties outraged by windfalls to arbitrators. On the other hand, the ICC's administrative charge may seem excessive in large cases, particularly when the arbitration takes place far from Paris, and the tribunal appoints its own secretary to be paid by the parties. (If the dispute involves US $1 million, the administrative charge will be $16,800 and the fee of one arbitrator will range from a minimum of $11,250 to a maximum of $53,500. If the case involves $50 million, the administrative charge is $57,800 and the range of arbitrator's fee from $48,750 to 204,000. With three arbitrators, the total fees may be increased to three times these amounts.) In 1986, the formerly open-ended scale for administrative charges was capped; as of 1998, the cap is fixed at $75,800 whenever the sum in dispute exceeds $80 million.

10–19 In the past, the ICC has insisted on immediate payment at the outset of an arbitration of an amount representing an estimate of the total costs and fees of the proceedings. As a result, in large cases hundreds of thousands of dollars were collected a full year before the arbitrators began to spend substantial time on the case. (As will be seen in paragraph 10–144 below, exchanges of written submissions are very important in international arbitration; their preparation implies much work over many months by the parties, while the arbitrators typically do not consecrate much studying time until the case approaches the stage of hearings.) Interest on these deposits is not credited to the parties. In recent years, however, the ICC has appropriately accepted bank guarantees in lieu of a portion of cash deposits for major cases. More importantly, since 1986, only one-half of the advance on cost is payable at the outset of the proceedings, the second half becoming due when the terms of reference (see above) have been finalised. As of 1998, a more flexible system of "provisional advances", payable by the claimant alone but credited toward the subsequent shared advances, has been introduced to speed up the process.

[6] D. Hascher, "Scrutiny of Draft Awards by The Court: 1994 Overview", *The ICC International Court of Arbitration Bulletin*, May 1995, at p. 51.

Pre-arbitral reference procedure

An interesting innovation was the ICC's adoption of Rules for a Pre-arbitral Referee Procedure in 1990. If parties agree to the application of these rules, they may obtain exceptionally rapid (30 days) provisional relief (*e.g.* directing the making of progress payments into an escrow account) in the form of a decision which, whilst not enforceable as an award. has the strength of a contractual provision. Its non-observance may then be sanctioned by the downstream arbitrators. 10–20

It must be said that this new mechanism has not yet got off to a fast start, judging from the paucity of applications. 10–21

LCIA Arbitration

The London Court of International Arbitration has roughly one-tenth of the case load of the ICC.[7] The LCIA should doubtless not be thought of as competing with the ICC, but rather as providing an alternative to the ICC system of arbitration. There are cases in which one system is more appropriate than the other. For example, the LCIA staff cannot match the linguistic proficiency of the ICC Court's secretariat, which handles correspondence in English, French, German and Spanish as a matter of routine. On the other hand, the LCIA—which has no activities apart from the organisation of arbitrations and which needs to consult no national committees—has a greater potential for institutional flexibility. 10–22

Since 1985, the LCIA has shed its original heavily English coloration to become resolutely international. Three-quarters of the members of the Court are from countries other than the United Kingdom, including Argentina, India, Japan, Russia, and the People's Republic of China. Since 1995, the President of the LCIA is an internationally renowned arbitration specialist from Germany. Like the ICC Court, the LCIA can administer arbitrations anywhere in the world. On the other hand, if the parties have not stipulated another place of arbitration—and unless the LCIA determines that there is some reason why another venue should be chosen—London will be the place of arbitration. (default position) 10–23

This factor, in addition to the fact that so many contracts calling for LCIA arbitration also stipulate English governing law, doubtless goes far to explain why the great majority of arbitrators appointed by the LCIA remain English. It does nevertheless happen that non-English arbitrators are appointed by the LCIA 10–24

[7] Craig, Park and Paulsson, *op. cit.*, p. 5.

even for cases heard in London. Indeed, that *must* be the case if a United Kingdom party is involved, because Article 3.3 of the 1985 LCIA Rules provides that "sole arbitrators or chairmen are not to be appointed if they have the same nationality as any party".

Presumption of sole arbitrator

10–25 Subject to a contrary agreement by the parties, the LCIA Rules establish a presumption in favour of sole arbitrators rather than three-member tribunals. Experience shows that international cases are particularly likely to result in greater delay and cost if three arbitrators must cooperate. Nevertheless, if a United Kingdom party is involved, and if, in view of the issues raised, it is desirable to appoint as arbitrator an English lawyer specialised in the field, a three-member tribunal is required to avoid transgression of Article 3.3.

10–26 The LCIA Rules contain a rigorous scheme designed to prevent abuse of the party-nomination process. As a commentary on the 1985 LCIA Rules puts it[8]:

> "The rules are designed to dissuade parties from abusing opportunities to nominate arbitrators. In cases where such an opportunity exists (generally because the parties have agreed that there shall be three arbitrators, of whom two are to be nominated by the parties), it is waived unless it is exercised within 30 days of receipt by the respondent of the Request of Arbitration (Article 3.4).
>
> Furthermore, when making such nominations, the parties are discouraged from proposing arbitrators who are not independent or impartial, or who are otherwise unsuitable, because the Court may refuse to appoint such nominees (Article 3.3). Indeed, if an unacceptable nomination has been made (or perhaps more likely if consecutive unacceptable nominations have been made), the Court retains discretion to refuse to allow the party to make a new nomination, and to make the appointment itself (Article 3.5).
>
> If an arbitrator is to be replaced after he has been appointed (whether because he resigned or because he was removed for cause), the Court also retains the discretion not to follow the original nominating procedure (Article 3.5).
>
> Practitioners having experience of cases where respondents have used the opportunity of naming arbitrators as a dilatory tactic—or, worse, as a chance to designate someone who will reveal everything about the tribunal's deliberations to his "client"—will recognize that these Rules have a lot of teeth. The LCIA hopes that the Rules will seldom have to be applied in their full severity, and that their very existence will cause all parties to

[8] J.M.H. Hunter and J. Paulsson, in *Yearbook of Commercial Arbitration 157* (1985).

behave reasonably, and in the process contribute to the development of a generally acceptable deontology of international arbitration.''

Like the ICC Rules, the LCIA Rules give the parties and the arbitrators maximum freedom to establish rules of procedure as they see fit, and to choose the law applicable to the merits of the dispute with or without reference to the law of the place of arbitration. The 1985 LCIA Rules contain a number of provisions inspired by UNCITRAL's work on the Model Law for International Commercial Arbitration, for example with respect to procedures for challenging arbitrators, the jurisdiction of the arbitral tribunal, and the use of experts appointed by the arbitrators. **10–27**

The LCIA process does not include the preparation of terms of reference; nor is the LCIA's approval of award required. Instead, the parties have 30 days within which to ask the arbitrators to correct awards containing mistakes of a clerical nature, or to ''make an additional award as to claims presented in the arbitral proceedings but not dealt with in the award'' (Article 17.3). **10–28**

The LCIA Rules provide that arbitrators are to be remunerated on the basis of time. As of August 1994, rates were estimated as falling within the range of £600–2,000 per day for meetings or hearings; and £100–£250 per hour for ''other time spent on the arbitration''. Time spent by the LCIA secretariat in the administration of the arbitration was charged at £150 per hour for the Registrar and Deputy Registrar, £75 per hour for the secretariat. Deposits may be called for; interest thereon is ''accumulated to the deposits'' (Article 15.1). **10–29**

Security for costs

LCIA arbitrators may order one of the parties to furnish security for the legal costs of its adversary; the LCIA Rules forbid application to ordinary courts for such orders. LCIA arbitrators may also order security for the amount in dispute in the arbitration, but this does not affect such rights as the parties may have to obtain pre-award conservatory measures relating to the merits of the dispute. **10–30**

Under Article 13 of the LCIA Rules, the arbitrators have power to order the production of evidence; by agreeing to LCIA arbitration, the parties waive the right to apply to the ordinary courts for such measures. **10–31**

The LCIA Rules are designed to discourage most interlocutory applications to the courts, since such applications have been abused by obstreperous defendants. Moreover, the English Act of 1996 has reduced the opportunity for such applications. **10–32**

LCIA arbitrators may express their award in any currency, and may award simple or compound interest at any rate they consider to be appropriate, without being bound by legal rates of interest (Article 16.5). This last provision is intended to prevent undeserving parties from insisting on going through with the arbitration only because doing so provides them with cheap money—at the expense of the deserving party. **10–33**

ICSID Arbitration

10–34 The International Centre for the Settlement of Investment Disputes (ICSID) was created in 1966 pursuant to the 1965 Washington Convention on the Settlement of Investment Disputes between States and Nationals of Other States ("the ICSID Convention"). As the name of the Convention implies, ICSID arbitration is available only with respect to disputes to which a State is a party. However, a State may designate one of its agencies as being sufficiently identified with the State as to qualify as "the State" for the purposes of the Convention.

10–35 The ICSID Convention has been a remarkable success in terms of its worldwide acceptance; it has been signed by 130 states, and ratified by 113 (as of the end of 1994). It should be emphasised that only parties who are nationals of signatory States may avail themselves of the ICSID mechanism. The formalities required when dealing with States, as well as in a number of instances where ICSID is bound by its unique constitutional requirements, are such that competent advice is essential.

10–36 ICSID operates under the aegis of the World Bank. Its Secretary- General *ex officio* is the General Counsel of the World Bank; ICSID is staffed by World Bank personnel. Unless the parties have agreed otherwise, the place of arbitration for ICSID proceedings will be Washington D.C. In practice, however, Paris has been the venue for more ICSID proceedings than any other place.

Exclusion of challenge

10–37 There is no possibility of challenging an ICSID award before the courts of the place of arbitration. All States signatory to the ICSID Convention have bound themselves to recognise and enforce ICSID awards to the same extent as if they were final national court judgments. This does not mean that ICSID awards are given higher dignity than a national court judgment; if the latter could not be enforced against a particular kind of State property due to national rules or sovereign immunity, the Convention does not require that an ICSID award fare better.

Small numbers but great importance

10–38 During its 30-year existence, ICSID has had but 30 arbitrations; only 10 have resulted in final awards. This modest caseload should not be allowed to obscure ICSID's considerable importance. First, the volume of ICSID cases is naturally reduced by virtue of the fact that this is by its nature not a forum for small routine matters. Contracts signed with States, or with State agencies formally designated by the State, tend to imply transactions of considerable significance, which in turn give rise to significant disputes. They are not myriad.

Secondly, it is quite plain that although there have not been many ICSID cases, a vast number of international contracts do refer to ICSID arbitration. This observation is consonant not only with the great number of States that have signed the ICSID Convention, but also with the frequent reference to the ICSID mechanism in bilateral treaties or national statutes designed to promote and protect investment. 10–39

Finally, most specialists would agree that ICSID arbitration is an intrinsically superior mechanism in certain contexts. An ICSID award, rendered in accordance with one of the most universally accepted international treaties, may be expected to have an exceptionally high degree of authority. Investors may be reassured by the reflection that apart from whatever legal means of enforcement exist, it must be politically costly for the host State, in terms of its relationship with all investors, to disregard an ICSID award when a central tenet of its investment law is that disputes are to be settled in this neutral international forum. Moreover, one can readily imagine that the World Bank itself would exercise moral persuasion, if for no other reason than the fact that it would be difficult for the World Bank, as a leader in project financing, to suggest that the contractual relationships essential to a major investment be subject to ICSID arbitration when it is common knowledge that the host State has failed to respect a prior award. 10–40

Review by ad hoc committee

Although, as mentioned above, ICSID awards may not be challenged before national courts, disappointed parties have a right to ask the Chairman of ICSID's Administrative Council (*i.e.* the President of the World Bank) to appoint a three-member committee to review awards. It had originally been thought that this power of review was very limited in scope, as indeed is suggested by the adjectives used in the definition of the grounds of annulment: *e.g.* "the Tribunal has manifestly exceeded its powers", or "there has been a serious departure from a fundamental rule or procedure". Nevertheless, in each of the first three cases where awards have been challenged, they were indeed annulled, thus setting the stage for further arbitral proceedings.[9] 10–41

Subsequent reassuring developments suggest that these initial annulments should be accepted as part of the natural evolution of a relatively new institution.[10] 10–42

[9] See D.A. Redfern, "ICSID—Losing its Appeal?" (1987) 3 *Arbitration International 98.*

[10] See J. Paulsson, "ICSID's Achievements and Prospects" (1991) 6 *ICSID Review—Foreign Investment Law Journal* 380.

WIPO Arbitration

10–43 Inaugurated in 1994, the World Intellectual Property Organization's Arbitration Center (located in Geneva) was created for the resolution of intellectual property disputes. Its Arbitration Rules are particularly comprehensive and up-to-date. As one might anticipate given the subject matter of the disputes expected to be brought before the WIPO Center, the Arbitration Rules contain unique and elaborate rules regarding confidentiality and the communication of trade secrets and other confidential information.

Expedited arbitration

10–44 The WIPO Center has also promulgated so-called Expedited Arbitration Rules for contractual disputes that might require especially rapid resolution. Under the Expedited Arbitration Rules, there will always be a sole arbitrator; all deadlines are compressed; and if hearings are to be held they may ordinarily not exceed three days' duration. Both parties must specifically agree to participate in expedited arbitration.

Administrative arrangements

10–45 The WIPO Center is an ''administrative unit'' of WIPO, a specialised agency of the United Nations located in Geneva. WIPO has 150 member States. It has a history of over 110 years, going back to the Paris Convention for the Protection of Industrial Property. The staff of the WIPO Secretariat—around 500 persons—administers 16 multilateral treaties dealing with intellectual property.

10–46 The WIPO Center maintains a list of arbitrators (and mediators) particularly qualified to deal with intellectual property disputes. While the Center's own infrastructure is in Geneva, and it may therefore be practical to choose Geneva as a venue for WIPO arbitrations, the Rules are designed to be usable anywhere in the world. The WIPO Center fulfils the traditional roles of a full-service arbitration institution: appointment/removal of arbitrators, establishment of fees, administration of advance deposits, and handling the communication of pleadings as well as the final award.

10–47 In order to ensure its autonomy in matters of both overall policy and specific case management, the WIPO Center has established two bodies, the Arbitration Council (to provide advice and recommendation, particularly with respect to the evolution of the Rules) and the Arbitration Consultative Commission, made up of ''leading experts in the areas of arbitration and intellectual property'' from whose midst ad hoc committees of three members are set up to consider matters such as the ''challenge, release or replacement of an arbitrator'' or issues relating to arbitrators' fees.

Wide competence

Although the WIPO Arbitration Center is brand new and untested in practice, it is mentioned here because of the credibility of its sponsoring organisation and the significant planning and resources that were committed to its creation. It may be that WIPO has a natural constituency of businesses for which intellectual property rights are crucial, and who feel more at home with a specialised institution. On the other hand, the fact of the matter is that there are very few "pure" intellectual property disputes. For example, while the purpose of a joint venture may have been the development of patentable products, a dispute between the partners is likely to raise contractual issues that would be familiar in the context of any troubled joint venture. The WIPO Center has understood this very well, and to avoid unfortunate and interminable debates about its statutory competence has been careful not to restrict the categories of cases that may be brought under its Rules. 10–48

Was it necessary or useful to create the WIPO Center? This undiplomatic question must be asked, because of course international intellectual property disputes were submitted to arbitration before the launching of the Center. For example, 16 per cent of the cases brought to the ICC in 1994 were intellectual property disputes. The WIPO Center would not fulfil its objectives if it merely has the effect of reducing the ICC's market share; the real test is whether it can expand the market by giving new reasons for potential users to go to arbitration. 10–49

Ad Hoc Arbitrations

An ad hoc arbitration is one conducted pursuant to an agreement which does not refer to an institution charged with setting up the arbitral tribunal and administering the proceedings, but is rather intended to be self-executing. If a party should fail to co-operate in setting the arbitral mechanism in motion, its adversary cannot rely on an arbitration institution to step in, but must ultimately apply to a court (which is presumably just what parties intend to avoid when agreeing to arbitration). The legal framework for the arbitration will be that defined in the arbitration agreement and in such arbitration law as may be applicable. 10–50

Difficulties of ad hoc arbitration in international disputes

In international cases, the difficulty in making an ad hoc arbitration work is compounded by the fact that due to the typically disparate nationalities of the 10–51 parties, jurisdictional issues may arise. In addition, ''neutral'' national authorities may be reluctant to become involved in heated conflicts that do not concern them. For example, many international contracts dating from the 1960s called for ad hoc arbitration with the chairman of the arbitral tribunal to be named by the President of the Swiss Federal Tribunal. It later transpired in several cases that the magistrate occupying that office refused to make such an appointment unless both parties wished him to do so. A recalcitrant defendant thus needed only to challenge the validity of the arbitration agreement to stymie the claim.

10–52 Another problem is that ad hoc arbitration agreements, since they are intended to be self-contained, require that draftsmen—often possessed of little knowledge of international arbitration—attempt something which most often turns out to be impossible: to set forth a comprehensive set of rules for the arbitration. With remarkable frequency, the arbitration agreement is revealed to contain lacunae—and unerringly the proceedings head straight for the problem area. The UNCITRAL Arbitration Rules of 1976 represent an attempt to make life easier for parties desiring ad hoc clauses. They contain a comprehensive set of rules, sufficient to steer the parties and the arbitrators through. The UNCITRAL Rules were prepared with the input of lawyers from round the world, and are therefore thought to be more acceptable to parties from developing countries than the rules of institutions perceived as inspired by the Western capitalist ethos. (In fact one would be hard-pressed to find any distinction of an ideological or cultural nature when comparing the arbitration rules of, say, UNCITRAL and the ICC.) For this reason, in the interest of facilitating negotiations the UNCITRAL Rules may also be adopted within a modified institutional arbitration agreement; the LCIA, for one, has made clear that it is prepared to administer arbitrations in which the parties ask that the UNCITRAL Rules rather than the LCIA Rules apply. The UNCITRAL Rules (available at the LCIA) are by and large perfectly acceptable. (The present author quarrels only with the rule that majority decisions are required; in cases where three arbitrators disagree, the chairman cannot decide alone but must compromise with one of his colleagues.)

Appointment arrangements

10–53 If the UNCITRAL Rules are referred to in a purely ad hoc arbitration agreement, the question remains who will appoint arbitrators (if the parties fail to agree), decide challenges to arbitrators, and advise the arbitrators with respect to fixing their fees. Under the UNCITRAL Rules, one of the parties would have to request that the Secretary-General of the Permanent Court of Arbitration at the Hague designate an authority to make the appointment. This system creates a potential for delay as well as great uncertainty with respect to the choice of arbitrators. Parties are therefore better advised to agree in advance (*i.e.* in the arbitration agreement) to the identity of the appointing authority, and to choose an authority that is willing and able to make wise appointments. Indeed the present author believes that most specialists would agree with him that an arbitration clause referring to the UNCITRAL Rules without identifying an appointing authority is purely and simply defective. The ICC Court and the LCIA are both willing to act as such appointing authorities, and have published descriptions of the manner in which they perceive their role as appointing authority, along with model clauses.

Fee problems

One seemingly irreducible problem with ad hoc arbitrations is that the arbitrators set their own fees. This results in often uncomfortable discussions between the parties and the arbitrators at the very outset of the proceedings, when the issues of method of compensation and payments on account arise. Even though well-crafted ad hoc rules try to deal with this matter (in the case of the UNCITRAL Rules, by providing for the possible intervention of the appointing authority in an *advisory* capacity) there is considerable pressure on a litigant who is distressed by the tribunal's fee proposal to grin and bear it in view of the higher stakes. This leaves a bitter aftertaste, and is harmful to the international arbitral process. While experienced professionals are sufficiently careful of their reputation that they stay within acceptable bounds, occasionally arbitrators appear who seem to have extravagant notions of their worth. When that happens, the parties are better off within an institutional framework, where the arbitrators must address their fee requests to the institution, not to the parties. 10–54

For this and other reasons, many practitioners (including the present author) advise against the inclusion of ad hoc arbitration clauses in international contracts (unless perhaps they are advising parties who confidently expect they would be defendants if any dispute were to arise). Such clauses are fertile grounds for mischief and abuse by wily defendants. Parties seeking to rely on the arbitral mechanism, are almost always better served by having an institutional backstop to ensure that the case will move forward on a reasonably predictable schedule. The apparent saving of the administrative charges of the institution is generally illusory; ad hoc arbitrators frequently end up establishing their own mini-administration, and the hesitations of the non-institutional setting may result in delays that are far more costly than the avoided institutional charges. 10–55

Once a dispute has arisen, the question is seen in a new light. An ad hoc mechanism can readily be negotiated if the claimant perceives that his adversary is reasonable. Then the parties, who at that stage take specialist expert advice, are in a position to draft a careful special submission agreement, tailor-made to their dispute, approved by both sets of litigating counsel, which will replace by novation the original arbitration clause. 10–56

If the defendant turns out not to be reasonable, the claimant can congratulate himself for being able to rely on an institutional clause which assures him that the matter will be handled by an organisation which has faced trouble before, and developed institutional responses. 10–57

Drafting an International Arbitration Agreement

10–58 Whether one is drafting a clause to be inserted into a contract, or a special submission agreement concerning an existing dispute; whether one is contemplating institutional or ad hoc arbitration, a number of points should be borne in mind.

Indispensable elements

10–59 A first set of considerations relates to those elements that are indispensable in the fashioning of a workable international arbitration clause. There are two: an unambiguous reference to the system of arbitration that has been chosen (it is astonishing how often contracts refer to non-existing institutions, or to institutions that have no arbitration rules, or to a known institution but using an incorrect appellation) and a clear definition of the scope of the disputes to be arbitrated. In most cases, the parties want the widest possible range of issues arising from their relationship to be covered by the arbitration agreement. Moreover, they want finality. The most recent model clause suggested by an international institution—the clause published with the 1994 Arbitration Rules of the World Intellectual Property Organization—is drafted in this spirit:

> "Any dispute, controversy or claim arising under, out of or relating to this contract and any subsequent amendments of this contract, including, without limitation, its formation, validity, binding effect, interpretation, performance, breach or termination, as well as non-contractual claims, shall be referred to and finally determined by arbitration in accordance with the WIPO Arbitration Rules."

Recommended elements

10–60 A second category of elements to be considered are those which, although not indispensable, are generally to be recommended. They include features of the arbitral process which are of capital importance, but whose advisability differs from case to case, thereby making it inappropriate to freeze them in a general set of rules intended for all types of cases. For example, it is generally wise to specify (i) the number of arbitrators, and in certain cases to agree to certain requirements as to their nationalities and qualifications. It is even more important to attempt to obtain stipulations of (ii) the place of arbitration and (iii) the law to be applied to the merits of the dispute (the governing law of the contract).

Elements occasionally useful

A third series of considerations relate to elements that are occasionally useful. They may be divided into two sub-categories: 10–61

(1) provisions that are in principle uncontroversial but which, when inserted before any dispute has arisen, tend to lead to useless complications: making negotiation, conciliation, or mediation a precondition to arbitration; defining the law applicable to the arbitration clause (as distinct from the governing law of the contract in which it appears); defining the applicable rules of conflict of laws; and setting forth procedural rules in greater detail than those contained in the general rules of arbitration to which the arbitration clause refers; and
(2) provisions that are useful in particular cases, but inappropriate in others: waiver of sovereign immunity; giving the arbitrators authority to decide as amiable compositors without reference to rules of law; giving the arbitrators authority to modify the contract; establishing powers and procedures for provisional relief or discovery of evidence; defining principles of apportioning costs of arbitration; accommodating the arbitral procedure to potential multiparty disputes (often an exceptionally difficult task), including an entry-of-judgment stipulation to the effect that the courts may convert the award into a judgment (unnecessary in most cases in most jurisdictions); and waiving appeal (generally unnecessary if the general arbitral rules referred to themselves contain such a waiver—as do the ICC Rules and the LCIA Rules).

This broad brush summary is no substitute for rigorous analysis at the time of concluding an arbitration agreement, particularly if an unusual departure from the various major institutional model clauses is envisaged. 10–62

Pitfalls to be avoided

One might imagine a fourth series of considerations, relating to *pathological elements* of the arbitration clause. Here are five types of sins to be avoided: 10–63

(i) Uninformed tinkering with model clauses. The ICC has a Model Clause comprised of one simple declarative sentence. It has been drafted and refined by experts, and appears in widely-disseminated ICC brochures. Yet, when a study was conducted in 1987 of 400 pending ICC arbitrations, only one instance was found in which the parties had managed to copy the Model Clause perfectly. (Of course there were some intentional variations, but most deviations appeared the product of nonchalance.) Draftsmen who are tempted to improve model clauses often achieve the opposite effect. The deceptively simple language of the ICC Model Clause ("all disputes arising out of or in connection with the present contract") covers issues of formation, termination, and quasi-contractual torts; attempts at ostensible sophistication, such as referring to "issues regarding the interpretation and performance of this contract", may be interpreted as restrictive and lead to arguments about the jurisdiction of the arbitrators.

(ii) Equivocation. There are a surprising number of instances of a non-choice, with clauses like the following: "In case of arbitration, the Rules of Arbitration shall apply; in case of litigation, any dispute shall be brought before the courts of [ ]". This is nonsense and insufficient to create reliable arbitral jurisdiction.

(iii) Insufficient specification of the arbitral institution (see above).

(iv) Designation of authorities intended to appoint arbitrators without verifying whether they are in fact willing to accept such a responsibility.

(v) Combining irreconcilable procedural laws. Quite often, negotiators reach unfortunate compromises, such as accepting a venue in country X in return for application of the procedural law of country Y. If the law of country X contains mandatory provisions with respect to any arbitrations taking place within that country, and those are inconsistent with the laws of country Y, intractable problems may arise.

The Importance of Treaties

10–64 One of the greatest advantages of international arbitration is seldom perceived: the fact that by and large arbitration awards have greater transnational currency than municipal court decisions. Contract negotiators often assume that an ideal result would be to talk the other side into accepting their own national courts (but, for the reasons explained in paragraph 10–03 above, realise that such a suggestion is likely to be rejected as lacking in neutrality). The initial assumption is often quite wrong.

10–65 Take for example an actual case involving a German financial institution dealing with a Spanish company. The Germans were in a strong negotiating position because they were the financiers. They therefore insisted on a contractual clause establishing the jurisdiction of German courts. Not only was this an advantage in the nationalistic sense, but the German party also reasoned that arbitration was an inappropriate mechanism in a context where a clear-cut financial obligation was at stake. A procedure requiring the time-consuming appointment of arbitrators, including perhaps a Spanish nominee, who would seek to delay matters, and the needless expense of private justice, was obviously wrong. Or so it seemed.

In the event, the German party won the battle but lost the war. After a dispute had arisen, it sought and obtained a quick judgment in a German court. This judgment was never paid, however, and it could not be enforced in Spain. In the absence at that time of a treaty between Spain and Germany for the recognition of judgments, Spanish law would recognise and enforce a German judgment only if it could be proved that German courts treated Spanish judgments with the same favour. As the German party was unable to do so, it ended up with the least attractive alternative of all; having to bring a new action on the merits before a Spanish court. **10–66**

A surer avenue for the German party—which for purposes of argument we will assume had a valid claim—would have been to opt for arbitration and then seek execution under the 1958 New York (United Nations) Convention for the Recognition and Enforcement of Foreign Arbitral Awards, which Spain has ratified. Indeed, the very fact that the Convention is in force in Spain would to some degree have operated as an inventive for the Spanish party to comply with the award on the ground that resistance would in all likelihood ultimately lead to failure. **10–67**

Multilateral treaties

The 1958 New York Convention has been remarkably successful, because it has been signed by over 90 states on all continents (the Latin American countries being the most reluctant). The Convention has two major effects: **10–68**

(1) it obligates the courts of signatory States to defer to the arbitral jurisdiction whenever an action is brought under a contract containing an arbitration clause (Article II); and
(2) it obligates the courts to enforce a foreign award without reviewing the merits of the arbitrators' decision (Article V); the only possible defences—with respect to which the resisting party has the burden of proof—are quite limited, such as the arbitrators' having exceeded their jurisdiction or failed to give the complaining party an opportunity to present its case, or the award having been set aside by a court in the country where it was rendered.

The New York Convention is immensely important. Indeed, the first question when negotiating a disputes clause in an international contract is whether the country where one would be likely to seek to enforce an award has ratified the New York Convention. If that is so, a second question is whether the ratification was subject to either one of the two reservations that may be made under the Convention: limiting its application to awards relating to "commercial relation- **10–69** ships'' (which tends not to be a problem, in most international contracts) or to awards rendered in another State that has ratified the Convention. The second reservation (known as the reciprocity reservation) is of considerable practical significance, because it means that if one seeks to give maximum effect to the award, the place of arbitration should be in a country where the Convention is in force. This includes nearly all European States (including those of the former USSR).

Other important international treaties

10–70 There are at least three additional treaties of worldwide importance dealing with international arbitration. The Geneva Convention of 1927 has been largely supplanted by The New York Convention. The Washington Convention of 1965 has already been discussed in paragraph 10–34 above. That leaves the European Convention on International Commercial Arbitration, often referred to as the 1961 Geneva Convention, which was designed to complement the New York Convention, and particularly to facilitate East–West trade.

10–71 The scope of the 1961 Geneva Convention, which applies only when disputing parties are resident in contracting States, is narrower than that of the New York Convention, which is focused not on the parties, but on the place of arbitration.

10–72 The 1961 Geneva Convention's enforcement scheme, however, is more rigorous. A foreign award set aside in the country where it was rendered may be refused recognition only if it had been annulled on one of the grounds enumerated in the Geneva Convention. For example, French courts applying the 1961 Geneva Convention may refuse recognition to a Swiss award annulled by the Swiss courts for lack of a valid arbitration agreement, but not an award annulled by the Swiss courts for ''arbitrariness'', since the latter is not a ground for annulment recognised by the Convention.

10–73 Although it is open to non-European signatories, the 1961 Geneva Convention has not yet had the widespread success of the New York Convention. It has been ratified by 18 countries, including, among the major trading nations, France, the Federal Republic of Germany, Italy, and the USSR.

10–74 It should be noted that the 1968 Brussels Convention on Jurisdiction and Judgments (dealing with the attribution of competence and the enforcement of court judgments within the European Economic Community), does not apply to arbitral awards.

10–75 This discussion of multilateral treaties has so far focused on the enforcement of awards. But there are also multilateral treaties that create a right for private parties of one signatory state to bring arbitration against another signatory state on the grounds that the latter has violated provisions of the treaty in a manner that has caused harm to the private party. This is an interesting new development, which has materialised in the North American Free Trade Agreement and the 1994 Energy Charter Treaty and in essence creates access to international arbitration for private third-party beneficiaries of the treaty's dispute resolution provision.[11]

Finally, it might be mentioned that neither of the two great efforts in the area of international arbitration that have been made by the United Nations Commission for International Trade Law (UNCITRAL) has taken the form of a treaty. The 1976 UNCITRAL Arbitration Rules, considered especially appropriate for cases involving parties from different politico-cultural backgrounds because they were prepared with the input of specialists from all around the world, simply constitute a set of voluntary rules to which parties may find it useful to refer in their international contracts (see paragraph 10–52 above). The UNCITRAL Model Law on International Commercial Arbitration, the text of which became final in 1985, is suggested to individual legislatures as a means of modernising their laws relating to international arbitration, with the added intended effect of harmonising the various national legal systems. **10–76**

Bilateral treaties

The achievements of the New York Convention should not be allowed to obscure the fact that in particular cases bilateral treaties may play a crucial role—either instead of a wider treaty, or as a complement to it. **10–77**

The following example, which may no longer be valid in light of subsequent Turkish legislation, was given in a study of ICC arbitration and was based on actual cases. It illustrates the usefulness of being aware of bilateral treaty stipulations: **10–78**

> "The U.S. company AmInc. wants to enter into a long-term agreement with a Turkish company for a major investment project in Turkey. In the early years, substantial outlays will be made by AmInc. which, if all goes well, is to recoup its investment by sharing profits in later years. It is therefore critical for AmInc. to examine its ability to enforce its rights.
>
> Since each party is reluctant to accept the national courts of the other, ICC arbitration is agreed upon in principle. But which location is to be the situs of the arbitration? The Turkish party urges Istanbul or Ankara, insisting that this is in AmInc.'s own interest. Turkey is not a signatory to the New York Convention, so AmInc. would have to worry about the enforceability in Turkey of an ICC award rendered, let us say, in Copenhagen. And, says the Turkish company, arbitration is recognised in Turkey. All the parties have to do is choose the neutral ICC rules, which means the tribunal would be chaired by an arbitrator of a third nationality.
>
> It is at this point that AmInc. should be aware of the fact that the Turkish Supreme Court has shown itself to be exceedingly hostile to ICC arbi-

[11] See J. Paulsson, "Arbitration without Privity", 10 *ICSID Review—Foreign Investment Law Journal* 232 (1995).

tration. In the so-called Keban Arbitration, named for the Turkish dam whose construction by French and Italian contractors gave rise to the dispute, an ICC award was rendered in Lausanne. The Turkish Supreme Court became seized of the matter when the award was sought to be relied upon in Turkey. It held that because of the role of the ICC Court, ICC proceedings simply did not constitute arbitration as understood under Turkish law. Referring to the ICC Court's function of approving awards proposed by the arbitral tribunals, the Turkish Supreme Court found it aberrant that the award be formally issued by an institution other than the tribunal that actually tried the case. Indeed, it concluded that the enforcement of an ICC award in Turkey would be contrary to public policy.

In this context, it becomes useful to know that Austria has a treaty with Turkey under which arbitral awards rendered in one country are to be recognized and enforced in the other. It does not appear necessary that the party relying on the award have either Austrian or Turkish nationality. Hence, under the treaty, one would appear to have at least as good a chance of enforcing an award in Turkey if it had been rendered in Vienna as if it had been rendered in Ankara or Istanbul. Meanwhile, one benefits from Austria's complete network of international treaties. Accordingly, the award would be enforceable in London or Paris or in a great number of other places where the Turkish company might have assets.

Were the award to be rendered in Turkey, the result might be disastrous. Not only would a Turkish court, following in the footsteps of its Supreme Court, annul the award in Turkey, but the fact that it was set aside in the country where it was rendered might—depending upon the rules of the potential enforcement jurisdictions—make it useless internationally.

The analysis of this situation depends to a considerable degree upon the position of the adversary. If it is a small Turkish company with no off-shore activities or assets, it may well be that international arbitration is simply an inappropriate mechanism. And, in fact, one's reluctance to refer to the local courts of one's adversary decreases when one is faced with an enterprise whose importance, and therefore influence, on the national scale is marginal.''

10–79 The development discussed in paragraph 10–75 above of third party beneficiary claims under multilateral treaties is also in evidence in bilateral treaties, most significantly in the context of so-called BITs (bilateral investment treaties). There are many BITs—perhaps nearly one thousand. Many of them provide for the right of private parties who are nationals of one signatory state to initiate arbitration—most often under the UNCITRAL or the ICSID Rules—against the other state if they feel they have suffered as the result of violations of the treaty. The emergence of BITs and their third-party beneficiary mechanisms is a relatively recent phenomenon of vast potential effect, but is beyond the scope of this discussion.[12]

[12] See Paulsson, ''Arbitration Without Privity'', *loc. cit.*

Importance of the Place of Arbitration

Although an award rendered in country A may be effective in country B irrespective of the view of the award that might be taken by the courts of country A,[13] the long and the short of it is that one should always pay attention to the arbitration law of the place of arbitration. 10–80

As has been noted in paragraph 10–72 above, the 1961 Geneva Convention obliges courts to enforce foreign awards unless it is proven that they comport at least one of a limited number of defects, which are exhaustively defined in the Convention. An award is not necessarily defective under the 1961 Geneva Convention because it has been set aside in the country where it was rendered. Thus, if an award rendered in country A is set aside because only two of the three arbitrators signed it, country B is still bound to enforce the award (unless it is flawed in some other way) because the Convention does not consider such an award to be defective. 10–81

Nevertheless, in view of the limited applicability of the Geneva Convention, and the understandable reluctance of judges to enforce awards that have been rejected in their countries of origin, the practical rule is to consider that the mandatory provisions of the arbitration law in force at the place of arbitration should always be respected. 10–82

The New York Convention of 1958, which is the dominant international instrument in this area, gives judges the discretion to decline to enforce foreign awards on the grounds that they have been set aside in the country where they were made whether or not the cause of annulment is also recognised by the law of the enforcement forum. Experience and common sense indicate that judges tend to avail themselves of this discretion. (It may be noted that the UNCITRAL Model Law embraces this concept of the New York Convention—and indeed copies its language.) It is in this connection that one might best understand the significance of Article 35 of the ICC Rules and Article 20(2) of the LCIA Rules, which call upon arbitrators to "make every reasonable effort to ensure that the award is legally enforceable". 10–83

A corollary of the rule that one should always respect the mandatory law of the place of arbitration is that one should avoid venues where the arbitration law is unfavourable. 10–84

While adherence to the New York Convention is almost always a necessary attribute for an acceptable venue, it is not sufficient on its own. Not all countries are safe havens for international arbitration. Some cling to wide powers of judicial review. Others have unclear legislation. Yet others have apparently adequate legislation but their courts seem to misapply the law—for example by adopting an over-elastic interpretation of "violation of public policy" as grounds for setting aside awards. Legal systems allowing extensive judicial interference with 10–85

[13] See, *e.g.* J. Paulsson, "Arbitration Unbound" (1981) 30 I.C.L.Q. 358; and by the same author, "Delocalisation of International Commercial Arbitration: When and Why it Matters" (1983) 32 I.C.L.Q. 53 as well as "Arbitration Unbound in Belgium" (1986) 2 *Arbitration International* 68.

arbitral awards should be avoided. The modern international consensus—as reflected in the 1985 UNCITRAL Model Law on International Commercial Arbitration—is that the courts at the place of arbitration should limit their review of international arbitral awards to the grounds of excess of jurisdiction, failure to give a party an adequate opportunity to present its case, or violation of public policy. Errors of fact or law should not be appropriate grounds for review by national courts. The parties contracted for arbitration and should accept the arbitral tribunal's decision as final.

10–86 A final group of unfavourable judicial systems comprises those where the aware is likely to be upheld in the end, but only after extraordinary complications and delays during which the award under challenge might not be enforceable elsewhere. (Under the New York Convention, a judge may suspend enforcement while a review procedure is pending in the courts at the place of arbitration.)

Leading venues

10–87 The author participated in a survey of the practice of the ICC court for the period of 1980 to 1988. There were 586 cases in which the place of arbitration was chosen by the ICC court because the parties had not done so by agreement. It may be assumed that a crucial factor in the choice of the place of arbitration is the attitude of the local courts. (The ICC has an institutional stake in avoiding countries whose courts appear to be too ready to set aside its awards.)

10–88 The leading choices by region, and in order of frequency, were:

Western Europe
France
Switzerland
Belgium
United Kingdom
Germany
Netherlands
Asia
Eastern Europe
Greece
Cyprus
North Africa
Tunisia
Sub-Saharan Africa
Ivory Coast
Asia
India
Pakistan
Jordan

North America
United States

The relatively low position of the United Kingdom in the Western Europe list (considering the importance of London as a trading and financial centre) appears to be largely due to the fact that, prior to 1979, English arbitration law was considered unacceptable to international practitioners because of the availability of appeals to the court on questions of law. Since 1979, predispute "exclusion agreements" are effective in international contracts except in the insurance, maritime and commodities fields. The international community has gradually become comfortable with judicial application of this reform, having regard in particular to the case law which establishes that waivers of rights of appeal are sufficient if they are contained in a set of printed arbitration rules (*e.g.* those of the ICC or the LCIA) to which the arbitration clause refers. **10–89**

Belgium
By comparison, the relatively high incidence of Belgium as a place of arbitration may have to do with its extreme "hands off" position. Provided that there is no Belgian party, the Belgian courts have no jurisdiction to review arbitral awards—even if it alleged that there has been excess of jurisdiction or corruption of an arbitrator. All objections have to be raised as to defense to enforcement actions wherever they might be initiated; no positive action for setting aside the award may be brought. Some practitioners like this regime, at least for certain cases; others believe it goes too far. **10–90**

Japan
Japan has always been out of favour for ICC arbitrations because the appearance of foreign lawyers in arbitration was severely restricted by local practice rules. These restrictions were relaxed in 1996. **10–91**

Colombia
Colombia is likely to fall into disfavour as a result of a Supreme Court decision which interpreted that country's constitution as requiring that all arbitrators in cases conducted within the country must be of Colombian nationality. **10–92**

Finally, when choosing the place of arbitration, it should be borne in mind that the proceedings are likely to be conducted by an arbitrator from that country—acting either as sole or presiding arbitrator. It is therefore desirable to choose a place of arbitration where there is an adequate pool of experienced arbitrators with experience of determining complex international disputes in a given area of specialisation or in a given language. With bad luck, the members of a small pool may all be eliminated by conflicts of interest or unavailability, in which case there is a risk of ending up with a mediocre arbitral tribunal. **10–93**

Advantages of traditional situs (place, jurisdiction)

10–94 The lesson here is clear: when in doubt, stipulate a traditional situs. Routine transactions are generally best served by routine solutions, which do not require complex analysis. Unusual situations require extensive technical expertise to find tailor-made solutions. A pathological arbitration clause imperils the whole foundation of the contract no matter how carefully the rest of the document has been drafted. Great attention at the time of contracting is merited.

10–95 In cases where one is considering an arbitration venue for the first time, it should be recalled that institutions such as the ICC or the LCIA have experience in supervising arbitrations in many locales, and are pleased to respond to enquiries about the advisability of a particular venue.

10–96 In the future, it is to be hoped that national arbitration laws will converge, and avoid creating pitfalls such as those that appear when peculiar local rules are applied to international arbitration. Such a harmonisation may well be inspired by the 1985 UNCITRAL Model Law on International Commercial Arbitration, which has already been wholly or partially enacted in over 25 jurisdictions, from Australia and Bulgaria to Scotland and Russia.[14] Countries that wish to attract international arbitrations can hardly do better than to adopt the Model Law.

Choice of Law

10–97 At least five different systems of law may become relevant during the course of an international arbitration:

- the law that determines the capacity of the parties,
- the law that determines the validity of the arbitration agreement,
- the law governing the arbitration itself and in particular the procedure,
- the law applicable to the substance of the dispute, and
- if there is a conflict of applicable substantive laws, the law under which that conflict is to be resolved.

10–98 In general, the parties cannot make a choice of the law applicable to capacity, except (for instance) by incorporating a company in a particular country. The

[14] See P. Sanders, "Unity and Diversity in The Adoption of The Model Law" (1995) 11 *Arbitration International* 1.

parties generally need not make an express choice in relation either to the law governing the validity of the arbitration agreement or the law governing the procedure of the arbitration itself. This will usually follow naturally from the circumstances; the proper law of the arbitration agreement is generally that of the contract of which it is a part, and the law governing the conduct of the arbitration is generally that of the place of arbitration. Parties wishing to make explicit exceptions in either respect should seek expert advice before doing so.

In practice, parties occasionally fail to choose any substantive law, thus leaving it to be determined by the arbitral tribunal. This may lead to the application of a system of law which is inappropriate to the language of the contract or to the intention of the parties. The parties should therefore try to resolve the question of the substantive (or proper) law at the time of negotiating the contract. **10–99**

The many important consequences of the choice of applicable law are beyond the scope of this chapter. It is, however, likely that, in the absence of a provision to the contrary, the proper law of the contract will also be deemed to determine the validity, scope and effect of the arbitration clause. Accordingly, that law should be studied not only as to its law of obligations, but also in relation to its effect on the agreement to arbitrate. **10–100**

To take a dramatic example, the Indian Supreme Court held in May 1992 that if Indian law applied to the arbitration clause, applications to set aside an award could be heard in India even if the place of arbitration was outside India, and the Indian courts could enjoin the enforcement of the award anywhere.[15] In other words, an acceptance of Indian law in a contract with an Indian party would ultimately lead to the Indian courts irrespective of the choice of a neutral venue. This case illustrates the need to verify the legal foundation of the dispute resolution mechanism. **10–101**

National law

It is wrong to assume that the choice of applicable law is immaterial if a detailed contract has been drafted, setting out the parties' rights and obligations *in extenso*. There will often be gaps to be filled. **10–102**

Moreover, some nationals laws contain mandatory provisions that add to the rights or obligations contained in the contract, or override explicit contractual stipulations. Some laws are particularly favourable to purchasers. Others allow an acknowledged debtor of a liquidated sum to suspend payment by seeking to set off a non liquidated claim in court or arbitration proceedings. Some laws allow judges or arbitrators to revise contractual terms they find unreasonable, while others vigorously take the opposite position. **10–103**

The 1980 Rome Convention on the Law Applicable to Contractual Obligations is increasingly accepted throughout Europe, and often influences arbitrators **10–104**

[15] *National Thermal Power Corp. v. The Singer Co.*, 3 *Supreme Court Cases* 91992, 551–573, XVIII *Yearbook of Commercial Arbitration* 403 (1993).

who view it as an expression of internationally agreed concepts. Broadly, the Convention provides that a contract shall be governed by the law chosen by the parties and that the choice must be made expressly or demonstrated with reasonable certainty. If no such choice is made, the contract is treated as being governed by the law of the country with which it is most closely connected.

10–105 There is a presumption that such a connection is most readily established with the law of the corporate seat and principal seat of business of the party whose performance characterises the contract. This points, for example, to the law of the seller in a sales contract, to that of the distributor in a distribution agreement, and to that of the manager in a management agreement.

10–106 Negotiators should be aware of this important development, which suggests what will happen if there is no choice of law in the contract. Some negotiators have the impression that by opting for arbitration in country X, they have chosen the law of country X to govern the merits of any dispute. This is a mistake, attributable perhaps to the traditional notion in some legal systems that submission to a *national court* implied acceptance of its substantive law. This concept is foreign to contemporary international arbitration, where the law of the place of arbitration has a strong claim to govern the conduct of the proceedings; a claim of influence (but no more) with respect to the resolution of conflict of laws; and no claim at all to govern substantive issues.

10–107 The idiosyncrasies of applicable national laws are often neutralised, at least to some extent, in international arbitrations by the following factors:

- most arbitration rules require the arbitral tribunal in all cases to take account of the terms of the contract and of trade usages;
- arbitration is founded in contract; arbitral tribunals are therefore reluctant to disregard contractual provisions, recognizing that parties operating internationally are often less aware of the provisions of various national laws than those of their home country, and that their legitimate expectations are best fulfilled if they are held to their bargain;
- the contract law of many countries has often been influenced by consumer transactions and other situations involving parties whose lack of sophistication understandably provokes legislators to protect the weak; such situations are far less prevalent with respect to international contracts involving large amounts of money and drafted by skilled negotiators.

10–108 Subject to identifying any particular characteristics of the kind indicated above, the interests of certainty usually require that the parties choose the national law of the country most closely associated with the transaction; or, alternatively, a neutral law with rules of contractual interpretation which are well developed and accessible to foreigners (preferably in the language of the contract).

10–109 In the course of negotiations there is often a trade-off between a national law favoured by one party and a place of arbitration favoured by another. In such a situation particular care should be taken to ensure that the place of arbitration is suitable for determining a dispute *governed by the national law chosen.*

General principles of law

The best hope of reaching an agreement on the governing law is sometimes to avoid reference to a national law altogether. General principles of law are frequently referred to in choice of law clauses, whether alone or in conjunction with some national system of law or as forming part of international trade law. Some arbitral awards have been founded on general principles of law. **10–110**

The problem, for the lawyer as much as for the businessman, is that the general principles of law are just that—they are general principles, not a developed code of law. The concepts that contracts must be obeyed (*pacta sunt servanda*), that good faith is important in commercial relationships, that a breach of a contractual commitment involves an obligation to make reparation, that a person should not enrich himself or herself unjustly at the expense of another—and other, similar, principles—are a valuable source of law, but often do not provide definite answers to particular questions. **10–111**

If the general principles of law are to be referred to in a choice of law clause, then—because of their necessarily general nature—they are better used in conjunction with a defined system of national law. This creates a concurrence of laws. **10–112**

Concurrent laws

Where one party to a contract is a state or state agency, principles of international law (or alternatively the general principles of law) are often coupled with a national law, so as to create a system of concurrent laws. Public international law (or alternatively, the general principles) then acts as a regulator of the national law, ensuring that it does not fall below a minimum international standard. **10–113**

The 1965 Washington Convention provides a striking example of this tendency in relation to disputes between states and nationals of other states in connection with disputes submission to ICSID arbitration. Article 42(1) of the Convention provides that, in the absence of any express choice of law by the parties, an arbitral tribunal shall apply the law of the contracting state and "such rules of international law as may be applicable." The law of the contracting state is recognised as paramount within its own territory, but is nevertheless subjected to international control. In this way, international law sets a minimum standard which the arbitral tribunal is mandated to uphold in its award. **10–114**

Clauses freezing the law

Contracts made between a state or state agency on the one hand and a private entity on the other are generally known as "state contracts." The private entity is often under considerable commercial pressure to agree that the law governing **10–115** the contract shall be that of the state concerned. This raises the fear that the state party may subsequently use its legislative powers to alter the law, and hence the contractual regime, without the consent of the private party. For example, a state, having granted a concession to the private party to construct and run a railway, or to build and operate a gas liquefaction plant, might, once the operation is on track, decree an increase of its share of revenue beyond that agreed, or levy taxes, or act in some other fashion that diminishes the return to the private party.

10–116 One technique sometimes used as a measure of protection against arbitrary legislation by the state party—such as nationalisation without compensation—is to couple the law of the state party with public international law. Another is to "freeze" the law of the state party. The relevant law is expressed to be the law in force at the date of the contract—thus (theoretically at least) preventing any subsequent change in the law to the detriment of the private party. If freezing the whole law is unacceptable to the state party, an appropriate move in this direction might nevertheless be agreed in the form of a "stabilisation clause", under which the state party would, for instance, undertake that benefits granted under the contract would not be affected by supervening legislative or regulatory changes.

10–117 Provisions of this kind may be worth considering in appropriate cases. However, there is considerable controversy as to whether a state can restrict its future legislative policy by means of a private contract, as opposed to a treaty. At best, the effect of such clauses may be to give a special right to compensation if the law is changed so as to affect adversely the private party's interests.

The lex mercatoria

10–118 The increasing complexity and internationalisation of modern trade and commerce have led some lawyers to conclude that what is needed to govern contractual relationships is not a particular national system of law but a modern law merchant. Such a law, it is said, would meet the requirements of international commerce in much the same way as the *lex mercatoria* met the requirements of traders living under the Roman Empire, or as enactments of customary law (such as the celebrated Consulato del Mare) met the needs of sailors and merchants in the Mediterranean in the 14th century.

10–119 This modern law merchant goes under various descriptions, including "transnational law", "the international law of contracts", "international *lex mercatoria*", and "international trade law". Whatever the description, the purpose is clear; it is to regulate international commercial transactions by a uniform system of law. The problem, as with the general principles of law (see above), lies in the vagueness of the *lex mercatoria*.

10–120 Nevertheless, arbitral tribunals have on occasion decided cases according to the *lex mercatoria* (equating it, perhaps, with concepts drawn from their own legal experience or commercial background) and their awards have been held to be enforceable in both France and England (where the significant test cases have arisen).

Trade usage

Article 13.5 of the ICC Rules requires arbitrators to take account not only of the applicable law but also of the provisions of the contract and the relevant "trade usage". A similar provision is to be found in Article 33(3) of the UNCITRAL Arbitration Rules and Article 28(4) of the UNCITRAL Model Law. It may also be found in national arbitration laws such as the Netherlands Arbitration Act of 1986, which provides in Article 1054 that: "In all cases the arbitral tribunal shall take into account any applicable trade usages." **10–121**

Indeed, reference to trade usages as an aid to interpreting contractual provisions is commonplace in all types of legal systems. The question then arises as to whether there are usages that apply to specific types of international transactions. **10–122**

Trade usage must usually be established by evidence in any given case (unless it is common ground that the arbitral tribunal are familiar with the trade in question). However, organisations such as the ICC have been prominent in attempting to establish a commonly understood meaning for terms which are in frequent use in international trade contracts. Terms such as "ex works", "c.i.f.", "f.o.b.", and so on are intended to establish a single international definition of rights and obligations. The precise extent of these rights and obligations is spelled out in an ICC booklet known as "Incoterms" (or "International Rules for the Interpretation of Trade Terms"), the 1990 version of which has sold in excess of 250,000 copies. An arbitral tribunal may in appropriate cases take these rules into account. **10–123**

In much the same way, the ICC's Uniform Customs and Practice for Documentary Credits (formulated as long ago as 1933) have proved valuable in moving towards a single international standard for the interpretation of these important instruments of world trade. **10–124**

These are examples of a general tendency for international standards and rules to become established in any significant service, trade or industry which crosses national frontiers. Standard form contracts are commonplace in the shipping trade, in the commodity markets and in the oil industry. It is only a small step from the establishment of uniform rules for the interpretation of these terms and conditions. If such rules are uniformly applied by many different national courts, or by arbitral tribunals, the basis is laid for the establishment of an international customary law created by merchants and traders. **10–125**

Amiable composition and equity clauses

Amiable composition and equity clauses are intended to produce a binding and enforceable award, but one which the arbitral tribunal may reach without apply- **10–126** ing strict legal principles if these appear unjust. It is sometimes said that an arbitral tribunal engaged in amiable composition is motivated by considerations of equity rather than strict law, but it should be emphasised that equity in this context does not refer to any system of specific rules and remedies, as that term is understood in the common law countries. It encompasses a looser and broader concept. An arbitral tribunal given powers of *amiable composition*, or, as it is sometimes put, the power to decide *ex aequo et bono* (in equity and good conscience) produces a binding decision which seeks to reflect the expectations of the parties at the time of entering into the contract, and what is fair in a general sense at the time the dispute arises.

10–127 In cases where the parties have for pragmatic reasons chosen a law to govern the contract which is not the "home" law of either of them, the decision of an arbitral tribunal based squarely in fairness or equity may be preferable to one based on law, particularly where the contract provides for a long-term, developing relationship. An equity clause may allow for the selection of arbitrators who are not lawyers but who are knowledgeable about the specific subject matter in dispute.

10–128 Furthermore, giving the arbitral tribunal power to act as amiable compositeurs often fits well in situations in which the parties to a long-term agreement wish to provide for a third party to have the power to take account of new or changing circumstances in resolving disputes which may arise between them. Authorising arbitrators to act as amiable compositeurs does not, however, necessarily give them power to fill gaps or revise the terms of the contract in respect to unforeseen developments. If required, it is best to confer such a power expressly in the arbitration clause or submission agreement.

10–129 It is almost impossible to frame a definition of the term *amiable composition* in a form which would be fully accepted by all authorities. It is probably best understood in France, where it originated and is given express statutory recognition.

10–130 The distinctive difference between arbitrators and amiable compositeurs is that the latter need not apply strict legal rules of interpretation to the obligations of the parties, contractual or otherwise, if they consider that a strict legal approach would lead to an inequitable result. In particular, amiable compositeurs may take a more flexible approach to the quantification of damages in order to reflect commercial fairness and reality, rather than regarding themselves as bound by rules of law governing standards of compensation.

10–131 Nonetheless, the powers of amiable compositeurs are not unlimited, nor should they be. They must observe due process in giving equality of treatment to the parties, and they are bound by rules of public policy as well as any applicable mandatory provisions of law.

International Arbitration in Practice

Arbitration is founded on consent, and the parties therefore are free to agree on the procedure to be followed. It should never be forgotten, however, that irrespective of the method the parties may have foisted upon them, the arbitrators have unfettered discretion to determine the relevance, materiality, and weight of any evidence. 10–132

It would appear that some advocates, perhaps a bit unsure when venturing outside their habitual jurisdiction, become over-eager to win contests over what procedural rule should apply. In so doing, they lose sight of the simple fact that at the end of the day, success awaits not the party which has won debating points regarding procedural arcana, but the one whose case convinced the arbitrators. It should not be hard to understand that arbitrators tend to be convinced by cases presented in a manner with which they are familiar and comfortable. In other words, a common-law advocate may be well advised to think twice before he insists on the right to week-long examination of witnesses before a tribunal presided by a retired continental judge who has never heard witnesses speak for more than 40 minutes and who believes that oral testimony results in nothing but a futile and disagreeable exposure to incoherence and prevarication. 10–133

Need for flexibility

Effective participation in international arbitration calls for flexibility. Perhaps more than most people, lawyers are creatures of habit, so the effort required is not negligible. The English lawyer facing an international arbitration should be prepared to live more by his wits than by the Rules of the Supreme Court. He would of course be much happier if the case were heard before the High Court, but he should compare what he is getting—an admittedly imperfect, largely unpredictable, occasionally maddening system which is, however, neutral—not with what he wished, but with what he avoided, which might have been litigation before the District Court of Yokohama. Now there is doubtless much to be said in favour of the rules and practice of Japanese courts, but from the English lawyer's professional point of view it would be the end of the road: it is a game he cannot play. 10–134

If flexibility commends itself to the advocate, the same is true for arbitrators. In international proceedings, the parties' nationalities tend to be different from that of the presiding arbitrator. In the case of a three-member tribunal, the arbitrators and the counsel appearing before them may very well represent five different legal systems. An arbitrator who insists woodenly on applying his own procedural rules without regard for the litigants' expectations, and without a trace of tolerance for their respective idiosyncrasies, will cramp their style and not be asked back. 10–135

International norms

10–136 When conceptions clash, however, rulings must be made one way or the other. Are there norms that may be accepted as the appropriate reflection of a hoped-for consensus in international arbitration? One may usefully look to the following major sources of international norms for arbitral practice:

(1) the 1976 UNCITRAL Arbitration Rules;
(2) the 1994 WIPO Arbitration Rules
(3) the ICC Rules of Arbitration as amended and effective as of January 1, 1998;
(4) the 1985 Rules of the LCIA;
(5) the ICSID Rules of Arbitration; and
(6) the International Bar Association Supplementary Rules Governing the Presentation and Reception of Evidence in International Arbitration (''the IBA Rules of Evidence'') adopted in 1983. Appearing in a four-page booklet, these Rules comprise a remarkable synthesis of international arbitral practice intended to be applied as a complement to other rules, prevailing ''solely as regards the presentation and reception of evidence''.

10–137 UNCITRAL's most recent contribution to the field is a document entitled Notes on Organizing Arbitral Proceedings. Beyond the innocuous definition of their purpose (''to assist arbitration practitioners by listing and briefly describing questions on which appropriately timed procedural decisions may be useful''), the Notes contain a veritable primer on the procedural issues that may have to be resolved in an international arbitration—particularly of the *ad hoc* kind. Whether as a checklist or as a means of alerting arbitrators and advocates to the need to anticipate a wide range of procedural options, this text is well worth studying.

Predominant rules

10–138 The search for predominant rules is concentrated for present purposes on the following major topics: (1) the object and preparation of hearings; (2) the order of proceedings; (3) the role of witnesses; (4) admissibility of evidence; (5) demonstrative evidence; and (6) use of experts.

Hearings

10–139 There does not seem to be much controversy as to whether or not hearings are to be held in international arbitration. The prevailing view is that a documents-only arbitration may be held, but it requires the agreement of all parties.[16] Any party thus has the right to insist on a hearing whatever the arbitrators may think. In international arbitration under the aegis of the main institutions, the number of documents-only cases is negligible.

What is of much greater concern is what takes place at hearings. More specifically, the fundamental issue is whether the case is caused to take shape prior to hearings by the formal submission of evidence in addition to pleadings. **10–140**

Those trained in the common law should realise something that may be painful, and it is this: the traditional forms of trial evolved by the common law, whose vestiges mark Anglo-American judicial practice even today, is wrong for international arbitration. **10–141**

It is inappropriate to transpose a system in which a central role is played by the illiterate juror, who must find the facts to which the judge will apply the law, but who at all times must be protected from manipulation by crafty lawyers. In international arbitration, the trier of fact also applies the law; moreover, he does not appear as the result of a random choice among the reluctant population at large; international arbitrators are hand-picked, willing and able specialists. **10–142**

The evolution of modern arbitral practice as opposed to the historical mode of trials under the Anglo-Saxon jury system is beyond the scope of this chapter; the distinctions to be made pertain to all arbitrations, and not just international ones. Nevertheless, the point should be made that emphasis on prior written submissions is particularly appropriate in international arbitration. When three arbitrators, not to mention the parties, their counsel and witnesses, live far apart and are fully occupied by other professional obligations, it would be a nightmare to force them to learn everything about the case in the course of interminable hearings, held in a hotel conference room far away from most participants' habitual place of work. **10–143**

A recent study of ICC practice reached the following conclusions with regard to ICC practice: **10–144**

> "The continental system of proof is characterized by the exchange of documents between the parties. Hearings serve principally as an occasion for arguments based on facts revealed in written evidence already submitted. The common-law system, on the other hand, uses hearings to develop facts and to introduce documents into evidence.
>
> The governing principles of the ICC Rules and the particularities of international disputes, where the parties and the arbitrators may be domiciled in different countries, favour the continental approach. Pursuant to Articles 3 and 4 of the ICC Rules, the Request for arbitration and the Answer should contain not only the particulars of the claim and defense, but also the agreements relied on and other documents necessary to establish clearly the circumstances of the case. . . .
>
> Many experienced international arbitrators consider that a witness's

[16] *cf.* ICC Rules, Art. 20(2); LCIA Rules, Art. 10(1).

essential contribution to the establishment of facts rarely requires more than a few hours of testimony. Arbitrators sceptical of the value of lengthy testimony in commercial cases would maintain that when all is said and done, after many days of observing an intelligent witness on the stand, one knows little more than whether or not one likes him.

In any event, full-blown oral hearings are very lengthy. Examination of witnesses in a major commercial case in English courts frequently takes many weeks, sometimes months. The process is somewhat less time-consuming in the United States, where there is extensive pre-trial deposition of witnesses by counsel prior to hearings. But even such depositions demand enormous amounts of time of witnesses and counsel, although not of the court.

In international arbitration, such extensive hearings are not practical. The site of arbitration will be foreign to at least one of the parties and usually to some or all of the arbitrators. The problems of arranging facilities for the hearing, hotel rooms, translators and stenographers (where required) and the discomfort for counsel working away from home offices contribute to make long hearings an unpleasant chore. The arbitrators usually have other functions which make it impossible for them to be exclusively available for long periods of time. As a result, hearings are seldom scheduled for a period of more than one or two weeks. If further hearings are required, they ordinarily have to be separated in time.

It should not be forgotten that documents are of primary importance in commercial matters. They are relied on heavily even in court litigation. Whatever may be the arguments in favour of oral proceedings in criminal litigation or in tort cases, they are far less relevant to an efficient system for the settlement of international commercial disputes by arbitration''.[17]

ICSID Rules

10–145 The ICSID Arbitration Rules, which explicitly attempt to harmonise procedures having evolved in the various major legal systems, contain the most detailed description of a process designed to allow the case to take shape before any hearings. Rule 30 describes ''The Written Procedure'', which precedes ''The Oral Procedure'', defined in rule 31. As explanatory note E to rule 30 makes clear, the scope of the memorials comprising the written procedure ''represents an adaptation of common law practice to the procedure of the civil law''.

10–146 This trend toward pre-hearing submissions of evidence is evident in the 1985 Rules of the LCIA. Article 6 provides for submission of a series of written statements containing detailed allegations of facts and contentions of law. Moreover, Article 6(5) makes clear that such statements are to be accompanied by copies (or, of they are especially voluminous, lists) of all essential documents

[17] Craig, Park and Paulsson, *op. cit.*, pp. 387–389.

on which the party concerned relies—and even, if relevant and practicable, by samples.

The oral hearing thus ceases to have the all-embracing function that it necessarily has in trial by jury. It becomes one of the procedures, or part of the procedure, available to the arbitrator and the parties in the effort to find the optimum combination of speed, quality and economy of dispute resolution. **10–147**

Time is a valuable commodity

The recognition that time is a valuable commodity to be allocated with great care is especially important in an international context, given the practical difficulties of coordinating the schedules and travels of participants located far apart. For example, the UNCITRAL Notes on Organizing Arbitral Proceedings say the following: **10–148**

> "*Whether one period of hearings should be held or separate periods of hearings*
>
> 77. Attitudes vary as to whether hearings should be held in a single period of hearings or in separate periods, especially when more than a few days are needed to complete the hearings. According to some arbitrators, the entire hearings should normally be held in a single period, even if the hearings are to last for more than a week. Other arbitrators in such cases tend to schedule separate periods of hearings. Advantages of one period of hearings are that it involves less travel costs, memory will not fade, and it is unlikely that people representing a party will change. On the other hand, the longer the hearings, the more difficult it may be to find early dates acceptable to all participants. Separate periods of hearings are easier to schedule and they leave time for analysing the records and for negotiations between the parties aimed at narrowing the points at issue by agreement.
>
> *Limiting time for oral arguments and questioning witnesses*
>
> 79. Some arbitrators consider it useful to limit the aggregate amount of time each party has for any of the following: (a) making oral statements, (b) questioning its witnesses, and (c) questioning the witnesses of the other party. In general, the same aggregate amount of time is considered appropriate for each party, unless the arbitral tribunal considers that a different allocation is justified. Before deciding, the arbitral tribunal may wish to consult the parties as to how much time they think they will need.
>
> 80. Such planning of time, provided it is realistic, fair and subject to judiciously firm control by the arbitral tribunal, will make it easier for the parties to plan the presentation of the various items of evidence and

arguments, reduce the likelihood of running out of time towards the end of the hearings, and avoid that one party would unfairly use up a disproportionate amount of time.''

The Order of Proceedings

10–149 The normal course of proceedings in a jury trial is for the plaintiff to present all his evidence, then the defendant to present all his evidence, and counsel to make final arguments. After the judge's summing up with respect to all issues, the jury makes its findings—also on all issues. Departures from this course are rare, because of the risk of confusing the jury. The arbitrator, on the other hand, is altogether free to depart from it if he thinks there is good reason to do so. If he thinks he is best educated by evidence taken issue by issue rather than party by party, that should settle the matter. He can, much more readily than a judge in a jury trial, hear all the evidence on a particular issue, adjourn for a few days or weeks, make and announce his decision on it, and then proceed with the case.

10–150 The UNCITRAL Notes on Organizing Arbitral Proceedings have the following to say on the subject of the order in which the parties present arguments and evidence:

''81. Arbitration rules and national laws on arbitral procedure typically give broad latitude to the arbitral tribunal to determine the order of presentations at the hearings. Procedural patterns differ, for example, as to whether opening or closing statements are heard and their level of detail; the sequence in which the claimant and the defendant are to present their opening statements, arguments, witnesses and other evidence; and whether the defendant or the claimant should have the last word. In view of such differences, it may foster efficiency of the proceedings if the arbitral tribunal clarifies to the parties, in advance of the hearings, the manner of conducting oral hearings, at least in broad lines.''

Witnesses

10–151 The following rules are to be recommended:

(1) A party should always have the right to be heard in support of its own case.

(2) Written affidavits signed by a witness (whether or not under oath)

should be accepted as evidence, provided that the arbitrator or any party other than the one presenting the witness shall have the right to ask the witness to appear personally to be questioned with respect to the affidavit, failing which the affidavit may be wholly or partially disregarded.

(3) As for witnesses called for by a party, their identity and the subject of their testimony should be disclosed in advance and the arbitrator should have the full authority to limit their appearance on the grounds of irrelevance or redundance.

(4) The arbitrator should have full authority to control the taking of oral testimony, including the right to limit or deny the right of a party to examine, cross-examine or re-examine a witness if he determines it to be unlikely to serve any further relevant purpose.

These concepts appear consonant with the ICSID, LCIA and ICC Rules, if not always expressly required or tolerated by them. In other words, they remain to some extent unwritten and cause controversy. **10–152**

For that reason, it is most interesting to examine the Rules of Evidence produced in 1983 by Committee D (Procedures for Settling Disputes) of the IBA's Section on Business Law. These Rules were promulgated by a Committee representing some 350 litigation lawyers from all continents, and reflect a commendable attempt to distil a unified procedural system out of the vast patchwork of national concepts. **10–153**

The IBA Rules of Evidence make explicit the four rules suggested above, and in addition reveal that civil lawyers were able to accept three controversial notions that are usually thought to be hallmarks of the common law approach: **10–154**

(1) any witness that appears is subject to cross-examination (Article 5(9));
(2) it is proper for a lawyer to interview witnesses or potential witnesses (Article 5(8)); and
(3) under the heading ''Production of Documents'' (Article 4), a right to a form of discovery is recognised. One may wonder how European lawyers, who tend to loathe the very thought of American-style discovery, ever accepted this concept. The answer is that there was a compromise, as a result of which the discovery mechanism is subject to two important limitations: First, there is no procedure for the deposition of adverse witnesses. Secondly, documents requested must be ''identified with reasonable particularity'' and cannot be purely internal documents—they must have ''passed to or from (the) other party from or to a third party who is not a party to the arbitration''.

Rules of admissibility

Anyone who cannot differentiate in value between first-hand and second-hand evidence should not be sitting as an arbitrator at all. The arbitrator should refuse **10–155** to allow a hearing to be dominated by strict adherence to rules of evidence designed primarily for trial by jury.

10–156 It is therefore hardly surprising to find the following provision in rule 33(1) of the ICSID Rules, entitled "Evidence: General Principles": "The Tribunal shall be the judge of the admissibility of any evidence adduced and of its probative value". As note A under this Rule 33 points out, this provision

> "reflects long-standing international practice. It confers on the Tribunal the power to determine the admissibility, relevance and materiality of evidence. Hence the Tribunal has full power to decide whether particular evidence (e.g. documents, interrogatories, written depositions, oral evidence by witnesses and experts given before the Tribunal or before a commissioner) should be admitted."

10–157 Similarly, Article 14(3) of the 1985 LCIA Rules authorises the arbitral tribunal to "receive and take into account such written and oral evidence as he shall determine to be relevant, whether or not strictly admissible in law."

Use of experts

10–158 In common-law court cases involving technical matters, any party may call expert witnesses on its own behalf to provide evidence on technical questions in issue. "Battles of experts" ensue, with detailed examination and cross-examination by counsel. Oral testimony of experts presented by the parties is rare in civil-law countries, where tradition and applicable procedural codes provide for the appointment of one or more neutral experts by the court.

10–159 Under Article 12 of the LCIA Rules and Article 20(4) of the ICC Rules, arbitrators may appoint neutral experts. With reference to less specific institutional rules, such as those of ICSID, one may conclude that authority to make such appointments is encompassed in more general powers to resolve the dispute expeditiously. Such is certainly the trend, as witnessed by Article 27 of the UNCITRAL Rules; Article 7 of the IBA Rules of Evidence; and Article 26 of the UNCITRAL Model Law. In major cases involving technical issues, however, both parties frequently wish to present evidence and testimony by experts whom they have consulted, whether the tribunal desires to be aided by a neutral expert or not. This occurs irrespective of whether the parties come from civil-law or common-law jurisdictions. In fact, when the issues in dispute include the evaluation of construction, engineering, design or mechanical and chemical processes, it is often indispensable for a party to consult experts outside its own organisation. Such experts, while paid for their work, do not have the same interest in the outcome of the litigation as a party's employee. Detached from the dispute, they can evaluate the issues more objectively. Their testimony may lend additional credibility to the party's case.

10–160 Even if they intend to appoint a neutral expert, arbitrators are not well-advised to reject the presentation of expert testimony by the parties. In particular, parties from common-law countries view with great misgiving a procedure whereby the arbitrators receive all their technical briefing from someone who, perhaps by unfortunate accident, may turn out to be incompetent: such an "expert" could not easily be challenged because, while perfectly mistaken, he is also perfectly neutral in the sense that his erroneous conclusions were not intended to benefit either side.

Since the information to be given by a party's expert is ordinarily both detailed and technical, the expert's report is generally filed as a document with other written evidence in the case. The consultation should provide a resumé of the qualifications of the expert as well as a summary of his *modus operandi* and the evidence examined in preparing his report. **10–161**

The written report is the foundation upon which the expert's oral examination is built. He should be able to defend his views in response to questions from both the tribunal and opposing counsel. The flexible procedure of international arbitration and its relaxation of evidentiary rules provide a receptive framework for hearing party-produced experts, who can make significant contributions to the resolution of complex technical disputes. **10–162**

The rules of ICSID and the ICC are flexible in allowing the parties to present expert witnesses, and allowing the arbitral tribunal to be assisted by its own appointed expert, but they do not guarantee that such an opportunity will be available, nor that a tribunal-appointed expert would be subject to questioning. As just stated, this is a matter of concern to many common lawyers, worried that the arbitrators may pick a mediocre but unchallengeable expert. (One might of course consider that if one casts one's fate with the chosen arbitrator, who may admittedly turn out to be honestly mistaken with respect to many matters, one of the things one entrusts him with is the choice of an expert.) The best solution to this problem is to ensure that the tribunal-appointed expert may be questioned, and this is precisely what the 1976 UNCITRAL Arbitration Rules provide for in Article 27(4): **10–163**

> "At the request of either party the expert, after delivery of the report, may be heard at a hearing where the parties shall have the opportunity to be present and to interrogate the expert. At this hearing either party may present expert witnesses in order to testify on the points at issue".

This concept, by and large reflected in Article 26(2) of the UNCITRAL Model Law, as well as in Article 12(2) of the LCIA Rules, would appear to be best suited to international cases. If a technical issue is important enough that the tribunal decides to appoint an expert, it is important enough that the parties should have full opportunity to examine and if necessary challenge the views of that expert. **10–164**

Multi-Party Arbitrations

10–165 Many international arbitrations involve more than two parties; for example, this was the case with respect to one-fifth of the requests for arbitration submitted to the ICC in 1994. Multi-party arbitrations have given rise to great procedural difficulties, starting with the appointment of arbitrators: how can one reconcile the need to have two co-arbitrators with the right of each of three parties to nominate its preferred appointee?

10–166 The time to consider these difficulties is when the relevant contracts are being negotiated, whether it is a "vertical" multi-party situation such as that of a main contractor who wishes the subcontractor to be implicated in any action brought by the owner or a "horizontal" one such as that of a consortium. There are now easy answers. As the Final Report on Multi-Party Arbitration approved by the ICC Commission on International Arbitration in 1994 demonstrates, this is not a task for amateurs:

> "In a multilateral relationship, whether involving a single contract or several related contracts, it may be appropriate or necessary to have a multi-party arbitration clause. . . . In general, the following precautions should be taken:
>
> — The contracting parties may wish to enable any signatory of the clause to take part voluntarily in a proceeding initiated only as between some of the parties, or to authorise any party to the proceeding to join any other contracting party. Such clauses must be drafted very carefully. In particular, it is important to determine a time limit after which voluntary or compulsory participation may no longer be requested. Moreover, it will be desirable to determine whether such participation will affect the constitution of the arbitral tribunal given the identity of its members and the possibility that they may have a relationship with a participating party.
>
> — The parties may wish to modify the composition of the arbitral tribunal depending on the number of parties involved in a dispute. Thus, for example, they may wish to provide for the constitution of an arbitral tribunal of four or five arbitrators where three or four parties are involved. This solution harbours major pitfalls and should be discouraged. It will be recalled that the ICC Rules of Arbitration only envisage the constitution of a tribunal of one or three arbitrators and that in any case the provisions of the Rules relating to the taking of decisions within the arbitral tribunal will have to be complied with. At a practical level, the preparation of a timetable will be all the more difficult if more arbitrators and lawyers are involved. Lastly, this solution will increase the cost of the proceeding.
>
> — In contrast with the foregoing solution, the arbitration agreement may provide that in any event (*i.e.* whether the tribunal comprises

one or three arbitrators), the arbitrators are all to be appointed by the ICC International Court of Arbitration. Although this solution is attractive by virtue of its simplicity, many arbitration users may consider that it depersonalises an arbitration too much.

— Another solution, although less frequently encountered, consists in the parties agreeing in advance on the identities of the arbitrators who are to decide any dispute. This solution appears risky—particularly when long-term contracts are involved—because the arbitrators initially foreseen may no longer be available, independent or in a position to carry out their appointment when invited to do so.

— In any event, the clause should also deal with the question of the effect of an arbitral award upon parties who have not participated in or been brought into the proceeding.

— Where several proceedings resulting from related contracts are consolidated, any formula suggested by practitioners . . . should be considered in the light of the circumstances of the case in question. Advice should be taken from lawyers with proper experience of arbitration procedure and of the ICC Rules in particular''.[18]

Even with specialist advice, there may be no ideal solution; without it, disaster looms over the horizon. Even when a multi-party arbitration argument proves effective to create jurisdiction before a single tribunal, specific challenges arise that are germane to the multiplicity of participants. As the draft UNCITRAL Notes on Organizing Proceedings put it: **10–167**

''89. In multi-party disputes it is often possible to identify issues that are interdependent in that a decision on one issue influences the outcome regarding another issue. For example, liability of a party found to exist vis-à-vis one claimant may affect the decision in another dispute in the multi-party setting. When such interdependence exists, it might be useful to divide the multi-party proceedings into stages that will deal with the issues in the appropriate order. It is, however, important to bear in mind that, since a decision on one issue may affect the position of a party in another issue, each interested party must be given an opportunity to present its arguments on the issues affecting that party.''

[18] *The ICC International Court of Arbitration Bulletin* 26 (May 1995) at p. 40. Art. 10 of the 1998 ICC Rules deals with the problem of ''multiple parties'' by providing that in the absence of joint appointments by multiple claimants or defendants all three arbitrators shall be named by the ICC Court. A similar (but arguably better) solution is contained in Art. 18 of the WIPO Arbitration Rules.

Conclusions

10–168 With the vast quantitative evolution of the international arbitral caseload over the past two decades, there has been a corresponding qualitative development. Arbitrators and counsel have seen that it is possible to marry the best elements of disparate traditions relating to the taking of evidence, and to do so in an efficient way that also conforms to legitimate expectations.

10–169 As one can see throughout their explanatory Notes, the ICSID Arbitration Rules reflect a conscious attempt to combine features of the major legal systems with respect to procedural rules. The same is true for the Rules of the new WIPO Arbitration Centre. The ICC Rules and the LCIA Rules are not as detailed, but clearly allow for an intelligent integration of various modes for trying cases that should leave all parties with the feeling they have been given full opportunity to present their case in a manner with which they are comfortable.

10–170 The 1983 IBA Rules of Evidence show that the effort of harmonisation need not require extensive and obscure definitions, but can be put as a short series of simple and concrete propositions covering the major issues that have long caused controversy with respect to the taking of evidence in international arbitration.

10–171 Thus, the right of the tribunal to appoint an independent expert need not be perceived as a denial of the philosophy and traditions of the adversarial process as long as an opportunity is given to question and challenge the findings of the expert, including the use of party-produced expert testimony.

10–172 Likewise, of submissions prior to hearings, and a corresponding de-emphasis of tedious formalities regarding the ''introduction'' of evidence at oral hearings, have been understood as indispensable in most international arbitral proceedings.

10–173 On the other hand, civil lawyers have been able to accept the concept that it is important for witnesses to appear, and that the parties should be given an opportunity to question them. Whether or not this questioning is called ''cross-examination'' is merely cosmetic. Lawyers unfamiliar with the techniques of cross-examination are understandably reluctant to accept a situation where their adversary may destroy their witnesses but they are unable to retaliate; in addition, they often justifiably feel that cross-examination in international arbitration with witnesses expressing themselves in a second language may degenerate into a humiliating and unseemly exercise. Accordingly, a middle ground can be found in the concept that ''questioning'' by parties takes place under the control of the arbitrators, who would curtail abuse.

10–174 Similarly, discovery may be tailored to the realities and requirements of international arbitration. It is perfectly possible to accept the notion that a party has the right to identify documents in the probable possession of an adversary and request the arbitral tribunal to order the production of these documents. The objection that arbitrators have no powers of coercion is not persuasive; the threat of drawing adverse inferences from the fact of non-production is not an idle one. On the other hand, proponents of the adversarial process are unlikely to get their way if they want to go on fishing expeditions on the basis of vague and over-comprehensive definitions of the documents they seek. They are also likely to have to accept the fact that they will not be able to obtain orders for the production of purely internal documents from the adversary; practitioners in most countries feel this is overreaching. Moreover, it is hard for the arbitrator to know whether party responding to such an order is really complying, given the totally hypothetical existence of many internal documents. It would hardly be appropriate to penalise parties who keep good records and whose personnel are unwilling to engage in selective shredding. Finally, deposition of adverse witnesses is unlikely to become commonplace in international arbitration.

The unavailability of discovery of internal documents or the deposition of **10–175** adverse witnesses is not to be deplored. Whatever the merits of these discovery techniques in domestic litigation, they are impractical in international arbitration, where in most cases one party will be in a superior position in terms of its ability to resist discovery. If the language of the arbitration is French, what would be the practical value of being allowed to depose witnesses who refuse to speak anything but Greek (as practitioners who have tried to cross-examine a witness through an interpreter well know) or to be told one may have access to documents located in Piraeus and written in Greek, and, most importantly, the revelation of which ultimately depends on the good faith of the producing party? More likely than not, one will get exactly what one did not want to see, and be carefully steered away from smoking guns.

Perfect homogeneity in the international arbitral process is not going to be **10–176** brought about in the near future. A case conducted by an English arbitrator in London will continue to have an English flavour, and the advocate will indeed notice a difference if the next month he is involved in a case heard under the direction of a chairman from Zurich. But the various approaches to the taking of evidence may in fact be successfully combined. This should not be surprising since the purpose—namely the objective establishment of the circumstances of the case—is always the same. Furthermore, bringing to bear some of the rigors of the adversarial process may often allow a greater depth of critical inquiry than the continental system, while the freedom of the arbitrator to take inquisitorial initiatives may happily steer the case out of the doldrums of evidentiary overkill occasionally permitted under the common-law system, and so unsuitable to international arbitration.

Part 11

ALTERNATIVE DISPUTE RESOLUTION

By Arthur L. Marriott, Q.C., F.C.I. Arb.

ADR Defined

It has long been a principle of English public policy to encourage and promote the settlement of disputes. Indeed, this policy is by no means confined to England and is reflected in the approach to settlement taken in many and diverse jurisdictions throughout the world. The policy was well summarised in *Cutt's v. Head*,[1] a case on privilege, in which Oliver L.J. (as he then was) said: 11–01

> "Public policy is clear from many authorities that parties should be encouraged so far as possible to settle their disputes without reference to litigation."

The promotion of settlement is the essence of ADR accomplished by structured negotiation which may take many forms. ADR may be defined as "the range of procedures which serve as alternatives to the adjudicatory procedures of litigation and arbitration for the resolution of disputes, generally but not necessarily involving the intercession and assistance of a neutral third party who helps to facilitate such resolution".[2]

Differences between ADR and arbitration.

ADR differs from arbitration in a number of important ways. Whilst both ADR and arbitration rest on agreement, agreements to arbitrate will as a general rule be enforced by the courts both here and elsewhere, but it is by no means yet settled that agreements to mediate will be enforced. In English law, two factors may be determinative; the first, as laid down by Lord Justice Kerr in the *Tubeworkers* case,[3] is that effect should be given to the dispute resolution mechanisms agreed upon by the parties. This also finds statutory expression in the Arbitration 1966 Act (see section 9(2)). 11–02

The second is by way of an *obiter dictum* in *Walford v. Miles*[4] (which expressly rejected the notion of good faith negotiation in an adversarial context), 11–03

[1] [1984] Ch. 290.
[2] Brown and Marriott, *ADR Principles and Practice*.
[3] *Tubeworkers and Tilbury* (1985) 30 B.L.R. 67.
[4] [1992] 2 A.C. 128.

which is Lord Ackner's reference to best endeavours as giving rise to enforceable obligations. In this, as in many other respects, the jurisprudence is more developed in Australia where, for example, Giles J. held in a case called *Hooper Bailie*[5] that an agreement to conciliate could be given effect to in law where it had the certainty necessary for legal enforceability. The judge defined what is enforced as

> "not cooperation and consent but participation in a process from which cooperation and consent might come".

The judge held that

> "an agreement to conciliate or mediate is not to be likened . . . to an agreement to agree. nor is it an agreement to negotiate, or negotiate in good faith, perhaps necessarily lacking certainty and obliging a party to act contrary to its interest. Depending upon its express terms and any terms to be implied, it may require of the parties participation in the process by conduct of sufficient certainty for legal recognition of the agreement."

A similar approach has been taken in jurisdictions in the United States.

11–04 A second difference between arbitration and ADR is that the object of arbitration is a final and binding award, but a binding agreement is by no means an automatic consequence of mediation. Whilst the arbitrator is empowered to make the binding award, a mediator has no power to make binding decision.

11–05 A third difference is that, so far, mediation is not subject to any statutory regime in England, unlike arbitration. There there are examples of statutory provisions for specific mediation and more generally in other jurisdictions as, for example, is found in section 2B of the Hong Kong Arbitration Ordinance 1989 and in the new statutes in Bermuda and Singapore.

11–06 A further difference is in the procedures to be followed for arbitration and mediation which are radically different. Arbitrators must act in accordance with the rules of natural justice, but mediators would be inhibited in their function if they were to do so. Procedures must be fair and free from abuse, but mediators must be free to see the parties independently and privately and subject to duties of confidentiality which may preclude them from disclosing to one party what they have been told by the other.

11–07 A final point of comparison is that arbitral decisions are to be reached on the basis of application of the law or, in the words of section 46 of the 1996 Act, "such other considerations as the parties may have agreed upon". The recommendations of a mediator are subject to no such constraints and in reaching a settlement both the mediator and the parties are free to ignore or to override substantive contractual provisions, though it is clear, as one American comment-

[5] *Hooper Bailie Associated Ltd v. Nation Group Pty Ltd* (1992) 28 N.S.W.L.R. 194.

ator has said, that mediation takes place in "the shadow of the law". It is a substantial advantage of mediation that the mediator can fashion solutions which are beyond the power of an arbitrator (or, for that matter, a judge).

Mediation and Negotiation

The essence of mediation is negotiation which has been defined as "the process we use to satisfy our needs when someone else controls what we want". The same author argues that negotiation normally occurs because "one has something the other wants and is willing to bargain to get it".[6] As we all know, negotiation is a feature of everyday life and is very much a practical skill learned pragmatically. 11–08

There are various theories of negotiation which have been the subject of various classifications, though most commentators agree that there is one basic distinction, namely between the problem solving approach to negotiation and the competitive approach. One American commentator has defined one type of negotiation as distributive, meaning, the more one party gets, the less the other party gets, as distinct from integrative, where there are a number of issues to be resolved which can be integrated to arrive at the best result, creating joint gains for both or all parties. The problem solving approach perhaps puts more emphasis on parties' interests rather than on parties' rights, but both approaches necessarily involve the consideration of the alternatives to a negotiated agreement, *i.e.* the consideration of the likely outcome and cost of an adjudicatory procedure such as litigation or arbitration. 11–09

Facilitative and evaluative

A further distinction in the same vein is made between facilitative and evaluative mediation. Broadly, facilitative mediation means interest based negotiation in which the mediator helps the parties to explore options and enhance their mutual interest. On the other hand, evaluative mediation tends to be more rights based, where the mediator makes or obtains an assessment and expresses a view on the merits of the dispute. Many mediators shy away from an evaluative role and the debate as to the proper role of mediators is one of some controversy. But the test must surely be that the mediator should work with the parties in the way most likely to bring about a settlement. 11–10

[6] Robert Maddoc, *Successful Negotiation*, (1988), at p. 14.

Balance of power

11–11 The balance of power between the parties to a negotiation is of cardinal importance. Critics of ADR often point out that excessive power in the hands of one party may result in unfair or unmeritorious settlements. This is contrasted with the position of parties to an action in the courts where (so it is said) all are equal before the law. But this is unreal, as one of the great criticisms of our current system of litigation is that it favours those with the deepest pockets. In the old cliché, justice is like the Ritz hotel, open to all, but, in reality, only to those who can pay the bill. But mediation can work even in situations where the balance of power is titled heavily in favour of one party. To take a simple and obvious example, it does not avail a creditor to refuse to negotiate a settlement other than on a basis of full and immediate payment, if the consequence would be the immediate bankruptcy of the debtor.

Good faith in negotiation

11–12 Central also to mediation is the principle of good faith in negotiation. In some civil law systems, there is an over-riding principle of good faith in the formation and performance of contracts. Precontractual liability can sometimes attach to parties where there has been a failure to negotiate and transact in good faith. In England and in the United States, parties are able to negotiate, if they wish, without risk of precontractual liability, though concepts of good faith and fair dealing have played a more pronounced role in US contract law than in English law. The position in English law has been summarised by Bingham L.J. in *Interfoto Library Ltd v. Stiletto Ltd*[7]:

> ''English law has, characteristically, committed itself to no such overriding principle [of good faith] but has developed solutions in response to demonstrated problems of unfairness.''

11–13 However, the professional ethics rules of some professions may well impose duties akin to good faith on their members when conducting negotiations. Thus, for example, a solicitor or barrister conducting a negotiation should not lie or mislead if asked a question, nor put forward a proposition which he knows to be false. The general law of misrepresentation, deceit and duress applies to the conduct of negotiations.

Voluntary nature

11–14 The conventional wisdom has it that mediation can only be voluntary, as the process is essentially consensual in nature. Parties must agree to enter into medi-

[7] [1989} Q.B. 433; [1988] 2 W.L.R. 615.

ation and must agree upon any settlement which results. However, the voluntary concept has been modified in that some contracts provide for compulsory mediation, so that, if one party insists upon it, the other is obliged to comply. The Hong Kong Government contracts for the new airport project are a major case in point. Some court systems have compulsory mediation as part of or an adjunct to the procedures of the court. At the core of the reform of family law in this country is compulsory mediation. Many states in the United States have compulsory mediation in certain kinds of cases.

The Attitude of the Mediator

Attempts to put mediation into various different straitjackets are sterile and to be deprecated. What matters is to achieve settlement by fair and proper negotiation. The role of the mediator will of course be influenced by the mediator's experience and personality. Some mediators are interventionist, actively promoting settlement and seeking to persuade parties of the advantgages of a particular course. Others are more passive, preferring the parties themselves to take the leading role. **11–15**

Mediation is not always conducted by sole mediators and co-mediators, particularly in family cases, are becoming widely used. Nor is the use of mediation confined to disputes between two parties only. There is considerable experience (particularly in the United States) with multi-party mediation, often of highly complicated cases. **11–16**

The stages of mediation

Mediation can be divided into a number of stages, though clearly these can differ according to the demands of different kinds of dispute and the particular requirements of a particular dispute. The stages can be generally defined as: **11–17**

- the initial inquiry—engaging the parties;
- the contract to mediate;
- preliminary communications and preparation;
- meeting the parties;
- the parties' presentations;
- information gathering;
- facilitating negotiations;
- impasse strategies;

- terminating mediation and recording agreements;
- post-termination phase.

11–18 All these stages are important, though clearly some are more important than others. Thus, for example, it is vital to have a very clear agreement with the parties as to the nature of the mediation and the way it is to be conducted. The limits of the mediator's authority must be clearly defined. Does the mediator, for example, have authority to disclose to one party documents given to him by the other? What information given to the mediator must remain confidential? How are the costs of the mediation to be funded? There is a range of practical matters which should be taken into account when preparing the agreement to mediate.

Conduct of the Mediation

11–19 The conduct of the mediation is essentially one of building the confidence of the parties in the mediator and in the process and, ultimately, to the point where the parties have sufficient confidence to make concessions and seek compromises. The mediator must be deft and adroit in the presentation of arguments and ideas and in the generation of options which may be necessary in order to avoid or find a way out of some impasse. The mediator must guard against abuse of the process by a party and must not hesitate to stop the mediation if it is clear that one party is not playing fair.

The settlement agreement

11–20 Sometimes the settlement agreement can be incorporated in an arbitral award, and enforceable as such, if the mediation is taking place in the context of an existing arbitration. Sometimes the settlement agreement can be an order of the court if the mediation has served to settle a pending action. It must be remembered that the settlement agreement gives rise to legally binding obligations and must be a clear record of what has been negotiated and agreed. Care needs to be taken in reducing any agreement reached to writing and the mediator will need to decide with the parties whether he should prepare the draft agreement himself, or whether it should be drafted by the parties. It may well be that particular attention should be paid to the post-termination phase, if, for example, the dispute has been one between partners or joint venturers and the unravelling of the relationship may take time and involve a whole series of transactions such as transfer or disposal of property. In these circumstances it may be desirable for the mediator to have a continuing role to ensure that problems which may arise in the implementation of the agreement are solved.

Mediation in the United Kingdom

Experience with mediation in the United Kingdom has been largely confined to labour disputes and family disputes. Both are special procedures of great importance. Recent years have seen considerable development in divorce and family mediation, given the increasing breakdown of marriage and co-habitation in this country. 11–21

Family mediation

Experience in this country with court-attached ADR is limited, even in family cases. Conciliation involving children, for example, has only been in force since 1983. Mediation has for some years taken place in relation to family matters, where courts have either dealt with conciliation appointments themselves (by the district judge or by a court welfare officer) or have adjourned cases for independent mediation outside the court. In-court mediation has tended to relate primarily to children's issues, whereas out of court mediation has covered children's issues and often financial issues as well (''all-issues mediation''). This is being further developed by the Family Law Act and the ancillary relief pilot scheme. 11–22

As regards family mediation, the principal organisations are the Family Mediators' Association and National Family Mediation, which have recently combined with National Family Mediation (Scotland) to form the United Kingdom College of Family Mediators under the presidency of Dame Margaret Booth. The Solicitors' Family Law Association also plays a significant role in training mediators and offering mediation services. Other organisations offering training and resources in family mediation include BALM (the British Association of Lawyer Mediators), Resolve and the Law Group, an association of 69 firms of solicitors. 11–23

Commercial and civil

11–24 But there has been growing interest in mediation of civil and commercial matters. Various organisations have been founded which offer mediation services to the private sector. In the civil and commercial field, perhaps the best known is CEDR, which started in 1990 with the support of the CBI and many leading professional firms. CEDR has mediated several hundred cases of varying size and complexity and has trained several hundred mediators. But the use of mediation in the private sector in civil and commercial disputes is very much in its infancy. It is clear that mediation of such disputes in the private sector in this country is more talked about than practised and that (justifiably) complaint is made that far more mediators have been trained than there is work for them to do.

11–25 In the commercial and civil field, the main experience has been with certain pilot schemes (although in some county courts, district judges may have helped to encourage and facilitate settlement, but that process should not be confused with mediation as such). One such scheme was set up in 1994 by the Bristol Law Society, in conjunction with CEDR and ADR Group. Consideration was initially given to its being an in-court pilot scheme, but the L.C.D. preferred it to be run as an out of court scheme. In the event, the referral rate and the take-up rate proved to be very low. Various reasons have been attributed to this, including lack of knowledge, reservations by solicitors about the value of the process, about mediators' skills, or about possible loss of revenue, tactical considerations and concerns about costs. There was disappointment about restraints placed on the scheme by the L.C.D. The scheme has recently been revived.

11–26 In London there are two pilot schemes in existence at the Central London County Court and Civil Trial Centre. One is concerned with patent and trademark issues and has been established by H.H. Judge Ford, the patent and trademark judge. The other focuses on general common law cases and has been promoted by H.H. Judge Neil Butter, Q.C. with the very active support and encouragement of the senior judge, Sir Frank White. Judge Butter, Q.C.'s scheme is being carefully monitored by a committee, with a statistical analysis being made by Professor Hazel Genn, Professor of Socio-legal Studies at University College London.

11–27 The Commercial Court issued a Practice Direction in 1993 which was of very limited scope and merely indicated that the court maintained a list of organisations and persons offering mediation services and that parties were encouraged to explore ADR as a means of resolving their disputes. In 1996 a further Practice Direction was issued, which indicated that the commercial judges would adjourn selected cases to enable ADR to take place. Anecdotal evidence suggests that the commercial judges are making such orders in several cases and as a matter of course. There are also plans for an appellate mediation scheme to try to ease the work load of the Court of Appeal.

Legal aid

A major difficulty is that legal aid has not been available for mediation. The accepted wisdom is that legal aid is not available for mediation as part of the litigation process, though legal aid will be available in family law disputes under the new Act. Legal aid will be required for mediation in civil and commercial disputes to enable many disputants to use ADR at all. For pilot scheme purposes[8] there may be ways around the problem if, to take personal injury cases as an example, the trade unions on the one hand and the insurance companies on the other are prepared to finance the mediation costs. Indeed, it may well be that some insurers would be prepared to pay the cost of both parties to attend a three or four hour mediation session as part of a pilot scheme. There are indications that some insurers may be prepared to do so. There needs to be consultation with the T.U.C. and individual trade unions. 11–28

Although legal aid will need to be extended to cover the costs of representation of disputants, some of the cost of providing services can be borne by the private sector. Initially, it is clear that the private sector will have to provide services *pro bono* in order to demonstrate that mediation works and that substantial cost savings to both the private and public purse are possible. In some civil and most (if not all) commercial cases, there is no reason why, if such schemes become permanent, disputants should not pay the market rate. If the system works, then commercial concerns will be prepared to do so. But in other cases where disputants lack means, the service will need to be provided free or at low cost. The civil magistrates system, envisaged by Lord Woolf, may well provide an opportunity for public service which many will take up. This is the experience in the U.S. where, for example, practising lawyers sometimes provide mediation services free (as in the Washington D.C. federal court system). In due course, if the system is seen to work, then this will encourage a transfer of public resources within the civil dispute system so that support is given to mediation as a real and effective alternative to litigation and in order the better to promote fair and prompt settlement. 11–29

Conclusions will also need to be drawn from the Bristol scheme and the two pilot schemes introduced in 1996 in the Central London County Court and Civil Trial Centre. Some of the matters that will need to be covered are as follows: 11–30

(a) More information about mediation will have to be given to disputants, and in a way that will enable them to choose and use it effectively.

(b) Solicitors acting for parties will have to be better informed about the mediation process and the qualifications of mediators and how the additional dynamic of a third party neutral changes the negotiation. They may need to be given an opportunity before any new pilot scheme is established, to air their concerns so that these can be addressed.

[8] Some legal aid provision has been made for the pilot scheme at the Central London County Court.

(c) The Law Society and other solicitors' bodies will need to consider arranging training for solicitors on how best to represent clients effectively in ADR processes, especially mediation. There are seldom good tactical reasons inhibiting the use of ADR processes, as lawyers will realise if they have a better understanding of it. Training may have to be extended to law schools, where the exclusive focus on litigation will need to be reviewed. As mediation becomes increasingly used, law schools will need to teach it to students from an earlier stage.

(d) In particular, lawyers should be able to explain to clients why participation in mediation does not indicate weakness (and the scheme should be structured so that no such implication could arise), Similarly, parties who feel that their cases are so strong that they see no point in negotiating should be advised of the merits of resolving disputes quickly without the costs and risks of litigation, and would be able to hold out for better terms than they could if they were less confident on the merits.

(e) Mediation organisations will need to address some of the questions raised by the Bristol research, in particular, about the extent to which mediators can, and should, help parties to form a better view of the merits of the case. This turns on the issue of whether a mediator should offer any form of evaluation. Most mediators do not consider this an appropriate part of their role and would resist doing so. However, in relation to in-court mediation, the expectations of the parties and their solicitors must be met and a better definition of what is on offer (and can be delivered) needs to be made. Mediation can help parties to re-assess strengths and weaknesses, but how this is done, and whether by the mediator directly, needs to be clearly established.

(f) The courts and the L.C.D. should support the pilot schemes in whatever way may be reasonably necessary and appropriate. This should be discussed with those providing mediation.

Arbitral Institutions and Mediation

11–31 Some arbitral institutions and others concerned with dispute resolution offer mediation services and have mediation rules. Thus, for example, the LCIA, though primarily a body specialising in international commercial arbitration, will provide mediation services, either by use of the UNCITRAL conciliation rules or by virtue of its arrangement with CEDR. The Chartered Institute also has a mediation service. The City Disputes Panel, designed to provide a service for the resolution of disputes within the financial services industry, has mediation rules and will administer mediations. A feature of the CDP's service is that in the arbitration rules there is a requirement that periodically the arbitrators should inquire of the parties whether they have considered settlement and whether the arbitrators can in any way assist them to achieve it.

The International Chamber of Commerce has conciliation rules, amended a few years ago to make them simpler and more streamlined. However, as is apparent from published statistics, the conciliation procedures of the ICC have rarely been used. The Zürich Chamber of Commerce has had for many years a mini-trial system which has hardly been used. The Netherlands Arbitration Institute published in 1995 mini-trial rules as a first stage, depending on reaction of the users, towards a more comprehensive system of mediation. **11–32**

Anecdotal evidence suggests that there is some experience in this country and elsewhere with ad hoc conciliation, sometimes using the UNCITRAL conciliation rules, though such evidence would again suggest that the use of the UNCITRAL arbitration rules, even putting to one side their use in the Iran Tribunal, has been far more widespread. **11–33**

So, while mediation and conciliation (the terms are now used interchangeably) have yet to challenge arbitration in this country as the primary means of dispute resolution in certain fields of commercial activity, arbitral institutions are increasingly recognising that they cannot confine their services to the provision of arbitral services, but must broaden the spectrum of resolution to include mediation. **11–34**

Other ADR processes

While mediation is at the heart of ADR, there are a number of processes which can be used as part of the general concept of alternative dispute resolution. It is one of the advantages of ADR that the experienced practitioner can devise special procedures, unfettered by formal rules of arbitration or of litigation. Such special procedures may utilise a number of techniques such as the following: **11–35**

- Fact gathering, by obtaining relevant information and documents from the parties and/or from third parties.
- Presentations by each party in a written, oral, audio-visual or any other form
- Examining the merits of the issues, whether of fact, law or technicality.
- Binding adjudication by the neutral.
- Non-binding adjudication, in which the neutral considers the parties' respective contentions and furnishes a non-binding opinion on the merits.
- Evaluation, by furnishing an informal and perhaps limited view on some or all of the issues.
- Expert intervention, by arranging for an expert in the subject-matter of the dispute to give a neutral opinion, technical or otherwise.
- Conducting joint and/or separate meetings with the parties.

- Facilitation of dispute resolution in various ways.
- Deciding upon the sequence in which steps are taken, and whether there may be parallel action in different fora; the timetable; the agenda; the power, authority and role of the neutral; the number of neutrals involved, and if more than one, their respective functions; the degree of confidentiality; the extent to which and stage at which the parties' own lawyers are involved; and other matters of a practical and management nature.

ADR and the Courts

11–36 The interim and final reports produced by Lord Woolf's Working Party have served to focus public attention on how to settle disputes which are either about to be litigated, or are already before the courts. In 1992, when the second edition of this book was published, there was little sign that we stood on the threshold of innovative and radical procedural reform of civil dispute resolution in this country. Lord Woolf had not been appointed and no draft of a new Arbitration Act had yet emerged from the Departmental Advisory Committee. The ADR movement, if it can be described as such, was in its infancy, being regarded somewhat warily by practising lawyers and judges.

11–37 Five years later, we have crossed the threshold of radical change in all aspects of civil dispute resolution. Lord Woolf, following the investigation by his working party and an extensive process of consultation with the legal profession and others concerned with civil dispute resolution, has published two reports. The first steps have been taken towards implementation of his reforms. Modern methods of case management will in due course become the order of the day. Judges, administrators and practitioners will need to change and face the reality, that neither the public purse nor private interest will tolerate any longer the conduct of litigation in its current, expensive and wasteful fashion. Whether all of Lord Woolf's reforms will work, only experience will tell us, but it is clear that the introduction of case management, fast-track procedures and stringent limitations on costs will change a system which has remained fundamentally the same since late Victorian times.

11–38 A further impetus to reform is that it appears that no Government of whatever political persuasion will deploy additional money or other resources to expand or improve the existing system of civil litigation. Self-help by lawyers and judges is required.

11–39 Some of Lord Woolf's reforms, such as the use of civil magistrates, can be accomplished without additional expenditure or the deployment of other resources. But Lord Woolf's central objective of promoting the settlement of disputes and his adoption of case management techniques can only be achieved without substantial extra expense if existing public resources are better deployed and those of the private sector are harnessed. There is a clear opportunity for private organisations which hold themselves out as providing arbitration and ADR services, as well as individuals drawn from a variety of professions and trades who would be prepared to devote their time and expertise to assist in the resolution of civil disputes by acting as arbitrators, mediators and adjudicators. Existing systems of litigation are too expensive and too long delayed. Access to justice is denied to the vast majority of citizens. Only the very rich or the very poor are able to go to law. The cost of commercial litigation is a matter of great concern not only to small and medium-sized companies but to large ones as well.

The statistics show that the majority of cases before the courts ultimately **11–40**
settle, but the cost and delay in achieving such settlements is often the primary motive for settlement with the consequence that justice is not necessarily done. The same is true in arbitration, where although statistical evidence is limited, anecdotal evidence suggests that most arbitration cases settle. Lord Woolf's proposals for radical procedural reform of the courts are based on the assumption that, by effective case management by judges, ways can be found to promote and encourage settlement at a very early stage and in any event before an expensive trial. While Lord Woolf makes no recommendations for the introduction of ADR schemes attached to the courts, he does encourage the use of ADR as a means of promoting settlement.

Government policy

It is Government policy to encourage mediation, particularly in family matters, **11–41**
though hitherto Government has been reluctant to provide finance for ADR schemes whether by direct contribution to the cost of court attached schemes, or by the provision of legal aid. However, it is clear that pressure on the public purse and limitations on the amount to be spent on the civil disputes system will lead to increasing emphasis on mediation within the court system as a means of improving access to justice and getting better value for public money. Some believe that it is only a matter of time (and probably not very long at that) before financial pressures cause the introduction of mandatory court attached mediation and arbitration.

Although there is a burgeoning interest in court attached schemes, at present **11–42**
there are limitations to what such schemes can achieve. The primary limitation is that they are essentially voluntary. It is quite clear, for example, from the work already undertaken, that there is considerable scepticism,and in some instances hostility, on the part of some solicitors to the idea of court attached mediation. Some solicitors appear concerned at the potential loss of revenue from their litigation work. If these schemes are to fulfill their promise of achieving settlements and, particularly if Lord Woolf's objective of promoting early settlement

is to be realised, some form of mandatory court attached mediation may well need to be introduced.

11–43 It may well be that court-attached schemes will develop along the lines of the interesting approach taken by the ancilary relief pilot scheme in family proceedings. Here, couples have the option either to have mediation, at this stage offered privately outside the court, or to participate in FDR (financial dispute resolution) in a privileged forum, conducted by a district judge, who will specifically try to facilitate a settlement, and who will not hear the case if it has to proceed to a formal hearing. Guidelines have been established for the way in which district judges should conduct those privileged hearings, and there may be guidelines as well to indicate how lawyers should represent parties to such proceedings.

11–44 The FDR could form a model for developing a partnership between the courts and the private sector, giving disputants in the civil and commercial fields the option of having a form of in-court facilitation, or out of court mediation. Obviously, these options would have to be carefully considered and developed, but the basis for further pilot schemes clearly exists.

Use of ADR in courts elsewhere

11–45 The use of ADR in courts abroad is now well-established. It is a feature of court procedures in many jurisdictions, that there is an obligation upon the judge to raise the possibility of settlement with both parties at various stages of the litigation. Indeed, in some jurisdictions, such as Germany, the obligation extends to the judge notifying the parties on a preliminary basis as to the views he has formed as to the likely outcome of the case and the basis upon which it could be settled.

11–46 In other jurisdictions such as the United States and Australia there is a whole panoply of ADR measures attached to the courts. It is commonplace to find compulsory references to mediation and to arbitration and such devices as early neutral evaluation which requires a neutral evaluator to meet parties at an early stage of a case in order to make a confidential assessment of the dispute, partly to help them to narrow and define the issues, and partly to promote efforts to arrive at a settlement; and neutral fact finding, which involves an investigation by a neutral expert into certain specific issues of fact, technicality and or law, and thereafter, if required, a mediatory role, and eventually participation in an adjudicatory process if required. Another technique has been the use of settlement weeks where the court, with the aid of outside mediators, suspends operations for a week and tries to settle all cases on the docket.

11–47 Appellate mediation is also used, particularly in the United States, and there are schemes in both the state and federal courts.

11–48 Whilst there is now considerable experience elsewhere with court-attached ADR, there is still a lack of statistical information as to the precise effects in terms of improving access to justice and in either saving money, or the reallocation of funding and human resources, or more efficient operation of the court system. But such evidence as exists (and it is primarily from the United States) does indicate that cases are settling at an earlier stage than they might otherwise do, and in many instances there is a very considerable saving of cost. There are also indications in the United States that a greater percentage of cases at appellate level may be settling than would otherwise be the case.

Not all cases are suitable for mediation and as a general rule issues which **11–49**
involve the rights of the citizen against the state or judicial review of administrative action would not in this country be considered suitable for ADR. Some commercial matters also require adjudication as, for example, where a standard form contract, or the working of a market, requires a binding decision of principle by a court or arbitrator to enable other similar contracts to be performed in a consistent manner, or to enable the market to function properly.

Court-attached schemes in the private sector

It is clear that if ADR is developed in England the principal impetus will come **11–50**
from court-attached schemes. Based on that precedent, private sector use will increase. However, private sector use could increase significantly, if both central and local government were, as a matter of course, to put in contracts for construction, procurement and supply, mandatory mediation clauses as the first stage of dispute resolution procedures. The attitude of the Government is by no means hostile to the use of ADR in government contracts. Government departments and agencies are aware of ADR for dispute resolution and have the discretion whether or not to stipulate ADR in contracts. But there is little evidence that government lawyers actually do so. Experience in Hong Kong has shown, particularly in the construction industry, that the use of ADR as a mechanism to prevent disputes getting to court at all requires the active support and participation of the Government. Government had to give the lead and set the example of including these clauses in government contracts. The Government should do so in the United Kingdom, perhaps on an experimental basis at first.

Experience outside England has been essentially to the same effect. Private **11–51**
sector organisations in the United States have taken some time to become commercially viable, though indications now are that the leaders in the field are extremely active and have substantial case-loads. The same is true in Australia where there is some anecdotal evidence to suggest that mediation, particularly in the construction industry, may be replacing arbitration or the courts as the primary means of dispute resolution.

That is almost certainly true of Hong Kong where the introduction by the **11–52**
Government in the mid-1980s, under persuasion from the private sector, of mediation provisions in government construction contracts has undoubtedly provoked an increase in the use of mediation of construction industry disputes. Hong Kong Government statistics indicate that certainly as regards government contracts, mediation is now the primary means of dispute resolution. It is signi-

ficant that in the contracts for the construction of the new airport, mediation is a compulsory and first stage of the dispute resolution procedure. But as yet in Hong Kong, unlike Australia or the United States, there is no move to have court-attached schemes for ADR,[9] despite the recommendations of a committee which reported to the Chief Justice to that effect.

ADR and Arbitration

11–53 Hitherto, arbitration has been the only real alternative to resolution by litigation. London has maintained its pre-eminent position as the leading centre for international commercial arbitration, particularly in such specialist fields as commodity and maritime disputes. Arbitration has continued to play a vital role in domestic dispute resolution, particularly in relation to the construction industry and in the commercial real property business. But private sector arbitration has itself fallen victim to the same criticism as applies to litigation. In recent years arbitration has been conducted in very similar fashion to High Court litigation and has been prone to the same problems of expense and delay. A welcome sign, however, has been the growth of the County Court arbitration scheme introduced in 1986 which appears to offer litigants precisely what they want, namely fast, inexpensive and final decisions.

11–54 The problems of delay, cost and denial of access which bedevil the courts in this country also afflict arbitration, perhaps indeed more so, for the cost of much English arbitration conducted in traditional fashion exceeds the cost of equivalent court proceedings, given that, unlike the judge, the arbitrator has to be paid by the parties and, unlike the court facilities which are provided by the state, the parties must provide hearing rooms and other physical facilities at their own expense. There is therefore scope for the introduction of radical procedural reform in arbitration, utilising ADR methods which may streamline the process, rendering it less costly and permit early and fair settlement.

11–55 The conventional wisdom in England has always been that the arbitrator is quite distinct from the mediator and the two functions should never be combined. This reflects the attitude of the judges who, whilst prepared to encourage settlement as a matter of public policy, have never descended into the arena to help bring it about. Indeed, an elaborate and complicated system of confidentiality and privilege has been created in order to prevent judges from having essen-

[9] There are indications that the new Chief Justice may be more favourably disposed to court-attached ADR than was his predecessor.

tial information as to the terms upon which parties might be encouraged to settle. So too in arbitration.

"Med-Arb"

However, in other parts of the world the combination of the role of judge or arbitrator and mediator is well known. Perhaps the leading example is that of China, where the same person can fulfil the two functions. The American Arbitration Association, the largest arbitral institution in the world, with over 60,000 cases in 1996, has long had rules for mediation combined with arbitration, known in the jargon as "med-arb". Similar schemes have existed in South Africa in the construction industry and there is increasing experience with this manner of proceeding. The conceptual objections are obvious, it being said that the parties would be very reluctant to talk frankly and fully to the mediator about the strengths and weaknesses of their case, if the mediation were then to fail and the same person proceeded to arbitrate the dispute. But many feel this objection is more apparent than real, first, because the chances of early settlement are increased by the process and, secondly, because a long drawn out battle in arbitration will usually reveal to the experienced arbitrator sooner or later where the strengths and weaknesses are to be found. Experienced and robust arbitrators often have more than an inkling of the strengths and weaknesses at a very early stage, merely from reading the relevant documents and the respective statements of case. **11–56**

It is to be hoped, that given the 1996 Act, with its express encouragement of party autonomy and the freedom of arbitrators and the parties to develop procedures best suited to the economic and expeditious dispatch of the case, those concerned will develop procedures which combine arbitration and mediation in various ways. They might commence by agreeing that the arbitrator should, as a matter of good practice, inquire regularly of the parties as to settlement and be prepared, if it would be of assistance, to give preliminary, informal and non-binding indications of his views, whether on legal, contractual or technical aspects of the dispute, or upon the basis upon which it appears to him that a settlement may be possible. **11–57**

Secondly, arbitrators and parties might look at some of the existing ADR procedures, such as referring matters to an early neutral evaluator, or to a neutral fact-finder, or to introducing at an appropriate stage in the procedure the use of the mini-trial. There is some difference of view between experts as to whether a mini-trial is only really suitable at a comparatively late stage of a dispute when it has been properly pleaded, the relevant documents disclosed and the issues defined. There are those who say that it can be used at an earlier stage; but that must be a matter for individual judgment. Unquestionably, experience tells us that the use of a mini-trial at an appropriate stage particularly of a complicated and lengthy dispute can often break the deadlock between the parties and produce a settlement. It should also not be forgotten that whilst an overall settlement **11–58** might not result, there can be a partial settlement, or a narrowing of issues and a saving thereby of time and cost.

The Supporting and Supervisory Role of the Courts in ADR

11–59 There is some controversy as to the role of the courts in relation to ADR. Clearly, where ADR takes place as an adjunct to litigation, the court must have a role to play of both support and supervision, but there are those who believe that that role should be limited. In the case of private sector ADR where mediation has not been ordered or compelled by a court, there are those who believe that the court has no role to play at all. However, one role for the court is the enforcement of agreements to use ADR and another role is the prevention of abuse by intervening to uphold ethical standards, or to protect confidentiality, privilege or privacy. Another is intervening in the public interest where iniquity is disclosed in the course of a mediation process. This can give rise to difficult ethical questions, particularly in family mediation, where it may become apparent in the course of proceedings that there has been (for example) child abuse or other domestic violence, or in commercial cases where it may be apparent that there has been wholesale fraud or other criminal conduct.

Conclusion

11–60 ADR is not a panacea. It is not suitable for all disputes which go before the courts, particularly those arising from the relationship between the citizen and the state. ADR is in its infancy, but we can derive confidence in its efficacy from its use in labour relations and in the increasingly important field of family breakdown. The case for radical change in our traditional systems of civil dispute resolution in the courts and by arbitration is unanswerable. Lord Woolf's proposals are the most important recommendations for procedural change in the courts since the great reforms of 1872 to 1875. The Arbitration Act 1996 also marks a radical change in the approach to arbitration in this country. For the first time, the legislature has imposed statutory duties upon arbitrators and parties to arbitration to find procedural solutions which are not only fair, but which promote economy and expedition. Extensive powers have been given to arbitrators to achieve these ends and the role of the court confined to essential supervision and powerful support of the proper exercise of arbitrators' powers.

There is a role for ADR, both as part of the processes of adjudication whether in the courts or by arbitration and as a system in its own independent right. Seen in the context of civil dispute resolution generally, ADR offers ways of improving the systems of adjudication and, more importantly, of broadening and improving access to justice. It also provides an opportunity to those concerned with civil dispute resolution and drawn from many professions other than the law to exploit their talents in the public interest. Much will have to be done *pro bono*, certainly to demonstrate the viability of ADR schemes and in recognition of the fact that public expenditure on the civil disputes system cannot be unlimited. But there are also considerable opportunities for private reward and such schemes function best when the public and private interests co-exist. **11–61**

Further reading

Brown and Marriott, *ADR Principles and Practice* (Sweet & Maxwell, 1993).

Dr Karl Mackie, David Miles and William Marsh, *Commercial Dispute Resolution: An ADR Practice Guide* (Butterworths, 1995).

ADR – *ADR For Financial Institutions.*

Arthur L. Marriott—"Tell it to the judge . . . but only if you feel you must" (1995 Freshfields Lecture), *Arbitration International*. Vol. 12, No. 1, 1996.

Freshfields booklet on ADR.

Stephen B. Goldberg, Eric D. Green and Frank E. A. Sander—*Dispute Resolution* (Little Brown, 1989).

APPENDICES

List of Appendices

Appendix 1
Precedents and Drafting Suggestions

LIST OF PRECEDENTS AND DRAFTING SUGGESTIONS

70. Final award without reasons
71. Final award with reasons
72. Final award—reasons to be annexed—consumer dispute
73. Interim award
74. Interim awards reserving costs for later decision
75. Clause reserving costs and giving directions
76. Clause reserving costs but making an award "*nisi*" as to costs and giving directions
77. Final award incorporating alternative final award
78. Award by umpire
79. Clauses for awards—rent review—declaration that landlord has unreasonably withheld consent
80. Award for the delivery up of property, with alternative money award
81. Letter publishing award
82. Specimen letter—arbitrator's charges
83. ICC—arbitrator's declaration of acceptance and statement of independence
84. Possible terms of engagement for a barrister/arbitrator

PRECEDENTS AND DRAFTING SUGGESTIONS

INTRODUCTION

A health warning for your insurance policy

One of the areas where thought is most needed and least given is in the adaptation of precedents for the case in hand. Another is in the drafting of dispute resolution clauses. In the hope of encouraging adaptation rather than unthinking adoption, the title of this section of the Handbook has been changed to "Precedents and Drafting Suggestions".

Thought is particularly necessary in two situations.[1] One is where the rules of an institution are being incorporated. These should not be incorporated blind; they should be read by the draughtsman; and can conveniently be annexed to the agreement. Even then, it is necessary to consider, which no drafting suggestion can, whether or not to provide for the automatic incorporation of changes in the rules made after the contract; or to incorporate only those rules as are extant at the date of the contract. In no circumstances should the draughtsman set out to redraft a set of rules. A situation that requires a redrafting requires a set of rules drafted from scratch.

The other is when dealing with the inclusions or exclusion of powers provided under the Act. The drafting suggestion herewith refers the draughtsman to Appendix 20. It would be a great waste of space, and also unnecessary (if the draughtsman is actually thinking as he should be) to set out individual drafting suggestions for as many times as there are powers to be included or excluded. And even that would not begin to address the vast range of combinations of powers that are available. Accordingly, here again, the draughtsman is well advised to set out in the clause, or even better in an annex to the clause, the express powers in full that are either incorporated or excluded. Where there are both inclusions and exclusions, he should then check specifically to make sure that one power or another has not got into both his inclusion and exclusion lists.

Another area which requires careful consideration is where the parties desire to have a form of dispute resolution prior to a formal arbitration. There are ADR drafting suggestions in the pages that follow; but linking them to formal arbitration clauses requires thought. It is recommended that any such procedure should be part of the arbitration clause procedure; and that there should be a limit on the time allowed to achieve an ADR solution, after which the time limits, if any, in the formal arbitration should kick in. This is to prevent a recalcitrant party from using the ADR procedure purely as a means of delay.

It should be borne in mind that even an unsuccessful ADR procedure may bring benefits, particularly in a complicated dispute. This can come about, for example, by way of clarification of the issues; identifying who are the parties more likely to carry responsibility; and who are the less potentially productive parties; which parties, if any have relevant finance and even, possibly, insurance; and so forth.

There are some footnotes to these drafting suggestions by way of comment. However, the principal texts of this book are where fuller discussions are to be found. The footnotes

[1] But in that case what is one doing drafting such clauses at all?

do not even begin to substitute them; and the absence of a footnote makes consulting the principal texts even more important.

Many, indeed most, of the suggestions that follow are grouped under headings relevant to an industry. It is of course permissible to use them, in whole or in part, for purposes other than those to which they have been allocated in these suggestions—but it needs thought, of course.

DRAFTING SUGGESTIONS

ADR CLAUSES

1. ADR clause combined with arbitration clause

If any dispute or difference shall arise between the parties to this agreement from or in connection with this agreement or its performance, construction or interpretation, the parties shall endeavour to resolve it by agreement through negotiations [conducted in good faith].[2] If they are unable to agree, the issues shall in the first instance be dealt with by mediation with a mediator to be chosen jointly by them [*or* to be appointed by . . .]. Both parties reserve all their rights in the event that no agreed resolution shall be reached in the mediation [and neither party shall be deemed precluded from taking such interim formal steps as may be considered necessary to protect such party's position while the mediation or other procedure is pending]. If the dispute has not been resolved by mediation within [28] days of initiation thereof, or such extended period as the parties may agree, the dispute shall be referred to arbitration by a single arbitrator in accordance with the provisions of the Arbitration Act 1996, or any amendment thereto, whose decision in relation to any such dispute or difference shall be final and binding on the parties hereto.

2. Short form of ADR clause—CEDR

This Agreement will be governed by the [laws of England]. The parties will with the help of the Centre for Dispute Resolution (CEDR) seek to resolve disputes between them by alternative dispute resolution. If the parties fail to agree within [ ] days of the initiation [commencement] of the procedure the dispute shall be referred to arbitration in accordance with [*as appropriate*]/or litigation.

3. A second form of short ADR clause—also CEDR

This Agreement will be governed by the [laws of England]. The parties will attempt in good faith to negotiate a settlement to any claim or dispute between them arising out of or in connection with this Agreement. If the matter is not resolved by negotiation the parties will refer the dispute to mediation in accordance with CEDR (Centre for Dispute Resolution) procedures. If the parties fail to agree within [ ] days of the initiation [com-

[2] As to the effect of contracting to negotiate "in good faith", see Chap. 5 in Brown & Marriott's *ADR Principles & Practice* under the sub-heading "Good faith in negotiation", with particular reference to the House of Lords decision in *Walford v. Miles* [1992] 2 W.L.R 174. However, the position remains to be resolved where the negotiation is expressed to take place within an ADR rather than traditional adversarial context. Arguably, in such event *Walford v. Miles* will not be applicable because the parties have specifically agreed to work within a consensual process. There would also seem to be a distinction between conducting negotiations in good faith (importing certain principles of good faith into the substance of the negotiations) and attempting in good faith to arrive at a settlement agreement (which may require no more than a genuine good faith attempt to arrive at a settlement, even if the negotiations are conducted with individual self-interest).

mencement] of the procedure the dispute shall be referred to arbitration in accordance with [*as appropriate*]/or litigation.

4. A third form of ADR clause—also CEDR

This Agreement will be governed by the [laws of England]. Unless settled by prior negotiation a claim or dispute arising out of or in connection with this Agreement shall be submitted to mediation by CEDR (Centre for Dispute Resolution) within [ ] days of one side giving written notice to the other of such dispute and their intention to refer it to mediation by CEDR.

5. CEDR middle length clause

1.1 The parties will attempt in good faith to resolve any dispute or claim arising out of or relating to this Agreement promptly through negotiations between the respective senior executives of the parties who have authority to settle the same.

1.2 If the matter is not resolved through negotiation, the parties will attempt in good faith to resolve the dispute or claim through an Alternative Dispute Resolution (ADR) procedure as recommended to the parties by the Centre for Dispute Resolution.

1.3 If the matter has not been resolved by an ADR procedure within [ ] days of the initiation of such procedure, or if either party will not participate in an ADR procedure, the dispute shall be referred to arbitration in accordance with [*as appropriate*]/or litigation.

1.4 The construction performance and validity of this Agreement shall in all respects be governed by the [laws of England].

6. CEDR long form

The following long form of a sample dispute resolution provision is recommended by CEDR, subject to such amendment or adaptation as may be appropriate to the individual requirements of each contract.

1.1 In the event of any dispute or difference arising between the parties in connection with this Agreement, [senior representatives/members of the board of directors] of the parties shall, within [10] days of a written request from either party to the other addressed to [the managing director], meet in a good faith effort to resolve the dispute without recourse to legal proceedings.

1.2 If the dispute or difference is not resolved as a result of such meetings, either party may (at such meeting or within 14 days from its conclusion) propose to the other in writing that structured negotiations be entered into with the assistance of a neutral advisor or mediator (''Neutral Advisor'').

1.3 If the parties are unable to agree on a Neutral Advisor or if the Neutral Advisor agreed upon is unable or unwilling to act, either party may within 14 days from the date of the proposal to appoint a Neutral Advisor or within 14 days of notice to either party that he or she is unable or unwilling to act, apply to the Centre for Dispute Resolution (''CEDR'') to appoint a Neutral Advisor.

1.4 The parties shall within 14 days of the appointment of the Neutral Advisor meet with him/her in order to agree a programme for the exchange of any relevant information and the structure to be adopted for the negotiations [to be held in London]. If considered appropriate, the parties may at any stage seek assistance from [CEDR] to provide guidance on a suitable procedure.

1.5 Unless concluded with a written legally binding agreement all negotiations connected with the dispute shall be conducted in confidence and without prejudice to the rights of the parties in any future proceedings.

1.6 If the parties accept the Neutral Advisor's recommendations or otherwise reach agreement on the resolution of the dispute, such agreement shall be reduced to writing and, once it is signed by their duly authorised representatives, shall be binding on the parties. [Such agreement shall be implemented in full within [ ] days of signature failing which it shall be rendered null and void (and may not be referred to in any subsequent legal proceedings) unless legal proceedings have been initiated to enforce it by either party within a further [ ] days].

1.7 Failing agreement, either of the parties may invite the Neutral Advisor to provide a non-binding but informative opinion in writing. [Such opinion shall be provided on a without prejudice basis and shall not be used in evidence in any proceedings commenced pursuant to the terms of this Agreement without the prior written consent of both parties].

1.8 If the parties fail to reach agreement in the structured negotiations within 60 days of the Neutral Advisor being appointed then any dispute or difference between them may be referred to the courts unless within [such period/a further period of 30 days] the parties agree to refer the matter to arbitration before an arbitrator whose method of appointment is agreed between them.

1.9 The construction performance and validity of this Agreement shall in all respects be governed by the [laws of England].

ARBITRATION AGREEMENTS—BEFORE A DISPUTE HAS ARISEN

7. General arbitration clause—short form

In the event of any dispute or difference arising between the parties to this agreement from or in connection with this agreement or its performance, construction or interpretation, such dispute shall be referred to arbitration by a single arbitrator in accordance with the provisions of the Arbitration Act 1996, or any amendments thereto, whose decision in relation to any such dispute or difference shall be final and binding on all the parties hereto.

8. Another longer form of general arbitration clause

Any dispute or difference arising out of or in connection with this contract shall be determined by the arbitration of:

A single arbitrator who failing agreement shall be appointed by the President or a Vice-President for the time being[3] of the [Chartered Institute of Arbitrators].[4]

OR

One arbitrator to be appointed by each party together (if they disagree) with an umpire who failing agreement between such arbitrators shall be appointed by the President or a Vice-President for the time being of the [Chartered Institute of Arbitrators](Ftnt3) on the application of either party or either arbitrator.

OR

One arbitrator to be appointed by each party together with a third arbitrator (the chairman) who shall be appointed by such arbitrators or (if they cannot agree upon the

[3] It is wise to check that the chosen body does indeed have a President or Vice-President.

[4] Or other appointing institution as appropriate.

appointment) by the President or a Vice-President for the time being of the [Chartered Institute of Arbitrators].[5] If on any matter in dispute the three arbitrators are not unanimous, the decision shall be given by the majority. If there is no majority the decision shall be given by the chairman.

Optional clauses that may be added to any of the clauses of 7 or 8 above are as follows:

9. Tailoring the powers of the tribunal to the wishes of the parties

In the conduct of any arbitration under this arbitration agreement, the arbitrator[6] [shall have][7] [shall not have] the following powers.[8]

10. Diminishing or enhancing the role of the court

In respect of any arbitration arising under this agreement the role of the court[9] [shall not extend to the exercise of any of the following powers][10] [shall be enlarged as follows].[11]

11. Scott v. Avery clause

Where by this clause any dispute or difference is to be referred to arbitration the making of an award shall be a condition precedent to any right of action by either party against the other.

12. Time limit

Any claim for damages for breach of this agreement shall be made in writing and shall be served upon the party whom the claim is made not more than X months from the date of the breach and in default any such claim shall be deemed to have been abandoned and shall be absolutely barred.

[5] See n.3 above.

[6] Or "the Tribunal".

[7] If the parties intend simply to enlarge or reduce the powers of the tribunal, then the appropriate formulation should be used. If they desire to enlarge the powers in some respects and reduce them in others, separate clauses should be used—see the following footnotes for further comments.

[8] Under the 1996 Act, the arbitrator or tribunal will have all the powers listed in the text of Part 2. Accordingly, if the parties do not wish the arbitrator or tribunal to have any of these powers they will have to be expressly and specifically excluded. If the parties desire to give the arbitrator or tribunal further powers, the arbitration agreement will have to say so specifically. It is to be noted that the rules of most, but not all, arbitration institutions will address these matters. If, therefore, it is intended to incorporate such rules, they should be examined to see what powers they provide; and whether the "package" is what the parties desire. And see n.11 and Appendix 20 below.

[9] Or, where the context is international, "the High Court of England and Wales under the 1996 Arbitration Act".

[10] See n.7 above.

[11] Appendix 20 sets out in tabular form the role of the Courts under the 1996 Act. The parties may wish to exclude some of these powers. The powers marked with an * may be excluded. If they are to be excluded, they should be specifically identified. *N.B.* Some of the powers of the courts are mandatory—those are the ones marked •. There is no point in attempting to exclude them. If it is wished to enhance the powers of the court, *e.g.* by an automatic right of appeal, not dependent on the leave of the court, again, this must be specifically set out.

13. Place and law of the arbitration

The arbitration shall be held in . . .[12] and the dispute shall be decided in accordance with [English] law.

14. Incorporating institutional rules[13]

The arbitration shall be conducted in accordance with the:
(Rules of the Chartered Institute of Arbitrators)
(Rules of the London Court of International Arbitration)
(Rules of the London Maritime Arbitrators' Association)
(London Bar Arbitration Scheme)
(Rules of [Conciliation and][14] Arbitration of the International Chamber of Commerce)
(Other scheme)[15]

15. Chartered Institute of Arbitrators clause

Any dispute arising out of or in connection with this contract shall be referred to and finally resolved by arbitration under the Rules of the Chartered Institute of Arbitrators, which Rules are deemed to be incorporated by reference into this clause.

16. London Court of International Arbitration clause

Any dispute arising out of or in connection with this contract, including any question regarding its existence, validity or termination, shall be referred to and finally resolved by arbitration under the Rules of the London Court of International Arbitration which Rules are deemed to be incorporated by reference into this clause.

17. London Bar Arbitration Scheme clause

Any dispute or difference of any kind whatsoever arising out of or in connection with this agreement shall be referred to arbitration in London under the rules of the London Bar Arbitration Scheme for determination in accordance with the law of England and Wales by a single arbitrator to be appointed by or on behalf of the Chairman for the time being of the London Common Law and Commercial Bar Association.

18. London Maritime Arbitrators' Association clauses

If any dispute should arise in connection with the interpretation and fulfilment of this contract, same shall be decided by arbitration in the city of . . .[16] and shall be referred to a single arbitrator to be appointed by the parties hereto. If the parties cannot agree upon the appointment of the single arbitrator, the dispute shall be settled by three arbitrators, each party appointing one arbitrator, the third being appointed by . . .[17]

[12] A venue needs to be filled in and it is sensible to opt for one where the local rules governing the conduct of arbitration are known by the draftsman to be acceptable to the parties.

[13] See the third paragraph in the Introduction to this section. Parties are strongly advised against tinkering with an existing set of Rules.

[14] Delete if not required.

[15] The Institution and the correct name of the rules should be specified. Check that the Institution does in fact have a set of rules.

[16] If this line is not filled in, it is likely that it will be taken that the arbitration will take place in London in accordance with English law. However, such gaps should *always* be filled in.

[17] If this line is not filled in it is understood that the third arbitrator shall be appointed by the President for the time being of the London Maritime Arbitrator's Association in London. However, such gaps should *always* be filled in.

All disputes or differences arising out of or under this contract which cannot be amicably resolved shall be referred to arbitration in London.

Unless the parties agree upon a sole arbitrator, one arbitrator shall be appointed by each party. In the case of an arbitration on documents, if the two arbitrators so appointed are in agreement their decision shall be final. In all other cases the arbitrators so appointed shall appoint a third arbitrator and the reference shall be to the three-man tribunal thus constituted.

If either of the appointed arbitrators refuses to act or is incapable of acting, the party who appointed him shall appoint a new arbitrator in his place.

If one party fails to appoint an arbitrator, whether originally or by way of substitution for two weeks after the other party, having appointed his arbitrator, has (by telex, fax or letter) called upon the defaulting party to make the appointment, the President for the time being of the London Maritime Arbitrators Association shall, upon application of the other party, appoint an arbitrator on behalf of the defaulting party and that arbitrator shall have the like powers to act in the reference and make an award (and, if the case so requires, the like duty in relation to the appointment of a third arbitrator) as if he had been appointed in accordance with the terms of the agreement. This contract is governed by English law and there shall apply to all proceedings under this clause the Terms of the London Maritime Arbitrators Association current at the time when the arbitration proceedings were commenced. All appointees shall be members of the Association.

Provided that where the amount in dispute does not exceed the sum of US$50,000 (or such other sum as the parties may agree) any dispute shall be resolved in accordance with the Small Claims Procedure of the London Maritime Arbitrators Association.

19. Clause referring disputes to arbitration by the Court of Arbitration of the International Chamber of Commerce

All disputes arising in connection with the present contract shall be finally settled under the Rules of Conciliation and Arbitration of the International Chamber of Commerce by one or more arbitrators appointed in accordance with the said Rules[18]

20. UNCITRAL Arbitration Rules—model clause

Any dispute, controversy or claim arising out of or relating to this contract, or the breach, termination, or invalidity thereof, shall be settled by arbitration in accordance with the UNCITRAL Arbitration Rules as at present in force.[19]

[18] ICC comment: "Parties are reminded that it may be desirable for them to stipulate in the arbitration clause itself the law governing the contract, the number of arbitrators and the place and language of the arbitration. The parties' free choice of the law governing the contract and of the place and language of the arbitration is not limited by the ICC Rules of Arbitration. Attention is called to the fact that the laws of certain countries expressly accept arbitration clauses, sometimes in a precise and particular manner."

[19] UNCITRAL:
The parties may wish to consider adding:
(a) the appointing authority shall be .... (name of institution or person);
(b) the number of arbitrators shall be .... (one or three);
(c) the place of arbitration shall be .... (town *and* country; if you simply put Paris, somebody with a desperate case or much in need of medical assistance will argue that you mean Paris, Texas!);
(d) the language(s) to be used in the arbitral proceedings shall be ....

21. Western Circuit Arbitration

All disputes or differences arising out of or in connection with this contract including its validity shall be referred for determination by arbitration according to the Rules of Western Circuit Arbitration, by an Arbitrator appointed thereunder.

22. Northern Arbitration Association

Any dispute or difference between the parties hereto arising out of or in connection with this agreement shall be referred to arbitration by a single Arbitrator [in *insert place in which arbitration to be conducted*] under the Rules of the Northern Arbitration Association which shall be incorporated in this agreement.

23. "Ad Hoc" Agreement

By this agreement AB of   and XY of   hereby agree to refer [all disputes and differences between them[20]]
[all disputes and differences between them arising out of a contract dated *insert date*][21]
[the disputes and differences set out in the Schedule to this agreement][22] to arbitration by a single arbitrator [in *insert place in which arbitration to be conducted*] [under the Rules of   ].

24. American Arbitration Association[23]

1.1 Any controversy or claim arising out of or relating to this contract, or the breach thereof, shall be settled by arbitration administered by the American Arbitration Association in accordance with its [applicable] rules and judgment on the award rendered by the arbitrator may be entered in any court having jurisdiction thereof.

1.2 [24]We, the undersigned parties, hereby agree to submit to arbitration administered by the American Arbitration Association under its [applicable] rules the following controversy [cite briefly]. We further agree that we will faithfully observe this agreement and the rules, that we will abide by the perform any award rendered by the arbitrator(s) and that a judgment of the court having jurisdiction may be entered upon the award.[25]

20 Delete as appropriate.

21 Delete as appropriate.

22 Delete as appropriate.

23 AAA comment: "It is not enough to state that 'disputes arising under the agreement shall be settled by arbitration'. While that language indicates the parties' intention to arbitrate and may authorize a court to enforce the clause it leaves many issues unresolved. Issues such as to when, where, how, and before whom a dispute will be arbitrated are subject to disagreement, with no way to resolve them except to go to court. The standard arbitration clause suggested by the American Arbitration Association addresses those questions. It has proven highly effective in over a million disputes. The parties can provide for arbitration of future disputes by inserting the following into their contracts."

24 Arbitration of existing disputes may be accomplished by use of this clause; and see [29] below.

25 AAA comment: "The preceding clauses, which refer to the time-tested rules of the AAA, have consistently received judicial support. The standard clause is often the best to include in a contract. . . ."

24. Kuala Lumpur Regional Centre for Arbitration

Any dispute, controversy or claim arising out of or relating to this contract, or the breach, termination or invalidity thereof, shall be decided by arbitration in accordance with the Rules for Arbitration of the Kuala Lumpur Regional Centre for Arbitration.[26]

26. Indian Council of Arbitration

Any dispute or differences whatsoever arising between the parties out of or relating to the construction, meaning and operation or effect of this contract or the breach thereof shall be settled by arbitration in accordance with the rules of arbitration of the Indian Council of Arbitration and the award made in pursuance thereof shall be binding on the parties.

27. Singapore International Arbitration Centre

Any dispute arising out of or in connection with this contract, including any question regarding its existence, validity or termination, shall be referred to and finally resolved by arbitration in Singapore in accordance with the Arbitration Rules of the Singapore International Arbitration Centre (''SIAC Rules'') for the time being in force which rules are deemed to be incorporated by reference into this clause.[27]

28. Hong Kong International Arbitration Centre

Any dispute, controversy or claim arising out of or relating to this contract, or the breach termination or invalidity thereof, shall be settled by arbitration in accordance with the UNCITRAL Arbitration Rules as at present in force and as may be amended by the rest of this clause. The appointing authority shall be Hong Kong International Arbitration Centre. The place of arbitration shall be in Hong Kong at Hong Kong International Arbitration Centre (HKIAC). There shall be only one arbitrator.[28] Any such arbitration shall be administered by HKIAC in accordance with HKIAC Procedures for Arbitration in force at the date of this contract including such additions to the UNCITRAL Arbitration Rules as are therein contained.[29]

[26] K.L.R.C.A. comment: ''NOTE: Parties may wish to consider adding:
0.1 The appointing authority shall be the Kuala Lumpur Regional Centre for Arbitration.
0.2 The number of arbitrators shall be .... (one or three).
0.3 The place of arbitration shall be .... (town or country).
0.4 The language(s) to be used in the arbitration proceedings shall be ....
0.5 The law applicable to this contract shall be that of ....''

[27] SIAC comment: ''Parties may add:
The Tribunal shall consist of .... arbitrator(s) to be appointed by the Chairman of SLAC.
The governing law of this contract shall be the substantive law of ....
The language of the arbitration shall be ....''

[28] This sentence must be amended if a panel of three arbitrators is required.

[29] HKIAC notes that this sentence may be deleted if administration by HKIAC is not required. If it is retained the Centre will then act as a clearing house for communications between the parties and the arbitral tribunal and will liaise with the arbitral tribunal and the parties on timing of meetings, etc. will hold deposits from the parties and assist the tribunal with any other matters required. HKIAC notes that if the language to be used in arbitration proceedings is likely to be in question, it may also be useful to include in contracts: ''The language(s) to be used in the arbitral proceedings shall be ....''.

ARBITRATION AGREEMENTS—AFTER A DISPUTE HAS ARISEN

29. General form

BY THIS AGREEMENT
a.b. of .... and
x.y. of ....
HEREBY AGREE TO REFER
all disputes and differences whatsoever between them

OR

all disputes and differences between them arising out of or in connection with a contract between them dated the ....

OR

the disputes and differences set out in the Schedule to this Agreement to the arbitration of Mr John Smith

OR

A single arbitrator who failing agreement shall be appointed by the President of the .... on the application of either party

OR

Mr John Smith and Mr George Jones together, if they disagree, with an umpire to be appointed by them or, if they should disagree, by the President or a Vice-President for the time being of ....

OR

Mr John Smith, Mr George Jones and Mr Robert Robinson
Dated this .... day of .... 19 ....

Signed on behalf of a.b	Signed on behalf of x.y.
(By)	(By) ....
(Name)	(Name) ....

30. To tailor an arbitration agreement to the wishes of the parties—see the suggestion at 9 above and the footnote to it

31. To diminish or enhance the role of the court in the contract for arbitration—see the suggestion at 10 above and the footnotes thereto

32. Agreement in advance (but post-dispute) for equal sharing of costs

Each party shall bear its own costs of the arbitration and the costs of the arbitrator/arbitration tribunal shall be borne by the parties equally.

33. Agreement varying the existing arbitration agreement[30]

WHEREAS by clause XXX of a contract dated the .... and made between .... (hereinafter called the Vendor) and .... (Hereinafter called the Purchaser) certain differences or disputes therein mentioned were referred to arbitration.
AND WHEREAS certain disputes having arisen between the parties Mr A. N. OTHER has been appointed as arbitrator to determine them.
NOW THE PARTIES HEREBY AGREE to submit to the arbitration of the said arbitrator

[30] If the variation requires some adjustment (*e.g.*, an enlargement of the Tribunal's powers) that needs to be put in here.

(in addition to the matters already referred to him) the following further matters, that is to say:
(example): Whether the said contract accurately sets out the terms agreed between the parties and intended to be contained in the said contract and if not whether and in what way the said contract should be rectified.
DATED THIS .... DAY OF ....

SUBSIDIARY FORMS—APPOINTMENT—FORMS

34. Joint appointment of a sole arbitrator
To a.b. of ....
Disputes[31] have arisen between us arising out of or in connection with a contract between us dated the .... a copy of which is enclosed. We wish to have determined by arbitration by you all such disputes. We therefore nominate and appoint[32] you as sole arbitrator in respect of the said disputes.
Dated ....
(Signed) ....

Signed) ....
(Name) ....

(Name) ....
for P.Q. plc of ....

for L.M. plc of ....

35 Appointment of an arbitrator by a party
To a.b. of ....
By an agreement dated the .... and made between .... of the one part and .... of the other part it was agreed (inter alia) that any dispute or difference arising out of or in relation to the agreement should be referred to the arbitration of two arbitrators, one to be appointed by each party, together (if they disagree) with an umpire to be appointed by them. Disputes have arisen between the said parties. We, P.Q. plc hereby appoint[33] you as an arbitrator in accordance with the provisions of the said agreement.
Dated ....
(Signed) .... for P.Q. plc

36. Notice to concur in the appointment of a sole arbitrator
To: a.b. plc of [etc.]
In pursuance of the provision for arbitration contained in clause .... of the agreement between us dated the .... we now require you to concur in the appointment of an arbitrator to resolve the disputes[34] that have arisen between us, namely .... Unless

[31] These should be identified, *e.g.* by an annex, referred to in the clause thus: "Disputes as summarized on the attached annex".
[32] The appointee should insist on seeing the arbitration clause before accepting the appointment. Also if he accepts without agreeing fees, he may be unable to recover cancellation fees and the like as of right.
[33] See previous footnote.
[34] Which should be specified in same manner, *e.g.* by an annex referred to in this notice.

within seven clear days after this notice is served upon you an arbitrator has been agreed between us we intend without further notice to apply to ....[35] for an appointment.
Dated ....
(Signed)..
(Name)..
For and on behalf of X.Y. plc

37. Notice requiring other party to appoint an arbitrator in the situation where the third arbitrator is an umpire

To c.d. plc
The agreement between us dated the .... provides that any dispute or difference arising out of or in relation to the agreement shall be determined by two arbitrators, one to be appointed by each of us together (if they disagree) with an umpire to be appointed by them. We have today appointed Mr A.B. to act as arbitrator. We now require you, within seven clear days after the service of this notice upon you, to appoint an arbitrator to determine the following dispute .... If you fail so to do we will appoint the said A.B. as sole arbitrator under the agreement.
Dated ....
(Signed)..
(Name)..
For and on behalf of E.F. plc

38. Appointment as sole arbitrator where other party fails to appoint to determine disputes currently existing

To a.b.
We enclose a copy of a notice that was served on C.D. plc on .... day the .... They acknowledged receipt by a (letter) (telex) (telefax) dated the .... (OR They have not acknowledged receipt; a copy of our letter/telex is enclosed). They have not appointed an arbitrator. Pursuant to the power conferred upon us by section [ ] of the Arbitration Act 1996 we hereby appoint you as sole arbitrator.
Dated ....
(Signed)..
(Name)..
For and on behalf of E.F. plc

39. Appointment by two arbitrators of umpire or third arbitrator

To: L.M. Esq
Under the provision for arbitration contained in the agreement made the .... between P.Q. plc of the one part and R.S. plc of the other party we the undersigned were appointed as arbitrators, with provision for [an umpire] OR [third arbitrator] to be appointed[36] by us. We hereby appoint you under the said provisions.
Dated ....
(Signed)..
(Name)..

[35] Insert name of appointor if one is specified in the arbitration agreement.
[36] See n.32 above.

(Signed) ....
(Name)...

40. Joint appointment of a substitute sole arbitrator

By an appointment in writing dated the .... we the undersigned appointed A.B. To be the sole arbitrator to determine certain disputes under the agreement therein mentioned. A.B. has (died) (refused to act) (become incapable of acting). We hereby appoint C.D. to be the arbitrator in place of the said A.B.

Dated ....
(Signed) ....
(Name)...
For and on behalf of L.M. plc

(Signed) ....
(Name)...
For and on behalf of P.Q. plc

41. Appointment by an appointing body or person

To C.D. plc of ....
and to E.F. plc of ....

By the arbitration clause contained in an agreement in writing dated the .... and made (Between you) (between G.H. plc of the one part and the said E.F. plc of the other part) it was provided that any dispute arising out of or in relation to the agreement should be referred to the arbitration of a person who failing agreement should be appointed (by me) (by the President of the ....). By the letter dated the .... the said E.F. plc asserted that the disputes identified on the attached form had arisen between you and notified me that no person had been agreed between you and requested me to appoint an arbitrator. Now I W.Y. (The person named as appointor as aforesaid) (being the President for the time being of the said ....) Do hereby appoint[37] A.B. of .... as arbitrator pursuant to the said agreement.

Dated ....
(Signed) ....

42. List of matters for possible consideration in organising arbitral proceedings[38]

1. Set of arbitration rules

   If the parties have not agreed on a set of arbitration rules, would they wish to do so
2. Language of proceedings

   (a) Possible need for translation of documents, in full or in part
   (b) Possible need for interpretation of oral presentations
   (c) Cost of translation and interpretation

[37] See discussion at para. 2–213 re the question of the terms the arbitrator is appointed under. The appointing institute must determine whether this is a complete and immediately effective appointment, a provisional appointment or a nomination. The appointee and the parties should also be clear about this.

[38] This list is part of the *UNCITRAL Notes on Organizing Arbitral Proceedings*, which the United Nations Commission on International Trade Law (UNCITRAL) adopted in 1996. The *Notes*, published as United Nations document V.96-84935, contain introductory explanations and annotations to the items that appear in this list (see Appendix 5 below).

3. Place of arbitration

    (a) Determination of the place of arbitration, if not already agreed upon by the parties
    (b) Possibility of meetings outside the place of arbitration

4. Administrative services that may be needed for the arbitral tribunal to carry out its functions
5. Deposits in respect of costs

    (a) Amount to be deposited
    (b) Management of deposits
    (c) Supplementary deposits

6. Confidentiality of information relating to arbitration; possible agreement thereon
7. Routing of writing communications among the parties and the arbitrators
8. Telefax and other electronic means of sending documents

    (a) Telefax
    (b) Other electronic means (*e.g.* electronic mail and magnetic or optical disk)

9. Arrangements for the exchange of written submissions

    (a) Scheduling of written submissions
    (b) Consecutive or simultaneous submissions

10. Practical details concerning written submissions and evidence (*e.g.* method of submission, copies, numbering, references)
11. Defining points at issue; order of deciding issues; defining relief or remedy sought

    (a) Should a list of points at issue be prepared
    (b) In which order should the points at issue be decided
    (c) Is there a need to define more precisely the relief or remedy sought

12. Possible settlement negotiations and their effect on scheduling procedures
13. Documentary evidence

    (a) Time-limits for submission of documentary evidence intended to be submitted by the parties; consequences of late submission
    (b) Whether the arbitral tribunal intends to require a party to produce documentary evidence
    (c) Should assertions about the origin and receipt of documents and about the correctness of photocopies be assumed as accurate
    (d) Are the parties willing to submit jointly a single set of documentary evidence
    (e) Should voluminous and complicated documentary evidence be presented through summaries, tabulations, charts, extracts or samples

14. Physical evidence other than documents

(a) What arrangements should be made if physical evidence will be submitted
(b) What arrangements should be made if an on-site inspection is necessary

15. Witnesses

(a) Advance notice about a witness whom a party intends to present; written witnesses' statements
(b) Manner or taking oral evidence of witnesses
(c) Order in which questions will be asked and the manner in which the hearing of witnesses will be conducted
(d) Whether oral testimony will be given under oath or affirmation and, if so, in what form an oath or affirmation should be made
(e) May witnesses be in the hearing room when they are not testifying
(f) The order in which the witnesses will be called
(g) Interviewing witnesses prior to their appearance at a hearing
(h) Hearing representatives of a party

16. Experts and expert witnesses

(a) Expert appointed by the arbitral tribunal
(b) The expert's terms of reference

INITIAL ACTION BY ARBITRATOR

43. Initial letter from sole arbitrator to the parties

Messrs	Messrs
Name & address of party Representative	Name & address of party Representative
[Means of communication][39]	
Reference	Reference
For the attention of	For the attention of
....	....

Dear [ ][40]

My Reference ....

Arbitration between AB plc and CD plc

I have been appointed[41] by (the President of the ....) to act in this arbitration. I have been sent the following documents:

....

....

Unless I am told in writing by both parties that they do not wish me to proceed for the time being, I propose convening a preliminary meeting at (this office). However, I am willing to arrange a telephone conference call if both parties think that we may thereby

[39] The arbitrator should determine upon a specific method of communication (*e.g.* by fax and post) at an early stage, and stick to it, unless agreed otherwise with the parties.
[40] As appropriate.
[41] See n.32 above re agreeing fees.

be able to dispense with a preliminary meeting. I would also be happy to deal with matters in writing provided that I am assured by both parties that this is very unlikely to lead to delay.

[*If writing to principal*]

If it is your intention to instruct representatives to act on your behalf, kindly ask them to get in touch with me.

OR

[*If writing to solicitor or other agent*]

Would you please confirm that you are authorised to deal with this arbitration on behalf of .... Please ensure that no document which is, or which refers to, a "without prejudice" matter is put before me, and that all other communications to me are copied to the other party. I enclose a Schedule setting out the fee basis[42] on which I propose to charge.

Yours faithfully,

Arbitrator

44. Schedule of Fees

SCHEDULE OF FEES OF Mr (or Ms) ....

1.1 *Acceptance fee*:

(to include one preliminary meeting and up to five hours preliminary reading).

Payable:

On taking up the award, or three months after appointment, whichever is the earlier.

1.2 *Fees for hearing*:

£ .... per usual sitting day.

Part days charged at £ .... per hour with a minimum of £ ....

Payable:

On taking up the award, or 10 days after notification that the award is ready for collection, or 10 days after notice to the arbitrator that no award is required; whichever first occurs.

1.3 *Additional hours worked outside hearing*:

e.g. preliminary reading and interlocutory hearings not included in 1 above; views (if any): preparation of award: £ .... per hour.

Payable:

As in 2, or three months after the fee is earned (whichever is earlier).

1.4 *Cancellation fees*:

When a hearing date has been fixed I enter it into my diary, together with the appropriate number of additional days for the preparation of my award. If those dates are cancelled at less than .... months' notice, I reserve the right to charge a cancellation fee of the following proportions of the fees that would have been payable had it proceeded:

If cancelled at more than .... month's notice .... %

If cancelled at less than .... month's notice .... %

This fee will be payable 10 days after the first of the cancelled days.[43]

[42] See n.32 above re agreeing fees.

[43] Some arbitrators include the following clause: "In deciding whether to exercise this right I will have regard (*inter alia*) to whether I can fill the vacated days with remunerated work, and to whether the arbitration is abandoned or is to continue". However applying such a clause can be very difficult indeed. It is suggested that if an arbitrator is minded to waive these fees he do so on a voluntary ad hoc basis rather than make it a term in the agreement.

1.5 Travelling and hotel expenses, and all proper disbursements, will be charged at cost. [Air Travel will be .... class.]

1.6 VAT on the above as appropriate.

45. Letter appointing a preliminary meeting

First Representative

....

....

.... *For the attention of*

and

Second Representative

....

....

.... *For the attention of*

Gentlemen,

Arbitration between .... and .... re ....

From the responses of both parties to my letter of .... it appears that they do not wish to have time for negotiations. I have not received from either party the confirmation requested in the second paragraph of my letter.[44] I propose to hold a preliminary meeting with the parties in the week commencing or .... in the week commencing .... If there are any dates or times during these weeks which would be inconvenient to you would you please let me know before .... At the preliminary meeting I would expect to ascertain the wishes of the parties so as to enable me to issue directions governing such matters as:

1.1 Whether the proceedings are to be by written representations only or whether there is to be an oral hearing.

1.2 The arrangements for either the submission of written representations or an oral hearing.

1.3 The nature of expert and any other evidence which the parties intend to submit or to call.

1.4 The preparation and the contents of a Statement of Agreed Facts relating to the issues in dispute or any of them.

1.5 Whether it may be desirable for a legal assessor to be appointed. If a party intends to be represented in the proceedings by solicitor or counsel it is highlydesirable that the solicitor be present at the preliminary meeting.[45]

Please inform me and the other party of the names and status of those you will expect to attend the preliminary meeting; I should like to have this information by not later than ....

Yours truly,

EXAMPLES OF INITIAL SETS OF DIRECTIONS

46. Order for Directions No. 1

Upon hearing Counsel for both parties herein, I hereby direct as follows:

1.1 Claimant to prepare a bundle of principal documents and to include therein such documents as Respondent requests to be included.

[44] Confirmation that they do not wish the arbitrator to proceed—see suggestion [No. 42] on page [18].

[45] This clause is optional. Numerous firms of solicitors regard themselves as more than able to discuss preliminary directions without the help of counsel.

1.2 Claimant to serve a comprehensive Statement of Case on liability. To the Case should be annexed a list of all documents relied upon by the Claimant. The Case is to be served by or before the [*date*]. The Case should finally identify who is or are said by the Claimant to be the Respondent/s. In so far as the Claimant does not accept that .... is the only proper Respondent, the Claimant should fully set out in the Case its submissions in support of its contentions.
1.3 Claimant may, if it so wishes, set out its case on Quantum in full.
1.4 Respondent to serve a comprehensive Statement of Defence (and of Counterclaim if so advised) by or before the expiry of six weeks from receipt of the statement of Case. Respondent to annex to the Defence (and Counterclaim, if any) a list of the documents relied upon. The Statement of Defence (and Counterclaim, if any) shall include full submissions on the proper construction of any clause in the contract relied upon by the Respondent to defeat the claim. The Statement of Defence should also respond fully to any submissions to the effect that .... is not the proper Respondent or is not the only proper Respondent.
1.5 The Respondent may if it so wishes respond to the case on Quantum if such is put forward by the Claimant.
1.6 Claimant to serve a comprehensive Reply to the Defence (and a comprehensive Defence to the Counterclaim if a Counterclaim is served) by or before the expiry of six weeks from the date of receipt of the Defence (and Counterclaim). A list of any documents which are relied upon by the Claimant in connection with the Reply (and Defence to Counterclaim, if any) and which are not already listed shall be annexed.
1.7 At the same time as the Reply is served, the Claimant shall deliver to me, and to the Respondent if it so desires, a chronological bundle of the documents listed as relied upon by the parties. This bundle need not be finally paginated, since other documents may be added later.
1.8 Liberty to Restore.
1.9 Costs in the Reference.

47. Another Order for Directions No. 1

Having considered the correspondence and written and oral submissions in this matter the Tribunal hereby makes the following directions[46]:

BY CONSENT

TERMINOLOGY

1.1 The .... Centre for Arbitration is hereinafter and in subsequent directions referred to as the ''Centre''.
1.2 The Uncitral Arbitration Rules, as amended for the use of the Centre are hereinafter and in subsequent directions referred to as the ''Rules''.
1.3 The amendments themselves are herein and hereafter referred to as the ''Centre's Rules''.[47]

[46] Obviously this is just an exemplar of the kind of order for directions that might be generated. The matters which are consensual and the matters which are contested and require a decision will vary from arbitration to arbitration. Indeed they may all be contested or they may all be consensual.

[47] Some such distinction may be necessary where an institution has taken a standard set of rules and has added to them but has not adjusted the numbering.

TIME FOR ARBITRATION

1.4 The parties agreed to the exercise by the Tribunal of the powers to extend for the completion of this arbitration by Rule 6 of the Centre's Rules. The Tribunal hereby extends the time for the completion of this arbitration under Rule 6 to [*date*].

PLEADINGS

1.5 Each party is to file with the Tribunal and the other party a response to the claim of the other party by or before 18.00 hours on the [*date*].

EVIDENCE

1.6 Each party is to file its evidence in chief, including witness statements containing the substance of the witness' evidence in chief and documentary evidence relied upon by or before 18.00 hours on the [*date*].

1.7 Along with its evidence in chief each party will file an initial Dramatis Personae identifying each individual and company referred to in its evidence in chief and the capacity and/or role of that individual or company. Likewise each party will file at the same time what it contends is a chronology of relevant events.

1.8 If either party is minded to file evidence in response, then the same is to be filed with the Tribunal and the other party by or before 18.00 hours on the [*date*].

1.9 If either party is minded to file evidence in reply, then the same is to be filed with the Tribunal and the other party by or before 18.00 hours on the [*date*]. Such evidence is to be limited to that necessary to deal with new matters contained in the evidence in response of the other party.

1.10 Where a witness statement in the evidence in chief, in response or in reply refers to a document or documents, the place or places in the annexed or previously served files where the same can be found will also be indicated. If not previously served, the document will be served with the evidence referring to it, or an explanation given for non service.

1.11 Once evidence, if any, in reply has been filed, the parties will seek to agree the Dramatis Personae and Chronology, taking into account any further matters arising from the evidence in response and in reply. The same will be served on the Tribunal on or before the [*date*], so far as agreed.

1.12 The evidence to be filed may include both factual and expert evidence.

DISCOVERY

1.13 Either party may seek discovery or class of documents at any time up to the [*date*]. Thereafter such an application may only be made by leave of the Tribunal.

1.14 Good cause for the discovery must be shown in all cases: and good cause for the lateness of the application must also be shown where the application is made after the [*date*].

HARD AND SOFT COPIES

1.15 As much as possible of the documentation supplied in accordance with the above orders should be supplied both in hard and soft form. The word processing facilities of the Tribunal are as follows:

—Microsoft Word
—Word Perfect 6.1
—Word Perfect 7

LEGAL MATERIALS AND AUTHORITIES

1.16 Legal Materials and Authorities must be filed with the other party and the Tribunal by or before 18.00 hours on the [*date*].

DOSSIER

1.17 The documents filed in accordance with the above directions shall constitute the dossier for the principal hearings. Save for demonstrative exhibits, no new documents will be allowed to be introduced to the principal hearings save by leave of the Tribunal and for good cause.

INTERLOCUTORY APPLICATIONS

1.18 Save for any matters which can conveniently be raised at the pre hearing review—as to which, see below at 1.19(d)—and subject to the liberty to apply provided for below at 1.34, all interlocutory matters will be dealt with in writing. The parties should indicate whether they wish the decision on the application to be a decision of the whole Tribunal. In the absence of any such indication the matter will be dealt with by the chairman alone unless he sees fit to consult the co-arbitrators.

PRINCIPAL HEARINGS

1.19 The principal hearings will be as follows:

(a) [*date*]–[*date*]—Evidence led by the Claimant and all relevant cross examination and examination in reply.
(b) [*date*]–[*date*]—Evidence led by the Respondent and all relevant cross examination and examination in reply.
(c) [*date*]–[*date*]—Closing oral submissions.
(d) Details of venue and organisation of the hearings will be determined in due course. However it should be noted that:
   (i) it is proposed to sit a five day week, and a five hour day;
   (ii) it is proposed to divide the available time between the parties;
   (iii) it is proposed to permit each party to make a short opening statement at the commencement of the first principal hearing;
   (iv) it is proposed to permit each party to lodge with the Tribunal a written opening, if it so desires;
   (v) examination in chief will be permitted but on a limited basis;
   (vi) it is proposed to direct the parties to identify the order in which witnesses will be called (without affecting the right to call them or not, as the party desires); and to seek a detailed schedule of how the hearing time will be expended;

(vii) for the avoidance of doubt it is proposed to dispense with the common law rule that evidence not challenged is accepted; and to replace it by the principle that the weight to be given to any evidence of whatever nature is wholly a matter for the discretion of the Tribunal;

(viii) there will be no extension of any of the hearing times save in very exceptional circumstances;

(ix) it is to be hoped that a chronological bundle of the documentation to be used at the hearings will be put together; in the event that this is done, the references in witness statements to documents will have to have this chronological bundle reference added in due course;

(x) it is to be hoped that a core bundle will be assembled.

(e) The parties are to consider the question of transcribing the proceedings at the principal hearings.

ADMINISTRATIVE

1.20 The parties have agreed to dispense with the requirement of Rule 5 of the Centre's Rules which provides for the Presiding Arbitrator to furnish records to the Director of the Centre.

1.21 All correspondence between the parties and the Tribunal shall be referenced and transmitted as follows:

(a) The Tribunal's letters to the parties will have the reference 186. The letter commenting on these directions is 001. Each party will choose its own reference and then give each letter a consecutive number. Whether each party gives the letters to the Tribunal an independent sequence to that used for letters between the parties, or uses the same sequence for both series of letters is a matter for each party.

(b) Communications shall be effected by fax in the first place, and copied by air mail post. Important documents and ones where bulk militates against the use of the fax shall be transmitted by courier. Documents which are not in themselves letters shall have a covering letter.[48]

1.22 The proceedings and all documents shall be in the English language.

BY DECISION save where indicated by asterisk.

NUMBER OF ARBITRATIONS

1.23 There is to be a single arbitration.

RELEVANT COMPANIES

1.24 The companies constituting the parties to the said arbitration will be specifically identified in the second Order for Directions to be issued in due course.

[48] And one can into great detail—files to be two hole ring binders, all stapling to be at top left and parallel to the long side of the page, and so on.

1.25 *The parties are to provide written submissions to the Tribunal and each other on the question of the identity of the parties to the arbitration as follows:

(a) All initial submissions by or before 18.00 hours on the [*date*].
(b) If so minded a submission in reply to the other party's initial submission by or before 18.00 hours on the [*date*].

CLAIMANT

1.26 In any event, ... will be Claimant.

APPLICATIONS FOR PRELIMINARY ISSUES AND INTERIM RELIEF

1.27 The Tribunal does not accede to the applications for the hearing of preliminary issues, for the ordering of an audit or for the ordering of pre hearing oral examinations of third party witnesses.

ANCILLARY

1.28 For brevity and convenience, the Claimant may be referred to as .... and the Respondent as the ....
1.29 Where there is any reference to a time of day in these Directions, it is to be taken as the time of day in ....
1.30 Save where it is impracticable to do so, the parties should use 2 ring lever arch files for filings with the Tribunal.
1.31 When serving its evidence in chief the Claimant will nominate its expert or, if there is more than one, then one of them, as its principal expert.
1.32 It will be the function of the principal expert to propose, once the evidence is complete, and seek to arrange, meetings between the various experts of like disciplines with a view to recording agreement where such agreement can be obtained; and isolating the principal issues of a technical nature. Such meetings will be without prejudice unless the parties agree otherwise. Once a statement, whether of agreement or principal issues or both, has been signed by the relevant experts for both parties, then the same is to be treated as an open document without the necessity for the agreement of the parties.
1.33 Unless the parties agree otherwise, discovery shall be effected by the transmission of copies by the discovering party to the inspecting party by whatever means chosen by and at the (reasonable according to the means chosen) cost of the inspecting party. At the instance and cost of the inspecting party, the copies can be notarised as true copies.

GENERAL

1.34 Liberty to apply generally.
1.35 Costs in cause.

48. Draft directions for consideration at preliminary meeting

1.1 .... plc shall be claimant and .... plc shall be respondent.

PLEADINGS

1.2 Claimant to serve points of claim by the ....

(a) Respondent to serve point of defence within .... days after service of points of claim.
(b) Claimant to serve points of reply (if so desired) within .... days after service of points of defence.
(c) A copy of each pleading to be sent to the arbitrator concurrently with service on the other party.

OR

STATEMENTS OF CASE

1.3 Claimant to serve Statement of Case by the ....

(a) Respondent to serve Statement of Case within .... days after service of Claimant's Statement of Case.
(b) Claimant to serve Reply (if so desired) within .... days after service of Respondent's Statement of Case.
(c) Statements of Case shall [not exceed .... words],[49] and Statements in Reply shall [not exceed .... words].
(d) Each Statement shall be accompanied by a copy of every document intended to be relied upon and not already delivered.

OR

(e) Claimant and Respondent each to serve on the other a Statement of Case, such Statements to be exchanged by the ....
(f) Claimant and Respondent may each (if so desired) serve on the other a Statement in Reply, such Statements to be exchanged within .... days of exchange of Statements of Case.
(g) Statements in Reply may contain evidence and submissions in rebuttal of material contained in the opposing party's Statements of Case, but may not otherwise introduce new material.
(h) Each Statement is to be served in duplicate. The party receiving it shall within 4 working days either deliver to the arbitrator one copy thereof or apply to the arbitrator to strike out all or part of the same. Any such application shall state in broad terms the grounds of objection, e.g. that the same discloses without prejudice discussions.
(i) Statements of Case shall not exceed .... words and Statements in Reply shall not exceed .... words.
(j) as 1.3(d) above.

[49] A limitation is not essential, and should only be introduced when there is some justification for believing it to be necessary.

1.4 The parties agree that the arbitration shall proceed on documents only, with no oral evidence or oral submissions. But the arbitrator reserves the right to convene a meeting and/or a hearing if the documents when lodged raise issues which in his opinion cannot be satisfactorily resolved on documents only.

OR

1.5 A Statement of Agreed Facts shall be prepared by (Counsel) (Solicitors) (expert Witnesses) on each side, and a copy delivered to the arbitrator by the ....

1.6 A copy of the written proof of any expert witness intended to be called shall be served on the other party by way of exchange by the ....

1.7 Where the proofs of experts conflict, a meeting shall be arranged between the experts concerned. It shall take place within .... days after exchange of proofs. It shall take place (with any legal adviser that a party wishes to be present) OR (without legal advisers). The discussions at such meeting shall be without prejudice. Before the end of such meeting the experts shall prepare, date and sign a note of the facts and opinions on which they are agreed and of the issues on which they cannot agree. This note will NOT be ''without prejudice'' and a copy of such note shall be delivered to the arbitrator within .... days.

1.8 The provisional date for commencing the hearing is .... The parties shall on or before the .... 19 .... send to the arbitrator an agreed estimate, or failing agreement each party's estimate, of the time required for the hearing and the numbers likely to attend the hearing.

1.9 The evidence will be given on oath or affirmation. If a party intends to call as a witness a person who wishes to take the oath otherwise than upon the Old or New Testaments, he shall make the appropriate arrangements to enable such witness to be sworn. If the party intends to call a witness to give evidence in a language other than English, he shall give notice to the arbitrator so that the attendance of a suitable interpreter can be arranged.

1.10 A shorthand transcript of the hearing (will not be required) (will be required and will be arranged by the (claimant's) solicitors.) Unless the arbitrator otherwise orders the expense thereof shall be borne equally by the parties.

1.11 (Discovery?[50]).

1.12 The arbitrator will make an interim award (dealing with the issue of liability only, and will thereafter arrange a further meeting to consider what further directions are needed).

OR

(dealing with all issues raised in the arbitration other than costs, and will thereafter take no action until one or both parties ask him to do so.)

1.13 Without prejudice discussions or correspondence are not to be disclosed to the arbitrator in any form.

1.14 Communications to the arbitrator should where possible be made by telex/fax. In any event a copy of any communication to the arbitrator should be sent to the other party/parties.

1.15 If any party wishes to ask for any other directions, he should give the maximum possible notice in writing to the other party/parties and to the arbitrator. The costs

[50] If there is to be an order for discovery, it should go here. The extent of the desired discovery should be considered—ranging from the old fashioned full common law style discovery to discovery limited to documents which can be specifically identified by the party seeking discovery and in respect of which that party can make out a strong case for the discovery.

of any adjournment necessitated by a party's avoidable failure to give reasonable notice are likely to be borne by that party.

49. Specimen letter following preliminary meeting sending [draft] directions[51]

Gentlemen,

In the matter of an Arbitration
between ....

I have noted for the record the following matters discussed at the Preliminary Meeting held at .... on ....

1.1 The lessors of the premises are .... and they will be regarded as the Claimant in the proceedings.

1.2 The lessees of the premises are .... and they will be regarded as the Respondent in the proceedings.

1.3 The Claimant and the Respondent have retained Counsel.

1.4 Neither party has any point to raise on the rent review notice dated .... a copy of which was handed to me by the Respondent's solicitor.

1.5 Neither party has any point of law or matter of construction to be raised or which, at this stage, seems likely to arise and neither party thinks it necessary for a legal assessor to be appointed.

1.6 The parties agreed that pleadings are not necessary.

1.7 Both parties requested that there should be an oral Hearing and asked that the matter should not be dealt with by written representations.

1.8 At an oral Hearing each part would expect to call an expert valuation witness and, at this stage, neither part expects it to be necessary to call additional witnesses.

1.9 The Claimant thought that one day, possibly two days, would be sufficient for the Hearing. The Claimant's Counsel would be available on .... 19 .... for any two days. It was not known whether the Respondent's Counsel would be available. The parties' solicitors would liaise to reserve two consecutive days.

1.10 The Claimant's Solicitors would provide the Arbitrator with certified copies of the Underlease and any licences or other relevant documents, neither party thought it necessary for there to be an order for discovery.

1.11 The Respondent's view was that a transcript of the hearing was unnecessary. Counsel for the Claimant said that he would take instructions.

1.12 The Respondent requested that evidence should be taken on oath and the Claimant raised no objection.

1.13 Before the Preliminary Meeting the parties had discussed a timetable for the proceedings and, after further discussion the following timetable was agreed:

(a) Statement of Agreed Facts relating to the subject premises. ....

(b) Agreement of schedule of improvements and alterations and whether they should be disregarded or taken into account when determining the fair yearly rent. ....

(c) Exchange of Schedule of comparable transactions. ....

(d) Exchange of Reports ....

(e) Exchange of replies to Reports ....

[51] These are of course from a rent review arbitration.

1.14 It was agreed that the Claimant's expert witness should prepare a draft of the Statement of Agreed Facts and deliver it to the Respondent's expert witness within the two weeks following the date of the Preliminary Meeting and that the Statement should include the floor areas of the subject premises (and the method of measurement used to ascertain them) and such other matters as the respective expert witnesses considered to be relevant to the determination of the fair yearly rent and upon which they were able to agree, together with a set of agreed drawings of the subject premises.

1.15 It was agreed that the respective expert witnesses should each prepare a draft schedule of improvements and alterations and then endeavour to agree a Schedule.

1.16 It was agreed that the respective expert witnesses should each prepare a draft schedule of comparable transactions included in the schedules. To the extent that relevant facts could not be agreed each party would be responsible for proving those facts at the Hearing. In respect of each transaction included in a Schedule there would be provided particulars of the premises; the lease covenants including term and rent payable; the floor areas (computed using the same method of measurement as used for the subject premises); a description of the premises; whether the rent thereof arose out of a market transaction or a rent review agreement or determination; and such other matters as were thought likely to affect the rental value of, or the rent payable for, the premises.

1.17 The parties agreed that they would like the Arbitrator to make a preliminary inspection which the Arbitrator would wish to make after the Hearing. The Arbitrator would wish to be accompanied by one representative of each party at both inspections.

1.18 It was not thought necessary for arrangements to be made for another preliminary Meetings.

1.19 It was agreed that the Claimant's Solicitor would be responsible for making arrangements for the reservation of accommodation for the Hearing, in liaison with the Respondent's Solicitor, and would in due course inform the Arbitrator of the agreed arrangements for him to confirm.

1.20 Both parties requested that the Arbitrator should make a reasoned Award.

1.21 [It was agreed that the Arbitrator would send draft directions to the parties' Solicitors for comment.][52]

2.1 I enclose [a draft of] directions [which I propose to issue] to give effect to these arrangements. [Please let me know by not later than noon on .... whether you have any comments to make on the draft.]

2.2 It was indicated at the Preliminary Meeting that I would give consideration to the Arbitrator's costs of the Reference in the light of what transpired at that Meeting. I have now done so and propose to charge a basic fee of .... and, additionally, a time charge at a rate of .... per day and proportionately for part thereof. This would be exclusive of out-of-pocket expenses and disbursements and exclusive of VAT.[53]

2.3 Any costs incidental to the proceedings e.g. hire of rooms; the taking of legal or other professional advice etc. would be charged additionally as incurred.

[52] In complicated cases para. 21 of the letter would be included and directions in draft form issued.

[53] The part of the letter on fees could be varied to meet different circumstances. The amounts of the basic fee and the daily rate of charge are matters of judgment for the arbitrator having regard to all the facts.

2.4 In the event that the parties are themselves able to reach agreement at any stage before an Award is made my charges would be as follows:

(a)	Agreement reached at this stage with no further action required of the Arbitrator	£ .... Plus time charge
(b)	Agreement reached before exchange of Reports	One quarter of basic fee plus time charge
(c)	Agreement reached after exchange of Reports but before commencement of Hearing	One half of basic fee plus time charge
(d)	Agreement reached after completion of Hearing but before making my second inspection of the subject premises and any comparables	Three-quarters of basic fee plus time charge

Out of pocket expenses; costs incidental to the proceedings and VAT would be additional to the amounts mentioned in 2.4(a), 2.4(b), 2.4(c) and 2.4(d) above.
Would you please confirm that this basis is acceptable.
I enclose a copy of the Attendance List for the Preliminary Meeting.
Yours truly
Enclosure

[Draft] Directions
Gentlemen,

In the matter of an Arbitration
between ....

In accordance with the arrangements made at the Preliminary Meeting held on .... I now direct as follows:

3.1 That is these Arbitration proceedings the lessors, ..., shall be designated the Claimant and the lessees, ... , shall be designated the Respondent.

3.2 That there shall be an oral Hearing commencing on .... and continuing through to .... and if not then concluded to stand adjourned to such date as may then be agreed with the parties or determined by me and that the Claimant's Solicitors shall be responsible for liaison with the Respondent's Solicitor to agree and make provisional agreements for the venue for the Hearing.

3.3 That evidence given at the Hearing shall be given on oath.

3.4 That the parties shall each be permitted to call an expert valuation witness to give evidence at the Hearing.

3.5 That the Claimant's Solicitors shall provide me with certified copies of the Underlease and any licences or other documents relating to that Underlease.

3.6 That the parties expert witnesses shall each prepare a schedule describing the nature and extent of any improvements and of any alterations which have been carried out to the demised premises since the grant of the Underlease thereof indicating whether any such improvements or alterations have been carried out at the expense of the lessor or the lessee and whether they are to be disregarded or taken into account in assessing the fair yearly rent and indicating those items in respect of which the parties are in agreement such schedules to be settled by not later than noon on .... and copies thereof lodged with me by not later than one week thereafter.

3.7 That the Claimant's expert witness shall prepare the draft of a Statement of Agreed Facts relating to the demised premises and the parties' expert witnesses shall agree so much thereof as they are able by noon on .... and a copy of the Statement of Agreed Facts shall be signed by them on behalf of the parties and lodged with me by not later than one week thereafter.

3.8 That the Statement of Agreed Facts shall incorporate the floor areas of the subject premises and a statement of the method of measurement used to compute those areas and such other matters as the expert witnesses consider to be relevant to the determination of the fair yearly rent and that there shall be appended to that Statement a set of agreed plans of the subject premises.

3.9 That by not later than noon on .... the parties' expert witnesses shall exchange their Schedules of comparable transactions and shall thereafter, as soon as may be, endeavour to agree the facts contained in such Schedules so far as they are able.

3.10 That the schedules of comparable transactions shall, as far as is practicable, include particulars and a description of each property; the lease covenants including terms and rent payable and the floor areas thereof (computed using the same method of measurement as has been used for the subject premises) and whether the rent payable results from a market transaction or a rent review agreement or determination in such other matters as the expert witnesses consider likely to affect the rental value of, or the rent payable for, the premises listed in the schedules.

3.11 That the parties shall exchange copies of their expert witnesses' Reports by not later than noon on .... and that such reports shall contain copies of all valuations, plans, documents and correspondence upon which a party intends to rely at the hearing and each party shall lodge with me a copy of such Report not later than one week thereafter.

3.12 That the parties shall exchange their replies, if any, to such Reports by not later than noon on .... and each party shall lodge with me a copy of any such reply by not later than one week thereafter.

3.13 That each party shall be responsible for sending to the other party a copy of every letter, document, drawing or other material or communication sent by the party to me.

I reserve the right to issue further directions as may appear to me to necessary or desirable, with liberty to the parties to apply.

Yours truly,

50. Notice to arbitrator of an application for leave to amend pleading or statement of case

A.B.

Dear Sir,

.... plc v .... plc

The claimant desires to amend the Statement of Case dated the .... (by substituting for the words "By a contract in writing made on the 27th April 1981" the words "by a contract made partly in writing on the 27th April and partly in two telephone conversations between John Smith on behalf of the Claimants and Mark Brown on behalf of the Respondents on the 28th April 1981")

OR

(as shown on the draft enclosed herewith.) The Respondents have declined to consent to this amendment. We therefore request an appointment for making the necessary application. Our clients will be represented by ...., and he/she considers that .... (minutes) (hours) should be allowed.
Yours faithfully,
for the Claimant.

51. Notice of intention to proceed *ex parte* after failure to comply with directions

RECORDED DELIVERY OR BY MESSENGER[54–55]

To: L.M. plc

In the matter of an arbitration between
.... plc and yourselves

I refer to my Directions herein dated the .... 19 .... and my letter to you dated the ....
You have failed to comply with the directions in that ....[56] and you have failed to give any effective answer to my letter dated [ ] which [ ].[57]
The hearing is now fixed for the .... 19 .... in Room No .... at .... 10.00 hours.
If you fail to attend at the hearing it is my intention to proceed with the arbitration in your absence. In that event I will notify you when the award is ready for collection.[58]
Yours, etc.
Arbitrator

52. Notice of intention to proceed *ex parte* after failure to attend hearing

RECORDED DELIVERY OR BY MESSENGER

To: L.M. plc

In the matter of an arbitration between
J.K. plc and yourselves

I refer to my (letter) (Directions) dated the .... 19 .... in which I notified you that the hearing would take place at 10.00 hrs at .... You failed to attendthat hearing. I accordingly adjourned it to the same place and time on .... day the .... 19 .... .
If you do not attend the adjourned hearing it is my intention to proceed in your absence.
In that event I will notify you when my award is ready for collection.
If you wish to attend an adjourned hearing but the date is inconvenient it is open to you

[54–55] A receipt is essential.
[56] The direction and the failure must be spelt out.
[57] Purpose of letter.
[58] Of course the appropriate sanction for failure to comply with a direction may well not be for the arbitrator to proceed with a hearing—which may cause the defaulting party no inconvenience at all. Accordingly the text of the paragraph should relate sanction to disobedience—making the punishment fit the crime along the principle if not the particular style of the Mikado.

to apply to me to change it. Any such application should be made promptly; notice of the application should be served upon me and upon J.K. plc; and you will be asked to explain why the date presently fixed is inconvenient. You should not assume in advance that any such application will be granted.

Yours, etc.

Arbitrator

53 Calderbank offer by a respondent[59]

To: ....

....

....

Your reference ....

WITHOUT PREJUDICE SAVE AS TO COSTS

Dear Sirs,

In the matter of an Arbitration

between

....

and

....

[We] [our clients] hereby offer to pay [you] [your clients], in full and final settlement of [all claims in this arbitration] OR [that part of your claim in this arbitration which relates to ....] the sum of £ .... [plus interest].[60]

OR

[including interest] together with your costs [of this arbitration]

OR

[of the said part of your claim] incurred up to the date of acceptance of this offer, such costs to be taxed by the court unless otherwise agreed.

Thereafter, unless expressly withdrawn it may be accepted subject to the following conditions.

1.1 Payment by [you] [your clients] of [our] [our clients'] costs from the date of this letter, such costs to be taxed if not agreed.

1.2 [The] [our] right [of our clients] to withhold a reasonable sum from the principal to cover the costs due under 1.1 above until such costs are taxed or agreed.

This offer will remain open for a period of [21] days from delivery to you of this letter. If you want an extension of that period, you should write to us appropriately.

This offer is made without prejudice to all matters in the arbitration save those as to costs, and its existence is not to be communicated to the arbitrator until all issues in the arbitration, other than those as to costs, have been disposed of.

Yours faithfully,

[59] This Calderbank offer is only suitable for the very simplest of cases. For complicated cases these offers need especially careful drafting, well beyond the scope of a drafting suggestion section.

[60] It may be easier to include interest in the sum offered: if not consideration should be given to specifying the period and the rate. A single reference to interest, separate from the principal, without specification creates a problem for the claimant and any court subsequently reviewing it. How much is the interest worth for example, is the question that will arise? An inability to answer this clearly is likely to deprive the letter of any effect.

54. Possible statement of case directions

ORDER FOR DIRECTIONS

Upon [hearing Counsel for both parties] [upon reading the written submissions] herein, I hereby direct as follows:

1.1 Claimant to prepare a bundle of principal documents and to include therein such documents as Respondent requests to be included.

1.2 Claimant to serve a comprehensive Statement of Case on liability. To the Case should be annexed a list of all documents relied upon by the Claimant. The Case is to be served by or before the [*date*]. The Case should finally identify who is or are said by the Claimant to be the Respondent/s. In so far as the Claimant does not accept that .... is the only proper Respondent, the Claimant should fully set out in the Case its submissions in support of its contentions.

1.3 Claimant may, if it so wishes, set out its case on Quantum in full.

1.4 Respondent to serve a comprehensive Statement of Defence (and of Counterclaim if so advised) by or before the expiry of six weeks from receipt of the Statement of Case. Respondent to annex to the Defence (and Counterclaim, if any) a list of the documents relied upon. The Statement of Defence (and Counterclaim, if any) shall include full submissions on the proper construction of any clause in the contract relied upon by the Respondent to defeat the claim. The Statement of Defence should also respond fully to any submissions to the effect that .... is not the proper Respondent or is not the only proper Respondent.

1.5 The Respondent may if it so wishes respond to the case on Quantum if such is put forward by the Claimant.

1.6 Claimant to serve a comprehensive Reply to the Defence (and a comprehensive Defence to the Counterclaim if a Counterclaim is served) by or before the expiry of six weeks from the date of receipt of the Defence (and Counterclaim). A list of any documents which are relied upon by the Claimant in connection with the Reply (and Defence to Counterclaim, if any) and which are not already listed shall be annexed.

1.7 At the same time as the Reply is served, the Claimant shall deliver to me, and to the Respondent if it so desires, a chronological bundle of the documents listed as relied upon by the parties. This bundle need not be finally paginated, since other documents may be added later.

1.8 Liberty to Restore.

1.9 Costs in the Reference.

ARBITRATION CLAUSES RELEVANT TO THE CONSTRUCTION INDUSTRY

55. Clause for main or principal contract which also provides for determination of related subcontract issues[61]

1.1 In the following provisions of this clause ''Head Arbitration'' means an arbitration under this contract; ''Related Arbitration'' means an arbitration under any contract

[61] These provisions follow on a clause referring disputes to arbitration.

("Related Contract") by one of the parties under this contract and a third party for the carrying out of, or services in connection with, any part of the works the subject of this contract; and "Head Arbitrator" means the arbitrator or the arbitration tribunal appointed in the Head Arbitration.

1.2 If within .... weeks prior to or after the commencement of a Head Arbitration, either party to a Related Contract commences a Related-Arbitration in which the issues substantially overlap with issues raised or to be raised in the Head Arbitration the party to this contract who is also a party to the Related Contract may by notice in writing to the other party to this contract and to the party to the Related Arbitration require that the Related-Arbitration be referred to the arbitration of the Head Arbitration and be consolidated with or heard together with the Head Arbitration. The other party to this contract shall consent to such a requirement.

1.3 Any dispute as to whether the Related-Arbitration raises issues which substantially overlap issues raised in the Head Arbitration and any questions as to the order or manner in which the arbitrations or any issue in either of them are to be determined shall be decided by the Head Arbitrator.

56. Provision in subcontract requiring concurrence with head arbitration if required

1.1 In the following provisions of this clause "Head Arbitration" means an arbitration under .... "Head Arbitrator" means the arbitration tribunal appointed in a "Head Arbitration"; and "Arbitration" means an arbitration under this contract.

1.2 Any arbitration under this contract shall be commenced by notice in writing to the other party.

1.3 If prior to or within .... weeks of the service of such notice a Head Arbitration is commenced in which the issues raised substantially overlap with the issues raised in the Arbitration the party to the Head Arbitration who is a party under this contract may by notice to the other party under this contract require that the Arbitration be referred to the determination of the Head Arbitrator and be consolidated with or heard together with the Head Arbitration and the other party shall consent to such a requirement.

1.4 Any dispute as to whether the issues respectively raised in the Arbitration and the Head Arbitration substantially overlap or as to whether the two arbitrations shall be heard or determined separately or together or as to the order or manner in which the two arbitrations or any issue in either of them shall be determined by the Head Arbitrator.

57. Construction Directions

IN THE MATTER OF THE ARBITRATION ACT 1996 AND IN THE MATTER OF AN ARBITRATION BETWEEN:

Claimants

and

Respondents

Upon hearing (Counsel) (the Solicitors) (on both sides) (and by consent) the following Directions are hereby given and it is Ordered that:

1.1 There be Pleadings in this Arbitration as follows:

(a) Points of Claim to be delivered to me and to the Respondent(s) Solicitor(s) within .... (days)/(weeks) from the date hereof;
(b) Points of Defence (and Counterclaim if any) to be delivered to me and to the Claimant(s) Solicitor(s) within .... (days)/(weeks) from the delivery of the Points of Claim; and
(c) Points of Reply (and Defence to Counterclaim) are to be delivered to me and to the Respondent(s) Solicitor(s) within .... (days)/(weeks) from delivery of the Points of Defence and Counterclaim; and
(d) Points of Reply of Defence to Counterclaim are to be delivered to me and to the Claimant(s) Solicitor(s) within .... (days)/(weeks) from the delivery of Points of Defence to Counterclaim; and
(e) Requests for Further and Better Particulars to be made within .... days from the receipt of any Pleading and to be answered within a further .... days; and
(f) Any such request for Further and Better Particulars will automatically extend the time for the delivery of the following Pleadings by a time equal to that which elapses between the request for such particulars and the Reply; and

1.2 After the close of the Pleadings the Claimants and the Respondents do respectively within .... (days)/(weeks) deliver to the other a List of Documents which are or have been in their possession or power relating to the matters in question in this Arbitration and that inspection be given within .... (days)/(weeks) thereafter; and

1.3 Correspondence, plans, photographs and figures be agreed as such as far as possible; and

1.4 Further Directions will be issued in due course controlling the preparation of ''Agreed Bundles'' but the Parties are advised now that such Agreed bundles should consist solely of those documents which are relevant to the issues pleased; and

1.5 The Parties are to consider the possibility of agreeing a limitation on the number of expert witnesses to be called and I am to be advised of the decision of the Parties on this point not later than .... (days) (weeks) after the close of Pleadings; and

1.6 The Parties do mutually disclose experts reports within .... (days) (weeks) (of the close of Pleadings) (prior to the start of the Hearing) and such reports be agreed if possible. Only such experts whose reports have been so disclosed may be called to give evidence at the Hearing; and

1.7 The Parties are to consider the possibility of agreeing to exchange proofs of evidence of witnesses of fact by some predetermined date prior to the Hearing and I am to be advised of the decision of the Parties on this possibility not later than 28 days after close of Pleadings; and

1.8 Not later than 28 days after the close of Pleadings the Claimants are to serve on the Respondents a Notice to Admit Facts in Accordance with Practice Form 60 and the Respondents within a further 28 days are to reply to the Notice and if so advised, to serve their own Notice to Admit Facts such Notice to be replied to within 14 days; and

1.9 Not later than .... (weeks) after (close of Pleadings) (completion of discovery of documents) the Parties are to prepare and submit to me a statement setting forth in numbered paragraphs the various issues which I am called upon to decide such statement to be agreed if possible, failing which each Party to produce their own statement; and

1.10 (After the completion of the inspection of documents referred to in paragraph 2 above) (after the close of the Pleadings) the Parties are to consider and are to advise me as soon as possible thereafter of their best estimate of the direction of the Hearing and of dates when it is known that their witnesses etc. will not be available together with an expression of any preference a party may have regarding the venue for the Hearing; and

1.11 The Parties are to consider the necessity for a shorthand record of the Hearing being taken and of the extent and distribution of any transcript and I am to be advised of the decision of the Parties on this point not later than the close of the Pleadings (not less than .... (weeks) (months) before the start of the Hearing); and

1.12 If any communication is made to me by either Party a copy thereof is simultaneously to be sent to the other Party; and

1.13 Each Party is to advise the other Party if it is their intention to engage Counsel; and

1.14 BY CONSENT,[62] the Parties are to advise me not later than .... (weeks) before the commencement of the Hearing if they require me to issue a reasoned Award and are to state the purpose for such request so that my Reasoned Award is directed to the appropriate object; and

1.15 The Parties are to consider the desirability of agreeing that Counsel's closing addresses be made in writing after the close of the Hearing, with a further Hearing after such written addresses have been received at which each party may make oral summaries not exceeding one half day in duration; and

1.16 The costs of this Order are costs in the cause; and

1.17 Liberty to either Party to apply.

Arbitrator.

Dated this .... day of .... 19 ....

58. Another form of construction directions

ORDER FOR DIRECTIONS NO. 1

UPON CONSIDERING the matters raised at the initial interlocutory meeting in this matter and BY CONSENT, I direct as follows:

1.1 Save as hereinafter expressly provided for, and subject to the liberty to apply hereinafter provided for, Rule 6 of the JCT Arbitration Rules 1988 is to apply to the conduct of this arbitration.

1.2 The Rules of Western Circuit Arbitration, and in particular Rule 4 thereof, do not apply to this arbitration.

1.3 The Claimant shall serve, by or before the [*date*], a detailed Statement of Case.

1.4 The Respondents shall serve, by or before the [*date*], a detailed Statement of Defence, and any Statement of Counterclaim that they may be minded to make.

1.5 The Claimant shall be at liberty to serve a Statement of Reply to any duly served

[62] Obviously this only goes in to this form if the matter is indeed agreed by the parties.

Statement of Defence, provided the same is served within 14 days of the service of the Statement of Defence.

1.6 If the Respondents duly serve a Statement of Counterclaim, the Claimant shall serve a Statement of Defence to Counterclaim within 28 days of service of the Statement of Counterclaim.

1.7 The Respondents shall be at liberty to serve a Statement of Reply to any Statement of Defence to Counterclaim that the Claimant may serve, provided the same is served within 14 days of the service of the Statement of Defence to Counterclaim.

1.8 With each of the above Statements, but principally with the Statements of Case, Defence and Counterclaim, the parties will include a list of any documents considered necessary by the serving party to support any part of the relevant Statement. In addition, each party shall serve of each of the principal documents upon which that party wishes to rely, save for any such document that has already been served by either party.

1.9 Save as aforesaid, Rules 6.4, 6.5, 6.8 and 6.9 of the JCT Arbitration Rules shall apply in their standard form. For convenience of reference the said rules are set out in an endnote to these directions.

1.10 Detailed directions for the conduct of the hearing are to be agreed by the parties by or before the [*date*]. Such directions must be constructed so as to ensure that the hearing finishes within the allotted time. If not agreed by the said date, specific directions on the matter will be issued.

1.11 Statements containing the evidence in chief of any witness whom it is proposed to call by either party shall be served by or before the [*date*]. These statements shall stand as evidence in chief. Oral evidence in chief from witnesses of fact will only be permitted on application, showing good cause. No statement so served shall be relied upon in the proceedings by either party until the witness is called and has formally proved the statement.

1.12 Liberty to the parties to adduce expert evidence. The identity of each expert whom a party proposes to call must be notified in writing to me and to the other party no later than the [*date*]. The notification must identify his or her discipline and enclose a copy of the relevant CV.

1.13 In respect of the following directions which deal with meetings and the like between the expert witnesses, the principal expert witness for the Claimant is to take on administrative responsibility for arranging or attempting to arrange the same; and is to chair any such meetings, and prepare the documents for circulation hereinafter referred to. The Claimant is to nominate his principal expert witness when identifying his experts.

1.14 The expert witnesses are to arrange at least one without prejudice meeting before exchange of their reports and to be at liberty to arrange more than one. No reference to be made to the proceedings in such meetings, save by way of a written memorandum signed by each expert present, and containing such statements as all the signatories are content to have circulated.

1.15 Statements containing a full account of the relevant's expert's proposed evidence in chief are to be served by or before the [*date*].

1.16 After service of the said statements, the experts are to meet on a without prejudice basis at least once before the [*date*] in an endeavour to reduce the issues and to clarify the contentious matters. The experts are to be at liberty to meet more than once. No reference to be made to the proceedings in such meetings, save by way of a written memorandum signed by each expert present, and containing such statements as all the signatories are content to have circulated. Any such memorandum to be produced by or before the [*date*].

1.17 A bundle to be agreed and served by or before the [*date*].

1.18 A written opening by the Claimant is to be served no later than [*date*].

1.19 A Site visit is to take place on the [*date*].

1.20 The Claimant is to organize the venue of the hearing. The Claimant may utilize its own offices for this purpose only if the Respondents agree.

1.21 There will be no transcript of the hearing.

1.22 Communications between the parties and myself will normally be by DX, but can be by fax in case of urgency.

1.23 Interlocutory applications will so far as possible be dealt with on paper and not by oral hearings.

1.24 Liberty to apply generally; and specifically by way of an application for specific discovery.

1.25 Costs in cause.

59. Construction Scott Schedule Claim for extra work—stage one

SCOTT (or OFFICIAL REFEREE'S) SCHEDULE

Served pursuant to Order of the Arbitrator
Dated the .... day of .... 19 ....

SCHEDULE

Part One

1. No. of Item	2. Full particulars of each item of extra work ordered by respondent and done by claimant	3. Date when order given and by whom on part of the respondent	4. Amount claimed by claimant	5. Amount, if any, admitted by respondent	6. Respondent's observations	7. For use of the arbitrator

60. Check list for preliminary meeting

Item No.	Item	Notes
1.1	Confirm that arbitration is under the 1996 Act and not the 1950 Act.[63]	
1.2	Is there a binding arbitration agreement (see section 8 of the 1996 Act)? Obtain copies of all documents relied upon.	
1.3	Does the arbitration agreement contain any conditions precedent to an arbitration? (*e.g.*: that work must be completed.) If so, have they been complied with?	
1.4	Have I seen a copy of the notice to concur or any other relevant document commencing the arbitration?	
1.5	Are there any grounds for disputing my jurisdiction? If so, how and when should I resolve them (section 30 of the 1996 Act)?[64]	
1.6	Are the terms of my appointment (including fees) agreed by the parties and have they signed my letter of appointment?	
1.7	What is this dispute about? 1. Who is the claimant? 2. Very brief review of nature of claim. 3. Very brief review of nature of likely defence if known to respondent. 4. Is there likely to be a counterclaim?	
1.8	General procedure for the arbitration 1. Does the arbitration agreement provide that the arbitration shall be in accordance with specified procedural rules (*e.g.*: J.C.T. Arbitration Rules)? 2. If there is choice of procedure, what sort of procedure do I think would be appropriate for this arbitration? 3. Do the parties have any view on overall procedure that I should take into account at this stage?	
1.9	My powers—what powers do the parties agree that I shall have and shall not have under the 1996 Act? What other powers do I have irrespective?	

[63] It is unlikely that arbitrations with preliminary meetings being held now will be under the 1950 Act. Therefore references in this table are to the 1996 Act.

[64] The arbitrator may have to look at jurisdiction again later in the arbitration in relation to individual claims/counterclaims once they are known.

1.10	Points of claim: what form should these take? When should they be served? Should the claimant attach any documents that they rely upon?[65]	
1.11	Points of defence/counterclaim.	
1.12	Reply to counterclaim.	
1.13	Is a Scott Schedule appropriate? If so, what should the headings be? Dates for completion.	
1.14	Discovery: should there be full discovery or not? Should discovery be by lists or by simply attaching documents relied upon in the pleading? If there is not to be a full discovery, what shall I shall say about applications for specific discovery for particular documents?	
1.15	Date for exchange of list of documents/other mechanism for discovery.	
1.16	Arrangements for inspection of documents.	
1.17	Expert witnesses—number and discipline, date for exchange of reports.	
1.18	Should I order without prejudice experts' meetings in order to try to limit issues for the hearing?	
1.19	Witness statements—anticipated number for each side, dates for exchange.	
1.20	Should I make an order for rebuttal statements now?	
1.21	Parties to try to agree plans and photographs.	
1.22	Parties to try to agree figures as figures.	
1.23	Anticipated length of hearing.	
1.24	Date of hearing.	
1.25	Venue of hearing—where and whom to arrange.	
1.26	Will parties be represented at hearing? If so, by counsel or solicitor?	
1.27	Will any transcript be required?	
1.28	Will evidence be on oath?	
1.29	Claimants to prepare agreed bundle by given date.	
1.30	Should parties provide written opening statements in advance of hearing? If so, set dates.	

[65] The arbitrator may wish to raise this issue now but postpone discussing it until he deals with discovery later on in the hearing.

1.31	At the hearing, will evidence be on oath?	
1.32	Should parties provide written closing submissions?	
1.33	Contact between parties and arbitrator other than at hearings to be by fax or letter only, copy to be provided to the other side immediately and arbitrator's copy to be marked as having been so copied.	
1.34	Cost of the preliminary hearing to be costs in the arbitration.	

ARBITRATION CLAUSES RELEVANT TO RENT REVIEW

63. Provision enabling rent review under underlease to be referred to same arbitrator as rent review under head lease

1.1 In the following provisions of this clause ''Head Arbitration'' means as arbitration under this lease; ''Head Arbitrator'' means the arbitrator or arbitration tribunal appointed in the Head Arbitration; and ''Sub-arbitration'' means an arbitration under any sub-lease created out of this lease.

1.2 Any Head Arbitration shall be commenced by written notice to the lessor or lessee requiring arbitration.

1.3 If whether before or after a Head Arbitration has commenced a Sub-arbitration is commenced in which the issues substantially overlap issues raised in the Head Arbitration or which in the opinion of the lessee are likely to be raised in a Head Arbitration the lessee may be notice in writing to the lessor and to the underlessee served within .... months of the written notice last mentioned required that the sub-arbitration be referred to the arbitration of the Head Arbitrator.

1.4 Any dispute as to whether the Sub-arbitration raises issues which substantially overlap issues raised in the Head Arbitration or as to whether the two arbitrations shall be heard or determined separately or together or as to the order or manner in which the two arbitrations or any issue in either of them shall be determined by the Head Arbitrator.

1.5 Save for any dispute under 1.3 above, the Head Arbitrator shall be at liberty to treat the dispute or disputes under this lease and the dispute or disputes under the sub-lease or sub-lease as if they arose under the in this lease arbitration clause; to give directions accordingly; in particular, but without derogating from the generality of the foregoing, he shall be at liberty to hear all relevant parties at the same hearing, and to take into account any evidence led by any party so present when determining any of the said disputes.

61. Claimant's Scott Schedule of defects—Stage 1. Headings only

Scott Schedule item No.	Location of defect	Particulars of breach	Terms of contract/ specification breached	Remedial work required	Cost of remedial work required	Respondent's comments	Arbitrator's comments
1.							
2.							

1. This example Schedule adopts headings relevant to a defects claim in a construction case. The headings will not, however, be the same for every arbitration. Thought should always be given to what headings would be the most useful given the issues in dispute.

2. The Schedule should always be completed in stages. The headings should preferably be considered at the preliminary meeting and may be the subject of an Order. The Claimant should then complete his part of the Schedule. The Respondents should then fill in their comments. Finally, the Arbitrator can add his own comments.

62. Claimant's Scott Schedule of defects—Stage 2. Claimant's comments

	Location of defect		Particulars of breach	Terms of contract specification breached	Remedial work required	Cost of remedial work required	Respondent's comments	Arbitrator's comments
1.1	Room AB-2	V1214, jacket drain valve on V303	The jacket drain valve is difficult to access, which will cause operational problems.	Clause 3.2 of the General Conditions, requiring that the plant shall conform to good engineering service practice.	Extend and modifying piping.	£1,500		
2.1	Room AB-2	Line 3016	The line does not fall continuously to V1215 as required by the ELD. It will not be fully drainable and this will compromise cleaning and sterilization operations.	Clause 2 Section D of the Specification, requiring that the plant comply with European and American guidelines on GMP for Pharmaceuticals, which requires that system design facilitates cleaning and sterilization.	Modify piping/ supports.	£3,000		

64. Provision in underlease of part enabling rent review to be referred to same arbitrator as rent review under head lease

1.1 In the following provisions of this clause "Head Arbitration" means an arbitration under the rent review provisions of the head lease out of which the estate hereby granted is created: "Head Arbitrator" means the arbitrator or arbitration tribunal appointed in the Head Arbitration; and "Sub-arbitration" means an arbitration under the rent review provision of this underlease.

1.2 Any Sub-arbitration shall be commenced by written notice requiring arbitration.

1.3 If whether before or after a Head Arbitration has commenced a sub-arbitration is commenced under this sub-lease in which the issues substantially overlap issues raised in the Head Arbitration the under lessee may by notice in writing to the underlessee require that the sub-arbitration be referred to the arbitration of the Head Arbitrator.

1.4 Any dispute as to whether the Sub-arbitration raises issues which substantially overlap issues in the Head Arbitration or as to whether the two arbitrations shall be heard together or separately or as to the order or manner in which the two arbitrations or any issue in either of them shall be determined by the Head Arbitrator.

65. Directions for proceeding by written representations without a hearing

Messrs	Messrs
Name and Address	Name and Address
For the attention of:	*For the attention of*:

Gentlemen,

In the matter of an Arbitration
between

....

and

....

In respect of

....

1.1 At the preliminary meeting which was held .... on .... the Landlord, ..., was represented by .... the Tenant, ... by ....

1.2 It was agreed that the matter should be dealt with by written representations and I enclose with each letter a copy of the Procedure Notes for Written Representations.

1.3 I direct that the matters referred to in the procedure Notes shall be compiled with as follows:

(a) A copy of the Statement of Agreed Facts (Note 1.1)[66] is to be delivered to me by ....;

(b) Copies of the Lists of Comparable Transactions (Note 1.2) are to be exchanged by ....;

(c) Copies of the Schedules of Particulars of the Comparable Transactions in the Lists (Note 1.3) are to be prepared in draft by each representative and exchanged by .... for approval by and agreement of the other representative by .... ;

(d) Copies of the Lists of Comparable Transactions (Note 2) and the Schedules of Particulars relating thereto (Note 3) are to be delivered to me by each representative by ....;

[66] Please see the following Suggestion for the Notes.

(e) A copy of the agreed Schedule of Improvements and Alteration to the subject premises, if any, (Note 1.4) is to be delivered to me by ....;
(f) Copies of the Statements of Submissions (Notes 1.5 and 1.6) are to be exchanged by .... and copies delivered to me one week later;
(g) Copies of written responses to the other party's submissions (Notes 1.7 and 1.8) are to be exchanged or lodged with the other party's representative by .... and copies delivered to me one week later;
(h) The Tenant's representative is to provide me with a certified copy of the lease dated ....;
(i) The Landlord's representative is to provide me with (i) certified copies of the Licence to Assign and the Assignment; (ii) copies of any other Licences which have been granted and (iii) copies of any other documents pertinent to the arbitration proceedings;
(j) Any plans incorporated or referred to are to be coloured as described in the lease, licences and other documents;
(k) All letters, documents, drawings and other materials sent to me by one party are to be copied by that party to the other party;
(l) The time by which action is to take place on a day and date specified in (a) to (g) inclusive above is to be noon on all such days and dates.

1.4 I have noted the request of both parties for a reasoned award.

OR

I have noted that .... reserves the .... position as to whether a reasoned award will be requested.

1.5 Both parties have asked that I should make an Interim Award which would be final except as to costs and that the parties should be given an opportunity to make submissions on costs before I make a Final Award.

OR

Both parties have reserved the position as to whether I should be asked to make an Interim Award which would be final except as to costs.

1.6 I have noted that the landlord/lessor served a rent review notice on .... and that the tenant/lessee served a counter-notice on ....

1.7 I shall wish to inspect the demised premises and will in due course issue directions regarding the inspections. As intimated at the meeting I will expect to make a preliminary inspection shortly after receiving the counter-representations (Note 1.7) followed later by a full inspection at the time when the comparable properties are to be inspected.

1.8 I shall make inspections of the interiors of the properties which have been included in the Lists of Comparable Transactions only if the representative putting forward such properties is able to make arrangements with the occupiers for inspections.

1.9 At all inspections I will expect to be accompanied by a representative of each party.

1.10 I reserve the right to direct that the proceedings shall be supplemented by or changed to an oral hearing if it appears to me to be appropriate so to do.

1.11 I also reserve the right to issue further directions as may appear to me to be necessary or desirable with liberty to the parties to apply.

A separate letter has been sent to the parties' representatives on the subject of costs.

Yours truly,

66. Procedure notes for written representations

1.1 The parties' representatives are to submit to the arbitrator a signed Statement of Agreed Facts in respect of the demised premises including such matters as floor areas; rating assessments and descriptions; planning history and any relevant planning decision mains and other services; service charges and such other facts as may be relevant to the assessment of the annual rental value of the property together with all plans, maps and other documents which are to be relied upon by the parties including a certified copy of the lease or under-lease and copies of any licences granted in connection therewith. The statement should indicate (where such be the case) any matters of fact which the representatives are unable to agree and, if possible, the reason for the disagreement. The statement is to be prepared in draft by the Landlord's representative and submitted to the Tenant's representative for approval.

1.2 The representatives are to exchange their respective Lists of Comparable Transactions intended to be used in evidence.

1.3 The representatives are to exchange Schedule of Particulars of the Comparable Transactions in the Lists. The particulars are to include, as far as practicable, a description of each property listed therein; the relevant lease covenants including the term and the rent payable thereunder; the floor areas of the premises; whether the rent payable results from a market transaction or a rent review agreement or determination and all other matters that may affect the open market rental value of or the rent payable for the property. The representatives are to agree the facts contained in the Schedules so far as they are able.

1.4 The representatives are to submit to the arbitrator a signed Schedule of Improvements and Alternations, if any, to the demised premises made by the landlord or by the tenant indicating whether any such improvements or alterations are to be taken into account or are to be disregarded in assessing the annual rental value. The schedule is to be prepared by the Tenant's representative and submitted to the Landlord's representative for approval.

1.5 Each representative is to lodge with the other representative two copies of a Statement of Submissions in the form of a Report or Proof of Evidence. The statement should include every valuation which is to be relied upon as evidence.

1.6 One week after exchanging the documents referred to in Note (1.5) above one of the two copies is to be transmitted by each representative to the arbitrator.

1.7 If it is so desired representative may then submit to the other representative two copies of a document comprising representations on the other representative's Statement of Submissions. The representations should be confined to matters raised in the other representative's submissions. Evidence on new matters should not be introduced.

1.8 One week after receiving the documents referred to in Note (1.7) above one of the two copies is to be transmitted by each representative to the arbitrator.

1.9 The arbitrator may direct written questions to one representative or both representatives on their Statements of Submissions and their Representations. The other party's representative will be informed of any such questions and the replies thereto. The arbitrator may also require the parties or their representatives to attend at an oral hearing if he considers it desirable to do so.

1.10 So that long drawn out proceedings may be avoided responses to representations will not normally be permitted.

1.11 Both representatives are expected to take care in the making of any submissions, representations, replies to questions, correspondence and other exchanges to avoid disclosing any privileged material. The purpose of allowing one week following exchange of submissions and representations is to enable a representative to object to the inclusion of material or otherwise to challenge the admissibility of evidence submitted and to resolve the matter with the other representative before that material has been disclosed to the arbitrator.

1.12 Factual evidence relating to comparable property and transactions in respect thereof will require to be strictly proved except to the extent that such facts are agreed by or accepted unchallenged by the other party.

1.13 Floor areas and other dimensions of the demised premises and comparable properties are to be in common form ascertained and expressed in accordance with the Code of Measuring Practice published jointly by the Royal Institution of Chartered Surveyors and the Incorporated Society of Valuers and Auctioneers.

67. Directions for oral hearing

Messrs	Messrs
Name and Address	Name and Address
For the attention of	*For the attention of*

Gentlemen,[67]

In the matter of an Arbitration
between
....
and
....
in respect of
....

1.1 At the preliminary meeting which was held .... on .... the Landlord, ... was represented by ...., and the Tenant, ... by ....

1.2 It was agreed that the matter should be dealt with at an oral hearing and I enclose with each letter a copy of the Procedure Notes for an oral hearing.

1.3 I now direct as follows:

(a) that in these arbitration proceedings .... shall be designated the claimant and .... shall be designated the respondent;

(b) that there shall be an oral hearing commencing on .... 19 .... and that the claimant's solicitors shall be responsible for making arrangements for the venue of the hearing in consultation with the respondent's solicitors;

(c) that evidence at the hearing shall be given on oath;

(d) that the parties shall each be permitted to call one valuation expert witness [and one accountancy expert] to give evidence at the hearing;

(e) that the parties are to comply with the Procedure Notes in accordance with the undermentioned timetable:

(i) The signed Statement of Agreed Facts (Notes 1.1 and 1.2)[68] is to be delivered to the arbitrator by the claimant's representative by .... day .... 19 .... ;

(ii) The certified copies of documents (Note 1.3) are to be delivered to the arbitrator by the claimant's solicitors/representative by .... day .... 19 .... ;

[67] Obviously adjust as appropriate.

[68] Please see the following suggestion for the notes.

(iii) Lists of comparable Transactions (Note 1.4) are to be exchanged by .... day .... 19.... ;

(iv) Schedules of Particulars of the Comparable Transactions (Note 1.5) are to be exchanged by .... day .... 19 .... ;

(v) Copies of the List of Comparable Transactions (Note 1.4) and copies of the Schedules of Particulars of the Comparable Transactions (Note 1.5) as exchanged are to be delivered to the arbitrator by each party's representative by .... day .... 19 .... ;

(vi) A copy of the Schedule of Improvements and Alterations (Note 1.6) is to be delivered to the arbitrator by the .... representative by .... day .... 19 .... ;

(vii) Exchanges of Reports by expert witnesses (Note 1.8) is/are to take place by .... day .... 19 .... ;

(viii) Delivery of Reports to the arbitrator where there has not been an exchange of Reports (Note 1.9) is to take place by .... day .... 19 .... ;

(ix) Exchange(s) of Responses by expert witnesses (Note 1.10) is/are to take place by .... day .... 19 .... ;

(x) Delivery of Responses to the arbitrator where there has not been an exchange of Responses (Note 1.11) is to take place by .... day .... 19 .... ;

(xi) The time by which action is to be take place on a day and date specified in 1.3(e)(i)–(x) inclusive above is to be noon on all such days and dates;

(xii) That each party shall be responsible for sending to the other party a copy of every letter, document, drawing or other material and communication sent by the party to me.

1.4 Both parties have asked that I should make an Interim Award which would be final except as to costs and that the parties should be given an opportunity to make submissions on costs before I make a Final Award.

OR

Both parties have reserved the position as to whether I should be asked to make an Interim Award which would be final except as to costs.

1.5 I have noted that the Claimant/Respondent served a rent review notice on .... and that the Claimant/Respondent served a counter-notice on ....

1.6 I shall wish to inspect the demised premises and will in due course issue directions regarding the inspections. As intimated at the meeting I will expect to make a preliminary inspection in the week preceding the commencement of the hearing followed by a full inspection at the time when the comparable properties are to be inspected.

1.7 I shall make inspections of the interiors of the properties which have been included in the Lists of Comparable Transactions only if the representative putting forward such properties is able to make arrangements with the occupiers for inspections.

1.8 At all inspections I will expect to be accompanied by a representative of each party.

1.9 I reserve the right to issue further directions as may appear to me to be necessary or desirable, with liberty to the parties to apply.

1.10 A separate letter has been sent to the parties' representatives on the subject of costs.

Yours truly,

68. Procedure notes for an oral hearing

1.1 The parties' representatives are to submit to the arbitrator a signed Statement of Agreed Facts in respect of the demised premises. The statement is to be prepared in draft by the .... representative and submitted to the .... representative for approval. The Statement is to include such matters as floor areas; rating assessments and descriptions; Planning history and any relevant planning decisions; availability of mains and other services; service charges and such other facts as may be thought to be relevant to the assessment of the open market rental value of the demised premises. The statement should indicate (where such be the case) any matters of fact upon which the parties' representatives are unable to agree and, if possible, the reasons for the disagreement.

1.2 Appended to the Agreed Statement of Facts there is to be an agreed set of copies of all plans, maps, photographs and documents to be relied upon by the representatives.

1.3 The .... representative is to prepare and agree with the .... representative and submit to the arbitrator certified copies of the lease (or its counterpart) of all licences, notices and other relevant documents.

1.4 The representatives are to exchange their respective Lists of Comparable Transactions intended to be used in evidence.

1.5 The representatives are to exchange Schedules of Particulars of the Comparable Transactions in the Lists. The particulars are to include, so far as practicable, a description of each property listed therein; the relevant lease covenants including the term and the rent payable; the floor areas of the premises; whether the rent payable results from a market transaction, a rent review agreement or a rent review determination and such other matters as are considered likely to affect the open market rental value of or the rent payable for the property. The representatives are to agree the facts contained in the Schedules so far as they are able.

1.6 The representatives are to deliver to the arbitrator a signed Schedule of Improvements and Alterations, if any, to the demised premises made by the landlord or the tenant indicating whether any such improvements or alterations are to be taken into account or are to be disregarded in assessing the open market rental value. The schedule is to be prepared by the Tenant's representative and submitted to the Landlord's representative for approval before delivering to the arbitrator.

1.7 For the purpose of the preceding Notes (1.1) to (1.6) inclusive a party's representative is to be taken to be the party's valuation expert witness and if more than one valuation expert witness is to be called then a party's representative is to be the party's principal valuation expert witness as nominated by that party.

1.8 Each party's expert witness is to exchange Reports with the corresponding expert witness of the other party. In the case of valuation expert witnesses the Report is to contain all valuations upon which that expert witness intends to rely at the hearing. Similarly, an accountancy expert witness is to include in the Report all accounts, returns, records, assessments and other statistical evidence upon which that expert witness intends to rely and so, too, for other expert witnesses as regards their Reports and the fields in which they have experience and expertise. Ten working days after Reports have been exchanged each expert witness is to deliver a copy thereof to the arbitrator.

1.9 In the event that a part intends not to call an expert witness in all or any of the fields in which the other party will be calling an expert witness then two copies of the Report of that expert witness are to be delivered to the arbitrator who will subsequently deliver one of the copies to the party who has not called an expert witness in a particular field.

1.10 If it is desired so to do an expert witness may exchange Responses with the counterpart expert witness controverting by way of criticism or observation or otherwise the content of the Report of the other's expert witness. Ten working days after Responses have been exchanged each expert witness is to deliver a copy thereof to the arbitrator.

1.11 Where one party has not called an expert witness the procedure set out in Note 1.9 above as to Reports is to apply to Responses in like manner *mutatis mutandis*.

1.12 Factual evidence relating to comparable property and transactions in respect thereof will require to be strictly proved except to the extent that such facts are agreed by or accepted unchallenged by the other party.

1.13 Floor areas and other dimensions of the demised premises and comparable properties are to be in common form ascertained and expresses in accordance with the Code of Measuring Practice published jointly by the Royal Institution of chartered Surveyors and the Incorporated Society of Valuers and Auctioneers.

69. Agreement to refer point of law for the decision of counsel

IN THE MATTER OF AN ARBITRATION

BETWEEN

L.M. plc — Claimants

and

P.Q. plc — Respondents

1.1 A contract between the above parties dated the .... 19 .... contained, in clause 6, provision for arbitration.

1.2 On the .... 19 .... Mr A.B. was appointed arbitrator (OR Mr A.B. and Mr C.D. have been appointed arbitrators by the claimants and the respondents respectively).

1.3 The matters in issue between the parties include the issue set out in the Schedule hereto.

1.4 The parties hereby agree:

(a) that the said issue shall be submitted, in the form of a Joint Case, for the Opinion of (Mr Y.Z. of Counsel)

OR

(b) (Counsel to be chosen by the Arbitrator(s) from a list of four names of which two shall be nominated by each party);

(c) that the Arbitrator(s) shall be bound to accept the Opinion of Counsel as correctly stating the law on the issue referred to him;

(d) (to be deleted if inapplicable) that any right of appeal under the Arbitration Act 1996 is hereby excluded in relation to the said issue;

(e) that the costs of obtaining the said opinion shall be in the discretion of the Arbitrator(s);

Dated ....

(Signed)	(Signed) ....
(Name)	(Name) ....
For L.M. plc	For P.Q. plc

70. Final award without reasons[69]

IN THE MATTER OF AN ARBITRATION
BETWEEN
P.Q. plc Claimants
and
L.M. plc Respondents

FINAL AWARD

1.1 I .... was appointed
(By letters respectively from the claimant dated the .... and from the respondent dated the .... 19 ....)
OR
(By letter from the President of the .... dated the .... 19 ....) to act as arbitrator under (an arbitration clause contained in a contract dated the .... 19 ....)
OR
(an arbitration agreement dated the .... 19 ....)

1.2 I have received and studied (a) the contract between the parties dated .... 19 .... and (b) the submissions of the parties hereto (made to me in written Statements of Case and Statements of Reply)
OR
(at a hearing on the .... and the .... 19 ....)

1.3 I have inspected ....

1.4 Neither party has asked for a reasoned award.

1.5 I DO HEREBY AWARD AND DETERMINE that the Respondent do pay to the claimant the sum of £ .... with interest thereon from the .... at the rate of .... per cent.

1.6 I further AWARD AND DIRECT
(that the .... do pay the .... my fees for this arbitration and award (which I hereby assess at £ ....) and the .... costs of the arbitration to be taxed (if not agreed))
OR
(that there be no order as to costs save that my fees for this arbitration and award shall be borne by the parties equally, and that if either party shall in the first instance pay more than one-half of my said fees the other party shall pay to him the amount of the excess.)

1.7 I further award and direct that any taxation under the above provisions of my award shall be (by me)[70]
OR
(by the High Court) and shall be (on an indemnity basis)
OR
(on a party and party basis)

Dated ....
(Signed) ....
Arbitrator

[69] An unmotivated award should be a very rare animal post the 1996 Act.
[70] To be preferred.

71. Final award with reasons

IN THE MATTER OF AN ARBITRATION
BETWEEN
P.Q. plc Claimant
and
L.M. plc Respondent
FINAL AWARD

1.1 I, A.B., was appointed by letters respectively from the claimant dated .... 19 .... and from the respondent dated the .... 19 ....

OR

by letter from the President of the .... dated the .... 19 .... to act as arbitrator under an arbitration clause contained in a contract dated .... 19 ....

OR

an arbitration agreement dated the .... 19 .... .

1.2 The submissions of the parties hereto were made to me (in writing, by the claimant personally and by .... on behalf of the respondents)

OR

(at a hearing on the .... and the .... 19 .... at which the claimants were represented by Miss X.Y. of Counsel and the respondents by Mr W.R., a chartered quantity surveyor).

1.3 Three issues were put to me for determination. They were formulated (by Counsel) (by the advocates) (by the parties, with my assistance), as follows:
ISSUE 1: ....
ISSUE 2: ....
ISSUE 3: ....

1.4 (A Statement of Agreed Facts was put before me. It is annexed to and forms part of this Award)

OR

(The following facts were not in dispute)

1.5 As to Issue 1: The case for the claimants was ....
The case for the respondents was ....
....
In my judgment .... therefore decide this issue in favour of the ....

1.6 As to Issue 2: [etc. as for Issue 1]

1.7 As to Issue 3: [etc. as for Issue 1]

1.8 The overall result of my determinations on these issues is ....

1.9 I therefore DO HEREBY AWARD AND DETERMINE that the Respondent pay to the claimant the sum of £ .... with interest thereon from the .... 19 .... at the rate of .... per cent.

1.10 I further AWARD AND DIRECT
(that the respondent do pay to the claimant my fees for this arbitration and award (which I hereby assess at £ ....) And the claimant's costs of the arbitration to be taxed (if not agreed)

OR

(by me with the assistance if I think necessary of a Costs Assessor to be selected by me from the Costs Panel of the Chartered Institute of Arbitrators)

OR

(that there be no order as to costs save that my fees for this arbitration and award shall be borne by the parties equally, and that if either party shall in the first instance pay more than one-half of my said fees the other party shall pay to him the amount of the excess)
the taxation to be (on the standard basis)

OR

(on the indemnity basis)[71]

Dated ....
(Signed) ....
Arbitrator

72. Final award—reasons to be annexed—consumer dispute

(Reference No.)
IN THE MATTER OF THE ARBITRATION ACT 1996
and
IN THE MATTER OF AN ARBITRATION UNDER THE RULES OF THE .... SCHEME FOR THE .... INDUSTRY (EDITION)
BETWEEN:

(Name and address) Claimant

and

(Name and address) Respondent

ARBITRATOR'S AWARD

WHEREAS:

1.1 (On or about .... the Claimant entered into a contract with the Respondent whereby the Claimant would pay the total sum of £ and the Respondent would provide ....).

1.2 During the [*relevant circumstances and dates*] certain events occurred which resulted in a dispute arising between the parties.

1.3 Such dispute has not been amicably resolved and has been referred to arbitration in accordance with the Chartered Institute of Arbitrators' Arbitration Scheme for the .... Industry.

1.4 The parties to the arbitration have agreed to the Arbitrator deciding the case solely on documents which have been submitted by them.

1.5 On [*date of appointment*] the [*President or Vice President*] of the Chartered Institute of Arbitrators appoint me [*name, qualifications and reference to the particular panel of which arbitrator is a member*] to act as arbitrator in the Reference. This appointment I accepted on [*date*].

1.6 My reasons are set out in the annex to my Award, but they form part of my Award.

Now I, the said (name), having carefully considered the submissions of the parties as set out in the documents provided to me, HEREBY AWARD AND DIRECT as follows:
(Alternative forms of Award)

(A)

(a) The Claimant's claim succeeds.
(b) The Respondent shall pay to the Claimant in full and final settlement of his claim the sum of [£x] provided that if the Claimant has accepted all or any of

[71] See para. 2–842 re taxing costs, and who should do it.

the *ex gratis* payment offered by the Respondent the amount shall be reduced accordingly. For the avoidance of doubt, the sum of [£x] is to be paid net).

(c) The Respondent shall pay to the Claimant the sum of [£x] which sum represents the amount of the Claimant's Registration Fee payable under the Rules of the Scheme

(B)

(d) The Claimant's claim fails.

(e) The Claimant shall pay to the Respondent the sum of [£x] being the amount representing the Respondent's Registration Fee payable under the Rules of the Scheme.

Given under my hand this ( ) day of ( ) 199

....

(Signature of arbitrator)

Witnessed by: ....

NOTES

1.7 It may not be necessary to specify the time within which payment is to be made since usually code arbitration Rules provide that payment is to be made within 21 days. The arbitrator should check the situation. The wording in parenthesis in note 1.6(b) will be appropriate in cases where the Respondent has already made an *ex gratia* payment.

1.8 In those exceptional cases where the arbitrator decides that a successful party should NOT recover his registration fee, the relevant paragraph would be omitted and the arbitrator would explain in his reasons why he has exercised his discretion in the way he has.

1.9 The annex referred to in paragraph 1.6 above would be headed "These reasons are given with and form part of my Award".

73. Interim award

[*Heading as in suggestion [54] but change "final award" to "interim award"*]

[*Paragraphs 1, 2, 3 and 4 as in suggestion [54], then continue:*]

1.1 (At the hearing) OR (By letters from the parties dated [*etc.*]) it was agreed between the parties that I should determine as a preliminary issue Issue 1, and publish an interim award upon it.

1.2 The case for the claimants on this issue was ....

1.3 The Case for the respondents was ....

1.4 In my judgment ....

1.5 I therefore determine this preliminary issue in favour of the (claimants) (respondents) and I therefore DO AWARD AND DETERMINE that (*e.g.* the respondents are liable to the claimants for damages for the breach of contract alleged in paragraph .... of the Claimant's Statement of Case).

1.6 This award is made as my interim award. The question of the costs of this preliminary issue and of this interim award is reserved, as are all other issues in the arbitration.

Dated ....

(Signed) ....

74. Interim awards reserving costs for later decision

Interim award, final as to all matters except costs

[*Heading as in suggestion [54], but change "final award" to "interim award"*]

[*Paragraphs 1 to 9 as in suggestion 54, then continue:*]

1.1 The parties have agreed that this award should be final as to all matters other than costs. I reserve my award as to the costs of the reference including liability for my fees as between the parties. In all other respects this award is my final award.

Dated ....

(Signed) ....

Arbitrator

75. Clause reserving costs and giving directions

[*Heading of award as in suggestion [54] but change "final award" to "interim award (Final except as to costs)"*]

[*Paragraphs 1 to 9 as in Suggestion [54], then continue:*]

1.1 This award is final as to all matters except costs.

1.2 I shall now proceed to make an award as to costs.

If either party wishes me to convene a hearing to receive submissions as to costs it should notify me, and the other party, in writing within [10] days of the date of this award. If neither party so notifies me, I will consider any written submissions as to costs (including information as to any Calderbank offer intender to be relied upon) received at the above address within a further 10 days.

76. Clause reserving costs but making an award "nisi" as to costs and giving directions

[*Heading of award as in suggestion [54], but change "final award" to "interim award (Final except as to costs)"*]

[*Paragraphs 1 to 9 as in Suggestion [54], then continue:*]

1.1 This award is final as to all matters except costs.

1.2 As to costs:

1.3 If neither party made any submissions to me as to costs I would determine and award that

....

....

1.4 If either party wishes to submit to me that I should make some order different from that indicated, or no order, it should notify me, and the other party, in writing within [10] days of the date of this award. Such notification should state what order it contends for, and

either written submissions (including information as to any Calderbank offer intended to be relied upon) showing why I should make the order asked for

or notice requesting me to arrange an oral hearing on the question of costs.

If upon the expiry of 10 days from the publication of this award I have not received such a notification, I will issue a final award in the terms set out in paragraph A above.

77. Final award incorporating alternative final award

[*Heading and paragraph 1 as suggestion [54], then continue:*]

1.1 I held a hearing on the .... 19 .... at which the claimants were represented by Mr R.S. of Counsel and the respondents by Miss T.V. of Messrs. Smith and Jones, Solicitors. During the hearing a point of law was raised, which was formulated by agreement between the advocates as follows:
"Whether on a true construction of the contract dated the 27 June 1991 the obligation of the respondents was to deliver 220 tons not later than 1st November 1991 and the balance of 230 tons not later than 1st January 1992 (as the claimants contend) or whether the said obligation was to deliver 450 tons not later than 1st January 1992 (as the respondents contend)"
The parties intimated that the unsuccessful party might wish to appeal against my decision on this issue, and they therefore requested me to make a final award but to include also an alternative final award to take effect if my decision upon the above issue was reversed by the Court.

1.2 The other issues put for my determination were agreed as follows:
Issue 2: ....
Issue 3: ....

1.3 [*From here onwards as in paragraphs [ ] in suggestion [ ]*]

1.4 If I had decided the first issue in favour of the .... I would have determined and awarded that .... and I would have award that the costs of this arbitration and award ....

Dated ....

(Signed) ....

Arbitrator

78. Award by umpire

IN THE MATTER OF AN ARBITRATION

BETWEEN

L.M. plc

and

P.Q. plc

FINAL AWARD TO E.F. UMPIRE

1.1 By an arbitration clause in a contract made the .... 19 .... between the above named parties

OR

(By an arbitration agreement made the .... 19 .... between the above named parties) it was provided that (copy from contract or agreement, e.g.: "Any dispute or difference should be referred to the arbitration of an arbitrator to be appointed by each party or if they disagreed by an umpire to be appointed by the arbitrators.")

1.2 By letter dated the .... 19 .... L.M. plc appointed Mr A.B. as arbitrator and by letter dated the .... 19 .... P.Q. plc appointed Mr C.D. as arbitrator.

1.3 By a letter of appointment dated the .... 19 .... A.B. and C.D. having disagreed appointed me as Umpire pursuant to the said agreement.

[*Then continue as in award of single arbitrator, as appropriate.*]

79. Clauses for awards—rent review—declaration that landlord has unreasonably withheld consent

I DO HEREBY AWARD AND DECLARE that the respondent has unreasonably withheld its consent to the assignment to A.N. Other plc mentioned in paragraph X of the claimants Statement of Case.

AND I DO FURTHER AWARD AND DECLARE that the claimants are now entitled to proceed with the assignment therein mentioned without the consent of the respondents.

80. Award for the delivery up of property, with alternative money award

I DO HEREBY AWARD AND DIRECT that the respondents do deliver up to the claimants not later than the .... 19 .... (or on such later date as the claimants may in their discretion allow) the property specified in paragraph X of the Statement of Claim, and that in default thereof the respondents do pay to the claimants the sum of £ .... .

81. Letter publishing award

Dear Sirs,

Arbitration between L.M. plc and P.Q. plc

I have now made my award in this arbitration. It may be taken up by either party at my office, on payment of my charges set out in the attached fee note. On the award being taken up by one party only, I will unless otherwise requested despatch a copy by first class post to the other party.

Yours faithfully,

Arbitrator

L.M. plc	P.Q. plc
Copy to: their (Solicitors)	Copy to: their (Solicitors)
(Other Representative)	(Other Representative)
Messrs	Messrs ....

82. Specimen letter—arbitrator's charges

Messrs

....

....

.... *For the attention of*

and

Messrs

....

....

.... *For the attention of*

Gentlemen,

In the matter of an Arbitration

between

....

and

....

in respect of

....

It was indicated at the preliminary meeting which took place on .... that I would give consideration to the arbitrator's costs in the Reference in the light of what transpired at that meeting. I have now done so and propose to charge a fixed fee of .... . % of the mean of the .... rental values contended for by the parties plus a time charge of £ .... per day, pro rata for part of a day, in excess of .... days, subject to a minimum fee of £ ....

In the event that the parties are themselves able to reach agreement at any stage before an award is made my charge would be as follows, depending on the period within which the parties reach an accord:—

Period 1	Up to and including the date of the Preliminary Meeting	£
Period 2	From the day after the end of Period 1 up to and including the date for exchanging statements of submissions	£
Period 3	From the day after the end of Period 2 up to and including the date of the preliminary inspection .... of the full fee subject to a minimum of	£
Period 4	From the day after the end of Period 3 up to and including the date of the full inspection .... of the full fee subject to a minimum of	£
Period 5	From the day after the end of Period 4 the full fee subject to a minimum of	£

Out of pocket expenses and disbursements; costs incidental to the proceedings, *e.g.* the hiring of rooms and the taking of legal and other professional advice and VAT will be charged additionally to the amounts mentioned above.

Yours truly,

MISCELLANEOUS

83. ICC—arbitrator's declaration of acceptance and statement of independence[83]

I, the undersigned,

Name .... First Name ....

☐ hereby declare that I accept to serve as arbitrator under the ICC Rules of Arbitration in the instant case. In so declaring, I confirm that I have familiarised myself with the requirements of the ICC Rules of Arbitration and am able and available to serve as an arbitrator in accordance with all of the requirements of those Rules and accept to be remunerated in accordance therewith.

(If this box is checked, please also check one *of the two following boxes. The choice of which box to check will be determined after you have taken into account,* inter alia, *whether there exists any past or present relationship, direct or indirect, with any of the parties, their counsel, whether financial, professional or of another kind and whether the nature of any such relationship is such that disclosure is called for pursuant to the criteria set out below.* Any doubt should be resolved in favour of disclosure.)

☐ I am independent of each of the parties and intend to remain so; to the best of my knowledge, there are no facts or circumstances, past or present, that need be disclosed because they might be of such nature as to call into question my independence in the eyes of any of the parties.

☐ I am independent of each of the parties and intend to remain so; however, in consideration of Article 2, paragraph 7 of the ICC Rules of Arbitration,[73] I wish to call your

[72] Please mark the relevant box or boxes.

[73] Article 2(7) of the ICC Rules: "Every arbitrator appointed or confirmed by the Court must be and remain independent of the parties in the arbitration. Before appointment or confirmation by

attention to the following facts or circumstances which I hereafter disclose because they might be of such a nature as to call into question my independence in the eyes of any of the parties. (Use separate sheet if necessary.)

☐ hereby declare that I decline to serve as arbitrator in the subject case. (If you wish to state the reasons for checking this box, please do so.)

Place: ....Date: ....Signature: ....

84. Possible terms of engagement for a barrister/arbitrator

BASIS OF ENGAGEMENT

(January 1997 Edition)

To whom it may concern

1.1 *Fees and Disbursements*

I charge for my work by way of time charges. However, as will be seen from paragraph 3.1 below, I am happy to entertain different arrangements if preferred.

1.2 *The Hourly Rate*

Time expended on or in connection with this case is charged at the rate of £ per hour. The phrase "in connection with" is intended to include both time expended in directly working upon a case as well as time otherwise expended—*e.g.* in travel connected with the case.

This can be an onerous obligation in some cases, and I am happy to consider or to make alternative proposals. In particular, if it is possible to relate more than one item of work to a particular journey, then, provided the arrangements are made prior to commencement of the travel, the travel time will be disposed between the items of work in what I consider to be a reasonable manner, or as agreed in advance of departure.

1.3 *Validity of Rate*

The rate quoted above is valid for time expended in 1997 I reserve the right to vary the rate for time expended after [*date*]. This right may be exercised at any time, but if it is exercised after [*date*], then the varied rate will only apply to time expended after the date of variation. My right to charge the varied rate is not dependent upon prior notification to the client.

1.4 *Disbursements*

Disbursements are charged in addition. "Disbursements" includes such matters as travel and accommodation charges, and fax, Lexis, courier and photocopying expenses.

the Court, a prospective arbitrator shall disclose in writing to the Secretary General of the Court any facts or circumstances which might be of such a nature as to call into question the arbitrator's independence in the eyes of the parties. Upon receipt of such information the Secretary General of the Court shall provide it to the parties in writing and fix a time-limit for any comments from them. An arbitrator shall immediately disclose in writing to the Secretary General of the Court and the parties any facts or circumstances of a similar nature which may arise between the arbitrator's appointment or confirmation by the Court and the notification of the final award."

2.1 *Advance Bookings*

I am happy to book time in my diary in advance. I am unwilling to follow the practice of some clerks and double and treble book such time. Equally I am unhappy to have substantial amounts of time locked up which may never be used. Accordingly, booking charges will apply as follows:

2.2 The first five consecutive calendar days of the first booking in a case do not attract a booking fee at all. For any other period there is a booking fee of £ .... per week, payable prior to the booking being entered into the diary.

2.3 This booking fee is only returnable if I am unable to hold the booking. (Bookings are accepted on the basis that I am not liable for any costs of whatsoever nature of or occasioned by my inability to keep the booking. ''Inability'' includes but is not limited to illness and overrun of other cases.) If the relevant week is actually utilized in whole or in part the booking fee for that week is treated as a credit on account of the fees for that week. This provision applies whatever the method of charging.

3.1 *Charging other than by hourly rates*

If it is desired to have a more traditional arrangement with, for example, brief fees and refreshers rather than an hourly rate, please let me or my assistant know and we will be happy to give you a quotation. Please also let one of us know if a quotation in a different currency is required. Payment can be effected (perfectly legally so far as I am concerned!) to banks outside the UK if that too is desired.

4.1 *Arrangements through a Clerk*

If it is preferred to deal through a clerk, please communicate with the clerk to my [ ] Chambers, as follows: ....

5.1 *Queries*

I hope that the above is clear, but if it is not, please indicate the problem and I or my clerk (as appropriate) will endeavour to help.

6.1 *Value Added Tax*

Where appropriate Value Added Tax is added to the above fees at the rate in force at the time the work is billed.

7.1 *Billing*

7.2 Save as provided above and save as otherwise expressly agreed in writing, and whatever the method of charging, I reserve the right to bill fees and disbursements from time to time during the course of the case. Such billings will be in arrear, but will not be more frequently than monthly. Fees are payable within 28 days of billing and if not so paid give rise to a right on my part to cease further work on the case. This right is in addition to any other that I may have under these terms and/or the general law.

7.3 Interest will be charges on fees paid late at the rate of 15% per annum with quarterly rests.

7.4 When sitting as an arbitrator, each party is jointly and severally liable to me for all fees and disbursements and I shall be entitled to order, at any time, the provision of reasonable security.

8.1 *Signifying agreement*

A second copy of these terms is attached. I would be obliged if each party would sign and return that copy to signify their agreement to them.

Appendix 2
Statutes and Orders

COURTS AND LEGAL SERVICES ACT 1990 (c. 41)

PART I

Evidence

....

Evidence given in arbitrations on small claims

6. In section 64 of the County Courts Act 1984 (references to arbitration) the following subsections shall be inserted after subsection (2)—

"(2A) County court rules may prescribe the procedures and rules of evidence to be followed on any reference under subsection (1) or (2).

(2B) Rules made under subsection (2A) may, in particular, make provision with respect to the manner of taking and questioning evidence."

....

PART V

Arbitration

Arbitration by official referee

99. For section 11 of the Arbitration Act 1950 (reference to official referee) there shall be substituted—

"**Power of official referee to take arbitrations**

11.—(1) An official referee may, if in all the circumstances he thinks fit, accept appointment as sole arbitrator, or as umpire, by or by virtue of an arbitration agreement.

(2) An official referee shall not accept appointment as arbitrator or umpire unless the Lord Chief Justice has informed him that, having regard to the state of official referees' business, he can be made available to do so.

(3) The fees payable for the services of an official referee as arbitrator or umpire shall be taken in the High Court.

(4) Schedule 3 to the Administration of Justice Act 1970 (which modifies this

Act in relation to arbitration by judges, in particular by substituting the Court of Appeal for the High Court in provisions whereby arbitrators and umpires, their proceedings and awards are subject to control and review by the court) shall have effect in relation to official referees appointed as arbitrators or umpires as it has effect in relation to judge-arbitrators and judge-umpires (within the meaning of that Schedule).

(5) Any jurisdiction which is exercisable by the High Court in relation to arbitrators and umpires otherwise than under this Act shall, in relation to an official referee appointed as arbitrator or umpire, be exercisable instead by the Court of Appeal.

(6) In this section ''official referee'' means any person nominated under section 68(1)(a) of the Supreme Court Act 1981 to deal with official referees' business.

(7) Rules of the Supreme Court may make provision for—

(a) cases in which it is necessary to allocate references made under or by virtue of arbitration agreements to official referees;

(b) the transfer of references from one official referee to another.''

Specific powers of arbitration exercisable by High Court

100. After section 43 of the Supreme Court Act 1981 there shall be inserted the following section—

''Specific powers of arbitration exercisable by High Court

43A. In any cause or matter proceeding in the High Court in connection with any contract incorporating an arbitration agreement which confers specific powers upon the arbitrator, the High Court may, if all parties to the agreement agree, exercise any such powers.''

Power of parties in certain cases to fill vacancy

101.—(1) In section 10 of the Arbitration Act 1950 (power of court in certain cases to appoint an arbitrator or umpire), the following shall be substituted for subsection (3)—

''(3) In any case where—

(a) an arbitration agreement provides that the reference shall be to three arbitrators, one to be appointed by each party and the third to be appointed by the two appointed by the parties or in some other manner specified in the agreement; and

(b) one of the parties (''the party in default'') refuses to appoint an arbitrator or does not do so within the time specified in the agreement or, if no time is specified, within a reasonable time,

the other party to the agreement, having appointed his arbitrator, may serve the party in default with a written notice to appoint an arbitrator.

(3A) A notice under subsection (3) must indicate whether it is served for the purposes of subsection (3B) or for the purposes of subsection (3C).

(3B) Where a notice is served for the purposes of this subsection, then unless a contrary intention is expressed in the agreement, if the required appointment is not made within seven clear days after the service of the notice—

(a) the party who gave the notice may appoint his arbitrator to act as sole arbitrator in the reference; and

(b) his award shall be binding on both parties as if he had been appointed by consent

(3C) Where a notice is served for the purposes of this subsection, then, if the required appointment is not made within seven clear days after the service of the notice, the High Court or a judge thereof may, on the application of the party who gave the notice, appoint an arbitrator on behalf of the party in default who shall have the like powers to act in the reference and make an award (and, if the case so requires, the like duty in relation to the appointment of a third arbitrator) as if he had been appointed in accordance with the terms of the agreement.

(3D) The High Court or a judge thereof may set aside any appointment made by virtue of subsection (3B).''

(2) Section 10 of the Act of 1950 shall continue to apply in relation to any arbitration agreement entered into before the commencement of this section as if this section had not been enacted.

(3) Subsection (2) does not apply if a contrary intention is expressed in the arbitration agreement, whether or not as the result of a variation made after the commencement of this section.

Want of prosecution

102. After section 13 of the Arbitration Act 1950 (time for making an award) there shall be inserted—

''Want of prosecution

13A.—(1) Unless a contrary intention is expressed in the arbitration agreement, the arbitrator or umpire shall have power to make an award dismissing any claim in a dispute referred to him if it appears to him that the conditions mentioned in subsection (2) are satisfied.

(2) The conditions are—

(a) that there has been inordinate and inexcusable delay on the part of the claimant in pursuing the claim; and

(b) that the delay—

(i) will give rise to a substantial risk that it is not possible to have a fair resolution of the issues in that claim, or

(ii) has caused, or is likely to cause or to have caused, serious prejudice to the respondent.

(3) For the purpose of keeping the provision made by this section and the corresponding provision which applies in relation to proceedings in the High Court in step, the Secretary of State may by order made by statutory instrument amend subsection (2) above.

(4) Before making any such order the Secretary of State shall consult the Lord Chancellor and such other persons as he considers appropriate.

(5) No such order shall be made unless a draft of the order has been laid before, and approved by resolution of, each House of Parliament.''

Repeal of High Court's power to order discovery etc.

103. Section 12(6)(b) of the Arbitration Act 1950 (power of High Court to order discovery of documents and interrogatories) shall cease to have effect.

CIVIL EVIDENCE ACT 1995 (c. 38)

An Act to provide for the admissibility of hearsay evidence, the proof of certain documentary evidence and the admissibility and proof of official actuarial tables in civil proceedings; and for connected purposes. [8th November 1995]

BE IT ENACTED by the Queen's most Excellent Majesty, by and with the advice and consent of the Lords Spiritual and Temporal, and Commons, in this present Parliament assembled, and by the authority of the same, as follows:—

Admissibility of hearsay evidence

1.—(1) In civil proceedings evidence shall not be excluded on the ground that it is hearsay.

(2) In this Act—

(a) "hearsay" means a statement made otherwise than by a person while giving oral evidence in the proceedings which is tendered as evidence of the matters stated; and
(b) references to hearsay include hearsay of whatever degree.

(3) Nothing in this Act affects the admissibility of evidence admissible apart from this section.

(4) The provisions of sections 2 to 6 (safeguards and supplementary provisions relating to hearsay evidence) do not apply in relation to hearsay evidence admissible apart from this section, notwithstanding that it may also be admissible by virtue of this section.

Safeguards in relation to heresay evidence

2.—(1) A party proposing to adduce hearsay evidence in civil proceedings shall, subject to the following provisions of this section, give to the other party or parties to the proceedings—

(a) such notice (if any) of that fact, and
(b) on request, such particulars of or relating to the evidence, as is reasonable and practicable in the circumstances for the purpose of enabling him or them to deal with any matters arising from its being hearsay.

(2) Provision may be made by rules of court—

(a) specifying classes of proceedings or evidence in relation to which subsection (1) does not apply, and
(b) as to the manner in which (including the time within which) the duties imposed by that subsection are to be complied with in the cases where it does apply

(3) Subsection (1) may also be excluded by agreement of the parties; and compliance

with the duty to give notice may in any case be waived by the person to whom notice is required to be given.

(4) A failure to comply with subsection (1), or with rules under subsection (2)(b), does not affect the admissibility of the evidence but may be taken into account by the court—

(a) in considering the exercise of its powers with respect to the course of proceedings and costs, and
(b) as a matter adversely affecting the weight to be given to the evidence in accordance with section 4.

3.—Rules of court may provide that where a party to civil proceedings adduces hearsay evidence of a statement made by a person and does not call that person as a witness, any other party to the proceedings may, with the leave of the court, call that person as a witness and cross-examine him on the statement as if he had been called by the first-mentioned party and as if the hearsay statement were his evidence in chief.

4.—(1) In estimating the weight (if any) to be given to hearsay evidence in civil proceedings the court shall have regard to any circumstances from which any inference can reasonably be drawn as to the reliability or otherwise of the evidence.

(2) Regard may be had, in particular, to the following—

(a) whether it would have been reasonable and practicable for the party by whom the evidence was adduced to have produced the maker of the original statement as a witness;
(b) whether the original statement was made contemporaneously with the occurrence or existence of the matters stated;
(c) whether the evidence involves multiple hearsay;
(d) whether any person involved had any motive to conceal or misrepresent matters;
(e) whether the original statement was an edited account, or was made in collaboration with another or for a particular purpose;
(f) whether the circumstances in which the evidence is adduced as hearsay are such as to suggest an attempt to prevent proper evaluation of its weight.

Supplementary provisions as to hearsay evidence

5.—(1) Hearsay evidence shall not be admitted in civil proceedings if or to the extent that it is shown to consist of, or to be proved by means of, a statement made by a person who at the time he made the statement was not competent as a witness.

For this purpose "not competent as a witness" means suffering from such mental or physical infirmity, or lack of understanding, as would render a person incompetent as a witness in civil proceedings; but a child shall be treated as competent as a witness if he satisfies the requirements of section 96(2)(a) and (b) of the Children Act 1989 (conditions for reception of unsworn evidence of child).

(2) Where in civil proceedings hearsay evidence is adduced and the maker of the original statement, or of any statement relied upon to prove another statement, is not called as a witness—

(a) evidence which if he had been so called would be admissible for the purpose of attacking or supporting his credibility as a witness is admissible for that purpose in the proceedings; and

(b) evidence tending to prove that, whether before or after he made the statement, he made any other statement inconsistent with it is admissible for the purpose of showing that he had contradicted himself.

Provided that evidence may not be given of any matter of which, if he had been called as a witness and had denied that matter in cross-examination, evidence could not have been adduced by the cross-examining party.

6.—(1) Subject as follows, the provisions of this Act as to hearsay evidence in civil proceedings apply equally (but with any necessary modifications) in relation to a previous statement made by a person called as a witness in the proceedings.

(2) A party who has called or intends to call a person as a witness in civil proceedings may not in those proceedings adduce evidence of a previous statement made by that person, except—

(a) with the leave of the court, or
(b) for the purpose of rebutting a suggestion that his evidence has been fabricated.

This shall not be construed as preventing a witness statement (that is, a written statement of oral evidence which a party to the proceedings intends to lead) from being adopted by a witness in giving evidence or treated as his evidence.

(3) Where in the case of civil proceedings section 3, 4 or 5 of the Criminal Procedure Act 1865 applies, which make provision as to—

(a) how far a witness may be discredited by the party producing him,
(b) the proof of contradictory statements made by a witness, and
(c) cross-examination as to previous statements in writing,

this Act does not authorise the adducing of evidence of a previous inconsistent or contradictory statement otherwise than in accordance with those sections.

This is without prejudice to any provision made by rules of court under section 3 above (power to call witness for cross-examination on hearsay statement).

(4) Nothing in this Act affects any of the rules of law as to the circumstances in which, where a person called as a witness in civil proceedings is cross-examined on a document used by him to refresh his memory, that document may be made evidence in the proceedings.

(5) Nothing in this section shall be construed as preventing a statement of any description referred to above from being admissible by virtue of section 1 as evidence of the matters stated.

7.—(1) The common law rule effectively preserved by section 9(1) and (2)(a) of the Civil Evidence Act 1968 (admissibility of admissions adverse to a party) is superseded by the provisions of this Act.

(2) The common law rules effectively preserved by section 9(l) and (2)(b) to (d) of the Civil Evidence Act 1968, that is, any rule of law whereby in civil proceedings—

(a) published works dealing with matters of a public nature (for example, histories, scientific works, dictionaries and maps) are admissible as evidence of facts of a public nature stated in them,
(b) public documents (for example, public registers, and returns made under public

authority with respect to matters of public interest) are admissible as evidence of facts stated in them, or

(c) records (for example, the records of certain courts, treaties, Crown grants, pardons and commissions) are admissible as evidence of facts stated in them,

shall continue to have effect.

(3) The common law rules effectively preserved by section 9(3) and (4) of the Civil Evidence Act 1968, that is, any rule of law whereby in civil proceedings—

(a) evidence of a person's reputation is admissible for the purpose of proving his good or bad character, or

(b) evidence of reputation or family tradition is admissible—

(i) for the purpose of proving or disproving pedigree or the existence of a marriage, or

(ii) for the purpose of proving or disproving the existence of any public or general right or of identifying any person or thing,

shall continue to have effect in so far as they authorise the court to treat such evidence as proving or disproving that matter.

Where any such rule applies, reputation or family tradition shall be treated for the purposes of this Act as a fact and not as a statement or multiplicity of statements about the matter in question.

(4) The words in which a rule of law mentioned in this section is described are intended only to identify the rule and shall not be construed as altering it in anyway.

Other matters

8.—(1) Where a statement contained in a document is admissible as evidence in civil proceedings, it may be proved—

(a) by the production of that document, or

(b) whether or not that document is still in existence, by the production of a copy of that document or of the material part of it,

authenticated in such manner as the court may approve.

(2) It is immaterial for this purpose how many removes there are between a copy and the original.

9.—(1) A document which is shown to form part of the records of a business or public authority may be received in evidence in civil proceedings without further proof.

(2) A document shall be taken to form part of the records of a business or public authority if there is produced to the court a certificate to that effect signed by an officer of the business or authority to which the records belong.

For this purpose—

(a) a document purporting to be a certificate signed by an officer of a business or public authority shall be deemed to have been duly given by such an officer and signed by him; and

(b) a certificate shall be treated as signed by a person if it purports to bear a facsimile of his signature.

(3) The absence of an entry in the records of a business or public authority may be proved in civil proceedings by affidavit of an officer of the business or authority to which the records belong.

(4) In this section—

''records'' means records in whatever form;

''business'' includes any activity regularly carried on over a period of time, whether for profit or not, by any body (whether corporate or not) or by an individual;

''officer'' includes any person occupying a responsible position in relation to the relevant activities of the business or public authority or in relation to its records; and

''public authority'' includes any public or statutory undertaking, any government department and any person holding office under Her Majesty.

(5) The court may, having regard to the circumstances of the case, direct that all or any of the above provisions of this section do not apply in relation to a particular document or record, or description of documents or records.

10. [Admissibility and proof of Ogden Tables.]

General

11. In this Act ''civil proceedings'' means civil proceedings, before any tribunal, in relation to which the strict rules of evidence apply, whether as a matter of law or by agreement of the parties.

References to ''the court'' and ''rules of court'' shall be construed accordingly.

Provisions as to rules of court

12.—(1) Any power to make rules of court regulating the practice or procedure of the court in relation to civil proceedings includes power to make such provision as may be necessary or expedient for carrying into effect the provisions of this Act.

(2) Any rules of court made for the purposes of this Act as it applies in relation to proceedings in the High Court apply, except in so far as their operation is excluded by agreement, to arbitration proceedings to which this Act applies, subject to such modifications as may be appropriate.

Any question arising as to what modifications are appropriate shall be determined, in default of agreement, by the arbitrator or umpire, as the case may be.

13. In this Act—

''civil proceedings'' has the meaning given by section 11 and ''court'' and ''rules of court'' shall be construed in accordance with that section;

''document'' means anything in which information of any description is recorded, and ''copy'', in relation to a document, means anything onto which information recorded in the document has been copied, by whatever means and whether directly or indirectly;

''hearsay'' shall be construed in accordance with section 1(2);

''oral evidence'' includes evidence which, by reason of a defect of speech or hearing, a person called as a witness gives in writing or by signs;

''the original statement'', in relation to hearsay evidence, means the underlying statement (if any) by—

(a) in the case of evidence of fact, a person having personal knowledge of that fact, or

(b) in the case of evidence of opinion, the person whose opinion it is; and "statement" means any representation of fact or opinion, however made.

Savings

14.—(1) Nothing in this Act affects the exclusion of evidence on grounds other than that it is hearsay.

This applies whether the evidence falls to be excluded in pursuance of any enactment or rule of law, for failure to comply with rules of court or an order of the court, or otherwise.

(2) Nothing in this Act affects the proof of documents by means other than those specified in section 8 or 9.

(3) Nothing in this Act affects the operation of the following enactments—

(a) section 2 of the Documentary, Evidence Act 1868 (mode of proving certain official documents);

(b) section 2 of the Documentary Evidence Act 1882 (documents printed under the superintendence of Stationery Office)

(c) section 1 of the Evidence (Colonial Statutes) Act 1907 (proof of statutes of certain legislatures);

(d) section 1 of the Evidence (Foreign, Dominion and Colonial Documents) Act 1933 (proof and effect of registers and official certificates of certain countries);

(e) section 5 of the Oaths and Evidence (Overseas Authorities and Countries) Act 1963 (provision in respect of public registers of other countries).

15. [Consequential amendments and repeals.]

16.—(1) This Act may be cited as the Civil Evidence Act 1995.

(2) The provisions of this Act come into force on such day as the Lord Chancellor may appoint by order made by statutory instrument, and different days may be appointed for different provisions and for different purposes.

(3) An order under subsection (2) may contain such transitional provisions as appear to the Lord Chancellor to be appropriate; and subject to any such provision, the provisions of this Act shall not apply in relation to proceedings begun before commencement.

(4) This Act extends to England and Wales.

(5) [Provisions applying in Northern Ireland.]

(6) [Extent of amending or repealing provisions.]

[Schedules 1 and 2 contain consequential amendments and repeals and are not reproduced here.]

ARBITRATION ACT 1996 (c. 23)

An Act to restate and improve the law relating to arbitration pursuant to an arbitration agreement; to make other provision relating to arbitration and arbitration awards; and for connected purposes. [17th June 1996]

PART I

ARBITRATION PURSUANT TO AN ARBITRATION AGREEMENT

Introductory

General principles

1. The provisions of this Part are founded on the following principles, and shall be construed accordingly—

(a) the object of arbitration is to obtain the fair resolution of disputes by an impartial tribunal without unnecessary delay or expense;

(b) the parties should be free to agree how their disputes are resolved, subject only to such safeguards as are necessary in the public interest;

(c) in matters governed by this Part the court should not intervene except as provided by this Part.

Scope of application of provisions

2.—(1) The provisions of this Part apply where the seat of the arbitration is in England and Wales or Northern Ireland.

(2) The following sections apply even if the seat of the arbitration is outside England and Wales or Northern Ireland or no seat has been designated or determined]—

(a) sections 9 to 11 (stay of legal proceedings, &c.), and

(b) section 66 (enforcement of arbitral awards).

(3) The powers conferred by the following sections apply even if the seat of the arbitration is outside England and Wales or Northern Ireland or no seat has been designated or determined]—

(a) section 43 (securing the attendance of witnesses), and

(b) section 44 (court powers exercisable in support of arbitral proceedings);

but the court may refuse to exercise any such power if, in the opinion of the court, the fact that the seat of the arbitration is outside England and Wales or Northern Ireland, or that when designated or determined the seat is likely to be outside England and Wales or Northern Ireland, makes it inappropriate to do so.

(4) The court may exercise a power conferred by any provision of this Part not mentioned in subsection (2) or (3) for the purpose of supporting the arbitral process where—

(a) no seat of the arbitration has been designated or determined, and

(b) by reason of a connection with England and Wales or Northern Ireland the court is satisfied that it is appropriate to do so.

(5) Section 7 (separability of arbitration agreement) and section 8 (death of a party) apply where the law applicable to the arbitration agreement is the law of England and Wales or Northern Ireland even if the seat of the arbitration is outside England and Wales or Northern Ireland or has not been designated or determined.

The seat of the arbitration

3. In this Part "the seat of the arbitration" means the juridical seat of the arbitration designated—

(a) by the parties to the arbitration agreement, or
(b) by any arbitral or other institution or person vested by the parties with powers in that regard, or
(c) by the arbitral tribunal if so authorised by the parties,

or determined, in the absence of any such designation, having regard to the parties' agreement and all the relevant circumstances.

Mandatory and non-mandatory provisions

4.—(1) The mandatory provisions of this Part are listed in Schedule 1 and have effect notwithstanding any agreement to the contrary.

(2) The other provisions of this Part (the "non-mandatory provisions") allow the parties to make their own arrangements by agreement but provide rules which apply in the absence of such agreement.

(3) The parties may make such arrangements by agreeing to the application of institutional rules or providing any other means by which a matter may be decided.

(4) It is immaterial whether or not the law applicable to the parties' agreement is the law of England and Wales or, as the case may be, Northern Ireland.

(5) The choice of a law other than the law of England and Wales or Northern Ireland as the applicable law in respect of a matter provided for by a non-mandatory provision of this Part is equivalent to an agreement making provision about that matter.

For this purpose an applicable law determined in accordance with the parties' agreement, or which is objectively determined in the absence of any express or implied choice, shall be treated as chosen by the parties.

Agreements to be in writing

5.—(1) The provisions of this Part apply only where the arbitration agreement is in writing, and any other agreement between the parties as to any matter is effective for the purposes of this Part only if in writing.

The expressions "agreement", "agree" and "agreed" shall be construed accordingly.

(2) There is an agreement in writing

(a) if the agreement is made in writing (whether or not it is signed by the parties),
(b) if the agreement is made by exchange of communications in writing, or
(c) if the agreement is evidenced in writing.

(3) Where parties agree otherwise than in writing by reference to terms which are in writing, they make an agreement in writing.

(4) An agreement is evidenced in writing if an agreement made otherwise than in writing is recorded by one of the parties, or by a third party, with the authority of the parties to the agreement.

(5) An exchange of written submissions in arbitral or legal proceedings in which the existence of an agreement otherwise than in writing is alleged by one party against another party and not denied by the other party in his response constitutes as between those parties an agreement in writing to the effect alleged.

(6) References in this Part to anything being written or in writing include its being recorded by any means.

The arbitration agreement

Definition of arbitration agreement

6.—(1) In this Part an "arbitration agreement" means an agreement to submit to arbitration present or future disputes (whether they are contractual or not).

(2) The reference in an agreement to a written form of arbitration clause or to a document containing an arbitration clause constitutes an arbitration agreement if the reference is such as to make that clause part of the agreement.

Separability of arbitration agreement

7. Unless otherwise agreed by the parties, an arbitration agreement which forms or was intended to form part of another agreement (whether or not in writing) shall not be regarded as invalid, non-existent or ineffective because that other agreement is invalid, or did not come into existence or has become ineffective, and it shall for that purpose be treated as a distinct agreement.

Whether agreement discharged by death of a party

9.—(1) Unless otherwise agreed by the parties, an arbitration agreement is not discharged by the death of a party and may be enforced by or against the personal representatives of that party.

(2) Subsection (1) does not affect the operation of any enactment or rule of law by virtue of which a substantive right or obligation is extinguished by death.

Stay of legal proceedings

Stay of legal proceedings

8.—(1) A party to an arbitration agreement against whom legal proceedings are brought (whether by way of claim or counterclaim) in respect of a matter which under the agreement is to be referred to arbitration may (upon notice to the other parties to the proceedings) apply to the court in which the proceedings have been brought to stay the proceedings so far as they concern that matter.

(2) An application may be made notwithstanding that the matter is to be referred to arbitration only after the exhaustion of other dispute resolution procedures.

(3) An application may not be made by a person before taking the appropriate procedural step (if any) to acknowledge the legal proceedings against him or after he has taken any step in those proceedings to answer the substantive claim.

(4) on an application under this section the court shall grant a stay unless satisfied that the arbitration agreement is null and void, inoperative, or incapable of being performed.

(5) If the court refuses to stay the legal proceedings, any provision that an award is a condition precedent to the bringing of legal proceedings in respect of any matter is of no effect in relation to those proceedings.

Reference of interpleader issue to arbitration

10.—(1) Where in legal proceedings relief by way of interpleader is we granted and any issue between the claimants is one in respect of which there is an arbitration agreement between them, the court granting the relief shall direct that the issue be determined in accordance with the agreement unless the circumstances are such that proceedings brought by a claimant in respect of the matter would not be stayed.

(2) Where subsection (1) applies but the court does not direct that the issue be determined in accordance with the arbitration agreement, any provision that an award is a condition precedent to the bringing of legal proceedings in respect of any matter shall not affect the determination of that issue by the court.

Retention of security where Admiralty proceedings stayed

11.—(1) Where Admiralty proceedings are stayed on the ground that the dispute in question should be submitted to arbitration, the court granting the stay may, if in those proceedings property has been arrested or bail or other security has been given to prevent or obtain release from arrest—

(a) order that the property arrested be retained as security for the satisfaction of any award given in the arbitration in respect of that dispute, or
(b) order that the stay of those proceedings be conditional on the provision of equivalent security for the satisfaction of any such award.

(2) Subject to any provision made by rules of court and to any necessary modifications, the same law and practice shall apply in relation to property retained in pursuance of an order as would apply if it were held for the purposes of proceedings in the court making the order.

Commencement of arbitral proceedings

Power of court to extend time for beginning arbitral proceedings etc.

12.—(1) Where an arbitration agreement to refer future disputes to arbitration provides that a claim shall be barred, or the claimant's right extinguished, unless the claimant takes within a time fixed by the agreement some step—

(a) to begin arbitral proceedings, or
(b) to begin other dispute resolution procedures which must be exhausted before arbitral proceedings can be begun,

the court may by order extend the time for taking that step.

(2) Any party to the arbitration agreement may apply for such an order (upon notice to the other parties), but only after a claim has arisen and after exhausting any available arbitral process for obtaining an extension of time.

(3) The court shall make an order only if satisfied—

(a) that the circumstances are such as were outside the reasonable contemplation of the parties when they agreed the provision in question, and that it would be just to extend the time, or

(b) that the conduct of one party makes it unjust to hold the other party to the strict terms of the provision in question.

(4) The court may extend the time for such period and on such terms as it thinks fit, and may do so whether or not the time previously fixed (by agreement or by a previous order) has expired.

(5) An order under this section does not affect the operation of the Limitation Acts (see section 13).

(6) The leave of the court is required for any appeal from a decision of the court under this section.

Application of Limitation Acts

13.—(1) The Limitation Acts apply to arbitral proceedings as they apply to legal proceedings.

(2) The court may order that in computing the time prescribed by the Limitation Acts for the commencement of proceedings (including arbitral proceedings) in respect of a dispute which was the subject matter—

(a) of an award which the court orders to be set aside or declares to be of no effect, or

(b) of the affected part of an award which the court orders to be set aside in part, or declares to be in part of no effect,

the period between the commencement of the arbitration and the date of the order referred to in paragraph (a) or (b) shall be excluded.

(3) In determining for the purposes of the Limitation Acts when a cause of action accrued, any provision that an award is a condition precedent to the bringing of legal proceedings in respect of a matter to which an arbitration agreement applies shall be disregarded.

(4) In this Part ''the Limitation Acts'' means—

(a) in England and Wales, the Limitation Act 1980, the Foreign Limitation Periods Act 1984 and any other enactment (whenever passed) relating to the limitation of actions;

(b) in Northern Ireland, the Limitation (Northern Ireland) Order 1989, the Foreign Limitation Periods (Northern Ireland) Order 1985 and any other enactment (whenever passed) relating to the limitation of actions.

Commencement of arbitral proceeding

14.—(1) The parties are free to agree when arbitral proceedings are to be regarded as commenced for the purposes of this Part and for the purposes of the Limitation Acts.

(2) If there is no such agreement the following provisions apply.

(3) Where the arbitrator is named or designated in the arbitration agreement, arbitral proceedings are commenced in respect of a matter when one party serves on the other party or parties a notice in writing requiring him or them to submit that matter to the person so named or designated.

(4) Where the arbitrator or arbitrators are to be appointed by the parties, arbitral pro-

ceedings are commenced in respect of a matter when one party serves on the other party or parties notice in writing requiring him or them to appoint an arbitrator or to agree to the appointment of an arbitrator in respect of that matter.

(5) Where the arbitrator or arbitrators are to be appointed by a person other than a party to the proceedings, arbitral proceedings are commenced in respect of a matter when one party gives notice in writing to that person requesting him to make the appointment in respect of that matter.

The arbitral tribunal

The arbitral tribunal

15.—(1) The parties are free to agree on the number of arbitrators to form the tribunal and whether there is to be a chairman or umpire.

(2) Unless otherwise agreed by the parties, an agreement that the number of arbitrators shall be two or any other even number shall be understood as requiring the appointment of an additional arbitrator as chairman of the tribunal.

(3) If there is no agreement as to the number of arbitrators, the tribunal shall consist of a sole arbitrator.

Procedure for appointment of arbitrators

16.—(1) The parties are free to agree on the procedure for appointing the arbitrator or arbitrators, including the procedure for appointing any chairman or umpire.

(2) If or to the extent that there is no such agreement, the following provisions apply.

(3) If the tribunal is to consist of a sole arbitrator, the parties shall jointly appoint the arbitrator not later than 28 days after service of a request in writing by either party to do so.

(4) If the tribunal is to consist of two arbitrators, each party shall appoint one arbitrator not later than 14 days after service of a request in writing by either party to do so.

(5) If the tribunal is to consist of three arbitrators—

(a) each party shall appoint one arbitrator not later than 14 days after service of a request in writing by either party to do so, and
(b) the two so appointed shall forthwith appoint a third arbitrator as the chairman of the tribunal.

(6) If the tribunal is to consist of two arbitrators and an umpire—

(a) each party shall appoint one arbitrator not later than 14 days after service of a request 4 in writing by either party to do so, and
(b) the two so appointed may appoint an umpire at any time after they themselves are appointed and shall do so before any substantive hearing or forthwith if they cannot agree on a matter relating to the arbitration.

(7) In any other case (in particular, if there are more than two parties) section 18 applies as in the case of a failure of the agreed appointment procedure.

Power in case of default to appoint sole arbitrator

17.—(1) Unless the parties otherwise agree, where each of two parties to an arbitration agreement is to appoint an arbitrator and one party ("the party in default") refuses to do so, or fails to do so within the time specified, the other party, having duly appointed his arbitrator, may give notice in writing to the party in default that he proposes to appoint his arbitrator to act as sole arbitrator.

(2) If the party in default does not within 7 clear days of that notice being given—

(a) make the required appointment, and
(b) notify the other party that he has done so,

the other party may appoint his arbitrator as sole arbitrator whose award shall be binding on both parties as if he had been so appointed by agreement.

(3) Where a sole arbitrator has been appointed under subsection (2), the party in default may (upon notice to the appointing party) apply to the court which may set aside the appointment.

(4) The leave of the court is required for any appeal from a decision of the court under this section.

Failure of appointment procedure

18.—(1) The parties are free to agree what is to happen in the event of a failure of the procedure for the appointment of the arbitral tribunal.

There is no failure if an appointment is duly made under section 17 (power in case of default to appoint sole arbitrator), unless that appointment is set aside.

(2) If or to the extent that there is no such agreement any party to the arbitration agreement may (upon notice to the other parties) apply to the court to exercise its powers under this section.

(3) Those powers are—

(a) to give directions as to the making of any necessary appointments;
(b) to direct that the tribunal shall be constituted by such appointments (or any one or more of them) as have been made;
(c) to revoke any appointments already made;
(d) to make any necessary appointments itself.

(4) An appointment made by the court under this section has effect as if made with the agreement of the parties.

(5) The leave of the court is required for any appeal from a decision of the court under this section.

Court to have regard to agreed qualifications

19.—(1) In deciding whether to exercise, and in considering how to exercise, any of its powers under section 16 (procedure for appointment of arbitrators) or section 18 (failure of appointment procedure), the court shall have due regard to any agreement of the parties as to the qualifications required of the arbitrators.

Chairman

20.—(1) Where the parties have agreed that there is to be a chairman, they are free to agree what the functions of the chairman are to be in relation to the making of decisions, orders and awards.

(2) If or to the extent that there is no such agreement, the following provisions apply.

(3) Decisions, orders and awards shall be made by all or a majority of the arbitrators (including the chairman).

(4) The view of the chairman shall prevail in relation to a decision, order or award in respect of which there is neither unanimity nor a majority under subsection (3).

Umpire

21.—(1) Where the parties have agreed that there is to be an umpire, they are free to agree what the functions of the umpire are to be, and in particular—

(a) whether he is to attend the proceedings, and
(b) when he is to replace the other arbitrators as the tribunal with power to make decisions, orders and awards.

(2) If or to the extent that there is no such agreement, the following provisions apply.

(3) The umpire shall attend the proceedings and be supplied with the same documents and other materials as are supplied to the other arbitrators.

(4) Decisions, orders and awards shall be made by the other arbitrators unless and until they cannot agree on a matter relating to the arbitration.

In that event they shall forthwith give notice in writing to the parties and the umpire, whereupon the umpire shall replace them as the tribunal with power to make decisions, orders and awards as if he were sole arbitrator.

(5) If the arbitrators cannot agree but fail to give notice of that fact, or if any of them fails to join in the giving of notice, any party to the arbitral proceedings may (upon notice to the other parties and to the tribunal) apply to the court which may order that the umpire shall replace the other arbitrators as the tribunal with power to make decisions, orders and awards as if he were sole arbitrator.

(6) The leave of the court is required for any appeal from a decision of the court under this section.

Decision-making where no chairman or umpire

22.—(1) Where the parties agree that there shall be two or more arbitrators with no chairman or umpire, the parties are free to agree how the tribunal is to make decisions, orders and awards.

(2) If there is no such agreement, decisions, orders and awards shall be made by all or a majority of the arbitrators.

Revocation of arbitrator's authority

23.—(1) The parties are free to agree in what circumstances the authority of an arbitrator may be revoked.

(2) If or to the extent that there is no such agreement the following provisions apply.

(3) The authority of an arbitrator may not be revoked except—

(a) by the parties acting jointly, or
(b) by an arbitral or other institution or person vested by the parties with powers in that regard.

(4) Revocation of the authority of an arbitrator by the parties acting jointly must be agreed in writing unless the parties also agree (whether or not in writing) to terminate the arbitration agreement.

(5) Nothing in this section affects the power of the court—

(a) to revoke an appointment under section 18 (powers exercisable in case of failure of appointment procedure), or
(b) to remove an arbitrator on the grounds specified in section 24.

Power of court to remove arbitrator

24.—(1) A party to arbitral proceedings may (upon notice to the other parties, to the arbitrator concerned and to any other arbitrator) apply to the court to remove an arbitrator on any of the following grounds—

(a) that circumstances exist that give rise to justifiable doubts as to his impartiality;
(b) that he does not possess the qualifications required by the arbitration agreement;
(c) that he is physically or mentally incapable of conducting the proceedings or there are justifiable doubts as to his capacity to do so;
(d) that he has refused or failed—
   (i) properly to conduct the proceedings, or
   (ii) to use all reasonable despatch in conducting the proceedings or making an award,

and that substantial injustice has been or will be caused to the applicant.

(2) If there is an arbitral or other institution or person vested by the parties with power to remove an arbitrator, the court shall not exercise its power of removal unless satisfied that the applicant has first exhausted any available recourse to that institution or person.

(3) The arbitral tribunal may continue the arbitral proceedings and application to the court under this section is pending.

(4) Where the court removes an arbitrator, it may make such order as it thinks fit with respect to his entitlement (if any) to fees or expenses, or the repayment of any fees or expenses already paid.

(5) The arbitrator concerned is entitled to appear and be heard by the court before it makes any order under this section.

(6) The leave of the court is required for any appeal from a decision of the court under this section.

Resignation of arbitrator

25.—(1) The parties are free to agree with an arbitrator as to the consequences of his resignation as regards—

(a) his entitlement (if any) to fees or expenses, and
(b) any liability thereby incurred by him.

(2) If or to the extent that there is no such agreement the following provisions apply.

(3) An arbitrator who resigns his appointment may (upon notice to the parties) apply to the court—

(a) to grant him relief from any liability thereby incurred by him, and
(b) to make such order as it thinks fit with respect to his entitlement (if any) to fees or expenses or the repayment of any fees or expenses already paid.

(4) If the court is satisfied that in all the circumstances it was reasonable for the arbitrator to resign, it may grant such relief as is mentioned in subsection (3)(a) on such terms as it thinks fit.

(5) The leave of the court is required for any appeal from a decision of the court under this section.

Death of arbitrator or person appointing him

26.—(1) The authority of an arbitrator is personal and ceases on his death.

(2) Unless otherwise agreed by the parties, the death of the person by whom an arbitrator was appointed does not revoke the arbitrator's authority.

Filling of vacancy, etc.

27.—(1) Where an arbitrator ceases to hold office, the parties are free to agree—

(a) whether and if so how the vacancy is to be filled,
(b) whether and if so to what extent the previous proceedings should stand, and
(c) what effect (if any) his ceasing to hold office has on any appointment made by him (alone or jointly)

(2) If or to the extent that there is no such agreement, the following provisions apply.

(3) The provisions of sections 16 (procedure for appointment of arbitrators) and 18 (failure of appointment procedure) apply in relation to the filling of the vacancy as in relation to an original appointment.

(4) The tribunal (when reconstituted) shall determine whether and if so to what extent the previous proceedings should stand.

This does not affect any right of a party to challenge those proceedings on any ground which had arisen before the arbitrator ceased to hold office.

(5) His ceasing to hold office does not affect any appointment by him (alone or jointly) of another arbitrator, in particular any appointment of a chairman or umpire.

Joint and several liability of parties to arbitrators for fees and expenses

28.—(1) The parties are jointly and severally liable to pay to the arbitrators such reasonable fees and expenses (if any) as are appropriate in the circumstances.

(2) Any party may apply to the court (upon notice to the other parties and to the arbitrators) which may order that the amount of the arbitrators' fees and expenses shall be considered and adjusted by such means and upon such terms as it may direct.

(3) If the application is made after any amount has been paid to the arbitrators by way of fees or expenses, the court may order the repayment of such amount (if any) as is shown to be excessive, but shall not do so unless it is shown that it is reasonable in the circumstances to order repayment.

(4) The above provisions have effect subject to any order of the court under section 24(4) or 25(3)(b) (order as to entitlement to fees or expenses in case of removal or resignation of arbitrator).

(5) Nothing in this section affects any liability of a party to any other party to pay all or any of the costs of the arbitration (see sections 59 to 65) or any contractual right of an arbitrator to payment of his fees and expenses.

(6) In this section references to arbitrators include an arbitrator who has ceased to act and an umpire who has not replaced the other arbitrators.

Immunity of arbitrator

29.—(1) An arbitrator is not liable for anything done or omitted in the discharge or purported discharge of his functions as arbitrator unless the act or omission is shown to have been in bad faith.

(2) Subsection (1) applies to an employee or agent of an arbitrator as it applies to the arbitrator himself.

(3) This section does not affect any liability incurred by an arbitrator by reason of his resigning (but see section 25).

Jurisdiction of the arbitral tribunal

Competence of tribunal to rule on its own jurisdiction

30.—(1) Unless otherwise agreed by the parties, the arbitral tribunal may rule on its own substantive jurisdiction, that is, as to—

(a) whether there is a valid arbitration agreement,
(b) whether the tribunal is properly constituted, and
(c) what matters have been submitted to arbitration in accordance with the arbitration agreement.

(2) Any such ruling may be challenged by any available arbitral process of appeal or review or in accordance with the provisions of this Part.

Objection to substantive jurisdiction of tribunal

31.—(1) An objection that the arbitral tribunal lacks substantive jurisdiction at the outset of the proceedings must be raised by a party not later than the time he takes the first step in the proceedings to contest the merits of any matter in relation to which he challenges the tribunal's jurisdiction.

A party is not precluded from raising such an objection by the fact that he has appointed or participated in the appointment of an arbitrator.

(2) Any objection during the course of the arbitral proceedings that the arbitral tribunal is exceeding its substantive jurisdiction must be made as soon as possible after the matter alleged to be beyond its jurisdiction is raised.

(3) The arbitral tribunal may admit an objection later than the time specified in subsection (1) or (2) if it considers the delay justified.

(4) Where an objection is duly taken to the tribunal's substantive jurisdiction and the tribunal has power to rule on its own jurisdiction, it may—

(a) rule on the matter in an award as to jurisdiction, or
(b) deal with the objection in its award on the merits.

If the parties agree which of these courses the tribunal should take, the tribunal shall proceed accordingly.

(5) The tribunal may in any case, and shall if the parties so agree, stay proceedings whilst an application is made to the court under section 32 (determination of preliminary point of jurisdiction).

Determination of preliminary point of jurisdiction

32.—(1) The court may, on the application of a party to arbitral proceedings (upon notice to the other parties), determine any question as to the substantive jurisdiction of the tribunal.

A party may lose the right to object (see section 73).

(2) An application under this section shall not be considered unless—

(a) it is made with the agreement in writing of all the other parties to the proceedings, or

(b) it is made with the permission of the tribunal and the court is satisfied—

(i) that the determination of the question is likely to produce substantial savings in costs,

(ii) that the application was made without delay, and

(iii) that there is good reason why the matter should be decided by the court.

(3) An application under this section, unless made with the agreement of all the other parties to the proceedings, shall state the grounds on which it is said that the matter should be decided by the court.

(4) Unless otherwise agreed by the parties, the arbitral tribunal may continue the arbitral proceedings and make an award while an application to the court under this section is pending.

(5) Unless the court gives leave, no appeal lies from a decision of the court whether the conditions specified in subsection (2) are met.

(6) The decision of the court on the question of jurisdiction shall be treated as a judgment of the court for the purposes of an appeal.

But no appeal lies without the leave of the court which shall not be given unless the court considers that the question involves a point of law which is one of general importance or is one which for some other special reason should be considered by the Court of Appeal.

The arbitral proceedings

General duty of the tribunal

33.—(1) The tribunal shall—

(a) act fairly and impartially as between the parties, giving each party a reasonable opportunity of putting his case and dealing with that of his opponent, and

(b) adopt procedures suitable to the circumstances of the particular case, avoiding unnecessary delay or expense, so as to provide a fair means for the resolution of the matters falling to be determined.

(2) The tribunal shall comply with that general duty in conducting the arbitral proceedings, in its decisions on matters of procedure and evidence and in the exercise of all other powers conferred on it.

Procedural evidential matters

34.—(1) It shall be for the tribunal to decide all procedural and evidential matters, subject to the right of the parties to agree any matter.

(2) Procedural and evidential matters include—

(a) when and where any part of the proceedings is to be held;
(b) the language or languages to be used in the proceedings and whether translations of any relevant documents are to be supplied;
(c) whether any and if so what form of written statements of claim and defence are to be used, when these should be supplied and the extent to which such statements can be later amended;
(d) whether any and if so which documents or classes of documents should be disclosed between and produced by the parties and at what stage;
(e) whether any and if so what questions should be put to and answered by the respective parties and when and in what form this should be done;
(f) whether to apply strict rules of evidence (or any other rules) as to the admissibility, relevance or weight of any material (oral, written or other) sought to be tendered on any matters of fact or opinion, and the time, manner and form in which such material should be exchanged and presented;
(g) whether and to what extent the tribunal should itself take the initiative in ascertaining the facts and the law;
(h) whether and to what extent there should be oral or written evidence or submissions.

(3) The tribunal may fix the time within which any directions given by it are to be complied with, and may if it thinks fit extend the time so fixed (whether or not it has expired).

Consolidation of proceedings and concurrent hearings

35.—(1) The parties are free to agree—

(a) that the arbitral proceedings shall be consolidated with other arbitral proceedings, or
(b) that concurrent hearings shall be held,

on such terms as may be agreed.

(2) Unless the parties agree to confer such power on the tribunal, the tribunal has no power to order consolidation of proceedings or concurrent hearings.

Legal or other representation

36. Unless otherwise agreed by the parties, a party to arbitral proceedings may be represented in the ''proceedings by a lawyer or other person chosen by him.

Power to appoint experts, legal advisers or assessors

37.—(1) Unless otherwise agreed by the parties—

(a) the tribunal may—
    (i) appoint experts or legal advisers to report to it and the parties, or
    (ii) appoint assessors to assist it on technical matters,

    and may allow any such expert, legal adviser or assessor to attend the proceedings and
(b) the parties shall be given a reasonable opportunity to comment on any information, opinion or advice offered by any such person.

(2) The fees and expenses of an expert, legal adviser or assessor appointed by the tribunal for which the arbitrators are liable are expenses of the arbitrators for the purposes of this Part.

General powers exercisable by the tribunal

38.—(1) The parties are free to agree on the powers exercisable by the arbitral tribunal for the purposes of and in relation to the proceedings.

(2) Unless otherwise agreed by the parties the tribunal has the following powers.

(3) The tribunal may order a claimant to provide security for the costs of the arbitration.

This power shall not be exercised on the ground that the claimant is—

(a) an individual ordinarily resident outside the United Kingdom, or
(b) a corporation or association incorporated or formed under the law of a country outside the United Kingdom, or whose central management and control is exercised outside the United Kingdom.

(4) The tribunal may give directions in relation to any property which is the subject of the proceedings or as to which any question arises in the proceedings, and which is owned by or is in the possession of a party to the proceedings—

(a) for the inspection, photographing, preservation, custody or detention of the property by the tribunal, an expert or a party, or
(b) ordering that samples be taken from, or any observation be made of or experiment conducted upon, the property.

(5) The tribunal may direct that a party or witness shall be examined on oath or affirmation, and may for that purpose administer any necessary oath or take any necessary affirmation.

(6) The tribunal may give directions to a party for the preservation for the purposes of the proceedings of any evidence in his custody or control.

Power to make provisional awards

39.—(1) The parties are free to agree that the tribunal shall have power to order on a provisional basis any relief which it would have power to grant in a final award.

(2) This includes, for instance, making—

(a) a provisional order for the payment of money or the disposition of property as between the parties, or
(b) an order to make an interim payment on account of the costs of the arbitration.

(3) Any such order shall be subject to the tribunal's final adjudication; and the tribunal's final award, on the merits or as to costs, shall take account of any such order.

(4) Unless the parties agree to confer such power on the tribunal, the tribunal has no such power. This does not affect its powers under section 47 (awards on different issues, &c.).

General duty of parties

40.—(1) The parties shall do all things necessary for the proper and expeditious conduct of the arbitral proceedings.

(2) This includes—

(a) complying without delay with any determination of the tribunal as to procedural or evidential matters, or with any order or directions of the tribunal, and
(b) where appropriate, taking without delay any necessary steps to obtain a decision of the court on a preliminary question of jurisdiction or law (see sections 32 and 45).

Power of tribunal in case of party's default

41.—(1) The parties are free to agree on the powers of the tribunal in case of a party's failure to do something necessary for the proper and expeditious conduct of the arbitration.

(2) Unless otherwise agreed by the parties, the following provisions apply.

(3) If the tribunal is satisfied that there has been inordinate and inexcusable delay on the part of the claimant in pursuing his claim and that the delay—

(a) gives rise, or is likely to give rise, to a substantial risk that it is not possible to have a fair resolution of the issues in that claim, or
(b) has caused, or is likely to cause, serious prejudice to the respondent,

the tribunal may make an award dismissing the claim.

(4) If without showing sufficient cause a party—

(a) fails to attend or be represented at an oral hearing of which due notice was given, or
(b) where matters are to be dealt with in writing, fails after due notice to submit written evidence or make written submissions,

the tribunal may continue the proceedings in the absence of that party or, as the case may be, without any written evidence or submissions on his behalf, and may make an award on the basis of the evidence before it.

(5) If without showing sufficient cause a party fails to comply with any order or directions of the tribunal, the tribunal may make a peremptory order to the same effect, prescribing such time for compliance with it as the tribunal considers appropriate.

(6) If a claimant fails to comply with a peremptory order of the tribunal to provide security for costs, the tribunal may make an award dismissing his claim.

(7) If a party fails to comply with any other kind of peremptory order, then, without prejudice to section 42 (enforcement by court of tribunal's peremptory orders), the tribunal may do any of the following—

(a) direct that the party in default shall not be entitled to rely upon any allegation or material which was the subject matter of the order;
(b) draw such adverse inferences from the act of non-compliance as the circumstances justify;
(c) proceed to an award on the basis of such materials as have been properly provided to it;

(d) make such order as it thinks fit as to the payment of costs of the arbitration incurred in consequence of the non-compliance.

Powers of court in relation to arbitral proceedings

Enforcement of peremptory orders of tribunal

42.—(1) Unless otherwise agreed by the parties, the court may make an order requiring a party to comply with a peremptory order made by the tribunal.

(2) An application for an order under this section may be made—

(a) by the tribunal (upon notice to the parties),
(b) by a party to the arbitral proceedings with the permission of the tribunal (and upon notice to the other parties), or
(c) where the parties have agreed that the powers of the court under this section shall be available.

(3) The court shall not act unless it is satisfied that the applicant has exhausted any available arbitral process in respect of failure to comply with the tribunal's order.

(4) No order shall be made under this section unless the court is satisfied that the person to whom the tribunal's order was directed has failed to comply with it within the time prescribed in the order or, if no time was prescribed, within a reasonable time.

(5) The leave of the court is required for any appeal from a decision of the court under this section.

Securing the attendance of witnesses

43.—(1) A party to arbitral proceedings may use the same court procedures as are available in relation to legal proceedings to secure the attendance before the tribunal of a witness in order to give oral testimony or to produce documents or other material evidence.

(2) This may only be done with the permission of the tribunal or the agreement of the other parties.

(3) The court procedures may only be used if—

(a) the witness is in the United Kingdom, and
(b) the arbitral proceedings are being conducted in England and Wales or, as the case may be, Northern Ireland.

(4) A person shall not be compelled by virtue of this section to produce any document or other material evidence which he could not be compelled to produce in legal proceedings.

Court powers exercisable in support of arbitral proceedings

44.—(1) Unless otherwise agreed by the parties, the court has for the purposes of and in relation to arbitral proceedings the same power of making orders about the matters listed below as it has for the purposes of and in relation to legal proceedings.

(2) Those matters are—

(a) the taking of the evidence of witnesses;

(b) the preservation of evidence;

(c) making orders relating to property which is the subject of the proceedings or as to which any question arises in the proceedings—

(i) for the inspection, photographing, preservation, custody or detention of the property, or

(ii) ordering that samples be taken from, or any observation be made of or experiment conducted upon, the property;

and for that purpose authorising any person to enter any premises in the possession or control of a party to the arbitration;

(d) the sale of any goods the subject of the proceedings;

(e) the granting of an interim injunction or the appointment of a receiver.

(3) If the case is one of urgency, the court may, on the application of a party or proposed party to the arbitral proceedings, make such orders as it thinks necessary for the purpose of preserving evidence or assets.

(4) If the case is not one of urgency, the court shall act only on the application of a party to the arbitral proceedings (upon notice to the other parties and to the tribunal) made with the permission of the tribunal or the agreement in writing of the other parties.

(5) In any case the court shall act only if or to the extent that the arbitral tribunal, and any arbitral or other institution or person vested by the parties with power in that regard, has no power or is unable for the time being to act effectively.

(6) If the court so orders, an order made by it under this section shall cease to have effect in whole or in part on the order of the tribunal or of any such arbitral or other institution or person having power to act in relation to the subject-matter of the order.

(7) The leave of the court is required for any appeal from a decision of the court under this section.

Determination of preliminary point of law

45.—(1) Unless otherwise agreed by the parties, the court may on the application of a party to arbitral proceedings (upon notice to the other parties) determine any question of law arising in the course of the proceedings which the court is satisfied substantially affects the rights of one or more of the parties.

An agreement to dispense with reasons for the tribunal's award shall be considered an agreement to exclude the court's jurisdiction under this section.

(2) An application under this section shall not be considered unless—

(a) it is made with the agreement of all the other parties to the proceedings, or

(b) it is made with the permission of the tribunal and the court is satisfied

(i) that the determination of the question is likely to produce substantial savings in costs, and

(ii) that the application was made without delay.

(3) The application shall identify the question of law to be determined and, unless made with the agreement of all the other parties to the proceedings, shall state the grounds on which it is said that the question should be decided by the court.

(4) Unless otherwise agreed by the parties, the arbitral tribunal may continue the arbitral proceedings and make an award while an application to the court under this section is pending.

(5) Unless the court gives leave, no appeal lies from a decision of the court whether the conditions specified in subsection (2) are met.

(6) The decision of the court on the question of law shall be treated as a judgment of the court for the purposes of an appeal.

But no appeal lies without the leave of the court which shall not be given unless the court considers that the question is one of general importance, or is one which for some other special reason should be considered by the Court of Appeal.

The award

Rules applicable to substance of dispute

46.—(1) The arbitral tribunal shall decide the dispute—

(a) in accordance with the law chosen by the parties as applicable to the substance of the dispute, or

(b) if the parties so agree, in accordance with such other considerations as are agreed by them or determined by the tribunal.

(2) For this purpose the choice of the laws of a country shall be understood to refer to the substantive laws of that country and not its conflict of laws rules.

(3) If or to the extent that there is no such choice or agreement, the tribunal shall apply the law determined by the conflict of laws rules which it considers applicable.

Awards on different issues, etc.

47.—(1) Unless otherwise agreed by the parties, the tribunal may make more than one award at different times on different aspects of the matters to be determined.

(2) The tribunal may, in particular, make an award relating—

(a) to an issue affecting the whole claim, or

(b) to a part only of the claims or cross-claims submitted to it for decision.

(3) If the tribunal does so, it shall specify in its award the issue, or the claim or part of a claim, which is the subject matter of the award.

Remedies

48.—(1) The parties are free to agree on the powers exercisable by the arbitral tribunal as regards remedies.

(2) Unless otherwise agreed by the parties, the tribunal has the following powers.

(3) The tribunal may make a declaration as to any matter to be determined in the proceedings.

(4) The tribunal may order the payment of a sum of money, in any currency.

(5) The tribunal has the same powers as the court—

(a) to order a party to do or refrain from doing anything;

(b) to order specific performance of a contract (other than a contract relating to land);

(c) to order the rectification, setting aside or cancellation of a deed or other document.

Interest

49.—(1) The parties are free to agree on the powers of the tribunal as regards the award of interest.

(2) Unless otherwise agreed by the parties the following provisions apply.

(3) The tribunal may award simple or compound interest from such dates, at such rates and with such rests as it considers meets the justice of the case—

(a) on the whole or part of any amount awarded by the tribunal, in respect of any period up to the date of the award;
(b) on the whole or part of any amount claimed in the arbitration and outstanding at the commencement of the arbitral proceedings but paid before the award was made, in respect of any period up to the date of payment.

(4) The tribunal may award simple or compound interest from the date of the award (or any later date) until payment, at such rates and with such rests as it considers meets the justice of the case, on the outstanding amount of any award (including any award of interest under subsection (3) and any award as to costs).

(5) References in this section to an amount awarded by the tribunal include an amount payable in consequence of a declaratory award by the tribunal.

(6) The above provisions do not affect any other power of the tribunal to award interest.

Extension of time for making award

50.—(1) Where the time for making an award is limited by or in pursuance of the arbitration agreement, then, unless otherwise agreed by the parties, the court may in accordance with the following provisions by order extend that time.

(2) An application for an order under this section may be made—

(a) by the tribunal (upon notice to the parties), or
(b) by any party to the proceedings (upon notice to the tribunal and the other parties),

but only after exhausting any available arbitral process for obtaining an extension of time.

(3) The court shall only make an order if satisfied that a substantial injustice would otherwise be done.

(4) The court may extend the time for such period and on such terms as it thinks fit, and may do so whether or not the time previously fixed (by or under the agreement or by a previous order) has expired.

(5) The leave of the court is required for any appeal from a decision of the court under this section.

Settlement

51.—(1) If during arbitral proceedings the parties settle the dispute, the following provisions apply unless otherwise agreed by the parties.

(2) The tribunal shall terminate the substantive proceedings and, if so requested by the parties and not objected to by the tribunal, shall record the settlement in the form of an agreed award.

(3) An agreed award shall state that it is an award of the tribunal and shall have the same status and effect as any other award on the merits of the case.

(4) The following provisions of this Part relating to awards (sections 52 to 58) apply to an agreed award.

(5) Unless the parties have also settled the matter of the payment of the costs of the arbitration, the provisions of this Part relating to costs (sections 59 to 65) continue to apply.

Form of award

52.—(1) The parties are free to agree on the form of an award.

(2) If or to the extent that there is no such agreement, the following provisions apply.

(3) The award shall be in writing signed by all the arbitrators or all those assenting to the award.

(4) The award shall contain the reasons for the award unless it is an agreed award or the parties have agreed to dispense with reasons.

(5) The award shall state the seat of the arbitration and the date when the award is made.

Place where award is made

53. Unless otherwise agreed by the parties, where the seat of the arbitration is in England and Wales or Northern Ireland, any award in the proceedings shall be treated as made there, regardless of where it was signed, despatched or delivered to any of the parties.

Date of award

54.—(1) Unless otherwise agreed by the parties, the tribunal may decide what is to be taken to be the date on which the award was made.

(2) In the absence of any such decision, the date of the award shall be taken to be the date on which it is signed by the arbitrator or, where more than one arbitrator signs the award, by the last of them.

Notification of award

55.—(1) The parties are free to agree on the requirements as to notification of the award to the parties.

(2) If there is no such agreement, the award shall be notified to the parties by service on them of copies of the award, which shall be done without delay after the award is made.

(3) Nothing in this section affects section 56 (power to withhold award in case of non-payment).

Power to withhold award in case of non-payment

56.—(1) The tribunal may refuse to deliver an award to the parties except upon full payment of the fees and expenses of the arbitrators.

(2) If the tribunal refuses on that ground to deliver an award, a party to the arbitral proceedings may (upon notice to the other parties and the tribunal) apply to the court, which may order that—

(a) the tribunal shall deliver the award on the payment into court by the applicant of the fees and expenses demanded, or such lesser amount as the court may specify,

(b) the amount of the fees and expenses properly payable shall be determined by such means and upon such terms as the court may direct, and

(c) out of the money paid into court there shall be paid out such fees and expenses as may be found to be properly payable and the balance of the money (if any) shall be paid out to the applicant.

(3) For this purpose the amount of fees and expenses properly payable is the amount the applicant is liable to pay under section 28 or any agreement relating to the payment of the arbitrators.

(4) No application to the court may be made where there is any available arbitral process for appeal or review of the amount of the fees or expenses demanded.

(5) References in this section to arbitrators include an arbitrator who has ceased to act and an umpire who has not replaced the other arbitrators.

(6) The above provisions of this section also apply in relation to any arbitral or other institution or person vested by the parties with powers in relation to the delivery of the tribunal's award.

As they so apply, the references to the fees and expenses of the arbitrators shall be construed as including the fees and expenses of that institution or person.

(7) The leave of the court is required for any appeal from a decision of the court under this section.

(8) Nothing in this section shall be construed as excluding an application under section 28 where payment has been made to the arbitrators in order to obtain the award.

Correction of award or additional award

57.—(1) The parties are free to agree on the powers of the tribunal to correct an award or make an additional award.

(2) If or to the extent there is no such agreement, the following provisions apply.

(3) The tribunal may on its own initiative or on the application of a party—

(a) correct an award so as to remove any clerical mistake or error arising from an accidental slip or omission or clarify or remove any ambiguity in the award, or

(b) make an additional award in respect of any claim (including a claim for interest or costs) which was presented to the tribunal but was not dealt with in the award.

These powers shall not be exercised without first affording the other parties a reasonable opportunity to make representations to the tribunal.

(4) Any application for the exercise of those powers must be made within 28 days of the date of the award or such longer period as the parties may agree.

(5) Any correction of an award shall be made within 28 days of the date the application was received by the tribunal or, where the correction is made by the tribunal on its own initiative, within 28 days of the date of the award or, in either case, such longer period as the parties may agree.

(6) Any additional award shall be made within 56 days of the date of the original award or such longer period as the parties may agree.

(7) Any correction of an award shall form part of the award.

Effect of award

58.—(1) Unless otherwise agreed by the parties, an award made by the tribunal pursuant to an arbitration agreement is final and binding both on the parties and on any persons claiming through or under them.

(2) This does not affect the right of a person to challenge the award by any available arbitral process of appeal or review or in accordance with the provisions of this Part.

Costs of the arbitration

Costs of the arbitration

59.—(1) References in this Part to the costs of the arbitration are to—

(a) the arbitrators' fees and expenses,
(b) the fees and expenses of any arbitral institution concerned, and
(c) the legal or other costs of the parties.

(2) Any such reference includes the costs of or incidental to any proceedings to determine the amount of the recoverable costs of the arbitration (see section 63).

Agreement to pay costs in any event

60. An agreement which has the effect that a party is to pay the whole or part of the costs of the arbitration in any event is only valid if made c after the dispute in question has arisen.

Award of costs

61.—(1) The tribunal may make an award allocating the costs of the arbitration as between the parties, subject to any agreement of the parties.

(2) Unless the parties otherwise agree, the tribunal shall award costs on the general principle that costs should follow the event except where it appears to the tribunal that in the circumstances this is not appropriate in relation to the whole or part of the costs.

Effect of agreement or award about costs

62. Unless the parties otherwise agree, any obligation under an agreement between them as to how the costs of the arbitration are to be borne, or under an award allocating the costs of the arbitration, extends only to such costs as are recoverable.

The recoverable costs of the arbitration

63.—(1) The parties are free to agree what costs of the arbitration are recoverable.

(2) If or to the extent there is no such agreement, the following provisions apply.

(3) The tribunal may determine by award the recoverable costs of the arbitration on such basis as it thinks fit.

If it does so, it shall specify—

(a) the basis on which it has acted, and
(b) the items of recoverable costs and the amount referable to each.

(4) If the tribunal does not determine the recoverable costs of the arbitration, any party to the arbitral proceedings may apply to the court (upon notice to the other parties) which may—

(a) determine the recoverable costs of the arbitration on such basis as it thinks fit, or
(b) order that they shall be determined by such means and upon such terms as it may specify.

(5) Unless the tribunal or the court determines otherwise—

(a) the recoverable costs of the arbitration shall be determined on the basis that there shall be allowed a reasonable amount in respect of all costs reasonably incurred, and
(b) any doubt as to whether costs were reasonably incurred or were reasonable in amount shall be resolved in favour of the paying party.

(6) The above provisions have effect subject to section 64 (recoverable fees and expenses of arbitrators).

(7) Nothing in this section affects any right of the arbitrators, any expert, legal adviser or assessor appointed by the tribunal, or any arbitral institution, to payment of their fees and expenses.

Recoverable fees and expenses of arbitrators

64.—(1) Unless otherwise agreed by the parties, the recoverable costs of the arbitration shall include in respect of the fees and expenses of the arbitrators only such reasonable fees and expenses as are appropriate in the circumstances.

(2) If there is any question as to what reasonable fees and expenses are appropriate in the circumstances, and the matter is not already before the court on an application under section 63(4), the court may on the application of any party (upon notice to the other parties)—

(a) determine the matter, or
(b) order that it be determined by such means and upon such terms as the court may specify.

(3) Subsection (1) has effect subject to any order of the court under section 24(4) or 25(3)(b) (order as to entitlement to fees or expenses in case of removal or resignation of arbitrator).

(4) Nothing in this section affects any right of the arbitrator to payment of his fees and expenses.

Power to limit recoverable costs

65.—(1) Unless otherwise agreed by the parties, the tribunal may direct that the recoverable costs of the arbitration, or of any part of the arbitral proceedings, shall be limited to a specified amount.

(2) Any direction may be made or varied at any stage, but this must be done sufficiently in advance of the incurring of costs to which it relates, or the taking of any steps in the proceedings which may be affected by it, for the limit to be taken into account.

Powers of the court in relation to award

Enforcement of the award

66.—(1) An award made by the tribunal pursuant to an arbitration agreement may, by leave of the court, be enforced in the same manner as a judgment or order of the court to the same effect.

(2) Where leave is so given, judgment may be entered in terms of the award.

(3) Leave to enforce an award shall not be given where, or to the extent that, the person against whom it is sought to be enforced shows that the tribunal lacked substantive jurisdiction to make the award.

The right to raise such an objection may have been lost (see section 73).

(4) Nothing in this section affects the recognition or enforcement of an award under any other enactment or rule of law, in particular under Part II of the Arbitration Act 1950 (enforcement of awards under Geneva Convention) or the provisions of Part III of this Act relating to the recognition and enforcement of awards under the New York Convention or by an action on the award.

Challenging the award: substantive jurisdiction

67.—(1) A party to arbitral proceedings may (upon notice to the other parties and to the tribunal) apply to the court—

(a) challenging any award of the arbitral tribunal as to its substantive jurisdiction; or
(b) for an order declaring an award made by the tribunal on the merits to be of no effect, in whole or in part, because the tribunal did not have substantive jurisdiction.

A party may lose the right to object (see section 73) and the right to apply is subject to the restrictions in section 70(2) and (3).

(2) The arbitral tribunal may continue the arbitral proceedings and make a further award while an application to the court under this section is pending in relation to an award as to jurisdiction.

(3) On an application under this section challenging an award of the arbitral tribunal as to its substantive jurisdiction, the court may by order—

(a) confirm the award,
(b) vary the award, or
(c) set aside the award in whole or in part.

(4) The leave of the court is required for any appeal from a decision of the court under this section.

Challenging the award: serious irregularity

68.—(1) A party to arbitral proceedings may (upon notice to the other parties and to the tribunal) apply to the court challenging an award in the proceedings on the ground of serious irregularity affecting the tribunal, the proceedings or the award.

A party may lose the right to object (see section 73) and the right to apply is subject to the restrictions in section 70(2) and (3).

(2) Serious irregularity means an irregularity of one or more of the following kinds which the court considers has caused or will cause substantial injustice to the applicant—

(a) failure by the tribunal to comply with section 33 (general duty of tribunal);
(b) the tribunal exceeding its powers (otherwise than by exceeding its substantive jurisdiction: see section 67);

(c) failure by the tribunal to conduct the proceedings in accordance with the procedure agreed by the parties;
(d) failure by the tribunal to deal with all the issues that were put to it;
(e) any arbitral or other institution or person vested by the parties with powers in relation to the proceedings or the award exceeding its powers;
(f) uncertainty or ambiguity as to the effect of the award;
(g) the award being obtained by fraud or the award or the way in which it was procured being contrary to public policy;
(h) failure to comply with the requirements as to the form of the award; or
(i) any irregularity in the conduct of the proceedings or in the award which is admitted by the tribunal or by any arbitral or other institution or person vested by the parties with powers in relation to the proceedings or the award.

(3) If there is shown to be serious irregularity affecting the tribunal, the proceedings or the award, the court may—

(a) remit the-award to the tribunal, in whole or in part, for reconsideration,
(b) set the award aside in whole or in part, or
(c) declare the award to be of no effect, in whole or in part.

The court shall not exercise its power to set aside or to declare an award to be of no effect, in whole or in part, unless it is satisfied that it would be inappropriate to remit the matters in question to the tribunal for reconsideration.

(4) The leave of the court is required for any appeal from a decision of the court under this section.

Appeal on point of law

69.—(1) Unless otherwise agreed by the parties, a party to arbitral proceedings may (upon notice to the other parties and to the tribunal) appeal to the court on a question of law arising out of an award made in the proceedings.

An agreement to dispense with reasons for the tribunal's award shall be considered an agreement to exclude the court's jurisdiction under this section.

(2) An appeal shall not be brought under this section except—

(a) with the agreement of all the other parties to the proceedings, or
(b) with the leave of the court.

The right to appeal is also subject to the restrictions in section 70(2) and (3).

(3) Leave to appeal shall be given only if the court is satisfied—

(a) that the determination of the question will substantially affect the rights of one or more of the parties,
(b) that the question is one which the tribunal was asked to determine,
(c) that, on the basis of the findings of fact in the award—
  (i) the decision of the tribunal on the question is obviously wrong, or
  (ii) the question is one of general public importance and the decision of the c tribunal is at least open to serious doubt, and
(d) that, despite the agreement of the parties to resolve the matter by arbitration,

it is just and proper in all the circumstances for the court to determine the question.

(4) An application for leave to appeal under this section shall identify the question of law to be determined and state the grounds on which it is alleged that leave to appeal should be granted.

(5) The court shall determine an application for leave to appeal under this section without a hearing unless it appears to the court that a hearing is required.

(6) The leave of the court is required for any appeal from a decision of the court under this section to grant or refuse leave to appeal.

(7) On an appeal under this section the court may by order—

(a) confirm the award,
(b) vary the award,
(c) remit the award to the tribunal, in whole or in part, for reconsideration in the light of the court's determination, or
(d) set aside the award in whole or in part.

The court shall not exercise its power to set aside an award, in whole or in part, unless it is satisfied that it would be inappropriate to remit the matters in question to the tribunal for reconsideration.

(8) The decision of the court on an appeal under this section shall be treated as a judgment of the court for the purposes of a further appeal.

But no such appeal lies without the leave of the court which shall not be given unless the court considers that the question is one of general importance or is one which for some other special reason should be considered by the Court of Appeal.

Challenge or appeal: supplementary provisions

70.—(1) The following provisions apply to an application or appeal under section 67, 68 or 69.

(2) An application or appeal may not be brought if the applicant or pros appellant has not first exhausted—

(a) any available arbitral process of appeal or review, and
(b) any available recourse under section 57 (correction of award or additional award).

(3) Any application or appeal must be brought within 28 days of the date of the award or, if there has been any arbitral process of appeal or review, of the date when the applicant or appellant was notified of the result of that process.

(4) If on an application or appeal it appears to the court that the award—

(a) does not contain the tribunal's reasons, or
(b) does not set out the tribunal's reasons in sufficient detail to enable the court properly to consider the application or appeal,

the court may order the tribunal to state the reasons for its award in sufficient detail for that purpose.

(5) Where the court makes an order under subsection (4), it may make such further

order as it thinks fit with respect to any additional costs of the arbitration resulting from its order.

(6) The court may order the applicant or appellant to provide security for the costs of the application or appeal, and may direct that the application or appeal be dismissed if the order is not complied with.

The power to order security for costs shall not be exercised on the ground that the applicant or appellant—

(a) an individual ordinarily resident outside the United Kingdom, or
(b) a corporation or association incorporated or formed under the law of a country outside the United Kingdom, or whose central management and control is exercised outside the United Kingdom.

(7) The court may order that any money payable under the award shall be brought into court or otherwise secured pending the determination of the application or appeal, and may direct that the application or appeal be dismissed if the order is not complied with.

(8) The court may grant leave to appeal subject to conditions to the same or similar effect as an order under subsection (6) or (7).

This does not affect the general discretion of the court to grant leave subject to conditions.

Challenge or appeal: effect of order of court

71.—(1) The following provisions have effect where the court makes an order under section 67, 68 or 69 with respect to an award.

(2) Where the award is varied, the variation has effect as part of the tribunal's award.

(3) Where the award is remitted to the tribunal, in whole or in part, for reconsideration, the tribunal shall make a fresh award in respect of the matters remitted within three months of the date of the order for remission or such longer or shorter period as the court may direct.

(4) Where the award is set aside or declared to be of no effect, in whole or in part, the court may also order that any provision that an award is a condition precedent to the bringing of legal proceedings in respect of a matter to which the arbitration agreement applies, is of no effect as regards the subject matter of the award or, as the case may be, the relevant part of the award.

Miscellaneous

Saving for rights of person who takes no part in proceedings

72.—(1) A person alleged to be a party to arbitral proceedings but who takes no part in the proceedings may question—

(a) whether there is a valid arbitration agreement,
(b) whether the tribunal is properly constituted, or
(c) what matters have been submitted to arbitration in accordance with the arbitration agreement,

by proceedings in the court for a declaration or injunction or other appropriate relief.

(2) He also has the same right as a party to the arbitral proceedings to challenge an award—

(a) by an application under section 67 on the ground of lack of substantive jurisdiction in relation to him, or
(b) by an application under section 68 on the ground of serious irregularity (within the meaning of that section) affecting him;

and section 70(2) (duty to exhaust arbitral procedures) does not apply in his case.

Loss of rights to object

73.—(1) If a party to arbitral proceedings takes part, or continues to take part, in the proceedings without making, either forthwith or within such time as is allowed by the arbitration agreement or the tribunal or by any provision of this Part, any objection—

(a) that the tribunal lacks substantive jurisdiction,
(b) that the proceedings have been improperly conducted,
(c) that there has been a failure to comply with the arbitration agreement or with any provision of this Part, or
(d) that there has been any other irregularity affecting the tribunal or the proceedings,

he may not raise that objection later, before the tribunal or the court, unless he shows that, at the time he took part or continued to take part in the proceedings, he did not know and could not with reasonable diligence have discovered the grounds for the objection.

(2) Where the arbitral tribunal rules that it has substantive jurisdiction and a party to arbitral proceedings who could have questioned that ruling—

(a) by any available arbitral process of appeal or review, or
(b) by challenging the award,

does not do so, or does not do so within the time allowed by the arbitration agreement or any provision of this Part, he may not object later to the tribunal's substantive jurisdiction on any ground which was the subject of that ruling.

Immunity of arbitral institutions, etc.

74.—(1) An arbitral or other institution or person designated or requested by the parties to appoint or nominate an arbitrator is not liable for anything done or omitted in the discharge or purported discharge of that function unless the act or omission is shown to have been in bad faith.

(2) An arbitral or other institution or person by whom an arbitrator is appointed or nominated is not liable, by reason of having appointed or nominated him, for anything done or omitted by the arbitrator (or his employees or agents) in the discharge or purported discharge of his functions as arbitrator.

(3) The above provisions apply to an employee or agent of an arbitral or other institution or person as they apply to the institution or person himself.

Charge to secure payment of solicitors' costs

75.—The powers of the court to make declarations and orders under section 73 of the Solicitors Act 1974 or Article 71H of the Solicitors (Northern Ireland) Order 1976 (power to charge property recovered in the proceedings with the payment of solicitors' costs) may be exercised in relation to arbitral proceedings as if those proceedings were proceedings in the court.

Supplementary

Service of notices, etc.

76.—(1) The parties are free to agree on the manner of service of any notice or other document required or authorised to be given or served in pursuance of the arbitration agreement or for the purposes of the arbitral proceedings.

(2) If or to the extent that there is no such agreement the following provisions apply.

(3) A notice or other document may be served on a person by any effective means.

(4) If a notice or other document is addressed, pre-paid and delivered by post—

(a) to the addressee's last known principal residence or, if he is or has been carrying on a trade, profession or business, his last known principal business address, or

(b) where the addressee is a body corporate, to the body's registered or principal office,

it shall be treated as effectively served.

(5) This section does not apply to the service of documents for the purposes of legal proceedings, for which provision is made by rules of court.

(6) References in this Part to a notice or other document include any form of communication in writing and references to giving or serving a notice or other document shall be construed accordingly.

Powers of court in relation to service of documents

77.—(1) This section applies where service of a document on a person in the manner agreed by the parties, or in accordance with provisions of section 76 having effect in default of agreement, is not reasonably practicable.

(2) Unless otherwise agreed by the parties, the court may make such order as it thinks fit—

(a) for service in such manner as the court may direct, or

(b) dispensing with service of the document.

(3) Any party to the arbitration agreement may apply for an order, but only after exhausting any available arbitral process for resolving the matter.

(4) The leave of the court is required for any appeal from a decision of the court under this section.

Reckoning periods of time

78.—(1) The parties are free to agree on the method of reckoning periods of time for the purposes of any provision agreed by them or any provision of this Part having effect in default of such agreement.

(2) If or to the extent there is no such agreement, periods of time shall be reckoned in accordance with the following provisions.

(3) Where the act is required to be done within a specified period after or from a specified date, the period begins immediately after that date.

(4) Where the act is required to be done a specified number of clear days after a specified date, at least that number of days must intervene between the day on which the act is done and that date.

(5) Where the period is a period of seven days or less which would include a Saturday, Sunday or a public holiday in the place where anything which has to be done within the period falls to be done, that day shall be excluded.

In relation to England and Wales or Northern Ireland, a ''public holiday'' means Christmas Day, Good Friday or a day which under the Banking and Financial Dealings Act 1971 is a bank holiday.

Power of court to extend time limits relating to arbitral proceedings

79.—(1) Unless the parties otherwise agree, the court may by order extend any time limit agreed by them in relation to any matter relating to the arbitral proceedings or specified in any provision of this Part having effect in default of such agreement.

This section does not apply to a time limit to which section 12 applies (power of court to extend time for beginning arbitral proceedings, &c.).

(2) An application for an order may be made—

(a) by any party to the arbitral proceedings (upon notice to the other parties and to the tribunal), or
(b) by the arbitral tribunal (upon notice to the parties).

(3) The court shall not exercise its power to extend a time limit unless it is satisfied—

(a) that any available recourse to the tribunal, or to any arbitral or other institution or person vested by the parties with power in that regard, has first been exhausted, and
(b) that a substantial injustice would otherwise be done.

(4) The court's power under this section may be exercised whether or not the time has already expired.

(5) An order under this section may be made on such terms as the court thinks fit.

(6) The leave of the court is required for any appeal from a decision of the court under this section.

Notice and other requirements in connection with legal proceedings

80.—(1) References in this Part to an application, appeal or other step in relation to legal proceedings being taken ''upon notice'' to the other parties to the arbitral proceedings, or to the tribunal, are to such notice of the originating process as is required by rules of court and do not impose any separate requirement.

(2) Rules of court shall be made—

(a) requiring such notice to be given as indicated by any provision of this Part, and
(b) as to the manner, form and content of any such notice.

(3) Subject to any provision made by rules of court, a requirement to give notice to the tribunal of legal proceedings shall be construed—

(a) if there is more than one arbitrator, as a requirement to give notice to each of them; and
(b) if the tribunal is not fully constituted, as a requirement to give notice to any arbitrator who has been appointed.

(4) References in this Part to making an application or appeal to the court within a specified period are to the issue within that period of the appropriate originating process in accordance with rules of court.

(5) Where any provision of this Part requires an application or appeal to be made to the court within a specified time, the rules of court relating to the reckoning of periods, the extending or abridging of periods, and the consequences of not taking a step within the period prescribed by the rules, apply in relation to that requirement.

(6) Provision may be made by rules of court amending the provisions of this Part—

(a) with respect to the time within which any application or appeal to the court must be made,
(b) so as to keep any provision made by this Part in relation to arbitral proceedings in step with the corresponding provision of rules of court applying in relation to proceedings in the court, or
(c) so as to keep any provision made by this Part in relation to legal proceedings in step with the corresponding provision of rules of court applying generally in relation to proceedings in the court.

(7) Nothing in this section affects the generality of the power to make rules of court.

Saving for certain matters governed by common law

81.—(1) Nothing in this Part shall be construed as excluding the operation of any rule of law consistent with the provisions of this Part, in particular, any rule of law as to—

(a) matters which are not capable of settlement by arbitration;
(b) the effect of an oral arbitration agreement; or
(c) the refusal of recognition or enforcement of an arbitral award on grounds of public policy.

(2) Nothing in this Act shall be construed as reviving any jurisdiction of the court to set aside or remit an award on the ground of errors of fact or law on the face of the award.

Minor definitions

82.—(1) In this Part—

''arbitrator'', unless the context otherwise requires, includes an umpire;

''available arbitral process'', in relation to any matter, includes any process of appeal to or review by an arbitral or other institution or person vested by the parties with powers in relation to that matter;

"claimant", unless the context otherwise requires, includes a counterclaimant, and related expressions shall be construed accordingly;

"dispute" includes any difference;

"enactment" includes an enactment contained in Northern Ireland legislation;

"legal proceedings" means civil proceedings in the High Court or a county court;

"peremptory order" means an order made under section 41(5) or made in exercise of any corresponding power conferred by the parties;

"premises" includes land, buildings, moveable structures, vehicles, vessels, aircraft and hovercraft;

"question of law" means—

(a) for a court in England and Wales, a question of the law of England and Wales, and

(b) for a court in Northern Ireland, a question of the law of Northern Ireland;

"substantive jurisdiction", in relation to an arbitral tribunal, refers to the matters specified in section 30(1)(a) to (c), and references to the tribunal exceeding its substantive jurisdiction shall be construed accordingly.

(2) References in this Part to a party to an arbitration agreement include any person claiming under or through a party to the agreement.

Index of defined expressions: Part I

83.—(1) In this Part the expressions listed below are defined or otherwise explained by the provisions indicated—

agreement, agree and agreed	section 5(1)
agreement in writing	section 5(2) to (5)
arbitration agreement	sections 6 and S(t)
arbitrator	section 82(1)
available arbitral process	section 82(1)
claimant	section 82(1)
commencement (in relation to arbitral proceedings)	section 14
costs of the arbitration	section 59
the court	section 105
dispute	section 82(1)
enactment	section 82(1)
legal proceedings	section 82(1)
Limitation Acts	section 13(4)
notice (or other document),	section 76(6)
party—	
—in relation to an arbitration agreement	section 82(2)
—where section 106(2) or (3) applies	section 106(4)
peremptory order	section 82(1) (and see section 41(5))
premises	section 82(1)
question of law	section 82(1)
recoverable costs	sections 63 and 64
seat of the arbitration	section 3

serve and service (of notice or other document	section 76(6)
substantive jurisdiction (in relation to an arbitral tribunal)	section 82(1) (and see section 30(1)(a) to (c))
upon notice (to the parties or the tribunal)	section 80
written and in writing	section 5(6)

Transitional provisions

84.—(1) The provisions of this Part do not apply to arbitral proceedings commenced before the date on which this Part comes into force.

(2) They apply to arbitral proceedings commenced on or after that date under an arbitration agreement whenever made.

(3) The above provisions have effect subject to any transitional provision made by an order under section 109(2) (Power to include transitional provisions in commencement order).

PART II

OTHER PROVISIONS RELATING TO ARBITRATION

Domestic arbitration agreements

Modifications of Part 1 in relation to domestic arbitration agreement

85.—(1) In the case of a domestic arbitration agreement the provisions of Part I are modified in accordance with the following sections.

(2) For this purpose a "domestic arbitration agreement" means an arbitration agreement to which none of the parties is—

(a) an individual who is a national of, or habitually resident in, a state other than the United Kingdom, or

(b) a body corporate which is incorporated in, or whose central control and management is exercised in, a state other than the United Kingdom,

and under which the seat of the arbitration (if the seat has been designated or determined) is in the United Kingdom.

(3) In subsection (2) "arbitration agreement" and "seat of the arbitration" have the same meaning as in Part I (see sections 3, 5(1) and 6).

Staying of legal proceedings

86.—(1) In section 9 (stay of legal proceedings), subsection (4) (stay unless the arbitration agreement is null and void, inoperative, or incapable of being performed) does not apply to a domestic arbitration agreement.

(2) on an application under that section in relation to a domestic arbitration agreement the court shall grant a stay unless satisfied—

(a) that the arbitration agreement is null and void, inoperative, or incapable of being performed, or

(b) that there are other sufficient grounds for not requiring the parties to abide by the arbitration agreement.

(3) The court may treat as a sufficient ground under subsection (2)(b) the fact that the applicant is or was at any material time not ready and willing to do all things necessary for the proper conduct of the arbitration or of any other dispute resolution procedures required to be exhausted before resorting to arbitration.

(4) For the purposes of this section the question whether an arbitration agreement is a domestic arbitration agreement shall be determined by reference to the facts at the time the legal proceedings are commenced.

Effectiveness of agreement to exclude court's jurisdiction

87.—(1) In the case of a domestic arbitration agreement any agreement to exclude the jurisdiction of the court under—

(a) section 45 (determination of preliminary point of law), or
(b) section 69 (challenging the award: appeal on point of law), is not effective unless entered into after the commencement of the arbitral proceedings in which the question arises or the award is made.

(2) For this purpose the commencement of the arbitral proceedings has the same meaning as in Part I (see section 14).

(3) For the purposes of this section the question whether an arbitration agreement is a domestic arbitration agreement shall be determined by reference to the facts at the time the agreement is entered into.

Power to repeal or amend sections 85 to 87

88.—(1) The Secretary of State may by order repeal or amend the provisions of sections 85 to 87.

(2) An order under this section may contain such supplementary, incidental and transitional provisions as appear to the Secretary of State to be appropriate.

(3) An order under this section shall be made by statutory instrument and no such order shall be made unless a draft of it has been laid before and approved by a resolution of each House of Parliament.

Application of unfair terms regulations to consumer arbitration agreements

89.—(1) The following sections extend the application of the Unfair Terms in Consumer Contracts Regulations 1994 in relation to a term which constitutes an arbitration agreement.

For this purpose "arbitration agreement" means an agreement to submit to arbitration present or future disputes or differences (whether or not contractual).

(2) In those sections "the Regulations" means those regulations and includes any regulations amending or replacing those regulations.

(3) Those sections apply whatever the law applicable to the arbitration agreement.

Regulations apply where consumer is a legal person

90. The Regulations apply where the consumer is a legal person as they apply where the consumer is a natural person.

Arbitration agreement unfair where modest amount sought

91.—(1) A term which constitutes an arbitration agreement is unfair for the purposes of the Regulations so far as it relates to a claim for a pecuniary remedy which does not exceed the amount specified by order for the purposes of this section.

(2) Orders under this section may make different provision for different cases and for different purposes.

(3) The power to make orders under this section is exercisable—

(a) for England and Wales, by the Secretary of State with the concurrence of the Lord Chancellor,
(b) for Scotland, by the Secretary of State with the concurrence of the Lord Advocate, and
(c) for Northern Ireland, by the Department of Economic Development for Northern Ireland with the concurrence of the Lord Chancellor.

(4) Any such order for England and Wales or Scotland shall be made by statutory instrument which shall be subject to annulment in pursuance of a resolution of either House of Parliament.

(5) Any such order for Northern Ireland shall be a statutory rule for the purposes of the Statutory Rules (Northern Ireland) Order 1979 and shall be subject to negative resolution, within the meaning of section 41(6) of the Interpretation Act (Northern Ireland) 1954.

Small claims arbitration in the county court

Exclusion of Part 1 in relation to small claims arbitration in the county court

92. Nothing in Part I of this Act applies to arbitration under section 64 of the County Courts Act 1984.

Appointment of judges as arbitrators

Appointment of judges as arbitrators

93.—(1) A judge of the Commercial Court or an official referee may, if in all the circumstances he thinks fit, accept appointment as a sole arbitrator or as umpire by or by virtue of an arbitration agreement.

(2) A judge of the Commercial Court shall not do so unless the Lord Chief Justice has informed him that, having regard to the state of business in the High Court and the Crown Court, he can be made available.

(3) An official referee shall not do so unless the Lord Chief Justice has informed him that, having regard to the state of official referees' business, he can be made available.

(4) The fees payable for the services of a judge of the Commercial Court or official referee as arbitrator or umpire shall be taken in the High Court.

(5) In this section—

"arbitration agreement" has the same meaning as in Part I, and
"official referee" means a person nominated under section 68(1)(a) of the Supreme Court Act 1981 to deal with official referees' business.

(6) The provisions of Part I of this Act apply to arbitration before a person appointed under this section with the modifications specified in Schedule 2.

Statutory arbitrations

Application of Part I to statutory arbitrations

94.—(1) The provisions of Part I apply to every arbitration under an enactment (a "statutory arbitration"), or whether the enactment was passed or made before or after the commencement of this Act, subject to the adaptations and exclusions specified in sections 95 to 98.

(2) The provisions of Part I do not apply to a statutory arbitration if or to the extent that their application—

(a) is inconsistent with the provisions of the enactment concerned, with any rules or procedure authorised or recognised by it, or

(b) is excluded by any other enactment.

(3) In this section and the following provisions of this Part "enactment"—

(a) in England and Wales, includes an enactment contained in subordinate legislation within the meaning of the Interpretation Act 1978;

(b) in Northern Ireland, means a statutory provision within the meaning of section 1(f) of the Interpretation Act (Northern Ireland) 1954.

General adaptation of provisions in relation to statutory arbitrations

95.—(1) The provisions of Part I apply to a statutory arbitration—

(a) as if the arbitration were pursuant to an arbitration agreement and as if the enactment were that agreement, and

(b) as if the persons by and against whom a claim subject to arbitration in pursuance of the enactment may be or has been made were parties to that agreement.

(2) Every statutory arbitration shall be taken to have its seat in England and Wales or, as the case may be, in Northern Ireland.

Specific adaptations of provisions in relation to statutory arbitrations

96.—(1) The following provisions of Part I apply to a statutory arbitration with the following adaptations.

(2) In section 30(1) (competence of tribunal to rule on its own jurisdiction), the reference in paragraph (a) to whether there is a valid arbitration agreement shall be construed as a reference to whether the enactment applies to the dispute or difference in question.

(3) Section 35 (consolidation of proceedings and concurrent hearings) applies only so as to authorise the consolidation of proceedings, or concurrent hearings in proceedings, under the same enactment.

(4) Section 46 (rules applicable to substance of dispute) applies with the omission of subsection (1)(b) (determination in accordance with considerations agreed by parties).

Provisions excluded from applying to statutory arbitrations

97.—(1) The following provisions of Part I do not apply in relation to a statutory arbitration—

(a) section 8 (whether agreement discharged by death of a party);
(b) section 12 (power of court to extend agreed time limits);
(c) sections 9(5), 10(2) and 71(4) (restrictions on effect of provision that award condition precedent to right to bring legal proceedings).

Power to make further provision by regulations

98.—(1) The Secretary of State may make provision by regulations for adapting or excluding any provision of Part I in relation to statutory arbitrations in general or statutory arbitrations of any particular description.

(2) The power is exercisable whether the enactment concerned is passed or made before or after the commencement of this Act.

(3) Regulations under this section shall be made by statutory instrument which shall be subject to annulment in pursuance of a resolution of either House of Parliament.

PART III

RECOGNITION AND ENFORCEMENT OF CERTAIN FOREIGN AWARDS

Enforcement of Geneva Convention awards

Continuation of Part II of the Arbitration Act 1950

99. Part II of the Arbitration Act 1950 (enforcement of certain foreign awards) continues to apply in relation to foreign awards within the meaning of that Part which are not also New York Convention awards.

Recognition and enforcement of New York Convention awards

New York Convention awards

100.—(1) In this Part a "New York Convention award" means an award made, in pursuance of an arbitration agreement, in the territory of a state (other than the United Kingdom) which is a party to the New York Convention.

(2) For the purposes of subsection (1) and of the provisions of this Part relating to such awards—

(a) "arbitration agreement" means an arbitration agreement in writing, and
(b) an award shall be treated as made at the seat of the arbitration, regardless of where it was signed, despatched or delivered to any of the parties.

In this subsection "agreement in writing" and "seat of the arbitration" have the same meaning as in Part I.

(3) If Her Majesty by Order in Council declares that a state specified in the Order is a party to the New York Convention, or is a party in respect of any territory so specified, the Order shall, while in force, be conclusive evidence of that fact.

(4) In this section "the New York Convention" means the Convention on the Recognition and Enforcement of Foreign Arbitral Awards adopted by the United Nations Conference on International Commercial Arbitration on 10th June 1958.

Recognition and enforcement of awards

101.—(1) A New York Convention award shall be recognised as binding on the persons as between whom it was made, and may accordingly be relied on by those persons by way of defence, set-off or otherwise in any legal proceedings in England and Wales or Northern Ireland.

(2) A New York Convention award may, by leave of the court, be enforced in the same manner as a judgment or order of the court to the same effect.

As to the meaning of "the court" see section 105.

(3) Where leave is so given, judgment may be entered in terms of the award.

Evidence to be produced by party seeking recognition or enforcement

102.—(1) A party seeking the recognition or enforcement of a New York Convention award must produce—

(a) the duly authenticated original award or a duly certified copy of it, and
(b) the original arbitration agreement or a duly certified copy of it.

(2) If the award or agreement is in a foreign language, the party must also produce a translation of it certified by an official or sworn translator or by a diplomatic or consular agent.

Refusal of recognition or enforcement

103.—(1) Recognition or enforcement of a New York Convention award shall not be refused except in the following cases.

(2) Recognition or enforcement of the award may be refused if the person against whom it is invoked proves—

(a) that a party to the arbitration agreement was (under the law applicable to him) under some incapacity;
(b) that the arbitration agreement was not valid under the law to which the parties subjected it or, failing any indication thereon, under the law of the country where the award was made;
(c) that he was not given proper notice of the appointment of the arbitrator or of the arbitration proceedings or was otherwise unable to present his case;
(d) that the award deals with a difference not contemplated by or not falling within the terms of the submission to arbitration or contains decisions on matters beyond the scope of the submission to arbitration (but see subsection (4));
(e) that the composition of the arbitral tribunal or the arbitral procedure was not in accordance with the agreement of the parties or, failing such agreement, with the law of the country in which the arbitration took place;
(f) that the award has not yet become binding on the parties, or has been set aside or suspended by a competent authority of the country in which, or under the law of which, it was made.

(3) Recognition or enforcement of the award may also be refused if the award is in

respect of a matter which is not capable of settlement by arbitration, or if it would be contrary to public policy to recognise or enforce the award.

(4) An award which contains decisions on matters not submitted to arbitration may be recognised or enforced to the extent that it contains decisions on matters submitted to arbitration which can be separated from those on matters not so submitted.

(5) Where an application for the setting aside or suspension of the award has been made to such a competent authority as is mentioned in subsection (2)(f), the court before which the award is sought to be relied upon may, if it considers it proper, adjourn the decision on the recognition or enforcement of the award.

It may also on the application of the party claiming recognition or enforcement of the award order the other party to give suitable security.

Saving for other bases of recognition or enforcement

104. Nothing in the preceding provisions of this Part affects any right to rely upon or enforce a New York Convention award at common law or under section 66.

PART IV

GENERAL PROVISIONS

Meaning of "the court" jurisdiction of High Court and county court

105.—(1) In this Act "the court" means the High Court or a county court, subject to the following provisions.

(2) The Lord Chancellor may by order make provision—

(a) allocating proceedings under this Act to the High Court or to county courts; or
(b) specifying proceedings under this Act which may be commenced or taken only in the High Court or in a county court.

(3) The Lord Chancellor may by order make provision requiring proceedings of any specified description under this Act in relation to which a county court has jurisdiction to be commenced or taken in one or more specified county courts.

Any jurisdiction so exercisable by a specified county court is exercisable throughout England and Wales or, as the case may be, Northern Ireland.

(4) An order under this section—

(a) may differentiate between categories of proceedings by reference to such criteria as the Lord Chancellor sees fit to specify, and
(b) may make such incidental or transitional provision as the Lord Chancellor considers necessary or expedient.

(5) An order under this section for England and Wales shall be made by statutory instrument which shall be subject to annulment in pursuance of a resolution of either House of Parliament.

(6) An order under this section for Northern Ireland shall be a statutory rule for the purposes of the Statutory Rules (Northern Ireland) Order 1979 which shall be subject to annulment in pursuance of a resolution of either House of Parliament in like manner as

a statutory instrument and section 5 of the Statutory Instruments Act 1946 shall apply accordingly.

Crown application

106.—(1) Part I of this Act applies to any arbitration agreement to which Her Majesty, either in right of the Crown or of the Duchy of Lancaster or otherwise, or the Duke of Cornwall, is a party.

(2) Where Her Majesty is party to an arbitration agreement otherwise than in right of the Crown, Her Majesty shall be represented for the purposes of any arbitral proceedings—

(a) where the agreement was entered into by Her Majesty in right of the Duchy of Lancaster, by the Chancellor of the Duchy or such person as he may appoint, and

(b) in any other case, by such person as Her Majesty may appoint in writing under the Royal Sign Manual.

(3) Where the Duke of Cornwall is party to an arbitration agreement, he shall be represented for the purposes of any arbitral proceedings by such person as he may appoint.

(4) References in Part I to a party or the parties to the arbitration agreement or to arbitral proceedings shall be construed, where subsection (2) or (3) applies, as references to the person representing Her Majesty or the Duke of Cornwall.

Consequential amendments and repeals

107.—(1) The enactments specified in Schedule 3 are amended in accordance with that Schedule, the amendments being consequential on the provisions of this Act.

(2) The enactments specified in Schedule 4 are repealed to the extent specified.

Extent

108.—(1) The provisions of this Act extend to England and Wales and, except as mentioned below, to Northern Ireland.

(2) The following provisions of Part II do not extend to Northern Ireland—

section 92 (exclusion of Part I in relation to small claims arbitration in the county court), and

section 93 and Schedule 2 (appointment of judges as arbitrators).

(3) Sections 89, 90 and 91 (consumer arbitration agreements) extend to Scotland and the provisions of Schedules 3 and 4 (consequential amendments and repeals) extend to Scotland so far as they relate to enactments which so extend, subject as follows.

(4) The repeal of the Arbitration Act 1975 extends only to England and Wales and Northern Ireland.

Commencement

109.—(1) The provisions of this Act come into force on such day as the Secretary of State may appoint by order made by statutory instrument, and different days may be appointed for different purposes.

(2) An order under subsection (1) may contain such transitional provisions as appear to the Secretary of State to be appropriate.

Short title

110. This Act may be cited as the Arbitration Act 1996.

SCHEDULES

SCHEDULE 1

MANDATORY PROVISIONS OF PART I

sections 9 to 11 (stay of legal proceedings);
section 12 (power of court to extend agreed time limits);
section 13 (application of Limitation Acts);
section 24 (power of court to remove arbitrator);
section 26(1) (effect of death of arbitrator);
section 28 (liability of parties for fees and expenses of arbitrators);
section 29 (immunity of arbitrator);
section 31 (objection to substantive jurisdiction of tribunal);
section 32 (determination of preliminary point of jurisdiction);
section 33 (general duty of tribunal);
section 37(2) (items to be treated as expenses of arbitrators);
section 40 (general duty of parties);
section 43 (securing the attendance of witnesses);
section 56 (power to withhold award in case of non-payment);
section 60 (effectiveness of agreement for payment of costs in any event);
section 66 (enforcement of award);
sections 67 and 68 (challenging the award: substantive jurisdiction and serious irregularity), and sections 70 and 71 (supplementary provisions; effect of order of court) so far as relating to those sections;
section 72 (saving for rights of person who takes no part in proceedings);
section 73 (loss of right to object);
section 74 (immunity of arbitral institutions, &c.);
section 75 (charge to secure payment of solicitors' costs).

SCHEDULE 2

MODIFICATIONS OF PART I IN RELATION TO JUDGE-ARBITRATORS

Introductory

1. In this Schedule ''judge-arbitrator'' means a judge of the Commercial Court or official referee appointed as arbitrator or umpire under section 93.

General

2.—(1) Subject to the following provisions of this Schedule, references in Part I to the court shall be construed in relation to a judge-arbitrator, or in relation to the appointment of a judge-arbitrator, as references to the Court of Appeal.

(2) The references in sections 32(6), 45(6) and 69(8) to the Court of Appeal shall in such a case be construed as references to the House of Lords.

Arbitrator's fees

3.—(1) The power of the court in section 28(2) to order consideration and adjustment of the liability of a party for the fees of an arbitrator may be exercised by a judge-arbitrator.

(2) Any such exercise of the power is subject to the powers of the Court of Appeal under sections 24(4) and 25(3)(b) (directions as to entitlement to fees or expenses in case of removal or resignation).

Exercise of court powers in support of arbitration

4.—(1) Where the arbitral tribunal consists of or includes a judge-arbitrator the powers of the court under sections 42 to 44 (enforcement of peremptory orders, summoning witnesses, and other court powers) are exercis-able by the High Court and also by the judge-arbitrator himself.

(2) Anything done by a judge-arbitrator in the exercise of those powers shall be regarded as done by him in his capacity as judge of the High Court and have effect as if done by that court.

Nothing in this sub-paragraph prejudices any power vested in him as arbitrator or umpire.

Extension of time for making award

5.—(1) The power conferred by section 50 (extension of time for making award) is exercisable by the judge-arbitrator himself.

(2) Any appeal from a decision of a judge-arbitrator under that section lies to the Court of Appeal with the leave of that court.

Withholding award in case of non-payment

6.—(1) The provisions of paragraph 7 apply in place of the provisions of section 56 (power to withhold award in the case of non-payment) in relation to the withholding of an award for non-payment of the fees and expenses of a judge-arbitrator.

(2) This does not affect the application of section 56 in relation to the delivery of such an award by an arbitral or other institution or person vested by the parties with powers in relation to the delivery of the award.

7.—(1) A judge-arbitrator may refuse to deliver an award except upon payment of the fees and expenses mentioned in section 56(1).

(2) The judge-arbitrator may, on an application by a party to the arbitral proceedings,

order that if he pays into the High Court the fees and expenses demanded, or such lesser amount as the judge-arbitrator may specify—

(a) the award shall be delivered,
(b) the amount of the fees and expenses. properly payable shall be determined by such means and upon such terms as he may direct, and
(c) out of the money paid into court there shall be paid out such fees and expenses as may be found to be properly payable and the balance of the money (if any) shall be paid out to the applicant.

(3) For this purpose the amount of fees and expenses properly payable is the amount the applicant is liable to pay under section 28 or any agreement relating to the payment of the arbitrator.

(4) No application to the judge-arbitrator under this paragraph may be made where there is any available arbitral process for appeal or review of the amount of the fees or expenses demanded.

(5) Any appeal from a decision of a judge-arbitrator under this paragraph lies to the Court of Appeal with the leave of that court.

(6) Where a party to arbitral proceedings appeals under sub-paragraph (5), an arbitrator is entitled to appear and be heard.

Correction of award or additional award

Subsections (4) to (6) of section 57 (correction of award or additional award: time limit for application or exercise of power) do not apply to a judge-arbitrator.

Costs

9. Where the arbitral tribunal consists of or includes a judge-arbitrator the powers of the court under section 63(4) (determination of recoverable costs) shall be exercised by the High Court.

10.—(1) The power of the court under section 64 to determine an arbitrator's reasonable fees and expenses may be exercised by a judge-arbitrator.

(2) Any such exercise of the power is subJect to the powers of the Court of Appeal under sections 24(4) and 25(3)(b) (directions as to entitlement to fees or expenses in case of removal or resignation).

Enforcement of award

11. The leave of the court required by section 66 (enforcement of award) may in the case of an award of a judge-arbitrator be given by the judge-arbitrator himself.

Solicitors' costs

12. The powers of the court to make declarations and orders under the provisions applied by section 75 (power to charge property recovered in arbitral proceedings with the payment of solicitors' costs) may be exercised by the judge-arbitrator.

Powers of court in relation to service of documents

13.—(1) The power of the court under section 77(2) (powers of court in relation to service of documents) is exercisable by the judge-arbitrator.

(2) Any appeal from a decision of a judge-arbitrator under that section lies to the Court of Appeal with the leave of that court.

Powers of court to extend time limits relating to arbitral proceedings

14.—(1) The power conferred by section 79 (power of court to extend time limits relating to arbitral proceedings) is exercisable by the judge-arbitrator himself.

(2) Any appeal from a decision of a judge-arbitrator under that section lies to the Court of Appeal with the leave of that court.

[Schedules 3 and 4 are not reproduced here.]

RULES OF THE SUPREME COURT

ORDER 73

ARBITRATION PROCEEDINGS

Arbitration proceedings not to be assigned to Chancery Division

1. [*Revoked by R.S.C. (Amendment. No. 2) 1983 (S.I. 1983 No 1181).*]

Matters for a judge in court

2.—(1) Every application to the Court—

(a) to remit an award under section 22 of the Arbitration Act 1950, or
(b) to remove an arbitrator or umpire under section 23(1) of that Act, or
(c) to set aside an award under section 23(2) thereof, or
(d) [*Revoked by R.S.C. (Amendment. No.2) 1983 (S.I. 1983 No.1181).*]
(e) to determine, under section 2(1) of the Arbitration Act 1979, any question of law arising in the course of a reference,

must be made by originating motion to a single judge in court.

(2) Any appeal to the High Court under section 1(2) of the Arbitration Act 1979 shall be made by originating motion to a single judge in court.

(3) An application for a declaration that an award made by an arbitrator or umpire is not binding on a party to the award on the ground that it was made without jurisdiction may be made by originating motion to a single judge in court, but the foregoing provision shall not be taken as affecting the judge's power to refuse to make such a declaration in proceedings begun by motion.

Matters for judge in chambers or master

3.—(1) Subject to the foregoing provisions of this Order and the provisions of this rule, the jurisdiction of the High Court or a judge thereof under the Arbitration Act 1950 and the jurisdiction of the High Court under the Arbitration Act 1975 and the Arbitration Act 1979 may be exercised by a judge in chambers, a master or the Admiralty Registrar.

(2) Any application

(a) for leave to appeal under section 1(2) of the Arbitration Act 1979, or
(b) under section 1(5) of that Act (including any application for leave), or
(c) under section 5 of that Act,

shall be made to a judge in chambers.

(3) Any application to which this rule applies shall, where an action is pending, be made by summons in the action, and in any other case by an originating summons which shall be in Form No.10 in Appendix A.

(4) Where an application is made under section 1(5) of the Arbitration Act 1979 (including any application for leave) the summons must be served on the arbitrator or umpire and on any other party to the reference.

Applications in district registries

4. An application under section 12(4) of the Arbitration Act 1950 for an order that a writ of subpoena ad testificandum or of subpoena duces tecum shall issue to compel the attendance before an arbitrator or umpire of a witness may, if the attendance of the witness is required within the district of any district registry, be made at that registry, instead of at the Admiralty and Commercial Registry, at the option of the applicant.

Time-limits and other special provisions as to appeals and applications under the Arbitration Acts

5.—(1) An application to the Court—

(a) to remit an award under section 22 of the Arbitration Act 1950, or
(b) to set aside an award under section 23(2) of that Act or otherwise, or
(c) to direct an arbitrator or umpire to state the reasons for an award under section 1(5) of the Arbitration Act 1979,

must be made, and the summons or notice must be served, within 21 days after the award has been made and published to the parties.

(2) In the case of an appeal to the Court under section 1(2) of the Arbitration Act 1979, the summons for leave to appeal, where leave is required, and the notice of originating motion must be served and the appeal entered, within 21 days after the award has been made and published to the parties:

Provided that, where reasons material to the appeal are given on a date subsequent to the publication of the award, the period of 21 days shall run from the date on which the reasons are given.

(3) An application, under section 2(1) of the Arbitration Act 1979, to determine any question of law arising in the course of a reference, must be made, and notice thereof served, within 14 days after the arbitrator or umpire has consented to the application being made, or the other parties have so consented.

(4) For the purpose of paragraph (3) the consent must be given in writing.

(5) In the case of every appeal or application to which this rule applies, the notice of originating motion, the originating summons or the summons, as the case may be, must state the grounds of the appeal or application and, where the appeal or application is founded on evidence by affidavit, or is made with the consent of the arbitrator or umpire or of the other parties, a copy of every affidavit intended to be used. or, as the case may be, of every consent given in writing, must be served with that notice.

(6) Without prejudice to paragraph (5), in an appeal under section 1(2) of the Arbitration Act 1979 the statement of the grounds of the appeal shall specify the relevant parts of the award and reasons, and a copy of the award and reasons, or the relevant parts thereof, shall be lodged with the court and served with the notice of originating motion.

(7) Without prejudice to paragraph (5), in an application for leave to appeal under section 1(2) of the Arbitration Act 1979, any affidavit verifying the facts in support of a

contention that the question of law concerns a term of a contract or an event which is not a one-off term or event must be lodged with the court and served with the notice of originating motion.

(8) Any affidavit in reply to an affidavit under paragraph (7) shall be lodged with the court and served on the applicant not less than two clear days before the hearing of the application.

(9) A respondent to an application for leave to appeal under section 1(2) of the Arbitration Act 1979 who desires to contend that the award should be upheld on grounds not expressed or not fully expressed in the award and reasons shall not less than two clear days before the hearing of the application lodge with the court and serve on the applicant a notice specifying the grounds of his contention.

Applications and appeals to be heard by Commercial Judges

6.—(1) Any matter which is required, by rule 2 or 3, to be heard by a judge shall be heard by a Commercial Judge, unless any such judge otherwise directs.

(2) Nothing in the foregoing paragraph shall be construed as preventing the powers of a Commercial judge from being exercised by any judge of the High Court.

Service out of the jurisdiction of summons, notice, etc.

7.—(1) Subject to paragraph (1A), service out of the jurisdiction of—

(a) any originating summons or notice of originating motion under the arbitration Act 1950 or the Arbitration Act 1979, or

(b) any order made on such a summons or motion as aforesaid,

is permissible with the leave of the Court provided that the arbitration to which the summons, motion or order relates is governed by English law or has been, is being, or is to be held within the jurisdiction.

(1A) Service out of the jurisdiction of an originating summons for leave to enforce an award is permissible with the leave of the Court whether or not the arbitration is governed by English law.

(2) An application for the grant of leave under this rule must be supported by an affidavit stating the grounds on which the application is made and showing in what place or country the person to be served is, or probably may be found; and no such leave shall be granted unless it shall be made sufficiently to appear to the Court that the case is a proper one for service out of the jurisdiction under this rule.

(3) Order 11, rules 5 to 8, shall apply in relation to any such summons, notice or order as is referred to in paragraph (1) as they apply in relation to a writ.

Registration in High Court of foreign awards

8. Where an award is made in proceedings on an arbitration in any part of Her Majesty's dominions or other territory to which Part I of the Foreign Judgments (Reciprocal Enforcement) Act 1933 extends, being a part to which Part II of the Administration of Justice Act 1920 extended immediately before the said Part I was extended thereto, then, if the award has, in pursuance of the law in force in the place where it was made, become enforceable in the same manner as a judgment given by a court in that place, Order 71 shall apply in relation to the award as it applies in relation to a judgment given by that court, subject, however, to the following modifications:—

(a) for references to the country of the original court there shall be substituted references to the place where the award was made; and
(b) the affidavit required by rule 3 of the said Order must state (in addition to the other matters required by that rule) that to the best of the information or belief of the deponent the award has, in pursuance of the law in force in the place where it was made, become enforceable in the same manner as a judgment given by a court in that place.

Registration of awards under Arbitration (International Investment Disputes) Act 1966

9.—(1) In this rule and in any provision of these rules as applied by this rule—

"the Act of 1966" means the Arbitration (International Investment Disputes) Act 1966;
"award" means an award rendered pursuant to the Convention;
"the Convention" means the Convention referred to in section 1(1) of the Act of 1966;
"judgment creditor" and "judgment debtor" means respectively the person seeking recognition or enforcement of an award and the other party to the award.

(2) Subject to the provisions of this rule, the following provisions of Order 71, namely, rules 1, 3(1) (except sub-paragraphs (c) (iv) and (d) thereof) 7 (except paragraph (3) (c) and (d) thereof), and 10 (3) shall apply with the necessary modifications in relation to an award as they apply in relation to a Judgment to which Part II of the Foreign Judgments (Reciprocal Enforcement) Act 1933 applies.

(3) An application to have an award registered in the High Court under section 1 of the Act of 1966 shall be made by originating summons which shall be in Form No.10 in Appendix A.

(4) The affidavit required by Order 71, rule 3, in support of an application for registration shall—

(a) in lieu of exhibiting the judgment or a copy thereof, exhibit a copy of the award certified pursuant to the Convention, and
(b) in addition to stating the matters mentioned in paragraph 3(1) (c) (i) and (ii) of the said rule 3, state whether at the date of the application the enforcement of the award has been stayed (provisionally or otherwise) pursuant to the Convention and whether any, and if so what, application has been made pursuant to the Convention, which, if granted, might result in a stay of the enforcement of the award.

(5) There shall be kept in the Admiralty and Commercial Registry under the direction of the Senior Master a register of the awards ordered to be registered under the Act of 1966 and particulars shall be entered in the register of any execution issued on such an award.

(6) Where it appears to the court on granting leave to register an award or on an application made by the judgment debtor after an award has been registered—

(a) that the enforcement of the award has been stayed (whether provisionally or otherwise) pursuant to the Convention or

(b) that an application has been made pursuant to the Convention which, if granted, might result in a stay of the enforcement of the award,

the court shall, or, in the case referred to in sub-paragraph (b) may, stay execution of the award for such time as it considers appropriate in the circumstances.

(7) An application by the judgment debtor under paragraph (6) shall be made by summons and supported by affidavit.

Registration of awards under Multilateral Investment Guarantee Agency Act 1988

9A. Rule 9 shall apply, with the necessary modifications, in relation to an award rendered pursuant to the convention referred to in section 1(1) of the Multilateral Guarantee Agency Act 1988 as it applies in relation to an award rendered pursuant to the convention referred to in section 1(1) of the Arbitration (International Investment Disputes) Act 1966.

Enforcement of arbitration awards

10.—(1) An application for leave under section 96 of the Arbitration Act 1950 or under section 3(1) (a) of the Arbitration Act 1975 to enforce an award on an arbitration agreement in the same manner as a judgment or order may be made ex parte but the Court hearing the application may direct a summons to be issued.

(2) If the Court directs a summons to be issued, the summons shall be an originating summons which shall be in Form No.10 in Appendix A.

(3) An application for leave must be supported by affidavit—

(a) exhibiting—
   (i) where the application is under section 96 of the Arbitration Act 1950, the arbitration agreement and the original award or, in either case, a copy thereof
   (ii) where the application is under section 3(1) (a) of the Arbitration Act 1975, the documents required to be produced by section 4 of that Act.

(b) stating the name and the usual or last known place of abode or business of the applicant (hereinafter referred to as ''the creditor'') and the person against whom it is sought to enforce the award (hereinafter referred to as ''the debtor'') respectively,

(c) as the case may require, either that the award has not been complied with or the extent to which it has not been complied with at the date of the application

(4) An order giving leave must be drawn up by or on behalf of the creditor and must be served on the debtor by delivering a copy to him personally or by sending a copy to him at his usual or last known place of abode or business or in such other manner as the Court may direct.

(5) Service of the order out of the jurisdiction is permissible without leave, and Order 11, rules 5, 6 and 8, shall apply in relation to such an order as they apply in relation to a writ.

(6) Within 14 days after service of the order or, if the order is to be served out of the jurisdiction, within such other period as the Court may fix, the debtor may apply to set aside the order and the award shall not be enforced until after the expiration of that

period or, if the debtor applies within that period to set aside the order, until after the application is finally disposed of.

(7) The copy of the order served on the debtor shall state the effect of paragraph (6).

(8) In relation to a body corporate this rule shall have effect as if for any reference to the place of abode or business of the creditor or the debtor there were substituted a reference to the registered or principal address of the body corporate; so, however, that nothing in this rule shall affect any enactment which provides for the manner in which a document may be served on a body corporate.

Appendix 3

UNCI TRAL MODEL LAW ON INTERNATIONAL COMMERCIAL ARBITRATION

(United Nations document A/40/17, Annex 1)

(As adopted by the United Nations Commission on International Trade Law on June 21, 1985)

C HAPTER I

General provisions

Article 1 Scope of application*

1. This Law applies to international commercial** arbitration, subject to any agreement in force between this State and any other State or States.

2. The provisions of this Law, except Articles 8, 9, 35 and 36, apply only if the place of arbitration is in the territory of this State.

3. An arbitration is international if:

(a) the parties to an arbitration agreement have, at the time of the conclusion of that agreement, their places of business in different States; or

(b) one of the following places is situated outside the State in which the parties have their places of business:

* Article headings are for reference purposes only and are not to be used for purposes of interpretation.

** The term ''commercial'' should be given a wide interpretation so as to cover matters arising from all relationships of a commercial nature, whether contractual or not. Relationships of a commercial nature include, but are not limited to, the following transactions: any trade transaction for the supply or exchange of goods or services; distribution agreement; commercial representation or agency; factoring; leasing; construction of works; consulting; engineering; licensing; investment; financing; banking; insurance; exploitation agreement or concession; joint venture and other forms of industrial or business co-operation; carriage of goods or passengers by air, sea, rail or road.

(i) the place of arbitration if determined in, or pursuant to, the arbitration agreement;

(ii) any place where a substantial part of the obligations of the commercial relationship is to be performed or the place with which the subject-matter of the dispute is most closely connected; or

(c) the parties have expressly agreed that the subject-matter of the arbitration agreement relates to more than one country.

4. For the purposes of paragraph (3) of this article:

(a) if a party has more than one place of business, the place of business is that which has the closest relationship to the arbitration agreement;

(b) if a party does not have a place of business, reference is to be made to his habitual residence.

5. This Law shall not affect any other law of this State by virtue of which certain disputes may not be submitted to arbitration or may be submitted to arbitration only according to provisions other than those of this Law.)

Article 2 Definitions and rules of interpretation

For the purposes of this Law:

(a) "arbitration" means any arbitration whether or not administered by a permanent arbitral institution;

(b) "arbitral tribunal" means a sole arbitrator or a panel of arbitrators;

(c) "court" means a body or organ of the judicial system of a State;

(d) where a provision of this Law, except article 28, leaves the parties free to determine a certain issue, such freedom includes the right of the parties to authorize a third party, including an institution, to make that determination;

(e) where a provision of this Law refers to the fact that the parties have agreed or that they may agree or in any other way refers to an agreement of the parties, such agreement includes any arbitration rules referred to in that agreement;

(f) where a provision of this Law, other than in articles 25(a) and 32(2)(a), refers to a claim, it also applies to a counter-claim, and where it refers to a defence, it also applies to a defence to such counter-claim.

Article 3 Receipt of written communications

1. Unless otherwise agreed by the parties:

(a) any written communication is deemed to have been received if it is delivered to the addressee personally or if it is delivered at his place of business, habitual residence or mailing address; if none of these can be found after making a reasonable inquiry, a written communication is deemed to have been received if it is sent to the addressee's last-known place of business, habitual residence or mailing address by registered letter or any other means which provides a record of the attempt to deliver it;

(b) the communication is deemed to have been received on the day it is so delivered.

2. The provisions of this article do not apply to communications in court proceedings.

Article 4 Waiver of right to object

A party who knows that any provision of this Law from which the parties may derogate or any requirement under the arbitration agreement has not been complied with and yet proceeds with the arbitration without stating his objection to such non-compliance without undue delay or, if a time-limit is provided therefor, within such period of time, shall be deemed to have waived his right to object.

Article 5 Extent of court intervention

In matters governed by this Law, no court shall intervene except where so provided in this Law.

Article 6 Court or other authority for certain functions of arbitration assistance and supervision

The functions referred to in Articles 11(3), 11(4), 13(3), 14, 16(3) and 34(2) shall be performed by .... [Each State enacting this model law specifies the court, courts or, where referred to therein, other authority competent to perform these functions.]

CHAPTER II

Arbitration agreement

Article 7 Definition and form of arbitration agreement

1. "Arbitration agreement" is an agreement by the parties to submit to arbitration all or certain disputes which have arisen or which may arise between them in respect of a defined legal relationship, whether contractual or not. An arbitration agreement may be in the form of an arbitration clause in a contract or in the form of a separate agreement.

2. The arbitration agreement shall be in writing. An agreement is in writing if it is contained in a document signed by the parties or in an exchange of letters, telex, telegrams or other means of telecommunication which provide a record of the agreement, or in an exchange of statements of claim and defence in which the existence of an agreement is alleged by one party and not denied by another. The reference in a contract to a document containing an arbitration clause constitutes an arbitration agreement provided that the contract is in writing and the reference is such as to make that clause part of the contract.

Article 8 Arbitration agreement and substantive claim before court

1. A court before which an action is brought in a matter which is the subject of an arbitration agreement shall, if a party so requests not later than when submitting his first statement on the substance of the dispute, refer the parties to arbitration unless it finds that the agreement is null and void, inoperative or incapable of being performed.

2. Where an action referred to in paragraph (1) of this article has been brought, arbitral proceedings may nevertheless be commenced or continued, and an award may be made, while the issue is pending before the court.

Article 9 Arbitration agreement and interim measures by court

It is not incompatible with an arbitration agreement for a party to request, before or during arbitral proceedings, from a court an interim measure of protection and for a court to grant such measure.

CHAPTER III

Composition of arbitral tribunal

Article 10 Number of arbitrators

1. The parties are free to determine the number of arbitrators.

2. Failing such determination, the number of arbitrators shall be three.

Article 11 Appointment of arbitrators

1. No person shall be precluded by reason of his nationality from acting as an arbitrator, unless otherwise agreed by the parties.

2. The parties are free to agree on a procedure of appointing the arbitrator or arbitrators, subject to the provisions of paragraphs (4) and (5) of this article

3. Failing such agreement,

(a) in an arbitration with three arbitrators, each party shall appoint one arbitrator, and the two arbitrators thus appointed shall appoint the third arbitrator; if a party fails to appoint the arbitrator within thirty days of receipt of a request to do so from the other party, or if the two arbitrators fail to agree on the third arbitrator within thirty days of their appointment, the appointment shall be made, upon request of a party, by the court or other authority specified in Article 6;

(b) in an arbitration with a sole arbitrator, if the parties are unable to agree on the arbitrator, he shall be appointed, upon request of a party, by the court or other authority specified in Article 6.

4. Where, under an appointment procedure agreed upon by the parties,

(a) a party fails to act as required under such procedure, or

(b) the parties, or two arbitrators, are unable to reach an agreement expected of them under such procedure, or

(c) a third party, including an institution, fails to perform any function entrusted to it under such procedure, or

any party may request the court or other authority specified in Article 6 to take the necessary measure, unless the agreement on the appointment procedure provides other means for securing the appointment.

5. A decision on a matter entrusted by paragraph (3) or (4) of this article to the court or other authority specified in Article 6 shall be subject to no appeal. The court or other authority, in appointing an arbitrator, shall have due regard to any qualifications required of the arbitrator by the agreement of the parties and to such considerations as are likely to secure the appointment of an independent and impartial arbitrator and, in the case of a sole or third arbitrator, shall take into account as well the advisability of appointing an arbitrator of a nationality other than those of the parties.

Article 12 Grounds for challenge

1. When a person is approached in connection with his possible appointment as an arbitrator, he shall disclose any circumstances likely to give rise to justifiable doubts as to his impartiality or independence. An arbitrator, from the time of his appointment and throughout the arbitral proceedings, shall without delay disclose any such circumstances to the parties unless they have already been informed of them by him.

2. An arbitrator may be challenged only if circumstances exist that give rise to justifiable doubts as to his impartiality or independence, or if he does not possess qualifications agreed to by the parties. A party may challenge an arbitrator appointed by him, or in whose appointment he has participated, only for reasons of which he becomes aware after the appointment has been made.

Article 13 Challenge procedure

1. The parties are free to agree on a procedure for challenging an arbitrator, subject to the provisions of paragraph (3) of this article.

2. Failing such agreement, a party who intends to challenge an arbitrator shall, within fifteen days after becoming aware of the constitution of the arbitral tribunal or after becoming aware of any circumstance referred to in Article 12(2), send a written statement of the reasons for the challenge to the arbitral tribunal. Unless the challenged arbitrator withdraws from his office or the other party agrees to the challenge, the arbitral tribunal shall decide on the challenge.

3. If a challenge under any procedure agreed upon by the parties or under the procedure of paragraph (2) of this article is not successful, the challenging party may request, within thirty days after having received notice of the decision rejecting the challenge, the court or other authority specified in Article 6 to decide on the challenge, which decision shall be subject to no appeal; while such a request is pending, the arbitral tribunal, including the challenged arbitrator, may continue the arbitral proceedings and make an award.

Article 14 Failure or impossibility to act

1. If an arbitrator becomes *de jure* or *de facto* unable to perform his functions or for other reasons fails to act without undue delay, his mandate terminates if he withdraws from his office or if the parties agree on the termination. Otherwise, if a controversy remains concerning any of these grounds, any party may request the court or other authority specified in article 6 to decide on the termination of the mandate, which decision shall be subject to no appeal.

2. If, under this Article or Article 13(2), an arbitrator withdraws from his office or a party agrees to the termination other mandate of an arbitrator, this does not imply acceptance of the validity of any ground referred to in this article or Article 12(2).

Article 15 Appointment of substitute arbitrator

Where the mandate of an arbitrator terminates under Article 13 or 14 or because of his withdrawal from office for any other reason or because of the revocation of his mandate by agreement of the parties or in any other case of termination of his mandate, a subsitute arbitrator shall be appointed according to the rules that were applicable to the appointment of the arbitrator being replaced.

CHAPTER IV

Jurisdiction of arbital tribunal

Article 16 Competence of arbitral tribunal to rule on its jurisdiction

1. The arbitral tribunal may rule on its own jurisdiction, including any objections with respect to the existence or validity of the arbitration agreement. For that purpose, an arbitration clause which forms part of a contract shall be treated as an agreement independent of the other terms of the contract. A decision by the arbitral tribunal that the contract is null and void shall not entail *ipso jure* the invalidity of the arbitration clause.

2. A plea that the arbitral tribunal does not have jurisdiction shall be raised not later than the submission of the statement of defence. A party is not precluded from raising such a plea by the fact that he has appointed, or participated in the appointment of, an arbitrator. A plea that the arbitral tribunal is exceeding the scope of its authority shall be raised as soon as the matter alleged to be beyond the scope of its authority is raised during the arbitral proceedings. The arbitral tribunal may, in either case, admit a later plea if it considers the delay jusfified.

3. The arbitral tribunal may rule on a plea referred to in paragraph (2) of this Article either as a preliminary question or in an award on the merits. If the arbitral tribunal rules as a preliminary question that it has jurisdiction, any party may request, within thirty days after having received notice of that ruling, the court specified in Article 6 to decide the matter, which decision shall be subject to no appeal; while such a request is pending, the arbitral tribunal may continue the arbitral proceedings and make an award.

Article 17 Power of arbitral tribunal to order interim measures

Unless otherwise agreed by the parties, the arbitral tribunal may, at the request of a party, order any party to take such interim measure of protection as the arbitral tribunal may consider necessary in respect of the subject-matter of the dispute. The arbitral tribunal may require any party to provide appropriate security in connection with such measure.

CHAPTER V

Conduct of arbitral proceedings

Article 18 Equal treatment of parties

The parties shall be treated with equality and each party shall be given a full opportunity of presenting his case.

Article 19 Determination of rules of procedure

1. Subject to the provisions of this Law, the parties are free to agree on the procedure to be followed by the arbitral tribunal in conducting the proceedings.

2. Failing such agreement, the arbitral tribunal may, subject to the provisions of this Law, conduct the arbitration in such manner as it considers appropriate. The power conferred upon the arbitral tribunal includes the power to determine the admissibility, relevance, materiality and weight of any evidence.

Article 20 Place of arbitration

1. The parties are free to agree on the place of arbitration. Failing such agreement, the place of arbitration shall be determined by the arbitral tribunal having regard to the circumstances of the case, including the convenience of the parties.

2. Notwithstanding the provisions of paragraph (1) of this article, the arbitral tribunal may, unless otherwise agreed by the parties, meet at any place it considers appropriate for consultation among its members, for hearing witnesses, experts or the parties, or for inspection of goods, other property or documents.

Article 21 Commencement of arbitral proceedings

Unless otherwise agreed by the parties, the arbitral proceedings in respect of a particular dispute commence on the date on which a request for that dispute to be referred to arbitration is received by the respondent.

Article 22 Language

1. The parties are free to agree on the language or languages to be used in the arbitral proceedings. Failing such agreement, the arbitral tribunal shall determine the language or languages to be used in the proceedings. This agreement or determination, unless otherwise specified therein, shall apply to any written statement by a party, any hearing and any award, decision or other communication by the arbitral tribunal.

2. The arbitral tribunal may order that any documentary evidence shall be accompanied by a translation into the language or languages agreed upon by the parties or determined by the arbitral tribunal.

Article 23 Statements of claim and defence

1. Within the period of time agreed by the parties or determined by the arbitral tribunal, the claimant shall state the facts supporting his claim, the points at issue and the relief or remedy sought, and the respondent shall state his defence in respect of these particulars, unless the parties have otherwise agreed as to the required elements of such statements. The parties may submit with their statements all documents they consider to be relevant or may add a reference to the documents or other evidence they will submit.

2. Unless otherwise agreed by the parties, either party may amend or supplement his claim or defence during the course of the arbitral proceedings, unless the arbitral tribunal considers it inappropriate to allow such amendment having regard to the delay in making it.

Article 24 Hearings and written proceedings

1. Subject to any contrary agreement by the parties, the arbitral tribunal shall decide whether to hold oral hearings for the presentation of evidence or for oral argument, or whether the proceedings shall be conducted on the basis of documents and other materials. However, unless the parties have agreed that no hearings shall be held, the arbitral tribunal shall hold such hearings at an appropriate stage of the proceedings, if so requested by a party.

2. The parties shall be given sufficient advance notice of any hearing and of any meeting of the arbitral tribunal for the purposes of inspection of goods, other property or documents.

3. All statements, documents or other information supplied to the arbitral tribunal by one party shall be communicated to the other party. Also any expert report or evidentiary document on which the arbitral tribunal may rely in making its decision shall be communicated to the parties.

Article 25 Default of a party
Unless otherwise agreed by the parties, if, without showing sufficient cause,

(a) the claimant fails to communicate his statement of claim in accordance with Article 23(1), the arbitral tribunal shall terminate the proceedings;
(b) the respondent fails to communicate his statement of defence in accordance with Article 23(1), the arbitral tribunal shall continue the proceedings without treating such failure in itself as an admission of the claimant's allegations;
(c) any party fails to appear at a hearing or to produce documentary evidence, the arbitral tribunal may continue the proceedings and make the award on the evidence before it.

Article 26 Expert appointed by arbitral tribunal
1. Unless otherwise agreed by the parties, the arbitral tribunal

(a) may appoint one or more experts to report to it on specific issues to be determined by the arbitral tribunal;
(b) may require a party to give the expert any relevant information or to produce, or to provide access to, any relevant documents, goods or other property for his inspection.

2. Unless otherwise agreed by the parties, if a party so requests or if the arbitral tribunal considers it necessary, the expert shall, after delivery of his written or oral report, participate in a hearing where the parties have the opportunity to put questions to him and to present expert witnesses in order to testify on the points at issue.

Article 27 Court assistance in taking evidence
The arbitral tribunal or a party with the approval of the arbitral tribunal may request from a competent court of this State assistance in taking evidence. The court may execute the request within its competence and according to its rules on taking evidence.

CHAPTER VI

Making of award and termination of proceedings

Article 28 Rules applicable to substance of dispute
1. The arbitral tribunal shall decide the dispute in accordance with such rules of law as are chosen by the parties as applicable to the substance of the dispute. Any designation of the law or legal system of a given State shall be construed, unless otherwise expressed, as directly referring to the substantive law of that State and not to its conflict of laws rules.
2. Failing any designation by the parties, the arbitral tribunal shall apply the law determined by the conflict of laws rules which it considers applicable.
3. The arbitral tribunal shall decide *ex aequo et bono* or as *amiable compositeur* only if the parties have expressly authorized it to do so.

4. In all cases, the arbitral tribunal shall decide in accordance with the terms of the contract and shall take into account the usages of the trade applicable to the transaction.

Article 29 Decision making by panel of arbitrators
In arbitral proceedings with more than one arbitrator, any decision of the arbitral tribunal shall be made, unless otherwise agreed by the parties, by a majority of all its members. However, questions of procedure may be decided by a presiding arbitrator, if so authorized by the parties or all members of the arbitral tribunal.

Article 30 Settlement
1. If, during arbitral proceedings, the parties settle the dispute, the arbitral tribunal shall terminate the proceedings and, if requested by the parties and not objected to by the arbitral tribunal, record the settlement in the form of an arbitral award on agreed terms.

2. An award on agreed terms shall be made in accordance with the provisions of Article 31 and shall state that it is an award. Such an award has the same status and effect as any other award on the merits of the case.

Article 31 Form and contents of award
1. The award shall be made in writing and shall be signed by the arbtrator or arbitrators. In arbitral proceedings with more than one arbitrator, the signatures of the majority of all members of the arbitral tribunal shall suffice, provided that the reason for any omitted signature is stated.

2. The award shall state the reasons upon which it is based, unless the parties have agreed that no reasons are to be given or the award is an award on agreed terms under Article 30.

3. The award shall state its date and the place of arbitration as determined in accordance with Article 20(1). This award shall be deemed to have been made at that place.

4. After the award is made, a copy signed by the arbitrators in accordance with paragraph (1) of this Article shall be delivered to each party.

Article 32 Termination of proceedings
1. The arbitral proceedings are terminated by the final award or by an order of the arbitral tribunal in accordance with paragraph (2) of this Article.

2. The arbitral tribunal shall issue an order for the termination of the arbitral proceedings when:

(a) the claimant withdraws his claim, unless the respondent objects thereto and the arbitral tribunal recognizes a legimate interest on his part in obtaining a final settlement of the dispute;
(b) the parties agree on the termination of the proceedings;
(c) the arbitral tribunal finds that the continuation of the proceedings has for any other reason become unnecessary or impossible.

3. The mandate of the arbitral tribunal terminates with the termination of the arbitral proceedings, subject to the provisions of Articles 33 and 34(4).

Article 33 Correction and interpretation of award: additional award

1. Wthin thirty days of receipt of the award, unless another period of time has been agreed upon by the parties:

(a) a party, with notice to the other party, may request the arbitral tribunal to correct in the award any errors in computation, any clerical or typographical errors or any errors of similar nature;
(b) if so agreed by the parties, a party, with notice to the other party, may request the arbitral tribunal to give an interpretation of a specific point or part of the award.

If the arbitral tribunal considers the request to be justified, it shall make the correction or give the interpretation within thirty days of receipt of the request. The interpretation shall form part of the award.

2. The arbitral tribunal may correct any error of the type referred to in paragraph (1)(a) of this Article on its own initiative within thirty days of the date of the award.

3. Unless otherwise agreed by the parties, a party, with notice to the other party, may request, within thirty days a receipt of the award, the arbitral tribunal to make an additional award as to claims presented in the arbitral proceedings but omitted from the award. If the arbitral tribunal considers the request to be justified, it shall make the additional award within sixty days.

4. The arbitral tribunal may extend, if necessary, the period of time within which it shall make a correction, intepretation or an additional award under paragraph (1) or (3) of this Article.

5. The provisions of Article 31 shall apply to a correction or interpretation of the award or to an additional award.

CHAPTER VII

Recourse against award

Article 34 Application for setting aside as exclusive recourse against arbitral award

1. Recourse to a court against an arbitral award may be made only by an application for setting aside in accordance with paragraphs (2) and (3) of this Article.

2. An arbitral award may be set aside by the court specified in Article 6 only if:

(a) the party making the application furnishes proof that:
  (i) a party to the arbitration agreement referred to in Article 7 was under some incapacity; or the said agreement is not valid under the law to which the parties have subjected it or, failing any indication thereon, under the law of this State; or
  (ii) the party making the application was not given proper notice of the appointment of an arbitrator or of the arbitral proceedings or was otherwise unable to present his case; or
  (iii) the award deals with a dispute not contemplated by or not falling within the terms of the submission to arbitration, or contains decisions on matters

beyond the scope of the submission to arbitration, provided that, if the decisions on matters submitted to arbitration can be separated from those not so submitted, only that part of the award which contains decisions on matters not submitted to arbitration may be set aside; or

(iv) the composition of the arbitral tribunal or the arbitral procedure was not in accordance with the agreement of the parties, unless such agreement was in conflict with a provision of this Law from which the parties cannot derogate, or, failing such agreement, was not in accordance with this Law; or

(b) the court finds that:

(i) the subject-matter of the dispute is not capable of settlement by arbitration under the law of this State; or

(ii) the award is in conflict with the public policy of this State.

3. An application for setting aside may not be made after three months have elapsed from the date on which the party making that application had received the award or, if a request had been made under Article 33, from the date on which that request had been disposed of by the arbitral tribunal.

4. The court, when asked to set aside an award, may, where appropriate and so requested by a party, suspend the setting aside proceedings for a period of time determined by it in order to give the arbitral tribunal an opportunity to resume the arbitral proceedings or to take such other action as in the arbitral tribunal's opinion will eliminate the grounds for setting aside.

CHAPTER VII

Recognition and enforcement of awards

Article 35 Recognition and enforcement

1. An arbitral award, irrespective of the county in which it was made, shall be recognized as binding and, upon application in wrtiing to the competent court, shall be enforced subject to the provisions of this Article and of Article 36.

2. The party relying on an award or applying for its enforcement shall supply the duly authenticated original award or a duly certified copy thereof, and the original arbitration agreement referred to in Article 7 or a duly certified copy thereof. If the award or agreement is not made in an of official language of this State, the party shall supply a duly certified translation thereof into such language.***

Article 36 Grounds for refusing recognition of enforcement

1. Recognition or enforcement of an arbitral award, irrespective of the country in which it was made, may be refused only:

(a) at the request of the party against whom it is invoked, if that party furnishes to the competent court where recognition or enforcement is sought proof that:

*** The conditions set forth in this paragraph are intended to set maximum standards. It would, thus, not be contrary to the harmonization to be achieved by the model law if a State retained even less onerous conditions.

(i) a parly to the arbitration agreement referred to in Article 7 was under some incapacity; or the said agreement is not valid under the law to which the parties have subjected it or, failing any indication thereon, under the law of the country where the award was made; or

(ii) the party against whom the award is invoked was not given proper notice of the appointment of an arbitrator or of the arbitral proceedings or was otherwise unable to present his case; or

(iii) the award deals with a dispute not contemplated by or not falling within the terms of the submission to arbitration, or it contains decisions on matters beyond the scope of the submission to arbitration, provided that, if the decisions on matters submitted to arbitration can be separated from those not so submitted, that part of the award which contains decisions on matters submitted to arbitration may be recognized and enforced; or

(iv) the composition of the arbitral tribunal or the arbitral procedure was not in accordance with the agreement of the parties or, failing such agreement, was not in accordance with the law of the country where the arbitration took place; or

(v) the award has not yet become binding on the parties or has been set aside or suspended by a court of the country in which, or under the law of which, that award was made; or

(b) if the court finds that:

(i) the subject-matter of the dispute is not capable of settlement by arbitration under the law of this State; or

(ii) the recognition or enforcement of the award would be contrary to the public policy of this State.

2. If an application for setting aside or suspension of an award has been made to a court referred to in paragraph (1)(a)(v) of this article, the court where recognition or enforcement is sought may, if it considers it proper, adjoun its decision and may also, on the application of the party claiming recognition or enforcement of the award, order the other party to provide appropriate security.

Explanatory Note by the UNCITRAL Secretariat on the Model Law on International Commercial Arbitration*

1. The UNCITRAL Model Law on International Commercial Arbitration was adopted by the United Natons Commission on International Trade Law (UNCITRAL) on 21 June 1985, at the close of the Commission's 18th annual session. The General Assembly, in its Resolution 40/72 of 11 December 1985, recommended "that all States give due consideration to the Model Law on International Commercial Arbitration, in view of the desirability of uniformity of the law of arbitral procedures and the specific needs of international commercial arbitration practice".

2. The Model Law constitutes a sound and promising basis for the desired harmoniza-

* This note has been prepared by the Secretariat of the United Nations Commission on International Trade Law (UNCITRAL) for informational purposes only; it is not an official commentary on the Model Law. A commentary prepared by the Secretariat on an earlier draft of the Model Law appears in document A/CN.9/264 (reproduced in *UNCITRAL Yearbook*, Vol. XVI, 1985) (United Nations Publication, Sales No. E.87.V.4).

tion and improvement of national laws. It covers all stages of the arbitral process from the arbitration agreement to the recognition and enforcement of the arbitral award and reflects a worldwide consensus on the principles and important issues of international arbitration practice. It is acceptable to States of all regions and the different legal or economic systems of the world.

3. The form of a model law was chosen as the vehicle for harmonization and improvement in view of the flexibility it gives to States in preparing new arbitration laws. It is advisable to follow the model as closely as possible since that would be the best contribution to the desired harmonization and in the best interest of the users of international arbitration, who are primarily foreign parties and their lawyers.

A. BACKGROUND TO THE MODEL LAW

4. The Model Law is designed to meet concerns relating to the current state of national laws on arbitration. The need for improvement and harmonization is based on findings that domestic laws are often inappropriate for international cases and that considerable disparity exists between them.

1. Inadequacy of domestic laws

5. A global survey of national laws on arbitration revealed considerable disparities not only as regards individual provisions and solutions but also in terms of development and refinement. Some laws may be regarded as outdated, sometimes going back to the nineteenth century and often equating the arbitral process with court litigation. Other laws may be said to be fragmentary in that they do not address all relevant issues. Even most of those laws which appear to be up-to-date and comprehensive were drafted with domestic arbitration primarily, if not exclusively, in mind. While this approach is understandable in view of the fact that even today the bulk of cases governed by a general arbitration law would be of a purely domestic nature, the unfortunate consequence is that traditional local concepts are imposed on international cases and the needs of modern practice are often not met.

6. The expectations of the parties as expressed in a chosen set of arbitration rules or a "one-off" arbitration agreement may be frustrated, especially by a mandatory provision of the applicable law. Unexpected and undesired restrictions found in national laws relate, for example, to the parties' ability effectively to submit future disputes to arbitration, to their power to select the arbitrator freely, or to their interest in having the arbitral proceedings conducted according to the agreed rules of procedure and with no more court involvement than is appropriate. Frustrations may also ensue from non-mandatory provisions which may impose undesired requirements on unwary parties who did not provide otherwise. Even the absence of non-mandatory provisions may cause difficulties by not providing answers to the many procedural issues relevant in an arbitration and not always settled in the arbitration agreement.

2. Disparity between national laws

7. Problems and undesired consequences, whether emanating from mandatory or non-mandatory provisions or from a lack of pertinent provisions, are aggravated by the fact that national laws on arbitral procedure differ widely. The differences are a frequent source of concern in international arbitration, where at least one of the parties is, and often both parties are, confronted with foreign and unfamiliar provisions and procedures.

For such a party it may be expensive, impractical or impossible to obtain a full and precise account of the law applicable to the arbitration.

8. Uncertainty about the local law with the inherent risk of frustration may adversely affect not only the functioning of the arbitral process but already the selection of the place of arbitration. A party may well for those reasons hesitate or refuse to agree to a place which otherwise, for practical reasons, would be appropriate in the case at hand. The choice of places of arbitration would thus be widened and the smooth functioning of the arbitral proceedings would be enhanced if States were to adopt the Model Law which is easily recognizable, meets the specific needs of international commercial arbitration and provides an international standard with solutions acceptable to parties from different States and legal systems.

B. SALIENT FEATURES OF THE MODEL LAW

1. Special procedural regime for international commercial arbitration

9. The principles and individual solutions adopted in the Model Law aim at reducing or eliminating the above concerns and difficulties. As a response to the inadequacies and disparities of national laws, the Model Law presents a special legal regime geared to international commercial arbitration, without affecting any relevant treaty in force in the State adopting the Model Law. While the need for uniformity exists only in respect of international cases, the desire of updating and improving the arbitration law may be felt by a State also in respect of non-international cases and could be met by enacting modern legislation based on the Model Law for both categories of cases.

a. Substantive and territorial scope of application

10. The Model Law defines an arbitration as international if ''the parties to an arbitration agreement have, at the time of the conclusion of that agreement, their places of business in different States'' (Article 1(3)). The vast majority of situations commonly regarded as international will fall under this criterion. In addition, an arbitration is international if the place of arbitration, the place of contract performance, or the place of the subject-matter of the dispute is situated in a State other than where the parties have their place of business, or if the parties have expressly agreed that the subject-matter of the arbitration agreement relates to more than one country.

11. As regards the term ''commercial'', no hard and fast definition could be provided. Article 1 contains a note calling for ''a wide interpretation so as to cover matters arising from all relationships of a commercial nature, whether contractual or not''. The footnote to Article 1 then provides an illustrative list of relationships that are to be considered commercial, thus emphasizing the width of the suggested interpretation and indicating that the determinative test is not based on what the national law may regard as ''commercial''.

12. Another aspect of applicability is what one may call the territorial scope of application According to Article 1(2), the Model Law as enacted in a given State would apply only if the place of arbitration is in the territory of that State. However, there is an important and reasonable exception. Articles 8(1) and 9 which deal with recognition of arbitration agreements, including their compatibility with interim measures of protection, and Articles 35 and 36 on recognition and enforcement of arbitral awards are given a global scope, *i.e.* they apply irrespective of whether the place of arbitration is in that State or in another State and, as regards Articles 8 and 9, even if the place of arbitration is not yet determined.

13. The strict territorial criterion, governing the bulk of the provisions of the Model Law, was adopted for the sake of certainty and in view of the following facts. The place of arbitration is used as the exclusive criterion by the great majority of national laws and, where national laws allow parties to choose the procedural law of a State other than that where the arbitration takes place, experience shows that parties in practice rarely make use of that facility. The Model Law, by its liberal contents, further reduces the need for such choice of a ''foreign'' law in lieu of the (Model) Law of the place of arbitration, not the least because it grants parties wide freedom in shaping the rules of the arbitral proceedings. This includes the possibility of incorporating into the arbitration agreement procedural provisions of a ''foreign'' law, provided there is no conflict with the few mandatory provisions of the Model Law. Furthermore, the strict territorial criterion is of considerable practical benefit in respect of Articles 11, 13, 14, 16, 27 and 34, which entrust the courts of the respective State with functions of arbitration assistance and supervision.

b. Delimitation of court assistance and supervision

14. As evidenced by recent amendments to arbitration laws, there exists a trend in favour of limiting court involvement in international commercial arbitration. This seems justified in view of the fact that the parties to an arbitration agreement make a conscious decision to exclude court jurisdiction and, in particular in commercial cases, prefer expediency and finality to protracted battles in court.

15. In this spirit, the Model Law envisages court involvement in the following instances. A first group comprises appointment, challenge and termination of the mandate of an arbitrator (Articles 11, 13 and 14), jurisdiction of the arbitral tribunal (Article 16) and setting aside of the arbitral award (Article 34). These instances are listed in Article 6 as functions which should be entrusted, for the sake of centralization, specialization and acceleration, to a specially designated court or, as regards Articles 11, 13 and 14, possibly to another authority (*e.g.* arbitral institution, chamber of commerce). A second group comprises court assistance in taking evidence (Article 27), recognition of the arbitration agreement, including its compatibility with court-ordered interim measures of protection (Articles 8 and 9), and recognition and enforcement of arbitral awards (Articles 35 and 36).

16. Beyond the instances in these two groups, ''no court shall intervene, in matters governed by this Law''. This is stated in the innovative Article 5, which by itself does not take a stand on what is the appropriate role of the courts but guarantees the reader and user that he will find all instances of possible court intervention in this Law, except for matters not regulated by it (*e.g.* consolidation of arbitral proceedings, contractual relationship between arbitrators and parties or arbitral institutions, or fixing of costs and fees, including deposits). Especially foreign readers and users, who constitute the majority of potential users and may be viewed as the primary addressees of any special law on international commercial arbitration, will appreciate that they do not have to search outside this Law.

2. Arbitration agreement

17. Chapter II of the Model Law deals with the arbitration agreement, including its recognition by courts. The provisions follow closely Article 11 of the Convention on the Recognition and Enforcement of Foreign Arbitral Awards (New York, 1958) (hereafter referred to as ''1958 New York Convention'), with a number of useful clarifications

a. Definition and form of arbitration agreement

18. Article 7(1) recognizes the validity and effect of a commitment by the parties to submit to arbitration an existing dispute (''compromise'') or a future dispute (''clause compromissoire''). The latter type of agreement is presently not given full effect under certain national laws.

19. While oral arbitration agreements are found in practice and are recognized by some national laws, Article 7(2) follows the 1958 New York Convention in requiring written form. It widens and clarifies the definition of written form of Article 11(2) of that Convention by adding ''telex or other means of telecommunication which provide a record of the agreement, by covering the submission-type situation of ''an exchange of statements of claim and defence in which the existence of an agreement is alleged by one party and not denied by another'', and by providing that ''the reference in a contract to a document'' (*e.g.* general conditions) ''containing an arbitration clause constitutes an arbitration agreement provided that the contract is in writing and the reference is such as to make that clause part of the contract''.

b. Arbitration agreement and the courts

20. Articles 8 and 9 deal with two important aspects of the complex issue of the relationship between the arbitration agreement and resort to courts. Modelled on Article 11(3) of the 1958 New York Convention, Article 8(1) of the Model Law obliges any court to refer the parties to arbitration if seized with a claim on the same subject-matter unless it finds that the arbitration agreement is null and void, inoperative or incapable of being performed. The referral is dependent on a request which a party may make not later than when submitting his first statement on the substance of the dispute. While this provision, where adopted by a State when it adopts the Model Law, by its nature binds merely the courts of that State, it is not restricted to agreements providing for arbitration in that State and, thus, helps to give universal recognition and effect to international commercial arbitration agreements.

21. Article 9 expresses the principle that any interim measures of protection that may be obtained from courts under their procedural law (*e.g.* pre-award attachments) are compatible with an arbitration agreement. Like Article 8, this provision is addressed to the courts of a given State, insofar as it determines their granting of interim measures as being compatible with an arbitration agreement, irrespective of the place of arbitration Insofar as it declares it to be compatible with an arbitration agreement for a party to request such measure from a court, the provision would apply irrespective of whether the request is made to a court of the given State or of any other country. Wherever such request may be made, it may not be relied upon, under the Model Law, as an objection against the existence or effect of an arbitration agreement.

3. Composition of arbitral tribunal

22. Chapter III contains a number of detailed provisions on appointment, challenge, termination of mandate and replacement of an arbitrator. The chapter illustrates the approach of the Model Law in eliminating difficulties arising from inappropriate or fragmentary laws or rules. The approach consists, first, of recognizing the freedom of the parties to determine, by reference to an existing set of arbitration rules or by an ad hoc agreement, the procedure to be followed, subject to fundamental requirements of fairness and justice Secondly, where the parties have not used their freedom to lay down the rules of procedure or a particular issue has not been covered, the Model Law ensures, by

providing a set of suppletive rules, that the arbitration may commence and proceed effectively to the resolution of the dispute.

23. Where under any procedure, agreed upon by the parties or based upon the suppletive rules of the Model Law, difficulties arise in the process of appointment, challenge or termination of the mandate of an arbitrator, Articles 11, 13 and 14 provide for assistance by courts or other authorities. In view of the urgency of the matter and in order to reduce the risk and effect of any dilatory tactics, instant resort may be had by a party within a short period of time and the decision is not appealable.

4. *Jurisdiction of arbitral tribunal*

a. Competence to rule on own jurisdiction

24. Article 16(1) adopts the two important (not yet generally recognized) principles of "*Kompetenz-Kompetenz*" and of separability or autonomy of the arbitration clause. The arbitral tribunal may rule on his own jurisdiction, including any objections with respect to the existence or validity of the arbitration agreement. For that purpose, an arbitration clause shall be treated as an agreement independent of the other terms of the contract, and a decision by the arbitral tribunal that the contract is null and void shall not entail *ipso jure* the invalidity of the arbitration clause. Detailed provisions in paragraph (2) require that any objections relating to the arbitrators' jurisdiction be made at the earliest possible time.

25. The arbitral tribunal's competence to rule on his own jurisdiction, *i.e.* on the very foundation of its mandate and power, is, of course, subject to court control. Where the arbitral tribunal rules as a preliminary question that it has jurisdiction, Article 16(3) provides for instant court control in order to avoid unnecessary waste of money and time. However, three procedural safeguards are added to reduce the risk and effect of dilatory tactics: short time-period for resort to court (30 days), court decision is not appealable, and discretion of the arbitral tribunal to continue the proceedings and make an award while the matter is pending with the court. In those less common cases where the arbitral tribunal combines its decision on jurisdiction with an award on the merits, judicial review on the question of jurisdiction is available in setting aside proceedings under Article 34 or in enforcement proceedings under Article 36.

b. Power to order interim measures

26. Unlike some national laws, the Model Law empowers the arbitral tribunal, unless otherwise agreed by the parties, to order any party to take an interim measure of protection in respect of the subject-matter of the dispute, if so requested by a party (Article 17). It may be noted that the article does not deal with enforcement of such measures; any State adopting the Model Law would be free to provide court assistance in this regard.

5. *Conduct of arbitral proceedings*

27. Chapter V provides the legal framework for a fair and effective conduct of the arbitral proceedings. It opens with two provisions expressing basic principles that permeate the arbitral procedure governed by the Model Law. Article 18 lays down fundamental requirements of procedural justice and Article 19 the rights and powers to determine the rules of procedure.

a. Fundamental procedural rights of a party

28. Article 18 embodies the basic principle that the parties shall be treated with equally and each party shall be given a full opportunity of presenting his case. Other provisions implement and specify the basic principle in respect of certain fundamental rights of a party. Article 24(1) provides that, unless the parties have validly agreed that no oral hearings for the presentation of evidence or for oral argument be held, the arbitral tribunal shall hold such hearings at an appropriate stage of the proceedings, if so requested by a party. It should be noted that Article 24(1) deals only with the general right of a party to oral hearings (as an alternative to conducting the proceedings on the basis of documents and other materials) and not with the procedural aspects such as the length, number or timing of hearings.

29. Another fundamental right of a party of being heard and being able to present his case relates to evidence by an expert appointed by the arbitral tribunal. Article 26(2) obliges the expert, after having delivered his written or oral report, to participating a hearing where the parties may put questions to him and present expert witnesses in order to testify on the points at issue, if such a hearing is requested by a party or deemed necessary by the arbitral tribunal. As another provision aimed at ensuring fairness, objectively and impartiality, Article 24(3) provides that all statements, documents and other information supplied to the arbitral tribunal by one party shall be communicated to the other party, and that any expert report or evidentiary document on which the arbitral tribunal may rely in making its decision shall be communicated to the parties. In order to enable the parties to be present at any hearing and at any meeting of the arbitral tribunal for inspection purposes, they shall be given sufficient notice in advance (Article 24(2)).

b. Determination of rules of procedure

30. Article 19 guarantees the parties' freedom to agree on the procedure to be followed by the arbitral tribunal in conducting the proceedings, subject to a few mandatory provisions on procedure, and empowers the arbitral tribunal, failing agreement by the parties, to conduct the arbitration in such a manner as it considers appropriate. The power conferred upon the arbitral tribunal includes the power to determine the admissibility, relevance, materially and weight of any evidence.

31. Autonomy of the parties to determine the rules of procedure is of special importance in international cases since it allows the parties to select or tailor the rules according to their specific wishes and needs, unimpeded by traditional domestic concepts and without the earlier mentioned risk of frustration. The supplementary discretion of the arbitral tribunal is equally important in that it allows the tribunal to tailor the conduct of the proceedings to the specific features of the case without restraints of the traditional local law, including any domestic rules on evidence. Moreover, it provides a means for solving any procedural questions not regulated in the arbitration agreement or the Model Law.

32. In addition to the general provisions of Article 19, there are some special provisions using the same approach of granting the parties autonomy and, failing agreement, empowering the arbitral tribunal to decide the matter. Examples of particular practices importance in international cases are Article 20 on the place of arbitration and Article 22 on the language of the proceedings.

c. Default of a party

33. Only if due notice was given, may the arbitral proceedings be continued in the absence of a party. This applies, in particular, to the failure of a party to appear at a

hearing or to produce documentary evidence without showing sufficient cause for the failure (Article 25(c)). The arbitral tribunal may also continue the proceedings where the respondent fails to communicate his statement of defence, while there is no need for continuing the proceedings if the claimant fails to submit his statement of claim (Article 25(a), (b)).

34. Provisions which empower the arbitral tribunal to carry out its task even if one of the parties does not participate are of considerable practical importance since, as experience shows, it is not uncommon that one of the parties has little interest in co-operating and in expediting matters. They would, thus, give international commercial arbitration its necessary effectiveness, within the limits of fundamental requirements of procedural justice.

6. Making of award and termination of proceedings

a. Rules applicable to substance of dispute

35. Article 28 deals with the substantive law aspects of arbitration. Under paragraph (1), the arbitral tribunal decides the dispute in accordance with such rules of law as may be agreed by the parties. This provision is significant in two respects. It grants the parties the freedom to choose the applicable substantive law, which is important in view of the fact that a number of national laws do not clearly or fully recognize that right. In addition, by referring to the choice of "rules of law" instead of "law", the Model Law gives the parties a wider range of opbons as regards the designation of the law applicable to the substance of the dispute in that they may, for example, agree on rules of law that have been elaborated by an international forum but have not yet been incorporated into any national legal system. The power of the arbitral tribunal, on the other hand, follows more traditional lines. When the parties have not designated the applicable law, the arbitral tribunal shall apply the law, i.e. the national law, determined by the conflict of laws rules which it considers applicable.

36. According to Article 28(3), the parties may authorize the arbitral tribunal to decide the dispute *ex aequo et bono* or as *amiables compositeurs*. This type of arbitration is currently not known or used in all legal systems and there exists no uniform understanding as regards the precise scope of the power of the arbitral tribunal. When parties anticipate an uncertainty in this respect, they may wish to provide a clarification in the arbitration agreement by a more specific authorization to the arbitral tribunal. Paragraph (4) makes clear that in all cases, i.e including an arbitration *ex aequo et bono*, the arbitral tribunal must decide in accordance with the terms of the contract and shall take into account the usages of the trade applicable to the transaction.

b. Making of award and other decisions

37. In its rules on the making of the award (Articles 29–31), the Model Law pays special attention to the rather common case that the arbitral tribunal consists of a plurality of arbitrators (in particular, three). It provides that, in such case, any award and other decision shall be made by a majority of the arbitrators, except on questions of procedure, which may be left to a presiding arbitrator The majority principle applies also to the signing of the award, provided that the reason for any omitted signature is stated.

38. Article 31(3) provides that the award shall state the place of arbitration and that it shall be deemed to have been made at that place. As to this presumption, it may be noted that the final making of the award constitutes a legal act, which in practice is not necessarily one factual act but may be done in deliberations at various places, by tele-

phone conversation or correspondence; above all, the award need not be signed by the arbitrators at the same place.

39. The arbitral award must be in writing and state its date. It must also state the reasons on which it is based, unless the parties have agreed otherwise or the award is an award on agreed terms, *i.e.* an award which records the terms of an amicable settlement by the parties. It may be added that the Model Law neither requires nor prohibits "dissenting opinions".

7. *Recourse against award*

40. National laws on arbitration, often equating awards with court decisions, provide a variety of means of recourse against arbitral awards, with varying and often long time-periods and with extensive lists of grounds that differ widely in the various legal systems. The Model Law attempts to ameliorate this situation, which is of considerable concern to those involved in international commercial arbitration.

a. Application for setting aside as exclusive recourse

41. The first measure of improvement is to allow only one type of recourse, to the exclusion of any other means of recourse regulated in another procedural law of the State in question. An application for setting aside under Article 34 must be made within three months of receipt of the award. It should be noted that "recourse" means actively "attacking" the award; a party is, of course, not precluded from seeking court control by way of defence in enforcement proceedings (Article 36). Furthermore, "recourse" means resort to a court, *i.e.* an organ of the judicial system of a State; a party is not precluded from resorting to an arbitral tribunal of second instance if such a possibility has been agreed upon by the parties (as is common in certain commodity trades).

b. Grounds for setting aside

42. As a further measure of improvement, the Model Law contains an exclusive list of limited grounds on which an award may be set aside. This list is essentially the same as the one in Article 36(1), taken from Article V of the 1958 New York Convention: lack of capacity of parties to conclude arbitration agreement or lack of valid arbitration agreement; lack of notice of appointment of an arbitrator or of the arbitral proceedings or inability of a party to present his case; award deals with matters not covered by submission to arbitration; composition of arbitral tribunal or conduct of arbitral proceedings contrary to effective agreement of parties or, failing agreement, to the Model Law; non-arbitrability of subject-matter of dispute and violation of public policy, which would include serious departures from fundamental notions of procedural justice.

43. Such a parallelism of the grounds for setting aside with those provided in Article V of the 1958 New York Convention for refusal of recognition and enforcement was already adopted in the European Convention on International Commercial Arbitration (Geneva, 1961). Under its Article IX, the decision of a foreign court setting aside an award for a reason other than the ones listed in Article V of the 1958 New York Convention does not constitute a ground for refusing enforcement. The Model Law takes this philosophy one step further by directly limiting the reasons for setting aside.

44. Although the grounds for setting aside are almost identical to those for refusing recognition or enforcement, two practical differences should be noted. Firstly, the grounds relating to public policy, including non-arbitrability, may be different in substance, depending on the State in question (*i.e.* State of setting aside or State of enforcement). Secondly, and more importantly, the grounds for refusal of recognition or

enforcement are valid and effective only in the State (or States) where the winning party seeks recognition and enforcement, while the grounds for setting aside have a different impact: The setting aside of an award at the place of origin prevents enforcement ,of that award in all other countries by virtue of Article V(1)(e) of the 1958 New York Convention and Article 36(1)(a)(v) of the Model Law.

8. Recognition and enforcement of awards

45. The eighth and last chapter of the Model Law deals with recognition and enforcement of awards. Its provisions reflect the significant policy decision that the same rules should apply to arbitral awards whether made in the country of enforcement or abroad, and that those rules should follow closely the 1958 New York Convention.

a. Towards uniform treatment of all awards irrespective of country of origin

46. By treating awards rendered in international commercial arbitration in a uniform manner irrespective of where they were made, the Model Law draws a new demarcation line between "international" and "non-international" awards instead of the traditional line between "foreign" and "domestic" awards. This new line is based on substantive grounds rather than territorial borders, which are inappropriate in view of the limited importance of the place of arbitration in international cases. The place of arbitration is often chosen for reasons of convenience of the parties and the dispute may have little or no connection with the State where the arbitration takes place. Consequently, the recognition and enforcement of "international" awards, whether "foreign" or "domestic", should be governed by the same provisions.

47. By modelling the recognition and enforcement rules on the relevant provisions of the 1958 New York Convention, the Model Law supplements, without conflicting with, the regime of recognition and enforcement created by that successful Convention.

b. Procedural conditions of recognition and enforcement

48. Under Article 35(1) any arbitral award, irrespective of the country in which it was made, shall be recognized as binding and enforceable, subject to the provisions of Article 35(2) and of Article 36 (which sets forth the grounds on which recognition or enforcement may be refused). Based on the above consideration of the limited importance of the place of arbitration in international cases and the desire of overcoming territorial restrictions, reciprocity is not included as a condition for recognition and enforcement.

49. The Model Law does not lay down procedural details of recognition and enforcement since there is no practical need for unifying them, and since they form an intrinsic part of the national procedural law and practice. The Model Law merely sets certain conditions for obtaining enforcement: application in writing, accompanied by the award and the arbitration agreement (Article 35(2)).

c. Grounds for refusing recognition or enforcement

50. As noted earlier, the grounds on which recognition or enforcement may be refused under the Model Law are identical to those listed in Article V of the New York Convention. Only, under the Model Law, they are relevant not merely to foreign awards but to all awards rendered in international commercial arbitration. While some provisions of that Convention, in particular as regards their drafting, may have called for improvement, only the first ground on the list (*i.e.* "the parties to the arbitration agreement were, under the law applicable to them, under some incapacity" was modified since it was viewed as containing an incomplete and potentially misleading conflicts rule. Generally, it was

deemed desirable to adopt, for the sake of harmony, the same approach and wording as this important Convention.

Further information on the Model Law may be obtained from:

UNCITRAL Secretariat
Vienna International Centre
P.O. Box 500
A-1400 Vienna Austria

Telex: 135612 uno a
Tel.: (43)(1) 21345-4060
Fax: (43)(1) 21345-5813

Appendix 4

UNITED NATIONS COMMISSION ON INTERNATIONAL TRADE LAW ARBITRATION RULES

(Resolution 31/98 adopted by the General Assembly on December 15, 1976)

The General Assembly

Recognising the value of arbitration as a method of settling disputes arising in the context of international commercial relations,

Being convinced that the establishment of rules for *ad hoc* arbitration that are acceptable in countries with different legal, social and economic systems would significantly contribute to the development of harmonious international economic relations,

Bearing in mind that the Arbitration Rules of the United Nations Commission on International Trade Law have been prepared after extensive consultation with arbitral institutions and centres of international commercial arbitration,

Noting that the Arbitration Rules were adopted by the United Nations Commission on International Trade Law at its ninth session after due deliberation,

1. *Recommends* the use of the Arbitration Rules of the United Nations Commission of International Trade Law in the settlement of disputes arising in the context of international commercial relations, particularly by reference to the Arbitration Rules in commercial contracts;

2. *Requests* the Secretary-General to arrange for the widest possible distribution of the Arbitration Rules.

SECTION I. INTRODUCTORY RULES

Scope of application

Article 1

1. Where the parties to a contract have agreed in writing that disputes in relation to that contract shall be referred to arbitration under the UNCITRAL Arbitration Rules, then such disputes shall be settled in accordance with these Rules subject to such modification as the parties may agree in writing.

2. These Rules shall govern the arbitration except that where any of these Rules is in conflict with a provision of the law applicable to the arbitration from which the parties cannot derogate, that provision shall prevail.

Notice, calculation of periods of time

Article 2

1. For the purposes of these Rules, any notice, including a notification, communication or proposal, is deemed to have been received if it is physically delivered to the addressee or if it is delivered at his habitual residence, place of business or mailing address, or, if none of these can be found after making reasonable inquiry, then at the addressee's last-known residence or place of business. Notice shall be deemed to have been received on the day it is so delivered.

2. For the purposes of calculating a period of time under these Rules, such period shall begin to run on the day following the day when a notice, notification, communication or proposal is received. If the last day of such period is an official holiday or a non-business day at the residence or place of business of the addressee, the period is extended until the first business day which follows. Official holidays or non-business days occurring during the running of the period of time are included in calculating the period.

Notice of arbitration

Article 3

1. The party initiating recourse to arbitration (hereinafter called the "claimant") shall give to the other party (hereinafter called the "respondent") a notice of arbitration.

2. Arbitral proceedings shall be deemed to commence on the date on which the notice of arbitration is received by the respondent.

3. The notice of arbitration shall include the following:

(a) A demand that the dispute be referred to arbitration;
(b) The names and addresses of the parties;
(c) A reference to the arbitration clause or the separate arbitration agreement that is invoked;
(d) A reference to the contract out of or in relation to which the dispute arises;
(e) The general nature of the claim and an indication of the amount involved, if any;
(f) The relief or remedy sought;
(g) A proposal as to the number of arbitrators (*i.e.* one or three), if the parties have not previously agreed thereon.

4. The notice of arbitration may also include:

(a) The proposals for the appointments of a sole arbitrator and an appointing authority referred to in Article 6, paragraph 1;
(b) The notification of the appointment of an arbitrator referred to in Article 7;
(c) The statement of claim referred to in Article 18.

Representation and assistance

Article 4

The parties may be represented or assisted by persons of their choice. The names and addresses of such persons must be communicated in writing to the other party; such communication must specify whether the appointment is being made for purposes of representation or assistance.

SECTION II. COMPOSITION OF THE ARBITRAL TRIBUNAL

Number of arbitrators

Article 5

If the parties have not previously agreed on the number of arbitrators (*i.e.* one or three) and if within fifteen days after the receipt by the respondent of the notice of arbitration the parties have not agreed that there shall be only one arbitrator, three arbitrators shall be appointed.

Appointment of Arbitrators (Articles 6–8)

Article 6

1. If a sole arbitrator is to be appointed, either party may propose to the other:

(a) The names of one or more persons, one of whom would serve as the sole arbitrator; and
(b) If no appointing authority has been agreed upon by the parties, the name or names of one or more institutions or persons, one of whom would serve as appointing authority.

2. If within thirty days after receipt by a party of a proposal made in accordance with paragraph 1 the parties have not reached agreement on the choice of a sole arbitrator, the sole arbitrator shall be appointed by the appointing authority agreed on by the parties. If no appointing authority has been agreed upon by the parties, if the appointing authority agreed upon refuses to act or fails to appoint the arbitrator within sixty days of the receipt of a party's request therefore, either party lay request the Secretary-General of the Permanent Court of Arbitration at The Hague to designate an appointing authority.

3. The appointing authority shall, at the request of one of the parties, appoint the sole arbitrator as promptly as possible. In making the appointment the appointing authority shall use the following list-procedure, unless both parties agree that the list-procedure should not be used or unless the appointing authority determines in its discretion that the use of the list-procedure is not appropriate for the case:

(a) At the request of one of the parties the appointing authority shall communicate to both parties an identical list containing at least three names;
(b) Within fifteen days after the receipt of this list, each party may return the list to the appointing authority after having deleted the name or names to which he objects and numbered the remaining names on the list in the order of his preference;

(c) After the expiration of the above period of time the appointing authority shall appoint the sole arbitrator from among the names approved on the lists returned to it and in accordance with the order of preference indicated by the parties;

(d) If for any reason the appointment cannot be made according to this procedure, the appointing authority may exercise its discretion in appointing the sole arbitrator.

4. In making the appointment, the appointing authority shall have regard to such considerations as are likely to secure the appointment of an independent and impartial arbitrator and shall take into account as well the advisability of appointing an arbitrator of a nationality other than the nationalities of the parties.

Article 7

1. If three arbitrators are to be appointed, each party shall appoint one arbitrator. The two arbitrators thus appointed shall choose the third arbitrator who will act as the presiding arbitrator of the tribunal.

2. If within thirty days after the receipt of a party's notification of the appointment of an arbitrator the other party has not notified the first party of the arbitrator he has appointed:

(a) The first party may request the appointing authority previously designated by the parties to appoint the second arbitrator; or

(b) If no such authority has been previously designated by the parties, or if the appointing authority previously designated refuses to act or fails to appoint the arbitrator within thirty days after receipt of a party's request therefor, the first party may request the Secretary-General of the Permanent Court of Arbitration at The Hague to designate the appointing authority. The first party may then request the appointing authority so designated to appoint the second arbitrator. In either case, the appointing authority may exercise its discretion in appointing the arbitrator.

3. If within thirty days after the appointment of the second arbitrator the two arbitrators have not agreed on the choice of the presiding arbitrator, the presiding arbitrator shall be appointed by an appointing authority in the same way as a sole arbitrator would be appointed under Article 6.

Article 8

1. When an appointing authority is requested to appoint an arbitrator pursuant to Article 6 or Article 7, the party which makes the request shall send to the appointing authority a copy of the notice of arbitration, a copy of the contract out of or in a relation to which the dispute has arisen and a copy of the arbitration agreement if it is not contained in the contract. The appointing authority may require from either party such information as it deems necessary to fulfil its functions.

2. Where the names of one or more persons are proposed for appointment as arbitrators, their full names, addresses and nationalities shall be indicated, together with a description of their qualifications.

Challenge of arbitrators (Articles 9–12)

Article 9

A prospective arbitrator shall disclose to those who approach him in connection with his possible appointment any circumstances likely to give rise to justifiable doubts as to his impartiality or independence. An arbitrator, once appointed or chosen, shall disclose such circumstances to the parties unless they have already been informed by him of these circumstances.

Article 10

1. Any arbitrator may be challenged if circumstances exist that give rise to justifiable doubts as to the arbitrator's impartiality or independence.

2. A party may challenge the arbitrator appointed by him only for reasons of which he becomes aware after the appointment has been made.

Article 11

1. A party who intends to challenge an arbitrator shall send notice of his challenge within fifteen days after the appointment of the challenged arbitrator has been notified to the challenging party or within fifteen days after the circumstances mentioned in Articles 9 and 10 became known to that party.

2. The challenge shall be notified to the other party, to the arbitrator who is challenged and to the other members of the arbitral tribunal. The notification shall be in writing and shall state the reasons for the challenge.

3. When an arbitrator has been challenged by one party, the other party may agree to the challenge. The arbitrator may also, after the challenge, withdraw from his office. In neither case does this imply acceptance of the validity of the grounds for the challenge. In both cases the procedure provided in Article 6 or 7 shall be used in full for the appointment of the substitute arbitrator, even if during the process of appointing the challenged arbitrator a party had failed to exercise his right to appoint or to participate in the appointment.

Article 12

1. If the other party does not agree to the challenge and the challenged arbitrator does not withdraw, the decision on the challenge will be made:

(a) When the initial appointment was made by an appointing authority, by that authority;

(b) When the initial appointment was not made by an appointing authority, but an appointing authority has been previously designated, by that authority;

(c) In all other cases, by the appointing authority to be designated in accordance with the procedure for designating an appointing authority as provided for in Article 6.

2. If the appointing authority sustains the challenge, a substitute arbitrator shall be appointed or chosen pursuant to the procedure applicable to the appointment or choice of an arbitrator as provided in Articles 6–9 except that, when this procedure would call for the designation of an appointing authority, the appointment of the arbitrator shall be made by the appointing authority which decided on the challenge.

Replacement of an arbitrator

Article 13

1. In the event of the death or resignation of an arbitrator during the course of the arbitral proceedings, a substitute arbitrator shall be appointed or chosen pursuant to the procedure provided for in Articles 6–9 that was applicable to the appointment or choice of the arbitrator being replaced.

2. In the event that an arbitrator fails to act or in the event of the *de jure* or *de facto* impossibility of his performing his functions, the procedure in respect of the challenge and replacement of an arbitrator as provided in the preceding articles shall apply.

Repetition of hearings in the event of the replacement of an arbitrator

Article 14

If under Articles 11–13 the sole or presiding arbitrator is replaced, any hearings held previously shall be repeated; if any other arbitrator is replaced, such prior hearings may be repeated at the discretion of the arbitral tribunal.

SECTION III. ARBITRAL PROCEEDINGS

General provisions

Article 15

1. Subject to these Rules, the arbitral tribunal may conduct the arbitration in such manner as it considers appropriate, provided that the parties are treated with equality and that at any stage of the proceedings each party is given a full opportunity of presenting his case.

2. If either party so requests at any stage of the proceedings, the arbitral tribunal shall hold hearings for the presentation of evidence by witnesses, including expert witnesses, or for oral argument. In the absence of such a request, the arbitral tribunal shall decide whether to hold such hearings or whether the proceedings shall be conducted on the basis of documents and other materials.

3. All documents or information supplied to the arbitral tribunal by one party shall at the same time be communicated by that party to the other party.

Place of arbitration

Article 16

1. Unless the parties have agreed upon the place where the arbitration is to be held, such place shall be determined by the arbitral tribunal, having regard to the circumstances of the arbitration.

2. The arbitral tribunal may determine the locale of the arbitration within the country agreed upon by the parties. It may hear witnesses and hold meetings for consultation among its members at any place it deems appropriate, having regard to the circumstances of the arbitration.

3. The arbitral tribunal may meet at any place it deems appropriate for the inspection of goods, other property or documents. The parties shall be given sufficient notice to enable them to be present at such inspection.

4. The award shall be made at the place of arbitration.

Language

Article 17

1. Subject to an agreement by the parties, the arbitral tribunal shall, promptly after its appointment, determine the language or languages to be used in the proceedings. This determination shall apply to the statement of claim, the statement of defence, and any further written statements and, if oral hearings take place, to the language or languages to be used in such hearings.

2. The arbitral tribunal may order that any documents annexed to the statement of claim or statement of defence, and any supplementary documents or exhibits submitted in the course of the proceedings, delivered in their original language, shall be accompanied by a translation into the language or languages agreed upon by the parties or determined by the arbitral tribunal.

Statement of claim

Article 18

1. Unless the statement of claim was contained in the notice of arbitration, within a period of time to be determined by the arbitral tribunal, the claimant shall communicate his statement of claim in writing to the respondent and to each of the arbitrators. A copy of the contract, and of the arbitration agreement if not contained in the contract, shall be annexed thereto.

2. The statement of claim shall include the following particulars:

(a) The names and addresses of the parties;
(b) A statement of the facts supporting the claim;
(c) The points at issue;
(d) The relief or remedy sought.

The claimant may annex to his statement of claim all documents he deems relevant or may add a reference to the documents or other evidence he will submit.

Statement of defence

Article 19

1. Within a period of time to be determined by the arbitral tribunal, the respondent shall communicate his statement of defence in writing to the claimant and to each of the arbitrators.

2. The statement of defence shall reply to the particulars (b), (c) and (d) of the statement of claim (Article 18, paragraph 2). The respondent may annex to his statement the documents on which he relies for his defence or may add a reference to the documents or other evidence he will submit.

3. In his statement of defence, or at a later stage in the arbitral proceedings if the arbitral tribunal decides that the delay was justified under the circumstances, the respondent may make a counter-claim arising out of the same contract or rely on a claim arising out of the same contract for the purpose of a set-off.

4. The provisions of Article 18, paragraph 3, shall apply to a counter-claim and a claim relied on for the purpose of a set-off.

Amendments to the claim or defence

Article 20

During the course of the arbitral proceedings either party may amend or supplement his claim or defence unless the arbitral tribunal considers it inappropriate to allow such amendment having regard to the delay in making it or prejudice to the other party or any other circumstances. However, a claim may not be amended in such a manner that the amended claim falls outside the scope of the arbitrator clause or separate arbitration agreement.

Pleas as to the jurisdiction of the arbitral tribunal

Article 21

1. The arbitral tribunal shall have the power to rule on objections that it has no jurisdiction, including any objections with respect to the existence or validity of the arbitration clause or of the separate arbitration agreement.

2. The arbitral tribunal shall have the power to determine the existence or the validity of the contract of which an arbitration clause forms a part. For the purposes of article 21, an arbitration clause which forms part of a contract and which provides for arbitration under these Rules shall be treated as an agreement independent of the other terms of the contract. A decision by the arbitral tribunal that the contract is null and void shall not entail *ipso jure* the invalidity of the arbitration clause.

3. A plea that the arbitral tribunal does not have jurisdiction shall be raised not later than in the statement of defence or, with respect to a counter-claim, in the reply to the counter-claim.

4. In general, the arbitral tribunal should rule on a plea concerning its jurisdiction as preliminary question. However, the arbitral tribunal may proceed with the arbitration and rule on such a plea in their final award.

Further written statements

Article 22

The arbitral tribunal shall decide which further written statements, in addition to the statement of claim and the statement of defence, shall be required from the parties or may be presented by them and shall fix the periods of time for communicating such statements.

Periods of time

Article 23

The periods of time fixed by the arbitral tribunal for the communication of written statements (including the statement of claim and statement of defence) should not exceed forty-five days. However, the arbitral tribunal may extend the time-limits if it concludes that an extension is justified.

Evidence and hearings (Articles 24 and 25)

Article 24

1. Each party shall have the burden of proving the facts relied on to support his claim or defence.

2. The arbitral tribunal may, if it considers it appropriate. require a party to deliver to the tribunal and to the other party, within such a period of time as the arbitral tribunal shall decide, a summary of the documents and other evidence which that party intends to present in support of the facts in issue set out in his statement of claim or statement of defence.

3. At any time during the arbitral proceedings the arbitral tribunal may require the parties to produce documents, exhibits or other evidence within such a period of time as the tribunal shall determine.

Article 25

1. In the event of an oral hearing, the arbitral tribunal shall give the parties adequate advance notice of the date, time and place thereof.

2. If witnesses are to be heard, at least fifteen days before the hearing each party shall communicate to the arbitral tribunal and to the other party the names and addresses of the witnesses he intends to present, the subject upon and the languages in which such witnesses will give their testimony.

3. The arbitral tribunal shall make arrangements for the translation of oral statements made at a hearing and for a record of the hearing if either is deemed necessary by the tribunal under the circumstances of the case, or if the parties have agreed thereto and have communicated such agreement to the tribunal at least fifteen days before the hearing.

4. Hearings shall be held *in camera* unless the parties agree otherwise. The arbitral tribunal may require the retirement of any witness or witnesses during the testimony of other witnesses. The arbitral tribunal is free to determine the manner in which witnesses are examined.

5. Evidence of witnesses may also be presented in the form of written statements signed by them.

6. The arbitral tribunal shall determine the admissibility, relevance, materiality and weight of the evidence offered.

Interim measures of protection

Article 26

1. At the request of either party, the arbitral tribunal may take any interim measures it deems necessary in respect of the subject-matter of the dispute, including measures for the conservation of the goods forming the subject-matter in dispute, such as ordering their deposit with a third person or the sale of perishable goods.

2. Such interim measures may be established in the form of an interim award. The arbitral tribunal shall be entitled to require security for the costs of such measures.

3. A request for interim measures addressed by any party to a judicial authority shall not be deemed incompatible with the agreement to arbitrate or as a waiver of that agreement.

Experts

Article 27

1. The arbitral tribunal may appoint one or more experts to report to it, in writing, on specific issues to be determined by the tribunal. A copy of the expert's terms of reference, established by the arbitral tribunal, shall be communicated to the parties.

2. The parties shall give the expert any relevant information or produce for his inspection any relevant documents or goods that he may require of them. Any dispute between a party and such expert as to the relevance of the required information or production shall be referred to the arbitral tribunal for decision.

3. Upon receipt of the expert's report, the arbitral tribunal shall communicate a copy of the report to the parties who shall be given the opportunity to express, in writing, their opinion on the report. A party shall be entitled to examine any document on which the expert has relied in his report.

4. At the request of either party the expert, after delivery of the report, may be heard at a hearing where the parties shall have the opportunity to be present and to interrogate the expert. At this hearing either party may present expert witnesses in order to testify on the points at issue. The provisions of Article 25 shall be applicable to such proceedings.

Default

Article 28

1. If, within the period of time fixed by the arbitral tribunal, the claimant has failed to communicate his claim without showing sufficient cause for such failure, the arbitral tribunal shall issue an order for the termination of the arbitral proceedings. If, within the period of time fixed by the arbitral tribunal, the respondent has failed to communicate his statement of defence without showing sufficient cause for such failure, the arbitral tribunal shall order that the proceedings continue.

2. If one of the parties, duly notified under these Rules, fails to appear at a hearing, without showing sufficient cause for such failure, the arbitral tribunal may proceed with the arbitration.

4. If one of the parties, duly invited to produce documentary evidence, fails to do so within the established period of time, without showing sufficient cause for such failure, the arbitral tribunal may make the award on the evidence before it.

Closure of hearings

Article 29

1. The arbitral tribunal may inquire of the parties if they have any further proof to offer or witnesses to be heard or submissions to make and, if there are none, it may declare the hearings closed.

2. The arbitral tribunal may, if it considers it necessary owing to exceptional circumstances, decide, on its own motion or upon application of a party, to reopen the hearings at any time before the award is made.

Waiver of rules

Article 30

A party who knows that any provision of, or requirement under, these Rules has not been complied with and yet proceeds with the arbitration without promptly stating his objection to such non-compliance, shall be deemed to have waived his right to object.

SECTION IV. THE AWARD

Decisions

Article 31

1. When there are three arbitrators, any award or other decision of the arbitral tribunal shall be made by a majority of the arbitrators.

2. In the case of questions of procedure, when there is no majority or when the arbitral tribunal so authorises, the presiding arbitrator may decide on his own, subject to revision, if any, by the arbitral tribunal.

Form and effect of the award

Article 32

1. In addition to making a final award, the arbitral tribunal shall be entitled to make interim, interlocutory, or partial awards.

2. The award shall be made in writing and shall be final and binding on the parties. The parties undertake to carry out the award without delay.

3. The arbitral tribunal shall state the reasons upon which the award is based, unless the parties have agreed that no reasons are to be given.

4. An award shall be signed by the arbitrators and it shall contain the date on which and the place where the award was made. Where there are three arbitrators and one of them fails to sign, the award shall state the reason for the absence of the signature.

5. The award may be made public only with the consent of both parties.

6. Copies of the award signed by the arbitrators shall be communicated to the parties by the arbitral tribunal.

7. If the arbitration law of the country where the award is made requires that the award be filed or registered by the arbitral tribunal, the tribunal shall comply with this requirement within the period of time required by law.

Applicable law, amiable compositeur

Article 33

1. The arbitral tribunal shall apply the law designated by the parties as applicable to the substance of the dispute. Failing such designation by the parties, the arbitral tribunal shall apply the law determined by the conflict of laws rules which it considers applicable.

2. The arbitral tribunal shall decide as *amiable compositeur* or *ex aequo et bono* only if the parties have expressly authorised the arbitral tribunal to do so and if the law applicable to the arbitral procedure permits such arbitration.

3. In all cases, the arbitral tribunal shall decide in accordance with the terms of the contract and shall take into account the usages of the trade applicable to the transaction.

Settlement or other grounds for termination

Article 34

1. If, before the award is made, the parties agree on a settlement of the dispute, the arbitral tribunal shall either issue an order for the termination of the arbitral proceedings or, if requested by both parties and accepted by the tribunal, record the settlement in the form of an arbitral award on agreed terms. The arbitral tribunal is not obliged to give reasons for such an award.

2. If, before the award is made, the continuation of the arbitral proceedings becomes unnecessary or impossible for any reason not mentioned in paragraph 1, the arbitral tribunal shall inform the parties of its intention to issue an order for the termination of the proceedings. The arbitral tribunal shall have the power to issue such an order unless a party raises justifiable grounds for objection.

3. Copies of the order for termination of the arbitral proceedings or of the arbitral award on agreed terms, signed by the arbitrators, shall be communicated by the arbitral tribunal to the parties. Where an arbitral award on agreed terms is made, the provisions of Article 32, paragraphs 2 and 4–7, shall apply.

Interpretation of the award

Article 35

1. Within thirty days after the receipt of the award, either party, with notice to the other party, may request that the arbitral tribunal give an interpretation of the award.

2. The interpretation shall be given in writing within forty-five days after the receipt of the request. The interpretation shall form part of the award and the provisions of article 32, paragraphs 2–7, shall apply.

Correction of the award

Article 36

1. Within thirty days after the receipt of the award, either party, with notice to the other party, may request the arbitral tribunal to correct in the award any errors in computation, any clerical or typographical errors, or any errors of similar nature. The arbitral tribunal may within thirty days after the communication of the award make such corrections on is own initiative.

2. Such corrections shall be in writing, and the provisions of Article 32, paragraphs 2–7, shall apply.

Additional award

Article 37

1. Within thirty days after the receipt of the award, either party, with notice to the other party, may request the arbitral tribunal to make an additional award as to claims presented in the arbitral proceedings but omitted from the award.

2. If the arbitral tribunal considers the request for an additional award to be justified and considers that the omission can be rectified without any further hearings or evidence, it shall complete its award within sixty days after the receipt of the request.

3. When an additional award is made, the provisions of Article 32, paragraphs 2–7, shall apply.

Costs (Articles 38–40)

Article 38

The arbitral tribunal shall fix the costs of arbitration in its award. The term "costs" includes only:

(a) The fees of the arbitral tribunal to be stated separately as to each arbitrator and to be fixed by the tribunal itself in accordance with article 39;
(b) The travel and other expenses incurred by the arbitrators;
(c) The costs of expert advice and of other assistance required by the arbitral tribunal;
(d) The travel and other expenses of witnesses to the extent such expenses are approved by the arbitral tribunal;
(e) The costs for legal representation and assistance of the successful party if such costs were claimed during the arbitral proceedings, and only to the extent that the arbitral tribunal determines that the amount of such costs is reasonable;
(f) Any fees and expenses of the appointing authority as well as the expenses of the Secretary-General of the Permanent Court of Arbitration at The Hague.

Article 39

1. The fees of the arbitral tribunal shall be reasonable in amount, taking into account the amount in dispute. the complexity of the subject-matter, the time spent by the arbitrators and any other relevant circumstances of the case.

2. If an appointing authority has been agreed upon by the parties or designated by the Secretary-General of the Permanent Court of Arbitration at The Hague, and if that authority has issued a schedule of fees for arbitrators in international cases which it administers, the arbitral tribunal in fixing its fees shall take that schedule of fees into account to the extent that it considers appropriate in the circumstances of the case.

3. If such appointing authority has not issued a schedule of fees for arbitrators in international cases, any party may at any time request the appointing authority to furnish a statement setting forth the basis for establishing fees which is customarily followed in international cases in which the authority appoints arbitrators. If the appointing authority consents to provide such a statement, the arbitral tribunal in fixing its fees shall take such information into account to the extent that it considers appropriate in the circumstances of the case.

4. In cases referred to in paragraphs 2 and 3, when a party so requests and the appointing authority consents to perform the function, the arbitral tribunal shall fix its fees only after consultation with the appointing authority which may make any comment it deems appropriate to the arbitral tribunal concerning the fees.

Article 40

1. Except as provided in paragraph 2, the costs of arbitration shall in principle be borne by the unsuccessful party. However, the arbitral tribunal may apportion each of such costs between the parties if it determines that apportionment is reasonable, taking into account the circumstances of the case.

2. With respect to the costs of legal representation and assistance referred to in Article 38, paragraph (e), the arbitral tribunal, taking into account the circumstances of the case, shall be free to determine which party shall bear such costs or may apportion such costs between the parties if it determines that apportionment is reasonable.

3. When the arbitral tribunal issues an order for the termination of the arbitral proceedings or makes an award on agreed terms, it shall fix the costs of arbitration referred to in Article 38 and Article 39, paragraph 1, in the text of that order or award.

4. No additional fees may be charged by an arbitral tribunal for interpretation or correction or completion of its award under Articles 35–37.

Deposit of costs

Article 41

1. The arbitral tribunal, on its establishment, may request each party to deposit an equal amount as an advance for the costs referred to in Article 38, paragraphs (a), (b) and (c).

2. During the course of the arbitral proceedings the arbitral tribunal may request supplementary deposits from the parties.

3. If an appointing authority has been agreed upon by the parties or designated by the Secretary-General of the Permanent Court of Arbitration at The Hague, and when a party so requests and the appointing authority consents to perform the function, the arbitral tribunal shall fix the amounts of any deposits or supplementary deposits only after consultation with the appointing authority which may make any comments to the arbitral tribunal which it deems appropriate concerning the amount of such deposits and supplementary deposits.

4. If the required deposits are not paid in full within thirty days after the receipt of the request, the arbitral tribunal shall so inform the parties in order that one or another of them may make the required payment. If such payment is not made, the arbitral tribunal may order the suspension or termination of the arbitral proceedings.

5. After the award has been made, the arbitral tribunal shall render an accounting to the parties of the deposits received and return any unexpended balance to the parties.

Appendix 5

UNICITRAL NOTES ON ORGANIZING ARBITRAL PROCEEDINGS

(United Nations, Vienna, 1996)

PREFACE

The United Nations Commission on International Trade Law (UNCITRAL) finalized the Notes at its twenty-ninth session (New York, May 28–June 14 1996). In addition to the 36 member States of the Commission, representatives of many other States and of a number of international organizations participated in the deliberations. In preparing the draft materials, the Secretariat consulted with experts from various legal systems, with national arbitration bodies and with international professional associations.

The Commission, after an initial discussion on the project in 1993, considered in 1994 a draft entitled "Draft Guidelines for Preparatory Conferences in Arbitral Proceedings". That draft was also discussed at several meetings of arbitration practitioners, including the XIIth International Arbitration Congress, held by the International Council for Commercial Arbitration (ICCA) at Vienna from November 3 to 6 1994. On the basis of those discussions in the Commission and elsewhere, the Secretariat prepared draft Notes on Organizing Arbitral Proceedings. The Commission considered the draft Notes in 1995, and a revised draft in 1996, when the Notes were finalized.

INTRODUCTION

Purpose of the notes

1. The purpose of the Notes is to assist arbitration practitioners by listing and briefly describing questions on which appropriately timed decisions on organizing arbitral proceedings may be useful. The text, prepared with a particular view to international arbitrations, may be used whether or not the arbitration is administered by an arbitral institution.

Non-binding character of the Notes

2. No legal requirement binding on the arbitrators or the parties is imposed by the Notes. The arbitral tribunal remains free to use the Notes as it sees fit and is not required to give reasons for disregarding them.

3. The Notes are not suitable to be used as arbitration rules, since they do not establish any obligation of the arbitral tribunal or the parties to act in a particular way. Accordingly, the use of the Notes cannot imply any modification of the arbitration rules that the parties may have agreed upon.

Discretion in conduct of proceedings and usefulness of timely decisions on organizing proceedings

4. Laws governing the arbitral procedure and arbitration rules that parties may agree upon typically allow the arbitral tribunal broad discretion and flexibility in the conduct of arbitral proceedings. This is useful in that it enables the arbitral tribunal to take decisions on the organization of proceedings that take into account the circumstances of the case, the expectations of the parties and of the members of the arbitral tribunal, and the need for a just cost-efficient resolution of the dispute.

5. Such discretion may make it desirable for the arbitral tribunal to give the parties a timely indication as to the organization of the proceedings and the manner in which the tribunal intends to proceed. This is particularly desirable in international arbitrations, where the participants may be accustomed to differing styles of conducting arbitrations. Without such guidance, a party may find aspects of the proceedings unpredictable and difficult to prepare for. That may lead to misunderstandings, delays and increased costs.

Multi-party arbitration

6. These Notes are intended for use not only in arbitrations with two parties but also in arbitrations with three or more parties. Use of the Notes in multi-party arbitration is referred to below in paragraphs 86–88 (item 18).

Process of making decisions on organizing arbitral proceedings

7. Decisions by the arbitral tribunal on organizing arbitral proceedings may be taken with or without previous consultations with the parties. The method chosen depends on whether, in view of the type of the question to be decided, the arbitral tribunal considers that consultations are not necessary or that hearing the views of the parties would be beneficial for increasing the predictability of the proceedings or improving the procedural atmosphere.

8. The consultations, whether they involve only the arbitrators or also the parties, can be held in one or more meetings, or can be carried out by correspondence or telecommunications such as telefax or conference telephone calls or other electronic means. Meetings may be held at the venue of arbitration or at some other appropriate location.

9. In some arbitrations a special meeting may be devoted exclusively to such procedural consultations; alternatively, the consultations may be held in conjunction with a hearing on the substance of the dispute. Practices differ as to whether such special meetings should be held and how they should be organized. Special procedural meetings of the arbitrators and the parties separate from hearings are in practice referred to by expressions such as "preliminary meeting", "pre-hearing conference", "preparatory conference", "pre-hearing review", or terms of similar meaning. The terms used partly depend on the stage of the proceedings at which the meeting is taking place.

List of matters for possible consideration in organizing arbitral proceedings

10. The Notes provide a list, followed by annotations, of matters on which the arbitral tribunal may wish to formulate decisions on organizing arbitral proceedings.

11. Given that procedural styles and practices in arbitration vary widely, that the purpose of the Notes is not to promote any practice as best practice, and that the Notes are designed for universal use, it is not attempted in the Notes to describe in detail different arbitral practices or express a preference for any of them.

12. The list, while not exhaustive, covers a broad range of situations that may arise in an arbitration. In many arbitrations, however, only a limited number of the matters mentioned in the list need to be considered. It also depends on the circumstances of the case at which stage or stages of the proceedings it would be useful to consider matters concerning the organization of the proceedings. Generally, in order not to create opportunities for unnecessary discussions and delay, it is advisable not to raise a matter prematurely, *i.e.* before it is clear that a decision is needed.

13. When the Notes are used, it should be borne in mind that the discretion of the arbitral tribunal in organizing the proceedings may be limited by arbitration rules, by other provisions agreed to by the parties and by the law applicable to the arbitral procedure. When an arbitration is administered by an arbitral institution, various matters discussed in the Notes may be covered by the rules and practices of that institution.

LIST OF MATTERS FOR POSSIBLE CONSIDERATION IN ORGANIZING ARBITRAL PROCEEDINGS

Paragraphs

ANNOTATIONS

1. Set of arbitration rules

If the parties have not agreed on a set of arbitration rules, would they wish to do so

14. Sometimes parties who have not included in their arbitration agreement a stipulation that a set of arbitration rules will govern their arbitral proceedings might wish to do so after the arbitration has begun. If that occurs, the UNCITRAL Arbitration Rules may be used either without modification or with such modifications as the parties might wish to agree upon. In the altemative, the parties might wish to adopt the rules of an arbitral institution; in that case, it may be necessary to secure the agreement of that institution and to stipulate the terms under which the arbitration could be carried out in accordance with the rules of that institution.

15. However, caution is advised as consideration of a set of arbitration rules might delay the proceedings or give rise to unnecessary controversy.

16. It should be noted that agreement on arbitration rules not a necessity and that, if the parties do not agree on a set of arbitration rules, the arbitral tribunal has the power to continue the proceedings and determine how the case will be conducted.

2. Language of proceedings

17. Many rules and laws on arbitral procedure empower the arbitral tribunal to determine the language or languages to be used in the proceedings, ir the parties have not reached an agreement thereon.

(a) Possible need for translation of documents, in full or in part

18. Some documents annexed to the statements of claim and defence or submitted later may not be in the language of the proceedings. Bearing in mind the needs of the proceedings and economy, it may be considered whether the arbitral tribunal should order that any of those documents or parts thereof should be accompanied by a translation into the language of the proceedings.

(b) Possible need for interpretation of oral presentations

19. If interpretation will be necessary during oral hearings. it is advisable to consider whether the interpretation will be simultaneous or consecutive and whether the arrangements should be the responsibility of a party or the arbitral tribunal. In an arbitration administered by an institution, interpretation as well as translation services are often arranged by the arbitral institution.

(c) Cost of translation and interpretation

20. In taking decisions about translation or interpretation, it is advisable to decide whether any or all of the costs are to be paid directly by a pany or whether they will be paid out of the deposits and apportioned between the parties along with the other arbitration costs.

3. Place of arbitration

(a) Determination of the place of arbitration, if not already agreed upon by the parties

21. Arbitration rules usually allow the parties to agree on the place of arbitration, subject to the requirement of some arbitral institutions that arbitrations under their mles be conducted at a particular place, usually the location of the institution. If the place has not been so agreed upon, the rules governing the arbitration typically provide that it is in the power of the arbitral tribunal or the institution administering the arbitration to determine the place. If the arbitral tribunal is to make that determination, it may wish to hear the views of the parties before doing so.

22. Various factual and legal factors influence the ace of the place of arbitration and their relative importance varies from case to case. Among the more prominent factors are: (a) suitability of the law on arbitral procedure of the place of arbitration: (b) whether there is a multilateral or bilateral treaty on enforcement of arbitral awards between the State where the arbitration takes place and the State or States where the award may have to be enforced; (c) convenience of the parties and the arbitrators, including the travel distances; (d) availability and cost of support services needed; and (e) location of the subject-matter in dispute and proximity of evidence.

(b) Possibility of meetings outside the place of arbitration

23. Many sets of arbitration rules and laws on arbitral procedure expressly allow the arbitral tribunal to hold meetings elsewhere than at the place of arbitration. For example, under the UNCITRAL Model Law on International Commercial Arbitration ''the arbitral tribunal may, unless otherwise agreed by the parties, meet at any place it considers appropriate for consultation among its members, for hearing witnesses, experts or the parties, or for inspection of goods, other property or documents'' (Article 20(2)). The purpose of this discretion is to permit arbitral proceedings to be carried out in a manner that is most efficient and economical.

4. *Administrative services that may be needed for the arbitral tribunal to carry out its functions*

24. Various administrative services (*e.g.* hearing rooms or secretarial services) may need to be procured for the arbitral tribunal to be able to carry out its functions. When the arbitration is administered by an arbitral institution, the institution will usually provide all or a good part of the required administrative support to the arbitral tribunal. When an arbitration administered by an arbitral institution takes place away from the seat of the institution, the institution may be able to arrange for administrative services to be obtained from another source, often an arbitral institution; some arbitral institutions have entered into cooperation agreements with a view to providing mutual assistance in servicing arbitral proceedings.

25. When the case is not administered by an institution, or the involvement of the institution does not include providing administrative support, usually the administrative arrangements for the proceedings will be made by the arbitral tribunal or the presiding arbitrator; it may also be acceptable to leave some of the arrangements to the parties, or to one of the parties subject to agreement of the other party or parties. Even in such cases, a convenient source of administrative support might be found in arbitral institutions, which often offer their facilities to arbitrations not governed by the rules of the institution. Otherwise, some services could be procured from entities such as chambers of commerce, hotels or specialized firms providing secretarial or other support services.

26. Administrative services might be secured by engaging a secretary of the arbitral tribunal (also referred to as registrar, clerk, administrator or rapporteur), who carries out the tasks under the direction of the arbitral tribunal. Some arbitral institutions routinely assign such persons to the cases administered by them. In arbitrations not administered by an institution or where the arbitral institution does not appoint a secretary, some arbitrators frequently engage such persons, at least in certain types of cases, whereas many others normally conduct the proceedings without them.

27. To the extent the tasks of the secretary are purely organizational (*e.g.* obtaining meeting rooms and providing or coordinating secretarial services), this is usually not controversial. Differences in views, however, may arise if the tasks include legal research and other professional assistance to the arbitral tribunal (*e.g.* collecting case law or published commentaries on legal issues defined by the arbitral tribunal, preparing summaries from case law and publications, and sometimes also preparing drafts of procedural decisions or drafts of certain parts of the award, in particular those concerning the facts of the case). Views or expectations may differ especially where a task of the secretary is similar to professional functions of the arbitrators. Such a role of the secretary is in the view of some commentators inappropriate or is appropriate only under certain conditions, such as that the parties agree thereto. However, it is typically recognized that it is important to ensure that the secretary does not perform any decision-making function of the arbitral tribunal.

5. *Deposits in respect of costs*

(a) Amount to be deposited

28. In an arbitration administered by an institution, the Institution often sets, on the basis of an estimate of the costs of the proceedings, the amount to be deposited as an advance for the costs of the arbitration. In other cases it is customary for the arbitral tribunal to make such an estimate and request a deposit. The estimate typically includes travel and other expenses by the arbitrators, expenditures for administrative assistance required by the arbitral tribunal, costs of any expert advice required by the arbitral tribunal, and the fees for the arbitrators. Many arbitration rules have provisions on this matter, including on whether the deposit should be made by the two parties (or all parties in a multi-party case) or only by the claimant.

(b) Management of deposits

29. When the arbitration is administered by an institution, the institution's services may include managing and accounting for the deposited money. Where that is not the case, it might be useful to clarify matters such as the type and location of the account in which the money will be kept and how the deposits will be managed.

(c) Supplementary deposits

30. If during the course of proceedings it emerges that the costs will be higher than anticipated, supplementary deposits may be required (*e.g.* because the arbitral tribunal decides pursuant to the arbitration rules to appoint an expert).

6. Confidentiality of information relating to the arbitration; possible agreement thereon

31. It is widely viewed that confidentiality is one of the advantageous and helpful features of arbitration. Nevertheless, there is no uniform answer in national laws as to the extent to which the participants in an arbitration are under the duty to observe the confidentiality of information relating to the case. Moreover, parties that have agreed on arbitration rules or other provisions that do not expressly address the issue of confidentiality cannot assume that all jurisdictions would recognize an implied commitment to confidentiality. Furthermore, the participants in an arbitration might not have the same understanding as regards the extent of confidentiality that is expected. Therefore, the arbitral tribunal might wish to discuss that with the parties and, if considered appropriate, record any agreed principles on the duty of confidentiality.

32. An agreement on confidentiality might cover, for example, one or more of the following matters: the material or information that is to be kept confidential (*e.g.* pieces of evidence, written and oral arguments, the fact that the arbitration is taking place, identity of the arbitrators, content of the award); measures for maintaining confidentiality of such information and hearings; whether any special procedures should be employed for maintaining the confidentiality of information transmitted by electronic means (*e.g.* because communication equipment is shared by several users, or because electronic mail over public networks is considered not sufficiently protected against unauthorized access); circumstances in which confidential information may be disclosed in part or in whole (*e.g.* in the context of disclosures of information in the public domain, or if required by law or a regulatory body).

7. Routing of written communications among the parties and the arbitrators

33. To the extent the question how documents and other written communications should be routed among the parties and the arbitrators is not settled by the agreed rules, or, if an institution administers the case, by the practices of the institution, it is useful for the arbitral tribunal to clarify the question suitably early so as to avoid misunderstandings and delays.

34. Among various possible patterns of routing, one example is that a party transmits the appropriate number of copies to the arbitral tribunal, or to the arbitral institution, if one is involved, which then forwards them as appropriate. Another example is that a party is to send copies simultaneously to the arbitrators and the other party or parties. Documents and other written communications directed by the arbitral tribunal or the presiding arbitrator to one or more parties may also follow a determined pattern, such as through the arbitral institution or by direct transmission. For some communications, in particular those on organizational matters (*e.g.* dates for hearings), more direct routes of communication may be agreed, even if, for example, the arbitral institution acts as an intermediary for documents such as the statements of claim and defence, evidence or written arguments.

8. Telefax and other electronic means of sending documents

(a) Telefax

35. Telefax, which offers many advantages over traditional means of communication, is widely used in arbitral proceedings. Nevertheless, should it be thought that, because of the characteristics of the equipment used, it would be preferable not to rely only on a telefacsimile of a document, special arrangements may be considered, such as that a particular piece of written evidence should be mailed or otherwise physically delivered, or that certain telefax messages should be confirmed by mailing or otherwise delivering documents whose facsimile were transmitted by electronic means. When a document should not be sent by telefax, it may, however, be appropriate, in order to avoid an unnecessarily rigid procedure, for the arbitral tribunal to retain discretion to accept an advance copy of a document by telefax for the purposes of meeting a deadline, provided that the document itself is received within a reasonable time thereafter.

(b) Other electronic means (*e.g.* electronic mail and magnetic or optical disk)

36. It might be agreed that documents, or some of them, will be exchanged not only in paper-based form, but in addition also in an electronic form other than telefax (*e.g.* as electronic mail, or on a magnetic or optical disk), or only in electronic form. Since the use of electronic means depends on the aptitude of the persons involved and the availability of equipment and computer programs, agreement is necessary for such means to be used. If both paper-based and electronic means are to be used, it is advisable to decide which one is controlling and, if there is a time-limit for submitting a document, which act constitutes submission.

37. When the exchange of documents in electronic form is planned, it is useful, in order to avoid technical difficulties, to agree on matters such as: data carriers (*e.g.* electronic mail or computer disks) and their technical characteristics; computer programs to be used in preparing the electronic records; instructions for transforming the electronic records into human-readable form; keeping of logs and back-up records of communications sent and received; information in human-readable form that should accompany the disks (*e.g.* the names of the originator and recipient, computer program, titles of the electronic files and the back-up methods used); procedures when a message is lost or the communication system otherwise fails; and identification of persons who can be contacted if a problem occurs.

9. *Arrangements for the exchange of written submissions*

38. After the parties have initially stated their claims defences, they may wish, or the arbitral tribunal might request them, to present further written submissions so as to prepare for the hearings or to provide the basis for a decision without hearings. In such submissions, the parties, for example, present or comment on allegations and evidence, cite or explain law, or make or react to proposals. In practice such submissions are referred to variously as, for example, statement, memorial, counter-memorial, brief, counter-brief, reply, *répliqué*, *dupliqué*, rebuttal or rejoinder; the terminology is a matter of linguistic usage and the scope or sequence of the submission.

(a) Scheduling of written submissions

39. It is advisable that the arbitral tribunal set time-limits for written submissions. In enforcing the time-limits, the arbitral tribunal may wish, on the one hand, to make sure that the case is not unduly protracted and, on the other hand, to reserve a degree of discretion and allow late submissions if appropriate under the circumstances. In some cases the arbitral tribunal might prefer not to plan the written submissions in advance, thus leaving such matters, including time-limits, to be decided in light of the developments in the proceedings. In other cases, the arbitral tribunal may wish to determine, when scheduling the first written submissions, the number of subsequent submissions.

40. Practices differ as to whether, after the hearings have been held, written submissions are still acceptable. While some arbitral tribunals consider post-hearing submissions unacceptable, others might request or allow them on a particular issue. Some arbitral tribunals follow the procedure according to which the parties are not requested to present written evidence and legal arguments to the arbitral tribunal before the hearings; in such a case, the arbitral tribunal may regard it as appropriate that written submissions be made after the hearings.

(b) Consecutive or simultaneous submissions

41. Written submissions on an issue may be made consecutively, *i.e.* the party who receives a submission is given a period of time to react with its counter-submission. Another possibility is to request each party to make the submission within the same time period to the arbitral tribunal or the institution administering the case; the received submissions are then forwarded simultaneously to the respective other party or parties. The approach used may depend on the type of issues to be commented upon and the time in which the views should be clarified. With consecutive submissions, it may take longer than with simultaneous ones to obtain views of the parties on a given issue. Consecutive submissions, however, allow the reacting party to comment on all points raised by the other party or parties, which simultaneous submissions do not; thus, simultaneous submissions might possibly necessitate further submissions.

10. *Practical details concerning written submissions and evidence (e.g. method of submission, copies, numbering, references)*

42. Depending on the volume and kind of documents be handled, it might be considered whether practical arrangements on details such as the following would be helpful:

- Whether the submissions will be made as paper documents or by electronic means, or both (see paragraphs 35-37);

- The number of copies in which each document is to be submitted;
- A system for numbering documents and items of evidence, and a method for marking them, including by tabs;
- The form of references to documents (*e.g.* by the heading and the number assigned to the document or its date);
- Paragraph numbering in written submissions, in order to facilitate precise references to parts of a text;
- When translations are to be submitted as paper documents, whether the translations are to be contained in the same volume as the original texts or included in separate volumes.

11. Defining points at issue; order of deciding issues; defining relief or remedy sought

(a) Should a list of points at issue be prepared

43. In considering the parties' allegations and arguments, the arbitral tribunal may come to the conclusion that it would be useful for it or for the parties to prepare, for analytical purposes and for ease of discussion, a list of the points at issue, as opposed to those that are undisputed. If the arbitral tribunal determines that the advantages of working on the basis of such a list outweigh the disadvantages, it chooses the appropriate stage of the proceedings for preparing a list, bearing in mind also that subsequent developments in the proceedings may require a revision of the points at issue. Such an identification of points at issue might help to concentrate on the essential matters, to reduce the number of points at issue by agreement of the parties, and to select the best and most economical process for resolving the dispute. However, possible disadvantages of preparing such a list include delay, adverse effect on the flexibility of the proceedings, or unnecessary disagreements about whether the arbitral tribunal has decided all issues submitted to it or whether the award contains decisions on matters beyond the scope of the submission to arbitration. The terms of reference required under some arbitration rules, or in agreements of parties, may serve the same purpose as the above-described list of points at issue.

(b) In which order should the points at issue be decided

44. While it is often appropriate to deal with all the points at issue collectively, the arbitral tribunal might decide to take them up during the proceedings in a particular order. The order may be due to a point being preliminary relative to another (*e.g.* a decision on the jurisdiction of the arbitral tribunal is preliminary to consideration of substantive issues, or the issue of responsibility for a breach of contract is preliminary to the issue of the resulting damages). A particular order may be decided also when the breach of various contracts is in dispute or when damages arising from various events are claimed.

45. If the arbitral tribunal has adopted a particular order of deciding points at issue, it might consider it appropriate to issue a decision on one of the points earlier than on the other ones. This might be done, for example, when a discrete part of a claim is ready for decision while the other parts still require extensive consideration, or when it is expected that after deciding certain issues the parties might be more inclined to settle the remaining ones. Such earlier decisions are referred to by expressions such as "partial", "interlocutory" or "interim" awards or decisions, depending on the type of issue dealt with and on whether the decision is final with respect to the issue it resolves. Questions that might be the subject of such decisions are, for example, jurisdiction of the arbitral tribunal, interim measures of protection, or the liability of a party.

(c) Is there a need to define more precisely the relief or remedy sought

46. If the arbitral tribunal considers that the relief or remedy sought is insufficiently definite, it may wish to explain to the parties the degree of definiteness with which their claims should be formulated. Such an explanation may be useful since criteria are not uniform as to how specific the claimant must be in formulating a relief or remedy.

12. Possible settlement negotiations and their effect on scheduling proceedings

47. Attitudes differ as to whether it is appropriate for the arbitral tribunal to bring up the possibility of settlement. Given the divergence of practices in this regard, the arbitral tribunal should only suggest settlement negotiations with caution. However, it may be opportune for the arbitral tribunal to schedule the proceedings in a way that might facilitate the continuation or initiation of settlement negotiations.

13. Documentary evidence

(a) Time-limits for submission of documentary evidence intended to be submitted by the parties; consequences of late submission

48. Often the written submissions of the parties contain sufficient information for the arbitral tribunal to fix the time-limit for submitting evidence. Otherwise, in order to set realistic time periods, the arbitral tribunal may wish to consult with the parties about the time that they would reasonably need.

49. The arbitral tribunal may wish to clarify that evidence submitted late will as a rule not be accepted. It may wish not to preclude itself from accepting a late submission of evidence if the party shows sufficient cause for the delay.

(b) Whether the arbitral tribunal intends to require a party to produce documentary evidence

50. Procedures and practices differ widely as to the conditions under which the arbitral tribunal may require a party to produce documents. Therefore, the arbitral tribunal might consider it useful, when the agreed arbitration rules do not provide specific conditions, to clarify to the parties the manner in which it intends to proceed.

51. The arbitral tribunal may wish to establish time-limits for the production of documents. The parties might be reminded that, if the requested party duly invited to produce documentary evidence fails to do so within the established period of time. without showing sufficient cause for such failure, the arbitral tribunal is free to draw its conclusions from the failure and may make the award on the evidence before it.

(c) Should assertions about the origin and receipt of documents and about the correctness of photocopies be assumed as accurate

52. It may be helpful for the arbitral tribunal to inform parties that it intends to conduct the proceedings on the basis that, unless a party raises an objection to any of the following conclusions within a specified period of time: (a) a document is accepted as having originated from the source indicated in the document; (b) a copy of a dispatched communication (*e.g.* letter, telex, telefax or other electronic message) is accepted without further proof as having been received by the addressee; and (c) a copy is accepted as correct. A statement by the arbitral tribunal to that effect can simplify the introduction of documentary evidence and discourage unfounded and dilatory objections, at a late stage of the proceedings, to the probative value of documents. It is advisable to provide that the time-limit for objections will not be enforced if the arbitral tribunal considers the delay justified.

(d) Are the parties willing to submit jointly a single set of documentary evidence

53. The parties may consider submitting jointly a single set of documentary evidence whose authenticity is not disputed. The purpose would be to avoid duplicate submissions and unnecessary discussions concerning the authenticity of documents, without prejudicing the position of the parties concerning the content of the documents. Additional documents may be inserted later if the parties agree. When a single set of documents would be too voluminous to be easily manageable, it might be practical to select a number of frequently used documents and establish a set of "working" documents. A convenient arrangement of documents in the set may be according to chronological order or subject-matter. It is useful to keep a table of contents of the documents, for example, by their short headings and dates, and to provide that the parties will refer to documents by those headings and dates.

(e) Should voluminous and complicated documentary evidence be presented through summaries, tabulations, charts, extracts or samples

54. When documentary evidence is voluminous and complicated, it may save time and costs if such evidence is presented by a report of a person competent in the relevant field (*e.g.* public accountant or consulting engineer). The report may present the information in the form of summaries, tabulations, charts, extracts or samples. Such presentation of evidence should be combined with arrangements that given the interested party the opportunity to review the underlying data and the methodology of preparing the report.

14. Physical evidence other than documents

55. In some arbitrations the arbitral tribunal is called upon to assess physical evidence other than documents, for example, by inspecting samples of goods, viewing a video recording or observing the functioning of a machine.

(a) What arrangements should be made if physical evidence will be submitted

56. If physical evidence will be submitted, the arbitral tribunal may wish to fix the time schedule for presenting the evidence, make arrangements for the other party or parties to have a suitable opportunity to prepare itself for the presentation of the evidence, and possibly take measures for safekeeping the items of evidence.

(b) What arrangements should be made if an on-site inspection is necessary

57. If an on-site inspection of property or goods will take place, the arbitral tribunal may consider matters such as timing, meeting places, other arrangements to provide the opportunity for all parties to be present, and the need to avoid communications between arbitrators and a party about points at issue without the presence of the other party or parties.

58. The site to be inspected is often under the control of one of the parties, which typically means that employees or representatives of that party will be present to give guidance and explanations. It should be borne in mind that statements of those representatives or employees made during an on-site inspection, as contrasted with statements those persons might make as witnesses in a hearing, should not be treated as evidence in the proceedings.

15. Witnesses

59. While laws and rules on arbitral procedure typically leave broad freedom concerning the manner of taking evidence of witnesses, practices on procedural points are varied. In order to facilitate the preparations of the parties for the hearings, the arbitral tribunal may consider it appropriate to clarify, in advance of the hearings, some or all of the following issues.

(a) Advance notice about a witness whom a party intends to present; written witnesses' statements

60. To the extent the applicable arbitration rules do not deal with the matter, the arbitral tribunal may wish to require that each party give advance notice to the arbitral tribunal and the other party or parties of any witness it intends to present. As to the content of the notice, the following is an example of what might be required, in addition to the names and addresses of the witnesses: (a) the subject upon which the witnesses will testify; (b) the language in which the witnesses will testify; and (c) the nature of the relationship with any of the parties, qualifications and experience of the witnesses if and to the extent these are relevant to the dispute or the testimony, and how the witnesses learned about the facts on which they will testify. However, it may not be necessary to require such a notice, in particular if the thrust of the testimony can be clearly ascertained from the party's allegations.

61. Some practitioners favour the procedure according to which the party presenting witness evidence submits a signed witness's statement containing testimony itself. It should be noted, however, that such practice, which implies interviewing the witness by the party presenting the testimony, is not known in all parts of the world and, moreover, that some practitioners disapprove of it on the ground that such contacts between the party and the witness may compromise the credibility of the testimony and are therefore improper (see paragraph 67). Notwithstanding these reservations, signed witness's testimony has advantages in that it may expedite the proceedings by making it easier for the other party or parties to prepare for the hearings or for the parties to identify uncontested matters. However, those advantages might be outweighed by the time and expense involved in obtaining the written testimony.

62. If a signed witness's statement should be made under oath or similar affirmation of truthfulness, it may be necessary to clarify by whom the oath or affirmation should be administered and whether any formal authentication will be required by the arbitral tribunal.

(b) Manner of taking oral evidence of witnesses

(i) Order in which questions will be asked and the manner in which the hearing of witnesses will be conducted

63. To the extent that the applicable rules do not provide an answer, it may be useful for the arbitral tribunal to clarify how witnesses will be heard. One of the various possibilities is that a witness is first questioned by the arbitral tribunal, whereupon questions are asked by the parties, first by the parties who called the witness. Another possibility is for the witness to be questioned by the party presenting the witness and then by the other party or parties, while the arbitral tribunal might pose questions during the questioning or after the parties on points that in the tribunal's view have not been sufficiently clarified. Differences exist also as to the degree of control the arbitral tribunal exercises over the hearing of witnesses. For example, some arbitrators prefer to permit the parties to pose questions freely and directly to the witness, but may disallow a question if a party objects; other arbitrators tend to exercise more control and may disallow a question on their initiative or even require that questions from the parties be asked through the arbitral tribunal.

(ii) Whether oral testimony will be given under oath or affirmation and, if so, in what form an oath or affirmation should be made

64. Practices and laws differ as to whether or not oral testimony is to be given under oath or affirmation. In some legal systems, the arbitrators are empowered to put witnesses on oath, but it is usually in their discretion whether they want to do so. In other systems, oral testimony under oath is either unknown or may even be considered improper as only an official such as a judge or notary may have the authority to administer oaths.

(iii) May witnesses be in the hearing room when they are not testifying

65. Some arbitrators favour the procedure that, except if the circumstances suggest otherwise, the presence of a witness in the hearing room is limited to the time the witness is testifying; the purpose is to prevent the witness from being influenced by what is said in the hearing room, or to prevent that the presence of the witness would influence another witness. Other arbitrators consider that the presence of a witness during the testimony of other witnesses may be beneficial in that possible contradictions may be readily clarified or that their presence may act as a deterrent against untrue statements. Other possible approaches may be that witnesses are not present in the hearing room before their testimony, but stay in the room after they have testified, or that the arbitral tribunal decides the question for each witness individually depending on what the arbitral tribunal considers most appropriate. The arbitral tribunal may leave the procedure to be decided during the hearings, or may give guidance on the question in advance of the hearings.

(c) The order in which the witnesses will be called

66. When several witnesses are to be heard and longer testimony is expected, it is likely to reduce costs if the order in which they will be called is known in advance and their presence can be scheduled accordingly. Each party might be invited to suggest the order in which it intends to present the witnesses, while it would be up to the arbitral tribunal to approve the scheduling and to make departures from it.

(d) Interviewing witnesses prior to their appearance at a hearing

67. In some legal systems, parties or their representatives are permitted to interview witnesses, prior to their appearance at the hearing, as to such matters as their recollection of the relevant events, their experience, qualifications or relation with a participant in the proceedings. In those legal systems such contacts are usually not permitted once the witness's oral testimony has begun. In other systems such contacts with witnesses are considered improper. In order to avoid misunderstandings, the arbitral tribunal may consider it useful to clarify what kind of contacts a party is permitted to have with a witness in the preparations for the hearings.

(e) Hearing representatives of a party

68. According to some legal systems, certain persons affiliated with a party may only be heard as representatives of the party but not as witnesses. In such a case, it may be necessary to consider ground rules for determining which persons may not testify as witnesses (*e.g.* certain executives, employees or agents) and for hearing statements of those persons and for questioning them.

16. Experts and expert witnesses

69. Many arbitration rules and laws on arbitral procedure address the participation of experts in arbitral proceedings. A frequent solution is that the arbitral tribunal has the power to appoint an expert to report on issues determined by the tribunal; in addition, the parties may be permitted to present expert witnesses on points at issue. In other cases. it is for the parties to present expert testimony, and it is not expected that the arbitral tribunal will appoint an expert.

(a) Expert appointed by the arbitral tribunal

70. If the arbitral tribunal is empowered to appoint an expert, one possible approach is for the tribunal to proceed directly to selecting the expert. Another possibility is to consult the parties as to who should be the expert; this may be done, for example, without mentioning a candidate, by presenting to the parties a list of candidates, soliciting proposals from the parties, or by discussing with the parties the ''profile'' of the expert the arbitral tribunal intends to appoint, *i.e.* the qualifications, experience and abilities of the expert.

(i) The expert's terms of reference

71. The purpose of the expert's terms of reference is to indicate the questions on which the expert is to provide clarification, to avoid opinions on points that are not for the expert to assess and to commit the expert to a time schedule. While the discretion to appoint an expert normally includes the determination of the expert's terms of reference, the arbitral tribunal may decide to consult the parties before finalizing the terms. It might also be useful to determine details about how the expert will receive from the parties any relevant information or have access to any relevant documents, goods or other propeny, so as to enable the expert to prepare the report. In order to facilitate the evaluation of the expert's report, it is advisable to require the expert to include in the report information on the method used in arriving at the conclusions and the evidence and information used in preparing the report.

(ii) The opportunity of the parties to comment on the expert's report, including by presenting expert testimony

72. Arbitration rules that contain provisions on experts usually also have provisions on the right of a party to comment on the report of the expert appointed by the arbitral tribunal. If no such provisions apply or more specific procedures than those prescribed are deemed necessary, the arbitral tribunal may, in light of those provisions, consider it opportune to determine, for example, the time period for presenting written comments of the parties, or, if hearings are to be held for the purpose of hearing the expert, the procedures for interrogating the expert by the parties or for the participation of any expert witnesses presented by the parties.

(b) Expert opinion presented by a party (expert witness)

73. If a party presents an expert opinion, the arbitral tribunal might consider requiring, for example, that the opinion be in writing, that the expert should be available to answer questions at hearings, and that, if a party will present an expert witness at a hearing, advance notice must be given or that the written opinion must be presented in advance, as in the case of other witnesses (see paragraphs 60-62).

17. Hearings

(a) Decision whether to hold hearings

74. Laws on arbitral procedure and arbitration rules often have provisions as to the cases in which oral hearings must be held and as to when the arbitral tribunal has discretion to decide whether to hold hearings.

75. If it is up to the arbitral tribunal to decide whether to hold hearings, the decision is likely to be influenced by factors such as, on the one hand, that it is usually quicker and easier to clarify points at issue pursuant to a direct confrontation of arguments than on the basis of correspondence and, on the other hand, the travel and other cost of holding hearings, and that the need of finding acceptable dates for the hearings might delay the proceedings. The arbitral tribunal may wish to consult the parties on this matter.

(b) Whether one period of hearings should be held or separate periods of hearings

76. Attitudes vary as to whether hearings should be held in a single period of hearings or in separate periods, especially when more than a few days are needed to complete the hearings. According to some arbitrators, the entire hearings should normally be held in a single period, even if the hearings are to last for more than a week. Other arbitrators in such cases tend to schedule separate periods of hearings. In some cases issues to be decided are separated, and separate hearings set for those issues, with the aim that oral presentation on those issues will be completed within the allotted time. Among the advantages of one period of hearings are that it involves less travel costs, memory will not fade, and it is unlikely that people representing a party will change. On the other hand, the longer the hearings, the more difficult it may be to find early dates acceptable to all participants. Furthermore, separate periods of hearings may be easier to schedule, the subsequent hearings may be tailored to the development of the case, and the period between the hearings leaves time for analysing the records and negotiations between the parties aimed at narrowing the points at issue by agreement.

(c) Setting dates for hearings

77. Typically, firm dates will be fixed for hearings. Exceptionally, the arbitral tribunal may initially wish to set only ''target dates'' as opposed to definitive dates. This may be done at a stage of the proceedings when not all information necessary to schedule hearings is yet available, with the understanding that the target dates will either be confirmed or rescheduled within a reasonably short period. Such provisional planning can be useful to participants who are generally not available on short notice.

(d) Whether there should be a limit on the aggregate amount of time each party will have for oral arguments and questioning witnesses

78. Some arbitrators consider it useful to limit the aggregate amount of time each party has for any of the following: (a) making oral statements; (b) questioning its witnesses; and (c) questioning the witnesses of the other party or parties. In general, the same aggregate amount of time is considered appropriate for each party, unless the arbitral tribunal considers that a different allocation is justified. Before deciding, the arbitral tribunal may wish to consult the parties as to how much time they think they will need.

79. Such planning of time, provided it is realistic, fair and subject to judiciously firm control by the arbitral tribunal, will make it easier for the parties to plan the presentation of the various items of evidence and arguments, reduce the likelihood of running out of time towards the end of the hearings and avoid that one party would unfairly use up a disproportionate amount of tlme.

(e) The order in which the parties will present their arguments and evidence

80. Arbitration rules typically give broad latitude to the arbitral tribunal to determine the order of presentations at the hearings. Within that latitude, practices differ, for example, as to whether opening or closing statements are heard and their level of detail; the sequence in which the claimant and the respondent present their opening statements. arguments, witnesses and other evidence; and whether the respondent or the claimant has the last word. In view of such differences, or when no arbitration rules apply, it may foster efficiency of the proceedings if the arbitral tribunal clarifies to the parties, in advance of the hearings, the manner in which it will conduct the hearings, at least in broad lines.

(f) Length of hearings

81. The length of a hearing primarily depends on the complexity of the issues to be argued and the amount of witness evidence to be presented. The length also depends on the procedural style used in the arbitration. Some practitioners prefer to have written evidence and written arguments presented before the hearings, which thus can focus on the issues that have not been sufficiently clarified. Those practitioners generally tend to plan shorter hearings than those practitioners who prefer that most if not all evidence and arguments are presented to the arbitral tribunal orally and in full detail. In order to facilitate the parties' preparations and avoid misunderstandings, the arbitral tribunal may wish to clarify to the parties, in advance of the hearings, the intended use of time and style of work at the hearings.

(g) Arrangements for a record of the hearings

82. The arbitral tribunal should decide, possibly after consulting with the parties, on the method of preparing a record of oral statements and testimony during hearings. Among different possibilities, one method is that the members of the arbitral tribunal take personal notes. Another is that the presiding arbitrator during the hearing dictates to a typist a summary of oral statements and testimony. A further method, possible when a secretary of the arbitral tribunal has been appointed, may be to leave to that person the preparation of a summary record. A useful, though costly, method is for professional stenographers to prepare verbatim transcripts, often within the next day or a similarly short time period. A written record may be combined with tape-recording, so as to enable reference to the tape in case of a disagreement over the written record.

83. If transcripts are to be produced, it may be considered how the persons who made the statements will be given an opportunity to check the transcripts. For example, it may be determined that the changes to the record would be approved by the parties or, failing their agreement, would be referred for decision to the arbitral tribunal.

(h) Whether and when the parties are permitted to submit notes summarizing their oral arguments

84. Some legal counsel are accustomed to giving notes summarizing their oral arguments to the arbitral tribunal and to the other party or parties. If such notes are presented, this is usually done during the hearings or shortly thereafter; in some cases, the notes are sent before the hearing. In order to avoid surprise, foster equal treatment of the parties and facilitate preparations for the hearings, advance clarification is advisable as to whether submitting such notes is accceptable and the time for doing so.

85. In closing the hearings the arbitral tribunal will normally assume that no further proof is to be offered or submission to be made. Therefore, if notes are to be presented to be read after the closure of the hearings, the arbitral tribunal may find it worthwhile to stress that the notes should be limited to summarizing what was said orally and in particular should not refer to new evidence or new argument.

18. Multi-party arbitration

86. When a single arbitration involves more than two parties (multi-party arbitration), considerations regarding the need to organize arbitral proceedings, and matters that may be considered in that connection, are generally not different from two-party arbitrations. A possible difference may be that, because of the need to deal with more than two parties, multi-party proceedings can be more complicated to manage than bilateral proceedings. The Notes, notwithstanding a possible greater complexity of multi-party arbitration, can be used in multi-party as well as in two-party proceedings.

87. The areas of possibly increased complexity in multi-party arbitration are, for example, the flow of communications among the parties and the arbitral tribunal (see paragraphs 33, 34 and 38-41); if points at issue are to be decided at different points in time, the order of deciding them (paragraphs 44–45); the manner in which the parties will participate in hearing witnesses (paragraph 63); the appointment of experts and the participation of the parties in considering their reports (paragraphs 70–72); the scheduling of hearings (paragraph 76); the order in which the parties will present their arguments and evidence at hearings (paragraph 80).

88. The Notes, which are limited to pointing out matters that may be considered in organizing arbitral proceedings in general, do not cover the drafting of the arbitration agreement or the constitution of the arbitral tribunal, both issues that give rise to special questions in multi-party arbitration as compared to two-party arbitration.

19. Possible requirements concerning filing or delivering the award

89. Some national laws require that arbitral awards be filed or registered with a court or similar authority, or that they be delivered in a particular manner or through a particular authority. Those laws differ with respect to, for example, the type of award to which the requirement applies (*e.g.* to all awards or only to awards not rendered under auspices of an arbitral institution); time periods for filing, registering or delivering the award (in some cases those time periods may be rather short); or consequences for failing to comply with the requirement (which might be, for example, invalidity of the award or inability to enforce it in a particular manner).

Who should take steps to fulfil any requirement

90. If such a requirement exists, it is useful, some time before the award is to be issued, to plan who should take the necessary steps to meet the requirement and how the costs are to be borne.

Appendix 6

THE NEW YORK CONVENTION ON THE RECOGNITION AND ENFORCEMENT OF FOREIGN ARBITRAL AWARDS

(June 10, 1958)

Article I

1. This Convention shall apply to the recognition and enforcement of arbitral awards made in the territory of a State other than the State where the recognition and enforcement of such awards are sought, and arising out of differences between persons, whether physical or legal. It shall also apply to arbitral awards not considered as domestic awards in the State where their recognition and enforcement are sought.

2. The term ''arbitral awards'' shall include not only awards made by arbitrators appointed for each case but also those made by permanent arbitral bodies to which the parties have submitted.

3. When signing, ratifying or acceding to this Convention, or notifying extension under Article X hereof, any State may on the basis of reciprocity declare that it will apply the Convention to the recognition and enforcement of awards made only in the territory of another Contracting State. It may also declare that it will apply the Convention only to differences arising out of legal relationships, whether contractual or not, which are considered as commercial under the national law of the State making such declaration.

Article II

1. Each Contracting State shall recognise an agreement in writing under which the parties undertake to submit to arbitration all or any differences which have arisen or which may arise between them in respect of a defined legal relationship, whether contractual or not, concerning a subject-matter capable of settlement by arbitration.

2. The term ''agreement in writing'' shall include an arbitral clause in a contract or an arbitration agreement, signed by the parties or contained in an exchange of letters or telegrams.

3. The court of a Contracting State, when seized of an action in a matter in respect of which the parties have made an agreement within the meaning of this article shall, at the request of one of the parties, refer the parties to arbitration, unless it finds that the said agreement is null and void, inoperative or incapable of being performed.

Article III

Each Contracting State shall recognise arbitral awards as binding and enforce them in accordance with the rules of procedure of the territory where the award is relied upon, under the conditions laid down in the following articles. There shall not be imposed substantially more onerous conditions or higher fees or charges on the recognition or enforcement of arbitral awards to which this Convention applies than are imposed on the recognition or enforcement of domestic arbitral awards.

Article IV

1. To obtain the recognition and enforcement mentioned in the preceding article, the party applying for recognition and enforcement shall, at the time of the application, supply:

(a) The duly authenticated original award or a duly certified copy thereof;
(b) The original agreement referred to in Article II or a duly certified copy thereof.

2. If the said award or agreement is not made in an official language of the country in which the award is relied upon, the party applying for recognition and enforcement of the award shall produce a translation of these documents into such language. The translation shall be certified by an official or sworn translator or by a diplomatic or consular agent.

Article V

1. Recognition and enforcement of the award may be refused, at the request of the party against whom it is invoked, only if that party furnishes to the competent authority where the recognition and enforcement is sought, proof that:

(a) The parties to the agreement referred to in Article II were, under the law applicable to them, under some incapacity, or the said agreement is not valid under the law to which the parties have subjected it or, failing any indication thereon, under the law of the country where the award was made; or
(b) The party against whom the award is invoked was not given proper notice of the appointment of the arbitrator or of the arbitration proceedings or was otherwise unable to present his case; or
(c) The award deals with a difference not contemplated by or not falling within the terms of the submission to arbitration, or it contains decisions on matters beyond the scope of the submission to arbitration, provided that, if the decisions on matters submitted to arbitration can be separated from those not so submitted, that part of the award which contains decisions on matters submitted to arbitration may be recognised and enforced; or
(d) The composition of the arbitral authority or the arbitral procedure was not in accordance with the agreement of the parties, or, failing such agreement, was not in accordance with the law of the country where the arbitration took place; or
(e) The award has not yet become binding on the parties, or has been set aside or suspended by a competent authority of the country in which, or under the law of which, that award was made.

2. Recognition and enforcement of an arbitral award may also be refused if the competent authority in the country where recognition and enforcement is sought finds that:

(a) The subject-matter of the difference is not capable of settlement by arbitration under the law of that country; or
(b) The recognition or enforcement of the award would be contrary to the public policy of that country.

Article VI

If an application for the setting aside or suspension of the award has been made to a competent authority referred to in Article V(1)(e), the authority before which the award is sought to be relied upon may, if it considers it proper, adjourn the decision on the enforcement of the award and may also, on the application of the party claiming enforcement of the award, order the other party to give suitable security.

Article VII

1. The provisions of the present Convention shall not affect the validity of multilateral or bilateral agreements concerning the recognition and enforcement of arbitral awards entered into by the Contracting States nor deprive any interested party of any right he may have to avail himself of an arbitral award in the manner and to the extent allowed by the law or the treaties of the country where such award is sought to be relied upon.

2. The Geneva Protocol on Arbitration Clauses of 1923 and the Geneva Convention on the Execution of Foreign Arbitral Awards of 1927 shall cease to have effect between Contracting States on their becoming bound and to the extent that they become bound, by this Convention.

Article VII

1. This Convention shall be open until December 31, 1958 for signature on behalf of any Member of the United Nations and also on behalf of any other State which is or hereafter becomes a member of any specialised agency of the United Nations, or which is or hereafter becomes a party to the Statute of the International Court of Justice, or any other State to which an invitation has been addressed by the General Assembly of the United Nations.

2. This Convention shall be ratified and the instrument of ratification shall be deposited with the Secretary-General of the United Nations.

Article IX

1. This Convention shall be open for accession to all States referred to in Article VIII.

2. Accession shall be effected by the deposit of an instrument of accession with the Secretary-General of the United Nations.

Article X

1. Any State may, at the time of signature, ratification or accession, declare that this Convention shall extend to all or any of the territories for the international relations of which it is responsible. Such a declaration shall take effect when the convention enters into force for the State concerned.

2. At any time thereafter any such extension shall be made by notification addressed to the Secretary-General of the United Nations and shall take effect as from the ninetieth day after the day of receipt by the Secretary-General of the United Nations of this notification, or as from the date of entry into force of the Convention for the State concerned, whichever is the later.

3. With respect to those territories to which this Convention is not extended at the Time of signature, ratification or accession, each State concerned shall consider the possibility of taking the necessary steps in order to extend the application of this Convention to such territories, subject, where necessary for constitutional reasons, the consent of the Governments of such territories.

Article XI

In the case of a federal or non-unitary State, the following provisions shall apply:

(a) With respect to those articles of this Convention that come within the legislative jurisdiction of the federal authority, the obligations of the federal Government shall to this extent be the same as those of Contracting States which are not federal States;

(b) With respect to those articles of this Convention that come within the legislative jurisdiction of constituent states or provinces which are not, under the institutional system of the federation, bound to take legislative action, the federal government shall bring such articles with a favourable recommendation to the notice of the appropriate authorities of constituent states or provinces at the earliest possible moment.

(c) A federal State Party to this Convention shall, at the request of any other Contracting State transmitted through the Secretary-General of the United Nations, supply a statement of the law and practice of the federation and its constituent units in regard to any particular provision of this Convention, showing the extent to which effect has been given to that provision by legislative or other action.

Article XII

1. This Convention shall come into force on the ninetieth day following the date of deposit of the third instrument of ratification or accession.

2. For each State ratifying or acceding to this Convention after the deposit of the instrument of ratification or accession, this Convention shall enter into force on ninetieth day after deposit of such State of its instrument of ratification or accession.

Article XIII

1. Any Contracting State may denounce this Convention by a written notification to the Secretary-General of the United Nations. Denunciation shall take effect one year after the date of receipt of the notification by the Secretary-General.

2. Any State which has made a declaration or notification under Article X may, at any time thereafter, by notification to the Secretary-General of the United Nations, declare that this Convention shall cease to extend to the territory concerned one year after the date of the receipt of the notification by the Secretary-General.

3. This Convention shall continue to be applicable to arbitral awards in respect of which recognition or enforcement proceedings have been instituted before the denunciation takes effect.

Article XIV

A Contracting State shall not be entitled to avail itself of the present Convention against other Contracting States except to the extent that it is itself bound to apply the Convention.

Article XV

The Secretary-General of the United Nations shall notify the States contemplated in Article VIII of the following:

(a) Signatures and ratifications in accordance with Article VIII;
(b) Accessions in accordance with Article IX;
(c) Declarations and notifications under Articles I, X and XI;
(d) The date upon which this Convention enters into force in accordance with Article XII;
(e) Denunciations and notifications in accordance with Article XIII.

Article XVI

1. This Convention, of which the Chinese, English, French, Russian and Spanish texts shall be equally authentic, shall be deposited in the archives of the United Nations.

2. The Secretary-General of the United Nations shall transmit a certified copy of this Convention to the States contemplated in Article VIII.

Appendix 7

THE CHARTERED INSTITUTE OF ARBITRATORS ARBITRATION RULES*

These Rules are published by the Chartered Institute of Arbitrators, to help parties and arbitrators take maximum advantage of the flexible procedures available in arbitration for the resolution of disputes quickly and economically. The Rules provide that the wishes of the parties regarding procedure will be respected so far as possible, but they also seek to ensure that the Arbitrator will have sufficient powers to direct the proceedings if the parties cannot agree on procedure or will not co-operate. The Rules may be used without reference to the Institute (unless the Institute is required to act as Appointing Authority in accordance with Article 2.1).
The Arbitration Rules of the Chartered Institute of Arbitrators are not intended for use in arbitrations relating to international contracts or disputes (*i.e.* where the parties come from different countries). In such cases, reference should be made to the Rules of the London Court of International Arbitration.

The Chartered Institute of Arbitrators

The Chartered Institute of Arbitrators was founded in 1915 and granted a Royal Charter in 1979. The aims of the Institute are to establish and maintain professional standards for arbitrators, and to promote the wider use of arbitration in the resolution of disputes. Its members come from a wide range of professional disciplines, both in the United Kingdom and internationally. Training programmes, leading to professional qualification as an arbitrator, are an important aspect of the Institute's activities. The Institute acts as an appointing authority, appointing arbitrators when authorised to do so by parties in dispute. It also provides a wide range of additional arbitration services. For further information please contact:

* These Rules are an amended version of the C.I.A. Arbitration Rules (effective January 1, 1988) and are provisional only. A revised version of the Rules will be available from the C.I.A. in 1998.

International Arbitration Centre
24 Angel Gate
City Road
London ECIV 2RS
Telephone: 0171-837 4483
Facsimile: 0171-837 4185
Secretary General:
K. R. K. Harding, MIPD, FRSA, M.Inst.D., F.C.I.Arb.

Suggested clauses

1. Parties to a contract who wish to have any *future* disputes referred to arbitration under the Rules of the Chartered Institute of Arbitrators may insert in the contract an arbitration clause in the following form:

"Any dispute arising out of or in connection with this contract shall be referred to and finally resolved by arbitration under the Rules of the Chartered Institute of Arbitrators, which Rules are deemed to be incorporated by reference into this clause."

2. Parties to an *existing* dispute who wish to refer it to arbitration under the Rules of the Chartered Institute of Arbitrators may agree to do so in the following terms:

"We, the undersigned, agree to refer to arbitration under the Rules of the Chartered Institute of Arbitrators the following dispute which has arisen between us:

(Brief description of matters to be referred to arbitration)
Signed ____________________ (Claimant)
Signed ____________________ (Respondent)
Date ____________________ "

3. Where the Rules of the Chartered Institute of Arbitrators apply:

(a) The parties may if they wish specify an Appointing Authority to appoint the arbitrator (or arbitrators) if the parties fail to do so or cannot agree. If no Appointing Authority is specified, then the Rules provide the President or a Vice-President for the time being of the Chartered Institute of Arbitrators will act as Appointing Authority. The following provision may be suitable if some other Appointing Authority is required:

"The Appointing Authority shall be (name of institution or person)."

(b) The Rules provide a sole arbitrator will be appointed unless the parties agree otherwise. If the parties wish to specify a three-man tribunal, the following provision may be suitable:

"The arbitral tribunal shall consist of three arbitrators one of whom shall be appointed by each party and the third by the Appointing Authority."

Arbitation rules

Where any agreement, submission or reference provides for arbitration under the Rules of the Chartered Institute of Arbitrators, the parties shall be taken to have agreed that the arbitration shall be conducted in accordance with the following Rules, or such amended Rules as the Chartered Institute of Arbitrators may have adopted to take effect before the commencement of the arbitration.

Article 1 Commencement of arbitration

1.1 Any party wishing to commence an arbitration under these Rules (''the Claimant'') shall send to the other party (''the Respondent'') a written request for arbitration (''the Request'') which shall include, or be accompanied by:

(a) the names and addresses of the parties to the arbitration;
(b) copies of the contractual documents in which the arbitration clause is contained or under which the arbitration arises;
(c) a brief statement describing the nature and circumstances of the dispute, and specifying the relief claimed;
(d) a statement of any matters (such as the Appointing Authority, the number of arbitrators, or their qualifications or identities) with respect to which the requesting party wishes to make a proposal;
(e) if the arbitration agreement calls for each party to appoint an arbitrator, the name and address (and telephone, telex and fax numbers, if known) of the arbitrator appointed by the Claimant.

The arbitration shall be deemed to commence on the date of receipt by the Respondent of the Request for Arbitration.

1.2 For the purpose of facilitating the choice of arbitrators, within 30 days of receipt of the Request for Arbitration, the Respondent may send to the Claimant a Response containing:

(a) confirmation or denial of all or part of the claims;
(b) a brief statement of the nature and circumstances of any envisaged counterclaims;
(c) comment (including confirmation of agreement) in response to any proposals contained in the Request, as called for under Article 1.1(d), on matters relating to the conduct of the arbitration;
(d) if the arbitration agreement calls for each party to appoint an arbitrator, the name and address (and telephone, telex and fax numbers if known) of the arbitrator appointed by the Respondent.

1.3 Failure to send a Response shall not preclude the Respondent from denying the claim nor from setting out a counterclaim in its Statement of Defence. However, if the arbitration agreement calls for each party to appoint an arbitrator, failure to send a Response or to name an appointed arbitrator in it within the time specified in Article 1.2 shall constitute a waiver of the right to appoint an arbitrator.

Article 2 Appointing Authority

2.1 The parties may agree to nominate an Appointing Authority. Failing such nomination the Appointing Authority shall be the President or a Vice-President for the time being of the Chartered Institute of Arbitrators.

2.2 Any application to the Appointing Authority to act in accordance with these Rules shall be accompanied by:

(a) Copies of the Request and Response and any other related correspondence;
(b) Confirmation that a copy of the application has been received by the other party;
(c) Particulars of any method or criteria of selection of arbitrators agreed by the parties.

The Appointing Authority may require payment of a fee for its services.

Article 3 Appointment of Arbitrator

3.1 Provided that the final member is uneven, the parties may agree on the number of arbitrators in the Tribunal. Failing such agreement there shall be a σsole arbitrator. In these Rules, the expression "the Arbitrator" includes a sole arbitrator or all the arbitrators where more than one is appointed.

3.2 The Arbitrator shall act fairly and impartially, and shall not act as advocate for any party. Before appointment if so requested by either party or the Appointing Authority any proposed arbitrator shall furnish a resume of his past and present professional activities (which will be communicated to the parties). In any event any arbitrator if so requested by either party or the Appointing Authority shall sign a declaration to the effect that there are no circumstances likely to give rise to any justified doubts as to his impartiality and that he will forthwith disclose any such circumstances to the parties if they should arise after that time and before the arbitration is concluded.

3.3 The Arbitrator may be appointed by agreement of the parties. Failing such agreement within 28 days of the commencement of the arbitration in accordance with Article 1, the Arbitrator shall upon the application of either party be appointed by the Appointing Authority.

3.4 Where the parties have agreed there shall be three arbitrators, they may also agree that each party shall appoint an arbitrator. If either party fails to make and notify the other party of such appointment within 14 days of the commencement of the arbitration under Article 1, that appointment shall be made by the Appointing Authority.

3.5 Where the parties have agreed that each shall appoint an arbitrator then, unless otherwise agreed by the parties, a third arbitrator shall be appointed to act as chairman by the two arbitrators and failing agreement by the Appointing Authority.

3.6 If any arbitrator, after appointment, dies, is unable to act, or refuses to act, the Appointing Authority will, upon request by a party or by the remaining arbitrals, appoint another arbitrator.

Article 4 Communications between parties and the Arbitrator

4.1 Where the Arbitrator sends any communication to one party, he shall send a copy to the other party.

4.2 Where a party sends any communication (including Statements under Article 6) to the Arbitrator, it shall be copied to the other party and be shown to the Arbitrator to have been so copied.

4.3 The addresses of the parties for the purpose of all communications during the proceedings shall be those set out in the Request, or as either party may at any time notify to the Arbitrator and to the other party. Any communication by post shall be deemed to be received in the ordinary course of mail unless the contrary is proved.

4.4 With the agreement the parties, the Arbitrator may appoint the Secretary General of the Chartered Institute of Arbitrators to act as arbitration administrator (whether or not the Chartered Institute of Arbitrators is acting as Appointing Authority). Where the Secretary General is so appointed, all communications and notices between a party and the Arbitrator in the course of the arbitration (except at meetings and hearings) will be addressed through the Secretary General and in the case of communications to the Arbitrator will be deemed received by him when received by the Secretary General.

Article 5 Conduct of the proceedings

5.1 In the absence of procedural rules agreed by the parties or contained herein, the arbitrator shall have the widest discretion allowed by law to ensure the just, expeditious, economical, and final determination of the dispute.

5.2 Any party wishing the Arbitrator to adopt a simplified or expedited procedure should apply to the Arbitrator for this within 15 days of notification of the Arbitrator's acceptance of his appointment

5.3 In the case of a three-member tribunal the Chairman may, after consulting the other arbitrators, make procedural rulings alone.

Article 6 Submission of written statements and documents

6.1 Subject to any procedural rules agreed by the parties or determined by or requested from the Arbitrator under Article 5, the written stage of the proceedings shall be as set out in the Article (and in accordance with Article 4).

6.2 Within 28 days of receipt by the Claimant of notification of the Arbitrator's acceptance of the appointment, the Claimant shall send to the Arbitrator a Statement of Case setting out in sufficient detail the facts and any contentions of law on which it relies and the relief claimed.

6.3 Within 28 days of receipt of the Statement of Case, the Respondent shall send to the Arbitrator a Statement of Defence stating in sufficient detail which of the facts and contentions of law in the Statement of Case it admits or denies, on what grounds, and on what other facts and contentions of law it relies. Any Counterclaims shall be submitted with the Statement of Defence in the same manner as claims set out in the Statement of Case.

6.4 Within 28 days of receipt of the Statement of Defence, the Claimant may send to the Arbitrator a Statement of Reply which, where there are Counterclaims, shall include a Defence to Counterclaims.

6.5 If the Statement of Reply contains a Defence to Counterclaims, the Respondent may within a further 28 days send to the Arbitrator a Statement of Reply regarding Counterclaims.

6.6 All Statements referred to in this Article shall be accompanied by copies (or, if they are especially voluminous, lists) of all essential documents on which the party concerned relies and which have not previously been submitted by any party, and (where appropriate) by any relevant samples.

6.7 As soon as practicable following completion of the submission of the Statements specified in this Article, the Arbitrator shall proceed in such manner as has been agreed by the parties, or pursuant to his authority under these Rules.

Article 7 Party representatives

Any party may be represented by persons of their choice, subject to such proof of authority as the Arbitrator may require. The names and addresses of such representatives must be notified to the other party.

Article 8 Hearings

8.1 Subject to Article 12, and any agreement to the contrary by the parties, the Arbitrator has the right to decide whether there should be a hearing or the arbitration should be by documents only.

8.2 The Arbitrator shall fix the date, time and place of any meetings and hearings in the arbitration, and shall give the parties reasonable notice thereof.

8.3 The Arbitrator may in advance of hearings provide the parties with a list of matters or questions to which he wishes them to give special consideration.

8.4 All meetings and hearings shall be in private unless the parties agree otherwise.

Article 9 Witnesses

9.1 The Arbitrator may require each party to give notice of the identity of witnesses it intends to call. The Arbitrator may also require before a hearing the exchange of witnesses statements and of expert reports.

9.2 The Arbitrator has discretion to allow, limit, or (subject to Article 10.2) refuse to allow the appearance of witnesses, whether witnesses of fact or expert witnesses.

9.3 Any witness who gives oral evidence may be questioned by each party or its representative, under the control of the Arbitrator, and may be required by the Arbitrator to testify under oath or affirmation in accordance with the Arbitration Act 1996. The Arbitrator may put questions at any stage of the examination of the witnesses.

9.4 The testimony of witnesses may be presented in written form, either as signed statements or by duly sworn affidavits. Subject to Article 9.2 any party may request that such a witness should attend for oral examination at a hearing. If the witness fails to attend, the Arbitrator may place such weight on the written testimony as he thinks fit, or may exclude it altogether.

Article 10 Experts appointed by the Arbitrator

10.1 Unless otherwise agreed by the parties, the Arbitrator:

(a) may appoint one or more experts to report to the Arbitrator on specific issues;
(b) may require a party to give any such expert any relevant information or to produce, or to provide access to, any relevant documents goods or property for inspection by the expert.

10.2 Unless otherwise agreed by the parties, if a party so requests or if the Arbitrator considers it necessary, the expert shall, after delivery of his written or oral report, participate in a hearing, at which the parties shall have the opportunity to question him and to present expert witnesses in order to testify on the points at issue.

10.3 The provisions of Article 10.2 shall not apply to an assessor appointed by agreement of the parties, nor to an expert appointed by the Arbitrator to advise him solely in relation to procedural matters.

Article 11 Additional powers of the Arbitrator

11.1 Unless the parties at any time agree otherwise, the Arbitrator shall have the power to:

(a) allow any party, upon such terms (as to costs and otherwise) as he shall determine, to amend claims or counterclaims;
(b) extend or abbreviate any time limits provided by these Rules or by his directions;
(c) conduct such enquiries as may appear to the Arbitrator to be necessary or expedient;
(d) order the parties to make any property or thing available for inspection, in their presence, by the arbitrator or any expert;
(e) order any party to produce to the Arbitrator, and to the other parties for inspection, and to supply copies of any documents or classes of documents in their possession, custody or power which the Arbitrator determines to be relevant;
(f) order the rectification in any contract or arbitration agreement of any mistake which he determines to be common to the parties;
(g) rule on the existence, validity or determination of the contract;
(h) rule on his own jurisdiction, including any objections with respect to the existence or validity of the arbitration agreement or to his terms of reference.

Article 12 Jurisdiction of the Arbitrator

12.1 In addition to the jurisdiction to exercise the powers defined elsewhere in these Rules, the Arbitrator shall have jurisdiction to:

(a) determine any question of law arising in the arbitration;
(b) receive and take into account such written or oral evidence as he shall determine to be relevant, whether or not strictly admissible in law:
(c) proceed in the arbitration and make an award notwithstanding the failure or refusal of any party to comply with these Rules or with the Arbitrator's written orders or written directions, or to exercise its right to present its case, but only after giving that party written notice that he intends to do so.

12.2 If the Claimant fails to attend any hearing of which due notice has been given, the Arbitrator may make an award on the substantive issue and an award as to costs, with or without a hearing, but such an award must be an Interim Award with the provision that it shall become a Final Award after 42 days if no application for a hearing is made by the Claimant during that period. If the Respondent fails to submit a Statement of Defence or to attend any bearing after due notice has been given, the Arbitrator may conduct the hearing in the absence of the Respondent and make an Award.

Article 13 Deposits and security

13.1 The Arbitrator may direct the parties, in such proportions as he deems just, to make one or more deposits to secure the Arbitrator's fees and expenses. Such deposits shall be made to and held by the Arbitrator, or the Chartered Institute of Arbitrators or some other person or body to the order of the Arbitrator, as the Arbitrator may direct, and may be drawn from as required by the Arbitrator. Interest on sums deposited, if any, shall be accumulated to the deposits.

13.2 The Arbitrator shall have the power to order a claimant or counter-claimant to provide security for the legal or other costs of the other party by way of deposit or bank guarantee or in any other manner the Arbitrator thinks fit.

13.3 The Arbitrator shall also have the power to order any party to provide for all or part of any amount in dispute in the arbitration.

Article 14 The award

14.1 The Arbitrator shall make his award in writing and, unless all the parties agree otherwise, shall state the reasons upon which his award is based. The award shall state its date and shall be signed by the Arbitrator.

14.2 Where there is more than one arbitrator and they fail to agree on any issue, they shall decide by a majority. Failing a majority decision on any issue, the Chairman of the tribunal shall make the award alone as if he were sole arbitrator. If an arbitrator refuses or fails to sign the award, the signatures of the majority shall be sufficient, provided that the reason for the omitted signature is stated.

14.3 The Arbitrator shall be responsible for delivering the award or certified copies thereof to the parties, provided that he has been paid his fees and expenses.

14.4 The Arbitrator may make separate awards on different issues at different times.

14.5 If, before the award is made, the parties agree on a settlement of the dispute, the Arbitrator shall either, issue an order for termination of the reference to arbitration or, if requested by both parties and accepted by the Arbitrator, record the settlement in the form of a consent award. The Arbitrator shall then be discharged and the reference to arbitration concluded, subject to payment by the parties of any outstanding fees and expenses of the Arbitrator.

Article 15 Correction of awards and additional awards

15.1 Within 28 days of receiving an award, unless another period of time has been agreed upon by the parties, a party may by notice to the Arbitrator request the Arbitrator to correct in the award any errors in computation, any clerical or typographical errors or any errors of similar nature. If the Arbitrator considers the request to be justified he shall make the corrections within 28 days of receiving the request. Any correction shall be notified in writing to the parties and shall become part of the award.

15.2 The Arbitrator may correct any error of the type referred to in Article 15.1 on his own initiative within 28 days of the date of the award.

15.3 Unless otherwise agreed by the parties, a party may request the Arbitrator within 28 days of the date of the award, and with notice to the other party, to make an additional award as to claims presented in the reference to arbitration but not dealt with in the award. If the Arbitrator considers the request to be justified, he shall notify the parties within 7 days and shall make the additional award within 50 days of the date of the original award.

15.4 The provisions of Article 14 shall apply to any correction of the award and to any additional award.

Article 16 Costs

16.1 The Arbitrator shall specify in the award the total amount of his fees and expenses, including the charges of the arbitration administrator (if any). Unless the parties shall agree otherwise after the dispute has arisen, the Arbitrator shall determine the proportions which the parties shall pay such fees and expenses, provided that the parties will be jointly and severally liable to the Arbitrator for payment of all such fees and expenses until they have been paid in full. If the Arbitrator has determined that all or any of his fees and expenses shall be paid by any party other than a party which has already paid them to the Arbitrator, the latter party shall have the right to recover the appropriate amount from the former.

16.2 The Arbitrator has power to order in his award that all or a part of the legal or other costs of one party shall be paid by the other party. The Arbitrator also has power to determine the amount of these costs and may do so if requested by the parties.

16.3 If the Arbitration is abandoned, suspended or concluded, by agreement or otherwise, before the final award is made, the parties shall be jointly and severally liable to pay to the Arbitrator his fees and expenses as determined by him together with the charges of the arbitration administrator (if any).

Article 17 Exclusion of liability

17.1 The Arbitrator, the Appointing Authority and the arbitration administrator (if any) shall not be liable for anything done or omitted in the discharge or purported discharge of their functions as arbitrator appointing authority or arbitration administrator unless the act or omission is shown to have been in bad faith.

17.2 After the award has been made and the possibilities of correction and additional awards referred to in Article 15 have lapsed or been exhausted, the Arbitrator, the Appointing Authority (and the arbitration administrator if any) shall not be under any obligation to make any statement to any person about any matter concerning the arbitration, and no party shall seek to make any arbitrator or the Appointing Authority or the arbitration administrator a witness in any legal proceedings arising out of the arbitration.

Article 18 Waiver

A party which is aware of non-compliance with these Rules and yet proceeds with the arbitration without promptly stating its objection to such non-compliance, shall be deemed to have waived its right to object.

Appendix 8

THE CHARTERED INSTITUTE OF ARBITRATORS

SHORT FORM ARBITRATION RULES 1991

(February 1995)

Preliminary

1. These Rules shall apply to arbitrations which the parties intend to be conducted according to shortened forms of procedure, whether on the basis of:

1.1 written submission and documentary evidence only, without a hearing; or
1.2 a hearing for the purpose of receiving oral submissions and evidence.

The parties may vary any of the provisions of these Rules by agreement.

Commencement of arbitration

2. An application for arbitration shall be made to the Appointing Authority by the parties on the Appointing Authority's form, accompanied by the prescribed registration fee. At such time as the Appointing Authority thinks fit, it shall appoint an Arbitrator.

Jurisdiction and powers of the Arbitrator

3. Without prejudice to the jurisdictions and powers set out in the Schedule to these Rules, the Arbitrator shall have the widest discretion permitted by law to ensure the just, expeditious, economical and final determination of the dispute.

4. Without prejudice to any powers conferred on the Arbitrator by law or by the contract between the parties, the Arbitrator may exercise the powers set out in the Schedule to these Rules.

Procedure

5. The parties shall, if possible, agree whether the arbitration is to proceed on the basis of written submissions and documentary evidence only, without a hearing, or whether a hearing is required for the purpose of receiving oral submissions and evidence. If the parties fail to agree, the Arbitrator shall decide which procedure is to be followed and may, if he considers it desirable, call a meeting with the parties to consider the matter. The Arbitrator shall in any case confirm which procedure is to be followed by directions issued to the parties in writing.

6. Within 21 days of the Arbitrator's directions under Article 5, the party making the claim ("the Claimant") shall submit to the Arbitrator and to the other party ("the Respondent") a brief statement of claim.

7. Within 21 days of receipt of the Claimant's statement of its claim, the Respondent shall submit to the Arbitrator and to the Claimant:

7.1 a brief statement of its defence to the claim;
7.2 a brief statement of any counterclaim.

8. 14 days of receipt of the Respondent's (statement(s) under Article 7, the Claimant shall submit to the Arbitrator and to the Respondent:

8.1 a brief statement of any reply to the defence which it wishes to make;
8.2 a brief statement of its defence to any counterclaim.

9. Where the Claimant submits a defence to the Respondent's counterclaim, the Respondent may, within 14 days of receipt of the defence to the counterclaim, submit to the Arbitrator and to the Claimant a brief statement of its reply to that defence.

10. All statements submitted under Articles 6 to 9 above shall include a brief statement of:

10.1 the party's principal arguments of fact and law;
10.2 in the case of the claim and of any counterclaim, the remedies sought;

and shall be accompanied by copies of all documents on which the party seeks to rely in support of its case and detailed calculations of any sums claimed.

11. Submissions will normally be closed on completion of the procedure set out in Articles 6–10. However, the Arbitrator may, in his discretion, permit the parties to make further replies to each other's cases, but shall in every case have the power to determine when the submissions are closed.

12. The Arbitrator may require the parties to submit to him and to each other:

12.1 on application to the Arbitrator, such documents as are properly discoverable to help the parties in preparing their submissions;
12.2 in any case, such further submissions, documents or information as he considers to be necessary.

13. Within 14 days of the close of submissions or at such other time as he thinks fit, the Arbitrator may in appropriate cases conduct an inspection of the subject-matter of the arbitration. Either party or both parties shall be entitled to attend, but only for the purpose of identifying for the Arbitrator the subject-matter of the dispute or any relevant part(s).

14. Where, under Article 5, the Arbitrator has directed that a hearing be held, he shall, in consultation with the parties, fix a date and venue for the hearing at the earliest opportunity.

15. Where, under Article 5, the Arbitrator has directed that the arbitration is to proceed on the basis of written submissions and documentary evidence only, the Arbitrator may nevertheless call the parties to an informal hearing solely for the purpose of seeking clarification of any matters arising from the parties' statements and supporting evidence.

16. If, during the course of the arbitration, the Arbitrator concludes that the dispute is incapable of proper resolution in accordance with these Rules, or if, having directed otherwise under Article 5, he considers that a full formal hearing is after all required, he shall advise the parties of his alternative proposals for the conduct of the arbitration. The arbitration shall, unless otherwise directed by the Arbitrator, continue from the point already reached.

17. The parties may, by agreement at any time, serve notice on the Arbitrator that the arbitration shall no longer be conducted in accordance with these Rules.

18. The Arbitrator shall have the power to extend or vary any of the time limits stipulated in these Rules.

Costs

19. In making his award under these Rules, the Arbitrator shall, at his discretion, which shall be exercised judicially, order by whom and in what proportion the parties shall pay his fees and expenses. He shall also decide who shall pay the parties' own costs.

20. In determining the parties' liability for their own costs under Article 19, the Arbitrator shall award all costs which have been reasonably incurred, having received representations as to costs from the parties.

Miscellaneous

21. The Appointing Authority reserves the right to appoint a substitute arbitrator if the original appointee dies, is incapacitated or is for any reason unable to deal expeditiously with the dispute following acceptance of the appointment.

22. Awards made under these Rules shall be final and binding on the parties.

23. Neither the Appointing Authority nor the Arbitrator shall be liable to any party for any act or omission in connection with any arbitration conducted under these Rules.

24. The Short Form Arbitration Rules 1990 are hereby revoked.

SCHEDULE—JURISDICTION AND POWERS OF THE ARBITRATOR

Jurisdiction

The Arbitrator shall have jurisdiction to:

1. determine any question as to the existence, validity or termination of any contract between the parties;

2. order the rectification of any contract or the arbitration agreement, but only to the extent required to rectify any manifest error, mistake or omission σwhich he determines to be common to all the parties.

3. determine any question of law arising in the arbitration;

4. determine any question as to his own jurisdiction, including any objections with respect to the existence or validity of the arbitration agreement or to his terms of reference;

5. determine any question of good faith, dishonesty or fraud arising in the dispute, if specifically pleaded by a party.

Powers

6. The Arbitrator shall, without prejudice to any powers conferred by these Rules, have power to:

(a) allow any party, upon such terms (as to costs and otherwise) as he shall determine, to amend any statement of case, counterclaim, defence to counterclaim and reply, or any other submissions;
(b) order the parties to produce relevant information, documents, goods or property for inspection, in their presence, by the Arbitrator;
(c) order any party to produce to the Arbitrator and to the other party, a list of relevant documents for inspection, and to supply copies of any documents or classes of documents in their possession, custody or power which the arbitrator determines to be relevant;
(d) allow, limit or refuse to allow the appearance of witnesses, whether witnesses of tact or expert witnesses;
(e) require, prior to any hearing, the exchange of witnesses' statements and of experts' reports;
(f) appoint one or more experts to report to the Arbitrator on specific issues and to order a party to produce relevant information, documents, and (so far as is practicable) goods or property or samples thereof for inspection by the expert;
(g) seek legal advice in such form as he thinks fit;
(h) direct the parties, in such proportions as he deems just and in any manner he thinks fit, to make one or more deposits to secure the Arbitrator's fees and expenses;
(i) order any party to provide security for the legal or other costs of any other party by way of deposit or bank guarantee or in any other manner the Arbitrator thinks fit;
(j) order any party to provide security for all or part of any amount in dispute in the arbitration;
(k) proceed in the arbitration notwithstanding the failure or refusal of any party to comply with these Rules or with his orders or directions, or to attend any meeting or hearing, but only after giving that party written notice that he intends to do so;
(l) express awards in any currency;
(m) issue an order for termination of the reference to arbitration if the parties agree to settle the dispute before an award is made or, if required by both parties, record the settlement in the form of a consent award.

7. If the parties agree, following an explanation by the Arbitrator of the consequences, the Arbitrator may exercise the following additional powers;

(a) to conduct such enquiries as may appear to him to be necessary or expedient;
(b) to order the preservation, storage, sale or other disposal of any property or thing under the control of any party;
(c) to receive oral or written evidence from any party which he considers relevant, whether or not strictly admissible in law. In particular the Arbitrator may, at his discretion, receive secondary evidence and/or draw appropriate inferences from a party's conduct where that party fails to comply with an order made by the Arbitrator;
(d) to make an award on the basis of fairness and reasonableness, without necessarily being bound by mandatory rules of law.

Appendix 9

THE LONDON COURT OF INTERNATIONAL ARBITRATION RULES

(adopted to take effect from January 1, 1998)

Where any agreement, submission or reference provides in whatsoever manner for arbitration under the rules of the London Court of International Arbitration ("the LCIA") or by the Court of the LCIA ("the LCIA Court"), the parties shall be taken to have agreed in writing that the arbitration shall be conducted in accordance with the following rules ("the LCIA Rules") or such amended rules as the LCIA may have adopted hereafter to take effect before the commencement of the arbitration. The LCIA Rules include the Schedule of Costs in effect at the commencement of the arbitration, as separately amended from time to time by the LCIA Court.

Article 1 The Claimant's request for arbitration

1.1 Any party wishing to commence an arbitration under these LCIA Rules ("the Claimant") shall send to the Registrar of the LCIA Court ("the Registrar") a written request for arbitration ("the Request") which should include, or be accompanied by:

(a) the names, addresses, telephone, facsimile, telex and e-mail numbers (if known) of the parties to the arbitration and of their legal representatives;
(b) a copy of the written arbitration clause or separate written arbitration agreement invoked by the Claimant ("the Arbitration Agreement"), together with a copy of the contractual documentation in which the arbitration clause is contained or in respect of which the arbitration arises;
(c) a brief statement describing the nature and circumstances of the dispute, and specifying the claims advanced by the Claimant against another party to the arbitration ("the Respondent").
(d) a statement of any matters (such as the seat or language(s) of the arbitration, or the number of arbitrators, or their qualifications or identities) on which the parties have already agreed in writing for the arbitration or in respect of which the Claimant wishes to make a proposal;
(e) if the Arbitration Agreement calls for party nomination of arbitrators, the name, address, telephone, facsimile, telex and e-mail numbers (if known) of the Claimant's nominee;
(f) the fee prescribed in the Schedule of Costs;

(g) confirmation to the Registrar that copies of the Request (including all accompanying documents) have been or are being served simultaneously on all other parties to the arbitration by one or more means of service to be identified in such confirmation.

1.2 The date of receipt by the Registrar of the Request shall be treated as the date on which the arbitration has commenced for all purposes. The Request (including all accompanying documents) shall be submitted to the Registrar in two copies where a sole arbitrator should be appointed, or, if the parties have agreed or the Claimant considers that three arbitrators should be appointed,]in four copies.

Article 2 The Respondent's response

2.1 Within 30 days of service of the Request on the Respondent (or such lesser period fixed by the LCIA Court), the Respondent should send to the Registrar a written response to the Request (''the Response'') containing:

(a) confirmation or denial of all or part of the claims advanced by the Claimant in the Request;
(b) a brief statement of the nature and circumstances of any counterclaims advanced by the Respondent against the Claimant;
(c) comment in response to any statements contained in the Request, as called for under Article 1(d), on matters relating to the conduct of the arbitration;
(d) if the Arbitration Agreement calls for party nomination of arbitrators, the name, address, telephone, facsimile, telex and e-mail numbers (if known) of the Respondent's nominee;
(e) confirmation to the Registrar that copies have been or are being served simultaneously on all other parties to the arbitration.

2.2 The Response shall be submitted in duplicate, or if the parties have agreed or the Respondent considers that three arbitrators should be appointed, in quadruplicate.

2.3 Failure to send a Response shall not preclude the Respondent from denying any claim or from advancing a counterclaim in its Statement of Defence. However, if the Arbitration Agreement calls for party nomination of arbitrators, failure to send a Response or to nominate an arbitrator timeously or at all shall constitute a waiver of that party 's opportunity to nominate an arbitrator.

Article 3 The LCIA court and registrar

3.1 The functions of the LCIA Court under these LCIA Rules shall be performed in its name by the President or a Vice-President of the LCIA or by a division of three or five members of the LCIA Court appointed by the President or a Vice-President of the LCIA, as determined by the President.

3.2 The functions of the Registrar under these LCIA Rules shall be performed by the Registrar or Deputy Registrar of the LCIA Court under the supervision of the LCIA Court.

3.3 All communications from any party to the LCIA Court shall be addressed to the Registrar.

Article 4 Notices and periods of time

4.1 Any notice or other communication that may be or is required to be given by a party under these LCIA Rules shall be in writing and shall be delivered by registered postal or courier service or transmitted by facsimile, telex, e-mail or any other means of telecommunication that provide a record of its transmission.

4.2 A party's last-known residence or place of business during the arbitration shall be a valid address for the purpose of any notice or other communication in the absence of any notification of a change to such address by that party to the other parties, the Arbitral Tribunal and the Registrar.

4.3 For the purpose of determining the date of commencement of a time limit, a notice or other communication shall be treated as having been received on the day it is delivered or, in the case of telecommunications, transmitted in accordance with Articles 4.1 and 4.2.

4.4 For the purpose of determining compliance with a time limit, a notice or other communication shall be treated as having been sent, made or transmitted if it is dispatched in accordance with Articles 4.1 and 4.2 prior to or on the date of the expiration of the time-limit.

4.5 Notwithstanding the above, any notice or communication by one party may be addressed to another party in the manner agreed in writing between them or, failing such agreement, according to the practice followed in the course of their previous dealings or in whatever manner ordered by the Arbitral Tribunal.

4.6 For the purpose of calculating a period of time under these LCIA Rules, such period shall begin to run on the day following the day when a notice or other communication is received. If the last day of such period is an official holiday or a non-business day at the residence or place of business of the addressee, the period is extended until the first business day which follows. Official holidays or non-business days occurring during the running of the period of time are included in calculating that period.

4.7 The Arbitral Tribunal may at any time extend or abridge any period of time prescribed under these LCIA Rules or under the Arbitration Agreement for the conduct of the arbitration, including any notice or communication to be served by one party on any other party.

Article 5 Formation of the Arbitral Tribunal

5.1 The expression "the Arbitral Tribunal" in the LCIA Rules includes a sole arbitrator or all the arbitrators where more than one. All references to an arbitrator, an expert, the President or Vice-President of the LCIA Court, the Registrar or Deputy Registrar shall include the masculine and feminine.

5.2 All arbitrators conducting an arbitration under these LCIA Rules shall be and remain at all times impartial and independent of the parties; and none shall act in the arbitration as advocates for any party. No arbitrator, whether before or after appointment, shall advise any party on the merits or outcome of the dispute.

5.3 Before appointment by the LCIA Court, each arbitrator shall furnish to the Registrar a written résumé of his past and present professional positions; he shall agree in writing upon fee rates conforming to the Schedule of Costs; and he shall sign a declaration to the effect that there are no circumstances known to him likely to give rise to any justified doubts as to his impartiality or independence, other than any circumstances disclosed by him in the declaration, and that he will forthwith disclose any such circumstances to the LCIA Court, to any other members of the Arbitral Tribunal and to all the parties if such circumstances should arise after that the date of such declaration and before the arbitration is concluded.

5.4 The LCIA Court shall appoint the Arbitral Tribunal as soon as practicable after receipt by the Registrar of the Response or after the expiry of 30 days following service of the Request upon the Respondent if no Response is received by the Registrar (or such lesser period fixed by the LCIA Court). The LCIA Court may proceed with the formation of the Tribunal notwithstanding that the Request or Response is missing or incomplete. A sole arbitrator will be appointed unless the parties have agreed in writing otherwise, or unless the LCIA Court determines that in view of all the circumstances of the case a three-member tribunal is appropriate.

5.5 The LCIA Court alone is empowered to appoint arbitrators. The LCIA Court will appoint arbitrators with due regard for any particular method or criteria of selection agreed in writing by the parties. In selecting arbitrators consideration will be given to the nature of the transaction, the nature and circumstances of the dispute, the nationality, location and languages of the parties and (if more than two) the number of parties.

5.6 In the case of a three-member Arbitral Tribunal, the LCIA Court shall appoint the chairman (who will not be a party-nominated arbitrator).

Article 6 Nationality of arbitrators

6.1 Where the parties are of different nationalities, a sole arbitrator or chairman of the Arbitral Tribunal shall not have the same nationality as any party unless the parties who are not of the same nationality as the proposed appointee all agree in writing otherwise.

6.2 The nationality of parties shall be understood to include that of controlling shareholders or interests. For the purpose of this Article, citizens of the European Union shall be treated as nationals of its different Member States.

Article 7 Party and other nominations

7.1 If the parties have agreed that any party or third person is to appoint any arbitrator, that agreement shall be treated as a written agreement to nominate an arbitrator for all purposes. In such circumstances or where the parties have agreed that any party or third person is to nominate an arbitrator, such arbitrator shall only be appointed subject to his prior compliance with Article 5.3. The LCIA Court may refuse to appoint any such nominee if it determines that he is not suitable or independent or impartial.

7.2 Where the parties have howsoever agreed that the Respondent is to nominate an arbitrator and the Respondent fails to make a nomination timeously, the LCIA Court may appoint an arbitrator without regard to any nomination by the Respondent. Likewise, if the Request for Arbitration does not contain a nomination by the Claimant where the parties have howsoever agreed that the Claimant is to nominate an arbitrator, the LCIA Court may appoint an arbitrator without regard for any nomination by the Claimant.

Article 8 Three or more parties

8.1 Where the Arbitration Agreement entitles each party howsoever to nominate an arbitrator, the parties to the dispute number more than two and such parties have not all agreed in writing that the disputant parties represent two separate sides for the formation of the Arbitral Tribunal as Claimant and Respondent respectively, the LCIA Court shall appoint the Arbitral Tribunal without regard to any party's nomination.

8.2 In such circumstances, the Arbitration Agreement shall be treated for all purposes as a written agreement by the parties for the appointment of the Arbitral Tribunal by the LCIA Court.

Article 9 Expedited formation

9.1 In exceptional urgency, on or after the commencement of the arbitration, any party may apply to the LCIA Court for the expedited formation of the Arbitral Tribunal, including the appointment of a Replacement Arbitrator.

9.2 Such an application shall be made in writing to the Registrar, copied to all other parties to the arbitration; and it shall set out the specific grounds for exceptional urgency in the formation of the Arbitral Tribunal.

9.3 The LCIA Court may, in its complete discretion, abridge or curtail any time-limit under these LCIA Rules for the formation of the Arbitral Tribunal, including service of the Response and of any matters or documents adjudged to be missing from the Request. The LCIA Court shall not be entitled to abridge or curtail any other time-limit.

Article 10 Revocation of arbitrator's appointment

10.1 If any arbitrator dies, falls seriously ill, refuses, or becomes unable or unfit to act, upon challenge by a party or at the request of the remaining arbitrators or (as the case may be) by the arbitrator himself, the LCIA Court may revoke his appointment and appoint another arbitrator. The LCIA Court shall decide upon the amount of fees and expenses to be paid for the former arbitrator's services as it may consider appropriate in all the circumstances.

10.2 If any arbitrator acts in deliberate violation of the Arbitration Agreement (including these LCIA Rules) or does not act fairly and impartially as between the parties or does not conduct or participate in the arbitration proceedings with reasonable diligence, avoiding unnecessary delay or expense, that arbitrator may be considered unfit in the opinion of the LCIA Court.

10.3 An arbitrator may be challenged by any party if circumstances exist that give rise to justifiable doubts as to his impartiality or independence. A party may challenge an arbitrator it has nominated, or in whose appointment it has participated, only for reasons of which it becomes aware after the appointment has been made.

10.4 A party who intends to challenge an arbitrator shall, within 15 days of the formation of the Arbitral Tribunal or (if later) after becoming aware of any circumstances referred to in Article 10.1, 10.2 or 10.3, send a written statement of the reasons for its challenge to the LCIA Court, the Arbitral Tribunal and all other parties. Unless the challenged arbitrator withdraws or all other parties agree to the challenge within 15 days of receipt of the written statement, the LCIA Court shall decide on the challenge.

Article 11 Nomination and replacement arbitrators

11.1 In the event that the LCIA Court determines that any nominee is not suitable or independent or impartial or if an appointed arbitrator is to be replaced for any reason, the LCIA Court shall have a complete discretion to decide whether or not to follow the original nominating process.

11.2 If the LCIA Court should so decide, any opportunity given to a party to make a re-nomination shall be waived if not exercised within 15 days (or such lesser time as the LCIA Court may fix), after which the LCIA Court shall appoint the replacement arbitrator.

Article 12 Truncated Arbitral Tribunal

12.1 If any arbitrator on a three-member Arbitral Tribunal refuses to participate in the arbitration, the two other arbitrators shall have the power, upon notice to the parties and the Registrar of such refusal and unless the parties have agreed otherwise in writing, to continue the arbitration (including the making of any decision, ruling or award), notwithstanding the absence of the third recalcitrant arbitrator.

12.2 In determining whether to continue the arbitration, the two other arbitrators shall take into account the stage of the arbitration, any excuse expressed by the third arbitrator for his non-participation and such other matters as they consider appropriate in the circumstances of the case. The reasons for such determination shall be stated in any award, order or other decision made by the two arbitrators without the participation of the third arbitrator.

12.3 In the event that the two other arbitrators determine not to continue the arbitration without the participation of the third arbitrator, the two arbitrators shall notify the parties and the Registrar of their determination; and in that event, the two arbitrators or any party may refer the matter to the LCIA Court for the revocation of that third arbitrator's appointment under Article 10.

Article 13 Communications between parties and the Arbitral Tribunal

13.1 Until the Arbitral Tribunal is formed, all communications between parties and arbitrators shall be made through the Registrar.

13.2 Thereafter, unless and until the LCIA Court directs that communications shall take place directly between the Arbitral Tribunal and the parties (with simultaneous copies to the Registrar), all written communications between the parties and the Arbitral Tribunal shall continue to be made through the Registrar.

13.3 Where the Registrar sends any written communication to one party on behalf of the Arbitral Tribunal, he shall send a copy of each of the other parties. Where any party sends to the Registrar any communication (including Statements and Documents under Article 15), it shall include a copy for each arbitrator; and if shall also send copies direct to all other parties and confirm to the Registrar in writing that it has done or is doing so.

Article 14 Conduct of the proceedings

14.1 The parties may agree on the conduct of their arbitral proceedings and they are encouraged to do so, consistent with the Arbitral Tribunal's general duties at all times:

(i) to act fairly and impartially as between all parties, giving each a reasonable opportunity of putting its case and dealing with that of its opponent; and
(ii) to adopt procedures suitable to the circumstances of the arbitration, avoiding unnecessary delay or expense, so as to provide a fair and efficient means for the final resolution of the parties' dispute.

Such agreements shall be made by the parties in writing or recorded in writing by the Arbitral Tribunal at the request of and with the authority of the parties.

14.2 Unless otherwise agreed by the parties under Article 14.1, the Arbitral Tribunal shall have the widest discretion allowed under such law as may be applicable to discharge its general duties; and at all times the parties shall do everything necessary for the proper and expeditious conduct of the arbitration.

14.3 In the case of a three-member Arbitral Tribunal the chairman may, with the prior consent of the other two arbitrators, make procedural rulings alone.

Article 15 Submission of written statements and documents

15.1 Unless the parties have agreed otherwise under Article 14.1 or the Arbitral Tribunal should determine differently, the written stage of the proceedings shall be as set out below.

15.2 Within 30 days of receipt of notification from the Registrar of the formation of the Arbitral Tribunal, the Claimant shall send to the Registrar a Statement of Case setting out in sufficient detail the facts and any contentions of law on which it relies, together with the relief claimed against all other parties, save and insofar as such matters have not been set out in its Request.

12.2 Within 30 days of receipt of the Statement of Case or written notice from the Claimant that it elects to treat the Request as its Statement of Case, the Respondent shall send to the Registrar a Statement of Defence setting out in sufficient detail which of the facts and contentions of law in the Statement of Case or Request (as the case may be) it admits or denies, on what grounds and on what other facts and contentions of law it relies. Any counterclaims shall be submitted with the Statement of Defence in the same manner as claims are to be set out in the Statement of Case.

15.4 Within 30 days of receipt of the Statement of Defence, the Claimant may send to the Registrar a Statement of Reply which, where there are any counterclaims, shall include a Defence to Counterclaim in the same manner as a defence is to be set out in the Statement of Defence.

15.5 If the Statement of Reply contains a Defence to Counterclaim, within 30 days of its receipt the Respondent may send to the Registrar a Statement of Reply to Counterclaim.

15.6 All Statements referred to in this Article shall be accompanied by copies (or, if they are especially voluminous, lists) of all essential documents on which the party concerned relies and which have not previously been submitted by any party, and (where appropriate) by any relevant samples and exhibits.

15.7 As soon as practicable following receipt of the Statements specified in this Article, the Arbitral Tribunal shall proceed in such manner as has been agreed in writing by the parties or pursuant to its authority under these LCIA Rules.

15.8 If the Respondent fails to submit a Statement of Defence or the Claimant a Statement of Defence to Counterclaim, or if at any point any party fails to avail itself of the opportunity to present its case in the manner directed by the Arbitral Tribunal, the Tribunal may nevertheless proceed with the arbitration and make an award.

Article 16 Seat of arbitration and place of hearings

16.1 The parties may agree in writing the seat (or legal place) of their arbitration. Failing such a choice, the seat of arbitration shall be London, unless and until the LCIA Court determines in view of all the circumstances, and after having given the parties an opportunity to make written comment, that another seat is more appropriate.

16.2 The Arbitral Tribunal may hold hearings, meetings and deliberations at any convenient geographical place in its discretion; and if elsewhere than the seat of the arbitration, the arbitration shall be treated as an arbitration conducted at the seat of the arbitration and any award as an award made at the seat of the arbitration for all purposes.

16.3 The law applicable to the arbitration shall be the arbitration law of the seat of arbitration, unless the parties have expressly agreed in writing on the application of another arbitration law and such agreement is permitted by the law of the arbitral seat.

Article 17 Language of arbitration

17.1 The initial language of the arbitration shall be that of the Arbitration Agreement, unless the parties have agreed in writing otherwise and providing always that a defaulting party shall have no cause for complaint if communications to and from the Registrar and the arbitration proceedings are conducted in the English language.

17.2 In the event that the Arbitration Agreement is agreed in more than one language, the LCIA Court may, unless the Arbitration Agreement provides that the arbitration proceedings shall be conducted in more than one language, decide which of those languages shall be the initial language of the arbitration.

17.3 Upon the formation of the Arbitral Tribunal and unless the parties have agreed upon the language or languages of the arbitration, the Arbitration Tribunal shall decide upon the language(s) of the arbitration, after giving the parties an opportunity to make written comment and taking into account the initial language of the arbitration and any other matter it may consider appropriate in all the circumstances of the case.

17.4 If any document is expressed in a language other than the language(s) of the arbitration and no translation of such document is submitted by the party relying upon the document, the Arbitral Tribunal or (if the Arbitral Tribunal has not been formed) the LCIA Court may order that party to submit a translation in a form to be determined by the Arbitral Tribunal or the LCIA Court, as the case may be.

Article 18 Party representation

18.1 Any party may be represented by legal practitioners or any other representatives.

18.2 At any time the Arbitral Tribunal may require from any party proof of authority granted to its representative(s) in such form as the Arbitral Tribunal may determine.

Article 19 Hearings

19.1 Any party which expresses a desire to that effect has the right to be heard orally before the Arbitral Tribunal on the merits of the dispute, unless the parties have agreed in writing on documents-only arbitration.

19.2 The Arbitral Tribunal shall fix the date, time and geographical place of any meetings and hearings in the arbitration, and shall give the parties reasonable notice thereof.

19.3 The Arbitral Tribunal may in advance of any hearing submit to the parties a list of questions which it wishes them to answer with special attention.

19.4 All meetings and hearings shall be in private unless the parties agree otherwise in writing or the Arbitral Tribunal directs otherwise.

19.5 The Arbitral Tribunal shall have the fullest authority to establish time-limits for meetings and hearings, or for any parts thereof.

Article 20 Witnesses

20.1 Before any hearing, the Arbitral Tribunal may require any party to give notice of the identity of each witness that party wishes to call (including rebuttal witnesses), as well as the subject matter of that witness's testimony, its content and its relevance to the issues in the arbitration.

20.2 The Arbitral Tribunal may also determine the time, manner and form in which such materials should be exchanged between the parties and presented to the Arbitral Tribunal; and it has a discretion to allow, refuse, or limit the appearance of witnesses (whether witness of fact or expert witness).

20.3 Subject to any order otherwise by the Arbitral Tribunal, the testimony of a witness may be presented by a party in written form, either as a duly signed statement or as a duly sworn affidavit.

20.4 Subject to Article 14.1 and 14.2, any party may request that a witness, on whose testimony another party seeks to rely, should attend for oral questioning at a hearing before the Arbitral Tribunal. If the Arbitral Tribunal orders that other party to produce the witness and the witness fails to attend the oral hearing without good cause, the Arbitral Tribunal may place such weight on the written testimony (or exclude the same altogether) as it considers appropriate in the circumstances of the case.

20.5 Any witness who gives oral evidence at a hearing before the Arbitral Tribunal may be questioned by each of the parties under the control of the Arbitral Tribunal. The Arbitral Tribunal may put questions at any stage of the examination of an oral witness.

20.6 Subject to the mandatory provisions of any applicable law, it shall not be improper for any party or its legal representatives to interview any witness or potential witness for the purpose of presenting his testimony in written form or producing him as an oral witness for examination at any hearing of the arbitration.

20.7 Any individual intending to testify to the Arbitral Tribunal on any issue of fact or expertise shall be treated as a witness under these LCIA Rules notwithstanding that the individual is a party to the arbitration or was or is an officer, employee or shareholder of any party.

Article 21 Experts to the Arbitral Tribunal

21.1 Unless otherwise agreed by the parties in writing, the Arbitral Tribunal:

(a) may appoint one or more experts to report to the Arbitral Tribunal on specific issues, who shall be impartial and independent of the parties; and
(b) may require a party to give any such expert any relevant information or to provide access to any relevant documents, goods, samples, property or site for inspection by the expert.

21.2 Unless otherwise agreed by the parties in writing, if a party so requests or if the Arbitral Tribunal considers it necessary, the expert shall, after delivery of his written or oral report to the Arbitral Tribunal and the parties, participate in one or more hearings at which the parties shall have the opportunity to question the expert on his report and to present expert witnesses in order to testify on the points at issue.

21.3 The fees and expenses of any expert appointed by the Arbitral Tribunal under this Article shall be paid out of the deposits payable under Article 24 and shall form part of the costs of the arbitration.

Article 22 Additional powers of the Arbitral Tribunal

22.1 Unless the parties at any time agree otherwise in writing and to subject to any mandatory limitations of any applicable law, the Arbitral Tribunal shall have the power, on the application of any party or of its own motion, but in either case only after giving the parties a reasonable opportunity to state their views:

(a) to determine what are the law(s) or rules of law applicable to the Arbitration Agreement and the arbitration;
(b) to order the correction of any contract between the parties or the Arbitration Agreement, but only to the extent required to rectify any mistake which it determines to be common to the parties and then only if and to the extent to which the law or rules of law applicable to the contract or Arbitration Agreement permit such correction;
(c) to allow, only upon the application of a party, one or more third persons to be joined in the arbitration as a party provided any such third person and the applicant party have consented thereto in writing, and thereafter to make a

single final award, or separate awards, in respect of all parties so implicated in the arbitration;

(d) to allow any party, upon such terms (as to costs and otherwise) as it shall determine, to amend any claim, counterclaim and defence and reply;

(e) to extend or abbreviate any time-limit provided by the Arbitration Agreement or these Rules for the conduct of the arbitration or by the Arbitral Tribunal's own orders;

(f) to conduct such enquiries as may appear to the Arbitral Tribunal to be necessary or expedient, including whether and to what extent the Arbitral Tribunal should itself take the initiative in identifying the issues and ascertaining the relevant facts and the applicable law(s) or rules of law;

(g) to order any party to make any property, site or thing under its control and relating to the subject matter of the arbitration available for inspection by the Arbitral Tribunal, any other party, its expert or any expert to the Arbitral Tribunal;

(h) to order the preservation, storage, sale or other disposal of any property or thing under the control of any party and relating to the subject matter of the arbitration;

(i) to order any party to produce to the Arbitral Tribunal, and to the other parties for inspection, and to supply copies of, any documents or classes of documents in their possession, custody or power which the Arbitral Tribunal determines to be relevant;

(j) to order on a provisional basis, subject to final determination in an award, any relief which the Arbitral Tribunal would have power to grant in an award, including a provisional order for the payment of money or the disposition of property as between any parties; and

(k) to decide whether or not to apply any strict rules of evidence (or any other rules) as to the admissibility, relevance or weight of any material tendered by a party on any matter of fact or expert opinion; and to determine the time, manner and form in which such material should be exchanged between the parties and presented to the Arbitral Tribunal.

22.2 The Arbitral Tribunal shall decide the parties' dispute in accordance with the law(s) or rules of law chosen by the parties as applicable to the merits of their dispute. If and to the extent that the Arbitral Tribunal determines that the parties have made no such choice, the Arbitral Tribunal shall apply the law(s) which it considers appropriate.

22.3 The Arbitral Tribunal shall only apply to the merits of the dispute other principles deriving from "ex aequo et bono", "amiable composition" or "honourable engagement" where the parties have so agreed expressly in writing.

22.4 By agreeing to arbitration under these LCIA Rules, the parties shall be treated as having agreed not to apply to any state court or other judicial authority after the formation of the Arbitral Tribunal for any order under paragraphs (g), (h) or (i) of Article 22.1, except with the agreement in writing of all parties or the prior authorisation of the Arbitral Tribunal.

Article 23 Jurisdiction of the Arbitral Tribunal

23.1 The Arbitral Tribunal shall have the power to rule on its own jurisdiction, including any objection to the existence or validity of the Arbitration Agreement. For that purpose, an arbitration clause which forms or was intended to form part of another agreement shall be treated as an arbitration agreement independent of that other agreement. A decision by the Arbitral Tribunal that such other agreement is invalid, non-existent or ineffective shall not entail ipso jure the invalidity, non-existence or ineffectiveness of the arbitration clause.

23.2 A plea by a Respondent that the Arbitral Tribunal does not have jurisdiction shall be raised not later than in the Statement of Defence and a like plea by a Respondent to Counterclaim no later than in the Statement of Defence to Counterclaim. A plea that the Arbitral Tribunal is exceeding the scope of its authority shall be raised promptly after the Arbitral Tribunal has indicated its intention to decide on the matter alleged by any party to be beyond the scope of its authority. In either case the Arbitral Tribunal may nevertheless admit an untimely plea if it considers the delay justified in the particular circumstances.

23.3 The Arbitral Tribunal may determine the plea to its jurisdiction or authority in an award as to jurisdiction or later in an award on ther]merits, as it considers appropriate in the circumstances.

23.4 By agreeing to arbitration under these LCIA Rules, the parties shall be treated as having agreed not to apply to any state court or other judicial authority for any relief regarding the Arbitral Tribunal's jurisdiction or authority, except with the agreement in writing of all parties to the arbitration, or the prior authorisation of the Arbitral Tribunal, or the latter's award finally determining the plea impugning its jurisdiction or authority.

Article 24 Deposits

24.1 The LCIA Court may direct the parties, in such proportions as it thinks appropriate, to make one or several interim or final payments on account of the costs of the arbitration. Such deposits shall be made to and held by the LCIA and from time to time may be released by the LCIA Court to the arbitrator(s), any expert appointed by the Arbitral Tribunal and the LCIA itself as the arbitration progresses.

24.2 The Arbitral Tribunal shall not proceed with the arbitration without ascertaining at all times from the Registrar that the LCIA is in requisite funds.

24.3 In the event that a party fails or refuses to provide any deposit as instructed by the LCIA Court, the LCIA Court may invite the other party or parties to effect a substitute payment to allow the arbitration to proceed (subject to any award on costs). In such circumstances, the party paying the substitute payment shall be entitled to recover that amount as a debt immediately due from the defaulting party.

24.4 Failure by a claimant or counterclaiming party to provide timeously and in full the required deposit may be treated by the LCIA Court as a withdrawal of the claim or counterclaim respectively.

Article 25 Security

25.1 The Arbitral Tribunal shall have the power to order any respondent party to a claim or counterclaim to provide security for all or part of the amount in dispute, by way of deposit or bank guarantee or in any other manner and upon such terms as the Arbitral Tribunal considers appropriate. Such terms may include the provision by the claiming or counterclaiming party of a cross-indemnity, itself secured in such manner as the Arbitral Tribunal considers appropriate, for any costs or losses incurred by such respondent in providing security. The amount of any costs and losses payable under such cross-indemnity may be determined by the Arbitral Tribunal in one or more awards.

25.2 Such power shall not prejudice any party's right to apply to any state court or other judicial authority for interim or conservatory measures before the formation of the

Arbitral Tribunal and, in exceptional cases, thereafter. Any order for such measures after the formation of the Arbitral Tribunal shall be promptly communicated by the applicant to the Arbitral Tribunal and all other parties.

25.3 The Arbitral Tribunal shall have the power to order any claiming or counterclaiming party to provide security for the legal or other costs of any other party by way of deposit or bank guarantee or in any other manner and upon such terms as the Arbitral Tribunal considers appropriate. Such terms may also include the provision by that other party of a cross-indemnity, itself secured in such manner as the Arbitral Tribunal considers appropriate, for any costs and losses incurred by such claimant or counterclaimant in providing security. The amount of any costs and losses payable under such cross-indemnity may be determined by the Arbitral Tribunal in one or more awards. In the event that a claiming or counterclaiming party does not comply with any order to provide security, the Arbitral Tribunal may stay that party's claims or counterclaims or dismiss them in an award.

25.4 By agreeing to arbitration under these LCIA Rules, the parties shall be taken to have agreed not to apply to any state court or other judicial authority for any order for security for its legal or other costs.

Article 26 The award

26.1 The Arbitral Tribunal shall make its award in writing and, unless all the parties agree in writing otherwise, shall state the reasons upon which its award is based. The award shall also state the date when the award is made and the seat of the arbitration; and it shall be signed by the sole arbitrator or (where there are three arbitrators) the members of the Arbitral Tribunal or those assenting to the award.

26.2 If any arbitrator fails to comply with the mandatory provisions of any applicable law relating to the making of the award, having been given a reasonable opportunity to do so, the remaining arbitrators may proceed in his absence and state in their award the circumstances of the other arbitrator's failure to participate in the making of the award.

26.3 Where there are three arbitrators and the Arbitral Tribunal fails to agree on any issue, the arbitrators shall decide that issue by a majority. Failing a majority decision on any issue, the chairman of the Arbitral Tribunal shall decide that issue. If any arbitrator refuses or fails to sign the award, the signatures of the majority or (failing a majority) of the chairman shall be sufficient, provided that the reason for the omitted signature is stated by the majority or chairman.

26.4 The sole arbitrator or chairman shall be responsible for delivering true copies of the award (one more than the number of parties) to the LCIA Court, which shall transmit certified copies to the parties provided that the costs of arbitration have been paid to the LCIA in accordance with Article 28.

26.5 An award may be expressed in any currency. The Arbitral Tribunal may order that simple or compound interest shall be paid by any party on any sum awarded at such rates as the Arbitral Tribunal determines to be appropriate, without being bound by legal rates of interest imposed by any state court, in respect of any period which the Arbitral Tribunal determines to be appropriate ending not later than the date upon which the award is complied with.

26.6 The Arbitral Tribunal may make separate awards on different issues at different times. Such awards shall have the same status and effect as any other award made by the Arbitral Tribunal.

26.7 In the event of a settlement of the parties' dispute, the Arbitral Tribunal may render an award recording the settlement if the parties so request in writing (a "Consent

Award"), provided always that the Consent Award indicates that it is an award made by the parties' consent. If the parties do not require a consent award, then on written confirmation by the parties to the LCIA Court that a settlement has been reached, the Arbitral Tribunal shall be discharged and the arbitration proceedings concluded, subject to payment by the parties of any outstanding costs of the arbitration under Article 28.

26.8 All awards shall be final and binding on the parties. By agreeing to arbitration under these LCIA Rules, the parties undertake to carry out any award immediately, without any delay, and waive their right to any form of appeal, review or recourse to any state court or other judicial authority, insofar as such waiver may be validly made.

Article 27 Correction of awards and additional awards

27.1 Within 30 days of receipt of any award, a party may by written notice to the Registrar (copied to all other parties) request the Arbitral Tribunal to correct in the award any errors in computation, clerical or typographical errors or any errors of a similar nature. If the Arbitral Tribunal considers the request to be justified, it shall make the corrections within 30 days of receipt of the request. Any correction shall take the form of separate memorandum dated and signed by the Arbitral Tribunal or (if three arbitrators) those of its members assenting to it; and such memorandum shall become part of the award for all purposes.

27.2 The Arbitral Tribunal may likewise correct any error of the nature described in Article 27.1 on its own initiative within 30 days of the date of the award, to the same effect.

27.3 Within 30 days of receipt of the final award, a party may by written notice to the Registrar (copied to all other parties), request the Arbitral Tribunal to make an additional award as to claims or counterclaims presented in the arbitration but not determined in the any award. If the Arbitral Tribunal considers the request to be justified, it shall make the additional award within 60 days of receipt of the request. The provisions of Article 26 shall apply to any additional award.

Article 28 Arbitration and legal costs

28.1 The costs of the arbitration (other than the legal or other costs incurred by the parties themselves) shall be determined by the LCIA Court in accordance with the Schedule of Costs. The parties shall be jointly and severally liable to the LCIA for such arbitration costs.

28.2 The Arbitral Tribunal shall specify in the award the total amount of the costs of the arbitration as determined by the LCIA Court. Unless the parties agree otherwise in writing, the Arbitral Tribunal shall determine the proportions in which the parties shall bear all or part of such arbitration costs. If the Arbitral Tribunal has determined that all or any part of the arbitration costs shall be borne by a party other than a party which has already paid them to the LCIA, the latter party shall have the right to recover the appropriate amount from the former party.

28.3 The Arbitral Tribunal shall have the power to order in its award that all or part of the legal or other costs of a party (apart from the costs of the arbitration) be paid by another party. The Arbitral Tribunal shall determine and fix the amount of each item comprising such costs on such reasonable basis as it thinks fit.

28.4 Unless the parties otherwise agree in writing, the Arbitral Tribunal shall make its orders on both arbitration and legal costs on the general principle that costs should follow the result of the award or arbitration except where it appears to the Arbitral

Tribunal that in the particular circumstances this approach is inappropriate. Any such order for costs shall be made with reasons in the award.

28.5 If the arbitration is abandoned, suspended or concluded, by agreement or otherwise, before the final award is made, the parties shall remain jointly and severally liable to pay to the LCIA the costs of the arbitration as determined by the LCIA Court in accordance with the Schedule of Costs. In the event that such arbitration costs are less than the deposits made by the parties, there shall be a refund by the LCIA in such proportion as the parties may agree in writing, or failing such agreement, in the same proportions as the deposits were made by the parties to the LCIA.

Article 29 Decisions by the LCIA Court

29.1 The decisions of the LCIA Court with respect to all matters relating to the arbitration shall be conclusive and binding upon the parties and the Arbitral Tribunal. Such decisions are to be treated as administrative in nature and the LCIA Court shall not be required to give any reasons.

29.2 To the extent permitted by the law of the seat of the arbitration, the parties shall be taken to have waived any right of appeal or review in respect of any such decisions of the LCIA Court to any state court or other judicial authority. If such appeals or review remain possible due to mandatory provisions of any applicable law, the LCIA Court shall, subject to the provisions of that applicable law, decide whether the arbitral proceedings are to continue, notwithstanding an appeal or review.

Article 30 Confidentiality

30.1 By submitting to arbitration under these LCIA Rules, unless the parties expressly agree in writing to the contrary, the parties undertake as a general principle to keep all awards confidential (together with all other materials introduced by another party into the proceedings not otherwise in the public domain), save and to the extent that disclosure may be required of a party by legal duty, to protect or pursue a legal right or to enforce or impugn an award in legal proceedings before a state court or other judicial authority.

30.2 The deliberations of the Arbitral Tribunal are likewise confidential to its members, save and to the extent that disclosure of an arbitrator's refusal to participate in the arbitration is required of the other members of the Arbitral Tribunal under Articles 10, 12, 26.2 and 26.3.

30.3 It is the policy of the LCIA Court not to publish any award or any part of an award without the prior written consent of all parties and the Arbitral Tribunal.

Article 31 Exclusion of liability

31.1 None of the LCIA, the LCIA Court (including its President, Vice-Presidents and individual members), the Registrar, the Deputy Registrar, any arbitrator and any expert to the Arbitral Tribunal shall be liable to any party howsoever for any act or omission in connection with any arbitration conducted by reference to these LCIA Rules, save where the act or omission is shown by that party to constitute conscious and deliberate wrongdoing committed by the body or person alleged to be liable to that party.

31.2 After the award has been made and the possibilities of correction and additional awards referred to in Article 27 have lapsed or been exhausted, neither the LCIA, the LCIA Court including its President, Vice-Presidents and individual members), the Registrar, the Deputy Registrar, any arbitrator or expert to the Arbitral Tribunal shall be under any legal obligation to make any statement to any person about any matter concerning the arbitration, nor shall any party seek to make any of these persons a witness in any legal or other proceedings arising out of the arbitration.

Article 32 General rules

32.1 A party who knows that any provision of the Arbitration Agreement (including these LCIA Rules) has not been complied with and yet proceeds with the arbitration without promptly stating its objection to such non-compliance, shall be treated as having waived its right to object.

30.2 In all matters not expressly provided for in these LCIA Rules, the LCIA Court, the Arbitral Tribunal and the parties shall act in the spirit of the LCIA Rules and shall make every reasonable effort to ensure that an award is legally enforceable.

Appendix 10

RULES OF ARBITRATION OF THE INTERNATIONAL CHAMBER OF COMMERCE*

A. Introductory provisions

Article 1 International Court of Arbitration

1. The International Court of Arbitration (''the Court'') of the International Chamber of commerce (''the ICC'') is the arbitration body attached to the ICC. The statutes of the Court are set forth in Appendix I. Members of the Court are appointed by the Council of the ICC. The function of the Court is to provide for the settlement by arbitration of business disputes of an international character in accordance with these Rules. If so empowered by an arbitration agreement, the Court shall also provide for the settlement by arbitration in accordance with these Rules of business disputes not of an international character.

2. The Court does not itself settle disputes. It has the function of ensuring the application of these Rules. It draws up its own Internal Rules (Appendix II).

3. The Chairman of the Court, or in the Chairman's absence or otherwise at his request, one of its Vice Chairmen shall have the power to take urgent decisions on behalf of the Court, provided that any such decision shall be reported to the Court at its next session.

4. As provided for in its Internal Rules, the Court may delegate to one or more committees composed of its members the power to take certain decisions, provided that any such decision shall be reported to the Court at its next session.

5. The Secretariat of the Court (''the Secretariat'') under the direction of its Secretary General (''the Secretary General'') shall have its seat at the headquarters of the ICC.

Article 2 Definitions

In these Rules:

(i) ''Arbitral Tribunal'' includes one or more arbitrators, as the case may be.

* ICC Rules of Arbitration (1998)—ICC Rules of Conciliation (1988). ICC Publication No. 581—ISBN 9 2842 1239 1 (E); ISBN 9 8422 1239 (F). Published in its official English version by the International Chamber of Commerce. Copyright © 1997—International Chamber of Commerce (ICC), Paris. Available from: The ICC Court of Arbitration, 38 Count Albert 1er, 75008 Paris, France.

(ii) "Claimant" includes one or more claimants and "Respondent" includes one or more respondents, as the case may be.
(iii) "Award" includes, *inter alia*, an interim, partial or final Award, as the case may be.

Article 3 Written notifications or communications; time limits

1. All pleadings and other written communications submitted by any party, as well as all documents annexed thereto, shall be supplied in a number of copies sufficient to provide one copy for each party, plus one for each arbitrator, and one for the Secretariat. A copy of any communication from the Arbitral Tribunal to the parties shall be sent to the Secretariat.

2. All notifications or communications from the Secretariat and the Arbitral Tribunal shall be made to the address or last known address of the party or its representative for whom the same are intended, as notified either by the party in question or by the other party as appropriate. Such notification or communication may be made by delivery against receipt, registered post, courier, facsimile transmission, telex, telegram or any other means of telecommunication that provides a record of the sending thereof.

3. A notification or communication shall be deemed to have been effected on the day when it was received by the party itself or by its representative, or would have so been received if made in accordance with the preceding paragraph.

4. Periods of time specified in or fixed under the present Rules shall start to run on the day following the date a notification or communication is deemed to have been effected in accordance with the preceding paragraph. When the day next following such date is an official holiday or a non business day in the country where the notification or communication is deemed to have been effected, the period of time shall commence on the first following business day. Official holidays and non business days are included in the calculation of the period of time. If the last day of the relevant period of time granted is an official holiday or a non business day in the country where the notification or communication is deemed to have been effected, the period of time shall expire at the end of the first following business day.

B. Commencing the arbitration

Article 4 Request for arbitration

1. A party wishing to have recourse to arbitration under these Rules shall submit its Request for Arbitration ("the Request") to the Secretariat, which shall notify the Claimant and Respondent of the receipt of the Request and the date of such receipt.

2. The date when the Request is received by the Secretariat shall, for all purposes, be deemed to be the date of the commencement of the arbitral proceedings.

3. The request shall, *inter alia*, contain the following information:

(a) names in full, description and addresses of each of the parties;
(b) a description of the nature and circumstances of the dispute giving rise to the claims;
(c) a statement of the relief sought including, to the extent possible, an indication of any amounts claimed;
(d) the relevant agreements and, in particular, the arbitration agreement;
(e) all relevant particulars concerning the number of arbitrators and their choice in

accordance with the provisions of Articles 8, 9 and 10, and any nomination of an arbitrator required thereby; and,

(f) any comments as to the place of arbitration, the applicable rules of law and the language of the arbitration.

4. Together with the Request, the Claimant shall submit the number of copies thereof required by Article 3(1) and shall make the advance payment on administrative expenses required by the Schedule of Costs (Appendix III) in force on the date the Request is submitted. In the event that the Claimant fails to comply with either of these requirements, the Secretariat may fix a time limit within which the Claimant must comply, failing which the file shall be closed without prejudice to the right of the Claimant to submit the same claims at a later date in another Request.

5. The Secretariat shall send a copy of the Request and the documents annexed thereto to the Respondent for its Answer once the Secretariat has sufficient copies of the Request to do so and the required advance payment.

6. When a party submits a Request in connection with a legal relationship in respect of which arbitration proceedings between the same parties are already pending under these Rules, the Court may, at the request of a party, decide to include the claims contained in the Request in the pending proceedings, provided that the Terms of Reference have not yet been signed or approved by the Court. Once the Terms of Reference have been signed or approved by the Court, claims may only be included in the pending proceedings subject to the provisions of Article 19.

Article 5 Answer to the Request; counterclaims

1. Within 30 days from the receipt of the Request from the Secretariat, the Respondent shall file an Answer (''the Answer'' which shall, *inter alia*, contain the following information:

(a) its name in full, description and address;

(b) its comments as to the nature and circumstances of the dispute giving rise to the claims;

(c) its position as to the relief sought;

(d) any comments concerning the number of arbitrators and their choice in light of the Claimant's proposals and in accordance with the provisions of Articles 8, 9 and 10, and any nomination of an arbitrator required thereby; and,

(e) any comments as to the place of arbitration, the applicable rules of law and the language of the arbitration.

2. The Secretariat may grant the Respondent an extension of the time for filing the Answer, provided the application for such an extension contains the Respondent's comments concerning the number of arbitrators and their choice, and where required by Articles 8, 9 and 10, the nomination of an arbitrator. If the Respondent fails to do so, the Court shall proceed in accordance with these Rules.

3. The Answer shall be supplied to the Secretariat in the number of copies specified by Article 3(1).

4. A copy of the Answer and the documents annexed thereto shall be communicated by the Secretariat to the Claimant.

5. Any counterclaims made by the Respondent shall be filed with its Answer and shall provide:

(a) A description of the nature and circumstances of the dispute giving rise to the counterclaims; and,

(b) a statement of the relief sought including, to the extent possible, an indication of any amounts counterclaimed.

6. The Claimant shall file a Reply to any counterclaim within 30 days from the date of receipt of the counterclaims communicated by the Secretariat. The Secretariat may grant the Claimant an extension of time for filing the Reply.

Article 6 Effect of the arbitration agreement

1. Where the parties have agreed to submit to arbitration under the Rules of Arbitration of the ICC, they shall be deemed thereby to have submitted *ipso facto* to the Rules in effect on the date of commencement of the arbitration proceedings, unless they have agreed to submit to the Rules in effect on the date of their arbitration agreement.

2. If the Respondent does not file an Answer, as provided by Article 5, or if any party raises one or more pleas concerning the existence, validity or scope of the arbitration agreement, the Court may decide, without prejudice to the admissibility or merits of the plea or pleas, that the arbitration shall proceed if it is prima facie satisfied that an arbitration agreement under the Rules of Arbitration of the ICC may exist. In such a case, any decision as to the jurisdiction of the Arbitral Tribunal shall be taken by the Arbitral Tribunal itself. If the Court is not so satisfied, the parties shall be notified that the arbitration cannot proceed. In such a case, any party retains the right to ask any court having jurisdiction whether or not there is a binding arbitration agreement.

3. If any of the parties refuses or fails to take part in the arbitration or any stage thereof, the arbitration shall proceed notwithstanding such refusal or failure.

4. Unless otherwise agreed, the Arbitral Tribunal shall not cease to have jurisdiction by reason of any claim that the contract is null and void or allegation that it is non-existent provided that the Arbitral Tribunal upholds the validity of the arbitration agreement. The Arbitral Tribunal shall continue to have jurisdiction to determine the respective rights of the parties and to adjudicate upon their claims and pleas, even though the contract itself may be nonexistent or null and void.

C. The Arbitral Tribunal

Article 7 General provisions

1. Any arbitrator must be and remain independent of the parties involved in the arbitration.

2. Before appointment or confirmation, a prospective arbitrator shall sign a statement of independence and disclose in writing to the Secretariat any facts or circumstances which might be of such a nature as to call into question the arbitrator's independence in the eyes of the parties. The Secretariat shall provide such information to the parties in writing and fix a time-limit for any comments from them.

3. An arbitrator shall immediately disclose in writing to the Secretariat and to the parties any facts or circumstances of similar nature which may arise during the arbitration.

4. The decisions of the Court as to the appointment, confirmation, challenge or replacement of an arbitrator, shall be final and the reasons for such decisions shall not be communicated.

5. By accepting to serve every arbitrator undertakes to carry out his responsibilities in accordance with these Rules.

6. Insofar as the parties shall not have provided otherwise, the Arbitral Tribunal shall be constituted in accordance with the provisions of Articles 8 to 10.

Article 8 Number of arbitrators

1. The disputes shall be decided by a sole arbitrator or by three arbitrators.

2. Where the parties have not agreed upon the number of arbitrators, the Court shall appoint a sole arbitrator, save where it appears to the Court that the dispute is such as to warrant the appointment of three arbitrators. In such case, the Claimant shall nominate an arbitrator within a period of 15 days from the receipt of the notification of the decision of the Court, and the Respondent shall nominate an arbitrator within a period of 15 days from the receipt of the notification of the nomination made by the Claimant.

3. Where the parties have agreed that the dispute shall be settled by a sole arbitrator, they may, by agreement, nominate the sole arbitrator for confirmation. If the parties fail so to nominate a sole arbitrator within 30 days from the date when the Claimant's Request for Arbitration has been received by the other party, or within such additional time as may be allowed by the Secretariat, the sole arbitrator shall be appointed by the Court.

4. Where the dispute is to be referred to three arbitrators, each party shall nominate in the Request and the Answer respectively one arbitrator for confirmation by the Court. If a party fails to nominate an arbitrator, the appointment shall be made by the Court. The third arbitrator, who will act as Chairman of the Arbitral Tribunal, shall be appointed by the Court, unless the parties have agreed upon another procedure for such appointment, in which case the nomination will be subject to confirmation pursuant to Article 9. Should such procedure not result in a nomination, within the time-limit fixed by the parties or the Court, the third arbitrator shall be appointed by the Court.

Article 9 Appointment and confirmation of the arbitrators

1. In confirming or appointing arbitrators, the Court shall have regard to the prospective arbitrator's nationality, residence and other relationships with the countries of which the parties or the other arbitrators are nationals and the prospective arbitrators availability and ability to conduct the arbitration in accordance with these Rules. The same shall apply where the Secretary General confirms arbitrators pursuant to Article 9(2).

2. The Secretary General may confirm as co-arbitrators, sole arbitrators and chairmen of Arbitral Tribunals persons nominated by the parties or pursuant to their particular agreements, provided they have filed a statement of independence without qualification or a qualified statement of independence has not given rise to objections. Such confirmation shall be reported to the Court at its next session. If the Secretary General considers that a co-arbitrator, sole arbitrator or chairman of an Arbitral Tribunal should not be confirmed, the matter shall be submitted to the Court.

3. Where the Court is to appoint a sole arbitrator or the chairman of an Arbitral Tribunal, it shall make the appointment upon a proposal of a National Committee of the ICC that is considers to be appropriate. If the Court does not accept the proposal made, or if the National Committee fails to make the proposal requested within the time-limit fixed by the Court, the Court may repeat its request or may request a proposal from another National Committee that it considers appropriate.

4. Where the Court considers that the circumstances so demand, it may choose the sole arbitrator or the chairman of the Arbitral Tribunal from a country where there is no National Committee, provided that neither of the parties objects within the time-limit fixed by the Court.

5. The sole arbitrator or the chairman of the Arbitral Tribunal shall be of a nationality other than those of the parties. However, in suitable circumstances and provided that neither of the parties objects within the time-limit fixed by the Court, the sole arbitrator or the chairman of the Arbitral Tribunal may be chosen from a country of which any of the parties is a national.

6. Where the court is to appoint an arbitrator on behalf of a party which has failed to nominate one, it shall make the appointment upon a proposal of the National Committee of the country of which that party is a national. If the Court does not accept the proposal made, or if the National Committee fails to make the proposal requested within the time-limit fixed by the Court, or if the country of which the said party is a national has no National Committee, the Court shall be at liberty to choose any person whom it regards as suitable. The Secretariat shall inform the National Committee of the country of which such person is a national, if one exists, of such choice.

Article 10 Multiple parties

1. Where there are multiple parties, whether as Claimant or as Respondent, and where the dispute is to be referred to three arbitrators, the multiple Claimants, jointly, and the multiple Respondents, jointly, shall nominate an arbitrator for confirmation pursuant to Article 9.

2. In the absence of such a joint nomination and where all parties are unable to agree to a method for the constitution of the Arbitral Tribunal, the Court may appoint each member of the Arbitral Tribunal and shall designate one of them to act as chairman. In such case, the Court shall be at liberty to choose any person whom it regards as suitable to act as arbitrator, applying Article 9 when it considers it appropriate.

Article 11 Challenge of arbitrators

1. A challenge of an arbitrator, whether for an alleged lack of independence or otherwise, shall be made by the submission to the Secretariat of a written statement specifying the facts and circumstances on which the challenge is based.

2. For a challenge to be admissible, it must be sent by a party either within 30 days from receipt by that party of the notification of the appointment or confirmation of the arbitrator, or within 30 days from the date when the party making the challenge was informed of the facts and circumstances on which the challenge is based if such date is subsequent to the receipt of such notification.

3. The Court shall decide on the admissibility, and, at the same time, if need be, on the merits of a challenge after the Secretariat has afforded an opportunity for the arbitrator concerned, the other party or parties and any other members of the Arbitral Tribunal to comment in writing within a suitable period of time. Such comments shall be communicated to the parties and to the arbitrators.

Article 12 Replacement of arbitrators

1. An arbitrator shall be replaced upon his death, upon the acceptance by the Court of the arbitrator's resignation, upon acceptance by the Court of a challenge or upon the request of all the parties.

2. An arbitrator shall also be replaced on the Court's own initiative when it decides that he is prevented *de jure* or *de facto* from fulfilling his functions, or that he is not fulfilling his functions in accordance with the Rules or within the prescribed time-limits.

3. When, on the basis of information that has come to its attention, the Court considers applying Article 12(2), it shall decide on the matter after the arbitrator concerned, the parties and any other members of the Arbitral Tribunal have had an opportunity to comment in writing within a suitable period of time. Such comments shall be communicated to the parties and to the arbitrators.

4. When an arbitrator is to be replaced, the Court has discretion to decide whether or not to follow the original nominating process. Once reconstituted, and after having invited the parties to comment, the Arbitral Tribunal shall determine if and to what extent prior proceedings shall be repeated before the reconstituted Arbitral Tribunal.

5. Subsequent to the closing of the proceedings, instead of replacing an arbitrator who has died or been removed by the Court pursuant to Articles 12(1) and 12(2), the Court may decide, when it considers it appropriate, that the remaining arbitrators shall continue the arbitration. In making such determination, the Court shall take into account the views of the remaining arbitrators and of the parties and such other matters that it considers appropriate in the circumstances.

D. The arbitral proceedings

Article 13 Transmission of the file to the Arbitral Tribunal

The Secretariat shall transmit the file to the Arbitral Tribunal as soon as it has been constituted, provided the advances on costs required by the Secretariat at this stage have been paid.

Article 14 Place of the arbitration

1. The place of the arbitration shall be fixed by the Court, unless agreed upon by the parties.

2. The Arbitral Tribunal may, after consultation with the parties, conduct hearings and meetings at any location it considers appropriate, unless otherwise agreed by the parties.

3. The Arbitral Tribunal may deliberate at any location it considers appropriate.

Article 15 Rules governing the proceedings

1. The proceedings before the Arbitral Tribunal shall be governed by these Rules and, where these Rules are silent, any rules which the parties or, failing them, the Arbitral Tribunal may settle, whether or not reference is thereby made to the rules of procedure of a national law to be applied to the arbitration.

2. In all cases, the Arbitral Tribunal shall act fairly and impartially and ensure that each party as a reasonable opportunity to present its case.

Article 16 Language of the arbitration

In the absence of an agreement by the parties, the Arbitral Tribunal shall determine the language or languages of the arbitration, due regard being given to all relevant circumstances, including the language of the contract.

Article 17 Applicable rules of law

1. The parties shall be free to agree upon the rules of law to be applied by the Arbitral Tribunal to the merits of the dispute. In the absence of any such agreement, the Arbitral Tribunal shall apply the rules of law which it determines to be appropriate.

2. In all cases, the Arbitral Tribunal shall take account of the provisions of the contract and relevant trade usages.

3. The Arbitral Tribunal shall assume the powers of an amiable compositeur or decide *ex aequo et bono* only if the parties have agreed to give it such powers.

Article 18 Terms of reference; procedural timetable

1. As soon as it has received the file from the Secretariat, the Arbitral Tribunal shall draw up, on the basis of documents or in the presence of the parties and in the light of their most recent submissions, a document defining its Terms of Reference. This document shall include the following particulars:

(a) the full names and descriptions of the parties;
(b) the addresses of the parties to which notifications and communications arising in the course of the arbitration may be made;
(c) a summary of the parties respective claims and of the relief sought by each party with an indication to the extent possible of the amounts claimed or counterclaimed;
(d) unless the Arbitral Tribunal considers it inappropriate, a list of issues to be determined;
(e) the full names, descriptions and addresses of the arbitrators;
(f) the place of the arbitration; and
(g) particulars of the applicable procedural rules and, if such is the case, reference to the power conferred upon the Arbitral Tribunal to act as amiable compositeur or to decide *ex aequo et bono*.

2. The Terms of Reference shall be signed by the parties and the Arbitral Tribunal. Within two months of the date when the file has been transmitted to it, the Arbitral Tribunal shall transmit to the Court the Terms of Reference signed by it and by the parties. The Court may extend this time-limit, pursuant to a reasoned request from the Arbitral Tribunal or on its own initiative if it decides it is necessary to do so.

3. If any of the parties refuses to take part in the drawing up of the Terms of Reference or to sign the same, they shall be submitted to the Court for approval. When the Terms of Reference are signed in accordance with Article 18(2) or approved by the Court, the arbitration shall proceed.

4. When drawing up the Terms of Reference, or as soon as possible thereafter, the Arbitral Tribunal, after having consulted the parties, shall establish in a separate document a provisional timetable that it intends to follow for the conduct of the arbitration and communicate it to the Court and the parties. Any subsequent modifications of the provisional timetable shall be communicated to the Court and the parties.

Article 19 New claims

After the Terms of Reference have been signed or approved by the Court, no party shall make new claims or counterclaims which fall outside the limits of the Terms of Reference unless it has been authorised to do so by the Arbitral Tribunal, which shall have regard to the nature of such new claims or counterclaims, the stage of the arbitration and other relevant circumstances.

Article 20 Establishing the facts of the case

1. The Arbitral Tribunal shall proceed within as short a time as possible to establish the facts of case by all appropriate means.

2. After study of the written submissions of the parties and of all documents relied upon, the Arbitral Tribunal shall hear the parties together in person if any of them so requests or failing such a request, it may of its own motion decide to hear them.

3. The Arbitral Tribunal may decide to hear witnesses, experts appointed by the parties or any other person, in the presence of the parties, or in their absence provided they have been duly summoned.

4. The Arbitral Tribunal after having consulted the parties, may appoint one or more experts, define their terms of reference and receive their reports. At the request of a party, the parties shall be given the opportunity to question at a hearing my such expert appointed by the Tribunal.

5. At any time during the proceedings, the Arbitral Tribunal may summon any party to provide additional evidence.

6. The Arbitral Tribunal may decide the case solely on the documents submitted by the parties unless any of the parties requests a hearing.

7. The Arbitral Tribunal may take measures for protecting trade secrets and confidential information.

Article 21 Hearings

1. When a hearing is to be held, the Arbitral Tribunal, giving reasonable notice, shall summon the parties to appear before it on the day and at the place fixed by it.

2. If any of the parties, although duly summoned, fails to appear without valid excuse, the Arbitral Tribunal shall have the power to proceed with the hearing.

3. The Arbitral Tribunal shall be in full charge of the hearings, at which all the parties shall be entitled to be present. Save with the approval of the Arbitral Tribunal and the parties, persons not involved in the proceedings shall not be admitted.

4. The parties may appear in person or through duly authorised representatives. In addition, they may be assisted by advisers.

Article 22 Closing of the proceedings

1. When it is satisfied that the parties have had a reasonable opportunity to present their cases, the Arbitral Tribunal shall declare the proceedings closed. Thereafter, no further submission or argument may be made or evidence produced, unless requested or authorized by the Arbitral Tribunal.

2. When the Arbitral Tribunal has declared the proceedings closed, it shall indicate to the Secretariat an approximate date by which the draft Award will be submitted to the Court for approval pursuant to Article 27. Any postponement of that date shall be communicated to the Secretariat by the Arbitral Tribunal.

Article 23 Conservatory and interim measures

1. Unless the parties have otherwise agreed, as soon as the file has been transmitted to it, the Arbitral Tribunal may, at the request of a party, order any interim or conservatory measure it deems appropriate. The Arbitral Tribunal may make the granting of any such measure subject to appropriate security being furnished by the requesting party. Any such measure shall take the form of an order, giving reasons, or an Award, as the Arbitral Tribunal considers appropriate.

2. Before the file is transmitted to the Arbitral Tribunal, and in appropriate circumstances even thereafter, the parties may apply to any competent judicial authority for interim or conservatory measures. The application of a party to a judicial authority for such measures or for the implementation of any such measures ordered by an Arbitral Tribunal shall not be deemed to be an infringement or a waiver of the arbitration agreement and shall not affect the relevant powers reserved to the Arbitral Tribunal. Any such application and any measures taken by the judicial authority must be notified without delay to the Secretariat. The Secretariat shall inform the Arbitral Tribunal thereof.

E. Awards

Article 24 Time-limit for the Award

1. The time-limit within which the Arbitral Tribunal must render its final Award is six months. Such time-limit shall start to run from the date of the last signature by the Arbitral Tribunal or of the parties of the Terms of Reference, or, in the case of application of Article 18(3), the date of the notification to the Arbitral Tribunal by the Secretariat of the approval of the Terms of Reference by the Court.

2. The Court may extend this time-limit, pursuant to a reasoned request from the Arbitral Tribunal or on its own initiative, if it decides it is necessary to do so.

Article 25 Making of the Award

1. When the Arbitral Tribunal is composed of more than one arbitrator, an Award is given by a majority decision. If there be no majority, the Award shall be made by the chairman of the Arbitral Tribunal alone.

2. The Award shall state the reasons upon which it is based.

3. The Award shall be deemed to be made at the place of the arbitration and on the date stated therein.

Article 26 Award by consent

If the parties reach a settlement after the file has been transmitted to the Arbitral Tribunal in accordance with Article 13, the settlement shall be recorded in the form of an Award made by consent of the parties if so requested by the parties and the Arbitral Tribunal agrees to do so.

Article 27 Scrutiny of the Award by the Court

Before signing any Award, the Arbitral Tribunal shall submit it in draft form to the Court. The Court may lay down modifications as to the form of the Award and, without affecting the Arbitral Tribunal's liberty of decision, may also draw its attention to points of substance. No Award shall be rendered by the Arbitral Tribunal until it has been approved by the Court as to its form.

Article 28 Notification, deposit and enforceability of the Award

1. Once an Award has been made, the Secretariat shall notify to the parties the text signed by the Arbitral Tribunal, provided always that the costs of the arbitration have been fully paid to the ICC by the parties or by one of them.

2. Additional copies certified true by the Secretary General shall be made available on request and at any time, to the parties but to no one else.

3. By virtue of the notification made in accordance with Paragraph 1 of this Article, the parties waive any other form of notification or deposit on the part of the Arbitral Tribunal.

4. An original of each Award made in accordance with the present Rules shall be deposited with the Secretariat.

5. The Arbitral Tribunal and the Secretariat shall assist the parties in complying with whatever further formalities may be necessary.

6. Every Award shall be binding on the parties. By submitting the dispute to arbitration under these Rules, the parties undertake to carry out any Award without delay and shall be deemed to have waived their right to any form of recourse insofar as such waiver can validly be made.

Article 29 Correction and interpretation of the award

1. On its own initiative, the Arbitral Tribunal may correct a clerical, computational or typographical error, or any errors of similar nature contained in an Award, provided such correction is submitted for approval to the Court within 30 days of the date of such Award.

2. Any application of a party for the correction of an error of the kind referred to in Article 29(1), or for the interpretation of an Award, must be made to the Secretariat within 30 days of the receipt of the Award by such party. Copies of such application shall be supplied to the Arbitral Tribunal and to the other party in accordance with Article 3(1). The Arbitral Tribunal shall grant the other party a short time-limit, normally not exceeding 30 days, from the receipt of the application by that party to submit any comments thereon. If the Arbitral Tribunal decides to correct or interpret the Award, it shall submit its decision in draft form to the Court not later than 30 days following the expiration of the time limit for the receipt of any comments from the other party or within such other period as the Court may decide.

3. The decision to correct or to interpret the Award shall take the form of an addendum and shall constitute part of the Award. The provisions of Articles 25, 27 and 28 shall apply *mutatis mutandis*.

F. Costs

Article 30 Advance to cover the costs of the arbitration

1. After receipt of the Request, the Secretary General may request the Claimant to pay a provisional advance in an amount intended to cover the costs of arbitration until the Terms of Reference have been drawn up.

2. As soon as practicable, the Court shall fix the advance on costs in an amount likely to cover the fees and expenses of the arbitrators and the ICC administrative costs for the claims and counterclaims which have been referred to it by the parties. This amount may be subject to readjustment at any time during the arbitration. Where, apart from the claims, counterclaims are submitted, the Court may fix separate advances on costs for the claims and the counterclaims.

3. The advance on costs fixed by the Court shall be payable in equal shares by the Claimant and the Respondent. Any provisional advance paid on the basis of Article 30(1) will be considered as a partial payment thereof. However, any one party shall be free to pay the whole of the advance on costs in respect of the principal claim or the counterclaim, should the other party fail to pay its share. When the Court has set separate advances on costs in accordance with Article 30(2), each of the parties shall pay the advance on costs corresponding to its claims.

4. When a request for an advance on costs has not been complied with, and after consultation with the Arbitral Tribunal, the Secretary General may direct the Arbitral Tribunal to suspend its work and set a time-limit, which must be not less than 15 days, on the expiry of which the relevant claims, or counterclaims, shall be considered as withdrawn. Should the party in question wish to object to this measure it must make a request within the aforementioned period for the matter to be decided by the Court. Such party shall not be prevented on the ground of such withdrawal from reintroducing the same claims or counterclaims at a later date in another proceeding.

5. If one of the parties claims a right to a set-off with regard to either claims or counterclaims, such set-off shall be taken into account in determining the advance to cover the costs of arbitration, in the same way as a separate claim, insofar as it may require the Arbitral Tribunal to consider additional matters.

Article 31 The costs of the arbitration

1. The costs of the arbitration shall include the fees and expenses of the arbitrators and the ICC administrative costs fixed by the Court, in accordance with the scale in force at the time of the commencement of the arbitral proceedings, as well as the fees and expenses of any experts appointed by the Arbitral Tribunal and the reasonable legal and other costs incurred by the parties for the arbitration.

2. The Court may fix the fees of the arbitrators at a figure higher or lower than that which would result from the application of the relevant scale should this be deemed necessary due to the exceptional circumstances of the case. Decisions on costs other than those fixed by the Court may be taken by the Arbitral Tribunal at any time during the proceedings.

3. The final Award shall fix the costs of the arbitration and decide which of the parties shall bear them or in what proportions they shall be borne by the parties.

G. Miscellaneous

Article 32 Modified time-limits

1. The parties may agree to shorten the various time-limits set out in these Rules. Any such agreement entered into subsequent to the constitution of an Arbitral Tribunal shall become effective only upon the approval of the Arbitral Tribunal.

2. The Court may extend any time-limit which has been modified pursuant to Article 32(1) on its own initiative if it decides that it is necessary to do so in order that the Arbitral Tribunal or the Court may fulfil their responsibilities in accordance with these Rules.

Article 33 Waiver

A party which proceeds with the arbitration without raising its objection to a failure to comply with any provisions of these Rules or any other rules applicable to the proceedings, any direction given by the Arbitral Tribunal or any requirement under the arbitration agreement relating to the constitution of the Arbitral Tribunal or to the conduct of the proceedings, shall be deemed to have waived its right to object.

Article 34 Exclusion of the liability

Neither the arbitrators, nor the Court and its members, nor the ICC and its employees, nor the ICC National Committees shall be liable to any person for any act or omission in connection with the arbitration.

Article 35 General rule

In all matters not expressly provided for in these Rules, the Court and the Arbitral Tribunal shall act in the spirit of these Rules and shall make every effort to make sure that the Award is enforceable in law.

Appendix I—Statutes of the International Court of Arbitration of the ICC

1. Function

The function of the International Court of Arbitration of the International Chamber of Commerce (the Court) is to ensure the application of the Rules of Arbitration and of the

Rules of Conciliation of the International Chamber of Commerce and it has all the necessary powers for that purpose.

2. Composition of the Court

The Court shall consist of a Chairman, Vice-Chairmen and members and alternate members (collectively designated at members). In its work it is assisted by its Secretariat (Secretariat of the International Court of Arbitration of the International Chamber of Commerce).

3. Appointment

—The Chairman is elected by the ICC Council upon recommendation of the Executive Board of the ICC.

—The ICC Council appoints the Vice-Chairmen of the Court from among the members of the Court or otherwise.

—Its members are appointed by the ICC Council on the proposal of National Committees, one member for each Committee.

—On the proposal of the Chairman of the Court, the Council may appoint alternate members.

—The term of office of all members is three years. If a member is no longer in a position to exercise his functions, his successor is appointed by the Council for the remainder of the term.

4. Plenary Session of the Court

The Plenary Sessions of the Court are presided by the Chairman, in his absence by one of the Vice-Chairmen designated by him. The deliberations shall be valid when at least six members are present. Decisions are taken by a majority vote, the Chairman having a casting vote in the event of a tie.

5. Committees

The Court may set up one or more Committees and lay down the functions and organisation of such Committees.

6. Confidentiality

The work of the Court is of a confidential character which must be respected by everyone who participates in that work in whatever capacity. The Court lays down the rules regarding the persons who can attend the meetings of the Court and its Committees and who are entitled to have access to the material submitted to the Court and its Secretariat.

7. Modification of the Rules of Arbitration

Any proposals of the Court for a modification of the Rules are laid before the Commission on International Arbitration before submission to the Executive Board and the Council of the ICC for approval.

Appendix II—Internal Rules of the International Court of Arbitration

Confidential character of the work of the International Court of Arbitration

1. The sessions of the International Court of Arbitration of the International Chamber of Commerce (''the Court''), whether plenary or those of a Committee of the Court, are open only to its members and to the Secretariat.

However, in exceptional circumstances the Chairman of the Court may invite other persons to attend. Such persons must respect the confidential character of the work of the Court.

2. The documents submitted to the Court or drawn up by it in the course of its proceedings are communicated only to the members of the Court and to the Secretariat and to persons authorized by the Chairman to attend Court sessions.

The Chairman or the Secretary General of the Court may authorize researchers undertaking work of a scientific nature on international trade law to acquaint themselves with awards and other documents of general interest, with the exception of memoranda, notes, statements and documents remitted by the parties within the framework of arbitration proceedings.

Such authorization shall not be given unless the beneficiary has undertaken to respect the confidential character of the documents made available and to refrain from any publication in their respect without having previously submitted the text for approval to the Secretary General of the Court.

3. The Secretariat will in each case submitted to arbitration under the Rules of Arbitration of the International Chamber of Commerce (''the ICC Rules'') retain in the archives of the Court all awards, terms of reference, decisions of the Court as well as copies of the pertinent correspondence of the Secretariat.

Any documents, communications or correspondence submitted by the parties or the arbitrators may be destroyed unless a party or an arbitrator requests in writing within a period fixed by the Secretariat the return of such documents. All related costs and expenses shall be borne by such party or arbitrator.

Participation of members of the International Court of Arbitration in ICC arbitration

4. The Chairman and the members of the Secretariat of the Court may not act as arbitrators or as counsel in cases submitted to ICC arbitration.

The Court shall not appoint Vice-Chairmen or members of the Court as arbitration. They may, however, be proposed for such duties by one or more of the parties or pursuant to any other procedure agreed upon by the parties, subject to confirmation by the Court.

5. When the Chairman, a Vice-Chairman or a member of the Court or of the Secretariat is involved, in any capacity whatsoever, in proceedings pending before the Court, such person must inform the Secretary General of the Court upon becoming aware of such involvement.

Such person must refrain from participating in the discussions or in the decisions of the Court concerning the proceedings and must be absent from the courtroom whenever the matter is considered.

Such person will not receive any material documentation or information pertaining to such proceedings.

Relations between the members of the Court and the ICC National Committees

6. By virtue of their capacity, the members of the Court are independent of the ICC National Committees which proposed them for appointment by the ICC Council.

Furthermore, they must regard as confidential, *vis-à-vis* the said National Committees, any information concerning individual cases with which they have become acquainted in their capacity as members of the Court except when they have been requested, by the

Chairman or the Court or by its Secretary General, to communicate specific information to their respective National Committee.

Committee of the Court

7. In accordance with the provisions of Article 1(4) of the ICC Rules and Article 5 of its Statutes (Appendix I), the Court hereby establishes a Committee of the Court.

8. The members of the Committee consist of a Chairman and at least two other members. The Chairman of the Court acts as the Chairman of the Committee. If absent, the Chairman may designate a Vice-Chairman of the Court or, in exceptional circumstances, another member of the Court as Chairman of the Committee.

The other two members of the Committee are appointed by the Court from among the Vice-Chairmen or the other members of the Court. At each Plenary Session the Court appoints the members who are to attend the meetings of the Committee to be held before the next Plenary Session.

9. The Committee meets when convened by its Chairman. Two members constitute a quorum.

10.—(a) The Court shall issue directions determining the decisions that may be taken by the Committee.

(b) The decisions of the Committee are taken unanimously.

(c) When the Committee cannot reach a decision or deems it preferable to abstain, it transfers the case to the next Plenary Session, making any suggestions it deems appropriate.

(d) The Committee's decisions are brought to the notice of the Court at its next Plenary Session.

Court Secretariat

11. In case of absence, the Secretary General may delegate to the General Counsel and Deputy Secretary General the authority to confirm arbitrators, to certify true copies of awards and to request the payment of a provisional advance respectively provided for in Articles 9(2), 28(2) and 30(1) of the ICC Rules.

The Secretariat may, with the approval of the Court, issue notes and other documents for the information of the parties and the arbitrators or necessary for the proper conduct of the arbitral proceedings.

Scrutiny of Arbitral Awards

12. When the Court scrutinizes draft awards in accordance with Article 27 of the ICC Rules, it considers, to the extent practicable, the requirements of mandatory law at the place of arbitration.

Appendix III—Arbitration costs and fees

A—Advance on costs

1. Each request to commence an arbitration pursuant to the Rules of Arbitration of the International Chamber of Commerce (the "ICC Rules") must be accompanied by an advance payment of US $2,000 on the administrative expenses. Such payment is non-refundable, but shall be credited to the Claimant's portion of the advance on costs.

2. The provisional advance on costs fixed by the Secretary General according to Article 30(1) of the ICC Rules shall normally not exceed the amount obtained by adding together the administrative expenses, the minimum of the fees (as set out in the scale hereinafter) based upon the amount of the claim and the expected reimbursable expenses of the Arbitral Tribunal incurred in relation with the drafting of the Terms of Reference. If such amount is not quantified, the provisional advance shall be fixed at the discretion of the Secretary General Payment by the Claimant shall be credited to its share of the advance on costs fixed by the International Court of Arbitration of the International Chamber of Commerce (''the Court'').

3. In general, after the Terms of Reference have been signed or approved by the Court and the provisional timetable has been established, the Arbitral Tribunal shall in accordance with Article 30(4) of the ICC Rules proceed only in respect of those claims or counterclaims in regard to which the whole of the advance on costs has been paid.

4. The advances on costs fixed by the Court according to Article 30(2) of the ICC Rules comprises the fees of the arbitrator(s), any expenses of the arbitrator(s) and the administrative expenses.

5. Each party shall pay in cash its share of the total advance on costs. However, if its share exceeds an amount fixed from time to time by the Court, a party may post a bank guarantee for this additional amount.

6. A party having already paid in full its share on costs fixed by the Court may in accordance with Article 30(3) of the ICC Rules pay the unpaid portion of the advance owed by the defaulting party by posting a bank guarantee.

7. When the Court has fixed separate advances on costs pursuant to Article 30(2) of the ICC Rules, the Secretariat shall invite each party to pay the amount of the advance corresponding to its respective claims.

8. When, as a result of the fixing of separate advances on costs, the separate advance fixed for the claim of either party exceeds one-half of such global advance as was previously fixed (in respect of the same claims and counterclaims that are the object of separate advances), a bank guarantee may be posted to cover any such excess amount. In the event that the amount of the separate advance is subsequently increased, at least one-half of the increase shall be paid in cash.

9. The Secretariat shall establish the terms governing all bank guarantees which the parties may post pursuant to the above provisions.

10. As provided in Article 30(2) of the ICC Rules, the advance on costs may be subject to readjustment at any time during the arbitration, in particular to take account of the fluctuations in the amount in dispute, changes in the amount of the estimated expenses of the arbitrator(s) or of the evolving difficulty or complexity of arbitration proceedings.

11. Before any expertise ordered by the Arbitral Tribunal can be commenced, the parties, or one of them, shall pay an advance on costs fixed by the Arbitral Tribunal sufficient to cover the expected fees and expenses of the expert as determined by the Arbitral Tribunal. The Arbitral Tribunal shall be responsible for ensuring the payment by the parties of such fees and expenses.

B—Costs and fees

1. Subject to Article 31(2) of the ICC Rule, the Court shall fix the fee(s) of the arbitrator(s) in accordance with the scale hereinafter set out or, where the sum in dispute is not stated, at its discretion.

2. In setting the arbitrators' fees, the Court takes into consideration the diligence of arbitrators, the time spent, the rapidity of the proceedings, and the complexity of the dispute, so as to arrive at a figure within the limits specified, or, in exceptional circumstances (Article 31(2) of the ICC Rules), at a figure higher or lower than those limits.

3. When a case is submitted to more than one arbitrator, the Court, at its discretion, shall have the right to increase the total fees up to a maximum which shall normally not exceed three times the fee of one arbitrator.

4. Arbitrators' fees and expenses shall be fixed exclusively by the Court as required by the ICC Rules. Separate fee arrangements between the parties and the arbitrators are contrary to the ICC Rules.

5. The Court shall fix the administrative expenses of each arbitration in accordance with the scale hereinafter set out or, where the sum in dispute is not stated, at its discretion. In exceptional circumstances, the Court may fix the administrative expenses at a lower or higher figure than that which would result from the application of such scale, provided that such expenses shall normally not exceed the maximum amount of the scale. Further, the Court may require the payment of administrative expenses in addition to those provided in the scale of administrative expenses as a condition to holding an arbitration in abeyance at the request of the parties or one of them with the acquiescence of the other(s).

6. If an arbitration terminates before the rendering of a final award, the Court shall fix the costs of the arbitration at its discretion, taking into account the stage attained by the arbitral proceedings and any other relevant circumstances.

7. In the case of an application under Article 29(2) of the ICC Rules, the Court may fix an advance to cover additional fees and expenses of the Arbitral Tribunal and subordinate the transmission of such application to the Arbitral Tribunal to the prior cash payment in full to the ICC of such an advance. The Court shall fix at its discretion any possible fees of the arbitrator(s) when approving the decision of the Arbitral Tribunal.

8. When an arbitration is preceded by attempted conciliation, one-half of the administrative expenses paid for such conciliation shall be credited to the administrative expenses of the arbitration.

9. Amounts paid to arbitrators do not include any possible value added taxes (VAT) or other taxes or charges and imposts applicable to arbitrator(s) fees. Parties are expected to acquit any such taxes or charges; however, the recovery of any such charges or taxes is a matter solely between an arbitrator and the parties.

C—Appointment of arbitrators

A registration fee normally not exceeding US $2,000 is payable by the requesting party in respect of each request made to the ICC to appoint an arbitrator for any arbitration not conducted under the ICC Rules. No request for appointment of an arbitrator will be entertained unless accompanied by said fee, which is not recoverable and becomes the property of the ICC.

Such fee shall cover any additional services rendered by the ICC regarding the appointment, such as decisions on a challenge of the arbitrator and the appointment of a substitute arbitrator.

D—Scales of administrative expenses and of arbitrator(s) fees

To calculate the administrative expenses and the arbitrator(s) fees, the amounts calculated for each successive slice of the sum in dispute must be added together, (*) (**) except that where the sum in dispute is over US $, a flat amount of US $ (*) shall constitute the entirety of the administrative expenses.

* The definite amounts will be fixed when the scales of administrative expenses and of arbitrators' fees have been finalized.

Appendix 11

THE LMAA TERMS (1997)

Preliminary

1. These terms may be referred to as "the LMAA Terms (1997)".

2. In these Terms, unless the context otherwise requires.

(i) "The Association" means the London Maritime Arbitrators Association; "Member of the Association" includes full, retired and supporting members; "President" means the President for the time being of the Association.

(ii) "Tribunal" includes a sole arbitrator, a tribunal of two or more arbitrators, and an umpire.

(iii) "Original arbitrator" means an arbitrator appointed (whether initially or by substitution) by or at the request of a party as its nominee and any arbitrator duly appointed so to act following failure of a party to make its own nomination.

3. The purpose of arbitration according to these Terms is to obtain the fair resolution of maritime and other disputes by an impartial tribunal without unnecessary delay or expense. The arbitrators at all times are under a duty to act fairly and impartially between the parties and an original arbitrator is in no sense to be considered as the representative of his appointer.

Application

4. These Terms apply to all arbitral proceedings commenced on or after 31 January 1997. Section 14 of the Arbitration Act 1996 ("the Act") shall apply for the purpose of determining on what date arbitral proceedings are to be regarded as having commenced.

5. These Terms shall apply to an arbitration agreement whenever the parties have agreed that they shall apply and the parties shall in particular be taken to have so agreed:

(a) whenever the dispute is referred to a sole arbitrator who is a full Member of the Association and whenever both the original arbitrators appointed by the parties are full Members of the Association, unless both parties have agreed or shall agree otherwise;

(b) whenever a sole arbitrator or both the original arbitrators have been appointed on the basis that these Terms apply to their appointment.

Whenever a sole arbitrator or both the original arbitrators have been appointed on the basis referred to at (b), such appointments or the conduct of the parties in taking part in the arbitration thereafter shall constitute between the parties an agreement that the arbitration agreement governing their dispute has been made or varied so as to incorporate these Terms and shall further constitute authority to their respective arbitrators so to confirm in writing on their behalf.

6. In the absence of any agreement to the contrary the parties to all arbitral proceedings to which these Terms apply agree:

(a) that the law applicable to their arbitration agreement is English law; and
(b) that the seat of the arbitration is in England.

7. (a) Subject to paragraph (b), the arbitral proceedings and the rights and obligations of the parties in connection therewith shall be in all respects governed by the Act save to the extent that the provisions of the Act are varied, modified or supplemented by these Terms.
(b) Where the seat of the arbitration is outside England and Wales the provisions of these Terms shall nevertheless apply to the arbitral proceedings, save to the extent that any mandatory provisions of the law applicable to the arbitration agreement otherwise provide.

The arbitral tribunal

8. If the tribunal is to consist of three arbitrators:

(a) each party shall appoint one arbitrator not later than 14 days after service of a request in writing by either party to do so;
(b) the two so appointed may at any time thereafter appoint a third arbitrator so long as they do so before any substantive hearing or forthwith if they cannot agree on any matter relating to the arbitration;
(c) the third arbitrator shall be the chairman unless the parties shall agree otherwise;
(d) before the third arbitrator has been appointed or if the position has become vacant, the two original arbitrators, if agreed on any matter, shall have the power to make decisions, orders and awards in relation thereto;
(e) after the appointment of the third arbitrator decisions, orders or awards shall be made by all or a majority of the arbitrators;
(f) the view of the chairman shall prevail in relation to a decision, order or award in respect of which there is neither unanimity nor a majority under paragraph (e).

9. If the tribunal is to consist of two arbitrators and an umpire:

(a) each party shall appoint one arbitrator not later than 14 days after service of a request in writing by either party to do so;
(b) the two so appointed may appoint an umpire at any time after they themselves are appointed and shall do so before any substantive hearing or forthwith if they cannot agree on any matter relating to the arbitration;
(c) the umpire shall attend any substantive hearing and shall following his appointment be supplied with the same documents and other materials as are supplied to the other arbitrators;

(d) the umpire may take part in the hearing and deliberate with the original arbitrators;

(e) decisions, orders and awards shall be made by the original arbitrators unless and until they cannot agree on a matter relating to the arbitration. In that event they shall forthwith give notice in writing to the parties and the umpire, whereupon the umpire shall replace them as the tribunal with power to make decisions, orders and awards as if he were the sole arbitrator.

Jurisdiction

10. The jurisdiction of the tribunal shall extend to determining all disputes arising under or in connection with the transaction the subject of the reference, and each part shall have the right before the tribunal has given notice of its intention to proceed to its award to refer to the tribunal for determination any further dispute(s) arising subsequent to the commencement of the arbitral proceedings.

Tribunal's fees

11. Provisions regulating fees payable to the tribunal and other related matters are set out in the First Schedule. Save as therein or herein otherwise provided, payment of the tribunal's fees and expenses is the joint and several responsibility of the parties.

Arbitration procedure

12. (a) It shall be for the tribunal to decide all procedural and evidential matters subject to the right of the parties to agree any matter.

(b) An application to the tribunal for directions as to procedural or evidential matters should, as a general rule, be made only after the other party has bee afforded a reasonable opportunity to agree the terms of the directions proposed.

(c) In the absence of agreement it shall be for the tribunal to decide whether and to what extent there should be oral or written evidence or submissions in the arbitration. The parties should however attempt to agree at an early stage whether the arbitration is to be on documents alone (*i.e.* without a hearing) or whether there is to be an oral hearing.

(d) If agreement is not reached, the applicant should apply to the tribunal, setting out the terms of the directions proposed. The application must be copied to the other party, who must respond to the tribunal (copy to the applicant) stating the grounds of objection. The response must be made within three working days, or such further time as the tribunal may allow on the application of the respondent party.

(e) Unless either party has requested a meeting with the arbitrators (see paragraph 16 relating to preliminary meetings), the tribunal will make its order following receipt of the response or, in default of response within the time allowed, upon expiry of that time.

(f) Communications regarding procedural matters should be made expeditiously.

Arbitration on documents

13. (a) If it is determined by the tribunal or agreed by the parties that an arbitration is to be on documents alone (*i.e.* without an oral hearing) it is the responsibility of the parties to agree the procedure to be followed and to inform the tribunal of the agreement reached. The procedure set out in the Second Schedule should normally be adopted, with any such modifications as maybe appropriate: and in default of agreement the tribunal will give appropriate directions.

(b) Applications for directions should not be necessary but, if required, they should be made in accordance with paragraph 12.

Preparation of cases involving oral hearings

14. (a) A timetable for preparation of the case for hearing should, wherever possible, be agreed between the parties and the tribunal should then be informed by the claimant of the agreement reached. In default of agreement, an application for directions should be made in accordance with paragraph 12.

(b) A hearing date will not be fixed, save in exceptional circumstances, until the preparation of a case is sufficiently advanced to enable the duration of the hearing to be properly estimated; this will normally be after discovery has been substantially completed.

(c) Unless the case calls for a preliminary meeting with the tribunal (see paragraph 16), it is the duty of the parties or their advisers, prior to application for a hearing date, to consult together (i) to assess the expected readiness and the likely duration of the hearing, (ii) to plan the preparatory work still to be done, and (iii) to consider whether any other directions are required from the tribunal when the hearing date is requested.

(d) Following such consultation, application for a hearing date must be made in writing, indicating the expected date of readiness and likely duration of the hearing.

(e) Following fixture of the hearing date a booking fee will be payable in accordance with the provisions of the Second Schedule.

Powers of the tribunal

15. In addition to the powers set out in the Act, the tribunal shall have the following specific powers to be exercised in a suitable case so as to avoid unnecessary delay or expense, and so as to provide a fair means for the resolution of the matters falling to be determined:

(a) The tribunal may limit the number of expert witnesses to be called by any party or may direct either that no expert be called on any issue(s) or that no expert evidence shall be called save with the leave of the tribunal.

(b) Where two or more arbitrations appear to raise common issues of fact or law, the tribunals may direct that the two or more arbitrations shall be heard concurrently. Where such an order is made, the tribunals may give such directions as the interests of fairness, economy and expedition require including:

(i) that the documents disclosed by the parties in one arbitration shall be made available to the parties to the other arbitration upon such conditions as the tribunals may determine;

(ii) that the evidence given in one arbitration shall be received and admitted in the other arbitration, subject to all parties being given a reasonable opportunity to comment upon it and subject to such other conditions as the tribunals may determine.

Preliminary meetings

16. (a) The tribunal may decide at any stage that the circumstances of the arbitration require that there should be a preliminary meeting to enable the parties and the tribunal to review the progress of the case; to reach agreement so far as possible upon further preparation for, and the conduct of the hearing; and, where agreement is not reached, to enable the tribunal to give such directions as it thinks fit.

(b) A preliminary meeting should be held in complex cases including most cases involving a hearing of more than five days' duration. Exceptionally more than one preliminary meeting may be required.

(c) All preliminary meetings (whether required by the tribunal or held on the application of the parties) should be preceded by a discussion between the parties' representatives who should attempt to identify matters for discussion with the tribunal, attempt to reach agreement so far as possible on the directions to be given, and prepare for submission to the tribunal an agenda of matters for approval or determination by it.

(d) Before the preliminary meeting takes place the parties should provide the tribunal with a bundle of appropriate documents, together with information sheets setting out the steps taken and to be taken in the arbitration, a list of any proposed directions whether agreed or not and an agenda of matters for discussion at the hearing. The information sheets should include estimates of readiness for the hearing and the likely duration of the hearing.

(e) There is set out in the Third Schedule a guidance document indicating topics which may be appropriate for consideration before and at the preliminary hearing.

Settlement

17. It is the duty of the parties

(a) to notify the tribunal immediately if the arbitration is settled or otherwise terminated;

(b) to make provision in any settlement for payment of the fees and expenses of the tribunal; and

(c) to inform the tribunal of the parties' agreement as to the manner in which payment will be made of any outstanding fees and expenses of the tribunal, *e.g.* for interlocutory work not covered by any booking fee paid. The same duty arises if the settlement takes place after an interim award has been made. Upon being notified of the settlement or termination of any matter the tribunal may dispose of the documents relating to it.

18. Any booking fee paid will be dealt with in accordance with the provisions of the paragraph (B)(1)(c) of the First Schedule. Any other fees and expenses of the tribunal shall be settled promptly and at latest within 28 days of presentation of the relevant account(s). The parties shall be jointly and severally responsible for such fees and expenses.

Adjournment

19. If a case is for any reason adjourned part-heard, the tribunal will be entitled to an interim payment, payable in equal shares or otherwise as the tribunal may direct, in respect of fees and expenses already incurred, appropriate credit being given for the booking fee.

Availability of arbitrators

20. (a) In cases where it is known at the outset that an early hearing is essential, the parties should consult and ensure the availability of the arbitrator(s) to be appointed by them.

(b) If, in cases when the tribunal has already been constituted, the fixture of an acceptable hearing date is precluded by the commitments of the original appointee(s) the provisions of the Fourth Schedule shall apply.

The award

21. The time required for preparation of an award must vary with the circumstances of the case. The award should normally be available within not more than six weeks from the close of the proceedings. In many cases, and in particular where the matter is one of urgency, the interval should be substantially shorter.

22. The members of a tribunal need not meet together for the purpose of signing their award or of effecting any corrections thereto.

23. (a) If before the award is made one or more parties to the reference shall give notice to the tribunal that a reasoned award is required, the award shall contain the reasons for the award.

(b) The parties agree to dispense with reasons in all cases where no notice shall have been given to the tribunal under paragraph (a) before the award is made. [Note: the effect of such agreement is to exclude the court's jurisdiction under section 69 of the Act to determine an appeal on a question of law arising out of the award; see section 69(1).]

(c) Where in accordance with paragraph (b) the parties have agreed to dispense with reasons the tribunal will issue an award without reasons together with a document which does not form part of the award but which gives, on a confidential basis, an outline of the reasons for the tribunal's decision (hereafter called "privileged reasons").

(d) Unless the court shall otherwise determine, the document containing privileged reasons (referred to in paragraph (c)) may not be relied upon or referred to by either party in any proceedings relating to the award.

24. As soon as possible after an award has been made it shall be notified to the parties by the tribunal serving on them a notice in writing which shall inform the parties of the amount of the fees and expenses of the tribunal and which shall indicate that the award is available for sending to or collection by the parties upon full payment of such amount. At the stage of notification neither the award nor any copy thereof need be served on the parties and the tribunal may thereafter refuse to deliver the award or any copy thereof to the parties except upon full payment of its fees and expenses.

25. If any award has not been paid for and collected within one month of the date of publication, the tribunal may give written notice to either party requiring payment of the costs of the award, whereupon such party shall be obliged to pay for and collect the award within fourteen days.

26. (a) In addition to the powers set out in Section 57 of the Act, the tribunal shall have the following powers to correct an award or to make an additional award:

(i) The tribunal may on its own initiative or on the application of a party correct any accidental mistake, commission or error of calculation in its award.

(ii) The tribunal may on the application of a party give an interpretation of a specific point or part of the award.

(b) An application for the exercise of the powers set out above and in Section 57 of the Act must be made within 28 days of the award unless the tribunal shall think fit to extend the time.

(c) The powers set out above shall not be exercised without first affording the other parties a reasonable opportunity to make representations to the tribunal.

(d) Any correction or interpretation of an award may be effected in writing on the original award or in a separate memorandum which shall become part of the award. It shall be effected within 90 days of the original award unless all parties shall agree a longer period.

27. If the tribunal considers that an arbitration decision merits publication and gives notice to the parties of its intention to release the award for publication, then unless either or both parties inform the tribunal of its or their objection to publication within 21 days of the notice, the award may be publicised under such arrangements as the Association may effect from time to time. The publication will be so drafted as to preserve anonymity as regards the identify of the parties, of their legal or other representatives, and of the tribunal.

Service of documents

28. Where a party is represented by a lawyer or other agent in connection with any arbitral proceedings, all notices to other documents required to be given or served for the purposes of the arbitral proceedings together with all decisions, orders and awards made or issued by the tribunal shall be treated as effectively served if served on that lawyer or agent.

General

29. Three months after the publication of a final award the tribunal may notify the parties of its intention to dispose of the documents and to close the file, and it will act accordingly unless otherwise requested within 21 days of such notice being given.

30. In relation to any matters not expressly provided for herein the tribunal shall act in accordance with the tenor of these Terms.

THE FIRST SCHEDULE

TRIBUNAL'S FEES

(A) Appointment fee

An appointment fee is payable on appointment by the appointing party or by the party at whose request the appointment is made. The appointment fee shall be a standard fee fixed by the Committee of the Association from time to time. Unless otherwise agreed, the appointment fee of an umpire or third arbitrator shall in the first instance be paid by the claimant.

(B) Booking fee

(1) (a) For a hearing of up to ten days' duration there shall be payable to the tribunal a booking fee of £250 per person or such other sum as the Committee of the Association may from time to time decide, for each day reserved. The booking fee will be invoiced to the party asking for the hearing date to be fixed or to the parties in equal shares if both parties ask for the hearing date to be fixed as the case may be and shall be paid within 14 days of confirmation of the reservation or six months in advance of the first date reserved (the start date), whichever date be the later. If the fee is not paid in full be the due date the tribunal will be entitled to cancel the reservation but either party may secure reinstatement of the reservation by payment within seven days of any balance outstanding.

(b) For hearings over ten days' duration the booking fee in sub-paragraph (1)(a) above all for each day reserved be increased by 30% in the case of a hearing of up to 15 days and 60% in the case of a hearing of up to 20 days and may, at the discretion of the tribunal, be subscribed in non-returnable instalment payments. For hearings in excess of 20 days the booking fee shall be at the rate for a hearing of 20 days plus such addition sum as may be agreed with the parties in the light of the length of the proposed hearing.

(c) Where the case proceeds to an award, or is settled subsequent to the start of the hearing, appropriate credit will be given for the booking fee in calculating the amount to be paid in order to collect the award, or as the case may be, the amount payable to the tribunal upon settlement of the case.

(d) Where at the request of one or both of the parties, a hearing is adjourned or a hearing date vacated prior to or on or after the start date, then, unless non-returnable instalment or other payments have been agreed, the booking fee will be retained by the tribunal (i) in full if the date is adjourned or vacated less than three months before the start date or on or after that date, (ii) as to 50 per cent if the date is adjourned or vacated three months or more before the start date. Any interlocutory fees and expenses incurred will also be payable or, as the case maybe, deductible from the refund under (ii).

(e) Where, at the request of one or both of the parties, a hearing is adjourned or a hearing date is vacated and a new hearing date is fixed, a further booking fee will be payable in accordance with paragraphs (a) and (b) above.

(2) An arbitrator or umpire who, following receipt of his booking fee or any part thereof, is for any reason replaced is, upon settlement of his fees for any interlocutory work, responsible for transfer of his booking fee to the person appointed to act in his place. In the event of death the personal representative shall have corresponding responsibility.

ACCOMMODATION

(1) If accommodation and/or catering is arranged by the tribunal, the cost will normally be recovered as part of the cost of the award, but where a case is adjourned part-heard

or in other special circumstances, the tribunal reserves the right to direct that the cost shall be provisionally paid by the parties in equal shares (or as the tribunal may direct) promptly upon issue of the relevant account. Prior to booking accommodation and/or catering the tribunal may, if they think fit, request that they be provided with security sufficient to cover their prospective liabilities in respect thereof.

(2) If accommodation is reserved and paid for by the parties and it is desired that the cost incurred be the subject of directions in the award, the information necessary for that purpose must be furnished promptly to the tribunal.

THE SECOND SCHEDULE

ARBITRATION ON DOCUMENTS

Recommended procedure

If it is determined by the tribunal or agreed by the parties that the dispute is to be decided without an oral hearing the procedure set out in paragraphs 1–5 below is recommended for adoption by agreement.

When this procedure (or any modification) has been agreed, the tribunal should be so informed. The tribunal must be promptly advised if, at a later stage, the parties or either of them wish to apply for an oral hearing.

The exchange of submissions, etc. will take place directly between the parties unless the case is being handled by others (*e.g.* by lawyers or a Club) on their behalf.

Copies of all submissions, comments and documents must be supplied simultaneously to the tribunal, and all communications with the tribunal must be copied to the other party.

All documents relied on must be legibly copied and translations supplied as necessary.

(1) Within 28 days of agreement by the parties to adopt the procedure or of the order of the tribunal, the claimants shall send to the respondents, with copies to the tribunal, their written claim submissions, together with copies of supporting documents.

(2) Within 28 days of the service of the claim submissions, the respondents shall send to the claimants, with copies to the tribunal, their written submissions (including those relating to any counterclaim) together with copies of the documents relied on additional to those already provided by the claimants.

(3) If there is no counterclaim, the claimant's final submissions (if any) on the claim shall be provided to the respondents and the tribunal within 21 days after receipt of the respondents' submissions and documents.

(4) If there is a counterclaim:

(a) The claimants shall furnish submissions and any additional documents relative to the counterclaim within 28 days after receipt of the respondents' submissions and documents;

(b) The respondents' final submissions (if any) on the counterclaim shall be provided within 21 days after receipt of the claimants' submissions and additional documents (if any).

(5) The tribunal will then give notice to the parties of its intention to proceed to its award and will so proceed unless either party within seven days requests, and is thereafter granted, leave to serve further submissions and/or documents.

THE THIRD SCHEDULE

PRELIMINARY MEETINGS

This Schedule sets out, in check-list form, the topics which may be appropriate or consideration when a preliminary meeting is to be held in accordance with paragraph 16 of the Terms.

The circumstances in which a preliminary meeting may be held vary very considerably. In some cases (including the more complex arbitrations and most cases involving a hearing of more than five days) a preliminary meeting is necessary and will be held on the initiative of the tribunal or at the request of the parties, after much of the preparatory work has been done, to review the progress of the case and to enable directions to be made or agreed for further preparation for, and the conduct of, the hearing. In other cases a dispute may have arisen as to some procedural matter (*e.g.* a failure to serve a pleading or to give adequate disclosure of documents) and a party may seek to persuade the tribunal to give appropriate directions (including, in a proper case, a peremptory order under section 41(5) of the Act) so as to resolve the matter.

Whatever the occasion for preliminary meeting with the arbitrators, two general principles apply; first, that an application to the arbitrators for a particular order should as a general rule be made only after the other party has been afforded a reasonable opportunity to agree the terms of the directions proposed (see paragraph 12(b) of the Terms); second, that, wherever possible, a preliminary meeting should be preceded by a discussion between the parties' representatives as to the future conduct of the case along the lines indicated in paragraph 16(c) and (d) of the Terms.

The check-list sets out some of the most important matters for consideration. It cannot attempt to be comprehensive. Inevitably, certain matters must be left to the discretion of the tribunal and the parties' advisers. The opportunity is taken to list the procedural matters which may need to be considered in a logical order from the commencement of the arbitration. It should however be possible in the majority of cases for the directions relating to at least the earlier stages of the arbitration to be agreed with the other party, or failing agreement to be dealt with on a written application to the arbitrators and without the need for a preliminary meeting (see paragraph 12 of the Terms).

1. Can the arbitration be decided on documents only?

The parties and their advisers should consider at the outset whether the case is suitable to be decided without an oral hearing (see paragraph 12(c) of the Terms) and whether the procedure set out in the Second Schedule is appropriate.

2. Pleadings and statements of cases

(i) A timetable should be ordered or agreed for the service of pleadings or statements (including letters) of claim and defence.

(ii) Once an initial exchange has taken place, it should be considered whether a reply is necessary and whether requests for further details (including particulars) of the other party's case are necessary and if made whether all such requests have been properly dealt with.

(iii) As the case proceeds and further documents become available, the pleadings or statements of case should be reviewed to see:

(a) whether amendments are required;

(b) whether all issues are still alive.

3. Disclosure of documents

(i) A timetable should be ordered or agreed either for the disclosure of all relevant documents or for the initial disclosure of such specified categories of documents as may be ordered or agreed.
(ii) Applications for further discovery should initially be made to the opposing party, and if not compiled with, by application to the tribunal.
(iii) Disputes as to outstanding discovery should not normally require a specific meeting with the arbitrators and applications can often best be reserved until a preliminary meeting is to take place in any event.
(iv) Consideration should always be given to whether it can be ordered or agreed that the ambit of discovery be limited so as avoid unnecessary delay and expense.

4. Factual evidence

(i) Can some facts/figures be agreed or admitted?
(ii) A timetable should be ordered or agreed for the exchange of statements (or affidavits) of witnesses of fact.
(iii) It should be ordered or agreed;
   (a) whether the statements or affidavits are to be admitted without calling the maker to give oral evidence at the hearing or
   (b) whether the statements are to stand as the evidence in chief of the witnesses subject to their attending to give oral evidence; and
   (c) whether the evidence of any witness is to be taken in advance or by means of a live telephone or video link or by use of a video recording.
(iv) In any case where it may be desired to seek the assistance of a Court (whether within or outside the United Kingdom) to secure the attendance of witnesses at the hearing, to obtain documentary or other evidence, to record oral testimony for presentation to the tribunal or to exercise other powers in support of the arbitral proceedings, the party intending to invoke the assistance of the Court should first where practicable seek the agreement of the other parties to the making of the application to the Court or, if agreement cannot be reached, should apply to the tribunal for permission to make the application (see sections 43 and 44 of the Act) and for directions as to when and how it is to be made.

5. Expert evidence

(i) It should be ordered or agreed whether or not the case requires expert evidence to be adduced and, if so, the subjects on which expert evidence is necessary and the number and disciplines of the experts.
(ii) If it is ordered or agreed that the case is one requiring expert evidence the order or agreement should provide
   (a) whether each party is to adduce expert evidence; and/or
   (b) whether the tribunal should appoint experts or assessors to assist it on technical matters (see section 37 of the Act).

(iii) Where expert evidence is to be adduced by the parties a timetable should be ordered or agreed for the following:
  (a) the exchange of experts' reports;
  (b) any "without prejudice" meeting of experts held to agree or narrow the issues;
  (c) the drawing up of a memorandum by the experts setting out what has been agreed and what remains in issue;
  (d) the service of supplementary experts' reports.

(iv) It should be ordered or agreed whether the tribunal will deal with the technical issues on the basis of the experts' reports, without the need for the authors to give oral evidence.

6. Preliminary issues/interim awards
Both the tribunal and the parties should consider at any preliminary meeting:

(i) what are the important matters in issue between the parties;
(ii) how are those issues best decided;
(iii) whether time and expense will be saved if one or more issues (*e.g.* interpretation of contract) are decided as preliminary issues;
(iv) whether liability and damages should be decided at one hearing or separately.

7. Questions to the parties
It may be considered whether one of the parties (or the tribunal) should put questions to a party and in what form this should be done.

8. Procedure at the hearing
Directions may be given as to:

(i) what if any rules of evidence will apply and generally as to the manner and form in which the evidence is to be presented at the hearing;
(ii) the length of time available for witnesses to give their evidence or for parties or their representatives to present their arguments;
(iii) whether arguments are to be in written or oral form or a combination the two.

9. Investigations by the tribunal
Would any investigations by the tribunal assist in ascertaining the facts?

10. Inspection
Would the tribunal be assisted by attending trials or experiments, or inspecting any object featuring in the dispute?

11. Documents

(i) If possible provide agreed chronology and *dramatis personae*;
(ii) arrangements of document (*e.g.* different bundles for different topics, or as appropriate) and dates by which bundles to be produced;
(iii) unnecessary inclusion of documents to be avoided;
(iv) when documents are voluminous, consider copying only key bundles and providing a core bundle.

12. Advance reading

(i) Provision of pleadings and other suitable material (*e.g.* experts' reports) to the tribunal as far in advance of the hearing as possible.
(ii) Should time be set aside during the hearing, after appropriate opening, for private reading of any documents by tribunal (to reduce time otherwise involved in reading documents out)?

13. Multi-party disputes

(i) Concurrent or consecutive hearings (see paragraph 15(b) of the Terms);
(ii) procedure generally.

14. Representation
Level of representation at the hearing to be appropriate to the case.

15. Hearing dates
(The fixing of dates will, in the majority of cases, be most usefully considered after discovery has been substantially completed. An application for a date to be fixed should not, however, be made until the parties are able to make a realistic estimate of how long the hearing is likely to last, and when the parties will be ready.)

(i) Estimated duration of hearing.
(ii) When can parties realistically be expected to be ready?
(iii) Any problems re availability of witnesses? (If so, can these be mitigated by taking evidence in advance, using proofs/affidavits at the hearing, by means of a live telephone or video link, or by use of a video recording?)
(iv) Availability of tribunal (see paragraph 20 of the Terms and the Fourth Schedule).
(v) Accommodation required and numbers attending.
(vi) Any special facilities (*e.g.* transcripts, interpreters, etc.)
(vii) Arrangements for accommodation, etc.: who to book/pay for?

THE FOURTH SCHEDULE

RECONSTRUCTION OF THE TRIBUNAL

The following provisions are directed to avoiding delay which the parties or either of them consider unacceptable, but if both parties prefer to retain a tribunal as already constituted they remain free so to agree.

1. The governing factor will be the ability of the tribunal to fix a hearing date within a reasonable time of the expected readiness date as notified by the parties on application for a date (see paragraph 14(d) of the Terms) or, if they are not agreed as to the expected readiness date, within a reasonable time of whichever forecast date the tribunal considers more realistic.

2. For hearings of up to 10 days' estimated duration, what constitutes a reasonable time will (unless the parties apply for a date further ahead) be determined by reference to the estimated length of hearing as follows:

	ESTIMATED DURATION	REASONABLE TIME
(i)	Up to 2 days	3 months
(ii)	3–5 days	6 months
(iii)	6–10 days	10 months

"Relevant timescale" is used below to mean whichever of the foregoing periods is applicable and, in cases of more than 10 days' duration, such corresponding timescale as the tribunal may consider appropriate.

3. A sole arbitrator who is unable to offer a date within the relevant timescale will offer to retire and, if so requested by the parties or either of them, will retire upon being satisfied that an appropriate substitute appointment has been effected by the parties; in event of their disagreement, either party may request the President to make the necessary substitute appointment.

4. In all other cases, unless all members of the tribunal are able to offer a matching date within the relevant timescale:

(A) The tribunal will have regard to any agreed preference of the parties, but if there is no agreed preference the tribunal will fix:
  (i) the earliest hearing date that can be given by any member(s) able to offer a guaranteed date within the relevant timescale;
  (ii) if a guaranteed date within the relevant timescale cannot be offered by any member of the tribunal, the earliest date thereafter which can be guaranteed by any member(s) of the tribunal; on the basis, in either case, that any member then unable (by reason of a prior commitment) to guarantee the date so fixed will (unless that prior commitment has meanwhile cleared) retire by notice given six clear weeks prior to the start date.

(B) Upon notification of any such retirement an appropriate substitution will be effected as follows:
  (i) If an original arbitrator retires the substitute shall be promptly appointed by his appointer; or failing such appointment at least 21 days prior to the start date the substitute will then be appointed by the umpire or third arbitrator or, if an umpire or third arbitrator has not yet been appointed, the substitute will be appointed by the President;
  (ii) If an umpire or third arbitrator retires the substitute will be appointed by the original arbitrators.

5. For the purpose of paragraph (4):

(a) "appropriate substitution" means appointment of a substitute able to match the hearing date established in accordance with subparagraph (A);
(b) "start date" means the first date reserved for the hearing;
(c) An umpire or third arbitrator will retain power to make any necessary substitution under subparagraph (B)(i) notwithstanding that he may himself have given notice of retirement under subparagraph (A) and an original arbitrator will retain the like power under subparagraph (B)(ii).

6. An arbitrator or umpire who retires as mentioned above shall:

(i) be entitled to immediate payment of his fees and expenses incurred up to the date of his retirement; and
(ii) incur no liability to any party by reason thereof.

Appendix 12

THE CHARTERED INSTITUTE OF ARBITRATORS

ARBITRATION SCHEME FOR THE ASSOCIATION OF BRITISH TRAVEL AGENTS

(1994 edition)

Introduction and scope of the Scheme

1. The Scheme applies to disputes arising out of the provision of any travel services by members of the Association of British Travel Agents (ABTA) to their customers. Claims may be made by or on behalf of any person named in the booking form or other contractual documents and in these Rules "customer" includes all persons on whose behalf a claim is made.

2. These Rules apply to applications for arbitration received on or after 1 September 1994.

3. No claim may be made under the Scheme:

(i) For compensation exceeding £1,500 per person and £7,500 per booking, whichever is the lower;
(ii) In respect of injury, illness or death or the consequences of any of these.

4. In considering the parties' cases, the arbitrator shall have regard to ABTA's Tour Operators' and/or its Travel Agents' Codes of Conduct. In the event of a conflict between a rule of law and a provision of either code, the interpretation most favourable to the customer shall prevail.

5. These Rules are designed primarily for arbitrations between two parties, that is to say, between a customer and a travel agent or a tour operator. However, a customer may also apply for arbitration against both a travel agent and a tour operator.

Institution of arbitration proceedings

6. The parties must make a joint application for arbitration to the Institute, accompanied by their registration fees.

7. In general, the parties' registration fees are charged on the scale set out in the Institute's application form, but:

(i) Where a travel agent and a tour operator are joined in the same application, each shall pay half the registration fee.

(ii) Where the only customer claiming is a child under the age of 12, a registration fee shall be payable by the person making a claim on his behalf.

Unless Rules 10(iii) or (v) apply, registration fees are non-returnable.

8. Unless there is a good reason for any delay the customer must return a completed application for arbitration to ABTA within nine months of completion of the return journey.

Procedure

The Institute will appoint a sole arbitrator to determine the dispute and notify the parties of the appointment. Subject to any directions given by the arbitrator, the arbitration procedure will be on documents only, as follows:

9. General

(i) The Institute will acknowledge receipt of the application to the parties and will also send the party making the claim ("the Claimant") a claim form.

(ii) The Claimant must return the completed claim form and supporting documents to the Institute within 28 days. Extra copies of the form and documents must be submitted to the Institute for each Respondent.

(iii) A claim exceeding the amount specified in the application form will not be permissible.

(iv) The Institute will send a copy of the claim documents to the other party/parties ("the Respondent(s)"), who must, within 28 days of receipt, send to the Institute a written defence, together with supporting documents. Extra copies of the defence and documents must be submitted to the Institute for the Claimant and for any other Respondent.

(v) The Institute will send a copy of each of the defence documents to the Claimant, who may send the Institute written comments on the defence(s), in duplicate/triplicate (as appropriate), within 14 days. No new matters or points of claim may be raised by the comments.

(vi) Where there are two Respondents, the Institute will send a copy of each Respondent's defence to the other for comment. Any such comments must be submitted within 28 days and must be restricted to points arising from the documents.

(vii) The arbitrator will give an award with reasons which the Institute will forward to the parties and forward a copy to ABTA.

(viii) Payment ordered by an award must be made within 21 days, unless directed otherwise in the award. It must be made directly between the parties and not through the arbitrator, the Institute or ABTA. Enforcement of the award is the parties'responsibility and the Institute is unable to assist. Enforcement should in the first instance be sought through ABTA.

(ix) Original documents will be returned to the parties after six weeks have elapsed from the date of the award if requested by the parties within this time, and only if the request is accompanied by a self addressed envelope of suitable size and appropriate prepaid postage.

10. Supplementary

(i) The arbitrator may, through the Institute, request the provision of any further documents/information or submissions which he considers would assist him in his decision. If these are not sent to the Institute within the time prescribed, the arbitrator will proceed only on the basis of the documents already before him.

(ii) Documents submitted by the parties otherwise than under Rules 9(i)–(iv) and 10(i) will not be admissible as of right but at the arbitrator's sole discretion. Where a party submits such documents, the arbitrator will decide whether or not they are admissible. Where the documents are held to be admissible, the other party will be sent copies and be entitled to comment on them before an award is made.

(iii) If the Claimant does not submit his claim within the time allowed and does not send one within 14 days of a reminder by the Institute, he will be treated as having abandoned his claim. The arbitration will not proceed and the Respondent's registration fee will be returned.

(iv) If a Respondent does not submit its defence within the time allowed and does not send one within 14 days of a reminder by the Institute, the arbitrator will be appointed and, subject to any directions he may give, the dispute will be decided by him by reference to the documents submitted by the Claimant.

(v) If, in the arbitrator's opinion (which shall be final), the dispute is not capable of proper resolution on documents only, he shall advise the parties, through the Institute. The arbitrator's appointment shall be revoked, the parties' application for arbitration withdrawn and their registration fees refunded. The Claimant may then pursue the matter through the courts.

Costs

11. The arbitrator's fees and expenses shall be paid by the Institute and are part of the administrative costs of the Scheme. The said costs are Subject to a separate agreement between the Institute and ABTA.

12. Each party shall bear its own costs of preparing and submitting its case (including legal costs).

13. The arbitrator may, at his discretion, direct the reimbursement by one party of the other's registration fee.

14. No legal proceedings may be brought by one party against the other for recovery of any of the costs set out in Rules 11 and 12 or any other costs incurred in pursuing the arbitration.

Miscellaneous

15. (i) The law to apply (English, Scots, etc.) shall be determined by the arbitrator if the parties fail to agree

(ii) Where Scots law applies, any reference in these Rules to an arbitrator shall be construed as a reference to an arbiter.

16. By applying for arbitration, the parties agree to the non disclosure of the proceedings, award, and reasons for the award to any stranger to the proceedings unless it is necessary to do so in order to enforce the award.

17. The Institute reserves the right to appoint a substitute arbitrator if the arbitrator originally appointed dies, is incapacitated or is for any reason unable to deal expeditiously with the dispute. The parties shall be notified of any substitution.

18. Awards made under the Scheme shall be final and binding on the parties.

19. Subject to the right of one party to request the Institute to draw the arbitrator's attention to any accidental slip or omission which he has power to correct by law, neither the Institute nor the arbitrator can enter into correspondence regarding an award made under the Scheme.

20. A party may make an application or appeal to the courts under the relevant Arbitration Acts but:

(i) The special provisions of Rules 11–13 shall not apply to any such application or appeal;

(ii) Either party making any such application or appeal (other than anapplication for leave to enforce the award) will bear its own and the other party's costs (including the cash of any resumed or fresh arbitration resulting from such proceedings) regardless of the outcome of those proceedings.

21. Neither the Institute nor the arbitrator shall be liable to any party for any act or omission in connection with any arbitration conducted under these Rules, save that the arbitrator (but not the Institute) shall be liable for any wrongdoing on his own part arising from bad faith.

Appendix 13

THE CONSTRUCTION INDUSTRY MODEL ARBITRATION RULES*

FOR USE WITH ARBITRATION AGREEMENTS UNDER THE ARBITRATION ACT 1996

(March 1997)

INTRODUCTION

The enactment of the Arbitration Act 1996 brings a unique opportunity to introduce a uniform procedural basis for arbitration in the construction industry.

The Construction Industry Model Arbitration Rules are the result of an extensive consultation with the industry over a period of a year commencing in January 1996.

These Rules as printed in March 1997 are offered as a draft for consideration for adoption by contract drafting bodies. They may also be incorporated into non-standard contracts and into agreements to refer specific disputes to arbitration.

Rule 1: objective and application

1.1 These Rules are to be read consistently with the Arbitration Act 1996 (the Act), with common expressions having the same meaning. Appendix I contains definitions of terms. Section numbers given in these Rules are references to the Act.

1.2 The objective of the Rules is to provide for the fair, impartial, speedy, cost-effective and binding resolution of construction disputes, with each party having a reasonable opportunity to put his case and to deal with that of his opponent. The parties and the arbitrator are to do all things necessary to achieve this objective: see sections 1 (General principles), 33 (General duty of tribunal) and 40 (General duty of parties).

1.3 The parties may not, without the agreement of the arbitrator, amend the Rules or impose procedures in conflict with them.

1.4 The arbitrator has all the powers and is subject to all the duties under the Act except where expressly modified by the Rules.

* The original Rules contained extracts from various sections of the Arbitration Act 1996. The Act is reproduced in full in Appendix 1 above.

1.5 Sections of the Act which need to be read with the Rules are printed with the text. Other sections referred to are printed in Appendix 2.

1.6 These Rules apply where:

(a) a single arbitrator is to be appointed;
(b) the seat of the arbitration is in England and Wales or Northern Ireland.

Rule 2: Beginning and appointment

2.1 Arbitral proceedings are begun in respect of a dispute when one party serves on the other a written notice of arbitration identifying the dispute and requiring him to agree to the appointment of an arbitrator; but see Rule 3.6 and Section 13 (limitation).

2.2 The party serving notice of arbitration should name any persons he proposes as arbitrator, with the notice or separately. The other party should respond and may propose other names.

2.3 If the parties fail to agree on the name of an arbitrator within 14 days of the notice of arbitration being served, or any agreed extension, either party may apply for the appointment of an arbitrator to the person so empowered.

2.4 The arbitrator's appointment takes effect upon his agreement to act or his appointment under Rule 2.3, whether or not there needs to be acceptance of his terms.

2.5 Where two or more related disputes fall under separate arbitration agreements (whether or not between the same parties) any person who is required to appoint an arbitrator must give due consideration as to whether

(i) the same arbitrator or
(ii) a different arbitrator

should be appointed in respect of those disputes and should appoint the same arbitrator unless sufficient grounds are shown for not doing so.

2.6 Where different persons are required to appoint an arbitrator in relation to disputes covered by Rule 2.5, due consideration includes consulting with every other such person. Where an arbitrator has already been appointed in relation to one such dispute, due consideration includes considering the appointment of that arbitrator.

2.7 As between any two or more persons who are required to appoint, the obligation to give due consideration under Rules 2.5 or 2.6 may be discharged by making arrangements for some other person or body to make the appointment in relation to disputes covered by Rule 2.5.

Rule 3: Joinder

3.1 A notice of arbitration may include two or more disputes if they fall under the same arbitration agreement.

3.2 A party served with a notice of arbitration may, at any time before an arbitrator is appointed, himself give a notice of arbitration in respect of any other disputes which fall under the same arbitration agreement, and those other disputes shall be consolidated with the arbitral proceedings.

3.3 After an arbitrator has been appointed, either party may give a further notice of arbitration to the other and to the arbitrator referring any other dispute which falls under the same arbitration agreement to those arbitral proceedings. If the other party does not consent to the other dispute being so referred the arbitrator may as he considers appropriate, order either:

(i) that the other dispute should be referred to and consolidated with the same arbitral proceedings; or
(ii) that the other dispute should not be so referred.

3.4 If the arbitrator makes an order under Rule 3.3(ii), Rule 2.3 then applies.

3.5 In relation to a notice of arbitration in respect of any other dispute under Rules 3.2 or 3.3, the arbitrator is empowered to:

(i) decide any matter which may be a condition precedent to bringing the other dispute before the arbitrator;
(ii) abrogate any condition precedent to the bringing of arbitral proceedings in respect of the other dispute.

3.6 Arbitral proceedings in respect of any other dispute are begun when the notice of arbitration for that other dispute is served: see section 13 (limitation).

3.7 Where the same arbitrator is appointed in two or more arbitral proceedings each of which involves some common issue, whether or not involving the same parties, the arbitrator may, if he considers it appropriate, order the concurrent hearing of any two or more such proceedings or of any claim or issue arising in such proceedings: see section 35.

3.8 If the arbitrator orders concurrent hearings he may give such other directions as are necessary or desirable for the purpose of such hearings but shall, unless the parties otherwise agree, deliver separate awards in each of such proceedings.

3.9 Where the same arbitrator is appointed in two or more arbitral proceedings each of which involves some common issue, whether or not involving the same parties, the arbitrator may, if the parties so agree, order that any two or more such proceedings shall be consolidated.

3.10 If the arbitrator orders the consolidation of two or more arbitral proceedings he may give such other directions as are appropriate for the purpose of such consolidated proceedings and shall, unless the parties otherwise agree, deliver a single award which shall be final and binding on all the parties to the consolidated proceedings.

3.11 Where an arbitrator has ordered concurrent hearings or consolidation under the foregoing rules, he may at any time revoke any orders so made, and may give such further orders or directions as are appropriate for the separate hearing and determination of the matters in issue.

3.12 Where two or more arbitral proceedings are ordered to be heard concurrently or to be consolidated, the arbitrator may exercise any or all of the powers in these Rules either separately or jointly in relation to the proceedings to which such order relates.

Rule 4: Particular powers

4.1 The arbitrator has the power set out in section 30(1) (ruling on substantive jurisdiction).

4.2 The arbitrator has the powers set out in section 37(1) (appointment of experts, advisers or assessors).

4.3 The arbitrator has the powers set out in section 38(4) to (6) (dealing with property, examination of witnesses and preservation of evidence).

4.4 The arbitrator may order the preservation of any work, goods or materials even though they form part of work which is continuing.

4.5 The arbitrator may direct the manner in which, by whom and when any test or experiment is to be carried out and may himself observe such test or experiment even though one or both parties is not present.

4.6 The arbitrator may order a claimant to give security for the whole or part of the costs likely to be incurred by his opponent in defending a claim if satisfied that the claimant is unlikely to be able to pay those costs (as well as his own costs) if the claim is unsuccessful. In exercising this power, the arbitrator should consider all the circumstances including the strength of the claim and any defence, and the stage at which the application is made. This power is subject to section 38(3).

4.7 The arbitrator shall give reasons for an order under Rule 4.6 if requested by one of the parties to do so.

4.8 The arbitrator has the power to order a claimant to give security for his own costs: see section 38(3).

4.9 If, without showing sufficient cause, a claimant fails to comply with an order for security for costs under Rule 4.6, the arbitrator may make a peremptory order to the same effect prescribing such time for compliance as he considers appropriate. If the peremptory order is not complied with, the arbitrator may make an award dismissing the claim: see Rules 11.4 and 11.6.

Rule 5: Evidence

5.1 Subject to these Rules, the arbitrator shall decide all procedural and evidential matters including those set out in section 34(2), subject to the right of the parties to agree any matter.

5.2 The arbitrator is not bound by the strict rules of evidence and shall determine the admissibility, relevance or weight of any material sought to be tendered on any matters of fact or opinion by any party.

5.3 The arbitrator shall determine which documents or classes of documents should be disclosed between and produced by the parties and at what stage.

5.4 Whether or not them are oral proceedings the arbitrator may determine the manner in which the parties and their witnesses are to be examined

5.5 The arbitrator may fix the time within which any order or direction is to be complied with and may extend or reduce the time at any stage

5.6 In any of the following cases:

(a) an application for security for costs;
(b) an application to strike out for want of prosecution;
(c) an application for a provisional order;
(d) any other instance where he considers it appropriate;

the arbitrator shall require that evidence be put on affidavit or that some other formal record of the evidence be made.

Rule 6: Procedure and directions

6.1 As soon as he is appointed the arbitrator must consider the form of procedure which is most appropriate to the dispute: see section 33.

6.2 For this purpose the parties shall, as soon as practicable after the arbitrator is appointed, provide to each other and to the arbitrator:

(a) estimates of the amounts in dispute;
(b) a view as to the need for and length of any hearing;
(c) proposals as to the form of procedure appropriate to the dispute.

6.3 The arbitrator shall convene a procedural meeting with the parties or their representatives at which, having regard to the information submitted under Rule 6.2, he shall give a direction as to the procedure to be followed. The direction may:

(a) adopt the procedure in Rules 7, 8 or 9;
(b) adopt any part of one or more of these procedures;
(c) adopt any other procedure which he considers to be appropriate;

and may be varied or amended from time to time.

6.4 The arbitrator shall give such directions as he considers appropriate in accordance with the procedure adopted. He shall also give such other directions under these Rules as he considers appropriate: see particularly Rules 4 and 5 and Rule 13.4.

6.5 The matters under Rules 6.3 and 6.4 may be dealt with without a meeting if the arbitrator considers a meeting to be unnecessary.

Rule 7: Short hearing

7.1 This procedure is appropriate where the matters in dispute are to be determined principally by the arbitrator inspecting work, materials, machinery or the like.

7.2 The parties shall, either at the same time or in sequence as the arbitrator may direct, submit written statements of their cases, including any documents and statements of witnesses relied on.

7.3 There shall be a hearing of not more than one day at which each party will have a reasonable opportunity to address the matters in dispute. The arbitrator's inspection may take place before or after the hearing, or may be combined with it. The parties may agree to extend the hearing.

7.4 The arbitrator may form his own opinion on the matters in dispute and need not inform the parties of his opinion before delivering his award.

7.5 Either party may adduce expert evidence but may not recover any costs so incurred unless the arbitrator decides that such evidence was necessary for coming to his decision.

7.6 The arbitrator shall make his award within one month of the last of the foregoing steps, or within such further time as he may require and notify to the parties.

7.7 The recovery of costs is subject to Rule 13.5; see section 65 (capping of costs).

Rule 8: Documents only

8.1 This procedure is appropriate where there is to be no hearing, for instance, because the issues do not require oral evidence, or because the sums in dispute do not warrant the cost of a hearing.

8.2 The parties shall, either at the same time or in sequence as the arbitrator may direct, submit written statements of their cases including:

(a) an account of the relevant facts or opinions relied on;
(b) statements of witnesses concerning those facts or opinions, signed or otherwise confirmed by the witness;
(c) the remedy or relief sought, for instance, a sum of money with interest.

8.3 Each party may submit a statement in reply to that of the other party.

8.4 After reading the parties' written statements, the arbitrator may

(a) put questions to or request a further written statement from either party;
(b) direct that there be a hearing of not more than one day at which he may put questions to the parties or to any witness. In this event the parties will also have a reasonable opportunity to comment on any additional information given to the arbitrator.

8.5 The arbitrator shall make his award within one month of the last of the foregoing steps, or within such further time as he may require and notify to the parties.

8.6 The recovery of costs is subject to Rule 13.5; see section 65 (capping of costs).

Rule 9: Full procedure

9.1 Where neither the Documents Only nor the Short Procedure is appropriate, the Full Procedure should be adopted, subject to such modification as is appropriate to the particular matters in issue.

9.2 The parties shall exchange statements of claim and defence in accordance with the following guidelines:

(a) each statement should contain the facts and matters of opinion which are intended to be established by evidence and may include a statement of any relevant point of law which will be contended for:
(b) a statement should contain sufficient particulars that the other party is able to answer each allegation without recourse to general denials;
(c) a statement may include or refer to evidence to be adduced if this will assist in defining the issues to be determined;
(d) the reliefs or remedies sought, for instance specific monetary losses, must be stated in such a way that they can be answered or admitted;
(e) all statements should adopt a common system of numbering or identification of sections to facilitate analysis of issues. Particulars given in schedule form should anticipate the need to incorporate replies.

9.3 The arbitrator may permit or direct the parties at any stage to amend, expand, summarise or reproduce in some other format any of the statements of claim or defence so as to identify the matters essentially in dispute, including preparing a list of the matters in issue.

9.4 The arbitrator should give detailed directions, with times or dates for all steps in the proceedings including

(a) further statements or particulars required;
(b) disclosure and production of documents between the parties;
(c) service of statements of witnesses of fact;
(d) the number of experts and service of their reports;
(e) meetings between experts and/or other persons;
(f) arrangements for any hearing.

9.5 The arbitrator should fix the length of each hearing including the time which will be available to each party to present its case and answer that of its opponent.

9.6 The arbitrator may at any time order the following to be delivered to him and to the other party in writing:

(a) any submission or speech by an advocate:
(b) questions intended to be put to any witness;
(c) answers by any witness to identified questions

Rule 10: Provisional relief

10.1 The arbitrator has power to order the following relief on a provisional basis (see Section 39):

(a) payment of a reasonable proportion of the sum which is likely to be awarded finally in respect of the claims to which the payment relates, after taking account of any defence or counterclaim that may be available;
(b) payment of a sum on account of any costs of the arbitration, including costs relating to an order under this Rule;
(c) any other relief claimed in the arbitral proceedings.

10.2 The arbitrator may exercise the powers under this Rule after application by a party or of his own motion after giving due notice to the parties.

10.3 A provisional order under this Rule must be based on formal evidence: see Rule 5.6. The arbitrator may give such reasons for his order as he thinks appropriate.

10.4 The arbitrator ay order any money or property which is the subject of a provisional order to be paid to or delivered to a stakeholder on such terms as he considers appropriate.

10.5 A provisional order is subject to the final adjudication of the arbitrator who makes it, or of any arbitrator who subsequently has jurisdiction over the dispute to which it relates.

Rule 11: Default powers and sanctions

11.1 The arbitrator has the power set out in section 41(3) to make an award dismissing a claim.

11.2 The arbitrator has the power set out in section 41(4) to proceed in the absence of a party or without any written evidence or submission from a party.

11.3 The arbitrator may by any order direct that if a party fails to comply with that order he will:

(a) refuse to allow the party in default to rely on any allegation or material which was the subject of the order;
(b) draw such adverse inferences from the act of non-compliance as the circumstances justify;

and may, if that party fails to comply without showing sufficient cause, refuse to allow such reliance or draw such adverse inferences and may proceed to make an award on the basis of such materials as have been properly provided and may make any order as to costs in consequence of such non-compliance

11.4 In addition to his power under Rule 11.3 the arbitrator has the powers set out in section 41(5), (6) and (7) (peremptory orders).

11.5 An application to the court for an order requiring a party to comply with a peremptory order may be made only by or with the permission of the arbitrator: see section 42(2) (enforcement of orders).

11.6 An application to dismiss a claim for inordinate and inexcusable delay or failure to comply with a peremptory order to provide security for costs must be based on formal evidence: see Rule 5.6. Where a claim is dismissed on such a ground, the claim is barred and may not be re-arbitrated.

Rule 12: Awards and remedies

12.1 The arbitrator has the powers set out in section 47 (awards on different issues).

12.2 Where the arbitrator directs or the parties agree to a hearing dealing with part of a dispute, then whether or not there is any agreement between the parties as to such matters, the arbitrator may do any of the following:

(a) decide what are the issues or questions to be determined;
(b) decide whether or not to give an award on part of the claims submitted;
(c) make a provisional order; but see Rule 10.2.

12.3 At the conclusion of a hearing, where the arbitrator is to deliver an award he shall inform the parties of the target date for its delivery. The arbitrator must take all possible steps to complete the award by that date and inform the parties of any reason which prevents him doing so. The award shall not deal with the allocation of costs and/or interest unless these have been addressed.

12.4 An award shall be in writing and signed by the arbitrator.

12.5 An award should contain sufficient reasons for the parties to understand why the arbitrator has reached the decisions contained in it.

12.6 The arbitrator has the powers set out in section 48(3), (4) and (5) (remedies).

12.7 Where an award orders that a party should do some act, for instance carry our specified work, the arbitrator has the power to supervise the performance or, if he thinks it appropriate, to appoint (and to re-appoint as may be necessary) a suitable person so to supervise and to fix the terms of his engagement, and retains all powers necessary to ensure compliance with the award.

12.8 The arbitrator has the powers set out in section 49(3) and (4) (award of simple or compound interest). This is in addition to any power to award contractual interest.

12.9 The arbitrator has the powers set out in section 57(3) to (6) (correction of award) which are to be exercised subject to the time limits stated.

12.10 The arbitrator may notify an award or any part of an award to the parties as a draft or proposal. In such case the arbitrator shall consider comments of the parties notified to him within such time as he may specify and thereafter complete the award.

Rule 13: Costs

13.1 The general principle is that costs should be borne by the losing party; see section 61 (award of costs). Subject to any agreement between the parties, the arbitrator has the widest discretion in awarding which party should bear what proportion of the costs of the arbitration.

13.2 In allocating costs the arbitrator shall have regard to all material circumstances, including such of the following as may be relevant:

(a) which of the claims has led to the incurring of substantial costs and whether they were successful;

(b) whether any claim which has succeeded was unreasonably exaggerated;
(c) the conduct of the party who succeeded on any claim and any concession made by the other party;
(d) the degree of success of each party.

See also Rule 13.6.

13.3 Where an award deals with both a claim and a counter-claim, the arbitrator should deal with the recovery of costs in relation to each of them separately unless he considers them to be so interconnected that they should be dealt with together.

13.4 The arbitrator may impose a limit on recoverable costs of the arbitration: see Section 65. In determining such limit the arbitrator shall have regard primarily to the amounts in dispute. Except in the case of proceedings subject to Rule 7 or Rule 8, the limit should not normally exceed 25% of the aggregate of amounts in dispute.

13.5 A direction under Rule 6.3 for the adoption of Rule 7 (Short Hearing) or Rule 8 (Documents Only) is subject to a further direction that the recoverable costs of that part of the arbitration subject to such procedure shall be limited to 10% of the aggregate of amounts in dispute, unless the parties agree or the arbitrator directs that a lesser figure should apply.

13.6 In allocating costs the arbitrator shall have regard to any offer of settlement or compromise from either party, whatever its description or form. The general principle which the arbitrator should follow is that a party who recovers less overall than was offered to him in settlement or compromise should recover the costs which he would otherwise have been entitled to recover only up to the date on which it was reasonable for him to have accepted the offer and the offeror should recover his costs thereafter.

13.7 Section 63(3) to (7) applies to the determination of the recoverable costs of the arbitration (determination by the arbitrator or by the court). Where the arbitrator is to determine recoverable costs, he may do so on such basis as he thinks fit. Section 59 (costs of the arbitration) also applies.

Rule 14: Miscellaneous

14.1 A party may be represented in the proceedings by any one or more persons of his choice and by different persons at different times: see Section 36 (representation).

14.2 The arbitrator shall establish and record postal addresses and other means, including facsimile or telex, by which communication in writing may be effected for the purposes of the arbitration. Section 76(3) to (6) (service of notices) shall apply in addition.

14.3 Section 78(3) to (5) apply to the reckoning of periods of time.

14.4 The parties shall promptly inform the arbitrator of any settlement. Section 51 (settlement) then applies.

14.5 The parties shall promptly inform the arbitrator of any intended application to the court and provide copies of any proceedings issued in relation.

Appendix I

Definition of terms

"Act" means the Arbitration Act 1996 (c. 23) including any amendment or re-enactment.

"claim" includes counterclaim.

"claimant" includes counterclaimant.

"concurrent hearing" means two or more arbitral proceedings being head together: see Rules 3.7 and 3.8.

"consolidation" means two or more arbitral proceedings being treated as one proceeding: see Rules 3.9 and 3.10.

"dispute" includes a difference which is subject to a condition precedent to arbitral proceedings being brought: see Rule 3.5.

"notice of arbitration" means the written notice which begins arbitral proceedings: see Rules 2.1 and 3.6.

"party" means one of the parties to arbitral proceedings.

"provisional order" means an order for provisional relief in accordance with Rule 10.

"Rule" refers to a separate section of the Rules or a part.

"Section" means a section of the Act.

Appendix II

[sections of the Arbitration Act 1996 reproduced at Appendix 2 above]

Appendix 14

THE CHARTERED INSTITUTE OF ARBITRATORS

SURVEYORS AND VALUERS ARBITRATION SCHEME

(1993 edition)

EXPLANATORY NOTES

Arbitration is the process by which two parties in dispute appoint or have appointed on their behalf a third, but independent, person to resolve the dispute. It is the only alternative to going to court if parties require a final and legally enforceable decision. The decision is legally binding so that the same matter cannot be pursued through the courts. An appeal lies against an arbitrator's award only on a point of law.

This Scheme provides for the settling by arbitration of disputes or differences between members of the Royal Institution of Chartered Surveyors, the Incorporated Society of Valuers & Auctioneers and their clients which they are unable to resolve amicably by themselves or with the assistance of the RICS or the ISVA.

The Scheme is intended for use primarily in disputes between chartered surveyors or incorporated valuers and their private clients. Chartered surveyors and incorporated valuers are also encouraged by their respective professional bodies to give serious consideration to the use of the Scheme when requested to do so by small business clients. The RICS and ISVA do not expect their members to agree to use the Scheme where they are in dispute with large commercial clients, who can afford to fund legal action themselves.

The client has the option of referring the dispute to arbitration after it has arisen instead of proceeding in the courts. Application must be made to the Institute on its application form. Each party is responsible for its own costs (including legal costs) and all other costs are paid by RICS and ISVA. One party may be ordered to reimburse the other's registration fee.

The procedure is simple, quick, informal and inexpensive. Each party presents a written statement of its arguments in the dispute, together with supporting documents, and comments on the arguments and evidence of the other party. The arbitrator makes a decision by reference to the documents alone and following a site inspection in appropriate cases.

The Scheme does not deal with issues of alleged dishonesty or other breaches of the relevant professional codes. Such allegations should be made in writing to the Professional Conduct Department of the RICS, 12 Great George Street, Parliament Square, London, SW1P 3AD or to the Professional Services Department, ISVA, 3 Cadogan Gate, London, SW1X 0AS. If any allegation of professional misconduct is also the subject of a claim for compensation under this Scheme, the RICS and ISVA may defer any disciplinary investigation until the arbitrator has made an award.

If the award involves a finding of liability on the part of the RICS or ISVA member, the member must inform its insurers of the arbitrator's decision.

The arbitrators selected for appointment by the President or a Vice President of the Institute are Fellows of the Institute and all appointments are within the Institute's exclusive control.

The law relating to the dispute and to arbitration procedure under this Scheme is that of England and Wales, unless the arbitrator directs the applicable law is to be that of Scotland, Northern Ireland, Jersey, Guernsey or the Isle of Man.

Introduction

1. These Rules apply to applications for arbitration made to the Chartered Institute of Arbitrators (''the Institute'') on or after 1 June 1993 in respect of disputes between members of the Royal Institution of Chartered Surveyors (''RICS''), *i.e.* chartered surveyors, the Incorporated Society of Valuers and Auctioneers (''ISVA''), *i.e.* incorporated valuers, and their clients. A dispute may only be referred to arbitration under the Scheme where both parties have agreed to do so after the dispute has arisen.

2. The Scheme applies to disputes involving:

(i) a chartered surveyor or incorporated valuer practising in England and Wales, Scotland, Northern Ireland, the Channel Islands or the Isle of Man;
(ii) a client who has instructed the chartered surveyor or incorporated valuer;
(iii) an allegation that chartered surveyor or incorporated valuer is liable in contract to that client for breach of professional duty.

For the purposes of this Rule, ''chartered surveyor or incorporated valuer'' includes a partnership, a limited company or an unlimited company carrying on practice as surveyors or valuers, of which at least one partner or director is a chartered surveyor or incorporated valuer.

3. No claim may be made under the Scheme:

(i) in respect of physical injury, illness or nervous shock or the consequences of any of these;
(ii) where the property or land to which the dispute relates is situated outside the territories listed in Rule 2(i);
(iii) if the issues are unusually complicated and their resolution is likely to require a hearing and oral evidence.

4. The Rules are designed primarily for arbitrations between the two parties only. With the agreement of the Institute and of all parties concerned, the Rules may be adapted for arbitrations between three or more parties.

5. A registration fee is payable by each party when an application for arbitration is submitted and is specified in the Institute's application form. It is non-returnable except as provided in Rules 9(v) and (vii) although either party may be required to reimburse the other's registration fee under Rule 12.

Commencing arbitration proceedings

6. A joint application for arbitration must be submitted to the Institute on its application form, signed by both parties and accompanied by the registration fee.

7. The arbitration commences under these Rules when the Institute sends the parties written notice of acceptance of the application. The notice sent to the client (''the Claimant'') will be accompanied by a claim form.

Procedure

GENERAL

8. The institute will appoint a sole arbitrator to decide the dispute and notify the parties of the appointment. Subject to any directions issued by the arbitrator and to the provisions of these Rules, the arbitration will be on documents only and the procedure will be as follows:

(i) The Claimant shall, within 28 days of receipt of the claim form, send the completed form together with the supporting documents, in duplicate, to the Institute.

(ii) The Claimant may not generally claim an amount greater than that specified on the application form. If he/she does, however, the arbitrator will have a discretion as to whether to allow this.

(iii) A copy of the claim documents will be sent by the Institute to the chartered surveyor or incorporated valuer (''the Respondent'') who shall, within 28 days of the receipt of the documents, send to the Institute a written defence to the claim, together with any supporting documents in duplicate. The Respondent may include with its defence a counterclaim in respect of any balance of payment alleged to be due on the contract between the parties. The Respondent may not make any other counterclaim against the Claimant unless:

(a) notice of it was contained in the parties' application for arbitration; and

(b) the arbitrator consents to the making of such counterclaim.

(iv) A copy of the defence documents will be sent by the Institute to the Claimant, who may send to the Institute any written comments which he/she wishes to make on them and a defence to any counterclaim within 14 days of their receipt. Such comments must be in duplicate and the Institute will send a copy to the Respondent. They must refer only to points arising from the defence and any counterclaim and may not introduce any new matters or points of claim.

(v) The arbitrator will make his/her award by reference to the documents submitted by the parties and his/her reasons will be set out or referred to in the award.

(vi) Any compensation ordered may include or be limited to any amount of fees owing to the Respondent for which a counterclaim has been made.

(vii) The Institute will send copies of the award to each party and to the RICS or ISVA (as appropriate).

(viii) Unless the award states otherwise, payment shall be made of any monies directed by the award to be paid within 21 days of despatch of the award. Such payment shall be made by the party liable direct to the party entitled, and not through the arbitrator, the Institute, the RICS or the ISVA. Enforcement of the award is the responsibility of the parties and the Institute cannot assist.

(ix) If either party has sent original documents in support of its case to the Institute that party may, within six weeks of despatch of the award, request the return of those documents. Subject to that, case papers will be retained by the Institute and may be disposed of.

SUPPLEMENTARY

9. (i) The arbitrator may require the parties to provide any further documents/information which he/she considers would assist him/her in his/her decision. If the documents/information are not supplied to the Institute within such time as it prescribes, the arbitrator may proceed with the reference on the basis of the documents already before him/her.

(ii) The arbitrator may make an examination of the land or property to which the dispute relates. The parties shall give the arbitrator all necessary assistance for the conduct of this examination.

(iii) The arbitrator may appoint an independent expert or call for expert evidence from the parties. The parties will be given an opportunity to comment on any evidence obtained.

(iv) The arbitrator may at his/her discretion appoint a legal or technical assessor to assist him/her in considering the documentary evidence submitted by the parties.

(v) If the Claimant does not submit his/her claim within the time allowed and fails to do so within 14 days of a reminder by the Institute, he/she will be treated as having abandoned his/her claim. The arbitration will not proceed and the Respondent's registration fee will be returned.

(vi) If the Respondent does not submit its defence within the time allowed and fails to do so within 14 days of a reminder by the Institute, the arbitrator may decide the dispute by reference to the documents submitted by the Claimant.

(vii) If the arbitrator concludes that the dispute is not capable of proper resolution under these Rules, he/she shall so advise the parties. Failing agreement as to how the arbitration should otherwise proceed (including proposals as to costs) the arbitrator's appointment shall be deemed revoked, the parties' application for arbitration shall be deemed withdrawn and their registration fees will be refunded. The Claimant will then be able to pursue the matter through the courts.

Costs

10. The administrative costs of the Scheme, including the fees and expenses of the arbitrator, any independent expert appointed by the arbitrator under Rule 9 (iii) and any assessor appointed under Rule 9 (iv), shall be paid by the RICS or ISVA (as appropriate). The maximum potential liability of an unsuccessful Claimant for costs under the Scheme will therefore by limited to his/her own and the other party's registration fee in accordance with Rule 12 below.

11. Each party bears its own legal and other costs of preparing and submitting its case (including legal costs), and may not recover them in court proceedings against the other party.

2. The arbitrator may, in the award, order one party to reimburse the other's registration fee.

Miscellaneous

13. (i) The applicable law (English, Scots, Northern Irish, etc.) shall be determined by the arbitrator if the parties fail to agree.

(ii) Where Scots law applies, any reference in these Rules to an "arbitrator" shall be construed as a reference to an "arbiter" and Scottish arbitration procedures shall apply.

14. The Institute may appoint a substitute arbitrator if the original appointee dies, is incapacitated or is for any reason unable to deal quickly with the dispute. The parties shall be notified of any substitution.

15. The arbitrator's award shall be final and binding on the parties. Subject to a party's right to draw attention to any accidental slip or omission which the arbitrator has power by law to correct, neither the Institute nor the arbitrator can enter into correspondence regarding awards made under the Scheme.

16. The parties may apply or appeal to the courts under the relevant Arbitration Acts, but:

(i) the special costs provisions of the Scheme shall not apply to any such application or appeal;

(ii) the party making an application or appeal (other than an application for leave to enforce the award) will bear its own and the other party's costs (including the costs of any resumed or fresh arbitration) regardless of the outcome of such proceedings, unless the relevant court orders otherwise.

17. Neither the Institute nor the arbitrator shall be liable to any party for any act or omission in connection with any arbitration conducted under these Rules. However, the arbitrator (but not the Institute) shall be liable for any wrongdoing on his/her own part arising from bad faith.

The Chartered Institute of Arbitrators
24 Angel Gate,
City Road,
London EC1V 2RS
Tel.: 0171-837 4483
Fax: 0171-837 4185

Appendix 15

GRAIN AND FEED TRADE ASSOCIATION

ARBITRATION RULES NO. 125

(Effective January 31, 1997)

DEFINITIONS

The following are definitions of the references contained in the Arbitration Rules.

''Arbitrator'': a Qualified Arbitrator Member of the Grain and Feed Trade Association pursuant to the Association's Members' Rules and Regulations.

''Association'': the Grain and Feed Trade Association.

''Tribunal'': a sole arbitrator or a tribunal of three arbitrators.

''The Claimant'': the party claiming arbitration.

''Appellant'': the party lodging an appeal.

''The Respondent'': the party against whom arbitration is claimed, and/or the other party named in a first tier award the subject of an appeal.

''Rye Terms'' Clause: those contract clauses whereby the obligations of the parties are defined by reference to the condition of the goods on arrival.

''Notices'': a notice in writing, served in accordance with Rule 21.

''Monies Due'': any debt payable pursuant to the contract, including liquidated damages.

References to the masculine include references to the feminine and also to companies, corporations or other legal persons.

Any dispute arising out of a contract which incorporates these Rules shall be referred to arbitration in accordance with the following provisions:

1. Preliminary

1.1 The provisions of the Arbitration Act 1996, and of any statutory amendment, modification or enactment thereof for the time being in force, shall apply to every arbitration and/or appeal under these Rules save insofar as such provisions are expressly modified by, or are inconsistent with, these Rules.

1.2 The juridical seat of the arbitration shall be, and is hereby designated pursuant to section 4 of the Arbitration Act 1996 as, England.

1.3 Arbitration shall take place at the registered offices of The Grain and Feed Trade Association (GAFTA), London, or (but without prejudice to Rules 1.1 and 1.2 above), elsewhere if agreed by the parties in writing.

2. Procedure and time limits for claiming arbitration

The claimant shall serve on the respondent a notice stating his intention to refer a dispute to arbitration within the following time limits.

2.1 *Disputes as to quality and/or condition*

(a) In respect of disputes arising out of the ''Rye Terms'' clause not later than the 10th consecutive day after the date of completion of final discharge. (See Rule 6).
(b) In respect of claims arising out of certificates of analysis in respect of which allowances are not fixed by the terms of the contract, not later than the 21st consecutive day after the date on which the claimant receives the final certificate of analysis.
(c) In respect of all other quality and/or condition disputes, not later than the 21st consecutive day after the date of completion of final discharge, or delivery, or the unstuffing of the container(s), as the case may be.

2.2 *Monies due*

In respect of disputes relating to monies due not later than the 90th consecutive day after the dispute has arisen.

2.3 *Other disputes*

In respect of all other disputes relating to the sale of goods,

(a) arising out of CIF, CIFFO, C & F and similar shipment contract terms, not later than the 90th consecutive day after (i) the expiry of the contract period of shipment, including extension if any, or (ii) the date of completion of final discharge of the ship at port of destination, whichever period shall last expire,
(b) arising out of FOB terms, not later than the 90th consecutive day after (i) the date of the last bill of lading or (ii) the expiry of the contract period of delivery, including extension if any, whichever period shall first expire,
(c) on any other terms, not later than the 90th consecutive day after the last day of the contractual delivery, collection or arrival period, as the case may be.

2.4 No award by the tribunal shall be questioned or set aside on appeal or otherwise on the ground that the claim was not made within the time limits stipulated in this Rule if the respondent to the claim did not raise the matter in their submissions so as to enable the tribunal to consider whether or not to exercise the discretion vested in it by Rule 22.

3. Appointment of the tribunal

The dispute shall be heard and determined by a tribunal of three arbitrators (appointed in accordance with Rule 3.2) or, if both parties agree, by a sole arbitrator (appointed in accordance with clause 3.1).

The time limits imposed by this Rule for the appointment of the tribunal shall run from the date of service pursuant to Rule 2 of a notice referring a dispute to arbitration.

This Rule is without prejudice to Rule 6, which governs the appointment of the tribunal in relation to disputes arising out of the Rye Terms clause, and Rule 5.3, which governs the appointment of a tribunal for examination of samples.

3.1 *Procedure for the appointment of a sole arbitrator*

(a) If he requires the appointment of a sole arbitrator the claimant shall, not later than the 9th consecutive day after service of the notice referring a claim to arbitration, serve a notice on the respondent seeking his agreement to the appointment of a sole arbitrator by the Association.

(b) Not later than the 9th consecutive day after service of the notice referred to in (a) above, the respondent shall either; (i) serve a notice on the claimant stating that he agrees to the appointment of a sole arbitrator by the Association, or (ii) appoint an arbitrator to a tribunal of three arbitrators and serve on the claimant a notice of the arbitrator so appointed, in which case Rule 3.2(c) shall apply.

(c) Where the parties have agreed to the appointment of a sole arbitrator the Association shall appoint an arbitrator on receipt of the first statements and evidence submitted in accordance with Rule 4, or, where interlocutory or interim decisions are required of the tribunal, upon the application of either party.

3.2 *Procedure for the appointment of a tribunal of three arbitrators*

(a) The claimant shall not later than the 9th consecutive day after service of the notice referring a claim to arbitration appoint an arbitrator and serve a notice on the respondent of the name of the arbitrator so appointed.

(b) The respondent shall, not later than the 9th consecutive day after service of the notice referred to at (a) above, appoint a second arbitrator and serve a notice on the claimant of the name of the arbitrator so appointed.

(c) If the respondent does not agree to the appointment of a sole arbitrator and has instead appointed an arbitrator and given written notice thereof pursuant to Rule 3.1 (b), the claimant shall not later than the 9th consecutive day after service of such notice of appointment, appoint a second arbitrator and serve a notice on the respondent of the name of the arbitrator so appointed.

(d) Where two arbitrators have been appointed, the Association shall appoint a third arbitrator on receipt of the first statements and evidence submitted in accordance with Rule 4, or, where interlocutory or interim decisions are required of a tribunal, upon the application of either party. The third arbitrator shall be the chairman of the tribunal so formed and his name shall be notified to the parties by the Association.

3.3 *Appointments of arbitrators by the Association*

If either party fails to appoint an arbitrator or to give notice thereof within the above time limits, the other party may apply to the Association for the appointment of an arbitrator. Notice of such application must be served on the party who has failed to appoint. Upon such application being made, the Association will appoint an arbitrator on behalf of the party who has failed to do so, and give notice of the name of the arbitrator appointed to the parties.

Where the claimant has already sought the respondent's agreement to the appointment of a sole arbitrator pursuant to Rule 3.1 then the Association will appoint a sole arbitrator. Where either party has already appointed an arbitrator, pursuant to Rule 3.1(b) or Rule 3.2, then the Association will appoint the second arbitrator of the tribunal.

3.4 Applications to the Association for the appointment of an arbitrator shall be accompanied by,

(a) prima facie evidence that the parties have entered into a contract subject to these Rules,
(b) copies of the notices (i) claiming arbitration and (ii) stating that an application has been made to the Association for the appointment of an arbitrator,
(c) the appropriate fee ruling at the date of application.

3.5 An arbitrator appointed under these Rules shall be a Qualified Arbitrator Member of the Association and shall not be interested in the transaction nor directly interested as a member of a company or firm named as a party to the arbitration, nor financially retained by any such company or firm, nor a member of nor financially retained by any company or firm financially associated with any party to the arbitration.

3.6 An appointment of an arbitrator shall be valid and effective for all purposes provided that he has signified his acceptance of the appointment to the party appointing him, or to the Association, as the case may be, at any time prior to the discharge of any arbitral function.

3.7 (a) If an arbitrator dies, refuses to act, resigns, or becomes incapable of acting, or if he fails to proceed with the arbitration, or is found to be ineligible, or his authority is revoked by the Association pursuant to the Association's Rules and Regulations, the party, or the Association as the case maybe, who originally appointed that arbitrator shall forthwith appoint a substitute and serve notice thereof on the other party.

(b) If a party fails, contrary to (a) above, to appoint a substitute arbitrator and to give notice thereof within 5 consecutive days of learning of the arbitrator's death, refusal to act, resignation, incapacity, failure to proceed, finding of ineligibility or revocation of authority, as the case may be, the Association shall, upon the application of either party, have the power to appoint a substitute arbitrator.

3.8 Any party making an application to the Association for the appointment of an arbitrator may be required by the Association to pay a deposit of such sum as the Association may require on account of any fees and expenses thereafter arising. In addition the tribunal may call upon either party to deposit with the Association such sum or sums as it considers appropriate on account of fees, costs and expenses prior to the commencement of the arbitration hearing.

4. Arbitration procedure

4.1 The claimant shall draw up a clear and concise statement of his case which, together with a copy of the contract and any supporting documents, shall be served as set out in Rule 4.4.

4.2 The respondent shall, on receipt of the claimant's case and documents, draw up a clear and concise statement of his defence (and counterclaim, if any) which, together with any supporting documents, shall be served as set out in Rule 4.4.

4.3 The claimant may submit further written comments and/or documents in reply, such to be served as set out in Rule 4.4.

4.4 All statements and evidence shall be served by sending them to the other party, with copies to the Association. In the case of a sole arbitrator 2 sets, or in the case of a tribunal of three arbitrators, 4 sets of statements and evidence, shall be delivered to the Association. Failure to send all sets to the Association will render the party responsible liable to the Association for the costs of copying such documents for forwarding to the arbitrators.

4.5 The tribunal may vary or depart from the above procedure in order to give each party a reasonable opportunity of putting his case and dealing with that of his opponent, and shall adopt procedures suitable to the circumstances of the particular case, avoiding unnecessary delay or expense, so as to provide a fair means for the resolution of the matters falling to be determined.

4.6 The timetable for the proceedings, including any steps to be taken pursuant to Rule 4 and/or determined by the tribunal, will be advised to the parties by the Association. It shall be the duty of the tribunal to ensure the prompt progress of the arbitration, including the making of orders where appropriate. Any delay in the proceedings may be notified to the Association.

4.7 Nothing in this Rule shall prevent the respondent from delivering his statement and documentary evidence before receiving documents/statements from the claimant.

4.8 Where the tribunal considers that an oral hearing is necessary, the date, time and place will be arranged by the Association.

4.9 *Lapse of claim*

If neither party submits any documentary evidence or submissions as set out in this Rule or as ordered by the tribunal, within 1 year from the date of the notice claiming arbitration, then, subject only to Rule 22, the claimant's claim shall be deemed to have lapsed on the expiry of the said period of 1 year unless before that date the claim is renewed:

(a) by a notice served by either party on the other, such notice to be served during the 30 consecutive days prior to the expiry date, or
(b) by the service of documentary evidence or submissions by either party,

in which case the claim and counterclaim are each renewed for a further year.

The claim may be thus renewed for successive periods of 1 year. Wherever a claim is renewed any counterclaim is also deemed to be renewed.

4.10 If the arbitration is abandoned, suspended or concluded, by agreement or otherwise, before the final award is made, the parties shall be jointly and severally liable to pay to the Association the tribunal's and the Association's costs, fees and expenses.

5. Samples

5.1 If either party wishes to submit samples for examination by the tribunal, those samples shall be drawn, sealed and despatched to the Association in accordance with the provisions of the Sampling Rules Form No. 124, and shall be held at the disposal of the tribunal.

5.2 As soon as possible after receipt (and if necessary prior to the completion of the exchange of submissions and documents pursuant to Rule 4 and/or the order of the tribunal), the samples shall be examined by the tribunal. In particular.

(a) in the case of claims arising out of the "rye terms" clause, the samples shall be examined not later than 21 consecutive days after the date of completion of final discharge of the ship at port of destination.

and

(b) where the claim involves comparison with a f.a.q. (fair average quality) standard, the samples shall be examined not later than 21 consecutive days after the date of publication by the Association that the standard has been, or will not be, made.

5.3 Upon the joint application of both parties, the Association may arrange for the examination of the contract goods to take place at the port of destination, by a sole arbitrator or (in the case of a dispute arising out of the "rye terms" clause) three arbitrators, such arbitrator or arbitrators to be appointed by the Association. This provision does not over-ride the parties' obligations to take, seal and despatch samples where required by the Sampling Rules Form No. 124. The tribunal so appointed shall determine all matters in dispute between the parties.

5.4 All samples sent to the Association for arbitration, testing and/or other purposes shall become and be the absolute property of the Association.

6. Arbitration procedure for claims arising out of the "rye terms" clause

6.1 When the claimant has served on the respondent notice of its intention to refer the dispute to arbitration in accordance with Rule 2.1(b), he shall send a copy of the notice to the Association, together with sufficient information to identify the samples relating to the claim.

6.2 Notwithstanding anything to the contrary in these Rules, upon receipt of the notice as above, the Association shall appoint a tribunal of three arbitrators.

6.3 Any documentary submissions or evidence to be submitted by the parties shall be provided in accordance with Rule 4.

6.4 An award made pursuant to this Rule shall be final and binding and no appeal shall lie to a board of appeal.

7. String arbitrations—consolidated arbitrations and concurrent hearings

7.1 *Quality and condition*

If a contract forms part of a string of contracts which contain materially identical terms (albeit that the price may vary under each contract), a single arbitration determining a dispute as to quality and/or condition may be held between the first seller and the last buyer in the string as though they were parties who had contracted with each other.

Any award made in such proceedings shall, subject only to any right of appeal pursuant to Rule 10, be ψbinding on all the parties in the string and may be enforced by an intermediate party against his immediate contracting party as though a separate award had been made pursuant to each contract.

7.2 *Other conditions*

In all other cases, if all parties concerned expressly agree, the tribunal may conduct arbitral proceedings concurrently with other arbitral proceedings, and, in particular, concurrent hearings may be held, but separate awards shall be made pursuant to each contract.

8. Issues of substantive jurisdiction, provisional orders and awards on different aspects

8.1 *Issues of substantive jurisdiction*

(a) The tribunal may rule on its own jurisdiction, that is, as to whether there is a valid arbitration agreement, whether the tribunal is properly constituted and what matters have been submitted to arbitration in accordance with the arbitration agreement.

(b) In the event that the tribunal determines it has no jurisdiction, the Association will notify the parties of the tribunal's decision. Such decision shall be final and binding upon the parties subject to any right of appeal to a board of appeal pursuant to Rule 10. The Association will invoice the claimant for any costs, fees and expenses incurred. In the event that the tribunal determines that it has jurisdiction, no appeal shall lie to a board of appeal.

(c) If the board of appeal upholds the tribunal's determination that it has no jurisdiction, the board of appeal shall order accordingly and the Association shall notify the parties and the tribunal and will invoice the appellants for any costs, fees and expenses incurred.

(d) If the board of appeal reverses the tribunal's determination that it has no jurisdiction, the board of appeal shall order accordingly and shall notify the parties, the tribunal and the Association, and shall order that the dispute be referred to arbitration afresh, whereupon:

   (i) The dispute shall be deemed to be one arising out of a contract embodying these Rules.

   (ii) The tribunal formerly appointed shall thereupon cease to act and shall not be re-appointed when the dispute is referred as aforesaid.

   (iii) The provisions of Rule 3 shall apply, the time limits for appointment running from the date of the board of appeal's order.

   (iv) The board of appeal may in its absolute discretion extend the time limits in these Rules, and no objection that time has expired shall be taken if the requirements of Rules were previously complied with.

8.2 *Provisional orders*

Where the tribunal decides at any time to order on a provisional basis any relief which it would have power to grant in a final award, no appeal shall lie to a board of appeal until the tribunal has issued a final award determining the issues between the parties.

8.3 *Awards on different aspects*

Where the tribunal decides during the course of an arbitration to make an award dealing finally with one or more aspects of the dispute, but which leaves to be decided by it other aspect(s) of the dispute, it may make an award which shall be final and binding as to the aspect(s) with which it deals, subject to any right of appeal pursuant to Rule 10.

9. Awards of arbitration

9.1 All awards shall be in writing and shall be signed by the sole arbitrator or, in the case of an award made by a three-man tribunal, by all three arbitrators. The tribunal shall have the power to assess and award the costs of and connected with the reference, including the Association's fees and/or expenses (which shall be those for the time being in force as prescribed by the Council) and also the fees and/or expenses incurred by the tribunal. The tribunal will assess and award costs at the conclusion of the arbitration.

9.2 The tribunal shall, on the application of either party, made before the arbitration award is made, have the power to extend the time for appealing in any case in which it considers it just or necessary so to do. Any such extension must be stated in the award.

9.3 The tribunal shall submit the award to the Association. The Association shall upon receipt of the signed award give notice to the parties named in the award, that the award is at their disposal upon payment of the fees and expenses incurred by the tribunal and the Association. If payment is not received by the Association within 14 days from such notice, the Association may call upon any one or more of the parties to take up the award and in such case the party or parties so called upon shall pay the fees and expenses as directed. Upon receipt of the fees and/or expenses, the Association shall date and issue the award to the parties, which date shall for the purpose of the Arbitration Act 1996 and these Rules be deemed to be the date on which the award was made.

9.4 Subject to any right of appeal pursuant to Rule 10 awards of arbitration shall be conclusive and binding on the parties with respect both to the matters in dispute and as to costs.

9.5 No award shall be questioned or invalidated on the ground that an arbitrator was not qualified to act unless such objection was made at the outset of the arbitration.

10. Right of appeal

10.1 Save as provided in Rules 6.4, 8.1(b), 8.2, 17 and 22, either party may appeal against an award to a board of appeal provided that the following conditions are complied with:

(a) Not later than 12 noon on the 30th consecutive day after the date on which the award was made the appellant shall:
  (i) ensure that a written notice of appeal is received by the Association,
  (ii) serve a notice of his intention to appeal on the other party and ensure receipt of a copy by the Association,
  (iii) and (subject to the provisions of Rule 20) make payment to the Association of the appeal fee stated on the award of arbitration on account of the costs, fees and expenses of the appeal.

(b) The fees and expenses of the arbitration award incurred by the tribunal and/or the Association, shall be paid to the Association before the appeal is heard.

(c) The appellants shall pay such further sum or sums on account of fees, costs and expenses as may be called for by the Association at any time after the lodging of the appeal (as defined in (a) and (b) above) and prior to the publication of the award by the board of appeal. The fees charged by the board of appeal shall be in accordance with the scale of fees laid down by the Council from time to time.

10.2 If appeals are lodged by both parties to the award the Association shall have the power to consolidate such appeals for hearing by the same board of appeal.

10.3 If neither the appeal fee required under Rule 10.1 nor evidence from a bank as required by Rule 20 has been received by the Association within 35 consecutive days of receipt of the notice of appeal, such notice shall be deemed to have been withdrawn and the right of appeal waived unless, prior to the expiry of that period of 35 consecutive days, the appellant has applied to the board of appeal for an extension, in which case the board of appeal may, in its absolute discretion on hearing evidence and/or submissions from each party, grant an extension.

11. Boards of appeal

11.1 Boards of appeal shall be elected and constituted in accordance with the Rules and Regulations of the Association and each board of appeal shall, when so elected, appoint one of its members to be chairman. Where the first tier arbitration award was made by a sole arbitrator the board of appeal will comprise of three Members. Where the first tier award was made by a tribunal of three arbitrators, then the board of appeal shall comprise of five members. The Association will notify the parties of the names of the members of the Board of Appeal.

11.2 If a member of the Board of Appeal dies, refuses to act, resigns, or becomes incapable of acting, or if he fails to proceed with the appeal, or is found to be ineligible, or his authority is revoked by the Association pursuant to the Association's Rules and Regulations, the next member of the Committee of Appeal duly appointed for this purpose shall thereupon become a member of the board of appeal in his place.

12. Appeal procedure

12.1 The parties shall serve their statements of case and documentary evidence in accordance with the following provisions or any other timetable which the board of appeal may order.

(a) The appellant shall draw up a concise statement of his case which, together with any supporting documents, shall be served as set out in Rule 12.2 within 28 consecutive days of lodging its appeal (as defined in Rule 10.1 (a)–(c)).

(b) The respondent shall draw up a concise statement of his case which, together with any supporting documents, shall be served as set out in Rule 12.2 within 28 consecutive days of service of the appellant's documents pursuant to (a) above.

(c) The appellant may serve further submissions or documents in response, such to be served as set out in Rule 12.2 within 14 consecutive days of service of the respondent's documents pursuant to (b) above.

12.2 Statements of case and documentary evidence (which may include new evidence not before the arbitrators) shall be served by sending them to the other party with copies to the Association. Where the appeal is against the award of a sole arbitrator 3 copies, or where the appeal is against the award of a tribunal of three arbitrators 5 copies, shall be sent to the Association. Failure to send all copies to the Association will render the party responsible liable to the Association for the costs of copying such documents for forwarding to the board of appeal.

12.3 The Association will set down the appeal for hearing having due regard to the above timetable, or any other time table which the board of appeal may decide.

12.4 An appeal involves a new hearing of the dispute and the board of appeal may confirm, vary, amend or set-aside the award of the tribunal. In particular (but not by way of restriction), the board of appeal may;

(a) vary an award by increasing or reducing, if the board shall see fit, the liability of either party,
(b) correct any errors in the award or otherwise alter or amend it,
(c) award the payment of interest,
(d) award the payment of costs, fees and expenses of and incidental to the hearing of the arbitration and the appeal; such costs, fees and expenses will normally follow the event.

12.5 An award shall be confirmed unless the board of appeal decide by a majority to vary, amend or set it aside.

12.6 The award of the board of appeal, whether confirming, varying, amending or setting aside the original award of arbitration, shall be signed by the chairman of the board of appeal, and, when so signed, shall be deemed to be the award of the board of appeal, and shall be final, conclusive and binding. Rule 9.3 shall apply to awards of the board of appeal.

12.7 (a) If the appellant, on receiving notice of the date fixed for the hearing of the appeal, requests a postponement of more than 14 days, or at the first or any subsequent hearing of the appeal requests an adjournment, then in such event the board of appeal may in its absolute discretion direct that as a condition of granting an adjournment all or any part of the money required by the terms of the award of arbitration to be paid by either party to the other shall be deposited in such bank and in such currency (either in the United Kingdom or abroad) as the board of appeal may direct. Such money shall be held by such bank in an account in the name of the Association, or on such terms as the board of appeal may direct. The board of appeal shall, where such money has been deposited, direct in its award how and to which of the parties the amount so held shall be paid out.

(b) If the appellant fails to make such payment as aforesaid in accordance with the directions of the board of appeal, and within such time as the board of appeal stipulates, then (subject to the provisions of Rule 20) the appeal shall be deemed to be withdrawn.

(c) If in the opinion of the board of appeal the appellant has been guilty of undue delay in proceeding with his appeal the board of appeal shall give due warning to the appellant that he should proceed with due despatch. If the appellant continues, thereafter, to delay the progress of the appeal, the board of appeal may (after giving both parties a reasonable opportunity to make submissions) order that the appeal is deemed to have been withdrawn, in which event the money on deposit (with interest if any, less any tax deductible) shall immediately become due and payable to the party and/or parties entitled thereto under the terms of the award of arbitration.

12.8 No award of a board of appeal or decision by a board of appeal on any issue or aspect, shall be questioned or invalidated on the ground that any of its members is not qualified to act unless objection is made within a reasonable period of the notification of the members of the board of appeal.

13. Withdrawal of appeals

13.1 The appellant shall have the right, at any time before the board of appeal makes an award, to withdraw his appeal by giving notice of such withdrawal to the Association, and in such case the Association shall forthwith notify all parties to the arbitration that the appeal has been withdrawn. If notice of withdrawal is received by the Association within 10 consecutive days of the date on which the appeal was lodged in accordance with Rule 10.1, half of the fees shall be returned. If notice of withdrawal is received by the Association not later than 48 hours before the time fixed for the hearing of the appeal a quarter of the fees shall be returned. No part of the fees shall be returned following receipt of notice of withdrawal at any later date.

13.2 In the event of withdrawal the respondent shall continue to have the right of appeal against the award to a board of appeal in accordance with the provisions of Rule 10, save that the time limit laid down in Rule 10.1 shall be 12 noon on the 30th consecutive day after the date of service of the Association's notice to that party of the aforesaid withdrawal.

14. Appeals on string contracts—quality and/or condition

14.1 Where a "string" award is made pursuant to Rule 7.1, then, unless it is an award determining a dispute arising out of the "Rye Terms" clause, each party in the string shall be entitled to appeal against that award to a board of appeal, provided that each of the following provisions, in addition to the provisions of Rule 10, are complied with:

(a) If the appellant is an intermediate party he shall state in his notice of appeal whether he is appealing as a buyer or as seller.

(b) If the appellant is the first seller or the last buyer he shall, within the time limits set out in Rule 10.1(a)(ii), serve written notice of his intention to appeal on the party in immediate contractual relationship with him.

(c) If the appellant is an intermediate party and is appealing as buyer or seller he shall, within the time limits set out in Rule 10.l(a)(ii), serve notice of his intention to appeal on both the respondent to the appeal and also his own immediate seller or buyer.

(d) The recipient of a notice served pursuant to the above provisions may, if it wishes to commence appeal proceedings against its own immediate contracting party, pass on a like notice upon the next party in the string. Such notice shall be passed on with due despatch, in which case the time limit in Rule 10 shall be deemed to have been complied with.

14.2 All appeals to which this Rule applies and to all awards made pursuant to this Rule shall be binding on every appellant and respondent. Non-compliance with any provisions of Rule 14.1(d) shall in no way limit or affect the jurisdiction of the board of appeal.

15. Appeal awards

The Association may call upon either of the disputing parties to take up the award of the board of appeal and in such case the party so called upon shall take up the award and pay the fees, costs and expenses of the board of appeal and/or the Association. Upon receipt of the fees, costs and expenses by the Association, the Association shall then date and issue the award to the parties, which date shall, for the purposes of the Arbitration Act 1996, be deemed to be the date upon which the award is made.

16. Legal representation and costs

16.1 The parties may expressly agree that they may engage legal representatives (*i.e.* solicitors, and/or a barrister or other legally qualified advocate) to represent them in the arbitration and/or in any appeal roceedings and to appear on their behalf at any oral hearings.

16.2 Where there is no such agreement between the parties they are nevertheless free to engage legal representatives to represent them in the written proceedings but not to appear on their behalf at oral hearings. The costs of engaging legal representatives in such circumstances shall not be recoverable unless the tribunal considers that such costs were reasonably incurred. This provision shall not apply to single track arbitrations pursuant to Rule 17.

17. "Single track" arbitration

Where both parties agree in writing, they may dispense with the two tier arbitration system provided by these Rules in favour of a single tier arbitration, in which case (a) a tribunal of three arbitrators will be appointed in accordance with Rule 3.2, (b) no appeal shall lie to a board of appeal, and either party may appeal directly to the Court if leave is granted pursuant to section 69 of the Arbitration Act 1996.

18. Tribunal's or board of appeal's own evidence

If at any time prior to the close of the proceedings the tribunal or the board of appeal deem it appropriate, they may take steps to ascertain the facts and the law on their own initiative, provided that they give both parties reasonable opportunity to comment on and/or provide evidence in response.

19. Fees and expenses

Each party engaging in an arbitration or an appeal pursuant to these Rules, whether or not a Member of the Association, is deemed thereby to agree to abide by these Rules and to agree with the Association to be liable to the Association (jointly and severally with the other parties to the arbitration or appeal) for all fees and expenses incurred in connection with the arbitration or appeal or any remissions, which said fees and expenses shall, upon notification by the Association be and become a debt due to the Association.

20. Currency regulations

If an appellant is precluded by currency regulations from paying any money due to be paid by him as required under Rule 10, and notifies the Association in writing (a) in the case of inability to pay the appeal fee when giving notice of appeal, and (b) in the case of inability to pay any further sum directed to be paid under Rules 10 and/or 12, within 9 consecutive days of the money being demanded, accompanied in every case by evidence from a bank that he has already made application for the transfer of the required sum, he shall be entitled to an extension of up to 35 consecutive days from the date when the said payment became due in which to pay such sum.

21. Notices

21.1 *Service on parties*

All notices to be served on the parties pursuant to these Rules shall be served by letter, telex, telegram or by other method of rapid written communication. For the purposes of time limits, the date of despatch shall, unless otherwise stated, be deemed to be the date of service.

Service on the brokers or agents named in the contract shall be deemed proper service under these Rules. So far as concerns such notices, this Rule over-rides any other provisions of the contract.

21.2 *Service on tribunals and appeal boards*

Unless the tribunal or board of appeal otherwise directs, all notices, proceedings and documents to be served on arbitrators and members of a board of appeal pursuant to these Rules shall be served by letter, telex, telegram or other method of rapid written communication on the Secretary of the Association at the Association's Offices. For the purposes of any time limits receipt of such notices by the Association shall be deemed to be the date of service.

21.3 *Computation of time*

Where these Rules require service not later than a specified number of consecutive days after a specified date or occurrence, that specified date or occurrence shall not count as one of the consecutive days.

22. Non-compliance with time limits and rules

If any time limit or provisions imposed by these Rules are not complied with then, subject only to the discretion of the tribunal or board of appeal conferred by this Rule, the claimant's claims and/or appellant's appeal as the case may be, shall be deemed to be waived and absolutely barred, except that:

(a) such matters shall be raised as a defence to the arbitration claim, whereupon the tribunal may in its absolute discretion admit a claim upon such terms as it may think fit, or it may determine that the claim is waived and barred and refuse to admit it. There shall be no appeal to the board of appeal against the decision of the tribunal to exercise its discretion to admit a claim. If a tribunal decides not to admit the claim, then the claimant shall have the right to appeal pursuant to Rule 10, and the board of appeal shall have the power in its absolute discretion to overturn that decision and to admit the claim;

(b) upon appeal if any of the provisions of Rules 10 to 21 have have not been complied with, then the board of appeal may in its absolute discretion extend the time for compliance (notwithstanding that the time may already have expired) or dispense with the necessity for compliance and may proceed to hear and determine the appeal as if each and all of those Rules had been complied with. Any decision made pursuant to this Rule shall be final, conclusive and binding.

23. Defaulters

23.1 In the event of any party to an arbitration or an appeal held under these Rules neglecting or refusing to carry out or abide by a final award of the tribunal or board of appeal made under these Rules, the Council of the Association may post on the Association's Notice Board and/or circulate amongst Members in any way thought fit notification to that effect. The parties to any such arbitration or appeal shall be deemed to have consented to the Council taking such action as aforesaid.

23.2 In the event that parties do not pay the costs, fees or expenses of the arbitration or appeal when called upon to do so by the Association in accordance with these Rules, the Council may post on the Association's Notice Board and/or circulate amongst Members in any way thought fit notification to that effect. The parties to any such arbitration or appeal shall be deemed to have consented to the Council taking such action as aforesaid.

THE GRAIN AND FEED TRADE ASSOCIATION
GAFTA House, 6 Chapel Place, Rivington Street,
London EC2A 3DQ

Appendix 16

INTERNATIONAL BAR ASSOCIATION SUPPLEMENTARY RULES GOVERNING THE PRESENTATION AND RECEPTION OF EVIDENCE IN INTERNATIONAL COMMERCIAL ARBITRATION

(May 28, 1993)

Article 1—Scope of application

1. These are procedural Rules governing the presentation of evidence (''the Rules of Evidence'') intended to supplement any other rules applicable to the arbitration (''the General Rules''). If the parties have so agreed in writing the Rules of Evidence shall govern the arbitration if and so far as they are not in conflict with mandatory applicable provisions of law. The parties may at any time agree in writing to amend, add to or delete any provision contained in the Rules of Evidence.

2. In so far as the Rules of Evidence and the General Rules applicable to the arbitration are silent, the Arbitrator may in his discretion conduct the taking of evidence as he thinks fit.

3. In case of conflict between any provisions of the Rules of Evidence and the General Rules, the Rules of Evidence shall prevail unless the parties shall otherwise agree in writing.

Article 2—Definitions

''*Arbitrator*'' means a single arbitrator, or the panel of arbitrators or a majority of them as the case may be and shall include an umpire;

''*Claimant*'' means the party or parties who commenced the arbitration or made the first claim therein;

''*Defendant*'' means the party or parties against whom the Claimant made his claim and includes a party making a counter-claim;

''*General Rules*'' means the specific rules of Arbitration agreed upon by the parties except in so far as evidence is concerned;

''*Introductory Submissions*'' means any Request for Arbitration or Statement of Claim or similar document produced by the Claimant, any Answer or Statement of Defence or similar document produced by the Defendant and any other or further documents in the nature of pleadings or submissions, however they may be denominated, produced by the parties in accordance with the General Rules, as well as any further submissions which the General Rules may require to be made before the hearings;

''*Production of Documents*'' means the listing of documents relevant to the subject matter of the claims and defences in issue in the possession, custody, or control of a party and the delivery of the List and of copies of such documents to the other parties to the arbitration and to the Arbitrator in accordance with the provisions of these Rules;

"*Witness Statement*" means a written statement complying with the provisions of Article 5(2) below.

Article 3—Introductory Submissions

The Introductory Submissions made by any party shall contain (*inter alia*) the means by which the facts relevant to the dispute are intended to be proved by that party, including, for each of such facts, the names of witnesses and reference to documents.

Article 4—Production of Documents

1. Each party shall make Production of Documents in respect of all documentation on which such party desires to rely.

2. No later than 60 days after delivery of the last Introductory Submission made by the Defendant or by the date agreed between the parties or determined by the Arbitrator, each party shall exchange his List with every other party and deliver his List to the Arbitrator. Unless a document has been so listed it shall not be produced at the hearing without the consent of the Arbitrator. All documents in the List shall be numbered consecutively, and shall be produced in their entirety unless otherwise agreed or ordered. Each party shall provide the Arbitrator with a copy of each document in his List.

3. A party shall at any time be entitled to a copy of any document listed by another party upon offer of payment of the reasonable copying charge. Such document shall be supplied within 15 days of the request.

4. A party may by Notice to Produce a Document request any other party to provide him with any document relevant to the dispute between the parties and not listed, provided such document is identified with reasonable particularity and provided further that it passed to or from such other party from or to a third party who is not a party to the arbitration. If a party refuses to comply with a Notice to Produce a Document he may be ordered to do so by the Arbitrator.

5. The Arbitrator shall have the power, upon application by one of the parties or of his own volition, to order a party to produce any relevant document within such party's possession, custody or control.

6. If a party fails to comply with the Arbitrator's order to produce any relevant document within such party's possession, custody or control, the Arbitrator shall draw his conclusions from such failure.

Article 5—Witnesses

1. Within 60 days of the delivery of the last Introductory Submission made by the Defendant or by the date agreed between the parties or determined by the Arbitrator, all parties shall deliver their Witness Statements to the Arbitrator only.

2. Each Witness Statement shall:

(a) contain the full names and address of the Witness, his relationship to or connection with any of the parties, and a description of his background qualifications, training and experience if these are relevant to the dispute or to the contents of his Statement

(b) contain a full statement of the evidence it is desired by that party to present through the testimony of that Witness;

(c) reflect whether the Witness is a witness of fact or an expert, and whether the Witness is testifying from his own knowledge, observation or experience, or from information and belief, and if the latter, the source of his knowledge, and
(d) be signed by the Witness, and give the date and place of signature.

3. When the Arbitrator has received the Witness Statement(s) of each party he shall simultaneously deliver copies of all the Witness Statement(s) to all the other parties to the arbitration.

4. Within 40 days of the receipt of any Witness Statement from another party a party may submit further or supplementary Witness Statements or Oral Evidence Notices in response to evidence submitted by such other party.

5. Within 20 days of the receipt of any Witness Statement any party may by notice to the Arbitrator and all other parties (an "Oral Evidence Notice") request the right himself to give oral evidence at the hearing or for any of his own witnesses or the witnesses of any other party to give oral evidence at the hearing. An Oral Evidence Notice shall stipulate the issues to which that evidence is to relate.

6. Within 20 days of the receipt of any Oral Evidence Notice all parties shall reply thereto. If a party fails to reply he shall be deemed to have agreed to the request contained in that Oral Evidence Notice. If all parties agree, or are deemed to have agreed, to a particular Oral Evidence Notice, the Witness named therein shall give oral evidence at the hearing in accordance with the Oral Evidence Notice. The Arbitrator may himself order that any witness gives oral evidence.

7. If a party objects to an Oral Evidence Notice he shall state his reasons, and the question whether the Witness shall give oral evidence and, if so, the issues upon which the evidence shall be given, shall be determinated by the Arbitrator in his discretion. The Arbitrator may give his decision on this question on the basis of the documents submitted or after hearing the parties, as he may decide.

8. A Party may be heard in support of his own case. It shall be proper for a Party or his legal advisers to interview witnesses or potential witnesses.

9. Any witness who gives oral evidence shall in the first place be questioned by the Arbitrator. and thereafter submit to examination by the party calling him, cross-examination by all other parties and re-examination by the party calling him.

10. The Arbitrator shall at all times have complete control over the procedure in relation to a witness giving oral evidence, including the right to limit or deny the right of a party to examine, cross-examine or re-examine a Witness when it appears to the Arbitrator that such evidence or examination is unlikely to serve any further relevant purpose.

11. The testimony of any witness not giving oral evidence or of a Witness in respect of any portion of his evidence not subject to oral testimony, shall be taken by means of his Witness Statement only.

12. A party shall be entitled to stipulate the name of a witness in his Oral Evidence Notice even if no Witness Statement has been produced for that Witness, provided that the party states in writing that he has requested the Witness to give a Witness Statement but that the Witness has refused to do so and that the party has no power to compel him to provide such Statement. If the Witness has given the party an informal or partial statement or other document (whether signed or not) the party shall deliver a copy thereof to the Arbitrator and to the other parties at the time he delivers the Oral Evidence Notice relating to that witness.

13. The Arbitrator shall decide what weight to attach to the evidence or Statements of any witness or party.

14. Nothing herein shall preclude the Arbitrator in his discretion from permitting any witness to give oral or written evidence.

Article 6—Scope of proceedings

1. Whenever Terms of Reference or the like are provided for in the General Rules or the parties so agree or the Arbitrator so directs, a list of those witnesses shall be included who will be called to give oral evidence at the hearing and the issues upon which each witness will testify.

2. The Arbitrator may provide for such other matters concerning evidence as he considers advisable with a view to facilitating the conduct of the arbitration.

Article 7—Arbitrator's powers

In addition to the powers available to him under the applicable procedural law and the General Rules under which the arbitration is conducted, the Arbitrator shall have the following powers:

(a) to vary, extend or limit any time-periods provided in the Rules of Evidence, or previously ordered by him;
(b) to order that a witness whose Witness Statement has been delivered be available to be called by any party;
(c) to call witnesses to testify orally or in writing, whether the parties agree thereto or not;
(d) to rule that a witness' evidence be ignored if the witness fails to appear without good cause;
(e) to rely on his own expert knowledge;
(f) to appoint experts to assist him or to give expert evidence or reports in the arbitration;
(g) to regulate the right of the parties to call expert witnesses and to make provisions with regard to their activities and the presentation of their evidence; and
(h) to exercise all the powers he deems necessary to make the arbitration effective and its conduct efficient as regards the taking of evidence.

Appendix 17

CITY DISPUTES PANEL

ARBITRATION RULES

(September 1997)

The City Disputes Panel is a body sponsored by the Corporation of London, Faculty of Advocates, Bank of England, The Securities and Investments Board, Lloyd's of London, Confederation of British Industry, States of Jersey and by a substantial membership of the financial institutions, professional bodies, industrial companies, legal and accounting firms, barristers, solicitors and private individuals.

CDP provides dispute resolution services for the wholesale financial services industry.

CDP arbitration is governed by the Arbitration Act 1996 and the CDP's Arbitration Rules 1997. CDP arbitration is designed to be fast, and cost effective. A CDP tribunal expects swift and positive co-operation from the parties. Tactical manoeuverings are discouraged. CDP arbitration aims to solve conflicts quickly, definitively, justly, fairly and economically.

Further information about CDP can be obtained from the City Disputes Panel, Fifth Floor, 3 London Wall Buildings, London EC2M 5PD.

The aim

1. The aim of every tribunal appointed under these Rules shall be to resolve the dispute fairly, within the shortest time commensurate with the nature of the dispute and the wishes of the parties. To facilitate this aim these Rules (rule 22) empower the parties to request the tribunal to adjourn or stay the proceedings at any time should they wish to consider alternative procedures.

Request for arbitration

2. Where parties to a dispute in the financial services sector (other than a dispute to which rule 3 applies) have agreed that it shall be referred to the City Disputes Panel (''the CDP'') for arbitration any party may request the CDP to appoint a tribunal under this rule. Where it is desired that the dispute shall be determined within a certain period the request shall so state. The requesting party shall confirm that copies of the request have been served on the other parties.

3. Where all the parties to a dispute are agreed that rapid decision is required they may jointly request the CDP to appoint a tribunal, stating that the request is made under this rule and specifying why rapid resolution of the dispute is needed and the date by which a decision is sought.

4. A request under rules 2 or 3 above shall be in writing and shall comprise the names, addresses, telephone and fax numbers of the parties, and brief details of the nature of the dispute and the relief claimed.

Commencement of the arbitration

5. An arbitration shall be deemed to commence on the date when the request for arbitration is received by the CDP.

The arbitral tribunal

6. On receipt of a request for arbitration the CDP will appoint a tribunal from its panel of arbitrators. The tribunal will usually consist of a legally qualified chairman and two experienced financial services practitioners. However, a sole arbitrator may be appointed if the circumstances of the case so warrant.

7. Where the request for arbitration has been made under rule 2, the CDP will appoint a tribunal and notify the parties of its membership within 7 days of the commencement of the arbitration. Where the request has been made under rule 3 the CDP will appoint a tribunal and notify the parties of its membership within the shortest time possible.

Impartiality of arbitrators

8. Before agreeing to be appointed to a tribunal under these Rules each arbitrator shall sign a declaration to the effect that to the best of his knowledge and belief no circumstances exist which might give rise to justified doubts as to his impartiality or independence and if such circumstances arise subsequently the arbitrator concerned shall at once disclose them to the CDP and to the parties.

Completion of the tribunal's appointment

9. As soon as the CDP has received the declarations required by rule 8 it shall send to the parties for signature an agreement to submit their dispute to arbitration and on receipt from the parties of this agreement the CDP will notify them that the tribunal is duly constituted.

Communication

10. The parties shall communicate with the tribunal through the CDP unless the parties, the tribunal and the CDP otherwise agree.

Challenge, revocation or cessation of an arbitrator's authority

11. If, at any time after the tribunal has been duly constituted under rule 9, a party believes that there are justifiable reasons to doubt the impartiality or independence of one or more of its members, or believes that he has some other reasonable ground for objecting to the continued involvement of that member or those members, he shall so inform the CDP within 7 days of becoming aware of such reasons or ground. The member or members thus challenged may thereupon withdraw, and shall do so if another party agrees with the challenge, but if he or they do not the CDP will rule upon the validity of the challenge as soon as possible and in any event within 3 working days. If the CDP accepts the validity of the challenge, the challenged member or members shall withdraw and the CDP will thereupon fill the vacancy or vacancies on the tribunal. Any decision of the CDP under this rule shall be final, subject to rule 12 below.

12. The provisions of rule 11 are subject to any statutory rights a party may have to apply to a court to remove an arbitrator.

13. The CDP shall have power to revoke the authority of an arbitrator and remove and replace him if justifiable doubts arise as to his impartiality, or he becomes physically or mentally incapable of conducting the proceedings or there are justifiable doubts as to his capacity to do so, or if he has refused or failed properly to conduct the proceedings or to use all reasonable despatch in so doing or in making an award. On the death of an arbitrator his authority ceases and the CDP shall thereupon appoint a successor to him.

14. If during the course of the proceedings a member of the tribunal is replaced, no hearing which has already taken place shall be repeated save in so far as the new tribunal considers repetition is necessary.

Jurisdiction of the tribunal

15. The tribunal shall have power to rule on any question regarding its own jurisdiction or the existence or validity of the arbitration agreement, as to whether the tribunal is properly constituted, and as to what matters have been submitted to arbitration in accordance with the agreement. Where the arbitration agreement forms part of a contract it shall be treated as an agreement independent of the contract. A challenge to the tribunal's jurisdiction made at the outset of the proceedings must be raised by a party not later than the time when he takes the first step in the proceedings to contest the merits of the matter in relation to which the challenge arises and a challenge during the proceedings must be made as soon as possible after the matter giving rise to the challenge is raised. The tribunal will rule on the objection in an award as to jurisdiction unless the parties expressly request it to deal with the objection in its award on the merits.

Additional powers of the tribunal

16. In addition to the powers conferred on the tribunal by any other rule, and unless the parties at any time agree otherwise, the tribunal shall have the power to:

(a) order the rectification of any mistake which the tribunal determines to be common to the parties in any contract or arbitration agreement;
(b) give directions to a party for the preservation for the purposes of the proceedings of any evidence in his custody or control;
(c) give directions for the inspection, photographing, preservation, custody or detention by the tribunal, an expert, or a party of any property the subject of the proceedings and which is owned by or in the possession of a party;
(d) direct the parties to provide security for the costs of the arbitration in one or more payments and in such proportions as it deems just. This power shall not be exercised on the ground that the party is ordinarily resident outside the United Kingdom or is a corporation or association incorporated or formed under the law of a country outside the United Kingdom, or whose central management or control is outside the United Kingdom. Any sums provided by way of security shall be deposited with the CDP and may be drawn on by the tribunal as required. Any interest earned on deposits will be added to those deposits;
(e) direct any party to provide security for any other party's costs of the reference, to the extent permitted by the applicable procedural law.

Duty of the tribunal

17. The tribunal shall adopt procedures appropriate to the case and to the aim of achieving the just, speedy, economical and final resolution of the dispute. To that end it shall act fairly and impartially between the parties, giving each party a reasonable opportunity of presenting his case and dealing with that of his opponent including the opportunity if he so desires of an oral hearing for the presentation of evidence and argument.

Procedural freedom of the tribunal

18. Subject to the tribunal's duty under rule 17 the parties may agree on the arbitral procedure or any part thereof. When they do not, the tribunal shall determine all procedural matters in its absolute discretion including in particular the admissibility, relevance, materiality and weight of any evidence. In a three-member tribunal the Chairman alone may give directions and make procedural rulings and orders provided he is authorised to do so by the other members.

Duty of the parties

19. It shall be the duty of the parties to do all things necessary for the proper and expeditious conduct of the proceedings. If a Claimant fails to prosecute his claim within the time laid down by the tribunal without showing sufficient cause for such failure, the tribunal may make an award dismissing the claim. If a party fails to participate in the proceedings at any stage without showing sufficient cause, the tribunal may direct that the proceedings shall continue despite his failure and may make an award on the basis of the evidence before it.

First management meeting

20. This rule shall apply except where the parties have requested rapid decision under rule 3 when rule 21 shall apply. Immediately after the tribunal has been duly constituted each party shall be invited to make written representations regarding appropriate procedures for the future conduct of the arbitration. The tribunal shall then call the parties to a meeting ("the first management meeting") to consider such procedures within 14 days after it has been duly constituted or within such further time as the tribunal shall determine, unless all the parties and the tribunal agree that such a meeting is not required. At this meeting, or following the parties' written representations if no meeting is required, the tribunal may give directions upon the following specific matters and any other matters, including those referred to in rule 22 below, upon which any party may request the tribunal or the tribunal may deem it desirable to give directions:

(a) the manner in which and the times within which the issues in the arbitration shall be defined;
(b) whether a simplified hearing procedure, such as that set out in Appendix 1, should be adopted;
(c) whether, with the agreement of the parties, the dispute should be determined upon the basis of documents only under the procedure set out in Appendix II;
(d) the production of documents;
(e) a timetable.

At the first management meeting the tribunal shall also ask the parties whether they wish to exclude any right of appeal.

First management meeting (rapid decision)

21. Where the parties have requested a rapid decision under rule 3 a first management meeting shall be called immediately after the tribunal has been duly constituted under rule 9 unless all the parties and the tribunal agree that such a meeting is not required. Having considered any representations made by the parties, at the first management meeting or otherwise, the tribunal shall give such directions for the future conduct of the proceedings as may be appropriate to secure the rapid determination of the dispute.

Alternative resolution procedures

22. The tribunal itself will not employ alternative dispute resolution procedures. However, should the parties at any stage of the proceedings wish to consider the possibility of resolving the dispute, or certain issues, by alternative procedures they may request the tribunal to adjourn or stay the proceedings and to give appropriate directions, if required. The tribunal will enquire at the first management meeting and at any subsequent management meeting whether any possibilities exist for the settlement of the dispute, or of some part of it, and whether the parties wish to consider resolving the dispute, or certain issues, by alternative procedures.

Defining the issues

23. Unless the parties agree or the tribunal directs otherwise, the parties shall set out their cases in writing in accordance with (a) to (d) below:

(a) within 14 days of the directions referred to in rule 20 the Claimant shall serve a statement setting out the substance of his case and the contentions of law on which he relies and the damages or other relief he claims.
(b) within 21 days of receipt of the Claimant's statement the Respondent shall serve a statement setting out the substance of his defence and the contentions of law on which he relies by way of defence to the claim and including any counterclaim.
(c) within 21 days of receipt of the statement of the Respondent the Claimant may serve a statement in reply which shall include a defence to counterclaim, if appropriate.
(d) all such statements shall be accompanied by copies of the documents upon which the party relies or, if these are numerous, by copies of the principal documents on which he relies together with a list of his further documents. "Documents" includes transcripts of tapes, disks or computer records and any other record which is capable of being printed out or transcribed.

Further management meetings

24. Whenever subsequently to the first management meeting the tribunal considers it appropriate to do so, the tribunal may invite the parties to make written representations as to the future conduct of the arbitration and the directions to be given and may call a further management meeting to consider such directions.

25. At the further management meeting the tribunal will give directions for the further conduct of the arbitration and will consider among other matters:

(a) whether any matters hitherto at issue may now be agreed;
(b) whether any party should give more details of his case on any issue;

(c) whether there should be discovery of documents either generally or in relation to any issue;
(d) whether there should be a hearing to determine whether any allegation should be struck out as disclosing no reasonable cause of action or defence;
(e) whether any issue should be determined by way of interim award;
(f) whether an expert or adviser should be appointed to investigate and report to the tribunal on any matter or issue of fact or law.

Witnesses

26. The tribunal may require each party to notify the tribunal and the other parties of the identities of all witnesses the party intends to call and may require the parties to exchange signed witnesses' statements and experts' reports before the hearing. A party may request the attendance at the hearing of a witness whose evidence has been submitted in written form and any witness who gives oral evidence may be questioned by or on behalf of the party which calls him and any other party. The testimony of witnesses may be presented in affidavit form, with the leave of the tribunal. Unless the parties agree the contrary, evidence shall not be on oath.

Experts appointed by the tribunal

27. The tribunal may appoint an expert or experts to report to it on specific issues. The parties shall give such expert any relevant information, document or thing he may require of them. The tribunal shall provide the parties with a copy of any expert's report and of any document referred to therein and shall give the parties an opportunity to comment upon such report and to question the expert thereon.

Hearings

28. The tribunal shall fix the date, time and place of any meeting or hearing, of which the parties will be given reasonable notice.

29. Hearings shall take place in London or Edinburgh as appropriate unless the parties, with the leave of the tribunal, or the tribunal, choose otherwise. All the parties and their representatives shall be entitled to be present throughout but, save with the consent of the tribunal and the parties, persons not involved in the proceedings shall not be admitted. The proceedings and any award shall remain confidential unless the tribunal, with the consent of the parties, directs otherwise or disclosure is required by law, by a court of competent jurisdiction or by any governmental agency or regulatory authority to which a party making disclosure is subject.

30. Any party may be legally represented or may, with the leave of the tribunal, appear by some other representative.

The award

31. Unless the parties expressly agree otherwise the tribunal shall make any award in writing and shall state the reasons upon which it is based.

32. Any award or other decision of a tribunal of three may be made by a majority of the members of the tribunal and failing a majority decision on any issue the chairman of the tribunal shall make the award alone, as if he were the sole arbitrator.

33. If any member of the tribunal should fail to join in the making of an award, having been given a reasonable opportunity to do so, the remaining member or members of the tribunal may proceed in his absence.

34. The award shall be made on the date when the CDP sends it to the parties.

35. If at any time the parties settle their differences it shall be their joint and several duty to inform the tribunal immediately in writing. The tribunal shall thereupon be discharged and the reference to arbitration concluded, subject to the payment by the parties of any outstanding fees and costs. However, the tribunal will render an award recording the settlement if requested by any party to do so.

36. The tribunal may add to, vary or amend an award to correct any clerical or arithmetical mistake or error arising from any accidental slip or omission. The tribunal may also add to, vary or amend an award to clarify any aspect of the award or to remove any ambiguity in its wording, provided the parties have been given an opportunity to make representations regarding the proposed addition, variation or amendment and all parties have assented thereto.

37. The tribunal shall decide all matters according to law, unless expressly authorised in writing by the parties to decide in accordance with such other considerations as are agreed by the parties or determined by the tribunal.

Remedies

38. Unless the parties expressly agree otherwise the tribunal may:

(a) make a declaration as to any matter to be determined in the proceedings;
(b) order the payment of a sum of money in any currency;
(c) to the extent permitted by the applicable procedural law, (i) order a party to do or refrain from doing anything, (ii) order specific performance of a contract, (iii) order the rectification, setting aside or cancellation of a deed or other document.

Interest

39. Unless the parties expressly agree otherwise the tribunal may award simple or compound interest from such dates at such rates and with such rests as it considers appropriate:

(a) on the whole or part of any amount awarded by the tribunal, in respect of any period up to the date of the award;
(b) on the whole or part of any amount claimed in the arbitration and outstanding at the commencement of the proceedings but paid before the award was made, in respect of any period up to the date of payment;
(c) from the date of the award until payment on the outstanding amount of any award, including any award of interest under (a) or (b) above and any award as to costs.

Costs

40. The tribunal will specify in its award the costs of the arbitration which shall include the fees and expenses of the tribunal and of any experts employed by the tribunal under rule 27 and the registration fees of the CDP.

41. The tribunal will direct in its award whether a party shall pay the whole or any part of another party's costs, which may include legal fees and disbursements, experts' fees and disbursements and witnesses' expenses and the tribunal shall determine the amount of the recoverable costs if these are not agreed, unless the parties are agreed that the costs shall be determined in some other way.

42. If the arbitration is abandoned, suspended or concluded by agreement or otherwise before an award is made, the parties shall be jointly and severally liable for all the costs of the arbitration as determined by the tribunal.

Exclusion of liability

43. Neither the CDP nor any arbitrator shall be liable for anything done or omitted in purported discharge of its or his functions unless the act or omission is shown to have been in bad faith.

Scotland

44. Where the place of arbitration is in Scotland:

(a) the tribunal may, unless the parties expressly agree otherwise, make an award in respect of delictual damages, if appropriate, and may award interest in respect of the whole or any part of any award for such period prior to the date of the award as it considers just;
(b) the parties will not, unless they expressly agree otherwise, apply at any stage to the tribunal to state a case for the opinion of the Court of Session.

Appendix I

The simplified hearing procedure

1. Where the tribunal has directed that the simplified hearing procedure shall be followed:

(a) the Claimant shall, within such period as the tribunal may direct, formulate his case in writing in sufficient detail to identify the matters in dispute and serve it together with copies of any documents on which he relies upon the Respondent and the members of the tribunal;
(b) the Respondent shall, within such period as the tribunal may direct, formulate his defence, and counterclaim if any, in sufficient detail to identify which matters if any in the Claimant's case he accepts and which matters he denies and shall serve it together with copies of any documents on which he relies upon the Respondent and the members of the tribunal; and
(c) the tribunal shall give directions as to service of a reply to any counterclaim under paragraph 2 below.

2. If any party requires further directions he shall specify his requirements in writing to the tribunal within 7 days of the date for service of the Respondent's defence and after this 7 day period has elapsed the tribunal shall give directions either in writing or at an oral hearing as to the future conduct of the arbitration or, if no further directions are required, shall so state.

3. Subject to any directions given under paragraph 2, the tribunal shall, within 21 days of service by the Respondent of his defence, proceed to a hearing of the dispute at which no evidence shall be adduced save for the documents appended to the statements of case and defence, except as the tribunal may otherwise direct or permit.

4. The tribunal shall publish its award within 7 days of the hearing.

Appendix II

Decision without a hearing

1. Where parties agree that their dispute shall be decided on the basis of documents only the issues shall be defined in accordance with rule 23, unless the parties agree that they shall be defined in accordance with a different procedure or in some other way.

2. The tribunal will thereafter hold a management meeting, unless the parties and the tribunal agree that such a meeting is not required, and will give such directions as may be required, including:

(a) directions as to any submissions as to fact and law which the parties may wish to make before the tribunal proceeds to its award;
(b) the time within which such submissions are to be made; and
(c) the time after the expiry of which the tribunal may make its award.

Appendix 18

THE CHARTERED INSTITUTE OF ARBITRATORS CONSUMER ARBITRATION SCHEME FOR FIMBRA RULES

(1992 edition—amended)

These Rules will apply to arbitrations commenced under the Scheme on and after March 23, 1992.

Introduction

1. These Rules apply to arbitration in respect of disputes between a member or a former member of the Financial Intermediates, Managers and Brokers Regulatory Association (FIMBRA) and a private client (as defined in the FIMBRA Rules) arising out of or in connection with any investment business with which FIMBRA is concerned. For the purposes of these Rules, "member" shall include a former member.

2. A dispute may be referred to arbitration by the client under this Scheme if:

(i) Neither the client's claim against the member nor any counterclaim by the member (which must be directly related to the circumstances of the claim) exceed £50,000; and

(ii) The dispute arises from an event which occurred:

(a) On or after 29 April 1988; and

(b) After the member became a member of FIMBRA or became interim authorised under Schedule 15 of the Financial Services Act 1986 pending membership of FIMBRA; and

(c) Prior to the cessation of membership of a former member. In such a case, the client must have notified his complaint to FIMBRA within 12 months of the cessation of membership; and

(iii) The dispute has been the subject of attempts at conciliation undertaken by FIMBRA's Complaints Department which has certified that, following attempted conciliation, the dispute has not been resolved; and

(iv) The client applies for arbitration before the expiry of three years from the date on which he knew or ought reasonably to have known of the event giving rise to the claim. An Arbitrator under the Scheme may at his discretion disapply this limitation period by reason of exceptional circumstances.

2A. A dispute, which is otherwise referable to arbitration by the client under this Scheme, may not be so referred where:

(i) FIMBRA certifies that it falls within the jurisdiction of the Personal Investment Authority Ombudsman or the dispute resolution scheme of another recognised self-regulating organisation or recognised body, or
(ii) Investors Compensation Scheme Ltd has notified the Chartered Institute of Arbitrators (''the Institute'') in writing that it has determined the FIMBRA member or former member who is a party to the dispute to be in default under Rule 2.01.1 of the Financial Services (Compensation of Investors) Rules 1994 or any Rule amending or replacing it.

3. In Rule 2(ii) above, ''event'' shall mean the alleged breach by a FIMBRA member of any duty arising out of one or more of the following:

(i) A client agreement, including a terms of business letter;
(ii) The FIMBRA Rules;
(iii) Ther Financial Services Act 1986 as amended and any delegated legislation made under that Act;
(iv) Any rule of law.

4. The resolution of disputes by an Arbitrator under this Scheme shall be entirely in accordance with the applicable law.

Institution of arbitration proceedings

5. A joint application for arbitration must be made to the Institute on the prescribed application form, signed by both parties and by an authorised officer of FIMBRA. By signing the application form, FIMBRA becomes a party to the arbitration for the purposes of Rules 13 and 15 below and certifies that, following attempted conciliation, the dispute has not been resolved.

6. A FIMBRA member is required by the FIMBRA Rules to join in any application for arbitration. For the avoidance of doubt, an application for arbitration which has not been signed by a FIMBRA member will be accepted as valid if signed by the Claimant and by an authorised officer of FIMBRA, provided that FIMBRA shall certify to the Institute that the FIMBRA member has been given adequate opportunity to sign the form.

7. The arbitration commences for the purposes of these Rules when the Institute notifies the parties in writing of acceptance of the application. The notice sent to the party making the claim will be accompanied by a claim form.

Procedure

8. *General*

The Institute will appoint a sole Arbitrator to decide the dispute and will notify the parties of the appointment. Subject to any directions issued by the Arbitrator and to the provisions of Rule 8(v) and 9(iv)–(vi) below, the arbitration will be on documents only and the procedure will be as follows:

(i) The client making the claim (the "Claimant") is required within 28 days of receipt of the claim form, to send the completed form together with the supporting documents, in duplicate, to the Institute.

(ii) The Claimant may not, without the consent of the Arbitrator, claim an amount greater than that specified on the application for arbitration;

(iii) A copy of the claim documents be sent by the Institute to the FIMBRA member (the "Respondent") which is required within 28 days of receipt of the documents, to send to the Institute its written defence to the claim together with any supporting documents in duplicate. The Respondent may include with the defence a counterclaim which is directly related to the circumstances of the claim.

(iv) A copy of the defence documents will be sent by the Institute to the Claimant, who is entitled to send to the Institute any written comments which he wishes to make on them, together with a defence to any counterclaim, within 14 days of their receipt. Such comments should be in duplicate and should address only points arising from the defence and/or counterclaim. The Claimant may not introduce any new matters or points of claim.

(v) An oral hearing may be held, at the discretion of the Arbitrator, if any party requests it or if the Arbitrator considers the issues cannot be determined on the basis of documents only. The procedure for any hearing, which will be at the discretion of the Arbitrator, shall permit the full presentation of the evidence and arguments of the parties. The Arbitrator shall not permit legal representation except where he considers it just and expeditious to do so.

(vi) The strict rules of evidence will not apply to any arbitration conducted under this Scheme.

(vii) In making the award, the Arbitrator shall state the reasons on which it is based.

(viii) The Institute will publish the award by sending copies to each of the parties. (A copy will also be sent to FIMBRA.)

(ix) Unless directed otherwise in the award, within 21 days of despatch to the parties of the copy award, payment shall be made of any monies directed by the award to be paid. Such payment shall be made by the party liable direct to the party entitled, and not through the Institute, the Arbitrator or FIMBRA. (Enforcement of the award is the responsibility of the parties and the Institute is unable to assist.)

(x) If either party has sent original documents in support of its case to the Institute, that party may, within six weeks of publication of the award, request the return of those documents. Subject to that, case papers will be retained by the Institute and may in due course be disposed of.

8A. Notwithstanding Rule 8(ix) above, where, in a claim for compensation arising out of or in connection with investment business relating to pension transfers, opt-out and non-joiners within the scope of any Direction issued under FIMBRA Rule 7.1A, the Arbitrator makes an award in favour of a Claimant the following directions may be made with the consent of the Claimant:

(i) payment of an appropriate sum to the trustee of the occupational scheme as the agreed consideration for the reinstatement of the Claimant in such scheme, or

(ii) if reinstatement is refused or offered on unreasonable terms, payment of an appropriate sum to the provider if the relevant personal pension policy or s.32

policy or the trustees of such policies (as the case may be) for the purpose only of augmenting the benefits of such policies by way of redress, or

(iii) such other relief in the form or forms of redress set out in the Personal Investment Authority's Guidance for Review of Past Business in respect of Pension Transfers, Opt-out and Non Joiners (1995) and any further related guidance issued by the Personal Investment Authority.

9. *Supplementary*

(i) The Arbitrator may at any time make such orders and directions as are necessary for the just and expeditious determination of the reference including (but not limited to) orders for the production to him of any relevant documents within the possession or control of the parties. The parties to the dispute shall be given an opportunity to inspect, if required, and to comment on any document so produced. If any order and direction is not complied with in the time prescribed the Arbitrator may proceed with the reference on the evidence already before him and may draw his own conclusions in addition to inviting the other party to submit oral or other evidence.

(ii) Where the Arbitrator is of the opinion that expert evidence or further expert evidence is required, he may call for such evidence as he thinks necessary to the determination of the dispute. The parties will be given an opportunity to comment on this evidence.

(iii) If the Claimant does not submit his claim within the time allowed and fails to do so within 14 days of a reminder by the Institute, he will be treated as having abandoned his claim.

(iv) If the Respondent does not submit its defence within the time allowed and fails to do so within 14 days of a reminder by the Institute, the Arbitrator may decide the dispute by reference to the documents submitted by the Claimant, unless he directs otherwise.

(v) The Arbitrator shall have power, at his discretion, to strike out all or part of any claim, defence, counterclaim or comments made in the proceedings on any one or more of the following grounds:

(a) Wilful breach of these Rules;
(b) Deliberate non-compliance by a party with any directions of the Arbitrator;
(c) Inordinate and/or inexcusable delay on the part of any party;
(d) That the claim, defence, counterclaim or comments are scandalous, frivolous or vexatious.

The Arbitrator may make a striking out order under grounds (a)–(c) above only if he is of the opinion that there is a probable risk that a fair determination of the dispute will not be possible.

(vi) If in the Arbitrator's opinion (which shall be final), the dispute is not capable of proper resolution under this Scheme, he shall so advise the parties, through the Institute.

Interim awards

10. (i) Where FIMBRA certifies that the dispute arises out of or in connection with an Equity Home Income Scheme as defined by FIMBRA Guidance Note dated

October 1991 the Arbitrator shall make an interim award as to liability to compensate only and, if in favour of the Claimant, defer the making of any final award until provided with any evidence of relevant awards or decisions, if any, by other regulatory bodies or persons in possible mitigation of damage. The Arbitrator, upon making such interim award, shall communicate the terms of the award to FIMBRA for consideration by other regulatory bodies or persons having responsibility for compensation of investors.

(ii) Where at any time in the course of any arbitration proceedings before the making of a final award Investors Compensation Scheme Ltd has given written notice to the Institute that it has determined the Respondent to be "in default" under Rule 2.01.1 of the Financial Services (Compensation of Investors) Rules 1994 or any Rule amending or replacing it, the Arbitrator shall be so informed by the Institute forthwith. The Arbitrator shall thereafter make an award as to liability to compensate only.

Confidentiality and disclosure of information

11. (i) Confidential information which becomes available in the course of the arbitration may not, subject to (ii) below, be disclosed by either the Arbitrator or any party to other persons except by the agreement of the Arbitrator and the parties.

(ii) Not withstanding (i) above the Arbitrator may disclose such confidential information to a regulatory or prosecuting authority or to the police where he has reason to believe that:

(a) A serious crime may be involved; or

(b) A serious breach of the FIMBRA Rules has been committed; or

(c) He is under a legal duty to disclose the information and the disclosure is made in good faith to the appropriate authority.

(iii) The Arbitrator shall be entitled to disclose any information which becomes available in the course of the arbitration to any regulatory body or to persons having responsibility for compensation of investors.

Costs

12. Subject to Rules 13 and 15 below, the Arbitrator's fees and expenses, the Institute's administration costs and the costs of an expert appointed by the Arbitrator under Rule 9(ii) above shall be paid by FIMBRA.

13. The Arbitrator may, at his discretion, order the payment by the Respondent to FIMBRA in any case of any costs payable under Rule 12 above, up to a limit of £1,000.

14. Subject to Rule 15 below, neither party may recover its costs (including legal costs) from the other party.

15. Where the Arbitrator is satisfied that any claim, defence or comments are scandalous frivolous or vexatious, he may award part of any of the costs set out in Rules 12 and/or 14 above against the party he considers to be at fault and in favour of the other party or FIMBRA as the case may be. If the party at fault is a private Claimant, any such award of costs shall be limited to £1,000.

Miscellaneous

16. The law applicable to the dispute and to any arbitration under this Scheme shall (unless the Arbitrator directs otherwise) be the law of England and Wales, unless the Arbitrator directs that the applicable law shall be that of Scotland or Northern Ireland.

17. The Institute reserves the right to appoint a substitute Arbitrator if the Arbitrator originally appointed dies, is incapacitated or, having accepted the appointment, subsequently finds that he is for any reason unable to deal expeditiously with the dispute. The parties shall be notified of any substitution.

18. Awards made under the Scheme are final and binding on the parties. Subject to the right of a party to request the Institute to draw the Arbitrator's attention to any accidental slip or omission which he has power by law to correct neither the Institute nor the Arbitrator can enter into correspondence regarding awards made under the Scheme.

19. The parties may make an application or appeal to the Courts under the relevant Arbitration Acts, but:

(i) The special costs provisions of Rules 12 and 14 shall not appear to any such application or appeal;

(ii) The party making any such application or appeal (other than an application for leave to enforce the award) will bear its own and the other party's costs (including the costs of any resumed or fresh arbitration resulting from such proceeds) irrespective of the outcome of such proceedings, unless otherwise directed by the court.

20. Neither the Institute nor the Arbitrator shall be liable to any party for any act or omission in connection with any arbitration conducted under these Rules, save that the Arbitrator (but not the Institute) shall be liable for any act or omission of the Arbitrator which is shown to have been in bad faith.

The Chartered Institute of Arbitrators
24 Angel Gate,
City Road,
London EC1V 2RS
Tel: 0171-837 4483
Fax: 0171-837 4185

Appendix 19

CHESS CLOCK ARBITRATIONS

CHESS CLOCK ARBITRATIONS

These are so called because each party is allocated a specific amount of time for its activities: and the time taken for any particular activity is deducted from the allocation. Theoretically a party can run out of time before its opponent and thus be left helpless to intervene while the opponent continues on. However, despite extensive experience of the procedure, none of the authors has seen this happen, although it has come close.

The Tribunal must always retain the power to revise the timings, even after they have started to run. However, this is difficult to do without creating actual unfairness or at least an appearance of unfairness. Therefore revision should only be entertained for some very good reason, such as a quite unforeseeable turn of events in the hearing.

The form of the chess clock agreement can be as complicated or as simple as the parties wish. At one end is a simple agreement to split the hearing time equally between the parties. At the other is the complicated procedure set out below. In between there is an infinite number of possibilities.

This commentary will focus on the complicated procedure, since the discussion of these extensive provisions will throw up most of the points that are likely to occur in a less complicated arrangement.

The earlier the issues in the case can be identified and a draft bundle of working documents assembled, the better this type of arbitration works.

It is necessary to begin with some important points that apply to all forms of limited time arbitration and particularly hearings.

1. The primary benefits

1.1 It enables parties to estimate the extent and timing of their liability for costs with greater accuracy than is normally the case.

1.2 Likewise for the Tribunal who may be prepared to quote a lump sum payable in stages.

1.3 It avoids the (potentially very serious) diary problem, generated by over-runs of hearings.

1.4 It provides a date at which an award can confidently be expected and permits a commercial organization to plan its affairs appropriately.

2. Tribunal responsibilities

It is essential that the Tribunal understands that a limited time hearing places very great strain on the advocates presenting the case. The Tribunal must conduct itself in such a way as to mitigate rather than enhance that strain.

The Tribunal must be aware that even not very bright witnesses quickly realise that a long answer puts more pressure on the questioner than a short answer. Accordingly the Tribunal should make clear early on and repeat if necessary the warning that gratuitously long answers may damage credibility. The Tribunal must be prepared to intervene if even this does not work.

3. Recording the time

In the case of a hearing that lasts longer than a day the time taken up during a day must be agreed at the end of the day and any dispute ruled on immediately. Each morning the parties should be told by the Tribunal the amount of time each one has left. To facilitate this exercise a particular individual on each side should be invested with the responsibility for noting the time taken and for agreeing it at the end of the day.

When there is to be a timed hearing the sitting hours and break timing must be spelt out and adhered to. Interlocutory disputes should be dealt with outside the appointed sitting hours.

A division of the time available to the parties, leaving them to decide how to use it is, perhaps, fairer than rather arbitrary decisions as to how long one can cross-examine for—*e.g.* the hour and a half for factual witnesses and the day for expert witnesses quoted elsewhere in the text.

4. The directions

4.1 These directions focus on a case with (by most standards) a very long hearing. However, in principle they work equally well for four days or 40: and indeed a very modified form would work for four hours.

They also start after the statement of case. Many such directions apply only to the hearing or hearings. On the other hand, a complete set of directions would include the statement of case and defence and would deal with other matters such as meetings of expert witnesses.

The original drafting work which led to these directions was done for a 90-day hearing in London in 1987. Those involved were Simon Tuckey, Q.C. (now Mr Justice Tuckey), then instructed by Mr Park of Linklater & Paines, Fred Bennett and Dan Kolkey, both of Gibson Dunn and Crutcher in Los Angeles, and one of the authors.

5. Draft order of directions

Recitals

Whereas

5.1 *40 working days commencing on [date] have been appointed for the hearing of this matter*

40 days is a very long time, and many jurisdictions would be horrified by the prospect of such a long hearing. However, as noted above, the directions work as well with a short hearing: and the longer the hearing the more important it is have the control given by this type of direction.

5.2 *A period of 40 working days is a reasonable period to dispose of such elements of the claim as justify debate at a full oral hearing*

This recital is useful if, in the relevant jurisdiction, there is any doubt about the power of the arbitrator to impose this kind of timescale. It is also useful to discourage later back sliding.

In a long hearing a key aim is to prevent the re-invention of the case of one side the other as matters continue. This can easily happen if one has a lot of good minds inadequately stretched by the proceedings. The re-invention leads to an application to amend. This is justified by the argument that it all sounds in costs and should therefore be allowed. The argument is flawed. It does not all sound in costs if the result is an award on a basis never floated before the hearing. Management time and resources for a company and the strain on an individual are not recoverable from a taxing master. Even more so do costs fail to meet the situation if the result of the amendment/s is to force the parties into a further hearing. In a controlled time hearing there is little room for the traditional approach of Anglo-Saxon jurisdictions to amendment of cases.

5.3 *In order that the hearing may be effective to dispose of all issues save those as to costs it is necessary to allocate the time available to the parties in a fair and equitable manner*

5.4 *It is also necessary to make ancillary arrangements to ensure that all matters in dispute can properly be dealt with*

These two recitals state the obvious but there is no harm in that.

5.5 *The following directions are made in order to achieve the above aims*

NOW I [JOHN ANTONY TACKABERRY] the duly appointed arbitrator in this matter, in the exercise of all relevant powers which I may have whether by operation of law or the agreement of the parties hereto, do DIRECT as follows:

Pre-hearing

5.6 *Each party shall deliver to the other party and to each member of the Tribunal the written proof of any witness which it may wish to call*

This direction deals with all witnesses—factual and expert.

Very often separate directions are used for the two different types of witness. In that event, the arbitrator should consider, by reference to the formulated cases, whether the expert or the factual evidence is likely to be the more important; and whether the expert evidence is likely to be affected by the factual evidence. If the expert evidence is both more important than and largely independent of the factual evidence, the exchange of that evidence should come first. If the expert evidence may be affected appreciably by the factual evidence, then the latter should come first and sufficiently in front of the expert evidence to afford the experts a good opportunity to consider it before finalizing their evidence. In many other cases the direction above does nicely. See below for experts' meetings.

5.7 *Such delivery shall be effected by or before 1600 hours on [date]*

It is sensible to have a specific time. It is important to have a specific time if the parties are in different time zones. In that event the direction could add "local time at point of delivery'' or ''local time at seat of arbitration'' or ''local time at [*Chairman*]'s office at . . .''.

5.8 *Such proofs shall not exceed a total of [100,000] words in length*

There is no harm in restricting proofs to a set maximum. It is also worth asking for an index or other guide to long proofs.

The Tribunal should also consider whether documents may or must or must not be annexed to the proof. The suggested course is to get all documents relied upon into or referred to in the initial case formulation. This should reduce the number of new documents appearing at this stage. However more documents are likely to be identified as matters progress. Therefore give liberty to apply for the addition of the new ones.

As noted above, the formulation of a draft bundle a.s.a.p. is important for the smooth running of the arbitration.

5.9 *The delivery of a proof shall not oblige a party to call the witness who made it*

The direction is a straightforward one. What is more difficult to resolve, and has to be resolved straight away, is the status of the proofs prior to the calling of the witnesses. Court systems that call for delivery of proofs prior to calling the witnesses usually regard the proof as privileged until the witness is called. Thus the proof of a witness who is not called is always privileged whatever it says. This is therefore a respectable route that a Tribunal can take. However it can seem very artificial: and it is equally possible to say that the proof once served is to be treated as an open document, to which reference can be made by either party at any time.

It is suggested that this latter course is the more practical and down to earth which is what arbitration should be. It also forces parties to consider carefully what they put in their proofs. Also the less discovery the Tribunal orders, the more it ought to ensure that the parties are committed to their position in the documents that they do produce before the hearing.

A necessary concomitant of this approach is the outlawing of oral evidence in chief. If, on seeing the other side's evidence, or for some other good reason, a party decides it needs more evidence in chief, it should have to apply for leave to introduce it, in writing, at least a set time before the beginning of the hearing.

5.10 *If a party decides not to call as a witness any person whose proof has been delivered that party shall forthwith notify the other party of that decision*

Otherwise the opposing party, who may be relying on potential cross-examination of the particular witness, may be taken by surprise. However, the direction is difficult to police. How will you *know* that the notification is indeed at time of decision? In any case, a formal decision can be put off even though the likely course of conduct is well established. Of course a Tribunal can usually rely on the integrity of the advocates.

There is also the *subpoena* route if the liberty given by the direction is used and a party is genuinely taken by surprise. Likewise there is the possibility of evidence on commission.

An alternative direction would be to direct that any witness whose statement is served shall be tendered for cross-examination, if not being otherwise formally called.

5.11 *Each party shall list the documents upon which it proposes to rely or to which it proposes to refer. A copy of such list shall be served upon the other party and upon me by or before 1600 hours on the [date]*

These directions do not deal with the initial formulation of the case by either or both sides.

This direction does not involve discovery Anglo-Saxon style. The Tribunal must consider the question of documentation very carefully indeed if the case is paper-heavy. This direction is the least burdensome variant that can properly be formulated. It probably does not go far enough: and it is suggested that the parties should be at liberty to call for specific documents for whose existence a reasonable case can be made out.

If such documents are called for and not produced, the Tribunal should consider carefully whether it goes down the "peremptory order" route. It may well be preferable simply to draw the most damaging inferences from the non production rather than have a head-on collision with a party about papers that may well be seen as very confidential—*e.g.* internal management records, profit details, techniques and methods of work or production, etc.

Once documents have been identified and produced, the sooner there is a draft bundle in existence the better. There should be an agreed bundle: and the parties must agree on the method by which it is to be presented to the Tribunal. The Tribunal should insist on this being addressed at an early stage, otherwise there is the small but real danger of each side constructing its bundle differently—*e.g.* one chronologically and one by topic. This makes the conduct of any hearing very tiresome.

5.12 *The hearing will commence upon* [date] *and shall continue for 40 working days thereafter. The sitting hours shall be 10.00 to 17.00 each day [with one hour for lunch and a morning and afternoon break of 15 minutes each]*

It is very important that the precise timing upon which the hearing has been planned is very clearly spelt out. Otherwise the parties will not be too clear as to what exactly is available to them. This is made worse if the Tribunal is relaxed about running into the lunch hour, or sitting late to finish a piece of evidence, or sitting early to accommodate someone's schedule. If the basic structure is uncertain such anomalies will provide a fruitful source of friction.

It is also important not to have too long a sitting day. Limited time hearings put a great strain on the presenting advocate: and he must have adequate time out of the hearing to rest, to prepare, to consult, to discuss. The continental habit of sitting hours such as 8 a.m. to 6 p.m. or even to 8 p.m. only works in the context of one or two day hearings.

5.13 *Time during the hearing shall be allotted as follows*

(a) The Claimant shall have a total of 8 working days for its opening and closing speeches, to be allocated as the Claimant sees fit.
(b) The Respondent shall have a total of 6 days for any opening statement it may wish to make and for its closing speech.

This was an old style hearing. Such "speeches" would now usually be in writing before/after the hearing as appropriate. The Tribunal should consider the order of delivery of such written openings and closings. Should they be consecutive or simultaneous? There is a good deal to be said for simultaneous: but if this route is adopted, each party should have a short opportunity for a brief written response to the other side's principal submission/s.

5.14 *The oral evidence time shall be divided into two equal halves—the first half for the presentation of the Claimant's evidence and the second half for the presentation of the Respondent's evidence*

5.15 *Within each such half, and subject to direction 16 below, each party shall have a maximum time of 13 days or [ ] working hours available for:*

(a) its evidence in chief and re-examination
and
(b) its cross-examination.

Again—an old style direction. Nowadays one would hope not to have any evidence in chief.

5.16 *Each party may deploy each said [ ] hours available to it as it sees fit*
This direction is the simplest one: and Directions 5.17 to 5.21 inclusive can be ignored. However, if the Tribunal or parties desire to have a tight control on all stages of the exercise the following directions can be considered.

5.17 *In the event that presentation of the Claimant's evidence takes less than half the witness time to complete, then the shortfall can be calculated*

5.18 *That shortfall shall be added to the time which would otherwise have been available to the Claimant during the presentation of the Respondent's evidence*

5.19 *In the event that during the presentation of the Respondent's evidence either party takes less than the total time which would in the event have been available to it (i.e. including any shortfall as provided for at Directions 5.17 and 5.18 above) then the saving by that party shall be added to the time available to that party for its closing speech.*

5.20 *In the administration and calculation of the matters herein before provided for at Directions 5.16–5.18 inclusive, time re-allocated from closing speeches (as hereinafter provided for) shall be wholly ignored.*

5.21 *Either party may utilise the time hereinbefore provided for its speech or speeches to supplement the time otherwise available to it (pursuant to Directions 5.13 to 5.19 inclusive above) during the oral evidence stage. Such utilisation may be effected only after the time otherwise available to that party pursuant to the said Directions has been wholly used up.*
See above, the comment in Direction 5.13.

Written submissions supplementing or in substitution for closing speeches

5.22 *Such written submissions may or shall be utilised (as the case may be) subject to the following Direction.*

5.23 *Either party may deliver a submission in writing in substitution for or supplementing its closing speech. No such submission shall exceed 75,000 words in length. Such delivery shall be to me and to the other party and shall be by or before [16.45] hours on [date]*

No particular comment is necessary. Most such directions have no limit or length. Note the point above in the comment on Direction about simultaneous or consecutive addresses.

Matters ancilllary to the hearing

5.24 *Time taken during the working day, regarding procedural matters (which in any event are to be kept to a minimum and dealt with as far as possible outside the working day) and time taken in the questioning (if any) of witnesses by me at the end of the witnesses' testimony are to be allocated equally between the parties. Time taken in the questioning of witnesses by me during their testimony is to be treated as time taken by the party who was questioning the witness immediately prior to my question/s*

There are very few interlocutory matters indeed which HAVE to be dealt with the moment they arise. Nearly all of them can be adjourned until the normal working day hours have expired. What is more advocates should be strongly discouraged from interrupting each other more often than is absolutely essential. If admissibility of evidence is the problem, admit the material *de bene esse* and press on.

Another advantage of taking interlocutory disputes after the main work of the day is over is that, usually, few people will want to make a meal of the matter. Nonetheless it is wise to limit argument to an hour at maximum.

A rather different rule is necessary if the questioning is done by the Tribunal. In such a case it should allocate itself a specific time per witness or per side AND KEEP TO IT.

If the main questioning is done by the parties, the Tribunal should leave its questions right to the end of the re-examination, if there is such a stage; and should afford both sides the opportunity to follow up (but *only* to follow up) the Tribunal's question.

5.25 *A record of time taken by each party shall be kept and agreed at the end of each day. A note of such agreements is to be supplied to me from time to time*

Ensuring this is done each day is critical to the success of the exercise.

5.26 *Failure formally to challenge any evidence shall not be regarded as acceptance of that evidence*

If there is one direction that is essential to a chess-clock hearing it is this one. However it is only necessary at all where the procedural law treats as accepted any evidence that is not specifically challenged.

Such is the rule in England. In commercial matters, particularly paper-heavy matters, it is almost certainly otiose. It is quite out of place where time is limited and the aim is to get the parties to focus on the issues that actually matter.

The direction will also assist a party (and the Tribunal) faced with a situation where huge proofs of evidence are served, which deal at length with matters which appear peripheral to the issues.

Another version of this problem is the witness who is verbose beyond belief under cross-examination and admirably laconic when answering his own side.

A Tribunal should be astute to intervene if this is clearly happening—perhaps by way of polite hints that the time allocation may be challenged if it continues. Meanwhile the direction means that the questioner does not have to follow up the menagerie of hares, red herrings and wild geese started by the witness, or the other side's legal team.

The award

5.27 *My award dealing with all matters remaining in dispute in the reference (save as to any matter of costs) shall be published by or before the [date]*

This is a good discipline for the Tribunal and should be of assistance to the parties.

Parties should insist upon it: and upon the Tribunal reserving time to achieve it. Of course such time, if reserved, may give rise to cancellation charges if the matter settles.

5.28 *The said award shall be a reasoned one*

This should be obligatory. It is now under English law, unless the parties agree otherwise. They should not so agree. A reasoned award is a good discipline for the Tribunal and enables the losing parties in particular to understand what happened.

Arbitrators should not be concerned about being appealed. Judges are appealed every day without the self confidence of the judiciary being much affected—at least to judge by appearances.

5.29 *I may by notice in writing (such notice to be of not less than one calendar month) seek the assistance of the parties on any matter relevant to the said award at any time prior to the [date].*

5.30 *As and when all matters in dispute between the parties (save as to costs) have been finally determined (whether by settlement, award or court decision) either party may give written notice (such notice to be not less than one month) of its intention to seek directions as to the determination of all outstanding issues of costs*

5.31 *The costs of the hearing on [date] and of these Directions shall be costs in the cause. Lest it be relevant. the said hearing was fit for two counsel on each side*

5.32 *There shall be liberty to apply*

Save for direction 5.32 these directions do not need comment. Direction 5.32 does. It is very important to the Tribunal to retain, and to be seen to retain, control of the procedure, even to altering the time allocation half way through, albeit only in very unusual circumstances.

General

6. Fairness

In discussing directions, particularly where there are advocates from different countries and disciplines and even different cultures, the Tribunal should be astute to find a formula or procedure which all involved can see is reasonably fair. Any advocate who makes the leap (as some still do) from what he is used to what the best system is should be firmly reproved.

7. The equal split of hearing time

The tendency is always to go for an equal split. This is both easy and looks equitable. However, the Tribunal should keep in mind the following points:

- If one side has to open a case orally, there will be an imbalance which may need correcting (*e.g.* a 3:2 or 7:6 split).
- In a case without an oral opening and without oral evidence in chief, the side that cross-examines first will have the harder task.
- By the time the other side of the case is cross-examining them the Parties and the

Tribunal will (or should) be very much more familiar with the issue and the whole thing goes faster.

- A defendant may simply be concentrating on knocking down the claim without raising its own claim. This may be a shorter exercise than establishing the claim.
- It is sensible to keep a day in reserve, unallocated, for emergencies.

Appendix 20

THE ROLE OF THE COURTS IN ARBITRATION

Powers of the Court	UNCI-TRAL Model Law Article	New York Conven-tion 1958	1950 Act, section	1975 Act, section	1979 Act, section	1996 Act section
Staying proceedings in court in order to give effect to an arbitration agreement	8		4(1) 5	1		9● 10● 11● 86
Extension of time for commencement of arbitral proceedings			27			12●+
Setting aside a "default" appoint-ment of a sole arbi-trator			7(b) 10(2b)			17+
Power in support of the constitution of the arbit-ral tribunal including revocation of an appointment	11(4)		10(1), (2) and (3c) 25			18+
Power to substitute an umpire for the original members of the tri-bunal			8(2), (3)			21+
Power to remove an arbitrator	12–14		13(3) 23 24(1)			24●+
Powers consequential upon the resignation of an arbitrator	14					25(3) and (4)+
Powers to consider and adjust arbitration fees and expenses						28(2) to (4)●+
Power to determine any questionas to the sub-stantive jurisdiction of the tribunal		2				32●# (+)

Powers of the Court	UNCITRAL Model Law Article	New York Convention 1958	1950 Act, section	1975 Act, section	1979 Act, section	1996 Act section
Power to require a party to comply with a peremptory order made by the tribunal					5	42+*
Power to secure the attendance of witnesses before the tribunal	27		12(4), (5)			43●+
General power in support of the arbitral proceedings	9 27	2	12(6)			44+*
Power to determine a preliminary point of law					2	45*(+)#
Power to extend the time for the making of the award			13(2)			50+*
Power to require delivery of a withheld award			19			56●+
Powers in connection with the determination of the amount of the recoverable costs of the arbitration and to disputes as to the recoverable costs part of fees and expenses of the tribunal			18(1), (2) 19			63 64*
Powers in connection with the enforcement of the award	35	3 5 6	26(1)			66●
Powers in connection with a challenge to an award on the basis of substantive jurisdiction or serious irregularity	16 34	5	22 23			67+ 68●+
Power to hear an appeal					1 3	69*(+)#
Powers to order a tribunal to state reasons for its award, to vary, remit or set aside awards or declaring them to be no effect			23(3) 22(2)		1(5), (6) 1(8)	70# 71●
Power in respect of challenge by person taking no part in the arbitral proceedings						72●

Powers of the Court	**UNCITRAL Model Law Article**	**New York Convention 1958**	**1950 Act, section**	**1975 Act, section**	**1979 Act, section**	**1996 Act section**
Power to make orders securing the payment of solicitors' costs						
Powers in relation to service of documents						77+*
Power to extend time limits within the arbitral proceedings						79*+ 79(3)#
Stay of proceedings in the context of a domestic arbitration agreement			4(1)	1(1)		86
Enforcement of New York Convention awards		1		3		101

KEY:● Mandatory provisions under the 1996 Act.
* Power of the court may be excluded by agreement of the parties.
+ Leave required to get to Court of First Instance.
# Certificate required for appeal to Court of Appeal.
Leave required for appeal to Court of Appeal.
All remedies must be exhausted before seeking to invoke Court's jurisdiction.
(+ Leave required to appeal to Court of Appeal in one subsection.

Appendix 21

CURRICULA VITAE OF THE AUTHORS AND CONTRIBUTORS

RONALD BERNSTEIN, D.F.C., Q.C., F.C.I.Arb.

A Bencher of the Middle Temple
Hon. Assoc. Royal Institution of Chartered Surveyors
Hon. Fellow, Incorporated Society of Valuers and Auctioneers
Vice-President (Emeritus) Chartered Institute of Arbitrators

From 1975 to 1985
Head of Chambers at 11 King's Bench Walk (now Falcon Chambers), Temple, London, specializing in property law

From 1980 to 1990
Deputy Official Referee and Deputy High Court Judge

From 1992 to 1994
Chairman of the Panel of Arbitrators of the Securities and Futures Association

Other works
Handbook of Rent Review (1982) (looseleaf); *Essentials of Rent Review* (1995)

ANTHONY BUNCH

Current position
Managing Partner of Masons
Chairman of the Management Board
Partner in Construction Department

Education and professional activities
B.A. (Hons) Law, Nottingham
Associate Chartered Institute of Arbitrators
Member of Official Referees Solicitors Association
Member of Chartered Institute of Arbitrators ADR Committee
Member of the Department Advisory Committee on the New Arbitration Act
Co-Author of National report on Hong Kong in the *International Handbook on Commercial Arbitration*
Member of the International Advisory Board to the Arbitration Institute of the Stockholm Chamber of Commerce

Professional career

Articles at Masons	1976–1978
Admitted as Solicitor	1978
Salaried Partner	1980
Equity Partner	1982
Admitted as Solicitor in Hong Kong	1985
Senior resident Partner in Hong Kong Office	1985–1990
Managing Partner	1991

Experience
Since qualifying, Tony Bunch has specialised in issues relating to or arising from the construction and engineering industries, including contentious and non-contentious and both international and domestic matters.

Tony Bunch has drafted a full range of contracts for major projects (including B.O.T. schemes) in the United Kingdom and the Far East on behalf of employers, major contractors and international consultants.

He has conducted and assisted in a large number of proceedings in the United Kingdom at all levels, to include the House of Lords. He has also conducted proceedings in a number of other countries, to include in particular Hong Kong, Singapore and the People's Republic of China.

He has promoted alternative dispute resolution as a means of achieving an amicable and pragmatic resolution of construction disputes, establishing Masons' ADR Unit in 1990.

Tony Bunch has represented various professional bodies including the Civil Engineering Committee of the Hong Kong Construction Association in policy discussions with the Hong Kong Government, drafted and revised Model Arbitration Rules and Mediation Rules.

Other responsibilities and positions
Associate, Chartered Institute of Arbitrators
Steering Committee member for the new Arbitration Act
Member of Official Referees Solicitors Association
Member of Chartered Institute of Arbitrators ADR Committee
Member of the International Advisory Board to the Arbitration Institute of the Stockholm Chamber of Commerce

Other professional activities
Lectured widely and prepared papers upon issues affecting the construction industry and in particular alternative dispute resolution.

PHILLIP CAPPER

Professor Phillip Capper is a Partner in Masons international law firm and a recognised authority on legal aspects of engineering design and construction risks. As well as advising international corporations, he is frequently called upon to advise government departments and national agencies on the management of risk and practical contractual frameworks and forms.

He is Head of Masons' International Arbitration Group, with substantial experience of arbitration from the point of view of adviser, advocate and arbitrator.

A great deal of his experience relates to complex engineering and infrastructure projects, and high technology in electrical and mechanical procurement. He has advised on projects for defence, highways, rail, transportation, power, process plant and construction procurement in many countries world-wide. Since 1989 he has represented T.M.L., the Channel Tunnel contractor consortium.

For the United Kingdom Institution of Civil Engineers, Phillip drafted the new Adjudication and Disputes clauses and other aspects of the 2nd edition of the New Engineering Contract. He is also retained by the ICE to draft and advise on the revised disputes and arbitration provisions for the 7th edition of the ICE Conditions of Contract. For the United Kingdom Construction Industry Research and Information Association he prepared the legal risk management aspects of its report "A Client's Guide to Risk in Construction." He has considerable working experience of the FIDIC forms of contract.

He is a member of the ICC Commission on International Arbitration and of the United Kingdom ICC Arbitration national committee. He is also a member of the European Advisory Committee of the CPR Institute for Dispute Resolution, based in New York.

Phillip has specialized in contractual risk management for over 20 years. He was author of the Contract section of the final series of the *Annual Survey* of Commonwealth law, and was founding Editor of the *Construction Industry Law Letter*.

Phillip is a visiting Professor in Construction Law and Arbitration at King's College, London and before joining Masons in 1988 he was Chairman of the Faculty of Law at the University of Oxford. He remains a Fellow by special election of Keble College, Oxford.

Phillip's international lectures have included: in 1993 the inaugural Lloyds Register Lecture for the Royal Academy of Engineering on "Practical Management of Legal Risks"; in 1994 at the USA DART (Dispute Avoidance and Resolution Task Force) Conference as special invited speaker; in 1995 at the XVIIth Annual Meeting of the ICC Institute of International Business Law and Practice in Brussels on dispute resolution within the performance of contracts; in 1996 at the International Dispute Resolution

Conference of the Hong Kong International Arbitration Centre, City University and C.I.Arb.

He also advised, for example, the British Government Department of Trade and Industry study on professional liability in construction, and for the Lord Chancellor's Department he lectured to Her Majesty's judges on liability arising on construction projects.

RICHARD (DICK) GREENSLADE, C.B.E., LL.B.

Registrar/District Judge since 1977 at Clerkenwell, Croydon and Gloucester. Retired April 1997.
Member, County Court Rule Committee 1987–93
Member, Legal Aid Advisory Committee 1992–94
Assessor, Woolf Inquiry 1994–96
President, Association of District Judges, 1996–97
Author, *Matrimonial Litigation and Advocacy* (Butterworths)
General Editor, *Greenslade on Costs* (FT Law and Tax)
Editor, *Civil Court Practice* (Butterworths)
Joint Editor, *County Court Practice* (Butterworths)

BRUCE HARRIS

Address
104 Ledbury Road, London, W11 2AH

Date of Birth
April 19, 1945

1963–1973
With Richards Butler & Co. (now Richards Butler), major City of London solicitors, assisting litigation partner in general commercial litigation and arbitration with substantial emphasis on shipping (charterparty, bill of lading, sale contract, insurance) and related disputes.

1973–1980
With Thos. R. Miller & Son (now Thomas Miller & Co.) as executive handling P&I and Defence claims, negotiating terms of entry, public and member relations and managing Defence Club.

Work involved substantial claims handling, occasional travelling to investigate disputes or negotiate settlements and to further member relations and negotiate terms; supervision of Defence Club matters generally including preparation for and presentation to directors of cases for consideration. Particular responsibility for relations with French members and correspondents.

1980 to date

Practising as full-time commercial arbitrator (having started part-time in 1975) dealing with all kinds of commercial and trading disputes, particularly maritime matters, predominantly in London arbitrations but also elsewhere, both as member of tribunal and a sole arbitrator (including umpire). Involved in well over 7,000 references to date and signatory to well over 1,400 awards.

Languages

English, French

Publications

Various articles in sundry publications including:
Le Droit Maritime Francais; *Arbitration*; *Arbitration International*; *Lloyd's List*; *The Shipbroker*; *Arbitration & Dispute Resolution Law Journal International Journal of Shipping Law*, etc., on matters related to shipping and arbitration law.
Joint author of *The Arbitration Act 1966—A Commentary* (Blackwell Science)
Editor and main author of Thos. R. Miller & Sons's *Legal Decisions*, 1977–80.

Lectures

Various lectures/tutorial sessions for Chartered Institute of Arbitrators Evening Courses, Advanced Studies Weekends, etc.; sundry lectures on arbitration in various public and academic fora around the world; lectures to potential arbitrators in LMAA Short Course and to UNC Seminar on International Arbitration.

Societies

Chartered Institute of Arbitrators, Chairman, 1993–94; Fellow; Council Member; Vice-President, 1990–94.
London Maritime Arbitrators Association, Honorary Secretary, 1978–79; Committee Member, 1980–89; 1993–; President, 1991–93.
Association Francaise du Droit Maritime
Chambre Arbitrale Maritime de Paris
The Association of Maritime Arbitrators of Canada
ICC Commission d'Arbitrage
IMAO Steering Committee

DEREK KIRBY JOHNSON, M.A. (CANTAB.) F.C.I.Arb.

Derek Kirby Johnson was born in Scotland in 1926 and educated at The King's School, Canterbury during the Second World War years.

He was commissioned into The Royal Engineers and served in India and the Middle East before going up to Corpus Christi College Cambridge to read Natural Sciences, quickly changing to read Part I English Tripos and Part II Law, and rowing for the College at Henley.

After articles in New Square, Lincoln's Inn, he qualified as a solicitor in 1953 and joined Randall Monier-Williams in the firm eventually known as Monier-Williams, of which in due course he became senior partner for some years before retiring in 1993.

While there, he came to act for many Trade Associations in areas as diverse as wines and spirits at one end and cattle feed at the other, mainly as Legal Assessor to Boards of Appeal in Special Case arbitrations. As solicitor for The Cattle Food Trade Association, he drew up the Memorandum and Articles of Association of the new body formed on the merger in 1971 with the London Corn Trade Association, called the Grain and Feed Trade Association, or GAFTA.

In 1973 came the big flood on the Mississippi River which led to the U.S. embargo on exports which in turn caused literally thousands of disputes over broken contracts for the deliver to Rotterdam of U.S. soyabean meal, on the terms of GAFTA Contract Form No. 100. All these disputes were arbitrated in London under GAFTA Arbitration Rules so that each week for several years several special case hearings were held at GAFTA's offices and, as assessor, he wrote some hundreds of awards, many of which form the basis of reported law on prohibition, *force majeure* and the computation of damages for non-fulfilment.

Since then, he has lectured widely on sale of goods and contract law, and, as a speciality, arbitration matters, particularly in the context of commodity trade disputes. He was solicitor not only for GAFTA, but also for the Cocoa Association of London and also sat as assessor in arbitrations held at the Refined Sugar Association and the London Oil and Tallow Trades Association, later merged into FOSFA, the Federation of Oils, Seeds and Fats Associations. On retiring from Monier-Williams, he took up a consultancy with Hill Taylor Dickinson specializing in arbitration matters.

He has written the chapter on Commodity Trade Arbitration in all three editions of the *Handbook of Arbitration Practice* and is the author of *International Commodity Arbitration*, the only textbook covering arbitration practice under the principal London based commodity trade associations. He is a Fellow of the Chartered Institute of Arbitrators and an arbitrator for the Securities and Futures Authority, for whom he has just drafted new rules under the new Act. He chaired the Law Society working party of the Consumer and Commercial Law Committee on the draft Arbitration Bill and sat on the Chartered Institute of Arbitrator's Committee for the same. He has also written a number of articles on the Bill and the Act for the *Law Society Gazette* and lectured widely on the subject.

ARTHUR LESLIE MARRIOTT, Q.C.

Address
Debevoise & Plimpton, 1 Creed Court, 5 Ludgate Hill, London EC4M 7AA, United Kingdom. Tel.: [44] (171) 329 0779; fax: [44] (171) 329 0860.

Nationality
British

Date of birth
March 30, 1943
Solicitor of the Supreme Court of England and Wales since 1966
Solicitor of the Supreme Court of Hong King since 1976
Partner, Debevoise & Plimpton
Assistant recorder (part-time judge)
Queen's Counsel 1997
Deputy High Court Judge (part-time)

Principal areas of specialisation
International commercial arbitration, mediation, oil and gas law and practice, joint venture agreements and civil engineering construction law and practice

Associations and memberships
Chairman of the Private Group engaged in the preparation of a new English arbitration statute
Member of Departmental Advisory Committee on Arbitration
member of Council of International Council for Commercial Arbitration (ICCA)
Member of Board of Hong Kong International Arbitration Centre (HKIAC) and of London Court of International Arbitration (LCIA)
Fellow of Chartered Institute of Arbitrators
High Courts (Civil Proceedings) rights of audience qualification—June 1994

Publications
Numerous articles; and co-author with Henry Brown of *ADR Principles and Practice* (Sweet & Maxwell, 1993)

Languages
English, German and some French

IAN V. ODDY, FRICS, F.C.I.Arb.

Ian V. Oddy, FRCS, F.C.I.Arb. is the Honorary Secretary of the Royal Institution of Chartered Surveyors (RICS) and an Equity Partner in St Quintin. He was President of the General Practice Division of the RICS in 1984–85. He has specialised in rent review work over the last 20 years, accepting numerous appointments as an arbitrator or independent expert. He was the arbitrator in *National Westminster Bank v. Arthur Young McClelland Moores*. He has been a Blundell Memorial Lecturer on two occasions.

JAN PAULSSON

Date and place of birth
November 5, 1959, Nyköping, Sweden

Professional address
Freshfields, 69 Boulevard Haussmann, 75008 Paris, France. Tel.: 44 56 44 56 Fax: 44 56 44 00.

Present position
Avocat of the Bar of Paris; Head of the Freshfields Arbitration Group

Languages
English, French and Swedish

Education
Harvard University (A.B. 1971)
Yale Law School (J.D. 1975) (Editor, *Yale Law Journal*)
University of Paris (*Diplôme d'études supérieures spécialisées* 1977)

Professional experience
Coudert Frères, Paris, 1975–89
Freshfields, Paris, 1989–present

Professional associations
Vice-President, London Court of International Arbitration
Member, International Olympic Committee's *Tribunal arbitral du sport* (Lausanne)
Member, International Council for Commercial Arbitration

Arbitration experience
Specialised in arbitration since 1975. Counsel or arbitrator in some 250 arbitral proceedings conducted in all major venues in Europe, as well as in Asia and the United States,

mostly under the Rules of the ICC but also notably under those of the LCIA, UNCITRAL, and various *ad hoc* arrangements. Counsel in seven ICSID arbitrations (on the side of the investor as well as the host State).

Most frequently recurring subject matters: joint ventures, investments, pricing mechanisms in long-term commodity supply agreements, construction projects, intellectual property, sports.

Some cases in the public domain: *State of Qatar v. State of Bahrain*; *Ken-Ren v. Voest* et al; *Republic of Cameroon v. Klöckner*; *SPP v. Republic of Egypt* (''Pyramids Oasis'' case); *Atlantic Triton v. Republic of Guinea*; *French Nuclear Energy Commission (CEA/EURODIF) v. State of Iran*; *LIAMCO (Atlantic Richfield) v. State of Libya.*

Related activities

General Editor, *Arbitration International* (1985–)

Chairman, LCIA Rules Revision Committee (1985–)

Member, Drafting Committee for 1994 World Intellectual Property Organization Rules of Arbitration

Co-Chairman, International Bar Association Sub-Committee on Enforcement of Arbitral Awards (1992–)

Member, Expert Consultative Group on International Commercial Arbitration, UNCITRAL (Vienna) (1994–95)

Senior Special Fellow, United Nations Institute for Training and Research, UNITAR (Geneva) (1995–)

Panel of Arbitrators, China International Economic and Trade Commission (Beijing, 1997–)

Adviser to a number of Governments with regard to legislation or treaties in the area of arbitration

Publications (a partial list)

Books

International Chamber of Commerce Arbitration, Oceana (1st ed., 1983; 2nd ed., 1990; 3rd ed. 1998) (with W. L. Craig and W. W. Park); *The Freshfields Guide to Arbitration and ADR Clauses* (1993) (with J. M. H. Hunter, N. K. Rawding and D. A. Redfern); *International Commercial Arbitration*, Foundation Press; 1997 (with W. M. Reisman, W. L. Craig and W. W. Park)

Articles

''Rediscovering the N.Y. Convention: Further Reflections on Chromalloy,'' Mealey's *International Arbitration Report*, April 1997, at p. 20

''Arbitration without Privity'', 10 ICSID Review (1995) *Foreign Investment Law Journal* 232

''La réforme de l'arbitrage en Inde'' (1996) *Revue de l'arbitrage* 597

''Contrats en Asie: Kuala Lumpur comme lieu d'arbitrage'' (1994) *Droit des affaires internatinales* 248

''1994 Revision of CIETAC Rules Promises Increased Neutrality In Arbitration in China'', Mealey's *International Arbitration Report*, June 1994, p. 1 (with Alastair Crawford)

''Arbitration of International Sports Disputes'', *The Entertainment and Sports Lawyer*, Winter 1994, at p. 12

"The Trouble with Confidentiality", *The ICC International Court of Arbitration Bulletin*, May 1994, at p. 48 (with N. K. Rawding)
"Standards of Conduct for Counsel in International Arbitration" (Essays in Honor of Hans Smit), (1992) *The American Review of International Arbitration* 214
"ICSID's Achievements and Prospects" (1991) *Foreign Investment Law Journal* 104
"La *lex mercatoria* dans l'arbitrage CCI", in (1990) *Revue de l'Arbitrage* 55
"Arbitrage international et voices de recours: La Cour suprême de Suède dans le sillage des solutions belges et helvétiques", (1990) *Journal du Droit International* 589
"Means of Recourse Against Arbitral Awards Under U.S. Law" (1989) *Journal of International Arbitration* 2
"Third World Participation in International Investment Arbitration" (1987) *Foreign Investment Law Journal* 19
"May a State Invoke its Internal Law to Repudiate Consent to International Commercial Arbitration?" (1986) *Arbitration International* 90
"Arbitration Unbound in Belgium" (1986) *Arbitration International* 68
"A Commentary on the 1985 Rules of the London Court of International Arbitration (1985) *Yearbook of Commercial Arbitration* 167 (with J. M. H. Hunter)
"A code of Ethics for Arbitrators in International Commercial Arbitration?" (1985) *International Business Lawyer* 153 (with J. M. H. Hunter)
"Sovereign Immunity from Execution: French Caselaw Revisited" (1985) *International Lawyer* 277
"L'arbitre et le contrat: l'adaptation due contrat", (1984) *Revue de l'Arbitrage* 249
"La réforme de la loi de l'arbitrage à Hong Kong" (1984) *Revue de l'Arbitrage* 325
"L'immunité restreinte entérinée par la jurisprudence suédoise dans le cadre de l'exequatur d'une sentence arbitrale étrangre rendue à l'encontre d'un Etat" (1981) *Journal du Droit International* 544
"French codification of a Legal Framework for International Commercial Arbitration" (1981) *Law and Policy in International Business* 727 (with W. Laurence Craig and W. W. Park)
"The Role of Swedish Courts in Transnational Commercial Arbitration" (1981) *Virginia Journal of International Law* 211

MARGARET RUTHERFORD, Q.C., LL.B., F.C.I.Arb.

Margaret Rutherford, Q.C., LL.B., F.C.I.Arb., a Past Chairman of the Chartered Institute of Abitrators, is a Chairman of the Registered Homes Tribunal, a President of the Mental Health Review Tribunal and a Chairman of the Independent Schools Tribunal. She is practising arbitrator, a lecturer (formerly of the College of Law), and writer. Together with John Sims she is author of *The Arbitration Act 1996: A Practical Guide* and a Joint Consultant Editor of *The Practical Arbitration Journal* (FT Law & Tax).

JOHN TACKABERRY

Address

Arbitration Chambers, 22 Willes Road, London NW5 3DS. DX 46454/Kentish Town. Tel.: 44 (0) 171 267 2137; fax 44 (0) 171 482 1018.

Arbitration and litigation

Extensive experience in building and civil engineering work and in international disputes throughout Europe, the USA, West Indies, Africa, Middle and Far East

Born Dublin, Ireland, November 13, 1939; Admitted 1963. Hon. Society of Gray's Inn, 1982; (*ad hoc*) Bar of Malaysia, 1987; Bar of the Irish Republic, 1988; (*ad hoc*) Hong Kong Bar, 1988; Bar of California, 1990; New South Wales Bar (Q.C.). 1967, called to Bar of England and Wales; 1982 Appointed one of Her Majesty's Counsel (England & Wales).

Education

Trinity College Dublin, Ireland, Downing College Cambridge, England. M.A., LL.M., Q.C., F.C.I.Arb.

Past and present member

American Arbitration Association, Arbitral Panels of the Los Angeles Center for commercial Arbitration, Society of Construction Arbitrators, The Chartered Institute of Arbitrators (Past Chairman), Society of Construction Law (Past President), European Society of Construction Law (Past President), British Academy of Experts, Association of Independent Producers, Indian Council of Arbitration, Association of Arbitrators in South Africa, Singapore International Arbitration Council, Interpacific Bar Association Council, London Maritime Arbitrators Association.

Publications

Contributed to the *Construction Contract Dictionary*, *Contemporary Problems in International Arbitration* (Ed. by Julian Lew 1986); Liability of Contractors (Lloyd, ed., 1986; *Journees Jean Robert*, Quebec Arbitration Centre, August 1987; *Journal of International Arbitration*—Article on ''Elementary Economics and the Construction Dispute. An Outsider Look at the Swiss Law Remedies Available to the Unpaid Contractor'' (Jacques Werner, ed., Sept. 1990).

Resumé of experience

During career at the Bar has undertaken a wide range of work: but in more recent years as an advocate and as an arbitrator has had a substantial degree of specialization in building and civil engineering work. As well as work in the United Kingdom has a wide degree of experience in international disputes, having worked on the European Continent and the U.S. (East and West Coast), the West Indies, Africa and the Far East (all arbitration cases); and having been concerned in disputes arising in the Middle East and the Far East (arbitration and litigation).

DEREK WOOD, C.B.E., Q.C.

Date of birth
October 14, 1937

Academic qualifications
B.C.L., M.A. (Oxon)

Professional career
Called to the Bar 1964, appointed Q.C. 1978, Recorder of the Crown Court 1985, Bencher of the Middle Temple 1986. Sat as Deputy Official Referee and Deputy High Court Judge (Chancery Division).

Practice at the Bar
Real property litigation of all descriptions in court, and before public inquiries, tribunals and arbitrators: commercial and agricultural landlord and tenant disputes, including rent review; housing; conveyancing easements and boundaries; compulsory purchase, tax and planning; joint development agreements; building and engineering disputes; professional negligence in connection with real property.

Publications
Joint author (with R. H. Bernstein and specialist authors) of the *Handbook of Arbitration Practice* (2nd ed.) (Sweet & Maxwell and Chartered Institute of Arbitrators, 1993).

Public appointments
Department of the Environment: Member of Advisory Group on Commercial Property Development 1975–1978; Property Advisory Group 1978–1994; Working Party on New Forms of Social Ownership and Tenure in Housing 1976.
Chairman of Expert Committee on the Rating of Plant and Machinery 1991–1992. (Report published HMSO 1993.) Chairman of Committee on the Rating of Plant and Machinery in Prescribed Industries 1996–1997.
Greater London Council: Chairman of Inquiry into Heavy Lorries in London 1981–1983. (Report published GLC 1983.)
Department of Transport: Chairman of Standing Advisory Committee on Trunk Road Assessment (SACTRA) 1987–1994. (Reports published: "Assessing the Environmental Impact of Road Schemes", HMSO, 1992; "Trunk Roads and the Generation of Traffic", HMSO, 1994.)
Code of Practice: Chairman of property industry's working party on Code of Practice for Commercial Leases in England and Wales, published December 1995.
QECD: Chairman of European Ministers of Transport Round Table on Infrastructure-induced mobility, Paris, November 1996.

Public honours
Awarded CBE in New Year's Honours List 1995 for services to property law.

Election to professional bodies
Hon. Fellow of Central Association of Agricultural Valuers (FAAV) 1988; Hon. Associate of Royal Institution of Chartered Surveyors (Hon. ARICS) 1991; Fellow of Chartered Institute of Arbitrators (F.C.I.Arb.) by examination, 1993.

Present position
Principal of St Hugh's College, Oxford (since 1991) and in practice at Falcon Chambers, Falcon Court, London EC4Y 1AA.

Addresses
St Hugh's College, Oxford OX2 6LE. Tel.: 01865 274909; fax: 01865 274912 or 01865 274950
Falcon Chambers, Falcon Court, London EC4Y 1AA. Tel: 0171 353 2484; fax: 0171 353 1261. DX: 408 Lond/Chancery Lane

Appendix 22

THE INSTITUTION OF CIVIL ENGINEERS' ARBITRATION PROCEDURE (1997)*

PART A. OBJECTIVES, REFERENCE AND APPOINTMENT

Rule 1. Aims and objectives

1.1 The object of arbitration is to obtain the fair resolution of disputes by an impartial arbitrator without unnecessary delay or expense. The Parties and the Arbitrator shall do all things necessary to achieve this object. The Arbitrator shall give each party a reasonable opportunity of putting its case and dealing with that of its opponent. This Procedure shall be interpreted and the proceedings shall be conducted in a manner most conducive to achieving these objectives.

1.2 Where the Act applies the Rules of this Procedure are institutional rules for the purposes of s4(3).

1.3 Where the Act does not apply, no alterations shall be made to this Procedure without the consent of the Arbitrator, except where there are express modifications in the Contract, or in the arbitration agreement.

Rule 2. Commencement of arbitration

2.1 Unless otherwise provided in the Contract a dispute or difference shall be deemed to arise when a claim or assertion made by one party is rejected by the other party and that rejection is not accepted, or no response is received within a period of 28 days. Subject only to the due observance of any condition precedent in the Contract or the arbitration agreement either party may then invoke arbitration by serving a Notice to Refer on the other party.

2.2 The date upon which the Notice to Refer is served shall be regarded as the date upon which the arbitral proceedings are commenced.

* This Procedure (approved February 1997) has been prepared by The Institution of Civil Engineers principally for use with the ICE family of Conditions of Contract and the NEC family of Documents in England and Wales for arbitrations conducted under the Arbitration Act 1996. It may be suitable for use with other contracts and in other jurisdictions. For the purposes of the ICE family of Conditions of Contract this Procedure shall be deemed to be an amendment or modification to the ICE Procedure (1983).

Copies of the Arbitration Procedure are available, priced £10, from Thomas Telford Services Ltd, 1 Heron Quay, London E14 4JD Tel. 0171 665 2464; Fax. 0171 537 3631.

2.3 The Notice to Refer shall list the matters which the Party serving the Notice to Refer wishes to be referred to arbitration. Nothing stated in the Notice shall restrict that party as to the manner in which it subsequently presents its case.

Rule 3. Appointment of sole arbitrator by agreement

3.1 At the same time as or after serving the Notice to Refer either party may serve upon the other a Notice to Concur in the appointment of an Arbitrator listing therein the names addresses of one or more persons it proposes as Arbitrator.

3.2 Within 14 days thereafter the other party shall:

(a) agree in writing to the appointment of one of the persons listed in the Notice to Concur or
(b) propose in like manner an alternative person or persons.

3.3 Once agreement has been reached either party may write to the person so selected inviting him to accept the appointment enclosing a copy of the Notice to Refer and documentary evidence of the other party's agreement to his appointment.

3.4 If the person so invited accepts the appointment he shall notify both parties simultaneously in writing. The date of posting or service as the case may be of this notification shall be deemed to be the date on which the Arbitrator's appointment is completed.

Rule 4. Appointment of sole arbitrator by the President

4.1 If within one calendar month from the service of the Notice to Concur the parties fail to appoint an Arbitrator in accordance with Rule 3 either party may apply to the President to appoint an Arbitrator. Alternatively the parties may agree to apply to the President without a Notice to Concur.

4.2 The application shall be in writing and shall include:

(a) a copy of the Notice to Refer;
(b) a copy of the Notice to Concur or the agreement to dispense with same;
(c) the names and addresses of all parties to the arbitration;
(d) a brief statement of the nature and circumstances of the dispute;
(e) a copy of the arbitration clause in the Contract or of the arbitration agreement;
(f) the appropriate fee;
(g) confirmation that any conditions precedent to arbitration contained in the Contract or arbitration agreement have been complied with and
(h) any other relevant document.

A copy of the application, but not supporting documentation, shall be sent at the same time to the other party.

4.3 The President will within 28 days of receiving the application or within such further time as may be necessary make the appointment and the Arbitrator's appointment shall thereby be completed. The Institution will notify both parties and the Arbitrator in writing as soon as possible thereafter.

Provided always that no such appointment shall be invalidated merely because the time limits set out herein have not been observed.

Rule 5. Notice of further disputes or differences

5.1 At any time before the Arbitrator's appointment is completed either party may put forward further disputes or differences to be referred to him. This shall be done by serving upon the other party an additional Notice to Refer in accordance with Rule 2.

5.2 Once his appointment is completed the Arbitrator shall have jurisdiction over any issue connected with and necessary to the determination of any dispute or difference already referred to him whether or not any condition precedent to referring the matter to arbitration had been complied with.

PART B. ARRANGEMENTS FOR THE ARBITRATION

Rule 6. The preliminary meeting

6.1 As soon as possible after his appointment the Arbitrator may summon the parties to a preliminary meeting for the purpose of giving such directions about the procedure to be adopted in the arbitration as he considers necessary and to deal with the matters referred to in Rule 6.4.

6.2 The Arbitrator may require the parties to submit to him short statements expressing their perceptions of the disputes or differences. Such statements shall give sufficient detail of the nature of the issues to enable the Arbitrator and the parties to discuss procedures appropriate for their settlement at the preliminary meeting.

6.3 The parties shall designate the seat of the arbitration. In default of such designation it shall be designated by the Arbitrator.

6.4 The parties and the Arbitrator shall consider whether and to what extent:

(a) Part F (Short Procedure) or Part G (Special Procedure for Experts) of these Rules shall apply;
(b) the arbitration should proceed on documents only;
(c) progress may be facilitated and costs saved by determining some of the issues in advance of the main hearing;
(d) evidence of Experts may be necessary, or desirable;
(e) disclosure of documents should be ordered;
(f) there should be a limit put on recoverable costs;
(g) where the Act applies to the Arbitration, the parties should enter into an agreement (if they have not already done so) excluding the right to appeal in accordance with the Act;

and in general shall consider such other steps as may achieve the speedy and cost effective resolution of the disputes.

PART C. POWERS OF THE ARBITRATOR

Rule 7. Power to rule on his own jurisdiction

7.1 The Arbitrator shall have power to rule on his own substantive jurisdiction as to:

(a) whether there is a valid arbitration agreement;
(b) whether he is properly appointed;

(c) whether there is a dispute or difference capable of being referred to arbitration, and whether it has been validly referred;
(d) whether and to what extent the Procedure applies to the conduct of the arbitration;
(e) what matters have been submitted to him in accordance with the contract or the arbitration agreement and this Procedure.

7.2 Should any party refer a ruling under Rule 7.1 to the court the Arbitrator shall direct whether or not the arbitral proceedings shall continue pending a decision by the court.

Procedural and evidential matters

7.3 The Arbitrator shall have power to decide all procedural and evidential matters including, but not limited to:

(a) whether any and if so what form of written statements of claim and defence are to be used, when these should be supplied and the extent to which such statements can be later amended;
(b) whether any and if so which documents or classes of document should be disclosed between and produced by the parties and at what stage;
(c) whether any and if so what questions should be put to and answered by the respective parties in advance of a hearing and when and in what form this should be done;
(d) whether to apply the strict rules of evidence (or any other rules) as to the admissibility, relevance or weight of any material (oral, written or other) sought to be tendered on any matters of fact or opinion, and the time, manner and form in which such material should be exchanged and presented;
(e) whether and to what extent the Arbitrator should himself take the initiative in ascertaining the facts and the law;
(f) whether and to what extent he should rely upon his own knowledge and expertise;
(g) whether and to what extent there should be oral or written evidence or submissions;
(h) whether and to what extent expert evidence should be adduced;
(j) whether and to what extent evidence should be given under oath or affirmation;
(k) the manner in which the evidence of witnesses shall be taken;
(l) whether translations of any relevant documents are to be supplied;
(m) whether and to what extent enquiries tests or investigations should be conducted

and in default of agreement between the parties, shall have power to decide:

(n) when and where any part of the proceedings is to be held;
(p) the language or languages to be used in the proceedings.

The Arbitrator may fix the time within which any directions given by him are to be complied with and may if he thinks fit extend the time so fixed whether or not it has expired.

Power to limit recoverable costs

7.4 The Arbitrator may direct that the recoverable Costs of the Arbitration, or any part of the arbitral proceedings shall be limited to a specific amount. Any such direction shall be given in advance of incurring the costs to which it relates.

Power to order security

7.5 The Arbitrator shall have power to:

(a) make an order for security for costs in favour of one or more of the parties and
(b) order his own costs to be secured.

Money ordered to be paid under this Rule shall be paid as directed by the Arbitrator into a separate bank account in the name of a stakeholder to be appointed by and subject to the directions of the Arbitrator.

Power to order protective measures

7.6 The Arbitrator (and in the case of urgency the courts also) shall have power to:

(a) order the preservation of evidence;
(b) make orders relating to property which is the subject of the proceedings or as to which any question arises in the proceedings:
    (i) for the inspection, photographing, preservation, custody or detention of the property, or
    (ii) ordering that samples be taken from, or any observation be made of or experiment conducted upon, the property;

(c) give directions for the detention storage sale or disposal of the whole or any part of the subject matter of the dispute at the expense of one or both of the parties.

PART D. PROCEDURES BEFORE THE HEARING

Rule 8. Statements of case and disclosure of documents

8.1 To the extent that the Arbitrator directs, each party shall prepare in writing and shall serve upon the other party or parties and the Arbitrator a statement of its case comprising:

(a) a summary of that party's case;
(b) a summary of that party's evidence;
(c) a statement or summary of the issues between the parties;
(d) a list and/or a summary of the documents relied upon;
(e) any points of law with references to any authorities relied upon;
(f) a statement or summary of any other matters likely to assist the resolution of the disputes or differences between the parties;
(g) any other document or statement that the Arbitrator considers necessary.

The Arbitrator may order any party to answer the other party's case and to give reasons for any disagreement therewith.

8.2 The Arbitrator shall determine which documents or classes of documents should be disclosed between the parties and produced by the parties and at what stage.

8.3 Statements or answers shall contain sufficient detail for the other party to know the case it has to answer. If sufficient detail is not provided the Arbitrator may of his own motion or at the request of the other party order the provision of such further information, clarification or elaboration as the Arbitrator may think fit.

8.4 (a) If a party fails to comply with any order made under this Rule the Arbitrator may make a peremptory order to the same effect providing such time for compliance with it as the Arbitrator considers appropriate.

(b) If the defaulting party fails to comply with a peremptory order the Arbitrator shall have power to:

(i) debar that party from relying on the matters in respect of which it is in default;

(ii) draw such adverse inferences from the act of noncompliance as the circumstances justify;

(iii) proceed to an award on the basis of such materials as have been properly provided to him.

Provided that the Arbitrator shall first give notice to the party in default that he intends to proceed under this Rule.

8.5 If the Arbitrator is satisfied that there has been inordinate and inexcusable delay by either party in pursuing its claim and that delay:

(a) gives rise, or is likely to give rise, to substantial risk that it is not possible to have a fair resolution of the issues in that claim or

(b) has caused, or is likely to cause, serious prejudice to the other party

the Arbitrator may make an award dismissing the claim.

Rule 9. Power to order concurrent hearings

9.1 Where disputes or differences have arisen under two or more contracts each concerned wholly or mainly with the same subject matter and the resulting arbitrations have been referred to the same Arbitrator he may with the agreement of all the parties concerned or upon the application of one of the parties being a party to all the contracts involved order that the whole or any part of the matters at issue shall be heard together upon such terms or conditions as the Arbitrator thinks fit.

9.2 Where an order for concurrent hearings has been made under Rule 9.1 the Arbitrator shall nevertheless make separate awards unless all the parties otherwise agree but the Arbitrator may if he thinks fit prepare one combined set of reasons to cover all the awards.

Rule 10. Procedural meetings

10.1 The Arbitrator may at any time call such procedural meetings as he deems necessary to identify or clarify the issues to be decided and the procedures to be adopted. For this purpose the Arbitrator may request particular persons to attend on behalf of the parties.

10.2 Either party may at any time apply to the Arbitrator for leave to appear before him on any interlocutory matter. The Arbitrator may call a procedural meeting for the purpose or deal with the application in correspondence or otherwise as he thinks fit.

10.3 At any procedural meeting or otherwise the Arbitrator may give such directions as he thinks fit for the proper conduct of the arbitration.

Rule 11. Power to appoint assessors or to seek outside advice

11.1 The Arbitrator may:

(a) appoint a legal technical or other assessor to assist him in the conduct of the arbitration. The Arbitrator shall direct when such assessor is to attend hearings of the arbitration;

(b) seek legal technical or other advice on any matter arising out of or in connect on with the proceedings.

11.2 The parties shall be given reasonable opportunity to comment on any information, opinion or advice offered by any such person.

Rule 12. Preparation for the hearing

12.1 In addition to his other powers the Arbitrator shall also have power to:

(a) order that the parties shall agree facts as facts and figures as figures where possible;

(b) order the parties to prepare an agreed and paginated bundle of all documents relied upon by the parties. The agreed bundle shall thereby be deemed to have been entered in evidence without further proof and without being read out at the hearing. Provided always that either party may at the hearing challenge the admissibility of any document in the agreed bundle;

(c) order that any Experts whose reports have been exchanged should meet and prepare a joint report identifying the points in issue and any other matters covered by their reports upon which they are in agreement and those upon which they disagree, stating the reasons for any disagreement.

12.2 Before the hearing the Arbitrator may and if so requested by the parties shall read the documents to be used at the hearing. For this or any other purpose the Arbitrator may require all such documents to be delivered to him at such time and place as he may specify.

PART E. PROCEDURE AT THE HEARING

Rule 13. Powers at the hearing

13.1 The Arbitrator may hear the parties their representatives and/or witnesses at any time or place and may adjourn the arbitration for any period on the application of any party or as he thinks fit.

13.2 Any party may be represented by any person including in the case of a company or other legal entity a director officer employee or beneficiary of such company or entity. In particular, a person shall not be prevented from representing a party because he is or may be also a witness in the proceedings. Nothing shall prevent a party from being represented by different persons at different times.

13.3 Nothing in these Rules or in any other rule custom or practice shall prevent the Arbitrator from starting to hear the arbitration once his appointment is completed or at any time thereafter.

13.4 Any meeting with or summons before the Arbitrator at which both parties are represented may if the Arbitrator so directs be treated as part of the hearing.

13.5 At or before the hearing and after hearing representations on behalf of each party the Arbitrator may determine the order in which:

(a) the parties will present their cases;
(b) the order in which the issues will be heard and determined.

13.6 The Arbitrator may order any submission or speech by or on behalf of any party to be put into writing and delivered to him and to the other party. A party so ordered shall be entitled if it so wishes to enlarge upon or vary any such submission orally.

13.7 The Arbitrator may at any time (whether before or after the hearing has commenced) allocate the time available for the hearing between the parties and those representing the parties shall then adhere strictly to that allocation. Should a party's representative fail to complete the presentation of that party's case within the time so allowed further time shall only be afforded at the sole discretion of the Arbitrator and upon such conditions as to costs as the Arbitrator may see fit to impose.

13.8 The Arbitrator may on the application of either party or of his own motion hear and determine any issue or issues separately.

13.9 If a party fails to appear at the hearing and provided that the absent party has had notice of the hearing or the Arbitrator is satisfied that all reasonable steps have been taken to notify it of the hearing the Arbitrator may proceed with the hearing in its absence. The Arbitrator shall nevertheless take all reasonable steps to ensure that the disputes between the parties are determined justly and fairly.

Rule 14. Evidence

14.1 The Arbitrator may order a party to submit in advance of the hearing a list of the witnesses it intends to call. That party shall not thereby be bound to call any witness so listed and may add to the list so submitted at any time.

14.2 No expert evidence shall be admissible except by leave of the Arbitrator. Leave may be given on such terms and conditions as the Arbitrator thinks fit. Unless the Arbitrator otherwise orders such terms shall be deemed to include a requirement that a report from each Expert containing the substance of the evidence to be given shall be served upon the other party within a reasonable time before the hearing.

14.3 The Arbitrator may order that Experts appear before him separately or concurrently at the hearing or otherwise so that he may examine them inquisitorially provided always that at the conclusion of the questioning by the Arbitrator the parties or its representatives shall have the opportunity to put such further questions to any Expert as they may reasonably require.

14.4 The Arbitrator may order disclosure or exchange of proofs of evidence relating to factual issues. The Arbitrator may also order any party to prepare and disclose in writing in advance a list of points or questions to be put in cross-examination of any witness.

14.5 Where a list of questions is disclosed whether pursuant to an order of the Arbitrator or otherwise the party making disclosure shall not be bound to put any question therein to the witness unless the Arbitrator so orders. Where the party making disclosure puts a question not so listed in cross-examination the Arbitrator may disallow the costs thereby occasioned.

14.6 The Arbitrator may order that any witness statement or Expert's report which has been disclosed shall stand as the evidence in chief of that witness or Expert. The Arbitrator may also at any time before cross-examination order the witness or Expert to deliver written answers to questions arising out of any statement or report.

PART F. SHORT PROCEDURE

Rule 15. Short Procedure

15.1 Where the parties so agree (either of their own motion or at the invitation of the Arbitrator) the arbitration shall be conducted in accordance with the following Short Procedure or any variations thereto which the parties and the Arbitrator so agree.

15.2 Within 30 days after the preliminary meeting held under Rule 6.1 the claiming party shall set out its case in the form of a file containing:

(a) a statement as to the orders or awards it seeks;
(b) a statement of its reasons for being entitled to such orders or awards;
(c) copies of any documents on which it relies (including statements) identifying the origin and date of each document;

and shall deliver of the said file to the other party and to the Arbitrator in such manner and within such time as the Arbitrator may direct.

15.3 The other party shall either at the same time or within 30 days of receipt of the claiming party's statement as the Arbitrator may direct deliver to the claiming party and the Arbitrator its statement in the same form as in Rule 15.2.

15.4 The Arbitrator may view the site or the works and may in his sole discretion order, permit or require either or both parties to:

(a) submit further documents or information in writing;
(b) prepare or deliver further files by way of reply or response. Such files may include witness statements or expert reports.

Provided always that such further files shall not raise any issue not already included expressly or by necessary inference unless ordered by the Arbitrator in the files delivered in accordance with Rules 15.2 and 15.3.

15.5 Within 30 days of completing the foregoing steps the Arbitrator shall fix a day to meet the parties for the purpose of:

(a) receiving any oral submissions which either party may wish to make;
(b) the Arbitrator putting questions to the parties their representatives or witnesses.

For this purpose the Arbitrator shall give notice of any particular person he wishes to question but no person shall be bound to appear before him.

15.6 The time periods in Rules 15.2, 15.3 and 15.5 may be varied as the Arbitrator may think fit.

Documents only

15.7 Alternatively with the agreement of the parties the Arbitrator may dispense with the meeting and upon receipt of any further files or information under Rule 15.4 proceed directly to the award in accordance with Rule 15.8.

15.8 Within 30 days following the conclusion of the meeting under Rule 15.5, or in the absence of a meeting 30 days following receipt of the further files or information under Rule 15.4, or such further period as the Arbitrator may reasonably require the Arbitrator shall make his award.

Rule 16. Other matters

16.1 Unless the parties otherwise agree the Arbitrator shall have no power to award costs to either party and the Arbitrator's own fees and expenses shall be paid in equal shares by the parties. Where one party has agreed to the Arbitrator's fees and expenses the other party by agreeing to this Short Procedure shall be deemed to have agreed likewise to the Arbitrator's fees and expenses.

Provided always that this Rule shall not apply to any dispute which arises after the Short Procedure has been adopted or imposed by the Contract.

16.2 Either party may at any time before the Arbitrator has made his award under this Short Procedure require by written notice served on the Arbitrator and the other party that the arbitration shall cease to be conducted in accordance with this Short Procedure. Save only for Rule 16.3 the Short Procedure shall thereupon no longer apply or bind the parties but any evidence already laid before the Arbitrator shall be admissible in further proceedings as if it had been submitted as part of those proceedings and without further proof.

16.3 The party giving written notice under Rule 16.2 shall thereupon in any event become liable to pay:

(a) the whole of the Arbitrator's fees and expenses incurred up to the date of such notice and

(b) a sum to be assessed by the Arbitrator as reasonable compensation for the costs (including any legal costs) incurred by the other party up to the date of such notice.

Payment in full of such expenses shall be a condition precedent to that party's proceeding further in the arbitration unless the Arbitrator otherwise directs. Provided that non-payment of the said expenses shall not prevent the other party from proceeding in the arbitration.

PART G. SPECIAL PROCEDURE FOR EXPERTS

Rule 17. Special Procedure for Experts

17.1 Where the parties so agree (either of their own motion or at the invitation of the Arbitrator) the hearing and determination of any issues of fact which depend upon the evidence of Experts shall be conducted in accordance with the following Special Procedure.

17.2 Each party shall set out its case on such issues in the form of a file containing:

(a) a statement of the factual findings it seeks;

(b) a report or statement from and signed by each Expert upon whom that party relies;
(c) copies of any other documents referred to in each Expert's report or statement or on which the party relies identifying the origin and date of each document;

and shall deliver copies of the said file to the other party and to the Arbitrator in such manner and within such time as the Arbitrator may direct.

17.3 After reading the parties cases the Arbitrator may view the site or the works and may require either or both parties to submit further documents or information in writing.

17.4 Thereafter the Arbitrator shall fix a day when he shall meet the Experts whose reports or statements have been submitted. At the meeting each Expert may address the Arbitrator and put questions to any other Expert representing the other party. The Arbitrator shall so direct the meeting as to ensure that each Expert has an adequate opportunity to explain his opinion and to comment upon any opposing opinion. No other person shall be entitled to address the Arbitrator or question any Expert unless the parties and the Arbitrator so agree.

17.5 Thereafter the Arbitrator may make an award setting out with such details or particulars as may be necessary his decision upon the issues dealt with.

Rule 18. Costs

18.1 The Arbitrator may in his award make orders as to the payment of any costs relating to the foregoing matters including his own fees and expenses in connection therewith.

18.2 Unless the parties otherwise agree and so notify the Arbitrator neither party shall be entitled to any costs in respect of legal representation assistance or other legal work relating to the hearing and determination of factual issues by this Special Procedure.

PART H. AWARDS

Rule 19. Awards

19.1 The Arbitrator may at any time make an award, and may make more than one award at different times on different aspects of the matters to be determined.

19.2 An award may:

(a) order the payment of money to one or more of the parties;
(b) order a party to do or refrain from doing anything;
(c) order specific performance;
(d) make a declaration as to any matter to be determined;
(e) order rectification, setting aside or cancellation of a deed or other document;
(f) be a consent award in the event of a settlement, which shall include an allocation of the Costs of the Arbitration.

Provisional relief

19.3 The Arbitrator may also make a provisional order and for this purpose the Arbitrator shall have power to award payment by one party to another of a sum representing a reasonable proportion of the final net amount which in his opinion that party is likely to be ordered to pay after determination of all the issues in the arbitration and after taking into account any defence or counterclaim upon which the other party may be entitled to rely.

19.4 The Arbitrator shall have power to order the party against whom a provisional order is made to pay part or all of the sum awarded to a stakeholder. In default of compliance with such an order the Arbitrator may order payment of the whole sum in the provisional order to the other party.

19.5 A provisional order shall be final and binding upon the parties unless and until it is varied by any subsequent award made by the same Arbitrator or by any other Arbitrator having jurisdiction over the matters in dispute. Any such subsequent award may order repayment of monies paid in accordance with the provisional order.

Interest

19.6 In any award the Arbitrator shall have power to award interest either simple or compound at such rate and between such dates or such events as he thinks fit.

Costs

19.7 Unless otherwise provided in this Procedure, the Arbitrator shall have power to:

(a) make an award allocating the Costs of the Arbitration between the parties in such manner as he considers appropriate;
(b) direct the basis upon which the costs are to be determined;
(c) in default of agreement by the parties, determine the amount of the recoverable cost;
(d) order payment of costs in relation to a provisional order including power to order that such costs shall be paid forthwith.

Rule 20. Reasons

20.1 The Arbitrator shall include in his award reasons for the award unless it is a consent award or the parties have agreed to dispense with reasons.

Rule 21. Making the award

21.1 Upon the closing of the hearing (if any) and after having considered all the evidence and submissions the Arbitrator shall prepare and make his award.

21.2 When the Arbitrator has made his award (including a provisional order under Rule 19.3) he shall so inform the parties in writing and shall specify how and where it may be taken up upon full payment of his fees and expenses.

Power to correct an award

21.3 The Arbitrator may, within 28 days of the date of the award, correct an award so as to remove any clerical mistake, error or ambiguity, and may also make an additional award in respect of any matter which was not dealt with in the award.

Rule 22. Appeals

22.1 If any party applies to the court for leave to appeal against any award or decision or for any other purpose that party shall forthwith notify the Arbitrator of the application.

The Arbitrator may continue the arbitral proceedings, including making further awards, pending a decision by the court.

22.2 Once any award or decision has been made and taken up the Arbitrator shall be under no obligation to make any statement in connection therewith other than in compliance with an order of the court.

PART J. MISCELLANEOUS

Rule 23. Definitions

23.1 In these Rules the following definitions shall apply:

(a) "Arbitrator" includes a tribunal of two or more Arbitrators, an Umpire or Chairman;
(b) "Institution" means The Institution of Civil Engineers;
(c) "President" means the President for the time being of the Institution or any Vice-President acting on his behalf or such other person as may have been nominated in the arbitration agreement to appoint the Arbitrator in default of agreement between the Parties;
(d) "Procedure" means The Institution of Civil Engineers' Arbitration Procedure (1997) unless the context otherwise requires;
(e) "Contract" means the Contract between the parties which incorporates the arbitration agreement under which the dispute arises;
(f) "Expert" means an expert witness or person called to give expert opinion evidence;
(g) The "Act" means the Arbitration Act 1996 and when the Act applies words defined in it shall have the same meanings in this Procedure;
(h) "Costs of the Arbitration" shall include:
   (i) the Arbitrator's fees and expenses;
   (ii) the fees and expenses of any arbitral institution concerned;
   (iii) the legal or other costs of the parties and
   (iv) the costs of or incidental to any proceedings to determine the amount of the recoverable costs of the arbitration.

Rule 24. Application of the ICE Procedure

24.1 This Procedure shall apply to the conduct of the arbitration if:

(a) the Contract so provides;
(b) the parties at any time so agree or
(c) the Arbitrator so stipulates at the time of his appointment.

Provided that where this Procedure applies by virtue of the Arbitrator's stipulation under (c) above the parties may within 14 days of that appointment agree otherwise in which event the Arbitrator's appointment shall be terminated.

24.2 This Procedure shall not apply to arbitrations under the law of Scotland for which a separate ICE Arbitration Procedure (Scotland) is available.

24.3 Where the seat of the arbitration is in a country other than England and Wales or Northern Ireland this Procedure shall apply to the extent that the applicable law permits.

24.4 If after the appointment of the Arbitrator any agreement is reached between the parties which is inconsistent with this Procedure the Arbitrator shall be entitled upon giving reasonable notice to terminate his appointment, and shall be entitled to payment of his reasonable fees and expenses incurred up to the date of the termination.

Rule 25. Exclusion of liability

25.1 Neither the Institution nor its servants or agents nor the President shall be liable to any party for any act omission or misconduct in connection with any appointment made or any arbitration conducted under this Procedure.

Appendix 23

THE REFINED SUGAR ASSOCIATION RULES RELATING TO ARBITRATION

RECOMMENDED ARBITRATION CLAUSE

Parties to a White Sugar Contract who wish to have any disputes referred to arbitration under the following Rules are recommended to insert in the Contract an arbitration clause in the following form:

> "All disputes arising out of or in connection with this Contract shall be referred to The Refined Sugar Association for settlement in accordance with the Rules Relating to Arbitration. This Contract shall be governed by and construed in accordance with English Law".

RULES

1. Any dispute arising out of or in connection with a Contract which the Parties have agreed (either in the Contract or otherwise) to refer to arbitration by The Refined Sugar Association shall be determined in accordance with the following Rules.

2. Any party wishing to commence an arbitration concerning a dispute falling within Rule 1 shall give to the other party seven clear days notice of his intention to claim arbitration.

After the expiry of the seven clear days notice period a written request for arbitration shall be sent to the Secretary. The Arbitration Rules of the Association in force at the time such request is received will apply to the reference.

The Claimant shall, together with the request for arbitration or within 30 days thereafter, or such extended time as the Council shall in its absolute discretion allow, forward to the Secretary the following:

(a) a clear and concise statement of his case, in duplicate;

(b) copies of the contractual documents, in duplicate, in which the arbitration clause is contained or under which the arbitration arises;

(c) any supporting documentary evidence, in duplicate, it thinks proper;
(d) the names, addresses, telexes and facsimile numbers (if appropriate) of the parties to the arbitration;
(e) a non-returnable registration fee (see Rule 3);
(f) if required (and without prejudice to the provisions of the Arbitration Act 1996, relating to security for costs) an advance payment on account of the Association's fees, costs and expenses (see Rule 3).

The Council shall thereupon have power to determine, as hereinafter provided, any such matter in dispute. Without prejudice to the provisions of the Arbitration Act 1996 relating to jurisdiction, where both parties to a dispute are members the Council shall have the jurisdiction to determine whether a contract has been made, whether there is a valid arbitration agreement and what matters have been submitted to arbitration in accordance with such agreement.

The Respondent party shall, not later than thirty days after dispatch to his last known address by the Secretary of a copy of the Claimant's statement of case and supporting documents, or such extended time as the Council shall in its absolute discretion allow, submit in duplicate to the Secretary a clear and concise statement of his defence together with a copy of such other documentary evidence in duplicate as he thinks proper. A copy of this statement of defence and supporting documents shall be forwarded be the Secretary to the Claimant.

The Claimant and the Respondent will in turn be permitted a period of twenty-one days, or such extended time as the Council shall in its absolute discretion allow, within which to submit further written comments and/or documents in reply to the other party's last submission, until the Council shall in its absolute discretion decide to proceed to make its award.

All statements, contracts and documentary evidence must be submitted in the English language. Whenever documentary evidence is submitted in a foreign language this must be accompanied by an officially certified English translation.

3. A non-returnable registration fee of such amount as shall be decided by the Council from time to time shall be paid to the Secretary upon any reference to arbitration. The Council may if it thinks fit at any time order either party to the arbitration to make one or more advance payments on account of the Association's fees, costs and expenses in connection with or arising out of the arbitration. Such power shall be without prejudice to the power of the Council to order security for costs in accordance with the Arbitration Act 1996.

4. Any notice, document or other correspondence to be served on any party in connection with an arbitration under these Rules may be effected either by (a) courier, (b) first class post, (c) post in a registered letter, (d) telex, (e) cable or (f) facsimile in each case to the usual or last known address or place of business of any party. In the case of a facsimile such notice, document or correspondence shall also be served in accordance with one of the provisions under (a) to (e) above.

5. Should a party in dispute with another party refuse to concur in the reference to arbitration as herein provided, the party referring the matter to arbitration may forthwith obtain an award of the Council on the question in dispute. The Council may at its discretion refuse to arbitrate on any reference made by a Member who has been suspended from the Association or whose Membership has been revoked.

6. Unless the Council shall as hereinbefore provided have refused to arbitrate, neither the Buyer, Seller, Trustee in Bankruptcy, liquidator nor any other person claiming under any of them, shall bring any action against any party to the contract in respect of any dispute arising out of such contract, until such dispute shall have been adjudicated upon in arbitration under these Rules; and the obtaining of an award under these Rules shall be a condition precedent to the right of either contracting party to sue the other in respect of any claim arising out of the contract.

7. When the subject matter and terms of contract are identical, except as to date and price, arbitration may in the Council's absolute discretion and subject to the written agreement of all parties be held as between first Seller and last Buyer as though they were contracting parties and the award made in pursuance thereof shall be binding on all intermediate parties, provided that this Rule shall not apply where a question or dispute shall arise between intermediate parties, not affecting both first Seller and last Buyer, and in such case the arbitration may be held as between the two parties affected by the dispute or, subject as aforesaid in the event of there being more than two such parties, as between the first and last of such parties as though they were contracting parties, and the award made in pursuance thereof shall be binding on all parties affected by the dispute.

8. For the purpose of all proceedings in arbitration, the contract shall be deemed to have been made in England, any correspondence in reference to the offer, the acceptance, the place or payment or otherwise, notwithstanding, and England shall be regarded as the place of performance. Disputes shall be settled according to the law of England wherever the domicile, residence or place of business of the parties to the contract may be or become. The seat of the arbitration shall be England and all proceedings shall take place in England. It shall not be necessary for the award to state expressly the seat of the arbitration. Unless the contract contains any statement expressly to the contrary, the provisions of neither the Convention relating to a Uniform Law on the International Sale of Goods, of 1964, nor the United Nations Convention on Contracts for the International Sale of Goods, of 1980, shall apply thereto.

9. For determination of a dispute the Council shall appoint not less than three and no more than five persons from the Panel of Arbitrators to act on its behalf. The number of persons appointed to determine a dispute shall be in the absolute discretion of the Council. No such person shall act in an arbitration where he is, or becomes, directly or indirectly interested in the subject matter in dispute. In the event of a person becoming so interested, dying or becoming in any other way in the view of the Council incapacitated from acting prior to the first meeting, the Council may appoint another person from the Panel of Arbitrators to take his place, and the arbitration shall thereupon proceed as if that other person had been originally appointed in lieu of the first person. If subsequently an Arbitrator discovers that he is directly involved in the subject matter in dispute, dies or becomes in any other way in the view of the Council incapacitated from acting, then the hearing shall, unless the Council in its absolute discretion decides otherwise, proceed without the necessity of appointing another person from the Panel of Arbitrators. The decision of the persons so appointed to act on behalf of the Council shall be by a majority and, in the event of an equality of votes, the Chairman, who shall have been previously elected by such persons, shall have a second or casting vote. The award of such persons shall be signed by the said Chairman (and it shall not be necessary for any of the other persons appointed from the Panel of Arbitrators to sign it) and when so signed shall be deemed to be the award of the Council and shall be final and binding in all cases.

10. The Council may in its discretion decide the case on the written statements and documents submitted to it without an oral hearing (without the attendance of the parties or their representatives and witnesses). The Council may, however, call the parties before it, and request the attendance of witnesses, or the provision of further documents, or information in written form.

Should either or both parties require an oral hearing they shall make their request, in writing, to the Secretary. The Council may grant or refuse such request in their absolute discretion and without assigning any reason.

Without prejudice to the provisions of the Arbitration Act 1996 relating to legal representation, in the event of an oral hearing, with or without witnesses, each party shall appear either personally or by any agent duly appointed in writing and may be represented at the oral hearing by counsel or solicitor. One party shall not, however, make any oral statement in the absence of the other, excepting in the case of his opponent failing to appear after notice has been given to him by the Secretary.

The Council may also, on its own behalf, whether in relation to a case decided on documents or an oral hearing, consult the legal advisers of the Association and unless otherwise agreed by the Council any information, opinion or advice offered by such person/s whether or not in writing shall be for the sole use of the Council and shall not be made available to the parties.

Without prejudice to the provisions of section 34 of the Arbitration Act 1996, the Council shall not be bound by the strict rules of evidence and shall be at liberty to admit and consider any material whatsoever notwithstanding that it may not be admissible under the law of evidence.

Unless both parties notify the Secretary, in writing, to the contrary, the Council shall issue a Reasoned Award.

The Council shall have the power to make more than one award at different times on different issues in accordance with section 47 of the Arbitration Act 1996, but shall not have the power to make provisional awards pursuant to section 39 of the Arbitration Act 1996.

11. If a party wishes to withdraw a claim or counterclaim, he shall give notice to that effect to the Secretary. On receipt of such a notice, the Secretary shall inform the other party and shall cancel any arrangements for the hearing of that claim or counterclaim (unless any other claim or counterclaim remains to be dealt with at the same hearing). The other party shall be entitled to an award dismissing the withdrawn claim or counterclaim with costs, provided that a written request for such an award is received by the Secretary within 28 days after such other party has been informed by the Secretary of the withdrawal. If no such request is received by the Secretary within the said period of 28 days the arbitration shall be deemed to have been terminated by consent so far as it relates to such claim or counterclaim. Such award or termination shall not affect any other claim or counterclaim which is the subject of the same arbitration proceedings, or the Council's right to recover its own and the Association's fees, costs and expenses from either party.

12. Subject to any agreement to the contrary, the Council shall, in addition to the powers under section 49 of the Arbitration Act 1996, have the power if it thinks fit:

(a) to award interest on any sum which becomes due in respect of a contract whether by way of debt or damages and which is paid before the commencement of arbitration proceedings at such rate as it thinks fit and for such period as it thinks fit ending not later than the date of payment;
(b) where a sum is due in respect of a contract whether by way of debt or damages, to award general damages in respect of the late payment of such sum.

13. The arbitration fees shall be in the discretion of the Council in every case, and shall be paid by whom the Council shall determine.

Any expenses incurred by the Association or by the Council, including the expenses incurred in obtaining legal assistance, copies of documents or evidence, shorthand notes, etc., may be added to such fees.

The Council may also make an award or order as to payment of the costs of the parties to the arbitration. In accordance with section 63 of the Arbitration Act 1996, the Council may also determine by award the recoverable costs of the parties on such basis as it thinks fit.

14. A book shall be kept in which all cases shall be noted, together with the award and fees and expenses charged. The Secretary shall notify the parties as soon as the award is signed and it shall be held by the Secretary at the disposal of either party against payment of fees and expenses incurred by the Association or by the Council. A copy of the award shall be given so the party who does not take up the original. If the award is not taken up within ten days, the Council may order either of the parties to take up the award, and in such case the party so ordered shall take up the award and pay the fees and expenses as directed. The Council shall have the right to invoke arbitration Rule 16, if any party neglects or refuses to abide by any such order.

15. The award must be honoured within twenty-eight days from the date on which it is taken up.

16. In the event of a party to an arbitration neglecting or refusing to carry out or abide by any award or order made under arbitration Rule 14, the Council may circularise to Members of the Association in any way thought fit a notification to that effect. The parties to any such arbitration shall be deemed to have consented to the Council taking such action as aforesaid.

17. In the event of both parties consenting in writing to the publication to Members of the Association of an Award or any part thereof or summary of its contents, the Council may make available the same to its Members in a form approved by the Parties. The Council shall be entitled to charge a fee to Members for the provision of such information.

Index